SIXTH EDITION

UNDERSTANDING
Psychology

Charles G. Morris

UNIVERSITY OF MICHIGAN

Albert A. Maisto

UNIVERSITY OF NORTH CAROLINA AT CHARLOTTE

Prentice Hall, Upper Saddle River, New Jersey 07458

Library of Congress Cataloging-in-Publication Data

Morris, Charles G.
Understanding psychology / Charles G. Morris, Albert A. Maisto—6th ed.
   p. cm.
  Includes bibliographical references and indexes.
  ISBN 0–13–048037–1
    1. Psychology.   I. Maisto, Albert A. (Albert Anthony)   II. Title.
  BF139.M67 2003
  150—dc21

2002003696

Editor-in-Chief: *Leah Jewell*
Project Manager: *Stephanie Johnson*
Senior Development Editor: *Roberta Meyer*
VP, Director of Production
  and Manufacturing: *Barbara Kittle*
Production Liaison: *Fran Russello*
Editorial/Production Supervision: *Bruce Hobart*
  (*Pine Tree Composition*)
Manufacturing Manager: *Nick Sklitsis*
Prepress and Manufacturing Buyer: *Tricia Kenny*
Creative Design Director: *Leslie Osher*
Interior Design: *Kathryn Foot*

Cover Design: *Kathryn Foot*
Cover Art: *Susan LeVan*
Director, Image Resource Center: *Melinda Reo*
Manager, Rights & Permissions: *Zina Arabia*
Interior Image Specialist: *Beth Boyd-Brenzel*
Cover Image Specialist: *Karen Sanatar*
Image Permission Coordinator: *Michelina Viscusi*
Photo Researcher: *Julie Tesser*
Production/Formatting/Art Manager: *Guy Ruggiero*
Electronic Art Creation: *Mirella Signoretto*
Marketing Manager: *Jeff Hester*

Photo credits appear on pp. C-1, which constitute a continuation of the copyright page.

This book was set in 10/12 Meridien by Pine Tree Composition and was printed and bound by Von Hoffman Press, Inc. The cover was printed by Phoenix Color Corp.

Copyright © 2003, 2001, 1999, 1996, 1993, 1991
by Pearson Education
Upper Saddle River, New Jersey 07458

Printed in the United States of America
10 9 8 7 6 5

ISBN 0-13-048037-1

ISBN 0-13-175940-X (Value Pack)

Pearson Education Ltd., *London*
Pearson Education Australia Pte. Ltd., *Sydney*
Pearson Education Singapore, Pte. Ltd.
Pearson Education North Asia Ltd., *Hong Kong*
Pearson Education Canada, Ltd., *Toronto*
Pearson Educación de Mexico, S.A. de C.V.
Pearson Education—Japan, *Tokyo*
Pearson Education Malaysia, Pte. Ltd.
Pearson Education, *Upper Saddle River, New Jersey*

BRIEF CONTENTS

CONTENTS

7 COGNITION AND MENTAL ABILITIES   230

8 MOTIVATION AND EMOTION   276

SPECIAL FEATURES

UNDERSTANDING OURSELVES

11 STRESS AND HEALTH PSYCHOLOGY   394

SPECIAL FEATURES

UNDERSTANDING OURSELVES

UNDERSTANDING OURSELVES

UNDERSTANDING The World Around Us

12 PSYCHOLOGICAL DISORDERS   426

SPECIAL FEATURES

UNDERSTANDING OURSELVES

UNDERSTANDING The World Around Us

13 THERAPIES   460

SPECIAL FEATURES

14   SOCIAL PSYCHOLOGY   494

SPECIAL FEATURES

APPENDIX

Continued focus on *understanding* basic concepts

With each edition of this text, we are reminded just how rapidly the field of psychology is developing. Even as one edition is sent to the printer, we begin gathering materials for the next edition. After poring over a stack of file folders, we chose over five hundred new references to incorporate into this revision, with more than one hundred of them dated 2000 or later. Each one offers important new information in our never-ending search to understand behavior. But despite the changes, the original goals for this book remain unchanged: to present a scientific, accurate, and thorough overview of the essential concepts of psychology, in engaging language that the average student can easily comprehend; to be current without being trendy; and to write clearly about psychology and its applications without being condescending.

Pedagogy that makes material more accessible

Throughout every edition of this text we have kept in mind that our final audience consists primarily of college undergraduates. Having taught undergraduates for decades, we realize that it is essential to make a textbook as accessible and helpful as possible. The sixth edition includes a number of pedagogical features designed to help students understand the material and how it applies to their lives. The result is that students don't just process lists of unrelated facts, but instead have a cognitive map with which to contextualize, better understand, and more effectively relate and recall concepts.

■ New *Understanding Ourselves* boxes provide practical information on how students can apply psychology to their own lives. Examples include "The Slow (but lasting) Fix for Weight Gain" (Chapter 8); "Traumatic Stress: Recovering from Disasters and Other Traumatic Events" (Chapter 11); and "Recognizing Depression" (Chapter 12).

■ New *Understanding the World Around Us* boxes help students use psychology to understand issues in the news and events occurring in the world around them. Examples include "Eyewitness Testimony: Can We Trust It?" (Chapter 6); "What Motivates Rape?" (Chapter 8); and "Kids Who Kill" (Chapter 9).

UNDERSTANDING The World Around Us

What Motivates Rape?

Every 5 minutes, somewhere in the United States, a woman reports being raped. Although men can be victims of sexual assault, in fact the victims are nearly always women. Perhaps one in four women in this country has been raped (Koss & Boeschen, 2000). About 40 percent of rape victims receive injuries (not counting genital injuries) during the attack, and victims are at risk for long-term health problems such as gastrointestinal disorders and tension headaches (Koss & Boeschen, 2000).

What motivates this crime? Media publicity suggests that a woman is raped when a psychopathic stranger abducts her, perhaps while she is jogging through a park or traveling at night on a dark road. Although some rapes certainly do fit this scenario, it is far from typical. The facts are that:

• About one-third of rapes occur in the victim's home.
• About half of all rapes take place on a date.
• In approximately 80 percent of rapes, the victim knows the rapist.

Perhaps one in four women in this country has been raped.

What causes rape? Early attempts to answer this question focused on rapists in prison. These studies suggested that power, anger, and sadism were the principal motives for rape. More recent research, based on more representative samples of the population, paint a rather different picture. One study (Prentky, Knight, & Rosenberg, 1988) found that many rapists did want to hurt, degrade, or humiliate their victims, often as a way of exacting revenge for perceived wrongs committed against them by other women. But in nearly half of the cases, sexual gratification seemed to be the predominant motive. Many of the latter rapists tended to be very impulsive; they did not plan to rape but did so when they had the opportunity. Others who raped for sexual gratification were acting out a sexual fantasy; many of these men seemed to believe that their victims would eventually enjoy the experience and perhaps even fall in love with them.

Woman may be able to reduce the risk of rape by avoiding contact with men with certain characteristics: Men who act on impulse, especially in aggressive ways; men who feel that they have been wronged by women or who speak or act with contempt toward women; men who are manipulative or possessive toward women; and men with a history of violent behavior. However, even women who are very careful about the company they keep must remember that situational factors play a powerful role in most behavior. In one experiment, for example, viewing films simulating forced sex did not arouse most men at all (Barbaree & Marshall, 1991). But many of these same men did become sexually aroused by scenes of sexual violence if they had been drinking or if they had recently had an argument with a woman. Thus, although most men are not disposed to rape, certain situational factors may make some men more likely to rape.

■ New "talking graphics" clarify complex processes with step-by-step explanations, particularly in the areas of neuroscience (Chapter 2), Sensation and Perception (Chapter 3), and Memory (Chapter 6).

UNDERSTANDING OURSELVES

Traumatic Stress: Recovering From Disasters and Other Traumatic Events

The September 11, 2001, terrorist attacks in New York City and Washington, D.C., were the type of events that we thought could never happen. Like other types of disasters, they were unexpected, sudden, and overwhelming. In some cases, there are no outwardly visible signs of physical injury, but there is nonetheless a serious emotional toll. It is common for people who have experienced traumatic situations to have very strong emotional reactions. Understanding normal responses to these abnormal events can aid you in coping effectively with your feelings, thoughts, and behaviors, and can help you along the path to recovery.

What happens to people after a disaster or another kind of traumatic event?

Shock and denial are typical responses to terrorism, disasters, and other kinds of trauma, especially shortly after the event. Both shock and denial are normal protective reactions. Shock is a sudden and often an intense disturbance of your emotional state that may leave you feeling stunned or dazed. Denial involves your not acknowledging that something very stressful has happened, or not experiencing fully the intensity of the event. You may temporarily feel numb or disconnected from life. As the initial shock subsides, reactions vary from one person to another. The following, however, are normal responses to a traumatic event:

• Feelings become intense and sometimes *are* unpredictable. You may become more irritable than usual, and your mood may change back and forth dramatically. You might be especially anxious or nervous, or even become depressed.

• Thoughts and behavior patterns are affected by the trauma. You might have repeated and vivid memories of the event. These flashbacks may occur for no apparent reason and may lead to physical reactions such as rapid heartbeat or sweating. You may find it difficult to concentrate or make decisions, or become more easily confused. Sleep and eating patterns also may be disrupted.

• Recurring emotional reactions are common. Anniversaries of the event, such as at one month or one year, as well as reminders such as aftershocks from earthquakes or the sounds of sirens, can trigger upsetting memories of the traumatic experience. These triggers may be accompanied by fears that the stressful event will be repeated.

• Interpersonal relationships often become strained. Greater conflict, such as more frequent arguments with family members and coworkers, is common. On the other hand, you may become withdrawn and isolated and may avoid your usual activities.

• Physical symptoms may accompany the extreme stress. For example, headaches, nausea, and chest pain may result and may require medical attention. Preexisting medical conditions may worsen because of the stress.

How do people respond differently over time?

It is important for you to realize that there is not one standard pattern.

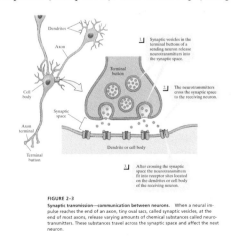

FIGURE 2–3
Synaptic transmission—communication between neurons. When a neural impulse reaches the end of an axon, tiny oval sacs, called synaptic vesicles, at the end of most axons, release varying amounts of chemical substances called neurotransmitters. These substances travel across the synaptic space and affect the next neuron.

■ *Check Your Understanding* quizzes at the end of each major section help students review and retain concepts before moving on to a new topic. These quizzes are also available in an interactive format on the Morris Companion Website.

WEB QUIZ 3.8

CHECK YOUR UNDERSTANDING

Match each term with the appropriate definition.

____ neuron | a. long cellular fibers carrying outgoing messages
____ dendrites | b. when a nerve cell cannot fire again
____ axons | c. affects emotions, arousal, and sleep
____ neural impulse | d. cell that transmits information
____ resting potential | e. chemicals that carry messages across synapses
____ absolute refractory period | f. short cellular fibers that pick up incoming messages
____ synapse | g. neurotransmitter with a role in schizophrenia
____ neurotransmitters | h. action potential
____ dopamine | i. terminal button, synaptic space, and dendrite of neighboring neuron
____ serotonin | j. electrical imbalance across a neural membrane at rest

- A chapter-opening **Overview** provides students with a road map for each chapter.

- **Questions** following each first- and second-level heading encourage students to be active readers and to critically evaluate the material that follows.

- **Summary Tables** provide concise reviews of the most important concepts.

- **Key terms** are printed in boldface and defined in the margin where they first appear.

- The **Chapter Review** provides a comprehensive summary of key concepts.

- **Critical Thinking** questions appear at the end of every chapter, and encourage students to consider the broader implications of major concepts.

Integrated Multimedia Focusing on the Basics

Our students never have enough time. Multimedia games might be fun, but what students really need are tools for understanding and retaining the basics. In this edition, we have streamlined and significantly enhanced the **Companion Website** to provide students with the tools to understand and master the basic concepts.

For each chapter, students will find numerous online quizzes with instant scoring and feedback, interactive lectures that help students review the key concepts, flashcards for drilling themselves on key terms, and an exciting new component called *Live!Psych* (described below). The website material is tightly integrated with the text through numbered icons in the text margins, which indicate when students should go to the website for quizzes, interactive lectures, and *Live!Psych* exercises that correspond to the concepts just covered in the chapter.

WEB QUIZ 3.2

INTERACTIVE LECTURE 3.2

3.2 *Live! psych*

Live!Psych is a series of highly interactive media simulations, animations, and assessments found on the Morris Companion Website. All *Live!Psych* modules were created in consultation with psychology instructors and carefully reviewed by a board of experts to ensure accuracy and pedagogical effectiveness (see list of contributers below under "Student Supplements: Live!Psych Modules"). The modules focus on the concepts students find most challenging, such as the major brain structures and functions; neurons and neural impulses; the structures of the human eye and ear; stages of sleep and brainwave patterns; the classical and operant conditioning processes; and many others. *Live!Psych* helps students master these difficult concepts by allowing them to see and experience them in a more interactive format than can be achieved in any textbook. All of the material on the Morris Companion Website, including the *Live!Psych* modules, can be accessed without restriction at www.prenhall.com/morris.

Increased Coverage of Culture and Diversity

For today's students and instructors of introductory psychology, diversity is more than simply an issue for discussion and debate; it is a daily reality. The challenge confronting any textbook author is to satisfy a heterogeneous audience without becoming trendy or unscientific. Over the last several years, the body of research examining issues of diversity has grown to significant levels. As a result, consideration of diversity is expanded in every new edition—both diversity within the North American population, and diversity across cultures worldwide. Material relating to diversity is incorporated throughout the Sixth Edition. Some of the new material includes: a major revision to the "Human Diversity" section in Chapter 1; an updated *Understanding Ourselves* box on "Cultural Diversity and Academic Performance" in Chapter 7; increased coverage of women in the workforce in Chapter 9; major changes in "Socioeconomic and Gender Differences in Coping with Stress" including the "tend-and-befriend" response among women in Chapter 11; new material on cultural differences in abnormal behavior in Chapter 12; new material on cultural differences in prevention programs, and updated statistics on gender differences in willingness to seek treatment in Chapter 13; a major revision of the racism discussion, new research on cross-cultural differences in attribution, and new information on cross-cultural replication of Milgram's research in Chapter 14.

Significant New Information

As we went about the revision, we looked for places where we could streamline the content of the chapters to make it flow more smoothly and clearly. We also integrated the new information we had gleaned over the previous two years. Consequently, revisions range from minor updates to major new discussions. Below is a list of the most significant changes in the Sixth Edition.

Chapter 1 The Science of Psychology

:: Reorganization of the history of psychology into three main stages: the emergence of a science of the mind, the behaviorist decades, and the cognitive revolution.

:: New discussions of evolutionary psychology and positive psychology.

:: Major revision of "Human Diversity."

Chapter 2 The Biological Basis of Behavior

:: *New topic*: Can the Brain and Nervous System Repair Themselves?

:: Updated and expanded coverage of language and the brain.

:: Updated section on molecular genetics and the human genome.

Chapter 3: Sensation and Perception

:: Updated and expanded coverage of pain.

Chapter 4 States of Consciousness

:: *New topic*: club drugs.

:: Expanded section on sleep and sleep deprivation.

:: Updated coverage of psychoactive drugs' effects.

:: Expanded discussions of drug dependence, abuse and addiction.

Chapter 5 Learning

:: *New topic*: Classical Conditioning of the Immune System.

:: Increased coverage of the evolutionary basis of fear.

Chapter 6 Memory

:: *New topics*: the biology of forgetting; childhood amnesia.

:: Reorganized and updated material on STM and LTM.

:: Thoroughly revised discussion of the biological basis of memory.

Chapter 7 Cognition and Mental Abilities

:: Newly organized section on "Language, Thought, and Culture."

:: Major updating of "Decision Making."

:: Extensive revision of "Heredity, Environment and Intelligence."

Chapter 8 Motivation and Emotion

:: Significantly increased coverage of Arousal Theory; Hunger.

:: Updated and increased coverage of Emotion; Aggression.

Chapter 9 Life-Span Development

:: New material on Teenage Pregnancy and Childbearing.

:: Increased coverage of women in the workforce.

:: New material on children in dual-career families.

:: Updated coverage of Alzheimer's disease.

Chapter 10 Personality

:: Major updating of "Big Five" trait theory.

:: New summary table showing for each group of personality theories the roots of personality and preferred methods of personality assessment.

:: Rewriting of objective and projective testing for greater clarity, brevity, and currency.

Chapter 11 Stress and Health Psychology

:: A new chapter opening vignette discussing the psychological impact of September 11.

:: A new "Understanding Ourselves" box on "Traumatic Stress: Recovering from Disasters and Other Traumatic Events."

:: Major revision to increase emphasis on health psychology; stress and health updated.

:: *New topic*: "Staying Healthy" despite inevitable stress.

:: New research on optimism/pessimism in section on "Stress and Individual Differences."

:: Greatly revised discussion of "hardiness" and new material on "resilience."

:: Major changes in "Socioeconomic and Gender Differences in Coping with Stress" including the "tend-and-befriend" response among women.

:: Extensive revision and updating on psychoneuroimmunology.

:: Major revision to "Bereavement."

Chapter 12 Psychological Disorders

:: New material on "Recognizing Depression." Using the criteria of DSM IV, discussion helps students distinguish between "normal" reactions to negative life events which may make one "feel depressed" and actual clinical depression.

:: New material on cultural differences in abnormal behavior.

Chapter 13 Therapies

:: New material on combining biological treatments with psychotherapy.

:: Updated discussion of prescribing psychoactive drugs for children.

:: New material on cultural differences in prevention programs.

Chapter 14 Social Psychology

- Major revision of discussion of racism.
- New research on cross-cultural differences in attribution.
- New information on cross-cultural replication of Stanley Milgram's research on obedience to authority.

Enhanced Supplements Package

It is increasingly true today that, as valuable as a good textbook is, it is still only one element of a comprehensive learning package. The supplements package that accompanies the Sixth Edition is the most comprehensive and integrated yet. We have made every effort to provide high-quality instructor supplements that will save you preparation time, and will enhance the time you spend in the classroom.

Print Supplements for the Instructor

Instructor's Resource Binder (0-13-045478-8): A new instructor's resource three-ring binder offers an exhaustive collection of resources prepared by Alan Swinkels of St. Edward's University. For each chapter, you'll find activities, exercises, assignments, handouts, and demos for in-class use, as well as guidelines on integrating the many Morris media resources into your classroom and syllabus. The material for each chapter is organized in an easy-to-use lecture outline format. This resource binder saves prep work and helps you make the maximum use of your classroom time.

Test Item File (0-13-045479-6): Developed by Gary Piggrem of DeVry Institute of Technology, this test file contains over 4400 multiple choice, true/false, and essay questions. To facilitate your selection of items, each question is page referenced to the textbook. All multiple choice questions are categorized as either factual, conceptual, or applied, and are identified as being new, revised, or from a previous edition. Many of the items also includes statistics indicating how many students answered that question correctly in class-testing at both 2-year and 4-year schools. In addition, the text author, Charles Morris, has carefully reviewed the test file and has indicated a number of "Author's Choice" questions because of their challenging nature or interesting focus.

PH Color Transparencies 2002 (0-13-041840-4): This set of over 130 full-color transparencies includes illustrations, figures, and graphs from the text, as well as images from a variety of other sources.

Media and Online Resources for Instructors

Instructor's CD-ROM (0-13-045474-5): This valuable, time-saving supplement brings all of the Sixth Edition's instructor resources together in one convenient place. The CD-rom offers presentation resources, including video clips from Prentice Hall's Video Classics CD-rom (in larger, presentation format), and PowerPoint presentations customized for the Morris text. It also includes the electronic files for the Instructor's Resource Binder materials and the Test Item File to help you customize your lecture notes.

PH Test Manager CD-rom: One of the best-selling test-generating software programs on the market, Test Manager is available in Windows and Macintosh formats, both of which are included on one CD-rom. The Test Manager includes a Gradebook, On-Line Network Testing, and many tools to help you edit and create tests quickly and easily.

PsychologyCentral **Website (www.prenhall.com/psychology):** This site is password-protected for instructors' use only, and allows you online access to all Prentice Hall Psychology supplements at any time. You'll find a multitude of resources (both text-specific and non-text-specific) for teaching introductory psychology—and many other psychology courses too. From this site, you can download any of the key supplements for the Sixth Edition: Instructor's Resource Binder, Test Item File, and PowerPoint presentations. Contact your local sales representative for the User ID and Password to access this site.

PowerPoint Presentations (on Instructor's CD-rom and *PsychologyCentral* website): Lynn Bradman of Metropolitan Community College has created two sets of PowerPoint presentations—one with graphics and one without—to give you even greater flexibility in using PowerPoint in your lectures. Both presentations highlight all of the key points in the text, and include easy-to-follow tips on how to customize and enhance your presentations.

On-Line Course Management: For instructors interested in using online course management, Prentice Hall offers fully customizable courses in BlackBoard, Course Compass, and WebCT to accompany this textbook. These online courses are preloaded with material for Morris 6e, including the test item file. Contact your local Prentice Hall representative or visit www.prenhall.com/demo for more information.

Video Resources for Instructors

NEW: Prentice Hall Custom Video for Introductory Psychology: Qualified adopters can receive this new videotape that includes five- to eight-minute clips covering all major topics in introductory psychology. The videos have been carefully selected from the *Films for Humanities and Sciences* library, and edited to provide brief and compelling video content for enhancing your lectures. Contact your local representative for a full list of video clips on this tape.

The Brain Video Series: Qualified adopters can select videos from this series of eight, one-hour programs that blend interviews with world-famous brain scientists and dramatic reenactments of landmark cases in medical history. Programs include *The Enlightened Machine; The Two Brains; Vision and Movement; Madness; Rhythms and Drives; States of Mind; Stress and Emotion;* and *Learning and Memory.* Contact your local representative for more details.

The *Discovering Psychology* Video Series: Qualified adopters can select videos from this series produced in association with the American Psychological Association. The series includes thirteen tapes, each containing two half-hour segments. Contact your local sales representative for a list of videos.

ABC News Videos for Introductory Psychology, Series III: Qualified adopters can obtain this series consisting of segments from the "ABC Nightly News with Peter Jennings," "Nightline," "20/20," "Prime Time Live," and "The Health Show."

Films for Humanities and Sciences Video Library: Qualified adopters can select videos on various topics in psychology from the extensive library of *Films for the Humanities and Sciences.* Contact your local sales representative for a list of videos.

Resources for Students:

Companion Website (www.prenhall.com/morris): Lynn Bradman of Metropolitan Community College has created and selected the resources on Companion Website to reinforce students' understanding of the concepts in the text. The Web resources are tightly integrated with the text through icons found in the text margins. These icons indicate when material on the website corresponds to material in the text. Students can take online quizzes and get immediate scoring and feedback, and go through an interactive lecture that helps review material from the text. An exciting new addition to the 6e website is *Live!Psych*, a series of interactive animations and demonstrations (described below). Access to the Morris Companion Website (www.prenhall.com/morris) is free and unrestricted to all students.

Live!Psych modules on the Companion Website: This series of highly interactive media simulations, animations, and assessments reinforces the more difficult concepts in instroductory psychology, making them more accessible to students with different learning styles. The modules are tightly integrated with the text through marginal icons, indicating when students should go to the Website for a *Live!Psych* module that corresponds to con-

cepts just covered in the text. All *Live!Psych* modules have been created in consultation with psychology instructors and carefully reviewed by a board of experts to ensure accuracy and pedagogical effectiveness. Lynne Blesz Vestal has served as the primary content provider, and the review board includes: Kim Ainsworth-Darnell (Georgia State University); Eric J. Chudler (University of Washington); Margaret Gatz (University of Southern California); Karen Hoblit (Victoria Community College); Gail Knapp (Mott Community College); John Krantz (Hanover College); Nancy Simpson (Trident Technical College); and Chuck Slem (Cal Poly-San Luis Obispo).

Video Classics in Psychology CD-ROM: Using the power of video to clarify key concepts in the text, this CDrom offers original footage of some of the best-known classic experiments in psychology, including Milgram's obedience study, Watson's Little Albert, Bandura's BoBo doll, Pavlov's dog, Harlow's monkey, and others. In addition, students can see interviews with renowned contributors to the field like B.F. Skinner, Carl Rogers, Erik Erickson, Carl Jung, and others. Each video is preceded by background information on the importance of that experiment or researcher to the field, and is followed by questions that connect the video to concepts presented in the text. The *Video Classics* CD-ROM can be packaged free with *Understanding Psychology, 6th Edition.* Contact your local sales representative for the value pack ISBN.

ContentSelect Research Database: Prentice Hall and EBSCO, the world leader in online journal subscription management, have developed a customized research database for students of psychology. The database provides unlimited access to the text of dozens of peer-reviewed psychology publications. Student access codes can be packaged free with *Understanding Psychology, 6th Edition.* To see for yourself how this site works, ask your local Prentice Hall representative for a free Instructor Access Code.

Mind Matters CD-ROM: Free when packaged with a new text, *Mind Matters* features interactive learning modules on history, methods, biological psychology, learning, memory, sensation and perception. Each module combines text, video, graphics, simulations, games and assessment to reinforce key psychological concepts.

Study Guide (0-13-045476-1): Created by Joyce Bishop and Jan Mendoza of Golden West College, the Sixth Edition study guide contains material to help reinforce students' understanding of the concepts covered in the text. Each chapter contains: an Overview to introduce students to the chapter; an Outline with space for students to take notes from the text and during lecture; a Learning Objectives exercise to test students' understanding of the main themes; a multiple choice Pretest and Posttest for gauging students' progress; Short Essay Questions to develop writing skills; Language Support Section for extra support in English; and Flash Cards of vocabulary terms.

Supplementary Texts

Any one of these texts can be packaged with Understanding Psychology, Fifth Edition at a reduced price:

The Psychology Major: Careers and Strategies for Success by Eric Landrum (Idaho State University), Stephen Davis (Emporia State University), and Terri Landrum (Idaho State University). This 160-page paperback provides valuable information on career options available to psychology majors, tips for improving academic performance, and a guide to the APA style of research reporting.

Experiencing Psychology by Gary Brannigan (State University of New York at Plattsburgh). This hands-on activity book contains thirty-nine active learning experiences corresponding to major topics in psychology to provide students with hands-on experience in "doing" psychology.

Forty Studies that Changed Psychology, Fourth Edition by Roger Hock (Mendocino College). Presenting the seminal research studies that have shaped modern psychological study, this brief supplement provides an overview of the environment that gave rise to each study, its experimental design, its findings, and its impact on current thinking in the discipline.

How to Think Like a Psychologist: Critical Thinking in Psychology, Second Edition by Donald McBurney (University of Pittsburgh). This unique supplementary text uses a question-answer format to explore some of the most common questions students ask about psychology.

Acknowledgments

We are deeply grateful for the assistance we received from the many people who reviewed the previous edition and suggested improvements for this edition. Reviewers of the 5th edition:

Cheryl Bluestone, Queensborough Community College

Dixon A. Bramblett, Lindenwood University

Jack Hartnett, Virginia Commonwealth University

Joseph Lao, Borough of Manhattan Community College

Laura Madson, New Mexico State University

Jennifer P. Peluso, Mercer University

Reviewers of prior editions:

Bobby Hutchinson, Modesto Junior College

Cheryl McFadden, York Technical College

Anita Rosenfield, DeVry Institute of Technology

Denys deCatanzaro, McMaster University

John Jahnke, Miami University

Philip S. Lasiter, Florida Atlantic University

Stephen Mayer, Oberlin College

Ronald Nowaczyk, Clemson University

Wesley Schultz, California State University, San Marcos

Steve Arnold, Northeast Community College

Susan K. Johnson, University of North Carolina, Charlotte

Don McCoy, University of Kentucky

Jerald S. Marshall, University of Central Florida

Michael Ruchs, Baker College

Morgan Slusher, Essex Community College

Harold G. Souheaver, East Arkansas Community College

We would also like to express our deep gratitude to the outstanding team of people at Prentice Hall, all of whom made major contributions. We are immensely grateful to Roberta Meyer, who served as Development Editor. Roberta's good judgment and eye for detail were invaluable to us throughout the revision process. Special thanks go to Wendy Dunn of Coe College, who consulted with us on several chapters and whose suggestions resulted in significant improvements over the last edition. Stephanie Johnson, Project Manager, helped guide the revision, and her Editorial Assistant, Catherine Fox, took care of the many administrative details involved in this project. The Companion Website for this edition was prepared by Lynn Bradman, Metropolitan Community College, with considerable help from Karen Branson, Media Editor. Al Maisto's graduate assistant, Cortney Hedman, provided invaluable help with many research tasks. The production of the Sixth Edition was managed by Fran Russello and directly supervised by Bruce Hobart. Thanks also to manufacturing buyer Tricia Kenny. Leslie Osher, Creative Design Director, and the Art Director, Kathryn Foot, did a super job on the design of both the interior and the cover. Special thanks to Jeff Hester, Marketing Manager, for directing the marketing campaign for this edition. Finally, our sincere thanks to the Prentice Hall sales staff for their enthusiastic support of our text, and for the excellent service they provide to our adopters.

Charles G. Morris

Albert A. Maisto

TO THE STUDENT

How does a nerve cell in the brain order a finger to move? What do genes have to do with intelligence? How do babies learn to talk? What is love? In this book, you will learn about the full range of human behavior, and how psychologists go about trying to answer questions like these. You will also learn about learning itself. Some of what psychologists know about learning can help you master the many topics covered in this text. To help you learn more effectively, we recommend that you follow a system of studying known as the SQ3R method—*Survey, Question, Read, Recite,* and *Review.* The text is embedded with a number of tools that will help you use this effective method of studying.

Survey: Surveying, or previewing, prepares your brain to receive information in an organized way. Properly done, it will help you read faster and comprehend better. Before you begin a chapter, survey the topics it covers by reading the **Overview** on the chapter title page.

Question: Be sure to read the **Questions** that appear after each major section in the chapter. These questions indicate what key ideas you should be looking for as you read that section.

Read: As you read each section, keep the opening question in mind and actively look for answers. The **Key Terms** in the margins provide clear definitions of the most important terms in the text, so study these as you go along rather than waiting until you have finished reading the chapter. **Figures** and **photos** will help you visualize concepts that are described in the text, and **summary tables** will aid in organizing the information.

Recite: After each main section, be sure to take the **Check Your Understanding** quiz. These brief quizzes will help you process the material you just read, to ensure that you understand it fully.

Review: At the end of each chapter is a list of **Key Terms** with page references. Review each term carefully, and refer back to the appropriate page if there are any you can't recall. Next, read through the detailed **Chapter Re-** view, which summarizes all of the key concepts in the chapter. Finally, try to answer the **Critical Thinking and Applications** questions to see if you've gained a true understanding of the material in the chapter.

Online Study Tools at www.prenhall.com/morris

In addition to the many learning aids in this text, you have at your disposal numerous online tools to help you master the concepts in this course. These include:

WEB QUIZ **3.2** ✓

Web Quizzes: As you go through the text, you'll notice numbered "Web Quiz" icons next to each of the "Check Your Understanding" section quizzes in the text. This indicates that these quizzes are also available in interactive versions on the Morris Website. The online quizzes offer instant scoring as well as feedback on any questions you answer incorrectly. In addition to the section quizzes, you'll find a practice "Chapter Exam" on the Website. This Chapter Exam tests you all of the main topics in the chapter, helping you to prepare for the actual exam that your instructor gives.

INTERACTIVE LECTURE **3.2** ➡️

Interactive Lectures: For more visual learners, an Interactive Lecture provides the chapter summary interspersed with additional visual aids.

3.2

Live!Psych: As you read your text, you'll notice *Live!Psych* icons in the margins of most chapters. *Live!Psych* is a series of highly interactive media simulations and animations found on the Morris Website. The modules focus on the concepts that many students find particularly challenging, like the major brain structures and functions, or neurons and neural impulses. *Live!Psych* can help you master these difficult concepts by allowing you to see and experience them in a more interactive format than can be achieved in any textbook.

1

The Science of Psychology

EY RAMOS GRADUATED FROM HARVARD UNIVERSITY, MAGNA CUM LAUDE, AND was accepted by Harvard Medical School—against all odds. Rey grew up in the South Bronx, an urban ghetto where young males are more likely to go to jail than they are to graduate from high school, and where early, violent death is not uncommon. All anyone asked of Rey was that he stay out of trouble and stay alive. As a young boy, he was considered a problem child, out of control. In the eighth grade, Rey's principal told Rey's mother that her son was being expelled and reassigned to a program for students with learning problems.

Rey: "My Mom just started crying, you know, in front of him, and I saw that. And I felt ashamed of myself."

Rey entered the ninth grade determined to turn his life around. His math teacher recognized his change in attitude—and his ability in math.

Math teacher: "When he got here, I knew he wasn't joking around anymore. He knew this was it. This was where it starts new."

Rey: "And I started feeling good about this one teacher who said good things about me, and that made me feel good."

Rey also excelled in science. But the high school he attended, considered one of the worst in New York City and since shut down, offered little. Rey enrolled in a special science program at a local college and graduated first in his class. It was his biology teacher who first suggested to Rey that he might be "Harvard material."

Biology teacher: "I was trying to push him to believe in himself and do something, because I felt he was incredible."

Rey accepted the challenge. In his Harvard application he wrote, "The four years I invest in Harvard will probably be the most important four years of my life. I will waste no time while I attend Harvard University." True to his word, Rey maintained a 3.4 grade point average, enlisted in ROTC, joined a Latino fraternity, and worked part-time. At graduation, he looked back.

Rey: "My father always said you can't change anything; destiny has everything written for you. And I told him no. I rebelled against that, and I told him I was going to make my own destiny, and so far I've never heard him say that line to me again."

Rey planned to marry Maiysha, his childhood sweetheart, that summer; to enter Harvard Medical School in the fall; and to fulfill his lifelong dream of returning to the South Bronx as a doctor.

Rey Ramos's story is the American Dream. Indeed, he was chosen to represent "The American Spirit" on *NBC Nightly News* (June 13, 1997). How did Rey Ramos escape from the "mean streets" to the Ivy League and a future as a physician? What can psychology tell us about his success story? What does it say about intelligence and motivation in general, and about the many factors that shape who we become?

What Is Psychology?

"Most psychologists study mental and emotional problems and work as psychotherapists." Is this statement true or false?

Psychology is the scientific study of behavior and mental processes. Some people might think that psychologists are interested only in problem or abnormal behaviors. In fact, they are interested in every aspect of human thought and behavior. In the late twentieth century, psychology expanded

---

Psychology
The scientific study of behavior and mental processes.

dramatically. New research technologies, new fields of inquiry, and new approaches to studying behavior and mental processes emerged. These advances led to greater specialization within psychology, more collaboration with other sciences—and the academic equivalent of an "identity crisis." As a result, psychology is continually redefining itself (Evans, 1999). Perhaps the best way to introduce psychology is to look at what topics interest psychologists. One way to grasp the breadth and depth of topics in psychology is to look at several major subdivisions of the field (see Table 1-1).

The Fields of Psychology

What are the major areas of study within the field of psychology?

TABLE 1-1   AMERICAN PSYCHOLOGICAL ASSOCIATION DIVISIONS (2001)

The two major organizations of psychologists in the United States are the American Psychological Association (APA), founded over 100 years ago, and the American Psychological Society (APS), founded in 1988. Members of both groups work in a wide variety of areas. The following list of divisions of the APA reflects the enormous diversity of the field of psychology.

Division*

1. Society for General Psychology
2. Society for the Teaching of Psychology
3. Experimental Psychology
5. Evaluation, Measurement, and Statistics
6. Behavioral Neuroscience and Comparative Psychology
7. Developmental Psychology
8. Society for Personality and Social Psychology
9. Society for the Psychological Study of Social Issues (SPSSI)
10. Psychology and the Arts
12. Society of Clinical Psychology
13. Society of Consulting Psychology
14. Society for Industrial and Organizational Psychology
15. Educational Psychology
16. School Psychology
17. Counseling Psychology
18. Psychologists in Public Service
19. Military Psychology
20. Adult Development and Aging
21. Applied Experimental and Engineering Psychology
22. Rehabilitation Psychology
23. Society for Consumer Psychology
24. Theoretical and Philosophical Psychology
25. Behavior Analysis
26. History of Psychology
27. Society for Community Research and Action: Division of Community Psychology
28. Psychopharmacology and Substance Abuse
29. Psychotherapy

30. Society of Psychological Hypnosis
31. State Psychological Association Affairs
32. Humanistic Psychology
33. Mental Retardation and Developmental Disabilities
34. Population and Environmental Psychology
35. Society for the Psychology of Women
36. Psychology of Religion
37. Child, Youth, and Family Services
38. Health Psychology
39. Psychoanalysis
40. Clinical Neuropsychology
41. American Psychology—Law Society
42. Psychologists in Independent Practice
43. Family Psychology
44. Society for the Psychological Study of Lesbian, Gay, and Bisexual Issues
45. Society for the Psychological Study of Ethnic Minority Issues
46. Media Psychology
47. Exercise and Sport Psychology
48. Society for the Study of Peace, Conflict, and Violence: Peace Psychology Division
49. Group Psychology and Group Psychotherapy
50. Addictions
51. Society for the Psychological Study of Men and Masculinity
52. International Psychology
53. Society of Clinical Child and Adolescent Psychology
54. Society of Pediatric Psychology
55. American Society for the Advancement of Pharmacotherapy

*There are no divisions 4 or 11.

For information on a division, e-mail the APA at division@apa.org, or locate them on the internet at http://www.apa.org/about/division.html.

Source: American Psychological Association Divisions (2002). Copyright © 2002 by the American Psychological Association. Reprinted by permission.

Child psychologists study many facets of childhood behavior including play, relating to other children, and creativity.

Developmental Psychology Developmental psychologists study human mental and physical growth from the prenatal period through childhood, adolescence, adulthood, and old age. *Child psychologists* focus on infants and children. They are concerned with such issues as whether babies are born with distinct personalities and temperaments, how infants become attached to their parents and caretakers, what the age is at which sex differences in behavior emerge, and what changes there are in the meaning and importance of friendship during childhood. *Adolescent psychologists*, who specialize in the teenage years, are concerned with how puberty, changes in relationships with peers and parents, and the search for identity can make this a difficult period for some young people. *Life-span psychologists*, who focus on the adult years, are concerned with the different ways that individuals adjust to partnership and parenting, middle age, retirement, and eventually death.

Developmental psychologists would see Rey Ramos's change of direction in the eighth grade in part as a reflection of his level of cognitive and emotional development. At earlier ages, the same experience would not have had the same impact. At age 3, he probably would have been frightened by his mother's bursting into tears. If he had been assigned to a slow-learner class at age 8, he might have known that he'd been "bad," but he would not have understood how or why. By age 12, his ability to analyze the connection between actions and consequences was much sharper. As a young adult now, Rey seems to have a strong sense of identity and purpose; he is ready to make a commitment to his girlfriend. But development does not suddenly stop at this point. Many chapters of his life story—establishing himself in his profession, experiencing parenthood, evaluating what he has made of his life in middle age, and facing the challenges of old age—have not yet been written.

Physiological Psychology Physiological psychologists investigate the biological basis of human behavior, thoughts, and emotions. *Neuropsychologists* are primarily interested in the brain and the nervous system. Why can't you taste food when you have a stuffy nose? What happens when a person has a stroke? *Psychobiologists* specialize in the body's biochemistry and in the way that hormones, psychoactive medications (such as antidepressants), and "social drugs" (such as alcohol, marijuana, and cocaine) affect people. Do changes in hormone levels—at puberty, before menstruation, at menopause—cause mood swings? Exactly how does alcohol act on the

Recent advances in neuroimaging techniques enable physiological psychologists to investigate how specific regions of the brain are involved in complex behaviors and mental processes.

brain? *Behavioral geneticists* investigate the impact of heredity on both normal and abnormal traits and behavior. To what degree is intelligence hereditary? What about shyness? Do illnesses such as alcoholism and depression run in families? To what extent are differences in the way men and women think, act, and respond to situations rooted in biology?

Some of the most exciting work in contemporary psychobiology concerns the effect of stress on health. We know that Rey Ramos grew up in a dangerous neighborhood; we can imagine that he faced many frustrations in his struggle to change directions as a teenager and that he had to adjust to an almost totally new environment at Harvard—all sources of stress. Will this stress eventually take a toll on his health? Research shows that some racial and ethnic groups are more vulnerable to certain conditions than others. For example, African Americans are at high risk for hypertension (high blood pressure). Is this tendency because of a genetic weakness (as is sickle-cell anemia, also more prevalent among African Americans)? because African Americans are more likely than other groups in the United States to be poor and live in unsafe neighborhoods like Rey's? or because even middle-class African-American professionals are viewed with suspicion and have direct experience of prejudice—ranging from small insults to police brutality—and so may live in a state of constant vigilance?

Experimental Psychology   Experimental psychologists conduct research on basic psychological processes, including learning, memory, sensation, perception, cognition, motivation, and emotion. They are interested in answering such questions as these: "How do people remember, and what makes them forget?" "How do people make decisions and solve problems?" "Do men and women go about solving complex problems in different ways?" "Why are some people more motivated than others?"

Rey Ramos apparently has a "flair for numbers," and he clearly excels at science. Experimental psychologists might be interested in discovering exactly how his style of thinking differs from that of other people. Does he process mathematical and scientific information in an unusual way? Does he perhaps have an unusually good memory for such information, and if so, how does his memory differ from yours and mine? During childhood and adolescence, Rey probably was given a number of aptitude, achievement, and intelligence tests. Do such tests actually measure important cognitive skills such as the ability to make decisions and solve problems, or are they more a measure of cultural knowledge? And finally, what motivates Rey to achieve and excel?

Personality Psychology   Personality psychologists study the differences among individuals in such traits as anxiety, sociability, self-esteem, need for achievement, and aggressiveness. Psychologists in this field attempt to determine what causes some people to be optimists and others to be pessimists, and why some people are outgoing and sociable whereas others are more reserved. They also study whether there are consistent differences between men and women in such characteristics as friendliness, anxiety, and conscientiousness.

From our brief introduction to Rey Ramos, we can infer that he is sociable: At Harvard, he made friends and deepened his relationship with his fiancée, Maiysha. He appears to have a strong need to achieve and a healthy level of self-esteem. Where did these characteristics come from? His early childhood experiences? The realization, in the ninth grade, that he could take control of "his destiny"? Is he as competitive in sports as he is in academics? as self-confident in an art gallery as he is in a laboratory? If he realizes his dream by returning to the Bronx with his M.D. and spends years trying to deal with the desperate needs of his patients, on the one hand,

and the lack of adequate funding and up-to-date facilities, on the other, will he remain an optimist? A major issue for personality psychologists is whether a given characteristic is a stable personality trait or simply a response to the social situation.

Clinical and Counseling Psychology   When asked to describe a "psychologist," most people think of a therapist who sees patients (or "clients") in his or her office, a clinic, or a hospital. This popular view is half-correct. About half of all psychologists specialize in clinical or counseling psychology. *Clinical psychologists* are interested primarily in the diagnosis, cause, and treatment of psychological disorders. *Counseling psychologists* are concerned primarily with "normal" problems of adjustment that most of us face at some point, such as choosing a career or coping with marital problems. Clinical and counseling psychologists often divide their time between treating patients and conducting research on the causes of psychological disorders and the effectiveness of different types of psychotherapy and counseling.

Social Psychology   Social psychologists study how people influence one another. They explore such issues as first impressions and interpersonal attraction; the way that attitudes are formed, maintained, or changed; prejudice; conformity; and whether people behave differently when they are part of a group or crowd than they would on their own.

As a teenager living in a tough, urban neighborhood, Rey Ramos no doubt experienced considerable peer pressure to become a member of a gang. Gangs seem to be an institution in poor neighborhoods. Why? Many of Rey's contemporaries probably gave in to this pressure; however, Rey didn't. Again, why not? As a Latino at one of America's most prestigious universities, Rey probably encountered prejudice. Classmates may have assumed that because he was a member of a minority group, he was admitted to Harvard as part of an affirmative action program, not because of his academic achievements. The Latino fraternity Rey joined probably helped him to maintain ethnic pride in the face of such prejudice. Do ethnically based social organizations promote mutual tolerance, or do they contribute to maintaining social distance?

Industrial and Organizational (I/O) Psychology   Industrial and organizational (I/O) psychologists are concerned with such practical issues as selecting and training personnel, improving productivity and working conditions, and the impact of computerization and automation on workers. Is it possible to determine in advance who will be an effective salesperson or airline pilot, and who will not? Do organizations tend to operate differently under female as opposed to male leadership? Research shows that work groups with high morale usually are more productive than those with low morale: Are there specific strategies that managers can use to improve group morale?

In medical school, Rey Ramos will spend much of his time in hospitals, on rotations, as an intern and, finally, as a resident. Hospitals and other large organizations frequently hire I/O psychologists as consultants to advise them on ways to increase efficiency, humanize a sterile environment, boost the morale of patients as well as of the staff, and so on.

Enduring Issues

Given this broad range of careers and interests, what holds psychology together?

What do psychologists who study organizations, psychological disorders, memory and cognition, behavioral genetics, or attachment in infants have in common? All psychologists share a common interest in five enduring

"Your father's a suit, and when you grow up you'll be just a suit, too."

issues that override their areas of specialization and that cut to the core of what it means to be human.

Person–Situation   To what extent is behavior caused by processes that occur inside the person (such as thoughts, emotions, motives, attitudes, values, personality, and genes)? In contrast, to what extent is behavior caused or triggered by factors outside the person (such as incentives, cues in the environment, and the presence of other people)? Put another way, are we masters of our fate or victims of circumstances? We will encounter these questions most directly in our consideration of behavior genetics, learning, emotion and motivation, personality, and social psychology.

Nature–Nurture   Is the person we become a product of innate, inborn tendencies, or a reflection of experiences and upbringing? This is the famous "nature versus nurture" debate. For decades, psychologists argued about the degree of influence that heredity or genes versus environment or experience have on thought and behavior. This issue appears in our discussions of behavior genetics, intelligence, development, personality, and abnormal psychology, though it will arise elsewhere as well.

Stability–Change   Are the characteristics we develop in childhood more or less permanent and fixed, or do we change in predictable (and unpredictable) ways over the course of our lives? Is the self a cognitive construct, a "fictional character" we create to maintain a sense of inner continuity in the face of varied, sometimes unpredictable experiences? Developmental psychologists are especially interested in these questions, as are psychologists who specialize in personality, adjustment, abnormal psychology, and therapy, as well as other areas.

Diversity–Universality   To what extent is every person in certain respects (a) like all other people, (b) like some other people, or (c) like no other person? (Adapted from Kluckhohn, Murray, & Schneider, 1961, p. 53.) Human diversity is a central concern for psychologists. Throughout the book we will encounter these questions: Does our understanding apply equally well to every human being? Or does it apply only to men or women, or only to particular racial or ethnic groups or particular societies

To understand human behavior, we must appreciate the rich diversity of culture throughout the world.

(especially our own)? Do we perhaps need "different psychologies" to account for the wide diversity of human behaviors?

Mind–Body   Finally, how are mind and body connected? Many psychologists are fascinated by the relationship between what we experience (such as thoughts and feelings) and what our biological processes are (such as activity in the nervous system). This mind–body issue will arise most clearly in our discussions of the biological basis of behavior, sensation and perception, altered states of consciousness, emotion and motivation, adjustment/health psychology, and disorders/therapy.

These five issues have been a running theme in the history of psychology. Depending on the times and the intellectual climate, one or another of these issues has assumed special prominence in the history of psychology. Depending on what subject they are studying, psychologists in one area or one school may emphasize the person or the situation, heredity or environment, stability or change, diversity or universality, or subjective experience or biological processes. Philosophers have pondered these issues for centuries; in contrast, psychologists look at these topics through a scientific lens.

Psychology as Science

What does psychology have in common with other sciences?

Earlier we defined psychology as the science of behavior and mental processes. The key word in this definition is *science*. Psychologists rely on the **scientific method** when seeking to answer questions. They collect data through careful, systematic observation; attempt to explain what they have observed by developing theories; make new predictions based on those theories; and then systematically test those predictions through additional observations and experiments to determine whether they are correct. Thus, like all scientists, psychologists use the scientific method to describe, understand, predict, and eventually, achieve some measure of control over what they study. (You can apply the principles of scientific thinking in your own life. See *Understanding Ourselves*.)

Take, for example, the issue of males, females, and aggression. Many people believe that males are naturally more aggressive than females. Others contend that boys learn to be aggressive because our society and culture encourages—indeed requires—males to be combative, even violent. How

Scientific method
An approach to knowledge that relies on collecting data, generating a theory to explain the data, producing testable hypotheses based on the theory, and testing those hypotheses empirically.

Males seem to be more physically aggressive than females. Different schools of psychology have different explanations for why this is the case.

would psychologists approach this issue? First, they would want to find out whether men and women actually differ in aggressive behavior. A number of research studies have addressed this question, and the evidence seems conclusive: Males are more aggressive than females, particularly when we're talking about physical aggression (Knight, Fabes, & Higgins, 1996; Wright, 1994). Perhaps girls and women make nasty remarks or yell, but boys and men are far more likely to fight. Now that we have established that there are sex differences in physical aggression and described those differences, the next step is to explain them. A number of explanations are possible. Physiological psychologists would probably ascribe these differences to genetics or body chemistry; developmental psychologists might look to the ways a child is taught to behave "like a boy" or "like a girl"; and social psychologists might explain the differences in terms of cultural norms, which require males to "stand up for themselves" and hold that physical aggression isn't "feminine."

Each of these explanations stands as a **theory** about the causes of sex differences in aggression; each attempts to distill a few principles from a large number of facts. And each theory allows us to make a number of new **hypotheses,** or predictions, about the phenomenon in question. If gender differences in aggression arise because males have higher levels of testosterone than females do, then we would predict that extremely violent men should have higher levels of testosterone than do men who are generally nonviolent. If sex differences in aggression stem from early training, then we would predict that there should be fewer sex differences in aggression in families where parents did not stress gender differences. Finally, if sex differences in aggression reflect cultural norms, then we would predict that in societies that do not prohibit girls and women from fighting, or those that consider physical aggression abnormal or improper for both sexes, the differences should be small.

Each of these predictions or hypotheses can be tested through research, and the results should indicate whether one theory is better than another at accounting for known facts and predicting new facts. If one or more of the theories is supported by research evidence, it should be possible to control aggressive behavior to a greater degree than was possible before.

Theory
Systematic explanation of a phenomenon; it organizes known facts, allows us to predict new facts, and permits us to exercise a degree of control over the phenomenon.

Hypotheses
Specific, testable predictions derived from a theory.

UNDERSTANDING OURSELVES

Critical Thinking: A Fringe Benefit of Studying Psychology

- Gifted children are less well adjusted than other children.
- Opposites attract.
- Subliminal messages on self-help audiotapes have beneficial effects.

Do you agree with these statements? Many people answer yes without a moment's hesitation on the grounds that "Everybody knows that." Critical thinkers, however, question common knowledge.

What exactly is critical thinking? It is the process of examining the information we have and then, based on this inquiry, making judgments and decisions. When we think critically, we define problems, examine evidence, analyze assumptions, consider alternatives, and ultimately find reasons to support or reject an argument. To think critically, you must adopt a certain state of mind, one characterized by objectivity, caution, a willingness to challenge other people's opinions, and—perhaps most difficult of all—a willingness to subject your deepest beliefs to scrutiny. In other words, you must think like a scientist.

Psychologists use a number of strategies in questioning assumptions and examining data. Here, we use the rules of psychological investigation to judge whether the second statement earlier, "Opposites attract," is correct.

- *Define the problem or the question you are investigating.* Do opposites attract each other?
- *Suggest a theory or a reasonable explanation for the problem.* People who are dissimilar balance each other out in a relationship.
- *Collect and examine all the available evidence.* In doing so, be skeptical of people's self-reports, as they may be subjectively biased. If data conflict, try to find more evidence. Research on attraction yields no support for the idea that opposites attract, whereas many studies confirm that people of similar looks, interests, age, family background, religion, values, and attitudes seek each other out.
- *Analyze assumptions.* Because balancing different people's strengths and weaknesses is a good way to form a group, it is probably a good basis for personal relationships as well, and that is why people of opposite temperaments are naturally attracted to each other. Yet research evidence shows that this assumption is false. Why should similars attract? One important reason is that they often belong to the same social circles. Research suggests proximity is a big factor in attraction.
- *Avoid oversimplifying.* Don't overlook the evidence that people of similar temperaments find living together rather difficult in some ways. For example, living with someone who is as tense as you are may be harder than living with someone of calm temperament—your opposite.
- *Draw conclusions carefully.* It seems safe to conclude that, in general, opposites don't attract, but there are specific exceptions to this general rule.
- *Consider every alternative interpretation.* People may cite cases that conflict with your conclusion. Remember, however, that their arguments are based on subjective observations and a far narrower database than attraction researchers have used.
- *Recognize the relevance of research to events and situations.* If you have been thinking of dating someone whose temperament seems quite different from yours, you may decide, on the basis of what you now know, not to rush into things but to go more slowly, testing your own observations against your knowledge of research findings.

By the way, psychological research has demonstrated that the other two statements are also false.

For example, if cultural norms are part of the reason for differences in aggression, then these differences should be smaller in situations in which individuals do not feel that they are being evaluated in terms of their masculinity or femininity. One research team tested this hypothesis with a computer war game (Lightdale & Prentice, 1994). When the researcher introduced participants in a way that made clear who was male or female, women played less aggressively than men; when women were told that they were anonymous to the researchers and other participants, however, women played just as aggressively as men did.

INTERACTIVE LECTURE **1.1**

WEB QUIZ **1.1**

CHECK YOUR UNDERSTANDING

1. Match each of the following major themes in psychology with its appropriate description.

____ personal–social

____ heredity–environment

____ stability–change

____ diversity–universality

____ mind–body

a. How much do we stay the same as we develop, and how much do we change?

b. In what ways do people differ in how they think and act?

c. What is the relationship between our internal experiences and our biological processes?

d. Is behavior caused more by inner traits or by external situations?

e. How do genes and experiences interact to influence people?

2. Indicate whether the following statements are true (T) or false (F).

____ a. Psychologists collect data through careful, systematic observation.

____ b. Psychologists try to explain their observations by developing theories.

____ c. Psychologists form hypotheses or predictions on the basis of theories.

____ d. Psychologists appeal to common sense in their arguments.

____ e. Psychologists systematically test hypotheses.

____ f. Psychologists base their conclusions on widely shared values.

Answers: 1. Personal–social (d); heredity–environment (e); stability–change (a); diversity–universality (b); mind–body (c). 2. a (T); b (T); c (T); d (F); e (T); f (F).

The Growth of Psychology

"Psychology has a long past, but a short history." What does that mean?

In the West, since the time of Plato and Aristotle, people have wondered and written about human behavior and mental processes. But not until the late 1800s did they begin to apply the scientific method to questions that had puzzled philosophers for centuries. Only then did psychology come into being as a formal, scientific discipline separate from philosophy. The history of psychology can be divided into three main stages: the emergence of a science of the mind, the behaviorist decades, and the "cognitive revolution."

The "New Psychology": A Science of the Mind

How did Wundt help to define psychology as a science of the mind? Why did James think that sensation and perception alone couldn't explain behavior? Why was Freud's theory of the unconscious shocking at the turn of the twentieth century?

At the beginning of the twentieth century, most psychology programs were located in philosophy departments. But the foundations of the "new psychology"—the science of psychology—had been laid.

Wilhelm Wundt and Edward Bradford Titchener: Structuralism By general agreement, psychology was born in 1879, the year that Wilhelm Wundt founded the first psychological laboratory at the University of Leipzig in Germany. In the public eye, a laboratory identified a field of inquiry as "science" (Benjamin, 2000). At the outset, Wundt did not attract much attention; only four students attended his first lecture. By the mid-1890s, however, his classes were filled to capacity.

Wilhelm Wundt

Wundt set about trying to explain immediate experience and to develop ways to study it scientifically, though he also believed that some mental processes could not be studied through scientific experiments (Blumenthal, 1975). Wundt was primarily interested in selective attention—the process by which we determine what we are going to attend to at any given moment. For Wundt, attention is actively controlled by intentions and motives. In turn, attention controls other psychological processes, such as perceptions, thoughts, and memories. We will examine the role of attention more closely in Chapter 4 (States of Consciousness) and Chapter 6 (Memory), but for the moment it is sufficient to note that in establishing a laboratory and insisting on measurement and experimentation, Wundt moved psychology out of the realm of philosophy into the world of science (Benjamin, 2000).

One important product of the Leipzig lab was its students, who carried new, scientific psychology to universities in other countries, including the United States. G. Stanley Hall, who established the first American psychology laboratory at Johns Hopkins University in 1883, studied with Wundt; so did J. M. Cattell, the first American to be called a "professor of psychology" (at the University of Pennsylvania in 1888). Yet another student, British-born Edward Bradford Titchener, went to Cornell University. Titchener's ideas in many respects differed sharply from those of his mentor. Titchener was impressed by recent advances in chemistry and physics, achieved by analyzing complex compounds (molecules) in terms of their basic elements (atoms). Similarly, Titchener reasoned, psychologists should analyze complex experiences in terms of their simplest components. For example, when people look at a banana they immediately think, "Here is a fruit, something to peel and eat." But this perception is based on associations with past experience; what are the most fundamental elements, or "atoms," of thought?

Titchener broke down consciousness into three basic elements: physical sensations (what we see), feelings (such as liking or disliking bananas), and images (memories of other bananas). Even the most complex thoughts and feelings, he argued, can be reduced to these simple elements. Titchener saw psychology's role as identifying these elements and showing how they can be combined and integrated — an approach known as **structuralism.** Although the structuralist school of psychology was relatively short-lived and has had little long-term effect, the study of perception and sensation continues to be very much a part of contemporary psychology (see Chapter 3, Sensation and Perception).

Structuralism
School of psychology that stresses the basic units of experience and the combinations in which they occur.

William James: Functionalism One of the first academics to challenge structuralism was an American, William James (son of the transcendentalist philosopher Henry James, Sr., and brother of novelist Henry James). As a young man, James earned a degree in physiology and also studied philosophy on his own, unable to decide which interested him more. In psychology he found the link between the two. In 1875, James offered a class in psychology at Harvard. He later commented that the first lecture he ever heard on the subject was his own.

James argued that Titchener's "atoms of experience"—pure sensations without associations—simply do not exist in real-life experience. Our minds are constantly weaving associations, revising experience, starting, stopping, and jumping back and forth in time. Perceptions, emotions, and images cannot be separated, James argued; consciousness flows in a continuous stream. If we could not recognize a banana, we would have to figure out what it was each time we saw one. Mental associations allow us to benefit from previous experience. When we get up in the morning, get dressed, open the door, and walk down the street, we don't have to think about

William James

Sigmund Freud

what we are doing; we act out of habit. James suggested that when we repeat something, our nervous systems are changed so that each repetition is easier than the last.

James developed a **functionalist theory** of mental processes and behavior that raised questions about learning, the complexities of mental life, the impact of experience on the brain, and humankind's place in the natural world that still seem current today. Although impatient with experiments, James shared Wundt and Tichener's belief that the goal of psychology was to analyze experience. Wundt was not impressed. After reading James's *The Principles of Psychology* (1890), he commented, "It is literature, it is beautiful, but it is not psychology" (in Hunt, 1994, p. 139).

Sigmund Freud: Psychodynamic Psychology   Of all psychology's pioneers, Sigmund Freud is by far the best known—and the most controversial. A medical doctor, unlike the other figures we have introduced, Freud was fascinated by the central nervous system. He spent many years conducting research in the physiology laboratory of the University of Vienna and only reluctantly became a practicing physician. After a trip to Paris, where he studied with a neurologist who was using hypnosis to treat nervous disorders, Freud established a private practice in Vienna. His work with patients convinced him that many nervous ailments are psychological rather than physiological in origin. Freud's clinical observations led him to develop a comprehensive theory of mental life that differed radically from the views of his predecessors.

Freud held that human beings are not as rational as they imagine and that "free will," which was so important to Wundt, is largely an illusion. Rather, we are motivated by unconscious instincts and urges that are not available to the rational, conscious part of our mind. Other psychologists had referred to the unconscious in passing, as a dusty warehouse of old experiences and information we could retrieve as needed. In contrast, Freud saw the unconscious as a dynamic cauldron of primitive sexual and aggressive drives, forbidden desires, nameless fears and wishes, and traumatic childhood memories. Although repressed (or hidden from awareness), unconscious impulses press on the conscious mind and find expression in disguised or altered form, including dreams, mannerisms, slips of the tongue, and symptoms of mental illness, as well as in socially acceptable pursuits such as art and literature. To uncover the unconscious, Freud developed the technique of *free association*, in which the patient lies on a couch, recounts dreams, and says whatever comes to mind.

Freud's psychodynamic theory was as controversial at the turn of the century as Darwin's theory of evolution had been twenty-five years earlier. His Victorian contemporaries were shocked, not only by his emphasis on sexuality but also by his suggestion that we are often unaware of our true motives and thus are not entirely in control of our thoughts and behavior. Despite (or perhaps because of) his notoriety, Freud's lectures and writings attracted considerable attention in the United States as well as in Europe; he had a profound impact on the arts and philosophy, as well as on psychology. However, Freud's theories and methods continue to inspire heated debate.

Psychodynamic theory, as expanded and revised by Freud's colleagues and successors, laid the foundation for the study of personality and psychological disorders, as we will discuss later in this book (Chapters 10, 12, and 13). His revolutionary notion of the unconscious and his portrayal of human beings as constantly at war with themselves are taken for granted today, at least in literary and artistic circles. Freud's theories were never totally accepted by mainstream psychology, however, and in recent decades his influence on clinical psychology and psychotherapy has declined (Robins, Gosling, & Craik, 1999; see also Westen, 1998).

Functionalism
Theory of mental life and behavior that is concerned with how an organism uses its perceptual abilities to function in its environment.

Psychodynamic theories
Personality theories contending that behavior results from psychological factors that interact within the individual, often outside conscious awareness.

Redefining Psychology: The Study of Behavior

How was Watson's approach to human behavior different from Freud's? How did Skinner expand behaviorism?

Until the beginning of the twentieth century, psychology saw itself as the study of mental processes, conscious or unconscious (psychodynamic psychology), viewed as discrete units and compounds (structuralism) or as an ever-changing flow (functionalism). The primary method of collecting data was introspection or self-observation, in a laboratory or on an analyst's couch. At the beginning of the twentieth century, however, a new generation of psychologists rebelled against this "soft" approach. The leader of the challenge was the American psychologist John B. Watson.

John B. Watson: Behaviorism   John B. Watson argued that the whole idea of mental life was superstition, a relic left over from the Middle Ages. In "Psychology as a Behaviorist Views It" (1913), Watson contended that you cannot see or even define consciousness any more than you can observe a soul. And if you cannot locate or measure something, it cannot be the object of scientific study. For Watson, psychology was the study of observable, measurable behavior—and nothing more.

John B. Watson

Watson's view of psychology, known as **behaviorism,** was based on the work of the Russian physiologist Ivan Pavlov, who had won a Nobel Prize for his research on digestion. In the course of his experiments, Pavlov noticed that the dogs in his laboratory began to salivate as soon as they heard their feeder coming, even before they could see their dinner. He decided to find out whether salivation, an automatic reflex, could be shaped by learning. He began by repeatedly pairing the sound of a buzzer with the presence of food. The next step was to observe what happened when the buzzer was sounded without introducing food. This experiment clearly demonstrated what Pavlov had noticed incidentally: after repeated pairings, the dogs salivated in response to the buzzer alone. Pavlov called this simple form of training *conditioning*. Thus a new school of psychology was inspired by a casual observation—followed by rigorous experiments.

Watson came to believe that all mental experiences—thinking, feeling, awareness of self—are nothing more than physiological changes in response to accumulated experiences of conditioning. An infant, he argued, is a *tabula rasa* (Latin for "blank slate") on which experience may write virtually anything:

> Give me a dozen healthy infants, well-formed, and my own specialized world to bring them up in, and I'll guarantee to take any one at random and train him to become any type of specialist I might select—doctor, lawyer, artist, merchant chief and, yes, even beggar man, and thief, regardless of his talents, penchants, tendencies, abilities, vocations, and race. (Watson, 1924, p. 104)

Watson attempted to demonstrate that all psychological phenomena—even Freud's unconscious motivations—are the result of conditioning (Rilling, 2000). In one of the most infamous experiments in psychology's history, Watson attempted to create a conditioned fear response in an 11-month-old boy. "Little Albert" was a secure, happy baby who enjoyed new places and experiences. On his first visit to Watson's laboratory, Albert was delighted by a tame, furry white rat, but he became visibly frightened when Watson banged a steel bar with a hammer just behind the infant's head. On his second visit, Watson placed the rat near Albert, and the moment the baby reached out and touched the rat, Watson banged the hammer. After half a dozen pairings, little Albert began crying the instant the rat was introduced,

Behaviorism
School of psychology that studies only observable and measurable behavior.

Mary Cover Jones

without any banging. Further experiments found that Alfred was frightened by anything white and furry—a rabbit, a dog, a scalskin coat, cotton wool, and Watson wearing a Santa Claus mask (Watson & Rayner, 1920). Freud labeled the transfer of emotions from one person or object to another "displacement," a neurotic response that he traced to the unconscious. Drawing on Pavlov, Watson called the same phenomenon "generalization," a simple matter of conditioning (Rilling, 2000). As far as Watson was concerned, psychodynamic theory and psychoanalysis were "voodooism."

Watson was also interested in showing that fears could be eliminated by conditioning. Mary Cover Jones (1924), one of his graduate students, successfully reconditioned a boy who showed a fear of rabbits (not caused by laboratory conditioning) to overcome this fear. Her technique, which involved presenting the rabbit at a great distance and then gradually bringing it closer while the child was eating, is similar to conditioning techniques used by psychologists today.

B. F. Skinner: Behaviorism Revisited   B. F. Skinner became one of the leaders of the behaviorist school of psychology. Like Watson, Skinner fervently believed that psychologists should study only observable and measurable behavior (Skinner, 1938, 1987, 1989, 1990). He, too, was primarily interested in changing behavior through conditioning—and in discovering natural laws of behavior in the process. But Skinner added a new element to the behaviorist repertoire: reinforcement. He rewarded his subjects for behaving the way he wanted them to behave. For example, an animal (rats and pigeons were Skinner's favorite subjects) was put into a special cage and allowed to explore it. Eventually, the animal reached up and pressed a lever or pecked at a disk on the wall, whereupon a food pellet dropped into the box. Gradually, the animal learned that pressing the bar or pecking at the disk always brought food. Why did the animal learn this? Because it was reinforced, or rewarded, for doing so. Skinner thus made the animal an active agent in its own conditioning. Behaviorism dominated academic psychology in the United States well into the 1960s.

The Cognitive Revolution

How did Gestalt psychologists influence the way we think about perception? How might existential psychology help us to feel less alienated? What aspects of life do humanistic psychologists stress?

In the 1960s, behaviorism began to loosen its grip on the field. On the one hand, research on perception, personality, child development, interpersonal relations, and other topics that behaviorists had ignored raised questions they couldn't readily explain. On the other hand, research in other fields (especially anthropology, linguistics, neurobiology, and computer science) was beginning to shed new light on the workings of the mind. Psychologists came to view behaviorism not as an all-encompassing theory or paradigm but as only one piece of the puzzle (Robins et al., 1999). They began to look into the black box and put more emphasis on humans (and other animals) as "sentient"—conscious, perceptive, and alert—beings, that is, as active learners, not passive recipients of life's lessons.

The Precursors: Gestalt and Humanistic Psychology   Not all psychologists had accepted behaviorist doctrines. Two schools that paved the way for the cognitive revolution were Gestalt psychology and humanistic psychology.

During the period that behaviorism dominated American psychology, a group of psychologists in Germany was attacking structuralism from another direction. Max Wertheimer, Wolfgang Köhler, and Kurt Koffka were all interested in perception, but particularly in certain tricks that the mind

B. F. Skinner

plays on itself. For example, when we see a series of still pictures flashed at a constant rate (for example, movies or "moving" neon signs), why do the pictures seem to move?

Phenomena like these launched a new school of thought, **Gestalt psychology.** Roughly translated from German, *Gestalt* means "whole" or "form." When applied to perception, it refers to our tendency to see patterns, to distinguish an object from its background, to complete a picture from a few cues. Like William James, the Gestalt psychologists rejected the structuralists' attempt to break down perception and thought into their elements. When we look at a tree, we see just that, a tree, not a series of isolated leaves and branches. Gestalt psychology paved the way for the modern study of perception (see Chapter 3).

During the same period, the American psychologist Abraham Maslow, who studied under Gestalt psychologist Max Wertheimer and anthropologist Ruth Benedict, developed a more holistic approach to psychology, in which feelings and yearnings play a key role. Maslow referred to **humanistic psychology** as the "third force"—beyond Freudian theory and behaviorism. Humanistic psychologists emphasize human potential and the importance of love, belonging, self-esteem and self-expression, peak experiences (when one becomes so involved in an activity that self-consciousness fades), and self-actualization (the spontaneity and creativity that result from focusing on problems outside oneself and looking beyond the boundaries of social conventions). They focus on mental health and well-being, on self-understanding and self-improvement, rather than on mental illness.

Existential psychology has made important contributions to the study of motivation and emotions (see Chapter 8), as well as to the subfields of personality and psychotherapy (Chapters 10 and 13). But it has never been totally accepted by mainstream psychology. Because humanistic psychology is interested in questions of meaning, values, and ethics, many people—including its own members—see this school of psychology more as a cultural and spiritual movement than as a branch of science (Rabasca, 2000). In recent years, however, positive psychologists (introduced later) have begun to reinvestigate some of the questions that humanistic psychologists raised a half century ago.

The Rise of Cognitive Psychology   In the 1960s, psychology began to come full circle. The field returned from a period in which consciousness was considered to be inaccessible to scientific inquiry and began to investigate and theorize about the mind—but now with new research methods and behaviorism's commitment to objective, empirical research. Even the definition of psychology changed. Psychology is still the study of human "behavior," but psychologists' concept of "behavior" has been expanded to include thoughts, feelings, and states of consciousness.

The phrase *cognitive revolution* refers to a general shift away from a limited focus on behavior toward a broad interest in mental processes. This new focus holds for both existing and new subfields of psychology. In developmental psychology, for example, the idea that a child is a blank slate, whose development is shaped entirely by his or her environment, was replaced by a new view of babies and children as aware, competent, social beings. In this new view, children actively seek to learn about and make sense of their world. Moreover, all healthy children are "equipped" with such distinctively human characteristics as the ability to acquire language, without formal education, through exposure. Developmental psychology is only one subfield that both contributed to and benefited from the emergence of cognitive psychology.

Cognitive psychology is the study of our mental processes in the broadest sense: thinking, feeling, learning, remembering, making decisions and judgments, and so on. If the behaviorist model of learning resembled an

Gestalt psychology
School of psychology that studies how people perceive and experience objects as whole patterns.

Humanistic psychology
School of psychology that emphasizes nonverbal experience and altered states of consciousness as a means of realizing one's full human potential.

Existential psychology
School of psychology that focuses on the meaninglessness and alienation of modern life, and how these factors lead to apathy and psychological problems.

Cognitive psychology
School of psychology devoted to the study of mental processes in the broadest sense.

old-fashioned telephone switchboard (a call or a stimulus comes in, is relayed along various circuits in the brain, and an answer or a response goes out), the cognitive model resembles a high-powered, modern computer. Cognitive psychologists are interested in the ways in which people "process information"—that is, how we acquire information, process or transform bits of information into programs, and use those programs to solve problems.

In contrast to behaviorists, cognitive psychologists believe that mental processes can and should be studied scientifically. Although we cannot observe memories or thoughts directly, we can observe behavior and make inferences about the kinds of cognitive processes that underlie that behavior. For example, we can read a lengthy story to people and then observe the kinds of things that they remember from that story, the ways in which their recollections change over time, and the sorts of errors in recall that they are prone to make. On the basis of systematic research of this kind, we can gain insight into the cognitive processes underlying human memory. Moreover, with the advent of new brain-imaging techniques (which we will discuss in Chapter 2), cognitive psychologists have begun to address questions about the neurological mechanisms that underlie such cognitive processes as learning, memory, intelligence, and emotion, giving rise to the rapidly expanding field of *cognitive neuroscience* (D'Esposito, Zarahn, & Aguirre, 1999; Schacter, 1999.)

In just a short time, cognitive psychology has had an enormous impact on almost every area of psychology (Sperry, 1988, 1995) and has become the most prominent school in contemporary scientific psychology (Johnson & Erneling, 1997; Robins et al., 1999).

New Directions

Where do evolutionary psychologists look for the roots of human behavior? What new focus is positive psychology bringing to the study of human behavior? Is there a single perspective dominating psychology today?

During much of the twentieth century, psychology was divided into competing theoretical schools. Crossing theoretical lines was considered intellectual heresy. Today, however, psychologists are more flexible in considering the merits of new approaches, combining elements of different perspectives as their interests or research findings dictate. As a result, new theories and initiatives are emerging.

Evolutionary Psychology   As the name indicates, **evolutionary psychology** focuses on the evolutionary origins of behavior patterns and mental processes, exploring what adaptive value they have or had and what functions they serve or served in our emergence as a distinct species (DeKay & Buss, 1992; Wright, 1994). All of the theoretical views we have discussed so far seek to explain modern humans, or *Homo sapiens*. In contrast, evolutionary psychologists ask, how did human beings get to be the way we are? They study such diverse topics as perception, language, helping others (altruism), parenting, happiness, sexual attraction and mate selection, jealousy, and violence (Buss, 2000; Buss & Schackelford, 1997). By studying such phenomena in different species, different habitats, different cultures, and in males and females, evolutionary psychologists seek to understand the basic programs that guide thinking and behavior (Archer, 1996; Buss & Malamuth, 1996; DeKay & Buss, 1992; Scarr, 1993).

Cognitive psychologists tend to see the human mind as a "general purpose" computer that requires software (experience) to process information. In contrast, many evolutionary psychologists see the mind as "hardwired," so that human beings are predisposed to think and act in certain ways (Cos-

Evolutionary psychology
An approach to, and subfield of, psychology that is concerned with the evolutionary origins of behaviors and mental process, their adaptive value, and the purposes they continue to serve.

Given the vast cultural difference between the environment in which humans evolved and the environment in which we live, psychologists disagree on whether evolutionary explanations can provide valid descriptions of our behavior today.

mides, Tooby, & Barkow, 1992; Goode, 2000). Further, they contend that these fixed programs evolved hundreds of thousands of years ago when our ancestors lived as hunter-gatherers and that the problem-solving strategies that benefited early humans may or may not be adaptive in the modern era. Whether evolutionary psychology finds a place among the major fields of psychology or stays on the sidelines remains to be seen.

Positive Psychology   Another emerging perspective is **positive psychology,** the view that psychology should devote more attention to "the good life": the study of subjective feelings of happiness and well-being; the development of such individual traits as intimacy, integrity, leadership, altruism, and wisdom; and the kinds of families, work settings, and communities that encourage individuals to flourish (Seligman & Csikszentmihalyi, 2000).

Positive psychologists argue that psychologists have learned a great deal about the origins, diagnosis, and treatment of mental illness but relatively little about the origins and nurturance of mental wellness. We have come to understand a lot about how individuals survive and endure under conditions of extreme adversity, but far less about how normal individuals find fulfillment under benign conditions. We know more about intelligence than about wisdom; more about conformity than originality; and more about stress than about tranquillity. There have been many studies of prejudice and intergroup hostility, for example, but very few about tolerance and intergroup harmony. In recent decades, psychologists have made great strides in understanding the neurology of depression, schizophrenia, and other disorders.

Today's positivists do not argue that psychologists should abandon their role in the science of healing. To the contrary, they support efforts to promote better, more widespread use of what psychologists have learned. But they argue that psychology has reached a point where building positive qualities should receive as much emphasis as repairing damage.

Multiple Perspectives of Psychology Today   As we've seen, contemporary psychologists tend to see different perspectives as complementary, with each perspective contributing to our understanding of human behavior (Friman, Allen, Kerwin, & Larzelere, 1993). When they study aggression, for example, psychologists no longer limit their explanations to the

Positive psychology
An emerging field of psychology that focuses on positive experiences, including subjective well-being, self-determination, the relationship between positive emotions and physical health, and the factors that allow individuals, communities, and societies to flourish.

Margaret Floy Washburn

behavioral view (aggressive behavior is learned as a consequence of reward and punishment) or the Freudian perspective (aggression is an expression of unconscious hostility toward a parent). Instead, most contemporary psychologists trace aggression to a number of factors, including long-standing adaptations to the environment (evolutionary psychology) and the influences of culture, gender, and socioeconomic status on how people perceive and interpret events—"That guy is making fun of me" or "She's asking for it"—(cognitive psychology). Likewise, physiological psychologists no longer limit themselves to identifying the genetic and biochemical roots of aggression. Instead, they study how heredity and the environment interact.

Sometimes these theoretical perspectives mesh beautifully, with each one enhancing the others; at other times, adherents of one approach challenge their peers, arguing for one viewpoint over all the others. But all psychologists agree that the field advances only with the addition of new evidence to support or challenge existing theories.

Where Are the Women?

In psychology's early years, why were relatively few women accepted in the field?

As you read the brief history of modern psychology, you may have concluded that the founders of the new discipline were all men. But did psychology really have only fathers and no mothers? If there were women pioneers, why are their names and accomplishments missing from historical accounts?

In fact, women have contributed to psychology from its beginnings. Women presented papers and joined the national professional association as soon as it was formed in 1892. Often, however, they faced discrimination. Some colleges and universities did not grant degrees to women, professional journals were reluctant to publish their work, and teaching positions were often closed to them (O'Connell & Russo, 1990; Russo & Denmark, 1987; Stevens & Gardner, 1982). Despite these barriers, a number of early women psychologists made important contributions and were acknowledged by at least some of the men in the growing discipline of psychology.

In 1906, James McKeen Cattell published *American Men of Science*, which, despite its title, included a number of women, among them 22 female psychologists. Cattell rated three of these women as among the 1,000 most distinguished scientists in the country: Mary Whiton Calkins (1863–1930), for her work in color vision; Christine Ladd-Franklin (1847–1930), for her analysis of how we learn verbal material and her contributions to self-psychology; and Margaret Floy Washburn (1871–1939) for her pioneering research examining the role of imagery in thought processes. In addition, Christine Ladd-Franklin was elected and served as the first female president of the American Psychological Association in 1905, a position also held by Margaret Floy Washburn in 1921. However, because the doors to an academic career remained closed, other early female psychologists found positions in therapeutic and other nonacademic settings; pursued careers in allied professions, such as child development and education, which were considered acceptable fields for women; or gained recognition by collaborating on research projects and books with their spouses (Evans, 1999).

Today women receive more than half of the Ph.D.'s granted in psychology (Pion et al., 1996), and they perform key research in all of the psychology subfields. You will find their work referred to throughout this text. Terry Amabile has studied creativity, in particular the positive effects that exposure to creative role models can have on people. Elizabeth Loftus's research on memory has uncovered how unreliable eyewitness accounts of a crime can be. Carol Nagy Jaklin has studied the role that parents' expectations can play in

Elizabeth Loftus

girls' (and boys') perceptions of the value of mathematics. Judith Rodin's research examines eating behavior, in particular bulimia and obesity. Eleanor Maccoby, Alice Eagly, and Jacqueline Eccles are prominent among the growing number of women and men who are studying sex differences in a variety of areas, such as emotionality, math and verbal ability, and helping behavior. Throughout this text we look at this work to see what part biology and society play in differences in the behavior of women and men.

The apparent absence of women from the history of psychology is only one aspect of a much bigger and more troubling concern: the relative inattention to human diversity that has characterized psychology through most of the twentieth century. Only recently have psychologists looked closely at the ways in which culture, gender, race, and ethnicity can affect virtually all aspects of human behavior. In the next section, we begin our examination of this important topic.

INTERACTIVE LECTURE 1.2

WEB QUIZ 1.2

CHECK YOUR UNDERSTANDING

1. It was not until the late _____ that psychology came into its own as a separate discipline.

2. Match the following schools of thought in psychology with the appropriate description.

   _____ structuralism

   _____ functionalism

   _____ behaviorism

   _____ psychodynamic psychology

   _____ existential psychology

   _____ humanistic psychology

   _____ Gestalt psychology

   _____ cognitive psychology

   _____ evolutionary psychology

   a. Explores the origins of human behavior and establishes links to the behavior of other animals.

   b. Stresses the whole character of perception.

   c. Is concerned with alienation in modern life and resulting psychological problems.

   d. Studies only observable and measurable behavior.

   e. Stresses the basic elements of experience and the way they combine.

   f. Emphasizes realizing one's full potential.

   g. Studies mental processes in the broadest sense.

   h. Maintains that hidden motives and unconscious desires govern much of our behavior.

   i. Is concerned with how an organism uses its perceptual abilities to function in its environment.

3. Match the following famous psychologists with their accomplishment.

   _____ Wilhelm Wundt

   _____ William James

   _____ Sigmund Freud

   _____ John B. Watson

   _____ B. F. Skinner

   a. Developed psychoanalysis and explored unconscious conflicts.

   b. Offered a psychology class at Harvard and developed a functionalist theory.

   c. Established the first psychological laboratory.

   d. Extensively studied the effects of rewards on behavior.

   e. Used conditioning principles to demonstrate the conditioning of fear.

Answers: 1. 1800s or nineteenth century. **2.** structuralism (e); functionalism (i); behaviorism (d); psychodynamic psychology (h); existential psychology (c); humanistic psychology (f); Gestalt psychology (b); cognitive psychology (g); evolutionary psychology (a). **3.** Wundt (c); James (b); Freud (a); Watson (e); Skinner (d).

Human Diversity

Why should you learn about human diversity?

For today's students—who will be tomorrow's citizens of the world—understanding human diversity is essential. The reason for that urgency is all around you. Our major cities are home to people from diverse backgrounds, with diverse values and goals, living side by side. But proximity does not always produce harmony; sometimes it leads to aggression, prejudice, and conflict. Understanding cultural, racial, and ethnic differences in thinking and behavior gives us the tools to reduce some of these interpersonal tensions. In the past, men and women led very different lives. Today, women in many societies are as likely as men to obtain higher education; to work full-time, pursue careers, and start businesses; and to be active in politics. And men are more likely to be more active parents and homemakers than their fathers were. Yet stereotypes about how the "typical male" looks and acts or the "accepted social roles" for females still lead to confusion and misunderstandings between the sexes. Looking at human diversity from a scientific perspective will allow you to separate fact from fiction in your daily interactions with people. Moreover, once you understand how and why groups differ in their values, behaviors, approaches to the world, thought processes, and responses to situations, you will be better able to savor the diversity around you. Finally, the more you comprehend human diversity, the more you will appreciate the many universal features of humanity.

In the early twentieth century, psychology was a white male profession with a distinctly American accent (Strickland, 2000). The great majority of research studies were conducted by white male professors at American universities, using white male American college students as participants. This arrangement was not a conscious or deliberate decision to study just one particular group. Like other sciences and prestigious professions in Europe and North America, psychology took for granted that what was true of white, Western males would be true for other people as well. One critical history of psychology during this period was entitled *Even the Rat Was White!* (Guthrie, 1976).

Examining and overcoming past assumptions and biases has been a slow and uneven process, but a new appreciation of human diversity is tak-

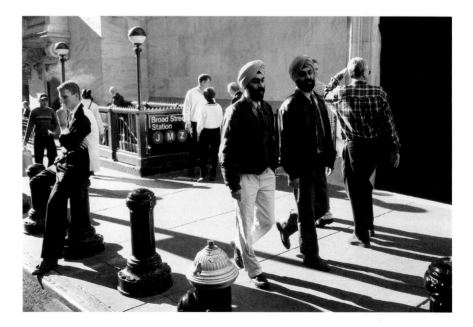

Within the dominant culture, members of subcultures share values, attitudes, rituals, and often, styles of dress.

ing shape (Phinney, 1996). Psychologists have begun to question assumptions that are explicitly based on gender, race, and culture. Are women more likely to help a person in distress than men are? Are African Americans more vulnerable to certain types of mental illness than European Americans, or vice versa? Do the Japanese view children's ability to learn in the same way Americans do? Do homosexuals have different motives and emotions than heterosexuals? Research indicates that the answer to such questions often is "no."

Gender

How are psychologists helping us to understand the differences between men and women?

Gender has many layers. The words *male* and *female* refer to one's biological makeup, the physical and genetic facts of being one sex or the other. Some scientists use the term *sex* to refer exclusively to biological differences in anatomy, genetics, or physical functioning, and **gender** to refer to the psychological and social meanings attached to being biologically male or female. Because distinguishing what is biologically produced from what is socially influenced is almost impossible, in our discussion of these issues, we will use the terms *sex* and *gender* interchangeably.

Gender Stereotypes "Women talk too much; men are strong and silent." "Men have pals; women have confidants." "Women worry about their looks and their children; men, about their jobs and their bank accounts." "Men monopolize the TV zapper; women monopolize the bathroom mirror." The list of gender stereotypes—characteristics that are assumed to be typical of each sex—is endless. In general, our culture holds that men are dominant, strong, and aggressive, whereas women are accommodating, emotional, and affectionate. As a result, many boys learn to hide their emotions, to deny feelings of weakness even to themselves, and to fight, whereas many girls learn to hide their ambitions, to deny their talents and strengths even to themselves, and perhaps to give in. Stereotypes are rarely benign. As we will see in Chapter 9 (Life Span Development), these particular stereotypes have significant negative effects on both boys and girls.

Beyond our stereotypes about what males and females "typically" are like, we have general beliefs about gender roles, that is, cultural expectations regarding acceptable behavior and activities for males and females, respectively. As a rule, cultural norms change more slowly than behavior patterns. Although most American families depend on two salaries today, the assumption that the husband should be the chief breadwinner and the wife should put her home and children first remains powerful. Working wives and mothers work a "second shift" (keeping house and caring for children) at home—as much because they feel that doing so is their responsibility and area of expertise as because their husbands still expect them to (Hochschild & Machung, 1989).

The study of gender similarities and differences has become part of mainstream psychology. Psychologists in virtually every subfield conduct research to determine whether their findings apply equally to males and females, and if not, why not. As we will see, **feminist theory** is not for women only.

Feminist Psychology In recent decades, the number of women who receive Ph.D's in psychology has grown dramatically (see **Figure 1–1**). Indeed, women have begun to outnumber men in psychology. According to the most recent American Psychological Association (APA) survey, women receive three-fourths of the baccalaureate degrees awarded in psychology; represent

Many women try to be both responsible mothers and workers at the same time, struggling to fill two demanding roles.

Gender
The psychological and social meanings attached to being biologically male or female.

Feminist theory
Feminist theories offer a wide variety of views on the social roles of women and men, the problems and rewards of those roles, and prescriptions for changing those roles.

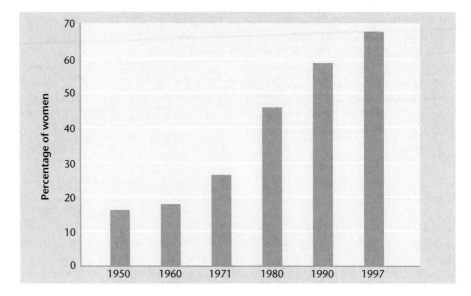

Figure 1–1

Percentage of women recipients of Ph.D.'s in psychology, 1950–1997

Source: Summary Report: Doctorate Recipients from United States Universities (Selected Years). National Research Council. Figure compiled by the APA Research Office. Copyright © 2000 by the American Psychological Association. Reprinted with permission.

just under three-fourths of psychology graduate students; and earned two out of three doctorate degrees in psychology awarded in 1997 (APA, 2000).

As the number of female psychologists has grown, so have their concerns about traditional psychological theories, research, and clinical practices. Feminist psychologists, such as Carol Gilligan make three main points. First, much of the research supporting key psychological theories, such as moral development, was based on all-male samples. Measured against "universal male" standards, females often were found "lacking." Second, reports of gender differences tend to focus on the extremes, exaggerating small differences and ignoring much greater similarities (Tavris, 1992). Third, the questions that psychologists ask and the topics that they study reflect what they consider to be important.

Beyond research and theory, contemporary feminist psychology has begun to influence every facet of psychological practice by seeking mechanisms to empower women in the community, by advocating action to establish policies that advance equality and social justice, and by increasing women's representation in global leadership. Feminists also took the lead in urging other psychologists to recognize sexual orientation as simply another aspect of human diversity.

Sexual Orientation   Sexual orientation refers to whether a person is sexually attracted to members of the opposite sex (heterosexuality), the same sex (homosexuality), or both sexes (bisexuality). Division 44 of the American Psychological Association, "Society for the Psychological Study of Lesbian, Gay, and Bisexual Issues," was founded in 1985 to promote research and education regarding sexual orientation, for psychologists as well as for the general public. Psychologists have only just begun to investigate the many sensitive issues associated with this dimension of human diversity—including such topics as the origins of sexual orientation (LeVay & Hamer, 1994), brain differences between heterosexual and homosexual men (Swaab & Hoffman, 1995), and the impact of allowing gays and lesbians to serve openly in the military (Jones & Koshes, 1995).

Race and Ethnicity

Why are psychologists interested in racial and ethnic differences?

One of the first things we notice about someone (along with sex) is that person's race or ethnicity (Omi & Winant, 1994). **Race** is a biological term

Race
A subpopulation of a species, defined according to an identifiable characteristic (that is, geographic location, skin color, hair texture, genes, facial features, and so forth).

used to refer to a subpopulation whose members have reproduced exclusively among themselves and therefore are genetically similar and distinct from other members of the same species (Betancourt & López, 1993; Diamond, 1994; Macionis, 1993). Most people simply take for granted the idea that the human species can be divided into a number of distinct races (Asians, Africans, Caucasians, Native Americans, and so on). However, human beings have migrated, intermarried, and commingled so frequently over time that it is impossible to identify biologically separate races. To a greater or lesser degree, all humans are "racial hybrids." Moreover, the criteria people use to differentiate among different races are arbitrary. In the United States, we assign people to different races primarily on the basis of skin color and facial features. In central Africa, members of the Tutsi and Hutu tribes see themselves as different races, although they are similar in skin color and facial features. In spite of these different definitions, most people continue to believe that racial categories are meaningful, and as a result, race shapes people's social identities, their sense of self, their experiences in their own and other societies, and even their health.

Whereas racial categories are based on physical differences, **ethnicity** is based on cultural characteristics. An ethnic group is a category of people who have migrated to another country but still see themselves—and are perceived by others—as distinctive because of a common homeland and history, language, religion, or traditional cultural beliefs and social practices. For example, Hispanic Americans may be black, white, or any shade in between. What unites them is their language and culture. By the mid-1980s, there was sufficient interest among psychologists in ethnicity that the American Psychological Association created a new division devoted to the psychological study of ethnic minority issues (Division 45). Increasing numbers of psychologists are now studying why ethnicity is so important both in our country and in others, and how individuals select or create an identity and respond to ethnic stereotypes.

Carol Gilligan.

Ethnicity
A common cultural heritage—including religion, language, or ancestry—that is shared by a group of individuals.

As psychologists study the origins of homosexuality, gay couples seek social acceptance as parents.

Kenneth Clark's research on the effects of segregation influenced the Supreme Court to outlaw segregated schools in *Brown v. Board of Education*.

Racial and Ethnic Minorities in Psychology Most ethnic minorities are still underrepresented among the ranks of psychologists. According to the APA, ethnic-minority students account for almost 25 percent of college entrants, but only 16 percent of graduates who majored in psychology, 14 percent of those who enroll in graduate school in psychology, 12 percent of those who receive master's degrees in psychology, and 9 percent of those who earn doctorates (Sleek, 1999). Why? One possibility is that when black, Hispanic American, Native American, and other students look at the history of psychology or at the psychology faculties of today's universities, they find few role models; likewise, when they look at psychological research, they find little about themselves and their realities (Strickland, 2000). As recently as the 1990s, a survey of psychology journals found that less than 2 percent of the articles focused on U.S. racial and ethnic minorities (Iwamasa & Smith, 1996). Nonetheless, their small numbers have not prevented them from achieving prominence and making significant contributions to the field. For example, Kenneth Clark, a former president of the American Psychological Association, received national recognition for the important work he and his wife, Mamie Clark, did on the effects of segregation on black children. This research was cited by the Supreme Court in the *Brown v. Board of Education* decision of 1954 that outlawed segregated schools in the United States.

In an effort to remedy the underrepresentation of ethnic minorities, the APA's Office of Ethnic Minority Affairs is sponsoring programs to attract ethnic-minority students to psychology (Rabasca, 2000). This initiative includes summer programs for high school students, recruitment at the high school and college levels, mentor and other guidance programs, and a clearinghouse for college students who meet the requirements for graduate programs.

Psychologists are also working to uncover and overcome biases in psychological research that are related to gender, race, and ethnicity. The field of psychology is broadening its scope to probe the full range and richness of human diversity, and this text mirrors that expansive and inclusive approach. We consider the problem of bias in psychological research later in the chapter.

Culture

How does culture contribute to human diversity?

Culture
The tangible goods and the values, attitudes, behaviors, and beliefs that are passed from one generation to another.

A classic definition of **culture** is a people's "design for living" (Kluckhohn, 1949). A culture provides modes of thinking, acting, and communicating; ideas about how the world works and why people behave as they do; beliefs and ideals that shape our individual dreams and desires; information about how to use and improve technology; and perhaps most important, criteria for evaluating what natural events, human actions, and life itself mean. All large, complex modern societies also include subcultures—groups whose values, attitudes, behavior, and vocabulary or accent distinguish them from the cultural mainstream. Most Americans participate in a number of subcultures as well as in mainstream culture.

Many of the traits we think of as defining us as

As they learn their academic lessons, these students in Xian, China are absorbing the values of their collectivist culture as well, where interdependence and fitting in contrast with individualistic cultures' emphasis on independence.

human—especially language, morals, and technology—are elements of culture. Even one's sense of self is dependent on culture and subculture (Segall, Lonner, & Berry, 1998). Thus psychology must take cultural influences into account. For example, cross-cultural research on motivation and emotions, personality and self-esteem, has called attention to a broad distinction between individualistic cultures (which value independence and personal achievement) and collectivist cultures (which value interdependence, fitting in, and harmonious relationships) (Kagitcibasi, 1997). Moreover, cross-cultural studies have had a significant impact on the study of gender. Anthropologist Margaret Mead's classic work, *Sex and Temperament in Three Primitive Societies* (1935), is still cited by feminists and others as showing that definitions of masculinity and femininity are not biological givens but are learned, cultural constructs and therefore subject to change. Finally, in our increasingly multicultural society, psychologists will be dealing with diverse clients, research participants, and students (Hall, 1997). To prepare for this future, psychology must begin educating and training "culturally competent" professionals.

Throughout this book we will explore similarities and differences among individuals and among groups of people. For example, we will examine differences in personality characteristics, intelligence, and levels of motivation; also, we will look at similarities in biological functioning and developmental stages. In almost every chapter, we will examine research on males and females, members of different racial and ethnic groups, and cross-cultural studies.

INTERACTIVE LECTURE 1.3

WEB QUIZ 1.3

CHECK YOUR UNDERSTANDING

1. Indicate whether the following reasons for studying human diversity are true (T) or false (F).

    ____a. Because our society is made up of so many different kinds of people.

    ____b. As a way of helping to solve interpersonal tensions based on misunderstandings of other people.

    ____ c. To help define what humans have in common.

    ____d. Because diversity psychology is one of the major subdivisions of psychology.

2. "A subculture is a group within a larger society that shares a certain set of values, beliefs, outlooks, and norms of behavior." Is this statement true (T) or false (F)?

3. Which of the following subcultures contribute to diversity in our own society?

    ____a. African Americans

    ____b. homosexual men and women

    ____ c. teenagers

    ____d. blue-eyed blondes

    ____e. the homeless

4. People who have ancestors from the same region of the world and who share a common language, religion, and set of social traditions are said to be part of the same ____ group.

5. "Minority groups are seriously underrepresented among psychologists." Is this statement true (T) or false (F)?

Answers: 1. a, b, c. 2. (T). 3. a, b, c, e. 4. ethnic. 5. (T).

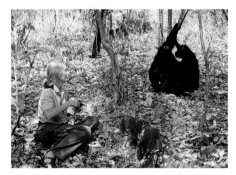

The world-famous primatologist Jane Goodall has spent most of her adult life observing chimpanzees in their natural environment in Africa.

Research Methods in Psychology

What are some of the research methods that psychologists use in their work?

All sciences—including psychology, sociology, economics, political science, biology, and physics—require evidence based on careful observation and experimentation. To collect data systematically and objectively, psychologists use a variety of research methods, including naturalistic observation, case studies, surveys, correlational research, and experimental research.

Naturalistic Observation

Why is a natural setting sometimes better than a laboratory for observing behavior?

Psychologists use **naturalistic observation** to study human or animal behavior in its natural context. One psychologist with this real-life orientation might observe behavior in a school or a factory; another might actually join a family to study the behavior of its members; still another might observe monkeys in the wild rather than in cages. The primary advantage of naturalistic observation is that the behavior observed in everyday life is likely to be more natural, spontaneous, and varied than that observed in a laboratory.

For example, naturalistic observation was used in a recent study (Hammen, Gitlin, & Altshuler, 2000) designed to understand why some patients with bipolar disorder (a mental disorder discussed more fully in Chapter 12, Psychological Disorders) are more likely to adjust successfully to the workplace than others. By carefully studying 52 people over a two-year period in their natural settings, these authors found that the people who displayed the most successful work adjustment were those who also had strong supportive personal relationships with other people. Surprisingly, stressful life events did not seem to play an important role in how well these people adjusted to work. Because simulating a genuine workplace environment in a laboratory would have been extremely difficult (especially over an extended period of time), naturalistic observation provided a practical alternative to exploring this issue.

Naturalistic observation is not without its drawbacks. Psychologists using naturalistic observation have to take behavior as it comes. They cannot suddenly yell, "Freeze!" when they want to study in more detail what is going on. Nor can psychologists tell people to stop what they are doing because it is not what the psychologists are interested in researching. Moreover, simply describing one's impressions of "a day in the life" of a particular group or the way that different people behave in the same setting is not science. Observers must measure behavior in a systematic way, for example, by devising a form that enables them to check at timed intervals what people are doing.

The main drawback in naturalistic observation is **observer bias.** As we will see in Chapter 6 (Memory), eyewitnesses to a crime are often very unreliable sources of information. Even psychologists who are trained observers may subtly distort what they see to make it conform to what they were hoping to see. For this reason, contemporary researchers often use videotapes that can be analyzed and scored by other researchers who do not know what the study is designed to find out. Another potential problem is that psychologists may not observe or record behavior that seems to be irrelevant. Therefore, many observational studies employ a team of trained observers who pool their notes. This strategy often generates a more complete picture than one observer could draw alone.

Unlike laboratory experiments that can be repeated over and over again, each natural situation is a one-time-only occurrence. Therefore, psy-

Naturalistic observation
Research method involving the systematic study of animal or human behavior in natural settings rather than in the laboratory.

Observer bias
Expectations or biases of the observer that might distort or influence his or her interpretation of what was actually observed.

When people are unaware that they are being watched, they behave naturally. A one-way mirror is therefore sometimes used for naturalistic observation.

chologists prefer not to make general statements based on information from naturalistic studies alone. Rather, they test the information from naturalistic observation under controlled conditions in the laboratory before they apply it to situations other than the original one.

Despite these disadvantages, naturalistic observation is a valuable tool. After all, real-life behavior is what psychology is all about. Naturalistic observation often provides new ideas and suggests new theories, which can then be studied more systematically and in more detail in the laboratory. This method also helps researchers maintain their perspective by reminding them of the larger world outside the lab.

Live! **psych 1.1**

Case Studies

When can a case study be most useful?

A second research method is the **case study:** a detailed description of one person or a few individuals. Although in some ways this method is similar to naturalistic observation, the researcher here uses a variety of methods to

Case study
Intensive description and analysis of a single individual or just a few individuals.

Jean Piaget based his theory of cognitive development on case studies of children.

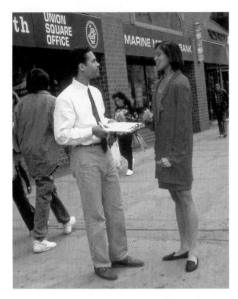

Surveys can generate a great deal of useful data, but only if the questions are clear and the people surveyed are carefully selected and answer the questions honestly.

collect information that yields a detailed, in-depth portrait of the individual. A case study usually includes real-life observation, interviews, scores on various psychological tests, and whatever other measures the researcher considers revealing. For example, the Swiss psychologist Jean Piaget developed a comprehensive theory of cognitive development by carefully studying each of his three children as they grew and changed during childhood. Other researchers have tested Piaget's theory with experiments involving larger numbers of children, both in our own culture and in others (see Chapter 9, Life-Span Development).

Like naturalistic observation, case studies can provide valuable insights but also have significant drawbacks. Observer bias is as much a problem here as it is with naturalistic observation. Moreover, because each person is unique, we cannot confidently draw general conclusions from a single case. Nevertheless, case studies figure prominently in psychological research. For example, the famous case of Phineas Gage, who suffered severe and unusual brain damage, led researchers to identify the front portion of the brain as important for the control of emotions and the ability to plan and carry out complex tasks (see Chapter 2, The Biological Basis of Behavior). The case study of another brain-damaged patient (Milner, 1959), called "H. M.," who could remember events that preceded his injury but nothing that happened after it, prompted psychologists to suggest that we have several distinct kinds of memory (see Chapter 6, Memory).

Surveys

What are some of the benefits of survey research?

In some respects, surveys address the shortcomings of naturalistic observation and case studies. In **survey research,** a carefully selected group of people is asked a set of predetermined questions in face-to-face interviews or in questionnaires. Surveys, even those with a low response rate, can generate a great deal of interesting and useful information at relatively low cost, but to be accurate, the survey questions must be unambiguous and clear, the people surveyed must be selected with great care, and the people must be motivated to respond to the survey thoughtfully and carefully (Krosnick, 1999). For example, asking parents, "Do you ever use physical punishment to discipline your children?" may elicit the socially correct answer, "No." Asking "When was the last time you spanked your child?" or "In what situations do you feel it is necessary to hit your child?" is more likely to elicit honest responses, because the questions are specific and imply that most parents use physical punishment; the researcher is merely asking when and why. At the same time, survey researchers must be careful not to ask leading questions, such as "Most Americans approve of physical punishment; do you?" Guaranteeing anonymity to participants in a survey can also be important.

Naturalistic observations, case studies, and surveys can provide a rich set of raw data that describes behaviors, beliefs, opinions, and attitudes. But these research methods are not ideal for making predictions, explaining, or determining the causes of behavior. For these purposes, psychologists use more powerful research methods, as we will see in the next two sections.

Correlational Research

What is the difference between correlation and cause and effect?

A psychologist, under contract to the U.S. Air Force, is asked to predict which applicants for a pilot-training program will make good pilots. An excellent approach to this problem would be **correlational research.** The psychologist might select several hundred trainees, give them a variety of

Survey research
Research technique in which questionnaires or interviews are administered to a selected group of people.

Correlational research
Research technique based on the naturally occurring relationship between two or more variables.

Can the experiences we have as children actually increase intelligence? Researchers might want to study the relationship between stimulating activities, such as frequent visits to science museums, and children's IQ scores. The relationship between the two may show a correlation, but researchers would not conclude from a correlational study that such experiences alone would cause a change in a child's IQ.

aptitude and personality tests, and then compare the results with their performance in training school. This approach would tell him whether some characteristic or set of characteristics is closely related to, or correlated with, eventual success as a pilot.

Suppose that the psychologist finds that the most successful trainees score higher than the unsuccessful trainees on mechanical aptitude tests and that they are also cautious people who do not like to take unnecessary risks. The psychologist has discovered that there is a *correlation*, or relationship, between these traits and success as a pilot trainee: High scores on tests of mechanical aptitude and caution predict success as a pilot trainee. If these correlations are confirmed in new groups of trainees, then the psychologist could recommend with some confidence that the Air Force consider using these tests to select future trainees.

Correlational data are useful for many purposes, but they do not permit the researcher to explain cause and effect. This important distinction is often overlooked. Correlation means that two phenomena seem to be related: When one goes up, the other goes up (or down). For example, young people with high IQ scores usually earn higher grades in school than do students with average or below-average scores. This correlation allows researchers to predict that children with high IQ scores will do well on tests and other classwork. But correlation does not identify the direction of influence. A high IQ might cause or enable a child to be a good student. But the reverse might also be true: Working hard in school might cause children to score higher on IQ tests. Or a third, unidentified factor might intervene. For example, growing up in a middle-class family that places a high value on education might cause both higher IQ scores and higher school grades (see Appendix for more on correlation).

So it is with our example. This psychologist has *described* a relationship between skill as a pilot and two other characteristics, and as a result he is able to use those relationships to predict with some accuracy which trainees will and will not become skilled pilots. But he has no basis for drawing conclusions about cause and effect. Does the tendency to shy away from risk-taking make a trainee a good pilot? Or is it the other way around: Learning to be a skillful pilot makes people cautious? Or is there some unknown factor that causes people to be both cautious and capable of acquiring the different skills needed in the cockpit?

Despite limitations, correlational research often sheds light on important psychological phenomena. In this book, you will come across many examples of correlational research: People who are experiencing severe stress are more prone to develop physical illnesses than people who are not; children whose parent(s) have schizophrenia are more likely to develop this disorder than are other children; and when someone needs help, the more bystanders there are, the less likely it is that any one of them will come forward to offer help. These interesting findings allow us to make some predictions, but psychologists want to move beyond simply making predictions. To explain the causes of psychological phenomena, psychologists most often use experimental research.

1.2

Experimental Research

What kinds of research questions are best studied by experimental research?

A psychology instructor notices that on Monday mornings, most students in her class do not remember materials as well as they do later in the week. She has discovered a correlation between the day of the week and memory for course-related material. On the basis of this correlation, she could predict that next Monday and every Monday thereafter, the students in her class will not absorb material as well as on other days. But she wants to go beyond simply predicting her students' behavior; she wants to understand or explain why their memories are poorer on Mondays than on other days of the week.

As a result of her own experiences and some informal interviews with students, she suspects that students stay up late on weekends and that their difficulty remembering facts and ideas presented on Mondays is due to lack of sleep. This hypothesis appears to make sense, but the psychologist wants to prove that it is correct. To gather evidence that lack of sleep actually causes memory deficits, she turns to the **experimental method.**

Her first step is to select **participants,** people whom she can observe to find out whether her hypothesis is correct. She decides to use student volunteers. To keep her results from being influenced by sex differences or intelligence levels, she chooses a group made up of equal numbers of men and women, all of whom scored between 520 and 550 on the verbal section of their College Board exams.

Next, she designs a memory task. She needs something that none of her participants will know in advance. If she chooses a chapter in a history book, for example, she runs the risk that some of her participants will be history buffs. Given the various possibilities, the psychologist decides to print a page of geometric shapes, each labeled with a nonsense word. Circles are "glucks," triangles are "rogs," and so on. She gives students half an hour to learn the names from this page, then takes it away and asks them to assign those same labels to geometric shapes on a new page.

The psychologist also needs to know which participants are sleep-deprived. Simply asking people whether they have slept well is not ideal: Some may say "no" so that they will have an excuse for doing poorly on the test, and others may say "yes" because they do not want a psychologist to think that they are so unstable they cannot sleep. And two people who both say they "slept well" may not mean the same thing by that phrase. So the psychologist decides to intervene—that is, to control the situation more closely. Everyone in the experiment, she decides, will spend the night in the same dormitory. They will be kept awake until 4:00 A.M., and then they will be awakened at 7:00 A.M. sharp. She and her colleagues will patrol the halls to make sure that no one falls asleep ahead of schedule. By manipulating the amount of time the participants sleep, the psychologist is introducing and

Experimental method
Research technique in which an investigator deliberately manipulates selected events or circumstances and then measures the effects of those manipulations on subsequent behavior.

Participants
Individuals whose reactions or responses are observed in an experiment.

controlling an essential element of the experimental method: an independent variable. The psychologist believes that the students' ability to learn and remember labels for geometric shapes will depend on their having had a good night's sleep. Performance on the memory task (the number of correct answers) thus becomes the dependent variable. According to the hypothesis, changing the **independent variable** (the amount of sleep) should also change the **dependent variable** (performance on the memory task). Her prediction is that this group of participants, who get no more than three hours of sleep, should do quite poorly on the memory test.

At this point, the experimenter begins looking for loopholes in her experimental design. How can she be sure that poor test results mean that the participants did less well than they would have done had they had more sleep? For example, their poor performance could simply be the result of knowing that they were being closely observed. To be sure that her experiment measures only the effects of inadequate sleep, the experimenter creates two groups, containing equal numbers of males and females of the same ages and with the same College Board scores. One of the groups, the **experimental group,** will be kept awake, as described, until 4:00 A.M. That is, they will be subjected to the experimenter's manipulation of the independent variable—amount of sleep. Members of the other group, the **control group,** will be allowed to go to sleep whenever they please. If the only consistent difference between the two groups is the amount of sleep they get, the experimenter can be much more confident that if the groups differ in their test performance, the difference is due to the length of time they slept the night before.

Finally, the psychologist questions her own objectivity. Because she believes that lack of sleep inhibits students' learning and memory, she does not want to prejudice the results of her experiment; that is, she wants to avoid **experimenter bias.** So she decides to ask a neutral person, someone who does not know which participants did or did not sleep all night, to score the tests.

The experimental method is a powerful tool, but it, too, has limitations. First, many intriguing psychological variables, such as love, hatred, or grief, do not readily lend themselves to experimental manipulation. And even if it were possible to induce such strong emotions as part of a psychological experiment, this treatment would raise serious ethical questions. In some cases, psychologists may use animals rather than humans for experiments. But some subjects, such as the emergence of language in children or the expression of emotions, cannot be studied with other species. Second, because experiments are conducted in an artificial setting, participants—whether human or nonhuman animals—may behave differently than they would in real life.

The accompanying Summary Table groups the main advantages and disadvantages of each of the research methods we have discussed. Because each method has drawbacks, psychologists often use more than one method to study a single problem.

Multimethod Research

What does multimethod research allow psychologists to do?

Suppose that a psychologist was interested in studying creativity. She might begin her research by giving a group of college students a creativity test that she had invented to measure their capacity to discover or produce something new. Next, she would compare the students' scores with their scores on intelligence tests and with their grades to see whether there is a correlation between them. Then, she would spend several weeks observing a college class and interviewing teachers, students, and parents to correlate

1.3

Independent variable
In an experiment, the variable that is manipulated to test its effects on the other, dependent variables.

Dependent variable
In an experiment, the variable that is measured to see how it is changed by manipulations in the independent variable.

Experimental group
In a controlled experiment, the group subjected to a change in the independent variable.

Control group
In a controlled experiment, the group not subjected to a change in the independent variable; used for comparison with the experimental group.

Experimenter bias
Expectations by the experimenter that might influence the results of an experiment or its interpretation.

BASIC METHODS OF RESEARCH

Research Method	Advantages	Limitations
Naturalistic Observation Behavior is observed in the environment in which it occurs natually.	Provides a great deal of firsthand behavioral information that is more likely to be accurate than reports after the fact. The participant's behavior is more natural, spontaneous, and varied than behaviors taking place in the laboratory. A rich source of hypotheses as well.	The presence of an observer may alter the participants' behavior; the observer's recording of the behavior may reflect a preexisting bias; and it is often unclear whether the observations can be generalized to other settings and other people.
Case Studies Behavior of one person or a few people is studied in depth.	Yields a great deal of detailed descriptive information. Useful for forming hypotheses.	The case(s) studied may not be a representative sample. This method can be time-consuming and expensive. Observer bias is a potential problem.
Surveys A large number of participants are asked a standard set of questions.	Enables an immense amount of data to be gathered quickly and inexpensively.	Sampling biases can skew results. Poorly constructed questions can result in answers that are ambiguous, so data are not clear. Accuracy depends on ability and willingness of participants to answer questions accurately.
Correlational Research This approach employs statistical methods to examine the relationship between two or more variables.	May clarify relationships between variables that cannot be examined by other research methods. Allows prediction of behavior.	This method does not permit researchers to draw conclusions regarding cause-and-effect relationships.
Experimental Research One or more variables are systematically manipulated, and the effect of that manipulation on other variables is studied.	Because of strict control of variables, offers researchers the opportunity to draw conclusions about cause-and-effect relationships.	The artificiality of the lab setting may influence subjects' behavior; unexpected and uncontrolled variables may confound results; many variables cannot be controlled and manipulated.

classroom behavior and the adults' evaluations with the students' scores on the creativity test. She would go on to test some of her ideas with an experiment using a group of students as participants. Finally, her findings might prompt her to revise the test, or they might give the teachers and parents new insight into particular students.

The Importance of Sampling

How can sampling affect the results of a research study?

One obvious drawback to every form of research is that it is usually impossible, or at least impractical, to measure every single occurrence of a characteristic. No one could expect to measure the memory of every human being, to study the responses of all individuals who suffer from phobias (irrational fears), or to record the maternal behavior of all female monkeys. No matter what research method is used, whenever researchers conduct a study, they examine only a relatively small number of people or animals of the population they seek to understand. In other words, researchers almost always study a small sample and then use the results of that limited study to generalize about larger populations. For example, the psychology instructor who studied the effect of lack of sleep on memory assumed that her results would apply to other students in her classes (past and future), as well as to students in other classes and at other colleges.

How realistic are these assumptions? How confident can researchers be that the results of research conducted on a relatively small sample of people apply to the much larger population from which the sample was drawn (see *Understanding the World Around Us*)? Social scientists have developed several techniques to deal with sampling error. One is to select participants at random from the larger population. For example, the researcher studying pilot trainees might begin with an alphabetical list of all trainees and then select every third name or every fifth name on the list to be in his study. These participants would constitute a **random sample** from the larger group of trainees, because every trainee had an equal chance of being chosen for the study.

Another way to make sure that conclusions apply to the larger population is to pick a **representative sample** of the population being studied. For example, researchers looking for a representative cross section of Americans would want to ensure that the proportion of males and females in the study matched the national proportion, that the number of participants from each state matched the national population distribution, and so on. Even with these precautions, however, unintended bias may influence psychological research. This issue has received a great deal of attention recently, particularly in relation to women and African Americans, as we discussed earlier.

Human Diversity and Research

Can we generalize about research findings from one group to another?

Historically, most psychological researchers have been white American males, and most participants used in psychological research have been white American male college students. For decades, hardly anyone thought about the underlying assumption that the results of these studies would also apply to women, to people of other racial and ethnic groups, and to people of different cultures. Psychologists have now begun to question that assumption explicitly. In fact, research indicates that people's gender, race, ethnic background, and culture often have a profound effect on their behavior. Studies have found consistent cultural differences in aggression (Triandis, 1994), memory (Mistry & Rogoff, 1994), some forms of nonverbal communication (Johnson, Ekman, & Friesen, 1975), and other behaviors. Similarly, men and women display differences in a variety of traits, including aggression (Eagly & Steffen, 1986) and their skill at perceiving or reading another person's expressions of emotion (Hall, 1984).

Unintended Biases in Research   The gender, race, or ethnicity of the experimenter may introduce subtle, unintended biases. For example, some early research concluded that women were more likely than men to conform to social pressure in the laboratory (e.g., Crutchfield, 1955). When the experimenter is female (Eagly & Carli, 1981), however, research now reveals no gender difference in this area. Similarly, evidence suggests that the results of research with African-American participants may be significantly affected by the race of the experimenter (Graham, 1992). Data on race and IQ scores have been widely misinterpreted as "demonstrating" innate racial inferiority. Advocates of this view rarely note that African Americans score higher on IQ and other tests when the person administering the test is also an African American (Graham, 1992). Similarly, do feminist theories, developed by and tested primarily with white, college-educated women, apply to women of color (Yoder & Kahn, 1993)?

Random sample
Sample in which each potential participant has an equal chance of being selected.

Representative sample
Sample carefully chosen so that the characteristics of the participants correspond closely to the characteristics of the larger population.

 INTERACTIVE LECTURE **1.4**

UNDERSTANDING The World Around Us

Internet Users: A Flawed Study?

"Sad, Lonely World Discovered in Cyberspace"

"Isolation Increases with Internet Use"

"Online and Bummed Out"

What's behind these headlines that appeared in various publications during the fall of 1998? Researchers had found that—as these publications phrased it—"using the Internet can cause isolation, loneliness, and depression"; "the Internet is actually bad for some people's psychological well-being"; and "greater use of the Internet leads to shrinking social support and happiness" (Kraut et al., 1998).

As a critical thinker, you would ask a number of questions about these headlines. Who was studied? How did the researchers determine Internet use? How did they measure such things as isolation, loneliness, depression, social support, and happiness? Did the researchers actually conduct a genuine experiment, manipulating the independent variable of Internet use and observing its effect on the dependent variables, or did they use some other, less powerful research design? If the latter, how do they know that Internet use caused any changes they might have observed?

The answers should cause you to be far more cautious than the headline writers about what the research actually showed. To begin with, the researchers studied 256 people from only 93 families in Pittsburgh, and 20 of the families and 87 of the people dropped out before the study was completed. The families were selected either because they had teenagers enrolled in high school journalism classes or because an adult was on the board of directors of a community development organization. Households with pre-existing Internet connections were excluded.

Thus, for most of the households, this was their first experience with a home computer. Would you consider this a representative sample of the population? Are you confident that the results from this

> The most that could be said is that heavier users of the Internet showed very slight declines in some . . . aspects of social involvement. . . .

sample can be generalized as broadly as the mass media did? Is it possible that the Internet users were already unusually lonely or isolated or depressed? If so, how might Internet use affect these individuals?

Going further, the researchers actually tracked Internet use through software on the computer. To measure social involvement and psychological well-being, however, they relied entirely on *self-report measures;* that is, the participants themselves supplied all the relevant data. The participants were asked to estimate the amount of time they spent communicating with other family members as well as the number of people they socialized with, talked to, or visited during an average month. In addition, they filled out questionnaires on social support, loneliness, stress, and depression in their lives.

Does this reliance on self-reports cause you to be cautious about the results of the research? How do we know whether these reports were accurate? For example, did loneli-ness actually increase as a result of Internet use, or did people simply become more willing to *say* that they were lonely as time went on? Did actual depression increase, or did people's *reports* of being depressed increase? Does Internet use "cause isolation, loneliness, and depression," or does it cause people to *say* that they are more "isolated, lonely, and depressed"?

If you relied solely on the headlines, you might conclude that the study found dramatic differences between Internet users and non-users. In fact, the changes in the dependent variable were *not* very large. The most that could be said is that heavier users of the Internet showed very slight declines in some aspects of social involvement and only slight increases in self-reported feelings of loneliness and depression.

Finally, you might ask whether anything happened during the period from March 1995 to March 1997 that might have increased Internet use and also have caused people to report more loneliness, isolation, and depression. For example, some of the participants were adolescents. Is it possible that they made greater use of the Internet and also withdrew somewhat from their families simply as part of growing up? In other words, could another variable have caused *both* greater Internet use and increased social withdrawal? We don't know the answer to this question, but it should be explored.

These are the kinds of questions you should ask yourself when you read accounts of psychological research in the mass media. And in fairness, they are among the questions the researchers themselves raised in their article.

WEB QUIZ **1.4**

CHECK YOUR UNDERSTANDING

1. A method of research known as ____ allows psychologists to study behavior as it occurs in real-life settings.

2. Psychologists use ____ research to examine relationships between two or more variables without manipulating any variable.

3. The experimental method is associated with all of the following except
   a. hypotheses.
   b. variables.
   c. experimenter bias.
   d. subjects or participants.

4. "Difficulty generalizing from observations is a major shortcoming of the case study method." Is this statement true (T) or false (F)?

5. The method of research best suited to explaining behavior is ____ research.

6. The ____ variable in an experiment is manipulated to see how it affects a second variable; the ____ variable is the one observed for any possible effects.

7. To ensure that the results of a particular study apply to a larger population, researchers use ____ or ____ samples.

Answers: 1. naturalistic observation. 2. correlational. 3. (c). 4. (T). 5. experimental. 6. independent, dependent. 7. random, representative.

Ethics and Psychology: Research on Humans and Animals

Are there ethical guidelines for conducting psychological research? What objections have been raised regarding research on animal subjects?

If the school you attend has a research facility, it is likely that you will have a chance to become a participant in an experiment in your psychology department. You will probably be offered a small sum of money or class credit to participate. But you may not learn the true purpose of the experiment until after it's over. Is this deception necessary to the success of psychology experiments? And what if the experiment causes you discomfort? Before answering, consider the ethical debate that flared up in 1963 when Stanley Milgram published the results of several experiments he had conducted.

Milgram hired people to participate in what he said was a learning experiment. When a participant arrived at the laboratory, he was met by a stern-faced researcher in a lab coat; another man in street clothes was sitting in the waiting room. The researcher explained that he was studying the effects of punishment on learning. When the two men drew slips out of the hat, the participant's slip said "teacher." The teacher watched as the "learner" was strapped into a chair and an electrode attached to his wrist. Then the teacher was taken into an adjacent room and seated at an impressive-looking "shock generator" with switches from 15 to 450 volts, labeled "Slight Shock," "Very Strong Shock" up to "Danger: Severe Shock," and finally "XXX." The teacher's job was to read a list of paired words, which the learner would attempt to memorize and repeat. The teacher was instructed to deliver a shock whenever the learner gave a wrong answer and to increase the intensity of the shock each time the learner made a mistake. At 90 volts, the learner began to grunt; at 120 volts, he shouted, "Hey, this really hurts!"; at 150 volts, he demanded to be released; at 270 volts, his protests became screams of agony. Beyond 330 volts, the learner

Stanley Milgram's Obedience Experiment. (A) The shock generator used in the experiment. (B) With electrodes attached to his wrists, the learner provides answers by pressing switches that light up on an answer box. (C) The subject administers a shock to the learner. (D) The subject breaks off the experiment. Milgram's study yielded interesting results, but it also raised serious questions about the ethics of such experimentation.

appeared to pass out. If the teacher became concerned and asked whether he could stop, the experimenter politely but firmly replied that he was expected to continue, that this experiment was being conducted in the interests of science.

In reality, Milgram was studying obedience, not learning. He wanted to find out whether ordinary people would obey orders to cause another person pain. As part of his research, Milgram (1974) described the experiment to 110 psychiatrists, college students, and middle-class adults, and he asked them at what point they thought participants would stop. Members of all three groups guessed that most people would refuse to continue beyond 130 volts and that no one would go beyond 300 volts. The psychiatrists estimated that only one in a thousand people would continue to the XXX shock panel. Astonishingly, 65 percent of Milgram's participants administered the highest level of shock, even though many worried aloud that the shocks might be causing serious damage to the learners.

To find out what he wanted to know, Milgram had to deceive his participants. The stated purpose of the experiment—to test learning—was a lie. The "learners" were Milgram's accomplices, who had been trained to act as though they were being hurt; the machines were fake; and the learners received no shocks at all (Milgram, 1963). But, critics argued, the "teachers"—the real subjects of the study—were hurt. Not only did most voice concern, but also they showed clear signs of stress: They sweated, bit their lips, trembled, stuttered, or in a few cases, broke into uncontrollable nervous laughter. Critics also worried about the effect of the experiment on the participants' self-esteem. How would you like to be compared with the people who ran the death camps in Nazi Germany?

Although the design of this experiment was not typical of the vast majority of psychological experiments, it sparked such a public uproar that the American Psychological Association (APA) reassessed its ethical guidelines, first published in 1953. A new code of ethics on psychological experimentation was approved. The code is assessed each year and periodically revised to ensure that it adequately protects participants in research studies. In addition to outlining the ethical principles guiding research and teaching, the code spells out a set of ethical standards for psychologists who offer therapy and other professional services, such as psychological testing.

The APA code of ethics requires that researchers obtain informed consent from participants and stipulates the following:

- Participants must be informed of the nature of research in clearly understandable language.
- Informed consent must be documented.
- Risks, possible adverse effects, and limitations on confidentiality must be spelled out in advance.
- If participation is a condition of course credit, equitable alternative activities must be offered.
- Participants cannot be deceived about aspects of the research that would affect their willingness to participate, such as risks or unpleasant emotional experiences.
- Deception about the goals of the research can be used only when absolutely necessary to the integrity of the research.

In addition, psychological researchers are required to follow the U.S. government's Code of Federal Regulations, which includes an extensive set of regulations concerning the protection of human participants in all kinds of research. Failure to abide by these federal regulations may result in the termination of federal funding for the researcher and penalties for the research institution.

The Science of Psychology   **39**

Despite these formal ethical and legal guidelines, controversy still rages about the ethics of psychological research on humans. Some people contend that research procedures should never be emotionally or physically distressing (Baumrind, 1985). Others assert that ethical guidelines that are too strict may undermine the scientific value of research or cripple future research (Gergen, 1973; Sears, 1994). Still others maintain that psychology, as a science, should base its ethical code on documented evidence about the effects of research procedures on participants, not on conjecture about what is "probably" a good way to conduct research (Trice, 1986). Still another view is that the explanations necessary to produce informed consent may foster a better understanding of the goals and methods of research (Blanck et al., 1992).

In recent years questions have also been raised about the ethics of using animals in psychological research (Herzog, 1995; Plous, 1996; Rowan & Shapiro, 1996; Shapiro, 1991).

Psychologists study animal behavior in order to shed light on human behavior. Crowding mice into small cages, for example, has yielded valuable insights into the effects of overcrowding on humans. Animals are used in experiments in which it would be clearly unethical to use human participants—for instance, studies involving brain lesions (requiring cutting into the brain) or electric stimulation of parts of the brain. In fact, much of what we know about sensation, perception, drugs, emotional attachment, and the neural basis of behavior is derived from animal research (Domjan & Purdy, 1995). Yet animal protectionists and others question whether it is ethical to use nonhuman animals, which cannot give their consent to serve as subjects, in psychological research.

Their opponents contend that the goals of scientific research—in essence, to reduce or eliminate human suffering—justify the means, even though they agree that animals should be made to suffer as little as possible (Gallistel, 1981; Novak, 1991). They argue that procedures now in place, including the use of anesthesia in many experiments, already minimize animal suffering.

The APA has addressed this issue in its ethical guidelines, noting that psychologists using animals in research must ensure "appropriate consideration of [the animal's] comfort, health, and humane treatment" (APA, 1992).

INTERACTIVE LECTURE **1.5**

CHECK YOUR UNDERSTANDING

WEB QUIZ **1.5**

1. "Controversy over ethical standards in psychology has almost disappeared." Is this statement true (T) or false (F)?
2. "The APA code of ethics used today is unchanged since 1953." True (T) or false (F)?
3. "Ethical questions in psychological research apply only to laboratory experiments." True (T) or false (F)?
4. "Getting the informed consent of participants in studies is central to the ethics of doing research on humans." True (T) or false (F)?
5. "Researchers who fail to follow the federal code of regulations are subject to penalties." True (T) or false (F)?
6. "Psychologists are much less concerned about ethical guidelines pertaining to animal research." True (T) or false (F)?

Answers: 1. (F). 2. (F). 3. (F). 4. (T). 5. (T). 6. (F).

Careers in Psychology

What can you do with a background in psychology or with an advanced degree?

Some readers may be studying psychology out of general interest; others may be considering careers in psychology. What kinds of careers are open to psychology graduates? People holding bachelor's degrees in psychology may find jobs assisting psychologists in mental-health centers, vocational rehabilitation facilities, and correctional centers. They may also take positions as research assistants, teach psychology in high school, or land jobs as trainees in government or business.

Community college graduates with associates degrees in psychology are well qualified for paraprofessional positions in state hospitals, mental health centers, and other human service settings. Job responsibilities may include screening and evaluating new patients, record keeping, and assisting in consultation sessions.

Many careers outside psychology draw on a person's knowledge of psychology without requiring postgraduate study. For example, personnel administrators deal with employee relations; vocational rehabilitation counselors help people with disabilities find employment; directors of volunteer services recruit and train volunteers; probation officers work with parolees; and supervisors of day care centers oversee the care of preschool children of working parents. Indeed, employers in areas such as business and finance seek out psychology majors because of their knowledge of the principles of human behavior and their skills in experimental design and data collection and analysis.

For those who pursue advanced degrees in psychology—a master's degree or a doctorate—career opportunities span a wide range. Many doctoral psychologists join the faculties of colleges and universities. Others work in applied settings such as school, health, industrial, commercial, and educational psychology. Nearly half of doctoral psychologists are clinicians or counselors who treat people experiencing mental, emotional, or adaptational problems. Master's graduates in psychology often work as researchers, collecting and analyzing data, at universities, in government, or for private companies. Others work in health, industry, and education. APA standards require that master's graduates who work in clinical, counseling, school, or testing and measurement settings be supervised by a doctoral-level psychologist.

Many students who major in psychology want to become therapists. For these students, there are five main career paths. A psychiatrist is a medical doctor who, in addition to four years of medical training, has completed three years of residency training in psychiatry, most of which is spent in supervised clinical practice. Psychiatrists specialize in the diagnosis and treatment of abnormal behavior. They are the only mental health professionals who are licensed to prescribe medications, in addition to providing psychotherapy. A psychoanalyst is a psychiatrist (or psychologist) who has received additional specialized training in psychoanalytic theory and practice, usually at a psychoanalytic institute that requires him or her to undergo psychoanalysis before practicing.

Clinical psychologists assess and treat mental, emotional, and behavioral disorders, ranging from short-term crises to chronic disorders such as schizophrenia. They hold advanced degrees in psychology (a Ph.D. or Psy.D.)—the result of a four- to six-year graduate program, plus a one-year internship in psychological assessment and psychotherapy and at least one more year of supervised practice. Counseling psychologists help people to cope

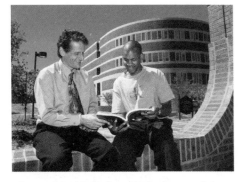

About one-third of psychologists work in colleges and universities. Here, Al Maisto, co-author of this text, talks with a student at the University of North Carolina, Charlotte.

with situational problems, such as adjusting to college, choosing a vocation, resolving marital problems, or dealing with the death of a loved one.

Finally, social workers may also offer treatment for psychological problems. Typically they have a master's degree (M.S.W.) or a doctorate (D.S.W.). Social workers often work under psychiatrists or clinical psychologists, though in some states they may be licensed to practice independently.

A free booklet, *Psychology: Scientific Problem Solvers, Careers for the Twenty-first Century*, is available by calling the Order Department of the American Psychological Association at 1-800-374-2721. The APA also maintains a Web site, http://www.apa.org/, that provides up-to-date information about employment opportunities, as well as a vast array of related material of interest to psychology students.

 INTERACTIVE LECTURE 1.6

 WEB QUIZ 1.6

CHECK YOUR UNDERSTANDING

1. "Careers in psychology are largely limited to people with Ph.D.'s." Is this statement true (T) or false (F)?
2. "Almost all the careers related to a knowledge of psychology are in the mental health field." True (T) or false (F)?
3. Which of the following are also medical doctors?
   ____ a. psychiatrists
   ____ b. some psychoanalysts
   ____ c. clinical psychologists
4. Psychologists can be found working in which of the following settings?
   ____ a. research laboratories
   ____ b. schools
   ____ c. government
   ____ d. corporations and other businesses
   ____ e. hospitals and clinics

Answers: 1. (F). 2. (F). 3. a, b. 4. a, b, c, d, e.

KEY TERMS

What is psychology?
psychology, p. 3
scientific method, p. 9
theory, p. 10
hypotheses, p. 10

The growth of psychology
structuralism, p. 13
functionalist theory, p. 14
psychodynamic theory, p. 14
behaviorism, p. 15
Gestalt psychology, p. 17

humanistic psychology, p. 17
existential psychology, p. 17
cognitive psychology, p. 17
evolutionary psychology, p. 18
positive psychology, p. 19

Human diversity
gender, p. 23
feminist theory, p. 23
race, p. 24
ethnicity, p. 25

culture, p. 26

Research methods in psychology
naturalistic observation, p. 28
observer bias, p. 28
case study, p. 29
survey research, p. 30
correlational research, p. 30
experimental method, p. 32
participants, p. 32

independent variable, p. 33
dependent variable, p. 33
experimental group, p. 33
control group, p. 33
experimenter bias, p. 33
random sample, p. 35
representative sample, p. 35

CHAPTER REVIEW

What Is Psychology?

"Most psychologists study mental and emotional problems and work as psychotherapists." Is this statement true or false? Psychology is the scientific study of behavior and mental processes. It seeks to both describe and explain every aspect of human thought, feelings, perceptions, and actions.

What are the major areas of study within the field of psychology? Psychology has many major subdivisions. Developmental psychology is concerned with processes of growth and change over the life course, from the prenatal period through old age and death. Physiological psychology focuses on the body's neural and chemical systems, studying how these affect thought and behavior. Experimental psychology investigates basic psychological processes, such as learning, memory, sensation, perception, cognition, motivation, and emotion. Personality psychology looks at differences among people in traits such as anxiety, aggressiveness, and self-esteem. Clinical and counseling psychology specializes in diagnosing and treating psychological disorders, while social psychology focuses on how people influence one another's thoughts and actions. Finally, industrial and organizational psychology studies problems in the workplace and other kinds of organizations.

Enduring Issues

Given this broad range of careers and interests, what holds psychology together? A number of fundamental questions cut across the various subfields of psychology, unifying them with similar themes. Five fundamental questions are: (1) PersonSituation: Is behavior caused more by inner traits or by external situations? (2) Nature-Nurture: How do genes and experiences interact to influence people? (3) Stability-Change: How much do we stay the same as we develop and how much do we change? (4) Diversity-Universality: In what ways do people differ in how they think and act? (5) Mind-Body: What is the relationship between our internal experiences and our biological processes?

What does psychology have in common with other sciences? Psychology is a science because it relies on the scientific method to find answers to questions. This method involves careful observation and collection of data, efforts to explain observations by developing theories about relationships and causes, and the systematic testing of hypotheses (or predictions) to rule out theories that aren't valid.

The Growth of Psychology

"Psychology has a long past, but a short history." What does that mean? As a subject of interest to people, psychology has a long past because humans have wondered about behavior and mental processes since ancient times. As a scientific discipline, however, psychology has a short history, dating back only to the late-nineteenth century.

How did Wundt help to define psychology as a science of the mind? Why did James think that sensation and perception alone couldn't explain behavior? Why was Freud's theory of the unconscious shocking at the turn of the twentieth century? Two leading psychological researchers were Wilhelm Wundt and Edward Titchener. Wundt established the first psychology laboratory in 1879 at the University of Leipzig in Germany. His use of experiment and measurement marked the beginnings of psychology as a science. One of Wundt's students, Edward Titchener, established a perspective called structuralism, which was based on the belief that psychology's role was to identify the basic elements of experience and how they combine.

The American psychologist William James criticized structuralism, arguing that sensations cannot be separated from the mental associations that allow us to benefit from past experiences. Our rich storehouse of ideas and memories is what enables us to function in our environment, James believed. His perspective became known as functionalism.

The theories of Sigmund Freud added another new dimension to psychology: the idea that much of our behavior is governed by unconscious conflicts, motives, and desires. Freud's work gave rise to psychodynamic theories.

How was Watson's approach to human behavior different from Freud's? How did Skinner expand behaviorism? John B. Watson, a spokesman for the school of thought called behaviorism, argued that psychology should concern itself only with observable, measurable behavior. Watson based much of his work on the conditioning experiments of Ivan Pavlov.

B. F. Skinner's beliefs were similar to Watson's, but he added the concept of reinforcement or rewards. In this way, he made the learner an active agent in the learning process. Skinner's views dominated American psychology into the 1960s.

How did Gestalt psychologists influence the way we think about perception? How might existential psychology help us to feel less alienated? What aspects of life do humanistic psychologists stress? According to Gestalt psychology, perception depends on the human tendency to see patterns, to distinguish objects from their backgrounds, and to complete pictures from a few clues. In this emphasis on wholeness the Gestalt school radically differed from structuralism.

Existential psychology is a school of thought that attributes psychological problems to feelings of alienation in modern life. The goal of existentialist psychology is to guide people toward an inner identity and the freedom to exercise their personal will. Humanistic psychology is another perspective, one that emphasizes the goal of reaching one's fullest potential.

Cognitive psychology is the study of mental processes in the broadest sense, focusing on how people perceive, interpret, store, and retrieve information. Unlike behaviorists, cognitive psychologists believe that mental processes can and should be studied scientifically. This view has dramatically changed American psychology from its previous behaviorist focus.

Where do evolutionary psychologists look for the roots of human behavior? What new focus is positive psychology bringing to the study of human behavior? Is there a single perspective dominating psychology today? Evolutionary psychology focuses on the functions and adaptive values of various human behaviors, trying to understand how they have evolved. Positive psychology studies subjective feelings of happiness and well-being; the development of individual traits such as integrity and leadership; and the settings that encourage individuals to flourish. In this way it seeks to add a new dimension to psychological research. Most contemporary psychologists do not adhere to just one school of thought. They believe that different theories can often complement one another and together enrich our understanding of human behavior.

In psychology's early years, why were relatively few women accepted in the field? Although psychology has profited from the contributions of women from its beginnings, women often faced discrimination: Some colleges and universities did not grant degrees to women, professional journals were often reluctant to publish their work, and teaching positions were often closed to them.

Human Diversity

Why should you learn about human diversity? A rich diversity of behavior and thought exists in the human species, among individuals and groups. A knowledge of this diversity can help reduce the tensions that arise when people misunderstand one another. It can also help us to define what humans have in common.

How are psychologists helping us to understand the differences between men and women? One area of research on diversity involves differences in thought and behavior between the two sexes or genders. Popular beliefs regarding these differences are called gender stereotypes. Psychologists are trying to determine the causes of gender differences—both the contributions of heredity to them and those of culturally learned gender roles. They have also begin to explore the sensitive issues associated with sexual orientation.

Why are psychologists interested in racial and ethnic differences? Race and ethnicity are two traditional dimensions of diversity in humans. Because it is so difficult to define race, most psychologists have abandoned the term as a scientific concept. Ethnicity and ethnic identity, however, remain meaningful. They involve a shared cultural heritage based on common ancestry, a shared heritage that can affect norms of behavior.

How does culture contribute to human diversity? The intangible aspects of culture—the beliefs, values, traditions, and norms of behavior that a particular people share—make an important contribution to human diversity. In a society as large and diversified as ours, there are also many subcultural groups with their own subcultural identities.

Research Methods in Psychology

What are some of the research methods that psychologists use in their work? Psychologists use a variety of methods to study behavior and mental processes. These include naturalistic observation, case studies, surveys, correlational research, and experiments. Each method has its own advantages and limitations.

Why is a natural setting sometimes better than a laboratory for observing behavior? Psychologists use naturalistic observation to study behavior in natural settings. Because there is minimal interference from the researcher, the behavior observed is likely to be more accurate, spontaneous, and varied than behavior studied in a laboratory. Researchers using this method must be careful to avoid observer bias.

When can a case study be most useful? Researchers conduct a case study to investigate the behavior of one person or a few persons in depth. This method can yield a great deal of detailed, descriptive information that is useful for forming hypotheses.

What are some of the benefits of survey research? Survey research generates a large amount of data quickly and inexpensively by asking a standard set of questions of a large number of people. Great care must be taken, however, in how the questions are worded.

What is the difference between correlation and cause and effect? Correlational research investigates the relation, or correlation, between two or more variables. But, while two variables may be *related* to each other, that does not imply that one *causes* the other.

What kinds of research questions are best studied by experimental research? An experiment is called for when a researcher wants to draw conclusions about cause and effect. In an experiment, the impact of one factor can be studied while all other factors are held constant. The factor whose effects are being studied is called the independent variable because the researcher is free to manipulate it at will. The factor on which there is apt to be an impact is called the dependent variable. Usually an experiment includes both an experimental group of subjects or participants and a control group for comparison purposes. Often a neutral person records data and scores results, so experimenter bias doesn't creep in.

What does multimethod research allow psychologists to do? Because each research method has benefits as well as limitations, many psychologists use multiple methods to study a single problem. Together they can give much fuller answers to questions.

How can sampling affect the results of a research study? Regardless of the particular research method used, psychologists almost always study a small sample of subjects and then generalize their results to larger populations. Proper sampling is critical to ensure that results have broader application. Random samples, in which subjects are chosen randomly, and representative samples, in which subjects are chosen to reflect the general characteristics of the population as a whole, are two ways of doing this.

Can we generalize about research findings from one group to another? Because of differences among people based on age, sex, ethnic background, culture, and so forth, findings from studies that use white, male, American college students as participants cannot always be generalized to other groups. In addition, the gender, race, and ethnic background of a psychologist can have a biasing impact on the outcome of research.

Ethics and Psychology: Research on Humans and Animals

Are there ethical guidelines for conducting psychological research? What objections have been raised regarding research on animal subjects? The American Psychological Association (APA) has a code of ethics for conducting research involving human participants or animal subjects. Researchers must obtain informed consent from participants in their studies. Participants must be told in advance about the nature of the research and the possible risks involved. People should not feel pressured to participate if they do not want to.

Although much of what we know about certain areas of psychology has come from animal research, the practice of experimenting on animals has strong opponents because of the pain and suffering that is sometimes involved. Although the American Psychological Association and the federal government have issued guidelines for the humane treatment of laboratory animals, many animal rights advocates argue that the only ethical research on animals is naturalistic observation.

Careers in Psychology

What can you do with a background in psychology or with an advanced degree? Psychology is one of the most popular majors in colleges and universities. A background in it is useful in a wide number of fields because so many jobs involve a basic understanding of people. Careers for those with advanced degrees in psychology include teaching, research, jobs in government and private business, and a number of occupations in the mental health field. Opportunities in the mental health field depend on one's degree of training. They include the occupations of psychiatrist which requires medical train-ing; the job of clinical psychologist, which involves getting a doctoral degree; and the jobs of counseling psychologist and social worker.

CRITICAL THINKING AND APPLICATIONS

1. What do we mean when we say that psychology is a science?

2. Choose an aspect of human behavior such as kindness, intelligence, or aggressiveness, and then describe how a contemporary psychologist might use multiple perspectives to understand it.

3. You notice that some students in your psychology class take many more notes than others do, and you wonder whether the amount of note-taking ultimately affects grades. What research methods might you use to find out? What would each of these methods tell you about the issue? What are the drawbacks of each? Be specific about the procedures you suggest.

4. How do you feel about animal research and experimentation in psychology? When, if ever, do you think that animal research is justified? Do you approve of the current regulations concerning it? Why, or why not?

WEB QUIZ **1.7** ✓ **Go to the Morris 6e Companion Website to take a practice chapter exam.**

2

The Biological Basis of Behavior

WHEN ALEX WAS BORN, THE LEFT SIDE OF HIS BRAIN, WHICH NORMALLY CONTROLS speech, was smothered by a tangle of abnormal blood vessels that left him unable to talk, half-blind, semiparalyzed, and prone to epileptic seizures. As Alex got older, the seizures became increasingly frequent and severe. Unable to control his epilepsy with medication, Alex's doctors recommended surgery to remove the entire left side of his brain. They were reasonably sure that this procedure would reduce Alex's seizures, but they warned his parents not to expect much other improvement. Alex was long past the age when a mute child could learn to talk.

The operation was a success; the seizures stopped. Then, ten months later, Alex stunned everyone by beginning to speak, first in single words and then in complete sentences. At age 11, he still pronounced some words incorrectly, as if he had a foreign accent; now at age 16, he is fluent. To date, more than fifty epileptic children have undergone successful *hemispherectomies* (removal of the left or right half of the brain). All are expected to be able to lead normal lives.

The brain is the master control center of everything we say and do. One would think that removing half a child's brain would leave him or her severely disabled. But Alex and others have shown that just the opposite is true. Children emerge from the operation with their memory, personality, and sense of humor intact. Like Alex, some show dramatic improvement in speech, coordination, and other areas. How can this be?

First, the human brain—the product of millions of years of evolution—is an extremely complex organ. Our brains contain billions of cells, arranged in countless overlapping pathways and networks, with many backup systems—far more "mental equipment" than we need. In addition, the two hemispheres of the brain are similar though not identical, like our right and left hands. Normally, the two work together. But if the left hemisphere is removed, the right hemisphere takes over most of the functions of the left as it did in Alex's case.

Second, the human brain demonstrates extraordinary *plasticity*, the ability to adapt to new environmental conditions. Although the brain may be the command center of our bodies, it also responds to feedback from the senses and surrounding environment, and so it changes as a result. One reason why children like Alex improve after a hemispherectomy is that their environment changes when their seizures stop and they no longer need antiseizure medications (powerful sedatives that make children groggy). Before the operation, the internal environment of their bodies is chaotic, and their ability to respond to the external environment is dulled. After the operation, their internal environment is calmer, and their awareness of the external environment is enhanced. All the organs of our body—and all our behavior—depend on intricate feedback-and-control patterns. We live surrounded by objects and events, and our biological systems are geared to make adjustments that keep us in tune with our surroundings.

This chapter introduces **psychobiology,** the branch of psychology that deals with the biological bases of behavior and mental processes. We begin by looking at the basic building blocks of the brain and nervous system: nerve cells, or neurons. Then we will explore the two major systems that integrate and coordinate our behavior, keeping us in constant touch with what is going on "out there." One is the *nervous system,* of which the brain is part. The other is the *endocrine system,* made up of glands that secrete chemical messages, called hormones, into the blood. Last, we examine the influence of heredity and human evolution on behavior.

Neurons: The Messengers

What types of cells are found in the nervous system?

The brain of an average human being contains as many as 100 billion nerve cells, or **neurons.** Billions more neurons are found in other parts of the nervous system. Neurons vary widely in size and shape, but they are all specialized to receive and transmit information. A typical neuron is shown in **Figure 2–1.** Like other cells, the neuron's cell body is made up of a nucleus, which contains a complete set of chromosomes and genes; cytoplasm, which keeps the cell alive; and a cell membrane, which encloses the whole cell. What makes a neuron different from other cells is the tiny fibers that extend out from the cell body, enabling a neuron to perform its special job: receiving and transmitting messages. The short fibers branching out around the cell body are **dendrites.** Their role is to pick up incoming messages from other neurons and transmit them to the cell body. The single long fiber extending from the cell body is an **axon.** The axon's job is to carry outgoing messages to neighboring neurons or to a muscle or gland. Axons vary in length from 1 or 2 millimeters (about the length of the word "or" in this sentence) to 3 feet. (In adults, a single axon may run from the brain to the base of the spinal cord or from the spinal cord to the tip of the thumb.) Although a neuron has only one axon, near its end the axon splits into many terminal branches. When we talk about a **nerve (or tract),** we are referring to a group of axons bundled together like wires in an electrical cable.

The axon in **Figure 2–1** is surrounded by a white, fatty covering called a **myelin sheath.** The myelin sheath is "pinched" at intervals, making the axon resemble a string of microscopic sausages. Not all axons have this covering, but myelinated axons are found in all parts of the body. (Because of this white covering, tissues made up primarily of myelinated axons are known as "white matter," whereas tissues made up primarily of unmyelinated axons are called "gray matter.") The myelin sheath has two functions: First, it provides insulation, so that signals from adjacent neurons do not interfere with each other; second, it increases the speed at which signals are transmitted.

Neurons that collect messages from sense organs and carry those messages to the spinal cord or the brain are called **sensory (or afferent) neurons.** Neurons that carry messages from the spinal cord or the brain to the muscles and glands are called **motor (or efferent) neurons.** And neurons that carry messages from one neuron to another are called **interneurons (or association neurons).**

The nervous system also contains a vast number of **glial cells,** or **glia** (the word *glia* means "glue"). Glial cells hold the neurons in place, provide nourishment and remove waste products, prevent harmful substances from passing from the bloodstream into the brain, and form the myelin sheath that insulates and protects neurons. Recent evidence suggests that glial cells may play an important role in learning and memory, and thereby may affect the brain's response to new experiences (Featherstone, Fleming, & Ivy, 2000; Roitbak, 1993).

The Neural Impulse

What "language" do neurons speak?

How do neurons "talk" to one another? What form do their messages take? Neurons speak in a language that all cells in the body understand: simple "yes-no," "on-off" electrochemical impulses.

When a neuron is at rest, the membrane surrounding the cell forms a partial barrier between the fluids that are inside and outside the neuron. Both solutions contain electrically charged particles, or **ions** (see

---

Psychobiology
The area of psychology that focuses on the biological foundations of behavior and mental processes.

Neurons
Individual cells that are the smallest unit of the nervous system.

Dendrites
Short fibers that branch out from the cell body and pick up incoming messages.

Axon
Single long fiber extending from the cell body; it carries outgoing messages.

Nerve (or tract)
Group of axons bundled together.

Myelin sheath
White fatty covering found on some axons.

Sensory (or afferent) neurons
Neurons that carry messages from sense organs to the spinal cord or brain.

Motor (or efferent) neurons
Neurons that carry messages from the spinal cord or brain to the muscles and glands.

Interneurons (or association neurons)
Neurons that carry messages from one neuron to another.

Glial cells (or glia)
Cells that insulate and support neurons by holding them together, provide nourishment and remove waste products, prevent harmful substances from passing into the brain, and form the myelin sheath.

Ions
Electrically charged particles found both inside and outside the neuron.

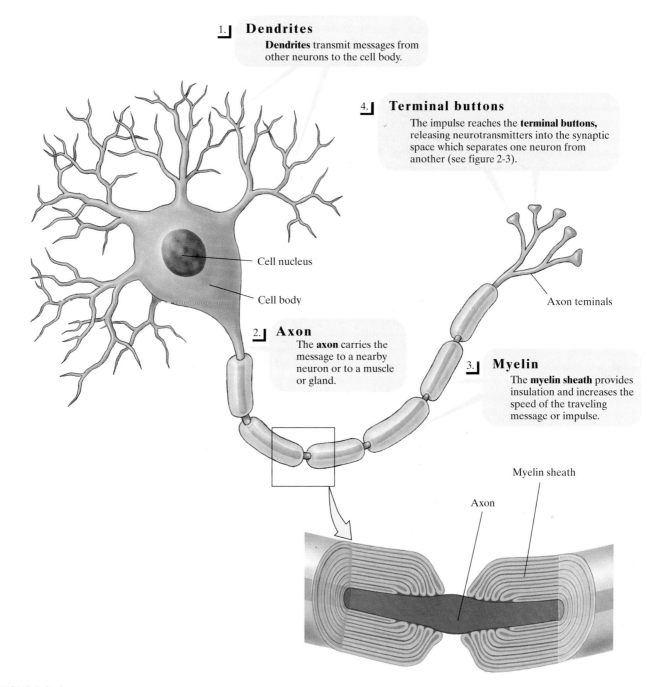

1. **Dendrites**

   Dendrites transmit messages from other neurons to the cell body.

4. **Terminal buttons**

   The impulse reaches the **terminal buttons,** releasing neurotransmitters into the synaptic space which separates one neuron from another (see figure 2-3).

Cell nucleus

Cell body

Axon teminals

2. **Axon**

   The **axon** carries the message to a nearby neuron or to a muscle or gland.

3. **Myelin**

   The **myelin sheath** provides insulation and increases the speed of the traveling message or impulse.

Myelin sheath

Axon

FIGURE 2–1

This typical myelinated neuron shows the cell body, dendrites, axon, myelin sheath, and terminal buttons.

Source: Adapted from *Fundamentals of Human Neuropsychology* (4/e), by Brian Kolb and Ian Q. Whishaw. Copyright © 1980, 1985, 1990, 1996 by W. H. Freeman and Company. Reprinted with permission.

Figure 2–2). Because there are more negative ions inside the neuron than outside, there is a small electrical charge (called the **resting potential**) across the cell membrane. Thus, the resting neuron is said to be in a state of **polarization.** A resting, or polarized, neuron is like a spring that has been compressed or a guitar string that has been pulled but not released. All that is needed to generate a neuron's signal is the release of this tension.

When a small area on the cell membrane is adequately stimulated by an incoming message, pores (or channels) in the membrane at the stimulated area open, allowing a sudden inflow of positively charged sodium ions. This

Resting potential
Electrical charge across a neuron membrane resulting from more positive ions concentrated on the outside and more negative ions on the inside.

Polarization
The condition of a neuron when the inside is negatively charged relative to the outside; for example, when the neuron is at rest.

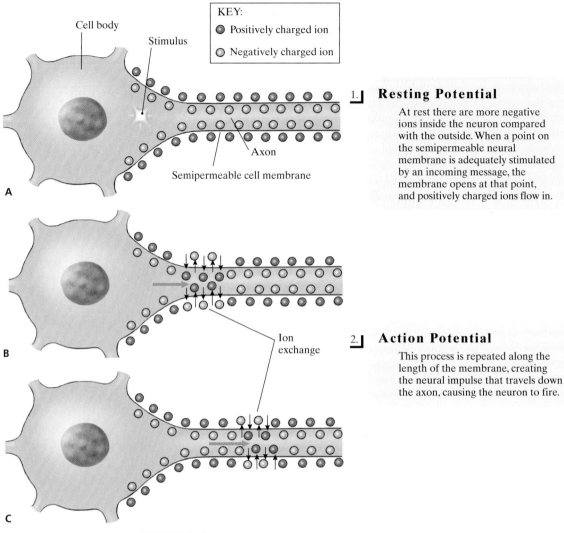

FIGURE 2–2
The neural impulse: communication within the neuron.

Figure labels:

Cell body

Stimulus

KEY:
- Positively charged ion
- Negatively charged ion

1. **Resting Potential**

At rest there are more negative ions inside the neuron compared with the outside. When a point on the semipermeable neural membrane is adequately stimulated by an incoming message, the membrane opens at that point, and positively charged ions flow in.

Axon

Semipermeable cell membrane

A

Ion exchange

2. **Action Potential**

This process is repeated along the length of the membrane, creating the neural impulse that travels down the axon, causing the neuron to fire.

B

C

process is called *depolarization;* now the inside of the neuron is positively charged relative to the outside. Depolarization sets off a chain reaction. When the membrane allows sodium to enter the neuron at one point, the next point on the membrane opens. More sodium ions flow into the neuron at the second spot and depolarize this part of the neuron, and so on, along the entire length of the neuron. As a result, an electrical charge, called a **neural impulse** or **action potential,** travels down the axon, much like a fuse burning from one end to the other (see **Figure 2–2**). When this happens, we say that the neuron has "fired." The speed at which neurons carry impulses varies widely, from as fast as nearly 400 feet per second on largely-myelinated axons to as slow as about 3 feet per second on those with no myelin.

As a rule, single impulses received from neighboring neurons do not make a neuron fire. The incoming message causes a small, temporary shift in the electrical charge, called a **graded potential,** which is transmitted along the cell membrane and may simply fade away, leaving the neuron in its normal polarized state. For a neuron to fire, graded potentials caused by impulses from many neighboring neurons—or from one neuron firing repeatedly—must exceed a certain minimum **threshold of excitation.** Just as a light switch requires a minimum amount of pressure to be turned on,

Neural impulse (or action potential)
The firing of a nerve cell.

Graded potential
A shift in the electrical charge in a tiny area of a neuron.

Threshold of excitation
The level an impulse must exceed to cause a neuron to fire.

an incoming message must be above the minimum threshold to make a neuron fire.

Either neurons fire, or they do not, and every firing of a particular neuron produces an impulse of the same strength. This is called the **all-or-none law.** However, the neuron is likely to fire *more often* when stimulated by a strong signal. The result is rapid neural firing that communicates the message "There's a very strong stimulus out here!" Immediately after firing, the neuron goes through an *absolute refractory period:* For about a thousandth of a second, the neuron will not fire again, no matter how strong the incoming messages may be. In the *relative refractory period,* when the cell is returning to the resting state, the neuron will fire, but only if the incoming message is considerably stronger than is normally necessary to make it fire. Finally, the neuron returns to its resting state, ready to fire again.

A single neuron may have many hundreds of dendrites, and its axon may branch out in numerous directions, so that it is in touch with hundreds or thousands of other cells at both its input end (dendrites) and its output end (axon). At any given moment, a neuron may be receiving messages from other neurons, some of which are primarily excitatory (telling it to "fire"), and from others, primarily inhibitory (telling it to "rest"). The constant interplay of excitation and inhibition determines whether the neuron is likely to fire or not.

 2.1

The Synapse

What happens as information moves from one neuron to the next?

Neurons are not directly connected like links in a chain. Rather, they are separated by a tiny gap, called a **synaptic space** or **synaptic cleft,** where the axon terminals of one neuron *almost* touch the dendrites or cell body of other neurons. The entire area composed of the axon terminals of one neuron, the synaptic space, and the dendrites and cell body of the next neuron is called the **synapse** (see **Figure 2–3**).

For the neural impulse to move on to the next neuron, it must somehow cross the synaptic space. It is tempting to imagine that the neural impulse simply leaps across the gap like an electrical spark, but in reality the transfer is made by chemicals. What actually happens is this: When a neuron fires, an impulse travels down the axon, out through the axon terminals, into a tiny swelling called a **terminal button,** or **synaptic knob.** Most terminal buttons contain a number of tiny oval sacs called **synaptic vesicles** (see **Figure 2–3**). When the neural impulse reaches the end of the terminals, it causes these vesicles to release varying amounts of chemicals called **neurotransmitters** into the synaptic space. Each neurotransmitter has specific matching **receptor sites** on the other side of the synaptic space. Neurotransmitters fit into their corresponding receptor sites just as a key fits into a lock. This lock-and-key system ensures that neurotransmitters do not randomly stimulate other neurons, but follow orderly pathways.

Once their job is complete, neurotransmitters detach from the receptor site. In most cases, they are either reabsorbed into the axon terminals to be used again, broken down and recycled to make new neurotransmitters, or disposed of by the body as waste. The synapse is cleared and returned to its normal state.

Neurotransmitters In recent decades, psychobiologists have identified hundreds of neurotransmitters; their exact functions are still being studied (see *Summary Table: Major Neurotransmitters and Their Effects*). However, a few brain chemicals are well known.

Acetylcholine (ACh) acts where neurons meet skeletal muscles. It also appears to play a critical role in arousal, attention, memory, and motivation

All-or-none law
Principle that the action potential in a neuron does not vary in strength; either the neuron fires at full strength, or it does not fire at all.

Synaptic space (or synaptic cleft)
Tiny gap between the axon terminal of one neuron and the dendrites or cell body of the next neuron.

Synapse
Area composed of the axon terminal of one neuron, the synaptic space, and the dendrite or cell body of the next neuron.

Terminal button (or synaptic knob)
Structure at the end of an axon terminal branch.

Synaptic vesicles
Tiny sacs in a terminal button that release chemicals into the synapse.

Neurotransmitters
Chemicals released by the synaptic vesicles that travel across the synaptic space and affect adjacent neurons.

Receptor sites
Locations on a receptor neuron into which a specific neurotransmitter fits like a key into a lock.

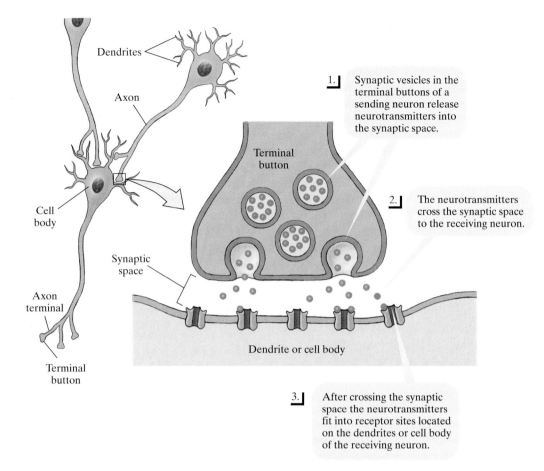

1. Synaptic vesicles in the terminal buttons of a sending neuron release neurotransmitters into the synaptic space.

2. The neurotransmitters cross the synaptic space to the receiving neuron.

3. After crossing the synaptic space the neurotransmitters fit into receptor sites located on the dendrites or cell body of the receiving neuron.

FIGURE 2–3

Synaptic transmission—communication between neurons. When a neural impulse reaches the end of an axon, tiny oval sacs, called synaptic vesicles, at the end of most axons, release varying amounts of chemical substances called neurotransmitters. These substances travel across the synaptic space and affect the next neuron.

> **SUMMARY TABLE**

MAJOR NEUROTRANSMITTERS AND THEIR EFFECTS

Acetylcholine (ACh)	Distributed widely throughout the central nervous system, where it is involved in arousal, attention, memory, motivation, and movement. Involved in muscle action through presence at neuromuscular junctions (specialized type of synapse where neurons connect to muscle cells). Degeneration of neurons that produce ACh has been linked to Alzheimer's disease. Too much ACh can lead to spasms and tremors; too little, to paralysis or torpor.
Dopamine	Involved in a wide variety of behaviors and emotions, including pleasure. Implicated in schizophrenia and Parkinson's disease.
Serotonin	Involved in the regulation of sleep, dreaming, mood, eating, pain, and aggressive behavior. Implicated in depression.
Norepinephrine Endorphins	Affects arousal, wakefulness, learning, memory, and mood. Involved in the inhibition of pain. Released during strenuous exercise. May be responsible for "runner's high."

(Panksepp, 1986). Alzheimer's disease, which involves loss of memory and severe language problems, has been linked to degeneration of the brain cells that produce and respond to ACh.

Dopamine generally affects neurons associated with voluntary movement, learning, memory, and emotions. The symptoms of Parkinson's disease—tremors, muscle spasms, and increasing muscular rigidity—have been traced to loss of the brain cells that produce dopamine. It may also play a role in schizophrenia, a serious mental illness.

Serotonin, popularly known as "the mood molecule," is an example of a neurotransmitter that has widespread effects. Serotonin is like a master key that opens many locks—that is, it attaches to as many as a dozen receptor sites. Serotonin is often involved in emotional experiences and may be a factor in some cases of depression.

Other brain chemicals regulate the sensitivity of large numbers of synapses, in effect "turning up" or "turning down" the activity level of whole portions of the nervous system. *Endorphins,* for example, appear to reduce pain by inhibiting, or "turning down," the neurons that transmit pain messages in the brain. One endorphin was found to be 48 times more potent than morphine when injected into the brain and 3 times more potent when injected into the bloodstream (S. H. Snyder, 1977).

Endorphins were discovered in the early 1970s. Researchers Candace Pert and Solomon Snyder (1973) were attempting to explain the effects of *opiates*—painkilling drugs such as morphine and heroin that are derived from the poppy plant—when they discovered that the central nervous system contained receptor sites for these substances. They reasoned that these receptor sites would not exist unless the body produced its own natural painkillers. Not long after, researchers discovered the endorphins. Morphine and other narcotics lock into the receptors for endorphins and have the same painkilling effects. Research on endorphins has provided clues to why people become addicted to morphine, heroin, and other opiates. When a person takes one of these drugs repeatedly, the body's production of *natural* painkillers slows down. As a result, an addict needs more of the artificial drug to feel "normal."

Imbalances in neurotransmitters appear to contribute to many types of mental illness. Schizophrenia, for example, has been associated with an overabundance of, or hypersensitivity to, dopamine. An undersupply of serotonin and norepinephrine has been linked to depression and other disorders. As in the case of endorphins, the design and testing of drugs has helped psychobiologists to identify the functions of neurotransmitters.

Drugs and Behavior   Most psychoactive drugs and toxins (or poisons) work by either blocking or enhancing the transmission of chemicals across synapses. For example, *botulism* (produced by the bacteria in improperly canned or frozen food) prevents the release of ACh, which carries signals to the muscles. The result is paralysis and, sometimes, rapid death. *Curare,* a poison that some native people of South America traditionally used to tip their arrows, instantly stuns and sometimes kills their prey or enemies. Curare blocks the ACh *receptors*—that is, it has the same effect as botulism but acts at the other side of the synapse. Likewise, the antipsychotic medications *chlorprozamine* (trade name Thorazine) and *clozapine* prevent dopamine from binding to receptor sites; this reduction in stimulation apparently reduces schizophrenic hallucinations.

Other substances do the opposite: they enhance the activity of neurotransmitters. Some do this by increasing the release of a transmitter. For example, the poison of the black widow spider causes ACh to spew into the synapses of the nervous system. As a result, neurons fire repeatedly, causing spasms and tremors. In a slightly more complex loop, *caffeine* increases

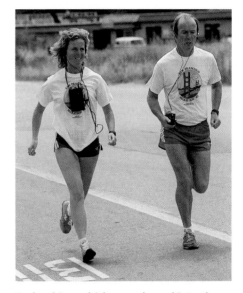

Endorphins, which are released into the brain and body during exercise, are neurotransmitters that act as natural painkillers.

  2.2

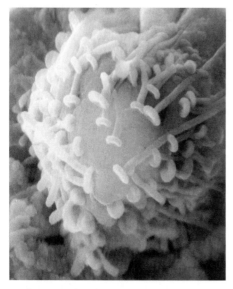

A photograph taken with a scanning electron microscope, showing the synaptic knobs at the ends of axons. Inside the knobs are the vesicles that contain neurotransmitters.

release of excitatory, arousing neurotransmitters by blocking the action of adenosine, a transmitter that inhibits the release of these substances (Nehlig, Daval, & Debry, 1992). Two or three cups of coffee contain enough caffeine to block half the adenosine receptors for several hours, producing a high state of arousal and, in some cases, anxiety and insomnia.

Other substances interfere with the removal of neurotransmitters from the synapse after they have done their job so that they continue to stimulate receptor neurons. *Cocaine*, for example, prevents dopamine from being reabsorbed. As a result, excess amounts of dopamine accumulate in the synapses, producing heightened arousal of the entire nervous system.

The same processes are used by antidepressant medications that reduce the hopeless/helpless symptoms of severe depression, and by antipsychotic medications that alleviate the hallucinations of schizophrenia. We will say more about these "miracle drugs" in Chapter 12, Psychological Disorders, and Chapter 13, Therapies.

Neural Plasticity and Neurogenesis

How does experience change the brain?

In a classic series of experiments, M. R. Rosenzweig (1984) demonstrated the importance of experience to neural development in the laboratory. Rosenzweig divided rats into several groups. Members of one group were isolated in barren cages (an impoverished environment); members of the second group were raised with other rats in cages equipped with a variety of toys, and hence opportunities for exploration, manipulation, and social interaction (an enriched environment). He found that the rats raised in enriched environments had larger neurons with more synaptic connections than those raised in impoverished environments (see **Figure 2–4**). In more

Dendrites of rats living in "enriched" cages showed more synaptic connections

Dendrites of rats living in bare cages

Figure 2–4

Brain growth and experience. In Rosenzweig's experiment, young rats lived in two kinds of cages: "impoverished," with nothing to manipulate or explore, or "enriched," with a variety of objects. When Rosenzweig examined the rats' brains, he found that the enriched group had larger neurons with more synaptic connections (shown as dendrites in the drawing) than the rats that lived in the bare cages. Experience, then, can actually affect the structure of the brain.

Source: From "Brain changes in response to experience" by M. R. Rosenzweig, E. L. Bennett, and M. C. Diamond. Copyright © 1972, Scientific American, Inc. All rights reserved. Adapted with permission of the estate of Bunji Tagawa.

UNDERSTANDING OURSELVES

Can the Brain and Nervous System Repair Themselves?

After a stroke in 1993, Sylvia Elam lost most of the sensation and movement on the right side of her body (Pollack, 2000). She recognized the benefits of an operation performed in 1999 almost as soon as she reached the recovery room. When she ate lunch, she could taste the food for the first time in years. Soon she was talking without stammering, walking without a cane some of the time, and even able to drive a car. "It was absolutely beyond our wildest dreams," said her husband, Ira (p. F1).

Traditionally, injuries to the brain and spinal cord have been considered permanent; treatment was limited to stabilizing the patient to prevent further damage, treating related infections, and using rehabilitation to maximize remaining capabilities (McDonald, 1999). Some individuals with brain damage recovered over time, but they were the exception. New discoveries have changed this prognosis. Specific treatments may take years to develop, but people suffering from neurological disorders such as Parkinson's and Alzheimer's diseases, as well as victims of spinal cord injuries and stroke, now have hope (Barinaga, 2000a; Gage, 2000; McMillan, Robertson, & Wilson, 1999).

The discovery of adult neurogenesis—the generation of new neurons—raises new possibilities. Could adult precursor cells grown in the laboratory be transplanted into patients with neurological damage? Sylvia Elam was one of the first people to volunteer for this procedure. Not all human trials have been as successful, and Mrs. Elam suffered a second, unrelated stroke several months after her operation.

> It was as if stem cells moved through the brain, going from one neuron to the next looking for damage.

Scientists have long known that embryos contain large numbers of stem cells: undifferentiated, precursor or "precells" that, under the right conditions, can give rise to any specialized cell in the body—liver, kidney, blood, heart, or neurons (Bjornson, Rietze, Reynolds, Magli, & Vescovi, 1999). Remarkably, in tests with animals, stem cells transplanted into a brain or spinal cord spontaneously migrated to damaged areas and began to generate specialized neurons for replacement (McKay, 1997). It was as if stem cells moved through the brain, going from one neuron to the next looking for damage. If damage was found, the stem cells began to divide and produce specialized neurons appropriate for that area of the brain.

In clinical trials with human patients suffering from Parkinson's disease, fetal nerve cell transplants have improved motor control for periods of five to ten years (Barinaga, 2000a). But the supply of fetal tissue is limited, and its harvest and use raise ethical questions.

Another potential use of new research findings is to stimulate the brain's own stem cells to provide "self-repair." Once the chemicals that regulate neurogenesis are more fully understood, it may be possible to increase the amounts of these substances in areas of the central nervous system where neural growth needs to occur (Gage, 2000). Some researchers have already begun to identify substances that show promise of stimulating neural regrowth (Rasika, Alvarez-Buylla, & Nottebohm, 1999).

To translate this discovery into treatment, scientists need to learn more about what causes (or blocks) the production of adult stem cells and what causes their "daughter cells" to become mature, specialized neurons and to migrate to different areas of the brain (Gage, 2000). But the groundwork has been laid.

recent experiments, Rosenzweig (1996) showed that similar changes occur in rats of any age. Other researchers have found that rats raised in stimulating environments perform better on a variety of problem-solving tests and develop more synapses when required to perform complex tasks (Kleim, Vig, Ballard, & Greenough, 1997). These combined results suggest that the brain changes in response to the experiences that the organism has, a principle called **neural plasticity.** Furthermore, they demonstrate that neural plasticity is a feedback loop: Experience leads to changes in the brain,

Neural plasticity
The ability of the brain to change in response to experience.

which, in turn, facilitate new learning, which leads to further neural change, and so on (Nelson, 1999).

Reorganization of the brain as a result of experience is not limited to rats. For example, violinists, cellists, and other string musicians spend years developing precise left-hand sensitivity and dexterity. Researchers have found that the area of the musicians' brains associated with left-hand sensation is larger than the area that represents the right hand (which string musicians use for bowing), and larger than the left-hand area in nonmusicians (Elbert, Pantev, Wienbruch, Rockstroh, & Taub, 1995). In deaf people, an area of the brain usually responsible for hearing rewires itself to read lips and sign language (Bosworth & Dobkins, 1999).

We have seen that experience can lead to dramatic changes in the number and complexity of synaptic connections in the brain; that is, in the connections between neurons. Might experience also produce new neurons? For many years, psychologists believed that organisms are born with all the brain cells they will ever have. New research appears to overturn this traditional view. A number of studies conducted in the 1990s showed that adult brains are capable of **neurogenesis,** the production of new brain cells. In the mid-1990s, some researchers demonstrated that human brain tissue (obtained from patients undergoing surgery for severe epilepsy) that was grown in a supportive environment in the laboratory produced functionally mature neurons (L. K. Altman, 1995), but most scientists at the time doubted that this process occurs in real life. A major breakthrough came in November 1998 when a group of American and Swedish researchers reported on autopsies of the brains of elderly patients who had died of cancer.

Neurogenesis
The growth of new neurons.

WEB QUIZ **2.1** ✓

CHECK YOUR UNDERSTANDING

Match each term with the appropriate definition.

_____ neuron
_____ neural plasticity
_____ dendrites
_____ axons
_____ neural impulse
_____ resting potential
_____ absolute refractory period
_____ neurogenesis
_____ synapse
_____ neurotransmitters
_____ dopamine
_____ serotonin
_____ all-or-none law

a. growth of new neurons
b. long cellular fibers carrying outgoing messages
c. when a nerve cell cannot fire again
d. affects emotions, arousal, and sleep
e. cell that transmits information
f. experience changes the brain
g. chemicals that carry messages across synapses
h. short cellular fibers that pick up incoming messages
i. neurotransmitter with a role in schizophrenia and Parkinson's disease
j. action potential
k. a neuron either fires at full strength or not at all
l. terminal button, synaptic space, and dendrite of neighboring neuron
m. electrical imbalance across a neural membrane at rest

Answers: neuron (e); neural plasticity (f); dendrites (h); axons (b); neural impulse (j); resting potential (m); absolute refractory period (c); neurogenesis (a); synapse (l); neurotransmitters (g); dopamine (i); serotonin (d); all-or-none law (k)

A substance injected into their tumors to monitor how fast the tumors were growing revealed that the patients' brains had continued to produce new neurons up to the end of their lives (Eriksson et al., 1998). The discovery of lifelong neurogenesis has widespread implications for treating neurological disorders (see *Understanding the World Around Us*).

INTERACTIVE LECTURE **2.1**

The Central Nervous System

The Organization of the Nervous System

How is the nervous system organized?

Every part of the nervous system is connected to every other part. To understand its anatomy and functions, however, it is useful to analyze the nervous system in terms of the divisions and subdivisions shown in **Figure 2–5.** The **central nervous system** includes the brain and spinal cord, which together contain more than 90 percent of the body's neurons. The **peripheral nervous system** consists of nerves that connect the brain and spinal cord to every other part of the body, carrying messages back and forth between the central nervous system and the sense organs, muscles, and glands. The peripheral nervous system is subdivided into the *somatic nervous system,* which transmits information about body movements and the external environment, and the *autonomic nervous system,* which transmits information to and from the internal organs and glands. (We will discuss the endocrine system, which works hand in hand with the nervous system, later in the chapter.)

The Brain

What are the major structures and areas of the brain, and what functions do they serve?

The brain is the seat of awareness and reason, the place where learning, memory, and emotions are centered. It is the part of us that decides what to do and whether that decision was right or wrong, and it imagines how things might have turned out if we had acted differently.

The human brain—our "crowning glory"—is the product of millions of years of evolution. As new, more complex structures were added, older structures were retained. One way to understand the brain is to look at three layers that evolved in different stages of evolution: (1) the primitive *central core;* (2) the *limbic system,* which evolved later; and (3) the *cerebral hemispheres,* which are in charge of higher mental processes such as problem-solving and language (see **Figure 2–6**). We will use these three basic divisions to describe the parts of the brain, what they do, and how they interact to influence our behavior (see *Summary Table: Parts of the Brain and Their Functions*).

The Central Core At the point where the spinal cord enters the skull, it becomes the hindbrain. Because the **hindbrain** is found in even the most primitive vertebrates, it is believed to have been the earliest part of the brain to evolve. The part of the hindbrain nearest to the spinal cord is the medulla, a narrow structure about 1.5 inches long. The medulla controls such bodily functions as breathing, heart rate, and blood pressure. The medulla is also the point

Central nervous system
Division of the nervous system that consists of the brain and spinal cord.

Peripheral nervous system
Division of the nervous system that connects the central nervous system to the rest of the body.

Hindbrain
Area containing the medulla, pons, and cerebellum.

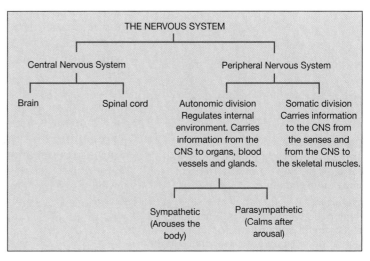

FIGURE 2–5

A schematic diagram of the divisions of the nervous system and their various subparts.

SUMMARY TABLE

PARTS OF THE BRAIN AND THEIR FUNCTIONS

Central Core	Medulla	Regulates respiration, heart rate, blood pressure
	Pons	Regulates sleep-wake cycles
	Cerebellum	Regulates reflexes and balance Coordinates movement
	Thalamus	Major sensory relay center Regulates higher brain centers and peripheral nervous system
	Hypothalamus	Influences emotion and motivation Governs stress reactions
	Reticular formation	Regulates attention and alertness
	Hippocampus	Regulates formation of new memories
	Amygdala	Governs emotions related to self-preservation
Cerebral Cortex	Frontal lobe	Goal-directed behavior Concentration Emotional control and temperament Voluntary movements Coordinates messages from other lobes Complex problem solving Involved in many aspects of personality
	Parietal lobe	Receives sensory information Visual/spatial abilities
	Occipital lobe	Receives and processes visual information
	Temporal lobe	Smell and hearing Balance and equilibrium Emotion and motivation Some language comprehension Complex visual processing and face recognition

Cerebellum
Structure in the hindbrain that controls certain reflexes and coordinates the body's movements.

Midbrain
Region between the hindbrain and the forebrain; it is important for hearing and sight, and it is one of several places in the brain where pain is registered.

Thalamus
Forebrain region that relays and translates incoming messages from the sense receptors, except those for smell.

at which many of the nerves from the body cross over on their way to and from the higher brain centers; nerves from the left part of the body cross to the right side of the brain and vice versa (a topic to which we will return). Near the medulla lies the pons, which produces chemicals that help maintain our sleep-wake cycle (discussed in Chapter 4, States of Consciousness). Both the medulla and the pons transmit messages to the upper areas of the brain.

The part of the hindbrain at the top and back of the brain stem is the **cerebellum** (or "little brain"), which is responsible for our sense of balance and for coordinating the body's actions to ensure that movements go together in efficient sequences. Damage to the cerebellum causes severe problems in movement, such as jerky motions and stumbling.

Above the cerebellum, the brain stem widens to form the **midbrain.** The midbrain is especially important for hearing and sight. It is also one of several places in the brain where pain is registered.

More or less directly over the brain stem are the two egg-shaped structures that make up the **thalamus.** The thalamus is often described as a relay station: Almost all sensory information passes through the thalamus on the way to higher levels of the brain, where it is translated and routed to the appropriate brain location. Directly below the thalamus is the smaller

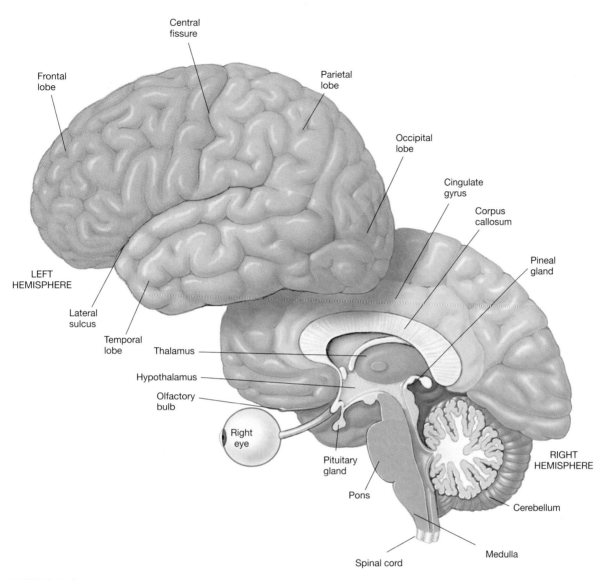

FIGURE 2–6
The divisions of the brain.

hypothalamus, which exerts an enormous influence on many kinds of motivation. Portions of the hypothalamus govern hunger, thirst, sexual drive, and body temperature (Winn, 1995) and are directly involved in emotional behavior such as experiencing rage, terror, or pleasure.

The **reticular formation (RF)** is a netlike system of neurons that weaves through all of these structures. Its main job seems to be to send "Alert!" signals to the higher parts of the brain in response to incoming messages. The RF can be subdued, however. During sleep, the RF is turned down; anesthetics work largely by temporarily shutting this system off; moreover, permanent damage to the RF can induce a coma.

The Cerebral Cortex Ballooning out over and around the central core, virtually hiding it, is the *cerebrum*. The cerebrum is divided into two hemispheres and covered by a thin layer of gray matter (unmyelinated cells) called the **cerebral cortex.** This is what most people think of first when they talk about "the brain"; it is the part of the brain that processes thought, vision, language, memory, and emotions. The cere-

Hypothalamus
Forebrain region that governs motivation and emotional responses.

Reticular formation (RF)
Network of neurons in the hindbrain, the midbrain, and part of the forebrain whose primary function is to alert and arouse the higher parts of the brain.

Cerebral cortex
The outer surface of the two cerebral hemispheres that regulates most complex behavior.

The human brain, viewed from the top. Its relatively small size belies its enormous complexity.

The skull of Phineas Gage, showing where the tamping iron passed through it, severely damaging his frontal lobes.

Association areas
Areas of the cerebral cortex where incoming messages from the separate senses are combined into meaningful impressions and outgoing messages from the motor areas are integrated.

Frontal lobe
Part of the cerebral cortex that is responsible for voluntary movement; it is also important for attention, goal-directed behavior, and appropriate emotional experiences.

Primary motor cortex
The section of the frontal lobe responsible for voluntary movement.

bral cortex takes up most of the room inside the skull, accounting for about 80 percent of the weight of the human brain and containing about 70 percent of the neurons in the central nervous system.

The cerebral cortex, which is the most recently evolved part of the nervous system, is more highly developed in humans than in any other animal. Spread out, the human cortex would cover 2 to 3 square feet and be about as thick as the letter T. To fit inside the skull, in humans the cerebral cortex has developed intricate folds—hills and valleys called *convolutions.* In each person, these convolutions form a pattern that is as unique as a fingerprint.

A number of landmarks on the cortex allow us to identify distinct areas each with different functions. The first is a deep cleft, running from front to back, that divides the brain into *right* and *left* hemispheres. As seen in **Figure 2–6,** each of these hemispheres can be divided into four *lobes* (described later), which are separated from one another by crevices, or fissures, such as the *central fissure.* In addition, there are large areas on the cortex of all four lobes called **association areas** that integrate information from diverse parts of the cortex and are involved in mental processes such as learning, thinking, and remembering.

The different lobes of the cerebral hemispheres are specialized for different functions (see **Figure 2–7**). The **frontal lobe,** located just behind the forehead, accounts for about half the volume of the human brain, yet it remains the most mysterious part of the brain. The frontal lobe receives and coordinates messages from the other three lobes of the cortex and seems to keep track of previous and future movements of the body. This ability to monitor and integrate the complex tasks that are going on in the rest of the brain has led some investigators to hypothesize that the frontal lobe serves as an "executive control center" for the brain (Kimberg, D'Esposito, & Farah, 1997; Waltz et al., 1999) and is involved in a wide range of problem-solving tasks, including answering both verbal and spatial IQ-test questions (Duncan et al., 2000). The section of the frontal lobe known as the **primary motor cortex** plays a key role in voluntary action. The frontal lobe also seems to play a key role in the behaviors we associate with personality, including motivation, persistence, affect (emotional responses), and even character (social and moral judgment).

Until recently, our knowledge of the frontal lobes was based on research with nonhuman animals, whose frontal lobes are relatively undeveloped, and on studies of rare cases of people with frontal lobe damage. One famous case, involving a bizarre accident, was reported in 1848. Phineas Gage, the foreman of a railroad construction gang, made a mistake while using some blasting powder. A 4-foot-long, 1/4-inch thick tamping iron tore through his cheek and severely damaged his frontal lobes. To the amazement of those who witnessed the accident, Gage remained conscious, walked part of the way to a doctor, and suffered few physical aftereffects. His memory and skills seemed to be as good as ever. However, Gage underwent major personality changes. Once a friendly, considerate fellow and a steady worker, he became increasingly profane and irreverent, lost interest in work, and drifted from job to job. Gage's personality changes were so radical that, in the view of his friends, he was no longer the same man.

A century later, most psychobiologists agree that personality change—especially loss of motivation and ability to concentrate—is the major outcome of frontal lobe damage. The frontal lobes are involved in goal-directed behavior and the ability to lead a mature emotional life. When adults suffer strokes or other traumas to the prefrontal cortex, their ability to make judgments is impaired.

Much more research needs to be done before psychologists can understand how this part of the cortex contributes to such a wide and subtle range of mental activities (see *Summary Table: Parts of the Brain and Their Functions*).

The **occipital lobe,** located at the very back of the cerebral hemispheres, receives and processes visual information. Damage to the occipital lobe can produce blindness, even though the eyes and their neural connections to the brain are perfectly healthy and intact (see **Figure 2–7**).

The **parietal lobe** occupies the top back half of each hemisphere. This lobe receives sensory information from all over the body—from sense receptors in the skin, muscles, joints, internal organs, and taste buds. Messages from these sense receptors are registered in the **primary somatosensory cortex.** The parietal lobe also seems to oversee spatial abilities, such as the ability to follow a map or to tell someone how to get from one place to another (A. Cohen & Raffal, 1991).

The **temporal lobe,** located in front of the occipital lobe, roughly behind the temples, plays an important role in complex visual tasks such as recognizing faces. The temporal lobe also receives and processes information from the ears, contributes to balance and equilibrium, and regulates

Occipital lobe
Part of the cerebral hemisphere that receives and interprets visual information.

Parietal lobe
Part of the cerebral cortex that receives sensory information from throughout the body.

Primary somatosensory cortex
Area of the parietal lobe where messages from the sense receptors are registered.

Temporal lobe
Part of the cerebral hemisphere that helps regulate hearing, balance and equilibrium, and certain emotions and motivations.

Central fissure
Separates the primary somatosensory cortex from the primary motor cortex

Primary somatosensory cortex
Registers sensory messages from the entire body

Primary motor cortex
Part of the frontal lobe; sends messages to muscles and glands; key role in voluntary movement

Parietal lobe
Receives sensory information from sense receptors all over the body (in the skin, muscles, joints, organs, taste buds); also involved in spatial abilities

Frontal lobe
Coordinates messages from the other cerebral lobes; involved in complex problem-solving tasks

Temporal lobe
Involved in complex visual tasks; balance; regulates emotions; strong role in understanding language

Occipital lobe
Receives and processes visual information

FIGURE 2–7
The four lobes of the cerebral cortex.   Deep fissures in the cortex separate these areas or lobes. Also shown are the primary somatosensory and motor areas.

Frontal lobe

Thalamus

Hippocampus

Amygdala

Hypothalamus

Olfactory bulb

FIGURE 2–8

The limbic system. A system of brain structures including the thalamus, hippocampus, amygdala, hypothalamus, and olfactory bulb. This system is primarily involved in regulating behaviors having to do with motivation and emotion.

2.3

emotions and motivations such as anxiety, pleasure, and anger. In addition, the ability to understand and comprehend language is thought to be concentrated primarily in the rear portion of the temporal lobes, though some language comprehension may also occur in the parietal and frontal lobes (Ojemann, Ojemann, Lettich, & Berger, 1989).

The Limbic System The **limbic system** is a ring of loosely connected structures located between the central core and the cerebral hemispheres (see **Figure 2–8**). In evolutionary terms, the limbic system is more recent than the central core and is fully developed only in mammals.

One part of the limbic system, the *hippocampus,* plays an essential role in the formation of new memories. People with severe damage to this area can still remember names, faces, and events that they recorded in memory before they were injured, but they cannot remember anything new. Another structure, the *amygdala,* along with the hippocampus governs emotions related to self-preservation (MacLean, 1970). When portions of these structures are damaged or removed, aggressive animals become tame and docile. In contrast, stimulation of some portions of these structures causes animals to exhibit signs of fear and panic, whereas stimulation of other portions triggers unprovoked attacks.

Other limbic structures heighten the experience of pleasure. Given the opportunity to press a bar that electrically stimulates one such region, animals do so endlessly, ignoring food and water. Humans also experience pleasure when some areas of the limbic system are electrically stimulated, though apparently not as intensely (Kupfermann, 1991; Olds & Forbes, 1981). (We will return to the limbic system in Chapter 8, Motivation and Emotion.) The limbic system also appears to play a central role in times of stress, coordinating and integrating the activity of the nervous system.

Hemispheric Specialization

How are the left and right hemispheres specialized for different functions?

The cerebrum, as noted earlier, consists of two separate cerebral hemispheres. Quite literally, humans have a "right half-brain" and a "left half-brain." The primary connection between the left and the right hemispheres is a thick, ribbonlike band of nerve fibers under the cortex called the **corpus callosum** (**Figure 2–9**).

Under normal conditions, the left and right cerebral hemispheres are in close communication through the corpus callosum and work together as a coordinated unit (Banich, 1998; Hellige, 1993; Hoptman & Davidson, 1994; Semrud-Clikeman & Hynd, 1990). But research suggests that the cerebral hemispheres are not really equivalent (see **Figure 2–9**).

The most dramatic evidence comes from "split-brain" patients. In some cases of severe epilepsy, surgeons cut the corpus callosum to stop the spread of epileptic seizures from one hemisphere to the other. In general, this procedure is successful: The patients' seizures are reduced and sometimes eliminated. But their two hemispheres are functionally isolated; in effect, their right brain doesn't know what their left brain is doing (and vice versa). Since sensory information typically is sent to both hemispheres, in everyday life, split-brain patients function quite normally. However, a series of ingenious experiments revealed what happens when the two hemispheres cannot communicate (Sperry, 1964, 1968, 1970).

In one such experiment, split-brain patients were asked to stare at a spot on a projection screen. When pictures of various objects were pro-

Limbic system
Ring of structures that plays a role in learning and emotional behavior.

Corpus callosum
A thick band of nerve fibers connecting the left and right cerebral cortex.

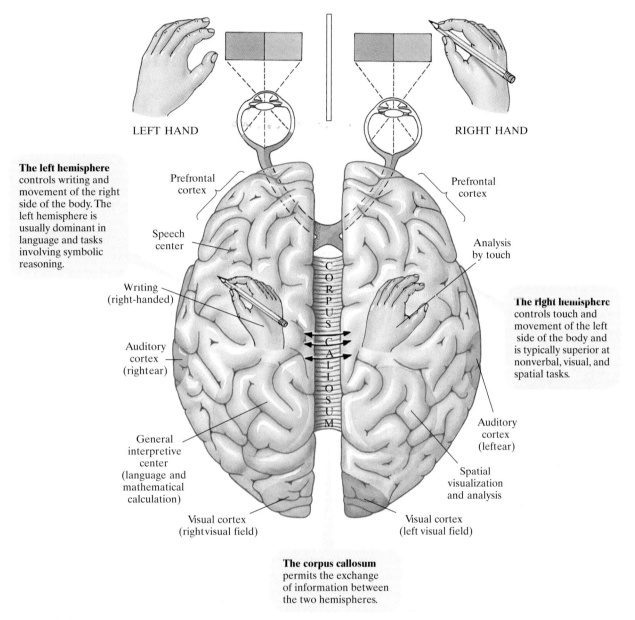

LEFT HAND

RIGHT HAND

The left hemisphere controls writing and movement of the right side of the body. The left hemisphere is usually dominant in language and tasks involving symbolic reasoning.

Prefrontal cortex

Prefrontal cortex

Speech center

Analysis by touch

Writing (right-handed)

The right hemisphere controls touch and movement of the left side of the body and is typically superior at nonverbal, visual, and spatial tasks.

Auditory cortex (right ear)

CORPUS CALLOSUM

General interpretive center (language and mathematical calculation)

Auditory cortex (left ear)

Spatial visualization and analysis

Visual cortex (right visual field)

Visual cortex (left visual field)

The corpus callosum permits the exchange of information between the two hemispheres.

FIGURE 2–9

The two cerebral hemispheres. Each hemisphere specializes in processing specific types of information, as shown on the diagram.

jected to the *right* of that spot, they could name the objects. And, with their right hands, they could pick them out of a group of hidden objects (see **Figure 2–10A**). However, when pictures of objects were shown on the *left* side of the screen, something changed. Patients could pick out the objects by feeling them with their left hands, but they couldn't say what the objects were! In fact, when asked what objects they saw on the left side of the screen, split-brain patients usually said "nothing" (see **Figure 2–10B**).

The explanation for these unusual results is found in the way each hemisphere of the brain operates. When the corpus callosum is cut, the *left hemisphere* receives information only from the right side of the body and the right half of the visual field. As a result, it can match an object shown in the right visual field with information received by touch from the right hand, but it is unaware of (and thus unable to identify) objects shown in the left

FIGURE 2–10

(A) When split-brain patients stare at the "X" in the center of the screen, visual information projected on the right side of the screen goes to the patient's left hemisphere, which controls language. When asked what they see, patients can reply correctly. (B) When split-brain patients stare at the "X" in the center of the screen, visual information projected on the left side of the screen goes to the patient's right hemisphere, which does not control language. When asked what they see, patients cannot name the object but can pick it out by touch with the left hand.

Source: Adapted from Carol Ward, © 1987, Discover Publications.

visual field or touched by the left hand. Conversely, the *right hemisphere* receives information only from the left side of the visual field and the left side of the body. Consequently, the right hemisphere can match an object shown in the left visual field with information received by touch from the left hand, but it is unaware of any objects shown in the right visual field or touched with the right hand.

But why can't the right hemisphere verbally identify an object that is shown in the left visual field? The answer is that for the great majority of people (even for most left-handers), language ability is concentrated primarily in the *left* hemisphere (Hellige, 1990, 1993). As a result, when an object is in the left visual field, the nonverbal right hemisphere can see the object but can't name it. The verbal left hemisphere, in contrast, can't see an object in this location, so when asked what it sees, it answers that nothing is on the screen.

Does the left hemisphere specialize in any other tasks besides language? Some researchers think that it may also operate more analytically, logically, rationally, and sequentially than the right hemisphere does (Kingstone, Enns, Mangun, & Gazzaniga, 1995). In contrast, the right hemisphere excels at visual and spatial tasks—nonverbal imagery, including music, face recognition, and the perception of emotions (Hellige, 1990, 1993; Metcalfe, Funnell, & Gazzaniga, 1995; Semrud-Clikeman & Hynd, 1990). Put another way, the left hemisphere specializes in analyzing sequences and details, whereas the right hemisphere specializes in holistic processing (Reuter-Lorenz & Miller, 1998).

The frontal lobes of the two hemispheres may also influence temperament in distinctive ways. People whose left frontal lobe is more active than the right tend to be more cheerful, sociable, ebullient, and self-confident, whereas people with more right frontal lobe activity are more easily stressed, frightened, and upset by unpleasant things. They also tend to be more suspicious and depressed than people with predominantly left frontal lobe activity (Henriques & Davidson, 1990; Tomarken et al., 1990).

Although such research is fascinating and fun to speculate about, it is necessary to be cautious in interpreting it. First, not everyone shows the same pattern of differences between the left and right hemispheres. In particular, the differences between the hemispheres may be greater in men than in women (Hellige, 1993; Seamon & Kenrick, 1992; Semrud-Clikeman & Hynd, 1990). Second, it is easy to oversimplify and exaggerate differences between the two sides of the brain. Split-brain research has given rise to several popular but misguided books that classify people as "right-brain" or "left-brain" thinkers. It is important to remember that under normal conditions, the right and left hemispheres are in close communication through the corpus callosum and so work together in a coordinated, integrated way (Hoptman & Davidson, 1994).

Language   The notion that human language is controlled primarily by the left cerebral hemisphere was first set forth in the 1860s by a French physician named Paul Broca. Broca's ideas were modified a decade later by the scientist Karl Wernicke. Thus, it should come as no surprise that the two major language areas in the brain have traditionally been called Broca's area and Wernicke's area (see **Figure 2–11**).

Wernicke's area lies toward the back of the temporal lobe. This area is crucial in processing and understanding what others are saying. By contrast, Broca's area, found in the frontal lobe, is considered to be essential to our ability to talk. To oversimplify a bit, Wernicke's area seems to be important for listening, and Broca's area seems to be important for talking. Support for these distinctions comes from patients who have suffered left-hemisphere strokes and resulting brain damage. Such strokes often produce predictable language problems, called *aphasias.* If the brain damage primarily affects Broca's area, the aphasia tends to be "expressive." That is, the patients' language difficulties lie predominantly in sequencing and producing language (talking). If the damage primarily affects Wernicke's area, the aphasia tends to be "receptive," and patients generally have profound difficulties understanding language (listening).

Tools for Studying the Brain

What methods have been developed to study the brain?

For centuries, our understanding of the brain depended entirely on observing patients who had suffered brain injury or from examining the brains of cadavers. Another approach (and one that is still in use) was to remove or damage the brains of nonhuman animals and study the effects. But the human cerebral cortex is far more complicated than that of any other animal. How can scientists study the living, fully functioning human brain? Contemporary neuroscientists have four basic techniques—microelectrodes, macroelectrodes, structural imaging, and functional imaging. New, more accurate techniques have appeared almost every year and are used for both diagnosis and research.

Microelectrode Techniques *Microelectrode* recording techniques are used to study the functions of single neurons. A microelectrode is a tiny glass or quartz pipette or tube (smaller in diameter than a human hair) that is filled with a conducting liquid. When technicians place the tip of this electrode inside a neuron, they can study changes in the electrical conditions of that neuron. Microelectrode techniques have been used to understand action potentials, the effects of drugs or toxins on neurons, and even processes that occur in the neural membrane.

Macroelectrode Techniques *Macroelectrode* recording techniques are used to obtain an overall picture of the activity in particular regions of the brain, which may contain millions of neurons. The first such device—the *electroencephalograph* (EEG) is still in use today. Flat electrodes, taped to the scalp, are linked by wires to a device that translates electrical activity into lines on a moving roll of paper (or, more recently, images on a computer screen). This graph of so-called brain waves provides an index of both the strength and the rhythm of neural activity. As we will see in Chapter 4, States of Consciousness, this technique has given researchers valuable insights into changes in brain waves during sleep and dreaming.

The macroelectrode technique enables researchers to "listen" to what is going on in the brain, but it does not allow them to *look* through the skull and see what is happening. Some newer techniques, however, do just that.

Structural Imaging When researchers want to map the structures in a living human brain, they turn to two newer techniques. *Computerized axial tomography* (CAT or CT) *scanning* allows scientists to create three-dimensional images of a human brain without performing surgery. To

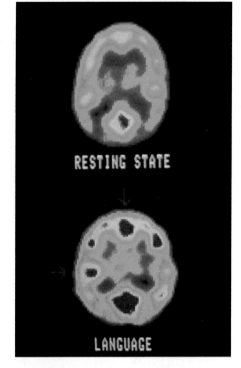

PET scans of a person at rest (top) and using language (bottom). The "hot" colors (red and yellow) indicate greater brain activity. These scans show that language activity is located primarily, but not exclusively, in the brain's left hemisphere.

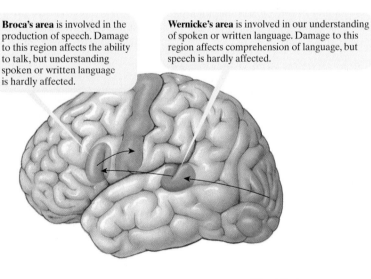

Motor Cortex

Broca's area is involved in the production of speech. Damage to this region affects the ability to talk, but understanding spoken or written language is hardly affected.

Wernicke's area is involved in our understanding of spoken or written language. Damage to this region affects comprehension of language, but speech is hardly affected.

Visual Cortex

FIGURE 2–11

Processing of speech and language.
Broca's and Wernicke's areas, generally found only on the left side of the brain, work together, enabling us to produce and understand speech and language.

MRI image of the human head.

EEG imaging of one person's alpha brain waves. Red and violet colors indicate greater alpha-wave activity.

produce a CAT scan, an X-ray photography unit rotates around the person, moving from the top of the head to the bottom; a computer then combines the resulting images. *Magnetic resonance imaging* (MRI) is even more successful at producing pictures of the inner regions of the brain, with its ridges, folds, and fissures. Here the person's head is surrounded by a magnetic field, and the brain is exposed to radio waves, which causes hydrogen atoms in the brain to release energy. The energy released by different structures in the brain generates an image that appears on a computer screen.

Functional Imaging   In many cases, researchers are interested in more than structure; they want to look at the brain's *activity* as it actually reacts to sensory stimuli such as pain, tones, and words. This is the goal of several functional *imaging* methods. EEG imaging measures brain activity "on a millisecond-by-millisecond basis" (Fischman, 1985, p. 18). In this technique, more than two dozen electrodes are placed at important locations on the scalp. These electrodes record brain activities, which are then converted by a computer into colored images on a television screen. This technique has been extremely useful in detecting abnormal cortical activity such as that observed during an epileptic seizure.

Two related techniques, called *magnetoencephalography* (MEG) and *magnetic source imaging* (MSI), take the procedure a step further. In standard EEG, electrical signals are distorted as they pass through the skull, and their exact source is difficult to determine. However, those same electrical signals create magnetic fields that are unaffected by bone. Both MEG and MSI measure the strength of the magnetic field and identify its source with considerable accuracy. Using these procedures, neuroscientists have begun to determine exactly which parts of the brain do most of the work in such psychological processes as memory (Gabrieli et al., 1996), language processing (Tulving et al., 1994), and reading. In turn, this research is beginning to shed new light on such disorders as amnesia and dyslexia (a reading disorder).

Another family of functional imaging techniques—including *positron emission tomography* (PET) *scanning*—uses radioactive energy to map brain activity. In these techniques, a person first receives an injection of a radioactive substance. Brain structures that are especially active immediately after the injection absorb most of the substance. When the substance starts to decay, it

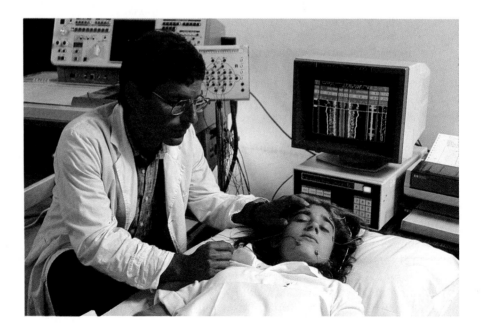

In an EEG, electrodes attached to the scalp are used to create a picture of neural activity in the brain.

releases subatomic particles. By studying where most of the particles come from, researchers can determine exactly which portions of the brain are most active. Some of the findings produced by these techniques have been surprising. For example, one study found that, in general, the brains of people with higher IQ scores are *less* active than those of people with lower IQ scores, perhaps because they process information more efficiently (Haier, 1993). Progress has also been made in locating the damaged brain region in Parkinson's disease. Other researchers have used these techniques to investigate how our memory for words and images is stored in the brain (Cabeza & Nyberg, 2000; Craik et al., 1999). These techniques also increase our knowledge of the effects of psychoactive drugs, such as antidepressants.

One of the newest and most powerful techniques for recording activity in the brain is called *functional magnetic resonance imaging* (fMRI). Functional MRI measures the movement of blood molecules (which is related to neuron activity) in the brain, permitting neuroscientists to pinpoint specific sites and details of neuronal activity. By comparing brain activity in normal learners with brain activity in children with learning problems, researchers have begun to identify the biological origins of attention-deficit/hyperactivity disorder (ADHD) (Vaidya et al., 1998); dyslexia (Shaywitz et al., 1998); and difficulties with math (Dehane, Spelke, Stanescu, Pinel, & Tsivkin, 1999). Because fMRI enables us to collect extremely precise images rapidly and does not require the injection of radioactive chemicals (making it less invasive), it is especially promising as a new research tool (Esposito, Zarahn, & Aguirre, 1999; Nelson et al., 2000).

By combining these various techniques, neuroscientists can simultaneously observe anatomical structures (from CAT and MRI), sites of energy use (PET and MEG), blood and water movement (fMRI), and areas of electrical activity in the brain (EEG). As a result, scientists have begun to study the impact of drugs on the brain, the formation of memories (Craik et al., 1999), and the sites of many other mental activities (Sarter, Berntson, & Cacioppo, 1996; Blood & Zatorre, 2001). They are also gaining insights into the role of the brain in schizophrenia (Thompson et al., 2001).

The Spinal Cord

What does the spinal cord do? How does it work with the brain to sense events and act on them?

We talk of the brain and the spinal cord as two distinct structures, but in fact, there is no clear boundary between them; at its upper end, the spinal cord enlarges into the brain stem (see **Figure 2–12**).

The **spinal cord** is our communications superhighway, connecting the brain to most of the rest of the body. Without it, we would be literally helpless. More than 400,000 Americans are partially or fully paralyzed—about half as a result of sudden traumas to the spinal cord (most often due to car crashes, gunshot wounds, falls, or sports injuries); and half as a result of tumors, infections, and such disorders as multiple sclerosis (McDonald, 1999). When the spinal cord is severed, parts of the body are literally disconnected from the brain. These victims lose all sensations from the parts of the body that can no longer send information to higher brain areas, and they can no longer control the movements of those body parts.

The spinal cord is made up of soft, jellylike bundles of long axons, wrapped in insulating myelin (white matter) and surrounded and protected by the bones in the spine. There are two major neural pathways in the spinal cord. One consists of motor neurons, descending from the brain, that control internal organs and muscles and help to regulate the autonomic nervous system (described later). The other consists of ascending, sensory neurons that carry information from the extremities and internal organs to

Severing the spinal cord at the neck typically causes paralysis of everything below the head because nerves connecting to the body's muscles no longer have a cable to the brain. Actor Christopher Reeve suffered this tragedy after being thrown from a horse. He and others may someday benefit from research on neurogenesis. (See the *Understanding the World Around Us* box on neurogenesis on p. 55.)

Spinal cord
Complex cable of neurons that runs down the spine, connecting the brain to most of the rest of the body.

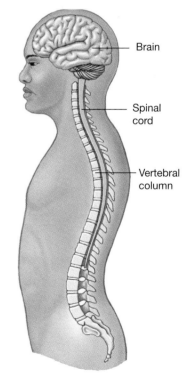

FIGURE 2–12
Brain and spinal cord.

Source: Human Physiology, An Integrated Approach by Silverthorn, © 1989. Reprinted by permission of Pearson Education, Inc., Upper Saddle River, NJ.

the brain. In addition, the spinal cord contains neural circuits that produce reflex movements (and control some aspects of walking). These circuits do not require input from the brain.

To understand how the spinal cord works, consider the simple act of burning your finger on a hot pan (see **Figure 2–13**). You pull your hand away without thinking, but that quick response was the last event in a series of reactions in your nervous system. First, special sensory cells pick up the message that your finger is burned. They pass this information along to *interneurons* located in the spinal cord. The interneurons, in turn, connect to motor neurons, triggering a quick withdrawal of your hand. (A similar reaction occurs when the doctor taps your knee with a rubber mallet.) At the same time, the message is being sent to other parts of your nervous system. Your body goes on "emergency alert": You breathe faster, your heart pounds, your entire body (including the endocrine system) mobilizes itself against the wound. Meanwhile, your brain is interpreting the messages it receives: You feel pain, you look at the burn, and you run cold water over your hand. A simple, small burn, then, triggers a complex, coordinated sequence of activities. This reaction began in the peripheral nervous system.

INTERACTIVE LECTURE **2.2**

WEB QUIZ **2.2**

CHECK YOUR UNDERSTANDING

1. Which brain structure is a vital center for the control of temperature, eating, drinking, and sexual behavior?
   a. cerebral cortex
   b. pons
   c. cerebellum
   d. hypothalamus
2. Match the lobes of the cerebral cortex with their functions.
   ____ frontal lobes   a. process language and information from the ears
   ____ occipital lobes   b. process body sensations and spatial information
   ____ temporal lobes   c. plan goal-directed behavior
   ____ parietal lobes   d. process visual information
3. Simple reflexes are controlled by the
   a. frontal cortex.
   b. cerebellum.
   c. spinal cord.
   d. somato sensory cortex.

Answers: 1. d. 2. frontal lobes (c); occipital lobes (d); temporal lobes (a); parietal lobes (b). 3. c.

The Peripheral Nervous System

How does the brain communicate with the rest of the body? How is the autonomic branch of the peripheral nervous system involved in controlling emotions?

Afferent neurons
Neurons that carry messages from sense organs to the spinal cord or brain.

Efferent neurons
Neurons that carry messages from the spinal cord or brain to the muscles and glands.

The peripheral nervous system (PNS) links the brain and spinal cord to the rest of the body, including the sensory receptors, glands, internal organs, and skeletal muscles (see **Figure 2–5**). It consists of both **afferent neurons,** which carry messages *to* the central nervous system (CNS), and **efferent neurons**, which carry messages *from* the CNS. The afferent neurons carry sensory information. All the things that register through your senses—sights, sounds, smells, temperature, pressure, and so on—travel to your brain via afferent neurons. The efferent neurons carry signals from the brain to the body's muscles and glands.

Some neurons belong to a part of the PNS called the **somatic nervous system.** Neurons in this system are involved in making voluntary movements of the skeletal muscles. Every deliberate action you make, from pedaling a bike to scratching a toe, involves neurons in the somatic nervous system. Other neurons belong to a part of the PNS called the autonomic nervous system. Neurons in the **autonomic nervous system** govern involuntary activities of your internal organs, from the beating of your heart to the hormone secretions of your glands.

The autonomic nervous system is of special interest to psychologists because it is involved not only in vital body functions, such as breathing and blood flow, but also in important emotions as well. To understand the workings of the autonomic nervous system, you must know about the system's two parts: the *sympathetic* and the *parasympathetic* divisions (see **Figure 2–14**).

The nerve fibers of the **sympathetic division** are busiest when you are intensely aroused, such as being enraged or very frightened. For example, if you were hiking through a woods and suddenly encountered a large, growling bear, your sympathetic division would be instantaneously triggered. In response to messages from it, your heart would begin to pound, your breathing would quicken, your pupils would enlarge, and your digestion would stop. All these changes would help direct your energy and attention to the emergency you faced, giving you the keen senses, stamina, and strength needed to flee from the danger or to stand and fight it. Your sympathetic division would also tell your glands to start pumping hormones into your blood to further strengthen your body's reactions. Sympathetic nerve fibers connect to every internal organ—a fact that explains why the body's response to sudden danger is so widespread.

Although sympathetic reactions are often sustained even after danger is passed, eventually even the most intense sympathetic division reaction fades, and the body calms down, returning to normal. This calming effect is promoted by the **parasympathetic division** of the autonomic nervous system. Parasympathetic nerve fibers connect to the same organs as sympathetic nerve fibers do, but they cause the opposite reaction. The parasympathetic division says, in effect, "OK, the heat's off, back to normal." The heart then goes back to beating at its regular rate, the stomach muscles relax, digestion resumes, breathing slows down, and the pupils contract. So whereas the sympathetic division arouses the body in response to danger and stress, the parasympathetic division calms the body once the threat has passed.

Traditionally, the autonomic nervous system was regarded as the "automatic" part of the body's response mechanism (hence its name). You could not, it was believed, tell your own autonomic nervous system when to speed up or slow down your heartbeat or when to stop or start your digestive processes. However, studies in the 1960s and 1970s showed that humans (and animals) have some control over the autonomic nervous

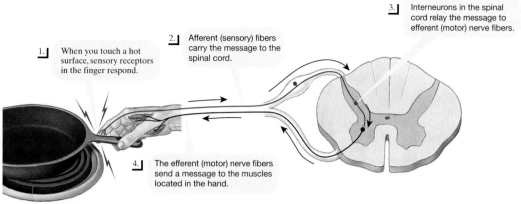

1. When you touch a hot surface, sensory receptors in the finger respond.

2. Afferent (sensory) fibers carry the message to the spinal cord.

3. Interneurons in the spinal cord relay the message to efferent (motor) nerve fibers.

4. The efferent (motor) nerve fibers send a message to the muscles located in the hand.

FIGURE 2–13
The spinal cord and reflex action.

When you are in a frightening situation, such as being confronted with an angry dog, the sympathetic division of the autonomic nervous system triggers a number of responses within your body. These responses give you the strength and stamina to either fight the danger or flee from it.

Somatic nervous system
The part of the peripheral nervous system that carries messages from the senses to the central nervous system and between the central nervous system and the skeletal muscles.

Autonomic nervous system
The part of the peripheral nervous system that carries messages between the central nervous system and the internal organs.

Sympathetic division
Branch of the autonomic nervous system; it prepares the body for quick action in an emergency.

Parasympathetic division
Branch of the autonomic nervous system; it calms and relaxes the body.

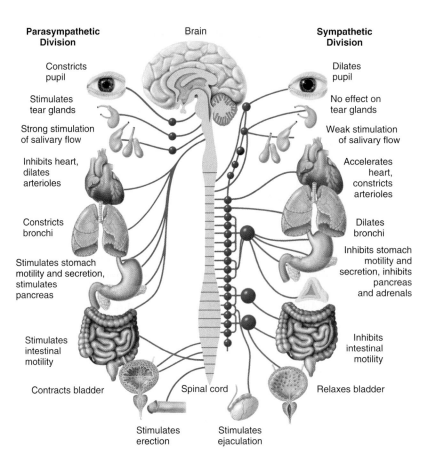

Figure 2–14

The sympathetic and parasympathetic divisions of the autonomic nervous system. The sympathetic division generally acts to arouse the body, preparing it for "fight or flight." The parasympathetic follows with messages to relax.

Source: Adapted from *General Biology*, revised edition, 1st edition by Willis Johnson, Richard A. Laubengayer, and Louis E. Delanney, Copyright © 1961. Reprinted with permission of Brooks/Cole, an imprint of the Wadsworth Group, a division of Thomson Learning. Fax 800 730-2215.

system. For example, people can learn to moderate the severity of high blood pressure or migraine headaches, and even to regulate their own heart rate and brain waves through *biofeedback*, a subject we will look at more closely in Chapter 5, Learning.

INTERACTIVE LECTURE **2.3**

WEB QUIZ **2.3**

CHECK YOUR UNDERSTANDING

Indicate whether each function is associated with the sympathetic (S) or the parasympathetic (P) division of the autonomic nervous system.

_____a. heartbeat increases

_____b. stomach starts digesting food

_____c. breathing speeds up

_____d. body recovers from an emergency situation

Answers: . a. (S), b. (P), c. (S), d. (P).

The Endocrine System

Why are psychologists interested in hormones?

The nervous system is not the only mechanism that regulates the functioning of our bodies. The endocrine system plays a key role in helping to coordinate and integrate complex psychological reactions. In fact, as we've noted throughout this chapter, the nervous system and the endocrine system work together in a constant chemical conversation. The **endocrine**

Endocrine glands

Glands of the endocrine system that release hormones into the bloodstream.

glands release chemical substances called **hormones** that are carried throughout your body by the bloodstream. Hormones serve a similar function to neurotransmitters: They carry messages. Indeed, the same substance—for example, norepinephrine—may serve both as a neurotransmitter and as a hormone. A main difference between the nervous and the endocrine systems is speed. A nerve impulse may travel through the body in a few hundredths of a second. Traveling through the bloodstream is a slower process: Hormones may take seconds, even minutes, to reach their target.

Hormones interest psychologists for two reasons. First, at certain stages of development, hormones *organize* the nervous system and body tissues. At puberty, for example, hormone surges trigger the development of secondary sex characteristics, including breasts in females, a deeper voice in males, and pubic and underarm hair in both sexes. Second, hormones *activate* behaviors. They affect such things as alertness or sleepiness, excitability, sexual behavior, ability to concentrate, aggressiveness, reactions to stress, even desire for companionship. Hormones can also have dramatic effects on mood, emotional reactivity, ability to learn, and ability to resist disease. Radical changes in some hormones may also contribute to serious psychological disorders such as depression. The locations of the endocrine glands are shown in **Figure 2–15.** Here we focus on those glands whose functions are best understood and that have the most impact on behavior and mental processes.

The **thyroid gland** is located just below the larynx, or voice box. It produces one primary hormone, *thyroxin,* which regulates the body's rate of metabolism and thus how alert and energetic people are and how fat or thin they tend to be. An overactive thyroid can produce a variety of symptoms: overexcitability, insomnia, reduced attention span, fatigue, agitation, acting out of character, and making snap decisions, as well as reduced concentration and difficulty focusing on a task. Too little thyroxin leads to the other extreme: the desire to sleep and sleep and yet feel constantly tired. It is not surprising that thyroid problems are often misdiagnosed as depression or simply as "problems in living."

Embedded in the thyroid gland are the **parathyroids**—four tiny organs that control and balance the levels of calcium and phosphate in the body, which in turn influence levels of excitability.

The pea-sized **pineal gland** is located in the middle of the brain. It secretes the hormone *melatonin,* which helps to regulate sleep–wake cycles. Disturbances in melatonin are responsible, in part, for "jet lag." We will discuss the biological clock in greater detail in Chapter 4, States of Consciousness.

The **pancreas** lies in a curve between the stomach and the small intestine. The pancreas controls the level of sugar in the blood by secreting two regulating hormones: *insulin* and *glucagon.* These two hormones work against each other to keep the blood-sugar level properly balanced. Underproduction of insulin leads to *diabetes mellitus,* a chronic disorder characterized by too much sugar in the blood and urine; oversecretion of insulin leads to the chronic fatigue of *hypoglycemia,* a condition in which there is too little sugar in the blood.

The **pituitary gland,** which is located on the underside of the brain, is connected to the hypothalamus. The pituitary produces the largest number of different hormones and thus has the widest range of effects on the body's functions. The pituitary influences blood pressure, thirst, contractions of the uterus during childbirth, milk production, sexual behavior and interest, body growth, the amount of water in the body's cells, and other functions as well. It is often called the "master gland" because of its influential role in regulating other endocrine glands.

Hormones
Chemical substances released by the endocrine glands; they help regulate bodily activities.

Thyroid gland
Endocrine gland located below the voice box; it produces the hormone thyroxin.

Parathyroids
Four tiny glands embedded in the thyroid; they secrete parathormone.

Pineal gland
A gland located roughly in the center of the brain that appears to regulate activity levels over the course of a day.

Pancreas
Organ lying between the stomach and small intestine; it secretes insulin and glucagon to regulate blood-sugar levels.

Pituitary gland
Gland located on the underside of the brain; it produces the largest number of the body's hormones.

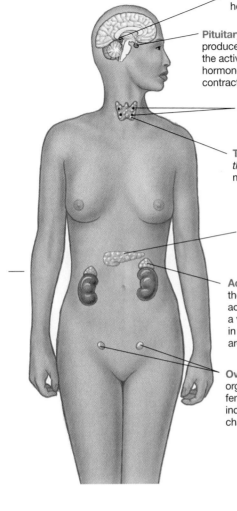

Pineal gland secretes *melatonin* which helps regulate sleep-wake cycles.

Pituitary gland, controlled by the hypothalamus, produces a wide variety of hormones that regulate the activities of several other glands. Pituitary hormones are also involved in growth, uterine contractions during childbirth and milk production.

Parathyroids regulate calcium and phosphate levels in the body influencing excitability.

Thyroid gland secretes the hormone *thyroxin*, which regulates the body's metabolic rate.

Pancreas regulates blood sugar levels with two hormones: *insulin* and *glucagon*.

Adrenal glands consist of two glands; the adrenal cortex (the outer layer) and adrenal medulla (the inner core) secrete a variety of hormones that are involved in the body's response to stress and arousal when physically threatened.

Ovaries secrete *estrogen*, which organizes the development of the female reproductive system, including the secondary sexual characteristics.

Testes secrete *testosterone*, which during prenatal growth regulates the development of the male reproductive system. Testosterone levels are also linked to sexual interest and sexual behavior in adults.

FIGURE 2–15

The glands of the endocrine system.   Endocrine glands secrete hormones that produce widespread effects on the body.

The **gonads**—the *testes* in males and the *ovaries* in females—secrete hormones that have traditionally been classified as masculine (the *androgens*) and feminine (the *estrogens*). (Both sexes produce both types of hormone, but androgens predominate in males, whereas estrogens predominate in females.) These hormones play a number of important organizing roles in human development. For example, in humans, if the hormone *testosterone* is present during the third and fourth month after conception, the fetus will develop as a male; otherwise, it will develop as a female (Kalat, 1988).

Testosterone has long been linked to aggressive behavior. For example, violence is greatest among males between the ages of 15 and 25, the years when testosterone levels are highest. However, recent studies suggest that estrogen also may be linked to aggressive behavior in both males and females (Angier, 1995; Ogawa et al., 1997). Estrogen also may be linked to a boost in cognitive abilities, such as manual dexterity, verbal skills, and perceptual speed. Women do better at these sorts of tasks during the ovulatory phase of their menstrual cycles, when estrogen levels are high, and postmenopausal women show improvement in them when they undergo re-

Gonads
The reproductive glands—testes in males and ovaries in females.

placement therapy (E. Hampson & Kimura, 1992; Kimura & Hampson, 1994). Finally, estrogen may serve a "protective" function in women, since their rate of strokes and heart attacks increases relative to men after menopause, when estrogen levels decline.

The two **adrenal glands** are located just above the kidneys. Each adrenal gland has two parts: an inner core, called the *adrenal medulla,* and an outer layer, called the *adrenal cortex.* Both the adrenal cortex and the adrenal medulla affect the body's reaction to stress. Stimulated by the autonomic nervous system, the adrenal cortex pours several hormones into the bloodstream. One, *epinephrine,* activates the sympathetic nervous system, making the heart beat faster, stopping digestion, enlarging the pupils of the eyes, sending more sugar into the bloodstream, and preparing the blood to clot fast, if necessary. Another hormone, *norepinephrine* (also a neurotransmitter) not only raises blood pressure by causing the blood vessels to become constricted but also is carried by the bloodstream to the anterior pituitary, where it triggers the release of still more hormones, thus prolonging the response to stress. This process is why it takes time for the body to return to normal after extreme emotional excitement. (We will see other examples of this interaction in Chapter 8, Motivation and Emotion.)

INTERACTIVE LECTURE **2.4**

WEB QUIZ **2.4**

CHECK YOUR UNDERSTANDING

1. Communication in the endocrine system depends on _____, which are chemicals secreted directly into the bloodstream.
2. Match each gland with its major function.

   _____ thyroid gland
   _____ parathyroid glands
   _____ pineal gland
   _____ pancreas
   _____ pituitary gland
   _____ gonads
   _____ adrenal glands

   a. balance calcium and phosphate in the body
   b. controls sugar level in the blood
   c. involved in stress response
   d. produce androgens and estrogens
   e. regulates rate of metabolism
   f. controls other endocrine glands
   g. controls daily cycle of activity levels

Answers: 1. hormones. 2. thyroid gland (e); parathyroid glands (a); pineal gland (g); pancreas (b); pituitary gland (f); gonads (d); adrenal glands (c).

Genes, Evolution, and Behavior

Our brain, nervous system, and endocrine system keep us aware of what is happening outside (and inside) our bodies; enable us to use language, think, and solve problems; affect our emotions; and thus guide our behavior. To understand why they function as they do, we need to look at our genetic heritage, as individuals and as members of the human species.

Two different but related fields address the influence of heredity on human behavior. **Behavior genetics** focuses on the extent to which heredity accounts for individual differences in behavior and thinking. **Evolutionary psychology** studies the evolutionary roots of behaviors and mental processes that all human beings share. To understand the contributions of these fields, we must first understand the process of inheritance.

Adrenal glands
Two endocrine glands located just above the kidneys.

Behavior genetics
Study of the relationship between heredity and behavior.

Evolutionary psychology
A subfield of psychology concerned with the origins of behaviors and mental processes, their adaptive value, and the purposes they continue to serve.

The 23 pairs of chromosomes found in every normal human cell. The two members of 22 of these pairs look exactly alike. The two members of the 23rd pair, the sex chromosomes, may or may not look alike. Females have equivalent X chromosomes, while males have one X and one Y chromosome (see above).

Genetics
Study of how traits are transmitted from one generation to the next.

Genes
Elements that control the transmission of traits; they are found on the chromosomes.

Chromosomes
Pairs of threadlike bodies within the cell nucleus that contain the genes.

Deoxyribonucleic acid (DNA)
Complex molecule in a double-helix configuration that is the main ingredient of chromosomes and genes and that forms the code for all genetic information.

Human genome
The full complement of genes within a human cell.

Dominant gene
Member of a gene pair that controls the appearance of a certain trait.

Recessive gene
Member of a gene pair that can control the appearance of a certain trait only if it is paired with another recessive gene.

Polygenic inheritance
Process by which several genes interact to produce a certain trait; responsible for our most important traits.

Genetics

How are traits passed from one generation to the next?

Genetics is the study of how living things pass on traits from one generation to the next. Offspring are not carbon copies or "clones" of their parents, yet some traits reappear from generation to generation in predictable patterns. At the turn of the century, scientists named the basic units of inheritance **genes.** But they did not know what genes were or how they were transmitted.

Today we know much more about genes and the way that they work. Genes are carried by **chromosomes,** tiny threadlike bodies found in the nucleus of all cells. Chromosomes vary in size and shape, and usually come in pairs. Each species has a constant number: Mice have 20 pairs, monkeys have 27, and peas have 7. Human beings have 23 pairs of chromosomes in every normal cell, except the sex cells (eggs and sperm), which have only half a set of chromosomes. At fertilization, the chromosomes from the father's sperm link to the chromosomes from the mother's egg, creating a new cell called a *zygote.* That single cell, and all of the billions of body cells that develop from it (except sperm and eggs), contain 46 chromosomes, arranged as 23 pairs.

The main ingredient of chromosomes is **deoxyribonucleic acid (DNA),** a complex organic molecule that looks like two chains twisted around each other in a double helix pattern. DNA is the only known molecule that can replicate or reproduce itself, which happens each time a cell divides. A gene is a small segment of DNA that carries directions for a particular trait or group of traits. Each human chromosome contains thousands of genes in fixed locations. The **human genome** (the sum total of all the genes in all human chromosomes) contains as many as 100,000 genes.

Genes, like chromosomes, occur in pairs. In some cases, such as eye color, one may be a **dominant gene** (B for brown eyes) and the other a **recessive gene** (b for blue eyes). A child who inherits the gene for blue eyes from both parents (bb) will have blue eyes (see **Figure 2–16**). A sibling who inherits the gene for brown eyes from both parents (BB) will have brown eyes; and so will a sibling who inherits the gene for brown eyes from one parent and the gene for blue eyes from the other (Bb or bB).

Examples of a single gene that controls a single trait are rare, however. In **polygenic inheritance,** a single gene contributes to more than one trait. Thus one trait depends on the actions of a number of genes. Weight, height, skin pigmentation, and countless other characteristics are polygenic. Just as each of the instruments in a symphony orchestra contributes separate notes to the sound that reaches the audience, each of the genes in a polygenic system contributes separately to the total effect (McClearn et al., 1991).

Heredity need not be immediately or fully apparent. In some cases, expression of a trait is delayed until later in life. For example, many men inherit "male-pattern baldness" that does not show up until middle age. Moreover, quite often genes may predispose a person to developing a particular trait, but full expression of the characteristic depends on environmental factors. For example, people with an inherited tendency to gain weight may or may not become obese, depending on their diet, exercise program, and overall health. Put another way, genes establish a range of potential outcomes. Height (and numerous other traits) depends on the interactions of many genes with the environment. Given the same environment, a person who inherits "tall" genes will be tall, and a person who inherits "short" genes, short. But if the first person is malnourished in childhood and the second person well nourished as a child, they may be the same height as adults. On average, Americans today are taller than their grandparents and great-grandparents, whose genes they share. The reason is that they enjoyed better food as children and were less likely to contract growth-stunting childhood diseases.

So far, we have used physical characteristics as examples. Behavior geneticists apply the same principles to *psychological* characteristics.

Behavior Genetics

What methods do psychologists use to study the effects of genes on behavior?

Behavior geneticists study the topics that interest all psychologists—perception, learning and memory, motivation and emotions, personality, and psychological disorders—but from a genetic perspective. Their goal is to identify what genes contribute to intelligence, temperament, talents, and other characteristics, as well as genetic predispositions to psychological and neurological disorders (Brunner, Nelen, Breakfield, Ropers, & Van Oost, 1993; D. Johnson, 1990; Loehlin, Willerman, & Horn, 1988; Plomin, 1999; Plomin, DeFries, & Mc-Clearn, 1990; Plomin & Rende, 1991). Of course, genes do not directly cause behavior. Rather, they affect both the development and operation of the nervous system and the endocrine system, which, in turn, influence the likelihood that a certain behavior will occur under certain circumstances (Wahlsten, 1999).

In the remainder of this chapter, we will look at some of the methods used by behavior geneticists as well as some of their more interesting discoveries. We will start with methods appropriate for animal studies and then examine the techniques used to study **behavior genetics** in humans.

Animal Behavior Genetics Much of what we know about behavior genetics comes from studies of nonhuman animals. Mice are favorite subjects because they breed quickly and have relatively complex behavior patterns. In *strain studies,* close relatives, such as siblings, are intensively inbred over many generations to create strains of animals that are genetically similar to one another but different from other strains. When animals from different strains are raised together in the same environment, differences between them largely reflect genetic differences in the strains. This method has shown that performance on learning tasks, as well as sense of smell and susceptibility to seizures, are affected by heredity.

Selection studies are another way to assess *heritability*, the degree to which a trait is inherited. If a trait is closely regulated by genes, when animals with the trait are interbred, more of their offspring should have the trait than one would find in the general population. Humans have practiced selective breeding for thousands of years to create breeds of dogs and other domesticated animals that have desirable traits. The evidence suggests that dogs resembled wolves until about 15,000 years ago, when humans began to establish permanent settlements. Through selective breeding, different traits—both physical and psychological—became associated with different breeds. Dogs bred to guard were aggressive and loyal to their master, whereas herding dogs developed the ability to concentrate intensely to keep large numbers of animals bigger than the dogs together in a group. Today, with more than 400 breeds, dogs are more variable in size and shape than any other species with the possible exception of humans.

FIGURE 2–16

Transmission of eye color by dominant (B) and recessive (b) genes. This figure represents the four possible combinations of eye-color genes in these parents' offspring. Because three out of the four combinations result in brown-eyed children, the chance that any child will have brown eyes is 75 percent.

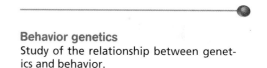

Behavior genetics
Study of the relationship between genetics and behavior.

The twisted chain of the long DNA molecule contains the genetic code.

People clearly do inherit physical traits from their parents. Whether—and to what extent—they also inherit behavioral traits remains uncertain.

Family studies
Studies of heritability in humans based on the assumption that if genes influence a certain trait, close relatives should be more similar on that trait than distant relatives.

Twin studies
Studies of identical and fraternal twins to determine the relative influence of heredity and environment on human behavior.

Identical twins
Twins developed from a single fertilized ovum and therefore identical in genetic makeup at the time of conception.

Fraternal twins
Twins developed from two separate fertilized ova and therefore different in genetic makeup.

Human Behavior Genetics   For obvious reasons, scientists cannot conduct strain or selection studies with human beings. But there are a number of ways to study behavioral techniques indirectly.

Family studies are based on the assumption that if genes influence a trait, close relatives should share that trait more often than distant relatives because close relatives have more genes in common. For example, overall, schizophrenia occurs in only 1 to 2 percent of the general population (Robins & Regier, 1991). Siblings of people with schizophrenia are about eight times more likely, and children of schizophrenic parents about ten times more likely, to develop the disorder than someone chosen randomly from the general population. Unfortunately, because family members share not only some genes but also similar environments, family studies alone cannot clearly distinguish the effects of heredity and environment (Plomin, DeFries, & McClearn, 1990).

To obtain a clearer picture of the influences of heredity and environment, psychologists often use **twin studies. Identical twins** develop from a single fertilized ovum and are therefore identical in genetic makeup. Any differences between them must be due to environmental influences. **Fraternal twins,** however, develop from two separate fertilized egg cells and are no more similar genetically than are other brothers and sisters. If twin pairs grow up in similar environments and if identical twins are no more alike in a particular characteristic than fraternal twins, then heredity cannot be very important for that trait.

Twin studies have provided evidence for the heritability of a number of behaviors, ranging from verbal skills (Eley, Bishop, et al., 1999), to aggressiveness (Eley, Lichenstein, & Stevenson, 1999), to mannerisms such as the strength of a handshake (Farber, 1981), to depression and anxiety (Eley & Stevenson, 1999; O'Connor, McGuire, Reiss, Hetherington, & Plomin, 1998). When one identical twin develops schizophrenia, the chances that the other twin will develop the disorder are about 50 percent. For fraternal twins, the chances are about 15 percent (Gottesman, 1991). The much higher rate exhibited by twins, particularly identical twins, suggests that heredity plays a crucial role in schizophrenia.

Similarities between twins, even identical twins, cannot automatically be attributed to genes, however; twins nearly always grow up together. Parents and others may treat them alike—or try to emphasize their differences, so that they grow up as separate individuals. In either case, the data for heritability may be biased. To avoid this problem, researchers attempt to locate identical twins who were separated at birth or in very early childhood and then raised in different homes. A University of Minnesota team led by Thomas Bouchard followed separated twins for more than ten years (Bouchard, 1984, 1996; Bouchard et al., 1990). They confirmed that genetics plays a major role in mental retardation, schizophrenia, depression, and intelligence. Bouchard and his colleagues have also found that complex personality traits, interests, and talents, and even the structure of brain waves, are guided by genetics.

Studies of twins separated shortly after birth do have some weaknesses. For example, the environment in the uterus may be more traumatic for one twin than the other (Phelps, Davis, & Schartz, 1997). Also, since adoption agencies usually try to place twins in similar families, their environments may not be much different (Ford, 1993; Wyatt, 1993). Finally, the number of twin pairs separated at birth is fairly small, so scientists sometimes rely on other types of studies to investigate the influence of heredity.

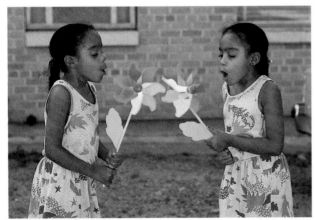

Identical twins develop from a single ovum and consequently start out with the same genetic material.

Adoption studies focus on children who were adopted at birth and brought up by parents not genetically related to them. Adoption studies provide additional evidence for the heritability of intelligence and some forms of mental illness (Horn, 1983; Scarr & Weinberg, 1983) and in behavior previously thought to be solely determined by environmental influences, even smoking (Boomsma, Koopman, Van Doornen, & Orlebeke, 1994; Heath & Martin, 1993; Lerman et al., 1999). By combining the results of *twin, adoption,* and *family* studies, psychologists have obtained a clearer picture of the role of heredity in many human characteristics, including schizophrenia. As shown in **Figure 2-17,** the average risk of schizophrenia steadily increases in direct relation to the closeness of one's biological relationship to an individual with the disorder.

So far, we have been talking about the environment as if it were something *out there,* something that happens *to* people, over which they have little control. But individuals also shape their environments. For example, people tend to seek out environments in which they feel comfortable. A shy child might prefer a quieter play group than would a child who is more outgoing. In addition, our own behavior causes others to respond in particular ways. A teacher's approach to correcting the behavior of a sensitive child might be quite different from how a more energetic child would be treated. Because genes and environments interact in so many intricate ways, trying to separate and isolate the effects of heredity and environment—nature and nurture—is artificial (Collins, Maccoby, Steinberg, Hetherington & Bornstein, 2000, 2001; McGuire, 2001; Plomin, 1997).

Molecular Genetics   Until recently, behavioral geneticists could study heritability only indirectly. But new molecular genetics techniques make it possible to study, and even change, the human genetic code directly. The goal of the Human Genome Project, launched in 1990, is to map all 23 pairs of human chromosomes and to determine which genes influence which characteristics (Johnson, 1990; Plomin & Rende, 1991). (See *Understanding the World Around Us*). In June 2000—ahead of schedule—researchers announced the first rough map of the entire **human genome,** the complete set of genes that defines a human being. Already, researchers have identified an individual gene on chromosome 19 that is associated with some forms of Alzheimer's disease (Corder et al., 1993), and other specific chromosome sites for alcoholism (Uhl, Blum, Nobel, & Smith, 1993), schizophrenia, (Blouin et al., 1998), suicide (Abbar, et al., 2001; Du et al., 1999), cognitive functioning (Gécz & Mulley, 2000), intelligence (Plomin et al., 1994), and even aging (Migliaccio et al., 1999). By using these genetic markers, researchers expect not only to prevent or reverse some genetic diseases but also to understand better the role of heredity in even the most complex behaviors (Plomin, DeFries, & McClearn, 1990; Wahlsten, 1999).

Evolutionary Psychology

How might the process of natural selection influence human social behaviors?

Much as behavior geneticists try to explain the individual differences in human behavior, evolutionary psychologists try to explain the behavioral traits that people have in common. The key to these shared characteristics, they feel, is the process of evolution by **natural selection,** first described by Charles Darwin in *On the Origin of Species* (1859).

Biological Relationship

General population	1%
First cousin	2%
Half-siblings	6%
Siblings	9%
Children	13%
Fraternal twins	17%
Identical twins	48%

Lifetime risk (in percentage) 0 10 20 30 40 50

FIGURE 2–17

Average risk of schizophrenia among biological relatives of people with schizophrenia.

Source: Biographical Relationship graph adapted from p. 96 from *Schizophrenia Genesis: The Origins of Madness* by Irving I. Gottesman, © 1991 by Irving I. Gottesman. Reprinted by permission of Henry Holt and Company, LLC..

Live! **psych** 2.5

Adoption studies
Research carried out on children, adopted at birth by parents not related to them, to determine the relative influence of heredity and environment on human behavior.

Human genome
The full complement of genes within a human cell.

Natural selection
The mechanism proposed by Darwin in his theory of evolution, which states that organisms best adapted to their environment tend to survive, transmitting their genetic characteristics to succeeding generations, whereas organisms with less adaptive characteristics tend to vanish from the earth.

UNDERSTANDING The World Around Us

In Search of the Human Genome

The term *genome* refers to the full complement of an organism's genetic material. Thus, the genome for any particular organism contains a complete blueprint for building all the structures and directing all the living processes for the lifetime of that organism. Scientists estimate that the human genome is made up of 80,000 to 100,000 individual genes, located on the 23 pairs of chromosomes that make up human DNA. These genes, contained within every cell of our body, distinguish us from other forms of life. Surprisingly minute variations in the human genome are responsible for the individual differences we see in the world's 6 billion people. Experts believe that the average variation in the human genetic code for any two different people is much less than 1 percent.

As we've noted, the Human Genome Project has yielded remarkable results with great promise for preventing and treating genetic diseases. Researchers have already begun to identify specific genes that contribute to the development of disorders such as cystic fibrosis, mental retardation, and some forms of cancer.

> The Human Genome Project has yielded remarkable results with great promise for preventing and treating genetic diseases.

Although rich with promise, the Human Genome Project raises many social and ethical questions. For example, will predicting the likelihood of cancer in an individual lead to discrimination from potential employers and insurers? Will the knowledge that a person has a 25 percent chance of producing a child with Parkinson's disease affect the choice of having children? How will the products of the Human Genome Project, such as medicines and diagnostic techniques, be shared by the international community, patented, and commercialized? Fortunately, committees made up of ethicists, physicians, researchers, and other concerned professionals have already begun to confront many of these issues. As our understanding of human genetic inheritance continues to grow, it will not, we hope, outpace our understanding of how to apply this knowledge in ways that are both effective and socially responsible.

According to the principle of natural selection, those organisms that are best adapted to their environments are most likely to survive and reproduce. If the traits that give them a survival advantage are genetically based, those same genetic characteristics are passed on to their offspring. Organisms that do not possess the adaptive traits tend to die off before they reproduce, and therefore the less-adaptive traits do not get passed along to future generations.

Natural selection therefore promotes the survival and reproduction of individuals who are genetically well adapted to their particular environment. If the environment changes or the individual moves into a new environment, the survival and reproductive value of inherited characteristics may also change, and so eventually may the frequency of genes in the population's gene pool.

As described in Chapter 1, evolutionary psychologists study the origins of behaviors and mental processes, emphasizing the adaptive or survival value of such traits. Rather than focusing on the *structural* changes in organisms, as evolutionary biologists do, evolutionary psychologists look at the role that natural selection might have played in selecting for adaptive *behaviors,* especially during the long period that our ancestors lived as hunter-gatherers. They argue that just as our hands and upright posture are products of natural selection, so are our brains. As a result, our brains are "prewired" to learn some things more easily than others, to analyze problems in certain ways, and to communicate in distinctively human ways.

Evolutionary psychologists cite language as a prime example (Pinker, 1994, 1997, 2000). As we will see in Chapter 9 (Life-Span Development), all normal children acquire language without specific instruction; children in different cultures acquire language at about the same ages and in predictable stages; and the underlying structure of all human languages (nouns and verbs, subjects and objects, questions and conditional phrases, and so on) is basically the same. Taken as a whole, evolutionary psychologists argue, the evidence strongly suggests that our human brains have a built-in "program" for language.

Evolutionary psychologists cite mate selection as another example. In choosing a partner, males and females tend to pursue different strategies. Why? Evolutionary psychologists answer this way: Human females usually have only one child at a time; moreover, they invest more in each child—going through pregnancy, caretaking, and providing nourishment—than men do. It would seem to be most adaptive for females to look for males who will provide the best genes, resources, and long term parental care. Males, on the other hand, are limited only by the number of prospective mates they can attract, because sperm are plentiful and quickly replaced. It may be most adaptive for males to seek to mate with as many females as they can and to compete with other males for access to females. Studies analyzing human behaviors associated with sexual selection have found that men and women do indeed take different approaches to sexuality, mate choice, and aggression, as predicted by evolutionary psychology (Buss, 1989, 2000; Callahan, 2000; Palwoski, Dunbar, & Lipowicz, 2000). In comparing evolutionary explanations with more traditional social learning explanations of sex differences in social behavior, it appears that evolutionary psychology does a much better job of accounting for overall patterns (Archer, 1996).

Some opponents argue that science is being used to justify perpetuating unjust social policies. These critics claim that simply by saying a trait is adaptive implies that it is both genetically determined and good. In the past, racists and fascists have misused biological theories to promote social injustices. In Nazi Germany, for example, Jews were considered genetically inferior, a view that was used to justify their extermination. Similarly, the evolutionary theory of male-female differences in mate selection could be seen as endorsing male promiscuity because it is biologically adaptive. In response, evolutionary psychologists are quick to point out that their aim is not to shape social policy but to understand the origins of human behavior. They argue further that behaviors that may have contributed to our adaptive success during the early years of human evolution may no longer be adaptive in our current environment and therefore should not be viewed as good and right simply because at one time they may have served an important adaptive function.

Other critics chide evolutionary psychologists for too hastily explaining behaviors from an evolutionary perspective rather than investigating other plausible origins of them. Just because a behavior occurs to some degree across a wide variety of cultures does not necessarily mean that it has evolutionary roots, they argue. Evolutionary psychologists answer that their goal is not to propose evolutionary theories that exclude all other possible explanations; instead, their aim is to offer an evolutionary perspective that may complement other points of view.

A relatively new approach in psychology, the evolutionary perspective has yet to take its place among psychology's most respected theoretical paradigms. Only the results of empirical research, which compare evolutionary

2.6

explanations with competing theoretical explanations of behavior, will determine the fate of this provocative and intriguing new perspective.

Social Implications

What are some of the ethical issues that arise as society gains more control over genetics?

Science is not simply a process that takes place in a laboratory; it can also have widespread effects on society at large. To the extent that we can trace individual differences in human behavior to chromosomes and genes, we have a potential biologically to control people's lives. This potential raises new ethical issues.

Modern techniques of prenatal screening now make it possible to detect many genetic defects even before a baby is born. *Chorionic villus sampling* and *amniocentesis* are two procedures for obtaining samples of cells from fetuses in order to analyze their genes. In the first, the cells are taken from membranes surrounding the fetus; in the second, the cells are harvested from the fluid in which the fetus grows. Using these procedures, genetic problems are detected in about 2 percent of pregnancies. Does the child in these cases nonetheless have a right to live? Do the parents have a right to abort the fetus? Should society protect all life no matter how imperfect it is in the eyes of some? If not, which defects are so unacceptable that abortion is justified? Most of these questions have a long history, but recent progress in behavior genetics and medicine has given them a new urgency. We are reaching the point at which we will be able to intervene in a fetus's development by replacing some of its genes with others. For which traits might this procedure be considered justified, and who has the right to make those decisions? If in tampering with genes we significantly change our society's gene pool, are future generations harmed or benefited? Such questions pose major ethical dilemmas (Baringaga, 2000a).

Another concern is one that centers on the difficulty in understanding the complex new genetic technologies and their implications. Although scientists are careful to report their research findings accurately and to use appropriate caution in suggesting how results might be applied, the mass media often report these findings in overly simplified, "either-or" sound bites ("scientists have discovered a gene for x"). As a result, the pendulum of popular opinion seems to have swung from an environmental (or a nurture) position, which holds that all people have significant potential, to a genetic (or nature) position, which holds that intelligence, temperament, and other qualities are inborn (deWaal, 1999). It is important to remember that human behavior is the result of the complex interplay of *both* heredity and environment.

The study of behavior genetics and evolutionary psychology makes many people uneasy. Some fear that it may lead to the conclusion that who we are is written in some kind of permanent ink before we are born. Some people also fear that research in these fields could be used to undermine movements toward social equality. But far from finding human behavior to be genetically predetermined, recent work in behavior genetics shows just how important the environment is in determining which genetic predispositions come to be expressed and which do not (Rutter, 1997). In other words, we may inherit predispositions, but we do not inherit destinies. The emerging picture confirms that both heredity and environment (nature and nurture) together shape most significant behaviors and traits.

INTERACTIVE LECTURE 2.5

CHECK YOUR UNDERSTANDING

1. "Individual differences in intelligence, emotional reactivity, and susceptibility to schizophrenia and depression may all be influenced by genes." Is this statement true (T) or false (F)?

2. Match each term with the appropriate definition.

____ nature	a. the study of how traits are passed from one generation to another
____ nurture	b. genetic influences on development and behavior
____ DNA	c. environmental influences on development and behavior
____ genetics	d. the total amount of genetic material in a cell
____ genome	e. complex molecule that carries genetic information

Answers: 1. T. 2. nature (b); nurture (c); DNA (e); genetics (a); genome (d).

KEY TERMS

psychobiology, p. 48

Neurons: the messengers
neurons, p. 48
dendrites, p. 48
axon, p. 48
nerve or tract, p. 48
myelin sheath, p. 48
sensory (afferent) neurons, p. 48
motor (efferent) neurons, p. 48
interneurons (association neurons), p. 48
glial cells/glia, p. 48
ions, p. 48
resting potential, p. 49
polarization, p. 49
neural impulse or action potential, p. 50
graded potential, p. 50
threshold of excitation, p. 50
all-or-none law, p. 51
synaptic space or synaptic cleft, p. 51
synapse, p. 51
terminal button or synaptic knob, p. 51

synaptic vesicles, p. 51
neurotransmitters, p. 51
receptor sites, p. 51
neural plasticity, p. 55
neurogenesis, p. 56

The central nervous system
central nervous system (CNS), p. 57
peripheral nervous system (PNS), p. 57
hindbrain, p. 57
cerebellum, p. 58
midbrain, p. 58
thalamus, p. 58
hypothalamus, p. 59
reticular formation, p. 59
cerebral cortex, p. 59
association areas, p. 60
frontal lobes, p. 60
primary motor cortex, p. 60
occipital lobes, p. 61
parietal lobes, p. 61
primary somatosensory cortex, p. 61

temporal lobes, p. 61
limbic system, p. 62
corpus callosum, p. 62
spinal cord, p. 67

The peripheral nervous system
afferent neurons, p. 68
efferent neurons, p. 68
somatic nervous system, p. 69
autonomic nervous system, p. 69
sympathetic division, p. 69
parasympathetic division, p. 69

The endocrine system
endocrine glands, p. 70
hormones, p. 71
thyroid gland, p. 71
parathyroids, p. 71
pineal gland, p. 71
pancreas, p. 71
pituitary gland, p. 71
gonads, p. 72

adrenal glands, p. 73

Genes, Evolution, and Behavior
behavior genetics, p. 73
evolutionary psychology, p. 73
genetics, p. 74
genes, p. 74
chromosomes, p. 74
deoxyribonucleic acid (DNA), p. 74
human genome, p. 74
dominant gene, p. 74
recessive gene, p. 74
polygenic inheritance, p. 74
behavior genetics, p. 75
family studies, p. 76
twin studies, p. 76
identical twins, p. 76
fraternal twins, p. 76
adoption studies, p. 77
human genome, p. 77
natural selection, p. 77

CHAPTER REVIEW

Biological processes are the basis of our thoughts, feelings, and actions. All of our behaviors are kept in tune with our surroundings and coordinated with one another through the work of two interacting systems: the nervous system and the endocrine system.

Neurons: The Messengers

What types of cells are found in the nervous system? The basic building block of the nervous system is the **neuron,** or nerve cell. Neurons have several characteristics that distinguish them from other cells. Neurons receive messages from other neurons through short fibers, called **dendrites.** A longer fiber, called an **axon,** carries outgoing messages from the cell. A group of axons bundled together forms a **nerve** or **tract.** Some axons are covered with a myelin sheath, made up of **glial cells;** this increases neuron efficiency and provides insulation.

What "language" do neurons speak? When a neuron is at rest, a state called the **resting potential,** there is a slightly higher concentration of negatively charged **ions** inside its membrane than there is outside. The membrane is said to be **polarized**—that is, the electrical charge inside it is negative relative to its outside. When an incoming message is strong enough, this electrical imbalance abruptly changes (the membrane is depolarized), and an **action potential (neural impulse)** is generated. Incoming messages cause **graded potentials,** which, when combined, may exceed the minimum **threshold of excitation** and make the neuron "fire." After firing, the neuron briefly goes through the **absolute refractory period,** when it will not fire again, and then through the **relative refractory period,** when firing will occur only if the incoming message is much stronger than usual. According to the **all-or-none law,** every firing of a particular neuron produces an impulse of equal strength. More rapid firing of neurons is what communicates the strength of a message.

What happens as information moves from one neuron to the next? **Neurotransmitter** molecules, released by **synaptic** vesicles, cross the tiny **synaptic space (or cleft)** between an **axon terminal (or terminal button)** of a sending neuron and a dendrite of a receiving neuron. Here they latch on to **receptor sites,** much as keys fit into locks, and pass on their excitatory or inhibitory messages. Psychologists need to understand how synapses function because neurotransmitters affect an enormous range of physical and emotional responses. Certain drugs produce psychological effects by increasing or decreasing the amount of neurotransmitters at **synapses.** Other drugs work on receptor sites, blocking the receptors or interfering with the removal or reabsorption of neurotransmitters.

How does experience change the brain? Research demonstrates that experiences in our environments can produce changes in the brain, a principle called **neural plasticity.** Human brains also are capable of **neurogenesis**—the production of new brain cells.

The Central Nervous System

How is the nervous system organized? The nervous system is organized into two parts: the **central nervous system (CNS),** which consists of the brain and spinal cord, and the **peripheral nervous system (PNS),** made up of nerves that radiate throughout the body, linking all of the body's parts to the CNS.

What are the major structures and areas of the brain, and what functions do they serve? Physically, the brain has three more or less distinct areas: the central core, the limbic system, and the cerebrum.

The central core consists of the hindbrain, cerebellum, midbrain, thalamus and hypothalamus, and reticular formation. The **hindbrain** is made up of the medulla, a narrow structure nearest the spinal cord that controls breathing, heart rate, and blood pressure, and the pons, which produces chemicals that maintain our sleep-wake cycle. The medulla is the point at which many of the nerves from the left part of the body cross to the right side of the brain and vice versa. The **cerebellum** controls the sense of balance and coordinates the body's actions. The **midbrain,** which is above the cerebellum, is important for hearing and sight and is one of the places in which pain is registered. The **thalamus** is a relay station that integrates and shapes incoming sensory signals before transmitting them to the higher levels of the brain. The **hypothalamus** is important to motivation and emotional behavior. The **reticular formation,** which is woven through all of these structures, alerts the higher parts of the brain to incoming messages.

The **limbic system,** a ring of structures located between the central core and the cerebral hemispheres, is a more recent evolutionary development than the central core. It includes the hippocampus, which is essential to the formation of new memories, and the amygdala, which together with the hippocampus governs emotions related to self-preservation. Other portions of the limbic system heighten the experience of pleasure. In times of stress, the limbic system coordinates and integrates the nervous system's response.

The cerebrum takes up most of the room inside the skull. The outer covering of the cerebral hemispheres is known as the **cerebral cortex.** They are the most recently evolved portion of the brain, and they regulate the most complex behavior. Each cerebral hemisphere is divided into four lobes, delineated by deep fissures on the surface of the brain. The **occipital lobe** of the cortex, located at the back of the head, receives and processes visual information. The **temporal lobe,** located roughly behind the temples, helps us perform complex visual tasks, such as recognizing faces. The **parietal lobe,** which sits on top of the temporal and occipital lobes, receives sensory information from all over the body and oversees in spatial abilities. Messages from sensory receptors are registered in **the primary somatosensory cortex.** The **frontal lobe** receives and coordinates messages from the other lobes and keeps track of past and future body movement. It is primarily responsible for goal-directed behavior and is key to the ability to lead a mature emotional life. The **primary motor cortex** is responsible for voluntary movement. The association areas—areas that are free to process all kinds of information—make up most of the cerebral cortex and enable the brain to produce behaviors requiring the coordination of many brain areas.

How are the left and right hemispheres specialized for different functions? The two cerebral hemispheres are linked by the **corpus callosum,** through which they communicate and coordinate their activities. Nevertheless, each hemisphere appears to specialize in certain tasks (although they also have overlapping functions). The right hemisphere excels at visual and spatial tasks, nonverbal imagery, and the perception of emotion, whereas the left hemisphere excels at language and perhaps analytical thinking, too. The right hemisphere controls the left side of the body, and the left hemisphere controls the right side.

What methods have been developed to study the brain? An increasingly sophisticated technology exists for investigating the brain. Among the most important tools are microelectrode techniques, macroelectrode techniques (EEG), structural imaging (CT scanning and MRI), and functional imaging (EEG imaging, MEG, and MSI). Two new functional imaging techniques, PET scanning and fMRI, allow us to observe not only the structure but also the functioning of parts of the brain. Scientists often combine these techniques to study brain activity in unprecedented detail—information that can help in the treatment of medical and psychological disorders.

What does the spinal cord do? How does it work with the brain to sense events and act on them? The **spinal cord** is a complex cable of nerves that connects the brain to most of the rest of the body. It is made up of bundles of long nerve fibers and has two basic functions: to permit some reflex movements and to carry messages to and from the brain. A break in the cord disrupts the flow of impulses from the brain below that point, causing paralysis.

The Peripheral Nervous System

How does the brain communicate with the rest of the body? How is the autonomic branch of the peripheral nervous system involved in controlling emotions? The peripheral nervous system (PNS) contains two types of neurons: **afferent neurons,** which carry sensory messages *to* the central nervous system, and **efferent neurons,** which carry messages *from* the CNS. Neurons involved in making voluntary movements of the skeletal muscles belong to a part of the PNS called the **somatic nervous system,** whereas neurons involved in governing the actions of internal organs belong to a part of the PNS called the autonomic nervous system. The **autonomic nervous system** is itself divided into two parts: the **sympathetic division,** which acts primarily to arouse the body when it is faced with threat, and the **parasympathetic division,** which acts to calm the body down, restoring it to normal levels of arousal.

The Endocrine System

Why are psychologists interested in hormones? The endocrine system is the other communication system in the body. It is made up of **endocrine glands** that produce **hormones,** chemical substances released into the bloodstream to either *trigger* developmental changes in the body or to activate certain behavioral responses. The **thyroid gland** secretes thyroxin, a hormone involved in regulating the body's rate of metabolism. Symptoms of an overactive thyroid are agitation and tension, whereas an underactive thyroid produces lethargy. The **parathyroids** control and balance the levels of calcium and phosphate in the blood and tissue fluids. This process in turn affects the excitability of the nervous system. The **pineal gland** regulates activity levels over the course of the day and also regulates the sleep-wake cycle. The **pancreas** controls the level of sugar in the blood by secreting insulin and glucagon. When the pancreas secretes too much insulin, the person can suffer *hypoglycemia*. Too little insulin can result in *diabetes mellitus*. Of all the endocrine glands, the **pituitary gland** regulates the largest number of different activities in the body. It affects blood pressure, thirst, uterine contractions in childbirth, milk production, sexual behavior and interest, and the amount and timing of body growth, among other functions. Because of its influences on other glands, it is often called the "master gland." The **gonads**—the testes in males and the ovaries in females—secrete hormones called androgens (including testosterone) and estrogens. Testosterone has long been linked to aggressive behavior, and recent research suggest that estrogen may also play a role in agression, as well as cognitive ability and cardiovascular health. Each of the two **adrenal glands** has two parts: an outer covering, the *adrenal cortex*, and an inner core, the *adrenal medulla*. Both affect our response to stress, although the adrenal cortex affects other body functions, too. One stress-related hormone of the adrenal medulla is epinephrine, which amplifies the effects of the sympathetic nervous system.

Genes, Evolution, and Behavior

How are traits passed from one generation to the next? The related fields of **behavior genetics** and **evolutionary psychology** explore the influences of heredity on human behavior. Both are helping to settle the nature-versus-nurture debate over the relative contributions of genes and the environment to human similarities and differences. **Genetics** is the study of how traits are passed on from one generation to the next via genes. This process is called heredity. Each gene is lined up on tiny threadlike bodies called **chromosomes,** which in turn are made up predominantly of **deoxyribonucleic acid (DNA).** Each member of a gene pair can be either **dominant** or **recessive.** In **polygenic inheritance** a number of genes interact to produce a trait.

What methods do psychologists use to study the effects of genes on behavior? Psychologists use a variety of methods to study heritability—that is, the contribution of genes in determining variations in certain traits. **Strain studies** approach the problem by observing strains of highly inbred genetically similar animals, whereas **selection studies** try to determine the extent to which an animal's traits can be passed on from one generation to another. In the study of humans, **family studies** tackle heritability by looking for similarities in traits as a function of biological closeness. Also useful in studying human heritability are **twin studies** and **adoption studies.** Molecular genetics focuses on mapping the genes on the chromosomes. The Human Genome Project has produced a rough map of the genes on the 23 pair of human chromosomes.

How might the process of natural selection influence human social behaviors? The theory of evolution by natural selection states that organisms best adapted to their environment tend to survive, transmitting their genetic characteristics to succeeding generations, whereas organisms with fewer adaptive characteristics tend to die off. **Evolutionary psychology** analyzes human behavioral tendencies by examining their adaptive value from an evolutionary perspective. It has proved useful in helping to explain some of the commonalities in human behavior that occur across cultures.

What are some of the ethical issues that arise as society gains more control over genetics? Manipulating human genes in an effort to change how people develop is a new technology that makes many people uneasy, but their concerns may be exaggerated because genes are not all-powerful. Both heredity and environment play a part in shaping most significant human behaviors and traits.

CRITICAL THINKING AND APPLICATIONS

1. Why are withdrawal symptoms from cocaine the opposite of the drug's effects?

2. Brain scans of men and women communicating show very different patterns of brain activity. What impact

might these differences have on relationships between the sexes?

3. Because the sympathetic division of the ANS is designed to help us deal with stress, why does long-term stimulation of it cause so many health problems?

4. A clinical psychologist refers a new client to a medical doctor because the client's psychological symptoms could indicate a problem with the thyroid gland. What symptoms might the psychologist be responding to?

5. How do twin studies help determine the relative contribution of genes and environment to human differences?

WEB QUIZ **2.6** ✔   **Go to the Morris 6e Companion Website to take a practice chapter exam.**

3 Sensation and Perception

ON A RAINY NIGHT, A 33-YEAR-OLD MATHEMATICIAN TOOK A FATEFUL AFTER-dinner stroll. His friends had always considered him a "gourmet's gourmet" because he had an uncanny ability to taste a dish and name all of its ingredients. One friend commented that he had "perfect pitch" for food. As the mathematician stepped into the street that night, a slow-moving van ran into him, and he fell to the sidewalk, hitting his head. When he got out of the hospital, he discovered, to his horror, that his sense of smell was gone. Because smell and taste are physiologically connected, his days as a gourmet were over.

His taste buds were working: He could tell whether food was salty, bitter, sour, or sweet. But without aromas, he could no longer experience the subtle mixtures of flavors that make food delicious and memorable. Eating became a chore.

Some years later, he sued the driver of the van, claiming, first, that his enjoyment of life had been damaged beyond repair, and second, that loss of the sense of smell was life-threatening. Indeed, he had failed to notice the smell of smoke when his apartment building caught fire; he had been poisoned when he didn't realize he was eating spoiled food; and he could not detect the smell of a gas leak. He won his case. The technical term for his disorder is *anosmia* (from the Latin/Greek combination "without smell") (Ackerman, 1995).

We take our sense of smell for granted, like the air we breathe. And, indeed, every breath we take is scented. Without the dark aroma of fresh brewed coffee, the salty tang of the ocean breeze, the clean aroma of fresh laundry, even the atmosphere of a stable, life would be extraordinarily bland. Ask the 2 million Americans who suffer from smell and taste disorders. "I feel empty, in a sort of limbo," the mathematician said (Ackerman, 1995, p. 41). A woman whose sense of smell was restored compared the day she realized she could taste food again to "the moment in 'The Wizard of Oz,' when the

world is transformed from black and white to Technicolor" (Ackerman, 1995, p. 42). Our sense of smell may not be as keen as that of other animals, such as dogs, yet aromas are part of our experience of life.

Sensations, which include smells, sights, sounds, tastes, balance, touch, and pain, are the raw data of experience. Our various sense organs are continuously bombarded by bits of information, all competing for attention and by themselves as meaningless as pieces of a giant jigsaw puzzle. Perception is the mental process of sorting, identifying, and arranging these bits into meaningful patterns. Sensation and perception are the foundation of consciousness; together, they tell us what is happening both inside and outside our bodies.

We begin this chapter by looking at the basic principles of sensation: how we acquire information from the outside (and inside) world. We will examine the body's different sense organs to see how each converts physical energy—light or sound waves, for example—into nerve impulses. But sensation is only half the story. Our eyes register only light, dark, and color, yet we "see" a tree. Our ears pick up sound waves, yet we distinguish between a baby's cry and a Bach fugue. We explore these issues in the last section of the chapter, which deals with perception.

The Nature of Sensation

What causes sensory experiences?

How is energy, such as light or sound, converted into a message to the brain?

Sensation begins when energy, either from an external source or from inside the body, stimulates a receptor cell in one of the sense organs, such as the eye or the ear. Each **receptor cell** responds to one particular form of energy—light waves in the case of vision, or vibration of air molecules in the case of hearing. When there is sufficient energy, the receptor cell "fires" and sends to the brain a coded signal that varies according to the characteristics of the stimulus. For instance, a very bright light might be coded by the rapid firing of a set of nerve cells, but a dim light would set off a much slower firing sequence. The neural signal is coded still further as it passes along the sensory nerves to the central nervous system, so the message that reaches the brain is precise and detailed. The coded signal that the brain receives from a flashing red light differs significantly from the message signaling a soft yellow haze. And both of these signals are coded in a much different way from a loud, piercing noise. The specific sensation produced, then, depends on *how many* neurons fire, *which* neurons fire, and *how rapidly* these neurons fire.

Each sensory experience—the color of a flower or the sound of a fire engine—is an illusion created in the brain by patterns of neural signals. The brain, isolated inside the skull, is bombarded by the "clicks," or "firings," of coded neural signals arriving on millions of nerve fibers. The clicks on the optic nerve reliably produce an experience we call vision, just as clicks moving along an auditory nerve produce the experience we call hearing, or audition. The one-to-one relationship between stimulation of a specific nerve and the resulting sensory experience is known as the *doctrine of specific nerve energies.* Even if the clicks on the optic nerve are caused by something other than light, the result is still a visual experience. Gentle pressure on an eye, for instance, results in signals from the optic nerve that the brain interprets as visual patterns—the visual pattern of "seeing stars" when we're hit in the eye is so familiar that even cartoons depict it.

Sensory Thresholds

What are the limits on our ability to sense stimuli in our environment?

To produce any sensation at all, the physical energy reaching a receptor cell must achieve a minimum intensity, or **absolute threshold.** Any stimulation below the absolute threshold will not be experienced. But how much sensory stimulation is enough? How loud must a sound be, for example, for a person to hear it? How bright does a blip on a radar screen have to be for the operator to see it?

To answer such questions, psychologists present a stimulus at different intensities and ask people whether they sense anything. You might expect that there would come a point at which people would suddenly say, "Now I see the flash" or "Now I hear a sound." But actually there is a range of intensities over which a person sometimes—but not always—can sense a stimulus. The absolute threshold is defined as the point at which a person can detect the stimulus 50 percent of the time that it is presented (see **Figure 3–1**).

Although there are differences among people—and even from moment to moment for the same person—the absolute threshold for each of our senses is remarkably low. The approximate absolute thresholds under ideal circumstances are as follows (McBurney & Collings, 1984):

Sensation
The basic experience of stimulating the body's senses.

Receptor cell
A specialized cell that responds to a particular type of energy.

Absolute threshold
The least amount of energy that can be detected as a stimulation 50 percent of the time.

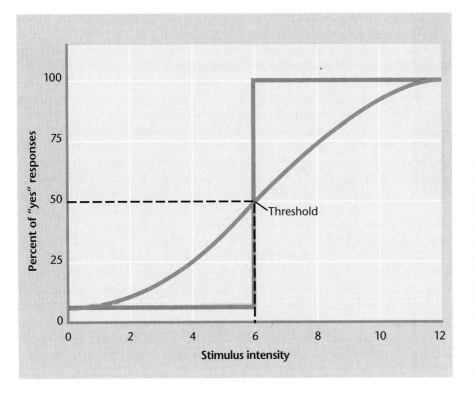

FIGURE 3–1

Determining a sensory threshold. The red line represents an ideal case: At all intensities below the threshold, the person reports no sensation or no change in intensity; at all intensities above the threshold, the person reports a sensation or a change in intensity. In reality however, we never come close to the ideal of the red line. The blue line shows the actual responses of a typical person. The threshold is taken as the point where a person reports a sensation or a change in intensity 50 percent of the time.

- Hearing: The tick of a watch from 6 meters (20 feet) in very quiet conditions
- Vision: A candle flame seen from 50 kilometers (30 miles) on a clear, dark night
- Taste: 1 gram (0.0356 ounce) of table salt in 500 liters (529 quarts) of water
- Smell: One drop of perfume diffused throughout a 3-room apartment
- Touch: The wing of a bee falling on the cheek from a height of 1 centimeter (0.39 inch)

Under normal conditions, absolute thresholds vary according to the level and nature of ongoing sensory stimulation. For example, your threshold for the taste of salt would be considerably higher after you eat salted peanuts, and your vision threshold would be much higher in the middle of a sunny day than at midnight on a moonless night. In both cases, the absolute threshold would rise because of sensory **adaptation,** in which our senses automatically adjust to the overall average level of stimulation in a particular setting. When confronted by a great deal of stimulation, they become much less sensitive than when the overall level of stimulation is low. Similarly, when the level of stimulation drops, our sensory apparatus becomes much more sensitive than under conditions of high stimulation. This process of adaptation allows all of our senses to be keenly attuned to a multitude of environmental cues without getting overloaded. We can hear the breathing of a sleeping baby when we enter a quiet room, but if we are on a city street during rush hour, the traffic noise would be deafening if our ears did not become less sensitive to stimulation. Similarly, we can go from a dark room into bright sunshine without experiencing great pain. (Later in this chapter we look more closely at adaptation.)

Imagine now that you can hear a particular sound. How much stronger must the sound become before you notice that it has grown louder? The smallest change in stimulation that you can detect 50 percent of the time is

Adaptation
An adjustment of the senses to the level of stimulation they are receiving.

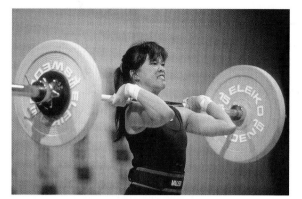

Adding 1 pound to this barbell would not produce a noticeable difference because 1 pound would fall below the difference threshold for this amount of weight.

called the **difference threshold, or the just noticeable difference (jnd).** Like the absolute threshold, the difference threshold varies from person to person and from moment to moment for the same person. And like absolute thresholds, difference thresholds tell us something about the flexibility of sensory systems. For example, adding 2 pounds to a 10-pound load will certainly be noticed, so we might assume that the difference threshold must be considerably less than 2 pounds. Yet adding 2 pounds to a 100-pound load probably would not make much of a difference, so we might conclude that the difference threshold must be considerably more than 2 pounds. But how can the difference threshold (jnd) be both less than and greater than 2 pounds? It turns out that the difference threshold varies according to the strength or intensity of the original stimulus. The greater the stimulus, the greater the change necessary to produce a jnd.

In the 1830s, Ernst Weber concluded that the difference threshold is a constant *fraction or proportion* of the original stimulus, a theory known as **Weber's law.** It is important to note that the values of these fractions vary significantly for the different senses. Hearing, for example, is very sensitive: We can detect a change in sound of 0.3 percent (1/3 of 1 percent). By contrast, producing a jnd in taste requires a 20 percent change. To return to our earlier example of weight, a change in weight of 2 percent is necessary to produce a jnd. So adding 1 pound to a 50-pound load would produce a noticeable difference half of the time; adding 1 pound to a 100-pound load would not.

Subliminal Perception

Under what circumstances might messages outside our awareness affect our behavior?

The idea of an absolute threshold implies that some events occur *subliminally*—below our level of awareness. Can subliminal messages used in advertisements and self-help tapes, for example, change people's behavior? For decades the story has circulated that refreshment sales increased dramatically when a movie theater in New Jersey flashed subliminal messages to "Drink Coca-Cola" and "Eat Popcorn." In fact, sales of Coke and popcorn did not change.

Similarly, audiotapes with subliminal self-help messages (which make up between one-quarter and one-third of all spoken-word audiocassette sales) often promise more than they deliver. In one series of studies, volunteers used such tapes for several weeks. About half said they had improved as a result of listening to the tapes, but objective tests detected no measurable change. Moreover, the perceived improvement had more to do with the label on the tape than its subliminal content: About half the people who received a tape labeled "Improve Memory" said that their memory had improved even though many of them had actually received a tape intended to boost self-esteem, and about one-third of the people who listened to tapes labeled "Increase Self-Esteem" said that their self-esteem had gone up, though many of them had actually been listening to tapes designed to improve memory (Greenwald et al., 1991).

Nevertheless, there is some evidence that under carefully controlled conditions, people can be influenced by information outside their awareness. In one study, for example, a group of people was shown a list of words related to competition, whereas a second group was exposed to a list of neutral words (Nuberg, 1988). Later, when playing a game, participants who had been shown the subliminal list of words with competitive overtones became especially competitive. In another study, one group of people was subliminally

Difference threshold or just noticeable difference (jnd)
The smallest change in stimulation that can be detected 50 percent of the time.

Weber's law
The principle that the jnd for any given sense is a constant fraction or proportion of the stimulation being judged.

exposed to words conveying honesty (a positive trait), whereas other people were subliminally exposed to words conveying hostility (a negative trait). Subsequently, all the participants read a description of a woman whose behavior could be looked at as either honest or hostile. When asked to assess various personality characteristics of the woman, the people who had been subliminally exposed to "honest" words rated her as more honest, and those who had been subliminally exposed to "hostile" words judged her as being hostile (Erdley & D'Agostino, 1988).

Studies like these indicate that *in a controlled laboratory setting*, people can process and respond to information outside of awareness. But the fact remains that there is no independent scientific evidence that subliminal messages in advertising or self-help tapes have any appreciable effect (Beatty & Hawkins, 1989; Greenwald et al., 1991; T. G. Russell, Rowe, & Smouse, 1991; Smith & Rogers, 1994; Underwood, 1994). Claims for extrasensory perception have also not been confirmed by scientific research (see *Understanding the World Around Us*).

UNDERSTANDING The World Around Us

Does Extrasensory Perception Exist?

Some people claim to have an extra power of perception, one beyond the powers of the normal senses. This unusual power, known as extrasensory perception, or ESP, has been defined as "a response to an unknown event not presented to any known sense" (McConnell, 1969). ESP refers to a variety of phenomena, including clairvoyance—awareness of an unknown object or event; telepathy—knowledge of someone else's thoughts or feelings; and precognition—foreknowledge of future events. The operation of ESP and other psychic phenomena is the focus of a field of study called *parapsychology.*

Much of the research into ESP has been criticized for poor experimental design, failure to control for dishonesty, selective reporting of results, or inability to obtain replicable results (Hansel, 1969). Nevertheless, psychologists continue to explore the possibility of psychic phenomena by using increasingly sophisticated procedures. For instance, Bem and Honorton (1994), using what has come to be known as the autoganzfeld procedure, re-ported encouraging results in their initial investigations of telepathy. In this procedure, a "sender," isolated in a soundproof room, concentrates on a picture or video segment randomly selected (by a computer) from a set of 80 photos or 80 videotape segments. A "receiver" is placed alone in another soundproof room. The receiver en-

Psychologists continue to explore the possibility of psychic phenomena by using increasingly sophisticated procedures.

gages in deep relaxation while wearing a half Ping-Pong ball over each eye and headphones playing a hissing sound (to provide uniform visual and auditory stimulation). The receiver then tries to experience any message or image coming from the sender. The experiment concludes with a test in which a computer displays four photos or videotape segments to the receiver, who rates them for similarity to impressions or images received during the sending phase of the experiment. Although receivers did not identify all the actual photos and videos that the senders were looking at, they performed significantly better than would be expected by chance alone.

Recent attempts to replicate Bem and Honorton's original findings have not generally met with success (Milton & Wiseman, 1999). Indeed, an extensive review of 30 studies, collectively testing over 1,100 participants, concluded that no convincing evidence for psychic functioning had emerged from the majority of studies that have used the autoganzfeld procedure (Milton & Wiseman, 1999).

Although research has failed to demonstrate clearly the existence of ESP, some psychologists and other scientists do not rule out entirely the idea that it might be a real phenomenon. Instead, they point out that experimentation has not yet given scientific support to its existence.

So far we have been talking about the general characteristics of sensation, but each of the body's sensory systems works a little differently. Individual sensory systems contain receptor cells that specialize in converting a particular kind of energy into neural signals. The threshold at which this conversion occurs varies from system to system. So do the mechanisms by which sensory data are sent to the brain for additional processing. We now turn to the unique features of each of the major sensory systems.

INTERACTIVE LECTURE **3.1**

WEB QUIZ **3.1**

CHECK YOUR UNDERSTANDING

Match the following terms with the appropriate definition.

1. ____ receptor cell
2. ____ absolute threshold
3. ____ difference threshold
4. ____ jnd
5. ____ Weber's law
6. ____ subliminal perception

a. just noticeable difference
b. perception of sensory information that is below the threshold of awareness
c. smallest stimulus detected 50 percent of the time
d. the difference threshold is a constant fraction of the stimulus
e. smallest change in stimulus detectable 50 percent of the time
f. converts energy into a neural signal

Answers: 1. f. 2. c. 3. a or e. 4. a or e. 5. d. 6. b.

Vision

Why have psychologists studied vision more than any other sense?

Different animal species depend more on some senses than on others. Dogs rely heavily on the sense of smell, bats on hearing, some fish on taste. But for humans, vision is the most important sense, so it has received the most attention from psychologists. To understand vision, we need to look first at the parts of the visual system, beginning with the structure of the eye.

The Visual System

How does light create a neural impulse?

The structure of the human eye, including the cellular path to the brain, is shown in **Figure 3–2.** Light enters the eye through the **cornea,** the transparent protective coating over the front part of the eye. It then passes through the **pupil,** the opening in the center of the **iris,** the colored part of the eye. In very bright light, the muscles in the iris contract to make the pupil smaller and thus protect the eye from damage. This contraction also helps us to see better in bright light. In dim light, the muscles relax to open the pupil wider and let in as much light as possible.

Inside the pupil, light moves through the **lens,** which focuses it onto the **retina,** the light-sensitive inner lining of the back of the eyeball. Normally the lens is focused on a middle distance, and it changes shape to focus on objects that are closer or farther away. To focus on a very close object, tiny muscles contract and make the lens rounder. To focus on something far away, the muscles flatten the lens. On the retina and directly behind the lens is a depressed spot called the **fovea** (see **Figure 3–3**). The fovea occupies the center of the visual field, and images that pass through

Cornea
The transparent protective coating over the front part of the eye.

Pupil
A small opening in the iris through which light enters the eye.

Iris
The colored part of the eye that regulates the size of the pupil.

Lens
The transparent part of the eye behind the pupil that focuses light onto the retina.

Retina
The lining of the eye containing receptor cells that are sensitive to light.

Fovea
The area of the retina that is the center of the visual field.

FIGURE 3–3

The retina. A view of the retina through an ophthalmoscope, an instrument used to inspect blood vessels in the eye. The small dark spot is the fovea. The yellow circle marks the blind spot, where the optic nerve leaves the eye.

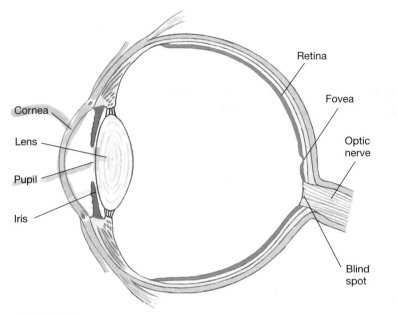

FIGURE 3–2

A cross section of the human eye. Light enters the eye through the cornea, passes through the pupil, and is focused by the lens onto the retina.

Source: Adapted from Hubel, 1963.

the lens are in sharpest focus here. Thus, the words you are now reading are hitting the fovea, while the rest of what you see—a desk, walls, or whatever—is striking other areas of the retina.

The Receptor Cells The retina contains the receptor cells responsible for vision. These cells are sensitive to only a fraction of the spectrum of electromagnetic energy, which includes *visible light* along with other energies (see **Figure 3–4**). Energies in the electromagnetic spectrum are referred to by their **wavelength.** Although we receive light waves from the full spectrum, the shortest wavelengths that we can see are experienced as violet-blue colors; the longest appear as reds.

Wavelengths
The different energies represented in the electromagnetic spectrum.

FIGURE 3–4

The electromagnetic spectrum. The eye is sensitive to only a very small segment of the spectrum, known as visible light.

FIGURE 3–5

Rods and cones.   As you can see from this photomicrograph, the rods and cones are named for their shape.

Source: E. R. Lewis, Y. Y. Zeevi, F. S. Werblin. *Brain Research 15* (1969): 559–562. Scanning electron microscopy of vertebrate receptors.

Rods
Receptor cells in the retina responsible for night vision and perception of brightness.

Cones
Receptor cells in the retina responsible for color vision.

Bipolar cells
Neurons that have only one axon and one dendrite; in the eye, these neurons connect the receptors on the retina to the ganglion cells.

Visual acuity
The ability to distinguish fine details visually.

There are two kinds of receptor cells in the retina—**rods** and **cones**—named for their characteristic shapes (see **Figure 3–5**). About 120 million rods and 8 million cones are present in the retina of each eye. Rods and cones differ from each other in a number of ways. Rods, chiefly responsible for *night vision*, respond only to varying degrees or intensities of light and dark. Cones, in contrast, allow us to see colors. Operating chiefly in daylight, cones are also less sensitive to light than rods are (MacLeod, 1978). In this regard, cones, like color film, work best in relatively bright light. The more sensitive rods, like black-and-white film, respond to much lower levels of illumination.

Cones are found mainly, but not exclusively, in the fovea, which contains no rods. The greatest density of cones is in the very center of the fovea, which is where images are projected onto the retina in sharpest focus. Rods predominate just outside the fovea. The greater the distance from the fovea, the sparser both rods and cones become until at the extreme edges of the retina, there are almost no cones and only a few rods.

Rods and cones also differ in the ways that they connect to the nerve cells leading to the brain. Both rods and cones connect to specialized neurons called **bipolar cells,** which have only one axon and one dendrite (see **Figure 3–6**). In the fovea, cones generally connect with only one bipolar cell—a sort of "private line" arrangement. In contrast, it is normal for several rods to share a single bipolar cell.

Also, outside the fovea, the number of rods and cones that connect to a single bipolar cell increases, and **visual acuity**—the ability visually to distinguish fine details—decreases. As a result, peripheral vision is somewhat blurred.

The one-to-one connection between cones and bipolar cells in the fovea allows for maximum visual acuity. To see this for yourself, hold this book about 18 inches from your eyes and look at the "X" in the center of the following line:

This is a test to show how visual **X** acuity varies across the retina.

Your fovea picks up the "X" and about four letters to each side. This is the area of greatest visual acuity. Notice how your vision drops off for words and letters toward the left or right end of the line.

In the dark, however, the fovea is almost useless because it contains no light-sensitive rods. To see an object, we have to look to one side so that the image falls outside the fovea where rods are present. Also, because rods normally pool their signals to the bipolar cells, a less-detailed message is sent to the brain. Outside the fovea, visual acuity drops by as much as 50 percent.

When we want to examine something closely, we move it into the sunlight or under a lamp. For activities such as reading, sewing, and writing, the more light, the better: Stronger light stimulates more cones, increasing the likelihood that bipolar cells will start a message to the brain.

Adaptation   Earlier in the chapter we introduced the term *adaptation,* the process by which our senses adjust to different levels of stimulation. In the case of vision, adaptation occurs as the sensitivity of rods and cones changes according to how much light is available. When you go from bright sunlight into a dimly lit theater, your cones are initially fairly insensitive to light, and you can see little as you look for a seat. During the first 10 minutes in the dark, the cones become increasingly sensitive to the dim light, and you will be able to see things directly in front of you, at least as well as you are going to: After about 10 minutes, the cones do not become any more sensitive. But the rods continue adapting until they reach their maximum sensitivity, about 30 minutes

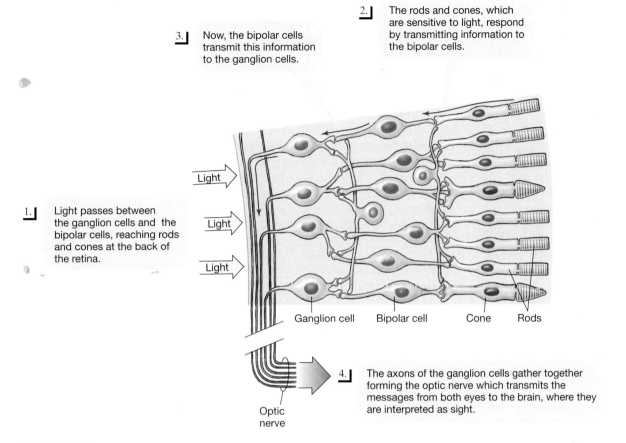

3.⌐ Now, the bipolar cells transmit this information to the ganglion cells.

2.⌐ The rods and cones, which are sensitive to light, respond by transmitting information to the bipolar cells.

1.⌐ Light passes between the ganglion cells and the bipolar cells, reaching rods and cones at the back of the retina.

Ganglion cell   Bipolar cell   Cone   Rods

Optic nerve

4.⌐ The axons of the ganglion cells gather together forming the optic nerve which transmits the messages from both eyes to the brain, where they are interpreted as sight.

FIGURE 3–6

A close-up of the layers of the retina.   Light must pass between the ganglion cells and the bipolar cells to reach the rods and cones. The sensory messages then travel back out from the receptor cells via the bipolar cells, to the ganglion cells. The axons of the ganglion cells gather together to form the optic nerve, which carries the messages from both eyes to the brain (see Figure 3–2).

after you enter a darkened room. The process by which rods and cones become more sensitive to light in response to lowered levels of illumination is called **dark adaptation.** But even with dark adaptation, there is usually not enough energy in very dim light to stimulate many cones, so you see the world in only black, white, and gray.

Problems with dark adaptation account in part for the much greater incidence of highway accidents at night (Leibowitz & Owens, 1977). When people drive at night, their eyes shift from the darkened interior of the car, to the road area illuminated by headlights, to the darker areas at the side of the road. Unlike the situation in a darkened movie theater, these changing night-driving conditions do not permit complete adaptation of either rods or cones, so neither system is operating at maximum efficiency. Because most drivers are generally unaware of the deterioration of their vision at night, they may overestimate their ability to stop in time to avoid an accident.

In the reverse process, **light adaptation,** the rods and cones become less sensitive to light. By the time you leave a movie theater, your rods and cones have grown very sensitive, and all the neurons fire at once when you go into bright outdoor light. You squint and shield your eyes, and your irises contract—all of which reduces the amount of light entering your pupils and striking your retinas. As light adaptation proceeds, the rods and

Dark adaptation
Increased sensitivity of rods and cones in darkness.

Light adaptation
Decreased sensitivity of rods and cones in bright light.

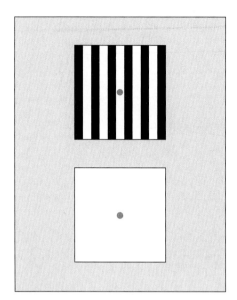

FIGURE 3–7

An afterimage. First stare continuously at the center of the upper square for about 20 seconds, then look at the dot in the lower square. Within a moment, a gray-and-white afterimage should appear inside the lower square.

Afterimage
Sense experience that occurs after a visual stimulus has been removed.

Ganglion cells
Neurons that connect the bipolar cells in the eyes to the brain.

Optic nerve
The bundle of axons of ganglion cells that carries neural messages from each eye to the brain.

Blind spot
The place on the retina where the axons of all the ganglion cells leave the eye and where there are no receptors.

Optic chiasm
The point near the base of the brain where some fibers in the optic nerve from each eye cross to the other side of the brain.

cones become less sensitive to stimulation by light. Within about a minute, both rods and cones are fully adapted to the light, and you no longer need to shield your eyes.

You can observe the effects of dark and light adaptation by staring continuously at the dot in the center of the upper square in **Figure 3–7** for about 20 seconds, then shifting your gaze to the dot in the lower square. A gray-and-white pattern should appear in the lower square. (When looking at the lower square, if you blink your eyes or shade the book from bright light, the illusion will be even stronger.) When you look at the lower square, the striped areas that were black in the upper square will now seem to be white, and the areas that were white in the upper square will now appear gray. This **afterimage** appeared because the part of the retina that was exposed to the dark stripes of the upper square became more sensitive (it dark-adapted), and the area exposed to the white part of the upper square became less sensitive (it light-adapted). When you shifted your eyes to the lower square, the less sensitive parts of the retina produced the sensation of gray rather than white. This afterimage fades within a minute as the retina adapts again, this time to the solid white square.

These examples show how visual adaptation is a partial back-and-forth process. The eyes adjust, but they never adapt completely. If the eyes did adapt completely, all the receptors would gradually become totally insensitive, and we would be unable to see anything at all. In the real world our eyes do not adapt completely, because light stimulation is rarely focused on the same receptor cells long enough for them to become totally insensitive. Rather, small involuntary eye movements keep the image moving slightly on the retina, so the receptor cells never have time to adapt completely.

From Eye to Brain   We have so far directed our attention to the eye, but messages from the eye must travel along multiple pathways to the brain in order for a visual experience to occur (see **Figure 3–6**). To begin with, rods and cones are connected to bipolar cells in many different numbers and combinations. In addition, sets of neurons called *interneurons* link receptor cells to one another and bipolar cells to one another. Eventually these bipolar cells hook up with the **ganglion cells,** leading out of the eye. The axons of the ganglion cells join to form the **optic nerve,** which carries messages from each eye to the brain. Although there are more than 125 million rods and cones in each retina, there are only about 1 million ganglion cells in the optic nerve. The information collected by the 125 million receptor cells must be combined and reduced to fit the mere 1 million "wires" that lead from each eye to the brain. Research indicates that most of this consolidation takes place in the interconnection between receptors and ganglion cells (Hubel & Livingstone, 1990; Livingstone & Hubel, 1988a, 1988b).

The place on the retina where the axons of all the ganglion cells join to form the optic nerve is called the **blind spot.** This area contains no receptor cells, so even when light from a small object is focused directly on the blind spot, the object will not be seen (see **Figure 3–8**). After the nerve fibers that make up the optic nerves leave the eyes, they separate, and some of them cross to the other side of the head at the **optic chiasm** (see **Figure 3–9**). The nerve fibers from the right side of each eye travel to the right hemisphere of the brain; those from the left side of each eye travel to the left hemisphere. Thus, as shown in **Figure 3–9,** visual information about any object in the left visual field, the area to the left of the viewer, will go to the right hemisphere (the pathway traced by the red line in **Figure 3–9**). Similarly, information about any object in the right visual field, the area to the right of the viewer, will go to the left hemisphere (the pathway traced by the blue line). (You can refer back to **Figures 2–9** and

FIGURE 3–8

Finding your blind spot.   To locate your blind spot, hold the book about a foot away from your eyes. Then close your right eye, stare at the "X," and slowly move the book toward you and away from you until the red dot disappears.

2–10 in Chapter 2, The Biological Basis of Behavior, to recall how researchers took advantage of the split-processing of the two visual fields to study split-brain patients.)

The optic nerves carry their messages to various parts of the brain. Some messages reach the area of the brain that controls the reflex movements that adjust the size of the pupil. Others go to the region that directs the eye muscles to change the shape of the lens. But the main destinations for messages from the retina are the visual projection areas of the cerebral cortex (see **Figure 2–7,** the occipital lobe), where the complex coded messages from the retina are registered and interpreted.

How does the brain register and interpret these signals, "translating" light into visual images? In research for which they received a Nobel Prize, David H. Hubel and Torsten N. Wiesel (1959, 1979) found that certain

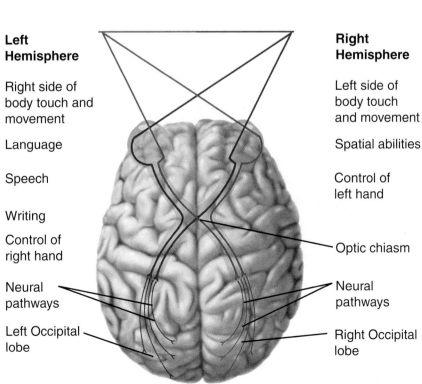

FIGURE 3–9

The neural connections of the visual system.   Messages about the red-colored area in the left visual field of each eye travel to the right occipital lobe; information about the blue area in the right visual field of each eye goes to the left occipital lobe. The crossover point is the optic chiasm.

Source: Adapted from "The Split Brain of Man," by Michael S. Gazzaniga. Copyright © 1967. Adapted with permission.

brain cells—called **feature detectors**—are highly specialized to detect particular elements of the visual field, such as horizontal or vertical lines. Other feature-detector cells register more complex information, with some being sensitive to movement, others to depth, and still others to color. These different types of feature detectors send messages to specific, but nearby, regions of the cortex. Visual experience, then, depends on the brain's ability to combine these pieces of information into a meaningful image.

Color Vision

How do we see color?

Humans, like many—but not all—other animals see in color, at least during the day. Color vision is highly adaptive for an animal that needs to know when fruit is ripe or how to avoid poisonous plants and berries (which tend to be brightly hued), as our ancestors did.

Properties of Color   Look at the color solid in **Figure 3–10.** What do you see? Most people report that they see some oranges, some yellows, some reds—a number of different colors. We call these different colors **hues,** and to a great extent, the hues you see depend on the wavelength of the light reaching your eyes (see **Figure 3–4**).

Now look at the triangle of green colors on the right side of **Figure 3–10.** Although each color patch on the triangle is the same hue, the green color is deepest or richest toward the left side of the triangle. The vividness or richness of a hue is its **saturation.**

Finally, notice that the colors near the top of the color patches are almost white, whereas those close to the bottom are almost black. This is the dimension of **brightness,** which depends largely on the strength of the light entering your eyes. If you squint and look at the color solid, you will reduce the apparent brightness of all the colors in the solid, and many of them will appear to become black.

Feature detectors
Specialized brain cells that only respond to particular elements in the visual field such as movement or lines of specific orientation.

Hues
The aspects of color that correspond to names such as red, green, and blue.

Saturation
The vividness or richness of a hue.

Brightness
The nearness of a color to white as opposed to black.

FIGURE 3–10

The color solid.   In the center portion of the figure, known as a color solid, the dimension of *hue* is represented around the circumference. *Saturation* ranges along the radius from the inside to the outside of the solid. *Brightness* varies along the vertical axis. The drawing at the left illustrates this arrangement schematically. The illustration at the right shows changes in saturation and brightness for the same hue.

FIGURE 3–11
Additive color mixing. Mixing light waves is an additive process. When red and green lights are combined, the resulting hue is yellow. Adding blue light to the other two yields white light.

Additive color mixing
The process of mixing lights of different wavelengths to create new hues.

Subtractive color mixing
The process of mixing pigments, each of which absorbs some wavelengths of light and reflects others.

Trichromatic theory
The theory of color vision that holds that all color perception derives from three different color receptors in the retina (usually red, green, and blue receptors).

Hue, saturation, and brightness are three separate aspects of our experience of color. Although people can distinguish only about 150 hues (Coren, Porac, & Ward, 1984), gradations of saturation and brightness within those 150 hues allow us to see more than 300,000 different colors (Hochberg, 1978; Kaufman, 1979). Some of this variety is captured in **Figure 3–10.**

Theories of Color Vision   If you look closely at a color television screen, you will see that the picture is actually made up of tiny red, green, and blue dots that blend together to give all possible hues. The same principle is at work in our own ability to see thousands of colors.

For centuries, scientists have known that they could produce all 150 basic hues by mixing together only a few lights of different colors (see **Figure 3–11**). Specifically, red, green, and blue lights—the primary colors for light mixtures—can be combined to create any hue. For example, red and green lights combine to give yellow; red and blue lights combine to make magenta. Combining red, green, and blue lights in equal intensities produces white. The process of mixing lights of different wavelengths is called **additive color mixing,** because each light adds additional wavelengths to the overall mix.

Color mixing with paint follows different rules than does color mixing with light. With light, different wavelengths add together, but the color of paint depends not on which wavelengths are *present,* but rather on which are *absorbed* and which are *reflected.* For example, red paint absorbs light from the blue end of the spectrum and reflects light from the red end. Since paint mixing depends on what colors are absorbed, or subtracted, the process is called **subtractive color mixing** (see **Figure 3–12**).

In the early 1800s, the German physiologist Hermann von Helmholtz proposed a theory of color vision based on additive color mixing. Helmholtz reasoned that since there are three primary colors of light, the eye must contain three types of cones: some that are sensitive to red light, others that pick up green, and still others that respond most strongly to blue-violet. According to this view, color experiences come from mixing the signals from the three receptors. Helmholtz's explanation of color vision is known as **trichromatic (or three-color) theory.**

Trichromatic theory explains how three primary colors can be combined to produce any other hue. In fact, people with normal color vision are

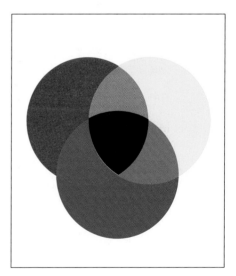

FIGURE 3–12
Subtractive color mixing. The process of mixing paint pigments rather than lights is a subtractive process, because the pigments absorb some wavelengths and reflect others. A mixture of the three primary pigments (red, yellow, and blue) absorbs all wavelengths, producing black.

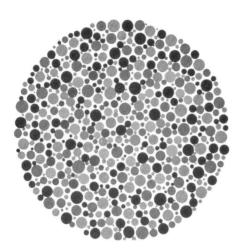

FIGURE 3–13

Experiencing colorblindness.
Perceiving the number 96 embedded in the mass of green circles is easy, except for people who have red-green color-blindness.

Source: Ishiharo, *Test for Color Deficiency.* Courtesy of the Isshinkai Foundation founded by Prof. Ishihara, Tokyo, Japan.

FIGURE 3–14

Afterimage.   Stare at the white spot in the center of the flag for about 30 seconds. Then look at a blank piece of white paper, and you will see an afterimage in complementary colors. Although the flag is printed in green, yellow, and black, its afterimage will appear in red, blue, and white.

Trichromats
People (and animals) that have normal color vision.

Color blindness
Partial or total inability to perceive hues.

Dichromats
People (and animals) that are blind to either red-green or yellow-blue.

Monochromats
Organisms that are totally color-blind.

called **trichromats.** Trichromats perceive all hues by combining the three primary colors. However, approximately 10 percent of men and 1 percent of women display some form of **color blindness,** which is not well explained by trichromatic theory. People with the two most common forms of color blindness are called **dichromats,** since they see the world in terms of only reds and greens (the red-green dichromats) or of blues and yellows (the blue-yellow dichromats) (see **Figure 3–13**). Among humans, **monochromats,** who see no color at all but respond only to shades of light and dark, are extremely rare.

Similarly, trichromatic theory does not explain some aspects of normal color vision. Why, for example, don't people with normal color vision ever see a light or a pigment that can be described as "reddish-green" or "yellowish-blue"? And what accounts for *color afterimages*? (See **Figure 3–14**.)

In the later nineteenth century, another German scientist, Edward Hering, proposed an alternative theory of color vision that can explain these phenomena. Hering proposed the existence of three *pairs* of color receptors: a yellow-blue pair and a red-green pair that determine the hue you see; and a black-white pair that determine the brightness of the colors you see. The yellow-blue pair can relay messages about yellow *or* blue, but not messages about yellow *and* blue light at the same time; the same is true for red-green receptors. Thus, the members of each pair work in opposition to each other, which explains why we never see yellowish-blue or reddish-green. Hering's theory is now known as the **opponent-process theory.**

Opponent-process theory also explains color afterimages. While you were looking at the green stripes in **Figure 3–14,** the red-green receptors were sending "green" messages to your brain; but they were also adapting to the stimulation by becoming less sensitive to green light. When you later looked at the white page (made up of light from all parts of the spectrum), the red-green receptors responded vigorously to wavelengths in the red portion of the spectrum, so you saw red stripes instead of green. Hering's opponent-process theory also explains the color experiences of dichromats. If the red-green system fails, then all that is left is the yellow-blue system, and vice versa.

Today psychologists believe that both the trichromatic and opponent-process theories are valid, but at different stages of the visual process. As trichromatic theory asserts, there are three kinds of cones for color (some are most sensitive to violet-blue light, others are most responsive to green light, and still others are most sensitive to yellow light—not red light, as Helmholtz contended). Thus, trichromatic theory corresponds fairly closely to the types of color receptors that actually exist in the retina. The opponent-process theory closely reflects what happens along the neural pathways that connect the eye and the brain. Together, trichromatic theory and opponent-process theory account for most color phenomena.

Color Vision in Other Species   Many animals—including some reptiles, fish, and insects (Neitz, Geist, & Jacobs, 1989; Rosenzweig & Leiman, 1982)—have color vision, but what colors they see varies. Humans and most other primates perceive a wide range of colors, but most other mammals experience the world only in reds and greens or blues and yellows (Abramov & Gordon, 1994; Jacobs, 1993). Hamsters, rats, squirrels, and other rodents are completely color-blind. So are owls, which are nocturnal birds of prey that have only rods in their eyes.

At the same time, however, other animals can see colors that we can't. Bees, for example, see ultraviolet light. To a bee's eyes, flowers with white petals that look drab to us flash like neon signs pointing the way to nectar. Birds, bats, and moths find red flowers irresistible, but bees pass them by. Tradition notwithstanding, bulls can't see red either; they are red-green color-blind. The matador's cape is bright red to excite the human audience, who find red arousing, perhaps especially when they expect to see blood, whether the bull's or the matador's. Given the roar of the crowd, confinement in the stadium, and the strange flapping, the bull would charge no matter what the cape's color.

Live! **psych** 3.1

INTERACTIVE LECTURE **3.2**

WEB QUIZ **3.2**

CHECK YOUR UNDERSTANDING

Match the following terms with the appropriate definitions.

1. ____ cornea   a. colored part of the eye
2. ____ pupil   b. center of the visual field
3. ____ iris   c. receptor cell responsible for color vision
4. ____ lens   d. protective layer over front part of the eye
5. ____ fovea   e. part that contains the receptor cells that respond to light
6. ____ retina   f. part that focuses light onto the retina
7. ____ rod   g. receptor cell most responsible for night vision
8. ____ cone   h. opening in the iris through which light enters
9. The place on the retina where the axons of all the ganglion cells come together to leave the eye is called the ____.
10. Trichromats can mix ____, ____, and ____ lights to create virtually any hue.

Answers: 1. d. 2. h. 3. a. 4. f. 5. b. 6. e. 7. g. 8. c. 9. blind spot. 10. red, green, blue.

Hearing

If a tree falls in the forest and no one is there, does the tree make a sound?

A psychologist would answer the philosopher's question about the tree falling in the forest this way: "There are sound waves, but there is no sound or noise." Sounds and noise are psychological experiences created by the brain in response to stimulation. In this section, we consider the kinds of stimuli that cause us to hear sounds. Then we focus on how those stimuli are converted into neural signals.

Sound

How do the characteristics of sound waves cause us to hear different sounds?

The sensation we call **sound** is our brain's interpretation of the ebb and flow of air molecules pounding on our eardrums. When something in the environment moves, pressure is caused when molecules of air or fluid collide with one another and then move apart again. This pressure transmits energy at every collision, creating **sound waves.** The simplest sound wave—what we hear as a pure tone—can be pictured as a sine wave (see **Figure 3–15**). The tuning fork vibrates, causing the molecules of air first to contract and then to expand. The **frequency** of the waves is measured in cycles per second, expressed in a unit called **hertz (Hz).** Frequency primarily determines the **pitch** of the sound—how high or how low it is. The

Opponent-process theory
Theory of color vision that holds that three sets of color receptors (yellow-blue, red-green, black-white) respond to determine the color you experience.

Sound
A psychological experience created by the brain in response to changes in air pressure that are received by the auditory system.

Sound waves
Changes in pressure caused when molecules of air or fluid collide with one another and then move apart again.

Frequency
The number of cycles per second in a wave; in sound, the primary determinant of pitch.

Hertz (Hz)
Cycles per second; unit of measurement for the frequency of sound waves.

Pitch
Auditory experience corresponding primarily to frequency of sound vibrations, resulting in a higher or lower tone.

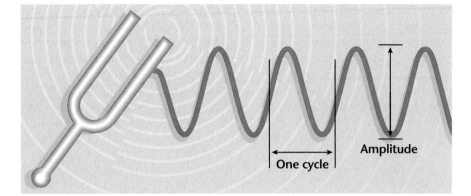

FIGURE 3–15

Sound waves. As the tuning fork vibrates, it alternately compresses and expands the molecules of air, creating a sound wave.

Amplitude
The magnitude of a wave; in sound, the primary determinant of loudness.

Decibel
Unit of measurement for the loudness of sounds.

human ear responds to frequencies from approximately 20 Hz to 20,000 Hz. A double bass can reach down to about 50 Hz; a piano can reach as high as 5,000 Hz.

The height of the sound wave represents its **amplitude (Figure 3–15)**, which, together with frequency, determines the perceived loudness of a sound. Sound intensity is measured in **decibels** (see **Figure 3–16**). As we grow older, we lose some of our ability to hear soft sounds, but we can hear loud sounds as well as ever.

The sounds that we hear seldom result from pure tones. Unlike a tuning fork, which can produce a tone that is almost pure, musical instruments

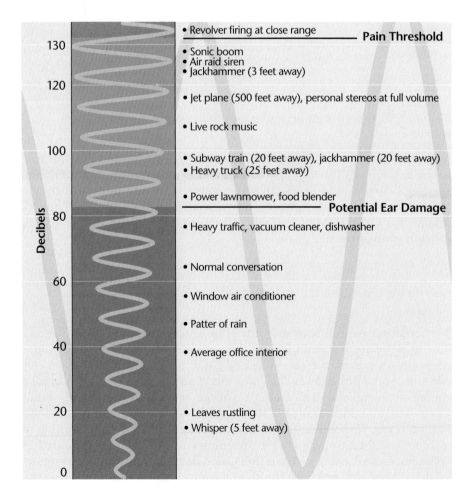

FIGURE 3–16

A decibel scale for several common sounds. Prolonged exposure to sounds above 85 decibels can cause permanent damage to the ears, as can even brief exposure to sounds near the pain threshold.

Source: Adapted from Dunkle, 1982.

produce **overtones**—accompanying sound waves that are different multiples of the frequency of the basic tone. This complex pattern of overtones determines the **timbre,** or texture, of the sound. When playing the same note, a piano sounds different from a violin because of differences in the overtones of the two instruments. Music synthesizers can mimic different instruments electronically because they produce not only pure tones but also the overtones that produce the timbre of different musical instruments.

Like our other senses, hearing undergoes adaptation and can function optimally under a wide variety of conditions. City residents enjoying a weekend in the country, for example, may be struck at first by how quiet everything seems. But after a while they may find that the country starts to sound very noisy because they have adapted to the quieted environment.

The Ear

What path does sound follow from the ear to the brain?

Hearing begins when sound waves are gathered by the *outer* ear and passed along to the eardrum (see **Figure 3–17**) causing it to vibrate. The quivering of the eardrum prompts three tiny bones in the *middle* ear—the *hammer,*

Overtones
Tones that result from sound waves that are multiples of the basic tone; primary determinant of timbre.

Timbre
The quality or texture of sound; caused by overtones.

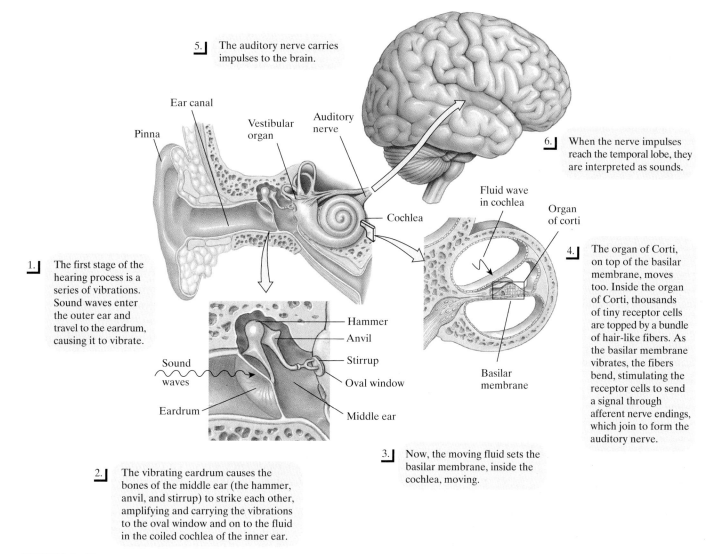

5. The auditory nerve carries impulses to the brain.

Ear canal

Pinna

Vestibular organ

Auditory nerve

6. When the nerve impulses reach the temporal lobe, they are interpreted as sounds.

Fluid wave in cochlea

Organ of corti

Cochlea

1. The first stage of the hearing process is a series of vibrations. Sound waves enter the outer ear and travel to the eardrum, causing it to vibrate.

4. The organ of Corti, on top of the basilar membrane, moves too. Inside the organ of Corti, thousands of tiny receptor cells are topped by a bundle of hair-like fibers. As the basilar membrane vibrates, the fibers bend, stimulating the receptor cells to send a signal through afferent nerve endings, which join to form the auditory nerve.

Hammer

Anvil

Stirrup

Oval window

Middle ear

Sound waves

Eardrum

Basilar membrane

3. Now, the moving fluid sets the basilar membrane, inside the cochlea, moving.

2. The vibrating eardrum causes the bones of the middle ear (the hammer, anvil, and stirrup) to strike each other, amplifying and carrying the vibrations to the oval window and on to the fluid in the coiled cochlea of the inner ear.

FIGURE 3–17
How we hear.

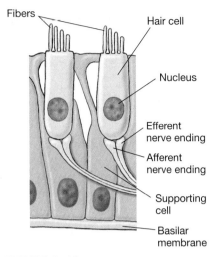

FIGURE 3–18

A detailed drawing of a hair cell. At the top of each hair cell is a bundle of fibers. If the fibers bend as much as 100 trillionths of a meter, the receptor cells transmit a sensory message to the brain.

Source: Adapted from "The Hair Cells of the Inner Ear," by A. J. Hudspeth, © 1983. Illustrated by Bunji Tagawa for Scientific American. Adapted with permission from the Estate of Bunji Tagawa.

Oval window
Membrane across the opening between the middle ear and inner ear that conducts vibrations to the cochlea.

Cochlea
Part of the inner ear containing fluid that vibrates, which in turn causes the basilar membrane to vibrate.

Basilar membrane
Vibrating membrane in the cochlea of the inner ear; it contains sense receptors for sound.

Organ of Corti
Structure on the surface of the basilar membrane that contains the receptor cells for hearing.

Auditory nerve
The bundle of axons that carries signals from each ear to the brain.

Place theory
Theory that pitch is determined by the location of greatest vibration on the basilar membrane.

Frequency theory
Theory that pitch is determined by the frequency with which hair cells in the cochlea fire.

Volley principle
Refinement of frequency theory; it suggests that receptors in the ear fire in sequence, with one group responding, then a second, then a third, and so on, so that the complete pattern of firing corresponds to the frequency of the sound wave.

the *anvil,* and the *stirrup*—to hit each other in sequence and thus carry the vibrations to the *inner* ear. The last of these three bones, the stirrup, is attached to a membrane called the **oval window.** Vibrations of the oval window, in turn, are transmitted to the fluid inside a snail-shaped structure called the **cochlea.** The cochlea is divided lengthwise by the **basilar membrane,** which is stiff near the oval window but gradually becomes more flexible toward its other end. When the fluid in the cochlea begins to move, the basilar membrane ripples in response.

Lying on top of the basilar membrane and moving in sync with it, is the **organ of Corti.** Here the messages from the sound waves finally reach the receptor cells for the sense of hearing: thousands of tiny hair cells that are embedded in the organ of Corti (Spoendlin & Schrott, 1989). As you can see in **Figure 3–18,** each hair cell is topped by a bundle of fibers. These fibers are pushed and pulled by the vibrations of the basilar membrane. When these fibers move, the receptor cells send a signal through the **auditory nerve** to the brain. The brain pools the information from thousands of hair cells to create sounds.

Neural Connections The sense of hearing is truly bilateral: Each ear sends messages to both cerebral hemispheres. The switching station where the nerve fibers from the ears cross over is in the medulla, part of the brain stem (see **Figure 2–6**). From the medulla, other nerve fibers carry the messages from the ears to the higher parts of the brain. Some messages go to the brain centers that coordinate the movements of the eyes, head, and ears. Others travel through the reticular formation (which we examined in Chapter 2). But the primary destinations for these auditory messages are the auditory areas in the temporal lobes of the two cerebral hemispheres (see **Figure 2–7**). En route to the temporal lobes, auditory messages pass through at least four lower brain centers where auditory information becomes more precisely coded.

Theories of Hearing

How do we distinguish low-frequency and high-frequency sounds?

Thousands of tiny hair cells send messages about the infinite variations in the frequency, amplitude, and overtones of sound waves. But how are the different sound-wave patterns coded into neural messages? One aspect of sound—loudness—seems to depend primarily on how many neurons are activated: The more cells that fire, the louder the sound seems to be. The coding of messages regarding pitch is more complicated. There are two basic views of pitch discrimination—place theory and frequency theory. According to **place theory,** the brain determines pitch by noting the place on the basilar membrane at which the message is strongest. High-frequency sounds cause the greatest vibration at the stiff base of the basilar membrane; low-frequency sounds resonate most strongly at the opposite end (Zwislocki, 1981). The brain detects the location of the most intense nerve-cell activity and uses this to determine the pitch of a sound.

The **frequency theory** of pitch discrimination holds that the frequency of vibrations of the basilar membrane as a whole—not just parts of it—is translated into an equivalent frequency of nerve impulses. Thus, if a hair bundle is pulled or pushed rapidly, its hair cell fires rapidly, sending a rush of signals to the brain. Because neurons cannot fire as rapidly as the frequency of the highest-pitched sound that can be heard, however, theorists have modified the frequency theory to include a **volley principle.** According to this view, auditory neurons can fire in sequence: One neuron fires, then a second one, then a third. By then the first neuron has had time to recover and can fire again. In this way, a set of neurons together, firing in sequence, can send a more rapid series of impulses to the brain than any single neuron could send by itself.

Because neither place theory nor frequency theory alone fully explains pitch discrimination, some combination of the two is necessary. Frequency theory appears to account for the ear's responses to frequencies up to about 4,000 Hz; above that, place theory provides a better explanation of what is happening.

Hearing Disorders   Because the mechanisms that allow us to hear are so complicated, there is a large number of possible problems that can interfere with hearing. Deafness, one of the most common concerns, may result from defects in the middle ear—for instance, the eardrum may be damaged, or the small bones of the middle ear may not work properly. Deafness may also occur because the basilar membrane, the hair cells, or the auditory nerve has been damaged, because of disease, infections, and even long-term exposure to loud noise.

Of the 28 million Americans with hearing loss, about 10 million are victims of exposure to noise. The chief culprits are leaf blowers, chain saws, snowmobiles, jet planes, and personal stereo systems (refer back to **Figure 3–16**) (Goldstein, 1999; Leary, 1990). Another hearing problem is *tinnitus*, a constant ringing in the ears. Tinnitus, which affects about 1 percent of the population, is due to irritation or damage to the hair cells. It is often the result of prolonged exposure to loud noise or toxins.

For people with irreversible hearing loss, a number of remedies are available. New digital technology has made hearing aids, which simply amplify sound, more precise by enhancing speech perception and reducing background noise. Surgery can help people with conductive hearing loss due to a stiffening of the connections between the bones (hammer, anvil, and stirrup) of the middle ear.

Implants offer hope to people who suffer from deafness due to cochlear damage (Clark, 1998). One or more platinum electrodes are inserted into the cochlea of one ear. The electrodes bypass the damaged hair cells and convey electrical signals from a miniature sound synthesizer directly to the auditory nerve, which convey an auditory message to the brain.

How many years will Aerosmith's Joe Perry be able to perform without causing damage to the sensitive structures of his ears?

 3.2

 INTERACTIVE LECTURE **3.3**

WEB QUIZ **3.3**

CHECK YOUR UNDERSTANDING

Number the following terms in the order in which a sound wave would reach them when traveling from the outer ear to the inner ear.

_____ 1. oval window   _____ 4. auditory nerve

_____ 2. anvil   _____ 5. eardrum

_____ 3. cochlea

Match the following theories with the appropriate definitions.

6. _____ frequency theory

7. _____ volley principle

8. _____ place theory

a. pitch is determined by groups of receptor cells firing in sequence, not individually

b. pitch is determined by the rate at which hair cells in the cochlea fire

c. pitch is determined by the location of the greatest vibration on the basilar membrane

Answers: 1. 3rd. 2. 2nd. 3. 4th. 4. 5th. 5. 1st. 6. b. 7. a. 8. c.

Certain animal species rely more on their sense of smell than humans do. This dog has been trained to use its keen sense of smell to detect bombs hidden in luggage at an airport.

The Other Senses

What are the chemical senses?

Researchers have focused most of their attention on vision and hearing because humans rely primarily on these two senses to gather information about their environment. Our other senses—including smell, taste, balance, motion, pressure, temperature, and pain—are also at play, even when we are less conscious of them. We turn first to the chemical senses: smell and taste.

Smell

What activates the sense of smell?

Although the sense of smell in humans is weaker than in most animals, it is still about 10,000 times as acute as that of taste (Moncrieff, 1951). Like our other senses, smell undergoes adaptation, so that odors that seem strong at first gradually become less noticeable.

Our sense of smell for common odors is activated by a complex protein produced in a nasal gland. As we breathe, a fine mist of this protein, called odorant binding protein (OBP), is sprayed through a duct in the tip of the nose. The protein binds with airborne molecules that then activate receptor cells for this sense, located high in each nasal cavity (see **Figure 3–19**). The

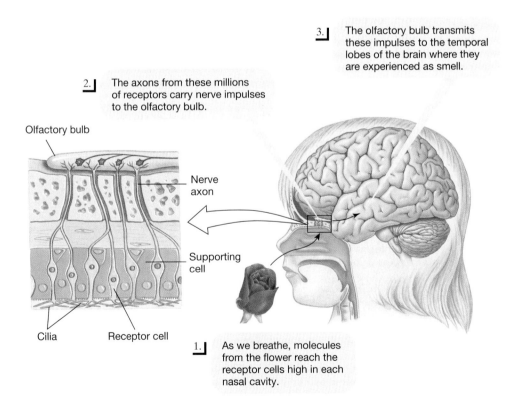

3. The olfactory bulb transmits these impulses to the temporal lobes of the brain where they are experienced as smell.

2. The axons from these millions of receptors carry nerve impulses to the olfactory bulb.

Olfactory bulb

Nerve axon

Supporting cell

Cilia   Receptor cell

1. As we breathe, molecules from the flower reach the receptor cells high in each nasal cavity.

FIGURE 3–19

The human olfactory system. The sense of smell is triggered when odor molecules in the air reach the olfactory receptors located inside the top of the nose. Inhaling and exhaling odor molecules from food does much to give food its flavorful "taste."

Source: From *Human Anatomy and Physiology* by Anthony J. Gaudin and Kenneth C. Jones. Copyright © 1989. Reprinted by permission.

axons from these millions of receptors go directly to the **olfactory bulb,** where some recoding takes place. Then messages are routed to the brain, resulting in our awareness of the smells.

Most mammals, including humans, have a second sensory system devoted to the sense of smell—which some animals use for communicating sexual, aggressive, or territorial signals. Receptors located in the roof of the nasal cavity detect chemicals called **pheromones,** which can have quite specific and powerful effects on behavior. For example, many animals, including dogs and wolves, use pheromones to mark their territory, identify sexually receptive mates, and recognize members of their group. Humans also have receptors for pheromones (Takami et al., 1993). Although the exact role that these receptors play in human behavior is not fully understood, recent research has shown that these receptors activate different areas of male and female brains when they are stimulated by the smell of testosterone and estrogen (Savic, Berglund, Gulyas, & Roland, 2001).

Taste

How do we detect the basic tastes?

To understand taste, we must distinguish it from flavor—a complex interaction of taste and smell. Try holding your nose when you eat. You will notice that most of the food's flavor will disappear, and you will experience only the basic taste qualities: *sweet, sour, salty,* and *bitter.* Most other tastes are derived from combinations of these.

The receptor cells for the sense of taste are housed in the **taste buds,** most of which are found on the tip, sides, and back of the tongue. The tip of the tongue is most sensitive to sweetness and saltiness; the back, to bitterness; and the sides, to sourness (see **Figure 3–20**), although each area can distinguish all four qualities to some degree (Bartoshuk & Beauchamp, 1994). Because the number of taste buds decreases with age, older people often lose interest in food—they simply cannot taste it as well as they used to.

The taste buds are embedded in the tongue's papillae, bumps that you can see if you look at your tongue in the mirror. When we eat something, the chemical substances in the food dissolve in saliva and go into the crevices between the papillae, where they come into contact with the taste

Olfactory bulb
The smell center in the brain.

Pheromones
Chemicals that communicate information to other organisms through smell.

Taste buds
Structures on the tongue that contain the receptor cells for taste.

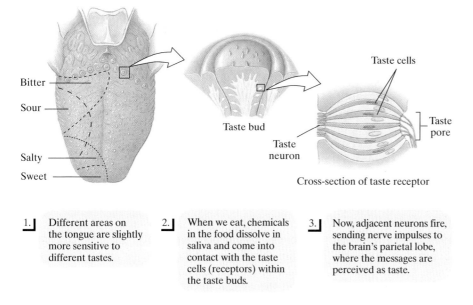

1. Different areas on the tongue are slightly more sensitive to different tastes.

2. When we eat, chemicals in the food dissolve in saliva and come into contact with the taste cells (receptors) within the taste buds.

3. Now, adjacent neurons fire, sending nerve impulses to the brain's parietal lobe, where the messages are perceived as taste.

FIGURE 3–20

The structure of a taste bud. The sensory receptors for taste are found primarily on the tongue. Taste cells can detect only sweet, sour, salty, and bitter qualities. All other tastes result from different combinations of these taste sensations.

This dancer is utilizing information provided by both her kinesthetic and her vestibular senses. Her kinesthetic senses are relaying messages pertaining to muscle strain and movements; her vestibular senses are supplying feedback about her body position in space.

Kinesthetic senses
Senses of muscle movement, posture, and strain on muscles and joints.

Stretch receptors
Receptors that sense muscle stretch and contraction.

Golgi tendon organs
Receptors that sense movement of the tendons, which connect muscle to bone.

Vestibular senses
The senses of equilibrium and body position in space.

receptors. The chemical interaction between food substances and the taste cells causes adjacent neurons to fire, sending a nerve impulse to the parietal lobe of the brain and to the limbic system.

Taste, like the other senses, experiences adaptation. When you first start eating salted peanuts or potato chips, the saltiness is quite strong, but after a while it becomes less noticeable. Furthermore, exposure to one quality of taste can modify other taste sensations—after brushing your teeth in the morning, for instance, you may notice that your orange juice has lost its sweetness.

Kinesthetic and Vestibular Senses

How do we know which way is up and whether we are moving or standing still?

The **kinesthetic senses** provide information about the speed and direction of our movement in space. More specifically, they relay information about muscle movement, changes in posture, and strain on muscles and joints. Specialized nerve endings called **stretch receptors** are attached to muscle fibers, and different nerve endings called **Golgi tendon organs** are attached to the tendons, which connect muscle to bones. Together these two types of receptors provide constant feedback from the stretching and contraction of individual muscles. The information from these receptors travels via the spinal cord to the cortex of the parietal lobes, the same brain area that perceives the sense of touch.

The **vestibular senses** provide information about our orientation or position in space (Leigh, 1994). We use this information to determine which way is up and which way is down. Birds and fish also rely on these senses to determine in which direction they are heading when they cannot see well. Like hearing, the vestibular senses originate in the inner ear, where hair cells serve as the sense organs. There are actually two kinds of vestibular sensation. The first one, which relays messages about the speed and direction of body rotation, arises in the three *semicircular canals* of the inner ear. As in the cochlea, each canal is filled with fluid that shifts hair bundles, which in turn stimulate hair cells, sending a message to the brain about the speed and direction of body rotation.

The second vestibular sense gives us information about gravitation and movement forward and backward, up and down. This sense arises from the two *vestibular sacs* that lie between the semicircular canals and the cochlea. Both sacs are filled with a jellylike fluid that contains millions of tiny crystals. When the body moves horizontally or vertically, the crystals bend hair bundles, prompting a sensory message.

The nerve impulses from both vestibular organs travel to the brain along the auditory nerve, but their ultimate destinations in the brain are still something of a mystery. Certain messages from the vestibular system go to the cerebellum, which controls many of the reflexes involved in coordinated movement. Others reach the areas that regulate the internal body organs, and some find their way to the parietal lobe of the cerebral cortex for analysis and response.

Perhaps we are most acutely aware of our vestibular senses when we experience *motion sickness.* Certain kinds of motion, such as riding in ships, cars, airplanes, even on camels and elephants, trigger strong reactions in some people. According to one theory, motion sickness stems from discrepancies between visual information and vestibular sensations (Stern & Koch, 1996). In other words, our eyes and our body are sending our brain contradictory information. The same thing occurs when we watch an automobile chase scene that was filmed from inside a moving car: Our eyes tell our brain that we are moving, but the organs in our inner ear insist that we are sitting still. Susceptibility to motion sickness appears to be related to both race and genetics: People of Asian ancestry are particularly susceptible to motion sickness, which also seems to be inherited (Muth et al., 1994).

The Skin Senses

What types of sensory messages are sent from the skin to the brain?

Our skin is our largest sense organ—a person 6 feet tall has about 21 square feet of skin. Our skin protects us from the environment, holds in body fluids, regulates our internal temperature, and contains receptors for our sense of touch, which plays an important role in human development and emotion (see *Understanding Ourselves*).

The skin's numerous nerve receptors, distributed in varying concentrations throughout its surface, send nerve fibers to the brain by two routes. Some information goes through the medulla and the thalamus and from there to the sensory cortex in the parietal lobe of the brain—which is presumably where our experiences of touch, pressure, and so on arise (see **Figure 2–7**). Other information goes through the thalamus and then on to the reticular formation, which, as we saw in Chapter 2, is responsible for arousing the nervous system or quieting it down.

Skin receptors give rise to sensations of pressure, temperature, and pain, but the relationship between the receptors and our sensory experiences is a subtle one. Researchers believe that our brains draw on complex information about the patterns of activity received from many different receptors to detect and discriminate among skin sensations. For example, our skin has "cold fibers" that increase their firing rate as the skin cools down and that slow their firing when the skin heats up. Conversely, we have "warm fibers" that accelerate their firing rate when the skin gets warm and that slow down when the skin cools. The brain may use the combined information from these two sets of fibers as the basis for determining skin temperature. If both sets are activated at once, the brain may read their combined pattern of firings as "hot" (Craig & Bushnell, 1994). Thus, you might sometimes think that you are touching something hot when you are really touching something warm and something cool at the same time, a phenomenon known as *paradoxical heat* (see **Figure 3–21**).

The skin senses are remarkably sensitive. For example, skin displacement of as little as 0.00004 of an inch can result in a sensation of pressure. Moreover, various parts of the body differ greatly in their sensitivity to pressure: Your face and fingertips are extremely sensitive, whereas your legs, feet, and back are much less so (Weinstein, 1968). It is this remarkable sensitivity in our fingertips that makes possible Braille touch reading, which requires identifying patterns of tiny raised dots distributed over a very small area.

Like other senses, the skin senses undergo various kinds of sensory adaptation. When we first get into a bath, it may be uncomfortably hot, but in a few minutes, we adapt to the heat, just as our eyes adapt to darkness. Skin senses are also influenced by our expectations. When someone tickles us, our skin senses respond with excitement, but tickling ourselves produces no effect. Clearly, the brain draws on many sources of information in interpreting the sense of touch.

Pain

What differences among people have an effect on the degree of pain they experience?

An old adage holds that pain is nature's way of telling you that something is wrong. It does seem reasonable to assume that damage to the body causes

FIGURE 3–21
Paradoxical heat. Touching a warm pipe and a cold pipe at the same time causes two sets of skin receptors to signal at once to the brain. The brain reads their combined pattern of firings as "hot," a phenomenon known as paradoxical heat.

UNDERSTANDING OURSELVES

The Importance of Touch

In most societies, hellos and good-byes are accompanied by shaking hands, hugging, and other gestures involving touch. And in most cultures, lovers express their affection by kissing, holding hands, and caressing. Touching and being touched by others bridges, at least momentarily, our isolation. Of all our senses, then, touch may be the most comforting.

Indeed, research such as psychologist Harry Harlow's classic experiments with monkeys shows that infant primates deprived of maternal contact suffer psychologically and physically (Harlow, 1958; Harlow & Zimmerman, 1959). (This research is explored in greater detail in Chapter 8, "Motivation and Emotion.") More recent studies suggest that the experience of being touched may directly affect the growth of an infant's mind and body and thus have significant implications for hospital care of premature infants. In one study premature infants who were massaged three times a day for fifteen minutes at a time gained weight much more quickly than did a control group that was left untouched in their incubators (Field, 1986). The massaged babies were subsequently more responsive to faces and rattles, and were generally more active than the other babies. Because of their comparatively rapid growth, the massaged infants were discharged from the hospital an average of six days earlier than the nonmassaged infants were. Eight months later the massaged infants maintained their weight advantage while performing better on tests of motor and mental ability. Significantly, the massaged infants did not eat more than the others: Their accelerated weight gain appears to be due solely to the effect of physical touch on their metabolism.

> Of all our senses, then, touch may be the most comforting.

Why does touch produce such beneficial effects? Studies of rats, whose basic neural and tactile (touch) systems are similar to those of humans, indicate that a specific pattern of touch inhibits the baby's manufacture of a chemical that reduces levels of growth hormone (Schanberg & Field, 1987). In related studies, when infant rats and monkeys were separated from their mothers, they showed a stress response that disappeared when maternal contact was resumed (S. Levine, Johnson, & Gonzales, 1985). According to the researchers,

The human response to touch may sometimes be therapeutic. Gentle massage tends to calm agitated premature babies, and by regularly massaging them, their growth rate can be increased. These findings agree with the common belief that touch is among our most comforting senses.

skin-to-skin contact may reduce the level of stress hormones, soothing all infants—not just premature babies. It may be that both mental and physical development of all infants could be enhanced if they were touched more (Jacobsen, Edelstein, & Hofmann, 1994; Wachs & Smitherman, 1985).

Each of us differs in the degree of physical contact we welcome. The uniqueness of our nervous systems may account for some of this difference, but our past experiences with touch undoubtedly play a role as well. Researchers suspect that those who have had little physical contact may become hypersensitive to touch, so much so that they find the experience of touching physically uncomfortable.

pain, but in many cases, actual physical injury is not accompanied by pain. Conversely, people may feel pain even though they have not suffered any physical harm. We might also assume that pain occurs when some kind of pain receptor is stimulated, but there is no simple relationship between pain receptors and the experience of pain. In fact, scientists have had great difficulty even finding pain receptors, although recent research indicates that free nerve endings may be involved (Dubner & Gold, 1998). People may feel pain even though they have not been injured or long after the injury has healed.

One of the most perplexing examples of this is the *phantom limb phenomenon* (Sherman, 1996). When people undergo amputation of an arm or a leg, they often continue to feel that the limb is still there. It may itch, tickle, or cramp; they may even forget that it is gone and try to move it. Often the missing limb is also a source of considerable pain. Phantom limb pain occurs in about 85 percent of amputees. Fortunately, the pain often subsides with time as the brain slowly reorganizes the neurons associated with the amputated limb (Flor, Elbert, Knecht, Weinbruch, & Pantev, 1995).

Individual Differences   Individuals vary widely in both their *pain threshold* (the amount of stimulation required to feel pain) and their *pain tolerance* (the amount of pain with which they can cope).

Culture and belief systems play an important role in how we cope with pain. How do psychologists explain why the experience of pain differs among individuals? One commonly accepted view is the **gate control theory** of pain (Melzack, 1980; Wall & Melzack, 1989). According to this theory, a "neurological gate" in the spinal cord controls the transmission of pain impulses to the brain. If the gate is open, we experience more pain than we do if it is closed. Whether the gate is closed or open depends on a complex competition between two different types of sensory nerve fibers—large fibers that tend to "close the gate" and small fibers that "open the gate" when they are stimulated, letting the pain messages get through to the brain. Moreover, certain areas of the brain stem can also close the gate from above by sending down signals to fibers in the spinal cord to close the gate.

Differences in how individuals experience pain may be due to the number of small and large fibers a person has. Also, some people may have faulty neurological gates, thereby experiencing more or less pain than others are.

Some psychologists believe that gate control theory oversimplifies the complex experience we call pain. **Biopsychosocial theory** holds that pain sensations involve three interrelated mechanisms. *Biological mechanisms* involve the degree to which tissue is injured and the way that our pain pathways have adapted. *Psychological mechanisms* involve our thoughts, beliefs, and emotions concerning pain. For example, when hospital patients were led to believe that a medical procedure was not painful, they actually reported experiencing less pain than people who had not been given this information (DiMatteo & Friedman, 1982).

Finally, *social mechanisms,* such as the degree of family support or cultural expectations, can influence our experience of pain. For example, when people believe that their pain is manageable and that they can cope, they often experience less pain, perhaps because these positive beliefs cause higher brain centers to reduce or block pain signals (Wall & Melzack, 1996).

Alternative Approaches   Increasingly, Americans are turning to so-called alternative medicine to treat chronic pain. Are people who use these approaches fooling themselves? Many studies have shown that if you give pain sufferers a chemically inert pill, or *placebo,* but tell them that it is an effective pain reducer, they often report some relief. No doubt many home remedies and secret cures rely on the **placebo effect.** Research indicates that both placebos and acupuncture, which involves the insertion of thin needles into parts of the body, work through the release of endorphins, the pain-blocking neurotransmitters that we examined in Chapter 2. Some other pain-reduction techniques, however—such as hypnosis or related concentration exercises (as in the Lamaze birth tech-

Glowing coals smolder under the feet of these participants in an annual ritual at Mt. Takao, Japan. How do they do it? Is it mind over matter—the human ability to sometimes "turn off" pain sensations? The secret in this case may actually lie more in the coals than in the men. Because wood is a poor conductor of heat, walking over wood coals quickly may not be that painful after all.

Gate control theory
The theory that a "neurological gate" in the spinal cord controls the transmission of pain messages to the brain.

Biopsychosocial theory
The theory that the interaction of biological, psychological, and cultural factors influence the intensity and duration of pain.

Placebo effect
Pain relief that occurs when a person believes a pill or procedure will reduce pain. The actual cause of the relief seems to come from endorphins.

Traditional Asian medicine has used acupuncture to reduce or eliminate pain. Studies indicate that acupuncture works by releasing endorphins into the body.

INTERACTIVE LECTURE **3.4**

nique)—appear to have nothing to do with endorphins, and rely on some other means of reducing the pain sensation. Further research is needed before we will fully understand the sensation of pain.

WEB QUIZ **3.4**

CHECK YOUR UNDERSTANDING

Match the following senses with the appropriate description.

1. ____ smell
2. ____ taste
3. ____ kinesthetic
4. ____ vestibular
5. ____ motion
6. ____ skin senses
7. ____ pain

a. controls awareness of body position
b. detected in vestibular organs
c. includes sweet, sour, salty, and bitter
d. react to pressure, temperature, and pain
e. explained by gate control theory
f. activated by airborne molecules
g. related to muscle movement

Answers: 1. f. 2. c. 3. g. 4. a. 5. b. 6. d. 7. e.

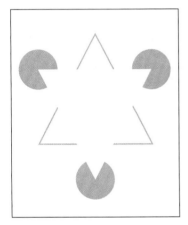

FIGURE 3–22

An illusory triangle.   When sensory information is incomplete, we tend to create a complete perception by supplying the missing details. In this figure we fill in the lines that let us perceive a white triangle in the center of the pattern.

Perception

How is perception different from sensation?

Our senses provide us with raw data about the external world. But unless we interpret this raw information, it is nothing more than what William James (1890) called a "booming, buzzing confusion." The eye records patterns of lightness and darkness, but it does not "see" a bird flittering from branch to branch. The eardrum vibrates in a particular fashion, but it does not "hear" a symphony. Deciphering *meaningful* patterns in the jumble of sensory information is what we mean by perception. But how does **perception** differ from sensation?

Perception takes place in the brain. Using sensory information as raw material, the brain creates perceptual experiences that go beyond what is sensed directly. For example, looking at **Figure 3–22**, we tend to perceive a white triangle in the center of the pattern, although the sensory input consists only of three circles from which "pie slices" have been cut and three 60-degree angles. Or take **Figure 3–23**. At first glance most people see only an assortment of black blotches. If you are told that the blotches represent a person riding a horse, suddenly your perceptual experience changes. What was meaningless sensory information now takes shape as a horse and rider.

Sometimes, as in certain optical illusions, you perceive things that could not possibly exist. The trident shown in **Figure 3–24** exemplifies such an "impossible" figure; on closer inspection, you discover that the object that you "recognized" is not really there. In all these cases, the brain actively creates and organizes perceptual experiences out of raw sensory data— sometimes even from data we are not aware of receiving. We now explore how perceptual processes organize sensory experience.

Perceptual Organization

How do we organize our perceptual experiences?

Early in this century, a group of German psychologists, calling themselves *Gestalt psychologists,* set out to discover the principles through which we in-

Perception
The brain's interpretation of sensory information so as to give it meaning.

terpret sensory information. The German word *Gestalt* has no exact English equivalent, but essentially it means "whole," "form," or "pattern." The Gestalt psychologists believed that the brain creates a coherent perceptual experience that is more than simply the sum of the available sensory information and that it does so in predictable ways.

In one important facet of the perceptual process, we distinguish *figures* from the *ground* against which they appear. A colorfully upholstered chair stands out from the bare walls of a room. A marble statue is perceived as a whole figure separate from the red brick wall behind it. The figure-ground distinction pertains to all of our senses, not just vision. We can distinguish a violin solo against the ground of a symphony orchestra, a single voice amid cocktail-party chatter, and the smell of roses in a florist's shop. In all these instances, we perceive some objects as "figures" and other sensory information as "background."

Sometimes, however, there are not enough cues in a pattern to permit us easily to distinguish a figure from its ground. The horse and rider in **Figure 3–23** illustrate this problem, as does **Figure 3–25,** which shows a spotted dog investigating shadowy surroundings. It is hard to distinguish the dog because it has few visible contours of its own, and as a result, it seems to have no more form than the background. This is the principle behind camouflage—to make a figure blend into its background.

Sometimes a figure with clear contours can be perceived in two very different ways because it is unclear which part of the stimulus is the figure

FIGURE 3–23

Perceiving a pattern.   Knowing beforehand that the black blotches in this figure represent a person riding a horse changes our perception of it.

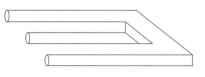

FIGURE 3–24

An optical illusion.   In the case of the trident, we go beyond what is sensed (blue lines on flat white paper) to perceive a three-dimensional object that isn't really there.

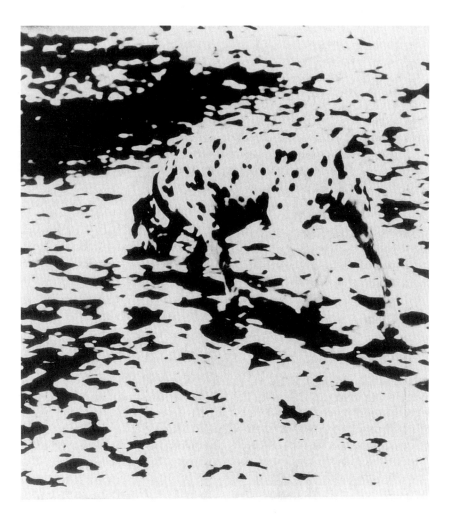

FIGURE 3–25

Random dots or something more?   This pattern does not give us enough cues to allow us easily to distinguish the figure of the Dalmatian dog from the ground behind it.

Source: Gregory, 1970.

FIGURE 3–26A

The reversible figure and ground in this M. C. Escher woodcut cause us first to see black devils and then to see white angels in each of the rings.

FIGURE 3–26B

Figure-ground relationship . . . How do you perceive this figure? Do you see a vase or the silhouettes of a man and a woman? Both interpretations are possible, but not at the same time. Reversible figures like this work because it is unclear which part of the stimulus is the figure and which is the neutral ground against which the figure is perceived.

and which is the ground (see **Figures 3–26A** and **3–26B**). At first glance you perceive figures against a specific background, but as you stare at the illustrations, you will discover that the figures and the ground reverse, making for two very different perceptions of the same illustration.

Figure 3–27 demonstrates some other important principles of perceptual organization. As these figures demonstrate, we use sensory information to create a perception that is more than just the sum of the parts. Although sometimes this process can cause problems, the perceptual tendency to "fill in the blanks" usually broadens our understanding of the world. As creatures searching for meaning, our brain tries to fill in missing information, to group various objects together, to see whole objects and hear meaningful sounds rather than just random bits and pieces of raw sensory data.

Perceptual Constancies

How do we perceive things as unchanging despite changing sensory information?

When anthropologist Colin Turnbull (1961) studied the Mbuti pygmies of Zaire, most of them had never left the dense Ituri rain forest and had rarely encountered objects that were more than a few feet away. On one occasion, Turnbull took a pygmy guide named Kenge on a trip onto the African plains. When Kenge looked across the plain and saw a distant herd of buffalo, he asked what kind of insects they were. He refused to believe that the tiny black spots he saw were buffalo. As he and Turnbull drove toward the herd, Kenge believed that magic was making the animals grow larger. Be-

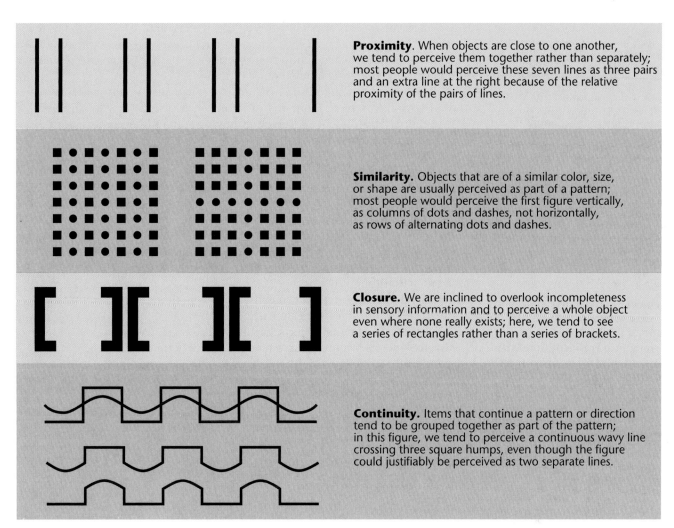

Proximity. When objects are close to one another, we tend to perceive them together rather than separately; most people would perceive these seven lines as three pairs and an extra line at the right because of the relative proximity of the pairs of lines.

Similarity. Objects that are of a similar color, size, or shape are usually perceived as part of a pattern; most people would perceive the first figure vertically, as columns of dots and dashes, not horizontally, as rows of alternating dots and dashes.

Closure. We are inclined to overlook incompleteness in sensory information and to perceive a whole object even where none really exists; here, we tend to see a series of rectangles rather than a series of brackets.

Continuity. Items that continue a pattern or direction tend to be grouped together as part of the pattern; in this figure, we tend to perceive a continuous wavy line crossing three square humps, even though the figure could justifiably be perceived as two separate lines.

FIGURE 3–27
Gestalt principles of perceptual organization. Size constancy.

It's not what it looks like.

cause he had no experience of distant objects, he could not perceive the buffalo as having constant size.

Perceptual constancy refers to the tendency to perceive objects as relatively stable and unchanging despite changing sensory information. Once we have formed a stable perception of an object, we can recognize it from almost any position, at almost any distance, under almost any illumination. A white house looks like a white house by day or by night and from any angle. We see it as the same house. The sensory information may change as illumination and perspective change, but the object is perceived as constant. Without this ability, we would find the world very confusing (as Kenge did).

Memory and experience play important roles in perceptual constancy, as shown in **Figure 3–28**. For example, we tend to perceive familiar objects at their true size regardless of the size of the image that they cast on the retina. As **Figure 3–29** shows, the farther away an object is from the lens of the eye, the smaller the retinal image it casts. We might guess that a woman some distance away is 5 feet 4 inches tall when she is really 5 feet 8 inches, but hardly anyone would perceive her as being 3 feet tall, no matter how far away she is. We know from experience that adults are seldom that short. **Size constancy** depends partly on experience—information about the relative sizes of objects stored in memory—and partly on distance cues.

Perceptual constancy
A tendency to perceive objects as stable and unchanging despite changes in sensory stimulation.

Size constancy
The perception of an object as the same size regardless of the distance from which it is viewed.

FIGURE 3–28

Look again! Context, hair style, and head shape lead us to believe that this is a picture of former President Clinton and former Vice President Gore when, in reality, Clinton's face is superimposed over the face of Gore.

Source: APA Monitor, 1997.

3.3 *Live!* **psych**

Shape constancy
A tendency to see an object as the same shape no matter what angle it is viewed from.

Color constancy
An inclination to perceive familiar objects as retaining their color despite changes in sensory information.

Brightness constancy
The perception of brightness as the same, even though the amount of light reaching the retina changes.

Monocular cues
Visual cues requiring the use of one eye.

Binocular cues
Visual cues requiring the use of both eyes.

Familiar objects also tend to be seen as having a constant shape, even though the retinal images they cast change as they are viewed from different angles (this is called **shape constancy**). A dinner plate is perceived as a circle even when it is tilted and the retinal image is oval. A rectangular door will project a rectangular image on the retina only when it is viewed directly from the front. From any other angle, it casts a trapezoidal image on the retina, but it is not perceived as having suddenly become a trapezoidal door (see **Figure 3–30**).

Similarly, we tend to perceive familiar objects as keeping their colors, regardless of information that reaches the eye. If you own a red automobile, you will see it as red whether it is on a brightly lit street or in a dark garage, where the low light may send your eye a message that it is closer to brown or black than red. But **color constancy** does not always hold true. When objects are unfamiliar or there are no customary color cues to guide us, color constancy may be distorted—as when you buy a sweater in a brightly lit store, only to discover that in ordinary daylight, it is not the shade you thought it was.

Brightness constancy means that even though the amount of light available to our eyes varies greatly over the course of a day, the perceived brightness of familiar objects hardly varies at all. We perceive a sheet of white paper as brighter than a piece of coal whether we see these objects in candlelight or under bright sunlight. Brightness constancy occurs because an object reflects the same percentage of the light falling on it whether that light is from a candle or the sun. Rather than basing our judgment of brightness on the absolute amount of light that the object reflects, we assess how the relative reflection compares with the surrounding objects.

Perception of Distance and Depth

How do we know how far away something is?

We are constantly judging the distance between ourselves and other objects. When we walk through a classroom, our perception of distance helps us to avoid bumping into desks or tripping over the wastebasket. If we reach out to pick up a pencil, we automatically judge how far to extend our hand. We also assess the depth of objects—how much total space they occupy. We use many cues to determine the distance and the depth of objects. Some of these cues depend on visual messages that one eye alone can transmit; these are called **monocular cues.** Others, known as **binocular cues,** require the use of both eyes. Having two eyes allows us to make more accurate judgments about distance and depth, particularly when objects are relatively close. But monocular cues alone are often sufficient to allow us to judge distance and depth quite accurately, as we see in the next section.

FIGURE 3–29

The relationship between distance and the size of the retinal image. Object A and object B are the same size, but A, being much closer to the eye, casts a much larger image on the retina.

FIGURE 3–30

Examples of shape constancy. Even though the image of the door on the retina changes greatly as the door opens, we still perceive the door as being rectangular.

Source: Boring, Langfeld, & Weld, 1976.

Monocular Cues One important monocular distance cue that provides us with information about relative position is called **interposition.** Interposition occurs when one object partly blocks a second object. The first object is perceived as being closer, the second as more distant (see **Figure 3–31**).

As art students learn, there are several ways in which perspective can help in estimating distance and depth. In **linear perspective,** two parallel lines that extend into the distance seem to come together at some point on the horizon. In **aerial perspective,** distant objects have a hazy appearance and a somewhat blurred outline. On a clear day, mountains often seem to be much closer than on a hazy day, when their outlines become blurred. The **elevation** of an object also serves as a perspective cue to depth: An object that is on a higher horizontal plane seems to be farther away than one on a lower plane (see **Figure 3–32**).

Another useful monocular cue to distance and depth is **texture gradient.** An object that is close seems to have a rough or detailed texture. As distance increases, the texture becomes finer, until finally the original texture cannot be distinguished clearly, if at all. For example, when standing on a pebbly beach, you can distinguish among the gray stones and the gravel in front of your feet. As you look down the beach, however, the stones appear to become smaller and finer until eventually you cannot make out individual stones at all. **Shadowing,** another important cue to the distance, depth, and solidity of an object is illustrated in **Figure 3–33**.

People traveling on buses or trains often notice that nearby trees or telephone poles seem to flash past the windows, whereas buildings and other objects farther away seem to move slowly. These differences in the speeds of movement of images across the retina as you move give an important cue to distance and depth. You can observe the same effect if you stand still and move your head from side to side as you focus your gaze on something in the middle distance: Objects close to you seem to move in the direction opposite to the direction in which your head is moving, whereas objects far away seem to move in the same direction as your head. This distance cue is known as **motion parallax.**

Binocular Cues All the visual cues examined so far depend on the action of only one eye. Many animals—such as horses, deer, and fish—rely entirely on monocular cues. Although they have two eyes, the two visual fields do not overlap, because their eyes are located on the sides of the head rather than in front. Humans, apes, and many predatory animals—such as lions, tigers, and wolves—have a distinct physical advantage over these other animals. Because both eyes are set in the front of

Interposition
Monocular distance cue in which one object, by partly blocking a second object, is perceived as being closer.

Linear perspective
Monocular cue to distance and depth based on the fact that two parallel lines seem to come together at the horizon.

Aerial perspective
Monocular cue to distance and depth based on the fact that more distant objects are likely to appear hazy and blurred.

Elevation
Monocular cue to distance and depth based on the fact that the higher on the horizontal plane an object is, the farther away it appears.

Texture gradient
Monocular cue to distance and depth based on the fact that objects seen at greater distances appear to be smoother and less textured.

Shadowing
Monocular cue to distance and depth based on the fact that shadows often appear on the parts of objects that are more distant.

Motion parallax
Monocular distance cue in which objects closer than the point of visual focus seem to move in the direction opposite to the viewer's moving head, and objects beyond the focus point appear to move in the same direction as the viewer's head.

FIGURE 3–31

Superposition. Because the king of clubs appears to have been superimposed on the king of spades, we perceive it to be closer to us.

3.4

the head, the visual fields overlap. The **stereoscopic vision** derived from combining the two retinal images—one from each eye—makes the perception of depth and distance more accurate.

Because our eyes are set approximately 2 1/2 inches apart, each one has a slightly different view of things. The difference between the two images that the eyes receive is known as **retinal disparity.** The left eye receives more information about the left side of an object, and the right eye receives more information about the right side. You can easily prove that each of your eyes receives a different image. Close one eye and line up a finger with some vertical line, like the edge of a door. Then open that eye and close the other one. Your finger will appear to have moved a great distance. When you look at the finger with both eyes, however, the two different images become one.

An important binocular cue to distance comes from the muscles that control the **convergence** of the eyes. When we look at objects that are fairly close to us, our eyes tend to *converge*—to turn slightly inward toward each other. The sensations from the muscles that control the movement of the eyes thus provide a cue to distance. If the object is very close, such as at the end of the nose, the eyes cannot converge, and two separate images are perceived. If the object is more than a few yards (meters) away, the sight lines of the eyes are more or less parallel, and there is no convergence.

Location of Sounds   Just as we use monocular and binocular cues to establish visual depth and distance, we draw on **monaural** (single-ear) and **binaural** (two-ear) **cues** to locate the source of sounds (see **Figure 3–34**). In one monaural cue, loud sounds are perceived as closer than faint sounds, with changes in loudness translating into changes in distance. Binaural cues work on the principle that because sounds off to one side of the head reach one ear slightly ahead of the other (in the range of 1/1,000th of a second), the time difference between sound

Stereoscopic vision
Combination of two retinal images to give a three-dimensional perceptual experience.

Retinal disparity
Binocular distance cue based on the difference between the images cast on the two retinas when both eyes are focused on the same object.

Convergence
A visual depth cue that comes from muscles controlling eye movement as the eyes turn inward to view a nearby stimulus.

Monaural cue
Cue to sound location that requires just one ear.

Binaural cue
Cue to sound location that involves both ears working together.

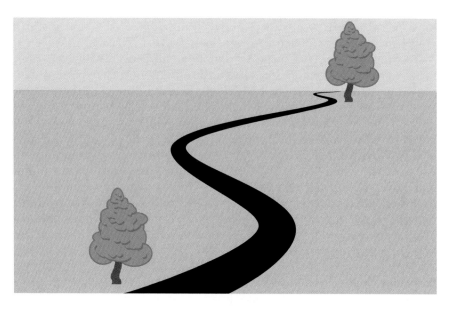

FIGURE 3–32

Elevation as a visual cue. Because of the higher elevation and the suggestion of depth provided by the road, the tree on the right is perceived as being more distant and about the same size as the tree at lower left. Actually, it is appreciably smaller, as you can see if you measure the heights of the two drawings.

waves reaching the two ears registers in the brain and helps us to make accurate judgments of location.

In a second binaural cue, sound signals arriving from a source off to one side of you are slightly louder in the nearer ear than in the ear farther from the source. The slight difference occurs because your head, in effect, blocks the sound, reducing the intensity of sound in the opposite ear. This relative loudness difference between signals heard separately by the two ears is enough for the brain to locate the sound source and to judge its distance. When sound engineers record your favorite musical group, they may place microphones at many different locations. On playback, the two speakers or headphones project sounds at slightly different instants to mimic the sound patterns you would hear if you were actually listening to the group perform right in front of you.

Most of us rely so heavily on visual cues that we seldom pay much attention to the rich array of auditory information available around us. Blind people, who often compensate for their lack of vision by sharpening their awareness of sounds (Arias, Curet, Moyano, Joekes, & Blanch, 1993), can figure out where obstacles lie in their paths by listening to the echoes from a cane, their own footsteps, and their own voices. Many blind people can judge the size and distance of one object in relation to another using nothing more than sound cues. They can also discriminate between contrasting surfaces, such as glass and fabric, by listening to the difference in the echo produced when sound strikes them.

Perception of Movement

How do we perceive movement?

The perception of movement is a complicated process involving both visual information from the retina and messages from the muscles around the eyes as they follow an object. On occasion, our perceptual processes play tricks on us, and we think we perceive movement when the objects that we are looking at are in fact stationary. We must distinguish, therefore, between real and apparent movement.

Real movement refers to the physical displacement of an object from one position to another. The perception of real movement depends only in part on movement of images across the retina of the eye. If you stand still and move your head to look around you, the images of all the objects in the room will pass across your retina. Yet you will probably perceive all of the objects as stationary. Even if you hold your head still and move only your eyes, the images will continue to pass across your retina. But the messages from the eye muscles seem to counteract those from the retina, so the objects in the room will be perceived as motionless.

The perception of real movement seems to be determined less by images moving across the retina than by how the position of objects changes in relation to a background that is perceived as stationary. When we perceive a car moving along a street, for example, we see the street, the buildings, and the sidewalk as a stationary background and the car as a moving object.

Apparent movement occurs when we perceive movement in objects that are actually standing still. One form of apparent movement is referred to as the **autokinetic illusion**—the perceived motion created by a single stationary object. If you stand in a room that is absolutely dark except for one tiny spot of light and stare at the light for a few seconds, you will begin to see the light drift. In the darkened room, your eyes have no visible framework; there are no cues telling you that the light is really stationary. The slight movements of the eye muscles, which go unnoticed most of the time, make the light appear to move.

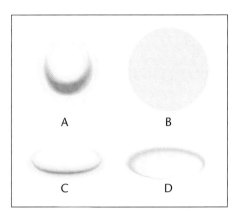

FIGURE 3–33

Shadowing. Shadowing on the outer edges of a spherical object, such as a ball or globe, gives it a three-dimensional quality (A). Without shadowing (B), it might be perceived as a flat disk. Shadowing can also affect our perception of the direction of depth. In the absence of other cues, we tend to assume overhead lighting, so image C appears to be a bump because its top edge is lit, whereas image D appears to be a dent. If you turn the book upside down, the direction of depth is reversed.

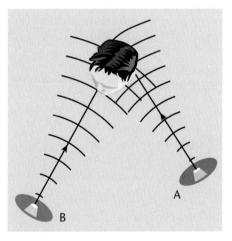

FIGURE 3–34

Cues used in sound localization. Sound waves coming from source B will reach both ears simultaneously. A sound wave from source A reaches the left ear first, where it is also louder. The head casts a "shadow" over the other ear, thus reducing the intensity of the delayed sound in that ear.

Source: Langfeld & Weld, 1976.

Autokinetic illusion
The perception that a stationary object is actually moving.

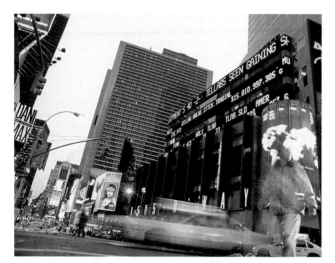

When we look at an electronic marquee such as this one, we see motion, even though the sign consists of stationary lights that are flashed on and off.

Another form of apparent movement is **stroboscopic motion**—the apparent motion created by a rapid series of still images. This form of apparent movement is illustrated best by a motion picture, which is not in motion at all. The film consists of a series of still pictures showing people and objects in slightly different positions. When the separate images are projected sequentially onto a screen at a specific rate of speed, the people and objects seem to be moving because of the rapid change from one still picture to the next.

Another common perceptual illusion, known as the **phi phenomenon,** occurs as a result of stroboscopic motion. When a light is flashed on at a certain point in a darkened room, then flashed off, and a second light is flashed on a split second later at a point a short distance away, most people will perceive these two separate lights as a single spot of light moving from one point to another. This perceptual process causes us to see motion in neon signs or theater marquees, where words appear to move across the sign, from one side to the other, as the different combinations of stationary lights are flashed on and off.

Visual Illusions

What causes visual illusions?

Visual illusions graphically demonstrate the ways in which we use a variety of sensory cues to create perceptual experiences that may (or may not) correspond to what is out there in the real world. By understanding how we are fooled into "seeing" something that isn't there, psychologists can figure out how perceptual processes work in the everyday world and under normal circumstances.

Psychologists generally distinguish between physical and perceptual illusions. One example of a *physical illusion* is the bent appearance of a stick when it is placed in water—an illusion easily understood because the water acts like a prism, bending the light waves before they reach our eyes. *Perceptual illusions* occur because the stimulus contains misleading cues that give rise to inaccurate or impossible perceptions.

The illusions in **Figure 3–35** result from false and misleading depth cues. For example, in **Figure 3–35F** both monsters cast the same size image on the retina in our eyes. But the depth cues in the tunnel suggest that we are looking at a three-dimensional scene and that therefore the top monster is much farther away. In the real world, this perception would mean that the top monster is actually much larger than the bottom monster. Therefore we "correct" for the distance and actually perceive the top monster as larger, despite other cues to the contrary. We know that the image is actually two-dimensional, but we still respond to it as if it were three-dimensional.

There are also "real world" illusions that illustrate how perceptual processes work, such as the illusion of *induced movement.* When you are sitting in a stationary train and the train next to you begins to move forward, you seem to be moving backward. Because you have no reference point by which to tell whether you are standing still, you are confused as to which train is actually moving. However, if you look down at the ground, you can establish an unambiguous frame of reference and make the situation clear to yourself.

Artists rely on many of these perceptual phenomena both to represent reality accurately and to distort it deliberately. In paintings and sketches drawn on a two-dimensional surface, it is almost always necessary to distort objects for them to be perceived correctly by viewers. For example, in

Stroboscopic motion
Apparent movement that results from flashing a series of still pictures in rapid succession, as in a motion picture.

Phi phenomenon
Apparent movement caused by flashing lights in sequence, as on theater marquees.

FIGURE 3–35

Reversible figures and misleading depth cues.   Images A, B, and C are examples of reversible figures—drawings that we can perceive two different ways, but not at the same time. Images D, E, and F show how, through the use of misleading depth cues, we misjudge the size of objects. The middle circles in image D are exactly the same size, as are the lines in image E and the monsters in image F.

representational art, the railroad tracks, sidewalks, and tunnels are always drawn closer together in the distance. Three-dimensional movies also work on the principle that the brain can be deceived into seeing three dimensions if slightly different images are presented to the left and right eyes (working on the principle of retinal disparity). Thus, our understanding of perceptual illusion enables us to manipulate images for deliberate effect—and to delight in the results.

 3.5

Observer Characteristics

What personal factors influence our perceptions?

We clearly draw on past experience and learning when it comes to perception, but our own motivations, values, expectations, cognitive style, and cultural preconceptions can also affect our perceptual experiences. Although the focus of this section is on differences among individuals, consider how a person's sensory and perceptual experiences are affected by race, culture, and gender.

Motivation   Our desires and needs shape our perceptions. People in need are likely to perceive something that they think will satisfy that need. For example, if people are deprived of food for some time and are then shown vague or ambiguous pictures, they are apt to perceive the pictures as being related to food (McClelland & Atkinson, 1948; Sanford, 1937).

Values   In an experiment that revealed how strongly perceptions can be affected by a person's values, nursery schoolchildren were shown a poker chip. Each child was asked to compare the size of the chip with the size of an adjustable circle of light until the child said that the chip and the circle of light were the same size. The children were then brought to a machine with a crank that, when turned, produced a poker chip that could be exchanged for candy. Thus, the children were taught to value the poker chips more highly than they had before. After the children had been rewarded with candy for the poker chips, they were again asked to compare the size of the chips with a circle of light. This time the chips seemed larger to the children (Lambert, Solomon, & Watson, 1949).

Expectations   Preconceptions about what we are supposed to perceive can influence perception by causing us to delete, insert, transpose, or otherwise modify what we see (Lachman, 1996). Lachman (1984) demonstrated this phenomenon by asking people to copy a group of stimuli similar to this one:

PARIS

IN THE

THE SPRING

Often, people tended to omit the "extra" words and to report seeing more familiar (and more normal) expressions, such as PARIS IN THE SPRING. This phenomenon reflects a strong tendency to see what we *expect* to see, even if our expectation conflicts with external reality.

Cognitive Style   As we mature, we develop a cognitive style—our own way of dealing with the environment—which also affects how we see the world. Some psychologists distinguish between two general approaches that people use in perceiving the world (Witkin et al., 1962). People taking the *field-dependent approach* tend to perceive the environment as a whole and do not clearly delineate in their minds the shape, color, size, or other qualities of individual items. If field-dependent people are asked to draw a human figure, they generally draw it so that it blends into the background. By contrast, people who are *field independent* are more likely to perceive the elements of the environment as separate and distinct from one another and to draw each element as standing out from the background.

Cognitive styles can also be viewed from the perspective of "levelers" and "sharpeners"—those who level out the distinctions among objects and those who magnify them. To investigate the differences between these two cognitive styles, G. S. Klein (1951) showed people sets of squares of varying sizes and asked them to estimate the size of each one. One group, the levelers, failed to perceive any differences in the size of the squares. The sharpeners, however, picked up the differences in the size of the squares and made their size estimates accordingly.

Experience and Culture   Cultural background also influences people's perceptions. As we will see in Chapter 7, Cognition and Mental Abilities, the language that people speak affects the ways in which they perceive their surroundings. Cultural differences in people's experiences can also influence how people use perceptual cues. For example, East African Masai, who depend on herding animals for their living, are more perceptive about the characteristics of individual animals in their herd than are Westerners. Similarly, professional dog breeders see championship qualities in a pup that most people would not recognize. And wine experts can distinguish subtle differences in the flavor of different vintages that most of us could not detect.

Personality   A number of researchers have shown that our individual personalities influence perception (for a review of the research, see Greenwald, 1992). For example, college students were compared with depressed students or students with an eating disorder in terms of their ability to identify words related to depression and food (von Hippel, Hawkins, & Narayan, 1994). All the words in this study were exposed very quickly (generally for less than 1/10th of a second). In general, students with an eating disorder were faster at identifying words that referred to foods that they commonly thought about than they were at identifying foods that they rarely thought about. Similarly, depressed students were faster at identifying adjectives describing personality traits that they commonly thought about (such as "quiet," "withdrawn," "hesitant," and "timid") than adjectives that described traits that they rarely thought about (such as "extrovert," "lively," and "bold"). These findings suggest that personality—along with the other factors explored in this chapter—may influence perception.

 INTERACTIVE LECTURE 3.5

 WEB QUIZ 3.5

CHECK YOUR UNDERSTANDING

1. The process by which we create meaningful experiences out of the jumble of sensory information is called ____.

Match the following principles of perception with the appropriate definitions.

2. ____ similarity
3. ____ continuity
4. ____ proximity
5. ____ closure

a. tendency to perceive a whole object even where none exists
b. elements that continue a pattern are likely to be seen as part of the pattern
c. objects that are like one another tending to be grouped together
d. elements found close together tending to be perceived as a unit

Answers: 1. perception. 2. c. 3. b. 4. d. 5. a.

KEY TERMS

CHAPTER REVIEW

The Nature of Sensation

What causes sensory experiences? Humans have sensory experiences of sight, hearing, smell, taste, touch, pain, and balance, which are known as **sensations.** These experiences begin when the body's sensory receptors are stimulated. In each case, some form of physical energy is converted into neural impulses that are carried to the brain.

How is energy, such as light or sound, converted into a message to the brain? The process of sending a sensory message to the brain begins when energy stimulates **receptor cells** in one of the sense organs. The receptor cells then send the brain a coded neural signal that varies according to the characteristics of the stimulus. Further coding occurs as the signal passes along sensory nerve fibers, so that the message finally reaching the brain is very detailed and precise.

What are the limits on our ability to sense stimuli in our environment? The amount of physical energy that reaches sensory receptors must be of a minimal intensity to produce a detectable sensation. The least amount of energy needed to produce a sensation 50 percent of the time is called the **absolute threshold.** For hearing, the absolute threshold is roughly the tick of a watch from 6 meters (20 feet) away in a very quiet room, and for vision, it is a candle flame seen from 50 kilometers (30 miles) on a clear, dark night. Absolute thresholds vary according to the intensity of the stimulus present at any given time—a process called **adaptation.** Also, we are very sensitive to *changes* in the stimulus intensity. The **difference threshold** or the **just noticeable difference (jnd)** is the smallest change in stimulation that can be detected 50 percent of the time.

Under what circumstances might messages outside our awareness affect our behavior? When people respond to sensory messages that are below their threshold level of awareness, they are said to be responding subliminally. Such subliminal processing can occur in controlled laboratory settings, but there is no scientific evidence that subliminal messages have any effect in everyday life.

Vision

Why have psychologists studied vision more than any other sense? Different animal species depend more on some senses than others. In bats, hearing is particularly important; in dogs, it is the sense of smell. In humans, vision is probably the most important sense, which is why it has received the most research attention.

How does light create a neural impulse? Light enters an eye through the **cornea** (a transparent protective coating) and passes through the **pupil** (the opening in the **iris**) as well as the **lens,** which focuses it onto the eye's light-sensitive inner lining called the **retina.** Neural impulses are generated in the retina by receptor cells known as **rods** and **cones.** The rods and cones connect to nerve cells called **bipolar cells,** which in turn connect to **ganglion cells.** The axons of ganglion cells converge to form the **optic nerve,** which carries to the brain the neural impulses triggered in the retina.

How do we see colors? One theory of color vision, the **trichromatic theory,** is based on the principles of **additive color mixing.** It holds that the eyes contain three different kinds of color receptors, one of which is most responsive to red, another to green, and another to blue. By combining signals from these three types of receptors, the brain can detect a wide range of shades. In contrast, the **opponent-process theory** of color vision maintains that receptors in the eyes are specialized to respond to one member of three basic color pairs: red-green, yellow-blue, and black-white (or light-dark). Research gives some support for both these theories. There are indeed three kinds of color receptors in the retinas, but the messages they initiate are coded by other neurons into opponent-process form.

Hearing

If a tree falls in the forest and no one is there, does the tree make a sound? A psychologist's answer to this age-old question is no; there isn't a **sound.** Although sound waves are produced by a falling tree, no sound can be heard without an ear to detect it.

How do the characteristics of sound waves cause us to hear different sounds? The physical stimuli for the sense of hearing are **sound waves,** which produce vibration in the eardrums. **Frequency,** the number of cycles per second in a sound wave, is the primary determinant of **pitch** (how high or low the tones seems to be). **Amplitude,** the magnitude of a wave, largely determines the loudness of a sound.

What path does sound follow from the ear to the brain? When sound waves strike an eardrum and cause it to vibrate, three bones in the middle ear—the hammer, the anvil, and the stirrup—are stimulated to vibrate in sequence. These vibrations are magnified in their passage through the middle ear and into the inner ear beyond it. In the inner ear, movement of the **basilar membrane** stimulates sensory receptors in the **organ of Corti.** This stimulation of the hair cells produces auditory signals that travel to the brain through the **auditory nerve.**

How do we distinguish low-frequency and high-frequency sounds? The **place theory** holds that the brain distinguishes low-frequency from high-frequency sounds by noting the place on the basilar membrane at which the greatest stimulation is occurring. For high-frequency sounds, this is the base of the basilar membrane; for low-frequency sounds, it is the membrane's opposite end. Another theory of pitch discrimination is the **frequency theory.** According to this theory, the frequency of vibrations on the basilar membrane as a whole is translated into an equivalent frequency of nerve impulses that travel to the brain. The frequency theory, with its associated **volley principle,** can account for pitch detection up to frequencies of about 4,000 Hz. Above that, the place theory seems to provide a better explanation.

The Other Senses

What are the chemical senses? Two of our senses are designed to detect the presence of various chemical substances in the air and in things that we eat. These two chemical senses are smell and taste.

What activates the sense of smell? Substances carried by airborne molecules into the nasal cavities activate highly specialized receptors for smell. From here messages are carried directly to the **olfactory bulb** in the brain, where they are sent to the brain's temporal lobe, resulting in our awareness of smell.

How do we detect the basic tastes? The overall flavor of something is a complex blend of taste and smell. When we consider taste alone, there are four basic ones—sweet, sour, salty, and bitter—and other tastes derive from combinations of these. The receptors for taste are housed in the **taste buds** on the tongue. When these receptors are activated by the chemical substances in food, their adjacent neurons fire, sending nerve impulses to the brain.

How do we know which way is up and whether we are moving or standing still? The **vestibular senses** provide information about our orientation or position in space, such as whether we are rightside up or upside down. The receptors for these senses are in two vestibular organs in the inner ear—the semicircular canals and the vestibular sacs. The kinesthetic senses provide information about the speed and direction of our movements. They rely on feedback from two sets of specialized nerve endings—**stretch receptors,** which are attached to muscle fibers, and **Golgi tendon organs,** which are attached to the tendons that connect muscle to bone. The vestibular organs are responsible for motion sickness. This queasy feeling may be triggered by discrepancies between visual information and vestibular sensations.

What types of sensory messages are sent from the skin to the brain? The skin is the largest sense organ, and sensations that arise from the receptors embedded in it produce our sensation of touch, which includes pressure, temperature, and pain. Research has not yet established a simple, direct connection between these three sensations and the various types of skin receptors whose nerve fibers lead to the brain.

What differences among people have an effect on the degree of pain they experience? People have varying degrees of sensitivity to pain based partly on their physiological makeup but also on their current mental and emotional state, their expectations about what they will experience, and their cultural beliefs and values. One commonly accepted explanation of pain is the **gate control theory,** which holds that a "neurological gate" in the spinal cord controls the transmission of pain messages to the brain. **Biopsychosocial theory** proposes that pain results from the interaction of biological, psychological, and social mechanisms.

Perception

How is perception different from sensation? Sensation refers to the raw sensory data that the brain receives from the senses of sight, hearing, smell, taste, balance, touch, and pain. **Perception,** which takes place in the brain, is the process of organizing, interpreting, and giving meaning to that raw data in order to understand what is going on around us.

How do we organize our perceptual experiences? Early in the twentieth century, a group of Gestalt psychologists in Germany set out to discover the principles through which we interpret sensory information. They believed that the brain creates a coherent perceptual experience that is more than simply the sum of the available sensory data. The brain imposes order on the data it receives partly by distinguishing patterns such as figure and ground, proximity, similarity, closure, and continuity.

How do we perceive things as unchanging despite changing sensory information? **Perceptual constancy** is our tendency to perceive objects as unchanging even given many changes in sensory stimulation. Once we have formed a stable perception of something, we see it as essentially the same regardless of differences in viewing angle, distance, lighting, and so forth. These **size, shape, brightness,** and **color constancies** help us better to understand and relate to the world.

How do we know how far away something is? We perceive distance and depth through both **monocular cues** (which can be received even by one eye alone) and **binocular cues** (which depend on the interaction of both eyes). Examples of monocular cues are **interposition** (in which one object partly covers another), **linear perspective, elevation** (or closeness of something to the horizon), **texture gradient** (from coarser to finer depending on distance), **shadowing,** and **motion parallax** (differences in the relative movement of close and distant objects as we change position). An important binocular cue is **stereoscopic vision,** which is derived from combining our two retinal images to produce a 3-D effect. Two other binocular cues are **retinal disparity** (the fact that each eye receives a slightly different view from the other) and **convergence** of the eyes as viewing distance decreases. Just as we use monocular and binocular cues to sense depth and distance, we use **monaural** (one-ear) and **binaural** (two-ear) cues to locate sound.

How do we perceive movement? Perception of movement is a complicated process involving both visual messages from the retina and messages from the muscles around the eyes as they shift to follow a moving object. At times our perceptual processes trick us into believing that an object is moving when in fact it is not. There is a difference, then, between real movement and apparent movement. Examples of apparent movement are the **autokinetic illusion** (caused by the absence of visual cues surrounding a stationary object), **stroboscopic motion** (produced by rapidly flashing a series of pictures), and the **phi phenomenon** (produced by a pattern of flashing lights).

What causes visual illusions? Visual illusions occur when we use a variety of sensory cues to create perceptual experiences that do not actually exist. Some are *physical illusions,* such as the bent appearance of a stick in water. Others are *perceptual illusions,* which occur because a stimulus contains misleading cues that lead to inaccurate perceptions.

What personal factors influence our perceptions? In addition to past experience and learning, several personal factors color our perceptions. For example, familiarity with an object affects our expectations about how that object should look, even if we observe subtle changes in its appearance. Our perceptions are also influenced by our motivation, values, expectations, cognitive style, experience and culture, and personality.

CRITICAL THINKING AND APPLICATIONS

1. Research on the effectiveness of subliminal perception is inconsistent. Suggest several explanations for those inconsistencies.

2. When we look directly at an object, the image is focused on each eye's fovea. Why is this ability advantageous?

3. When we are reading or studying, we often seem to be very aware of movements off to our sides. Why is it so easy to sense these events?

4. Why do you get different colors when you mix colored lights as compared with when you mix colored inks?

5. What is the difference between the vestibular sense and the kinesthetic sense? What kinds of activities require both?

6. "Flavor" is thought of as the combination of the sense of taste with the sense of smell. How could you demonstrate the difference between flavor and taste? between flavor and smell?

7. Why do people have such differences in pain tolerance?

8. In what ways can emotional or motivational factors affect our sense of pain? Do these same factors have similar effects on other senses?

9. Examine a few passages of your favorite song. Explain how the Gestalt principles of organization (proximity, similarity, closure, and so on) operate in the perception of music.

10. What principles do artists rely on to make a realistic drawing of a person?

WEB QUIZ **3.6** ✔ **Go to the Morris 6e Companion Website to take a practice chapter exam.**

4 States of Consciousness

OVERVIEW

Conscious Experience
- Daydreaming and Fantasy

Sleep
- Circadian Cycles: The Biological Clock
- The Rhythms of Sleep
- Inadequate Sleep
- Sleep Disorders

Dreams
- Why Do We Dream?

Drug-altered Consciousness
- Substance Use, Abuse, and Dependence
- Depressants: Alcohol, Barbiturates, and the Opiates

- Stimulants: Caffeine, Nicotine, Amphetamines, and Cocaine
- Hallucinogens and Marijuana
- Explaining Abuse and Addiction

Meditation and Hypnosis
- Meditation
- Hypnosis

O N AUGUST 18, 1993, A MILITARY CARGO PLANE CRASHED INTO THE GROUND JUST a quarter of a mile short of the runway at Guantanamo Bay, Cuba. All three crew members were seriously injured; the DC-8 freighter they were flying was destroyed by the impact and subsequent fire. Visibility was good and the plane was on course until the very last minute. What caused the crash? After an extensive review, the National Transportation Safety Board concluded that the accident was the result not of mechanical failure or pilot error but of "pilot fatigue."

This was the first (and only) time an aviation accident has been officially attributed to pilot fatigue. But the problem is more common than most of us recognize. According to NASA and federal aviation experts, one in seven pilots nods off in the cockpit. The problem is most acute on overnight international trips. Off the record, many pilots admit to waking up suddenly and not knowing where they are. This situation isn't dangerous if the copilot is awake. But flight attendants report going into the cabin and finding both pilots snoozing, which is why they regularly knock on the door and offer the crew refreshments. In the 1980s, a cargo plane missed the Los Angeles airport and flew out over the Pacific Ocean for nearly an hour before air controllers were able to rouse the sleeping pilots and bring them back. Even when pilots remain awake, they may be too groggy to react efficiently in an emergency, which is what happened at Guantanamo Bay. Estimates are that pilot fatigue contributes to as many as one-third of aviation accidents.

Ironically, the technological advances that have made it possible to safely fly larger planes greater distances contribute to pilot fatigue. Today's jetliners virtually fly themselves. Once a plane reaches cruising altitude and the autopilot turns on, pilots face long hours with little to do. Boredom and inactivity trigger daydreaming and drowsiness. A psychologist who studies pilot fatigue warns, "If we ignore this, it's going to get worse and worse" (Merzer, 1998, p. 4).

Sleep and wakefulness are both states of **consciousness.** In everyday conversation, we use the word *consciousness* to describe being alert. Psychologists define consciousness more broadly, as our awareness of various mental processes. On any given day, we engage in a great variety of cognitive activities—concentrating, making decisions, planning, remembering, daydreaming, reflecting, sleeping, and dreaming are but a few. Those cognitive activities vary in the extent to which we are aware of our mental processes. They fall into two broad groups. **Waking consciousness** includes all the thoughts, feelings, and perceptions that occur when we are awake and reasonably alert. Waking consciousness is usually action- or plan-oriented and tuned in to the external environment. **Altered states of consciousness** differ from our normal waking consciousness in that we're detached, in varying degrees, from our external environment. Certain altered states—such as sleep, daydreaming, and dreaming—occur routinely, even spontaneously. Others are induced by mind-altering drugs, such as alcohol, and even others by meditation and hypnosis.

In this chapter, we introduce the varieties of human consciousness, beginning with waking consciousness. Next, we look at how psychologists study and attempt to explain a natural state of altered consciousness, sleep, and dreams. Then, we turn to the ways in which people seek altered states of consciousness. We begin with psychoactive drugs, from caffeine to crack, with special attention to alcohol abuse. What do these drugs do *to* people? What do they do *for* people? Last, we consider meditation and hypnosis from a scientific perspective.

Conscious Experience

What problems could arise if we were constantly aware of all external and internal sensations?

Even when we are fully awake and alert, we are usually conscious of only a small portion of what is going on around us. At any given moment, we are exposed to a great variety of sounds, sights, and smells from the outside world. At the same time, we experience all sorts of internal sensations, such as heat and cold, touch, pressure, pain, and equilibrium, as well as an array of thoughts, memories, emotions, and needs. Normally, however, we are not aware of all these competing stimuli. To make sense of our environment, we must select only the most important information to attend to and then filter out everything else. At times we pay such close attention to what we are doing that we are oblivious to what is going on around us. How the process of attention works is examined at some length in Chapter 6, Memory. Here it is enough to note that the hallmark of normal waking consciousness is the highly selective nature of attention.

The selective nature of attention can be seen in the number of processes that go on without drawing our conscious attention. We are rarely attuned to such vital bodily processes as blood pressure and respiration, for example, and we can walk down the street or ride a bicycle without consciously thinking about every movement. In fact, we carry out certain tasks, such as signing our name, better when we are *not* consciously aware of performing each movement. Similarly, when we drive or walk along a familiar route that we always take to work or school, the process may be so automatic that we remain largely unaware of our surroundings.

Many psychologists believe that certain key mental processes, such as recognizing a word or a friend's face, also go on outside of normal waking consciousness. As we saw in the first chapter, Sigmund Freud thought that many of the most important influences on our behavior—such as erotic feelings for our parents—are screened from our consciousness and may be accessible only through states such as dreaming. We explore the notion of nonconscious mental processes as we consider various altered states of consciousness, beginning with natural ones such as daydreaming, and we return to them when we discuss behavioral disorders in Chapter 12.

Daydreaming and Fantasy

Do daydreams serve any useful function?

In James Thurber's classic short story "The Secret Life of Walter Mitty" (1942), the meek, painfully shy central character spends much of his time weaving elaborate fantasies in which he stars as a bold, dashing adventurer. Daydreams are his reality—and his waking-conscious experience something of a nightmare. Few people live in their imaginations to the extent that Walter Mitty does. Thurber deliberately used exaggeration to explore the secret life that all of us share but that few of us discuss: our fantasies. Everyone has **daydreams:** apparently effortless, spontaneous shifts in attention away from the here and now into a private world of make-believe.

The urge to daydream seems to come in waves, surging about every 90 minutes and peaking between noon and 2 P.M. (Ford-Mitchell, 1997). According to some estimates, the average person spends almost half of his or her waking hours fantasizing, though this proportion varies from person to person and situation to situation. Typically, we daydream when we would rather be somewhere else or be doing something else, so daydreaming is a momentary escape.

Consciousness
Our awareness of various cognitive processes, such as sleeping, dreaming, concentrating, and making decisions.

Waking consciousness
Mental state that encompasses the thoughts, feelings, and perceptions that occur when we are awake and reasonably alert.

Altered states of consciousness
Mental states that differ noticeably from normal waking consciousness.

Daydreams
Apparently effortless shifts in attention away from the here-and-now into a private world of make-believe.

"*Harry lives inside a beltway all his own.*"

Are daydreams random paths that your mind travels? Not at all. Studies show that most daydreams are variations on a central theme: thoughts and images of unfulfilled goals and wishes, accompanied by emotions arising from an appraisal of where we are now compared with where we want to be (Baars & McGovern, 1994). Daydreams—and daydreamers—fall into distinct categories: positive, negative, scattered, and purposeful (Singer, 1975). Some people—"happy daydreamers"—imagine pleasant, playful, entertaining scenarios, uncomplicated by guilt or worry. By contrast, people who are extremely achievement-oriented tend to experience recurring themes of frustration, guilt, fear of failure, and hostility, reflecting the self-doubt and competitive envy that accompanies great ambition. People who score high on measures of anxiety often have fleeting, loosely connected, worrisome daydreams, which give them little pleasure. Finally, people with high levels of curiosity tend to use daydreams to solve problems, think ahead, and develop insights.

Does daydreaming serve any useful function? Some psychologists view daydreaming as nothing more than a retreat from the real world, especially when that world is not meeting our needs. As such, daydreaming can interfere with productive activities and make those problems worse (the "Walter Mitty" syndrome). Clearly, people who have difficulty distinguishing between fantasy and reality and who begin replacing real-life relationships with imaginary family and friends need professional help.

Other psychologists stress the positive value of daydreaming and fantasy (Klinger, 1990). Daydreams may provide a refreshing break from a stressful day and serve to remind us of neglected personal needs. Freudian theorists tend to view daydreams as a harmless way of working through hostile feelings or satisfying guilty desires. Cognitive psychologists emphasize that daydreaming can build problem-solving and interpersonal skills, as well as encourage creativity. Moreover, daydreaming helps people endure difficult situations: Prisoners of war have used fantasies to survive torture and deprivation. Daydreaming and fantasy, then, may provide welcome relief from unpleasant reality and reduce internal tension and external aggression.

Sleep

How do evolutionary psychologists explain the need for sleep?

Human beings spend about one-third of their lives in the altered state of consciousness known as sleep: a natural state of rest characterized by a reduction in voluntary body movement and decreased awareness of the surroundings. No one who has tried to stay awake longer than 20 hours at a time could doubt the necessity of sleep. Some people claim they never sleep, but when observed under laboratory conditions, they actually sleep soundly without being aware of it. When people are sleep-deprived, they crave sleep just as strongly as they would food or water after a period of deprivation. Merely resting doesn't satisfy us.

All birds and mammals sleep—and although scientists are not sure about reptiles—frogs, fish, and even insects go into "rest states" similar to sleep. Indeed, Drosophila fruit flies, a favorite subject for genetic studies because they reproduce rapidly, are remarkably like us: They are active during the day and somnolent at night; when deprived of sleep, they need long naps to recover: and caffeine keeps them awake, whereas antihistamines make them drowsy (Shaw, Cirelli, Greenspan, & Tononi, 2000). How long organisms sleep, where, in what positions, and other details vary from species to species. In general, large animals sleep less than small animals, perhaps because eating enough to support their size requires more time awake.

Nobody knows exactly why we need to sleep. Evolutionary psychologists see sleep as an adaptive mechanism that evolved to allow organisms to conserve and restore energy (Tobler, 1997). In support of this theory, researchers have shown that people use less energy when they are asleep than when they are awake (Madsen, 1993). Another possibility is that some vital substance in the nervous system is resynthesized during sleep. But what that substance might be is still a mystery (Tobler, 1997). The naturally occurring chemical, adenosine, appears to trigger sleepiness (Porkka-Heiskanen et al., 1997). In one group of studies, cats kept awake an abnormally long time were found to have elevated levels of adenosine in their brains during wakefulness. When the cats were finally permitted to sleep, the adenosine levels dropped. To determine whether the adenosine buildup actually caused the sleepiness, the investigators injected adenosine

Sleep researchers monitor volunteers' brain waves, muscle tension, and other physiological changes during sleep.

into well-rested cats. These cats immediately became sleepy and began to exhibit the EEG patterns typical of drowsiness. Exactly why a high level of adenosine appears to trigger sleepiness is not known, but additional research along this line may soon provide us with a better understanding of the neurological processes underlying the need for sleep.

Circadian Cycles: The Biological Clock

What is the biological clock and what does it have to do with jet lag?

Like many other biological functions, sleep and waking follow a daily, or circadian, cycle (from the Latin expression *circa diem*, meaning "about a day") (Moore-Edea, Czeisler, & Richardson, 1983). Circadian rhythms are an ancient and a fundamental adaptation to the 24-hour solar cycle of light and dark, found not only in humans and other animals but also in plants and even one-celled organisms (Moore, 1999). The human biological clock is actually a tiny cluster of neurons in the hypothalamus that responds to levels of proteins in the body. When the protein supply gets low, these neurons "turn on" and stimulate production of more proteins. When the proteins reach a certain level, they "turn off" again (Young, 2000). In turn, these proteins are the building blocks of hormones, neurotransmitters, and other essential body chemicals.

Over the course of a day, metabolism, stomach acidity, alertness, body temperature, blood pressure, and the level of most hormones also vary predictably. But not all body cycles follow the same pattern. For example, the level of the hormone epinephrine (which causes the body to go on alert) reaches a peak in the late morning hours and then steadily declines until around midnight, when it suddenly drops to a very low level and remains there until morning. By contrast, levels of melatonin (which promotes sleep) surge at night and drop off during the day. Normally, the rhythms and chemistry of all these different cycles interact smoothly, so that a shift in one brings about a corresponding shift in others (Moore-Edea et al., 1983).

The biological clock is self-sustaining and continues to function in the absence of external cues to the cycle of day and night. For example, Czeisler, Duffy, and Shanahan (1999) studied twenty-four people who volunteered to live in an artificial environment for 3 weeks. The only time cues that participants had were a weak cycle of light and dark set at 28 hours and a bedtime signal. Even in this misleading environment, their body temperatures, hormone levels, and other biological processes showed that their bodies continued to function according to their own internal 24-hour cycle.

We rarely notice circadian rhythms until they are disturbed. Jet lag is a familiar example. Travelers who cross several time zones in one day often feel "out of it" for several days. The reason for jet lag is not so much lack of sleep as *desynchronization*. Sleep-and-wake cycles adapt quickly, but hormones, body temperature, and digestive cycles change more slowly. As a result, bodily functions are out of synch. Likewise, shift workers often lose weight and suffer from irritability, insomnia, and extreme drowsiness for some time after changing to a new shift (Richardson, Miner, & Czeisler, 1989–1990).

Researchers may have found a way to adjust our biological clocks. Light inhibits the production of melatonin, which goes up as the sun goes down. A small dose of melatonin taken in the morning (the time when the hormone is usually tapering off) sets back or slows down the biological clock (Liu et al., 1997). Taken in the evening, melatonin speeds up the biological clock, making the person fall asleep earlier than usual (Lewy, 1992). Applying this knowledge, melatonin has been successfully used as an aide to persons with blindness, who sometimes are unable to sense dark-light cycles, causing insomnia or daytime sleepiness. Carefully timed doses of melatonin seem to "reset" the biological clocks of such people, enabling them to sleep better at night and remain alert during the day (Sack, Brandes, Kendall, & Lewy, 2000).

The Rhythms of Sleep

What physical changes mark the rhythms of sleep?

To say that psychologists know more about sleep than about waking consciousness would only be a slight exaggeration. Over the years, researchers have accumulated a large body of observations about what happens in our bodies and brains during sleep. In a typical study, researchers recruit volunteers who spend one or more nights in a "sleep lab." With electrodes painlessly attached to their skulls, the volunteers sleep comfortably as their brain waves, eye movements, muscle tension, and other physiological functions are monitored. Data from such studies show that although there are significant individual differences in sleep behavior, almost everyone goes through the same stages of sleep (Anch et al., 1988). Each stage is marked by characteristic patterns of brain waves, muscular activity, blood pressure, and body temperature (Carlson, 2000). **Figure 4–1** illustrates the electrical activity related to the brain, heart, and facial muscles at each stage.

"Going to sleep" means losing awareness and failing to respond to a stimulus that would produce a response in the waking state. As measured by an EEG, brain waves during this "twilight" state are characterized by irregular, low-voltage alpha waves. This brain-wave pattern mirrors the sense of relaxed wakefulness that we experience while lying on a beach or in a hammock or when resting after a big meal. In this twilight state with the eyes closed, people often report seeing flashing lights and colors, geometric patterns, and visions of landscapes. Sometimes they also experience a floating or falling sensation, followed by a quick jolt back to consciousness.

After this initial twilight phase, the sleeper enters Stage 1 of sleep. Stage 1 brain waves are tight and of very low amplitude (height), resembling those recorded when a person is alert or excited. But, in contrast to normal waking consciousness, Stage 1 of the sleep cycle is marked by a slowing of the pulse, muscle relaxation, and side-to-side rolling movements of the eyes—the last being the most reliable indication of this first stage of sleep (Dement, 1974). Stage 1 usually lasts only a few moments. The sleeper is easily aroused at this stage and, once awake, may be unaware of having slept at all.

Stages 2 and 3 are characterized by progressively deeper sleep. During Stage 2, short rhythmic bursts of activity called *sleep spindles* periodically appear. In Stage 3, *delta waves*—slow waves with very high peaks—begin to emerge. During these stages, the sleeper is hard to awaken and does not re-

FIGURE 4–1

Waves of sleep. This series of printouts illustrates electrical activity in the brain, heart, and facial muscles during the various stages of sleep. Note the characteristic delta waves that begin to appear during Stage 3 and become more pronounced during Stage 4.

Awake   Stage 1   Stage 2

Stage 3   Stage 4   REM

spond to stimuli such as noises or lights. Heart rate, blood pressure, and temperature continue to drop.

In Stage 4 sleep, the brain emits very slow delta waves. Heart rate, breathing rate, blood pressure, and body temperature are as low as they will get during the night. In young adults, delta sleep occurs in 15- to 20-minute segments—interspersed with lighter sleep—mostly during the first half of the night. Delta sleep time lessens with age but continues to be the first sleep to be made up after sleep has been lost.

About an hour after falling asleep, the sleeper begins to ascend from Stage 4 sleep to Stage 3, Stage 2, and back to Stage 1—a process that takes about 40 minutes. The brain waves return to the low-amplitude, saw-toothed shape characteristic of Stage 1 sleep and waking alertness. Heart rate and blood pressure also increase, yet the muscles are more relaxed than at any other point in the sleep cycle, and the person is very difficult to awaken. The eyes move rapidly under closed eyelids. This **rapid eye movement (REM)** sleep stage is distinguished from all other stages of sleep (called **non-REM** or **NREM**) that precede and follow it.

REM sleep is also called **paradoxical sleep,** because although measures of brain activity, heart rate, blood pressure, and other physiological func-tions closely resemble those recorded during waking consciousness, the person in this stage appears to be deeply asleep and is incapable of moving; the body's voluntary muscles are essentially paralyzed. Some research sug-gests that REM sleep is also the stage when most dreaming occurs, though dreams take place during NREM sleep as well (Stickgold, Rittenhouse, & Hobson, 1994). The first Stage 1–REM period lasts about 10 minutes and is followed by Stages 2, 3, and 4 of NREM sleep. This sequence of sleep stages repeats itself all night, averaging 90 minutes from Stage 1–REM to Stage 4 and back again. Normally, a night's sleep consists of four to five sleep cycles of this sort. But the pattern of sleep changes as the night progresses. At first, Stages 3 and 4 dominate; but as time passes, the Stage 1–REM periods grad-ually become longer, and Stages 3 and 4 become shorter, eventually disap-pearing altogether. Over the course of a night, then, about 45 to 50 percent of the sleeper's time is spent in Stage 2, whereas REM sleep takes up an-other 20 to 25 percent of the total.

Sleep requirements and patterns vary considerably from person to person, though. Some adults need hardly any sleep. Researchers have documented the case of a Stanford University professor who slept for only 3 to 4 hours a night over the course of 50 years, and that of a woman who lived a healthy life on only 1 hour of sleep per night (Rosenzweig & Leiman, 1982). Sleep patterns also change with age (Sadeh, Raviv, & Gruber, 2000) (see **Figure 4–2**). Infants sleep much longer than adults—13 to 16 hours during the first year—and much more of their sleep is REM sleep (see **Figure 4–3**).

 4.1

Inadequate Sleep

What are the consequences of sleep deprivation?

Inadequate sleep has become a "national epidemic" in the United States (Angier, 1990). Between one-third and one-half of all adults regularly fail to get enough sleep. High school students report that they fall asleep in class about once a week (Maas, 1998). Moreover, the number of accredited sleep-disorder clinics in the United States has risen from 25 in 1980 to more than 337 in 1997, with still more on the way (Grady, 1997).

Extensive research shows that losing an hour or two of sleep every night, week after week, month after month, makes it more difficult for people to pay attention (especially to monotonous tasks) and to remember things. Reaction time slows down, behavior becomes unpredictable, and accidents and errors in judgment increase, while productivity and the ability to make decisions

REM (paradoxical) sleep
Sleep stage characterized by rapid eye movements and increased dreaming.

Non-REM (NREM) sleep
Non-rapid-eye-movement stages of sleep that alternate with REM stages during the sleep cycle.

FIGURE 4–2

A night's sleep across the life span. Sleep patterns change from childhood to young adulthood to old age. The red areas represent REM sleep, the stage of sleep that varies most dramatically across age groups.

Source: Adapted by permission of *The New England Journal of Medicine, 290,* p. 487, 1974. Copyright © 1974 Massachusetts Medical Society. All rights reserved.

decline (Babkoff et al., 1991; Blagrove & Akehurst, 2000; Webb & Levy, 1984). These findings have important implications. For example, experts estimate that sleep loss is a contributing factor in between 200,000 and 400,000 automobile accidents each year, resulting in approximately 1,500 deaths. Research suggests that driving while sleepy is just as dangerous as driving while drunk (Powell et al., 2001).

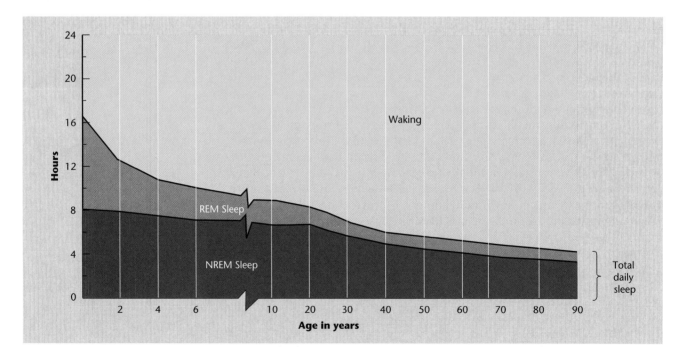

FIGURE 4–3

Changes in REM and NREM sleep. The amount of REM sleep people need declines sharply during the first few years of life. Newborns spend about 8 hours, or almost half of their total sleep time in REM sleep, whereas older children and adults spend just 1 to 2 hours or about 20 to 25 percent of their total sleep time in REM sleep.

Source: Adapted with permission from H. P. Roffwarg, "Ontogenetic Development of the Human Sleep-Dream Cycle," *Science, 152,* p. 604. Copyright © 1966 by the American Association for the Advancement of Science.

Sleep deprivation may also routinely affect the performance of people in high-risk positions, such as pilots (as we saw in the opening of this chapter). Hospital staff and nuclear power–plant operators, who often have to make critical decisions on short notice, are also at risk. In 1979, there was an accident at the nuclear power plant at Three Mile Island, Pennsylvania, in which human error transformed a minor mishap into a major nuclear disaster.

Awareness of the relationship between sleep deprivation and accidents has led to changes in the working patterns of people whose jobs can have life-and-death consequences. Several states have shortened the shifts of hospital residents to prevent errors caused by sleep deprivation. Similarly, the FAA has restricted the number of hours a pilot can fly without having time off to sleep.

Unfortunately, people do not always know when they are not getting enough sleep. Most truck drivers involved in accidents that resulted from their falling asleep at the wheel claimed that they felt rested at the time (Wald, 1995). In a laboratory study, one group of healthy college students who were getting 7 to 8 hours of sleep a night showed no apparent signs of sleep deprivation. Yet 20 percent of them fell asleep immediately when they were put into a dark room, a symptom of chronic sleep loss. Another group for a period of time went to bed 60 to 90 minutes earlier than their normal bedtime. These students reported that they felt much more vigorous and alert—indeed, they performed significantly better on tests of psychological and mental acuity (Carskadon & Dement, 1982).

According to a well-known sleep researcher, Dr. William Dement, one way to reduce your sleep debt is to take short naps. Unfortunately, while in many cultures midafternoon is seen as siesta time, in America we often reach for a cup of coffee to keep us going. Even a 20-minute nap can increase alertness, reduce irritability, and improve efficiency.

Sleep Disorders

Are prescription medicines the best way to treat occasional insomnia?

The scientific study of typical sleep patterns has yielded insights into sleep disorders, including sleepwalking and night terrors, insomnia, apnea, and narcolepsy.

Sleeptalking, Sleepwalking, and Night Terrors *Sleeptalking* and *sleepwalking* usually occur during Stage 4. Both are more common among children than adults: About 20 percent of children have at least one episode of either sleepwalking or sleeptalking. Boys are more likely to walk in their sleep than girls. Contrary to popular belief, waking a sleepwalker is not dangerous, but because sleepwalking commonly takes place during a very deep stage of sleep, waking a sleepwalker is not easy (Hobson, 1994).

Some people also experience *sleep terrors,* or *night terrors,* a form of nocturnal fright that makes them suddenly sit up in bed, often screaming out in fear. Sleep terrors are altogether different from nightmares (Zadra & Donderi, 2000). People generally cannot be awakened from sleep terrors and will push away anyone trying to comfort them. Unlike nightmares, sleep terrors cannot be recalled the next morning. They also occur more often if the person is very tired. Though sleep terrors are usually seen in children between 4 and 12 years old, they may continue into adulthood (Hartmann, 1983). Adults who have them are more likely to suffer from a personality disorder (Kales et al., 1980) or to abuse drugs or alcohol. Brain injuries associated with epilepsy may also contribute to night terrors in adults.

Neither nightmares nor night terrors alone indicate psychological problems. Anxious people have no more nightmares than other people do. And like night terrors, nightmares diminish with age (Wood & Bootzin, 1990).

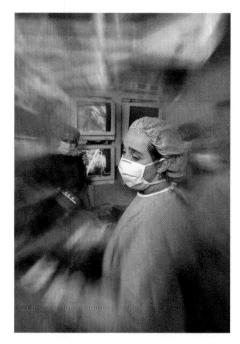

Sleep deprivation impairs cognitive skills to a greater extent than many people realize. When deprived of sleep we react more slowly, have more trouble focusing attention, and are more prone to making errors in judgment. Emergency room doctors often lose sleep because of the unpredictable and demanding nature of their work. This can be a serious problem when they are called on to make critical decisions quickly.

People whose nightmares stem from a traumatic experience, however, may be plagued by terrifying nighttime episodes for years.

Insomnia, Apnea, and Narcolepsy **Insomnia,** the inability to fall or remain asleep, afflicts as many as 35 million Americans. Most episodes of insomnia grow out of stressful events and are temporary (see *Understanding Ourselves*). But for some sufferers, insomnia is a persistent disruption. Treatments can create problems as well. Some prescription medications for insomnia can cause anxiety, memory loss, hallucinations, and violent behavior.

The causes of insomnia vary for different individuals (Lichstein, Wilson, & Johnson, 2000). For some people, insomnia is part of a larger psychological problem, such as depression, so its cure requires treating the underlying disorder. For others, insomnia results from an overaroused biological system. A physical predisposition to insomnia may combine with distress over chronic sleeplessness to create a cycle in which biological and emotional factors reinforce one another. People may worry so much about not sleeping that their bedtime rituals, such as brushing teeth and getting dressed for bed, "become harbingers of frustration, rather than stimuli for relaxation" (Hauri, 1982). Furthermore, bad sleep habits—such as varying bedtimes—and distracting sleep settings may aggravate or even cause insomnia.

Another sleep disorder, **apnea,** affects 10 to 12 million Americans, many of whom have inherited the condition (Kadotani et al., 2001). Apnea is associated with breathing difficulties at night: In severe cases, the victim actually stops breathing after falling asleep (Vgontzas & Kales, 1999). When the level of carbon dioxide in the blood rises to a certain point, apnea sufferers are spurred to a state of arousal just short of waking consciousness. Because this process may happen hundreds of times a night, apnea patients typically feel exhausted and fall asleep repeatedly the next day.

People suffering from insomnia and apnea may envy those who have no trouble sleeping. But too much sleep has serious repercussions as well. **Narcolepsy** is a hereditary disorder whose victims nod off without warning in the middle of a conversation or other alert activity. People with narcolepsy often experience a sudden loss of muscle tone upon expression of any sort of emotion. A joke, anger, sexual stimulation—all bring on the muscle paralysis associated with deep sleep. Suddenly, without warning, they collapse. Another symptom of the disorder is immediate entry into REM sleep, which produces frightening hallucinations that are, in fact, dreams that the person is experiencing while still partly awake. Narcolepsy is believed to arise from a defect in the central nervous system (Bassetti & Aldrich, 1996).

Insomnia
Sleep disorder characterized by difficulty in falling asleep or remaining asleep throughout the night.

Apnea
Sleep disorder characterized by breathing difficulty during the night and feelings of exhaustion during the day.

Narcolepsy
Hereditary sleep disorder characterized by sudden nodding off during the day and sudden loss of muscle tone following moments of emotional excitement.

Dreams
Vivid visual and auditory experiences that occur primarily during REM periods of sleep.

Dreams

What are dreams?

Every culture, including our own, attributes meaning to dreams. Some people believe that dreams contain messages from their gods; some, that dreams predict the future. Psychologists define **dreams** as visual and auditory experiences that our minds create during sleep. The average person has four or five dreams a night, accounting for about 1 to 2 hours of the total time spent sleeping. People awakened during REM sleep report graphic dreams about 80 to 85 percent of the time (Berger, 1969). Less striking dreamlike experiences that resemble normal wakeful consciousness are reported about 50 percent of the time during NREM sleep.

Most dreams last about as long as the events would in real life; they do not flash on your mental screen just before waking, as was once believed. Generally, dreams consist of a sequential story or a series of stories. Stimuli,

UNDERSTANDING OURSELVES

Coping with Occasional Insomnia

Like most people, you probably have had at least a few nights when you found it difficult to fall asleep. Episodes of even temporary or occasional insomnia can impair your ability to function during the day. So what can you do if you suddenly find yourself going through a period when you are unable to get a good night's sleep? Here are some tips that may help:

- Maintain regular bedtime hours; don't sleep late on weekends.
- Establish a regular bedtime routine that you follow each night before retiring, such as a warm bath, followed by a little reading or writing a letter.

- Abstain from drugs (including alcohol, caffeine, and nicotine, as well as the routine use of sleeping pills). Tryptophan, a substance that promotes sleep, may be taken as a sleep aid in the form of warm milk, confirming a folk remedy for sleeplessness.
- Adjust the temperature of the room if it is too cold or too warm.
- Avoid foods that may cause sleeplessness, such as chocolate.
- Establish a regular exercise program during the day, but never exercise within several hours of bedtime.

- Avoid anxious thoughts while in bed. Set aside regular times during the day—well before bedtime—to mull over your worries. This technique may be supplemented by relaxation training, using such methods as biofeedback, self-hypnosis, or meditation (Morin et al., 1994).
- Don't fight insomnia when it occurs. The old saying "If I can't sleep, I mop the kitchen floor" makes sense to sleep researchers, who counsel their clients to get out of bed and engage in an activity for an hour or so until they feel sleepy again.

both external (such as a train whistle or a low-flying airplane) and internal (say, hunger pangs), may modify an ongoing dream, but they do not initiate dreams. Often dreams are so vivid that it is difficult to distinguish them from reality.

Why Do We Dream?

Psychologists have long been fascinated by dream activity and the contents of dreams, and a number of explanations have been proposed.

Dreams as Unconscious Wishes   Sigmund Freud (1900), the first modern theorist to investigate this topic, called dreams the "royal road to the unconscious." Believing that dreams represent wishes that have not been fulfilled in reality, he asserted that people's dreams reflect the motives guiding their behavior—motives of which they may not be consciously aware. Freud distinguished between the *manifest,* or surface, *content* of dreams and their *latent content*—the hidden, unconscious thoughts or desires that he believed were expressed indirectly through dreams.

In dreams, according to Freud, people permit themselves to express primitive desires that are relatively free of moral controls. For example, someone who is not consciously aware of hostile feelings toward a sister may dream about murdering her. However, even in a dream, such hostile feelings may be censored and transformed into a symbolic form. For example, the desire to do away with one's sister (the dream's latent content) may be recast into the dream image of seeing her off at a train "terminal" (the dream's manifest content). According to Freud, this process of censorship and symbolic transformation accounts for the highly illogical nature of many dreams. Deciphering the disguised meanings of dreams is one of the principal tasks of psychoanalysts (Hill et al., 2000; Mazzoni, Lombardo,

The fanciful images of Marc Chagall's paintings capture the quality of many of our dreams. Is a dream of an entwined man and woman floating high above a city symbolic of some subconscious sexual desire, as Freud would have suggested? Or is it just an illogical image caused by random brain cell activity during sleep? As yet psychologists have no conclusive answer. Perhaps both views have merit.

Malvagia, & Loftus, 1999). Freud's pioneering work, focused on exploring the meaning of dreams, paved the way for contemporary investigations of dream content (Domhoff, 1996).

Dreams and Information Processing   Another explanation for dreaming holds that in our dreams we reprocess information gathered during the day as a way of strengthening the memory of information crucial to survival (Carpenter, 2001; Winson, 1990). During our waking hours, our brains are bombarded with sensory data. We need a "time out" to decide what information is valuable, whether it should be filed in long-term memory, where it should be filed (with which older memories, ideas, desires, and anxieties), and what information should be erased so that it doesn't clutter neural pathways (Crick & Mitchison, 1995). According to this view, dreams seem illogical because the brain is rapidly scanning old files and comparing them with new, unsorted "clippings."

In support of this view, research has demonstrated that both humans and nonhumans spend more time in REM sleep after learning difficult material; furthermore, interfering with REM sleep immediately after learning severely disrupts the memory for the newly learned material (Smith, 1985; Smith & Kelly, 1988; Smith & Lapp, 1986). Brain-imaging studies have also found that the specific area of the brain most active while learning new material is also active during subsequent REM sleep (Maquet et al., 2000).

Other psychologists see dreams as a form of emotional processing. In dreams, emotionally significant events may be integrated with previous experiences (Farthing, 1992). For example, children's first experience of a carnival or an amusement park is usually a blend of terror and excitement. Later in life, whenever they have experiences that are exciting but also somewhat frightening, carnival rides or images may dominate their dreams. Some psychologists (Cartwright, 1996) have suggested that we work through problems in our dreams—indeed, that dreams are part of the healing process after a divorce, the death of a loved one, or other emotional crises. But, critics argue that these breakthroughs may be more the result of foresight or hindsight than of dreams themselves (Domhoff, 1996).

Dreams and Waking Life   Still another theory maintains that dreams are an extension of the conscious concerns of daily life in altered (but not disguised) form (Domhoff, 1996). Research has shown that what people dream about is generally similar to what they think about and do while awake. That is, dream content commonly reflects an individual's unique conceptions, interests, and concerns. For example, a parent who's having problems with a child may dream about childhood confrontations with his or her own parents. Dream content also appears to be relatively "consistent" for most individuals, displaying similar themes across years and even decades (Domhoff, 1996). Moreover, many of our dreams seem realistic and coherent while they are occurring and even after we are awake (Squire & Domhoff, 1998).

Dreams and Neural Activity   New research, using advanced brain-imaging techniques, has indicated that the limbic system, which is involved with emotions, motivations, and memories, is "wildly" active during dreams; so, to a lesser extent, are the visual and auditory areas of the forebrain that process sensory information. However, areas of the forebrain involved in working memory, attention, logic, and self-monitoring are relatively inactive during dreams (Braun, 1998). This fact would explain the highly emotional texture of dreams, as well as bizarre imagery, and the loss of critical insight, logic, and self-reflection. This uncensored mixture of desires, fears, and memories comes very close to the psychoanalytic concept of unconscious wishes, suggesting that Freud may have come closer to the meaning of dreams than many contemporary psychologists have acknowledged.

INTERACTIVE LECTURE **4.1**

WEB QUIZ **4.1**

CHECK YOUR UNDERSTANDING

1. Our awareness of the mental processes of our everyday life is called _____.
2. Technological innovations such as _____ (_____) enable scientists to study brain activity during various states of consciousness.
3. The major characteristic of waking consciousness is _____ _____.
4. In humans, sleeping and waking follow a _____ cycle.
5. Most vivid dreaming takes place during the _____ stage of sleep.
6. We normally spend about _____ hours each night dreaming.
7. Freud distinguished between the _____ and _____ content of dreams.
8. Indicate whether the following statements are true (T) or false (F).
    _____ a. We do not really need to dream.
    _____ b. Sleep deprivation has been implicated in both industrial and driving accidents.

Match the following terms with the correct definition:

9. _____ circadian cycle   a. relaxed wakefulness
10. _____ alpha waves   b. hidden meaning
11. _____ latent content   c. daily cycle
12. _____ sleep deprivation   d. trouble getting to sleep or staying asleep
13. _____ insomnia   e. suddenly falling asleep during the day
14. _____ narcolepsy   f. national epidemic

Answers: 1. consciousness. **2.** electronencephalography (EEG). **3.** selective attention. **4.** circadian **5.** REM. **6.** two. **7.** manifest, latent. **8.** a. (F); b. (T). **9.** c. **10.** a. **11.** b. **12.** f. **13.** d. **14.** e.

Drug-Altered Consciousness

How is today's drug problem different from the drug use in other societies and times?

Drug-altered consciousness is not new. In nearly every known culture throughout history, people have sought ways to alter waking consciousness. The use of **psychoactive drugs**—substances that change people's moods, perceptions, mental functioning, or behavior—is almost universal. Many of the drugs available today, legally or illegally, have been used for thousands of years. For example, marijuana is mentioned in the herbal recipe book of a Chinese emperor, dating from 2737 B.C. Natives of the Andes Mountains in South America chew leaves of the coca plant (which contain cocaine) as a stimulant—a custom dating back at least to the Inca Empire of the fifteenth century.

In the nineteenth century, Europeans began adding coca to wine, tea, and lozenges (Platt, 1997). In the United States, *laudanum*—opium dissolved in alcohol—was the main ingredient in numerous over-the-counter (or patent) medicines. Following this trend, in 1886 an Atlanta pharmacist combined crushed coca leaves from the Andes, caffeine-rich cola nuts from West Africa, cane sugar syrup, and carbonated water in a patent medicine he called "Coca Cola."

Of all psychoactive substances, alcohol has the longest history of widespread use. Archaeological evidence suggests that Late Stone Age groups began producing mead (fermented honey, flavored with sap or fruit) about 10,000 years ago. The Egyptians and Babylonians, Greeks and Romans, viewed wine as a "gift from the gods." Wine is frequently praised in the Bible—and drinking water is hardly mentioned. In the Middle Ages, alcohol earned the title *aqua vitae*, the "water of life"—with good reason (Vallee, 1998). Wherever people settled down, water supplies quickly became contaminated with waste products. As recently as the nineteenth century, most people in Western civilizations drank alcohol with every meal (including breakfast) and between meals, as a "pick-me-up," as well as on social and religious occasions.

Is today's drug problem different from the drug use in other societies and times? In many ways, the answer is yes. First, motives for using psychoactive drugs have changed. In most cultures, psychoactive substances have been used as part of religious rituals, as medicines and tonics, as nutrient beverages, or as culturally approved stimulants (much as we drink coffee). The use of alcohol and other drugs in our society today is primarily recreational. For the most part, people do not raise their glasses in praise of God or inhale hallucinogens to get in touch with the spirit world, but to relax, have fun with friends (and strangers), and get high. Moreover, Americans most often imbibe and inhale in settings specifically designed for recreation and inebriation: bars, clubs, beer parties, cocktail parties, "raves" (large, all-night dance parties), and so-called crack houses. In addition, people use and abuse drugs privately and secretly in their homes, sometimes without the knowledge of their family and friends—leading to hidden addiction. Whether social or solitary, the use of psychoactive substances today is largely divorced from religious and family traditions.

Second, the drugs themselves have changed. Today's psychoactive substances often are stronger than those used in other cultures and times. For most of Western history, wine (12 percent alcohol) was often diluted with water. Hard liquor (40 to 75 percent alcohol) appeared only in the tenth century A.D. And the heroin available on the streets today is stronger and more addictive than that available in the 1930s and 1940s.

Psychoactive drugs
Chemical substances that change moods and perceptions.

In addition, new, synthetic drugs appear regularly, with unpredictable consequences. In the 1990s, the National Institute for Drug Abuse created a new category, "Club Drugs," for increasingly popular psychoactive substances manufactured in small laboratories or even home kitchens (from recipes available on the Internet). Because the source, psychoactive ingredients, and possible contaminants are unknown, the symptoms, toxicity, and short- or long-term consequences are also unknown—making these drugs especially dangerous. The fact that they are often consumed with alcohol multiplies the risks. Examples include "Ecstasy" (methylenedioxymethamphetamine [MDMA]), a combination of the stimulant amphetamine and an hallucinogen; "Grievous Bodily Harm" (gammahydroxybutyrate [GHB]), a combination of sedatives and growth hormone stimulant; "Special K" (ketamine), an anesthetic approved for veterinary use that induces dreamlike states and hallucinations in humans; and "Roofies" (flunitrazepam), a tasteless, odorless sedative/anesthesia that can cause temporary amnesia, which is why it is also known as "Forget-me Pill" and is associated with sexual assault.

Finally, scientists and the public know more about the effects of psychoactive drugs than in the past. Cigarettes are an obvious example. The Surgeon General's Report issued in 1964 confirmed a direct link between smoking and heart disease, as well as lung cancer. Subsequent research establishing that cigarettes are harmful not only to smokers but also to people around them (secondhand smoke) and to their unborn babies (Ness et al., 1999) transformed a personal health decision into a moral issue. Nonetheless, tens of millions of Americans still smoke, and millions of others use drugs they know to be harmful.

Excessive drinking and public drunkenness have been widely frowned on in many cultures. In this etching, *Gin Lane*, by the 18th-century English artist William Hogarth, a baby slips carelessly from the arms of a drunken mother.

Source: William Hogarth (1697–1765), *Gin Lane*. The Metropolitan Museum of Art, Harris Brisbane Dick Fund, 1932.

Substance Use, Abuse, and Dependence

How can we tell whether someone is dependent on a substance?

If we define drugs broadly, as we did earlier, to include caffeine, tobacco, and alcohol, then most people throughout the world use some type of drug on an occasional or a regular basis. The majority of these people use such drugs in moderation and do not suffer ill effects. But for many, substance use escalates into **substance abuse**—a pattern of drug use that diminishes a person's ability to fulfill responsibilities, that results in repeated use of the drug in dangerous situations, or that leads to legal difficulties related to drug use. For example, people whose drinking causes ill health and problems within their families or on their jobs are abusing alcohol (D. Smith, 2001). Substance abuse is America's leading health problem (Martin, 2001).

The ongoing abuse of drugs, including alcohol, may lead to compulsive use of the substance, or **substance dependence** (also known as addiction) (see **Table 4–1**). Although not everyone who abuses a substance develops dependence, dependence usually follows a period of abuse. Dependence often includes *tolerance*, the phenomenon whereby higher doses of the drug are required to produce its original effects or to prevent *withdrawal symptoms*, the unpleasant physical or psychological effects following discontinuance of the substance.

The causes of substance abuse and dependence are a complex combination of biological, psychological, and social factors that varies for each individual and for each substance. Also, the development of substance dependence does not follow an established timetable. One person might drink socially for years before abusing alcohol, whereas someone else might become addicted to cocaine in a matter of days. Before we examine specific drugs and their effects, we first look at how psychologists study drug-related behaviors.

Substance abuse
A pattern of drug use that diminishes the ability to fulfill responsibilities at home or at work or school, that results in repeated use of a drug in dangerous situations, or that leads to legal difficulties related to drug use.

Substance dependence
A pattern of compulsive drug-taking that results in tolerance, withdrawal symptoms, or other specific symptoms for at least a year.

TABLE 4-1 SIGNS OF SUBSTANCE DEPENDENCE

The most recent clinical definition of dependence (American Psychiatric Association, 1994) describes a broad pattern of drug-related behaviors characterized by at least three of the following seven symptoms over a 12-month period:

1. Developing tolerance, that is, needing increasing amounts of the substance to gain the desired effect or experiencing a diminished effect when using the same amount of the substance. For example, the person might have to drink an entire six-pack to get the same effect formerly experienced after drinking just one or two beers.

2. Experiencing withdrawal symptoms, which are physical and psychological problems that occur if the person tries to stop using the substance. Withdrawal symptoms range from anxiety and nausea to convulsions and hallucinations.

3. Using the substance for a longer period or in greater quantities than intended.

4. Having a persistent desire or making repeated efforts to cut back on the use of the substance.

5. Devoting a great deal of time to obtaining or using the substance.

6. Giving up or reducing social, occupational, or recreational activities as a result of drug use.

7. Continuing to use the substance even in the face of ongoing or recurring physical or psychological problems likely to be caused or made worse by the use of the substance.

How Drug Effects Are Studied   The effects of particular drugs are studied under carefully controlled scientific conditions. In most cases, experimenters compare people's behavior before the administration of the drug with their behavior afterward, taking special precautions to ensure that any observed changes in behavior are due to the drug alone.

To eliminate research errors based on subject or researcher expectations, most drug experiments use the **double-blind procedure,** in which some participants receive the active drug, while others take a neutral, inactive substance called a **placebo.** Neither the researchers nor the participants know who took the active drug and who got the placebo. If the behavior of the participants who actually received the drug differs from the behavior of those who got the placebo, the cause is likely to be the active ingredient in the drug.

Studying drug-altered consciousness is complicated by the fact that most drugs not only affect different people in different ways but also produce different effects in the same person at different times or in different settings. For example, some people are powerfully affected by even small amounts of alcohol, whereas others are not. And drinking alcohol in a convivial family setting usually produces somewhat different effects than does consuming alcohol under the watchful eyes of a scientist.

Recently, sophisticated neuroimaging procedures have proved useful for studying drug effects. Techniques such as PET imaging have enabled researchers to isolate specific differences between the brains of addicted and nonaddicted people. For example, the "addicted brain" has been found to differ qualitatively from the nonaddicted brain in a variety of ways, including metabolism and responsiveness to environmental cues (Leshner, 1996). Investigators have also focused on the role played by neurotransmitters in the addictive process—noting that every addictive drug causes dopamine levels in the brain to increase (Glassman & Koob, 1996). Results like these may lead to not only better understanding of the biological basis of addiction but also more effective treatments.

Double-blind procedure
Experimental design useful in studies of the effects of drugs, in which neither the subject nor the researcher knows at the time of administration which subjects are receiving an active drug and which are receiving an inactive substance.

Placebo
Chemically inactive substance used for comparison with active drugs in experiments on the effects of drugs.

SUMMARY TABLE

DRUGS: CHARACTERISTICS AND EFFECTS

	Typical Effects	Effects of Overdose	Tolerance/Dependence
Depressants			
Alcohol	Biphasic; tension-reduction "high," followed by depressed physical and psychological functioning.	Disorientation, loss of consciousness, death at extremely high blood-alcohol levels.	Tolerance; physical and psychological dependence; withdrawal symptoms.
Barbiturates Tranquilizers	Depressed reflexes and impaired motor functioning, tension reduction.	Shallow respiration, clammy skin, dilated pupils, weak and rapid pulse, coma, possible death.	Tolerance; high psychological and physical dependence on barbiturates, low to moderate physical dependence on such tranquilizers as Valium, although high psychological dependence; withdrawal symptoms.
Opiates	Euphoria, drowsiness, "rush" of pleasure, little impairment of psychological functions.	Slow shallow breathing, clammy skin, nausea, vomiting, pinpoint pupils, convulsions, coma, possible death.	High tolerance; physical and psychological dependence; severe withdrawal symptoms.
Stimulants			
Amphetamines Cocaine Caffeine Nicotine	Increased alertness, excitation, euphoria, increased pulse rate and blood pressure, sleeplessness.	For amphetamines and cocaine: agitation and, with chronic high doses, hallucinations (e.g., "cocaine bugs"), paranoid delusions, convulsions, death. For caffeine and nicotine: restlessness, insomnia, rambling thoughts, heart arrhythmia, possible circulatory failure. For nicotine: increased blood pressure.	For amphetamines, cocaine and nicotine: tolerance, psychological and physical dependence. For caffeine: physical and psychological dependence; withdrawal symptoms.
Hallucinogens			
LSD	Illusions, hallucinations, distortions in time perception, loss of contact with reality.	Psychotic reactions.	No physical dependence for LSD; degree of psychological dependence unknown for LSD.
Marijuana	Euphoria, relaxed inhibitions, increased appetite, possible disorientation.	Fatigue, disoriented behavior, possible psychosis.	Psychological dependence.

   In analyzing drugs and drug use, it is convenient to group psychoactive substances into three categories: depressants, stimulants, and hallucinogens (see Summary Table: Drugs: Characteristics and Effects). (We will look at a fourth category of psychoactive drugs, medications used in the treatment of mental illness, in Chapter 13, Therapies.) These categories are not rigid (the same drug may have multiple effects or different effects on different users), but this division helps organize our knowledge about drugs.

Depressants: Alcohol, Barbiturates, and the Opiates

Why does alcohol, a depressant, lead to higher rates of violence?

Depressants are chemicals that retard behavior and thinking by either speeding up or slowing down nerve impulses. Generally speaking, alcohol, barbiturates, and the opiates have depressant effects.

Alcohol   The most frequently used psychoactive drug in Western societies is **alcohol.** The effects of alcohol depend on the individual, the social setting, and cultural attitudes—but also on how much a person consumes and how fast (see **Table 4–2**).

Depressants
Chemicals that slow down behavior or cognitive processes.

Alcohol
Depressant that is the intoxicating ingredient in whiskey, beer, wine, and other fermented or distilled liquors.

TABLE 4-2   THE BEHAVIORAL EFFECTS OF BLOOD-ALCOHOL LEVELS

Levels of Alcohol in the Blood	Behavioral Effects
0.05%	Feels good; less alert
0.10%	Is slower to react; less cautious
0.15%	Reaction time is much slower
0.20%	Sensory-motor abilities are suppressed
0.25%	Is staggering (motor abilities severely impaired); perception is limited as well
0.30%	Is in semistupor
0.35%	Is at level for anesthesia; death is possible
0.40%	Death is likely (usually as a result of respiratory failure)

Source: Data from *Drugs, Society, and Human Behavior* (3rd ed.) by Oakey Ray, 1983, St. Louis: The C. V. Mosby Co.

In spite of, or perhaps because of, the fact that it is legal and socially approved, alcohol is America's number one drug problem. More than 50 percent of high school seniors say that they get drunk. And binge drinking has become a dangerous "tradition" on college campuses (See *Understanding the World Around Us*). Alcohol is a highly addictive drug with potentially devastating long-term effects. At least 14 million Americans (more than 7 percent of the population ages 18 and older) have problems with drinking, including more than 8 million alcoholics, who are addicted to alcohol. Three times as many men as women are problem drinkers. For both sexes, alcohol abuse and addiction is highest in the 18- to 29-year-old age group (see **Figure 4–4**) (National Institute on Alcohol Abuse and Alcoholism, 2000b). (See *Understanding Ourselves.*)

Heavy, chronic drinking can harm virtually every organ in the body, beginning with the brain. Chronic and excessive alcohol use is associated with impairments in perceptual-motor skills, visual-spatial processing, problem solving, and abstract reasoning (Nixon, 1999). Alcohol is the leading cause of liver disease and kidney damage; is a major factor in cardiovascular disease; increases the risk of certain cancers; and can lead to sexual dysfunction and infertility. Alcohol is particularly damaging to the nervous system during the teenage years. Areas of the brain that are not fully developed until age twenty-one are especially susceptible to damage from high levels of alcohol intoxication (Ballie, 2001). Approximately 100,000 Americans die each year as a result of using alcohol with other drugs or from alcohol-related problems, making it the third leading cause of preventable mortality, after tobacco and diet-activity patterns (Van Natta, Malin, Bertolucci, & Kaelbert, 1985).

The social costs of abusing alcohol are high. Alcohol is involved in a substantial proportion of violent and accidental deaths, including suicides, which makes it the leading contributor (after AIDS) to death among young people. Al-

This bereaved mother holds her daughter's photograph to publicize the tragic consequences of drinking and driving.

UNDERSTANDING The World Around Us

Binge Drinking on College Campuses

One of the few places today where drunkenness is tolerated, and often expected, is the American college campus. National surveys of 140 colleges and universities, conducted in 1993 and again in 1997 and 1999, found that almost half of college students engage in "binge drinking," defined as five or more drinks in a row for men, four or more drinks for women (Weschler, Dowdall, Davenport, & DeJong, 2000). The extent of binge drinking at different schools ranged from 1 percent to 70 percent, indicating that the campus environment is an important influence on drinking patterns. Many campuses are divided into two subcultures: one that emphasizes personal and social responsibility and considers drunkenness as deviant, and another that glamorizes being out of control and views abstinence as deviant.

The survey identified a number of factors that make it more likely that a student will engage in binge drinking. One of the most important factors was whether a student had engaged in binge drinking in high school. Others were as follows:

- *Race-ethnicity:* White students were more than twice as likely to be binge drinkers compared with other racial and ethnic groups.
- *Religion:* Students who said religion was not very important to them were twice as likely to be binge drinkers as other students.
- *Athletics:* Students who said that participation in athletics was important or very important to them were one-and-a-half times more likely to be binge drinkers.
- *Fraternity and sorority residence:* Students who lived in fraternity or sorority houses were four times more likely than other students to be binge drinkers.

> Frequent binge drinkers had more problems, and more serious problems, than other students.

About half of binge drinkers—one in five students overall—had gone on binges three or more times during the two weeks before the survey and been intoxicated three or more times over the past month. Most of these students cited getting drunk as their main reason for drinking. Regardless of how much they drank, very few (less than 1 percent) considered themselves "problem drinkers."

It is not surprising that frequent binge drinkers had more problems, and more serious problems, than other students. Many had missed classes, fallen behind in schoolwork, engaged in unplanned—and unprotected—sex, gotten in trouble with campus police, engaged in vandalism, or been hurt or injured. Bingers were more likely than other students to have used other drugs, especially cigarettes and marijuana. They were 10 times more likely to have driven a car after drinking and more than 15 times more likely to have ridden with a driver who was drunk or high.

The effects of binge drinking are not limited to students who participate. At schools with high binge rates, a majority of students report that they have been unable to study or sleep because of binge drinking. Many sober students have cared for drunken friends, endured drunken insults, and fended off unwanted sexual advances. Yet most are reluctant to report these problems to campus or other authorities.

The researchers emphasize that the majority of students at four-year institutions—56 percent nationally—abstain or drink in moderation, a strong foundation for change. Nevertheless, binge drinking is an extremely serious problem that not only interferes with education but also carries a high risk of disease, injury, and death. In Chapter 14, Social Psychology, we consider ways to change students' beliefs about binge drinking.

cohol is implicated in more than two-thirds of all fatal automobile accidents, two-thirds of all murders, two-thirds of all spouse beatings, and more than half of all cases of violent child abuse. Moreover, the use of alcohol during pregnancy has been linked to a variety of birth defects, the most notable being fetal alcohol syndrome (See Chapter 8, Life Span Development). More than 40 percent of all heavy drinkers die before the age of 65 (compared with less than 20 percent of nondrinkers). In addition, there is

In the past year:
  .... Used any illicit* drug
  ——— Used marijuana or hashish
  •••••••• Was drunk on alcohol

*Includes marijuana, LSD, other hallucinogens, cocaine, heroin, other opiates, stimulants, barbiturates, methaqualone, or tranquilizers not under a doctor's order.

FIGURE 4–4

Teenage drug use. A national survey found that the use of illegal drugs and alcohol by American teenagers held fairly steady in 1999. Before that year, it had diminished slightly after years of growth. Among high school seniors, 42 percent reported that they had used an illegal drug in the previous year. More than 20 percent of 8th graders admitted to drug use, up from 12 percent in 1991 but down slightly from the previous year. In this group, 18.5 percent reported getting drunk during the past year; among 12th graders, that number was 53 percent.

Source: L. D. Johnston, P. M. O'Malley, & J. G. Bachman. (December 1999). *Drug trends in 1999 are mixed.* University of Michigan News and Information Services: Ann Arbor, MI. Available on-line at: www.monitoringthe future.org; accessed 1/14/00. Reprinted with permission.

the untold cost in psychological trauma suffered by the nearly 30 million children of alcohol abusers.

What makes alcohol so powerful? Alcohol first affects the frontal lobes of the brain (Adams & Johnson-Greene, 1995), which figure prominently in inhibitions, impulse control, reasoning, and judgment. As consumption continues, alcohol impairs functions of the cerebellum, the center of motor control and balance (Johnson-Greene et al., 1997). Eventually, alcohol consumption affects the spinal cord and medulla, which regulate such involuntary functions as breathing, body temperature, and heart rate. A blood-alcohol level of 0.25 percent or more may cause this part of the nervous system to shut down and may severely impair functioning; slightly higher levels can cause death from alcohol poisoning (see **Table 4–2**).

Even in moderate quantities, alcohol affects perception, motor processes, memory, and judgment. It diminishes the ability to see clearly, to perceive depth, to distinguish the differences between bright lights and colors, and spatial-cognitive functioning—all clearly necessary for driving a car safely (Matthews, Best, White, Vandergriff, & Simson, 1996). Alcohol interferes with memory storage: Heavy drinkers may also experience *blackouts,* which make them unable to remember anything that occurred while they were drinking; but even long-term alcoholics show improvements in memory, attention, balance, and neurological functioning after three months of sobriety (Sullivan, Rosenbloom, Lim, & Pfefferbaum, 2000).

Heavy drinkers have difficulty focusing on relevant information and ignoring inaccurate, irrelevant information, thus leading to poor judgments (Nixon, 1999). For example, dozens of studies demonstrate that alcohol is correlated with increases in aggression, hostility, violence, and abusive behavior (Bushman, 1993; Bushman & Cooper, 1990; Ito, Miller, & Pollock, 1996). Thus, intoxication makes people less aware of and less concerned about the negative consequences of their actions. The same principle ap-

UNDERSTANDING OURSELVES

What Are the Signs of Alcoholism?

The following test is excerpted from a comprehensive self-test published by the National Council on Alcoholism. It will help you determine whether you or someone you know needs to find out more about alcoholism, but it should not be used to establish the diagnosis of alcoholism.

1. Do you ever drink heavily when you are disappointed, under pressure, or when you have had a quarrel with someone?
2. Can you handle more alcohol now than when you first started to drink?
3. Have you ever been unable to remember part of the previous evening, even though your friends say that you didn't pass out?
4. When drinking with other people, do you try to have a few extra drinks the others won't know about?

5. Has a family member or close friend ever expressed concern or complained about your drinking?
6. Have you been having memory "blackouts"?
7. Do you often want to continue drinking after your friends say that they've had enough?
8. Do you usually have a reason for the occasions when you drink heavily?
9. When you're sober, do you sometimes regret things you did or said while drinking?
10. Have you tried switching brands or drinks or following different plans to control your drinking?
11. Have you sometimes failed to keep promises you made to yourself about controlling or cutting down on your drinking?

If your answer to any of these questions is yes, you may be at risk for alcoholism. More than one yes may signal an alcohol-related problem and the need to consult with an alcoholism counselor. To find out more, contact the National Council on Alcoholism and Drug Dependence in your area.

For further information about drug dependence, contact the following organizations:

National Council on Alcoholism and Drug Dependence: (800) 622-2255

Psychiatric Institutes of America: (800) COCAINE

National Institute on Drug Abuse: (301) 443-6245

American Cancer Society (nicotine): (800) 227-2345

---

plies to potential victims. A recent study demonstrated that when women are intoxicated, their ability to accurately evaluate a dangerous situation with a potential male aggressor is diminished, so that their risk of being sexually assaulted increases (Testa, Livingston, & Collins, 2000). Similarly, people who are intoxicated are more likely to engage in unprotected sex than if they were sober (MacDonald, Fong, Zanna, & Martineau, 2000; MacDonald, MacDonald, Zanna, & Fong, 2000).

Women are especially vulnerable to the effects of alcohol (National Institute on Alcohol Abuse and Alcoholism, 2000c). Because women generally weigh less than men, the same dose of alcohol has a stronger effect on the average woman than on the average man (York & Welte, 1994). In addition, most women have lower levels of the stomach enzyme that regulates alcohol metabolism. The less of this enzyme in the stomach, the greater the amount of alcohol that passes into the bloodstream and spreads through the body. (This is the reason why drinking on an empty stomach has more pronounced effects than drinking with meals [Frezza et al., 1990].) As a rough measure, one drink is likely to have the same effects on a woman as two drinks have on a man.

The dangers of alcohol notwithstanding, alcohol continues to be popular because of its short-term effects. As a depressant, it calms the nervous system, much like a general anesthetic (McKim, 1997). Thus, people consume

Nineteenth-century immigrants to the United States are shown gambling and smoking opium pipes at a clubhouse in New York's Chinatown. Problems associated with abuse of this drug led to it being banned for nonmedical use early in the 20th century.

Barbiturates
Potentially deadly depressants, first used for their sedative and anticonvulsant properties, now used only to treat such conditions as epilepsy and arthritis.

Opiates
Drugs, such as opium and heroin, derived from the opium poppy, that dull the senses and induce feelings of euphoria, well-being, and relaxation. Synthetic drugs resembling opium derivatives are also classified as opiates.

alcohol to relax or to enhance their mood (Steele & Josephs, 1990). It is often experienced as a stimulant because it inhibits centers in the brain that govern critical judgment and impulsive behavior. Alcohol makes people feel more courageous, less inhibited, more spontaneous, and more entertaining (Steele & Josephs, 1990). To drinkers, the long-term negative consequences of alcoholism pale beside these short-term positive consequences.

Barbiturates **Barbiturates**, which are commonly known as "downers," include such medications as Amytal, Nembutal, and Seconal. Discovered about a century ago, this class of depressants was first prescribed for its sedative and anticonvulsant qualities. But after researchers recognized in the 1950s that barbiturates had potentially deadly effects—particularly in combination with alcohol—their use declined, though they are still sometimes prescribed to treat such diverse conditions as insomnia, anxiety, epilepsy, arthritis, and bed-wetting (Reinisch & Sanders, 1982). Though barbiturates such as Amytal, Nembutal, Seconal, and phenobarbital are often prescribed to help people sleep, they actually disrupt the body's natural sleep patterns and cause dependence when used for long periods. Frequently prescribed for elderly people, who tend to take them chronically along with their other medications, barbiturates may produce significant side effects such as confusion and anxiety (Celis, 1994).

The general effects of barbiturates are strikingly similar to those of alcohol: Taken on an empty stomach, a small dose causes light-headedness, silliness, and poor motor coordination (McKim, 1986, 1997), whereas larger doses may bring on slurred speech, loss of inhibition, and increases in aggression (Aston, 1972). When taken during pregnancy, barbiturates, like alcohol, produce such birth defects as a cleft palate and malformations of the heart, skeleton, and central nervous system (Wilder & Bruni, 1981).

Opiates Psychoactive substances derived from, or resembling, the seedpod of the opium poppy, **opiates** have a long history of use—though not always abuse. A Sumerian tablet from 4,000 B.C. refers to the "joy plant." Originating in Turkey, opium spread west around the Mediterranean and east through India into China, where it was used in pill or liquid form in folk medicines for thousands of years. But changes in the way opium and its derivative, morphine, were used opened the door to abuse. In the mid–seventeenth century, when the emperor of China banned tobacco and the Chinese began to smoke opium, addiction quickly followed. During the American Civil War, physicians used a new invention, the hypodermic needle, to administer morphine, a much-needed painkiller for soldiers. In this form, morphine was far more addictive than smoking opium. Heroin—introduced in 1898 as a cure for morphine addiction—created an even stronger dependency.

Morphine compounds are still used in painkillers and other medications, such as codeine cough syrups. When the nonmedicinal distribution of opiates was banned early in the twentieth century, a black market for heroin developed. In the public mind, the heroin addict became synonymous with the "dope fiend," the embodiment of social evil.

Heroin and other opiates resemble endorphins, the natural painkillers produced by the body, and occupy many of the same nerve-receptor sites (see Chapter 2, The Biological Basis of Behavior). Heroin users report a surge of euphoria soon after taking the drug, followed by a period of "nodding off" and clouded mental functioning. Regular use leads to tolerance; tolerance may lead to physical dependence. In advanced stages of addiction, heroin becomes primarily a painkiller to stave off withdrawal symptoms. These symptoms, which may begin within hours of the last dose, include profuse sweating; alternating hot flashes and chills with goose bumps resembling the texture of a plucked turkey (hence the term *cold turkey*); severe cramps, vomiting, and diarrhea; and convulsive shaking and kicking (as in "kicking the habit").

Heroin abuse is associated with serious health conditions, including fatal overdose, spontaneous abortion, collapsed veins, pulmonary problems, and infectious diseases, especially HIV/AIDS and hepatitis as a result of sharing needles (Bourgois, 1999). The mortality rate of heroin users is almost 15 times higher than that of nonusers (Inciardi & Harrison, 1998). No longer an inner-city problem, its use is growing in suburbs and among young people and women, who often inhale or smoke heroin in the mistaken belief that it is not dangerous in this form (Kantrowitz, Rosenberg, Rogers, Beachy, & Holmes, 1993; National Institute on Drug Abuse, 2000c).

Stimulants: Caffeine, Nicotine, Amphetamines, and Cocaine

How do people tend to feel after a stimulant wears off?

The drugs classified as **stimulants**—caffeine, nicotine, amphetamines, and cocaine—have legitimate uses, but because they produce feelings of optimism and boundless energy, the potential for abuse is high.

Caffeine　Caffeine, which occurs naturally in coffee, tea, and cocoa, belongs to a class of drugs known as *xanthine stimulants*. The primary ingredient in over-the-counter stimulants, caffeine is popularly believed to maintain wakefulness and alertness, but many of its stimulant effects are illusory. In one study, subjects performing motor and perceptual tasks thought that they were doing better when they were on caffeine, but their actual performance was no better than without it. In terms of wakefulness, caffeine reduces the total number of sleep minutes and increases the time it takes to fall asleep. It is interesting that it is the only stimulant that does not appear to alter sleep stages or cause REM rebound, making it much safer than amphetamines.

Caffeine is found in many beverages and nonprescription medications, including pain relievers and cold and allergy remedies (see **Figure 4–5**). It is generally considered a benign drug, although large doses—more than five or six cups of strong coffee, for example—may cause caffeinism, or "coffee nerves": anxiety, headaches, heart palpitations, insomnia, and diarrhea. Caffeine interferes with prescribed medications, such as tranquilizers and sedatives, and appears to aggravate the symptoms of many psychiatric disorders. It is not clear what percentage of coffee drinkers are dependent on caffeine. Those who are dependent experience tolerance, difficulty in giving it up, and physical and psychological distress, such as headaches, lethargy, and depression, whether the caffeine is in soda, coffee, or tea (Blakeslee, 1994).

Nicotine　Nicotine, the addictive ingredient in tobacco, is probably the most dangerous and addictive stimulant in use today. Recent studies have found that the neurochemical properties of nicotine are similar to those of cocaine, amphetamines, and morphine (Glassman & Koob, 1996; Pontieri, Tanda, Orzi, & DiChiara, 1996). When smoked, nicotine tends to arrive at the brain all at once following each puff—a rush similar to the "high" experienced by heroin users. The smoker's heart rate increases and blood vessels constrict, causing dull skin and cold hands and accelerating the process of wrinkling

Stimulants
Drugs, including amphetamines and cocaine, that stimulate the sympathetic nervous system and produce feelings of optimism and boundless energy.

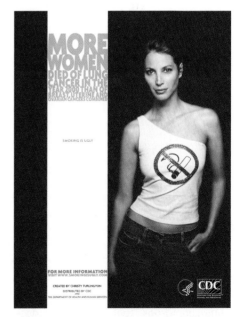

Supermodel Christie Turlington posed for a series of anti-smoking ads after her father died of lung cancer.

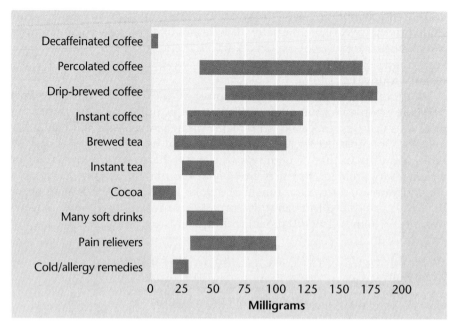

FIGURE 4–5

The amount of caffeine in some common preparations. Caffeine occurs in varying amounts in coffee, tea, soft drinks, and many nonprescription medications. On average, Americans consume about 200 mg of caffeine each day.

Source: Copyright © 1991 by the New York Times. Reprinted by permission.

and aging (Daniell, 1971). Nicotine affects levels of several neurotransmitters, including norepinephrine, dopamine, and serotonin, and depending on the time, the amount smoked, and other factors, may have sedating or stimulating effects. Symptoms of withdrawal from nicotine include nervousness, difficulty concentrating, both insomnia and drowsiness, headaches, irritability, and intense craving, which continue for weeks and may recur months or even years after a smoker has quit (Brandon, 1994). Despite well-known health risks and strong social pressures, millions of Americans continue to smoke, either for the pleasure of the combined stimulant-sedative effects or for preventing cravings and withdrawal symptoms. Particularly worrisome is that the number of teenagers who start smoking each year has hardly changed. Youth aged 12 to 17 who smoke are about twelve times more likely to use illicit drugs, and sixteen times more likely to drink heavily, than their nonsmoking peers and have an increased risk of depression (National Household Survey on Drug Abuse, 1998; D. Smith, 2001).

Amphetamines Amphetamines are powerful synthetic stimulants, first marketed in the 1930s as a nasal spray to relieve symptoms of asthma. At the chemical level, **amphetamines** resemble epinephrine, a hormone that stimulates the sympathetic nervous system (see Chapter 2, The Biological Basis of Behavior). During World War II, the military routinely gave soldiers amphetamines in pill form to relieve fatigue. After the war, the demand for "pep pills" grew among night workers, truck drivers, students, and athletes. Because amphetamines tend to suppress the appetite, they were widely prescribed as "diet pills."

Amphetamines not only increase alertness but also produce feelings of competence and well-being. People who inject them intravenously report a "rush" of euphoria. After the drug's effects wear off, however, users may "crash" into a state of exhaustion and depression (Gunne & Anggard, 1972). Amphetamines are habit-forming: Users may come to believe that they cannot function without them. High doses can cause sweating, tremors, heart palpitations, anxiety, and insomnia—which may lead people to take barbiturates or drugs to counteract these effects. Chronic, excessive use may cause personality changes, including paranoia, homicidal and sui-

Amphetamines
Stimulant drugs that initially produce "rushes" of euphoria often followed by sudden "crashes" and, sometimes, severe depression.

cidal thoughts, and aggressive, violent behavior (Leccese, 1991). Over time, chronic users may develop amphetamine psychosis, which resembles paranoid schizophrenia and is characterized by delusions, hallucinations, and paranoia. The label "dope fiend" more accurately describes the behavior of amphetamine addicts than that of heroin addicts!

Methamphetamine—known on the street as "speed" and "fire," or in a crystal, smokable form as "ice," "crystal," and "crank"—is easily produced in clandestine laboratories from ingredients available over the counter. An increasingly popular variation, Ecstasy (methylenedioxymethamphetamine, or MDMA), acts as both a stimulant and an hallucinogen. The name "Ecstasy" reflects the users' belief that the drug makes people love and trust one another, puts them in touch with their own emotions, and heightens sexual pleasure. Short-term physical effects include involuntary teeth clenching (which is why users often wear baby pacifiers around their neck or suck lollipops), faintness, and chills or sweating. Even short-term recreational use of MDMA may have long-term harmful consequences, affecting sleep, mood, appetite, and impulsiveness by damaging the neuroconnections between lower brain centers and the cortex (Kish, Furukawa, Ang, Vorce, & Kalasinsky, 2000; McCann, Slate, & Ricaurte, 1996; McCann, Szabo, Scheffel, Dannals, & Ricaurte, 1998). Moreover, the use of Ecstasy during pregnancy has been associated with birth defects (McElhatton, Bateman, Evan, Pughe, & Thomas, 1999). One recent study also found that the recreational use of Ecstasy may lead to a decrease in intelligence test scores (Gouzoulis-Mayfrank et al., 2000). Animal research going back more than 20 years shows that high doses of methamphetamine damage the axon terminals of dopamine- and serotonin-containing neurons, perhaps permanently (National Institute on Drug Abuse, 2000b). The only legitimate medical uses for amphetamines are to treat narcolepsy and attention deficit disorder (paradoxically, amphetamines have a calming effect on hyperactive children).

Cocaine   First isolated from cocoa leaves in 1885, **cocaine** came to be used widely as a topical anesthetic for minor surgery (and still is, for example, in the dental anesthetic Novocain). Around the turn of the century, many physicians believed that cocaine was beneficial as a general

Cocaine
Drug derived from the coca plant that, although producing a sense of euphoria by stimulating the sympathetic nervous system, also leads to anxiety, depression, and addictive cravings.

An 1885 American advertisement for Cocaine Toothache Drops, obviously intended for young children as well as adults. The addition of cocaine to everyday products, including Coca Cola, was quite common in the 19th century.

stimulant, as well as a cure for excessive use of alcohol and morphine addiction. Among the more famous cocaine users was Sigmund Freud. When he discovered how addictive cocaine was, Freud campaigned against it, as did many of his contemporaries, and ingesting the drug fell into disrepute.

Cocaine made a comeback in the 1970s in such unlikely places as Wall Street, among investment bankers who found that the drug not only made them high but also allowed them to wheel and deal around the clock with little sleep (Califano, 1999). In the white-powdered form that is snorted (street names "coke" and "snow"), it became a status drug, the amphetamine of the wealthy. In the 1980s, a cheaper, smokable, crystallized form known as "crack" (made from the by-products of cocaine extraction) appeared in inner-city neighborhoods. Crack reaches the brain in less than 10 seconds, producing a high that lasts from 5 to 20 minutes, followed by a swift and equally intense depression. Users report that crack leads to almost instantaneous addiction. Addiction to powdered cocaine, which has longer effects, is not inevitable but is likely. Babies born to women addicted to crack and cocaine often are premature or have low birth weight; may have withdrawal symptoms; and enter school with subtle deficits in intelligence and language skills (Inciardi, Surratt, & Saum, 1997).

On the biochemical level, cocaine blocks the reabsorption of the neurotransmitter dopamine, which is associated with awareness, motivation, and, most significantly, pleasure (Swan, 1998). From an evolutionary perspective, dopamine rewards such survival-related activities as eating, drinking, and engaging in sex. Excess dopamine intensifies and prolongs feelings of pleasure—hence the cocaine user's feelings of euphoria. Normally, dopamine is reabsorbed, leading to feelings of satiety or satisfaction; dopamine reabsorption tells the body, "That's enough." But cocaine short-circuits this feeling of satisfaction, in effect telling the body, "More!" On the structural level, crack and cocaine affect a pleasure center in the brain that governs emotions. Brain-imaging studies (Volkow et al., 1997) show that when cocaine users report euphoria, areas throughout the brain are activated; when the drug's effects wear off, a small number of neural circuits deep in the brain remain activated, hence the fierce craving for more cocaine.

Hallucinogens
Any of a number of drugs, such as LSD and mescaline, that distort visual and auditory perception.

Hallucinogens and Marijuana

How does marijuana affect memory?

The hallucinogens include lysergic acid diethylamide (LSD, also known as "acid"), mescaline, peyote, and psilocybin. Even in very small doses, these drugs can cause striking perceptual experiences that resemble hallucinations, hence the term *hallucinogen*. Marijuana is sometimes included in this group, although its effects are normally less powerful. In large enough doses, many other drugs bring on hallucinatory or delusional experiences, mimicking those that occur in severe mental illnesses; hallucinogens do so in small doses, usually without toxic effects.

Hallucinogens   **Hallucinogens** are natural or synthetic drugs that cause shifts in perception of the outside world or, in some cases, experience of imaginary landscapes, settings, and beings that may seem more real than the outside world. How many cultural groups have used hallucinogens is not known. Historians believe that Native Americans have used mescaline, a psychedelic substance found in the mushroom-shaped tops or "buttons" of peyote cactus, for at least 8,000 years.

These Native American women in Mexico are grinding dry peyote that will be mixed with water and drunk during an upcoming festival. Many Native American peoples have traditionally included peyote in their religious ceremonies.

By contrast, the story of **lysergic acid diethylamide (LSD),** the drug that triggered the current interest in the hallucinogens, begins in the twentieth century. In 1943, an American pharmacologist synthesized LSD, and after ingesting it, he reported experiencing "an uninterrupted stream of fantastic pictures and extraordinary shapes with an intense, kaleidoscopic play of colors." His report led others to experiment with LSD as an artificial form of psychosis, a painkiller for terminal cancer patients, and a cure for alcoholism in the 1950s (Ashley, 1975). LSD came to public attention in the 1960s, when Harvard psychologist Timothy Leary, after trying the related hallucinogen psilocybin, began spreading the "Turn On, Tune In, Drop Out" gospel of the hippie movement. Use of LSD and marijuana (see later) declined steadily in the 1970s but became popular once again in the 1990s, especially with high school and college students (Janofsky, 1994).

About an hour after ingesting LSD, people begin to experience an intensification of sensory perception, loss of control over their thoughts and emotions, and feelings of depersonalization and detachment, as if they were watching themselves from a distance. Some LSD users say that things never looked or sounded or smelled so beautiful; others have terrifying, nightmarish visions. Some users experience a sense of extraordinary mental lucidity; others become so confused that they fear they are losing their minds. The effects of LSD are highly variable, even for the same person on different occasions.

"Bad trips," or unpleasant experiences, may be set off by a change in dosage or an alteration in setting or mood. During a bad trip, the user may not realize that the experiences are being caused by the drug and thus may panic. Flashbacks, or recurrences of hallucinations, may occur weeks after ingesting LSD. Other consequences of frequent use may include memory loss, paranoia, panic attacks, nightmares, and aggression (Gold, 1994; Seligmann et al., 1992).

Unlike depressants and stimulants, LSD and the other hallucinogens do not appear to produce withdrawal effects. If LSD is taken repeatedly, tolerance builds up rapidly: After a few days, no amount of the drug will produce its usual effects, until its use is suspended for about a week (McKim, 1997). This effect acts as a built-in deterrent to continuous use, which helps explain why LSD is generally taken episodically rather than habitually. After a time, users seem to get tired of the experience and so decrease or discontinue their use of the drug, at least for a period of time.

Marijuana   **Marijuana** is a mixture of dried, shredded flowers and leaves of the hemp plant *Cannabis sativa* (which is also a source of fiber for rope and fabrics). Unlike LSD, marijuana usage has a long history. In China, cannabis has been cultivated for at least 5,000 years. The ancient Greeks knew about its psychoactive effects, and it has been used as an intoxicant in India for centuries. But only in the twentieth century did marijuana become popular in the United States. Today, marijuana is the most frequently used illegal drug in the United States, and the fourth most popular drug among students, after alcohol, caffeine, and nicotine (Treaster, 1994). **Figure 4–4** shows the increase in marijuana use by adolescents in recent years.

Although the active ingredient in marijuana, *tetrahydrocannabinol* (THC), shares some chemical properties with hallucinogens like LSD, it is far less potent. Marijuana smokers report feelings of relaxation; heightened enjoyment of food, music, and sex; a loss of awareness of time; and on occasion, dreamlike experiences. As with LSD, experiences are varied. Many users experience a sense of well-being, and some feel euphoric, but others become suspicious, anxious, and depressed.

Lysergic acid diethylamide (LSD)
Hallucinogenic or "psychedelic" drug that produces hallucinations and delusions similar to those occurring in a psychotic state.

Marijuana
A mild hallucinogen that produces a "high" often characterized by feelings of euphoria, a sense of well-being, and swings in mood from gaiety to relaxation; may also cause feelings of anxiety and paranoia.

Marijuana has direct physiological effects, including dilation of the blood vessels in the eyes, making the eyes appear bloodshot; a dry mouth and coughing (because it is generally smoked); increased thirst and hunger; and mild muscular weakness, often in the form of drooping eyelids (Donatelle & Davis, 1993). The major physiological dangers of marijuana are potential respiratory and cardiovascular damage, including triggering heart attacks (Mittleman, 2000; Sridhar, Ruab, & Weatherby, 1994). Among the drug's psychological effects is a distortion of time, which has been confirmed under experimental conditions (Chait & Pierri, 1992): Feelings that minutes occur in slow motion or that hours flash by in seconds are common. In addition, marijuana may produce alterations in short-term memory and attention.

While under the influence of marijuana, people often lose the ability to remember and coordinate information, a phenomenon known as *temporal disintegration*. For instance, someone who is "high" on marijuana may forget what he or she was talking about in midsentence. Such memory lapses may trigger anxiety and panic (Hollister, 1986; Leccese, 1991). While high, marijuana users have shortened attention spans and delayed reactions, which contribute to concerns about their ability to drive a car or to study or work effectively (Chait & Pierri, 1992; National Institute on Drug Abuse, 1998).

Is marijuana a "dangerous drug"? This question is the subject of much debate in scientific circles as well as public forums. On the one hand are those who hold that marijuana can be psychologically if not physiologically addictive; that frequent, long-term use has a negative impact on learning and motivation; and that legal prohibitions against marijuana should be continued. The evidence for cognitive or psychological damage is mixed. One study of college students showed that critical skills related to attention, memory, and learning are impaired among people who use marijuana heavily, even after discontinuing its use for at least twenty-four hours (National Institute on Drug Abuse, 2000a). On the other hand are those who maintain that marijuana is less harmful than the legal drugs, alcohol and nicotine. They argue that the criminalization of marijuana forces people to buy unregulated cannabis from illegal sources, which means that they might smoke "pot" contaminated with more harmful substances. Moreover, some evidence indicates that marijuana can relieve some of the unpleasant side effects of chemotherapy and can reduce suffering among terminal cancer patients. In short, the jury is still out, and the debate over marijuana is likely to continue.

So far we have been talking about the effects of individual drugs. In reality, most people who abuse drugs abuse more than one, and most addicts are polyaddicted (Califano, 2000). As a rule, young people who use "club drugs" also drink and smoke; likewise, college binge drinkers typically smoke cigarettes and marijuana as well. The same behavior is true of older drug abusers. In addition, people who use one drug (say, the stimulants amphetamine or cocaine) often use another drug (such depressants as alcohol, barbiturates, or minor tranquilizers) to counteract the effects of the first drug. This practice not only multiplies their risks as individuals but also makes efforts to diagnose and treat drug problems more difficult.

4.2

Explaining Abuse and Addiction

What combination of factors make it more likely that someone will abuse drugs?

Some people drink socially and never develop a problem with alcohol, whereas others become dependent or addicted. Some experiment with crack, which is known to be almost instantly addictive, or use "club drugs," which are known to be dangerous, whereas others "just say no." Each year, millions of Americans stop smoking cigarettes. Given the known hazards of smoking, why do a significant number of them relapse after months, even years, of not smoking?

The causes of substance abuse and dependence are complex, the result of a combination of biological, psychological, social, and cultural factors that varies from person to person, as well as what psychoactive drug or drugs are used (Finn, Sharkansky, Brandt, & Turcotte, 2000; Zucker & Gomberg, 1990). There is no "one-size-fits-all" explanation. But psychologists have identified a number of factors that, especially in combination, make it more likely that a person will abuse drugs.

Biological Factors   Are some individuals biologically vulnerable to drug abuse because of hereditary factors? There is evidence of a genetic basis for alcohol abuse. People whose biological parents have alcohol-abuse problems are more likely to abuse alcohol—even if they are adopted and raised by people who do not abuse alcohol. Identical twins are far more likely to have similar drink patterns relating to alcohol, tobacco, and marijuana use than are fraternal twins (Gordis, 1996; Lerman, et al., 1999; McGue, 1993; National Institute on Drug Abuse, 2000a).

Psychologists have not reached consensus on the exact role that heredity plays in a predisposition for alcoholism (or abuse of other substances). Some psychologists point to hereditary differences in levels of the stomach enzyme mentioned earlier, deducing that people born with higher levels of the enzyme have to drink more alcohol to achieve the same psychological effects as those with lower levels of the enzyme. People also appear to differ genetically in their tolerance for alcohol in the blood and in the ways they react to alcohol (Bolos et al., 1990; Gordis, 1996).

Is addiction a disease, like diabetes or high blood pressure? Alcoholics Anonymous (AA), the oldest and probably most successful self-help organization in this country, has long endorsed this view. According to the disease model, alcoholism is not a moral issue but a medical one, and alcohol abuse is not a sign of character flaws but is a symptom of a physiological condition. Furthermore, AA holds that accepting the disease model is an essential part of treatment.

The disease model has been applied to many addictions. For example, a new organization called *Nicotine Anonymous*, dedicated to helping smokers quit, now operates over 450 active groups nationwide (Lichtenstein, 1999). To some degree, the disease model has become part of conventional wisdom: Many Americans view substance abuse as a biological problem, often the result of "bad" genes, that requires medical treatment. Many health professionals share this viewpoint. Miller and Brown (1997) point out that clinical psychologists tend to view substance abuse as a medical problem, beyond their area of expertise, and either to refer clients to substance abuse programs or to focus on the consequences of substance abuse, rather than on the abuse itself.

Psychological, Social, and Cultural Factors   Whether a person uses a psychoactive drug and what effects that drug has also depend on the person's expectations, the social setting, and cultural beliefs and values.

A number of studies have shown that people use or abuse alcohol because they expect that drinking will help them to feel better (Cooper, Frone, Russell, & Mudar, 1995). During the 1960s and 1970s, members of the counterculture held similar expectations for marijuana, as do a significant number of young people today.

The setting in which drugs are taken is another important determinant of their effects. Every year thousands of hospital patients are given opiate-based painkillers before and after surgery. They may have experiences that a heroin or cocaine user would label as a "high," but they are more likely to consider them confusing than pleasant. In this setting, psychoactive substances are defined as medicine, dosage is supervised by physicians, and patients take them to get well, not to get high. In contrast, at teenage raves, college beer parties, and all-night clubs, people drink specifically to get drunk and take other drugs to get high. But even in these settings, some individuals participate without using or abusing drugs, and motives for using drugs vary. People who drink or smoke marijuana because they think that they need a drug to overcome social inhibitions and be accepted are more likely to slip into abuse than people who use the same substances in the same amounts because they want to have more fun.

The family in which a child grows up also shapes attitudes and beliefs about drugs. For example, children whose parents do not use alcohol tend to abstain or to drink only moderately; children whose parents abuse alcohol tend to drink heavily (Chassin, Pitts, Delucia, & Todd, 1999; Gordis, 1996; Harburg, Gleiberman, DiFranceisco, Schork, & Weissfeld, 1990). Such children are most likely to abuse alcohol if their family tolerates deviance in general or encourages excitement and pleasure seeking (Finn et al., 2000). Moreover, adolescents who have been physically assaulted or sexually abused in their homes are at increased risk for drug abuse (Kilpatrick et al., 2000). Parents are not the only family influence; some research indicates that siblings' and peers' attitudes and behavior have as much or more impact on young people than parents do (Ary, Duncan, Duncan, & Hops, 1999; also see Harris, 1998).

Culture, too, may steer people toward or away from alcoholism. Parents and spouses may introduce people to a pattern of heavy drinking. Alcohol is also more acceptable in some ethnic cultures than in others—for example, Orthodox Jews frown on the use of alcohol, and Muslims prohibit it.

Many researchers believe that a full understanding of the causes of alcoholism and other drug addictions will not be achieved unless we take account of a wide variety of factors: heredity, personality, social setting, and culture (Zucker & Gomberg, 1990). In Chapter 14, Social Psychology, we look at social influences on binge drinking, a major concern on college campuses across the United States.

INTERACTIVE LECTURE 4.2

WEB QUIZ 4.2

CHECK YOUR UNDERSTANDING

1. _____ _____ are chemical substances that change moods and perceptions.
2. The three major substances categorized as depressants are _____, _____, and _____.
3. The four major substances categorized as stimulants are _____, _____, _____, and _____.
4. Indicate whether the following statements are true (T) or false (F).
   _____ a. Alcohol is implicated in more than two-thirds of all automobile accidents.
   _____ b. Caffeine is not addictive.
   _____ c. Many users become dependent on crack cocaine almost immediately after beginning to use it.
   _____ d. Recurring hallucinations are common among users of hallucinogens.
   _____ e. Marijuana interferes with short-term memory.
5. Although alcohol is a _____, it is sometimes experienced subjectively as a _____.

Match the following categories of drugs with the appropriate descriptions:

6. _____ alcohol
7. _____ amphetamines
8. _____ barbiturates
9. _____ opiates
10. _____ cocaine
11. _____ hallucinogens

a. produce feelings of optimism and boundless energy

b. are addictive drugs that dull the senses

c. can produce euphoria, followed by anxiety, depression, and a craving for more

d. its use is associated with the most serious drug problem in the United States today

e. profoundly affect visual and auditory perception

f. are depressants that affect memory and perception of time

Answers: 1. psychoactive drugs. 2. alcohol, barbiturates, opiates. 3. caffeine, nicotine, amphetamines, cocaine. 4. a(T); b(F); c(T); d(T); e(T). 5. depressant, stimulant. 6. d. 7. a. 8. f. 9. b. 10. c. 11. e.

Meditation and Hypnosis

Can hypnosis help you overcome a problem, such as smoking or overeating?

At one time Western scientists viewed meditation and hypnosis with great skepticism. However, research has shown that both techniques can produce alterations in consciousness that can be measured through such sophisticated methods as brain imaging.

Meditation

What are the effects of meditation?

For centuries, people have used various forms of **meditation** to experience an alteration in consciousness (Benson, 1975). Each form of meditation focuses the meditator's attention in a slightly different way. *Zen meditation* concentrates on respiration, for example, whereas *Sufism* relies on frenzied dancing and prayer (Schwartz, 1974). In *transcendental meditation* (TM), practitioners intone a mantra, which is a sound, specially selected for each person, to keep all other images and problems at bay and to allow the meditator to relax more deeply (Deikman, 1973; Schwartz, 1974).

In all its forms, meditation suppresses the activity of the sympathetic nervous system, the part of the nervous system that prepares the body for strenuous activity during an emergency (see Chapter 2). Meditation also lowers the rate of metabolism, reduces heart and respiratory rates, and decreases blood lactate, a chemical linked to stress. Alpha brain waves (which accompany relaxed wakefulness) increase noticeably during meditation.

Meditation has been used to treat certain medical problems, especially so-called functional complaints (those for which no physical cause can be found). For example, stress often leads to muscle tension and, sometimes, to pressure on nerves—and pain. In other cases, pain leads to muscle tension, which makes the pain worse. Relaxation techniques such as meditation may bring relief (Blanchard et al., 1990). Several studies have also found that people stopped using drugs after taking up meditation (Alexander, Robinson, & Rainforth, 1994).

Besides physiological benefits, people who regularly practice some form of meditation report emotional and even spiritual gains, including increased sensory awareness and a sense of timelessness, well-being, and

Meditation can help relieve anxiety and promote peace of mind and a sense of well-being.

Meditation
Any of the various methods of concentration, reflection, or focusing of thoughts undertaken to suppress the activity of the sympathetic nervous system.

In this eighteenth century engraving, Anton Mesmer, attempts to relieve a woman's symptoms through the power of suggestion. As she holds one of the rods extending from a fluid-filled vat, Mesmer holds her wrist in one hand and a "magnetic wand" in the other. After Mesmer touched her body with the wand, the theory went, she would be cured.

being at peace with oneself and the universe (Hameroff, Kaszniak, & Scott, 1996; Lantz, Buchalter, & McBee, 1997).

Hypnosis

What clinical uses have been found for hypnosis?

In mid-eighteenth-century Europe, Anton Mesmer, a Viennese physician, fascinated audiences by putting patients into trances in order to cure their illnesses. Mesmerism—now known as **hypnosis**—was initially discredited by a French commission chaired by Benjamin Franklin. But some respectable nineteenth-century physicians revived interest in hypnosis when they discovered that it could be used to treat certain forms of mental illness. Nevertheless, even today considerable disagreement persists about how to define hypnosis and even about whether it is a valid altered state of consciousness.

One reason for the controversy is that from a behavioral standpoint, there is no simple definition of what it means to be hypnotized. Different people who are believed to have undergone hypnosis describe their experiences in very different ways (Farthing, 1992, p. 349):

> "Hypnosis is just one thing going on, like a thread . . . focusing on a single thread of one's existence. . . ."
>
> "I felt as if I were 'inside' myself; none of my body was touching anything. . . ."
>
> "I was very much aware of the split in my consciousness. One part of me was analytic and listening to you (the hypnotist). The other part was feeling the things that the analytic part decided I should have."

Hypnotic Suggestions   Individuals also vary in their susceptibility to hypnosis. One measure of susceptibility is whether people respond to hypnotic suggestion. Some people who are told that they cannot move their arms or that their pain has vanished do, in fact, experience paralysis or anesthesia; if told that they are hearing a certain piece of music or are unable to hear anything, they may hallucinate or become deaf temporarily (Montgomery, DuHamel, & Redd, 2000). When hypnotized subjects are told, "You will remember nothing that happened under hypnosis until I tell you," some people do experience amnesia. But, contrary to rumors, hypnotic suggestion cannot force people to do something foolish and embarrassing—or dangerous—against their will.

Another measure of the success of hypnosis is whether people respond to *posthypnotic commands*. For example, under hypnosis, a person suffering from back pain may be instructed that when he feels a twinge, he will imagine that he is floating on a cloud and his body is weightless, and the pain will stop—a technique also called "imaging." A runner may be told that when she pulls on her ear, she will block out the noise of the crowd and the runners on either side of her to heighten her concentration—a form of *self-hypnosis*. As the last example suggests, hypnosis has become increasingly popular among professional athletes and their weekend counterparts (Liggett, 2000).

Clinical Applications of Hypnosis   Because hypnotic susceptibility varies significantly from one person to another, its value in clinical and therapeutic settings is difficult to assess. Nevertheless, hypnosis is used in a variety of medical and counseling situations (Rhue, Lynn, & Kirsch, 1993). Some research indicates that it can enhance the effectiveness of traditional forms of psychotherapy (Kirsch, Montgomery, & Sapirstein, 1995), but psychologists do not agree on this issue. Hypnosis has been shown to be effective in controlling certain types of physical pain (Patterson & Ptacek, 1997). Dentists

Hypnosis
Trancelike state in which a person responds readily to suggestions.

have used it as an anesthetic for years. Hypnosis has also been used to alleviate pain in children with leukemia who have to undergo repeated bone-marrow biopsies (Hilgard, Hilgard, & Kaufmann, 1983).

Can hypnosis make someone change or eliminate bad habits? In some cases, posthypnotic commands temporarily diminish a person's desire to smoke or overeat (Green & Lynn, 2000; Griffiths & Channon-Little, 1995). But even certified hypnotists agree that this treatment is effective only if people are motivated to change their behavior. Hypnosis may shore up their will, but so might joining a support group, such as Nicotine Anonymous or Weight Watchers.

 INTERACTIVE LECTURE **4.3**

WEB QUIZ **4.3**

CHECK YOUR UNDERSTANDING

Match the following terms with the appropriate description:

1. _____ meditation
2. _____ hypnosis
3. _____ hypnotic susceptibility
   a. varies tremendously over time
   b. is a controversial altered state of consciousness
   c. suppresses sympathetic nervous system
4. Many psychologists believe that the effects of hypnosis can be accounted for by the variable of _____.

Answers: 1. c. 2. b. 3. a. 4. suggestibility.

KEY TERMS

CHAPTER REVIEW

Conscious Experience

What problems could arise if we were constantly aware of all external and internal sensations? To make sense of our complex environment, we choose what to absorb from the myriad happenings around us and filter out the rest. This process applies to both external stimuli such as sounds, sights, and smells, and internal sensations such as heat, cold, pressure, and pain. Even our thoughts, memories, emotions, and needs are subjected to this selective process. We also perform familiar tasks, such as signing our names, without deliberate attention. Many psychologists believe that important mental processes go on outside normal **waking consciousness.**

Do daydreams serve any useful function? Daydreaming occurs without effort, often when we seek briefly to escape the demands of the real world. Some psychologists see no positive or practical value in daydreaming. Others contend that daydreams and fantasies allow us to express and deal with hidden desires without guilt or anxiety. Still others believe that daydreams build cognitive and creative skills that helps us survive difficult situations—that they serve as a useful substitute for reality or a beneficial way of relieving tension.

Sleep

How do evolutionary psychologists explain the need for sleep? Evolutionary psychologists see sleep as an adaptation allowing organisms to conserve and restore energy.

What is the biological clock and what does it have to do with jet lag? The human biological clock is a cluster of neurons in the hypothalamus that responds to levels of proteins in the body. When those levels are low, these neurons stimulate production of more proteins. These proteins are the building blocks of chemicals that regulate biological functions such as metabolism and alertness.

Normally, the rhythms and chemistry of the body's cycles interact smoothly, but when we cross several time zones in one day, hormonal, temperature, and digestive cycles become desynchronized.

What physical changes mark the rhythms of sleep? Normal sleep consists of several stages. During Stage 1, the pulse slows, muscles relax, and the eyes move from side-to-side. The sleeper is easily awakened from *Stage 1* sleep. In *Stages 2 and 3* the sleeper is hard to awaken and does not respond to noise or light. Heart rate, blood

pressure, and temperature continue to drop. During *Stage 4* sleep, heart and breathing rates, blood pressure, and body temperature are at their lowest points of the night. About an hour after first falling asleep, the sleeper begins to ascend through the stages back to Stage 1—a process that takes about 40 minutes. At this stage in the sleep cycle, heart rate and blood pressure increase, the muscles become more relaxed than at any other time in the cycle, and the eyes move rapidly under closed eyelids. It is this **rapid eye movement (REM)** that gives this stage of sleep its name.

Are prescription medicines the best way to treat occasional insomnia? Sleep disorders include sleeptalking, sleepwalking, night terrors, **insomnia, apnea,** and **narcolepsy.** Most episodes of sleeptalking and sleepwalking occur during a deep stage of sleep. Unlike nightmares, night terrors, which are more common among children than adults, prove difficult to be awakened from and are rarely remembered the next morning. Insomnia is characterized by difficulty in falling asleep or remaining asleep throughout the night. Some prescription medicines can cause anxiety, memory loss, hallucinations, and violent behavior.

Dreams

What are dreams? Dreams are visual or auditory experiences that occur primarily during REM periods of sleep. Less vivid experiences that resemble conscious thinking tend to occur during NREM sleep.

Why do we dream? Several theories have been developed to explain the nature and content of dreams. According to Freud, dreams have two kinds of contents: manifest (the surface content of the dream itself) and latent (the disguised, unconscious meaning of the dream). One recent hypothesis suggests that dreams arise out of the mind's reprocessing of information absorbed during the day—information that is important to the survival of the organism. According to this theory, then, dreaming strengthens our memories of important information.

Drug-altered Consciousness

How is today's drug problem different from the drug use in other societies and times? Although many of the **psychoactive drugs** available today have been used for thousands of years, the motivation for using drugs is different today. Traditionally, these drugs were used in religious rituals, as nutrient beverages, or as culturally approved stimulants. Today, most psychoactive drug use is recreational, divorced from religious or family traditions.

How can we tell whether someone is dependent on a substance? **Substance abuse** is a pattern of drug use that diminishes the person's ability to fulfill responsibilities at home or at work or school, that results in repeated use of a drug in dangerous situations or that leads to legal difficulties related to drug use. Continued abuse over time can lead to **substance dependence,** a pattern of compulsive drug taking that is much more serious than substance abuse. It is often marked by tolerance, the need to take higher doses of a drug to produce its original effects or to prevent withdrawal symptoms. Withdrawal symptoms are the unpleasant physical or psychological effects that follow discontinuance of the psychoactive substance.

Why does alcohol, a depressant, lead to higher rates of violence? **Depressants** are chemicals that slow down behavior or cognitive processes. **Alcohol** calms down the nervous system, working like a general anesthetic. It is often experienced subjectively as a stimulant because it inhibits centers in the brain that govern critical judgment and impulsive behavior. That is why alcohol is involved in a substantial proportion of violent and accidental deaths.

How do people tend to feel after a stimulant wears off? **Stimulants** are drugs such as caffeine, nicotine, **amphetamines,** and **cocaine** that stimulate the sympathetic nervous system and produce feelings of optimism and boundless energy, making the potential for their abuse significant.

Caffeine occurs naturally in coffee, tea, and cocoa; nicotine occurs naturally only in tobacco. Caffeine is considered to be a benign drug, but in large doses it can cause anxiety, insomnia, and other unpleasant conditions. Although nicotine is a stimulant, it acts like a depressant when taken in large doses. **Amphetamines** are stimulants that initially produce "rushes" of euphoria often followed by sudden "crashes" and, sometimes, depression. Cocaine brings on a sense of euphoria by stimulating the sympathetic nervous system, but it can also cause anxiety, depression, and addictive cravings. Its crystalline form—crack—is highly addictive.

How does marijuana affect memory? **Hallucinogens** include drugs, such as **LSD,** psilocybin, and mescaline, that distort visual and auditory perception. **Marijuana** is a mild hallucinogen that is capable of producing feelings of euphoria, a sense of well-being, and swings in mood from gaiety to relaxation to paranoia. Though similar to hallucinogens in certain respects, marijuana is far less potent, and its effects on consciousness are far less profound. Marijuana can disrupt memory, causing people to forget what they are talking about in mid-sentence.

What combination of factors make it more likely that someone will abuse drugs? Several factors make it more likely that a person will abuse drugs. They include a possible genetic predisposition, the person's expectations, the social setting, and cultural beliefs and values.

Meditation and Hypnosis

What are the effects of meditation? **Meditation** refers to any of several methods of concentration, reflection, or focusing of thoughts intended to suppress the activity of the sympathetic nervous system. Meditation not only lowers the rate of metabolism but also reduces heart and respiratory rates. Brain activity during meditation resembles that experienced during relaxed wakefulness, and the accompanying decrease in blood lactate reduces stress.

What clinical uses have been found for hypnosis? **Hypnosis** is a trancelike state in which the person responds readily to suggestions. People's susceptibility to hypnosis depends on how suggestible they are. Hypnosis has several practical applications; for instance, it eases the pain of certain medical conditions and can help people stop smoking and break other habits.

WEB QUIZ **4.4** ✓   **Go to the Morris 6e Companion Website to take a practice chapter exam.**

5 Learning

OVERVIEW

AS UNLIKELY AS IT MAY SEEM, THE FOLLOWING ALL HAVE SOMETHING IN COMMON: Riding a bike, catching a ball, or passing an algebra test.

Feeling ill at the thought of an anchovy pizza or putting on oven gloves before picking up a hot casserole.

Teaching a squirrel to water-ski or a dog to give you his paw.

What all of these behaviors share is **learning,** the topic of this chapter. Although most people associate learning with classrooms and studying for tests, psychologists define it more broadly. To them, learning occurs whenever experience or practice results in a relatively permanent change in behavior or in potential behavior. This definition includes all the examples above, plus a great many more. When you remember which way to put the key into your front door lock, when you recall how to park a car or where the library water fountain is, you are showing just a small part of your enormous capacity for learning.

Human life would be impossible without learning. Learning is involved in virtually everything we do. You could not communicate with other people, recognize yourself as human, or even know what substances are appropriate to eat if you were unable to learn. In this chapter we explore several kinds of learning. One type is learning to associate one event with another. When lizards associate jumping and receiving food, or when a person associates a certain place and a certain strong emotion, they are engaging in two forms of learning called *operant* and *classical conditioning.* Because psychologists have studied these forms of learning so extensively, much of this chapter is devoted to them. But learning associations isn't all there is to human learning. Our learning also involves the formation of concepts, theories, ideas, and other mental abstractions. Psychologists call this cognitive learning, and we discuss it at the end of this chapter.

Our tour of learning begins in another time and place: the laboratory of a Nobel prize–winning Russian scientist at the turn of the twentieth century. His name is Ivan Pavlov, and his work is helping to revolutionize the study of learning. He has discovered classical conditioning.

Classical Conditioning

How did Pavlov discover classical conditioning?

Pavlov (1849–1936) discovered **classical conditioning** almost by accident. He was studying digestion, which begins when saliva mixes with food in the mouth. While measuring how much saliva dogs produce when given food, he noticed that they began to salivate even before they tasted the food. The mere sight of food made them drool. In fact, they even drooled at the sound of the experimenter's footsteps. This aroused Pavlov's curiosity. What was causing these responses? How had the dogs learned to salivate to sights and sounds?

To answer this question, Pavlov sounded a bell just before presenting his dogs with food. A ringing bell does not usually make a dog's mouth water, but after hearing the bell many times right before getting fed, Pavlov's dogs began to salivate as soon as the bell rang. It was as if they had learned that the bell signaled the appearance of food, and their mouths watered on cue even if no food followed. The dogs had been conditioned to

Learning
The process by which experience or practice results in a relatively permanent change in behavior or potential behavior.

Classical (or Pavlovian) conditioning
The type of learning in which a response naturally elicited by one stimulus comes to be elicited by a different, formerly neutral stimulus.

165

salivate in response to a new stimulus—the bell—that normally would not prompt salivation (Pavlov, 1927). **Figure 5–1** shows one of Pavlov's procedures in which the bell has been replaced by a touch to the dog's leg just before food is given.

Elements of Classical Conditioning

How might you classically condition a pet?

Figure 5–2 diagrams the four basic elements in classical conditioning: (1) the unconditioned stimulus, (2) the unconditioned response, (3) the conditioned stimulus, and (4) the conditioned response. The **unconditioned stimulus (US)** is an event that automatically elicits a certain reflex reaction, which is the **unconditioned response (UR).** In Pavlov's studies, food in the mouth was the unconditioned stimulus, and salivation to it was the unconditioned response. The third element in classical conditioning, the **conditioned stimulus (CS),** is an event that is repeatedly paired with the unconditioned stimulus. For a conditioned stimulus, Pavlov often used a bell. At first the conditioned stimulus does not elicit the desired response. But eventually, after repeatedly being paired with the unconditioned stimulus, the conditioned stimulus alone comes to trigger a reaction similar to the unconditioned response. This learned reaction is the **conditioned response (CR).**

Classical conditioning has been demonstrated in virtually every animal species, even squid and spiders (Krasne & Glanzman, 1995). You yourself

Unconditioned stimulus (US)
A stimulus that invariably causes an organism to respond in a specific way.

Unconditioned response (UR)
A response that takes place in an organism whenever an unconditioned stimulus occurs.

Conditioned stimulus (CS)
An originally neutral stimulus that is paired with an unconditioned stimulus and eventually produces the desired response in an organism when presented alone.

Conditioned response (CR)
After conditioning, the response an organism produces when a conditioned stimulus is presented.

FIGURE 5–1

Pavlov's apparatus for classically conditioning a dog to salivate. The experimenter sits behind a one-way mirror and controls the presentation of the conditioned stimulus (touch applied to the leg) and the unconditioned stimulus (food). A tube runs from the dog's salivary glands to a vial, where the drops of saliva are collected as a way of measuring the strength of the dog's response.

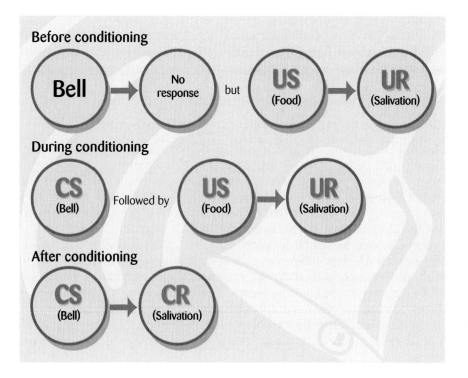

Before conditioning

During conditioning

After conditioning

FIGURE 5–2
A model of the classical conditioning process.

may have inadvertently classically conditioned one of your pets. For instance, you may have noticed that your cat begins to purr when it hears the sound of the can opener running. For a cat, the taste and smell of food are unconditioned stimuli for a purring response. By repeatedly pairing the can opener whirring with the delivery of food, you have turned this sound into a conditioned stimulus that triggers a conditioned response.

 5.1

Establishing a Classically Conditioned Response

If you once burned your finger on a match while listening to a certain song, why doesn't that song now make you reflexively jerk your hand away?

Certain procedures make it easier to establish a classically conditioned response. One is repeated pairings of the unconditioned stimulus and the cue that will eventually become the conditioned stimulus. The likelihood or strength of the conditioned response increases each time these two stimuli are paired. This learning, however, eventually reaches a point of diminishing returns. The amount of each increase gradually becomes smaller, until finally no further learning occurs. The conditioned response is now fully established.

It is fortunate that repeated pairings are usually needed for classical conditioning to take place (Schwartz, 1989). There are always a lot of environmental stimuli present whenever an unconditioned stimulus triggers an unconditioned response. If conditioning occurred on the basis of single pairings, all these usually irrelevant stimuli would generate some type of CR. Soon we would be overwhelmed by learned associations. Because a number of pairings are usually needed to produce a conditioned response, only a cue consistently related to the unconditioned stimulus typically becomes a conditioned stimulus.

The spacing of pairings is also important in establishing a classically conditioned response. If pairings of the CS and US follow each other very rapidly, or if they are very far apart, learning the association is slower. If the spacing of pairings is moderate—neither too far apart nor too close

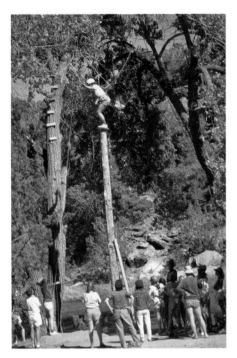

Desensitization therapy is based on the belief that we can overcome fears by learning to remain calm in the face of increasingly fear-arousing situations. Here people being desensitized for a fear of heights are able to swing high above the ground without panicking.

together—learning occurs more quickly. It is also important that the CS and US rarely, if ever, occur alone. Pairing the CS and US only once in a while, called **intermittent pairing,** reduces both the rate of learning and the final strength of the learned response.

Classical Conditioning in Humans

What is an example of classical conditioning in your own life?

Classical conditioning is as common in humans as it is in other animals. Some people learn phobias through classical conditioning. Phobias are intense, irrational fears of particular things or situations, such as spiders, snakes, flying, or being in enclosed places (claustrophobia). In Chapter 1, we discussed the study in which John Watson and his assistant Rosalie Rayner used classical conditioning to instill a phobia of white rats in a 1-year-old baby named Little Albert (Watson & Rayner, 1920). They started by showing Albert a white rat, which he happily tried to play with. But every time he approached the rat, the experimenters made a loud noise by striking a steel bar behind the baby's head. After a few attempts at pairing the rat and the frightening noise, Albert would cry in fear at the sight of the rat alone. By being paired with the unconditioned stimulus of the loud noise, the rat had become a conditioned stimulus for a conditioned fear response.

Several years later, psychologist Mary Cover Jones demonstrated a way that fears can be unlearned by means of classical conditioning (Jones, 1924). Her subject was a 3-year-old boy named Peter who, like Albert, had a fear of white rats. Jones paired the sight of a rat with an intrinsically pleasant experience—eating candy. While Peter sat alone in a room, a caged white rat was brought in and placed far enough away so that the boy would not be frightened. At this point Peter was given plenty of candy to eat. On each successive day the cage was moved closer to Peter, after which he was given candy. Eventually he showed no fear of the rat, even without any candy. By being repeatedly paired with a stimulus that evoked a pleasant emotional response, the rat had become a conditioned stimulus for pleasure.

In more recent times, psychiatrist Joseph Wolpe (1915–1997) adapted Jones's method to the treatment of certain kinds of anxiety (Wolpe, 1973, 1982). Wolpe reasoned that because irrational fears are learned or conditioned, they could also be unlearned through conditioning. He noted that it is not possible to be both fearful and relaxed at the same time. Therefore, if people could be taught to relax in fearful or anxious situations, their anxiety should disappear. Wolpe's **desensitization therapy** begins by teaching a system of deep-muscle relaxation. Then the person constructs a list of situations that prompt various degrees of fear or anxiety, from intensely frightening to only mildly so. A person with a fear of heights, for example, might construct a list that begins with standing on the edge of the Grand Canyon and ends with climbing two rungs on a ladder. While deeply relaxed, the person imagines the least distressing situation on the list first. If he or she succeeds in remaining relaxed, the person proceeds to the next item on the list, and so on until no anxiety is felt, even when imagining the most frightening situation. In this way, classical conditioning is used to change an undesired reaction: A fear-arousing thought is repeatedly paired with a muscular state that produces calmness until eventually the formerly fearful thought no longer triggers anxiety.

Intermittent pairing
Pairing the conditioned stimulus and the unconditioned stimulus on only a portion of the learning trials.

Desensitization therapy
A conditioning technique designed to gradually reduce anxiety about a particular object or situation.

Classical Conditioning and the Immune System   In another example of classical conditioning in humans, researchers have devised a novel way to treat autoimmune disorders, which cause the immune system to attack healthy organs or tissues. Although powerful drugs can be used to suppress the immune system and thus reduce the impact of the autoimmune disorder, these drugs often have dangerous side effects, so they must be administered sparingly. The challenge, then, was to find a treatment that could suppress the immune system without damaging vital organs. Researchers discovered that they could use formerly neutral stimuli either to increase or to suppress the activity of the immune system (Ader & Cohen, 1975; Hollis, 1997; Markovic, Dimitrijevic, & Jankovic, 1993). Here's how it works: The researchers use immune-suppressing drugs as USs and pair them with a specific CS, such as a distinctive smell or taste. After only a few pairings of the drug (US) with the smell or taste (CS), the CS alone suppresses the immune system (the CR) without any dangerous side effects! In this case, classical conditioning works on the mind but ultimately affects the body.

Classical Conditioning Is Selective

Why are people more likely to develop a phobia of snakes than of flowers?

If people can develop phobias through classical conditioning, as Little Albert did, why don't we acquire phobias of virtually everything that is paired with harm? For example, many people get shocks from electric sockets, but almost no one develops a socket phobia. Why should this be the case? Why shouldn't most carpenters have phobias of hammers because they have accidentally pounded their fingers with them?

Psychologist Martin Seligman has offered an answer. The key, he says, lies in the concept of **preparedness.** Some things readily become conditioned stimuli for fear responses because we are biologically prepared to learn those associations. Among the common objects of phobias are heights, snakes, and the dark. In our evolutionary past, fear of these potential dangers probably offered a survival advantage, and so a readiness to form such fears may have become "wired into" our species.

Preparedness also underlies **conditioned taste aversion,** a learned association between the taste of a certain food and a feeling of nausea and revulsion. Conditioned taste aversions are acquired very quickly. It usually takes only one pairing of a distinctive flavor and subsequent illness to develop a learned aversion to the taste of that food. Seligman calls this aversion the "sauce béarnaise effect," because he once suffered severe nausea after eating sauce béarnaise and ever since has abhorred the flavor. In one study, more than half the college students surveyed reported at least one such conditioned taste aversion (Logue, Ophir, & Strauss, 1981). Readily learning connections between distinctive flavors and illness has clear benefits. If we can quickly learn which foods are poisonous and avoid those foods in the future, we greatly increase our chances of survival. Other animals with a well-developed sense of taste, such as rats and mice, also readily develop conditioned taste aversions, just as humans do.

Even knowing that a certain food paired with nausea wasn't the cause of the illness doesn't spare us from developing a conditioned taste aversion. Seligman knew that his nausea was due to stomach flu, not to something he ate, but he acquired an aversion to sauce béarnaise just the same. Similarly, cancer patients often develop strong taste aversions to foods eaten right before nausea-inducing chemotherapy, even though they know that it is the drug that triggered their nauseous reaction. These patients can't prevent themselves from automatically learning a connection that they are biologically prepared to learn (Jacobsen et al., 1994).

Seligman's theory of preparedness argues that we are biologically prepared to associate certain stimuli, such as heights, the dark, and snakes, with fear responses. In our evolutionary past, fear of these potential dangers probably offered a survival advantage.

Preparedness
A biological readiness to learn certain associations because of their survival advantages.

Conditioned taste aversion
Conditioned avoidance of certain foods even if there is only one pairing of conditioned and unconditioned stimuli.

INTERACTIVE LECTURE **5.1**

WEB QUIZ **5.1**

CHECK YOUR UNDERSTANDING

1. The simplest type of learning is called _____ _____. It refers to the establishment of fairly predictable behavior in the presence of well-defined stimuli.

2. Match the following in Pavlov's experiment with dogs:

   ____ unconditioned stimulus   a. bell
   ____ unconditioned response   b. food
   ____ conditioned stimulus   c. salivating to bell
   ____ conditioned response   d. salivating to food

3. Which of the following are examples of classical conditioning?

   a. eating when not hungry just because we know it is lunchtime
   b. a specific smell triggering a bad memory
   c. a cat running into the kitchen to the sound of a can opener
   d. all of the above are examples of classical conditioning

4. The intense, irrational fears that we call phobias can be learned through classical conditioning. Is this statement true (T) or false (F)?

5. You have a cat that runs to the sound of the kitchen cabinet opening. The sound of the cabinet is the

   a. US
   b. CS
   c. CR

6. A learned association between the taste of a certain food and a feeling of nausea is called _____ _____ _____.

7. Teaching someone to relax even when he or she encounters a distressing situation is called _____ _____.

8. In the experiment with Little Albert, the unconditioned stimulus was _____ _____.

Answers: 1. classical conditioning. **2.** unconditioned stimulus—b; unconditioned response—d; conditioned stimulus—a; conditioned response—c. **3.** d. **4.** T. **5.** b. **6.** conditioned taste aversion. **7.** desensitization therapy. **8.** loud noises.

Operant Conditioning

How are operant behaviors different from the responses involved in classical conditioning?

Around the turn of the century, while Pavlov was busy with his dogs, the American psychologist Edward Lee Thorndike (1874–1949) was using a "puzzle box," or simple wooden cage, to study how cats learn (Thorndike, 1898). As illustrated in **Figure 5–3,** Thorndike confined a hungry cat in the puzzle box, with food just outside where the cat could see and smell it. To get to the food, the cat had to figure out how to open the latch on the box door, a process that Thorndike timed. In the beginning, it took the cat quite a while to discover how to open the door. But on each trial, it took the cat less time, until eventually it could escape from the box in almost no time at all. Thorndike was a pioneer in studying this kind of learning, which involves making a certain response because of the consequences it brings. This form of learning has come to be called **operant** or **instrumental conditioning.**

Elements of Operant Conditioning

What two essential elements are involved in operant conditioning?

One essential element in operant conditioning is *emitted behavior*. This is one way in which operant conditioning is different from classical conditioning.

Operant (or instrumental) conditioning The type of learning in which behaviors are emitted (in the presence of specific stimuli) to earn rewards or avoid punishments.

FIGURE 5–3

A cat in a Thorndike "puzzle box."   The cat can escape and be rewarded with food by tripping the bolt on the door. As the graph shows, Thorndike's cats learned to make the necessary response more rapidly after an increasing number of trials.

In classical conditioning, a response is automatically triggered by some stimulus. Food in the mouth automatically triggers salivation; a loud noise automatically triggers fear. In this sense, classical conditioning is passive. The behaviors are elicited by stimuli. This process is not true of the behaviors involved in operant conditioning. Thorndike's cats *spontaneously* tried to undo the latch on the door of the box. You *spontaneously* wave your hand to signal a taxi or bus to stop. You voluntarily study your teacher's assignments *by choice* in an effort to earn a good grade. You *voluntarily* put money into machines to obtain food, sodas, entertainment, or a chance to win a prize. These and similar actions are called **operant behaviors** because they involve "operating" on the environment.

A second essential element in operant conditioning is a *consequence* following a behavior. Thorndike's cats gained freedom and a piece of fish for escaping from the puzzle boxes; your dog may receive a food treat for sitting on command; a child may receive praise or a chance to watch television for helping to clear the table. Consequences like these that increase the likelihood that a behavior will be repeated are called **reinforcers.** In contrast, consequences that *decrease* the chances that a behavior will be repeated are called **punishers.** Imagine how Thorndike's cats might have acted had they been greeted by a large, snarling dog when they escaped from the puzzle boxes. Or consider what might happen if a dog that sits on command is scolded for doing so, or if a child who has helped to clear the table is sent to sit in a "time out" corner. Thorndike summarized the influence of consequences in his **law of effect:** Behavior that brings about a satisfying effect (reinforcement) is likely to be performed again, whereas behavior that brings about a negative effect (punishment) is likely to be suppressed. Contemporary psychologists often refer to the **principle of reinforcement** rather than the law of effect, but the two terms mean the same thing.

What Is Punishment?   We do not know whether something is reinforcing or punishing until we see whether it increases or decreases the occurrence of a response. We might assume that candy, for example, is a reinforcer for

Operant behavior
Behavior designed to operate on the environment in a way that will gain something desired or avoid something unpleasant.

Reinforcer
A stimulus that follows a behavior and increases the likelihood that the behavior will be repeated.

Punisher
A stimulus that follows a behavior and decreases the likelihood that the behavior will be repeated.

Law of effect (principle of reinforcement)
Thorndike's theory that behavior consistently rewarded will be "stamped in" as learned behavior, and behavior that brings about discomfort will be "stamped out."

children, but some children don't like candy. We might also assume that having to work alone rather than in a group of peers would be punishing, but some children prefer to work alone. Teachers must understand the children in their classes as individuals before they decide how to reward or punish them. Similarly, what is reinforcing for men may not be reinforcing for women, and what is reinforcing for people in one culture might not have the same effect for people in other cultures.

In addition, an event or object might not be consistently rewarding or punishing over time. So even if candy is initially reinforcing for some children, if they eat large amounts of it, it can become neutral or even punishing. We must therefore be very careful in labeling items or events as reinforcers or punishers.

Establishing an Operantly Conditioned Response

How might a speech therapist teach the sound of "s" to a child with a lisp?

Because the behaviors involved in operant conditioning are voluntary behaviors, it is not always easy to establish an operantly conditioned response. The desired behavior must first be performed spontaneously in order for it to be rewarded and strengthened. Sometimes you can simply wait for this action to happen. Thorndike, for example, waited for his cats to trip the latch that opened the door to his puzzle boxes. Then he rewarded them with fish.

But when there are many opportunities for making irrelevant responses, waiting can be slow and tedious. If you were an animal trainer for a circus, imagine how long you would have to wait for a tiger to decide to jump through a flaming hoop so you could reward it. One way to speed up the process is to increase motivation, as Thorndike did by allowing his cats to become hungry and by placing a piece of fish outside the box. Even without food in sight, a hungry animal is more active than a well-fed one and so is more likely, just by chance, to make the response you're looking for. Another strategy is to reduce opportunities for irrelevant responses, as Thorndike did by making his puzzle boxes small and bare.

Many researchers do the same thing by using Skinner boxes to train small animals in. A **Skinner box,** named after B. F. Skinner, another pioneer in the study of operant conditioning, is a small cage with solid walls that is relatively empty, except for a food cup and an activating device, such as a bar or a button (see **Figure 5–4**). In this simple environment, it doesn't take long for an active, hungry rat or a pigeon to press the bar or peck the button that releases food into the cup, thereby reinforcing the behavior.

Usually, however, the environment cannot be controlled so easily, so a different approach is called for. Another way to speed up operant conditioning is to reinforce successive approximations of the desired behavior. This approach is called **shaping.** In a Skinner box, for example, we might first reward a rat for turning toward the bar, then for moving toward it, then for touching the bar with its paw, and so on until it performs the desired behavior. The circus is a wonderful place to see the results of shaping. To teach a tiger to jump through a flaming hoop, the trainer might first reinforce the animal simply for jumping up on a pedestal. After that behavior has been learned, the tiger might be reinforced only for leaping from that pedestal to another. Next, the tiger might be required to jump through a hoop between the pedestals to gain a reward. And finally, the hoop is set on fire, and the tiger must leap through it to be rewarded. In much the same way, a speech therapist might reward a child with a lisp for closer and closer approximations of the correct sound of "s."

As in classical conditioning, the learning of an operantly conditioned response eventually reaches a point of diminishing returns. If you look back at **Figure 5–3,** you'll see that the first few reinforcements produced quite large improvements in performance, as indicated by the rapid drop in time required to escape from the puzzle box. But each successive reinforcement produced less of an effect until, eventually, continued reinforcement brought no evidence of further learning. After twenty-five trials, for instance, Thorndike's cats were escaping from the box no more quickly than they had been after fifteen trials. The operantly conditioned response has now been fully established. Can operant conditioning influence human behavior? See the *Understanding Ourselves* (p. 174) box to learn about how you can use operant conditioning to modify our own behavior.

Skinner box
A box often used in operant conditioning of animals; it limits the available responses and thus increases the likelihood that the desired response will occur.

Shaping
Reinforcing successive approximations to a desired behavior.

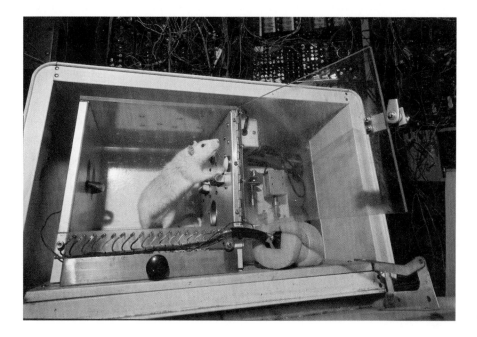

FIGURE 5–4

A rat in a Skinner box.   By pressing the bar, the rat releases food pellets into the box; this procedure reinforces its bar-pressing behavior.

UNDERSTANDING OURSELVES

Modifying Your Own Behavior

Can you modify your own undesirable behaviors by using operant conditioning techniques? Yes, but first you must observe your own actions, think about their implications, and plan a strategy of intervention.

Begin by *identifying the behavior you want to acquire:* This is called the "target" behavior. You will be more successful if you focus on acquiring a new behavior rather than on eliminating an existing one. For example, instead of setting a target of being less shy, you might define the target behavior as becoming more outgoing or more sociable. Other possible target behaviors might include behaving more assertively, studying more, and getting along better with your roommates. In each case, you have spotlighted the behavior that you want to acquire rather than the behavior that you want to eliminate.

The next step is *defining the target behavior precisely:* What exactly do you mean by "assertive" or "sociable"? Imagine situations in which the target behavior could be performed. Then describe in writing the way in which you now respond to these situations. For example, in the case of shyness, you might write, "When I am sitting in a lec-

ture hall, waiting for class to begin, I don't talk to the people around me." Next, write down how you would rather act in that situation: "In a lecture hall before class, I want to talk to at least one other person. I might ask the person sitting next to me how he or she likes the class or the professor, or simply comment on some aspect of the course."

The third step is *monitoring your present behavior:* You may do so by keeping a daily log of activities related to the target behavior. This will establish your current "base rate" and give you something concrete against which to gauge improvements. At the same time, try to figure out whether your present, undesirable behavior is being reinforced in some way. For example, if you find yourself unable to study, record what you do instead (Get a snack? Watch television?) and determine whether you are inadvertently rewarding your failure to study.

The next step—the basic principle of self-modification—is *providing yourself with a positive reinforcer that is contingent on specific improvements in the target behavior:* You may be able to use the same reinforcer that now maintains your undesir-

able behavior, or you may want to pick a new reinforcer. For example, if you want to increase the amount of time you spend studying, you might reward yourself with a token for each 30 minutes of study. Then, if your favorite pastime is watching movies, you might charge yourself three tokens for an hour of television, whereas the privilege of going to a movie might cost six.

Remember that the new, more desirable behavior need not be learned all at once. You can use shaping or successive approximations to change your behavior bit by bit. A person who wants to become more sociable might start by giving rewards just for sitting next to another person in a classroom rather than picking an isolated seat. The person could then work up to rewarding increasingly sociable behaviors, such as first saying hello to another person, then striking up a conversation.

If you would like to try a program of self-improvement, a book by David Watson and Roland Tharp, *Self-Directed Behavior: Self-Modification for Personal Adjustment* (1997), is a good place to start. It contains step-by-step instructions and exercises that provide a useful guide.

A Closer Look at Reinforcement

What is the difference between positive and negative reinforcement? What are some of the unintentional effects that reinforcement can have?

We have been talking about reinforcement as if all reinforcers are alike, but in fact this is not the case. Think about the kinds of consequences that would encourage you to perform some behavior. Certainly these include consequences that give you something positive, like praise, recognition, or money. But the removal of some negative stimulus is also a good reinforcer of behavior. When new parents discover that rocking a baby will stop the infant's persistent crying, they sit down and rock the baby deep into the night; the removal of the infant's crying is a powerful reinforcer.

These examples show that there are two kinds of reinforcers. **Positive reinforcers,** such as food, praise, or money, add something rewarding to a situation, whereas **negative reinforcers,** such as stopping an aversive noise, subtract something unpleasant. You might find it helpful to use a plus sign (+) to refer to a positive reinforcer that *adds* something rewarding and a minus sign (−) to refer to a negative reinforcer that *subtracts* something noxious. Animals will learn to press bars and open doors not only to obtain food and water (positive reinforcement) but also to turn off a loud buzzer or to avoid an electric shock (negative reinforcement).

Both positive and negative reinforcement result in the learning of new behaviors or the strengthening of existing ones. Remember, in everyday conversation when we say that we have "reinforced" something, we mean that we have strengthened it. "Reinforced concrete" is strengthened by the addition of steel rods or steel mesh; generals strengthen armies by sending in "reinforcements"; arguments are strengthened by being "reinforced" with facts. Similarly, in operant conditioning, reinforcement—whether positive or negative—always strengthens or encourages a behavior. A child might practice the piano because she or he receives praise for practicing (positive reinforcement) or because it gives her or him a break from doing tedious homework (negative reinforcement), but in either case the end result is a higher incidence of piano playing.

But what if a particular behavior is just *accidentally* reinforced because it happens by chance to be followed by some rewarding incident? Will the behavior still be more likely to occur again? B. F. Skinner showed that the answer is yes (1948). He put a pigeon in a Skinner box and at random intervals dropped a few grains of food into the food cup. The pigeon began repeating whatever it had been doing just before the food was given: standing on one foot, hopping around, or strutting with its neck stretched out. None of these actions had anything to do with getting the food, of course. But still the bird repeated them over and over again. Skinner called the bird's behavior superstitious, because it was learned in a way that is similar to how some human superstitions are learned. If you happen to be wearing an Albert Einstein T-shirt when you get your first A on an exam, you may come to believe that wearing this shirt was a factor. Even though the connection was pure coincidence, you may keep on wearing your "lucky" shirt to every test thereafter.

Shaping Behavioral Change Through Biofeedback Patrick, an 8-year-old third-grader, was diagnosed with attention deficit disorder (ADD). He was restless and unable to concentrate in school. An EEG showed increased numbers of slow brain waves. After a course of forty training sessions, using special computer equipment that allowed Patrick to monitor his brain-wave activities, he learned how to produce more of the fast waves that are associated with being calm and alert. As a result, Patrick became much more "clued in" to what was going on around him and much less likely to become frustrated when things didn't go his way (Fitzgerald, 1999).

Researchers studying women with sexual dysfunction identified a feedback loop involving both cognitive and physiological function. They were able to help women enhance their physiological response to sexual stimuli, as well as increase their cognitive expectations of sexual gratification (Palace, 1995). Results suggest that it may be possible for women to learn how to reverse dysfunctional sexual responses.

Biofeedback training is an operant conditioning technique in which instruments are used to give learners information about the strength of a biological response over which they seek to gain control. A biofeedback device records information about a particular biological response—muscle contrac-

How does an animal trainer get a tiger to jump through a flaming hoop so that behavior can be rewarded? The answer is usually through shaping. The trainer reinforces closer and closer approximations of the desired response until eventually the tiger leaps through the hoop on command.

Shaping can also be used for some types of human learning. A diver's movements are developed and perfected through a series of successive approximations.

Positive reinforcer
Any event whose presence increases the likelihood that ongoing behavior will recur.

Negative reinforcer
Any event whose reduction or termination increases the likelihood that ongoing behavior will recur.

Biofeedback
A technique that uses monitoring devices to provide precise information about internal physiological processes, such as heart rate or blood pressure, to teach people to gain voluntary control over these functions.

A person attached to a biofeedback machine. Biofeedback has become a well-established treatment for a number of medical problems, even though some people still reject it as quackery.

tions, blood pressure, heart rate, brain waves—that normally proceeds outside our conscious awareness. Variations in the strength of the response are reflected in the form of a light, a tone, or some other signal that varies according to the measured level of the response. Through the feedback information—the tone or light—the response is learned little by little, as with other shaping techniques. Patrick, the 8-year-old with ADD, learned to control the movement of a Superman icon on a computer screen.

Biofeedback training has been used for a wide variety of disorders. More recently, researchers have drawn on biofeedback techniques to treat a painful bowel condition in infants (Cox et al., 1994), incontinence in adults (Keck et al., 1994), as well as migraine (Wauquier et al., 1995) and post-traumatic headaches (Ham & Packard, 1996).

Biofeedback has become a well-established treatment for a number of medical problems, including tension headaches and migraine headaches, as well as asthma and peptic ulcers.

Biofeedback has also been used by athletes, musicians, and other performers to control the anxiety that can interfere with their performance. Marathon runners use it to help overcome the tight shoulders and shallow breathing that can prevent them from finishing races. Although most reports of the effectiveness of biofeedback in sports come from personal accounts rather than controlled studies, this anecdotal evidence strongly suggests that biofeedback offers real benefits (Peper & Crane-Cochley, 1990). It has even been used in space. NASA combined a program of biofeedback with cognitive therapy (such as mental messages) to reduce the motion sickness that astronauts experience at zero gravity.

Despite its successes, some still reject biofeedback as quackery (National Institute of Health Consensus Development Conference, 1996). Critics challenge the scientific rigor of studies that have evaluated biofeedback and the professional caliber of the technicians who operate the various biofeedback instruments (Middaugh, 1990). In addition, some conditions, such as high blood pressure, do not always respond well to biofeedback training (McGrady, 1996; Weaver & McGrady, 1995). Further research may reveal other conditions for which this type of treatment is not appropriate. Advocates of the technique argue that when biofeedback is viewed properly—as a way to learn self-regulation of biological processes rather than as a therapy—and when it's evaluated on those terms, it can stand up to the most rigorous scientific scrutiny (P. A. Norris, 1986).

In the case of forming superstitions, reinforcement has an illogical effect on behavior, but that effect is generally harmless. Are there any more negative results that rewards can sometimes inadvertently have? Some psychologists think there may be. They believe that offering certain kinds of reinforcers (candy, money, play time) for a task that could be intrinsically rewarding can undermine the intrinsic motivation to perform it. People may begin to think that they are working only for the reward and lose enthusiasm for what they are doing. They may no longer see their work as an intrinsically interesting challenge in which to invest creative effort and strive for excellence. Instead, they may see work as a chore that must be done to earn some tangible payoff. This warning can be applied to many situations, such as offering tangible rewards to students for their work in the classroom, or giving employees a "pay for performance" incentive to meet company goals (Kohn, 1993; Tagano, Moran, & Sawyers, 1991). Concern about tangible reinforcers may be exaggerated, however. Although the use of rewards may sometimes produce negative outcomes, this is not always the case. In fact, one extensive review of more than 100 studies showed that when used appropriately, rewards do not compromise intrinsic motivation, and they may even help to encourage creativity (Eisenberger & Cameron, 1996).

A Closer Look at Punishment

What problems can punishment create?

Although we all hate to be subjected to it, **punishment** is a powerful controller of behavior. After receiving a heavy fine for failing to report extra income to the IRS, we are less likely to make that mistake again. After being rudely turned down when we ask someone for a favor, we are less likely to ask that person for another favor. In both cases, an unpleasant consequence reduces the likelihood that we will repeat a behavior. This is the definition of punishment.

Punishment is different from negative reinforcement. Reinforcement of whatever kind *strengthens* (reinforces) behavior. Negative reinforcement strengthens behavior by removing something unpleasant from the environment. In contrast, punishment adds something unpleasant to the environment, and as a result, it tends to *weaken* the behavior that caused it. If going skiing for the weekend rather than studying for a test results in getting an F, the F is an unpleasant consequence (a punisher) that makes you less likely to give more importance to skiing than to homework again.

Is punishment effective? Does it always work? We can all think of instances when it doesn't seem to. Children often continue to misbehave even after they have been punished repeatedly for that particular misbehavior. Some drivers persist in driving recklessly despite repeated fines. The family dog may sleep on the couch at night despite being punished for being on the couch every morning. Why are there these seeming exceptions to the law of effect? Why, in these cases, isn't punishment having the result it is supposed to?

For punishment to be effective, it must be imposed properly. First, punishment should be *swift*. If it is delayed, it doesn't work as well. Sending a misbehaving child immediately to a time-out seat (even when it is not convenient to do so) is much more effective than waiting for a "better" time to punish. Punishment should also be *sufficient* without being cruel. If a parent briefly scolds a child for hitting other children, the effect will probably be less pronounced than if the child is sent to his or her room for the day. At the same time, punishment should be *consistent*. It should be imposed for all infractions of a rule, not just for some. If parents allow some acts of aggression to go unpunished, hitting and bullying other children is likely to persist.

Punishment is particularly useful in situations in which a behavior is dangerous and must be changed quickly. A child who likes to poke things into electric outlets must be stopped immediately, so punishment may be the best course of action. Similarly, punishment may be called for to stop severely disturbed children from repeatedly banging their heads against walls or hitting themselves in the face with their fists. Once this self-destructive behavior is under control, other forms of therapy can be more effective.

But even in situations like these, punishment has drawbacks (Skinner, 1953). First, it only *suppresses* the undesired behavior; it doesn't prompt someone to "unlearn" the behavior, and it doesn't teach a more desirable one. If the threat of punishment is removed, the negative behavior is likely to recur. This result is apparent on the highway. Speeders slow down when they see a police car (the threat of punishment) but speed up again as soon as the threat is passed. Punishment, then, rarely works when long-term changes in behavior are wanted. Second, punishment often stirs up negative feelings (frustration, resentment, self-doubt), which can impede the learning of new, more desirable behaviors. For example, when a child who is learning to read is scolded for every mispronounced word, the child may become very frustrated and hesitant. This frustration and doubt about ability can prompt more mispronunciations, which lead to more scolding. In time, the negative feelings that punishment has caused can become so unpleasant that the child avoids

Punishment
Any event whose presence decreases the likelihood that ongoing behavior will recur.

A punishment is any consequence that decreases the chances that a particular behavior will be repeated. This man being carried to the pillory in colonial New England will probably think twice before repeating whatever misdeed he committed, because public humiliation is a powerful form of punishment.

Live! psych 5.2

reading. A third drawback of punishment, when it is harsh, is the unintended lesson that it teaches: Harsh punishment may encourage the learner to copy that same harsh and aggressive behavior toward other people. In laboratory studies, monkeys that are harshly punished tend to attack other monkeys, pigeons other pigeons, and so on (B. Schwartz, 1989). In addition, punishment often makes people angry, and angry people frequently become more aggressive and hostile.

Because of these drawbacks, punishment should be used carefully, and always together with reinforcement of desirable behavior. Once a more desirable response is established, punishment should be removed to reinforce negatively that new behavior. Positive reinforcement (praise, rewards) should also be used to strengthen the desired behavior. This approach is more productive than punishment alone, because it teaches an alternative behavior to replace the punished one. Positive reinforcement also makes the learning environment less threatening.

Sometimes, after punishment has been administered a few times, it needn't be continued, because the mere threat of punishment is enough to induce the desired behavior. Psychologists call this **avoidance training** because the person is learning to avoid the possibility of a punishing consequence. Avoidance training is responsible for many everyday behaviors. It has taught you to carry an umbrella when it looks like rain to avoid the punishment of getting wet, and to keep your hand away from a hot iron to avoid the punishment of a burn. Avoidance training, however, doesn't always work in our favor. For instance, a child who has been repeatedly criticized for poor performance in math may learn to shun difficult math problems in order to avoid further punishment. Unfortunately, because of this avoidance, the child fails to develop math skills and therefore fails to improve any innate capabilities, and so a vicious cycle has set in. The avoidance must be unlearned through some positive experiences with math in order for this cycle to be broken.

Learned Helplessness

In what ways do some college students exhibit learned helplessness?

Through avoidance training, people learn to prevent themselves from being punished, but what happens when such avoidance of punishment for some reason isn't possible? The answer is often a "giving up" response that can generalize to other situations. This response is known as **learned helplessness.**

Martin Seligman and his colleagues first studied learned helplessness in experiments with dogs (Maier, Seligman, & Soloman, 1969). They placed two groups of dogs in chambers that delivered a series of electric shocks to the dogs' feet at random intervals. The dogs in the control group could turn off (escape) the shock by pushing a panel with their nose. The dogs in the experimental group could not turn off the shock—they were, in effect, helpless. Next, both the experimental and the control animals were placed in a different situation, one in which they could escape shock by jumping over a hurdle. A warning light always came on 10 seconds before each 50-second shock was given. The dogs in the control group quickly learned to jump the hurdle as soon as the warning light flashed, but the dogs in the experimental group didn't. These dogs, which had previously experienced unavoidable shocks, didn't even jump the hurdle *after* the shock started. They just lay there and accepted the pain. Also, many of these dogs were generally listless, suffered loss of appetite, and displayed other symptoms associated with depression.

Avoidance training
Learning a desirable behavior to prevent the occurrence of something unpleasant, such as punishment.

Learned helplessness
Failure to take steps to avoid or escape from an unpleasant or aversive stimulus that occurs as a result of previous exposure to unavoidable painful stimuli.

Many subsequent studies have shown that learned helplessness can occur both in animals and in humans (Maier & Seligman, 1976). Once established, the condition generalizes to new situations and can be very persistent, even given evidence that an unpleasant circumstance can now be avoided (Peterson, Maier, & Seligman, 1993). For example, when faced with a series of unsolvable problems, a college student may eventually give up trying and make only halfhearted efforts to solve new problems, even when the new problems are solvable. Moreover, success in solving new problems has little effect on the person's behavior. He or she continues to make only halfhearted tries, as if never experiencing *any* success at all. Similarly, children raised in an abusive family, where punishment is unrelated to behavior, often develop a feeling of helplessness. Even in relatively normal settings outside their home, they often appear listless, passive, and indifferent. They make little attempt either to seek rewards or to avoid discomfort.

INTERACTIVE LECTURE 5.2

WEB QUIZ 5.2

CHECK YOUR UNDERSTANDING

1. Match the following terms with their appropriate definition:

____ reinforcement
____ positive reinforcement
____ negative reinforcement
____ punishment

a. any event whose reduction or termination increases the likelihood that ongoing behavior will recur
b. any event whose presence increases the likelihood that ongoing behavior will recur
c. anything that decreases the likelihood that a behavior will recur
d. anything that increases the likelihood that a behavior will recur

2. A type of learning that involves reinforcing the desired response is known as ____ ____.

3. When a threat of punishment induces a change to more desirable behavior, it is called ____ ____.

4. Superstitious behavior can result when a behavior is rewarded by pure ____.

5. Which of the following is not an example of operantly learned behavior?
   a. eye blinking after a flash of light is presented
   b. a child studying in order to get a teacher's approval
   c. a rat pressing a bar after receiving food for this behavior
   d. a rat pressing a bar to avoid a shock for this behavior

6. Any stimulus that follows a behavior and decreases the likelihood that the behavior will be repeated is called a ____.
   a. cue
   b. situational stimulus
   c. punishment
   d. higher-order conditioner

7. Which of the following problems may result from avoidance training?
   a. A person may continue to avoid something that no longer needs to be avoided.
   b. The effects of avoidance training tend to last for only a short time.
   c. Avoidance training may produce latent learning.
   d. Avoidance training tends to take effect when it is too late to make a difference in avoiding the problem situation.

Answers: 1. reinforcement—d; positive reinforcement—b; negative reinforcement—a; punishment—c. 2. operant conditioning. 3. avoidance training. 4. coincidence. 5. a. 6. c. 7. a.

Factors Shared by Classical and Operant Conditioning

Can you think of any similarities between classical and operant conditioning?

Despite the differences between classical and operant conditioning, these two forms of learning have many things in common. First, they both involve the learning of associations. In classical conditioning, it is a learned association between one stimulus and another (between food and a bell, for instance), whereas in operant conditioning, it is a learned association between some action and a consequence. Second, the responses in both classical and operant conditioning are under the control of stimuli in the environment. A classically conditioned fear might be triggered by the sight of a white rat; an operantly conditioned jump might be cued by the flash of a red light. In both cases, moreover, the learned responses to a cue can generalize to similar stimuli. Third, neither classically nor operantly conditioned responses will last forever if they aren't periodically renewed. This doesn't necessarily mean that they are totally forgotten, however. Even after you think that these responses have long vanished, either one can suddenly reappear in the right situation. And fourth, in both kinds of learning—classical *and* operant conditioning—new behaviors can build on previously established ones.

The Importance of Contingencies

How can changes in the timing of a conditioned stimulus lead to unexpected learning? Why does intermittent reinforcement result in such persistent behavior?

Because classical and operant conditioning are both forms of associative learning, they both involve perceived contingencies. A **contingency** is a relationship in which one event *depends* on another. Graduating from college is *contingent* on passing a certain number of courses. Earning a paycheck is *contingent* on having a job. In both classical and operant conditioning, perceived contingencies are very important.

Contingencies in Classical Conditioning   In classical conditioning, a contingency is perceived between the CS and the US. The CS comes to be viewed as a signal that the US is about to happen. This is why, in classical conditioning, the CS not only must occur in close proximity to the US but also should precede the US and provide predictive information about it (Rescorla, 1966, 1967, 1988).

Imagine an experiment in which animals are exposed to a tone (the CS) and a mild electric shock (the US). One group always hear the tone a fraction of a second before they are shocked. Another group sometimes hear the tone first, but other times the tone sounds a fraction of a second *after* the shock, and still other times the tone and shock occur together. Soon the first group will show a fear response upon hearing the tone alone, but the second group will not. This is because the first group has learned a contingency between the tone and the shock. For them, the tone has always preceded the shock, so it has come to mean that the shock is about to be given. For the second group, in contrast, the tone has signaled little or nothing about the shock. Sometimes the tone has meant that a shock is coming, sometimes it has meant that the shock is here, and sometimes it has meant that the shock is over and "the coast is clear." Because the meaning of the tone has been ambiguous for the members of this group, they have not developed a conditioned fear response to it.

Although scientists once believed that no conditioning would occur if the CS *followed* the US, this belief turns out not to be true. The explanation again

Contingency
A reliable "if-then" relationship between two events such as a CS and a US.

lies in contingency learning. Imagine a situation in which a tone (the CS) always follows a shock (the US). This process is called *backward conditioning*. After a while, when the tone is sounded alone, the learner will not show a conditioned fear response to it. After all, the tone has never predicted that a shock is about to be given. But what the learner *does* show is a conditioned *relaxation* response to the sound of the tone, because the tone has served as a signal that the shock is over and will not occur again for some time. Again we see the importance of contingency learning: The learner responds to the tone on the basis of the information that it gives about what will happen next.

Other studies similarly show that predictive information is crucial in establishing a classically conditioned response. In one experiment with rats, for instance, a noise was repeatedly paired with a brief electric shock until the noise soon became a conditioned stimulus for a conditioned fear response (Kamin, 1969). Then a second stimulus—a light—was added right before the noise. You might expect that the rat came to show a fear of the light as well, because it, too, preceded the shock. But this is not what happened. Apparently, the noise-shock contingency that the rat had already learned had a **blocking** effect on additional learning. Once the rat had learned that the noise signaled the onset of shock, adding yet another cue (a light) provided no new predictive information about the shock's arrival, and so the rat paid little attention to the light. Classical conditioning, then, occurs only when a stimulus tells the learner something *new* or *additional* about the likelihood that a US will occur.

Contingencies in Operant Conditioning   Contingencies also figure prominently in operant conditioning. The learner must come to perceive a connection between performing a certain voluntary action and receiving a certain reward or punishment. If no contingency is perceived, there is no reason to increase or decrease the behavior.

But once a contingency is perceived, does it matter how often a consequence is actually delivered? When it comes to rewards, the answer is yes. Fewer rewards are often better than more. In the language of operant conditioning, *partial* or *intermittent reinforcement* results in behavior that will persist longer than behavior learned by *continuous reinforcement*. Why would this be the case? The answer has to do with expectations. When people receive only occasional reinforcement, they learn not to expect reinforcement with every response, so they continue responding in the hopes that eventually they will gain the desired reward. Vending machines and slot machines illustrate these different effects of continuous versus partial reinforcement. A vending machine offers continuous reinforcement. Each time you put in the right amount of money, you get something desired in return (reinforcement). If a vending machine is broken and you receive nothing for your coins, you are unlikely to put more money in it. In contrast, a casino slot machine pays off intermittently; only occasionally do you get something back for your investment. This intermittent payoff has a compelling effect on behavior. You might continue putting coins into a slot machine for a very long time even though you are getting nothing in return.

Psychologists refer to a pattern of reward payoffs as a **schedule of reinforcement.** Partial or intermittent reinforcement schedules are either fixed or variable, and they may be based on either the number of correct responses or the time elapsed between correct responses. **Table 5–1** gives some everyday examples of different reinforcement schedules.

On a **fixed-interval schedule** learners are reinforced for the first response after a certain amount of time has passed since that response was previously rewarded. That is, they have to wait for a set period before they will be reinforced again. With a fixed-interval schedule, performance tends to fall off immediately after each reinforcement and

Blocking
A process whereby prior conditioning prevents conditioning to a second stimulus even when the two stimuli are presented simultaneously.

Schedule of reinforcement
In operant conditioning, the rule for determining when and how often reinforcers will be delivered.

Fixed-interval schedule
A reinforcement schedule in which the correct response is reinforced after a fixed length of time since the last reinforcement.

TABLE 5-1   EXAMPLES OF REINFORCEMENT IN EVERYDAY LIFE

Continuous reinforcement (reinforcement every time the response is made)	Putting money in the parking meter to avoid getting a ticket. Putting coins in a vending machine to get candy or soda.
Fixed-ratio schedule (reinforcement after a fixed number of responses)	Being paid on a piecework basis. In the garment industry, for example, workers may be paid a fee per 100 dresses sewn.
Variable-ratio schedule (reinforcement after a varying number of responses)	Playing a slot machine. The machine is programmed to pay off after a certain number of responses have been made, but that number keeps changing. This type of schedule creates a steady rate of responding, because players know that if they play long enough, they will win. Sales commissions. You have to talk to many customers before you make a sale, and you never know whether the next one will buy. The number of sales calls you make, not how much time passes, will determine when you are reinforced by a sale, and the number of sales calls will vary.
Fixed-interval schedule (reinforcement of first response after a fixed amount of time has passed)	You have an exam coming up, and as time goes by and you haven't studied, you have to make up for it all by a certain time, and that means cramming. Picking up a salary check, which occurs every week or every two weeks.
Variable-interval schedule (reinforcement of first response after varying amounts of time)	Surprise quizzes in a course cause a steady rate of studying because you never know when they'll occur; you have to be prepared all the time. Watching a football game, waiting for a touchdown. It could happen anytime. If you leave the room, you may miss it, so you have to keep watching continuously.

Source: From Landy, 1987, p. 212. Adapted by permission.

then tends to pick up again as the time for the next reinforcement draws near. For example, when exams are given at fixed intervals—like midterms and finals—students tend to decrease their studying right after one test is over and then increase studying as the next test approaches (see **Figure 5–5**).

A **variable-interval schedule** reinforces correct responses after varying lengths of time following the last reinforcement. One reinforcement might be given after 6 minutes, the next after 4 minutes, the next after 5 minutes, and the next after 3 minutes. The learner typically gives a slow, steady pattern of responses, being careful not to be so slow as to miss all the rewards. For example, if exams are given during a semester at unpredictable intervals, students have to keep studying at a steady rate, because on any given day there might be a test.

On a **fixed-ratio schedule,** a certain number of correct responses must occur before reinforcement is provided, resulting in a high response rate because making many responses in a short time yields more rewards. Being paid on a piecework basis is an example of a fixed-ratio schedule. Farmworkers might get $3 for every ten baskets of cherries they pick. The more they pick, the more money they make. Under a fixed-ratio schedule, a brief pause after reinforcement is followed by a rapid and steady response rate until the next reinforcement (see **Figure 5–5**).

On a **variable-ratio schedule,** the number of correct responses needed to gain reinforcement is not constant. The casino slot machine is a good example of a variable-ratio schedule. It will eventually pay off, but you have no idea when. Because there is always a chance of hitting the jackpot, the temptation to keep playing is great. Learners on a variable-ratio schedule tend not to pause after reinforcement and have a high rate of response over a long period of time. Because they never know when reinforcement may come, they keep on testing for a reward.

Variable-interval schedule
A reinforcement schedule in which the correct response is reinforced after varying lengths of time following the last reinforcement.

Fixed-ratio schedule
A reinforcement schedule in which the correct response is reinforced after a fixed number of correct responses.

Variable-ratio schedule
A reinforcement schedule in which a varying number of correct responses must occur before reinforcement is presented.

Extinction and Spontaneous Recovery

Can you ever get rid of a conditioned response? Under what circumstances might old learned associations suddenly reappear?

Another factor shared by classical and operant conditioning is that learned responses sometimes weaken and may even disappear. If a CS and a US are never paired again, or if a consequence always stops following a certain behavior, the learned association will begin to fade until eventually the effects of prior learning are no longer seen. This outcome is called **extinction** of a conditioned response.

Extinction and Spontaneous Recovery in Classical Conditioning   For an example of extinction in classical conditioning, let's go back to Pavlov's dogs, which had learned to salivate upon hearing a bell. What would you predict happened over time when the dogs heard the bell (the CS) but food (the US) was no longer given? The conditioned response to the bell—salivation—gradually decreased until eventually it stopped altogether. The dogs no longer salivated when they heard the bell. Extinction had taken place. Extinction of classically conditioned responses also occurs in your own life. If scary music in films (a CS) is no longer paired with frightening events on the screen (a US), you will eventually stop becoming tense and anxious (a CR) when you hear that kind of music. Your classically conditioned response to the music has undergone extinction.

Once such a response has been extinguished, is the learning gone forever? Pavlov trained his dogs to salivate when they heard a bell, then extinguished this conditioned response. A few days later, the dogs were exposed to the bell again in the laboratory setting. As soon as they heard it,

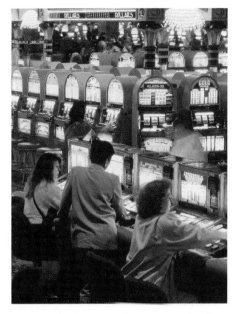

The slot machine is a classic example of a variable-ratio schedule of reinforcement. The machine eventually pays off, but always after a variable number of plays. Because people keep hoping that the next play will be rewarded, they maintain a high rate of response over a long period of time.

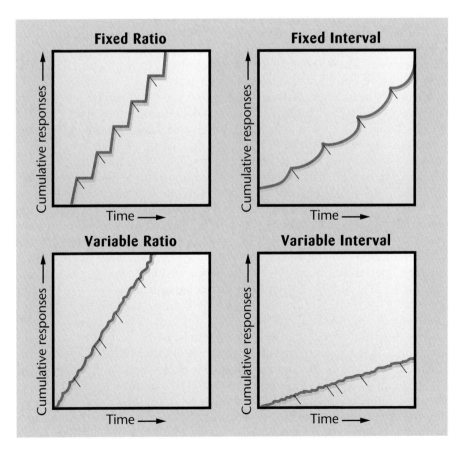

Extinction
A decrease in the strength or frequency, or stopping, of a learned response because of failure to continue pairing the US and CS (classical conditioning) or withholding of reinforcement (operant conditioning).

FIGURE 5–5

Response patterns to schedules of reinforcement. On a fixed-interval schedule, as the time for reinforcement approaches, the number of responses increases, and the slope becomes steeper. On a variable-interval schedule, the response rate is moderate and relatively constant. Notice that each tick mark on the graph represents one reinforcement. The fixed-ratio schedule is characterized by a high rate of response and a pause after each reinforcement. A variable-ratio schedule produces a high rate of response with little or no pause after each reinforcement.

When reinforcement has been frequent, a learned behavior tends to be retained even after reinforcement is reduced. A dog "shaking hands" is an excellent example. Many previous rewards for this response tend to keep the dog offering people its paw even when no reward follows.

their mouths began to water. The response that had been learned and then extinguished reappeared on its own with no retraining. This phenomenon is known as **spontaneous recovery.** The dogs' response was now only about half as strong as it had been before extinction, and it was very easy to extinguish a second time. Nevertheless, the fact that the response occurred at all indicated that the original learning was not completely forgotten. Similarly, if you stop going to the movies for a while, you may find that the next time you go, that scary music once again makes you tense and anxious. A response that was extinguished has returned spontaneously after the passage of time.

How can extinguished behavior disappear, then reappear later? According to Mark Bouton (1993, 1994), the explanation is that extinction does not erase learning. Rather, extinction occurs because new learning interferes with a previously learned response. New stimuli in other settings come to be paired with the conditioned stimulus, and these new stimuli may elicit responses different from (and sometimes incompatible with) the original conditioned response. For example, if you take a break from watching the latest horror movies in theaters and instead watch reruns of classic horror films on television, these classic films may seem so amateurish that they make you laugh rather than scare you. Here you are learning to associate the scary music in such films with laughter, which in effect opposes your original fear response. The result is interference and extinction. Spontaneous recovery consists of overcoming this interference. For instance, if you return to the theater to see the latest Stephen King movie, the conditioned response of fear to the scary music may suddenly reappear. It is as if the unconditioned stimulus of watching "up-to-date" horror acts as a reminder of your earlier learning and renews your previous classically conditioned response. Such "reminder" stimuli work particularly well when presented in the original conditioning setting.

Extinction and Spontaneous Recovery in Operant Conditioning Extinction and spontaneous recovery also occur in operant conditioning. In operant conditioning, extinction happens as a result of withholding reinforcement. The effect usually isn't immediate. In fact, when reinforcement is first discontinued, there is often a brief *increase* in the strength or frequency of responding before a decline sets in. For instance, if you put coins in a vending machine and it fails to deliver the goods, you may pull the lever more forcefully and in rapid succession before you finally give up.

Just as in classical conditioning, extinction in operant conditioning doesn't completely erase what has been learned. Even though much time has passed since a behavior was last rewarded and the behavior seems extinguished, it may suddenly reappear. This spontaneous recovery may again be understood in terms of interference from new behaviors. If a rat is no longer reinforced for pressing a lever, it will start to engage in other behaviors—turning away from the lever, biting at the corners of the Skinner box, attempting to escape, and so on. These new behaviors will interfere with the operant response of lever pressing, causing it to extinguish. Spontaneous recovery is a brief victory of the original learning over interfering responses. The rat decides to give the previous "reward" lever one more try, as if testing again for a reward.

The difficulty of extinguishing an operantly conditioned response depends on a number of factors. One is the strength of the original learning. The stronger the original learning, the longer it takes the response to extinguish. If you spend many hours training a puppy to sit on command, you will not need to reinforce this behavior very often once the dog grows up. The pattern of reinforcement matters also, however, as you learned earlier. Responses that were reinforced only occasionally when acquired are usually more resis-

Spontaneous recovery
The reappearance of an extinguished response after the passage of time, without training.

tant to extinction than responses that were reinforced every time they occurred. Another important factor is the variety of settings in which the original learning took place. The greater the variety of settings, the harder it is to extinguish the response. Rats trained to run several different types of alleys in order to reach a food reward will keep running longer after food is withdrawn than will rats trained in a single alley. Complex behavior, too, is much more difficult to extinguish than simple behavior is. Complex behavior consists of many actions put together, and each of those actions must be extinguished in order for the whole to be extinguished. Finally, behaviors learned through punishment rather than reinforcement are especially hard to extinguish. If you avoid jogging down a particular street because a vicious dog there attacked you, you may never venture down that street again, so your avoidance of the street may never extinguish.

One way to speed up the extinction of an operantly conditioned response is to put the learner in a situation that is different from the one in which the response was originally learned. The response is likely to be weaker in the new situation, and therefore it will extinguish more quickly. Of course, when the learner is returned to the original learning setting after extinction has occurred elsewhere, the response may undergo spontaneous recovery, just as in classical conditioning. But now the response is likely to be weaker than it was initially, and it should be relatively easy to extinguish once and for all. You may have experienced this phenomenon yourself when you returned home for the holidays after your first semester in college. A habit that you thought you had outgrown at school may have suddenly reappeared. The home setting worked as a "reminder" stimulus, encouraging the response, just as we mentioned when discussing classical conditioning. Because you have already extinguished the habit in another setting, however, extinguishing it here shouldn't be difficult.

Stimulus Control, Generalization, and Discrimination

How can anxiety about math in grade school affect a college student? Why do people often slap the wrong card when playing a game of slapjack?

The home setting acting as a "reminder" stimulus is just one example of how conditioned responses are influenced by surrounding cues in the environment. This outcome is called **stimulus control,** and it occurs in both classical and operant conditioning. In classical conditioning, the conditioned response (CR) is under the control of the conditioned stimulus (CS) that triggers it. Salivation, for example, might be controlled by the sound of a bell. In operant conditioning, the learned response is under the control of whatever stimuli come to be associated with delivery of reward or punishment. A leap to avoid electric shock might come under the control of a flashing light, for instance. In both classical and operant conditioning, moreover, the learner may respond to cues that are merely similar (but not identical) to the ones that prevailed during the original learning. This tendency to respond to similar cues is known as **stimulus generalization.**

Generalization and Discrimination in Classical Conditioning There are many examples of stimulus generalization in classical conditioning. One example is the case of Little Albert, who was conditioned to fear white rats. When the experimenters later showed him a white rabbit, he cried and tried to crawl away, even though he had not been taught to fear rabbits. He also showed fear of other white, furry objects—cotton balls, a fur coat, even a bearded Santa Claus mask. Similarly, Pavlov noticed that after his dogs had been conditioned to salivate when they heard a bell, their mouths would often water when they heard a buzzer or the ticking of a metronome. Both Pavlov's dogs and Albert had generalized their learned reactions from rats

Stimulus control
Control of conditioned responses by cues or stimuli in the environment.

Stimulus generalization
The transfer of a learned response to different but similar stimuli.

The skills a person learns in playing tennis may also be utilized in such sports as Ping-Pong, squash, and badmiton. This is an example of stimulus generalization in operant conditioning.

and bells to similar stimuli. In much the same way, a person who learned to feel anxious over math tests in grade school might come to feel anxious about any task involving numbers, even balancing a checkbook.

Stimulus generalization is not inevitable, however. Through a process called **stimulus discrimination,** learners can be trained not to generalize but rather to make a conditioned response only to a single specific stimulus. This process involves presenting several similar stimuli, only one of which is followed by the unconditioned stimulus. For instance, Albert might have been shown a rat, a rabbit, cotton balls, and other white, furry objects, but only the rat would be followed by a loud noise (the US). Given this procedure, Albert would have learned to discriminate the white rat from the other objects, and the fear response would not have generalized as it did.

Learning to discriminate is essential in everyday life. We prefer for children to learn not to fear *every* loud noise, *every* insect, *every* dog, and so forth, but only those that are potentially harmful. Through stimulus discrimination, behavior becomes more finely tuned to the demands of our environment.

Generalization and Discrimination in Operant Conditioning   Stimulus generalization also occurs in operant conditioning. A baby who is hugged and kissed for saying "Mama" when he sees his mother may begin to call everyone "Mama"—males and females alike. Although the person whom the baby sees—the stimulus—changes, he responds with the same word. Similarly, the skills you learn when playing tennis may be generalized to badminton, Ping-Pong, and squash.

In operant conditioning, responses, too, can be generalized, not just stimuli. For example, the baby who calls everyone "Mama" may also call people "Nana." His learning has generalized to other sounds that are similar to the correct response, "Mama." This is called **response generalization.** Response generalization doesn't occur in classical conditioning. If a dog is taught to salivate when it hears a high-pitched tone, it will salivate less when it hears a low-pitched tone, but the response is still salivation.

Just as discrimination is useful in classical conditioning, it is also useful in operant conditioning. Learning *what* to do has little value if you do not know *when* to do it. Learning that a response is triggered is pointless if you do not know which response is right. Discrimination training in operant conditioning consists of reinforcing *only* a specific, desired response and *only* in the presence of a specific stimulus. With this procedure, pigeons have been trained to peck at a red disk but not at a green one. First they are taught to peck at a disk. Then they are presented with two disks, one red and one green. They get food when they peck at the red one but not when they peck at the green. Eventually they learn to discriminate between the two colors, pecking only at the red. In much the same way, children learn to listen to exactly what the teacher is asking before they raise their hands.

New Learning Based on Original Learning

How might you build on a conditioned response to make an even more complex form of learning? Why is money such a good reinforcer for most people?

There are other ways, besides stimulus generalization and discrimination, that original learning can serve as the basis for new learning. In classical conditioning, an existing conditioned stimulus can be paired with a new stimulus to produce a new conditioned response. This is **called higher-order conditioning.** In operant conditioning, objects that have no intrinsic value can nevertheless become reinforcers because of their association with other, more basic reinforcers. These learned reinforcers are called *secondary reinforcers.*

Stimulus discrimination
Learning to respond to only one stimulus and to inhibit the response to all other stimuli.

Response generalization
Giving a response that is somewhat different from the response originally learned to that stimulus.

Higher-order conditioning
Conditioning based on previous learning; the conditioned stimulus serves as an unconditioned stimulus for further training.

Higher-order Conditioning   Pavlov demonstrated higher-order conditioning with his dogs. After the dogs had learned to salivate when they heard a bell, Pavlov used the bell (*without* food) to teach the dogs to salivate at the sight of a black square. Instead of showing them the square and following it with food, he showed them the square and followed it with the bell until the dogs learned to salivate when they saw the square alone. In effect, the bell served as a substitute unconditioned stimulus, and the black square became a new conditioned stimulus. This procedure is known as higher-order conditioning, not because it is more complex than other types of conditioning or because it incorporates any new principles; it is called higher-order simply because it is conditioning based on previous learning.

Higher-order conditioning is difficult to achieve because it is battling against extinction of the original conditioned response. The unconditioned stimulus no longer follows the original conditioned stimulus, and that is precisely the way to extinguish a classically conditioned response. During higher-order conditioning, Pavlov's dogs were exposed to the square followed by the bell, but no food was given. Thus, the square became a signal that the bell would not precede food, and soon all salivation stopped. For higher-order conditioning to succeed, the unconditioned stimulus must be occasionally reintroduced. Food must be given once in a while after the bell sounds so that the dogs will continue to salivate when they hear the bell.

Secondary Reinforcers   Some reinforcers, such as food, water, and sex, are intrinsically rewarding in and of themselves. These are called **primary reinforcers.** No prior learning is required to make them reinforcing. Other reinforcers have no intrinsic value. They have acquired value only through association with primary reinforcers. These are the **secondary reinforcers** we mentioned earlier. They are called secondary not because they are less important but because prior learning is needed before they will function as reinforcers. Suppose a rat learns to get food by pressing a bar; then a buzzer is sounded every time food drops into the dish. Even if the rat stops getting the food, it will continue to press the bar for a while just to hear the buzzer. Although the buzzer by itself has no intrinsic value to the rat, it has become a secondary reinforcer through association with food, a primary reinforcer.

Note how, in creating a secondary reinforcer, classical conditioning is involved. Because it has been paired with an intrinsically pleasurable stimulus, a formerly neutral stimulus comes to elicit pleasure, too. This stimulus can then serve as a reinforcer to establish an operantly conditioned response.

For humans, money is one of the best examples of a secondary reinforcer. Although money is just paper or metal, through its exchange value for food, clothing, and other primary reinforcers, it becomes a powerful reinforcer. Children come to value money only after they learn that it will buy such things as candy (a primary reinforcer). Then the money becomes a secondary reinforcer. And through the principles of higher-order conditioning, stimuli paired with a secondary reinforcer can acquire reinforcing properties. Checks and credit cards, for example, are one step removed from money, but they can also be highly reinforcing.

Summing Up

Does operant conditioning ever look like classical conditioning?

Classical and operant conditioning both entail forming associations between stimuli and responses, and perceiving contingencies between one event and another. Both are subject to extinction and spontaneous recovery, as well as to stimulus control, generalization, and discrimination. The main difference between the two is that in classical conditioning, the learner is passive and the behavior involved is usually involuntary, whereas

Primary reinforcer
A reinforcer that is rewarding in itself, such as food, water, and sex.

Secondary reinforcer
A reinforcer whose value is acquired through association with other primary or secondary reinforcers.

in operant conditioning, the learner is active and the behavior involved is usually voluntary. Some psychologists downplay these differences, however, suggesting that classical and operant conditioning are simply two different ways of bringing about the same kind of learning. For example, once an operant response becomes linked to a stimulus, it looks very much like a conditioned response in classical conditioning. If you have been reinforced repeatedly for stepping on the brake when a traffic light turns red, the red light comes to elicit braking just as the sound of a bell elicited salivation in Pavlov's dogs. Classical and operant conditioning, then, may simply be two different procedures for achieving the same end (Hearst, 1975). If so, psychologists may have overstressed the differences between them and paid too little attention to what they have in common.

INTERACTIVE LECTURE **5.3**

WEB QUIZ **5.3** ✓

CHECK YOUR UNDERSTANDING

1. Identify the following schedules of reinforcement as fixed interval (FI), variable interval (VI), fixed ratio (FR), and variable ratio (VR).
    a. Reinforcement comes on the first correct response after 2 minutes have passed since the last reinforcement. _____
    b. Reinforcement comes on every sixth correct response. _____
    c. Reinforcement comes after 4 correct responses, then after 6 more, then after 5 more. _____
    d. Reinforcement comes after varying lengths of time following the last reinforcement. _____
2. To extinguish a classically conditioned response, you must break the association between which pair?
    a. CS and US
    b. US and UR
    c. US and CR
3. After extinction and a period of rest, a conditioned response may suddenly reappear. This phenomenon is called _____ _____.
4. The process by which a learned response to a specific stimulus comes to be associated with different but similar stimuli is known as _____ _____.
5. Classify the following as primary (P) or secondary (S) reinforcers.
    a. food _____
    b. money _____
    c. college diploma _____
    d. sex _____

Answers: 1. a. (FI), b. (FR), c. (VR), d. (VI). 2. a. 3. spontaneous recovery. 4. stimulus generalization. 5. a. (P), b. (S), c. (S), d. (P).

Cognitive Learning

How would you study the kind of learning that occurs when you memorize the layout of a chessboard?

Some psychologists insist that because classical and operant conditioning can be *observed* and *measured*, they are the only legitimate kinds of learning to study scientifically. But others contend that mental activities are crucial to learning and so can't be ignored. How do you grasp the layout of a building from someone else's description of it? How do you know how to hold a tennis racket just from watching a game of tennis being played? How do you enter into memory abstract concepts like *conditioning* and *reinforcement*? You do all these things and many others through **cognitive learning**—the mental processes that go on inside us when we learn. Cognitive learning is impossible to observe and measure directly, but it can be *inferred* from behavior, and so it is also a legitimate topic for scientific study.

Latent Learning and Cognitive Maps

Did you learn your way around campus solely through operant conditioning (rewards for correct turns, punishments for wrong ones), or was something more involved?

Interest in cognitive learning began shortly after the earliest work in classical and operant conditioning. In the 1930s, Edward Chace Tolman, one of the pioneers in the study of cognitive learning, argued that we do not need to show our learning in order for learning to have occurred. Tolman called learning that isn't apparent because it is not yet demonstrated **latent learning.**

Tolman studied latent learning in a famous experiment (Tolman & Honzik, 1930). Two groups of hungry rats were placed in a maze and allowed to find their way from a start box to an end box. The first group found food pellets (a reward) in the end box; the second group found nothing there. According to the principles of operant conditioning, the first group would learn the maze better than the second group—which is, indeed, what happened. But when Tolman took some of the rats from the second, unreinforced group and started to give them food at the goal box, almost immediately they ran the maze as well as the rats in the first group (see **Figure 5–6**). Tolman argued that the unrewarded rats had actually learned a great deal about the maze as they wandered around inside it. In fact, they may have even learned *more* about it than the rats that had been trained with food rewards, but their learning was *latent*—stored internally but not yet reflected in their behavior. It was not until they were given a motivation to run the maze that they put their latent learning to use.

Since Tolman's time, much work has been done on the nature of latent learning regarding spatial layouts and relationships. From studies of how animals or humans find their way around a maze, a building, or a neighborhood with many available routes, psychologists have proposed that this kind of learning is stored in the form of a mental image, or **cognitive map.** When the proper time comes, the learner can call up the stored image and put it to use.

In response to Tolman's theory of latent learning, Thorndike proposed an experiment to test whether a rat could learn to run a maze and store a cognitive image of the maze without experiencing the maze firsthand. He envisioned researchers carrying each rat through the maze in a small wire-mesh container and then rewarding the rat at the end of each trial as if it had run the maze itself. He predicted that the rat would show little or no evidence of learning as compared with rats that had learned the same maze on their own through trial and error. Neither he nor Tolman ever conducted the experiment.

Two decades later, however, researchers at the University of Kansas did carry out Thorndike's idea (McNamara, Long, & Wike, 1956). But instead of taking the passive rats through the "correct" path, they carried them over the same path that a free-running rat had taken in that maze. Contrary to Thorndike's prediction, the passenger rats learned the maze just as well as the free-running rats. They did, however, need visual cues to learn the maze's layout. If carried through the maze only in the dark, they later showed little latent learning.

Cognitive learning
Learning that depends on mental processes that are not directly observable.

Latent learning
Learning that is not immediately reflected in a behavior change.

Cognitive map
A learned mental image of a spatial environment that may be called on to solve problems when stimuli in the environment change.

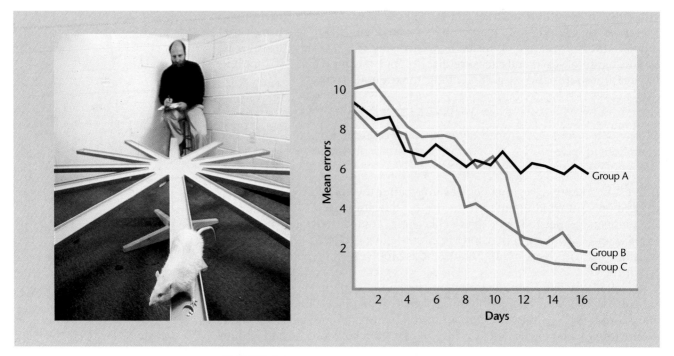

FIGURE 5–6

Maze used to study latent learning in rats. The results of the classic Tolman-Honzik study are revealed in the graph. Group A never received a food reward. Group B was rewarded each day. Group C was not rewarded until the eleventh day, but note the significant change in the rats' behavior on Day 12. The results suggest that Group C had been learning all along, although this learning was not reflected in their performance until they were rewarded with food for demonstrating the desired behaviors.

Source: From Tolman & Honzik, 1930.

More recent research confirms this picture of cognitive spatial learning. Animals show a great deal more flexibility in solving problems like mazes than can be explained by simple conditioning (Domjan, 1987). In a series of experiments with rats in a radial maze, the rats consistently recalled which arms they had previously traveled down and which they hadn't, even when scent cues were removed and all arms contained a reward. These rats had developed a cognitive map not only of the maze's layout but also of their experiences in it, too (Olton & Samuelson, 1976). Even in rats, learning involves more than just a new behavior "stamped in" through reinforcement. It also involves the formation of new mental images and constructs that may be reflected in future behavior.

Insight and Learning Sets

Do you have a learning set for writing a term paper?

During World War I, the German Gestalt psychologist Wolfgang Köhler conducted a series of studies into another aspect of cognitive learning—sudden **insight** into a problem's solution. Outside a chimpanzee's cage, Köhler placed a banana on the ground, not quite within the animal's reach. When the chimp realized that it couldn't reach the banana, it reacted with frustration. But then it started looking at what was in the cage, including a stick left there by Köhler. Sometimes quite suddenly the chimp would grab the stick, poke it through the bars of the cage, and drag the banana within

Insight
Learning that occurs rapidly as a result of understanding all the elements of a problem.

reach. The same kind of sudden insight occurred when the banana was hung from the roof of the cage, too high for the chimp to grasp. This time the cage contained some boxes, which the chimp quickly learned to stack up under the banana so that it could climb up to pull the fruit down. Subsequent studies have shown that even pigeons can solve the box-and-banana problem through insight if they are properly motivated, given the right tools, and taught how to use them (R. Epstein et al., 1984).

Previous learning can often be used to help solve problems through insight. This was demonstrated by Harry Harlow in a series of studies with rhesus monkeys (Harlow, 1949). Harlow presented each monkey with two boxes—say, a round green box on the left side of a tray and a square red box on the right side. A morsel of food was put under one of the boxes. The monkey was permitted to lift just one box; if it chose the correct box, it got the food. On the next trial, the food was put under the same box (which had been moved to a new position), and the monkey again got to choose just one box. Each monkey had six trials to figure out that the same box covered the food no matter where that box was located. Then the monkeys were given a new set of choices—say, between a blue triangular box and an orange oval one—and another six trials, and so on with other shapes and colors of boxes. The solution was always the same: The food was invariably under only one of the boxes. Initially the monkeys chose boxes randomly, sometimes finding the food, sometimes not. After a while, however, their behavior changed: In just one or two trials, they would find the correct box, which they chose consistently thereafter until the experimenter changed the boxes. They seemed to have learned the underlying principle—that the food would always be under the same box—and they used that learning to solve almost instantly each new set of choices given.

Harlow concluded that the monkeys "learned how to learn," that is, they had established a **learning set** regarding this problem: Within the limited range of choices available to them, they had discovered how to tell which box would give the reward. Similarly, Köhler's chimps could be said to have established a learning set regarding how to get food that was just out of reach. When presented with a new version of the problem, they simply called upon past learning in a slightly different situation (reaching a banana on the ground versus reaching one hanging from the ceiling). In both Harlow's and Köhler's studies, the animals seemed to have learned more than just specific behaviors—they had apparently learned *how* to learn. Whether this means that animals can think is an issue still being debated.

Human Insight Insightful learning is particularly important in humans, who must learn not only where to obtain food and how to escape from predators but also such complex ethical and cultural ideas as the value of working hard, helping others, overcoming addictions, or dealing with a life crisis. In Chapter 7 (Cognition and Mental Abilities), we will explore the role of insight in creative problem solving. As we will see, there are times when all other problem-solving techniques fail to produce a solution; in such cases, it is not unusual for the solution suddenly to "pop up" in a moment of insight. Moreover, once people gain insight into their own behavior, they should be capable of changing significantly over the course of their lives (Bornstein & Masling, 1998). Indeed, as we will see in Chapter 13 (Therapies), the common goal of the various insight therapies, such as psychoanalysis, is to give people a better awareness and understanding of their feelings, motivations, and actions in the hope that this will lead to better adjustment (Pine, 1998).

Köhler's experiments with chimpanzees illustrate learning through insight. In this photo one of the chimps has arranged a stack of boxes to reach bananas hanging from the ceiling. Insights gained in this problem-solving situation may transfer to similar ones.

Learning set
The ability to become increasingly more effective in solving problems as more problems are solved.

In observational or vicarious learning, we learn by watching a model perform a particular action and then trying to imitate that action correctly. Some actions would be very difficult to master without observational learning.

Learning by Observing

Why would it be harder to learn to drive a car if you had never been in one before? Why is it hard for deaf children to learn spoken language when they can easily be reinforced for correct speech sounds?

The first time you drove a car, you successfully turned the key in the ignition, put the car in gear, and pressed the gas pedal without having ever done any of those things before. How were you able to do that without step-by-step shaping of the correct behaviors? The answer is that you had often watched other people driving, a practice that made all the difference. There are countless things we learn by watching other people and listening to what they say. This process is called **observational** or **vicarious learning,** because although we are learning, we don't have to do the learned behaviors firsthand; we merely look or listen. Observational learning is a form of "social learning" because it involves interaction with other people. Psychologists who study it are known as **social learning theorists.**

Observational learning is very common. By watching other people who model new behaviors, we can learn such things as how to start a lawn mower and how to saw wood. We also learn how to show love or respect or concern, as well as how to show hostility and aggression. We can even learn bad habits, such as smoking. When the Federal Communications Commission (FCC) banned cigarette commercials on television, it was acting on the belief that providing models of smokers would prompt people to imitate smoking. The FCC removed the models to discourage the behavior.

Of course, we do not imitate *everything* that other people do. Why are we selective in our imitation? There are several reasons (Bandura, 1977, 1986). First, we can't pay attention to everything going on around us. The behaviors we are most likely to imitate are those that are modeled by someone who commands our attention (as does a famous or an attractive person or an expert). Second, we must remember what a model does in order to imitate it. If a behavior isn't memorable, it won't be learned. Third, we must make an effort to convert what we see into action. If we have no motivation to perform an observed behavior, we probably won't show what we've learned. This is a distinction between *learning* and *performance,* which is crucial to social learning theorists: We can learn without any change in overt behavior that demonstrates our learning. Whether or not we act depends on our motivation.

One important motivation for acting is the kind of consequences associated with an observed behavior—the rewards or punishments it appears to bring. These consequences do not necessarily have to happen to the observer. They may happen simply to the other people whom the observer is watching. This is called **vicarious reinforcement** or **vicarious punishment,** because the consequences aren't experienced firsthand by the learner; they are experienced *through* other people. If a young teenager sees adults drinking and they seem to be having a great deal of fun, the teenager is experiencing vicarious reinforcement of drinking and is much more likely to imitate it.

The foremost proponent of social learning theory is Albert Bandura, who refers to his perspective as a *social cognitive theory* (Bandura, 1986). In a classic experiment, Bandura (1965) showed that people can learn a behavior without being reinforced directly for it and that learning a behavior and performing it are not the same thing. Three groups of nursery schoolchildren watched a film in which an adult model walked up to an adult-size plastic inflated doll and ordered it to move out of the way. When the doll failed to obey, the model became aggressive, pushing the doll on its side, punching it in the nose, hitting it with a rubber mallet, kicking it around

Observational (or vicarious) learning
Learning by observing other people's behavior.

Social learning theorists
Psychologists whose view of learning emphasizes the ability to learn by observing a model or receiving instructions, without firsthand experience by the learner.

Vicarious reinforcement or vicarious punishment
Reinforcement or punishment experienced by models that affects the willingness of others to perform the behaviors they learned by observing those models.

the room, and throwing rubber balls at it. However, each group of children saw a film with a different ending. Those in the *model-rewarded condition* saw the model showered with candies, soft drinks, and praise by a second adult (vicarious reinforcement). Those in the *model-punished condition* saw the second adult shaking a finger at the model, scolding, and spanking him (vicarious punishment). And those in the *no-consequences condition* saw nothing happen to the model as a result of his aggressive behavior.

Immediately after seeing the film, the children were individually escorted into another room where they found the same large inflated doll, rubber balls, and mallet, as well as many other toys. Each child played alone for 10 minutes, while observers behind a one-way mirror recorded the number of imitated aggressive behaviors that the child spontaneously performed in the absence of any direct reinforcement for those actions. After 10 minutes, an experimenter entered the room and offered the child treats in return for imitating things the model had done. This was a measure of how much the child had previously learned from watching the model but perhaps hadn't yet displayed.

The green bars in **Figure 5–7** show that *all* the children had learned aggressive actions from watching the model, even though they were not overtly reinforced for that learning. When later offered treats to copy the model's actions, they all did so quite accurately. In addition, the yellow bars in the figure show that the children tended to suppress their inclination spontaneously to imitate an aggressive model when they had seen that model punished for aggression. This result was especially true of girls. Apparently, vicarious punishment provided the children with information about what might happen to them if they copied the "bad" behavior. Vicar-

Bandura's experiment in learned aggressive behavior.

After watching an adult behave aggressively toward an inflated doll, the children in Bandura's study imitated many of the aggressive acts of the adult model.

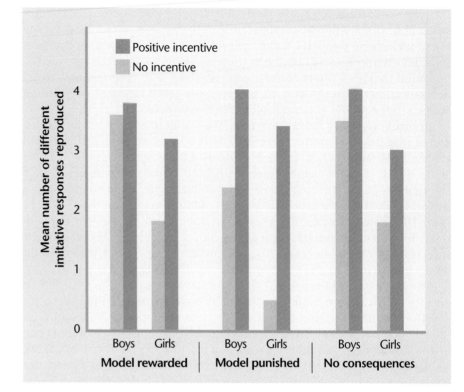

FIGURE 5–7

Results of Bandura's study. As the graph shows, even though all the children in Bandura's study of imitative aggression learned the model's behavior, they performed differently depending on whether the model whom they saw was rewarded or punished.

Source: A. Bandura, Influence of models' reinforcement contingencies on the acquisition of imitative responses, *Journal of Personality and Social Psychology, 1,* 592. Copyright © 1965 by the American Psychological Association. Reprinted by permission.

ious reinforcement similarly provides information about likely consequences, but in this study, its effects were not large. For children of this age (at least those not worried about punishment), imitating aggressive behavior toward a doll seems to have been considered "fun" in its own right, even without being associated with praise and candy. This outcome was especially true for boys.

This study has important implications regarding how not to teach aggression unintentionally to children. Suppose that you want to get a child to stop hitting other children. You might think that slapping the child as punishment would change the behavior, and it probably would suppress it to some extent. But slapping the child also demonstrates that hitting is an effective means of getting one's way. So slapping not only provides a model of aggression; it also provides a model associated with vicarious reinforcement. You and the child would both be better off if the punishment given for hitting was not a similar form of aggression and if the child could also be rewarded for showing appropriate interactions with others (Bandura, 1973, 1977).

Social learning theory's emphasis on expectations, insights, and information broadens our understanding of how people learn. According to social learning theory, humans use their powers of observation and thought to interpret their own experiences and those of others when deciding how to act (Bandura, 1962). This important perspective can be applied to the learning of many different things, from skills and behavioral tendencies to attitudes, values, and ideas.

INTERACTIVE LECTURE **5.4**

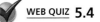
WEB QUIZ 5.4

CHECK YOUR UNDERSTANDING

1. An ape examines a problem and the tools available for solving it. Suddenly the animal leaps up and quickly executes a successful solution. This is an example of
   a. insight.
   b. operant conditioning.
   c. trial-and-error learning.

2. Match the following terms with the appropriate definition.

   ____ latent learning
   ____ insight
   ____ observational learning

   a. new, suddenly occurring idea to solve a problem
   b. learning by watching a model
   c. learning that has not yet been demonstrated in behavior

3. The view of learning that emphasizes the ability to learn through watching what happens to other people or by hearing about something is called _____ _____ _____.

4. If a person increases her behavior because she saw someone rewarded for that behavior, the reward is called _____ _____.

5. "Social learning theory broadens our understanding of how people learn skills and gain abilities by emphasizing expectations, insight, information, self-satisfaction, and self-criticism." Is this statement true (T) or false (F)?

6. "Social learning theory supports spanking as an effective way to teach children not to hit." Is this statement true (T) or false (F)?

Answers: 1. a. 2. latent learning (c); insight (a); observational learning (b). 3. social learning theory. 4. vicarious reinforcement. 5. (T). 6. (F).

KEY TERMS

learning, p. 165
classical (or Pavlovian) conditioning, p. 165

Classical conditioning
unconditioned stimulus (US), p. 166
unconditioned response (UR), p. 166
conditioned stimulus (CS), p. 166
conditioned response (CR), p. 166
intermittent pairing, p. 168
desensitization therapy, p. 168
preparedness, p. 169
conditioned taste aversion, p. 169

Operant conditioning
operant (or instrumental) conditioning, p. 170
operant behavior, p. 171
reinforcer, p. 171
punishers, p. 171
law of effect (principle of reinforcement), p. 171
Skinner box, p. 173
shaping, p. 173
positive reinforcer, p. 175
negative reinforcer, p. 175
biofeedback, p. 175
punishment, p. 177
avoidance training, p. 178
learned helplessness, p. 178

Factors shared by classical and operant conditioning
contingency, p. 180

blocking, p. 181
schedule of reinforcement, p. 181
fixed-interval schedule, p. 181
variable-interval schedule, p. 182
fixed-ratio schedule, p. 182
variable-ratio schedule, p. 182
extinction, p. 183
spontaneous recovery, p. 184
stimulus control, p. 185
stimulus generalization, p. 185
stimulus discrimination, p. 186
response generalization, p. 186

higher-order conditioning, p. 186
primary reinforcer, p. 187
secondary reinforcer, p. 187

Cognitive learning
cognitive learning, p. 189
latent learning, p. 189
cognitive map, p. 189
insight, p. 190
learning set, p. 191
observational (or vicarious) learning, p. 192
social learning theorists, p. 192
vicarious reinforcement or vicarious punishment, p. 192

CHAPTER REVIEW

Classical Conditioning

How did Pavlov discover classical conditioning? Learning is the process by which experience or practice produces a relatively permanent change in behavior or potential behavior. One basic form of learning involves learning to associate one event with another. **Classical conditioning** is a type of associative learning that Pavlov discovered while studying digestion. Pavlov trained a dog to salivate at the sound of a bell when he rang the bell just before food was given. The dog learned to associate the bell with food and began to salivate at the sound of the bell alone.

How might you classically condition a pet? Suppose you wanted to classically condition salivation in your own dog. You know that food is an **unconditioned stimulus (US)** that automatically evokes the **unconditioned response (UR)** of salivation. By repeatedly pairing food with a second, initially neutral stimulus (such as a bell) that doesn't at first cause salivation, the second stimulus would eventually become a **conditioned stimulus (CS)** for a **conditioned response (CR)** of salivation.

If you once burned your finger on a match while listening to a certain song, why doesn't that song now make you reflexively jerk your hand away? It is usually easier to establish a classically conditioned response if the US and CS are paired with each other repeatedly, rather than just being paired a single time, or even once in a while **(intermittent pairing).** That is why a single burn to your finger is not usually enough to produce a classically conditioned response. It is also important that the spacing of pairings be neither too far apart nor too close together.

What is an example of classical conditioning in your own life? John Watson conditioned a little boy, Albert, to fear white rats by making a loud, frightening noise every time the boy was shown a rat. In your own life you may have acquired a classically conditioned fear or anxiety (to the sound of a dentist's drill, for instance) in much the same way. Perhaps you have also unlearned a conditioned fear by repeatedly pairing the feared object with something pleasant. Mary Cover Jones pioneered this procedure by pairing the sight of a feared rat (at gradually decreasing distances) with a child's pleasant experience of eating candy. This procedure evolved into **desensitization therapy.**

Why are people more likely to develop a phobia of snakes than of flowers? Martin Seligman has used the concept of **preparedness** to account for the fact that certain conditioned responses are acquired very easily. The ease with which we develop **conditioned taste aversions** illustrates preparedness. Because animals are biologically prepared to learn them, conditioned taste aversions can occur with only one pairing of the taste of a tainted food and later illness, and even when there is a lengthy interval between eating the food and becoming ill. A fear of snakes may also be something that humans are prepared to learn.

Operant Conditioning

How are operant behaviors different from the responses involved in classical conditioning? Operant or **instrumental conditioning** is learning to make or withhold a certain response because of its consequences. **Operant behaviors** are different from the responses involved in classical conditioning because they are voluntarily emitted, whereas those involved in classical conditioning are elicited by stimuli.

What two essential elements are involved in operant conditioning? One essential element in operant conditioning is an operant behavior, or a behavior performed by one's own volition while "operating" on the environment. The second essential element is a consequence associated with that operant behavior. When a consequence increases the likelihood of an operant behavior's being emitted, it is called a **reinforcer.** When a consequence decreases the likelihood of an operant behavior, it is called a **punisher.** These relationships are the basis of the **law of effect,** or **principle of reinforcement:** Consistently rewarded behaviors are likely to be repeated, whereas consistently punished behaviors are likely to be suppressed.

How might a speech therapist teach the sound of "s" to a child with a lisp? To speed up establishing an operantly conditioned response in the laboratory, the number of potential responses may be reduced by restricting the environment, as in a **Skinner box.** For behaviors outside the laboratory, which cannot be controlled so conveniently, the process of **shaping** is often useful. In shaping, reinforcement is given for successive approximations to the desired response. A speech therapist might use shaping to teach a child to pronounce a certain sound correctly.

What is the difference between positive and negative reinforcement? What are some of the unintentional effects that reinforcement can have? There are several kinds of reinforcers, all of which strengthen behavior.

Positive reinforcers (like food) increase the likelihood of a behavior by adding something rewarding to a situation. **Negative reinforcers** (such as stopping an electric shock) increase the likelihood of a behavior by subtracting something unpleasant. When an action is followed closely by a reinforcer, we tend to repeat the action, even if it did not actually produce the reinforcement. Such behaviors are called superstitious.

What problems can punishment create? **Punishment** is any event that decreases the likelihood that the behavior that precedes it will occur again. Whereas negative reinforcement strengthens behavior, punishment weakens it. Although punishment can be effective, it also has drawbacks, such as stirring up negative feelings and sometimes modeling aggressive behavior. Also, punishment doesn't teach a more desirable response; it only suppresses an undesirable one. Sometimes, after punishment has been given a few times, it needn't be continued because the threat of it is enough. This process is called **avoidance training.**

In what ways do some college students exhibit learned helplessness? When people or other animals are unable to escape from a punishing situation, they may acquire a "giving up" response, called **learned helplessness.** Learned helplessness can generalize to new situations, causing resignation in the face of unpleasant outcomes, even when the outcomes can be avoided. A college student who gives up trying to do well in school after a few poor grades on tests is exhibiting learned helplessness.

Factors Shared by Classical and Operant Conditioning

Can you think of any similarities between classical and operant conditioning? A number of factors characterize both classical conditioning and operant conditioning: (1) both involve learned associations; (2) in both cases, responses come under control of stimuli in the environment; (3) in both cases, the responses will gradually disappear if they are not periodically renewed; and (4) in both cases, new behaviors can build upon previously established ones.

How can changes in the timing of a conditioned stimulus lead to unexpected learning? Why does intermittent reinforcement result in such persistent behavior? In both classical and operant conditioning, an "if-then" relationship, or **contingency,** exists either between two stimuli or between a stimulus and a response. In both these kinds of learning, perceived contingencies are very important.

In classical conditioning the contingency is between the CS and the US. The CS comes to be viewed as a signal that the US is about to happen. For that reason, the CS must not only occur in close proximity to the US but must also precede the US and provide predictive information about it. If the CS occurs *after* the US, it will come to serve as a signal that the US is over, not that the US is imminent.

In operant conditioning, contingencies exist between responses and consequences. Contingencies between responses and rewards are called **schedules of reinforcement.** *Partial reinforcement,* in which rewards are given for some correct responses but not for every one, generates behavior that persists longer than behavior learned by continuous reinforcement. This is the case because partial reinforcement encourages learners to keep "testing" for a reward. The type of partial reinforcement schedule also matters. A **fixed-interval schedule,** by which reinforcement is given for the first correct response after a fixed time period, tends to result in a flurry of responding right before a reward is due. A **variable-interval schedule,** which reinforces the first correct response after an unpredictable period of time, tends to result in a slow but steady pattern of responding as the learner keeps testing for the next payoff. In a **fixed-ratio schedule,** behavior is rewarded after a fixed number of correct responses, so the result is usually a high rate of responding because faster responses yield quicker payoffs. Finally, **a variable-ratio schedule** provides reinforcement after a varying number of correct responses. It encourages a high rate of response that is especially persistent because the person keeps harboring the hope that the next response will bring a reward.

Can you ever get rid of a conditioned response? Under what circumstances might old learned associations suddenly reappear? Another factor shared by classical and operant conditioning is that learned responses sometimes weaken and may even disappear, a phenomenon called **extinction.** The learning is not necessarily completely forgotten, however. Sometimes a **spontaneous recovery** occurs, in which the learned response suddenly reappears on its own, with no retraining.

Extinction is produced in classical conditioning by failure to continue pairing the CS and the US. The CS no longer serves as a signal that the US is about to happen, and so the conditioned response dies out. An important contributing factor is often new learned associations that interfere with the old one. In situations in which you are reminded of the old association, spontaneous recovery may occur.

Extinction occurs in operant conditioning when reinforcement is withheld until the learned response is no longer emitted. The ease with which an operantly conditioned behavior is extinguished varies according to several factors: the strength of the original learning, the variety of settings in which learning took place, and the schedule of reinforcement used during conditioning. Especially hard to extinguish is behavior learned through punishment.

How can anxiety about math in grade school affect a college student? Why do people often slap the wrong card when playing a game of slapjack? When conditioned responses are influenced by surrounding cues in the environment, **stimulus control** occurs. The tendency to respond to cues that are similar, but not identical, to those that prevailed during the original learning is known as **stimulus generalization. Stimulus discrimination** enables learners to perceive differences among cues so as not to respond to all of them.

In classical conditioning, the conditioned response (CR) is under the control of the conditioned stimulus (CS) that triggers it. An example of stimulus generalization in classical conditioning is a student's feeling anxious about studying math in college because he or she had a bad experience learning math in grade school.

In operant conditioning, the learned response is under the control of whatever cues come to be associated with delivery of reward or punishment. Learners often generalize about these cues, responding to others that are broadly similar to the ones that prevailed during the original learning. An example is slapping any face card in a game of slapjack. Learners may also generalize their responses by performing behaviors that are similar to the ones that were originally reinforced. This result is called **response generalization.** Discrimination in operant conditioning is taught by reinforcing only a certain response and only in the presence of a certain stimulus.

How might you build on a conditioned response to make an even more complex form of learning? Why is money such a good reinforcer for most people? In both classical and operant conditioning, original learning serves as a building block for new learning. In classical conditioning, an earlier conditioned stimulus can be used as an unconditioned stimulus for further training. For example, Pavlov used the bell to condition his dogs to salivate at the sight of a black square. This effect, which is called **higher-order conditioning,** is difficult to achieve because of extinction. Unless the original unconditioned stimulus is presented occasionally, the initial conditioned response will die out.

In operant conditioning, initially neutral stimuli can become reinforcers by being associated with other reinforcers. A **primary reinforcer** is one that, like food and water, is rewarding in and of itself. A **secondary reinforcer** is one whose value is learned through its association with primary reinforcers or with other secondary reinforcers. Money is such a good secondary reinforcer because it can be exchanged for so many different primary and secondary rewards.

Does operant conditioning ever look like classical conditioning? Despite their differences, classical and operant conditioning share many similarities: Both involve associations between stimuli and responses; both are subject to extinction and spontaneous recovery as well as generalization and discrimination; in both, new learning can be based on original learning. Many psychologists now wonder whether classical and operant conditioning aren't just two ways of bringing about the same kind of learning.

Cognitive Learning

How would you study the kind of learning that occurs when you memorize the layout of a chessboard? **Cognitive learning** refers to the mental processes that go on inside us when we learn. Some kinds of learning, such as memorizing the layout of a chessboard, seem to be purely cognitive, because the learner does not appear to be "behaving" while the learning takes place. Cognitive learning, however, can always affect future behavior, such as reproducing the layout of a memorized chessboard after it is cleared away. It is from such observable behavior that cognitive learning is inferred.

Did you learn your way around campus solely through operant conditioning (rewards for correct turns, punishments for wrong ones), or was something more involved? **Latent learning** is any knowledge we acquire that has not yet been demonstrated in behavior. Your knowledge of psychology is latent if you have not yet displayed it in what you say, write, and do. One kind of latent learning is knowledge of spatial layouts and relationships, which is usually stored in the form of a **cognitive map.** Rewards or punishments aren't essential for latent learning to take place. You did not need rewards and punishments to learn the layout of your campus, for example. You acquired this cognitive map simply by storing your visual perceptions.

Do you have a learning set for writing a term paper? A **learning set** is a concept or procedure that provides a key to solving a problem even when its demands are slightly different from those of problems you have solved in the past. As a student, you probably have a learning set for writing a term paper that allows you successfully to develop papers on many different topics. A learning set can sometimes encourage **insight,** or the sudden perception of a solution even to a problem that at first seems totally new. In this case, you are perceiving similarities between old and new problems that weren't initially apparent.

Why would it be harder to learn to drive a car if you had never been in one before? Why is it hard for deaf children to learn spoken language when they can easily be reinforced for correct speech sounds? **Social learning**

theorists argue that we learn much by observing other people who model a behavior or by simply hearing about something. This process is called **observational (or vicarious)** learning. It would be harder to learn to drive a car without ever having been in one because you would lack a model of "driving behavior." It is hard for deaf children to learn spoken language because they have no auditory model of correct speech.

The extent to which we imitate behaviors learned through observation depends on our motivation to do so. One important motivation is any reward or punishment that we have seen the behavior bring. When a consequence isn't experienced firsthand, but only occurs to other people, it is called **vicarious reinforcement** or **vicarious punishment.**

CRITICAL THINKING AND APPLICATIONS

1. Imagine biting into a slice of lemon. Your mouth probably starts to pucker, and you begin to secrete saliva, even though you are not actually experiencing the sour lemon taste. Use classical conditioning principles to explain this reaction.

2. Imagine that you want to keep your dog from barking and annoying the neighbors. What kind of reinforcement would you use to do this?

3. Think about your daily schedule. What kinds of things do you do every day that can be called operant behaviors?

4. Are secondary reinforcers the same for everyone? Explain your answer.

5. What attitudes about introductory psychology have you learned from observing your instructor? On the basis of what you have read, would you recommend biofeedback to someone who suffers from motion sickness or headaches? Why, or why not?

WEB QUIZ 5.5   Go to the Morris 6e Companion Website to take a practice chapter exam.

Memory

THE WORLD-RENOWNED CONDUCTOR ARTURO TOSCANINI MEMORIZED EVERY single note written for every instrument in some 250 symphonies and all the music and lyrics for more than 100 operas. Once, when he could not locate a score of Joachim Raff's Quartet No. 5, he sat down and reproduced it entirely from memory—even though he had not seen or played the score for decades. When a copy of the quartet turned up, people were astonished to discover that with the exception of a single note, Toscanini had reproduced it perfectly (Neisser, 1982).

A waiter named John Conrad routinely handled parties of 6 to 8 in a busy Colorado restaurant, remembering every order from soup to salad dressing, without writing them down. He once waited on a party of 19, serving 19 complete dinners to his customers without a single error (Singular, 1982).

Before being stricken with a viral illness, a 29-year-old woman known as MZ told researchers she could remember "the exact day of the week of future or past events of almost anything that touched my life . . . all personal telephone numbers . . . colors of interiors and what people wore . . . pieces of music . . . recalling a picture, as a painting in a museum, was like standing in the museum looking at it again" (Klatzky, 1980).

Accounts of people with extraordinary memories raise many questions about the nature of **memory** itself (see Wilding & Valentine, 1997): Why are some people so much better at remembering things than others? Are they simply born with this ability, or could any of us learn to remember as much as they do? And why is it that remembering may sometimes be so simple (think how effortlessly baseball fans remember the batting averages of their favorite players) and other times so difficult (as when we grope for answers on an exam)? Why do we find it so hard to remember something that happened only a few months back, yet we can recall in vivid detail some other event that happened 10, 20, even 30 years ago? Just how does memory work, and what makes it fail?

Among the first to seek scientific answers to these questions was the nineteenth-century German psychologist Hermann Ebbinghaus. Using himself as a subject, Ebbinghaus composed lists of "nonsense syllables," meaningless combinations of letters, such as PIB, WOL, or TEB. He memorized lists of 13 nonsense syllables each. Then, after varying amounts of time, he relearned each list of syllables. He found that the longer he waited after first learning a list, the longer it took to learn the list again. Most of the information was lost in the first few hours. Ebbinghaus's contributions dominated memory research for many years.

Today many psychologists find it useful to think about memory as a series of steps in which we process information, much as a computer stores and retrieves data (Massaro & Cowan, 1993). Together, these steps form what is known as the **information-processing model** of memory. In this chapter, you will find terms like *encoding, storage,* and *retrieval,* convenient ways of comparing human memory with computers. But we will also consider the social, emotional, and biological factors that make us human and that also distinguish our memories from those of computers.

Far more information bombards our senses than we can possibly process, so the first stage of information processing involves selecting some of this material to think about and remember. Therefore, we turn first to the sensory registers and to attention, the process that allows us to select incoming information for further processing.

The Sensory Registers

What is the role of sensory registers?

Look slowly around the room. Each glance takes in an enormous amount of visual information, including colors, shapes, textures, relative brightness, and shadows. At the same time, you pick up sounds, smells, and other kinds of sensory data. All of this raw information flows from your senses into what are known as the **sensory registers.** These registers are like waiting rooms in which information enters and stays for only a short time. Whether we remember any of this information depends on which operations we perform on it, as you will see throughout this chapter. Although there are registers for each of our senses, the visual and auditory registers have been studied most extensively.

Visual and Auditory Registers

What would happen if auditory information faded as quickly as visual information fades?

Although the sensory registers have virtually unlimited capacity (Cowan, 1988), information disappears from them quite rapidly. A simple experiment can demonstrate how much visual information we take in—and how quickly it is lost. Bring a camera into a darkened room, and then take a photograph using a flash. During the split second that the room is lit up by the flash, your visual register will absorb a surprising amount of information about the room and its contents. Try to hold on to that visual image, or *icon,* as long as you can. You will find that in a few seconds, it is gone. Then compare your remembered image of the room with what you actually saw, as captured in the photograph. You will discover that your visual register took in far more information than you were able to retain for even a few seconds.

Experiments by George Sperling (1960) clearly demonstrate how quickly information disappears from the visual register. Sperling flashed groups of letters, organized into three rows, on a screen for just a fraction of a second. When the letters were gone, he sounded a tone to tell his participants which row of letters to recall: A high-pitched tone indicated that they should try to remember the top row of letters, a low-pitched tone meant that they should recall the bottom row, and a medium-pitched tone signaled them to recall the middle row. Using this *partial-report technique,* Sperling found that if he sounded the tone immediately after the letters were flashed, people could usually recall 3 or 4 of the letters in *any* of the three rows; that is, they seemed to have at least 9 of the original 12 letters in their visual registers. But if he waited for even 1 second before sounding the tone, his participants were able to recall only 1 or 2 letters from any single row—in just 1 second, then, all but 4 or 5 of the original set of 12 letters had vanished from their visual registers.

Visual information may disappear from the visual register even more rapidly than Sperling thought (Cowan, 1988). In everyday life, new visual information keeps coming into the register, and this new information replaces the old information almost immediately, a process often called *masking.* This is just as well, because otherwise the visual information would simply pile up in the sensory register and get hopelessly scrambled. Under normal viewing conditions, visual information is erased from the

Memory
The ability to remember the things that we have experienced, imagined, and learned.

Information-processing model
A computerlike model used to describe the way humans encode, store, and retrieve information.

Sensory registers
Entry points for raw information from the senses.

If you were to walk into this room, your eyes and your other sense organs would pick up many impressions of what is to be found here. How much of this information would you remember later?

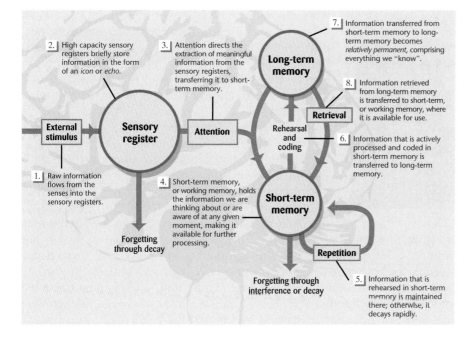

FIGURE 6-1
The sequence of information processing.

sensory register in about a quarter of a second as it is replaced by new information.

Auditory information fades more slowly than visual information. The auditory equivalent of the icon, the *echo,* tends to last for several seconds, which, given the nature of speech, is certainly lucky for us. Otherwise, *"You did it!"* would be indistinguishable from *"You did it!"* because we would be unable to remember the emphasis on the first words by the time the last words were registered.

Attention

Why does some information capture our attention, whereas other information goes unnoticed?

If information disappears from the sensory registers so rapidly, how do we remember *anything* for more than a second or two? One way is that we select some of the incoming information for further processing by means of **attention** (see **Figure 6–1**). Attention is the process of *selectively* looking, listening, smelling, tasting, and feeling. At the same time, we give meaning to the information that is coming in. Look at the page in front of you. You will see a series of black lines on a white page. Until you recognize these lines as letters and words, they are just meaningless marks. For you to make sense of this jumble of data, you process the information in the sensory registers for meaning.

How do we select what we are going to pay attention to at any given moment, and how do we give that information meaning? Donald Broadbent (1958) suggested that a filtering process at the entrance to the nervous system allows only those stimuli that meet certain requirements to pass through. Those stimuli that do get through the filter are compared with what we already know, so that we can recognize them and figure out what they mean. If you and a friend are sitting in a restaurant talking, you filter out all other conversations taking place around you, a process known as the *cocktail-party phenomenon* (Cherry, 1966; Wood & Cowan, 1995). Although you later might be able to describe certain characteristics of those other conversations, such as whether the people speaking were men or

Attention
The selection of some incoming information for further processing.

These children are working attentively in spite of the activity around them. If the teacher calls someone's name, though, that child's attention will be quickly diverted.

6.1 *Live! psych*

INTERACTIVE LECTURE **6.1**

WEB QUIZ **6.1** ✓

women and whether the words were spoken loudly or softly, according to Broadbent you normally cannot recall what was being discussed, even at neighboring tables. Because you filtered out those other conversations, the processing of that information did not proceed far enough for you to understand what you heard.

Broadbent's filtering theory helps explain some aspects of attention, but sometimes unattended stimuli do capture our attention. To return to the restaurant example, if someone nearby were to mention your name, your attention probably would shift to that conversation. Anne Treisman (1960, 1964) modified the filter theory to account for phenomena like this. She contended that the filter is not a simple on/off switch but rather a variable control, like the volume control on a radio, which can "turn down" unwanted signals without rejecting them entirely. According to this view, although we may be paying attention to only some incoming information, we monitor the other signals at a low volume. In this way, we can shift our attention if we pick up something particularly meaningful. This automatic processing works even when we are asleep: Parents often wake up immediately when they hear their baby crying but sleep through other, louder noises.

To summarize, we consciously attend to very little of the information in our sensory registers; instead, we select some information and process those signals further as we work to recognize and understand them. Unattended information receives at least some initial processing, however, so that we can shift our attention to any element of our surroundings that strikes us as potentially meaningful. The information that we do attend to enters our short-term memory.

CHECK YOUR UNDERSTANDING

1. Raw information from the senses reaches the _____ _____ before it disappears or is further processed.

2. Auditory information fades from the registers more slowly than _____ information.

3. The selection process that allows us to retain information after it has arrived from the senses is termed _____.

4. We are able to focus on some information while ignoring other information. This process is called the _____ _____ phenomenon.

5. We tend to shift our attention when we pick up on something that is particularly _____.

6. Indicate whether the following statements are true (T) or false (F).

    a. _____ The sensory registers have virtually unlimited capacity.

    b. _____ Some kinds of information are stored permanently in the sensory registers.

    c. _____ New visual information replaces old almost immediately through masking.

    d. _____ The filter theory as modified by Treisman holds that attention is like an on/off switch.

Answers: 1. sensory registers, 2. visual, 3. attention, 4. cocktail-party, 5. meaningful, 6. (a) T; (b) F; (c) T; (d) F.

Short-Term Memory

What are the two primary tasks of short-term memory?

Short-term memory (STM) holds the information that we are thinking about or are aware of at any given moment (Stern, 1985). When you listen to a conversation or a song on the radio, when you watch a television show or a football game, when you become aware of a leg cramp or a headache—in all these cases you are using STM both to hold onto and to think about new information coming in from the sensory registers. STM has two primary tasks: to store new information briefly and to work on that (and other) information. STM is sometimes called *working memory* to emphasize the active or working component of this memory system (Baddeley, 1986; Baddeley & Hitch, 1994).

The video-game fanatic is oblivious to the outside world. Chess masters at tournaments demand complete silence while they ponder their next move. You shut yourself in a quiet room to study for final exams. As these examples illustrate, STM can handle only so much information at any given moment. Research suggests that STM can hold about as much information as can be repeated or rehearsed in 1.5 to 2 seconds (Baddeley, 1986; Schweickert & Boruff, 1986).

To get a better idea of the limits of STM, read the first row of letters in the following list just once. Then close your eyes, and try to remember the letters in the correct sequence. Repeat the procedure for each subsequent row.

1. C X W
2. M N K T Y
3. R P J H B Z S
4. G B M P V Q F J D
5. E G Q W J P B R H K A

Like most other people, you probably found rows 1 and 2 fairly easy, row 3 a bit harder, row 4 extremely difficult, and row 5 impossible to remember after just one reading. You have just experienced the relatively limited capacity of STM.

Now try reading through the following set of 12 letters just once, and see whether you can repeat them.

TJYFAVMCFKIB

How many letters were you able to recall? In all likelihood, not all 12. But what if you had been asked to remember the following 12 letters instead?

TV FBI JFK YMCA

Could you remember them? Almost certainly the answer is yes. These are the same 12 letters as before, but here they are grouped into four separate "words." This way of grouping and organizing information so that it fits into meaningful units is called **chunking.** The 12 letters have been chunked into 4 meaningful elements that can readily be handled by STM—they can be repeated in less than 2 seconds. Now try to remember this list of numbers:

106619451812

Remembering 12 separate digits is usually very difficult, but try chunking the list into 3 groups of 4:

1066 1945 1812

Chess players demand complete silence as they consider their next move. This is because there is a definite limit to the amount of information STM can handle at any given moment.

Short-term memory (STM)
Working memory; briefly stores and processes selected information from the sensory registers.

Chunking
The grouping of information into meaningful units for easier handling by short-term memory.

"Hold on a second, Bob. I'm putting you on a stickie."

For those who take an interest in military history, these three chunks (which are dates of important battles) will be much easier to remember than 12 unrelated digits.

By chunking words into sentences or sentence fragments, we can process an even greater amount of information in STM (Aaronson & Scarborough, 1976, 1977; Baddeley, 1994). For example, suppose that you want to remember the following list of words: *tree, song, hat, sparrow, box, lilac, cat*. One strategy would be to cluster as many of them as possible into phrases or sentences: "The sparrow in the tree sings a song"; "a lilac hat in the box"; "the cat in the hat." But isn't there a limit to this strategy? Would 5 sentences be as easy to remember for a short time as 5 single words? No. As the size of any individual chunk increases, the number of chunks that can be held in STM declines (Simon, 1974). STM can easily handle 5 unrelated letters or words at once, but 5 unrelated sentences are much harder to remember.

Keep in mind that STM usually has to perform more than one task at a time (Baddeley & Hitch, 1994). During the brief moments you spent memorizing the preceding rows of letters, you probably gave them your full attention. But normally you have to attend to new incoming information while you work on whatever is already present in short-term memory. Competition between these two tasks for the limited work space in STM means that neither task will be done as well as it could be.

Encoding in STM

Do we store material in short-term memory as it sounds or as it looks?

We encode verbal information for storage in STM phonologically—that is, according to how it sounds. This is the case even if we see the word, letter, or number on a page rather than hear it spoken (Baddeley, 1986). Numerous experiments have shown that when people try to retrieve material from STM, they generally mix up items that sound alike (Sperling, 1960). A list of words such as *mad, man, mat, cap* is harder for most people to recall accurately than is a list such as *pit, day, cow, bar* (Baddeley, 1986).

But not all material in short-term memory is stored phonologically. At least some material is stored in visual form, and other information is retained on the basis of its meaning (Cowan, 1988; Matlin, 1989). For example, we don't have to convert visual data such as maps, diagrams, and paintings into sound before we can code them into STM and think about them. And deaf people rely primarily on shapes rather than sounds to retain information in STM (Conrad, 1972; Frumkin & Ainsfield, 1977). In fact, it appears that the capacity for visual encoding in STM exceeds that for phonological coding (Reed, 1992).

Maintaining STM

How can we hold information in STM?

As we have said, short-term memories are fleeting, generally lasting a matter of seconds. However, we can hold information in STM for longer periods through **rote rehearsal,** also called *maintenance rehearsal* (Greene,

Rote rehearsal
Retaining information in memory simply by repeating it over and over.

1987). Rote rehearsal consists of repeating information over and over, silently or out loud. Although this may not be the most efficient way to remember something permanently, it can be quite effective for a short time.

 INTERACTIVE LECTURE **6.2**

 WEB QUIZ **6.2**

CHECK YOUR UNDERSTANDING

1. ____ memory is what we are thinking about at any given moment. Its function is briefly to store new information and to work on that and other information.
2. ____ enables us to group items into meaningful units.
3. Strings of letters and numbers are encoded in short-term memory ____.
4. STM can hold, at most, about 2 seconds–worth of information. Is this statement true (T) or false (F)?
5. ____ rehearsal, or simply repeating information over and over, is an effective way of retaining information for just a minute or two.

Answers: 1. Short-term. 2. Chunking. 3. phonologically. 4. (T). 5. Rote.

Long-Term Memory

What types of information are retained in LTM?

Everything that we learn is stored in **long-term memory (LTM):** the words to a popular song; the results of the last election; the meaning of *justice*; the fact that George Washington was the first president of the United States; the meaning of abbreviations such as TV, FBI, JFK, and YMCA; what you ate for dinner last night; what presents you received at your sixth birthday party; how to roller skate or draw a face; your enjoyment of opera or your disgust at the sight of raw oysters; and what you are supposed to be doing tomorrow at 4 P.M.

Capacity of LTM

What is the limit of LTM?

We have seen that short-term memory can hold only a few items, normally only for a matter of seconds unless the items are maintained through rote rehearsal. By contrast, long-term memory can store a vast amount of information for many years. In one study, for example, adults who had graduated from high school more than 40 years earlier were still able to recognize the names of 75 percent of their classmates (Bahrick, Bahrick, & Wittlinger, 1974). And some people are able to remember their high school Spanish after fifty years, even if they have had little opportunity to practice it (Bahrick, 1984).

Encoding in LTM

How are most memories encoded in LTM?

Can you picture the shape of Florida? Do you know what a trumpet sounds like? Can you imagine the smell of a rose or the taste of coffee? When you answer the telephone, can you sometimes identify the caller immediately, just from the sound of the voice? Your ability to do most of these things means that at least some long-term memories are coded in terms of nonverbal images: shapes, sounds, smells, tastes, and so on (Cowan, 1988).

Long-term memory (LTM)
The portion of memory that is more or less permanent, corresponding to everything we "know."

Yet most of the information in LTM seems to be encoded in terms of *meaning*. If material is especially familiar (the words of the national anthem, say, or the opening of the Gettysburg Address), you may have stored it verbatim in LTM, and you can often retrieve it word for word when you need it. Generally speaking, however, we do not use verbatim storage in LTM. If someone tells you a long, rambling story, you may listen to every word, but you certainly will not try to remember the story verbatim. Instead, you will extract the main points of the story and try to remember those. Even simple sentences are usually encoded in terms of their meaning. Thus, when people are asked to remember that "Tom called John," they often find it impossible to remember later whether they were told "Tom called John" or "John was called by Tom." They usually remember the meaning of the message but not the exact words (Bourne, Dominowski, Loftus, & Healy, 1986).

Serial Position Effect

Which items in a list are hardest to remember?

When given a list of items to remember (such as a list of grocery items), people tend to do better at recalling the first items (*primacy effect*) and the last items (*recency effect*) in the list. They also tend to do poorest of all on the items in the middle of the list (see **Figure 6–2**).

The explanation for this **serial position effect** resides in understanding how short- and long-term memory work together. The *recency effect* occurs because the last items that were presented are still contained in STM and thus are available for recall. The *primacy effect*, on the other hand, reflects the opportunity to rehearse the first few items in the list—increasing their likelihood of being transferred to LTM.

Poor performance on the items in the middle of the list occurs because they were presented too long ago to still be in STM, and because so many items were presented before and after them that required attention, that there was little opportunity for rehearsal. The serial position effect has been shown to occur under a wide variety of conditions and situations (Neath, 1993). A version of the serial position effect has been demonstrated even in monkeys (Wright, 1998).

Serial position effect
The finding that when asked to recall a list of unrelated items, performance is better for the items at the beginning and end of the list.

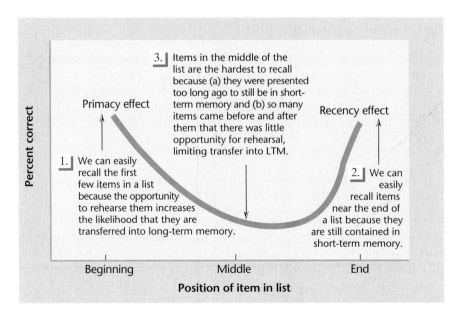

FIGURE 6–2

The serial position effect. The serial position effect demonstrates how short and long-term memory work together.

Maintaining LTM

What three ways are used to hold information in LTM?

Rote Rehearsal   Rote rehearsal, the principal tool for holding information in STM, is also useful for holding information in LTM. The old saying that practice makes perfect has some merit. Millions of students have learned the alphabet and multiplication tables by doggedly repeating letters and numbers. Rote rehearsal is probably the standard method of storing away largely meaningless material, such as phone numbers, Social Security numbers, security codes, computer passwords, birth dates, and people's names.

Indeed, although everyone hates rote drill, there seems to be no escaping its use in mastering a wide variety of skills, from memorizing the alphabet to playing a work of Mozart on the piano or doing a back flip on the balance beam. Mastering a skill means achieving *automaticity,* the word that researchers use to describe fluid, immediate performance. Expert typing, for example, means being able to hit the right keys accurately without having to think about it. And automaticity is achieved only through long, hard practice.

Research suggests, however, that repetition without any intention to learn generally has little effect on subsequent recall (Greene, 1987). You can probably prove this phenomenon to yourself: Stop here and try to imagine from memory the front side of a U.S. penny. Now look at **Figure 6–3,** and pick the illustration that matches your memory. For most people, this task is surprisingly difficult: Despite seeing thousands of pennies, most people cannot accurately draw one, or even pick one out from among other, similar objects (Nickerson & Adams, 1979).

Elaborative Rehearsal   As we have seen, rote rehearsal with the intent to learn is sometimes useful in storing information in LTM. But often, an even more effective procedure is **elaborative rehearsal** (Postman, 1975), the act of relating new information to something that we already know. Through elaborative rehearsal, you extract the meaning of the new information and then link it to as much of the material already in LTM as possible. The more links or associations you can make, the more likely you are to remember the new information later, just as it is easier to find a book in the library if it is cataloged under many headings rather than just one or two. Thus, we tend to remember meaningful material better than arbitrary facts: We can connect the meaningful material to more items already in LTM.

Clearly, elaborative rehearsal calls for a deeper and more meaningful processing of new data than does simple rote rehearsal (Craik & Lockhart, 1972). Unless we rehearse material in this way, we often soon forget it. For example, have you ever been in a group in which people were taking turns speaking up—perhaps on the first day of class when all present are asked to introduce themselves briefly, or at the beginning of a panel discussion when the speakers are asked to do the same in front of a large audience?

Elaborative rehearsal
The linking of new information in short-term memory to familiar material stored in long-term memory.

FIGURE 6–3

A penny for your thoughts.   Which of these accurately illustrates a real U.S. penny? The answer is on page 210.

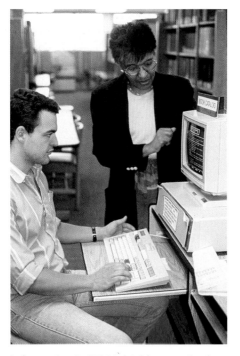

Information in LTM is highly organized and cross-referenced, like a cataloging system in a library. The more carefully we organize information, the more likely we will be to retrieve it later.

Did you notice that you forgot virtually everything that was said by the person who spoke just before you did? According to research, you failed to remember because you did not elaboratively rehearse what that person was saying (Bond, Pitre, & Van Leeuwen, 1991). That person's comments simply "went in one ear and out the other" while you were preoccupied with thinking about your own remarks.

Schemata   A variation on the idea of elaborative rehearsal is the concept of **schema** (plural: **schemata**). A schema is like a script that past experience has begun writing for you, with details to be filled in by your present experience. It is a mental representation of an event, an object, a situation, a person, a process, or a relationship that is stored in memory and that leads you to expect your experience to be organized in certain ways. For example, you may have a schema for going to the mall, for eating in a restaurant, for driving a car, or for attending a class lecture. A class lecture schema might include a large room, seating arranged in rows, a space in the front of the room where the professor or lecturer will stand, a podium or lectern, a chalkboard, a screen, and other characteristics common to your experience of attending lectures. You enter, sit down, open your notebook, and expect the professor or lecturer to come in and address the class from the front of the room.

Schemata such as these provide a framework into which incoming information is fitted. Schemata also may color what you recall by prompting you to form stereotypes, that is, to ascribe certain characteristics to all members of a particular group. (The process of stereotyping will be examined in Chapter 14, Social Psychology.) Finally, schemata may help you to fill in missing information or to draw inferences. If Bob was in a really bad mood one day and you found out later that he had a flat tire while rushing to an important appointment dressed in his best clothes, your schema or mental representation of what it is like to fix a tire in such a situation would help you understand why Bob was not his usual cheerful self that day.

To summarize, we have seen that long-term memory offers a vast storage space for information that we can retrieve in a variety of ways. Its capacity is immense, and material stored there may endure, more or less intact, for decades. By comparison, short-term memory has a sharply limited capacity; information may disappear from STM because it decays or simply because the storage space is full. To keep information in STM, we must refresh it constantly through rote rehearsal. If we want to retain information for a long time, we must transfer it to long-term memory, usually through elaborative rehearsal. The sensory registers can take in an enormous volume of less permanent information, but they have no ability to process memories. Together, these three stages of memory—the sensory registers, STM, and LTM—comprise the information-processing view of memory. (The accurate illustration of a penny in Figure 6–3 is the third from the left.)

Types of LTM

How do different types of LTM differ?

The information stored in LTM can take a myriad of forms. However, most long-term memories can be classified into one of several types.

Episodic memories (Tulving, 1985) are memories for events experienced in a specific time and place. These are *personal* memories, not historical facts. If you can recall what you ate for dinner last night, what presents you got at your sixteenth birthday party, or how you learned to ride a bike when

Schema
(skee-mah; plural: schemata) A set of beliefs or expectations about something that is based on past experience.

Episodic memory
The portion of long-term memory that stores personally experienced events.

you were little, then you are calling up episodic memories. We can think of episodic memory as a diary or daily journal that lets you "go back in time" (Wheeler, Stuss, & Tulving, 1997).

Semantic memories are facts and concepts not linked to a particular time. If episodic memory is like a daily journal, semantic memory is like a dictionary or an encyclopedia, filled with facts and concepts, such as the meaning of the word *semantic,* the name of the inventor of the light bulb, the location of the Empire State Building, the value of 2 times 7, and the identity of George Washington.

Procedural memories are motor skills and habits. They are not memories *about* skills and habits; they *are* the skills and habits. Procedural memories have to do with knowing *how*: how to ride a bicycle, swim, play a violin, type a letter, make coffee, write your name, comb your hair, walk across a room, or slam on a car's brakes. The information involved usually consists of a precise sequence of coordinated movements that are often difficult to describe in words. Repetition, and in many cases deliberate practice, are often required to master skills and habits, but once learned, they are rarely completely lost. The saying "You never forget how to ride a bicycle" illustrates the durability of procedural memories.

Emotional memories are learned emotional responses to various stimuli: all of our loves and hates, our rational and irrational fears, our feelings of disgust and anxiety. If you are afraid of flying insects, become enraged at the sight of a Nazi flag, or are ashamed of something you did, you have emotional memories.

Explicit and Implicit Memory

What are the differences between implicit and explicit memories?

Because of the differences among types of memories, psychologists distinguish between **explicit memory,** which includes episodic and semantic memories, and **implicit memory,** which includes procedural and emotional memories (Nelson, 1999). These terms reflect the fact that sometimes we are aware that we know something (explicit memory) and that sometimes we are not (implicit memory).

Serious interest in the distinction between explicit and implicit memory began as a result of experiments with amnesic patients. These patients had

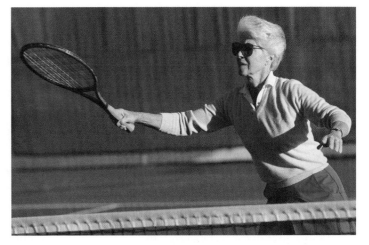

Once skills such as playing tennis have been stored in our procedural memory, they are seldom lost.

Semantic memory
The portion of long-term memory that stores general facts and information.

Procedural memory
The portion of long-term memory that stores information relating to skills, habits, and other perceptual-motor tasks.

Emotional memory
Learned emotional responses to various stimuli.

Explicit memory
Memory for information that we can readily express in words and are aware of having; these memories can be intentionally retrieved from memory.

Implicit memory
Memory for information that we cannot readily express in words and may not be aware of having; these memories cannot be intentionally retrieved from memory.

Graduating from college is a landmark day, an event filled with strong emotions. Years later, the memory of this day will be easily recalled.

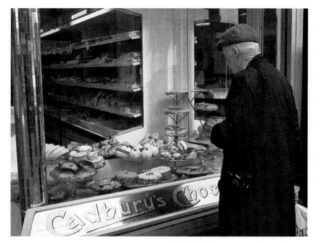

Looking into a bakery window, perhaps smelling the aromas of the cakes inside, may trigger distinct memories associated with those sights and smells, formed many years ago.

suffered brain damage that, it was thought, prevented them from forming new long-term memories. They could recall things learned prior to their injury, but not afterward.

For example, Brenda Milner (Milner, Corkin, & Teuber, 1968) studied the now famous case of patient H. M., a young man who had severe, uncontrollable epileptic seizures. The seizures became life-threatening, so that as a last resort, surgeons removed most of the afflicted area of his brain. The surgery greatly reduced the frequency and severity of seizures, but it left behind a new problem: H. M. could no longer form new memories. He could meet someone again and again, and each time it was as if he were meeting the person for the first time. He could read the same magazine day after day and not recall ever having seen it before. Old memories were intact: He could remember things that he had learned long before the operation, but he could not learn anything new. Or so it seemed!

Then one day Milner asked H. M. to trace the outline of a star while looking in a mirror. This simple task is surprisingly difficult, but with practice most people show steady progress. Surprisingly, so did H. M. Each day he got better and better at tracing the star, just as a person with an undamaged brain would do—yet each day he had no recollection of ever having attempted the task. H. M.'s performance demonstrated not only that he could learn but also that there are different kinds of memories. Some are explicit: We know things, and we know that we know them. And some are implicit: We know things, but that knowledge is unconscious (see **Table 6–1** for a summary of implicit and explicit memory).

Research on a phenomenon called *priming* also demonstrates the distinction between explicit and implicit memory. In priming, a person is exposed to a stimulus, usually a word or picture. Later, the person is shown a fragment of the stimulus (a few letters of a word or a piece of a picture) and is asked to complete it. The typical result is that people are more likely to complete fragments with items seen earlier than they are with other, equally plausible items. For example, you might be shown a list of words including the word *tour*. Later on, you might be shown a list of word fragments, including _____*ou*_____, and be asked to fill in the blanks to make a word. In comparison to others who had not been primed by seeing the word *tour*, you are far more likely to write *tour* than you are *four, pour,* or *sour,* all of which are just as acceptable as *tour.* The earlier exposure to *tour* primes you to write that word.

The distinction between explicit and implicit memories means that some knowledge is literally unconscious. Moreover, as we shall soon see,

TABLE 6-1 TYPES OF MEMORIES

Explicit		Implicit	
Semantic	**Episodic**	**Procedural**	**Emotional**
Memories of facts and concepts	Memories of personally experienced events	Motor skills and habits	Learned emotional reactions
Example: recalling that Albany is the capital of New York	*Example:* recalling a trip to Albany	*Example:* ice skating	*Example:* recoiling at the sight of a rat

explicit and implicit memories also seem to involve different neural structures and pathways. However, memories typically work together. When we remember going to a Chinese restaurant, we recall not only when and where we ate and whom we were with (episodic memory), but also the nature of the food we ate (semantic memory), the skills we learned such as eating with chopsticks (procedural memory), and the embarrassment we felt when we spilled the tea (emotional memory). When we recall events, we typically do not experience these kinds of memories as distinct and separate; rather, they are integrally connected, just as the original experiences were. Whether we will continue to remember the experiences accurately in the future depends to a large extent on what happens in our brain.

 6.2

 INTERACTIVE LECTURE 6.3

✓ **WEB QUIZ 6.3**

CHECK YOUR UNDERSTANDING

Match the following terms with the appropriate definitions.

1. ____ primacy effect
2. ____ recency effect
3. ____ serial position effect

   a. accounts for why we remember items at the end of a list

   b. accounts for why we remember items at the beginning of a list

   c. describes our lack of memory of the middle of the list

4. If information is learned through repetition, this process is _____ rehearsal; if it is learned by linking it to other memories, this process is _____ rehearsal.

5. A schema is a framework in memory into which new information is fit. Is this statement true (T) or false (F)?

Match the following terms with the appropriate definitions.

____ 6. procedural memories
____ 7. episodic memories
____ 8. emotional memories
____ 9. semantic memories

   a. memories specific to one's own experiences

   b. memories of facts and concepts

   c. memories of motor skills and habits

   d. fear, love, and hate, for example, associated with specific events

10. Implicit memories consist of _____ and _____ memories, whereas explicit memories consist of _____ and _____ memories.

11. An initial exposure to a word that you will later be asked to recall is the procedure used to demonstrate _____.

Answers: 1. b. 2. a. 3. c. 4. rote; elaborative. 5. T. 6. c. 7. a. 8. d. 9. b. 10. procedural and emotional; episodic and semantic. 11. priming.

The Biology of Memory

How and where are memories stored?

Research on the biology of memory focuses mainly on the question, How and where are memories stored? Simple as the question is, it has proved enormously difficult to answer. The tools used to search for the answer include studies of people who have suffered neurological damage through surgery, disease, or injury, and experimental studies of animals. Imaging tools for studying the nervous system (see Chapter 2, The Biological Basis of Behavior), especially PET and functional MRI imagining, have also been useful. Although our understanding of the biological basis of memory is incomplete, considerable progress has been made in the last two decades.

How Are Memories Formed?

What role do neurons play in memory?

Current research indicates that memories consist of changes in the synaptic connections among neurons (Squire & Kandel, 1999). Everything you learn is ultimately recorded in the brain in the form of changes in the size, shape, chemical functioning, and connectedness of neurons. When we learn new things, new connections are formed in the brain; when we review or practice previously learned things, old connections are strengthened. The nature of these changed connections seems to involve both chemical and structural changes that increase the number of connections among neurons and the likelihood that cells will excite one another through electrical discharges (see **Figure 2–3**). These changes in neurons are called *consolidation*. Although learning often occurs quickly, consolidation of memories is usually a slow process.

Where Are Memories Stored?

Are STM and LTM found in the same parts of the brain?

Not all memories are stored in one place (Brewer, Zhao, Desmond, Glover, & Gabriel, 1998). However, this characteristic does not mean that memories are randomly distributed throughout the brain. In fact, different parts of the brain are specialized for the storage of memories (Rolls, 2000).

Short-term memories, for example, seem to be located primarily in the prefrontal cortex and temporal lobe (Fuster, 1997; Rao, Rainer, & Miller, 1997; Rolls, Tovee, & Panzeri, 1999; see **Figure 6–4**). Damage to subcortical areas known to be important to the formation of long-term memory apparently does not affect short-term memory. This finding was illustrated by H. M., the amnesic patient discussed earlier. Although H. M. could not recognize the doctors he saw every day, his memory for events in his past was normal.

Long-term memories, on the other hand, seem to involve the participation of both subcortical and cortical structures, at least during the consolidation phase. Portions of the temporal lobe are especially important to the formation of new long-term memories. The hippocampus also plays a pivotal role in the formation of long-term semantic and episodic memories. If the hippocampus is damaged, people can remember events that have just occurred (and are in STM), but their long-term recall of those same events is impaired. Removal or total destruction of the hippocampus destroys the ability to remember new experiences. For example, the surgery that H. M. underwent to cure his epilepsy damaged his hippocampus.

But the fact that subcortical structures (such as the hippocampus) are essential to the formation of long-term memories does not necessarily mean that memories are stored there. Removal of the hippocampus, for example, prevents the formation of new semantic memories, but it does not prevent the recall of older ones; therefore, these memories are stored at least partly outside the hippocampus. So, where does the brain "put" the memories that it processes? Research suggests that they are widely dispersed throughout the brain; however, different kinds of memories tend to be concentrated in different locations.

Semantic memories seem to be located primarily in the frontal and temporal lobes of the cortex (see **Figure 6–4**). Research shows increased activity in a particular area of the left temporal lobe, for example, when people are asked to recall the names of people. A nearby area shows increased activity when they are asked to recall the names of animals, and another neighboring area becomes active when they are asked to recall the names

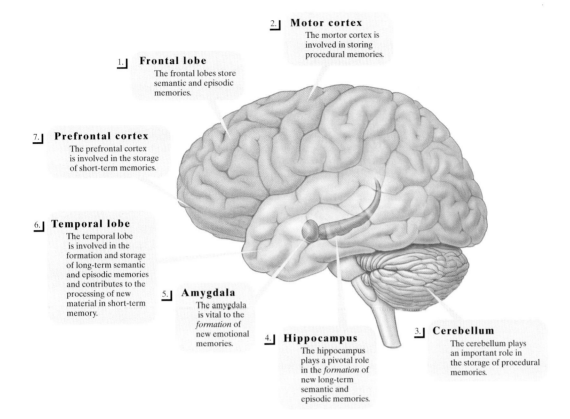

FIGURE 6–4

The biological basis of memory. Many different parts of the brain are specialized for the storage of memories.

of tools (Damasio, Grabowski, Tranel, Hichawa, & Damasio, 1996). Thus, it appears that semantic memories have their own special places, though this information may also be recorded partly in subcortical areas, especially the hippocampus, at least in the early stages of consolidation.

Like semantic memories, episodic memories find their home in the frontal and temporal lobes, which, interestingly, also seem to play a prominent role in consciousness and awareness (Wheeler, Stuss, & Tulving, 1997). But some evidence shows that episodic and semantic memories involve different brain structures. Wood and colleagues (1980) compared blood flow in the brain as people worked on two different kinds of tasks (blood flow to an area is associated with activity in that area). Some people performed a task involving episodic memory; others performed a task involving semantic memory. The researchers found that the two kinds of tasks resulted in increased blood flow to somewhat different areas of the brain.

Procedural memories appear to be located primarily in the cerebellum (an area required for balance and motor coordination) and in the motor cortex (see **Figure 6–4;** Gabrieli, 1998). When people perform a task that requires them to follow the motion of an object by tracing its path with a pencil, activity in their motor cortex increases (Grafton et al., 1992). Once again, however, the hippocampus also appears to be important.

Emotional memories are dependent on the amygdala (Cahill & McGaugh, 1998; Vazdarjanova & McGaugh, 1999), a structure that lies near the hippocampus. The amygdala seems to play a role in emotional memory that is similar to the role the hippocampus plays in episodic, semantic, and procedural memory. For example, damage to the amygdala reduces the ability to

INTERACTIVE LECTURE **6.4**

CHECK YOUR UNDERSTANDING

1. Consolidation of long-term memories occurs almost instantaneously. Is this statement true (T) or false (F)?

2. Consolidation of new memories seems to involve the growth of new branches on the dendrite of neurons. Is this statement true (T) or false (F)?

Match the following types of memory to the location in the brain where they appear to be stored.

3. ____ short-term memories   a. frontal and temporal lobes
4. ____ long-term semantic and   b. cerebellum and motor cortex
        episodic memories
5. ____ procedural memories   c. amygdala
6. ____ emotional memories   d. prefrontal cortex and temporal lobe

Answers: 1. F. 2. T. 3. d. 4. a. 5. b. 6. c.

recall new emotional experiences, but it does not prevent the recall of emotional events that occurred before the damage (see Nadel & Jacobs, 1998).

Forgetting

What factors explain why we sometimes forget?

Why do memories, once formed, not remain forever in the brain? Part of the answer has to do with the biology of memory, and another part has to do with the experiences that we have before and after learning.

The Biology of Forgetting

How does the deterioration of the brain help to explain forgetting?

Information that is stored in LTM also can be lost when consolidation is disrupted. Head injuries often result in **retrograde amnesia,** a condition in which people cannot remember what happened to them shortly before their injury. In such cases, forgetting may occur because memories are not fully consolidated in the brain. The problem is analogous to something that every computer user has experienced: A momentary power outage results in the loss of information that has not been saved to the hard drive. One moment the information is there before you, and readily accessed; in the next, it is gone.

Severe memory loss is invariably traced to brain damage caused by accidents, surgery, poor diet, or disease. For example, chronic alcoholism can lead to a form of amnesia called *Korsakoff's syndrome* caused by a vitamin deficiency in the poor diet typically eaten by people who abuse alcohol (Baddeley, 1987). Other studies show the importance of the hippocampus to long-term memory formation. Studies of elderly people who are having trouble remembering new material, for instance, show that the hippocampus is smaller than normal (Golomb et al., 1994). Brain scans also reveal a diminished hippocampus in people suffering from *Alzheimer's disease*, a neurological disorder that causes severe memory loss (Bennett & Knopman, 1994; see Chapter 9, Life-Span Development, for more information about Alzheimer's disease).

Retrograde amnesia
The inability to recall events preceding an accident or injury, but without loss of earlier memory.

Alzheimer's may also involve below-normal levels of the neurotransmitter acetylcholine in the brain. Indeed, some research suggests that drugs and surgical procedures that increase acetylcholine levels may serve as effective treatments for age-related memory problems (Li & Low, 1997; Parnetti, Senin, & Mecocci, 1997; D. E. Smith, Roberts, Gage, & Tuszynski, 1999).

Experience and Forgetting

What environmental factors contribute to our inability to remember?

Although sometimes caused by biological factors, forgetting can also result from inadequate learning. A lack of attention to critical cues, for example, is a cause of the forgetting commonly referred to as absentmindedness (Schacter, 1999). For example, if you can't remember where you parked your car, most likely you can't remember because you didn't pay attention to where you parked it.

Forgetting also occurs because, although we attended to the matter to be recalled, we did not rehearse the material enough. Merely "going through the motions" of rehearsal does little good. Prolonged, intense practice results in less forgetting than a few, half-hearted repetitions. Elaborative rehearsal can also help make new memories more durable. When you park your car in space G-47, you will be more likely to remember its location if you think, "G-47. My uncle *George* is about *47* years old." In short, we cannot expect to remember information for long if we have not learned it well in the first place.

Interference   Inadequate learning accounts for many memory failures, but learning itself can cause forgetting. This is the case because learning one thing can interfere with learning another. Information gets mixed up with, or pushed aside by, other information and thus becomes harder to remember. Such forgetting is said to be due to *interference.* There are two kinds of interference. In **retroactive interference,** new material interferes with information already in long-term memory. Retroactive interference occurs every day. For example, once you learn a new telephone number, you may find it difficult to recall your old number, even though you used that old number for years.

In the second kind of interference, old material interferes with new material being learned; this is called **proactive interference.** Like retroactive interference, proactive interference is an everyday phenomenon. Suppose you always park your car in the lot behind the building where you work, but one day all those spaces are full, so you have to park across the street. When you leave for the day, you are likely to head for the lot behind the building—and may even be surprised at first that your car is not there. Learning to look for your car behind the building has interfered with your memory that today you parked the car across the street.

The most important factor in determining the degree of interference is the similarity of the competing items. Learning to swing a golf club may interfere with your ability to hit a baseball but probably won't affect your ability to make a free throw on the basketball courts. The more dissimilar something is from other things that you have already learned, the less likely it will be to mingle and interfere with other material in memory (Bower & Mann, 1992).

Situational Factors   Whenever we try to memorize something, we are also unintentionally picking up information about the context in which the learning is taking place. That information becomes useful when we later try to retrieve the corresponding information from LTM. If those environmental cues are absent when we try to recall what we learned, the effort to remember is often unsuccessful. Context-dependent memory effects tend to

6.3

Retroactive interference
The process by which new information interferes with information already in memory.

Proactive interference
The process by which information already in memory interferes with new information.

UNDERSTANDING The World Around Us

Eyewitness Testimony: Can We Trust It?

I know what I saw!" When an eyewitness to a crime gives evidence in court, that testimony often overwhelms evidence to the contrary. Faced with conflicting or ambiguous testimony, jurors tend to put their faith in people who saw an event with their own eyes. However, there is now compelling evidence that this faith in eyewitnesses is often misplaced (Brodsky, 1999; McCloskey & Egeth, 1983; Wells & Bradfield, 1999). Although eyewitness accounts are essential to courtroom testimony, studies clearly show that people who say, "I know what I saw," often don't know.

For more than twenty years, Elizabeth Loftus (1993a; Loftus & Hoffman, 1989; Loftus & Pickrell, 1995) has been the most influential researcher into eyewitness memory. In a classic study, Loftus and Palmer (1974) showed experimental participants a film depicting a traffic accident. Some of the participants were asked, "About how fast were the cars going when they hit each other?" Other participants were asked the same question, but with the words *smashed into, collided with, bumped into,* or *contacted* in place of *hit.* The researchers discovered that people's reports of the cars' speed depended on which

word was inserted in the question. Those asked about cars that "smashed into" each other reported that the cars were going faster than those who were asked about cars that "contacted" each other. In another experiment, the participants were also shown a film of a collision and then were asked either "How fast were the cars going

> People who say, "I know what I saw," often mean, I don't know.

when they hit each other?" or "How fast were the cars going when they smashed into each other?" One week later, they were asked some additional questions about the accident that they had seen on film the week before. One of the questions was "Did you see any broken glass?" More of the participants who had been asked about cars that had "smashed into" each other reported that they had seen broken glass than did participants who had been asked the speed of cars that "hit" each other. These findings illustrate how police,

lawyers, and other investigators may, often unconsciously, sway witnesses and influence subsequent eyewitness accounts. On the basis of experiments like these, Loftus and Palmer concluded that eyewitness testimony is unreliable.

Why do eyewitnesses make mistakes? Some research suggests that the problem may be *source error:* People are sometimes unable to tell the difference between what they witnessed and what they merely heard about or imagined (Garry & Polaschek, 2000; Lindsay & Johnson, 1989; Reyna & Titcomb, 1997; Taylor, Pham, Rivkin, & Armor, 1998). We all know what it is like to imagine an event in a particularly vivid way and then later to have difficulty remembering whether the event really happened or we simply imagined it. Indeed, studies have shown that imagining an event sometimes makes people believe it actually happened (Garry & Polaschek, 2000; Henkel, Franklin, & Johnson, 2000). Similarly, if you hear information about an event you witnessed, you might later confuse your memory of that information with your memory of the original event. For instance, studies have shown that if an eyewitness receives confirming feedback after picking a suspect out of a

be small, so studying in the same classroom where you are scheduled to take an exam will probably not do too much to improve your grade. Nevertheless, contextual cues are occasionally used by police who sometimes take witnesses back to the scene of a crime in the hope that they will recall crucial details that can be used to solve the crime.

In addition to being influenced by environmental cues, our ability to accurately recall information is affected by internal cues. This phenomenon is known as *state-dependent memory.* State-dependent memory refers to the finding that people who learn material in a particular physiological state tend to recall that material better if they return to the same state they were in during learning.

police lineup, the feedback often increases the reported *certainty* of their recognition (Wells & Bradfield, 1999).

Even more disturbing, positive feedback following a lineup has been shown to change subsequent statements by witnesses with regard to "how good their view was" or "how much attention they paid to the crime" (Wells & Bradfield, 1998, 1999). The impact of subsequent information seems to be particularly strong when it is repeated several times (Zaragoza & Mitchell, 1996), as is often the case with extensive media coverage. Many psychologists (Lindsay, 1993; Zaragoza, Lane, Ackil, & Chambers, 1997) contend that if people paid more attention to the source of their memories, eyewitness accounts would be more reliable.

Whatever the reason for eyewitness errors, there is good evidence that such mistakes can send innocent people to jail. Increasingly, courts are recognizing the limits of eyewitness testimony (Kassin, Tubb, Hosch, & Memon, 2001). For example, judges instruct juries to be skeptical about eyewitness testimony and to evaluate it critically. But we still have a long way to go: A study of over 1,000 cases in which innocent people were con-

victed of crimes concludes that errors made by eyewitnesses were the single most persuasive element leading to false conviction (Wells, 1993). Consider the case of Father Bernard Pagano, a Roman Catholic priest who found himself accused of a series of armed robberies in Wilmington, Delaware. After one witness told police that Father

Pagano looked a lot like the man in a sketch being circulated by the local media, no less than seven eyewitnesses positively identified the priest as the perpetrator. In the middle of the trial, however, another man—whose resemblance to Father Pagano was not even close—confessed to the crime (see the accompanying photographs).

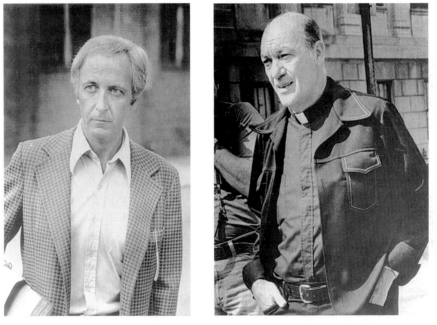

Father Bernard Pagano (right) was identified as an armed robber by seven eyewitnesses and was nearly convicted for crimes actually committed by the man on the left.

The Reconstructive Process   Forgetting also occurs because of what is called the "reconstructive" nature of remembering. Earlier we talked about how schemata are used in storing information in long-term memory. Bartlett proposed that people also use schemata to "reconstruct" memories (Bartlett, 1932; Schacter, Norman, & Koutstaal, 1998). This reconstructive process can lead to huge errors. Indeed, we are sometimes more likely to recall events that never happened than events that actually took place (Brainerd & Reyna, 1998)! The original memory is not destroyed; instead, people are sometimes unable to tell the difference between what actually happened and what they merely heard about or imagined (Garry & Polaschek, 2000; Lindsay & Johnson, 1989; Reyna & Titcomb, 1997; Taylor,

Pham, Rivkin, & Armor, 1998). In other words, sometimes people combine the elements of both real and imagined events (Henkel, Franklin, & Johnson, 2000). People also unknowingly "rewrite" past events to fit their current image or their desired image of themselves and their past decisions (Lyubomirsky & Ross, 1999; Mather, Shafir, & Johnson, 2000).

We may also reconstruct memories for social or personal self-defense. Each time you tell someone the story of an incident, you may unconsciously make subtle changes in the details of the story, with the result that these changes then become part of your memory of the event. When an experience doesn't fit our view of the world or ourselves, we tend, unconsciously, to adjust it or to blot it out of memory altogether (Bremner & Marmar, 1998). Such distortions of memory become critically important in criminal trials, in which a person's guilt or innocence may depend on the testimony of an eyewitness—a topic addressed in *Understanding the World Around Us*.

Improving Your Memory

What can you do to improve your memory?

The following steps can be taken to improve recall:

1. **Develop motivation.** Without a strong desire to learn or remember something, you probably won't. But if you find a way to keep yourself alert and stimulated, you will have an easier time learning and remembering things.

2. **Practice memory skills.** To stay sharp, memory skills, like all other skills, must be practiced and used. Memory experts recommend games such as crossword puzzles, acrostics, anagrams, Scrabble, Monopoly, Trivial Pursuit, and bridge. Or you might learn a new language or make a point of discussing current events regularly with friends.

3. **Be confident in your ability to remember.** If you're convinced that you won't remember something, you probably won't. Self-doubt often leads to anxiety, which, in turn, interferes with the ability to retrieve information from memory. Relaxation exercises, experts agree, may substantially boost your ability to retrieve information from memory.

4. **Minimize distractions.** Although some people can study for an exam and listen to the radio simultaneously, most people find that outside distractions interfere with both learning and remembering. If you are being distracted, look for a quiet, even secluded, setting before attempting to remember something.

5. **Stay focused.** Paying close attention to details, and focusing on your surroundings, emotions, and other elements associated with an event, will help you remember it clearly.

6. **Make connections between new material and other information already stored in your long-term memory.** One key to improving memory lies in organizing and encoding material more effectively when it first enters LTM. Discuss things that you want to remember with other people. Think about or write down ways in which the new information is related to things you already know. The more links you forge between new information and old information already in LTM, the more likely you are to remember the new material.

In some situations, special techniques called **mnemonics** (pronounced new-MON-iks) may help you to tie new material to information already in LTM. Some of the simplest mnemonic techniques are the rhymes and jingles that we often use to remember dates and other facts. "Thirty days hath September, April, June, and November . . ." enables us to recall how many days are in a month. We are also familiar

Mnemonics
Techniques that make material easier to remember.

with other simple mnemonic devices in which we make up words or sentences out of the material to be recalled. We can remember the colors of the visible spectrum—red, orange, yellow, green, blue, indigo, and violet—by using their first letters to form the name ROY G. BIV. In addition, several studies have shown that when you can relate a mnemonic to personal information, such as your hobbies or interests, you are even more likely to be able to recall it later (Symons & Johnson, 1997). Use mnemonics whenever you can.

The key to storing new material in LTM is to study actively. Simply reading a textbook chapter is not the same as learning it. To do that requires active participation, outlining, making notes, questioning, and reviewing as you go along.

7. **Use mental imagery.** Imagery works wonders as an aid to recalling information from memory. Whenever possible, form mental pictures of the items, people, words, or activities you want to remember. If you have a sequence of stops to make, picture yourself leaving each place and heading for the next. To memorize long speeches, Greek and Roman orators would go through the rooms of a building they knew well, placing images of material to be remembered in sequence at different spots. During a speech, the orators imagined themselves going through the rooms in order, and by association they would recall each point of the speech.

8. **Use retrieval cues.** The more retrieval cues that you have, the more likely it is that you will remember something. One way to establish automatic retrieval cues is to create routines and structure. For example, when you come in the door, put your house and car keys in the same place every time. Then when you ask yourself, "Where did I put my keys?" the fact that you have a special place for the keys serves as a retrieval cue. Sometimes something that is clearly not routine or structured can serve as a retrieval cue. For example, if you want to remember to do something before you go to bed, leave an unusual item on your bed (perhaps a shoe or a sock); when it's time to go to bed, you'll see the unusual object, and that sighting should help remind you of what you wanted to do.

9. **Rely on more than memory alone.** Use other tools. Write down the things you need to remember, and then post a list of those things somewhere obvious, such as on your bulletin board or refrigerator door. Put all the dates you want to remember on a calendar, and then put the calendar in a conspicuous place.

10. **Be aware that your own personal schemata may distort your recall of events.** As we've seen, people sometimes unknowingly "rewrite" past events to fit their current image or their desired image of themselves and their past decisions (Lyubomirsky & Ross, 1999; Mather, Shafir, & Johnson, 2000). Being on guard against such distortions may help you avoid them.

For more on improving memory, see *Understanding Ourselves.*

 6.4

Special Topics in Memory

What factors can influence how well you remember a specific incident?

Cultural Influences

Are the memory tasks in Western schools different from those in cultures that pass on oral traditions?

Remembering has practical consequences for our daily life and takes place within a particular context. It's not surprising, then, that many researchers believe that the values and customs of a given culture have a profound effect on what people remember and how easily they recall it (Mistry &

 INTERACTIVE LECTURE 6.5

UNDERSTANDING OURSELVES

Improving Your Memory for Textbook Material

You can use all the principles discussed in this chapter to help you remember material from textbooks in most of your courses. The key to storing new material in long-term memory is making associations between that material and information that is already in LTM. If you simply passively reread the chapter over and over, you are not likely to store, retain, or retrieve information effectively (McDaniel, Waddill, & Shakesby, 1996). Highlighting or underlining passages makes for a slight improvement, if only because you are at least thinking about which material is most important.

A more effective technique is to outline the chapter before you read it. Some textbooks (including this one) provide a ready-made outline at the beginning of the chapter, but creating one yourself forces you to start thinking about what the content of the chapter is and how one section relates to another. Then, as you read, write comments under the headings of your outline. Your personal summary will not only help you remember material as you are reading the chapter but will also be useful when you are reviewing the material for a test.

Another memory-enhancing technique is to rehearse the material as you read the chapter. You might write in the margin of the text as you go along, recording your reactions, questions, ideas about how the new material may relate to other material, thoughts about how you might apply what you are learning in your own life, and so on. Try to relate the new material to all sorts of things that you already know, expressing this relationship in your own words. You can also work with a friend, taking turns challenging each other with questions that draw on material from different sections or paragraphs. However you go about it, integrating and elaborating on the textual material forces you to process it and to form new associations among the pieces of information that you are storing.

Elaborative rehearsal offers two distinct benefits: It ties the new material to information already in memory, and it generates a large set of retrieval cues to help you recall the material when you need it. Even after you feel well prepared, continued rehearsal may improve your retention. In fact, studies have shown that if you overlearn a subject in school, such as a foreign language, you may be able to remember much of it for the rest of your life (Bahrick, 1984; Bahrick & Hall, 1991).

An even more effective system for studying is known by the letters of its five stages: SQRRR (or SQ3R, for short):

1. **Survey.** Before you start to read, look at the chapter outline, the headings of the various sections in the chapter, and the chapter summary. Doing so helps you organize and integrate the material as you read.

2. **Question.** Then translate each heading in the chapter into questions about the text to follow. Before reading this chapter, for example, you might have recast the heading "Short-Term Memory" on page 211 into questions such as "Why is it called 'short-term'?" and "Is there an-

other type of memory that lasts longer?"

3. **Read.** Now read the first section in the chapter, looking for answers to the questions you have posed. If you discover major points not directly related to your questions, either revise your old questions to encompass the new material, or make up new questions.

4. **Recite.** After reading a section, close the book and answer your questions. You can also jot down your answers in outline form. Then check to make sure that you have covered all the key points raised in the section. Repeat steps 3 and 4 for each section of the chapter.

5. **Review.** After reading the whole chapter, review your notes, and then recite or say mentally your questions and answers from memory. Relate the material either to other ideas or to experiences in your life. Try to think of particularly good examples or illustrations of key points or concepts in the chapter. Get involved.

The SQ3R method forces you to react—to enter into a dialogue with the text. This interaction makes the material more interesting and meaningful and improves your chances of recalling it. It also organizes the material and relates it to what you already know. This method certainly takes longer in the short run than does simply reading a chapter, but you will save time later on when studying for exams.

CHECK YOUR UNDERSTANDING

WEB QUIZ **6.5**

Match the following terms with their appropriate definitions

1. _____retrograde amnesia
2. _____retroactive interference
3. _____proactive interference

a. forgetting because new information makes it harder to remember information already in memory

b. forgetting because old information in memory makes it harder to learn new information

c. can result from head injury or electroconvulsive therapy

4. "Mnemonics are memory aids that make some types of material, such as lists, easier to remember." Is this statement true (T) or false (F)?

Answers: 1. c. 2. b. 3. a. 4. T.

Rogoff, 1994). In many Western cultures, for example, being able to recite a long list of words or numbers, to repeat the details of a scene, and to provide facts and figures about historical events are all signs of a "good memory." In fact, tasks such as these are often used to test people's memory abilities. What we should realize is that these kinds of memory tasks reflect the type of learning, memorization, and categorization skills taught in Western schools. Members of other cultures often perform poorly on such memory tests because the exercises seem so odd to them.

In contrast, consider the memory skills of a person living in a society in which cultural information is passed on from one generation to the next through a rich oral tradition. An individual here may be able to recite the deeds of the culture's heroes in verse or rattle off the lines of descent of families, larger lineage groups, and elders. Or perhaps the individual has a storehouse of information about the migration of animals or the life cycles of plants that help people to obtain food and to know when to harvest crops.

Autobiographical Memory

What kinds of events are most likely to be remembered?

Autobiographical memory refers to our recollection of events that happened in our life and when those events took place (Koriat, Goldsmith, & Pansky, 2000); as such, it is a form of episodic memory. Autobiographical memories are of fundamental importance. Indeed, Conway (1996) contends that "autobiographical memory is central to self, to identity, to emotional experience, and to all those attributes that define an individual" (p. 295).

In general, more recent life events are, of course, easier to recall than earlier ones. In a classic study of autobiographical memory, researchers asked young adults to report the earliest personal memory that came to mind when they saw each of twenty words and then to estimate how long ago each event had occurred. The words were all common nouns, such as *hall* and *oven*, for which people can easily create images. In general, most personal memories concerned relatively recent events: The longer ago an event occurred, the less likely people were to report it (Crovitz & Schiffman, 1974). Other research, however, shows that people over age 50 are more likely than younger people to recall events from relatively early in life, probably because many of the most critical choices we make in our

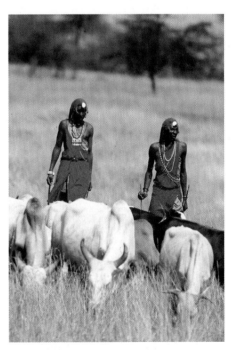

Look carefully at these cows and try to notice significant distinguishing characteristics of each animal. Is this task difficult for you? It probably is, unless you have been working closely with cattle all your life, as these two people have.

lives occur in late adolescence and early adulthood (Holland & Rabbitt, 1990; Mackavey, Malley, & Stewart, 1991).

Exactly how the vast amount of autobiographical information stored in memory is organized is not fully understood, but research in this area has supported two interesting theories. It may be that we store autobiographical information according to important events in our lives, such as beginning college, getting married, or experiencing the death of a loved one. This view explains why we can usually remember when events occurred relative to these major landmarks in our lives (Shum, 1998). We may also store autobiographical memories in *event clusters,* which are groups of memories on a related theme or that take place close together in time (Brown & Schopflocher, 1998).

Childhood Amnesia

Why do we have so few memories from the first two years of life?

Despite the richness of our autobigraphical memories, people rarely recall events that occurred before they were 2 years old. This phenomenon is sometimes called **childhood amnesia,** or *infantile amnesia.*

Exactly why people have difficulty remembering events from their first years of life is not well understood, although several explanations have been advanced. One hypothesis holds that childhood amnesia is a result of the child's brain not being fully developed at birth. An immature brain structure, such as the prefrontal cortex, may be incapable of efficiently processing and storing information in memory. In fact, the hippocampus, which is so important in the formation of episodic and semantic memories, is not fully formed until about age 2 (Jacobs and Nadel, 1998).

Childhood amnesia may also occur because young children lack a clear sense of self (Wheeler et al., 1997). According to this theory, without a sense of one's self, very young children find it difficult to organize and integrate their experiences into a coherent autobiographical memory scheme. However, with the emergence of self-concept and self-awareness near the end of the second year, childhood amnesia would be expected to lessen—which it does (Howe & Courage, 1993). Childhood amnesia may also be linked to language skills: Young children do not have the language skills necessary to strengthen and consolidate early experiences (Hudson & Sheffield, 1998).

In a twist on these theories, Patricia Bauer (1996) has shown that infants as young as 13 months can construct and maintain memories of specific events. Bauer contends that appropriate cues and repetition are the primary influences on efficient recall, not age. Childhood amnesia has to do with the inability of *adults* to remember early experiences, especially before the age of 2. And that, argue many psychologists, is a real phenomenon that needs to be explained (Eacott, 1999; Newcombe et al., 2000).

Flashbulb Memories

How can we explain the enduring vividness of flashbulb memories?

"I was standing by the stove getting dinner; my husband came in and told me." "I was fixing the fence. Mr. W. came along and told me. It was 9 or 10 o'clock in the morning." "It was in the forenoon; we were at work on the road by K's mills: A man driving past told us." These were three responses to the question "Do you recall where you were when you heard that Abraham Lincoln was shot?" Other accounts were even more detailed. In fact, of 179 people interviewed, 127 claimed to recall precisely the time and place at which they first heard of the assassination. That is a very high

Childhood amnesia
The difficulty adults have remembering experiences from their first 2 years of life.

percentage, considering that the researcher asked this question 33 years after the event (Colegrove, 1982).

A **flashbulb memory** is the experience of remembering vividly a certain event and the incidents surrounding it even after a long time has passed. We often remember events that are shocking or otherwise highly significant in this way. The death of a close relative, a birth, a graduation, or a wedding day may all elicit flashbulb memories. So can dramatic events in which we were not personally involved, such as the attack on the World Trade Center in New York City on September 11, 2001.

The assumptions that flashbulb memories are accurate, that they form at the time of an event, and that we remember them better because of their highly emotional content have all been questioned. First, flashbulb memories are certainly not always accurate. Although this is a difficult contention to test, let's consider just one case. Psychologist Ulric Neisser vividly recalled what he was doing on the day in 1941 when the Japanese bombed Pearl Harbor. He clearly remembered that he was listening to a professional baseball game on the radio, which was interrupted by the shocking announcement. But professional baseball is not played in December, when the attack took place, so this sharp flashbulb memory was simply incorrect (Neisser, 1982).

Even if an event is registered accurately, it may undergo periodic revision, just like other long-term memories (Schmolck, Buffalo, & Squire, 2000). We are bound to discuss and rethink a major event many times, and we probably also hear a great deal of additional information about that event in the weeks and months after it occurs. As a result, the flashbulb memory may undergo reconstruction and become less accurate over the years until it sometimes bears little or no resemblance to what actually happened.

Recovered Memories

Can people be persuaded to "create" new memories about events that never occurred?

In recent years a controversy has raged, both within the academic community and in society at large, about the validity of *recovered memories*. The idea is that people experience an event, then lose all memory of it, and then later recall it, often in the course of psychotherapy or under hypnosis. Frequently, the recovered memories concern physical or sexual abuse during childhood. The issue is important not only for theoretical reasons but also because of the fact that people have been imprisoned for abuse solely on the basis of the recovered memories of their "victims." No one denies the reality of childhood abuse or the damage that such experiences cause. But are the recovered memories real? Did the remembered abuse really occur?

The answer is by no means obvious. There is ample evidence that people can be induced to "remember" events that never happened. Loftus and her colleagues conducted experiments in which adults were asked to recall events that a close relative had supposedly mentioned (Loftus, Coan, & Pickrell, 1996; Loftus & Pickrell, 1995). Three events had actually occurred, the other (about getting lost in a shopping mall or other public place at the age of 5) had not. Twenty-five percent of the participants eventually "remembered" the fictitious event.

Other research confirms that it is relatively easy to implant memories of an experience merely by asking about it. The more times that people are asked about the event, the more likely they are to "remember" it. Sometimes these memories become quite real to the participant. In one experiment, 25 percent of adults "remembered" fictitious events by the third

Millions of people will forever have a vivid flashbulb memory of planes flying into the twin towers of the World Trade Center in New York City on September 11, 2001.

Flashbulb memory
A vivid memory of a certain event and the incidents surrounding it even after a long time has passed.

time they were interviewed about them. One of the fictitious events involved knocking over a punch bowl onto the parents of the bride at a wedding reception. At the first interview, one participant said that she had no recollection whatsoever of the event; by the second interview, she "remembered" that the reception was outdoors and that she had knocked over the bowl while running around. Some people even "remembered" details about the event, such as what people looked like and what they wore. Yet the researchers documented that these events never happened (Hyman, Husband, & Billings, 1995). Other research shows that people can even become convinced that they remember experiences from infancy (Spanos, 1996; Spanos, Burgess, Burgess, Samuels, & Blois, 1997).

The implication of this and similar research is that it is quite possible for people to "remember" abusive experiences that never happened. And some people who have "recovered" abuse memories have later realized that the events never occurred. Some of these people have brought suit against the therapists who, they came to believe, implanted the memories. In one case, a woman won such a suit and was awarded $850,000 (Imrie, 1999).

Yet there is reason to believe that not all recovered memories are merely the product of suggestion. There are numerous case studies of people who have lived through traumatic experiences, including natural disasters, accidents, combat, assault, and rape, who then apparently forgot these events for many years but who later remembered them (Arrigo & Pezdek, 1997). For example, Wilbur J. Scott, a sociologist, claimed to remember nothing of his tour of duty in Vietnam during 1968–1969, but during a divorce in 1983, he discovered his medals and souvenirs from Vietnam, and the memories then came back to him (Arrigo & Pezdek, 1997).

What is needed is a reliable way of separating real memories from false ones, but so far no such test is available. The sincerity and conviction of the person who "remembers" long-forgotten childhood abuse is no indication of the reality of that abuse. We are left with the conclusion that recovered memories are not, in themselves, sufficiently trustworthy to justify criminal convictions. There must also be corroborative evidence, since without corroboration, there is no way that even the most experienced examiner can separate real memories from false ones (Loftus, 1997). (See *Understanding the World Around You: Eyewitness Testimony: Can We Trust It?* on p. 218 for further discussion of memory distortion.)

INTERACTIVE LECTURE 6.6

WEB QUIZ 6.6

CHECK YOUR UNDERSTANDING

1. What people remember and how they recall it vary only a small amount from culture to culture. Is this statement true (T) or false (F)?

2. When older adults are asked to recall major life events, they tend to remember those that occurred in _____.

3. The phenomenon that we seldom remember events that occurred before our second birthday is called _____ _____.

4. A long-lasting and vivid memory for a certain event and the incidents surrounding it is called _____ _____.

5. Research demonstrates that it is nearly impossible to change a person's memory once that memory has been stored. Is this statement true (T) or false (F)?

Answers: 1. F. 2. late adolescence or early adulthood. 3. childhood amnesia. 4. flashbulb memory. 5. F.

KEY TERMS

CHAPTER REVIEW

The Sensory Registers

What is the role of sensory registers? Many psychologists view **memory** as a series of steps in which we encode, store, and retrieve information, much as a computer does. This is called **the information-processing** model of memory. The first step in the model is inputting data through our senses into temporary holding bins, called **sensory registers**. These registers give us a brief moment to decide whether something deserves our attention.

Visual and Auditory Registers

What would happen if auditory information faded as quickly as visual information fades? Information entering a sensory register disappears very quickly if it isn't processed further. Information in the visual register lasts for only about a quarter of a second before it is replaced by new information. If sounds faded from our auditory register as rapidly as this, spoken language would be more difficult to understand. Information in the auditory register can linger for several seconds.

Why does some information capture our attention, while other information goes unnoticed? The next step in the memory process is **attention**—selectively looking at, listening to, smelling, tasting, or feeling what we deem to be important. The nervous system seems automatically to filter out peripheral information, allowing us to zero in on what is essential at a particular time. Unattended information receives at least some processing, however, so that we can quickly shift attention to it if it suddenly strikes us as significant.

Short-Term Memory

What are the two primary tasks of short-term memory? **Short-term memory (STM)** holds whatever information we are actively attending to at any given time. Its two primary tasks are to store new information briefly and to "work" on information that we currently have in mind. This second function is why STM is also called *working memory.*

Do we store material in short-term memory as it sounds or as it looks? Information can be stored in STM according to the way it sounds, the way it looks, or its meaning. Verbal information is encoded by sound, even if we see the words written rather than hear them spoken. It is interesting that the capacity for visual encoding in STM seems to be greater than for encoding by sound.

How can we hold information in STM? Through **rote rehearsal,** or maintenance rehearsal, we retain information in STM for a minute or two by repeating it over and over again. However, rote memorization does not promote long-term memory.

Long-Term Memory

What types of information are retained in LTM? **Long-term memory (LTM)** is more or less permanent and stores everything we "know."

What is the limit of LTM? Long-term memory can store a vast amount of information that can last for many years.

How are most memories encoded in LTM? Most of the information in LTM seems to be encoded according to its meaning.

Which items in a list are hardest to remember? Short- and long-term memory work together to explain the **serial position effect,** the fact that when given a list of items to remember, people tend to recall the first and last items in the list better than words in the middle. The *recency effect* explains that end-words are still held in STM, whereas the *primacy effect* describes the extra LTM rehearsal given to first words in the list.

What three ways are used to hold information in LTM? Rote rehearsal is useful for holding information in LTM, particularly meaningless material such as phone numbers. Through **elaborative rehearsal,** we extract the meaning of information and link it to as much material that is already in LTM as possible. Elaborative rehearsal processes new data in a deeper and more meaningful way than simple rote repetition. The way in which we encode material for storage in LTM affects the ease with which we can retrieve it later on.

A **schema** is a mental representation of an object or event that is stored in memory. Schemata provide a framework into which incoming information is fitted. They may prompt the formation of stereotypes and the drawing of inferences.

How do different types of LTM differ? **Episodic memories** are memories for events experienced in a specific time and place. **Semantic memories** are facts and concepts not linked to a particular time. **Procedural memories** are motor skills and habits. **Emotional memories** are learned emotional responses to various stimuli.

What are the differences between implicit and explicit memories? **Explicit memory** refers to memories we are aware of, including episodic and semantic memories. **Implicit memory** refers to memories for information that either was not intentionally committed to LTM or is retrieved unintentionally from LTM, including procedural and emotional memories. This distinction is illustrated by research on *priming*, which finds that people are more likely to complete fragments with items seen earlier than with other, equally plausible items.

The Biology of Memory

How and where are memories stored? Memories are stored in various regions of the brain through a process called consolidation.

What role do neurons play in memory? Memories consist of changes in the chemistry and structure of neurons. The process by which these changes occur, called consolidation, is often very slow.

Are STM and LTM found in the same parts of the brain? There is no one place where all memories are stored, but research has shown that different parts of the brain are specialized for the storage of memories. Short-term memories seem to be located primarily in the prefrontal cortex and temporal lobe. Long-term memories seem to involve both subcortical and cortical structures. Semantic and episodic memories seem to be located primarily in the frontal and temporal lobes of the cortex, and procedural memories appear to be located primarily in the cerebellum and motor cortex. A brain structure called the hippocampus seems especially important in the consolidation of semantic, episodic, and procedural memories. Emotional memories are dependent on the amygdala.

Forgetting

What factors explain why we sometimes forget? Both biological and environmental factors can contribute to our inability to recall information.

How does the deterioration of the brain help to explain forgetting? Severe memory loss can be traced to brain damage caused by accidents, surgery, poor diet, or disease. Head injuries can cause **retrograde amnesia,** the inability of people to remember what happened shortly before their accident. Some studies have focused on the role of the hippocampus in long-term memory formation. Other research has emphasized the role of neurotransmitters, especially acetylcholine, in the memory process.

What environmental factors contribute to our inability to remember? To the extent that information is apparently lost from LTM, researchers attribute the cause to inadequate learning or to interference from competing information. Interference may come from two directions: In **retroactive interference,** new information interferes with old information already in LTM; **proactive interference** refers to the process by which old information already in LTM interferes with new information.

When environmental cues that were present during learning are absent during recall, context-dependent forgetting may occur. The ability to recall information is also affected by one's physiological state when the material was learned; this process is known *as state-dependent memory*.

Sometimes we "reconstruct" memories for social or personal self-defense as demonstrated in research about eyewitness testimony.

What can you do to improve your memory? A number of steps can be taken to improve recall: Develop motivation. Practice memory skills. Be confident in your ability to remember. Minimize distractions. Stay focused. Make connections between new material and other information already stored in your long-term memory, using such techniques as **mnemonics.** Use both mental imagery and retrieval cues. Rely on more than memory alone. Be aware that your own personal schemata may distort your recall of events.

Special Topics in Memory

What factors can influence how well you remember a specific incident? The values and customs of a given culture have a profound effect on what people remember and how easily they recall it. So do the emotions we attach to a memory, with some emotion-laden events being remembered for life. Also affecting how well we remember are the strategies we use to store and retrieve information.

Are the memory tasks in Western schools different from those in cultures that pass on oral traditions? Many Western schools stress being able to recall long lists of words, facts, and figures that are divorced from everyday life. In contrast, societies in which cultural information is passed on through a rich oral tradition may instead emphasize memory for events that directly affect people's lives.

What kinds of events are most likely to be remembered? Autobiographical memory refers to recollection of events from one's life. Not all of these events are recalled with equal clarity, of course, and some are not recalled at all. Autobiographical memories are typically strongest for events that had a major impact on our lives or that aroused strong emotion.

Why do we have so few memories from the first two years of life? People generally cannot remember events that occurred before age 2 (a phenomenon called **childhood amnesia**). Childhood amnesia may result from the incomplete development of brain structures before age 2, from the infants' lack of a clear sense of self, from the lack of language skills used to consolidate early experience; or childhood amnesia may be more related to an adult's inability to recall memories that were, in fact, stored during the first two years.

How can we explain the enduring vividness of flashbulb memories? Years after a dramatic or significant event occurs, people often have vivid memories of that event as well as the incidents surrounding it. These memories are known as **flashbulb memories.** Recent research has challenged the assumptions that flashbulb memories are accurate and stable.

Can people be persuaded to "create" new memories about events that never occurred? There are many cases of people who experience a traumatic event, lose all memory of it, but then later recall it. Such recovered memories are highly controversial, since research shows that people can be induced to "remember" events that never happened. So far there is no clear way to distinguish real recovered memories from false ones.

CRITICAL THINKING AND APPLICATIONS

1. How could our psychological state influence our attention?

2. What are three examples of elaborative rehearsal for course material that you need to learn now?

3. What impact can the phenomenon of reconstructive memory have on our judicial system? Do you think that recovered memories should be admissible in court? Why, or why not?

WEB QUIZ **6.7**   **Go to the Morris 6e Companion Website to take a practice chapter exam.**

7 Cognition and Mental Abilities

OVERVIEW

Building Blocks of Thought
:: Language
:: Images
:: Concepts

Language, Thought, and Culture

Problem Solving
:: The Interpretation of Problems
:: Producing Strategies and Evaluating Progress
:: Obstacles to Solving Problems

Decision Making
:: Logical Decision Making
:: Decision-Making Heuristics
:: Explaining Our Decisions

Intelligence and Mental Abilities
:: Theories of Intelligence
:: Intelligence Tests
:: What Makes a Good Test?

Heredity, Environment, and Intelligence
:: Heredity

:: Environment
:: The IQ Debate: A Useful Model
:: Mental Abilities and Human Diversity: Gender and Culture
:: Extremes of Intelligence

Creativity
:: Intelligence and Creativity
:: Creativity Tests

Answers to Problems in the Chapter

Answers to Intelligence Test Questions

"A T THE BRAEFIELD SCHOOL FOR THE DEAF, I MET JOSEPH, A BOY OF ELEVEN WHO had just entered school for the first time—an eleven-year-old with no language whatever. He had been born deaf, but this had not been realized until he was in his fourth year. His failure to talk, or understand speech, at the normal age was put down to 'retardation,' then to 'autism,' and these diagnoses had clung to him. When his deafness finally became apparent he was seen as 'deaf and dumb,' dumb not only literally, but metaphorically, and there was never any attempt to teach him language.

"Joseph longed to communicate, but could not. Neither speaking nor writing nor signing was available to him, only gestures and pantomimes, and a marked ability to draw. What has happened to him? I kept asking myself. What is going on inside, how has he come to such a pass? He looked alive and animated, but profoundly baffled: His eyes were attracted to speaking mouths and signing hands—they darted to our mouths and hands, inquisitively, uncomprehendingly, and, it seemed to me, yearningly. He perceived that something was 'going on' between us, but he could not comprehend what it was—he had, as yet, almost no idea of symbolic communication, of what it was to have a symbolic currency, to exchange meaning. . . .

"Joseph was unable, for example, to communicate how he had spent the weekend. . . . It was not only language that was missing: there was not, it was evident, a clear sense of the past, of 'a day ago' as distinct from 'a year ago.' There was a strange lack of historical sense, the feeling of a life that lacked autobiographical and historical dimension, . . . a life that only existed in the moment, in the present. . . .

"Joseph saw, distinguished, categorized, used; he had no problems with perceptual categorization or generalization, but he could not, it seemed, go much beyond this, hold abstract ideas in mind, reflect, play, plan. He seemed completely literal—unable to juggle images or hypotheses or possibilities, unable to enter an imaginative or figurative realm. And yet, one still felt, he was of normal intelligence, despite the manifest limitations of intellectual functioning. It was not that he lacked a mind, but that he was not using his mind fully. . . ." (Sacks, 2000, pp. 32–34)

As Sacks suggests, language and thought are intertwined. We find it difficult to imagine one without the other, and we consider both part of what it means to be human. Psychologists use the term **cognition** to refer to all the processes that we use to acquire and apply information. We have already considered the cognitive processes of perception, learning, and memory. In later chapters, we examine cognition's crucial relation to coping and adjustment, abnormal behavior, and interpersonal relations. In this chapter, we focus on three cognitive processes that we think of as characteristically human: thinking, problem solving, and decision making. We also discuss two mental abilities that psychologists have tried to measure: intelligence and creativity.

Building Blocks of Thought

What are the three most important building blocks of thought?

When you think about a close friend, you may have in mind complex statements about her, such as "I'd like to talk to her soon" or "I wish I could be more like her." You may also have an image of her—probably her face, but

Cognition
The processes whereby we acquire and use knowledge.

231

perhaps the sound of her voice as well. Or you may think of your friend by using various concepts or categories such as *woman, kind, strong, dynamic, gentle*. When we think, we make use of all these things—language, images, and concepts—often simultaneously. These are the three most important building blocks of thought.

Language

What steps do we go through to turn a thought into a statement?

Human **language** is a flexible system of symbols that enables us to communicate our ideas, thoughts, and feelings. Although all animals communicate with each other, human language is a far more complex system. It is a unique human ability that sets us apart from other animals (Savage-Rumbaugh & Brakke, 1996). Chimpanzes—our closest relatives in the animal kingdom—use some three dozen different vocalizations plus an array of gestures, postures, and facial expressions to communicate, a system that is far simpler than the speech of a normal three-year-old child.

One way to understand the uniquely human system of language is to consider its basic structure. Spoken language is based on units of sound called **phonemes.** The sounds of *t, th,* and *k,* for instance, are all phonemes in English. There are about 45 phonemes in the English language and as many as 85 in some other languages (Bourne, Dominowski, Loftus, & Healy, 1986). By themselves, phonemes are meaningless and seldom play an important role in helping us to think. The sound *b,* for example, has no inherent meaning. But phonemes can be grouped together to form words, prefixes (such as *un-* and *pre-*), and suffixes (such as *-ed* and *-ing*). These meaningful combinations of phonemes are known as **morphemes**—the smallest meaningful units in a language. Morphemes play a key role in human thought. They can represent important ideas such as "red" or "calm" or "hot." The suffix *-ed* captures the idea of "in the past" (as in *visited* or *liked*). The prefix *pre-* conveys the idea of "before" or "prior to" (as in *preview* or *predetermined*).

We can combine morphemes to create words that represent quite complex ideas, such as *pre-exist-ing, un-excell-ed, psycho-logy.* In turn, words can be joined into even more complex thoughts. Just as there are rules for combining phonemes and morphemes, there are also rules for structuring sentences and their meaning. These rules are what linguists call **grammar.** The two major components of grammar are *syntax* and *semantics. Syntax* is the system of rules that governs how we combine words to form meaningful phrases and sentences. For example, in English and many other languages, the meaning of a sentence often is determined by word order. "Sally hit the car" means one thing; "The car hit Sally" means something quite different; and "Hit Sally car the" is meaningless.

Semantics describes how we assign meaning to morphemes, words, phrases, and sentences—in other words, the content of language. When we are thinking about something—say, the ocean—our ideas usually consist of phrases and sentences, such as "The ocean is unusually calm tonight." Sentences have both a *surface structure*—the particular words and phrases—and a *deep structure*—the underlying meaning. The same deep structure can be conveyed by various different surface structures:

The ocean is unusually calm tonight.

Tonight the ocean is particularly calm.

Compared with most other nights, tonight the ocean is calm.

Syntax and semantics enable speakers and listeners to perform what linguist Noam Chomsky calls *transformations* between the surface and the deep

Language
A flexible system of communication that uses sounds, rules, gestures, or symbols to convey information.

Phonemes
The basic sounds that make up any language.

Morphemes
The smallest meaningful units of speech, such as simple words, prefixes, and suffixes.

Grammar
The language rules that determine how sounds and words can be combined and used to communicate meaning within a language.

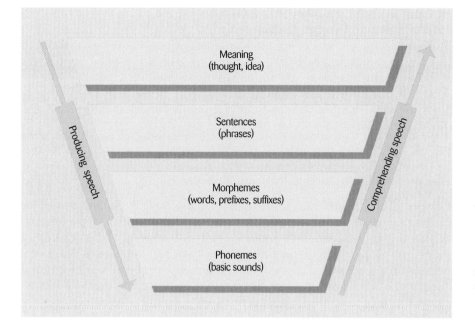

FIGURE 7–1

The direction of movement in speech production and comprehension.

Producing a sentence involves movement from thoughts and ideas to basic sounds; comprehending a sentence requires movement from basic sounds back to the underlying thoughts and ideas.

structure. According to Chomsky, when you want to communicate an idea, you start with a thought, then choose words and phrases that will express the idea, and finally produce the speech sounds that make up those words and phrases. Speaking requires *top-down processing,* and you can see from the left arrow in **Figure 7–1** that the movement is indeed from top to bottom. When you want to understand a sentence, your task is reversed. You must start with speech sounds and work your way up to the meaning of those sounds. This method is called *bottom-up processing,* as shown by the right arrow in **Figure 7–1**.

Images

What role do images play in thinking?

Think for a moment about Abraham Lincoln. Then think about being outside in a summer thunderstorm. Your thoughts of Lincoln may have included such phrases as "wrote the Gettysburg Address," "president during the Civil War," and "assassinated by John Wilkes Booth." You probably also had some mental images about him: bearded face, lanky body, or log cabin. When you thought about the thunderstorm, you probably formed mental images of wind, rain, and lightning—perhaps even the smell of wet leaves and earth. An **image** is a mental representation of some sensory experience, and it can be used to think about things. We can visualize the Statue of Liberty; we can smell Thanksgiving dinner or the scent of a Christmas tree; we can hear Martin Luther King, Jr., saying, "I have a dream!" In short, we can think by using images.

Images allow us to think about things in nonverbal ways. Albert Einstein relied heavily on his powers of visualization to understand phenomena he would later describe by using complex mathematical formulas. Einstein believed that his extraordinary genius resulted in part from his skill in visualizing possibilities (Shepard, 1978). Although few of us can match Einstein's brilliance, we all use images to think about and solve problems. We have all seen a teacher clarify a difficult concept by drawing a quick, simple sketch on a blackboard. Many times, when words make a tangled knot of an issue, a graphic image drawn on paper straightens out the confusion. Images also allow us to use concrete forms to represent com-

"Well, you don't look like an experimental psychologist to <u>me</u>."

Image
A mental representation of a sensory experience.

Pablo Picasso, the great twentieth century artist, developed a style of painting known as Cubism. In paintings such as *Nude with bunch of Irises and Mirror,* 1934, shown here, he reformed objects into basic geometric shapes. We recognize the figure in this painting as a woman because its shapes represent the "concept" of a female.

plex and abstract ideas, as when newspapers use pie charts and graphs to illustrate how people voted in an election.

Experiments using the brain imaging techniques that we learned about in Chapter 2 have shown that we often use the same brain centers for thinking about images as we do for visual perception (Kreiman, Koch, & Freid, 2000; Mosovich, Behrmann, & Winocur, 1994). This research supports the idea that we do not simply remember images; rather, we also think pictorially.

Concepts

How do concepts help us to think more efficiently?

Concepts are mental categories for classifying specific people, things, or events (Komatsu, 1992). *Dogs, books,* and *mountains* are all concepts for classifying things, whereas *fast, beautiful,* and *interesting* can classify things, events, or people. When you think about a specific thing—say, Mt. Everest—you usually think of the concepts that apply to it, such as *highest* and *dangerous to climb.* Concepts can also be used to create and organize hierarchies or groups of subordinate categories. For example, the general concept of *plants* can be broken down into the subordinate categories of *trees, bushes,* and *grasses,* just as the subordinate concept of *trees* can be further subdivided into *oaks, maples, pines,* and so forth (Reed, 1996). If we could not form concepts, we would need a different name for every object. Thus, concepts help us to think efficiently about things and how they relate to one another.

Concepts also give meaning to new experiences. We do not stop and form a new concept for every new experience that we have. We draw on concepts that we have already formed and place the new event into the appropriate categories. As we do so, we may modify some of our concepts to better match our experiences. Consider the concept of job interview. You probably have some concept of this process even before your first interview, but your concept will probably change somewhat after you actually look for a job. Once you have formed a concept of *job interview,* you will not have to respond to each interview as a totally new experience; you will know what to expect and how you are expected to behave. Conceptualizing, whether *job interview* or anything else, is a way of organizing experiences.

Although it is tempting to think of concepts as simple and clear-cut, most of the concepts that we use are rather "fuzzy": They overlap one another and are often poorly defined. For example, most people can tell a mouse from a rat, but listing the critical differences between the two would be difficult (Rosch, 1973, 1978).

If we cannot explain the difference between mouse and rat, how can we use these *fuzzy concepts* in our thinking? We may construct a model, or **prototype,** of a representative mouse and one of a representative rat, and then use those prototypes in our thinking (Rosch, 1978). Our concept of bird, for example, does not consist of a list of a bird's key attributes, like *feathered, winged, two-footed,* and *lives in trees.* Instead, most of us have a model bird, or prototype, in mind—such as a robin or a sparrow—that captures for us the essence of *bird.* When we encounter new objects, we compare them with this prototype to determine whether they are, in fact, birds. And when we think about birds, we usually think about our prototypical bird.

Concepts, then, like words and images, help us to formulate thoughts. But human cognition involves more than just passively thinking about things. It also involves actively using words, images, and concepts to fashion an understanding of the world, to solve problems, and to make decisions. In the next three sections, we see how this is done.

Concept
A mental category for classifying objects, people, or experiences.

Prototype
According to Rosch, a mental model containing the most typical features of a concept

INTERACTIVE LECTURE **7.1**

WEB QUIZ **7.1**

CHECK YOUR UNDERSTANDING

1. _____, _____, and _____ are the three most important building blocks of thought.

2. In language, units of sound, called _____, are combined to form the smallest units of meaning, called _____. These smallest meaningful units can then be combined to create words, which in turn can be used to build phrases and whole _____.

3. Language rules that specify how sounds and words can be combined into meaningful sentences are called rules of _____.

4. According to Chomsky, language users employ rules to allow them to go from the surface structure to the _____ _____ of language.

5. Categories for classifying specific people, things, or events are called
   a. concepts.
   b. images.
   c. phonemes.
   d. morphemes.

6. Indicate whether the following statements are true (T) or false (F).
   ____ a. Images help us to think about things because images use concrete forms to represent complex ideas.
   ____ b. People decide which objects belong to a concept by comparing the object's features to a model or prototype of the concept.
   ____ c. Concepts help us give meaning to new experiences.

Answers: 1. language, images, concepts. 2. phonemes, morphemes, sentences. 3. grammar. 4. deep structure 5. a. 6. a. (T); b. (T); c. (T).

Language, Thought, and Culture

How do language, thought, and culture influence each other?

Language is closely tied to the expression and understanding of thoughts. Words—such as *friend, family, airplane,* and *love*—correspond to concepts that are the building blocks of thought. By combining words into sentences, we can link concepts to other concepts and can express complex ideas. Is it possible that language also influences how we think and what we can think about? Benjamin Whorf (1956) strongly believed that it does. According to Whorf's **linguistic relativity hypothesis,** the language that we speak determines the pattern of our thinking and our view of the world. For Whorf, if a language lacks a particular expression, the thought to which the expression corresponds will probably not occur to the people who speak that language. For example, the Hopi, a Native American people of the southwestern United States, have only two nouns for things that fly. One noun refers to birds; the other is used for everything else. A plane and a dragonfly, for instance, are both referred to with the same noun. According to Whorf, Hopi speakers would not see as great a difference between planes and dragonflies as we do, because their language labels the two similarly.

The linguistic relativity hypothesis has intuitive appeal—it makes sense to think that limits of language will produce limits in thinking. However, researchers have found several flaws in Whorf's theory.

For example, the Dani people of New Guinea have only two words for colors—"dark" and "light"—yet they see and can easily learn to label other basic colors like red, yellow, and green. They also judge the similarity of colors much as English-speaking people do (E. R. Heider, 1972; E. R. Heider

Linguistic relativity hypothesis
Whorf's idea that patterns of thinking are determined by the specific language one speaks.

The Dani of New Guinea can perceive and remember the many colors of their world just as readily as you can, even though their language has only two color terms—"light" and "dark." Human thought is not limited to the words in a person's language. Language may indeed influence thought, but it doesn't seem to restrict thought to the extent that Whorf believed.

INTERACTIVE LECTURE **7.2**

& Oliver, 1972; Rosch, 1973). Thus, the ability to think about colors is quite similar across cultures, even when these cultures have quite different color terms in their languages.

Other critics say that it is the need to think about things differently that changes a language, not that language changes the way we think (Berlin & Kay, 1969). For example, English-speaking skiers, realizing that different textures of snow can affect their downhill run, refer to snow as *powder, corn,* and *ice.* The growth of personal computers and the Internet has inspired a vocabulary of its own, such as *hard drive, RAM, gigabytes, software, online,* and *CD-ROM.* In short, people create new words when they need them—experience shapes language.

Psychologists have not dismissed the Whorf hypothesis altogether but rather have softened it, recognizing that language, thought, and culture are intertwined (Matsumoto, 1996). This realization has caused us to examine more carefully how we use our language. Traditionally, the English language has used masculine terms such as "man" and "he" to describe people of both genders—"all 'men' are created equal." Research has shown, however, that when people are asked to make judgments about a person sometimes described as "he" and other times as "she," the particular word used *did* influence their behavior (Greenwald & Banaji, 1995; Hyde, 1984). Findings such as these have led many people (including textbook authors!) to refer to others in gender-neutral language (for example, "he or she").

People create words to capture important aspects of their experiences, and to some extent, words shape how people think and what they think about. People also can think about things for which they have no words. Finally, language and thought are both influenced by culture.

WEB QUIZ **7.2** ✔

CHECK YOUR UNDERSTANDING

1. According to Whorf's _____ _____ hypothesis, the language we speak shapes our thinking.
2. Which of the following does *not* support Whorf's hypothesis?
   a. Colors that are hard to name are also hard to recall.
   b. When society changes, language also changes.
   c. People make different judgments when another person is described as "he" rather than "she."
3. Indicate whether the following statements are true (T) or false (F).
   _____ a. Many words in our language correspond to concepts.
   _____ b. The more complex a society is, the more words that its language contains.
   _____ c. Thoughts are limited to the words in the language that a person speaks.

Answers: 1. linguistic relativity. 2. b. 3. a. (T). b. (T). c. (F).

Problem Solving

What are three general aspects of the problem-solving process?

Solve the following problems:

Problem 1 You have three measuring spoons (see **Figure 7–2**). One is filled with 8 teaspoons of salt; the other two are empty but have a capacity of 2 teaspoons each. Divide the salt among the spoons so that only 4 teaspoons of salt remain in the largest spoon.

Problem 2 You have a 5-minute hourglass and a 9-minute hourglass (see **Figure 7–3**). How can you use them to time a 14-minute barbecue? (Adapted from Sternberg, 1986.)

Most people find these problems very easy. But now try solving more elaborate versions of them (the answers are at the end of this chapter):

Problem 3 You have three measuring spoons (see **Figure 7–4**). One (spoon A) is filled with 8 teaspoons of salt. The second and third spoons are both empty. The second spoon (spoon B) can hold 5 teaspoons, and the third (spoon C) can hold 3 teaspoons. Divide the salt among the spoons so that spoon A and spoon B each have exactly 4 teaspoons of salt and spoon C is empty.

Problem 4 You have a 5-minute hourglass and a 9-minute hourglass (see **Figure 7–3**). How can you use them to time a 13-minute barbecue? (Adapted from Sternberg, 1986.)

Most people find these two problems much more difficult than the first two. Why? The answer lies in interpretation, strategy, and evaluation. Problems 1 and 2 are considered trivial because it's so easy to interpret what is called for, the strategies for solving them are simple, and you can effortlessly verify that each step you take moves you closer to a solution. Problems 3 and 4, in contrast, require some thought to interpret what is called for, the strategies for solving them are not immediately apparent, and it is harder to evaluate whether any given step has actually made progress toward your goal. These three aspects of problem solving—interpretation, strategy, and evaluation—provide a useful framework for investigating this topic.

The Interpretation of Problems

Why is representing the problem so important to finding an effective solution?

The first step in solving a problem is called **problem representation,** which means interpreting or defining the problem. It is tempting to leap ahead and try to solve a problem just as it is presented, but this impulse often leads to poor solutions. For example, if your business is losing money, you might define the problem as deciphering how to cut costs. But by defining the problem so narrowly, you have ruled out other options. A better representation of this problem would be to figure out ways to boost profits—by cutting costs, by increasing income, or both.

To see the importance of problem representation, consider these two problems:

Problem 5 You have four pieces of chain, each of which is made up of 3 links (see **Figure 7–5**). All links are closed at the beginning of the problem. It costs 2 cents to open a link and 3 cents to close a link. How can you

FIGURE 7–2

5 min.   9 min.

FIGURE 7–3

A

B

C

FIGURE 7–4

Problem representation
The first step in solving a problem; it involves interpreting or defining the problem.

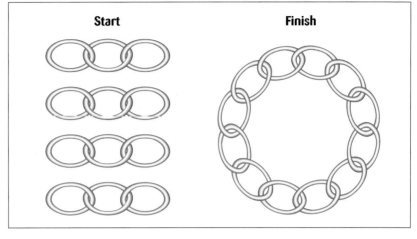

FIGURE 7–5

join all 12 links together into a single, continuous circle without paying more than 15 cents?

Problem 6 Arrange six kitchen matches into four equilateral triangles (see **Figure 7–6**). Each side of every triangle must be only one match in length.

These two problems are difficult because people tend to represent them in ways that impede solutions. For example, in Problem 5, most people assume that the best way to proceed is to open and close the end links on the pieces of chain. As long as they persist with this "conceptual block," they will be unable to solve the problem. If the problem is represented differently, the solution is almost immediately obvious. Similarly, for the kitchen match problem, most people assume that they can work only in two dimensions—that is, that the triangles must lie flat on a surface—or that one match cannot serve as the side of two triangles. When the problem is represented differently, the solution becomes much easier. (The solutions to both of these problems appear at the end of this chapter.)

If you have successfully interpreted Problems 5 and 6, give number 7 a try:

Problem 7 A monk wishes to get to a retreat at the top of a mountain. He starts climbing the mountain at sunrise and arrives at the top at sunset of the same day. During the course of his ascent, he travels at various speeds and stops often to rest. He spends the night engaged in meditation. The next day he starts his descent at sunrise, following the same narrow path that he used to climb the mountain. As before, he travels at various speeds and stops often to rest. Because he takes great care not to trip and fall on the way down, the descent takes as long as the ascent, and he does not arrive at the bottom until sunset. Prove that there is one place on the path that the monk passes at exactly the same time of day on the ascent and on the descent.

This problem is extremely difficult to solve if it is represented verbally or mathematically. It is considerably easier to solve if it is represented visually, as you can see from the explanation that appears at the end of this chapter.

Another aspect of successfully representing a problem is deciding which category the problem belongs to. Properly categorizing a problem can provide clues about how to solve it. In fact, once a problem has been properly categorized, its solution may be very easy. Quite often, people who seem to have a knack for solving problems are actually just very skilled at categorizing them in effective ways. Star chess players, for example, can readily cat-

FIGURE 7–6

The six-match problem. Arrange the six matches so that they form four equilateral triangles. The solution is given in Figure 7–12.

egorize a game situation by comparing it with various standard situations stored in their long-term memories. This strategy helps them interpret the current pattern of chess pieces with greater speed and precision than the novice chess player can. Similarly, a seasoned football coach may quickly call for a particular play because the coach has interpreted a situation on the field in terms of familiar categories. Gaining expertise in any field, from football to physics, consists primarily of increasing your ability to represent and categorize problems so that they can be solved quickly and effectively (Haberlandt, 1997).

Producing Strategies and Evaluating Progress

Why is an algorithm often better for solving a problem than is the process of trial and error?

Once you have properly interpreted a problem, the next steps needed are selecting a solution strategy and evaluating progress toward your goal. A solution strategy can be anything from simple trial and error, to information retrieval based on similar problems, to a set of step-by-step procedures guaranteed to work (called an algorithm), to rule-of-thumb approaches known as heuristics.

Trial and Error   Trial and error is a strategy that works best when there are only limited choices. For example, if you have only three or four keys to choose from, trial and error is the best way to find out which one unlocks your friend's garage door. In most cases, however, trial and error wastes time because there are so many different options to test. It is better to eliminate unproductive approaches and to zero in on an approach that will work. Let's consider some alternative strategies.

Information Retrieval   One approach is to retrieve from long-term memory information about how such a problem was solved in the past. Information retrieval is an especially important option when a solution is needed quickly. For example, pilots simply memorize the slowest speed at which a particular airplane can fly before it stalls.

Algorithms   More complex problems require more complex strategies. An **algorithm** is a problem-solving method that guarantees a solution if it is appropriate for the problem and is properly carried out. For example, to calculate the product of 323 and 546, we multiply the numbers according to the rules of multiplication (the algorithm). If we do it accurately, we are guaranteed to get the right answer. Similarly, to convert temperatures from Fahrenheit to Celsius, we use the algorithm $C = 5/9(F - 32)$.

Heuristics   Because we don't have algorithms for every kind of problem, we often turn to **heuristics,** or rules of thumb. Heuristics do not guarantee a solution, but they may bring it within reach. Part of problem solving is to decide which heuristic is most appropriate for a given problem (Bourne et al., 1986).

A very simple heuristic is **hill climbing:** We try to move continually closer to our goal without going backward. At each step, we evaluate how far "up the hill" we have come, how far we still have to go, and precisely what the next step should be. On a multiple-choice test, for example, one useful hill-climbing strategy is first to eliminate the alternatives that are obviously incorrect. In trying to balance a budget, each reduction in expenses brings you closer to the goal and leaves you with a smaller deficit.

An experienced football coach can analyze a situation on the field in terms of familiar categories. The coach can then call plays based on this knowledge. This is an example of how expertise can contribute to problem solving.

Algorithm
A step-by-step method of problem solving that guarantees a correct solution.

Heuristics
Rules of thumb that help in simplifying and solving problems, although they do not guarantee a correct solution.

Hill climbing
A heuristic problem-solving strategy in which each step moves you progressively closer to the final goal.

Another problem-solving heuristic is to create **subgoals.** By setting subgoals, we break a problem into smaller, more manageable pieces, each of which is easier to solve than the problem as a whole (Reed, 1996). Consider the problem of the Hobbits and the Orcs:

Problem 8 Three Hobbits and 3 Orcs are on the bank of a river. They all want to get to the other side, but their boat will carry only 2 creatures at a time. Moreover, if at any time the Orcs outnumber the Hobbits, the Orcs will attack the Hobbits. How can all the creatures get across the river without danger to the Hobbits?

The solution to this problem may be found by thinking of it in terms of a series of subgoals. What has to be done to get just one or two creatures across the river safely, temporarily leaving aside the main goal of getting everyone across? We could first send 2 of the Orcs across and have 1 of them return. That gets 1 Orc across the river. Now we can think about the next trip. It's clear that we can't then send a single Hobbit across with an Orc, because the Hobbit would be outnumbered as soon as the boat landed. Therefore, we have to send either 2 Hobbits or 2 Orcs. By working on the problem in this fashion—concentrating on subgoals—we can eventually get everyone across.

Once you have solved Problem 8, you might want to try Problem 9, which is considerably more difficult (the answers to both problems are at the end of the chapter):

Problem 9 This problem is identical to Problem 8, except that there are 5 Hobbits and 5 Orcs, and the boat can carry only 3 creatures at a time.

Subgoals are often helpful in solving a variety of everyday problems. For example, a student whose goal is to write a term paper might set subgoals by breaking the project into a series of separate tasks: choosing a topic, doing research and taking notes, preparing an outline, writing the first draft, editing, rewriting, and so on. Even the subgoals can sometimes be broken down into separate tasks: Writing the first draft of the paper might break down into the subgoals of writing the introduction, describing the position to be taken, supporting the position with evidence, drawing conclusions, writing a summary, and writing a bibliography. Subgoals make problem solving more manageable because they free us from the burden of having to "get to the other side of the river" all at once. Although the overall purpose of setting subgoals is still to reach the ultimate goal, this tactic allows us to set our sights on closer, more manageable objectives.

One of the most frequently used heuristics, called **means-end analysis,** combines hill climbing and subgoals. Like hill climbing, means-end analysis involves analyzing the difference between the current situation and the desired end, and then doing something to reduce that difference. But in contrast to hill climbing—which does not permit detours away from the final goal in order to solve the problem—means-end analysis takes into account the entire problem situation. It formulates subgoals in such a way as to allow us temporarily to take a step that appears to be backward in order to reach our goal in the end. One example is the pitcher's strategy in a baseball game when confronted with the best batter in the league. The pitcher might opt to walk this batter intentionally even though doing so moves away from the major subgoal of keeping runners off base. Intentional walking might enable the pitcher to keep a run from scoring and so contribute to the ultimate goal of winning the game. This flexibility in thinking is a major benefit of means-end analysis.

But means-end analysis also poses the danger of straying so far from the end goal that the goal disappears altogether. One way of avoiding this situation is to use the heuristic of **working backward** (Bourne et al., 1986).

Subgoals
Intermediate, more manageable goals used in one heuristic strategy to make it easier to reach the final goal.

Means-end analysis
A heuristic strategy that aims to reduce the discrepancy between the current situation and the desired goal at a number of intermediate points.

Working backward
A heuristic strategy in which one works backward from the desired goal to the given conditions.

With this strategy, the search for a solution begins at the goal and works backward toward the "givens." Working backward is often used when the goal has more information than the givens and when the operations involved can work in two directions. For example, if you wanted to spend exactly $100 on clothing, it would be difficult to reach that goal simply by buying some items and hoping that they totaled exactly $100. A better strategy would be to buy one item, subtract its cost from $100 to determine how much money you have left, then purchase another item, subtract its cost, and so on, until you have spent $100.

 7.1

Obstacles to Solving Problems

How can a "mental set" both help and hinder problem solving?

In everyday life, many factors can either help or hinder problem solving. One factor is a person's level of motivation, or emotional arousal. Generally, we must generate a certain surge of excitement to motivate ourselves to solve a problem, yet too much arousal can hamper our ability to find a solution (see Chapter 8, Motivation and Emotion).

Another factor that can either help or hinder problem solving is **mental set**—our tendency to perceive and to approach problems in certain ways. Set determines which information we tend to retrieve from memory to help us find a solution. Set can be helpful if we have learned operations that we can apply to the present situation. Much of our formal education involves learning sets and ways to solve problems (that is, learning heuristics and algorithms). But sets can also create obstacles, especially when a novel approach is needed. The most successful problem solvers have many different sets to choose from and can judge when to change sets or when to abandon them entirely. Great ideas and inventions come out of such flexibility.

One type of set that can seriously hinder problem solving is called **functional fixedness.** Consider **Figure 7–7.** Do you see a way to mount the candle on the wall? If not, you are probably stymied by functional fixedness. The more you use an object in only one way, the harder it is to

Mental Set
The tendency to perceive and to approach problems in certain ways.

Functional fixedness
The tendency to perceive only a limited number of uses for an object, thus interfering with the process of problem solving.

FIGURE 7–7

To test the effects of functional fixedness, participants might be given the items shown on the table and asked to mount a candle on the wall. See Figure 7–15 for a solution.

see new uses for it, because you have "assigned" the object to a fixed function. To some extent, part of the learning process is to assign correct functions to objects—this is how we form concepts. But we need to be open to seeing that an object can be used for an entirely different function. (The solution to this problem appears at the end of the chapter.) See *Understanding Ourselves* for techniques that will improve your problem-solving skills.

Because creative problem solving requires thinking up original ideas, deliberate strategies don't always help. Solutions to many problems rely on insight, often a seemingly arbitrary flash "out of the blue." (See Chapter 5, Learning.) Psychologists have only recently begun to investigate such spontaneous and unplanned problem-solving processes as insight and intuition (Bechara et al., 1997; see also Underwood, 1996).

You can't always sit back and wait for a flash of insight to solve a problem. When you need a quick solution, you can do some things that encourage creative answers. Sometimes we get so enmeshed in the details of a problem that we lose sight of the obvious. If we stop thinking about the problem for a while, we may return to it from a new angle (H. G. Murray & Denny, 1969). Then we may be able to redefine the problem, circumventing an unproductive mind-set.

The value of looking for new ways to represent a difficult problem cannot be overstressed. Ask yourself, "What is the real problem here? Can the

Divergent thinking
Thinking that meets the criteria of originality, inventiveness, and flexibility.

Convergent thinking
Thinking that is directed toward one correct solution to a problem.

UNDERSTANDING OURSELVES

Becoming a More Skillful Problem Solver

Even the best problem solvers occasionally get stumped, but you can do some things that will help you find a solution. These tactics encourage you to discard unproductive approaches and find strategies that are more effective.

1. **Eliminate poor choices.** When we are surer of what won't work than what will, the *tactic of elimination* can be very helpful. First, list all the possible solutions you can think of, and then discard all the solutions that seem to lead in the wrong direction. Now examine the list more closely. Some solutions seem to be ineffective but on closer examination may turn out to be good.

2. **Visualize a solution.** Sometimes people who are stumped by a problem can find a solution by using a basic building block of thought: visual images. *Visualiz-* *ing* often involves diagramming courses of action (J. L. Adams, 1980). For example, in the Hobbit and Orc problem, draw a picture of the river, and show the Hobbits and Orcs at each stage of the solution as they are ferried across. Drawing a diagram can help you grasp what a problem calls for. You also can visualize mentally.

3. **Develop expertise.** People get stumped on problems because they lack the knowledge to find a quick solution. Experts not only know more about a particular subject but also organize their information in larger "chunks" that are extensively interconnected, much like a cross-referencing system in a library.

4. **Think flexibly.** Striving to be more flexible and creative is an excellent tactic for becoming a better problem solver. Many problems require some original thinking. For example, how many unusual uses can you think of for a brick? Problems that have no single correct solution and that require a flexible, inventive approach call for **divergent thinking**—or thinking that involves generating many different possible answers. In contrast, **convergent thinking** is thinking that narrows its focus in a particular direction, assuming that there is only one solution, or at most a limited number of right solutions (Guilford, 1967). Many business and engineering schools stress divergent thinking skills to encourage more creative problem solving (Kaplan & Simon, 1990).

problem be interpreted in other ways?" Also be open to potential solutions that at first seem unproductive. The solution may turn out to be more effective, or it may suggest related solutions that will work. This is the rationale behind the technique called **brainstorming:** When solving a problem, generate a lot of ideas before you review and evaluate them (Haefele, 1962).

Finally, people often become more creative when exposed to creative peers and teachers (Amabile, 1983). Although some creative people work well alone, many others are stimulated by working in teams with other creative people.

Brainstorming
A problem-solving strategy in which an individual or a group produces numerous ideas and evaluates them only after all ideas have been collected.

psych 7.2

→ **INTERACTIVE LECTURE** 7.3

✓ **WEB QUIZ** 7.3

CHECK YOUR UNDERSTANDING

1. Match each problem-solving strategy with the appropriate definition.

   algorithm ____

   heuristic ____

   hill climbing ____

   means-end analysis ____

   working backward ____

   subgoal creation ____

   a. rule-of-thumb approach that helps in simplifying and solving problems, although it doesn't guarantee a correct solution

   b. strategy in which each step moves you closer to a solution

   c. step-by-step method that guarantees a solution

   d. strategy in which one moves from the goal to the starting point

   e. strategy that aims to reduce the discrepancy between the current situation and the desired goal at a number of intermediate points

   f. breaking down the solution to a larger problem into a set of smaller, more manageable steps

2. Which of the following can sometimes be an obstacle to problem solving?

   a. mental sets
   b. overexcitement
   c. functional fixedness
   d. all of the above

3. Match each form of thinking with its definition and the kind of problems to which it is suited.

   ____ divergent thinking

   ____ convergent thinking

   a. suited to problems for which there is one correct solution or a limited number of solutions

   b. thinking that involves generating many different ideas

   c. suited to problems that have no one right solution and require an inventive approach

   d. thinking that limits its focus to a particular direction

4. The first step in problem solving is problem ____.

5. ____ and ____ is a problem-solving strategy based on the successive elimination of incorrect solutions.

6. Producing many ideas without evaluating them prematurely is called ____.

7. Experts think differently from beginners in that they organize information into smaller, more detailed units. (T or F)

Answers: 1. Algorithm-c; heuristic-a; hill climbing-b; means-end analysis-e; working backward-d; subgoal creation-f; 2. d. 3. divergent thinking-b and c; convergent thinking-a and d. 4. representation (or interpretation). 5. trial and error. 6. brainstorming 7. F

If you were shopping for a new car, would you use a compensatory or a non-compensatory approach to making your decision?

Decision Making

How does decision making differ from problem solving?

Decision making is a special kind of problem solving in which we already know all the possible solutions or choices. The task is not to come up with new solutions but rather to identify the best available one based on whatever criteria we are using. This might sound like a fairly simple process, but sometimes we have to juggle a large and complex set of criteria as well as many possible options. For example, suppose that you are looking for an apartment and there are hundreds available. A reasonable rent is important to you, but so are good neighbors, a good location, a low noise level, and cleanliness. If you find a noisy apartment with undesirable neighbors but at a cheap rent, should you take it? Is it a better choice than an apartment in a better location with less noise but a higher rent? How can you weigh your various criteria and make the best choice?

Logical Decision Making

How would you go about making a truly logical decision?

The logical way to make a decision is to rate each of the available choices on all the criteria you are using, arriving at some overall measure of the extent to which each choice matches your criteria. For each choice, the attractive features can offset or compensate for the unattractive features. This approach to decision making is therefore called a **compensatory model**.

Table 7–1 illustrates one of the most useful compensatory models, applied to the car decision. The buyer has three criteria, which are weighted in terms of importance: price (not weighted heavily), gas mileage, and service record (both weighted more heavily). Each car is then rated from 1 (poor) to 5 (excellent) on each of the criteria. You can see that Car 1 has an excellent price (5) but relatively poor gas mileage (2) and service record (1); Car 2 has a less desirable price but fairly good mileage and service record. Each rating is then multiplied by the weight for that criterion (e.g., for Car 1, the price rating of 5 is multiplied by the weight of 4, and the result is put in parentheses next to the rating). Then, ratings are added to give a total for each car. Clearly Car 2 is the best choice: It has a less desirable price, but that disadvantage is offset by the fact that its mileage and service record are better, and these two criteria are more important than price to this particular buyer.

Using a table like this one allows individuals to evaluate a large number of choices on a large number of criteria. If the criteria are weighted properly and the choices rated correctly, the alternative with the highest total score is the most rational choice, given the information available. Does this outcome mean that most day-to-day decision making is rational? Not necessar-

---

Compensatory model
A rational decision-making model in which choices are systematically evaluated on various criteria.

TABLE 7-1 COMPENSATORY DECISION TABLE FOR PURCHASE OF A NEW CAR

	Price (weight = 4)	Gas Mileage (weight = 8)	Service Record (weight = 10)	Weighted Total
Car 1	5 (20)	2 (16)	1 (10)	(46)
Car 2	1 (4)	4 (32)	4 (40)	(76)

Ratings: 5 = excellent; 1 = poor

ily. Many, if not most, decisions—choosing a college, deciding whom to marry—involve a high degree of ambiguity (Mellers, Schwartz, & Cooke, 1998). Often we must rely on our intuition to make the right choice, taking a heuristic rather than a purely logical approach.

Decision Making Heuristics

How can heuristic approaches lead us to make bad decisions?

Research has identified a number of common heuristics that people use to make decisions. We use these because, for the most part, they have worked in the past and because they simplify decision making, even though they may lead to less-than-optimal decisions.

We use the **representativeness** heuristic whenever we make a decision on the basis of certain information that matches our model of the typical member of a category. For example, if every time you went shopping you bought the least expensive items, and if all of these items turned out to be poorly made, you might eventually decide not to buy anything that seems typical of the category "very cheap." Another common heuristic is **availability.** In the absence of full and accurate information, we often base decisions on whatever information is most readily available to memory, even though this information may not be accurate.

A familiar example of the availability heuristic is the so-called *subway effect* (Gilovich, 1991). It seems to be a law of nature that if you are waiting at a subway station, one train after another will come along headed in the opposite direction from the direction that you want to go. Similarly, if you need a taxi in a hurry, inevitably an unusually long string of occupied or off-duty taxis will pass by. The problem here is that once a subway train or a taxi does come along, we leave the scene, so we never get to see the opposite situation: several subway trains going in our direction before one comes the other way, or a long string of empty taxis. As a result, we tend to assume that those situations seldom or never occur, and so we make our decisions accordingly.

Another heuristic, closely related to availability, is **confirmation bias**—the tendency to notice and remember evidence that supports our beliefs and to ignore evidence that contradicts them (Myers, 1996). For example, individuals who believe that AIDS is something that happens to "other people" (homosexual men and intravenous drug-users, not middle-class heterosexuals) are more likely to remember articles about rates of HIV infection in these groups or in third-world countries than articles about AIDS cases among people like themselves (Fischhoff & Downs, 1997). Convinced that HIV is not something that they, personally, need to worry about, they ignore evidence to the contrary.

A related phenomenon is our tendency to see *connections* or *patterns of cause and effect* where none exist (Kahneman & Tversky, 1996; Rottenstreich & Tversky, 1997). For example, many people still believe that chocolate causes acne to flare up in susceptible teenagers, yet this myth was disproved almost half a century ago; acne is a bacterial infection, although the tendency to get acne has a strong genetic component (Kolata, 1996). Many parents strongly believe that sugar may cause hyperactivity in children—despite research evidence to the contrary. The list of commonsense beliefs that persist in the face of contrary evidence is long.

Explaining Our Decisions

How do we explain to ourselves the decisions we make?

Framing For the most part, people are reasonably satisfied with the decisions they make in the real world (Kleinmuntz, 1991). However, these

Representativeness
A heuristic by which a new situation is judged on the basis of its resemblance to a stereotypical model.

Availability
A heuristic by which a judgment or decision is based on information that is most easily retrieved from memory.

Confirmation bias
The tendency to look for evidence in support of a belief and to ignore evidence that would disprove a belief.

decisions can be intentionally or unintentially swayed by how the information provided to make the decision is presented, or *framed*. Psychologists use the term **framing** to refer to the perspective or phrasing of information that is used to make a decision. Numerous studies have shown that subtle changes in the way information is presented can dramatically affect the final decision (Detweiler, Bedell, Salovey, Pronin, & Rothman, 1999; Mellers, Schwartz, & Cooke, 1998; Slovic, 1995; Wolsko, Park, Judd, & Wittenbrink, 2000). A classic study illustrates how framing may influence a medical decision. In this study, experimental participants were asked to choose between surgery and radiation therapy to treat lung cancer. However, the framing of information provided to make this choice was manipulated. In the *survival frame,* the participants were given the statistical outcomes of both procedures in the form of survival statistics, thus emphasizing the number of people who would survive each procedure, one year and five years after treatment. In the *mortality frame,* the participants were given the same information, although this time it was presented (or framed) according to the number of people who would *die* after one year and after five years. It is interesting that although the actual number of deaths and survivors associated with each procedure was identical in both the survival and mortality frames, the percentage of participants who chose one procedure over another varied dramatically depending on how the information was framed. Probably most surprising was that this framing effect was found even when 424 experienced physicians with a specialty in radiology served as the experimental participants!

Hindsight Whether a choice is exceptionally good, extraordinarily foolish, or somewhere in between, most people think about their decisions after the fact. The term **hindsight bias** refers to the tendency to view outcomes as inevitable and predictable after we know the outcome, and to believe that we could have predicted what happened, or perhaps that we did (Azar, 1999; Fischoff, 1975). For example, physicians remember being more confident about their diagnoses when they learn that they were correct than they were at the time of the actual diagnoses.

Psychologists have long viewed the hindsight bias as a cognitive flaw—a way of explaining away bad decisions and maintaining our confidence (see Louie, Curren, & Harich, 2000). A team of researchers in Berlin, however, argues that the hindsight bias serves a useful function (Hoffrage, Hertwig, & Gigerenzer, 2000). "Correcting" memory is a quick and efficient way to replace misinformation or faulty assumptions, so that our future decisions and judgments will be closer to the mark. In a sense, hindsight functions like the "find and replace" function in a word processing program, eliminating extra, time-consuming keystrokes and mental effort.

"If Only" At times, everyone imagines alternatives to reality and mentally plays out the consequences. Psychologists refer to such thoughts about things that never happened as **counterfactual thinking**—the thoughts are counter to the facts (Roese, 1997; Spellman & Mandel, 1999). Counterfactual thinking often takes the form of "If only" constructions, in which we mentally revise the events or actions that led to a particular outcome: "If only I had studied harder"; "If only I had said no"; "If only I had driven straight home." Research shows that counterfactual thinking usually centers around a small number of themes: reversing a course of events that led to a negative experience; explaining unusual events by assigning responsibility to someone or something; and regaining a sense of personal control (Roese, 1997).

Framing
The perspective from which we interpret information before making a decision.

Hindsight
The tendency to vision outcomes as inevitable and predictable after we know the outcome.

Counterfactual thinking
Thinking about alternative realities and things that never happened.

INTERACTIVE LECTURE **7.4**

CHECK YOUR UNDERSTANDING

1. Matt is trying to decide between going camping in the Rockies or hiking in the Grand Canyon. To make the choice, he sets up some criteria for a good vacation and then rates the two alternatives on each criterion to see how they stack up against each other. Matt is using a _____ model of decision making.

2. Match each decision-making heuristic with the appropriate definition.

   _____ representativeness heuristic   a. making judgments on the basis of whatever information can be most readily retrieved from memory

   _____ availability heuristic   b. attending to evidence that supports your existing beliefs and ignoring other evidence

   _____ confirmation bias   c. making decisions on the basis of information that matches your model of what is "typical" of a certain category

3. The way a question is framed usually will not affect its answer. Is this statement true (T) or false (F)?

4. Julio's girlfriend gets a speeding ticket, and he blames himself, saying, "If only I hadn't let her borrow my car." His thinking is an example of _____ _____.

Answers: 1. compensatory. 2. representativeness heuristic—c; availability heuristics—a; confirmation bias—b. 3. F. 4. hindsight bias.

Intelligence and Mental Abilities

What types of questions are used to measure intelligence?

Answer the following questions:

1. Describe the difference between *laziness* and *idleness*.

2. Which direction would you have to face so that your right ear would be facing north?

3. What does *obliterate* mean?

4. In what way are an hour and a week alike?

5. Choose the lettered block that best completes the pattern in the following figure.

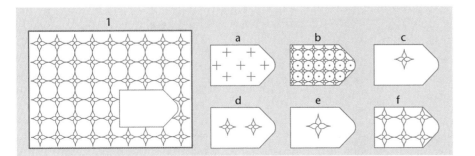

6. If three pencils cost 25 cents, how many pencils can you buy for 75 cents?

7. Select the lettered pair that best expresses a relationship similar to that expressed in the original pair:
CRUTCH: LOCOMOTION:
   (a) paddle: canoe
   (b) hero: worship
   (c) horse: carriage
   (d) spectacles: vision
   (e) statement: contention

8. Decide how the first two items in the following figure are related to each other. Then find the one item at the right that goes with the third item in the same way that the second item goes with the first.

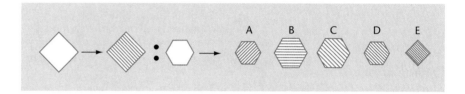

9. For each item in the following figure, decide whether it can be completely covered by using some or all of the given pieces without overlapping any.

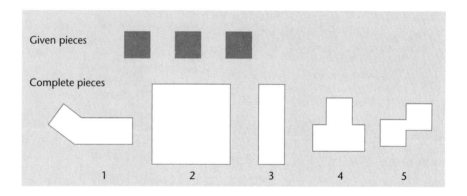

These questions were taken from various tests of **intelligence,** or general mental ability (the answers appear at the end of the chapter). Because intelligence is a fundamental human ability, it has long been the subject matter of psychology.

Theories of Intelligence

What are some of the major theories of intelligence?

For more than a century, psychologists have argued about what constitutes general intelligence—or even if "general" intelligence actually exists. One of their most basic questions is whether intelligence is a single, general mental ability or whether it is composed of many separate abilities (see Lubinski, 2000).

Early Theorists   Charles Spearman, an early-twentieth-century British psychologist, maintained that intelligence is quite general—a kind of well, or spring, of mental energy that flows through every action. Spearman believed that people who are bright in one area are often bright in other areas as well. The intelligent person understands things quickly, makes sound de-

Intelligence
A general term referring to the ability or abilities involved in learning and adaptive behavior.

cisions, carries on interesting conversations, and tends to behave intelligently in a variety of situations.

The American psychologist L. L. Thurstone disagreed with Spearman. Thurstone argued that intelligence is composed of seven distinct kinds of mental abilities (Thurstone, 1938): *spatial ability, memory, perceptual speed, word fluency, numerical ability, reasoning,* and *verbal meaning.* Unlike Spearman, Thurstone believed that these abilities are relatively independent of one another. Thus, a person with exceptional spatial ability (the ability to perceive distance, recognize shapes, and so on) might lack word fluency. To Thurstone, these primary mental abilities, taken together, make up general intelligence.

In contrast to Thurstone, the American psychologist R. B. Cattell (1971) identified just two clusters of mental abilities. The first cluster—*crystallized intelligence*—includes abilities such as reasoning, and verbal and numerical skills. These are the kinds of abilities stressed in school, and they tend to be greatly affected by experience and formal education. Cattell's second cluster of abilities—*fluid intelligence*—is made up of skills such as spatial and visual imagery, awareness of visual details, and a capacity for rote memory. Scores on tests of fluid intelligence are much less influenced by experience and education.

Contemporary Theorists   More recently, two American psychologists have proposed alternative theories of intelligence. Robert Sternberg's **triarchic theory of intelligence** concludes that human intelligence encompasses a much broader variety of skills than described by earlier theorists and that skills necessary for effective performance in the world are just as important as the more limited skills assessed by traditional intelligence tests (Sternberg, 1985, 1986). Sternberg illustrates his theory by comparing three graduate students he worked with at Yale, whom he calls Alice, Barbara, and Celia. Alice fit the standard definition of intelligence perfectly: She scored high on tests of intelligence and achieved nearly a 4.0 average as an undergraduate. Her analytical abilities were excellent. Alice excelled in her first year of graduate work, but in the second year, she was having trouble developing her own research ideas, and she dropped from the top of the class to the lower half. In contrast, Barbara's undergraduate record was poor, and her admission test scores were well below Yale's standards. Nevertheless, professors who had worked with her as an undergraduate described her as highly creative and able to do good research. Barbara proved to be the associate whom Sternberg had hoped for. In fact, he believes that some of his most important work has been done in collaboration with her. The third graduate student, Celia, was somewhere between the other two: She had good recommendations and fairly good admission test scores. She did skillful (but not great) research work, yet she had the easiest time finding a good job after graduate school.

These three students represent the three aspects of Sternberg's triarchic theory of intelligence. Alice was high in *componential intelligence*, which refers to the mental abilities emphasized in most theories of intelligence, such as the ability to learn how to do things or how to acquire new knowledge and carry out tasks effectively. Barbara was particularly strong in what Sternberg calls *experiential intelligence*—the ability to adjust to new tasks, to use new concepts, to respond effectively in new situations, to gain insight, and to think creatively. Celia had the easiest time finding a job because of her strong *contextual intelligence*—her ability to capitalize on her strengths and compensate for her weaknesses. People like Celia make the most of their talents by seeking situations that match their skills, by shaping those situations so they can use those skills to best advantage, and by knowing when to change situations better to fit their talents.

Triarchic theory of intelligence
Sternberg's theory that intelligence involves mental skills (componential aspect), insight and creative adaptability (experiential aspect), and environmental responsiveness (contextual aspect).

Author Toni Morrison, whose vivid, compelling prose has been likened to poetry, possesses an abundance of what Howard Gardner calls linguistic intelligence. In recognition of her exceptional talent, she was awarded a Nobel Prize in Literature.

An influential alternative to Sternberg's theory of intelligence is the **theory of multiple intelligences,** advanced by Howard Gardner and his associates at Harvard (Gardner, 1983a, 1993, 1999). Like Thurstone, Gardner argues that intelligence consists of many separate abilities, each relatively independent of the others. He lists seven: *logical-mathematical intelligence, linguistic intelligence, spatial intelligence, musical intelligence, bodily kinesthetic intelligence, interpersonal intelligence,* and *intrapersonal intelligence* (Gardner, 1993). The first two are included in the other theories of intelligence that we have discussed. Spatial intelligence, the ability to imagine the relative location of objects in space, is particularly prominent in people with artistic talent. Exceptional musical intelligence is demonstrated by people with an outstanding gift for music, where as outstanding athletes and dancers show strong bodily kinesthetic intelligence. People who are extraordinarily talented at understanding and communicating with others, such as exceptional teachers and parents, have strong interpersonal intelligence. Intrapersonal intelligence reflects the ancient adage "Know thyself." People who rank high in it understand themselves and use this knowledge effectively to reach their goals.

Recently, psychologist Daniel Goleman (1997) has proposed a new theory of **emotional intelligence,** which refers to how effectively people perceive and understand their own emotions and the emotions of others and can manage their emotional behavior. Goleman was puzzled about the fact that people with high IQ scores sometimes fail in life, whereas those with more modest intellectual skills prosper. He contends that one of the reasons IQ tests sometimes fail to predict success accurately is that they do not take into account an individual's emotional competence.

Five traits are generally recognized as contributing to one's emotional intelligence (Goleman, 1997; Mayer & Salovey, 1997):

1. **Knowing one's own emotions.** The ability to monitor and recognize our own feelings is of central importance to self-awareness and all other dimensions of emotional intelligence.

2. **Managing one's emotions.** The ability to control impulses; to cope effectively with sadness, depression, and minor setbacks, as well as to control how long emotions last.

3. **Using emotions to motivate oneself.** The capacity to marshal emotions toward achieving personal goals.

4. **Recognizing the emotions of other people.** The ability to read subtle, nonverbal cues that reveal what other people really want and need.

5. **Managing relationships.** The ability accurately to acknowledge and display one's own emotions as well as being sensitive to the emotions of others.

Because the concept of emotional intelligence is relatively new, researchers have only begun to evaluate its scientific merit (Mayer, 1999; Sternberg & Kaufman, 1998). Some studies have shown promising results. For example, Mayer and Gehr (1996) found that the ability of people to identify emotions accurately in other people does correlate with SAT scores. And, as you might expect, the ability to manage and regulate one's emotions in the workplace also appears to be important (Grandey, 2000).

Other investigators, however, remain more skeptical, arguing that emotional intelligence is no different from traits that are already assessed by more traditional measures of intelligence and personality (Davies, Stankov, & Roberts, 1998). More research is needed before we can assess the scientific validity and usefulness of this intriguing and potentially important new theory of intelligence (Mayer, 1999).

Theory of multiple intelligences
Howard Gardner's theory that there is not one intelligence, but rather many intelligences, each of which is relatively independent of the others.

Emotional intelligence
According to Goleman, a form of intelligence that refers to how effectively people perceive and understand their own emotions and the emotions of others, and can regulate and manage their emotional behavior.

Each of these theories has contributed to the techniques developed to measure intelligence, a topic to which we now turn.

Intelligence Tests

What kinds of intelligence tests are in use today?

The Stanford–Binet Intelligence Scale   The first test developed to measure intelligence was designed by two Frenchmen, Alfred Binet and Theodore Simon. The test, first used in Paris in 1905, was designed to identify children who might have difficulty in school.

The first *Binet–Simon Scale* consisted of 30 tests arranged in order of increasing difficulty. With each child the examiner started with the easiest tests and worked down the list until the child could no longer answer questions. By 1908, enough children had been tested to predict how the average child would perform at each age level. From these scores, Binet developed the concept of *mental age*. A child who scores as well as an average 4-year-old has a mental age of 4; a child who scores as well as an average 12-year-old has a mental age of 12.

A well-known adaptation of the *Binet–Simon Scale*, the *Stanford–Binet Intelligence Scale*, was prepared at Stanford University by L. M. Terman and published in 1916. Terman introduced the now famous term **intelligence quotient (IQ)** to establish a numerical value of intelligence, setting the score of 100 for a person of average intelligence. **Figure 7–8** shows an approximate distribution of IQ scores in the population.

The latest version of the Stanford–Binet, released in 1986, replaced items that had been found to be biased against members of ethnic groups or against males or females with neutral items. New items were added that permitted testers to identify mentally retarded and intellectually gifted people, as well as people with specific learning disabilities (Sattler, 1992).

The current Stanford–Binet Intelligence Scale is designed to measure four kinds of mental abilities that are almost universally considered to be part of intelligence: *verbal reasoning, abstract/visual reasoning, quantitative reasoning,* and *short-term memory.* Test items vary with the subject's age. For example, a 3-year-old might be asked to describe the purpose of a cup and to name objects such as a chair and a key. A 6-year-old might be asked to define words such as *orange* and *envelope* and to complete a sentence such as "An inch is short; a mile is _____." A 12-year-old might be asked to define *skill* and *juggler* and to complete the sentence "The streams are dry _____ there has been little rain" (Cronbach, 1990).

The Stanford–Binet test is given individually by a trained examiner. It is best suited for children, adolescents, and very young adults.

Intelligence quotient (IQ)
A numerical value given to intelligence that is determined from the scores on an intelligence test; based on a score of 100 for average intelligence.

FIGURE 7–8

The approximate distribution of IQ scores in the population.   Note that the greatest percentage of scores fall around 100. Very low percentages of people score at the two extremes of the curve.

The Wechsler Intelligence Scales, developed by David Wechsler, are individual intelligence tests administered to one person at a time. There are versions of the Wechsler Scales for both adults and children. Here a child and an adult are being asked to copy a pattern using blocks.

The Wechsler Intelligence Scales   The most commonly used individual test of intelligence for adults is the **Wechsler Adult Intelligence Scale—Third Edition (WAIS-III),** originally developed in the late 1930s by David Wechsler, a psychologist. The Stanford–Binet emphasizes verbal skills, but Wechsler felt that adult intelligence consists more of the ability to handle life situations than to solve verbal and abstract problems.

The WAIS-III is divided into two parts, one stressing verbal skills, the other performance skills. The verbal scale includes tests of information ("Who wrote *Paradise Lost*?"); tests of simple arithmetic ("Sam had three pieces of candy, and Joe gave him four more. How many pieces of candy did Sam have then?"); and tests of comprehension ("What should you do if you see someone forget a book on a bus?"). The performance scale also measures routine tasks. People are asked to "find the missing part" (buttonholes in a coat, for example), to copy patterns, and to arrange 3 to 5 pictures so that they tell a story.

Although the content of the WAIS-III is somewhat more sophisticated than that of the Stanford–Binet, Wechsler's chief innovation was in scoring. His test gives separate verbal and performance scores as well as an overall IQ score. On some items, one or two extra points can be earned, depending on the complexity of the answer given. This unique scoring system gives credit for the reflective qualities that we expect to find in intelligent adults. On some questions, both speed and accuracy affect the score.

Wechsler also developed a similar intelligence test for use with school-age children. Like the WAIS-III, the 1991 version of the **Wechsler Intelligence Scale for Children–Third Edition (WISC-III)** yields separate verbal and performance scores as well as an overall IQ score.

Group Tests   The Stanford–Binet, the WAIS-III, and the WISC-III are individual tests. The examiner takes a person to an isolated room, spreads the materials on a table, and spends from 30 to 90 minutes administering the test. The examiner may then take another hour or so to score the test according to detailed instructions in the manual. This is a time-consuming, costly operation, and the examiner's behavior can under some circumstances influence the score. For these reasons, test makers have devised **group tests.** These are written tests that a single examiner can administer to a large group of people at the same time. Instead of sitting across the

Wechsler Adult Intelligence Scale–Third Edition (WAIS-III)
An individual intelligence test developed especially for adults; measures both verbal and performance abilities.

Wechsler Intelligence Scale for Children–Third Edition (WISC-III)
An individual intelligence test developed especially for school-aged children; measures verbal and performance abilities and also yields an overall IQ score.

Group tests
Written intelligence tests administered by one examiner to many people at one time.

table from a person who asks you questions, you receive a test booklet that contains questions for you to answer within a certain amount of time.

When most people talk about "intelligence" tests, they are usually referring to group tests, because this is generally the means by which they were themselves tested in school. Schools are among the biggest users of group tests. From fourth grade through high school, tests such as the *California Test of Mental Maturity (CTMM)* are used to measure students' general abilities. Group tests are also widely used in different industries, the civil service, and the military.

Group tests have some distinct advantages over individualized tests. They eliminate bias on the part of the examiner. Answer sheets can be scored quickly and objectively. And because more people can be tested in this way, norms are easier to establish. But group tests also have some distinct disadvantages. The examiner is less likely to notice whether a person is tired, ill, or confused by the directions. People who are not used to being tested tend to do less well on group tests than on individual tests. Finally, emotionally disturbed children and children with learning disabilities often do better on individual tests than on group tests (Anastasi & Urbina, 1997).

Performance and Culture-Fair Tests   To perform well on the intelligence tests that we have discussed, people must be adept at the language in which the test is given. Standard intelligence tests simply cannot accurately assess cognitive abilities in children or adults who are not fluent in English. How, then, can we test these people? Psychologists have designed two general forms of tests for such situations: performance tests and culture-fair tests.

Performance tests consist of problems that minimize or eliminate the use of words. One of the earliest performance tests, the *Seguin Form Board,* was devised in 1866 to test people with mental retardation. The form board is essentially a puzzle. The examiner removes specifically designed cutouts, stacks them in a predetermined order, and asks the person to replace them as quickly as possible. A more recent performance test, the *Porteus Maze,* consists of a series of increasingly difficult printed mazes. People trace their way through the maze without lifting the pencil from the paper. Such tests require the test taker to pay close attention to a task for an extended period and continuously to plan ahead in order to make the correct choices.

Culture-fair tests are designed to measure the intelligence of people who are outside the culture in which the test was devised. Like performance tests, culture-fair tests minimize or eliminate the use of language. Culture-fair tests also try to downplay skills and values—such as the need for speed—that vary from culture to culture. In the *Goodenough–Harris Drawing Test,* people are asked to draw the best picture of a person that they can. Drawings are scored for proportions, correct and complete representation of the parts of the body, detail in clothing, and so on. An example of a culture-fair item from the *Progressive Matrices* is Question 5 on page 247. This test consists of 60 designs, each with a missing part. The person is given 6 to 8 possible choices to replace the part. The test involves various logical relationships, requires discrimination, and can be given to one person or to a group. *Cattell's Culture-Fair Intelligence Test* uses similar kinds of test items.

What Makes a Good Test?

What are some important characteristics of a good test?

How can we tell whether intelligence tests will produce consistent results no matter when they are given? And how can we tell whether they really measure what they claim to measure? Psychologists address these questions

Performance tests
Intelligence tests that minimize the use of language.

Culture-fair tests
Intelligence tests designed to eliminate cultural bias by minimizing skills and values that vary from one culture to another.

by referring to a test's reliability and validity. Issues of reliability and validity apply equally to all psychological tests, not just to tests of mental abilities. In Chapter 10, for example, we reexamine these issues as they apply to personality assessment.

Reliability   By **reliability,** psychologists mean the dependability and consistency of the scores that a test yields. If your alarm clock is set for 8:15 A.M. and it goes off at that time every morning, it is reliable. But if it is set for 8:15 and rings at 8:00 one morning and 8:40 the next, you cannot depend on it; it is unreliable. Similarly, a test has reliability when it yields consistent results.

How do we know whether a test is reliable? The simplest way to find out is to give the test to a group and then, after a short time, to give the same people the same test again. If they score approximately the same each time, the test is reliable.

There is a drawback, however. How do we know that people have not simply remembered the answers from the first testing and repeated them the second time around? To avoid this possibility, psychologists prefer to give two equivalent tests, both designed to measure the same thing. If people score the same on both forms, the tests are considered reliable. One way to create alternate forms is to split a single test into two parts—for example, to assign odd-numbered items to one part and even-numbered items to the other. If scores on the two halves agree, the test has **split-half reliability.** Most intelligence tests do, in fact, have alternate equivalent forms, just as each college admission test often has many versions.

How reliable are intelligence tests? In general, people's IQ scores on most intelligence tests are quite stable (see Meyer et al., 2001). Performance and culture-fair tests are somewhat less reliable. Scores on even the best tests, however, vary somewhat from one day to another. Therefore, many testing services now report a person's score along with a range of scores that allows for some day-to-day variation.

Validity   Generally, intelligence tests are quite reliable, but do these tests really measure "intelligence"? When psychologists ask this question, they are concerned with test validity. **Validity** refers to a test's ability to measure what it has been designed to measure. How do we know whether a given test actually measures what it claims to measure?

One measure of validity is known as **content validity**—whether the test contains an adequate sample of the skills or knowledge that it is supposed to measure. Most widely used intelligence tests, such as those from which the questions at the beginning of this chapter were taken, seem to measure at least some of the mental abilities that we think of as part of intelligence. These include planning, memory, understanding, reasoning, concentration, and the use of language. Although they may not adequately sample all aspects of intelligence equally well, they at least seem to have some content validity.

Another way to measure a test's validity is to see whether a person's score on that test closely matches his or her score on another test designed to measure the same thing. The two different scores should be very similar if they are both measures of the same ability. In fact, various intelligence test scores do relate well with one another despite the differences in test content: People who score high on one test tend to score high on others.

Still, this outcome doesn't necessarily mean that the two tests measure intelligence. Conceivably they could both be measuring the same thing, but that thing is not intelligence. To demonstrate that the tests are valid, we need an independent measure of intelligence against which to compare in-

Reliability
Ability of a test to produce consistent and stable scores.

Split-half reliability
A method of determining test reliability by dividing the test into two parts and checking the agreement of scores on both parts.

Validity
Ability of a test to measure what it has been designed to measure.

Content validity
Refers to a test's having an adequate sample of questions measuring the skills or knowledge it is supposed to measure.

telligence test scores. Determining test validity in this way is called **criterion-related validity.** Ever since Binet invented the intelligence test, the main criterion against which intelligence test scores have been compared has been school achievement. Even the strongest critics agree that IQ tests predict school achievement well (Aiken, 1988; Anastasi & Urbina, 1997).

Criterion-related validity
Validity of a test as measured by a comparison of the test score and independent measures of what the test is designed to measure.

Criticisms of IQ Tests   What is it about IQ tests, then, that makes them controversial? One major criticism concerns the narrowness of their content. Many critics believe that intelligence tests assess only a very limited set of skills: passive verbal understanding, the ability to follow instructions, common sense, and, at best, scholastic aptitude (Ginsberg, 1972; Sattler, 1975). One critic observes, "Intelligence tests measure how quickly people can solve relatively unimportant problems making as few errors as possible, rather than measuring how people grapple with relatively important problems, making as many productive errors as necessary with no time factor" (Blum, 1979, p. 83).

If there is one thing that all intelligence tests measure, it is the ability to take tests. This fact could explain why people who do well on one IQ test also tend to do well on other tests. And it could also explain why intelligence test scores correlate so closely with school performance: Academic grades also depend heavily on test-taking ability.

Other critics maintain that the content and administration of IQ tests discriminate against minorities. High scores on most IQ tests require considerable mastery of standard English, thus biasing the tests in favor of middle- and upper-class white people (Blum, 1979). Moreover, white middle-class examiners may not be familiar with the speech patterns of lower-income African-American children or children from homes in which English is not the primary language, a complication that may hamper good test performance (Sattler, 1992). In addition, certain questions may have very different meanings for children of different social classes. The WISC-III, for instance, asks, "What are you supposed to do if a child younger than you hits you?" The "correct" answer is "Walk away." But for a child who lives in an environment where survival depends on being tough, the "correct" answer might be "Hit him back." This answer, however, receives zero credit.

Even presumably culture-fair tests may accentuate the very cultural differences that they were designed to minimize, to the detriment of some test takers (Linn, 1982). For example, when given a picture of a head with the mouth missing, one group of Asian-American children responded by saying that the body was missing, thus receiving no credit. To them the absence of a body under the head was more remarkable than the absence of the mouth (Ortar, 1963). Although some investigations argue that the most widely used and thoroughly studied tests are not unfairly biased against minorities (Herrnstein & Murray, 1994; Reschly, 1981), others argue that a proper study of cultural bias in testing has yet to be made (Helms, 1992).

The issue of whether tests are unfair to minorities will be with us for some time. If IQ tests were used only for obscure research purposes, their results would not matter much, but because they are used for so many significant purposes, it is critical that we understand their strengths and their weaknesses.

Some people argue that intelligence tests largely measure test-taking skills, not a person's underlying mental capabilities. Others contend that the content of these tests and the ways in which they are administered discriminate against minorities.

IQ and Success   Alfred Binet developed the first IQ test to help the Paris public school system identify students who needed to be put in special classes. But the practice of using IQ tests to put a person into a "track" or "slot" in school may backfire. To the extent that children get low scores on

IQ tests because of test bias, language handicap, or their own lack of interest in test taking, putting them in special classes apart from "normal" students can lead them to doubt their abilities. Tracking may also have the opposite effect on high IQ scorers. In a self-fulfilling prophecy, such children may come to believe that they will be high achievers, and this expectation may figure prominently in their subsequent success (Dahlström, 1993). Teachers, too, may come to expect particular students to do well or poorly on the basis of IQ scores and so encourage or neglect those students. IQ scores, then, may not simply predict future achievement or failure; they may also contribute to it.

Of course, self-fulfilling prophecies are not the only reason why IQ tests can predict future school performance. It isn't surprising that scores on these tests correlate well with academic achievement, since both involve some intellectual activity and both stress verbal ability. Moreover, both academic achievement and high IQ scores require similar kinds of motivation, attention, perseverance, and test-taking ability.

Whatever the reason, IQ scores do predict success in school with some accuracy. In addition, people with high IQ scores tend to enter high-status occupations: Physicians and lawyers tend to have higher IQs than truck drivers and janitors. Critics point out, however, that this pattern can be explained in various ways. For one thing, because people with higher IQs tend to do better in school, they stay in school longer and earn advanced degrees, thereby opening the door to high-status jobs. Moreover, children from wealthy families are more likely to have the money needed for graduate school and advanced occupational training. They also tend to have helpful family connections. Perhaps most important, they grow up in environments that encourage academic success and reward good performance on tests (Blum, 1979; Ceci & Williams, 1997).

Still, higher grades and intelligence test scores do predict occupational success and performance on the job (Barret & Depinet, 1991; Ree & Earles, 1992). In response to these findings, some psychologists propose that job performance may be even better predicted by tests of tacit knowledge—the kind of practical knowledge that people need to be able to perform their jobs effectively.

Although there is much more research to be done, it does seem reasonable that abilities beyond those measured by intelligence tests contribute to success on the job and to success in school. One approach to expanding the usefulness of intelligence testing in schools is to use IQ scores in conjunction with other kinds of information that help us to interpret what these scores mean. One such approach is the System of Multicultural Pluralistic Adjustment (SOMPA). SOMPA involves collecting a wide range of data on a child, such as overall health status and socioeconomic background, which is used to provide a context within which intelligence test scores can be interpreted.

In any event, an IQ is not the same thing as intelligence. Tests measure our ability level at a certain point in time. Test scores do not tell us why someone performs poorly or well. Moreover, as we have seen, most psychologists today believe that intelligence is not a single entity but rather is a combination of abilities required for living effectively in the real world (Anastasi & Urbina, 1997; Sternberg, 1985, 1986, 1999). Clearly, these abilities will vary to some extent from culture to culture and with the age of the person (Berry, Portinga, Segall, & Dasen, 1992).

Finally, a test score is a very simplistic way of summing up an extremely complex set of abilities. Maloney and Ward (1976) point out that we do not describe a person's personality with a 2- or 3-digit number. Why, then, they ask, should we try to sum up something as complex as intelligence by labeling someone "90" or "110"?

INTERACTIVE LECTURE 7.5

CHECK YOUR UNDERSTANDING

1. Indicate whether the following statements are true (T) or false (F).
   ____ a. Intelligence is synonymous with problem-solving ability.
   ____ b. Cattell maintained that visual–spatial abilities were part of crystallized intelligence.
   ____ c. Intrapersonal intelligence reflects the adage "Know thyself."
   ____ d. Sternberg's and Gardner's theories of intelligence both emphasize practical abilities.

2. In 1916, the Stanford psychologist L. M. Terman introduced the term _____ _____, or _____, and set the score of _____ for a person of average intelligence.

3. _____ tests eliminate or minimize the use of words in assessing mental abilities. Like these tests, _____-_____ tests minimize the use of language, but they also include questions that minimize skills and values that vary across cultures.

4. If you take a test several times and score about the same each time you take it, your results suggest that the test has _____.

5. _____ is a test's ability to measure what it was designed to measure.

6. The test that includes information about a child's health and home environment along with an IQ assessment is _____.

Answers: 1. a. (F); b. (F); c. (T); d. (T). 2. intelligence quotient, I.Q., 100. 3. Performance, culture-fair. 4. reliability. 5. Validity 6. SOMPA.

Heredity, Environment, and Intelligence

What determines individual differences in intelligence?

Is intelligence inherited, or is it the product of the environment? Sorting out the importance of each factor as it contributes to intelligence is a complex task.

Heredity

Why are twin studies useful in studying intelligence?

As we saw in Chapter 2, The Biological Basis of Behavior, scientists can use studies of identical twins to measure the effects of heredity in humans. Twin studies of intelligence begin by comparing the IQ scores of identical twins who have been raised together. As **Figure 7–9** shows, the correlation between their IQ scores is very high. In addition to identical genes, however, these twins grew up in very similar environments: They shared parents, home, teachers, vacations, and probably friends, too. These common experiences could explain their similar IQ scores. To check this possibility, researchers have tested identical twins who were separated early in life—generally before they were 6 months old—and raised in different families. As **Figure 7–9** shows, even when identical twins are raised in different families, they tend to have very similar test scores; in fact, the similarity is much greater than that between siblings who grow up in the *same* environment.

These findings make a strong case for the heritability of intelligence. For reasons identified in Chapter 2, however, twin studies do not constitute "final proof," but other evidence also demonstrates the role of heredity. For example, adopted children have been found to have IQ scores that are more similar to those of their *biological* mothers than to those of the mothers who are raising them (Loehlin, Horn, & Willerman, 1997). Researcher

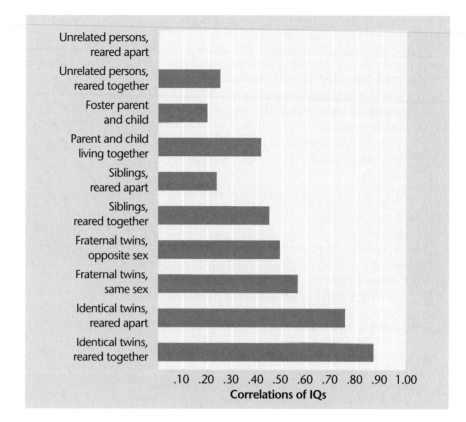

FIGURE 7–9

Correlations of IQ scores and family relationships. Identical twins who grow up in the same household have IQ scores that are almost identical to each other. Even when they are reared apart, their scores are highly correlated.

Source: Adapted from "Genetics and intelligence: A review," by Erienmeyer-Kimling and L. F. Jarvik 1963, *Science, 142,* pp. 1477–79. Copyright © 1963 by the American Association for the Advancement of Science. Reprinted with permission of the author.

John Loehlin finds these results particularly interesting because "[they] reflect genetic resemblance in the absence of shared environment: These birth mothers had no contact with their children after the first few days of life. . . ." (Loehlin et al., 1997, p. 113). Do psychologists, then, conclude that intelligence is an inherited trait and that environment plays little, if any, role?

Environment

What have we learned from early intervention programs about the influence of the environment on intellectual development?

Probably no psychologist denies that genes play a role in determining intelligence, but many believe that genes provide a base or starting point. Each of us inherits a certain body build from our parents, but our actual weight is greatly determined by what we eat and how much we exercise. Similarly, although we inherit certain mental capacities, the development of those inherited intellectual abilities depends on what we see around us as infants, how our parents respond to our first attempts to talk, what schools we attend, which books we read, which television programs we watch—even what we eat.

Environment affects children before birth as well, such as through prenatal nutrition (Hack et al., 1991). In one study of pregnant women who were economically deprived, half were given a dietary supplement, and half were given placebos. At ages 3 and 4, the children of the mothers who had taken the supplement scored significantly higher on intelligence tests than the other children (Harrell, Woodyard, & Gates, 1955). During infancy, malnutrition can lower IQ scores—in one study by an average 20 points (Stock & Smythe, 1963). Conversely, vitamin supplements can increase young children's IQ scores, possibly even among children who are not experiencing malnutrition (Benton & Roberts, 1988; Schoenthaler et al., 1991).

Quite by chance, psychologist H. M. Skeels found evidence in the 1930s that IQ scores among children also depend on environmental stimulation. While investigating orphanages for the state of Iowa, Skeels observed that the children lived in very overcrowded wards and that the few adults there had almost no time to play with the children, to talk to them, or to read them stories. Many of these children were classified as "subnormal" in intelligence. Skeels followed the cases of two girls who, after 18 months in an orphanage, were sent to a ward for women with severe retardation. Originally, the girls' IQs were in the range of retardation, but after a year on the adult ward, as if by magic, their IQs had risen to normal (Skeels, 1938). Skeels regarded this fact as quite remarkable—after all, the women with whom the girls had lived were themselves severely retarded. When he placed 13 other "slow" children as houseguests in such adult wards, within 18 months their mean IQ rose from 64 to 92 (within the normal range)—all because they had had someone (even someone of below-normal intelligence) to play with them, to read to them, to cheer them on when they took their first steps, and to encourage them to talk (Skeels, 1942). During the same period, the mean IQ of a group of children who had been left in orphanages dropped from 86 to 61. Thirty years later, Skeels found that all 13 of the children raised on adult wards were self-supporting, their occupations ranging from waiting on tables to real-estate sales. Of the contrasting group, half were unemployed, 4 were still in institutions, and all of those who had jobs were dishwashers (Skeels, 1966).

Later studies have reinforced Skeels's findings on the importance of intellectually stimulating surroundings as well as the importance of good nutrition (Capron & Duyme, 1989). The researchers found that the socioeconomic status (SES) of adoptive parents had an effect on their adopted children's IQs. Regardless of the socioeconomic status of the child's biological parents, those children adopted by high-SES parents had higher IQs than did those children adopted by low-SES parents, because high-SES families tend to provide children with better nutrition and heightened stimulation. Do such findings mean that intervention programs that enhance the environments of impoverished children can have a positive impact on their IQ?

Intervention Programs: How Much Can We Boost IQ?　In 1961 the Milwaukee Project was launched. Its purpose was to learn whether intervening in a child's family life could offset the negative effects of cultural and socioeconomic deprivation on IQ scores (Garber & Heber, 1982; Heber et al., 1972). The 40 women in the study, all from the Milwaukee area, were poor, pregnant, and primarily African-American. As a group, they averaged less than 75 on the Wechsler intelligence scale. They were split into two groups: One group received no special education or training; the other was sent to school, given job training, and instructed in child care, household management, and personal relationships.

After all the 40 women had their babies, the research team began to concentrate on the children. Starting when they were 3 months old and continuing for the next 6 years, the children in the experimental group—those whose mothers were being given special training—spent most of each day in an infant-education center, where they received nourishing meals, participated in an educational program, and were cared for by paraprofessionals who behaved like nonworking mothers in affluent families. The children in the control group—whose mothers were not receiving any special training—did not attend the education center.

Periodically, all the children were tested for IQ. The children in the experimental group achieved an average IQ score of 126—51 points higher than

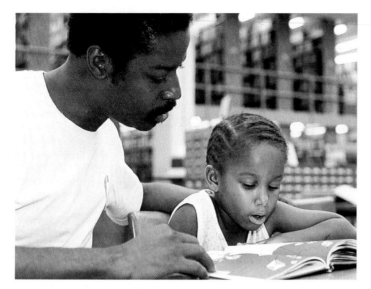

Individual differences in intelligence can be partly explained by differences in environmental stimulation and encouragement. The specific forms of stimulation given vary from culture to culture. Because our culture assigns importance to developing academic skills, the stimulation of reading and exploring information in books can give children an edge over those who are not so encouraged.

their mothers' average scores. In contrast, the children in the control group had an average IQ of 94—not as high as that of the experimental group but still much higher than their mothers' average scores, perhaps in part because they had become accustomed to taking tests, an experience that their mothers never had.

Head Start, the nation's largest intervention program, began in 1965. Today it provides comprehensive services for 739,000 children, lasting at least half a day up to two years (Kassebaum, 1994; Ripple, Gilliam, Chanana, & Zigler, 1999).). Head Start focuses on preschoolers between the ages of 3 and 5 from low-income families and has two key goals: to provide the children with some educational and social skills before they go to school, and to provide information about nutrition and health to both the children and their families. Head Start involves parents in all its aspects, from daily activities to administration of the program itself. This parental involvement has been crucial to Head Start's success (Cronan, Walen, & Cruz, 1994).

Several studies evaluating the long-term effects of Head Start have found that it boosts cognitive abilities (Barnett, 1998; B. Brown & Grotberg, 1981; Zigler, 1998; Zigler & Styfco, 2001), but some experts are concerned that these improvements may be modest or short-term. Nevertheless, children leaving Head Start are in a better position to profit from schooling than they would be otherwise (Zigler & Styfco, 1994). Head Start graduates followed until age 27 show several benefits, including higher academic achievement (Schweinhart, Barnes, & Weikart, 1993), a tendency to stay in school longer, and a greater likelihood of graduating from college. Even if the IQ gains owing to Head Start are temporary, the program still seems to provide long-term practical benefits.

Overall, the effectiveness of early intervention appears to depend on the quality of the particular program (Collins, 1993; Ramey, 1999; Zigler & Muenchow, 1992; Zigler & Styfco, 1993). Intervention programs that have clearly defined goals; that explicitly teach basic skills, such as counting, naming colors, and writing the alphabet; and that take into account the broad context of human development, including health care and other social services, achieve the biggest and most durable gains. Also, interventions that begin in the preschool years and include a high degree of parental involvement (to ensure continuity after the official program ends) are generally more successful (Cronan et al., 1994; Hart & Risley, 1995; Jaynes & Wlodkowski, 1990).

The IQ Debate: A Useful Model

How can the study of plants help us to understand the relationship between heredity and environment?

Head Start is a program designed to do just what its name implies: to give children from disadvantaged environments a head start in acquiring the skills and attitudes needed for success in school. Although researchers debate whether Head Start produces significant and lasting boosts in IQ, it does have many school-related benefits for those who participate in it.

Both heredity and environment have important effects on individual differences in intelligence, but is one of these factors more important than the other? The answer depends on whose IQs you are comparing. A useful analogy comes from studies of plants (Turkheimer, 1991). Suppose that you grow one group of randomly assigned plants in enriched soil, and another group in poor soil. The enriched group will grow to be taller and stronger than the nonenriched group; the difference between the two groups in this case is due entirely to differences in their environment. *Within* each group of plants, however, differences among individual plants are likely to be due primarily to genetics, because all plants in the same group share essentially the same environment. The height and strength of any single plant, then, reflects both heredity *and* environment.

Similarly, group differences in IQ scores might be due to environmental factors, but differences among people *within* groups could be due primarily to genetics. At the same time, the IQ scores of particular people would reflect the effects of both heredity *and* environment. Robert Plomin, an influential researcher in the field of human intelligence, concludes that "the world's literature suggests that about half of the total variance in IQ scores can be accounted for by genetic variance" (Plomin, 1997, p. 89). This finding means that environment accounts for the other half. Heredity and environment both contribute to human differences.

Mental Abilities and Human Diversity: Gender and Culture

Do culture and gender influence mental abilities?

Are there differences in mental abilities between males and females or among people from different cultures? Many people assume, for example, that males are naturally better at mathematics and that females excel in verbal skills. Others believe that the sexes are basically alike in mental abilities. Similarly, how do we account for the superior academic performance by students from certain countries and certain cultural backgrounds? Research offers some interesting insights into these controversial issues.

Gender Many occupations are dominated by one gender or the other. Engineering, for example, has traditionally been almost exclusively a male domain. Is it possible that this occupational difference and others like it reflect underlying gender differences in mental abilities?

In 1974, psychologists Eleanor Maccoby and Carol Jacklin published a review of psychological research on gender differences. They found no differences at all between males and females in most of the studies they examined. However, a few differences did appear in cognitive abilities: Girls tended to display greater verbal ability, and boys tended to exhibit stronger spatial and mathematical abilities. Largely as a result of this research, gender differences in verbal, spatial, and mathematical abilities became so widely accepted that they were often cited as one of the established facts of psychological research (Hyde, Fennema, & Lamon, 1990; Hyde & Linn, 1988).

Yet, a closer examination of the research literature, including more recent work, indicates that gender differences in math and verbal ability may be virtually nonexistent. For example, Janet Shibley Hyde and her colleagues analyzed 165 research studies, involving more than a million people, in which gender differences in verbal ability were examined. They concluded that "there are no gender differences in verbal ability, at least at this time, in American culture, in the standard ways that verbal ability has been measured" (Hyde & Linn, 1988, p. 62). In a similar analysis of studies examining mathematical ability, Hyde and her colleagues concluded that "females outperformed males by only a negligible amount. . . . Females are superior in computation, there are no gender differences in understanding of mathematical concepts, and gender differences favoring males do not emerge until the high school years" (Hyde et al., 1990, pp. 139, 151).

Males apparently do have an advantage over females in *spatial ability,* however (Halpern, 1992, 1997; Voyer, Voyer, & Bryden, 1995). Spatial tasks include mentally rotating an object and estimating horizontal and vertical dimensions (see the figures at the beginning of the chapter). These skills are particularly useful in solving certain engineering, architecture, and geometry problems. They are also handy in deciding how to arrange

Why do more males than females pursue careers in science? The reason is not that males have more innate aptitude for mathematics, because gender differences in math ability are negligible during childhood. The answer probably has more to do with cultural stereotypes about what girls are "good at" and what they are not.

A scene from a Japanese schoolroom. Studies have shown that Japanese students outperform their American peers on tests of mathematical proficiency. Some psychologists believe that cultural attitudes toward ability and effort might be partially responsible for these findings.

Mental retardation
Condition of significantly subaverage intelligence combined with deficiencies in adaptive behavior.

Down syndrome is a common biological cause of mental retardation, affecting 1 in 600 newborns. The prognosis for Down syndrome children today is much better than it was in the past. With adequate support, many children with the affliction can participate in regular classrooms and other childhood activities.

furniture in your new apartment or how to fit all those suitcases into the trunk of your car!

Men also differ from women in another way: They are much more likely than women to fall at the extremes of the intelligence range (Halpern, 1997). In one review of several large studies, Hedges and Nowell (1995) found that males accounted for 7 out of 8 people with extremely high IQ scores. These authors also reported that males represented an almost equally large proportion of the IQ scores within the range of mental retardation.

What should we conclude from these findings? First, the cognitive differences between males and females appear to be restricted to specific cognitive skills (Stumpf & Stanley, 1998). Scores on tests such as the Stanford–Binet or the WAIS reveal no gender differences in general intelligence (Halpern, 1992). Second, gender differences in specific cognitive abilities typically are small and in some cases appear to be diminishing—even when studied cross-culturally (Skaalvik & Rankin, 1994). Finally, we do not know whether the differences that do exist are a result of biological or cultural factors. Considerable research has identified several factors that discourage females from pursuing careers in mathematics and science. For example, one study found that women avoid careers in math and science partly because of *mathematics anxiety*. Girls and college women are more likely than males to agree with the statement "I dread mathematics class" (Chipman, Krantz, & Silver, 1992). Findings like these suggest that occupational and career differences may simply be an outgrowth of the ways that boys and girls are brought up.

Culture Many U.S. educators, policymakers, and parents are concerned that American students are falling behind students in other countries. Is this concern valid? And if it is, how can we explain it? Do these differences reflect differences in mental abilities, or is something else at work (Herrmstein & Murray, 1994; Jensen, 1969)? See *Understanding the World Around Us*, for some interesting answers.

Extremes of Intelligence

What do psychologists know about the two extremes of human intelligence: very high and very low?

The average IQ score on intelligence tests is 100. Nearly 70 percent of all people have IQs between 85 and 115, and all but 5 percent of the population have IQs between 70 and 130. In this section, we focus on people who score at the two extremes of intelligence—those with mental retardation and those who are intellectually gifted.

Mental Retardation **Mental retardation** encompasses a vast array of mental deficits with a wide variety of causes, treatments, and outcomes. The American Psychiatric Association (1994) defines mental retardation as "significantly subaverage general intellectual functioning . . . that is accompanied by significant limitations in adaptive functioning" and that appears before the age of 18 (p. 39). There are also various degrees of mental retardation. Mild retardation corresponds to Stanford–Binet IQ scores ranging from a high of about 70 to a low near 50. Moderate retardation corresponds to IQ scores from the low 50s to the middle 30s. People with IQ scores between the middle 30s and 20 are considered severely retarded, and the profoundly retarded are those whose scores are below 20 (see **Table 7–2**).

But a low IQ is not in itself sufficient for diagnosing mental retardation. The person must also be unable to perform the daily tasks needed to function independently (Wielkiewicz & Calvert, 1989). Thus, evaluations of people with mental retardation usually include tests of motor skills and so-

UNDERSTANDING The World Around Us

Smarter Students or Different Attitudes? Culture and Success in School

For years, U.S media have been reporting an achievement gap, especially in math, between American and Asian students. In the latest global survey, the results are no better: Asian students rank first, with Americans falling in the middle (C. Holden, 2000). Two decades ago, a team of researchers led by Harold Stevenson, were curious about differences in academic achievement. They began to study the performance of first- and fifth-grade children in American, Chinese, and Japanese elementary schools (Stevenson, Lee, & Stigler, 1986). At that time, the American students at both grade levels lagged far behind the other two countries in math and came in second in reading. A decade later, when the study was repeated with a new group of fifth-graders, the researchers discovered that the American students performed even worse than they had earlier. In 1990, the research team also studied the original first-graders from all three cultures, now in the eleventh grade. The result? The American students retained their low standing in mathematics compared with the Asian students. (Stevenson, 1992, 1993; Stevenson, Chen, & Lee, 1993).

The next question was, why? Stevenson's team wondered whether cultural attitudes toward ability and effort might, in part, explain the differences. To test this hypothesis, the researchers asked students, their parents, and their teachers in all three countries whether they thought effort or ability had a greater impact on academic performance. From first through eleventh grade, American students disagreed with the statement that "everyone in my class has about the same natural ability in math." In other words, the Americans thought that

> Stevenson's team wondered whether cultural attitudes toward ability and effort might, in part, explain the differences.

"studying hard" has little to do with performance. Their responses appear to reflect a belief that mathematical skill is primarily a function of innate ability. American mothers expressed a similar view. Moreover, 41 percent of the American eleventh-grade teachers thought "innate intelligence" is the most important factor in mathematics performance. By contrast, Asian students, parents, and teachers believed that effort and "studying hard" determined success in math (1993).

Such culturally influenced views of the relative importance of effort and innate ability may have profound consequences for the way that children, their parents, and their teachers approach the task of learning. Students who believe that learning is based on natural ability see little value in working hard to learn a difficult subject. In contrast, students who believe that academic success comes from studying are more likely to work hard, and in so doing, to succeed.

Attitudes toward what constitutes a sufficiently "good" education may also affect student performance in these cultures. For instance, 79 percent of the American mothers thought that their schools were doing a "good" or an "excellent" job of educating their children. Asian mothers were far more critical of their schools' performance, which could lead them to lobby for more challenging curriculums. Also, American mothers and students were generally satisfied with the students' academic performance, even though it was comparatively low. Such complacency does not contribute to high achievement.

Finally, all three groups of students scored the same on tests of information learned outside schools, emphasizing that cultural factors, not innate differences, were producing different levels of school success.

cial adaptation as well as tests of intelligence. Motor-skill tests, such as the widely used *Oseretsky Tests of Motor Proficiency,* measure the control of facial muscles, hand and finger coordination, and posture. Measures of social adaptation, such as the *Adaptive Behavior Scale (ABS)* and the *Vineland Adaptive Behavior Social Maturity Scale,* are based on observations of the person's behavior in everyday situations. People are scored in such areas as language development, understanding and use of number and time concepts,

TABLE 7-2	LEVELS OF MENTAL RETARDATION

Type of Retardation	IQ Range	Attainable Skill Level
Mild retardation	Low 50s–70s	People may be able to function adequately in society and learn skills comparable to a sixth-grader, but they need special help at times of unusual stress.
Moderate retardation	Mid-30s–low 50s	People profit from vocational training and may be able to travel alone. They learn on a second-grade level and perform skilled work in a sheltered workshop under supervision.
Severe retardation	Low 20s–mid-30s	People do not learn to talk or to practice basic hygiene until after age 6. They cannot learn vocational skills but can perform simple tasks under supervision.
Profound retardation	Below 20 or 25	Constant care is needed. Usually people have a diagnosed neurological disorder.

Source: Based on APA, DSM-IV, 1994.

domestic activity, responsibility, and social action. Another portion of the ABS focuses on the person's maladaptive behaviors, such as withdrawal, hyperactivity, and disturbing interpersonal behaviors.

What causes mental retardation? In most cases, the causes are unknown (Beirne-Smith, Patton, & Ittenbach, 1994)—especially in cases of mild retardation, which account for nearly 90 percent of all retardation. When causes can be identified, most often they stem from a wide variety of environmental, social, nutritional, and other risk factors (Scott & Carran, 1987).

About 25 percent of cases—especially the more severe forms of retardation—appear to involve genetic or biological disorders. Scientists have identified more than 100 forms of mental retardation caused by single defective genes (Plomin, 1997). One is the genetically based disease *phenylketonuria,* or *PKU,* which occurs in about 1 person out of 25,000 (Minton & Schneider, 1980). In people suffering from PKU, the liver fails to produce an enzyme necessary for early brain development. Fortunately, placing a PKU baby on a special diet can prevent mental retardation from developing. Another form of hereditary mental retardation is *fragile-X syndrome,* which affects about 1 in every 1,250 males and 1 in every 2,500 females (Plomin, 1997). A defect in the X chromosome, passed on between generations, seems to be caused by a specific gene (M. Hoffman, 1991). In the disorder known as *Down syndrome,* which affects 1 in 600 newborns, an extra 21st chromosome is the cause. Down syndrome, named for the physician who first described its symptoms, is marked by moderate to severe mental retardation.

Biologically caused mental retardation can be moderated through education and training. The prognosis for those with no underlying physical causes is even better. People whose retardation is due to a history of social and educational deprivation may respond dramatically to appropriate interventions. Today the majority of children with physical or mental disabilities are educated in local school systems (Lipsky & Gartner, 1996; Schroeder, Schroeder, & Landesman, 1987), a process called *mainstreaming,* which helps these students to socialize with their nondisabled peers. The principle of mainstreaming has also been applied to adults with mental retardation, by taking them out of large, impersonal institutions and placing them in smaller community homes that provide more normal life experiences (Conroy, 1996; Landesman & Butterfield, 1987; Maisto & Hughes, 1995; Stancliffe, 1997). Although the benefits of mainstreaming are debatable, most psychologists and educators support the effort (Zigler & Hodapp, 1991). To fully assess individuals and to place them in appropriate treatment and educational programs, mental health professionals need information on physical health and on emotional and social adjustment.

Like intelligence, mental retardation is a highly complex phenomenon. Just as intelligence tests do not measure certain abilities, such as artistic talent, people with mental retardation sometimes display exceptional skills in areas other than general intelligence. Probably the most dramatic and intriguing examples involve savant performance, in which a person with mental retardation displays remarkable abilities in some specialized area, such as numerical computation, memory, art, or music (O'Connor & Hermelin, 1987).

Giftedness   At the other extreme of the intelligence scale are "the gifted"—those with exceptional mental abilities, as measured by scores on standard intelligence tests. As with mental retardation, the causes of **giftedness** are largely unknown.

The first and now-classic study of giftedness was begun by Lewis Terman and his colleagues in the early 1920s. They defined giftedness in terms of academic talent and measured it by an IQ score in the top 2 percentile (1925). More recently, some experts have sought to broaden the definition of giftedness beyond that of simply high IQ (Csikszentmihalyi, Rathunde, & Whalen, 1993; Subotnik & Arnold, 1994). One view is that giftedness is often an interaction of above-average general intelligence, exceptional creativity, and high levels of commitment (Renzulli, 1978). Congress has defined gifted children as those with demonstrated achievement or potential ability in any of the following areas, singly or in combination: (1) general intellectual ability, (2) specific academic aptitude, (3) creative or productive thinking, (4) leadership ability, and (5) fine arts.

People have used various criteria to identify gifted students, including scores on intelligence tests, teacher recommendations, and achievement test results. School systems generally use diagnostic testing, interviews, and evaluation of academic and creative work (Sattler, 1992). These selection methods can identify students with a broad range of talent, but they can miss students with specific abilities, such as a talent for mathematics or music. This is an important factor because research suggests that most gifted individuals display special abilities in only a few areas. "Globally" gifted people are rare (Achter, Lubinski, & Benbow, 1996; Lubinski & Benbow, 2000; Winner, 1998, 2000).

A common view of the gifted is that they have poor social skills and are emotionally maladjusted. However, research does not support this stereotype (Robinson & Clinkenbeard, 1998). Indeed, one review (Janos & Robinson, 1985) concluded that "being intellectually gifted, at least at moderate levels of ability, is clearly an asset in terms of psychosocial adjustment in most situations" (p. 181). Nevertheless, children who are

Giftedness
Refers to superior IQ combined with demonstrated or potential ability in such areas as academic aptitude, creativity, and leadership.

Definitions of giftedness have recently broadened beyond high scores on IQ tests. These young people at the Moscow School of Music, for example, have demonstrated exceptional musical abilities. They are considered gifted in their own country, as they would be in ours.

INTERACTIVE LECTURE **7.6**

exceptionally gifted sometimes do experience difficulty "fitting in" with their peers.

WEB QUIZ **7.6**

CHECK YOUR UNDERSTANDING

1. Indicate whether the following statements are true (T) or false (F).

____ a. When identical twins are raised apart, their IQ scores are not highly correlated.

____ b. Environmental stimulation has little, if any, effect on IQ.

____ c. Head Start graduates are more likely than their peers to graduate from college.

2. Mental retardation and very high IQs are (more/less) common in males than in females. _____

3. Only about _____ percent of the population have IQs below 70 and above 130.

4. As psychologists learn more about giftedness, the definition of it has become (broader/narrower). _____

Answers: 1. a. (F); b. (F); c. (T); 2. more. 3. 5. 4. broader.

The Guggenheim Museum in Bilbao, Spain, is a feat of creative problem solving. The architect, Frank Gehry, gave the outside a dramatic shimmering effect by using a skin of titanium. The originality of the design is further heightened by its unusual juxtaposition of shapes. Divergent thinking underlies creative ideas like these.

Creativity
The ability to produce novel and socially valued ideas or objects.

Creativity

What is creativity?

Creativity is the ability to produce novel and socially valued ideas or objects ranging from philosophy to painting, from music to mousetraps (Mumford & Gustafson, 1988; Sternberg, 1996; Sternberg, 2001). Sternberg included creativity and insight as important elements in the experiential component of human intelligence. Most IQ tests, however, do not measure creativity, and many researchers would argue that intelligence and creativity are not the same thing. What, then, is the relationship between intelligence and creativity? Are people who score high on IQ tests likely to be more creative than those who score low?

Intelligence and Creativity

How is creativity related to intelligence?

Early studies typically found little or no relationship between creativity and intelligence (for example, Getzels & Jackson, 1962; Wing, 1969), but these studies examined only bright students. Perhaps creativity and intelligence are indeed linked, but only until IQ reaches a certain threshold level, after which higher intelligence isn't associated with higher creativity. There is considerable evidence for this threshold theory (Barron, 1963; Yamamoto & Chimbidis, 1966). All the research supporting it, however, has relied heavily on tests of creativity, and perhaps real-life creativity isn't the same as what these tests measure. Still, it makes sense that a certain minimum level of intelligence might be needed for creativity to develop but that other factors underlie creativity as well.

It is interesting that creative people are often perceived as being more intelligent than less creative people who have equivalent IQ scores. Perhaps some characteristic that creative people share—possibly "effectiveness" or some quality of social competence—conveys the impression of intelligence even though it is not measured by intelligence tests (Barron & Harrington, 1981).

In general, creative people are *problem finders* as well as problem solvers (Getzels, 1975; Mackworth, 1965). The more creative people are, the more they like to work on problems that they have set for themselves. Creative scientists (such as Charles Darwin and Albert Einstein) often work for years on a problem that has sprung from their own curiosity (Gruber & Wallace, 2001). Also, "greatness" rests not just on "talent" or "genius"; such people also have intense dedication, ambition, and perseverance.

Creativity Tests

Can creativity be measured?

Opinions differ about the best way to test creativity. Because creativity involves original responses to situations, questions that can be answered *true* or *false* or *a* or *b* are not good measures. More open-ended tests are better. Instead of asking for one predetermined answer to a problem, the examiner asks the test-takers to let their imaginations run free. Scores are based on the originality of a person's answers and often on the number of responses, too.

In one such test, the *Torrance Test of Creative Thinking*, people must explain what is happening in a picture, how the scene came about, and what its consequences are likely to be. In the *Christensen–Guilford Test*, they are to list as many words containing a given letter as possible, to name things belonging to a certain category (such as liquids that will burn), and to write four-word sentences beginning with the letters RDLS—"Rainy days look sad, Red dogs like soup, Renaissance dramas lack symmetry," and so on. One of the most widely used creativity tests, S. A. Mednick's (1962) *Remote Associates Test (RAT)*, asks people to relate three apparently unrelated words. For example, the three stimulus words might be *poke, go,* and *molasses,* and one response is to relate them through the word *slow:* "Slowpoke, go slow, slow as molasses." In the newer *Wallach and Kogan Creative Battery*, people form associative groupings. For instance, children are asked to "name all the round things you can think of" and to find similarities between objects, such as between a potato and a carrot.

Although people who do not have high IQs can score well on the Wallach and Kogan test, the Torrance test seems to require a reasonably high IQ for adequate performance. This finding raises the question of which of these tests is a valid measure of creativity. In general, current tests of creativity do not show a high degree of validity (Feldhusen & Goh, 1995), so measurements derived from them must be interpreted with caution.

 INTERACTIVE LECTURE **7.6**

CHECK YOUR UNDERSTANDING

WEB QUIZ **7.6**

1. The ability to produce novel and unique ideas or objects, ranging from philosophy to painting, from music to mousetraps, is termed
   a. creativity.
   b. IQ.
   c. fluid intelligence.
   d. contextual intelligence.

2. Two important features of creative people are that they
   a. take risks and like to work on problems that they invent themselves.
   b. are perceived as less intelligent and more irresponsible than other people.
   c. excel at art but are poor at science.

3. ____-____ tests are the best type for measuring creativity.
4. Indicate whether the following statements are true (T) or false (F).
____ a. Most IQ tests do not measure creativity.
____ b. Highly intelligent people are always highly creative.
____ c. A minimum level of intelligence is probably required for creativity.
____ d. Newly developed tests of creativity show a high degree of validity.

Answers: 1. a. 2. a. 3. Open-ended. 4. a. (T); b. (F); c. (T); d. (F).

A(8)   B(5)   C(3)

5   A to C   3
5   C to B 3
2   A to C   3
2   C to B 5   1
7   B to A 0   1
7   C to B 1   0
4   A to C 1   3
Goal: 4   C to B 4

FIGURE 7–10
Answer to Problem 3.

Answers to Problems in the Chapter

Problem 1   Fill each of the smaller spoons with salt from the larger spoon. That step will require 4 teaspoons of salt, leaving exactly 4 teaspoons of salt in the larger spoon.

Problem 2   Turn the 5-minute hourglass over; when it runs out, turn over the 9-minute hourglass. When it runs out, 14 minutes have passed.

Problem 3   As shown in **Figure 7–10,** fill spoon C with the salt from spoon A (now A has 5 teaspoons of salt and C has 3). Pour the salt from spoon C into spoon B (now A has 5 teaspoons of salt, and B has 3). Again fill spoon C with the salt from spoon A (leaving A with only 2 teaspoons of salt, while B and C each have 3). Fill spoon B with the salt from spoon C (this step leaves 1 teaspoon of salt in spoon C, while B has 5 teaspoons, and A has only 2). Pour all of the salt from spoon B into spoon A (now A has 7 teaspoons of salt, and C has 1). Pour all of the salt from spoon C into spoon B, and then fill spoon C from spoon A (this step leaves 4 teaspoons of salt in A, 1 teaspoon in B, and 3 teaspoons in C). Finally, pour all of the salt from spoon C into spoon B (this step leaves 4 teaspoons of salt in spoons A and B, which is the solution).

Problem 4   Start both hourglasses. When the 5-minute hourglass runs out, turn it over to start it again. When the 9-minute hourglass runs out, turn over the 5-minute hourglass. Because there is 1 minute left in the 5-minute hourglass when you turn it over, it will run for only 4 minutes. Those 4 minutes, together with the original 9 minutes, add up to the required 13 minutes for the barbecue.

Problem 5   Take one of the short pieces of chain shown in **Figure 7–11,** and open all three links (this step costs 6 cents). Use those three links to connect the remaining three pieces of chain (closing the three links costs 9 cents).

Problem 6   Join the matches to form a pyramid as seen in **Figure 7–12.**

Problem 7   One way to solve this problem is to draw a diagram of the ascent and the descent, as in **Figure 7–13.** From this drawing, you can see that indeed there is a point that the monk passes at exactly the same time on both days. Another way to approach this problem is to imagine that there are two monks on the mountain; one starts ascending at 7 A.M., while the other starts descending at 7 A.M. on the same day. Clearly, sometime during the day the monks must meet somewhere along the route.

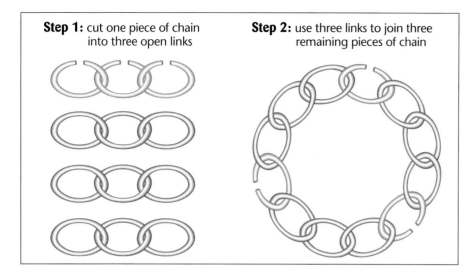

Step 1: cut one piece of chain into three open links

Step 2: use three links to join three remaining pieces of chain

FIGURE 7–11
Answer to Problem 5.

Problem 8   This problem has four possible solutions, one of which is shown in **Figure 7–14.**

Problem 9   There are 15 possible solutions to this problem, of which this is one: First, 1 Hobbit and 1 Orc cross the river in the boat; the Orc remains on the opposite side while the Hobbit rows back. Next, 3 Orcs cross the river; 2 of those Orcs remain on the other side (making a total of 3 Orcs on the opposite bank) while 1 Orc rows back. Now 3 Hobbits and 1 Orc row the boat back. Again, 3 Hobbits row across the river, at which point all 5 Hobbits are on the opposite bank with only 2 Orcs. Then, 1 of the Orcs rows back and forth across the river twice to transport the remaining Orcs to the opposite side.

FIGURE 7–12
Answer to Problem 6.

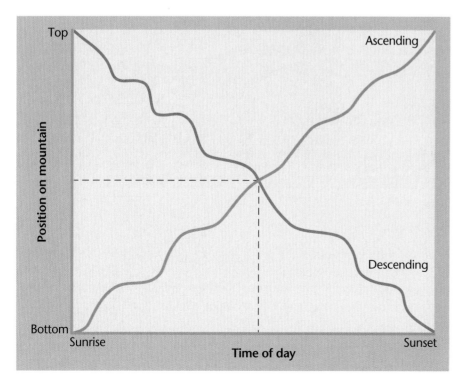

FIGURE 7–13
Answer to Problem 7.

FIGURE 7–14
Answer to Problem 8.

FIGURE 7–15
Solution to Figure 7–7. In solving the problem given in **Figure 7–7**, many people have trouble realizing that the box of tacks can also be used as a candle-holder, as shown in **Figure 7–15**.

Answers to Intelligence Test Questions

1. *Idleness* refers to the state of being inactive, not busy, unoccupied; *laziness* means an unwillingness or a reluctance to work. Laziness is one possible cause of idleness, but not the only cause.
2. If you face west, your right ear will face north.
3. *Obliterate* means to erase or destroy something completely.
4. Both an hour and a week are measures of time.
5. Alternative (f) is the correct pattern.
6. 75 cents will buy 9 pencils.
7. Alternative (d) is correct. A crutch is used to help someone who has difficulty with locomotion; spectacles are used to help someone who has difficulty with vision.
8. Alternative D is correct. The second figure is the same shape and size but with diagonal cross-hatching from upper left to lower right.
9. Figures 3, 4, and 5 can all be completely covered by using some or all of the given pieces.

KEY TERMS

CHAPTER REVIEW

Building Blocks of Thought

What are the three most important building blocks of thought? The three most important building blocks of thought are language, images, and concepts. Whatever we think about, we invariably use words, sensory "snapshots," and categories that classify things.

What steps do we go through to turn a thought into a statement? **Language** is a flexible system of symbols that allows us to communicate ideas to others. When we express thoughts as statements, we must conform to our language's rules. Every language has rules as to which sounds (or **phonemes**) are part of that particular language, how those sounds can be combined into meaningful units (or **morphemes**), and how those meaningful units can be ordered into phrases and sentences (rules of **grammar**). When we wish to communicate an idea, we start with a thought, then choose sounds, words, and phrases that will express the idea in an understandable way. To understand the speech of others, the task is reversed.

What role do images play in thinking? **Images** are mental representations of sensory experiences. Visual images in particular can be powerful aids in thinking about the relationships between things. Picturing things in our mind's eye can sometimes help us solve problems.

How do concepts help us to think more efficiently? **Concepts** are categories for classifying objects, people, and experiences based on their common elements. Without the ability to form concepts, we would need a different name for every new thing we encountered. Concepts also help clarify new experiences, as we can draw on them to anticipate what new experiences will be like.

Language, Thought, and Culture

How do language, thought, and culture influence each other? According to Benjamin Whorf's **linguistic relativity hypothesis,** thought is greatly influenced by the language a person speaks. But critics contend that Whorf overstated his case. Thought, they say, can shape and change a language as much as a language can shape and change thought.

Problem Solving

What are three general aspects of the problem-solving process? Interpreting a problem, formulating a strategy, and evaluating progress toward a solution are three general aspects of the problem-solving process. Each in its own way is critical to success at the task.

Why is representing the problem so important to finding an effective solution? **Problem representation**—defining or interpreting the problem—is the first step in problem solving. We must decide whether to view the problem verbally, mathematically, or visually, and we must decide what category of problems it belongs to in order to get clues about how to solve it. Representing a problem in an unproductive way can block progress completely.

Why is an algorithm often better for solving a problem than is the process of trial and error? Selecting a solution strategy and evaluating progress toward the goal are also important steps in the problem-solving process. A solution strategy can be anything from simple trial and error, to information retrieval based on similar problems, to a set of step-by-step procedures guaranteed to work (called an **algorithm**), to rule-of-thumb approaches known as **heuristics.** An algorithm is often preferable over trial and error because it guarantees a solution and does not waste time. But because there are so many things for which we don't have algorithms, heuristics are vital to human problem solving. Some useful heuristics are **hill climbing,** creating **subgoals,** means-end analysis, and **working backward.**

How can a "mental set" both help and hinder problem solving? A **mental set** is a tendency to perceive and approach a problem in a certain way. Although sets can enable us to draw on past experience to help solve problems, a strong set can also prevent us from using essential new approaches. One set that can seriously hamper problem solving is **functional fixedness**—the tendency to perceive only traditional uses for an object.

Decision Making

How does decision making differ from problem solving? Decision making is a special kind of problem solving in which we already know all the possible solutions or choices. The task is not to come up with new solutions but rather to identify the best available one based on whatever criteria we are using.

How would you go about making a truly logical decision? The logical way to make a decision is to rate each of the available choices in terms of criteria you have weighted based on how important they are to you. Then total the ratings for each choice to arrive at a "best" option. Because heavily weighted attractive features can compensate for lightly weighted unattractive ones, this decision-making approach is called a **compensatory model.**

How can heuristic approaches lead us to make bad decisions? When people use heuristics or rule-of-thumb approaches to help them make decisions, they can save a great deal of time and effort, but they do not always make the best choices. One example is errors in judgment based on the **representativeness** heuristic, which involves making decisions based on information that matches our model of the "typical" member of a category. Other examples are over-reliance on the **availability** heuristic (making choices based on whatever information we can most easily retrieve from memory, even though it may not be accurate) and the **confirmation bias** (the tendency to seek evidence in support of our existing beliefs and to ignore evidence that contradicts them).

How do we explain to ourselves the decisions we make? **Framing,** or setting the context in which a problem is presented, can also affect the outcome of a decision. And regardless of whether a decision proves to be good or bad, we often use **hindsight bias** to "correct" our memories so that the decision seems to be a good one. **Counterfactual thinking** involves revisiting our decisions by considering "what if" alternatives.

Intelligence and Mental Abilities

What types of questions are used to measure intelligence? Psychologists who study **intelligence** ask what intelligence entails and how it can be measured. They also wonder about the relationship between intelligence and creativity.

What are some of the major theories of intelligence? Intelligence theories fall into two categories: those that argue in favor of a "general intelligence," which affects all aspects of cognitive functioning, and those that say intelligence is composed of many separate abilities, with a person not necessarily scoring high in all of them.

Spearman's theory of intelligence is an example of the first category. The theories of Thurstone and Cattell are examples of the second category, as are Sternberg's **triarchic theory of intelligence** and Gardner's **theory of multiple intelligences.** Goleman's theory of **emotional intelligence** emphasizes skill in social relationships and awareness of others' and one's own emotions.

What kinds of intelligence tests are in use today? The *Binet–Simon Scale,* developed in France by Alfred Binet and Theodore Simon, was adapted by Stanford University's L. M. Terman to create a test that yields an **intelligence quotient (IQ),** the *Stanford–Binet Intelligence Scale.* **The Wechsler Adult Intelligence Scale** was developed by David Wechsler especially for adults. He also created the **Wechsler Intelligence Scale for Children.** In contrast to these individual intelligence tests, there are also **group tests** of intelligence, which are administered by one examiner to many people at a time. In addition, some psychologists who criticize traditional IQ tests have developed alternatives to them. Some are **performance tests** of mental abilities, which don't involve the use of language, and others are **culture-fair tests** that reduce cultural bias in a variety of ways.

What are some important characteristics of a good test? Reliability, the ability of a test to produce consistent and stable scores, and **validity,** the ability of a test to measure what it has been designed to measure, are two important characteristics of a good test. Although the reliability of IQ tests is seldom questioned, their validity is. Critics charge that these tests assess only a very limited set of mental skills—for instance, passive verbal understanding, the ability to follow instructions, and the ability to give correct answers in a limited time frame. They point out that some tests may be unfairly biased against members of some minority groups. Also poor school performance may be *the result of,* rather than caused by, low test scores, an example of a self-fulfilling prophecy. New tests are being developed to address these concerns.

Heredity, Environment, and Intelligence

What determines individual differences in intelligence? Why are twin studies useful in studying intelligence? Although there has been extended debate about the ex-

tent to which heredity and environment contribute to IQ, studies comparing the IQ scores of identical and fraternal twins raised in the same families and in different families indicate that approximately 50% of the differences in intelligence are due to genetics and the other half being due to differences in environment and education.

What have we learned from early intervention programs about the influence of the environment on intellectual development? With such a sizable percentage of the differences in IQ scores being attributable to the environment and education, many psychologists are strongly in favor of compensatory education programs for young children from disadvantaged homes. Two such programs are the Milwaukee Project and Head Start. Although they may not boost IQ scores greatly in the long run, such programs do seem to have significant education benefits.

Do gender and culture influence mental abilities? Many people believe that males and females are innately different in their verbal and mathematical abilities. Others believe that people from certain cultures have a natural tendency to excel at academic skills. Neither of these beliefs holds up under scientific scrutiny.

What do psychologists know about the two extremes of human intelligence: very high and very low? The IQs of nearly 70 percent of the general population fall between 85 and 115, and all but 5 percent of the population have IQs between 70 and 130. **Mental retardation** and **giftedness** are the two extremes of intelligence. About a quarter of the cases of mental retardation can be traced to biological causes, including Down syndrome, but the causes of the other 75 percent of cases are not fully understood. Neither are the causes of giftedness. Gifted people do not necessarily excel in all mental abilities. Sometimes they are gifted in one area without being gifted in others.

Creativity

What is creativity? Creativity is the ability to produce novel and socially valued ideas or objects, from philosophy to painting, from music to mousetraps.

How is creativity related to intelligence? The threshold theory holds that a certain minimum level of intelligence is needed for creativity, but above that threshold level, higher intelligence doesn't necessarily make for greater creativity. Apparently other factors, besides intelligence, contribute to creativity.

Can creativity be measured? A number of tests of creativity have been developed. These tests are scored on the originality of answers and frequently on the number of responses (divergent thinking). Some psychologists question how valid these tests are, however.

CRITICAL THINKING AND APPLICATIONS

1. Einstein believed his extraordinary genius resulted in part from his skill in visualizing the possibilities of abstract ideas. Could anyone become a genius by developing skills of visualization?

2. Think for a moment of the last time you were confronted with an important decision. What approach did you use in making your choice? Now that you have read this chapter, would you respond differently if you were faced with a similar decision today?

3. Because a performance test does not rely on language skills, it is necessarily culture-fair. Is this statement accurate? Why, or why not?

4. In what ways has intelligence testing had a profound influence on our lives? Do you think that this influence has been predominantly positive or negative? What could be done to improve intelligence tests and make their impact more positive?

WEB QUIZ 7.7 ✔   **Go to the Morris 6e Companion Website to take a practice chapter exam.**

8 Motivation and Emotion

the other is sleep. Sometimes behavior seems to be motivated by a desire to reduce the state of arousal; at other times, it appears to be motivated by a desire to increase the state of arousal. For example, when you are tired, you take a nap. When you are bored, you may watch television.

Arousal theory suggests that each of us has an optimum level of arousal that varies from one situation to another and over the course of the day. According to the theory, behavior is motivated by the desire to maintain the optimum level of arousal for a given moment. Students often take breaks from their studying to do something more stimulating. One student may study for 1 hour and then talk to a friend. Another may study for three hours without interruption and then take a walk. An "early bird" may jump out of bed in the morning and run a mile before dressing for work. A "night owl" might begin the day sipping coffee, reading the newspaper, and struggling to wake up. Each seeks the level of arousal that is optimum for him or her in a particular time and place.

It is not surprising that an individual's arousal level also affects how well she or he performs in different situations. Psychologists agree that there is no "best" level of arousal necessary to perform all tasks. Rather, it is largely a question of degree—of both the level of arousal and the complexity of the task. The **Yerkes-Dodson law** puts it this way: The more complex the task, the lower the level of arousal that can be tolerated without interfering with performance. Thus, higher levels of arousal are optimal when one is required to perform simple tasks, and relatively lower levels of arousal are best when performing complex tasks (see **Figure 8–1**).

But arousal theory may not account for all forms of stimulation. Extremely stimulating activities, such as rock climbing, skydiving, bungee jumping, and hang gliding do not seem to be done in pursuit of an optimal level of arousal (Zuckerman, 1979). A person may get up and go for a walk when she becomes bored or "restless," but if she makes an appointment to go skydiving next Tuesday, that action doesn't help her boredom today. Does skydiving each week somehow satisfy her need for stimulation all week? Zuckerman (1979, 1994) suggests that *sensation seeking* is itself a basic motivation that varies greatly from person to person. High-sensation seekers pursue high-risk, "thrill-seeking" activities (including dangerous sports and unsafe driving practices); low-sensation seekers avoid such activities.

Other theorists note that things going on outside the organism are also important in motivation. For example, bakery aromas may prompt us to eat, even if we have just finished a satisfying meal; a sample copy of a new magazine, a demonstration of a new product, or a store window display may lead us to buy something we would not have otherwise bought. In other words, objects in the environment—called **incentives**—can also motivate behavior (Bolles, 1972; Rescorla & Solomon, 1967). Advertisers are well aware of the lure of incentives.

We need not be aware of incentives for them to affect our behavior. A person may buy something without being aware that the purchase was triggered by an advertisement in the newspaper or a magazine. Similarly, we may enter a bakery without being aware that the aroma pulled us in.

Intrinsic and Extrinsic Motivation

Some psychologists distinguish between intrinsic and extrinsic motivation. **Intrinsic motivation** refers to rewards provided by an activity itself. In this case, we say that the behavior is intrinsically rewarding. Play is a good example. Children typically climb trees, finger paint, and play games for no other reward than the fun they get from the activity itself. In the same way, many adults solve crossword puzzles, play golf, and tinker in a workshop

Thrill-seeking behaviors cannot be explained by drive-reduction theory, because thrill seekers are trying to increase arousal, not reduce it. Everyone sometimes seeks to increase arousal, but thrill seekers seem to desire higher levels of arousal than most people do.

Arousal theory
Theory of motivation that proposes that organisms seek an optimal level of arousal.

Yerkes-Dodson law
States that there is an optimal level of arousal for the best performance of any task; the more complex the task, the lower the level of arousal that can be tolerated before performance deteriorates.

Incentive
External stimulus that prompts goal-directed behavior.

Intrinsic motivation
A desire to perform a behavior that stems from the behavior performed.

FIGURE 8–1

The Yerkes-Dodson law. A certain amount of arousal is needed to perform most tasks, but a very high level of arousal interferes with the performance of complicated activities. That is, the level of arousal that can be tolerated is higher for a simple task than for a complex one.
Source: After Hebb, 1955.

largely for the enjoyment they get from the activity. **Extrinsic motivation** refers to rewards that are obtained not from the activity, but as a *consequence* of the activity. For example, a child does chores to earn an allowance, and an adult who hates golf may play a round with a client because doing so may help to close a sale. Whether behavior is intrinsically or extrinsically motivated can have important consequences. For example, the National Advisory Mental Health Council (1995) writes as follows:

> When people pursue activities for their intrinsic interest they are especially likely to become and remain fascinated and absorbed by them and feel happy. Conversely, when people concentrate on the external rewards of particular tasks, they experience decreased emotional involvement and negative feelings. Studies have also revealed that higher intrinsic motivation is linked to higher school achievement and psychological adjustment in children, adolescents and college students. (p. 843)

It is interesting that intrinsic motivation can actually be decreased by rewards. For example, if parents offer a reward to their young daughter for writing to her grandparents, she may be less likely to write to them when rewards are no longer available. Research confirms this tendency. Among children, adolescents, and adults, when extrinsic rewards are offered for a behavior, intrinsic motivation and sense of personal responsibility for that behavior are likely to decrease, at least for a short time (Deci, Koestner, & Ryan, 1999). However, positive feedback (including praise) may actually increase intrinsic motivation (Chance, 1992; Deci et al., 1999).

Whether a behavior is intrinsically or extrinsically motivated is not always clear. Consider a child who spontaneously sits down and writes a letter to her grandparents. No one has asked her to do so or has offered her a reward; is her behavior intrinsically motivated? You might think so, but suppose she says, "Maybe if I write them a nice letter, they'll send me a present!" Now you might conclude that her behavior is extrinsically motivated, but had she kept quiet, you wouldn't know that. Now suppose she says nothing about her motives, but you learn that in the past, whenever she has written to her grandparents, they have replied with a card and some cash. Or suppose that the grandparents have merely replied but haven't sent money. As you can see, the distinction between intrinsic and extrinsic motivation is sometimes very difficult to make.

Extrinsic motivation
A desire to perform a behavior to obtain an external reward or avoid punishment.

A Hierarchy of Motives

Abraham Maslow (1954), a humanistic psychologist, arranged motives in a hierarchy, from lower to higher. The lower motives spring from bodily needs that must be satisfied. As we move higher in Maslow's hierarchy of needs, the motives have more subtle origins: the desire to live as comfortably as possible, to deal as well as we can with other human beings, and to make the best possible impression on others. Maslow believed that the highest motive in the hierarchy is self-actualization—the drive to realize one's full potential. Maslow's hierarchy of motives is illustrated in **Figure 8–2.**

According to Maslow's theory, higher motives emerge only after the more basic ones have been largely satisfied: A person who is starving doesn't care what people think of her table manners.

Maslow's model offers an appealing way to organize a wide range of motives into a coherent structure. But recent research challenges the universality of his views. Maslow based his hierarchical model on observations of historical figures, famous living individuals, and even friends whom he admired greatly. However, the majority of these people were white males living in Western society. In many simpler societies, people often live on the very edge of survival, yet they form strong and meaningful social ties and possess a firm sense of self-esteem (Neher, 1991). In fact, difficulty in meeting basic needs can actually foster the satisfaction of higher needs: A couple struggling financially to raise a family may grow closer as a result of the experience. In our discussion of development during adolescence and early adulthood (Chapter 9, Life-Span Development), we will examine some research indicating that males must have a firm sense of their own identity (and thus a degree of self-esteem) before they can successfully establish the kinds of close relationships with others that satisfy the need for belonging. As a result of such research findings, many psychologists now view Maslow's model with a measure of skepticism.

We have reviewed some basic concepts about motivation. With these concepts in mind, we now turn our attention to specific motives.

INTERACTIVE LECTURE 8.1

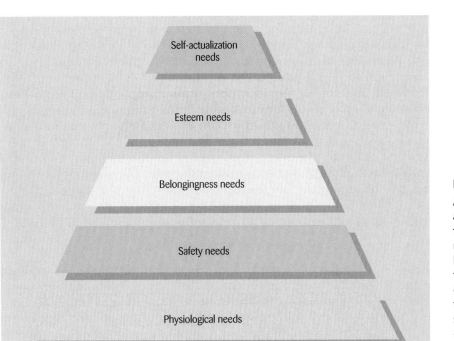

FIGURE 8–2

A pyramid representing Maslow's hierarchy of needs. From bottom to top, the stages correspond to how fundamental the motive is for survival and how early it appears in both the evolution of the species and the development of the individual. According to Maslow, the more basic needs must largely be satisfied before higher motives can emerge.

Source: After Maslow, 1954.

WEB QUIZ **8.1**

CHECK YOUR UNDERSTANDING

Match the following terms with the appropriate definition.

____ 1. drive

____ 2. drive reduction

____ 3. homeostasis

____ 4. incentive

____ 5. intrinsic motivation

____ 6. extrinsically motivated

a. external stimulus that prompts goal-directed behavior

b. state of balance in which the organism functions effectively

c. theory that motivated behavior is focused on reducing bodily tension

d. tending to perform behavior to receive some external reward or avoid punishment

e. state of tension brought on by biological needs

f. motivation arising from behavior itself

7. Indicate whether the following statements are true (T) or false (F).

___ a. Most significant human behavior is learned, not inborn.

___ b. Human behavior is rigidly unchanging and characteristic of our species.

___ c. Drive-reduction theory explains our attempts to increase arousal when we are bored.

Answers: 1. e. 2. c. 3. b. 4. a. 5. f. 6. d. 7. a. (T); b. (F); c. (F).

Hunger and Thirst

Why do people usually get hungry at mealtime?

When you are hungry, you eat. If you don't eat, your need for food will continue to increase, but your hunger may not. Suppose that you decide to skip lunch to study at the library. Your need for food will increase throughout the day, but your hunger will come and go. You will probably be hungry around lunchtime; then your hunger will likely abate while you are at the library. By dinnertime, no concern will seem as pressing as eating. The psychological state of hunger, then, is not the same as the biological need for food, although that need often sets the psychological state in motion.

Like hunger, *thirst* is stimulated by both internal and external cues. Internally, thirst is controlled by two regulators that monitor the level of fluids inside and outside the cells. Both of these regulators stimulate thirst when fluid levels are too low. Just as we become hungry in response to external cues, the experience of thirst can also be affected by environmental factors. We may get thirsty when we see a TV commercial featuring people savoring tall, cool drinks in a lush, tropical setting. Seasonal customs and weather conditions also affect our thirst-quenching habits: Ice-cold lemonade is a summer staple, whereas hot chocolate warms cold winter nights.

Biological and Emotional Factors

How can external cues influence our desire to eat?

Early research established the importance of the hypothalamus as the brain center involved in hunger and eating. Initially, researchers identified two regions in the hypothalamus as controlling our experience of hunger and satiety (satiety means being full to satisfaction). One of these centers appeared to act as the feeding center, because when it was stimulated, animals began to eat. When it was destroyed the animals stopped eating to the point of starvation. Another area of the hypothalamus was thought to be the satiety center: When it was stimulated, animals stopped eating; when it was destroyed, animals ate to the point of extreme obesity. The hypothalamus seemed to be a kind of "switch" that turned eating on or off, at least in rats.

However, more recent studies have challenged this simple "on-off" explanation for the control of eating by showing that a number of other areas of the brain are also involved (Winn, 1995). A third center in the hypothalamus appears to influence the drive to eat specific foods. Studies have also shown that regions of the cortex and spinal cord play an important role in regulating food intake. Moreover, the connections among brain centers that control hunger are now known to be considerably more complex than were once thought—involving more than a dozen different neurotransmitters (Flier & Maratos-Flier, 1998; Woods, Seeley, Porte, & Schwartz, 1998). Some of these neurotransmitters act to increase the consumption of specific foods such as carbohydrates or fats, whereas others suppress the appetite for these foods (Blundell & Halford, 1998; Lin, Umahara, York, & Bray, 1998).

How does the brain know when to stimulate hunger? The brain monitors the blood levels of *glucose* (a simple sugar used by the body for energy), fats, and carbohydrates, as well as insulin and other hormones that are released into the blood in response to these nutrients. Changes in the blood levels of these substances signal the need for food (Seeley & Schwartz, 1997).

The brain also monitors the amount and kind of food that you have eaten. Receptors in the stomach sense not only how much food the stomach is holding but also how many calories that food contains. Signals from these receptors travel to the brain. When food enters the small intestine, a hormone is released into the bloodstream and carried to the brain, where it serves as an additional source of information about the body's nutritional needs (Albus, 1989; Takaki, Nagai, Takaki, & Yanaihara, 1990).

But, as we noted earlier, a biological need for food does not always result in hunger. The sensation of hunger is the product not only of things going on in the body but also of things going on outside the body. The smell of a cake baking in the oven, for example, may trigger the desire to eat whether the body needs fuel or not. Sometimes just looking at the clock and realizing that it is dinnertime can make us feel hungry. One intriguing line of research suggests that such external cues set off internal biological processes that mimic those associated with the need for food. For example, the mere sight, smell, or thought of food causes an increase in insulin production, which, in turn, lowers glucose levels in the body's cells, mirroring the body's response to a physical need for food (Rodin, 1985). Thus, the aroma from a nearby restaurant may serve as more than an incentive to eat; it may actually trigger an apparent need for food.

How and when you satisfy hunger and thirst depends on social, psychological, environmental, and cultural influences as well as on physiological needs. For example, the Japanese tea ceremony is concerned more with restoring inner harmony than with satisfying thirst. Do you think the office worker is drinking coffee because she is thirsty?

The hunger drive is tied to emotions in complex ways. Some people head for the refrigerator whenever they are depressed, bored, anxious, or angry. Others lose all interest in food at these times and complain that they are "too upset to eat." One student studying for an important exam spends as much time eating as reading; another student studying for the same exam lives on coffee until the exam is over. Under emotionally arousing conditions, what one person craves may turn another person's stomach.

Cultural and Social Factors

How can the culture that you were raised in influence your desire to eat?

How you respond when you are hungry will vary according to your experiences with food, which are mostly governed by learning and social conditioning. The majority of Americans eat three meals a day at regular intervals. A typical American family eats breakfast at 7 A.M., lunch around noon, and dinner about 6 P.M. But in Europe, people often have dinner much later in the evening. Italians, for example, rarely eat dinner before 9 P.M. Numerous studies with both humans and animals have shown that regularly eating at particular times during the day leads to the release at those times of the hormones and neurotransmitters that cause hunger (see Woods, Schwartz, Baskin, & Seeley, 2000). In other words, we get hungry around noon partly because the body "learns" that if it's noon, it's time to eat.

Social situations also affect our motivation to eat. Say that you are at an important business lunch where you need to impress a prospective client. You may not feel very hungry, even though this lunch is taking place an hour past your usual lunchtime. Conversely, social situations may prompt you to eat even when you are not hungry. Imagine that on a day when you have slept late and eaten a large breakfast, you visit friends. When you arrive, you discover that a wonderful meal is being served in a few minutes. Although you are not at all hungry, you may decide to eat merely out of courtesy.

Culture influences what we choose to eat and how much. Although most Americans will not eat horsemeat, it is very popular in several European countries. Yet many Americans consume pork, which violates both Islamic and Jewish dietary laws (Scupin, 1995). So, although hunger is basically a biological drive, it is not merely an internal state that we satisfy when our body tells us to. Hunger is the product of the complex interaction of both environmental and biological forces.

Eating Disorders

How do people suffering from anorexia nervosa tend to view their bodies?

"When people told me I looked like someone from Auschwitz [the Nazi concentration camp], I thought that was the highest compliment anyone could give me." This confession comes from a young woman who as a teenager suffered from a serious eating disorder known as **anorexia nervosa.** She was 18 years old, 5 feet 3 inches tall, and weighed 68 pounds. This young woman was lucky. She managed to overcome the disorder and has since maintained normal body weight. Others are less fortunate. In 1983, the singer Karen Carpenter died of cardiac arrest following a long battle with anorexia. More recently, the world-class gymnast Christy Henrich succumbed to the disease, weighing just 61 pounds at her death (Pace, 1994).

People with anorexia nervosa perceive themselves as overweight and strive to lose weight, usually by severely limiting their intake of food. Even after they become very thin, they constantly worry about weight gain. The following four symptoms are used in the diagnosis of anorexia nervosa (APA, 1994):

Anorexia nervosa
A serious eating disorder that is associated with an intense fear of weight gain and a distorted body image.

1. Intense fear of becoming obese, which does not diminish as weight loss progresses.

2. Disturbance of body image (for example, claiming to "feel fat" even when emaciated).

3. Refusal to maintain body weight at or above a minimal normal weight for age and height.

4. In females, the absence of at least three consecutive menstrual cycles.

Approximately 1 percent of all adolescents suffer from anorexia nervosa; about 90 percent of these are white upper- or middle-class females (Brumberg, 1988; E. H. Gilbert & DeBlassie, 1984; Romeo, 1984). Before the development of more successful treatment methods in recent years, perhaps as many as 6 percent of people with anorexia died from the disorder (Agras & Kraemer, 1983). Generally, people suffering from anorexia enjoy an otherwise normal childhood and adolescence. They are usually successful students and cooperative, well-behaved children. They have an intense interest in food but view eating with disgust. They also have a very distorted view of their own body.

Anorexia is frequently compounded by another eating disorder known as **bulimia** (Fairburn & Wilson, 1993; Yanovski, 1993). The following criteria are used for the diagnosis of bulimia (APA, 1994):

1. Recurrent episodes of binge eating (rapid consumption of a large amount of food, usually in less than 2 hours).

2. Recurrent inappropriate behaviors to try to prevent weight gain, such as self-induced vomiting.

3. The binge eating and compensatory behaviors must occur at least twice a week for 3 months.

4. Body shape and weight excessively influence the person's self-image.

5. The above behaviors occur at least sometimes in the absence of anorexia.

Approximately 4 to 8 percent of all adolescent females and up to 2 percent of adolescent males suffer from bulimia (Gwirtsman, 1984; Heatherton & Baumeister, 1991; D. W. Johnson, Johnson, & Maruyama, 1984).

The binge-eating behavior usually begins at about age 18, when adolescents are facing the challenge of new life situations. It is not surprising that residence on a college campus is associated with a higher incidence of bulimia (Squire, 1983). The socioeconomic group at high risk for bulimia— again, primarily upper-middle-class and upper-class women—is highly represented on college campuses. Also, college campuses foster social as well as academic competition. Some evidence suggests that bulimia is more prevalent on campuses where dating is emphasized than on those where it is not (Rodin, Striegel-Moore, & Silberstein, 1985).

Although anorexia and bulimia are apparently much more prevalent among females than males, many more men are affected by these disorders than was once suspected. For example, in a 1992 survey of people who had graduated from Harvard University in 1982, reported cases of eating disorders had dropped by half for women over the decade but had doubled for men (Seligman, Rogers, & Annin, 1994).

Because studies of eating disorders have focused almost entirely on females, we know very little about what might predispose an adolescent male to develop such a disorder. Among adolescent women, several factors appear likely (Brooks-Gunn, 1993). The media promote the idea that a woman must be thin to be attractive (Crandall, 1994). How often have you seen a fashion magazine cover feature a well-proportioned woman of

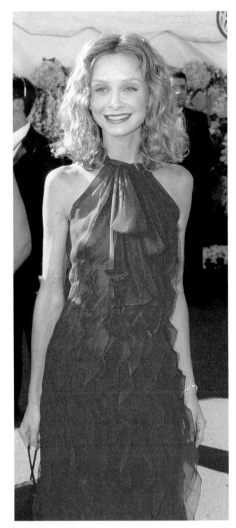

Does the American obsession with super-slimness lead adolescents to become anorexic? Popular models and actresses such as Calista Flockhart might deny it, but their status sets a standard that many young women try to follow, often to the detriment of their health.

Bulimia
An eating disorder characterized by binges of eating followed by self-induced vomiting.

UNDERSTANDING OURSELVES

The Slow but Lasting Fix for Weight Gain

Our current understanding of hunger and weight regulation suggests that a successful weight-control program must be long-term and must work with, rather than against, the body's normal tendency to maintain weight. It should be undertaken only after consultation with a doctor. On the basis of studies of the hunger drive and the relationship between eating and body weight, here is our formula for weight control:

1. First, check with your doctor before you start. People want quick fixes, so they often go overboard on dieting or exercise, sometimes with disastrous consequences. Make sure your weight-loss program will be safe.

2. Increase your body's metabolism through regular exercise. The most effective metabolism raiser is 20 to 30 minutes of moderate activity several times a week. Only about 200 to 300 calories are burned off during each exercise session (Craighead, 1990) but the exercise increases the resting metabolic rate, meaning that you burn more calories when not exercising. Thus, exercise is an important part of a weight reduction program (Wadden et al., 1997).

3. Modify your diet. A moderate reduction in calories is beneficial, but even more important is reducing the consumption of fats (particularly saturated fats) and sugars. Sugars trigger an increase in the body's level of insulin, and high levels of fat and insulin in the blood stimulate hunger.

4. Reduce, as much as possible, external cues that encourage you to eat undesirable foods. The mere sight or smell of food can increase the amount of insulin in the body, thus triggering hunger. If possible, don't bring food that is high in calories or fat into your home. Many people find that if they do their grocery shopping on a full stomach, they are less tempted to buy foods high in calories and fat.

5. Set realistic goals. Focus at least as much on preventing weight gain as on losing weight. If you must lose weight, try to shed just one pound a week for two or three months, then concentrate on maintaining that new, lower weight for several months before moving on to further weight loss.

6. Reward yourself—in ways unrelated to food—for small improvements. Use some of the behavior-modification techniques described in Chapter 5: Reward yourself not only for each pound of weight lost but also for each day or week that you maintain that weight loss. And remember, the only way you can keep the weight off is by continuing to adhere to a reasonable diet and exercise plan (McGuire, Wing, Klem, Lang, & Hill, 1999).

normal weight for her height? Perhaps because of this emphasis on weight, American women are prone to overestimate their body size (Bruch, 1980; Fallon & Rozin, 1985). One study found that over 95 percent of the female participants believed they were about one-fourth larger than they actually were in the waist, thighs, and hips (Thompson & Thompson, 1986).

A related phenomenon called muscle dysmorphia appears to be on the increase among young men (Pope, 2000). Muscle dysmorphia is an obsessive concern with one's muscle size. Men with muscle dysmorphia, many of whom are well-muscled, are distressed at their perceived puniness and so spend an inordinate amount of time fretting over their diet and exercising to increase their muscle mass.

Psychological factors also contribute to the risk of eating disorders (Walters & Kendler, 1995). An individual with an obsessive-compulsive disorder (see Chapter 12, Psychological Disorders) who feels personally ineffective and depends on others fits the portrait of an adolescent with an eating disorder (Phelps & Bajorek, 1991). Women with bulimia commonly have low self-esteem, are hypersensitive to social interactions (Steiger, Gauvin, Jabalpurwala, Seguin, & Stotland, 1999) and have experienced some form of clinical depression before developing the eating disorder (Klingenspor, 1994). Feelings of vulnerability and helplessness apparently dispose people to adopt inappropriate ways of controlling the world around them.

Eating disorders are notoriously hard to treat, and there is considerable disagreement on the most effective approach to therapy (Garfinkel & Garner, 1982). In fact, some psychologists doubt that we can ever eliminate eating disorders in a culture bombarded with the message that "thin is in." Regrettably, in many developing countries such as Taiwan, Singapore, and China, where dieting is becoming a fad, eating disorders, which were once little known, are now becoming a serious problem (Hsu, 1996).

Weight Control

Why is a quick weight-loss diet likely to fail in the long run?

The study of hunger and eating has led to some interesting insights into the problem of weight control. We know, for example, that the body interprets weight loss as a threat to survival and takes steps to prevent further weight loss. So, if you diet, you may lose a few pounds, but then your body will lower your metabolic rate and reduce the amount of energy you expend with the result that it will be harder to lose additional weight (Liebel, Rosenbaum, & Hirsch, 1995). For steps to successful weight control, see *Understanding Ourselves.*

 INTERACTIVE LECTURE **8.2**

 WEB QUIZ 8.2

CHECK YOUR UNDERSTANDING

1. The level of _____ in the blood signals hunger.
2. Hunger can be stimulated by both _____ and _____ cues.

Match the following terms with the appropriate definition.

_____ 3. hypothalamus

_____ 4. anorexia nervosa

_____ 5. bulimia

   a. recurrent episodes of binge eating, followed by vomiting, taking laxatives, or excessively exercising

   b. contains both a hunger center and a satiety center

   c. intense fear of obesity, disturbance of body image, and very little intake of food, with resulting weight well below normal minimums

Answers: 1. glucose. 2. internal, external. 3. b. 4. 4. c. 5. a.

Sex

How is the sex drive different from other primary drives?

Sex is the primary drive that motivates reproductive behavior. Like the other primary drives, it can be turned on and off by biological conditions in the body and by environmental cues. The human sexual response is also affected by social experience, sexual experience, nutrition, emotions—particularly feelings about one's sex partner—and age. In fact, just thinking

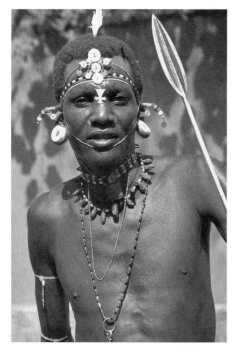

Do his elongated ear lobes and other bodily adornments enhance this young man's sexual attractiveness? It all depends on your cultural point of view. In the Samburu society of Kenya in which he lives, these particular adornments are considered highly attractive.

about or having fantasies about sex can lead to sexual arousal in humans (Laan, Everaerd, van Berlo, & Rijs, 1995; Leitenberg & Henning, 1995). Sex differs from other primary drives in one important way: Hunger and thirst are vital to the survival of the individual, but sex is vital only to the survival of the species. The sex drive, like hunger, is the result of both biological and environmental factors.

Biological Factors

How well do we understand the biology of the sex drive?

Biology clearly plays a major role in sexual motivation. At one time the level of hormones like *testosterone*—the male sex hormone—was believed to *determine* sex drive. Today scientists recognize that hormonal influences on human sexual arousal are considerably more complex. As we have seen in earlier chapters, testosterone does play a role in early sexual development (such as the onset of puberty), in differentiating male and female sex organs and, to some extent, in establishing characteristic patterns of adult sexual behavior (Kalat, 1988). But moment-to-moment fluctuations in testosterone levels are not necessarily linked to sex drive. In fact, adult males who have been castrated (resulting in a significant decrease in testosterone levels) often report little decrease in sex drive (Persky, 1983). Unlike lower animals, whose sexual activity is largely controlled by hormones and is tied to the female's reproductive cycle, humans are capable of sexual arousal at any time.

Many animals secrete substances called *pheromones* that promote sexual readiness in potential partners (see Chapter 3, Sensation and Perception). Some indirect evidence suggests that humans, too, secrete pheromones, in the sweat glands of the armpits and in the genitals and that they may influence human sexual attraction (Michael, Bonsall, & Warner, 1974; Wedeking, Seebeck, Bettens, & Paepke, 1995). The brain exerts a powerful influence on the sex drive, too. In particular, the limbic system, located deep within the brain, is involved in sexual excitement (see Chapter 2, Biological Basis of Behavior) (Heath, 1972; Hyden, 1982).

The biology of sexual behavior is better understood than that of the sex drive itself. Sex researchers William Masters and Virginia Johnson long ago identified a *sexual response cycle* that consists of four phases: *excitement, plateau, orgasm,* and *resolution* (Masters & Johnson, 1966). In the *excitement phase,* the genitals become engorged with blood. In the male, this causes erection of the penis; in the female, it causes erection of the clitoris and nipples. This engorgement of the sexual organs continues into the *plateau phase,* in which sexual tension levels off. During this phase, breathing becomes more rapid and genital secretions and muscle tension increase. During *orgasm,* the male ejaculates, and the woman's uterus contracts rhythmically, and both men and women experience some loss of muscle control. The *resolution phase* is one of relaxation in which muscle tension decreases and the engorged genitals return to normal. Heart rate, breathing, and blood pressure also return to normal. **Figure 8–3** displays the pattern of sexual responses for men and women.

Cultural and Environmental Factors

How does culture influence sexual behavior?

Although hormones and the nervous system do figure in the sex drive, human sexual motivation, especially in the early stages of excitement and arousal, is much more dependent on experience and learning than on biology.

What kind of stimuli activate the sex drive? It need not be anything as immediate as a sexual partner. The sight of one's lover, the smell of perfume or

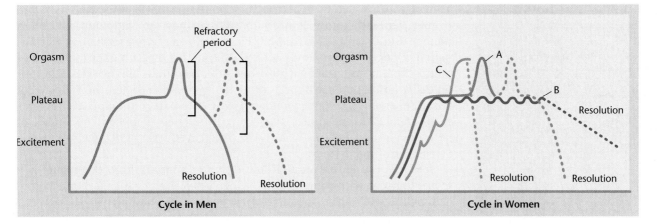

FIGURE 8–3

The sexual response cycle in males and females.   As the illustration shows, males typically go through one complete response cycle and are then capable of becoming excited again after a refractory period. Females have three characteristic patterns: one similar to the male cycle (A); one that includes a lengthy plateau phase with no orgasm (B); and a rapid cycle including several increases and decreases of excitement (C).

Source: Adapted from Masters & Johnson, 1966. Reprinted by permission of The Masters and Johnson Institute.

after-shave lotion—both of these can stimulate sexual excitement. Soft lights and music often have an aphrodisiac effect. One person may be unmoved by an explicit pornographic movie but aroused by a romantic love story, whereas another may respond in just the opposite way. Ideas about what is moral, appropriate, and pleasurable also influence our sexual behavior.

Just as society dictates standards for sexual conduct, culture guides our views of sexual attractiveness. Culture and experience may influence the extent to which we find particular articles of clothing or body shapes sexually arousing. In some cultures, most men prefer women with very large breasts, but in other cultures, small and delicate breasts are preferred. Among some African cultures, elongated earlobes are considered very attractive. In our own culture, what we find attractive often depends on the styles of the time.

As creatures grounded in individual societies and cultures, our primary biological drives, including sex, are strongly guided by environmental cues. By the same token, sexual dysfunctions—including diminished or nonexistent sexual drive—may be traced to both biological and psychological factors. We will examine sexual dysfunctions in depth in Chapter 12, Psychological Disorders.

Sexual Orientation

What are the arguments for and against a biological explanation of homosexuality?

Sexual orientation refers to the direction of an individual's sexual interest. People with a *heterosexual orientation* are sexually attracted to members of the opposite sex; those with a *homosexual orientation* are sexually attracted to members of their own sex; and *bisexuals* are attracted to members of both sexes. Recent studies indicate that about 2.8 percent of males and 1.4 percent of females have a homosexual orientation (Laumann, Gagnon, Michaels, & Michaels, 1994; Sell, Wells, & Wypij, 1995).

Why people display different sexual orientations has been argued for decades in the form of the classic nature-versus-nurture debate. Those on the nature side hold that sexual orientation is rooted in biology and is

Homosexual activity is common among animals. For example, male giraffes often engage in extreme necking, entwining, and rubbing, becoming sexually aroused as they do.

INTERACTIVE LECTURE 3.2

primarily influenced by genetics. They point out that homosexual men and women generally know before puberty that they are "different" and often remain "in the closet" regarding their sexual orientation for fear of recrimination. Evidence from family and twin studies shows a higher incidence of homosexuality in families with other gay men and a higher rate of homosexuality among men with a homosexual twin, even when the twins were raised separately (LeVay & Hamer, 1994). The nature position also derives some support from studies suggesting differences between the brains of homosexual and heterosexual men (Allen & Gorski, 1992; LeVay, 1991; Swaab & Hoffman, 1995).

It is interesting to note that among other animals, homosexual activity seems to occur with some degree of regularity. For instance, among pygmy chimpanzees, about 50 percent of all observed sexual activity is between members of the same sex. Even male giraffes commonly entwine their necks until both become sexually stimulated. And among some birds, such as greylag geese, homosexual unions have been found to last up to fifteen years (Bagemihl, 2000).

Those on the nurture side argue that sexual orientation is primarily a learned behavior, influenced by early experience and largely under voluntary control. They criticize research supporting the biological position as methodologically flawed—sometimes confusing what causes homosexuality with what results from homosexuality (Byne, 1994). Also, they contend that early socialization determines sexual orientation. Moreover, they find support for their position from cross-cultural studies that show sexual orientations occurring at different frequencies in various cultures.

To date, neither the biological nor the socialization theory has provided a completely satisfactory explanation for the origin of sexual orientation. As with most complex behaviors, a more likely explanation probably involves a combination of these two positions (Kelley & Dawson, 1994).

WEB QUIZ 8.3

CHECK YOUR UNDERSTANDING

1. _____ is the primary drive necessary for the survival of the species.
2. Culture plays a role in what is considered to be sexually attractive. Is this statement true (T) or false (F)?
3. The four stages of the sexual response cycle are _____, _____, _____, and _____.
4. Homosexuality has been observed in species other than humans. Is this statement true (T) or false (F)?

Match the following terms with the appropriate definitions.

____ 5. heterosexual orientation	a. a brain center involved in sexual excitement
____ 6. pheromones	b. sexual attraction to members of one's own sex
____ 7. homosexual orientation	c. the direction of an individual's sexual interest
____ 8. the limbic system	d. sexual attraction to members of the opposite sex
____ 9. sexual orientation	e. scents that may cause sexual attraction

Answers: 1. Sex. 2. T. 3. excitement, plateau, orgasm, and resolution. 4. T. 5. d. 6. e. 7. b. 8. a. 9. c.

Other Important Motives

How do stimulus motives and social motives differ from primary drives?

So far, we have moved from motives that depend on biological needs (hunger and thirst) to a motive that is far more sensitive to external cues—sex. Now we consider motives that are even more responsive to environmental stimuli. These motives, called **stimulus motives,** include exploration, curiosity, manipulation, and contact. They push us to investigate and often to change, our environment.

Exploration and Curiosity

What motives cause people to explore and change their environment?

Where does that road go? What is in that dark little shop? How does a television set work? Answering these questions has no obvious benefit: You do not expect the road to take you anywhere you need to go or the shop to contain anything you really want. Nor are you about to start a TV repair service. You just want to know. Exploration and curiosity are motives sparked by the new and unknown and are directed toward no more specific goal than "finding out." They are not unique to humans. The family dog will run around a new house, sniffing and checking things out, before it settles down to eat its dinner. Even rats, when given a choice, will opt to explore an unknown maze rather than run through a familiar one. But although curiosity is not uniquely human, it is perhaps particularly characteristic of humans.

Psychologists disagree about the nature and causes of curiosity (Loewenstein, 1994). William James viewed it as an emotion; Freud considered it a socially acceptable expression of the sex drive. Others have seen it as a response to the unexpected and as evidence of a human need to find meaning in life. We might assume that curiosity is a key component of intelligence, but studies attempting to establish a positive correlation between the two have been inconclusive. However, curiosity has been linked to creativity (Loewenstein, 1994).

Curiosity can also vary according to our familiarity with events and circumstances. As we continually explore and learn from our environment, we raise our threshold for the new and complex, and in turn our explorations and our curiosity become much more ambitious. In this respect, curiosity is linked to cognition. A gap in our understanding may stimulate our curiosity. But as our curiosity is satisfied and the unfamiliar becomes familiar, we tend to become bored. This outcome, in turn, prompts us to explore our surroundings further (Loewenstein, 1994).

Manipulation and Contact

Is the human need for contact universal?

Why do museums have Do Not Touch signs everywhere? It is because the staff knows from experience that the urge to touch is almost irresistible. Unlike curiosity and exploration, manipulation focuses on a specific object that must be touched, handled, played with, and felt before we are satisfied. Manipulation is a motive limited to primates, which have agile fingers and toes.

People also want to touch other people. The need for *contact* is more universal than the need for manipulation. Furthermore, it is not limited to touching with the fingers—it may involve the whole body. Manipulation is an active process, but contact may be passive.

In a classic series of experiments, Harry Harlow demonstrated how important is the need for contact (Harlow, 1958; Harlow & Zimmerman,

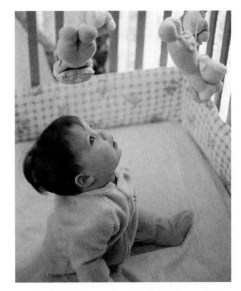

This infant is exhibiting curiosity, a stimulus motive.

Stimulus motive
Unlearned motive, such as curiosity or contact, that prompts us to explore or change the world around us.

An infant monkey with Harlow's surrogate "mothers"—one made of bare wire, the other covered with soft terry cloth. The baby monkey clings to the terry-cloth mother, even though the wire mother is heated and dispenses food. Apparently, there is contact comfort in the cuddly terry cloth that the bare wire mother can't provide.

1959). Newborn baby monkeys were separated from their mothers and given two "surrogate mothers." Both surrogate mothers were the same shape, but one was made of wire mesh and had no soft surfaces. The other was cuddly—layered with foam rubber and covered with terry cloth. Both surrogate mothers were warmed by means of an electric light placed inside them, but only the wire-mesh mother was equipped with a nursing bottle. Thus, the wire-mesh mother fulfilled two physiological needs for the infant monkeys: the need for food and the need for warmth. But baby monkeys most often gravitated to the terry-cloth mother, which did not provide food: When they were frightened, they would run and cling to it as they would to a real mother. Because both surrogate mothers were warm, the researchers concluded that the need for closeness goes deeper than a need for mere warmth. The importance of contact has also been demonstrated with premature infants. Low-birthweight babies who are held and massaged gain weight faster and are calmer than those who are seldom touched (Field, 1986).

Aggression

Is aggression a biological or a learned response?

Where people are concerned, the term **aggression** encompasses all behavior that is intended to inflict physical or psychological harm on others. Intent is a key element of aggression (R. Beck, 1983). Accidentally hitting a pedestrian with your car is not an act of aggression, but deliberately running down a person is.

Judging from the statistics (which often reflect underreporting of certain types of crimes), aggression is disturbingly common in this country. According to the *FBI's Uniform Crime Reports*, there were over 1.5 million violent crimes in the United States in 1998, including 18,000 murders, 96,000 forcible rapes, 446,000 robberies, and just over 1 million aggravated assaults. Family life also has a violent underside: One-quarter of families experience some form of violence. Some 3 to 4 million women are battered by their partners each year; more than 25 percent of these battered women seek medical attention for their injuries. In addition, over 1 million cases of child abuse are reported each year (National Research Council Panel on Child Abuse and Neglect, 1993), and more than 1,000 children die annually as a result of abuse.

Why are people aggressive? Freud considered aggression an innate drive, similar to hunger and thirst, that builds up until it is released. In his view, one important function of society is to channel the aggressive drive into constructive and socially acceptable avenues, such as sports, debating, and other forms of competition. If Freud's analysis is correct, then expressing aggression should reduce the aggressive drive. Research shows, however, that under some circumstances, venting one's anger is more likely to increase than to reduce future aggression (Bushman, Baumeister, & Stack, 1999).

According to another view, aggression is a vestige of our evolutionary past (see Buss & Shackelford, 1997) that is triggered by pain or frustration (Lorenz, 1968). Some evidence shows that pain can prompt aggressive behavior. In one experiment, for example, a pair of rats received electric shocks through the grid floor of their cage; they immediately attacked each other. As the frequency and intensity of the shocks increased, so did the fighting (Ulrich & Azrin, 1962).

Frustration also plays a role in aggression. In one experiment, researchers told people that they could earn money by soliciting charitable donations over the telephone (Kulik & Brown, 1979). Some participants were told that previous callers had been quite successful in eliciting

Aggression
Behavior aimed at doing harm to others; also, the motive to behave aggressively.

pledges; others were led to expect only scant success. Each group was given a list of prospective donors, all of whom were confederates of the experimenters and had instructions to refuse to pledge any money. The researchers assumed that people who expected to have an easy time would experience more frustration than those who anticipated difficulty. The results showed that the more frustrated group tended to argue with uncooperative respondents and even to slam down the phone. They expressed considerably more frustration than the other group.

Although studies like this one reveal a link between frustration and aggression, frustration does not always produce aggression. In fact, individuals have very different responses to frustration: Some seek help and support, others withdraw from the source of frustration, and some choose to escape into drugs or alcohol. Frustration seems to generate aggression only in people who have learned to be aggressive as a means of coping with unpleasant situations (Bandura, 1973).

One way we learn aggression is by observing aggressive models, especially those who get what they want (and avoid punishment) when they behave aggressively. For example, in contact sports, we often applaud acts of aggression (Bredemeier & Shields, 1985). In professional hockey, fistfights between players may elicit as much fan fervor as goal scoring.

Some psychologists believe that aggression is largely a learned behavior. Professional athletes in contact sports often serve as models of aggressive behavior.

But what if the aggressive model does not come out ahead or is even punished for aggressive actions? The ancient custom of public executions and painful punishments such as flogging and the stocks arose from the notion that punishing a person for aggressive acts would deter others from committing those acts. Observers usually will avoid imitating a model's behavior if it has negative consequences. However, as we saw in Chapter 5, Learning, children who viewed aggressive behavior learned aggressive behavior, regardless of whether the aggressive model was rewarded or punished. The same results were obtained in a study in which children were shown films of aggressive behavior. Those children who saw the aggressive model being punished were less aggressive than those who saw the aggressive model rewarded, but both groups of children were more aggressive than those who saw no aggressive model at all. These data are consistent with research showing that exposure to cinematic violence of any sort causes a small to moderate increase in aggressive behavior among children and adolescents (Wood, Wong, & Chachere, 1991). So, simply seeing an aggressive model seems to increase aggression among children, even if the model is punished; it also makes little difference whether the model is live or shown on film (e.g., C. A. Anderson, 1997).

Children who grow up in homes where aggression and violence are prevalent are at particular risk. As we mentioned earlier, domestic violence is rampant in the United States: One survey found that in a 12-month period, more than 3 percent of women (1.8 million) had been severely assaulted, with many of these assaults occurring at home (Browne, 1993). Children who witness domestic violence learn aggressive behavior and are more likely to behave aggressively in the future (Feldman et al., 1995).

Aggression and Culture   Cultures vary in how they handle aggression (Moghaddam, Taylor, & Wright, 1993; Smith & Bond, 1994; Triandis, 1994). For example, cultures such as the Semai of the Malaysian rain forest, the Tahitian Islanders of the Pacific, the Zuni and Blackfoot nations in North America, the Pygmies of Africa, and the residents of Japan and the Scandinavian nations place a premium on resolving conflicts peacefully. They tend to withdraw from confrontations rather than risk open conflict. In contrast, cultures such as the Yanomanö of South America, the Truk Islanders of Micronesia, and the Simbu of New Guinea encourage aggressive behavior among their members, particularly the males. Actually, we need not travel to exotic, faraway lands to find such diversity. Within the United States, subcultures such as Quakers, the Amish, the Mennonites, and the Hutterites have traditionally valued nonviolence and peaceful coexistence. This outlook contrasts markedly with attitudes and practices in the larger American culture.

Cultural differences in aggressiveness are reflected in statistics on violent crimes. The United States struggles with violent crime rates that are shockingly high compared with those of other nations. The murder rate in Norway, for example, is estimated at 0.9 per 100,000 people; in Finland and China, it is 1.1 per 100,000. In contrast, in the United States, the murder rate is 8.6 per 100,000 people—more than 7 times higher than in China and almost 10 times higher than in Norway (Triandis, 1994). Indeed, the murder rate in the United States is the highest among the industrialized nations of the world (Geen, 1998). The United States also reports higher rates of rape and vandalism.

These striking cultural differences in aggressive behavior suggest that aggression is very much influenced by the learning that takes place within a particular cultural context and by cultural norms and values. Consider the relatively nonaggressive cultures we just described. Most of them are collectivist societies that emphasize the good of the group over the desires of the individual. Members of collectivist societies are more likely to seek compromise or to withdraw from a threatening interaction because of their concern for maintaining group harmony. In contrast, members of individualist societies are more likely to follow the adage "Stand up for yourself."

Individualism and collectivism constitute an important and widely used dimension to describe cultures. Cultures high in individualism view the individual person as the basic unit of society and thus foster personal decision making and action. Members of individualist societies have social relationships with many different individuals and groups. In contrast, cultures high in collectivism see the group as the basic unit of society and thus foster group cohesion and input. Members of collectivist societies have close relationships only with those who share their circumstances, goals, and fate. Although there are some exceptions, the United States and most European societies emphasize individualism, whereas societies in Latin America, Asia, and Africa tend to be collectivist.

Some research evidence links the individualist/collectivist orientation of a culture with aggressive behavior (Bond, Wan, Leung, & Giacolone, 1985). In a study of verbal aggression, Chinese students in Hong Kong and American students in the United States heard a manager insult either a superior or a subordinate, who was either in that person's work group or outside it. Consistent with the more collectivist orientation of their culture, the Chinese students were more likely to perceive the high-status manager who insulted the subordinate as behaving legitimately in that situation. Also, the Chinese students were more likely to view an insult within the manager's group as more appropriate than one directed at someone in an out-group. These findings suggest that the interpretation of what is aggressive and what is not depends to a large extent on a person's cultural background.

Gender and Aggression   Across cultures and at every age, males are more likely than females to behave aggressively. In particular, men are more likely than women to murder, to use force to achieve their goals, and to prefer aggressive sports such as hockey, football, and boxing. Indeed, some acts of aggression, such as rape, are almost exclusively committed by males (see *Understanding the World Around Us*.)

Two metanalyses that reviewed more than 100 studies of aggression concluded that males are more aggressive than females both verbally (taunts, insults, threats) and, in particular, physically (hitting, kicking,

UNDERSTANDING The World Around Us

What Motivates Rape?

Every 5 minutes, somewhere in the United States, a woman reports being raped. Although men can be victims of sexual assault, in fact the victims are nearly always women. Perhaps one in four women in this country has been raped (Koss & Boeschen, 2000). About 40 percent of rape victims receive injuries (not counting genital injuries) during the attack, and victims are at risk for long-term health problems such as gastrointestinal disorders and tension headaches (Koss & Boeschen, 2000).

What motivates this crime? Media publicity suggests that a woman is raped when a psychopathic stranger abducts her, perhaps while she is jogging through a park or traveling at night on a dark road. Although some rapes certainly do fit this scenario, it is far from typical. The facts are that:

- About one-third of rapes occur in the victim's home.
- About half of all rapes take place on a date.
- In approximately 80 percent of rapes, the victim knows the rapist.

What causes rape? Early attempts to answer this question focused on rapists in prison. These studies suggested that power, anger, and sadism were the principal motives for rape. More recent research, based on more representative samples of the population,

> Perhaps one in four women in this country has been raped.

paint a rather different picture. One study (Prentky, Knight, & Rosenberg, 1988) found that many rapists did want to hurt, degrade, or humiliate their victims, often as a way of exacting revenge for perceived wrongs committed against them by other women. But in nearly half of the cases, sexual gratification seemed to be the predominant motive. Many of the latter rapists tended to be very impulsive; they did not plan to rape but did so when they had the opportunity. Others who raped for sexual gratification were acting out a sexual fan-

tasy; many of these men seemed to believe that their victims would eventually enjoy the experience and perhaps even fall in love with them.

Woman may be able to reduce the risk of rape by avoiding contact with men with certain characteristics: Men who act on impulse, especially in aggressive ways; men who feel that they have been wronged by women or who speak or act with contempt toward women; men who are manipulative or possessive toward women; and men with a history of violent behavior. However, even women who are very careful about the company they keep must remember that situational factors play a powerful role in most behavior. In one experiment, for example, viewing films simulating forced sex did not arouse most men at all (Barbaree & Marshall, 1991). But many of these same men did become sexually aroused by scenes of sexual violence if they had been drinking or if they had recently had an argument with a woman. Thus, although most men are not disposed to rape, certain situational factors may make some men more likely to rape.

fighting) (Eagly & Steffen, 1986; Hyde, 1986). These gender differences tend to be greater in natural settings than in controlled laboratory settings (Hyde, 1986) and appear to be remarkably stable (Knight, Fabes, & Higgins, 1996). Indeed, even historical data that go back to sixteenth-century Europe show that males committed more than three times as many violent crimes as females (see Ellis & Coontz, 1990).

Is the gender difference in aggression biological or social in origin? The answer is not simple. On the one hand, certain biological factors appear to contribute to aggressive behavior. As we saw in Chapter 2 (The Biological Basis of Behavior), low levels of testosterone and high levels of estrogen in both males and females are associated with aggressiveness and irritability. Moreover, exposure to high levels of testosterone during prenatal development is associated with increased aggressiveness (Reinisch, Ziemba-Davis,

Are males naturally more aggressive than females? Research suggests that both biology and culture encourage aggression in boys more than girls. Adults often look the other way when two boys are fighting, sending the message that violence is an acceptable way to settle disputes.

& Sanders, 1991). Other research suggests that human aggression has its roots in evolution and can be traced to defensive behaviors characteristic of our ancestors (Buss & Shackelford, 1997).

At the same time, our society clearly tolerates and even encourages greater aggressiveness in boys than in girls (Sommers-Flanagan, Sommers-Flanagan, & Davis, 1993). For example, we are more likely to give boys toy guns and to reward them for behaving aggressively; girls are more likely than boys to be taught to feel guilty for behaving aggressively or to expect parental disapproval for their aggressive behavior (Perry, Perry, & Weiss, 1989). Early socialization plays a key role in fostering aggression in boys, but other environmental factors can alter these gender differences. For example, when both sexes are subject to increased provocation, the difference in aggressiveness between males and females substantially decreases (Bettencourt & Miller, 1996).

Perhaps the most accurate conclusion is that both biological and social factors contribute to gender differences in aggressive behavior. Like most of the complex behaviors that we have reviewed, aggression undoubtedly depends on the interaction of nature and nurture (Geen, 1998).

Achievement

Is being highly competitive important to high achievement?

Climbing Mount Everest, sending rockets into space, making the dean's list, rising to the top of a giant corporation—all these actions may have mixed underlying motives. But in all of them there is a desire to excel, "to overcome obstacles, to exercise power, to strive to do something difficult as well and as quickly as possible" (Murray, 1938, pp. 80–81). It is this desire for achievement for its own sake that leads psychologists to suggest that there is a separate **achievement motive.**

As with all learned motives, the need for achievement varies widely from person to person. A number of years ago, David McClelland (1958) used responses to the Thematic Apperception Test (TAT) to measure achievement motivation. The TAT is a personality test in which a person looks at drawings of ambiguous situations and is asked to make up stories about them (see Chapter 10, Personality). For example, one picture used in the test shows an adolescent boy sitting at a classroom desk. A book lies open in front of him, but the boy's gaze is directed toward the viewer. Peo-

Achievement motive
The need to excel, to overcome obstacles.

ple's stories about this character are presumed to reflect their own motivations. Therefore, those whose stories involve the boy accomplishing something difficult or unique, setting high standards of excellence for himself, or taking significant pride in his success would score high on the need for achievement.

Using a self-report questionnaire called the Work and Family Orientation scale (WOFO) to study achievement motivation, some researchers discovered three separate but interrelated aspects of achievement-oriented behavior: *work orientation,* the desire to work hard and do a good job; *mastery,* the preference for difficult or challenging feats, with an emphasis on improving one's past performance; and *competitiveness,* the enjoyment of pitting one's skills against those of other people (Helmreich & Spence, 1978).

How do individual differences in the three aspects of achievement motivation relate to people's attainment of goals? In fact, having a high degree of competitiveness may actually interfere with achievement. In one study, students' grade-point averages (GPAs) were compared with their WOFO scores. As you might expect, students who scored low in work, mastery, and competitiveness had lower GPAs. But students who scored high in all three areas did not have the highest GPAs. It turned out that the students with the highest grades were those who had high work and mastery scores but low competitiveness scores. The counterproductive effect of competitiveness curbs achievement in other groups of people as well, including business people, elementary-school students, and scientists. What accounts for this phenomenon? No one knows for sure, but some researchers speculate that highly competitive people alienate the very people who would otherwise help them achieve their goals; others suggest that preoccupation with winning distracts them from taking the actions necessary to attain their goals.

From psychological tests and personal histories, psychologists have developed a profile of people with a high level of achievement motivation. These people are fast learners. They relish the opportunity to develop new strategies for unique and challenging tasks, whereas people with a low need for achievement rarely deviate from methods that worked for them in the past. Driven less by the desire for fame or fortune than by the need to live up to a high, self-imposed standard of performance (Carr, Borkowski, & Maxwell, 1991), they are self-confident, willingly take on responsibility, and do not readily bow to outside social pressures. Although they are energetic and allow few things to stand in the way of their goals, they are also apt to be tense and to suffer from stress-related ailments, such as headaches. They may also feel like impostors even—or especially—when they achieve their goals.

Affiliation

How do psychologists explain the human need to be with other people?

Generally, people have a need for affiliation—to be with other people. If they are isolated from social contact for a long time, they may become anxious. Why do human beings seek out one another?

For one thing, the **affiliation motive** is aroused when people feel threatened. Esprit de corps—the feeling of being part of a sympathetic group—is critical among troops going into a battle, just as a football coach's pregame pep talk fuels team spirit. Both are designed to make people feel they are working for a common cause or against a common foe.

But affiliation behavior often results from another motive entirely. For example, you may give a party to celebrate landing a job because you want to be praised for your achievement. Fear and anxiety may also be closely tied to the affiliation motive. When rats, monkeys, or humans are placed in anxiety-producing situations, the presence of a member of the same species

High achievement is partly a matter of great commitment and effort. Just as this student keeps working late into the night, so those who excel in any field are willing to work hard for success. The desire to excel not for tangible rewards but for the pleasure of being "one of the best" is called achievement motivation.

Affiliation motive
The need to be with others.

who remains calm will reduce the fear of the anxious ones. In the same way, if you are nervous on a plane during a bumpy flight, you may strike up a conversation with the calm-looking woman sitting next to you, especially if the agitation of the plane does not seem to be worrying her.

Some theorists have argued that our need for affiliation has an evolutionary basis (see Ainsworth, 1989; Baumeister & Leary, 1995; Buss, 1990, 1991). In this view, the formation and maintenance of social bonds provided our ancestors with both survival and reproductive benefits. Social groups can share resources such as food and shelter, provide opportunities for reproduction, and assist in the care of offspring. Children who chose to stay with adults were probably more likely to survive (and ultimately reproduce) than those who wandered away from their groups. Cues that signal danger, such as illness or catastrophe, also appear to increase our desire to be with others (Rofe, 1984). For example, patients with critical illnesses tend to prefer being with healthy people rather than with other seriously ill patients or by themselves (Rofe, Hoffman, & Lewin, 1985). The role that evolution may have played in the emergence of the affiliation motive has been summarized by Baumeister and Leary (1995):

> The likely result of this evolutionary selection would be a set of internal mechanisms that guide individual human beings into social groups and lasting relationships. These mechanisms would presumably include a tendency to orient toward other members of the species, a tendency to experience affective distress when deprived of social contact or relationships, and a tendency to feel pleasure or positive affect from social contact and relatedness. (p. 499)

Affiliation behavior (like most behavior) stems from a subtle interplay of biological and environmental factors. Whether you strike up a conversation with the person sitting next to you on a bumpy airplane flight depends on how friendly you normally are, as well as on how scared you feel at the moment, how calm your neighbor appears to be, and how turbulent the flight is.

INTERACTIVE LECTURE **8.4**

WEB QUIZ **8.4**

CHECK YOUR UNDERSTANDING

1. The category of wants or needs that is activated by external stimuli and pushes us to investigate our environment is called _____ motives.
2. _____ is all behavior in humans intended to inflict harm on others.
3. _____ societies emphasize the good of the group, whereas _____ societies emphasize the good of the individual.
4. A high degree of _____ may interfere with achievement.
5. A person who is willing to contend with the high risks of a career in sales is probably motivated by a high _____ motive.
6. The _____ motive is sometimes aroused when a person needs to be consoled or supported by a group of peers.
7. Indicate whether the following statements are true (T) or false (F).
   ____ a. Curiosity has been linked to creativity.
   ____ b. Research shows that low-birthweight babies gain weight faster with frequent physical contact.
   ____ c. Aggression may be a learned response to numerous stimuli.

Answers: 1. stimulus. 2. Aggression. 3. Collectivist, individualistic. 4. competitiveness. 5. achievement. 6. affiliation. 7. a. (T); b. (T); c. (T).

Emotions

How many basic emotions are there?

Ancient Greek rationalists thought that emotions, if not held in check, would wreak havoc on higher mental abilities such as rational thought and decision making (Cacioppo & Gardner, 1999). In the past, psychologists, too, often viewed emotions as a "base instinct"—a vestige of our evolutionary heritage that needed to be repressed.

More recently, however, scientists have begun to see emotions in a more positive light. Today they are thought of as essential to survival and a major source of personal enrichment (National Advisory Mental Health Council, 1995). Emotions are linked to variations in immune function and, thereby, to disease (Lazarus, 1999; O'Leary, 1990; see Chapter 11, Stress and Health Psychology). As we saw in Chapter 7 (Cognition and Mental Abilities), emotions may also influence how successful we are (Goleman, 1997). It is clear, then, that if we would understand human behavior, we must understand emotions. Unfortunately, that task is easier said than done. As you will soon see, even identifying how many emotions there are is difficult.

Basic Emotions

Are there basic emotions that all people experience regardless of their culture?

Many people have attempted to identify and describe the basic emotions experienced by humans (Ekman, 1980; Plutchik, 1980; also see Cornelius, 1996). Some years ago, Robert Plutchik (1980), for example, proposed that there are eight basic emotions: *fear, surprise, sadness, disgust, anger, anticipation, joy,* and *acceptance*. Each of these emotions helps us adjust to the demands of our environment, although in different ways. Fear, for example, underlies flight, which helps protect animals from their enemies; anger propels animals to attack or destroy.

Emotions adjacent to each other on Plutchik's emotion "circle" (see **Figure 8–4**) are more alike than those situated opposite each other or that are farther away from each other. Surprise is more closely related to fear than to anger; joy and acceptance are more similar to each other than either is to disgust. Moreover, according to Plutchik's model, different emotions may combine to produce an even wider and richer spectrum of experience. Occurring together, anticipation and joy, for example, yield optimism; joy and acceptance fuse into love; surprise and sadness make for disappointment. Within any of Plutchik's eight categories, emotions vary in intensity. Some scientists challenge Plutchik's model, noting that it may apply only to the emotional experience of English-speaking people. Anthropologists report enormous differences in the ways that other cultures view and categorize emotions. Some languages, in fact, do not even have a word for "emotion" (Russell, 1991). Languages also differ in the number of words that they have to name emotions. English includes over 2,000 words to describe emotional experiences, but Taiwanese Chinese has only 750 such descriptive words. One tribal language has only 7 words that could be translated into categories of emotion. Some cultures lack words for "anxiety" or "depression" or "guilt." Samoans have one word encompassing love, sympathy, pity, and liking—all distinct emotions in our own culture (Russell, 1991).

Of interest is that words used to name or describe an emotion may influence how that emotion is experienced. For example, the Tahitian

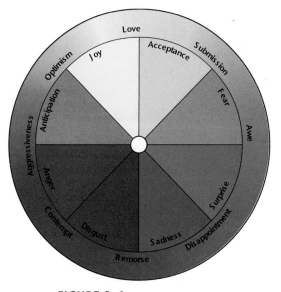

FIGURE 8–4

Plutchik's eight basic categories of emotion.

Source: Plutchik, 1980.

FIGURE 8–5

Display of anger in animal and human. Compare the facial expressions. The human face is that of a Kabuki player who is simulating anger. Note how the actor bares his teeth, copying the mandrill's display of emotion.

James-Lange theory
States that stimuli cause physiological changes in our bodies, and emotions result from those physiological changes.

language has no direct translation for the concept of sadness. Instead, Tahitians experience sadness in terms of physical illness. The sadness we feel over the departure of a close friend would be experienced by a Tahitian as, say, exhaustion.

Because of the differences in emotions from one culture to another, the tendency now is to distinguish between primary and secondary emotions. Primary emotions are those shared by people throughout the world, regardless of culture. They include, at a minimum, fear, anger, and pleasure, but may also include sadness, disgust, surprise, and other emotions. Most researchers use four criteria to identify primary emotions (see Plutchick, 1994): The emotion must (1) be evident in all cultures; (2) contribute to survival; (3) be associated with a distinct facial expression; and (4) be evident in nonhuman primates (see **Figure 8–5**). As yet no consensus exists about what emotions qualify as primary, but the number is small, very likely no more than a dozen.

Secondary emotions are those that are found throughout one or more cultures, but not throughout all cultures. They may be thought of as subtle amalgamations of the primary emotions. There are many more secondary emotions than primary emotions, but there is, again, no consensus about what those emotions are or how many they number.

Attempts to identify primary emotions have generally used cross-cultural studies (Ekman et al., 1987; Izard, 1994). For example, one group of researchers asked participants from ten countries to interpret photographs depicting various facial expressions of emotions (Ekman et al., 1987). The percentage of participants from each country who correctly identified the emotions ranged from 60 to 98 percent (see **Figure 8–6**). The researchers used this and other evidence to argue for the existence of six primary emotions—*happiness, surprise, sadness, fear, disgust,* and *anger* (see also Cornelius, 1996). Notice that love is not included in this list. Although Ekman did not find a universally recognized facial expression for love, many psychologists nevertheless hold that love is a primary emotion (Hazan & Shaver, 1987). Its outward expression, however, may owe much to the stereotypes promoted by a culture's media (Fehr, 1994). In one study in which American college students were asked to display a facial expression for love, the participants mimicked the conventional "Hollywood" prototypes such as sighing deeply, gazing skyward, and holding their hand over their heart (see Cornelius, 1996).

Theories of Emotion

What is the relationship among emotions, biological reactions, and thoughts?

In the 1880s the American psychologist William James formulated the first modern theory of emotion, and the Danish psychologist Carl Lange reached the same conclusions. According to the **James-Lange theory,** stimuli in the environment (say, seeing a large growling dog running toward us) cause physiological changes in our bodies (accelerated heart rate, enlarged pupils, deeper or shallower breathing, increased perspiration, goosebumps), and emotions arise from those physiological changes. The emotion of *fear,* then, would simply be the almost instantaneous and automatic awareness of physiological changes.

There has been some supporting evidence for this theory (Davidson, 1992; Levenson, 1992; McGeer & McGeer, 1980), but if you think back to the biology of the nervous system (Chapter 2), you should be able to identify a major flaw in the James-Lange theory. Recall that sensory information about bodily changes flows to the brain through the spinal cord. If bodily changes are the source of emotions, then people with severe spinal

Sadness: Brows' inner corners raised, mouth drawn out and down.

Interest: Brows raised or knit, mouth softly rounded, lips pursed.

Distress: Eyes tightly closed; mouth as in anger, squared and angular.

Joy: Mouth forms smile, cheeks lifted, twinkle in eyes.

FIGURE 8–6

Izard's universal emotions. Working from Charles Darwin's theory that certain emotional and facial expressions have an evolutionary basis, psychologist Caroll Izard believes he has isolated ten universal emotions that can be seen in the facial expressions of infants. Four are illustrated here.

cord injuries should experience fewer and less intense emotions, but this is not the case (Chwalisz, Diener, & Gallagher, 1988). Moreover, most emotions are accompanied by very similar physiological changes. Bodily changes, then, do not cause specific emotions and may not even be necessary for emotional experience.

Recognizing these facts, the **Cannon-Bard theory** holds that we mentally process emotions and physically respond simultaneously, not one after another. When you see the dog, you feel afraid *and* your heart races at the same time.

Cognitive Theories of Emotion Cognitive psychologists have taken Cannon-Bard's theory a step further. They argue that our emotional experience depends on our perception of a situation (Lazarus, 1982, 1991a, 1991b, 1991c). According to the **cognitive theory** of emotion, the situation gives us clues as to how we should interpret our state of arousal. When we see the dog, there are indeed bodily changes; we then use information about the situation to tell us how to respond to those changes. Only when we recognize that we are in danger do we experience those bodily changes as fear. (See **Figure 8–7** for a comparison of these three theories of emotion.)

Challenges to Cognitive Theory Although a cognitive theory of emotion makes a lot of sense, some critics reject the idea that feelings always stem from cognitions. Quoting the poet e. e. cummings, Zajonc (pronounced ZY-unz) argues that "feelings come first." Human infants, he points out, can imitate emotional expressions at 12 days of age, well before they acquire language. We have the ability to respond instantaneously to situations without taking time to interpret and evaluate them. But some emotional responses are not clear-cut. When we feel jit-

Cannon-Bard theory
States that the experience of emotion occurs simultaneously with biological changes.

Cognitive theory
States that emotional experience depends on one's perception or judgment of the situation one is in.

Psychologists disagree as to the ways that cognition and physiological processes contribute to emotions such as fear.

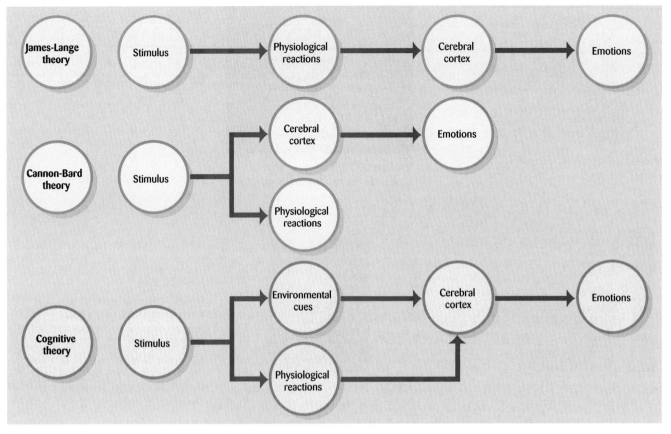

FIGURE 8–7

The three major theories of emotion. According to the James-Lange theory, the body first responds physiologically to a stimulus, and then the cerebral cortex determines which emotion is being experienced. The Cannon-Bard theory holds that impulses are sent simultaneously to the cerebral cortex and the peripheral nervous system; thus, the response to the stimulus and the processing of the emotion are experienced at the same time, but independently. Cognitive theorists assert that the cerebral cortex interprets physiological changes in the light of information about the situation to determine which emotions we feel.

tery, a cross between nervous and excited, we ask ourselves, "What's going on?" Zajonc (1984) believes that we invent explanations to label feelings: In his view, cognition follows emotion.

Another direct challenge to the cognitive theory claims that emotions can be experienced without the intervention of cognition (Izard, 1971). According to this view, a situation such as separation or pain provokes a unique pattern of unlearned facial movements and body postures that may be completely independent of conscious thought (Trotter, 1983). When information about our facial expressions and posture reaches the brain, we automatically experience the corresponding emotion. According to Carroll Izard, then, the James-Lange theory was essentially right in suggesting that emotional experience arises from bodily reactions. But Izard's theory stresses facial expression and body posture as crucial to the experience of emotion, whereas the James-Lange theory emphasized muscles, skin, and internal organs.

Considerable evidence supports Izard's view that facial expressions influence emotions (Adelmann & Zajonc, 1989; Cappella, 1993; Ekman & Davidson, 1993; Zajonc, Murphy, & Inglehart, 1989). If further research bolsters Izard's theory, we will be able to say with certainty that a key ele-

ment in determining our emotional experience is our own expressive behavior, the topic we turn to now.

INTERACTIVE LECTURE **8.5**

WEB QUIZ **8.5**

CHECK YOUR UNDERSTANDING

1. Robert Plutchik asserts that emotions vary in _____, a fact that accounts in part for the great range of emotions we experience.
2. Izard's theory of emotion stresses the importance of which element?
   a. cognition
   b. expressive behavior

Match the following theories with the appropriate description.

_____ 3. Cannon-Bard   a. states that physical reactions directly cause experienced emotions

_____ 4. cognitive theory   b. contends that emotions and bodily responses occur simultaneously

_____ 5. James-Lange   c. says that emotional experience depends on the perception of a given situation

Answers: 1. intensity. 2. b. 3. b. 4. c. 5. a.

Communicating Emotion

What is the most obvious signal of emotion?

Sometimes you are vaguely aware that a person makes you feel uncomfortable. When pressed to be more precise, you might say, "You never know what she is thinking." But you do not mean that you never know her opinion of a film or what she thought about the last election. It would probably be more accurate to say that you do not know what she is feeling. Almost all of us conceal our emotions to some extent, but usually people can tell what we are feeling. Although emotions can often be expressed in words, much of the time we communicate our feelings nonverbally. We do so through, among other things, voice quality, facial expression, body language, personal space, and explicit acts.

Voice Quality and Facial Expression

What role can voice and facial expression play in expressing emotion?

If your roommate is washing the dishes and says acidly, "I *hope* you're enjoying your novel," the literal meaning of his words is quite clear, but you probably know very well that he is not expressing a concern about your reading pleasure. He is really saying, "I am annoyed that you are not helping to clean up." Similarly, if you receive a phone call from someone who has had very good or very bad news, you will probably know how she feels before she has told you what happened. In the same way, we can literally hear fear in a person's voice, as we do when we listen to a nervous student give an oral report. Much of the information we convey is not contained in the words we use, but in the way those words are expressed.

Facial expressions are the most obvious emotional indicators. We can tell a good deal about a person's emotional state by observing whether that

FIGURE 8–8

People throughout the world use the "brow-raise" greeting when a friend approaches.

Source: Eibl-Eibesfeldt, 1972

When having a conversation, most Arabs stand closer to one another than most Americans do. In our society, two men would not usually stand as close together as these two Arabs unless they were very aggressively arguing with each other (a baseball player heatedly arguing with an umpire, for example).

person is laughing, crying, smiling, or frowning. Many facial expressions are innate, not learned (Ekman, 1994). Children who are born deaf and blind use the same facial expressions as do other children to express the same emotions. Charles Darwin first advanced the idea that most animals share a common pattern of muscular facial movements. For example, dogs, tigers, and humans all bare their teeth in rage. Darwin also observed that expressive behaviors serve a basic biological as well as social function. Darwin's notion that emotions have an evolutionary history and can be traced across cultures as part of our biological heritage laid the groundwork for many modern investigations of emotional expression (Izard, 1992, 1994; see **Figure 8–8**). Psychologists who take an evolutionary approach believe that facial expressions served an adaptive function, enabling our ancestors to compete successfully for status, to win mates, and to defend themselves (Ekman, 1992; Tooby & Cosmides, 1990).

Body Language, Personal Space, and Gestures

How can posture and personal space communicate emotion?

Body language is another way that we communicate messages nonverbally. How we hold our back, for example, communicates a great deal. When we are relaxed, we tend to stretch back into a chair; when we are tense, we sit more stiffly with our feet together.

The distance we maintain between ourselves and others is called *personal space.* This distance varies depending on the nature of the activity and the emotions felt. If someone stands closer to you than is customary, that proximity may indicate either anger or affection; if farther away than usual, it may indicate fear or dislike. The normal conversing distance between people varies from culture to culture. Two Swedes conversing would ordinarily stand much farther apart than would two Arabs or Greeks.

Explicit acts, of course, can also serve as nonverbal clues to emotions. A slammed door may tell us that the person who just left the room is angry. If friends drop in for a visit and you invite them into your living room, you are probably less at ease with them than with friends who generally sit down with you at the kitchen table. Gestures, such as a slap on the back or an embrace, can also indicate feelings. Whether people shake your hand briefly or for a long time, firmly or limply, tells you something about how they feel about you.

You can see from this discussion that nonverbal communication of emotions is important. However, a word of caution is needed here. Although nonverbal behavior may offer a clue to a person's feelings, it is not an *infallible* clue. Laughing and crying can sound alike, yet crying may signal sorrow, joy, anger, nostalgia—or that you are slicing an onion. Moreover, as with verbal reports, people sometimes "say" things nonverbally that they do not mean. We all have done things thoughtlessly—turned our backs, frowned when thinking about something else, laughed at the wrong time—that have given offense because our actions were interpreted as an expression of an emotion that we were not, in fact, feeling.

Also, many of us overestimate our ability to interpret nonverbal cues. For example, in one study of several hundred "professional lie catchers," including members of the Secret Service, government lie detector experts, judges, police officers, and psychiatrists, every group except for the psychiatrists rated themselves above average in their ability to tell whether another person was lying. Only the Secret Service agents managed to identify the liars at a better-than-chance rate (Ekman & O'Sullivan, 1991). Similar results have been obtained with other groups of people (e.g., DePaulo & Pfeifer, 1986).

Gender and Emotion

Are men less emotional than women?

Men are often said to be less emotional than women. But do men feel less emotion, or are they simply less likely to express the emotions they feel? And are there some emotions that men are more likely than women to express?

Research sheds some light on these issues. In one study, when men and women saw depictions of people in distress, the men showed little emotion, but the women expressed feelings of concern for those in distress (Eisenberg & Lennon, 1983). However, physiological measures of emotional arousal (such as heart rate and blood pressure) showed that the men in the study were actually just as affected as the women were. The men simply inhibited the expression of their emotions, whereas the women were more open about their feelings. Emotions such as sympathy, sadness, empathy, and distress are often considered "unmanly," and traditionally, in Western culture, boys are trained from an early age to suppress those emotions in public (O'Leary & Smith, 1988). The fact that men are less likely than women to seek help in dealing with emotional issues (Komiya, Good, & Sherrod, 2000) is probably a result of this early training. In addition, women tend to have stronger emotional reactions to self-generated thoughts and memories (Carter, 1998; see **Figure 8–9**).

Men and women are also likely to react with very different emotions to the same situation. For example, being betrayed or criticized by another person would make males feel angry, whereas females are more likely to feel hurt, sad, or disappointed (Brody, 1985). And, when men get angry, they generally turn their anger outward, against other people and against the situation in which they find themselves. Women, are more likely to see themselves as the source of the problem and to turn their anger inward, against themselves. These gender-specific reactions, are consistent with the fact that men are four times more likely than women to become violent in the face of life crises; women are much more likely to become depressed.

Men and women also differ in their ability to interpret nonverbal cues of emotion. Women are more skilled than men at decoding the facial expressions, body cues, and tones of voice of others (Hall, 1984). How can we explain these differences? One possibility is that because women tend to be the primary caregivers for preverbal infants, they need to become more attuned than men to the subtleties of emotional expressions. Some psychologists have even suggested that this skill may be genetically programmed into females. Consistent with this evolutionary perspective, research has shown that male and female infants do express and self-regulate emotions differently (McClure, 2000; Weinberg, Tronick, Cohn, & Olson, 1999).

Another explanation of gender differences in emotional sensitivity is based on the relative power of women and men. Because women historically have occupied less powerful positions, they may have felt the need to become acutely attuned to the emotional displays of others, particularly those in more powerful positions (namely, men). This idea is supported by evidence that, regardless of gender, followers are more sensitive to the emotions of leaders than vice versa (Snodgrass, 1992).

The fact that men are more likely than women to hold positions of power may affect emotional experience in other ways as well. In the types of jobs traditionally held by women, workers are often called on to regulate, manage, or otherwise alter their emotional expression. Sociologist Arlie

A

B

FIGURE 8–9

Emotion and brain activity in men and women. When asked to think of something sad, women (A) generate more activity in their brains than men (B).

Source: Carter, 1998, p. 100. Shading added.

Why do flight attendants always look happy? Because they must. Even while showing passengers how to use an oxygen mask, flight attendants are expected to trade genuine emotions—perhaps of fear or sadness—for an automatic, reassuring smile.

Hochschild (1983) described this process as emotional labor. In a study of flight attendants, the majority of whom were women, Hochschild found clear guidelines regarding which emotions were to be displayed, to whom, by whom, and how often. Most of the flight attendants felt that they were being robbed of genuine emotional experiences on the job: "… [I]n the flight attendant's work, smiling is separated from its usual function, which is to express a personal feeling, and attached to another one—expressing a company feeling" (p. 127). Hochschild also noted that jobs that are high in emotional labor—such as secretaries, registered nurses, cashiers, social workers, and bank tellers—tend to be filled by women.

Culture and Emotion

How can culture influence the way we express emotion?

Does where we live affect what we feel? And if so, why? For psychologists, the key issue is how cultures help shape emotional experiences. One defining element is whether a culture is predominantly individualist or collectivist—does its focus center mainly on the individual or on the group? Psychologists have only recently begun to study how individualism and collectivism affect emotional experience (Scherer & Wallbott, 1994). Most of the well-established findings in the psychology of emotions come from studies of emotional expression within a single culture.

Among nonverbal channels of communication, facial expressions seem to communicate the most specific information. Hand gestures or posture can communicate general emotional states (e.g., feeling bad), but the complexity of the muscles in the face allows facial expressions to communicate very specific feelings (e.g., feeling sad, angry, or fearful). Some researchers have argued that across cultures, peoples, and societies, the face looks the same whenever certain emotions are expressed; this phenomenon is known as the *universalist* position. Charles Darwin subscribed to this view, arguing that as part of our common evolutionary heritage, people use the same expressions to convey the same emotions. In contrast, other researchers support the *culture-learning* position, which holds that members of a culture learn the appropriate facial expressions for emotions. These expressions, then, can differ greatly from one culture to the next. Which view is more accurate?

As we saw earlier, Ekman and his colleagues have concluded from cross-cultural studies that at least six emotions are accompanied by universal facial expressions: happiness, sadness, anger, surprise, fear, and disgust. Carroll Izard (1980) conducted similar studies in England, Germany, Switzerland, France, Sweden, Greece, and Japan with similar results. These studies seem to support the universalist position: Regardless of culture, people tended to agree on which emotions that others were expressing facially. However, this research does not completely rule out the culture-learning view. Because the participants were all members of developed countries that likely had been exposed to one another through movies, magazines, and tourism, they might simply have become familiar with the facial expressions seen in other cultures. A stronger test was needed that reduced or eliminated this possibility.

Such a test was made possible by the discovery of several contemporary cultures that had been totally isolated from Western culture for most of their existence. Members of the Fore and the Dani cultures of New Guinea, for example, had their first contact with anthropologists only a few years before Ekman's research took place. They provided a nearly perfect opportunity to test the universalist/culture-learning debate. If members of these cultures gave the same interpretation of facial expressions and produced the same expressions on their own faces as people in Western cultures, there would be much stronger evidence for the universality of facial expressions of emotion. Ekman and his colleagues presented members of the Fore culture with three photographs of people from outside their culture and asked them to point to the picture that represented how they would feel in a certain situation. For example, if a participant was told "Your child has died, and you feel very sad," he or she would have the opportunity to choose which of the three pictures most closely corresponded to sadness. The results indicated very high rates of agreement on facial expressions of emotions (Ekman & Friesen, 1971; Ekman, Sorenson, & Friesen, 1969). Moreover, when photographs of the Fore and Dani posing the primary emotions were shown to college students in the United States, the same high agreement was found (Ekman & Friesen, 1975). This finding suggests that at least some emotional expressions are inborn.

Can you identify the emotions being expressed by this man from New Guinea? The finding that U.S. college students could recognize the emotional expressions of people who had been largely isolated from Western cultures—and vice versa—lent support to the *universalist* position of facial expression.

Source: From P. Ekman and W. V. Friesen, *Unmasking the Face*, Englewood Cliffs, N.J., Prentice Hall, 1975, p. 27.

If this is true, why are people so often confused about the emotions being expressed by people in other cultures? The answer lies in a principle called **display rules** (Ekman & Friesen, 1975). Display rules concern the circumstances under which it is appropriate for people to show emotion. Display rules differ substantially from culture to culture. In a study of Japanese and American college students, the participants watched graphic films of surgical procedures, either by themselves or in the presence of an experimenter. The students' facial expressions were secretly videotaped as they viewed the films. The results showed that when the students were by themselves, both the Japanese and the Americans showed facial expressions of disgust, as expected. But when the participants watched the films in the presence of an experimenter, the two groups displayed different responses. American students continued to show disgust on their faces, but the Japanese students showed facial expressions that were more neutral, even somewhat pleasant (Ekman, Friesen, & Ellsworth, 1972).

Why the sudden switch? The answer lies in the different display rules of the two cultures. The Japanese norm says "Don't display strong negative emotion in the presence of a respected elder" (in this case, the experimenter). Americans typically don't honor this display rule; hence, they expressed their true emotions whether they were alone or with someone else. To interpret what others are feeling, we need to understand both the universal expression of emotions and the particular rules operating in a culture.

 8.1

Display rules
Culture-specific rules that govern how, when, and why expressions of emotion are appropriate.

WEB QUIZ 8.6 ✓

CHECK YOUR UNDERSTANDING

1. Cultural differences, particularly _____, influence how we experience emotion.
2. Two important nonverbal cues to emotions are _____ _____ and _____ _____.
3. Men tend to interpret the source of their anger to be in their _____.
4. Research shows that some _____ _____ are recognized universally.
5. _____ _____ are the cultural circumstances under which it is appropriate to show emotions on the face.

Indicate whether the following statements are true (T) or false (F).

_____ 6. Overt behavior is an infallible clue to emotions.
_____ 7. Women are better than men at deciphering nonverbal cues.
_____ 8. Women experience emotions more deeply than men do.
_____ 9. Women express emotions more openly than men do.
_____10. Men are more likely than women to express violence in the face of life crises.

Answers: 1. language. 2. facial expression, body language. 3. environment. 4. facial expressions. 5. Display rules. 6. F. 7. T. 8. F. 9. T. 10. T.

KEY TERMS

motive, p. 278
emotion, p. 278

Perspectives on motivation
instinct, p. 278
drive, p. 278
drive-reduction theory, p. 278
homeostasis, p. 278

primary drive, p. 278
secondary drive, p. 278
arousal theory, p. 279
Yerkes-Dodson law, p. 279
incentives, p. 279
intrinsic motivation, p. 279
extrinsic motivation, p. 280

Hunger and Thirst
anorexia nervosa, p. 284
bulimia, p. 285

Other important motives
stimulus motives, p. 291
aggression, p. 292
achievement motive, p. 296
affiliation motive, p. 297

Emotions
James-Lange theory, p. 300
Cannon-Bard theory, p. 301
cognitive theory, p. 301

Communicating emotion
display rules, p. 307

CHAPTER REVIEW

Perspectives on Motivation

How can you use intrinsic and extrinsic motivation to help you succeed in college? There are many ways of viewing human motivation. The idea that our motivations are largely based on **instincts** was popular in the early twentieth century but has since fallen out of favor. Human motivation has also been viewed as an effort toward **drive reduction** and **homeostasis,** or balance in the body, as well as an effort to maintain an optimum level of arousal. Another perspective is that of motivational inducements or **incentives.** When inducements originate from within the person, they are called **intrinsic motivation,** and when they come from outside, they are called **extrinsic motivation.** Extrinsic motivation can certainly help you succeed in college, as when your parents offer to buy you an expensive present for good grades. Developing intrinsic motivation to succeed in college, however, will have a greater, more long-lasting effect.

Abraham Maslow suggested that human motives can be arranged in a hierarchy, with primitive ones based on physical needs positioned at the bottom, and higher ones such as self-esteem positioned toward the top. Maslow believed that the higher motives don't emerge until the more basic ones have been met, but recent research challenges his view. In some societies, difficulty in meeting basic needs can actually foster the satisfaction of higher motives.

Hunger and Thirst

Why do people usually get hungry at mealtime? How can external cues influence our desire to eat? How can the culture that you were raised in influence your desire to eat? Hunger is regulated by several centers within the brain. These centers are stimulated by receptors that monitor stomach contents, as well as by receptors that monitor the contents of the blood, especially its levels of glucose, fats, and carbohydrates. Hunger is stimulated by factors outside the body, such as cooking aromas, and by emotional, cultural, and social factors.

How do people suffering from anorexia nervosa tend to view their bodies? Eating disorders, particularly **anorexia nervosa** and **bulimia,** are more prevalent among females than among males. They are characterized by extreme preoccupation with body image and weight.

Why is a quick weight-loss diet likely to fail in the long run? The body interprets sudden weight loss as a threat to survival and takes steps to prevent further weight loss.

Sex

How is the sex drive different from other primary drives? Sex is a primary drive that gives rise to reproductive behavior essential for the survival of the species.

How well do we understand the biology of the sex drive? Although hormones are involved in human sexual responses, they don't play as dominant a role as they do in some other species. In humans, the brain exerts a powerful influence on the sex drive as well.

How does culture influence sexual behavior? Because people have different experiences, they also have different preferences for sexually arousing stimuli. What is sexually attractive is also influenced by culture.

What are the arguments for and against a biological explanation of homosexuality? People with a heterosexual orientation are sexually attracted to members of the opposite sex; those with a homosexual orientation are sexually attracted to members of their own sex. It is likely that both biological and environmental factors play a role in explaining homosexuality.

Other Important Motives

How do stimulus motives and social motives differ from primary drives? In contrast to primary drives, stimulus motives and social motives are less obviously associated with the survival of the organism or the species, even though they often help human beings adapt successfully to their environments. **Stimulus motives,** such as the urge to explore and manipulate things, are associated with obtaining information about the world. **Social motives,** such as the desire to affiliate with other people, center on human interactions with one another.

What motives cause people to explore and change their environment? Exploration and curiosity are two human motivations that encourage us both to explore our environment and often to change it.

Is the human need for contact universal? Another important stimulus motive in humans and other primates is to seek various forms of tactile stimulation. This contact motive can be seen in the child's urge to cling and cuddle.

Is aggression a biological or a learned response? Any behavior intended to inflict physical or psychological harm on others is an act of **aggression.** Some psychologists see aggression as an innate drive in humans that must be channeled to constructive ends, but others see it more as a learned response that is greatly influenced by modeling. The fact that levels of aggression differ markedly across cultures tends to support the view of human aggression as encouraged and shaped by learning. There are also gender differences in aggression, with males generally being more inclined than females to strike out at others and commit acts of violence. These gender differences probably depend on an interaction of nature and nurture.

Is being highly competitive important to high achievement? People who display a desire to excel, to overcome obstacles, and to accomplish difficult things score high in what psychologists call **achievement motive.** Although hard work and a strong desire to master challenges both contribute to achievement, competitiveness toward others often does not. In fact, competitiveness can actually interfere with achievement—perhaps by alienating other people, perhaps by becoming a preoccupation that distracts from the attainment of goals.

How do psychologists explain the human need to be with other people? The **affiliation motive,** or need to be with other people, is especially pronounced when we feel threatened or anxious. Affiliation with others in this situation can counteract fear and bolster spirits.

Emotions

How many basic emotions are there? Are there basic emotions that all people experience regardless of their culture? Robert Plutchik's classification system for **emotions** uses a circle to position eight basic emotional categories. But not all cultures categorize emotions the way that Plutchik does. Some do not even have a word for emotion. Others describe feelings by their physical sensations. A cross-cultural analysis of emotional expression has led Paul Ekman to argue for the universality of at least six emotions—happiness, surprise, sadness, fear, disgust, and anger. Many psychologists add love to this list.

What is the relationship among emotions, biological reactions, and thoughts? According to the **James-Lange theory,** certain stimuli in the environment can bring on physiological changes in the body, and emotions then arise from our awareness of those changes. In contrast, the **Cannon-Bard theory** holds that emotions and bodily responses occur simultaneously, not one after the other. A third perspective, the **cognitive theory** of emotion, contends that our perceptions and judgments of situations are essential to our emotional experiences. Without these cognitions we would have no idea how to label our feelings. Not everyone agrees with this view, however, because emotions sometimes seem to arise too quickly to depend on mental evaluations. C. E. Izard argues that it may not be cognitive assessments that give rise to emotions but rather certain inborn facial expressions and body postures that are automatically triggered in emotion-arousing situations and then "read" by the brain as particular feelings.

Communicating Emotion

What role can voice and facial expression play in expressing emotion? People sometimes express their emotions verbally through their words, tone of voice, exclamations, and other sounds. Facial expressions are the most obvious nonverbal indicators of emotion.

How can posture and personal space communicate emotion? Other indicators involve body language—our posture, the way we move, our preferred personal distance from others when talking to them, our degree of eye contact. Explicit acts, such as slamming a door, express emotions, too. People vary in their skill at reading these nonverbal cues.

Are men less emotional than women? Research confirms some gender differences in expressing and perceiving emotions. For instance, when confronted with a person in distress, women are more likely than men to express emotion, even though the levels of physiological arousal are the same for the two sexes. Also, in some stressful situations, such as being betrayed or criticized, men tend to report more anger, and women more disappointment and hurt. There is also some truth to the common stereotype that women are generally better than men at reading other people's emotions. This skill may be sharpened by their role as caretakers of infants and their traditional subordinate status to men.

How can culture influence the way we express emotion? The facial expressions associated with certain basic emotions appear to be universal: The expressions are the same regardless of a person's cultural background. This cross-cultural finding contradicts the culture-learning view, which suggests that facial expressions of emotion are learned within a particular culture. This is not to say that there are no cultural differences in emotional expression, however. Overlaying the universal expression of certain emotions are culturally varying **display rules** that govern when it is appropriate to show emotion—to whom, by whom, and under what circumstances. Other forms of nonverbal communication of emotion vary more from culture to culture than facial expressions do.

CRITICAL THINKING AND APPLICATIONS

1. People who get low grades in school or do poorly on the job are often viewed as lacking motivation. What are some other possible explanations for their substandard performance?

2. What would you recommend to someone who wanted to lose weight but had failed many times to do so?

3. Some research reveals that boredom inspires curiosity; other studies show that curiosity is piqued by the new and unknown. Explain why these findings do not contradict each other. How would you apply these concepts in a classroom?

4. Which theory of emotions do you prefer the most, and why?

5. Think about how you experience and handle feelings of love, anger, and sadness. Do you express all these emotions with equal ease? Do any of these emotions make you uncomfortable? Are your responses to these feelings typical of your gender and culture? In what ways?

WEB QUIZ 8.6 ✔ **Go to the Morris 6e Companion Website to take a practice chapter exam.**

9 Life-Span Development

K AY'S WAS A VERY UNUSUAL CHILDHOOD. BORN THE FOURTH OF FIVE CHILDREN IN a very wealthy family, she grew up in palatial houses tended by large staffs of servants. Yet oddly enough, she had no sense of being wealthy. Money was never talked about in her home, and she and her brother and sisters were never showered with expensive toys. From her earliest days, she saw herself as shy, passive, and lacking self-assurance, dowdy and never quite "measuring up." She envied her second sister's rebellious nature but didn't have the courage to be rebellious herself. Her mother, who did nothing to nurture greater self-confidence, set such high expectations for her children that reaching those heights seemed an impossible goal. The man Kay married was brilliant, witty, charming, and extremely successful. He dominated all the decisions in their family life. He was the creative thinker, she the implementer. He was the provider of excitement and zest, she the dutiful follower. And yet, after quietly suffering her husband's bouts of heavy drinking, his unpredictable anger, his long struggle with manic depression, and his eventual violent suicide, she went on to take over the family business and to become the talented and powerful head of a highly influential newspaper. This poor little rich girl so burdened with self-doubts was Katharine Graham (1917–2001), former publisher of *The Washington Post*. In her eighties, she won a Pulitzer Prize in 1997 for her autobiography (Graham, 1997).

The study of how people change from birth to old age is called **developmental psychology.** Because virtually everything about a person changes over the life span, developmental psychology includes all the other topics that psychologists study, such as thinking, language, intelligence, emotions, and social behavior. But developmental psychologists focus only on the changes that occur as people grow older.

Enduring Issues and Methods in Developmental Psychology

What are some of the limitations of the methods used to study development?

In trying to understand both the "what" and the "why" of human development, psychologists focus on three of the enduring issues we introduced in Chapter 1:

1. *individual characteristics versus shared human traits* Although there are many common patterns to human development, each person's development is also in some ways unique. Katharine Graham's life illustrates this well. Like so many other women, she progressed through the stages of childhood, adolescence, and adulthood; she married, had children, worked at a job, and eventually became a grandmother. These

Developmental psychology
The study of the changes that occur in people from birth through old age.

How did Katharine Graham's life illustrate several key issues in developmental psychology?

are all common developmental milestones. Yet in other ways, Katharine Graham's development was not like everyone else's. Not every woman is born into such a wealthy family, feels the shyness and insecurity that she did, has to cope with the early death of a husband, or achieves such heights in the business world. This combination of shared and distinctive elements is characteristic of all human development. We all take essentially the same developmental journey, but each of us travels somewhat different roads and experiences events in different ways.

2. *stability versus change* Human development is characterized by both major life transitions *and* continuities with the past. Again, Katharine Graham's life is an excellent example. The death of her husband and her takeover of his job at the family-owned *Post* was certainly a major turning point in her development. She went from being the dutiful, subordinate wife to becoming the accomplished head of a major American newspaper. And yet with all the changes that this transition brought, she still had ties to the person she had been before. Self-doubts about her job performance plagued her endlessly, even at the pinnacle of her success. She would lie awake at night reliving how she handled situations, wondering how she might have done better. The little girl fearful of never being "good enough" still lingered on inside her.

3. *heredity versus environment* This issue is central to developmental psychology. Human development can be explained by a combination of biological forces and environmental experiences. These two elements constantly interact to shape human growth. What made Katharine Graham into the person she became? She herself said that she lacked the "proper instincts" to be self-assured and daring, that what she was to some extent stemmed from her inherited makeup. And yet she recognized the crucial importance of environment. How different might she have been had she been born into a different family, married a different husband, or chosen a different life's work? People, she wrote, are "molded by the way they spend their days." This is an important concept in developmental psychology.

You will meet these three major issues often in this chapter as we journey through the human life course. As developmental psychologists study growth and change across the lifespan, they use the same research methods that psychologists in other areas use: naturalistic observations, correlational studies, and experiments (see Chapter 1). But because developmental psychologists are interested in processes of change over time, they use these methods in three special types of studies: cross-sectional, longitudinal, and biographical.

In a **cross-sectional study,** researchers examine developmental change by observing or testing people of different ages at the same time. For example, they might study the development of logical thought by testing a group of 6-year-olds, a group of 9-year-olds, and a group of 12-year-olds, and then looking for differences among the age groups. One problem with cross-sectional studies, however, is that they don't distinguish age differences from **cohort** differences. A cohort is a group of people born during the same period of history: All Americans born in 1940, for example, form a cohort. Cohort differences are differences between individuals stemming from the fact that they were born and grew up at different historical times. If we found that 40-year-olds were able to solve harder math problems than 80-year-olds, we wouldn't know whether this difference was due to better cognitive ability in younger people (an age difference) or to better math education 40 years ago than 80 (a cohort difference).

Cross-sectional study
A method of studying developmental changes by comparing people of different ages at about the same time.

Cohort
A group of people born during the same period in historical time.

Longitudinal studies address this problem by testing the same people two or more times as they grow older. For instance, researchers who are interested in the development of logical thought might begin their study by testing a group of 6-year-olds, then wait 3 years and test the same children again at age 9, then wait another 3 years to test them again at age 12. One problem with longitudinal studies, however, is that they don't distinguish age differences from differences that arise from improved assessment or measurement tools. For example, researchers retesting a cohort at age 9 might have access to a more sensitive measure of logical thought than they did when they tested that cohort at age 6. So if they found significant improvement in logical thought over this 3-year period, they wouldn't know to what extent it reflected the advance in age and to what extent it reflected the more sensitive measuring tool.

Another drawback to a longitudinal study is that it takes considerable time even when investigating childhood alone. When studying the entire course of adulthood, a longitudinal study can take 50 years or more. To avoid the huge expense of such a long study, researchers have devised a third way of studying adulthood: the **biographical study.** With this approach, the researcher might start with some 70-year-olds and pursue their lives backward. That is, the researchers would try to reconstruct their subjects' past by interviewing them and consulting various other sources. Biographical data are less trustworthy than either longitudinal or cross-sectional data, because people's recollections of the past may be inaccurate. Together, these research methods provide a wealth of information about human development, beginning well before birth.

Prenatal Development

Why can an organism or another substance cause devastating effects at one point in prenatal development but not at others?

During the earliest period of **prenatal development**—the stage of development from conception to birth—the fertilized egg divides, embarking on the process that will transform it, in just 9 months, from a one-celled organism into a complex human being. The dividing cells form a hollow ball, which implants itself in the wall of the uterus. Two weeks after conception, the cells begin to specialize: Some will form the baby's internal organs, others will form muscles and bones, and still others will form the skin and the nervous system. No longer an undifferentiated mass of cells, the developing organism is now called an **embryo.**

The embryo stage ends 3 months after conception, when the *fetal stage* begins. At this point, although it is only 1 inch long, the **fetus** roughly resembles a human being, with arms and legs, a large head, and a heart that has begun to beat. Although it can already move various parts of its body, another month is likely to pass before the mother feels those movements.

An organ called the *placenta* nourishes the embryo and the fetus. Within the placenta, the mother's blood vessels transmit nutritive substances to the embryo or fetus, and carry waste products away from it. Although the mother's blood never actually mingles with that of her unborn child, almost anything she eats, drinks, or inhales is capable of being transmitted through the placenta. If she develops an infection such as syphilis, rubella ("German measles"), or AIDS, the microorganisms that cause these diseases can cross the placenta and infect the fetus, often with disastrous results. If she inhales nicotine, drinks alcohol, or uses other drugs during pregnancy, these too can cross the placenta, compromising the baby's development (Brown, Bakeman, Coles, Sexson, & Demi, 1998; Harris & Liebert, 1991).

Longitudinal study
A method of studying developmental changes by evaluating the same people at different points in their lives.

Biographical (or retrospective) study
A method of studying developmental changes by reconstructing people's past through interviews and inferring the effects of past events on current behaviors.

Prenatal development
Development from conception to birth.

Embryo
A developing human between 2 weeks and 3 months after conception.

Fetus
A developing human between 3 months after conception and birth.

Children born with fetal alcohol syndrome often exhibit facial deformities, heart defects, stunted growth, and cognitive impairments that can last throughout life. The syndrome is entirely preventable but not curable.

Critical period
A time when certain internal and external influences have a major effect on development; at other periods, the same influences will have little or no effect.

Fetal alcohol syndrome (FAS)
A disorder that occurs in children of women who drink alcohol during pregnancy that is characterized by facial deformities, heart defects, stunted growth, and cognitive impairments.

INTERACTIVE LECTURE **9.1** ▶

WEB QUIZ **9.1** ✓

Many potentially harmful substances have a **critical period** when they are most likely to have a major effect on the fetus. At other times, the same substance may have no effect at all. For example, if a woman contracts rubella during the first 3 months of pregnancy, the effects can range from death of the fetus to a child who is born deaf. However, rubella contracted during the final 3 months of pregnancy is unlikely to cause severe damage to the fetus because the critical period for the formation of major body parts has passed.

Pregnancy is most likely to have a favorable outcome when the mother gets good nutrition and good medical care, and when she avoids exposure to substances that could be harmful to her baby, including alcohol. Alcohol is the drug most often abused by pregnant women, and with devastating consequences (Steinhausen, Willms, & Spohr, 1993). Pregnant women who consume large amounts of alcohol risk giving birth to a child with **fetal alcohol syndrome (FAS),** a condition characterized by facial deformities, heart defects, stunted growth, and cognitive impairments (Mattson, Riley, Gramling, Delis, & Jones, 1998; Shaffer, 1999). Even smaller amounts of alcohol can cause neurological problems (Hunt, Streissguth, Kerr, & Olson, 1995; Shriver & Piersel, 1994). For that reason, doctors recommend that pregnant women and those who are trying to become pregnant abstain from drinking alcohol altogether.

Pregnant women are also wise not to smoke. Smoking restricts the oxygen supply to the fetus, slows its breathing, and speeds up its heartbeat. These changes are associated with a significantly increased risk of miscarriage (Ness et al., 1999). In this country alone, smoking may cause over 100,000 miscarriages a year. Babies of mothers who smoke are also more likely to suffer low birth weight, which puts the child at risk for other developmental problems (DiFranza & Lew, 1995).

Increased psychological stress and the way that it is coped with during pregnancy also appear to be related to the health of a newborn. For instance, one study (Rini, Dunkel-Schetter, Wadhwa, & Sandman, 1999) found that the risks of prematurity and low birth weight were higher in mothers with low self-esteem who felt pessimistic, stressed, and anxious during pregnancy.

Differences in access to good nutrition and health care help explain why the infant death rate in this country is over twice as high for African Americans as it is for whites (see **Figure 9–1**; Singh & Yu, 1995). A much higher percentage of African Americans live in poverty, and it is much harder for the poor to eat a healthy diet and see a doctor regularly during pregnancy (Aved, Irwin, Cummings, & Findeisen, 1993).

CHECK YOUR UNDERSTANDING

1. The stage of development from conception to birth is called _____ _____.
2. During the first 3 months of human prenatal development, when all the major body parts are forming, the developing organism is called an _____.
3. During the final 6 months of human prenatal development, when rapid growth in size and weight occurs and the body is readied for life outside the womb, the developing organism is called a _____.
4. The organ that nourishes the developing embryo and fetus is known as the _____.
5. A time when an organism is especially susceptible to environmental influences related to a particular aspect of development is called a _____ period.

Answers: 1. prenatal development. 2. embryo. 3. fetus. 4. placenta. 5. critical.

The Newborn

How competent are newborns?

Research has disproved the old idea that **neonates,** or newborn babies, do nothing but eat, sleep, and cry, while remaining oblivious to the world. True, newborns can sleep up to 20 hours a day, but when awake they are much more aware and competent than they may seem at first glance.

Reflexes

What early reflexes enable newborns to respond to their environment?

Newborns come equipped with a number of useful reflexes. Many of these reflexes, such as those that control breathing, are essential to life outside the uterus. Some enable babies to nurse. The baby's tendency to turn his or her head toward anything that touches the cheek is called the *rooting reflex.* The rooting reflex is very useful in helping the baby find the mother's nipple. The *sucking reflex* is the tendency to suck on anything that enters the mouth, and the *swallowing reflex* enables the baby to swallow milk and other liquids without choking.

Other reflexes have purposes that are less obvious. The *grasping reflex* is the tendency to cling vigorously to an adult's finger or to any other object placed in the baby's hands. The *stepping reflex* refers to the fact that very young babies take what looks like walking steps if they are held upright with their feet just touching a flat surface. These two reflexes normally disappear after 2 or 3 months, reemerging later as voluntary grasping (at around 5 months of age) and real walking (at the end of the first year).

Very young babies are also capable of a surprisingly complex kind of behavior: imitating the facial expressions of adults. If an adult opens his or her mouth or sticks out his or her tongue, newborn babies often respond by opening their mouths or sticking out their tongues (McCall, 1979; Meltzoff & Moore, 1985). When this ability to imitate was first noted in newborns, psychologists could hardly believe it. How could babies carry out such complex responses at an age when they can have no idea how their own face looks, much less how to make specific facial expressions? It now appears that this early imitation is only a primitive reflex, like the grasping and stepping reflexes. The behavior disappears after a few weeks, and then reemerges in a more complex form many months later (Bjorklund, 1989; Wyrwicka, 1988).

Almost all newborns respond to the human face, the human voice, and the human touch. This behavior improves their chances of survival. After all, babies are totally dependent on the people who take care of them, so it is essential that their social relationships get off to a good start. From the very beginning, they have a means of communicating their needs to those they live with: They can cry. And very soon—in only about 6 weeks—they have an even better method of communication, one that serves as a thank you to the people who are working so hard to keep them happy: They can smile.

Temperament

Is your temperament the same as when you were a newborn?

We may be tempted to talk about babies as if they are all the same, but babies display individual differences in **temperament** (Goldsmith & Harman, 1994; Piontelli, 1989). Some cry much more than others; some are much

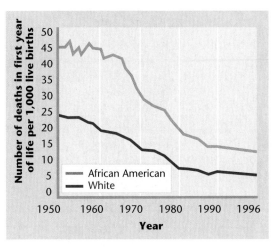

FIGURE 9–1

Mortality rates for white and African American infants.

Source: National Center for Health Statistics, 1995 (through 1990); BlackHealthCare.com, 2000 (for 1991–1996).

Neonates
Newborn babies.

Temperament
Characteristic patterns of emotional reactions and emotional self-regulation.

If they are raised in a compatible environment, easy, uninhibited babies will most likely grow to be outgoing children and adults.

more active. Some babies love to be cuddled; others seem to wriggle uncomfortably when held. Some are highly reactive to stimuli around them, whereas others are quite placid no matter what they see or hear.

In a classic study of infant temperament, Alexander Thomas and Stella Chess (1977) identified three types of babies: "easy," "difficult," and "slow-to-warm-up." "Easy" babies are good-natured and adaptable, easy to care for and please. "Difficult" babies are moody and intense, reacting to new people and new situations both negatively and strongly. "Slow-to-warm-up" babies are relatively inactive and slow to respond to new things, and when they do react, their reactions are mild. To these three types, Jerome Kagan and his associates (Kagan, Reznick, Snidman, Gibbons, & Johnson, 1988; Kagan & Snidman, 1991) have added a fourth: the "shy child." Shy children are timid and inhibited, fearful of anything new or strange. Their nervous systems react to stimuli in a characteristically hypersensitive way (Kagan, 1994). Kagan found interesting differences in the frequency with which various behaviors related to temperament appear in babies from different cultures. He and his colleagues have speculated that such differences may be due in large part to the effects of different gene pools and genetic predispositions (Kagan, Arcus, & Snidman, 1993).

Some evidence suggests, however, that differences in temperament also may be due to prenatal influences. In particular, maternal stress produces reliable changes in heartbeat and movement in the fetus, and these, in turn, are correlated with temperament in the child. Some psychologists believe that the mix of hormones in the womb may be as important as the genes that the child inherits in determining temperament (Azar, 1997b; DiPietro, Hodgson, Costigan, & Johnson, 1996).

Regardless of what initially causes a baby's temperament, it often remains quite stable over time. In one study that asked mothers to describe their children's temperaments, characteristics such as degree of irritability, flexibility, and persistence were all relatively stable from infancy through age 8 (Pedlow, Sanson, Prior, & Oberklaid, 1993). Other studies have found that fussy or difficult infants are likely to become "problem children" who are aggressive and have difficulties in school (Guérin, 1994; Patterson & Bank, 1989; Persson-Blennow & McNeil, 1988). A longitudinal study of shy children and some of their less inhibited peers showed that most shy infants continue to be relatively shy and inhibited in middle childhood, just as most uninhibited infants remained relatively outgoing and bold (Kagan & Snidman, 1991).

A combination of biological and environmental factors generally contributes to this stability in behavior. For instance, if a newborn has an innate predisposition to cry often and react negatively to things, the parents may find themselves tired, frustrated, and often angry. These reactions in the parents may serve to reinforce the baby's difficult behaviors, and so they tend to endure. Even if children are born with a particular temperament, then, they need not have that temperament for life. Each child's predispositions interact with his or her experiences, and how the child turns out is the result of that interaction (Kagan, 1989, 1994; Kagan, Snidman, & Arcus, 1992; Maccoby, 2000).

Perceptual Abilities

Which senses are the most developed at birth, and which are the least developed?

Newborns can see, hear, and understand far more than previous generations gave them credit for. Their senses work fairly well at birth and rapidly improve to near-adult levels. Neonates begin to absorb and process information from the outside world as soon as they enter it—or, in some cases, even before.

Vision Unlike puppies and kittens, human babies are born with their eyes open and functioning, even though the world looks a bit fuzzy to them at first. They see most clearly when faces or objects are only 8 to 10 inches away from them. Visual acuity (the clarity of vision) improves rapidly, however, and so does the ability to focus on objects at different distances. By 6 or 8 months of age, babies can see almost as well as the average college student, though their visual system takes another 3 or 4 years to develop fully (Maurer & Maurer, 1988).

Even very young babies already have visual preferences. They would rather look at a new picture or pattern than one they have seen many times before. If given a choice between two pictures or patterns, both of which are new to them, they generally prefer the one with the clearest contrasts. This preference explains why they choose to look at a black-and-white pattern more than a colored one, even though they are able to distinguish primary colors from gray. For a young baby, however, the pattern shouldn't be too complex: A large black-and-white checkerboard pattern is preferred to one with smaller squares because the smaller squares tend to blur in the baby's vision. As babies get older and their vision improves, they prefer more and more complex patterns, perhaps reflecting their need for an increasingly complex environment (Acredolo & Hake, 1982; Fantz, Fagan, & Miranda, 1975).

In general, infants find human faces and voices particularly interesting (see Flavell, 1999). They not only like to look at another person's face but also will follow the other person's gaze. Hood, Willen, and Driver (1998) presented a photograph of a human face on a video monitor. Sometimes the adult depicted looked straight ahead, sometimes to the left or right. The researchers found that infants as young as 3 months noticed the direction of the adult's gaze and shifted their gaze accordingly. Newborns also prefer to look at their own mother rather than at a stranger (Walton, Bower, & Bower, 1992). Because they see the mother so often, they acquire sets of different images of her (from various angles and so on). This visual familiarity makes the mother preferred (Walton & Bowen, 1993).

Depth Perception Depth perception is the ability to see the world in three dimensions, with some objects nearer, others farther away. Although researchers have been unable to find evidence of depth perception in babies younger than 4 months (Aslin & Smith, 1988), the ability to see the world in three dimensions is well developed by the time a baby learns to crawl, between 6 and 12 months of age.

This finding was demonstrated in a classic experiment using a device called a *visual cliff* (Walk & Gibson, 1961). Researchers divided a table into three parts. The center was a solid runway, raised above the rest of the table by about an inch. On one side of this runway was a solid surface decorated in a checkerboard pattern and covered with a sheet of clear glass. The other side was also covered with a thick sheet of clear glass, but on this side—the visual cliff—the checkerboard surface was not directly under the glass, but 40 inches below it. An infant of crawling age was placed on the center runway, and the mother stood on one side or the other, encouraging the baby to crawl toward her across the glass. All of the 6- to 14-month-old infants tested refused to crawl across the visual cliff, even though they were perfectly willing to cross the "shallow" side of the table. When the "deep" side separated the baby from the mother, some of the infants cried; others peered down at the surface below the glass or patted the glass with their hands. Their behaviors clearly showed that they could perceive depth.

Other Senses Even before babies are born, their ears are in working order. Fetuses in the uterus can hear sounds and will startle at a sudden, loud noise in the mother's environment. After birth, babies show signs that

When placed on a visual cliff, babies of crawling age (about 6 to 14 months) will not cross the deep side, even to reach their mothers. This classic experiment tells us that by the time they can crawl, babies can also perceive depth.

they remember sounds they heard in the womb. Babies also are born with the ability to tell the direction of a sound. They show this by turning their heads toward the source of a sound (Muir, 1985).

Infants are particularly tuned in to the sounds of human speech. One-month-olds can distinguish among similar speech sounds such as "pa-pa-pa" and "ba-ba-ba" (Eimas & Tartter, 1979). In some ways, young infants are even better at distinguishing speech sounds than older children and adults are. As children grow older, they often lose their ability to hear the difference between two very similar speech sounds that are not distinguished in their native language (Werker & Desjardins, 1995). For example, young Japanese infants have no trouble hearing the difference between "ra" and "la," sounds that are not distinguished in the Japanese language. By the time they are 1 year old, however, Japanese infants can no longer tell these two sounds apart (Werker, 1989).

With regard to taste and smell, newborns have clear-cut likes and dislikes. They like sweet flavors, a preference that persists through childhood. Babies only a few hours old will show pleasure at the taste of sweetened water but will screw up their faces in disgust at the taste of lemon juice (Steiner, 1979).

As infants grow older, their perceptions of the world become keener and more meaningful. Two factors are important in this development. One is physical maturation of the sense organs and the nervous system; the other is gaining experience in the world. Babies learn about the people and objects in their environment, and they experience a variety of sights, sounds, textures, smells, and tastes. As a result, a growing fund of memories and understanding increasingly enriches their perceptions.

INTERACTIVE LECTURE **9.2**

WEB QUIZ **9.2**

CHECK YOUR UNDERSTANDING

1. What are the four types of temperament?
2. Indicate whether the following statements are true (T) or false (F).
   ____a. The grasping reflex and the stepping reflex normally disappear at about 2 to 3 months.
   ____b. A newborn baby's ability to imitate facial expressions is best thought of as a reflex.
   ____c. The temperament of a newborn usually has no correspondence to later behavior.
   ____d. Babies prefer to look at familiar pictures rather than new ones.
   ____e. Newborns prefer to look at their mothers more than at strangers.
   ____f. A young infant may be better at distinguishing speech sounds than is an older child.
3. What device is used to determine whether or not babies can perceive depth?

Answers: 1. easy, difficult, slow-to-warm-up, shy. **2. a.** (T); **b.** (T); **c.** (F); **d.** (F); **e.** (T); **f.** (T). **3.** visual cliff.

Infancy and Childhood

What kinds of developmental changes occur during infancy and childhood?

During the first dozen or so years of life, a helpless baby becomes a competent member of society. Many important kinds of developments occur during these early years. Here we discuss physical and motor changes as well as cognitive and social ones.

Physical Development

Do children grow at a steady pace?

In the first year of life, the average baby grows 10 inches and gains 15 pounds. By 4 months, birth weight has doubled, and by the first birthday, birth weight has tripled. During the second year, physical growth slows considerably. Rapid increases in height and weight will not occur again until early adolescence.

An infant's growth does not occur in the smooth, continuous fashion depicted in growth charts. Rather, growth takes place in fits and starts (Lampl, Veidhuis, & Johnson, 1992). When babies are measured daily over their first 21 months, most show no growth 90 percent of the time, but when they do grow, they do so rapidly—sometimes startlingly so. Incredible though it may sound, some children gain as much as 1 inch in height overnight!

Marked changes in body proportions accompany changes in a baby's size. During the first 2 years after birth, children have heads that are large relative to their bodies as the brain undergoes rapid growth. A child's brain reaches three-quarters of its adult size by about the age of 2, at which point head growth slows down, and the body does most of the growing. Head growth is virtually complete by age 10, but the body continues to grow for several more years (see **Figure 9–2**).

The normal sequence of motor development. At birth babies have grasping and stepping reflexes. At about 2 months they can lift their head and shoulders. They can sit up by themselves at about 6½ months and can stand (while holding on to something) at about 9 months. Crawling begins, on average, at 10 months, and walking at 1 year.

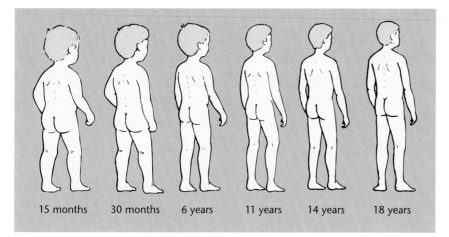

FIGURE 9–2

Body proportions at various ages.
Young children are top-heavy: They have large heads and small bodies. As they get older, the body and legs become longer, and the head is proportionately smaller.

Source: From Bayley, *Individual Patterns of Development.* Copyright © 1956 by the Society for Research in Child Development. Adapted with permission.

Motor Development

Is walking at an early age a sign of future athletic ability?

Motor development refers to the acquisition of skills involving movement, such as grasping, crawling, and walking. The *average ages* at which such skills are achieved are called *developmental norms.* By about 9 months, for example, the average infant can stand up while holding onto something. Crawling occurs, on average, at 10 months, and walking at about 1 year. However, some normal infants develop much faster than average, whereas others develop more slowly. A baby who is 3 or 4 months behind schedule may be perfectly normal, and one who is 3 or 4 months ahead is not necessarily destined to become a star athlete. To some extent, parents can accelerate the acquisition of motor skills in children by providing them with ample training, encouragement, and practice. Differences in these factors seem to account for most of the cross-cultural differences in the average age at which children reach certain milestones in motor development (Hopkins & Westra, 1989, 1990).

Much early motor development consists of substituting voluntary actions for reflexes (Clark, 1994). The newborn grasping and stepping reflexes, for instance, give way to voluntary grasping and walking in the older baby. Motor development proceeds in a *proximodistal* fashion—that is, from nearest the center of the body (proximal) to farthest from the center (distal). For example, the infant initially has much greater control over gross arm movements than over movements of the fingers. Babies start batting at nearby objects as early as 1 month, but they cannot reach accurately until they are about 4 months old. It takes them another month or two before they are consistently successful in grasping objects they reach for (von Hofsten & Fazel-Zandy, 1984). At first, they grasp with the whole hand, but by the end of the first year, they can pick up a tiny object with the thumb and forefinger.

Maturation refers to biological processes that unfold as a person grows older and that contribute to orderly sequences of developmental changes, such as the progression from crawling to toddling to walking. Psychologists used to believe that maturation of the central nervous system largely accounted for many of the changes in early motor skills—that environment and experience played only a minor part in their emergence. But this view has been changing (Thelen, 1994, 1995). Many researchers now see early motor development as arising from a combination of factors both within and outside the child. The child plays an active part in the process by exploring, discovering, and selecting solutions to the demands of new tasks. A baby who is learning to crawl, for example, must figure out how to position the body with belly off the ground and to coordinate arm and leg movements to maintain balance while managing to proceed forward (Bertenthal et al., 1994). What doesn't work must be discarded or adapted; what does work must be remembered and called on for future use. This process is a far cry from seeing the baby as one day starting to crawl simply because he or she has reached the point of maturational "readiness."

As coordination improves, children learn to run, skip, and climb. At 3 and 4, they begin to use their hands for increasingly complex tasks, learning how to put on mittens and shoes, then grappling with buttons, zippers, shoelaces, and pencils. Gradually, through a combination of practice and

Maturation
An automatic biological unfolding of development in an organism as a function of the passage of time.

the physical maturation of the body and the brain, they acquire increasingly complex motor abilities, such as bike riding, roller blading, and swimming. By the age of about 11, some children begin to be highly skilled at such tasks (Clark, 1994).

Cognitive Development

How does a child's ability to reason change over time?

Early cognitive development consists partly of changes in how children think about the world. The most influential theorist in this area was the Swiss psychologist Jean Piaget (1896–1980). Piaget's early training as a biologist had an important influence on his views. He became interested in cognitive development while working as a research assistant in the laboratory of Alfred Binet and Theodore Simon, creators of the first standardized intelligence test for children. Piaget became intrigued by the reasons that young children gave for answering certain questions incorrectly (Brainerd, 1996). Later, he observed and studied other children, including his own three. He watched them play games, solve problems, and perform everyday tasks, and he asked them questions and devised tests to learn how they thought.

Piaget believed that cognitive development is a way of adapting to the environment. Unlike other animals, human children do not have many built-in responses. This characteristic gives them more flexibility to adapt their thinking and behavior to "fit" the world as they experience it at a particular age. In Piaget's view, children are intrinsically motivated to explore and understand things. They are active participants in creating their own understandings of the world. This view is one of Piaget's major contributions (Fischer & Hencke, 1996; Flavell, 1996). Another contribution is his proposal of four basic stages of cognitive development. These are outlined in the accompanying Summary Table.

Sensory-Motor Stage (Birth to 2 Years) According to Piaget, babies spend the first 2 years of life in the **sensory-motor stage** of development. They start out by simply applying the skills they are born with—primarily sucking and grasping—to a broad range of activities. Young babies delight in taking things into their mouths—their mother's breast, their own thumb, or anything else within reach. Similarly, young babies will grasp a rattle reflexively. When they eventually realize that the noise comes from the rattle, they begin to shake everything they can get hold of in an effort to

Sensory-motor stage
In Piaget's theory, the stage of cognitive development between birth and 2 years of age in which the individual develops object permanence and acquires the ability to form mental representations.

SUMMARY TABLE

PIAGET'S STAGES OF COGNITIVE DEVELOPMENT

Stage	Approximate Age	Key Features
Sensory-motor	0–2 years	Object permanence Mental representations
Preoperational	2–7 years	Representational thought Fantasy play Symbolic gestures Egocentrism
Concrete-operational	7–11 years	Conservation Complex classification
Formal-operational	Adolescence–adulthood	Abstract and hypothetical thought

reproduce the sound. Eventually, they distinguish between things that make noise and things that do not. In this way, infants begin to organize their experiences, fitting them into rudimentary categories such as "suckable" and "not suckable," "noise making" and "not noise making."

Another important outcome of the sensory-motor stage, according to Piaget, is the development of **object permanence,** an awareness that objects continue to exist even when out of sight. For a newborn child, objects that disappear simply cease to exist—"out of sight, out of mind." But as children gain experience with the world, they develop a sense of object permanence. By the time they are 18 to 24 months old, they can even imagine the movement of an object that they do not actually see move. This last skill depends on the ability to form **mental representations** of objects and to manipulate those representations in their heads. This is a major achievement of the late sensory-motor stage.

By the end of the sensory-motor stage, toddlers have also developed a capacity for self-recognition—that is, they are able to recognize the child in the mirror as "myself." In one famous study, mothers put a dab of red paint on their child's nose while pretending to wipe the child's face. Then each child was placed in front of a mirror. Babies under 1 year of age stared in fascination at the red-nosed baby in the mirror; some of them even reached out to touch the nose's reflection. But babies between 21 and 24 months reached up and touched their own reddened noses, thereby showing that they knew the red-nosed baby in the mirror was "me" (Brooks-Gunn & Lewis, 1984).

Preoperational Stage (2 to 7 Years)   When children enter the **preoperational stage** of cognitive development, their thought is still tightly bound to their physical and perceptual experiences. But their increasing ability to use mental representations lays the groundwork for the development of language—using words as symbols to represent events and to describe, remember, and reason about experiences. (We will say much more about language development shortly.) Representational thought also lays the groundwork for two other hallmarks of this stage—engaging in *fantasy play* (a cardboard box becomes a castle) and using *symbolic gestures* (slashing the air with an imaginary sword to slay an imaginary dragon).

Although children of this age have made advances over sensory-motor thought, in many ways they don't yet think as do older children and adults. For example, preschool children are **egocentric.** They have difficulty seeing things from another person's point of view or putting themselves in someone else's place.

Children of this age are also easily misled by appearances (Flavell, 1986). They tend to concentrate on the most outstanding aspect of a display or an event, ignoring everything else. In a famous experiment, Piaget showed preoperational children two identical glasses, filled to the same level with juice. The children were asked which glass held more juice, and they replied (correctly) that both had the same amount. Then Piaget poured the juice from one glass into a taller, narrower glass (see photo). Again the children were asked which glass held more juice. They looked at the two glasses, saw that the level of the juice in the tall, narrow one was much higher, and then replied that the narrow glass had more. According to Piaget, children at this stage cannot consider the past (Piaget simply poured all the juice from one container into another) or the future (if he poured it back again, the levels of juice would be identical). Nor can they consider a container's height and width at the same time. Thus, they

Object permanence
The concept that things continue to exist even when they are out of sight.

Mental representations
Mental images or symbols (such as words) used to think about or remember an object, a person, or an event.

Preoperational stage
In Piaget's theory, the stage of cognitive development between 2 and 7 years of age in which the individual becomes able to use mental representations and language to describe, remember, and reason about the world, though only in an egocentric fashion.

Egocentric
Unable to see things from another's point of view.

In Piaget's famous experiment, the child has to judge which glass holds more liquid: the tall, thin one or the short, wide one. Although both glasses hold the same amount, children in the preoperational stage say that the taller glass holds more, because they focus their attention on only one thing—the height of the column of liquid.

can't understand how an increase in one dimension (height) might be offset by a decrease in another dimension (width).

Concrete Operational Stage (7 to 11 Years)   During the **concrete-operational stage,** children become more flexible in their thinking. They learn to consider more than one dimension of a problem at a time and to look at a situation from someone else's viewpoint. This is the age at which they become able to grasp **principles of conservation,** such as the idea that the volume of a liquid stays the same regardless of the size and shape of the container into which it is poured. Other related conservation concepts have to do with number, length, area, and mass. All involve an understanding that basic amounts remain constant despite superficial changes in appearance, which can always be reversed.

Another accomplishment of this stage is the ability to grasp complex classification schemes such as those involving superordinate and subordinate classes. For instance, if you show a preschooler four toy dogs and two toy cats and ask whether there are more dogs present or more animals, the child will almost always answer "more dogs." It is not until age 7 or 8 that children are able to think about objects as being simultaneously members of two classes, one more inclusive than the other. Yet even well into the elementary school years, children's thinking is still very much stuck in the "here and now." Often, they are unable to solve problems without concrete reference points that they can handle or imagine handling.

Formal Operational Stage (Adolescence–Adulthood)   This limitation is overcome in the **formal-operational stage** of cognitive development, often reached during adolescence. Youngsters at this stage can think in abstract terms. They can formulate hypotheses, test them mentally, and accept or reject them according to the outcome of these mental experiments. Therefore, they are capable of going beyond the here and now to understand things in terms of cause and effect, to consider possibilities as well as realities, and to develop and use general rules, principles, and theories.

Criticisms of Piaget's Theory   Piaget's work has produced a great deal of controversy. Many question his assumption that there are distinct stages in cognitive development that always progress in an orderly, sequential way, and that a child must pass through one stage before entering the next (Brainerd, 1978; Siegel, 1993). Some see cognitive development as a more gradual process, resulting from the slow acquisition of experience and practice rather than the abrupt emergence of distinctly higher levels of ability (Paris & Weissberg, 1986).

Piaget's theory has also sparked criticism for assuming that young infants understand very little about the world, such as the permanence of objects in it (see Gopnik, Meltzoff, & Kuhl, 1999; Meltzoff & Gopnik, 1997). When young babies are allowed to reveal their understanding of object permanence without being required to conduct a search for a missing object, they often seem to know perfectly well that objects continue to exist when hidden by other objects (Baillargeon, 1994). They also show other quite sophisticated knowledge of the world that Piaget thought they lacked, such as a rudimentary grasp of numbers (Wynn, 1995). At older ages, too, milestone cognitive achievements seem to be reached much sooner than Piaget believed (Gopnik, 1996).

Other critics have argued that Piaget underplayed the importance of social interaction in cognitive development. For instance, the influential Russian psychologist Lev Vygotsky contended that people who are more advanced in their thinking provide opportunities for cognitive growth for

Concrete-operational stage
In Piaget's theory, the stage of cognitive development between 7 and 11 years of age in which the individual can attend to more than one thing at a time and understand someone else's point of view, though thinking is limited to concrete matters.

Principle of conservation
The concept that the quantity of a substance is not altered by reversible changes in its appearance.

Formal-operational stage
In Piaget's theory, the stage of cognitive development between 11 and 15 years of age in which the individual becomes capable of abstract thought.

children whom they interact with (Vygotsky, 1978). These learning experiences greatly depend on a society's culture, another factor that Piaget ignored (Daehler, 1994).

Finally, although Piaget's theory gives a schematic road map of cognitive development, the interests and experiences of a particular child may influence the development of cognitive abilities in ways not accounted for in the theory. Thus, some critics argue, Piaget's theory does not adequately address human diversity.

9.1

Moral Development

How do gender and ethnic background affect moral development?

One of the important changes in thinking that occurs during childhood and adolescence is the development of moral reasoning. Lawrence Kohlberg (1979, 1981) studied this kind of development by telling his participants stories that illustrate complex moral issues. The "Heinz dilemma" is the best known of these stories:

> In Europe, a woman was near death from cancer. One drug might save her, a form of radium that a druggist in the same town had recently discovered. The druggist was charging $2,000, ten times what the drug cost him to make. The sick woman's husband, Heinz, went to everyone he knew to borrow the money, but he could only get together about half of what it cost. He told the druggist that his wife was dying and asked him to sell it cheaper or let him pay later. But the druggist said, "No." The husband got desperate and broke into the man's store to steal the drug for his wife. (Kohlberg, 1969, p. 379)

The children and adolescents who heard this story were asked, "Should the husband have done that? Why?"

On the basis of his participants' replies to these questions (particularly the second one, "Why?"), Kohlberg theorized that moral reasoning develops in stages, much like Piaget's account of cognitive development. Preadolescent children are at what Kohlberg called the *preconventional level* of moral reasoning: They tend to interpret behavior in terms of its concrete consequences. Younger children at this level base their judgments of "right" and "wrong" behavior on whether it is rewarded or punished. Somewhat older children, still at this level, guide their moral choices on the basis of what satisfies needs, particularly their own.

With the arrival of adolescence and the shift to formal-operational thought, the stage is set for progression to the second level of moral reasoning, the *conventional level*. At this level, the adolescent at first defines right behavior as that which pleases or helps others and is approved by them. Around mid-adolescence, there is a further shift toward considering various abstract social virtues, such as being a "good citizen" and respecting authority. Both forms of conventional moral reasoning require an ability to think about such abstract values as "duty" and "social order," to consider the intentions that lie behind behavior, and to put oneself in the "other person's shoes."

The third level of moral reasoning, the *postconventional level*, requires a still more abstract form of thought. This level is marked by an emphasis on abstract principles such as justice, liberty, and equality. Personal and strongly felt

What influences the development of compassionate behavior? Researchers in moral development want to understand why people make the moral choices they do. This young woman has volunteered to work in the Mother Teresa Home for the Dying in India.

moral standards become the guideposts for deciding what is right and wrong. Whether these decisions correspond to the rules and laws of a particular society at a particular time is irrelevant. For the first time, people may become aware of discrepancies between what they judge to be moral and what society has determined to be legal.

Kohlberg's views have been criticized on several counts. First, research indicates that many people in our society, adults as well as adolescents, never progress beyond the conventional level of moral reasoning (Conger & Petersen, 1991). Does this finding mean that these people are morally "underdeveloped," as Kohlberg's theory implies?

Second, Kohlberg's theory does not take account of cultural differences in moral values. Kohlberg put considerations of "justice" at the highest level of moral reasoning. In Nepal, however, researchers discovered that a group of adolescent Buddhist monks placed the highest moral value on alleviating suffering and showing compassion, concepts that have no place in Kohlberg's scheme of moral development (Huebner, Garrod, & Snarey, 1990).

Third, Kohlberg's theory has been criticized as sexist. Kohlberg found that boys usually scored higher than girls on his test of moral development. According to Carol Gilligan (1982, 1992), this was the case because boys are more inclined to base their moral judgments on the abstract concept of justice, whereas girls tend to base theirs more on the criteria of caring about other people and the importance of maintaining personal relationships. In Gilligan's view, there is no valid reason to assume that one of these perspectives is morally superior to the other. Although subsequent research has found that gender differences in moral thinking tend to diminish in adulthood (L. D. Cohn, 1991), concerns about gender bias in Kohlberg's theory still remain.

More recent research on moral development has moved in the direction of broadening Kohlberg's focus on changes in moral reasoning. These researchers are interested in the factors that influence moral choices in everyday life, and the extent to which those choices are actually put into action. In other words, they want to understand moral behavior as much as moral thinking (Power, 1994).

Language Development

How does a child develop language skills?

The development of language follows a predictable pattern. At about 2 months of age, an infant begins to *coo* (a nondescript word for nondescript sounds). In another month or two, the infant enters the **babbling** stage and starts to repeat sounds such as *da* or even meaningless sounds that developmental psychologists refer to as "grunts"; these sounds are the building blocks for later language development (Dill, 1994). A few months later, the infant may string together the same sound, as in *dadadada*. Finally, the baby will form combinations of different sounds, as in *dabamaga* (Ferguson & Macken, 1983).

Even deaf babies with deaf parents who communicate with sign language engage in a form of babbling (Pettito & Marentette, 1991). Like hearing infants, these babies begin to babble before they are 10 months old—but they babble with their hands! Just as hearing infants utter sounds over and over, deaf babies make repetitive movements of their hands, like those of sign language.

Gradually, an infant's babbling takes on certain features of adult language. At about age 4 to 6 months, the infant's vocalizations begin to show signs of *intonation*, the rising and lowering of pitch that allows adults to

Babbling
A baby's vocalizations, consisting of repetition of consonant-vowel combinations.

From 12 to 24 months babies typically point at and name, although not always correctly, whatever object interests them.

distinguish, for example, between questions ("You're tired?") and statements ("You're tired."). Also around this time, babies learn the basic sounds of their native language and can distinguish them from the sounds of other languages (Cheour et al., 1998). By 6 months, they may recognize commonly used words, such as their own names (Kuhl, Williams, & Lacerda, 1992; Mandel, Jusczyk, & Pisoni, 1995) and the words *mommy* and *daddy* (Tincoff & Jusczyk, 1999).

By around their first birthday, babies begin to use intonation to indicate commands and questions (Greenfield & Smith, 1976). At about the same age, they show signs of understanding what is said to them, and they begin not only to imitate what others say but also to use sounds to get attention. Vocalization also becomes more and more communicative and socially directed. Parents facilitate this process by speaking to their babies in what is called *motherese*. This "mother talk" is spoken slowly and uses simple sentences, a higher-pitched voice, repetition, and exaggerated intonations—all of which engage babies' attention and help them to distinguish the sounds of their language (Hampson & Nelson, 1993).

All this preparation leads up to the first word at about 12 months, usually *dada*. During the next 6 to 8 months, children build a vocabulary of one-word sentences called **holophrases:** "Up!"; "Out!"; "More!" Children may also use compound words such as *awgone* [all gone]. To these holophrases they add words used to address people—*Bye-bye* is a favorite— and a few exclamations, such as *Ouch!*

In the second year of life, children begin to distinguish between themselves and others. Possessive words become a big part of the vocabulary: [The shoes are] "Daddy's." But the overwhelming passion of children from 12 to 24 months old is naming. With little or no prompting, they will name virtually everything they see, though not always correctly! Children at this age are fascinated by objects. If they don't know the name of an object, they will simply invent one or use another word that is almost right. Feedback from parents ("No, that's not a dog, it's a cow") enhances vocabulary and helps children understand what names can and cannot be assigned to classes of things ("dog" is not used for big four-legged animals that live on farms and moo rather than bark).

During the third year of life, children begin to form two- and three-word sentences such as "See daddy," "Baby cry," "My ball," and "Dog go woof-woof." Recordings of mother-child conversations show that children from 24 to 36 months old noticeably omit auxiliary verbs and verb endings ([Can] "I have that?"; "I [am] eat[ing] it up"), as well as prepositions and articles ("It [is] time [for] Sarah [to] take [a] nap") (Bloom, 1970). Apparently, children this age seize on the most important parts of speech, those that contain the most meaning.

After 3 years of age, children begin to fill in their sentences ("Nick school" becomes "Nick goes to school"), and language production increases dramatically. Children start to use the past tense as well as the present. Sometimes they *overregularize* the past tense, by applying the regular form when an irregular one is called for (saying "goed" instead of "went," for example). Such mistakes are signs that the child has implicitly grasped the basic rules of language (Marcus, 1996). Preschoolers also ask more questions and learn to employ "Why?" effectively (sometimes monotonously

Holophrases
One-word sentences commonly used by children under 2 years of age.

so). By the age of 5 or 6, most children have a vocabulary of over 2,500 words and can construct sentences of 6 to 8 words.

Theories of Language Development Children readily pick up the vocabulary of their native language, as well as the complex rules for putting words together into sentences. Two very different theories explain how language develops. B. F. Skinner (1957) believed that parents and other people listen to the infant's cooing and babbling and reinforce those sounds that most resemble adult speech. If the infant says something that sounds like *mama*, mommy reinforces this behavior with smiles and attention. As children get older, the things they say must sound more and more like adult speech in order to be reinforced. Children who call the wrong person "mama" are less likely to be smiled at; they are praised only when they use the word appropriately. Skinner believed that an understanding of grammar, word construction, and so on are acquired in much the same way.

Most psychologists and linguists now believe that learning alone cannot explain the speed, accuracy, and originality with which children learn to use language (Chomsky, 1986; Jenkins, 2000; Pinker, 1994, 1999). Noam Chomsky (1965, 1986) has been the most influential critic of the notion that children must be *taught* language. Instead, he argues that children are born with a **language acquisition device,** an internal mechanism that is "wired into" the human brain, facilitating language learning and making it universal (Kuhl, Kuhl, & Williams, 1992). This language acquisition device is like an internal "map" of language: All the child has to do is to fill in the blanks with information supplied by the environment. An American child fills in the blanks with English words, a Mexican child with Spanish words, and so on. A more recent theory advanced by Steven Pinker (1994, 1999) holds that, to a large extent, evolutionary forces may have shaped language, providing humans with what he calls a *language instinct.*

But the environment must do more for children than provide words to fill in the blanks in their internal map of language. Without the social stimulus of people to talk to, children are slow to pick up words and grammatical rules. Babies reared in institutions, without smiling adults around to reward their efforts, babble like other children but take much longer to begin talking than children reared in families (Brown, 1958). The greater attention paid to first-born children may explain why these children tend to be more advanced in their language development than those born later (Jones & Adamson, 1987).

The importance of the social environment to language development was documented in a study by Betty Hart and Todd Risley (1995; see Chance, 1997, for a summary). These researchers compared the linguistic environment provided for preschool youngsters in their homes over a 3-year period. They found that both the quality and quantity of language experiences varied with the educational level of the parents. For example, the best-educated parents directed over three times as many words to their children as did the least-educated parents. The well-educated parents also did more explaining, asked more questions, and provided more feedback. The best educated parents were also far more likely to give positive feedback, such as, "That's right" or "Good." The least educated parents tended to comment negatively about a child's behavior (saying, "No" or "Stop that") than positively. These differences in environment predicted differences in academic achievement years later, especially in language skills.

Bilingualism and Success in School For almost 10 million school-aged children in the United States, English is not the primary language.

How can we maximize the school success of such children? Should these children be taught only in English, or should at least some of their

Language acquisition device
A hypothetical neural mechanism for acquiring language that is presumed to be "wired into" all humans.

Konrad Lorenz discovered that goslings will follow the first moving object they see, regardless of whether it is their mother, a mechanical toy, or a human. Here Lorenz is trailed by ducklings who have imprinted on him.

Imprinting
The tendency in certain species to follow the first moving thing (usually its mother) it sees after it is born or hatched.

Attachment
Emotional bond that develops in the first year of life that makes human babies cling to their caregivers for safety and comfort.

classes be taught in their primary language? One report on bilingual education in New York City showed that students who take most of their classes in English learn English better than those who are taught some subjects in their primary language. Also, students from groups that place a high value on learning English—such as Russian, Korean, and Chinese immigrants—pass through bilingual classes much faster than students from groups that place a lower value on English literacy (Dillon, 1994).

Social Development

How can parents help their children to become both securely attached and independent?

Learning to interact with others is an important aspect of development in childhood. Early in life, children's most important relationships are with their parents and other caregivers. But by the time they are 3, their important relationships have usually expanded to include siblings, playmates, and other children and adults outside the family. Their social world expands further when they start school. As we will see, social development involves both ongoing relationships and new or changing ones.

Parent-Child Relationships in Infancy: Development of Attachment   Young animals of many species follow their mothers around because of **imprinting.** Shortly after they are born or hatched, they form a strong bond to the first moving object they see. In nature, this object is normally the mother, the first source of nurturance and protection. But in laboratory experiments, certain species of animals, such as geese, have been hatched in incubators and have imprinted on decoys, mechanical toys, and even human beings (Hoffman & DePaulo, 1977; Lorenz, 1935). These goslings faithfully follow their human "mother," showing no interest whatever in adult females of their own species.

Human newborns do not imprint on first-seen moving objects, but they do gradually form an **attachment,** or emotional bond, to the people who take care of them (regardless of the caretaker's gender). As we saw in Chapter 8, classic studies of baby monkeys suggest that the sense of security engered by physical contact and closeness is one important root of attachment (Harlow, 1958; Harlow & Zimmerman, 1959).

In humans, of course, this attachment is built on many hours of interaction during which baby and parent come to form a close relationship. Signs of attachment are evident by the age of 6 months or even earlier. The baby will react with smiles and coos at the caregiver's appearance and with whimpers and doleful looks when the caregiver goes away. At around 7 months, attachment behavior becomes more intense. The infant will reach out to be picked up by the caregiver, and will cling to the caregiver, especially when tired, frightened, or hurt. The baby will also begin to be wary of strangers, sometimes reacting with loud wails at even the friendliest approach by an unfamiliar person. If separated from the caregiver even for a few minutes in an unfamiliar place, the baby will usually become quite upset.

Parents are often puzzled by this new behavior in their previously nonchalant infants, but it is perfectly normal. In fact, anxiety over separation from the mother indicates that the infant has developed a sense of "person permanence" along with a sense of object permanence. For 5-month-olds, it's still "out of sight, out of mind" when mother leaves the room, but for 9-month-olds, the memory of mother lingers, and they announce at the top of their lungs that they want her to come back!

Ideally, infants eventually learn that mother and other primary caregivers can be counted on to be there when needed. Psychologist Erik Erikson (1902–1994) called this result the development of *basic trust* (see Chapter 10). In his theory of psychosocial development, which spanned the entire life course from birth until old age, each stage of life presents a major task or challenge regarding the self and others, which people must somehow deal with, successfully or not (Erikson, 1963). The challenge of the first stage, which encompasses the first year of life, is to develop a basic trust in the world, especially of the people in it. If babies' needs are generally met, they come to acquire this view. They develop faith in other people and also in themselves. They see the world as a secure, dependable place and have optimism about the future. In contrast, babies whose needs are not usually met, perhaps because of an unresponsive or often absent caregiver, grow to be fearful and overly anxious about their own security. This view is supported by research showing that children who grow up in well-adjusted families generally form stronger attachments to their parents than do children who grow up in strife-filled families (Frosch, Mangelsdorf, & McHale, 2000). Erikson referred to these two possible outcomes as *trust versus mistrust*.

Studies have shown that working parents can instill feelings of trust and attachment in their infant children even when the infants are in full-time day care.

As infants develop basic trust, they are freed from preoccupation with the availability of the caregiver. They come to discover that there are other things of interest in the world. Cautiously at first, then more boldly, they venture away from the caregiver to investigate objects and other people around them. This exploration is a first indication of children's developing **autonomy,** or a sense of independence. Autonomy and attachment may seem to be opposites, but they are actually closely related. The child who has formed a secure attachment to a caregiver can explore the environment without fear. Such a child knows that the caregiver will be there when really needed, and so the caregiver serves as a "secure base" from which to venture forth (Ainsworth, 1977).

Children who are insecurely attached to their mothers are less likely to explore an unfamiliar environment, even when their mother is present. Moreover, if left in a strange place, most young children will cry and refuse to be comforted, but the insecurely attached child is more likely to continue crying even after the mother returns, either pushing her away angrily or ignoring her altogether. In contrast, a securely attached 12-month-old is more likely to rush to the returning mother for a hug and words of reassurance and then happily begin to play again (Ainsworth, Blehar, Waters, & Wall, 1978).

The importance of secure attachment early in life is evident for many years afterward. Studies of children from 1 through 6 years of age have shown that those who formed a secure attachment to their mothers by the age of 12 months later tended to be more at ease with other children, more interested in exploring new toys, and more enthusiastic and persistent when presented with new tasks (Harris & Liebert, 1991). Some researchers believe that a secure attachment instills in children a *positive inner working model* of the self and others (Belsky, Spritz, & Crnic, 1996; Bowlby, 1969, 1982). These children come to see themselves as basically lovable and

Autonomy
Sense of independence; a desire not to be controlled by others.

According to Erik Erikson, children between the ages of 3 and 6 take the initiative to try to master new skills.

competent and others as trustworthy and supportive (Thompson & Ganzel, 1994). This inner working model positively colors the children's responses toward much that they encounter as they grow older.

At about 2 years of age, children begin to assert their growing independence, becoming very negative when interfered with by parents. They refuse everything: getting dressed ("No!"), going to sleep ("No!"), using the potty ("No!"). The usual outcome of these first declarations of independence is that the parents begin to discipline the child. Children are told they have to eat and go to bed at a particular time, they must not pull the cat's tail or kick their sister, and they must respect other people's rights. The conflict between the parents' need for peace and order and the child's desire for autonomy often creates difficulties. But it is an essential first step in **socialization,** the process by which children learn the behaviors and attitudes appropriate to their family and their culture.

Erikson saw two possible outcomes of this early conflict: *autonomy versus shame and doubt.* If a toddler fails to acquire a sense of independence and separateness from others, self-doubt may take root. The child may begin to question his or her own ability to act effectively in the world. If parents and other adults belittle a toddler's efforts, the child may also begin to feel ashamed. The need for both autonomy and socialization can be met if parents allow the child a reasonable amount of independence, while insisting that the child follow certain rules.

Parent-Child Relationships in Childhood   As children grow older, their social world expands. They play with siblings and friends, they go off to nursery school or day care, and they eventually enter kindergarten. Erikson saw the stage between ages 3 and 6 as one of growing initiative, surrounded by a potential for guilt (*initiative versus guilt*). Children of this age become increasingly involved in independent efforts to accomplish goals—making plans, undertaking projects, mastering new skills—from bike riding to table setting to drawing, painting, and writing simple words. Parental encouragement of these initiatives leads to a sense of joy in taking on new tasks. But if children are repeatedly criticized and scolded for things they do wrong, they may develop strong feelings of unworthiness, resentment, and guilt. In Erikson's view, avoiding these negative feelings is the major challenge of this stage.

The effect of parenting style on a child's outlook and behavior has been the subject of extensive research. Diana Baumrind (1972) found that *authoritarian parents,* who control their children's behavior rigidly and insist on unquestioning obedience, are likely to produce children who are withdrawn and distrustful. But *permissive* parenting can also have negative effects: When parents exert too little control, their children tend to be overly dependent and lacking in self-control. The most successful parenting style is what Baumrind calls *authoritative.* Authoritative parents provide firm structure and guidance without being overly controlling. They listen to their children's opinions and give explanations for their decisions, but it is clear that they are the ones who make and enforce the rules. Parents who use this approach are most likely to have children who are self-reliant and socially responsible.

Of course, the parent does not determine a parent-child relationship on his or her own: Children also affect it (Collins, Maccoby, Steinberg, Hetherington, & Bornstein, 2000). Parents do not act the same way toward every child in the family (even though they may say they try to), because each child is a different individual. A thoughtful, responsible child is more likely

Socialization
Process by which children learn the behaviors and attitudes appropriate to their family and culture.

to elicit authoritative parenting, whereas an impulsive child who is difficult to reason with is more likely to elicit an authoritarian style. For instance, children with conduct disorders meet with controlling responses from a great many adults, even from those who do not behave toward their own children in a controlling way (O'Leary, 1995). Thus, children influence their caregivers at the same time that the caregivers are influencing them.

Some researchers have found that the characteristics of a child have an influence on which children end up being victims of child abuse. Children who in some way are difficult to care for—premature, colicky, physically and behaviorally handicapped, temperamentally irritable, or overactive—especially in combination with a mother who is depressed or a stepparent in the home, increase the risk of being abused (Carlson, 1994; Daly & Wilson, 1996; Knutson, 1995). This is not to say that children are responsible for their own mistreatment; child abuse is solely the responsibility of the adults involved. But the behavior of the child can be a stressor that makes abuse more likely. Other factors that make it more difficult for parents to care appropriately for their children include being young, unmarried (or in a conflict-ridden marriage), relatively less educated, financially troubled; living in overcrowded conditions; having health problems (physical or mental); and having a history of being abused as a child (Carlson, 1994; Melcher, 2000). Child abuse, in other words, is partly the product of a stressful environment, which is why programs aimed at preventing it often focus on offering various forms of support for high-risk parents. Educating these parents about more effective approaches to child rearing is another widely used tactic (Fagot, 1994; Irvine, Biglan, Smolkowski, Metzler, & Ary, 1999).

Relationships with Other Children   At a very early age, infants begin to show an interest in other children, but the social skills required to play with them develop only gradually (Pellegrini & Galda, 1994). Children first play alone; this activity is called *solitary play*. Then between 1½ and 2, they begin to engage in *parallel play*—that is, they play side by side, doing the same or similar things, but not interacting much with each other. Around the age of 2, imitation becomes a game: One child throws a toy into the air, the other does the same, and then they both giggle. At around 2½, children begin to use language to communicate with their playmates, and their play becomes increasingly imaginative. By age 3 or 3½, they are engaging in *cooperative play*, including games that involve group imagination such as "playing house" (Eckerman, Davis, & Didow, 1989).

When young children engage in *parallel play*, each plays alone, but near the other.

Among the first peers that most children encounter are their siblings. The quality of sibling relationships can have a major impact, especially on how children learn to relate to other peers. Sibling relations are usually most compatible when other relationships within the family are good, including between husband and wife and between parents and children (Brody, 1995). Siblings also influence one another indirectly, simply by their order of birth. In general, first-born children tend to be more anxious and fearful of physical injury, but also more intellectually able and more achievement oriented than their later-born siblings. Among boys, first-borns also tend to be more creative. These differences probably have to do with the extra attention (both negative and positive) that parents tend to give their first-born children (Eisenman, 1994).

Peer influences outside the family increase greatly when children start school. Now they are under a great deal of pressure to be part of a **peer group** of friends. In peer groups, children learn many valuable things, such

Peer group
A network of same-aged friends and acquaintances who give one another emotional and social support.

as how to engage in cooperative activities aimed at collective goals and how to negotiate the social roles of leader and follower (Rubin, Coplan, Chen, & McKinnon, 1994). Inability to get along well with classmates has long-lasting consequences. Children whose classmates dislike them are more likely to drop out of school, engage in criminal behavior, and become mentally ill. This tendency is particularly true of children who are disliked because they are aggressive (Parker & Asher, 1987).

As children get older, they develop a deeper understanding of the meaning of friendship (Rubin et al., 1994). For preschoolers, a friend is simply "someone I play with," but around age 7, children begin to realize that friends "do things" for one another. At this still egocentric age, however, friends are defined largely as people who "do things for *me*." Later, at about age 9, children come to understand that friendship is a two-way street and that, although friends do things for us, we are also expected to do things for them. During these early years, friendships often come and go at dizzying speed; they endure only as long as needs are being met. It is not until late childhood or early adolescence that friendship is viewed as a stable and continuing social relationship requiring mutual support, trust, and confidence (Selman, 1981).

Successfully making friends is one of the tasks that Erikson saw as centrally important to children between the ages of 7 and 11, the stage of *industry versus inferiority*. At this age, children must master many increasingly difficult skills, social interaction with peers being only one of them. Others have to do with mastering academic skills at school, meeting growing responsibilities placed on them at home, and learning to do various tasks that they will need as independent-living adults. In Erikson's view, if children become stifled in their efforts to prepare themselves for the adult world, they may conclude that they are inadequate or inferior and lose faith in their power to become self-sufficient. Those whose industry is rewarded develop a sense of competence and self-assurance.

Sex-Role Development   By about age 3, both boys and girls have developed a **gender identity**—that is, a little girl knows that she is a girl, and a little boy knows that he is a boy. At this point, however, children have little understanding of what that means. A 3-year-old boy might think that he could grow up to be a mommy or that if you put a dress on him and a bow in his hair, he will turn into a girl. By the age of 4 or 5, most children know that gender depends on what kind of genitals a person has (Bem, 1989). They have acquired **gender constancy,** the realization that gender cannot be changed.

At quite a young age, children also start to acquire **gender-role awareness,** a knowledge of what behaviors are expected of males and of females in their society (Lewin, 1996). As a result, they develop **gender stereotypes,** or oversimplified beliefs about what the "typical" male and female are like (Sinnott, 1994). Girls are supposed to be clean, neat, and careful, whereas boys are supposed to like rough, noisy, physical play; women are kind, caring, and emotional, whereas men are strong, dominant, and aggressive. There is much consistency across cultures regarding the gender stereotypes that children develop (Williams & Best, 1990). This is the case partly because gender roles tend to be similar in many different cultures and because gender stereotypes tend to "match" the tasks thought appropriate for the sexes.

Gender identity
A little girl's knowledge that she is a girl, and a little boy's knowledge that he is a boy.

Gender constancy
The realization that gender does not change with age.

Gender-role awareness
Knowledge of what behavior is appropriate for each gender.

Gender stereotypes
General beliefs about characteristics that men and women are presumed to have.

By school age, boys and girls tend to play by the rules of sex-typed behavior. Typically, girls play nonaggressive games, such as hopscotch, in pairs or small groups, whereas boys prefer more active group games.

At the same time that children acquire gender-role awareness and gender stereotypes, they also develop their own **sex-typed behavior:** Girls play with dolls, and boys play with trucks; girls put on pretty clothes and fuss with their hair, and boys run around and wrestle with each other. Although the behavioral differences between boys and girls are minimal in infancy, quite major differences tend to develop as children grow older (Prior, Smart, Sanson, & Oberklaid, 1993). Boys become more active and physically aggressive, and tend to play in larger groups. Girls talk more, shove less, and tend to interact in pairs. If aggression is displayed among girls, it is more likely to take the form of spiteful words and threats of social isolation (Zuger, 1998). Of course, there are some active, physically aggressive girls and some quiet, polite boys, but they are not in the majority. The source of such sex-typed behavior is a matter of considerable debate.

Because gender-related differences in styles of interaction appear very early in development (even before the age of 3), Eleanor Maccoby, a specialist in this area, believes that they are at least partly biological in origin. In addition to the influence of genes, some evidence suggests that prenatal exposure to hormones plays a part (Collaer & Hines, 1995). But Maccoby thinks that biologically based differences are small at first and later become exaggerated because of the different kinds of socialization experienced by boys and girls. She suggests that a lot of gender-typical behavior is the product of children playing with others of their sex (Maccoby, 1998). Undoubtedly, popular culture—especially as portrayed on television—also influences the norms of gender-appropriate behavior that develop in children's peer groups. And parents, too, can sometimes add input, especially during critical transitions in the child's life when parents feel it is important to behave in more sex-stereotyped ways (Fagot, 1994). The end result is substantial sex-typed behavior by middle childhood. Research on this topic continues, but the growing consensus is that both biology and experience contribute to gender differences in behavior (Collaer & Hines, 1995).

Television and Children

Is watching TV a good or bad influence on the development of children?

American children spend more time watching television than they do engaging in any other activity besides sleeping (Huston, Watkins, & Kunkel, 1989). On average, children between 2 and 5 years of age watch about four hours of TV each day (Lande, 1993). It is not surprising that psychologists, educators, and parents are very concerned about the influence TV has on children. Indeed, the American Academy of Pediatrics (1999) goes so far as to say that children under the age of 2 should not watch television at all and that older children should not have television sets in their bedrooms.

One concern is the violence that pervades much TV entertainment (Carter, 1996). Children who watch two hours of TV daily (well below our national average) will see about 8,000 murders and 100,000 other acts of violence by the time they leave elementary school (Kunkel et al., 1996). Even Saturday-morning cartoons average more than 20 acts of violence per hour (Seppa, 1997). Does witnessing this violence make children more aggressive, and if so, does TV violence account, at least in part, for the rapid rise in violent crime among adolescents (Lande, 1993)?

Children themselves think so. In one survey, most young people between the ages of 10 and 16 felt that TV violence was a factor in aggressive acts among their peers (Puig, 1995). Nevertheless, scientific answers concerning the effects of TV violence are still uncertain, because the causal links aren't clear. Although there is convincing evidence that children who frequently watch TV violence are more aggressive than other children

Sex-typed behavior
Socially prescribed ways of behaving that differ for boys and girls.

Studies confirm that watching television is associated with aggressive behavior in children, but only if the content of the shows is violent.

(Eron, 1982; Singer & Singer, 1983), this finding might simply mean that children who are prone to aggression are also drawn to violent shows (Aluja-Fabregat & Torrubia-Beltri, 1998).

Perhaps the best evidence that watching TV violence can encourage violent behavior comes from a study that compared rates of violence in three similar towns, one of which did not have television until 1973 (Will, 1993). Two years after television was introduced into that remote community, the rate of physical aggression soared by 45 percent for both boys and girls, whereas it did not change in the two other towns that already had television.

The most convincing theoretical argument that violent behavior is linked to television watching is based on social learning theory, which we discussed in Chapter 5, Learning. Social learning theory leads us to expect that children who see fictional characters on TV glamorized or rewarded for their violent behaviors will not only learn those behaviors but will also be more likely to perform them themselves when given the opportunity. Children need not be personally rewarded for a behavior in order to be encouraged to imitate it. They need only see an admired model being so rewarded.

Another concern about the effects of television viewing on children involves the extent to which it affects their cognitive development, IQs, and academic achievement. Scores on a number of standardized tests taken by American children and adolescents have been declining for years. Many educators blame these declines on the fact that children no longer read books; instead, they watch television (DeWitt, 1991). But a study of TV viewing by preschoolers found no correlation between their IQ scores and how much TV they watched (Plomin, Corley, DeFries, & Fulker, 1990). Also, despite the general increase in television viewing over the past few decades, IQ scores haven't declined. Rather, they have increased—all over the world (Flynn, 1987, 1999).

Another area of concern raised about children who watch too much television is that it can lead to a variety of sleep disturbances, including night wakings, daytime sleepiness, increased anxiety at bedtime, shortened sleep duration, and difficulty falling asleep. Children who watch television before bedtime or who have a television in their bedroom appear to have the highest risk for developing sleep problems (Owens et al., 1999).

But there is evidence that children can learn worthwhile things from watching television (Anderson, 1998; Wright et al., 1999). In one long-term study, the TV viewing habits of 5-year-olds was monitored and recorded by parents and electronic devices. Years later an examination of the high school records of these same children found that the more time they had spent viewing such educational programs as *Sesame Street* and *Mr. Rogers*, the higher their high school grades were. In contrast, children who watched a lot of noneducational and violent programming at the age of 5 had comparatively lower high school grades than their peers (Anderson, Huston, Wright, & Collins, 1998).

To summarize, television is a significant influence on children's development. It presents both "good" and "bad" models for them to copy, and it provides vast amounts of information. And every moment spent watching TV is a moment not engaging in other activities, such as chatting with friends or playing board games and sports, that may be more beneficial. In the end, whether television's influence is largely positive or largely negative may depend as much on what children watch as on how much.

INTERACTIVE LECTURE **9.3**

WEB QUIZ **9.3**

CHECK YOUR UNDERSTANDING

1. Early motor development in children (acquiring and refining the abilities to grasp, crawl, walk, and so forth) can best be explained
   a. entirely by biological maturation of the muscles and nervous system.
   b. by a combination of factors both within and outside the child.

2. Match each of Piaget's stages of cognitive development with the appropriate description(s).

   ____ sensory-motor stage   a. the ability to use representational thought expands

   ____ preoperational stage   b. thinking is still egocentric in many ways

   ____ concrete operational stage   c. the ability to think abstractly emerges

   ____ formal operational stage   d. the stage begins with applying reflex actions

         e. the ability to consider two dimensions at once emerges

         f. the ability to classify things in complex ways emerges

         g. awareness of object permanence emerges

3. Indicate the order in which the following language developments emerge.

   ____ a. holophrases   first

   ____ b. babbling   second

   ____ c. overregularization of verbs   third

   ____ d. two- and three-word sentences   fourth

4. Match each phase of childhood with its major challenge, according to Erik Erikson's theory.

   ____ infancy   a. industry versus inferiority

   ____ toddlerhood   b. trust versus mistrust

   ____ preschool years   c. autonomy versus shame and doubt

   ____ elementary school years   d. initiative versus guilt

Answers: 1. b. 2. sensory-motor stage: d and g; preoperational stage: a and b; concreate operations: e and f; formal operations: c. 3. a. second; b. first; d. third; c. fourth. 4. infancy: b; toddlerhood: c; preschool years: d; elementray school years: a.

Adolescence

Is adolescence characterized only by physical change?

Adolescence is the period of life between roughly ages 10 and 20 when a person is transformed from a child into an adult. This period involves not just the physical changes of a maturing body, but also many cognitive and social-emotional changes.

Physical Changes

What are the consequences of going through puberty early or late?

A series of dramatic physical milestones ushers in adolescence. The most obvious is the **growth spurt,** a rapid increase in height and weight that be-gins, on average, at about age 10½ in girls and 12½ in boys, and reaches its

Growth spurt
A rapid increase in height and weight that occurs during adolescence.

peak at age 12 in girls and 14 in boys. The typical adolescent attains his or her adult height about 6 years after the start of the growth spurt (Tanner, 1978).

The growth spurt begins with a lengthening of the hands, feet, arms, and legs, which produces the awkward, gangly look of young adolescents. This stage is followed by the growth of the torso, which brings the body back into proportion. In boys, the final stage of growth results in a broadening of the chest and shoulders and the development of heavier muscles. For girls, changes in body shape occur as the hips widen and as fat is deposited on the breasts, hips, buttocks, and thighs. All these changes result from an increase in hormones, which, as we saw in Chapter 2 (The Biological Basis of Behavior), are chemicals released by the endocrine system (Dyk, 1993).

In both sexes, changes also occur in the face. The chin and nose become more prominent, and the lips get fuller. Increases in the size of oil glands in the skin can contribute to acne; sweat glands produce a more odorous secretion. The heart, lungs, and digestive system all expand.

Sexual Development   The visible signs of **puberty**—the onset of sexual maturation—occur in a different sequence for boys and girls. In boys, the initial sign is growth of the testes, which starts, on average, at around 11½, about a year before the beginning of the growth spurt in height. Along with the growth spurt comes enlargement of the penis. Development of pubic hair takes a little longer, and development of facial hair longer still. Deepening of the voice is one of the last noticeable changes of male maturation.

In females, the beginning of the growth spurt is typically the first sign of approaching puberty. Shortly thereafter, the breasts begin to develop; some pubic hair appears at around the same time. **Menarche,** the first menstrual period, occurs about a year or so later—between 12½ and 13 for the average American girl (Powers, Hauser, & Kilner, 1989). The timing of menarche is affected by health and nutrition, with heavier girls maturing earlier than thinner ones. Smoking and drinking alcohol also are associated with early menarche (Danielle, Rose, Viken, & Kaprio, 2000).

The onset of menstruation does not necessarily mean that a girl is biologically capable of becoming a mother. It is uncommon (though not unheard of) for a girl to become pregnant during her first few menstrual cycles. Female fertility increases gradually during the first year after menarche. The same is true of male fertility. Boys achieve their first ejaculation at an average age of 13½, often during sleep. But first ejaculations contain relatively few sperm (Tanner, 1978). Nevertheless, adolescents are capable of producing babies long before they are mature enough to take care of them.

Psychologists used to believe that the beginnings of sexual attraction and desire in young people coincided with the physical changes of puberty, but recent research may be changing this view. Hundreds of case histories that researchers have collected tend to put the first stirrings of sexual interest in the fourth and fifth grade. The cause may be increases in an adrenal sex hormone that begin at age 6 and reach a critical level around age 10 (McClintock & Herdt, 1996). Other pubertal hormones may also begin their rise much earlier than we formerly knew (Marano, 1997). If so, the onset of the obvious physical changes that we now call puberty may actually be more of an ending to a process than a start.

Early and Late Developers   Individuals differ greatly in the age at which they go through the changes of puberty. Some 12-year-old girls and 14-year-old boys still look like children, whereas others their age already look like young women and men. Among boys, early maturing has psychologi-

Puberty
The onset of sexual maturation, with accompanying physical development.

Menarche
First menstrual period.

cal advantages. Boys who mature earlier do better in sports and in social activities and receive greater respect from their peers (Conger & Petersen, 1991). However, at least one study (Peskin, 1967) found that late-maturing boys develop a stronger sense of identity during early adulthood, perhaps because they do not feel pressured to "grow up" too quickly. For girls, early maturation appears to be a mixed blessing. A girl who matures early may be admired by other girls but is likely to be subjected to embarrassing treatment as a sex object by boys (Clausen, 1975).

As the students in this middle-school group show, the age at which adolescents reach sexual maturity varies widely. Differences can lead to problems for teenagers of both sexes.

Adolescent Sexual Activity   The achievement of the capacity to reproduce is probably the single most important development in adolescence. But sexuality is a confusing issue for adolescents in our society. Fifty years ago, young people were expected to postpone expressing their sexual needs until they were responsible, married adults. Since then, major changes have occurred in sexual customs. Three-fourths of all males and more than half of all females between the ages of 15 and 19 have had intercourse; the average age for first intercourse is 16 for boys and 17 for girls (Stodghill, 1998).

Boys and girls tend to view their early sexual behavior in significantly different ways (Lewin, 1994a). Fewer high school girls than boys report feeling good about their sexual experiences (46 percent versus 65 percent). Similarly, more girls than boys said that they should have waited until they were older before having sex (65 percent compared with 48 percent).

Teenage Pregnancy and Childbearing   The United States still has the highest teen birth rate in the industrialized world: nearly 7 times the rate in France and 13 times the rate in Japan. One reason for our higher teen birth rate may be ignorance of the most basic facts concerning reproduction among our young people. In countries such as England, Sweden, and the Netherlands, which have extensive programs of sex education, teenage pregnancy rates are much lower (Hechtman, 1989). Another explanation for some unwanted teenage pregnancies may be the adolescent tendency to believe that "nothing bad will happen to me." This sense of invulnerability may blind some teenagers to the possibility of pregnancy (Quadrel, Prouadrel, Fischoff, & Davis, 1993).

Whatever the causes of unmarried teenage pregnancy and teen childbearing, its consequences can be devastating. The entire future of a young unmarried mother is in jeopardy, particularly if she has no parental support or is living in poverty. She is less likely to graduate from high school, less likely to improve her economic status, and less likely to get married and stay married than a girl who postpones childbearing (see Coley & Chase-Lansdale, 1998). The babies of teen mothers are apt to suffer too. They are more likely to be of low birth weight, which is associated with learning disabilities and later problems in school, childhood illnesses, and neurological problems (Furstenberg, Brooks-Gunn, & Chase-Lansdale, 1989; Moore, Morrison, & Greene, 1997). In addition, children of teenage mothers are more likely to be neglected and abused than are children of older mothers (Coley & Chase-Lansdale, 1998; Goerge & Lee, 1997).

Cognitive Changes

What are two common fallacies that characterize adolescent thinking?

Just as bodies mature during adolescence, so do patterns of thought. Piaget (1969) saw the cognitive advances of adolescence as an increased ability to reason abstractly, called formal-operational thought. Adolescents can understand and manipulate abstract concepts, speculate about alternative possibilities, and reason in hypothetical terms. This process allows them to debate such problematical issues as abortion, sexual behavior, and AIDS. Of course, not all adolescents reach the stage of formal operations, and many of those who do fail to apply formal-operational thinking to the everyday problems they face (Gardner, 1982). Younger adolescents especially are unlikely to be objective about matters concerning themselves and have not yet achieved a deep understanding of the difficulties involved in moral judgments.

Moreover, in those who do achieve formal-operational thinking, this advance has its hazards, among them overconfidence in new mental abilities and a tendency to place too much importance on one's own thoughts. Some adolescents also fail to realize that not everyone thinks the way they do and that other people may hold different views (Harris & Liebert, 1991). Piaget called these tendencies the "egocentrism of formal operations" (Piaget, 1967).

David Elkind (1968, 1969) used Piaget's notion of adolescent egocentrism to account for two fallacies of thought that he noticed in this age group. The first is the **imaginary audience**—the tendency of teenagers to feel that they are constantly being observed by others, that people are always judging them on their appearance and behavior. This feeling of being perpetually "onstage" may be the source of much self-consciousness, concern about personal appearance, and showing off in adolescence.

The other fallacy of adolescent thinking is the **personal fable**—adolescents' unrealistic sense of their own uniqueness. For instance, a teenager might feel that others couldn't possibly understand the love that the teenager feels toward a boyfriend or girlfriend because that love is so unique and special. This view is related to the feeling of invulnerability we mentioned earlier. Many teenagers believe that they are so different from other people that they won't be touched by the negative things that happen to others. This feeling of invulnerability is consistent with the reckless risk-taking among people in this age group (Arnett, 1991). Of course, cultures vary in the degree to which they allow reckless behavior in teenagers. Those cultures that strongly inhibit it may create a safer, more orderly society, but they may also stifle some of the liveliness and spontaneity of adolescence (Arnett, 1995).

Personality and Social Development

What important tasks do adolescents face in their personal and social lives?

Adolescents are eager to establish independence from their parents, but at the same time, they fear the responsibilities of adulthood. They have many important tasks ahead of them and many important decisions to make. Particularly in a technologically advanced society like ours, this period of development is bound to involve some stress.

How "Stormy and Stressful" Is Adolescence?   Early this century many people saw adolescence as a time of great instability and strong emotions. For example, G. Stanley Hall (1904), one of the first developmental psychologists, portrayed adolescence as a period of "storm and stress," fraught with suffering, passion, and rebellion against adult authority. Recent research, however, suggests that the "storm and stress" view greatly exaggerates the experiences of most teenagers (Arnett, 1999). The great majority of adolescents do not describe their lives as rent by turmoil and chaos (Eccles et al., 1993). Most adolescents, particularly those whose childhood devel-

Imaginary audience
Elkind's term for adolescents' delusion that they are constantly being observed by others.

Personal fable
Elkind's term for adolescents' delusion that they are unique, very important, and invulnerable.

opment proceeded smoothly, manage to keep stress in check, and they experience little disruption in their everyday lives (Bronfenbrenner, 1986; Offer & Offer, 1975).

Still, adolescence is accompanied by some stress related to school, family, and peers, and this stress can at times be difficult to manage (Crystal et al., 1994). And some people find adolescence especially difficult. For instance, between 15 and 30 percent of adolescents drop out of high school, many regularly abuse drugs, and some are repeatedly in trouble with the law (teenagers have the highest arrest record of any age group) (Office of Educational Research and Improvement, 1988). Those whose prior development has been stressful are likely to experience a stressful adolescence.

Of course, individuals differ in their ability to cope with even the worst conditions. Some young people are particularly *resilient* and able to overcome great odds, partly because of a strong belief in their own ability to make things better (Werner, 1995). Thus, the degree of struggle growing up that any given adolescent faces is due to an interaction of developmental challenges on the one hand and factors that promote resilience on the other (Compas, Hinden, & Gerhardt, 1995).

Peer groups help adolescents develop identities apart from family influences. Cliques are small groups of friends that offer closeness but can also exert significant control over adolescents' lives.

Forming an Identity   To make the transition from dependence on parents to dependence on oneself, the adolescent must develop a stable sense of self. This process is called **identity formation,** a term derived from Erik Erikson's theory, which sees the major challenge of this stage of life as *identity versus role confusion* (Erikson, 1968). The overwhelming question for the young person becomes "Who am I?" In Erikson's view, the answer comes by integrating a number of different roles—say, talented math student, athlete, and artist or political liberal and aspiring architect—into a coherent whole that "fits" comfortably. Failure to form this coherent sense of identity leads to confusion about roles.

James Marcia (1980) believes that finding an identity requires a period of intense self-exploration called an **identity crisis.** He recognizes four possible outcomes of this process. One is *identity achievement.* Adolescents who have reached this status have passed through the identity crisis and succeeded in making personal choices about their beliefs and goals. They are comfortable with those choices because the choices are their own. In contrast are adolescents who have taken the path of *identity foreclosure.* They have prematurely settled on an identity that others provided for them. They have become what those others want them to be without ever going through an identity crisis. Other adolescents are in *moratorium* regarding the choice of an identity. They are in the process of actively exploring various role options, but they have not yet committed to any of them. Finally, there are teens who are experiencing *identity diffusion.* They avoid considering role options in any conscious way. Many are dissatisfied with this condition but are unable to start a search to "find themselves." Some of them resort to escapist activities such as drug or alcohol abuse (Adams & Gullota, 1983). Of course, any given adolescent's identity status can change over time as the person matures or even regresses. Some evidence suggests that identity development varies by social class or ethnic background. For instance, teens from poor families are often less likely to experience a period of identity moratorium, probably because financial constraints make it harder for them to explore many different role options (Holmbeck, 1994).

Identity formation
Erickson's term for the development of a stable sense of self necessary to make the transition from dependence on others to dependence on oneself.

Identity crisis
A period of intense self-examination and decision making; part of the process of identity formation.

Relationships with Peers For most adolescents, the peer group provides a network of social and emotional support that helps enable both the movement toward greater independence from adults and the search for personal identity. By choosing to associate with a particular group of friends, adolescents define themselves and create their own social style (P. R. Newman, 1982). Young teenagers feel an almost desperate need for their friends to approve of their choices, views, and behavior. The result is often a rigid conformity to peer group values that peaks around the ninth grade (Perry, 1990).

Peer relationships change during the adolescent years. Friendship groups in early adolescence tend to be small unisex groups, called **cliques,** of three to nine members. Especially among girls, these unisex friendships increasingly deepen and become more mutually self-disclosing as the teens develop the cognitive abilities better to understand themselves and one another (Holmbeck, 1994). Then, in midadolescence, unisex cliques generally break down and give way to mixed-sex groups. These, in turn, are usually replaced by groups consisting of couples. At first, adolescents tend to have short-term heterosexual relationships within the group that fulfill short-term needs without exacting the commitment of "going steady" (Sorensen, 1973). Such relationships do not demand love and can dissolve overnight. But between the ages of 16 and 19, most adolescents settle into more stable dating patterns.

Relationships with Parents While they are still searching for their own identity, striving toward independence, and learning to think through the long-term consequences of their actions, adolescents require guidance and structure from adults, especially from their parents. In their struggle for independence, adolescents question everything and test every rule. Unlike young children who believe that their parents know everything and are all-powerful and good, adolescents are all too aware of their parents' shortcomings. It takes many years for adolescents to see their mothers and fathers as real people with their own needs and strengths as well as weaknesses (Smollar & Youniss, 1989). In fact, the renewed perception of their strengths may come as a bit of a shock. Many young adults find themselves surprised that their parents have gotten so much smarter in the last seven or eight years!

The low point of parent-child relationships generally occurs in early adolescence, when the physical changes of puberty are occurring. Then the warmth of the parent-child relationship ebbs, and conflict rises. Warm and caring relationships with adults outside the home, such as those at school or at a supervised community center, are valuable to adolescents during this period (Eccles et al., 1993). However, conflicts with parents tend to be over minor issues and are usually not intense (Holmbeck, 1994). In only a small minority of families does the relationship between parents and children markedly deteriorate in adolescence (Paikoff & Brooks-Gunn, 1991).

Some Problems of Adolescence

What are some major problems faced by adolescents in our society?

Adolescence is a time of experimentation and risk taking, whether it be with sex, drugs, hair color, body piercing, or various kinds of rule breaking (Lerner & Galambos, 1998). It is also a time when certain kinds of developmental problems are apt to arise, especially problems that have to do with self-perceptions, feelings about the self, and negative emotions in general.

Declines in Self-Esteem Teenagers are acutely aware of the changes taking place in their bodies. Many become anxious about whether they are the "right" shape or size, and obsessively compare themselves with the models

Cliques
Groups of adolescents with similar interests and strong mutual attachment.

and actors they see on television and in magazines. Because few adolescents can match these ideals, it is not surprising that when young adolescents are asked what they most dislike about themselves, physical appearance is mentioned more often than anything else (Conger & Petersen, 1991). These concerns can lead to serious eating disorders, as we saw in Chapter 8, Motivation and Emotion. Satisfaction with one's appearance tends to be tied to satisfaction with oneself. Adolescents who are least satisfied with their physical appearance have the lowest self-esteem (Adams & Gullota, 1983; Altabe & Thompson, 1994).

Of course, negative body image is not the only thing that can cause self-esteem to drop in adolescence. Another is a negative view of one's school performance. In one study that found a sharp drop in self-esteem among girls during adolescence, the girls said that they felt this way largely because they were ignored by teachers, believed that they were not being given an equal chance at intellectual challenges, and found it hard to compete in the classroom with their more assertive male classmates. Boys' self-esteem drops too during adolescence, but not nearly as much. By midadolescence, the average boy has a much better opinion of himself than the average girl has of herself. (Kling, Hyde, Showers, & Buswell, 1999).

Why girls' self-esteem dips during adolescence is not clear.

"Is everything all right, Jeffrey? You never call me 'dude' anymore."

Depression and Suicide   Suicide is the third leading cause of death among adolescents, after accidents and homicides (Centers for Disease Control and Prevention, 1999; Hoyert, Kochanek, & Murphy, 1999). Although successful suicide is more common in males than in females, more females attempt suicide (Centers for Disease Control and Prevention, 1991). There is also a disturbing trend in our society toward suicide at younger ages. Between 1980 and 1992, the suicide rate among adolescents ages 10 to 14 rose by 120 percent and was especially high among black males in this age group (an increase of 300 percent) (Leary, 1995). A growing culture of youth violence and an increased accessibility to guns may contribute to these statistics.

Suicidal behavior in adolescents (including thinking about suicide as well as actually attempting it) is often linked to other psychological problems, such as depression, drug abuse, and disruptive behaviors (Andrews & Lewinsohn, 1992). The risk is higher too among females who have thought about suicide, who have a mental disorder (such as depression), and have a poorly educated father who is absent from the home. A history of physical or sexual abuse and poor family communication skills are also associated with suicide and suicide attempts. The research does not yet demonstrate that these factors play a causal role in self-injurious behavior (Wagner, 1997), but they do, at least in theory, allow us to identify people at risk.

Nevertheless, it is hard to predict which adolescents at higher-than-average risk will actually attempt suicide. Depression alone rarely leads to suicide (Connelly, Johnston, Brown, Mackay, & Blackstock, 1993). A combination of depression and other risk factors appears to make suicide more likely, but exactly which factors are most important and what kinds of intervention might reduce adolescent suicides are still unclear (Wagner, 1997).

Youth Violence   In April 1999, two boys, one 17 and the other 18, opened fire on their classmates at Columbine High School in Littleton, Colorado. Armed with two sawed-off shotguns, a semiautomatic rifle, and a semiautomatic pistol, they killed 13 fellow students and a teacher, and wounded 23 others

UNDERSTANDING The World Around Us

Kids Who Kill

Redlands, California . . . Blackville, South Carolina . . . Lynnville, Tennessee . . . Moses Lake, Washington . . . Bethel, Alaska . . . Pearl, Mississippi . . . West Paducah, Kentucky . . . Stamps, Arkansas . . . Jonesboro, Arkansas . . . Springfield, Oregon . . . Littleton, Colorado . . .

It is hard to imagine what such far-flung communities have in common, but they share at least one feature: They were the sites of killings by teenagers with guns between October 1995 and April 1999. When the gunfire ended, more than 40 people were dead, and many more were wounded.

Why did it happen? What causes boys as young as 11 to kill other people and, equally often, to kill themselves? Were they just "bad kids" from the start, or was their environment to blame? And if it was their environment, then why do other children not become violent when exposed to the same events? Although it is tempting to look for simple answers to these questions, in reality the causes of violence are quite complex. Our genes may affect the likelihood of violence. Our brain chemistry certainly does. And so does our environment. All of these factors influence one another in complex ways to lead to explosive violence.

Biology definitely plays a role, although its influence is certain to be much more complex than simply identifying a "murderer gene." More likely the genetic component, if any, is related to a lack of compassion or an inability to control strong emotions. Apart from genetics, the constant interplay between the brain and the environment ac-

In reality, the causes of violence are quite complex.

tually "rewires" the brain, sometimes with disastrous effects (Niehoff, 1999). For example, Bruce Perry and his colleagues at Baylor College of Medicine point out that repeated stress in the first 3 years of life gives rise to a steady flow of "stress chemicals" that can have two consequences. First, the normal "fight or flight" response may go on "hair-trigger alert," which can result in impulsive aggression. Alternatively, the person may become unresponsive and unfeeling, thereby leading in turn to a lack of empathy or sensitivity to the surrounding world, including an unresponsiveness to punishment (Perry & Pollard, 1998; Schwarz & Perry, 1994). In a similar vein, Daniel Amen has provided evidence that early trauma may cause a part of the brain called the cingulate gyrus to become hyperactive, leading individuals to become obsessed with a single thought (such as violence) at the same time that the prefrontal cortex becomes less able to control impulsive behavior (Amen, Stubblefield, Carmicheal, & Thisted, 1996).

But biology is only part of the story. Most psychologists also believe that an important factor in youth killings is the "gun culture" in which most of the youths were raised, along with the relatively easy availability of guns in their environments (Bushman & Baumeister, 1998; Jones & Krisberg, 1994). Most of the killers had extensive experience with guns. One relentlessly begged his parents for guns until they finally gave in. Another had a map over his bed with the

before killing themselves. Fortunately, 30 bombs filled with shrapnel and planted throughout the school were found and defused before they exploded. One of the shooters arrived at school that day wearing a favorite shirt that read "SERIAL KILLER."

In the days after the shootings, people throughout the country expressed their shock and outrage, and offered different theories as to the reasons for the tragedy. But well before these shootings took place, surveys had repeatedly shown that violence and crime are the issues of greatest concern to most Americans. And, despite an overall decrease in criminal activities in the 1990s, juvenile crime continues to rise (Waldman, 1996), as does violence directed toward children. (See *Understanding the World Around Us: Kids Who Kill*).

INTERACTIVE LECTURE 9.4

slogan "One Nation under My Gun" (Cloud, 1998).

Another environmental factor mentioned by many psychologists is severe neglect or rejection. All the killers indicated that they felt isolated from their family and from girls, outcast and abandoned by those who should have loved them. In turn, this condition led to feelings of powerlessness and injustice. Violence became a way of asserting power and saying "I matter." Luke Woodham, an overweight youth who at age 16 killed three people (including his mother) and injured seven others, said, "[My mother] always told me that I wouldn't amount to anything. She always told me that I was fat and stupid and lazy." Other rationales include the following: "The world has wronged me and I couldn't take it anymore." "I killed because people like me are mistreated every day. My whole life I felt outcasted, alone" (Cloud, 1998, p. 60; Lacayo, 1998, p. 38; Begley, 1999, p. 35). In other cases, a contributing factor appears to be a lack of adult supervision and support, often to the point of having no real attachment to at least one loving and reliable adult (Garbarino, 1999). With par-

ents missing because of work or divorce or other factors, and with no extended family to fill in the gap, increasing numbers of youths are "left to the mercies of a peer culture shaped by the media, the ultimate in crazed nannies" (Lacayo, 1998, p. 38).

Many youthful killers had also been exposed to a culture of violence reflected in role-playing games such as Doom and Mortal Kombat and in music by such artists as Nirvana, Rammstein, and Marilyn Manson (Bok, 1999). The American Psychiatric Association concluded in 1993 that media violence can promote not only desensitization and callousness but also aggression and an appetite for violence.

Are there any warning signs that might alert family and friends to potential violence? Indeed there are. Lack of connection, masking emotions, withdrawal (being habitually secretive and antisocial), silence, rage, increased lying, trouble with friends, hypervigilance, cruelty toward other children and animals—these factors should all be a cause for concern. This is especially true if they are exhibited by a boy who comes from a family with a

People gather outside Columbine High School in Littleton, Colorado, after two students opened fire on their classmates in April 1999. Youth violence has become an emotionally charged issue in the United States.

history of criminal violence, who has been abused, who belongs to a gang, who abuses drugs or alcohol, who has previously been arrested, or who has experienced problems at school.

CHECK YOUR UNDERSTANDING

WEB QUIZ **9.4**

1. The most obvious indication that adolescence is starting is a rapid increase in height and weight, known as the _____ _____. This is combined with a series of physical changes leading to sexual maturation, the onset of which is called _____.

2. Erikson's view of the major challenge in adolescence is one of _____ versus _____.

3. Match the following terms with their meanings.

____ menarche a. onset of the first menstrual period

____ imaginary audience b. social group of friends

____ personal fable c. unrealistic sense of one's own uniqueness

____ clique d. feeling of being constantly observed by others

4. Match each status regarding identity formation with the appropriate definition.

____ identity achievement a. prematurely settling on an identity that others provide

____ identity foreclosure b. success in making personal choices about beliefs and goals

____ identity moratorium c. avoiding consideration of role options

____ identity diffusion d. exploring role options but not yet committing to any

Indicate whether the following statement is true (T) or false (F).

5. True (T) or false (F). The most difficult time in the relationship between a teenager and parents is usually in late adolescence, when the young person is anxious to leave the family "nest."

Answers: 1. growth spurt; puberty. 2. identity; role confusion. 3. menarche: a. imaginary audience: d. personal fable: c. clique: b. 4. identity achievement: b; identity foreclosure: a; identity moratorium: d; identity diffusion: c. 5. (F).

Adulthood

Does personality change during adulthood?

Compared with adolescent development, development during adulthood is much less predictable, much more a function of the individual's decisions, circumstances, and even luck. In adulthood, as distinct from childhood and adolescence, developmental milestones do not occur at particular ages. Still, certain experiences and changes take place sooner or later in nearly everyone's life, and nearly every adult tries to fulfill certain needs, including nurturing partnerships and satisfying work.

Love, Partnerships, and Parenting

What factors are important in forming satisfying relationships in adulthood?

Like heterosexuals in successful relationships, gays in loving partnerships share decision making, trust, respect, and appreciation.

Nearly all adults form a long-term, loving partnership with another adult at some point in their lives. Such a partnership can happen at any stage in the life course, but it is especially common in young adulthood. According to Erik Erikson, the major challenge of young adulthood is *intimacy versus isolation*. Failure to form an intimate partnership with someone else can cause a young adult to feel painfully lonely and incomplete. Erikson believed that a person is not ready to commit to an intimate relationship until he or she has developed a firm sense of personal identity, the task of the preceding stage of life.

Forming Partnerships More than 90 percent of Americans eventually get married (Doherty & Jacobson, 1982), but those who marry are waiting longer to do so. In 1970, only 15 percent of men and women aged 25 to 29 had never married; by

1988, the percentage had increased to 36 percent (U.S. Bureau of the Census, 1990). This postponement of marriage is even greater among African Americans than among whites (Balaguer & Markman, 1994).

Most people marry someone of similar age, race, religion, education, and background (Michael, Gagnon, Laumann, & Kolata, 1994). This tendency is partly because people with similar characteristics and backgrounds are more likely to meet, and once they meet, they are more likely to discover shared interests and compatibility (Murstein, 1986). Choice of a partner for cohabitation (living together) seems to proceed in much the same way. Often, there is a spoken or an unspoken assumption among couples that "if things work out, then we'll marry." It is interesting that couples who live together before marriage are generally less satisfied with their marriages and more likely to divorce later than couples who married without first living together (DeMaris & Rao, 1992). One reason may be that many of those who decide to live together first are more tentative about their relationships than those who proceed directly to marriage (Balaguer & Markman, 1994).

Although heterosexual marriage is still the statistical norm in our society, other types of partnerships are increasingly meeting the needs of a diverse population. Long-term cohabiting relationships are one example. Contrary to popular belief, the greatest recent increase in cohabiting couples is not among the very young, but rather among people over age 35 (Steinhauer, 1997). Among elderly widows and widowers, cohabitation is increasingly seen as a way of enjoying a life together without financial complications and tax penalties.

Homosexual couples are another example of intimate partnerships outside the tradition of heterosexual marriage. Studies show that most gays and lesbians seek the same loving, committed, and meaningful partnerships as most heterosexuals do (Peplau & Cochran, 1990). Moreover, successful relationships among them have the same characteristics as successful relationships in the heterosexual world: high levels of mutual trust, respect, and appreciation; shared decision making; good communication; and good skills at resolving conflicts (Birchler & Fals-Stewart, 1994; Edwards, 1995; Kurdek, 1991, 1992). (See *Understanding Ourselves: Resolving Conflicts in Intimate Relationships*.)

Parenthood   For most parents, loving and being loved by their children is an unparalleled source of fulfillment. However, the birth of the first child is also a major turning point in a couple's relationship, one that requires many adjustments. Romance and fun often give way to duty and obligations. Since young children demand a lot of time and energy, parents may be left with little time or energy for each other.

Parenthood may also heighten conflicts between pursuit of careers and responsibilities at home. This outcome is especially likely among women who have had an active career outside the home. They may be torn between feelings of loss and resentment at the prospect of leaving their job, and anxiety or guilt over the idea of continuing to work. This conflict is added to the usual worries about being an adequate wife and mother (Warr & Perry, 1982). It is no wonder that women feel the need for their partner's cooperation more strongly during this period of life than men do (Belsky, Lang, & Rovine, 1985). Today's fathers spend more time with their children than their fathers did, but mothers still bear the greater responsibility for both child rearing and housework. Although homosexual couples as a group believe more strongly in equally dividing household duties than heterosexual couples do, homosexuals tend to make an exception when it comes to child rearing. After the arrival of a child (through adoption or artificial insemination), child-care responsibilities tend to fall more heavily on

UNDERSTANDING OURSELVES

Resolving Conflicts in Intimate Relationships

Even the closest, most loving couples have disagreements. People, after all, are different. They have different desires, different approaches, different priorities, different points of view. For those reasons, conflict is inevitable in every intimate relationship. But conflict does not necessarily mean destructive forms of fighting. Conflict can be resolved in constructive ways that don't tear a couple apart. Constructive fighting can actually bring people closer together in search of mutually satisfactory solutions.

Psychologists who have studied intimate relationships often suggest a number of steps that lead to constructive conflict resolution:

1. *Carefully choose the time and place for an argument.* People who start airing a grievance at some inappropriate time shouldn't be surprised when the outcome is unsatisfactory. Try not to begin a major disagreement while your partner is in the middle of completing some important task or is ready to fall asleep after a long, tiring day. Bring up the subject when there is ample time to discuss it fully.

2. *Be a good listener.* Don't go on the defensive as soon as your partner brings up a concern or complaint. Listen carefully without interrupting. Try to understand what your partner is saying from his or her point of view. Listening calmly, without anger, will help to get the discussion off to a good start. Don't let your body give nonverbal cues that contradict good listening. For instance, don't continue to do chores or watch television while your partner is speaking. Don't shrug your shoulders or roll your eyes as if discounting your partner's view.

3. *Give feedback regarding your understanding of the other person's grievance.* Restate what your partner has told you in your own words. Ask questions about anything you're not sure of. For instance, if a wife says she is fed up with the amount of time her husband spends watching television sports, he might respond by saying, "I know you don't like me watching sports a lot, but do you expect me to stop entirely?" Such feedback helps to clarify and avoid misunderstandings.

4. *Be candid. Level with your partner about your feelings.* Say what you really think. If you are angry, don't make your partner guess your feelings by giving the silent treatment or showing anger in indirect ways. Of course, being candid does not mean being tactless or hurtful. Don't engage in name calling, sarcasm, mockery, or insults. Such tactics are counterproductive.

5. *Use "I" rather than "you" statements.* For instance, if you're angry with your partner for being late, say, "I've been really worried and upset for the last hour" rather than "You're a whole hour late! Why couldn't you get here on time?" "You"

---

one member of a homosexual couple, whereas the other spends more time in paid employment (Patterson, 1994, 1995).

Given the demands of child rearing, it isn't surprising that marital satisfaction tends to decline after the arrival of the first child (Ruble, Fleming, Hackel, & Stangor, 1988; see **Figure 9–3**). But once children leave home, many parents experience renewed satisfaction in their relationship as a couple. Rather than lamenting over their "empty nests," most women breathe a sigh of relief (Rovner, 1990). For the first time in years, the husband and wife can be alone together and enjoy one another's company (Orbuch, Houser, Mero, & Webster, 1996).

Ending a Relationship   Intimate relationships frequently break up. Although this is the case for all types of couples—married and unmarried, heterosexual and homosexual—most of the research on ending relationships has focused on married, heterosexual couples. The U.S. divorce rate has risen substantially since the 1960s, as it has in many other developed nations (Lewin, 1995). Although the divorce rate appears to have stabistatements sound like accusations and tend to put people on the defensive. "I" statements sound more like efforts to communicate feelings in nonjudgmental ways.

6. *Focus on behavior, not on the person.* For example, focus on your partner's lateness as a problem, don't accuse your partner of being thoughtless and self-centered. People respond defensively to broadside attacks on their character. Such attacks threaten their self-esteem.

7. *Don't overstate the frequency of a problem or overgeneralize about it.* Don't tell your partner that he's always late or that she's exactly like her mother. Such exaggerations are annoying and tend to lead discussions away from legitimate complaints.

8. *Focus on a limited number of specific issues.* Don't overwhelm your partner with a barrage of grievances. Stick to current concerns of high priority. Don't get distracted by trivial matters that waste emotional energy. Don't dredge up a long list of complaints from the past.

9. *Don't find scapegoats for every grievance against you.* We all tend to explain away our shortcomings by blaming them on circumstances or sometimes on other people. Resist the temptation to offer excuses designed to get you "off the hook." Take responsibility for your actions and encourage your partner to do the same.

10. *Suggest specific, relevant changes to solve a problem.* Both participants in the conflict should propose at least one possible solution. A proposed solution should be reasonable and take into account the other person's viewpoint as well as your own.

11. *Be open to compromise.* Settling disputes successfully often involves negotiation. Both people must be willing to give in a little. Don't back your partner into a corner by giving an ultimatum: "Do what I want or else!" Partners need to be willing to change themselves to some extent in response to each other's feelings. This willingness is the essence of being in an intimate relationship. Being loved by your partner doesn't necessarily mean being accepted exactly as you are.

12. *Don't think in terms of winner and loser.* Popular books have been written on how always to win arguments. This competitive approach to conflict resolution is unfortunate in intimate relationships. If one partner is repeatedly the winner and the other repeatedly the loser, their relationship inevitably suffers. Strive for solutions that are satisfactory to both parties. Think of each other as allies attacking a mutual problem. In this way, your relationship will become stronger.

---

lized, it has stabilized at quite a high level. Almost half of American marriages eventually end in divorce (Darnton, 1992).

Rarely is the decision to separate a mutual one. Most often, one partner takes the initiative in ending the relationship after a long period of slowly increasing unhappiness. Making the decision does not necessarily bring relief. In the short term, it often brings turmoil, animosity, and apprehension. However, in the longer term, most divorced adults report that the divorce was a positive step that eventually resulted in greater personal contentment and healthier psychological functioning, although a substantial minority seem to suffer long-term negative effects (Kelly, 1982; Stack, 1994).

Divorce can have serious and far-reaching effects on children—especially on their school performance, self-esteem, gender-role development, emotional adjustment, relationships with others, and attitudes toward marriage (Barber & Eccles, 1992; Collins, Maccoby, Steinberg, Hetherington, & Bornstein, 2000; Forgatch & DeGarmo, 1999; Vaughn, 1993). And children who have been involved in multiple divorces are placed at an even greater risk (Kurdek, Fine, & Sinclair, 1995). Children adapt more success-

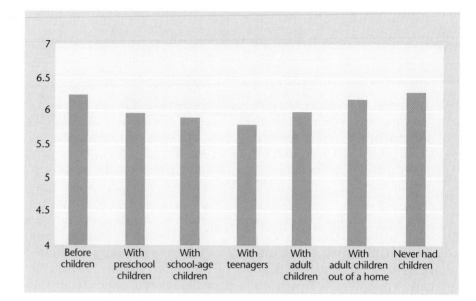

FIGURE 9–3

Marital satisfaction. This graph shows when married people are most and least content with their marriage, on a scale of 1 (very unhappy) to 7 (very happy).

Source: American Sociological Association; adapted from *USA Today*, August 12, 1997, p. D1.

fully to divorce when they have good support systems, when the divorcing parents maintain a good relationship, and when sufficient financial resources are made available to them. The effects of divorce also vary with the children themselves: Those who have easygoing temperaments and who were generally well behaved before the divorce usually have an easier time adjusting (Ahrons, 1994; Davies & Cummings, 1994; Edwards, 1995; Hetherington, Bridges, & Insabella, 1998; Miller, Kliewer, & Burkeman, 1993).

The World of Work

What are the satisfactions and stresses of adult work?

For many young people, the period from the late teens through the early twenties is crucial because it sets the stage for much of adult life. The educational achievements and training obtained during these transitional years often establish the foundation that will shape the income and occupational status for the remainder of adult life (Arnett, 2000).

Three or four generations ago, choosing a career was not an issue for most young adults. Men followed in their fathers' footsteps or took whatever apprenticeships were available in their communities. Women were occupied in child care, housework, and helping with the family farm or business, or they pursued such "female" careers as secretarial work, nursing, and teaching. Today, career choices are far more numerous for both men and women. In the 1990s, for example, women made up approximately 20 percent of full-time employed physicians and lawyers, and nearly 40 percent of college professors. All told, women accounted for about 39 percent of the labor force (Gilbert, 1994). However, on average, women get paid 30 percent less than men for doing the same work, and they are less likely than men to advance to managerial and executive positions (Valian, 1998; see **Figure 9–4**). Women hold 53 percent of the professional jobs in the United States, for example, but mostly in the less-well-paid fields, such as education. Only 28 percent of the professional jobs that paid over $40,000 in 1998 were held by women (Doyle, 2000). Moreover, many women experience discrimination and sexual harassment at work (Valian, 1998) and have fewer opportunities to change jobs or receive promotions (Aranya, Kushnir, & Valency, 1986).

The divorce rate in the United States has risen dramatically since the 1960s. Divorce can have serious and far-reaching effects on both the couple and the couple's children.

Dual-Career Families   Over the last fifty years, the number of married women in the paid labor force has increased dramatically: 71 percent of married women with school-aged children and 60 percent of women with children under 6 now have jobs outside the home (Gilbert, 1994; Harris & Liebert, 1991). The two-paycheck family is not always a matter of choice. This increasing role of women as economic providers is a worldwide trend (Lewin, 1995).

Balancing the demands of career and family is a problem in many families, especially for women. Even when the wife has a full-time job outside the home, she is likely to end up doing far more than half of the housework and child care. She is also likely to be aware of this imbalance and to resent it (Benin & Agostinelli, 1988). The "double shift"—one at paid work outside the home and another at unpaid household labor—is the common experience of millions of women throughout the world (Mednick, 1993). True equality—the hopeful goal of the dual-career movement—has yet to be achieved (Gilbert, 1994).

Despite the pressures associated with the double shift, most women report increases in self-esteem when they have a paid job (Baruch & Barnett, 1986). They also tend to experience less anxiety and depression than childless working women do (Barnett, 1994). The vast majority say that they would continue to work even if they didn't need the money (Schwartz, 1994). Those women most apt to feel stressed by a double shift are those who do not find satisfaction in their various roles (Barnett, 1994).

Children in Dual-Career Families   Most dual-career families must entrust their young children to the care of someone else for a sizable percentage of the children's waking hours. In America, over half of the children between birth and the third grade spend some time being regularly cared for by persons other than their parents (America's Children: Key National Indicators of Well-Being, 2000). Is it a good idea to leave infants and very young children with substitute caregivers?

Some research shows clear benefits for the children of mothers who work, even if the children are still very young (Greenstein, 1993). For example, the children of employed mothers tend to be more independent and self-confident and to have less stereotyped views of males and females (Harris & Liebert, 1991). Moreover, children of working mothers who are placed in a quality day care, even at very early ages, are no more likely to develop behavior problems or have problems with their self-esteem than children reared at home (Harvey, 1999). Nonetheless, there has been concern that being entrusted to caregivers outside the immediate family may interfere with the development of secure attachments and put children at greater risk for emotional maladjustment (Barglow, Vaughn, & Molitor, 1987; Belsky & Rovine, 1988). But according to the findings of a recent large-scale longitudinal study (NICHD, 1996), placing a baby in full-time day care even in the first few months of life doesn't in itself undermine attachment. Working parents and their babies still have ample opportunity to engage in the daily give-and-take of positive feelings on which secure attachments are built. When a mother provides generally insensitive and unresponsive care, however, her baby is even *more* likely to develop an insecure attachment to her if the child also experiences extensive day care, especially poor-quality care or changing day-care arrangements. One conclusion, then, is that *quality of care counts* (Brobert, Wessels, Lamb, & Hwang, 1997; Scarr, 1999). A secure, affectionate, stimulating environment is likely to produce children who are healthy, outgoing, and ready to learn,

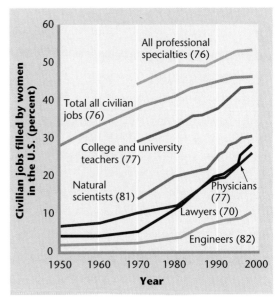

FIGURE 9–4

Percentage of selected jobs filled by women in the United States, 1950–2000. This graph shows the percentage of each job filled by women. The figures in parentheses indicate women's earnings as a percentage of men's in the given field.

Source: Scientific American, April 2000, p. 30; data from U.S. Bureau of the Census and Bureau of Labor Statistics. © 2000 Rodger Doyle. Reprinted with permission.

just as an environment that encourages fears and doubts is likely to stunt development.

Cognitive Changes

In what ways do adults think differently than adolescents?

Only recently have researchers begun to explore the ways in which an adult's thinking differs from that of an adolescent. Although adolescents are able to test alternatives and to arrive at what they see as the "correct" solution to a problem, adults gradually come to realize that there isn't a single correct solution to every problem—there may, in fact, be no correct solution, or there may be several. Adolescents rely on authorities to tell them what is "true," but adults realize that "truth" often varies according to the situation and one's viewpoint. Adults are also more practical: They know that a solution to a problem must be realistic as well as reasonable (Cavanaugh, 1990). No doubt these changes in adult thinking derive from greater experience of the world. Dealing with the kinds of complex problems that arise in adult life requires moving away from the literal, formal, and somewhat rigid thinking of adolescence and young adulthood (Labouvie-Vief, 1986).

And just as physical exercise is necessary for optimal physical development, so mental exercise is necessary for optimal cognitive development. Although some decline in cognitive skills is inevitable as people age, the decline can be minimized if people stay mentally active (Schaie, 1994).

Personality Changes

What changes in personality occur as adults move into midlife?

Psychological health generally increases in adulthood compared with adolescence. And those adolescents with greater psychological health tend to improve even further in adulthood (Jones & Meredith, 2000). Both men and women tend to become less self-centered and develop better coping skills with age (Neugarten, 1977). One longitudinal study found that people are more sympathetic, giving, productive, and dependable at 45 than they were at 20 (Block, 1971). Another found that people in their middle years feel an increasing commitment to and responsibility for others, develop new ways of adapting, and are more comfortable in interpersonal relationships (Vaillant, 1977). Such findings suggest that the majority of people are successfully meeting what Erik Erikson saw as the major challenge of middle adulthood: *generativity versus stagnation.* Generativity refers to the ability to continue being productive and creative, especially in ways that guide and encourage future generations. For those who fail to achieve this state, life becomes a drab and meaningless routine, and the person feels stagnant and bored.

Feelings of boredom and stagnation in middle adulthood may be part of what is called a **midlife crisis.** The person in midlife crisis feels painfully unfulfilled, ready for a radical, abrupt shift in career, personal relationships, or lifestyle. Research shows, however, that the midlife crisis is not typical; most people do not make sudden dramatic changes in their lives in midadulthood (Martino, 1995). In fact, many use this time to renew their commitments to marriage, work, and family (B. M. Newman, 1982).

Daniel Levinson, who studied personality development in men and women throughout adulthood (Levinson, 1978, 1986, 1987), preferred the term **midlife transition** for the period when people tend to take stock of their lives. Many of the men and women in his studies, confronted with the first signs of aging, began to think about the finite nature of life. They real-

Midlife crisis
A time when adults discover they no longer feel fulfilled in their jobs or personal lives and attempt to make a decisive shift in career or lifestyle.

Midlife transition
According to Levinson, a process whereby adults assess the past and formulate new goals for the future.

ized that they may never accomplish all that they had hoped to do, and they questioned the value of some of the things they had accomplished so far, wondering how meaningful they were. As a result, some gradually reset their life priorities, establishing new goals based on their new insights.

The "Change of Life"

What is menopause, and what changes accompany it?

A decline in the function of the reproductive organs occurs during middle age. In women, the amount of estrogen (the principal female hormone) produced by the ovaries drops sharply at around age 45, although the exact age varies considerably from woman to woman. Breasts, genital tissues, and the uterus begin to shrink, and menstrual periods become irregular and then cease altogether at around age 50. The cessation of menstruation is called **menopause.**

The hormonal changes that accompany menopause often cause certain physical symptoms; the most noticeable are "hot flashes." In some women, menopause also leads to a serious thinning of the bones, making them more vulnerable to fractures. Both of these symptoms can be prevented by estrogen replacement therapy (a pill or a skin patch that must be prescribed by a physician). Although this therapy may slightly increase a woman's risk for breast and uterine cancer (Steinberg et al., 1991), it appears to decrease significantly her risk for heart disease (Barrett-Connor & Bush, 1991). Some women are apprehensive about the "change of life," but others revel in their newfound freedom from fear of pregnancy.

Experts disagree about whether a "male menopause" exists. Men never experience as severe a drop in testosterone (the principal male hormone) as women do in estrogen. Instead, studies have found a more gradual decline—perhaps 30 to 40 percent—in testosterone in men between 48 and 70 (Angier, 1992). Recent evidence also confirms the common belief that with increasing age, male fertility slowly decreases as well (Ford et al., 2000).

Menopause
The time in a woman's life when menstruation ceases.

INTERACTIVE LECTURE 9.5

WEB QUIZ 9.5

CHECK YOUR UNDERSTANDING

1. According to Erik Erikson, the major challenge of young adulthood is _____ versus _____, whereas the major challenge of middle adulthood is _____ versus _____.

2. Indicate whether the following statements are true (T) or false (F).
   _____ a. The old saying "opposites attract" is an accurate description of how most people choose someone to marry.
   _____ b. Marital satisfaction generally increases with the arrival of the first child.
   _____ c. In comparison to childless working women, working women with children experience more anxiety and depression.
   _____ d. A significant decline in cognitive skills is inevitable after young adulthood.
   _____ e. The vast majority of middle-age people experience a midlife crisis in which they feel painfully unfulfilled.

3. The cessation of menstruation in middle-age women is called _____.

Answers: 1. intimacy, isolation; generativity, stagnation. 2. a. (F); b. (F); c. (F); d. (F); e. (F). 3. menopause.

Late Adulthood

What factors are related to life expectancy?

Older adults constitute the fastest-growing segments of the U.S. population. Indeed, during this century, the percentage of Americans over 65 has more than tripled, and those over 85 now represent the fastest-growing segment of the population (APA's Task Force on Diversity, 1998). At present, 35 million Americans are over age 65; by the year 2030, there may be more than 70 million in this age group (Kolata, 1992). This dramatic rise stems from the aging of the large baby boom generation, coupled with increases in life expectancy due primarily to better health care and nutrition (Downs, 1994; see **Figure 9–5**).

However, a sizable gender gap exists in life expectancy. The average woman today enjoys a life span that is seven years longer than that of the average male. The reasons for this gender gap are still unclear, but likely factors include differences in hormones, exposure to stress, health-related behaviors, and genetic makeup.

There is also a gap in life expectancy between whites and African Americans in this country. The average white American child is likely to live to age 76, whereas the average African American child is likely to live only to age 71. This difference seems to stem largely from disparities in socioeconomic well-being.

Because older adults are becoming an increasingly visible part of American society, it is important to understand their development. Unfortunately, our views of older adults are often heavily colored by myths. For example, many people believe that most older adults are lonely, poor, and troubled by ill health. Even health-care professionals sometimes assume that it is natural for elderly people to feel ill. As a result, symptoms that would indicate a treatable medical problem in younger people are taken as inevitable signs of decay in the elderly and thus frequently go untreated. The false belief that "senility" is inevitable in old age is another damaging myth, as is the belief that most older adults are helpless and dependent on their families for care and financial support. All the research on late adult-

FIGURE 9–5

Population age structure, 1999. The U.S. population will continue to age over the next several decades, as the huge baby boom generation moves through the population.

Source: U.S. Census Bureau. Available online at http://www.census.gov/population/www.dbna/db-aging-toc.html.

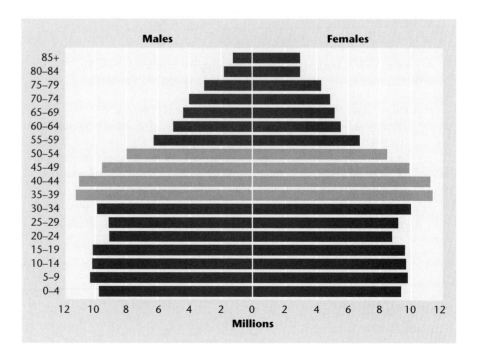

hood contradicts these stereotypes. Increasingly, people age 65 and over are healthy, productive, and able (Cutler, 2001; Kolata, 1996b; Manton & Gu, 2001).

Physical Changes

Why does the body deteriorate with age?

Beginning in middle adulthood and continuing through late adulthood, physical appearance and the functioning of every organ change. The hair thins and turns white or gray. The skin wrinkles. Bones become more fragile. Muscles lose power, and joints stiffen or wear out. Circulation slows, blood pressure rises, and because the lungs hold less oxygen, the older adult has less energy. Body shape and posture change, and the reproductive organs atrophy. Difficulties in falling asleep and staying asleep become more common, and reaction times are slower. Vision, hearing, and the sense of smell all become less acute (Cavanaugh, 1990; LaRue & Jarvik, 1982). Most people are at first unaware of these changes, because they occur gradually. But the decline eventually becomes undeniable.

It is curious, that we do not yet know why physical aging happens (Di-Giovanna, 1994). One theory is that genes may program our cells eventually to deteriorate and die. Alternatively, the genetic instructions for running the body may be capable of being read only a limited number of times before they begin to degrade and instructional errors (aging) result. The role that inheritance plays in aging is supported by a recent finding of a gene that appears to be related to exceptional longevity (Puca et al., 2001). Another explanation for aging is that the parts of the body simply wear out through repeated use, much as the parts of a car ultimately wear out after so many miles. Contributing to this wearing out process may be toxins that the body is exposed to, both external toxins in the environment (radiation, chemicals, viruses, and so forth) and toxins that accumulate as inevitable by-products of the body's own activities.

Whatever the ultimate explanation for physical decline, many factors affect the physical well-being of older adults, and some are things that they can control: particularly diet, exercise, health care, smoking, drug use, and overexposure to sun (Levenson & Aldwin, 1994). Attitudes and interests also matter. People who have a continuing sense of usefulness, who maintain old ties, investigate new ideas, take up new activities, and feel in control of their lives have the lowest rates of disease and the highest survival rates (Butler & Lewis, 1982; Caspi & Elder, 1986). Indeed, a survey of 2,724 people ranging in age from 25 to 74 years found that older adults reported experiencing more positive emotions during the past month than younger adults did (Mroczek & Kolarz, 1998). So there's a good deal of truth in the saying "You're only as old as you feel." In fact, psychologists are starting to use functional or psychological age, instead of chronological age, to predict an older adult's adaptability to life's demands.

Social Development

What kind of life style and sex life can be expected after age 65?

Far from being weak and dependent, most men and women over 65 live autonomous lives apart from their children and outside nursing homes, and most are very satisfied with their lifestyles. In one survey of people 65 years and older, more than half reported being just as happy as they were when younger. Three-quarters said they were involved in activities that were as interesting to them as any they had engaged in during their younger years (Birren, 1983).

Although physical changes are inevitable during late adulthood, how people respond to these changes has a major effect on their quality of life.

"Then it's moved and seconded that the compulsory retirement age be advanced to ninety-five."

Source: © The New Yorker Collection, 1963. Peter Arno from cartoonbank.com. All Rights Reserved.

Still, gradual social changes do take place in late adulthood. These changes have been described as occurring in three stages (Cumming & Henry, 1961). The first stage is *shrinkage of life space*: The older person starts to interact with fewer people and perform fewer social roles. The second stage is *increased individuality*: Behavior becomes less influenced by social rules and expectations than it was earlier in life. The third and final stage involves *acceptance* of the changes in the first two stages: The person steps back and assesses life, realizes there is a limit to the capacity for social involvement, and learns to live comfortably with those restrictions. This process does not necessarily entail a psychological "disengagement" from the social world, as some researchers have contended. Instead, older people may simply be making sensible choices that suit their more limited time frames and physical capabilities (Carstensen, 1995).

Retirement Another major change that most people experience in late adulthood is retiring from paid employment. People's reactions to retirement differ greatly, partly because society has no clear idea of what retirees are supposed to do. Should they sit in rocking chairs and watch life go by, or should they play golf, become foster grandparents, and study Greek? The advantage to this lack of clear social expectations is that older adults have the flexibility to structure their retirement as they please. Men and women often go about this process differently. Men generally see retirement as a time to slow down and do less, whereas women often view it as a time to learn new things and explore new possibilities (Helgesen, 1998). This difference can cause obvious problems for retired couples (also see Moen, Kim, & Hofmeister, 2001).

Of course, the nature and quality of retired life depend in part on financial status. If retirement means a major decline in a person's standard of living, that person will be less eager to retire and will lead a more limited life after retirement. Another factor in people's attitudes toward retirement is their feelings about work. People who are fulfilled by their jobs are usually less interested in retiring than people whose jobs are unrewarding (Atchley, 1982). Similarly, people who have very ambitious, hard-driving personalities tend to want to stay at work longer than those who are more relaxed.

Sexual Behavior A common misconception about the aged is that they have outlived their sexuality. This myth reflects our stereotypes. To the extent that we see the elderly as physically unattractive and frail, we find it difficult to believe that they are sexually active. True, older people respond more slowly and are less sexually active than younger people, but the majority of older adults can enjoy sex and have orgasms. One survey revealed that 37 percent of married people over 60 have sex at least once a week, 20 percent have sex outdoors, and 17 percent swim in the nude (Woodward & Springen, 1992). Another study of people ages 65 to 97 found that about half the men still viewed sex as important, and slightly over half of those in committed relationships were satisfied with the quality of their sex lives (Mark Clements Research, 1995).

Cognitive Changes

Is memory loss inevitable in old age?

Healthy people who remain intellectually active maintain a high level of mental functioning in old age (Schaie, 1984; Shimamura, Berry, Mangels, Rusting, & Jurica, 1995). Far from the common myth that the brain cells of elderly people are rapidly dying off, the brain of the average person shrinks only about 10 percent in size between the ages of 20 and 70 (Goleman,

1996). This finding means that, for a sizable number of older adults, cognitive abilities remain largely intact. True, the aging mind works a little more slowly (Birren & Fisher, 1995; Salthouse, 1991), and certain types of memories are a little more difficult to store and retrieve (Craik, 1994), but these changes are not serious enough to interfere with the ability to enjoy an active, independent life. Also, some mental abilities appear to decline more than others (Schaie, 1994), but training and practice can greatly reduce the decline in cognitive performance in later adulthood (Willis, 1985; Willis & Schaie, 1986).

Alzheimer's Disease   For people suffering from **Alzheimer's disease,** the picture is quite different. They forget the names of their children or are unable to find their way home from the store. Some even fail to recognize their husband or wife. Named for the German neurologist Alois Alzheimer, the disease causes progressive loss of the ability to communicate and reason resulting from changes in the brain (Glenner, 1994).

For many years, Alzheimer's disease was considered rare, and it was diagnosed only in people under 60 who developed symptoms of memory loss and confusion. But now Alzheimer's is recognized as a common disorder in older people who used to be called "senile." According to current estimates, about 10 percent of adults over 65 and nearly half of adults over 85 suffer from Alzheimer's disease (Bennett & Knopman, 1994). Factors that put people at risk for developing the disorder are having a family history of dementia (a general decline in physical and cognitive abilities), having Down syndrome or Parkinson's disease, being born to a woman over the age of 40, and suffering a head trauma (especially one that caused unconsciousness) (Kokmen, 1991; Myers, 1996). In addition, people who are not active, both physically and intellectually, during their middle years, increase their risk for the developing Alzheimer's disease (Friedland et al., 2001).

Alzheimer's usually begins with minor memory losses, such as difficulty in recalling words and names or in remembering where one put something. As it progresses—and this process may take anywhere from two to twenty years—personality changes are also likely. First, people may become emotionally withdrawn or flat. Later, they may suffer from delusions, such as thinking that relatives are stealing from them. These people become confused and may not know where they are or what time of day it is. Eventually, they lose the ability to speak, to care for themselves, and to recognize family members. If they do not die of other causes, Alzheimer's will eventually be fatal (Wolfson et al., 2001).

Early diagnosis of Alzheimer's disease is usually based on questions that healthy people typically have little difficulty answering but that give those in the early stages of Alzheimer's trouble (see Petersen et al., 2001; Solomon et al., 1998). At present there is no known cure for Alzheimer's, but breakthroughs in research are occurring so fast that a drug to slow the progress of the disorder or even a vaccine to prevent it may be developed in the near future (Henry, 1996; Novak, 1999; Pennisi, 1999).

Facing the End of Life

How well do most elderly people cope with the end of life?

Fear of death is seldom a central concern for people in later adulthood. In fact, such fear seems to be a greater problem in young adulthood or in middle age, when the first awareness of mortality coincides with a greater interest in living (Kimmel, 1974).

But the elderly do have some major fears associated with dying. They fear the pain, indignity, and depersonalization that they might experience during a terminal illness, as well as the possibility of dying alone. They also

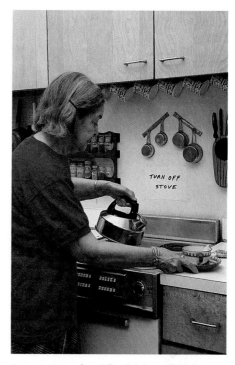

Because people with Alzheimer's disease suffer memory loss, signs can remind them to perform ordinary activities.

Alzheimer's disease
A neurological disorder, most commonly found in late adulthood, characterized by progressive losses in memory and cognition and by changes in personality.

worry about burdening their relatives with the expenses of their hospitalization or nursing care. Sometimes, too, relatives are not able to provide much support for the elderly as they decline, either because they live too far away or because they may be unable to cope either with the pain of watching a loved one die or with their own fears of mortality (Kübler-Ross, 1975).

Stages of Dying   Psychiatrist Elisabeth Kübler-Ross (1969) interviewed more than 200 dying people of all ages to try to understand the psychological aspects of dying. From these interviews, she described a sequence of five stages that she believed people pass through as they react to their own impending death.

1. *Denial:* The person denies the diagnosis, refuses to believe that death is approaching, insists that an error has been made, and seeks other, more acceptable opinions or alternatives.

2. *Anger:* The person now accepts the reality of the situation but expresses envy and resentment toward those who will live to fulfill a plan or dream. The question becomes "Why me?" Anger may be directed at the doctor or randomly in all directions. The patience and understanding of other people are particularly important at this stage.

3. *Bargaining:* The person desperately tries to buy time, negotiating with doctors, family members, clergy, and God in a healthy attempt to cope with the realization of death.

4. *Depression:* As bargaining fails and time is running out, the person may succumb to depression, lamenting failures and mistakes that can no longer be corrected.

5. *Acceptance:* Tired and weak, the person at last enters a state of "quiet expectation," submitting to fate.

According to Kübler-Ross, Americans have a greater problem coping with death than people in some other cultures. She observes that whereas some cultures are *death affirming,* American culture is *death denying:* "We are reluctant to reveal our age; we spend fortunes to hide our wrinkles; we prefer to send our old people to nursing homes" (1975, p. 28). We also shelter children from knowledge of death and dying. By trying to protect them from these unpleasant realities, however, we may actually make them more fearful of death.

Some observers have found fault with Kübler-Ross's model of dying. Most of the criticisms have focused on her methodology. She studied only a relatively small sample of people and provided little information about how they were selected and how often they were interviewed. Also, all her patients were suffering from cancer. Does her model apply as well to people dying from other causes? Finally, some critics question the universality of her model. Death itself is universal, but reactions to dying may differ greatly from one culture to another.

Despite these legitimate questions, there is nearly universal agreement that Kübler-Ross deserves credit for pioneering the study of the transitions that people undergo during the dying process. She was the first to investigate an area long considered taboo, and her research has made dying a more "understandable" experience, perhaps one that is easier to deal with.

Widowhood   The death of one's spouse may be the most severe challenge that people face during late adulthood. Especially if the death was unexpected, people respond to such a loss with

The loss of loved ones is one of the major challenges people face in late adulthood.

initial disbelief, followed by numbness. Only later is the full impact of the loss felt, and that can be severe. The incidence of depression rises significantly following the death of a spouse (Norris & Murrell, 1990). Moreover, a long-term study of several thousand widowers 55 years of age and older revealed that nearly 5 percent of them died in the 6-month period following their wife's death, a figure that is well above the expected death rate for men that age. Thereafter, the mortality rate of these men fell gradually to a more normal level (Butler & Lewis, 1982).

Perhaps because they are not as used to taking care of themselves, men seem to suffer more than women from the loss of a mate. But because women have a longer life expectancy, there are many more widows than widowers. Thus, men have a better chance of remarrying. More than half the women over 65 are widowed, and half of them will live another fifteen years without remarrying. For somewhat different reasons, then, the burden of widowhood is heavy for both men and women (Feinson, 1986).

 INTERACTIVE LECTURE 9.6

WEB QUIZ 9.6

CHECK YOUR UNDERSTANDING

1. Indicate whether the following statements are true (T) or false (F).
   ____ a. The average man lives as long as the average woman.
   ____ b. The physical changes of aging inevitably become incapacitating.
   ____ c. Most elderly people are dependent on their adult children.
   ____ d. Healthy people who remain intellectually involved maintain a high level of mental functioning in old age.
2. Match the following stages of dying with the appropriate definition.
   ____ denial   a. person submits to fate
   ____ anger   b. person expresses resentment toward others
   ____ bargaining   c. person refuses to believe the diagnosis
   ____ depression   d. person may lament mistakes
   ____ acceptance   e. person tries to buy time

Answers: 1. a. (F); b. (F); c. (F); d. (T) 2. denial: c; anger: b; bargaining: e; depression: d; acceptance: a.

KEY TERMS

developmental psychology, p. 313
cross-sectional study, p. 314
cohort, p. 314
longitudinal study, p. 315
biographical or retrospective study, p. 315

Prenatal development
prenatal development, p. 315
embryo, p. 315

fetus, p. 315
critical period, p. 316
fetal alcohol syndrome (FAS), p. 316

The newborn baby
neonate, p. 317
temperament, p. 317

Infancy and childhood
maturation, p. 322
sensory-motor stage, p. 323
object permanence, p. 324

mental representation, p. 324
preoperational stage, p. 324
egocentric, p. 324
concrete-operational stage, p. 325
principles of conservation, p. 325
formal-operational stage, p. 325
babbling, p. 327
holophrases, p. 328

language acquisition device, p. 329
imprinting, p. 330
attachment, p. 330
autonomy, p. 331
socialization, p. 332
peer group, p. 333
gender identity, p. 334
gender constancy, p. 334
gender-role awareness, p. 334

CHAPTER REVIEW

Enduring Issues and Methods in Developmental Psychology

What are some of the limitations of the methods used to study development? **Cross-sectional studies** involve studying different age-groups of people, whereas **longitudinal studies** study the same group of individuals at different times in their lives. Longitudinal studies are more time-consuming, but do account for **cohort** differences in the typical experiences of members of different generations. **Biographical,** or **retrospective,** studies involve reconstructing a person's past through interviews.

Prenatal Development

Why can an organism or another substance cause devastating effects at one point in prenatal development but not at others? The period of development from conception to birth is called **prenatal development.** During this time teratogens—disease-producing organisms or potentially harmful substances such as drugs—can pass through the placenta and cause irreparable harm to the **embryo** or **fetus.** This harm is greatest if the drug or other substance is introduced just at the time when some major developmental process that it interferes with is occurring. If the same substance is introduced outside this critical period, little or even no harm may result.

The Newborn

How competent are newborns? Although newborn babies appear helpless, they are much more competent and aware than they seem. Newborns see and hear, are capable of reflexive behavior, and are distinctly unique in their underlying temperaments.

What early reflexes enable newborns to respond to their environment? Newborns come equipped with a number of reflexes that help them to respond to their environments. Those that help them to breathe and nurse are critical to survival. For instance, the *rooting reflex* causes newborns, when touched on the cheek, to turn their head in that direction and grope around with their mouth. This helps them to locate a nipple. Nursing is further facilitated by the *sucking reflex*, which causes newborns to suck on anything placed in their mouth, and the *swallowing reflex*, which enables them to swallow liquids without choking.

Is your temperament the same as it was when you were a newborn? Babies are born with individual differences in personality called **temperament** differences. Often a baby's temperament remains quite stable over time due to a combination of genetic and environmental influences. But stability in temperament is not inevitable; changes in temperament can also take place. Your own temperament, therefore, may be both similar to and different from the temperament you displayed as a newborn.

Which senses are the most developed at birth, and which are the least developed? All of a baby's senses are functioning at birth: sight, hearing, taste, smell, and touch. Although it is hard to tell exactly what a baby's sensory world is like, newborns seem particularly adept at discriminating speech sounds, which suggests that their hearing is quite keen. Their least developed sense is probably vision, which takes 6 to 8 months to become as good as the average college student's.

Infancy and Childhood

What kinds of developmental changes occur during infancy and childhood? During the first dozen years of life a helpless infant becomes a competent older child. This transformation encompasses many important kinds of changes, including physical, motor, cognitive, and social developments.

Do children grow at a steady pace? Growth of the body is most rapid during the first year, with the average baby growing approximately 10 inches and gaining about 15 pounds. It then slows down considerably until early adolescence. When growth does occur, it happens suddenly—almost overnight—rather than through small, steady changes.

Is walking at an early age a sign of future athletic ability? This is a question about motor development, the acquisition of skills involving movement. Babies tend to reach the major milestones in early motor development at broadly similar ages, give or take a few months. The average ages are called developmental norms. Those who are somewhat ahead of their peers are not necessarily destined for athletic greatness. Motor development that is slower or faster than the norm tells us little or nothing about a child's future characteristics. **Maturation,** the biological process that lead to developmental changes, also is shaped by experiences with the environment.

How does a child's ability to reason change over time? According to the Swiss psychologist Jean Piaget, children undergo qualitative changes in thinking as they grow older. Piaget depicted these changes as a series of stages. During the **sensory-motor stage** (from birth to age 2) children acquire **object permanence,** the understanding that things continue to exist even when they are out of sight. In the **preoperational stage** (ages 2 to 7) they become increasingly adept at using mental representations, and language assumes an important role in describing, remembering, and reasoning about the world. Children in the **concrete-operational stage** (ages 7 to 11) are able to pay attention to more than one factor at a time and can understand someone else's point of view. Finally, in the **formal-operational stage** (adolescence–adulthood) teenagers acquire the ability to think abstractly and test ideas mentally using logic. Not all psychologists agree with Piaget's theory, however. His is one of several perspectives on children's cognitive development.

How do gender and ethnic background affect moral development? Like Piaget, Lawrence Kohlberg developed a stage theory about the development of thinking, but his focused exclusively on moral thinking. He proposed that children at different levels of moral reasoning base their moral choices on different factors: first a concern about physical consequences, then a concern about what other people think, and finally a concern about abstract principles. One problem with Kohlberg's view, however, is that it doesn't consider how gender and ethnic background affect moral development. The cultural values associated with being female, African American, Japanese, and so on may affect the ways in which people determine what is right and wrong, good and bad.

How does a child develop language skills? Some psychologists believe that childhood is a critical period for acquiring language, during which it is much easier to build a vocabulary, master the rules of grammar, and form intelligible sentences. If so, this would explain why learning a second language is also easier for children than for adults.

How can parents help their children to become both securely attached and independent? Developing a sense of independence is just one of the tasks that children face in their social development. It comes to the fore especially during the toddler period, when a growing awareness of being a separate person makes developing some autonomy from parents a very important issue. Parents can encourage independence in their children by allowing them to make choices and do things on their own within a framework of reasonable and consistently enforced limits. Other major social issues during the childhood years include forming a secure attachment toward and trust in other people (infancy), learning to take initiative in tackling new tasks (the preschool years), and mastering some of the many skills that will be needed in adulthood (middle and later childhood).

Socialization, the process by which children learn their cultures' behaviors and attitudes, is an important task of childhood. Play, which develops from *solitary play* (ages 1–2), to *parallel play* (age 2–3), to *cooperative play* (at age 3 or 3½), has an important role in socialization. Children develop **sex-typed behavior,** or behavior appropriate to their gender, through a process of **gender-role awareness** and the formation of **gender stereotypes** reflected in their culture.

Is watching TV a good or bad influence on the development of children? Watching television can be worthwhile when programs have educational context and provide positive role models. However, TV also reduces the time children could spend on other positive activities. When it contains aggressive content and negative role models, it can encourage aggressive behavior and can perhaps contribute to the decline in academic skills, especially reading.

Adolescence

Is adolescence characterized only by physical changes? The physical changes of adolescence—rapid growth and sexual maturation—are just part of the transformation that occurs during this period. The child turns into an adult not only physically but also cognitively, socially, and personally.

What are the consequences of going through puberty early or late? Although **puberty,** the onset of sexual maturation, starts earlier in girls than in boys, there are substantial individual differences in exactly when it begins. Very early maturing girls face both advantages and disadvantages. They may like the admiration they get from other girls but dislike the embarrassing sexual attention given to them by boys. Boys who mature early do better in sports and in social activities and receive greater respect from their peers, so it may seem that early maturation is preferable in males. Many late-maturing boys, however, may eventually develop a stronger sense of self-identity, perhaps because they don't feel pressured to "grow up" too quickly.

What are two common fallacies that characterize adolescent thinking? In terms of cognitive development, teenagers often reach the level of formal-operational thought, in which they can reason abstractly and speculate about alternatives. These newfound abilities may make them overconfident that their own ideas are right, turning adolescence into a time of cognitive egocentrism. Frequent focus on the self may also make teens prone to feeling constantly watched and judged by others, a phenomenon called the **imaginary audience.** In addition, adolescents may think of themselves as so unique as to be untouched by the negative things that happen to other people. This **personal fable** may encourage them to take needless risks.

What important tasks do adolescents face in their personal and social lives? Many adolescents undertake a search for personal identity in which they ideally acquire a solid sense of who they are. In Erik Erikson's theory, identity versus role confusion is the major challenge of this period. Teenagers also work toward developing romantic interests that can build a foundation for strong, intimate relationships in adulthood. Parent–child relationships may become temporarily rocky during adolescence as teenagers become aware of their parents' faults and question parental rules. These conflicts are most common during early adolescence and tend to resolve themselves by the later adolescent years.

What are some major problems among adolescents in our society? Developmental problems often show up for the first time during adolescence. A sizable number of adolescents think about committing suicide; a much smaller number attempt it. Statistics reflect a common decline in self-esteem during adolescence, especially among girls. In addition, teenagers have to cope with the demands of their new sexuality, the potential for early pregnancy, and the threat of violence in their peer groups.

Adulthood

Does personality change during adulthood? Reaching developmental milestones in adulthood is much less predictable than in earlier years, much more a function of the individual's decisions, circumstances, and even luck. Still, there are certain experiences and changes that take place sooner or later in nearly everyone's life and certain needs that nearly every adult tries to fulfill.

What factors are important in forming satisfying relationships in adulthood? Almost every adult forms a long-term loving partnership with at least one other adult at some point in life. According to Erik Erikson, the task of finding intimacy versus being isolated and lonely is especially important during young adulthood. Erikson believed that people are not ready for love until they have formed a firm sense of identity. But other psychologists, such as Carol Gilligan, suggest that intimacy can sometimes come before identity, especially in young women.

What are the satisfactions and stresses of adult work? The vast majority of adults are moderately or highly satisfied with their jobs and would continue to work even if they didn't need to for financial reasons. Balancing the demands of job and family is often difficult, however, especially for women, because they tend to have most of the responsibility for housework and child care. Yet despite this stress of a "double shift," a job outside the home is a positive, self-esteem–boosting factor in most women's lives.

In what ways do adults think differently than adolescents? An adult's thinking is more flexible and practical than an adolescent's. Whereas adolescents search for the one "correct" solution to a problem, adults realize that there may be several "right" solutions or none at all. Adults also place less faith in authorities than adolescents do.

What changes in personality occur as adults move into midlife? Certain broad patterns of personality change occur in adulthood. As people grow older, they tend to become less self-centered and more comfortable in interpersonal relationships. They also develop better coping skills and new ways of adapting. By middle age many adults feel an increasing commitment to, and responsibility for, others. This suggests that many adults are successfully meeting what Erik Erikson saw as the major challenge of middle adulthood: generativity (the ability to continue being productive and creative, especially in ways that guide and encourage future generations) versus stagnation (a sense of boredom or lack of fulfillment, sometimes called a **midlife crisis**). Most adults, however, do not experience dramatic upheaval in their middle years, and this period may be better thought of as one of **midlife transition.**

What is menopause, and what changes accompany it? Middle adulthood brings a decline in the functioning of the reproductive organs. In women this is marked by **menopause,** the cessation of menstruation, accompanied by a sharp drop in estrogen levels. Without estrogen-replacement therapy, some negative symptoms such as thinning bones and "hot flashes" can result. Men experience a slower decline in testosterone levels.

Late Adulthood

What factors are related to life expectancy? Over the past century life expectancy in America has increased mainly because of improved health care and nutrition. There is, however, a sizable gender gap, with women living an average of 7 years longer than men. There is also a sizable racial gap, with white Americans living an average of 5 years longer than blacks.

Why does the body deteriorate with age? The physical changes of late adulthood affect outward appearance and the functioning of every organ. We don't yet know why these changes happen. Perhaps our genes program cells to eventually deteriorate and die, or perhaps genetic instructions simply degrade over time. Another possible explanation is that body parts wear out after re-peated use, with environmental toxins contributing to the wearing-out process. Whatever the reason for it, physical aging is inevitable, although it can be slowed by a healthy lifestyle.

What kind of lifestyle and sex life can be expected after 65? Most older adults have an independent lifestyle and engage in activities that interest them. Although their sexual responses may be slowed, most continue to enjoy sex in their sixties and seventies. Still, gradual social changes occur in late adulthood. Older adults start to interact with fewer people and perform fewer social roles. They may also become less influenced by social rules and expectations. Realizing that there is a limit to the capacity for social involvement, they learn to live with some restrictions.

Is memory loss inevitable in old age? The aging mind works a little more slowly, and certain kinds of memories are more difficult to store and retrieve, but these changes are generally not extensive enough to interfere with most everyday tasks. Healthy older adults who engage in intellectually stimulating activities usually maintain a high level of mental functioning.

How well do most elderly people cope with the end of life? Most elderly people fear death less than younger people do. What they do fear are the pain, indignity, depersonalization, and loneliness associated with a terminal illness. They also worry about becoming a financial burden to their families. The death of a spouse may be the most severe challenge the elderly face.

CRITICAL THINKING AND APPLICATIONS

1. Does watching violent television lead to more violent behavior?

2. To what degree do you think that people maintain a stable and consistent identity throughout their life-time? To what degree do people change at each developmental stage of their life?

WEB QUIZ **9.7** ✔ **Go to the Morris 6e Companion Website to take a practice chapter exam.**

10 Personality

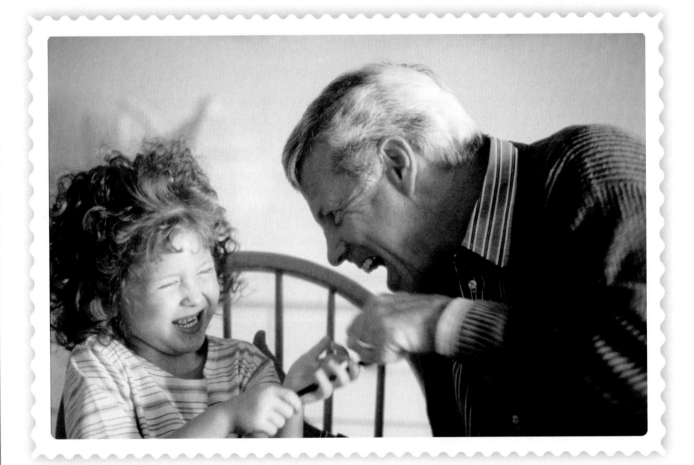

OVERVIEW

WE TALK ABOUT PERSONALITY ALL THE TIME. WE DESCRIBE OUR BEST FRIEND AS A "fun-loving but quiet personality" or "kind of a jock, but really gentle." Acquaintances whom we know less well may elicit a one-dimensional assessment: "He's really arrogant" or "She's a snob." These brief characterizations of people do not define their personalities, however, because personality is made up of not one or two outstanding characteristics or abilities but a whole range of them.

Many psychologists define **personality** as an individual's unique pattern of thoughts, feelings, and behaviors that persists over time and across situations. Notice that there are two important parts to this definition. On the one hand, personality refers to *unique differences*—those aspects that distinguish a person from everyone else. On the other hand, the definition asserts that personality is relatively *stable* and *enduring*—that these unique differences persist through time and across situations. If you have had the chance to view yourself at various ages in home movies or videos, you've probably noticed that at each age some of the same characteristics are evident. Maybe you are a natural "actor," always showing off for the camera, or you might be a director type who, at age 4 as well as at age 14, was telling the camera operator what to do. Because we expect people's personalities to be relatively consistent, we generally suspect that something is wrong with a person when that is not the case.

Psychologists approach the study of personality in a number of ways. Some set out to identify the most important characteristics of personality. Others seek to understand why there are differences in personality. Among the latter group, some psychologists identify the family as the most important factor in the development of the individual's personality. Others emphasize environmental influences outside the family, and still others see personality as the result of how we learn to think about ourselves and our experiences. Out of these various approaches have come four major categories of personality theories:

Psychodynamic theories place the origins of personality in unconscious, often sexual, motivations and conflicts.

Humanistic theories spotlight positive growth motives and the realization of potential in shaping personality.

Trait theories categorize and describe the ways in which people's personalities differ.

Cognitive–social learning theories find the roots of personality in the ways people think about, act on, and respond to their environment.

As we will see in this chapter, biological psychologists are now suggesting a fifth perspective—one emphasizing the *genetic basis* of personality traits. To varying degrees, each of these theoretical approaches contributes to our overall understanding of personality.

In this chapter, we explore the four approaches by examining some representative theories that each one has produced. We see how each theoretical paradigm sheds light on the personality of Jaylene Smith, a young doctor who is having trouble forming close and lasting relationships and who is described in the case that follows. Finally, we evaluate the strengths and weaknesses of each approach to the understanding of personality.

The Case of Jaylene Smith

Thirty-year-old Jaylene Smith is a talented physician who visits a psychologist because she is troubled by certain aspects of her social life. Acquaintances describe Jay in glowing terms—highly motivated, intelligent, attractive, and charming. But Jay feels terribly insecure and anxious. When asked by a psychologist to pick out some self-descriptive adjectives, she selected "introverted," "shy," "inadequate," and "unhappy."

Jay was the firstborn in a family of two boys and one girl. Her father is a quiet and gentle medical researcher. His work often allowed him to study at home, so he had extensive contact with his children when they were young. He loved all his children but clearly favored Jay. His ambitions and goals for her were extremely high, and as she matured, he responded to her every need and demand almost immediately and with full conviction. Their relationship remains as close today as it was during Jay's childhood.

Jay's mother worked long hours away from home as a store manager and consequently saw her children primarily at night and on an occasional free weekend. When she came home, Mrs. Smith was tired and had little energy for "nonessential" interactions with her children. She had always been career oriented, but she experienced considerable conflict and frustration trying to reconcile her roles as mother, housekeeper, and financial provider. Mrs. Smith was usually amiable toward all her children but tended to argue more with Jay, until the bickering subsided when Jay was about 6 or 7 years of age. Today their relationship is cordial but lacks the closeness apparent between Jay and Dr. Smith. Interactions between Dr. and Mrs. Smith were sometimes marred by stormy outbursts over seemingly trivial matters. These episodes were always followed by periods of mutual silence lasting for days.

Jay was very jealous of her first brother, born when she was 2 years old. Her parents recall that Jay sometimes staged temper tantrums when the new infant demanded and received a lot of attention (especially from Mrs. Smith). The temper tantrums intensified when Jay's second brother was born, just one year later. As time went on, the brothers formed an alliance to try to undermine Jay's supreme position with their father. Jay only became closer to her father, and her relationships with her brothers were marked by greater-than-average jealousy and rivalry from early childhood to the present.

Throughout elementary, junior high, and high school, Jay was popular and did well academically. Early on she decided on a career in medicine. Yet off and on between the ages of 8 and 17, she had strong feelings of loneliness, depression, insecurity, and confusion—feelings common enough during this age period, but stronger than in most youngsters and very distressing to Jay.

Jay's college days were a period of great personal growth, but several unsuccessful romantic involvements caused her much pain. The failure to achieve a stable and long-lasting relationship persisted after college and troubled Jay greatly. Although even-tempered in most circumstances, Jay often had an explosive fit of anger that ended each important romantic relationship that she had. "What is wrong with me?" she would ask herself. "Why do I find it impossible to maintain a serious relationship for any length of time?"

In medical school, her conflicts crept into her consciousness periodically: "I don't deserve to be a doctor"; "I won't pass my exams"; "Who am I, and what do I want from life?"

How can we describe and understand Jaylene Smith's personality? How did she become who she is? Why does she feel insecure and uncertain despite her obvious success? Why do her friends see her as charming and attractive, though she describes herself as introverted and inadequate? These

Personality
An individual's unique pattern of thoughts, feelings, and behaviors that persists over time and across situations.

are the kinds of questions that personality psychologists are likely to ask about Jay—and the kinds of questions we will try to answer in this chapter.

Psychodynamic Theories

What ideas do all psychodynamic theories have in common?

Psychodynamic theories see behavior as the product of psychological forces that interact within the individual, often outside conscious awareness. Freud drew on the physics of his day to coin the term *psychodynamics*: As thermodynamics is the study of heat and mechanical energy and the way that one may be transformed into the other, psychodynamics is the study of psychic energy and the way that it is transformed and expressed in behavior. Psychodynamic theorists disagreed among themselves about the exact nature of this psychic energy. Some, like Freud, traced it to sexual and aggressive urges; others, like Karen Horney, saw it as rooted in the individual's struggle to deal with dependency. But all psychodynamic theorists share the sense that unconscious processes primarily determine personality and can best be understood within the context of life-span development.

Some parts of psychodynamic theory, especially Freud's views of female sexuality, are out-of-date. The following five propositions, however, are central to all psychodynamic theories and have withstood the tests of time (Westen, 1998).

1. Much of mental life is unconscious, and as a result, people may behave in ways that they themselves do not understand.

2. Mental processes such as emotions, motivations, and thoughts operate in parallel and thus may lead to conflicting feelings.

3. Not only do stable personality patterns begin to form in childhood, but also early experiences strongly affect personality development.

4. Our mental representations of ourselves, of others, and of our relationships tend to guide our interactions with other people.

5. The development of personality involves learning to regulate sexual and aggressive feelings as well as becoming socially interdependent rather than dependent.

As we will see, these five propositions are implicit in the work of all the major psychodynamic theorists.

Sigmund Freud

When Freud proposed that sexual instinct is the basis of behavior, how was he defining "sexual instinct?"

To this day, Sigmund Freud (1856–1939) is the best known and most influential of the psychodynamic theorists. As we saw in Chapter 1, Freud created an entirely new perspective on the study of human behavior. Up to his time, psychology had focused on consciousness—that is, on those thoughts and feelings of which we are aware. In a radical departure, Freud stressed the **unconscious**—all the ideas, thoughts, and feelings of which we are *not* normally aware. Freud's ideas form the basis of **psychoanalysis,** a term that refers both to his theory of personality and to the form of therapy that he invented.

According to Freud, human behavior is based on unconscious instincts, or drives. Some instincts are aggressive and destructive; others, such as hunger, thirst, self-preservation, and sex, are necessary to the survival of

Psychodynamic theories
Personality theories contending that behavior results from psychological forces that interact within the individual, often outside conscious awareness.

Unconscious
In Freud's theory, all the ideas, thoughts, and feelings of which we are not and normally cannot become aware.

Psychoanalysis
The theory of personality Freud developed as well as the form of therapy he invented.

the individual and the species. Freud used the term *sexual instincts* to refer not just to erotic sexuality but also to the desire for virtually any form of pleasure. In this broad sense, Freud regarded the sexual instinct as the most critical factor in the development of personality.

How Personality Is Structured Freud theorized that personality is formed around three structures: the *id*, the *ego*, and the *superego*. The **id** is the only structure present at birth and is completely unconscious (see **Figure 10–1**). In Freud's view, the id consists of unconscious urges and desires that continually seek expression. It operates according to the **pleasure principle**— that is, it tries to obtain immediate pleasure and to avoid pain. As soon as an instinct arises, the id seeks to gratify it. Because the id is not in contact with the real world, however, it has only two ways of obtaining gratification. One way is by reflex actions, such as coughing, which relieve unpleasant sensations at once. The other is through fantasy, or what Freud referred to as *wish fulfillment*: A person forms a mental image of an object or a situation that partially satisfies the instinct and relieves the uncomfortable feeling. This kind of thought occurs most often in dreams and daydreams, but it may take other forms. For instance, if someone insults you and you spend the next half hour imagining clever retorts, you are engaging in wish fulfillment.

Mental images of this kind provide fleeting relief, but they cannot fully satisfy most needs. Just thinking about being with someone you love is a poor substitute for actually being with that person. Therefore, the id by itself is not very effective at gratifying instincts. It must link up with reality if it is to relieve its discomfort. The id's link to reality is the ego.

Freud conceived of the **ego** as the psychic mechanism that controls all thinking and reasoning activities. The ego operates partly consciously, partly *preconsciously*, and partly unconsciously. ("Preconscious" refers to material that is not currently in awareness but can easily be recalled.) The ego learns about the external world through the senses and sees to the satisfaction of the id's drives in the external world. But instead of acting according to the pleasure principle, the ego operates by the **reality principle**: By means of intelligent reasoning, the ego tries to delay satisfying the id's desires until it can do so safely and successfully. For example, if you are

---

Id
In Freud's theory of personality, the collection of unconscious urges and desires that continually seek expression.

Pleasure principle
According to Freud, the way in which the id seeks immediate gratification of an instinct.

Ego
Freud's term for the part of the personality that mediates between environmental demands (reality), conscience (superego), and instinctual needs (id); now often used as a synonym for "self."

Reality principle
According to Freud, the way in which the ego seeks to satisfy instinctual demands safely and effectively in the real world.

FIGURE 10–1

The structural relationship formed by the id, ego, and superego. Freud's conception of personality is often depicted as an iceberg to illustrate how the vast workings of the mind occur beneath its surface. Notice that the ego is partly conscious, partly unconscious, and partly preconscious; it derives knowledge of the external world through the senses. The superego also works at all three levels. But the id is an entirely unconscious structure.

Source: Adapted from *New Introductory Lectures on Psychoanalysis*, by Sigmund Freud, 1933, New York: Carlton House.

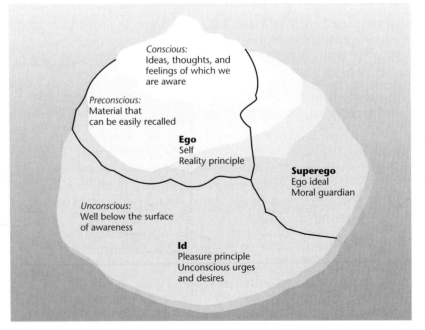

Conscious:
Ideas, thoughts, and feelings of which we are aware

Preconscious:
Material that can be easily recalled

Ego
Self
Reality principle

Superego
Ego ideal
Moral guardian

Unconscious:
Well below the surface of awareness

Id
Pleasure principle
Unconscious urges and desires

thirsty, your ego will attempt to determine how best to obtain something to quench your thirst effectively and safely (see **Figure 10–2**).

A personality that consisted only of ego and id would be completely selfish. It would behave effectively but unsociably. Fully adult behavior is governed not only by reality but also by morality—that is, by the individual's conscience or by the moral standards that the individual develops through interaction with parents and society. Freud called this moral watchdog the **superego.**

The superego is not present at birth. In fact, young children are amoral and do whatever is pleasurable. As we mature, however, we assimilate, or adopt as our own, the judgments of our parents about what is "good" and "bad." In time, the external restraint applied by our parents gives way to our own internal self-restraint. The superego, eventually acting as conscience, takes over the task of observing and guiding the ego, just as the parents once observed and guided the child. Like the ego, it works at the conscious, preconscious, and unconscious levels.

According to Freud, the superego also compares the ego's actions with an **ego ideal** of perfection and then rewards or punishes the ego accordingly. Unfortunately, the superego is sometimes too harsh in its judgments. An artist dominated by such a punishing superego, for example, may realize the impossibility of ever equaling Rembrandt and so give up painting in despair.

Ideally, our id, ego, and superego work in harmony, the ego satisfying the demands of the id in a reasonable, moral manner approved by the superego. We are then free to love and hate and to express our emotions sensibly and without guilt. When our id is dominant, our instincts are unbridled, and we are likely to endanger both ourselves and society. When our superego dominates, our behavior is checked too tightly, and we are inclined to judge ourselves too harshly or too quickly, impairing our ability to act on our own behalf and enjoy ourselves.

Superego
According to Freud, the social and parental standards the individual has internalized; the conscience and the ego ideal.

Ego ideal
The part of the superego that consists of standards of what one would like to be.

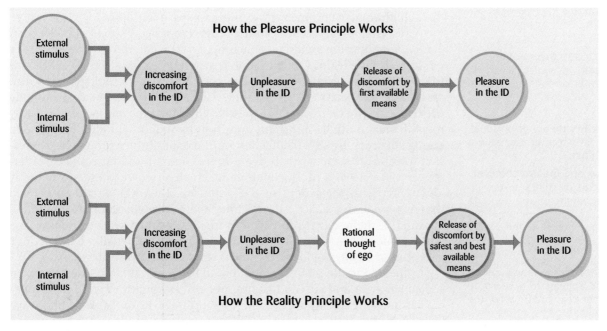

FIGURE 10–2

How Freud conceived the workings of the pleasure and reality principles.   Note that according to the reality principle, the ego uses rational thought to postpone the gratification of the id until its desires can be satisfied safely.

Freud believed that during the oral stage, when babies are dependent on others to fulfill their needs, they derive pleasure from the mouth, lips, and tongue.

Libido
According to Freud, the energy generated by the sexual instinct.

Fixation
According to Freud, a partial or complete halt at some point in the individual's psychosexual development.

Oral stage
First stage in Freud's theory of personality development, in which the infant's erotic feelings center on the mouth, lips, and tongue.

Anal stage
Second stage in Freud's theory of personality development, in which a child's erotic feelings center on the anus and on elimination.

Phallic stage
Third stage in Freud's theory of personality development, in which erotic feelings center on the genitals.

Oedipus complex and Electra complex
According to Freud, a child's sexual attachment to the parent of the opposite sex and jealousy toward the parent of the same sex; generally occurs in the phallic stage.

Latency period
In Freud's theory of personality, a period in which the child appears to have no interest in the other sex; occurs after the phallic stage.

Genital stage
In Freud's theory of personality development, the final stage of normal adult sexual development, which is usually marked by mature sexuality.

How Personality Develops Freud's theory of personality development focuses on the way in which we satisfy the sexual instinct during the course of life. Freud thought of the sexual instinct broadly, as a craving for sensual pleasure of all kinds. He called the energy generated by the sexual instinct **libido.** As infants mature, their libido becomes focused on different sensitive parts of the body. During the first 18 months of life, the dominant source of sensual pleasure is the mouth. At about 18 months, sensuality shifts to the anus; and at about age 3, it shifts again, this time to the genitals. According to Freud, children's experiences at each of these stages stamp their personality with tendencies that endure into adulthood. If a child is deprived of pleasure (or allowed too much gratification) from the part of the body that dominates a certain stage, some sexual energy may remain permanently tied to that part of the body, instead of moving on in normal sequence to give the individual a fully integrated personality. This is called **fixation,** and as we shall see, Freud believed that it leads to immature forms of sexuality and to certain characteristic personality traits. Let's look more closely at the psychosexual stages that Freud identified and their presumed relationship to personality development.

In the **oral stage** (birth to 18 months), infants, who depend completely on other people to satisfy their needs, relieve sexual tension by sucking and swallowing; when their baby teeth come in, they obtain oral pleasure from chewing and biting. According to Freud, infants who receive too much oral gratification at this stage grow into overly optimistic and dependent adults; those who receive too little may turn into pessimistic and hostile people later in life. Fixation at this stage is linked to such personality characteristics as lack of confidence, gullibility, sarcasm, and argumentativeness.

During the **anal stage** (roughly 18 months to 3½ years), the primary source of sexual pleasure shifts from the mouth to the anus. Just about the time children begin to derive pleasure from holding in and excreting feces, toilet training takes place, and they must learn to regulate this new pleasure. In Freud's view, if parents are too strict in toilet training, some children throw temper tantrums and may live in self-destructive ways as adults. Others become obstinate, stingy, and excessively orderly. If parents are too lenient, their children may become messy, unorganized, and sloppy.

When children reach the **phallic stage** (after age 3), they discover their genitals and develop a marked attachment to the parent of the opposite sex while becoming jealous of the same-sex parent. In boys, Freud called this the **Oedipus complex,** after the character in Greek mythology who killed his father and married his mother. Girls go through a corresponding **Electra complex,** involving possessive love for their father and jealousy toward their mother. A recent study found support for the idea that in young children, displays of affection for the opposite-sex parent and aggression toward the same-sex parent are more common than the reverse (Watson & Getz, 1990). Most children eventually resolve these conflicts by identifying with the parent of the same sex. However, Freud contended that fixation at this stage leads to vanity and egotism in adult life, with men boasting of their sexual prowess and treating women with contempt, and with women becoming flirtatious and promiscuous. Phallic fixation may also prompt feelings of low self-esteem, shyness, and worthlessness.

At the end of the phallic period, Freud believed, children lose interest in sexual behavior and enter a **latency period.** During this period, which begins around the age of 5 or 6 and lasts until age 12 or 13, boys play with boys, girls play with girls, and neither sex takes much interest in the other.

At puberty, the individual enters the last psychosexual stage, which Freud called the **genital stage.** At this time, sexual impulses reawaken. In lovemaking, the adolescent and the adult are able to satisfy unfulfilled desires from infancy and childhood. Ideally, immediate gratification of these desires yields to mature sexuality, in which postponed gratification, a sense of responsibility, and caring for others all play a part.

Feminists have assailed Freud's male-centered, phallic view of personality development, especially because he also hypothesized that all little girls feel inferior because they do not have a penis. Many people now see *penis envy* as much less central to female personality development than Freud thought it was (Gelman, 1990). In fact, the whole notion that male and female personality development proceeds along similar lines is being challenged. If this is the case, then the unique developmental tasks encountered by girls may leave them with important skills and abilities that were overlooked or minimized in Freud's theory.

Freud's beliefs, particularly his emphasis on sexuality, were not completely endorsed even by members of his own psychoanalytic school. Carl Jung and Alfred Adler, two early associates of Freud, eventually broke with him and formulated their own psychodynamic theories of personality. Jung expanded the scope of the unconscious well beyond the selfish satisfactions of the id. Adler believed that human beings have positive—and conscious— goals that guide their behavior. Other psychodynamic theorists put greater emphasis on the ego and its attempts to gain mastery over the world. These neo-Freudians, principally Karen Horney and Erik Erikson, also focused more on the influence of social interaction on personality.

Carl Jung

How did Carl Jung's view of the unconscious differ from Freud's?

Carl Jung (1875–1961) agreed with many of Freud's tenets, but he expanded the role of the unconscious. Jung contended that libido, or psychic energy, represents *all* the life forces, not just the sexual ones. Both Freud and Jung emphasized the role of the unconscious in determining human behavior. But where Freud viewed the id as a "cauldron of seething excitations" that the ego has to control, Jung saw the unconscious as the ego's source of strength and vitality. He also believed that the unconscious consists of the personal unconscious and the collective unconscious. The **personal unconscious** includes our repressed thoughts, forgotten experiences, and undeveloped ideas, which may enter consciousness if an incident or a sensation triggers their recall.

The **collective unconscious,** Jung's most original concept, comprises the memories and behavior patterns that are inherited from past generations and therefore are shared by all humans. Just as the human body is the product of millions of years of evolution, so too, according to Jung, is the human mind. Over millennia it has developed "thought forms," or collective memories, of experiences that people have had in common since prehistoric times. He called these thought forms **archetypes.** Archetypes appear in our thoughts as mental images. Because all people have mothers, for example, the archetype of "mother" is universally associated with the image of one's own mother, with Mother Earth, and with a protective presence.

Jung felt that specific archetypes play special roles in shaping personality. The **persona** (an archetype whose meaning stems from the Latin word for "mask") is the element of our personality that we project to other people—a shell that grows around our inner self. For some people, the public self so predominates that they lose touch with their inner feelings, leading to personality maladjustments.

Jung also divided people into two general attitude types—introverts and extroverts. **Extroverts** turn their attention to the external world. They are "joiners" who take an active interest in other people and in the events going on around them. **Introverts** are more caught up in their own private worlds. They tend to be unsociable and lack confidence in dealing with

According to Carl Jung, we all inherit from our ancestors collective memories or "thought forms" that people have had in common since the dawn of human evolution. The image of a motherlike figure with protective, embracing arms is one such primordial thought form that stems from the important, nurturing role of women throughout human history. This thought form is depicted here in this Bulgarian clay figure of a goddess that dates back some six or seven thousand years.

Personal unconscious
In Jung's theory of personality, one of the two levels of the unconscious; it contains the individual's repressed thoughts, forgotten experiences, and undeveloped ideas.

Collective unconscious
In Jung's theory of personality, the level of the unconscious that is inherited and common to all members of a species.

Archetypes
In Jung's theory of personality, thought forms common to all human beings, stored in the collective unconscious.

Persona
According to Jung, our public self, the mask we put on to represent ourselves to others.

Extrovert
According to Jung, a person who usually focuses on social life and the external world instead of on his or her internal experience.

Introvert
According to Jung, a person who usually focuses on his or her own thoughts and feelings.

Stevie Wonder, a blind man who became a highly successful musician, illustrates what Alfred Adler referred to as *compensation*.

other people. Everyone, Jung felt, possesses some aspects of both attitude types, but one is usually dominant.

Jung further divided people into *rational individuals*, who regulate their actions by thinking and feeling, and *irrational individuals*, who base their actions on perceptions, whether through the senses (sensation) or through unconscious processes (intuition). Most people exhibit all four psychological functions: thinking, feeling, sensing, and intuiting. Jung felt, however, that one or more of these functions is usually dominant. Thus, the thinking person is rational and logical, and decides on the basis of facts. The feeling person is sensitive to his or her surroundings, acts tactfully, and has a balanced sense of values. The sensing type relies primarily on surface perceptions and rarely uses imagination or deeper understanding. And the intuitive type sees beyond obvious solutions and facts to consider future possibilities.

While Freud emphasized the primacy of the sexual instincts, Jung stressed people's rational and spiritual qualities. And while Freud considered development to be shaped in childhood, Jung thought that psychic development comes to fruition only during middle age. Jung brought a sense of historical continuity to his theories, tracing the roots of human personality back through our ancestral past; yet he also contended that a person moves constantly toward self-realization—toward blending all parts of the personality into a harmonious whole.

Alfred Adler

What did Alfred Adler believe was the major determinant of personality?

Alfred Adler (1870–1937) disagreed sharply with Freud's concept of the conflict between selfish id and the morality-based superego. To Adler, people possess innate positive motives, and they strive for personal and social perfection. One of his earliest theories grew out of personal experience: As a child, Adler was frail and almost died of pneumonia at the age of 5. This early brush with death led him to believe that personality develops through the individual's attempt to overcome physical weaknesses, an effort he called **compensation.** The blind person who, like Stevie Wonder, cultivates particularly acute auditory abilities and the disabled child who, like the late Wilma Rudolph, surmounts the crippling effects of a disease and goes on to become an athlete, exemplify Adler's theory of compensation.

Later on, Adler modified and broadened his views, contending that people seek to overcome *feelings* of inferiority that may or may not have a basis in reality. Such feelings may spring from a child's sense of being inferior to parents, siblings, teachers, or peers. To Adler, birth order made a crucial difference in this sense of inferiority. That is, it does not matter whether second or third children are, in fact, inferior to their older siblings at athletics; what matters is that they tend to *believe* they are. In Adler's view, the attempt to overcome such feelings of inferiority is a principal force in human behavior and a major determinant of adult personality.

Adler did not consider the feeling of inferiority as a negative characteristic per se. Rather, he thought that such feelings often spark positive development and personal growth. Still, some people become so fixated on their feelings of inferiority that they become paralyzed and develop what Adler called an **inferiority complex.**

Later in his life, Adler again shifted his theoretical emphasis in a more positive direction when he concluded that strivings for superiority and perfection were more important to personality development than overcoming feelings of inferiority. He suggested that people strive both for personal perfection and for the perfection of the society to which they belong. In the course of doing so, they set important goals for themselves that guide their behavior.

Unlike Freud, Adler believed that individuals are not controlled by their environment; instead, he contended that we have the capacity to master

Compensation
According to Adler, the person's effort to overcome imagined or real personal weaknesses.

Inferiority complex
In Adler's theory, the fixation on feelings of personal inferiority that results in emotional and social paralysis.

our own fate. The emphasis Adler placed on positive, socially constructive goals and on striving for perfection is in marked contrast to Freud's pessimistic vision of the selfish person locked into eternal conflict with society. Because of this emphasis, Adler has been hailed by many psychologists as the father of humanistic psychology, a topic we will explore in greater depth later in this chapter.

Karen Horney

What major contributions did Karen Horney make to the psychodynamic perspective?

Karen Horney (1885–1952), another psychodynamic personality theorist greatly indebted to Freud, nevertheless took issue with some of his most prominent ideas, especially his analysis of women and his emphasis on sexual instincts. Based on her experience as a practicing therapist in Germany and the United States, Horney concluded that environmental and social factors are the most important influences in shaping personality, and among these, the most pivotal are the human relationships we experience as children.

In Horney's view, Freud overemphasized the sex drive, leading him to present a distorted picture of human relationships. Although Horney believed that sexuality does figure in the development of personality, she thought that nonsexual factors, such as the need for a sense of basic security and the person's response to real or imagined threats, play an even larger role. For example, all people share the need to feel loved and nurtured by their parents, regardless of any sexual feelings they might have about them. Conversely, parents' protective feelings toward their children emerge not only from biological forces but also from the value that society places on the nurturance of children.

For Horney, *anxiety*—an individual's reaction to real or imagined dangers—is a powerful motivating force. Whereas Freud believed that anxiety usually emerges from sexual conflicts, Horney stressed that feelings of anxiety also originate in a variety of nonsexual contexts. In childhood, anxiety arises because children depend on adults for their very survival. Insecure about receiving continued nurturance and protection, children develop inner protections, or defenses, that provide both satisfaction and security. They experience more anxiety when those defenses are threatened.

Anxious adults, according to Horney (1937), adopt one of three coping strategies, or **neurotic trends,** that help them deal with emotional problems and ensure safety, albeit at the expense of personal independence: moving toward people (submission), moving against people (aggression), and moving away from people (detachment). Each person's characteristic reliance on one or another of these strategies is reflected in his or her patterns of behavior, or personality type. A compliant type is an individual who has an overriding need to give in or submit to others and feels safe only when receiving their protection and guidance. This behavior is neurotic, according to Horney, because the resultant friendliness is superficial and masks feelings of aggression and anxiety. In contrast, the aggressive type masks his or her submissive feelings and relates to others in a hostile and domineering manner. The aggressive type, however, is also hiding basic feelings of insecurity and anxiety. Finally, the detached type copes with basic anxiety by withdrawing from other people. This person seems to be saying, "If I withdraw, nothing can hurt me."

Well-adjusted people also experience anxiety and threats to their basic security, but because their childhood environment enabled them to satisfy their basic emotional needs, they were able to develop without becoming trapped in neurotic lifestyles.

Parting company with Freud again, Horney held that cultural forces—including social status and social roles—shape our development more than

Karen Horney, a psychotherapist during the first half of the 20th century, disagreed with Freud's emphasis on sexual instincts. She considered environmental and social factors, especially the relationships we have as children, to be the most important influences on personality.

Neurotic trends
Horney's term for irrational strategies for coping with emotional problems and minimizing anxiety.

"I'm only a **good** dane."

Erik Erikson, another psychodynamic theorist, also stressed the importance of parent-child relationships for shaping personality. His eight-stage theory of personality development is still influential today.

do biological imperatives. She believed that adults can continue to develop and change throughout life. And if biology is not destiny, then personality differences between men and women would have more to do with culture than would anatomy. Horney was a forerunner of contemporary thinkers who believe that culture and society can be changed and, in the process, transform human relationships as well.

Erik Erikson

Erikson's theory focused less on unconscious conflict and more on what factors?

Erik Erikson (1902–1994) studied with Freud in Vienna and was psychoanalyzed by Freud's daughter, Anna. He was another psychodynamic theorist who took a socially oriented view of personality development. Erikson agreed with much of Freud's thinking on sexual development and the influence of libidinal needs on personality. But also important for Erikson was the quality of parent-child relationships, because the family constitutes the child's first brush with society. Only if children feel competent and valuable, in their own eyes and in society's, will they develop a secure sense of identity. In this way, Erikson shifted the focus of Freud's personality theory to ego development. Recent studies of Erikson's concepts of identity, intimacy, and generativity have reaffirmed the importance of these central ideas to personality development (Bradley, 1997; Marcia, 1994; Orlofsky, 1993).

In the last chapter, we examined how some aspects of Erikson's theory have been incorporated in the contemporary view of human development. Presented in the following list is a brief description of Erikson's eight stages of personality development (see **Figure 10–3**). Note especially how the first five of the eight stages correspond to Freud's stages of personality development. According to Erikson, success at each stage depends on the person's adjustments in previous stages:

1. *Trust versus mistrust.* During the first year of life, babies are torn between trusting and not trusting their parents. If their needs are generally met, infants come to trust the environment and themselves. This process leads to faith in the predictability of the environment and optimism about the future. Frustrated infants become suspicious, fearful, and overly concerned with security.

2. *Autonomy versus shame and doubt.* During their first 3 years, as physical development proceeds, children gain increasing autonomy and begin to explore their surroundings. They learn to walk, hold onto things, and control their excretory functions. If the child repeatedly fails to master these skills, self-doubt may take root. One response to self-doubt is the practice of abiding compulsively by fixed routines. At the other extreme is the hostile rejection of all controls, both internal and external. If parents and other adults belittle a child's efforts, the child may also begin to feel shame and may acquire a lasting sense of inferiority.

3. *Initiative versus guilt.* Between the ages of 3 and 6, children become increasingly active, undertaking new projects, manipulating things in the environment, making plans, and conquering new challenges. Parental support and encouragement for these initiatives lead to a sense of joy in exercising initiative and taking on new challenges. However, if the child is scolded for these initiatives, strong feelings of guilt, unworthiness, and resentment may take hold and persist.

4. *Industry versus inferiority.* During the next 6 or 7 years, children encounter a new set of expectations at home and at school. They must learn the skills needed to become well-rounded adults, including personal care, productive work, and independent social living. If children

Industry versus inferiority. A child's challenge during the school years is to begin acquiring the skills needed for a fulfilling adulthood. Success during these years builds confidence to face the future; continued failure or discouragement can fill a child with self-doubt.

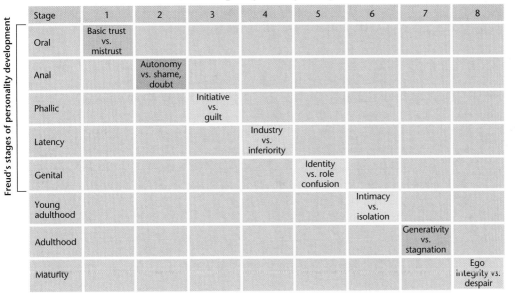

Erikson's stages of personality development

	Stage	1	2	3	4	5	6	7	8
Freud's stages of personality development	Oral	Basic trust vs. mistrust							
	Anal		Autonomy vs. shame, doubt						
	Phallic			Initiative vs. guilt					
	Latency				Industry vs. inferiority				
	Genital					Identity vs. role confusion			
	Young adulthood						Intimacy vs. isolation		
	Adulthood							Generativity vs. stagnation	
	Maturity								Ego integrity vs. despair

FIGURE 10–3

Erikson's 8 stages of personality development.   Each stage involves its own developmental crisis, whose resolution is crucial to adjustment in successive stages. The first 5 of the 8 stages correspond to Freud's stages of personality development.

Source: From *Childhood and Society,* by Erik H. Erikson. Copyright © 1950, 1963 by W. W. Norton & Company, Inc. Renewed 1978 by Erik H. Erikson. Used by permission of W. W. Norton & Company, Inc.

are stifled in their efforts to become part of the adult world, they may conclude that they are inadequate, mediocre, or inferior, and may lose faith in their power to become self-sufficient.

5. *Identity versus role confusion*. At puberty, childhood ends and the responsibilities of adulthood loom just ahead. The critical problem at this stage is to find one's identity. In Erikson's view, identity is achieved by integrating a number of roles—student, sister or brother, friend, and so on—into a coherent pattern that gives the young person a sense of inner continuity or identity. Failure to forge an identity leads to role confusion and despair.

6. *Intimacy versus isolation*. During young adulthood, men and women must resolve a critical new issue: the question of intimacy. To love someone else, Erikson argued, we must have resolved our earlier crises successfully and feel secure in our own identities. To form an intimate relationship, lovers must be trusting, autonomous, and capable of initiative, and must exhibit other hallmarks of maturity. Failure at intimacy brings a painful sense of loneliness and the feeling of being incomplete.

7. *Generativity versus stagnation*. During middle adulthood, roughly between the ages of 25 and 60, the challenge is to remain productive and creative in all aspects of one's life. People who have successfully negotiated the six earlier stages are likely to find meaning and joy in all the major activities of life—career, family, and community. For others, life becomes a drab routine, and they feel dull and resentful.

8. *Integrity versus despair*. With the onset of old age, people must try to come to terms with their approaching death. For some, this is a period of despair at the loss of former roles, such as employee and parent. Yet, according to Erikson, this stage also represents an opportunity to attain full selfhood. By this, he meant an acceptance of one's life, a sense that

it is complete and satisfactory. People who have gained full maturity by resolving the conflicts in all the earlier stages possess the integrity to face death with a minimum of fear.

A Psychodynamic View of Jaylene Smith

How would a psychodynamic theorist view the personality of Jaylene Smith?

According to Freud, personality characteristics such as insecurity, introversion, and feelings of inadequacy and worthlessness often arise from fixation at the phallic stage of development. Thus, had Freud been Jaylene's therapist, he would probably have concluded that Jay has not yet effectively resolved her Electra complex. Working from this premise, he would have hypothesized that Jay's relationship with her father was either very distant and unsatisfying or unusually close and gratifying. We know, of course, that it was the latter.

In all likelihood, Freud would also have asserted that at around age 5 or 6, Jay had become aware that she could not actually marry her father and do away with her mother, as he would say she wished to do. This possibility might account for the fact that fights between Jay and her mother subsided when Jay was about 6 or 7 years of age. Moreover, we know that shortly thereafter, Jay began to experience "strong feelings of loneliness, depression, insecurity, and confusion." Clearly, something important happened in Jay's life when she was 6 or 7.

Finally, the continued coolness of Jay's relationship with her mother and the unusual closeness with her father would probably have confirmed Freud's suspicion that Jay has still not satisfactorily resolved her Electra complex. Freud would have predicted that Jay would have problems making the progression to mature sexual relationships with other men. Jay, of course, is very much aware that she has problems relating to men, at least when these relationships get "serious."

And what does Erikson's theory tell us about Jaylene Smith's personality? Recall that for Erikson, one's success in dealing with later developmental crises depends on how effectively one has resolved earlier crises. Because Jay is having great difficulty in dealing with intimacy (Stage 6), he would have suggested that she is still struggling with problems from earlier developmental stages. Erikson would have looked for the source of these problems in the quality of Jay's relationship with others. We know that her mother subtly communicated her own frustration and dissatisfaction to her children and spent little time on "nonessential" interactions with them. These feelings and behavior patterns would not have instilled in a child the kind of basic trust and sense of security that Erikson believed are essential to the first stage of development. In addition, her relationship with her mother and brothers continued to be less than fully satisfactory. It is not surprising, then, that Jay had some difficulty working through subsequent developmental crises. Although she developed a close and caring relationship with her father, Jay was surely aware that his affection partly depended on her fulfilling the dreams, ambitions, and goals that he had for her.

Evaluating Psychodynamic Theories

How do modern psychologists view the contributions and limitations of the psychodynamic perspective?

Freud's emphasis on the fact that we are not always, or even often, aware of the real causes of our behavior has fundamentally changed the way people view themselves and others. Freud's ideas have also had a lasting impact on history, literature, and the arts. Yet Freud was a product of his time and place. Critics of his theories have pointed out that he was apparently unable to imagine a connection between his female patients' sense of inferiority and their subordinate position in society.

Psychodynamic views have also been criticized because they are based largely on retrospective (backward-looking) accounts of individuals who have sought treatment rather than on research with "healthy" individuals. And although it is often difficult to translate psychodynamic personality theories into hypotheses that can be tested experimentally (Cloninger, 1993), Freud's theory has received limited confirmation from research. For example, people who eat and drink too much tend to mention oral images when interpreting inkblot tests (Bertrand & Masling, 1969; Masling, Rabie, & Blondheim, 1967). Orally fixated people also seem to depend heavily on others, as Freud predicted (Fisher & Greenberg, 1985). Moreover, research confirms an association between specific personality types in childhood and later development of psychological problems. For example, in a longitudinal study, children who were described as inhibited at age 3 were more likely than a control group to be depressed at age 21 (Caspi, Moffitt, Newman, & Silva, 1996). The effectiveness of psychoanalysis as a therapy has also been cited as evidence in support of Freud's theories. Still, as we shall see in Chapter 13, Therapies, psychoanalysis does not seem to be any more or less effective than therapies based on other theories (Stiles, Shapiro, & Elliott, 1986).

Freud's theories have clearly expanded our understanding of personality, or they would not still be so vigorously debated today, more than one hundred years after he proposed them. Whatever their merit as science, psychodynamic theories attempt to explain the root causes of all human behavior. The sheer magnitude of this undertaking helps to account for their lasting attractiveness.

 INTERACTIVE LECTURE **10.1**

WEB QUIZ **10.1**

CHECK YOUR UNDERSTANDING

1. Personality is the pattern of thoughts, feelings, and behaviors that persists over _____ and _____ and that distinguishes one person from another.

Match the following of Freud's terms with the appropriate definition.

_____2. unconscious   a. energy that comes from the sexual instinct

_____3. superego   b. mediator between reality, the superego, and the id

_____4. id   c. unconscious urges seeking expression

_____5. ego   d. ideas and feelings of which we are normally not aware

_____6. libido   e. moral guardian of the ego

Match the following of Jung's terms with the appropriate definition.

_____7. persona   a. typical mental image or mythical representation

_____8. collective unconscious   b. memories and behavior patterns inherited from past generations

_____9. archetype   c. aspect of the personality by which one is known to other people

Match the following of Adler's terms with the appropriate definition.

_____10. inferiority complex   a. fixation on or belief in a negative characteristic

_____11. compensation   b. individual's effort to overcome weaknesses

12. Horney believed that _____ is a stronger source of emotional disturbance than sexual urges.

13. Erikson held a _____ oriented view of personality development.

Answers: 1. time, situations. 2. d. 3. e. 4. c. 5. b. 6. a. 7. c. 8. b. 9. a. 10. a. 11. b. 12. anxiety. 13. socially.

Humanistic Personality Theories

What are the major ways that humanistic personality theory differs from psychodynamic theories?

Freud believed that personality grows out of the resolution of unconscious conflicts and developmental crises. Many of his followers—including some who modified his theory and others who broke away from his circle—also embraced this basic viewpoint. But in the theory of Alfred Adler, we glimpsed at a very different view of human nature. Adler focused on forces that contribute to positive growth and a move toward personal perfection. For these reasons, Adler is sometimes called the first *humanistic* personality theorist.

Humanistic personality theory emphasizes that we are positively motivated and progress toward higher levels of functioning—in other words, that there is more to human existence than dealing with hidden conflicts. Humanistic psychologists believe that life is a process of opening ourselves to the world around us and experiencing joy in living. Humanists stress people's potential for growth and change as well as the ways that they subjectively experience their lives right now, rather than dwelling on how they felt or acted in the past. This approach holds all of us personally responsible for our lives. Finally, humanists also believe that given reasonable life conditions, people will develop in desirable directions (Cloninger, 1993). Adler's concept of striving for perfection laid the groundwork for later humanistic personality theorists such as Abraham Maslow and Carl Rogers. We discussed Maslow's theory of the hierarchy of needs leading to self-actualization in Chapter 8, Motivation and Emotion. We now turn to Rogers's theory of self-actualization.

Carl Rogers

According to Rogers, how can thinking of yourself as self-assured help you to become so?

One of the most prominent humanistic theorists, Carl Rogers (1902–1987), contended that men and women develop their personalities in the service of positive goals. According to Rogers, every organism is born with certain innate capacities, capabilities, or potentialities—"a sort of genetic blueprint, to which substance is added as life progresses" (Maddi, 1989, p. 102). The goal of life, Rogers believed, is to fulfill this genetic blueprint, to become the best of whatever each of us is inherently capable of becoming. Rogers called this biological push toward fulfillment the **actualizing tendency.** Although Rogers maintained that the actualizing tendency characterizes all organisms—plants, animals, and humans—he noted that human beings also form images of themselves, or *self-concepts*. Just as we try to fulfill our inborn biological potential, so, too, we attempt to fulfill our self-concept, our conscious sense of who we are and what we want to do with our lives. Rogers called this striving the **self-actualizing tendency.** If you think of yourself as "intelligent" and "athletic," for example, you will strive to live up to those images of yourself.

When our self-concept is closely matched with our inborn capacities, we are likely to become what Rogers called a **fully functioning person.** Such people are self-directed: They decide for themselves what it is they wish to do and to become, even though their choices may not always be sound ones. They are not unduly swayed by other people's expectations for them. Fully functioning people are also open to experience—to their own feelings as well as to the world and other people around them—and thus find themselves "increasingly willing to be, with greater accuracy and depth, that self which [they] most truly [are]" (Rogers, 1961, pp. 175–176).

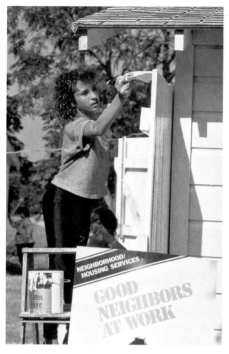

Carl Rogers believed that the goal of life is to fulfill our innate potential, which ideally comes to be reflected in the image we have of ourselves. This young woman's work painting houses for the poor suggests that she sees herself as kind and caring and is striving to reflect that image in her actions. In Rogers's view she may be on the way to becoming a self-actualized person.

Humanistic personality theory
Any personality theory that asserts the fundamental goodness of people and their striving toward higher levels of functioning.

Actualizing tendency
According to Rogers, the drive of every organism to fulfill its biological potential and become what it is inherently capable of becoming.

Self-actualizing tendency
According to Rogers, the drive of human beings to fulfill their self-concepts, or the images they have of themselves.

Fully functioning person
According to Rogers, an individual whose self-concept closely resembles his or her inborn capacities or potentials.

According to Rogers, people tend to become more fully functioning if they are brought up with **unconditional positive regard,** or the experience of being treated with warmth, respect, acceptance, and love regardless of their own feelings, attitudes, and behaviors.

But often parents and other adults offer children what Rogers called **conditional positive regard:** They value and accept only certain aspects of the child. The acceptance, warmth, and love that the child receives from others then depends on the child's behaving in certain ways and fulfilling certain conditions. In the process, self-concept comes to resemble the inborn capacity less and less, and the child's life deviates from the genetic blueprint.

When people lose sight of their inborn potential, they become constricted, rigid, and defensive. They feel threatened and anxious, and experience considerable discomfort and uneasiness. Because their lives are directed toward what other people want and value, they are unlikely to experience much real satisfaction in life. At some point, they may realize that they don't really know who they are or what they want.

A Humanistic View of Jaylene Smith

How would humanistic theorists view the development of Jaylene Smith's personality?

Humanistic personality theory would focus on the discrepancy between Jay's self-concept and her inborn capacities. For example, Rogers would point out that Jay is intelligent and achievement-oriented but nevertheless feels that she doesn't "deserve to be a doctor," worries about whether she will ever be "truly happy," and remembers that when she was 13, she never was able to be herself and really express her feelings, even with a good friend. Her unhappiness, fearfulness, loneliness, insecurity, and other dissatisfactions similarly stem from Jay's inability to become what she "most truly is." Rogers would suspect that other people in Jay's life made acceptance and love conditional on her living up to their ideas of what she should become. We know that for most of her life, Jay's father was her primary source of positive regard. Very possibly he conditioned his love for Jay on her living up to his goals for her.

Evaluating Humanistic Theories

What have humanistic theories contributed to our understanding of personality?

The central tenet of most humanistic personality theories—that the overriding purpose of the human condition is to realize one's potential—is difficult if not impossible to verify scientifically. The resulting lack of scientific evidence and rigor is one of the major criticisms of these theories. In addition, some critics claim that humanistic theories present an overly optimistic view of human beings and fail to take into account the evil in human nature. Others contend that the humanistic view fosters self-centeredness and narcissism, and reflects Western values of individual achievement rather than universal human potential.

Nonetheless, Maslow and, especially, Rogers did attempt to test some aspects of their theories scientifically. For example, Rogers studied the discrepancy between the way people perceived themselves and the way they ideally wanted to be. He discovered that people whose real selves differed considerably from their *ideal* selves were more likely to be unhappy and dissatisfied.

Unconditional positive regard
In Rogers's theory, the full acceptance and love of another person regardless of our behavior.

Conditional positive regard
In Rogers's theory, acceptance and love that are dependent on behaving in certain ways and on fulfilling certain conditions.

 INTERACTIVE LECTURE **10.2**

WEB QUIZ 10.2

CHECK YOUR UNDERSTANDING

1. Humanistic personality theory emphasizes that we are _____ _____, whereas psychodynamic personality theory emphasizes _____ _____.
2. Rogers believed that a person strives to live up to and fulfill a self-image; he called this a person's _____ - _____ tendency.
3. When children feel they are loved regardless of their behaviors, Rogers would say that they are receiving _____ _____ _____ from others.

Indicate whether the following are true (T) or false (F).

4. _____ The goal of life, Rogers believed, is to become the best of whatever each of us is inherently capable of becoming.
5. _____ Our self-concept is our inborn biological potential.
6. _____ When people lose sight of their inborn potential, they are unlikely to experience much satisfaction.

Answers: 1. positively motivated, hidden conflicts. **2.** self-actualizing. **3.** unconditional positive regard. **4.** (T). **5.** (F). **6.** (T).

Trait Theories

What is the key focus of trait theories?

The personality theories that we have examined so far all emphasize early childhood experiences, and all attempt to explain the varieties of human personality. Other personality theorists focus on the present, describing the ways in which already developed adult personalities differ from one another. These *trait theorists* assert that people differ according to the degree to which they possess certain **personality traits,** such as dependency, anxiety, aggressiveness, and sociability. Although traits cannot be observed directly, we can infer a trait from how a person behaves. If, for example, someone consistently throws parties and regularly participates in groups, we might conclude that the person possesses a high degree of sociability.

Psychologist Gordon Allport believed that traits—or "dispositions," as he called them—are literally encoded in the nervous system as structures that guide consistent behavior across a wide variety of situations. Allport also believed that whereas traits describe behaviors that are common to many people, each individual personality consists of a unique group of traits (Allport & Odbert, 1936). Raymond Cattell (1965), using a statistical technique called **factor analysis,** has demonstrated that various traits tend to cluster in groups. For example, a person who is described as persevering or determined is also likely to be thought of as responsible, ordered, attentive, and stable, and probably would not be described as frivolous, neglectful, and changeable (Cattell & Kline, 1977). According to Cattell, each individual personality consists of a relatively unique constellation of sixteen or so basic traits.

Other theorists thought that Cattell used too many traits to describe personality. Eysenck (1976) argued that personality could be reduced to three basic dimensions: *emotional stability, introversion-extroversion,* and *psychoticism*. According to Eysenck, *emotional stability* refers to how well a person controls emotions. On a continuum, individuals at one end of this trait would be seen as poised, calm, and composed,

Personality traits
Dimensions or characteristics on which people differ in distinctive ways.

Factor analysis
A statistical technique that identifies groups of related objects; used by Cattell to identify clusters of traits.

According to trait theorists, this woman would probably rate high on the traits of cheerfulness, extroversion, friendliness, and sociability. Trait theorists seek to identify sets of human characteristics on the basis of which personality can be assessed.

whereas people at the other end might be described as anxious, nervous, and excitable. *Introversion-extroversion* refers to the degree to which a person is inwardly or outwardly oriented. At one end of this dimension would be the socially outgoing, talkative, and affectionate people, known as *extroverts*. *Introverts*—generally described as reserved, silent, shy, and socially withdrawn—would be at the other extreme. Eysenck used the term *psychoticism* to describe people characterized by insensitivity and uncooperativeness at one end and warmth, tenderness, and helpfulness at the other end.

The Big Five

What five basic traits describe most differences in personality?

Although early trait studies have sometimes disagreed about the number of traits needed to describe personality, recently a consensus has emerged on the **"Big Five"** model of personality (Botwin & Buss, 1989; Goldberg, 1993; Tupes and Christal, 1961; Wiggins, 1996). According to this *five-factor* model, five traits, along with their various facets, are thought to capture the most important dimensions of human personality (Funder, 1991; Jang, Livesley, McCrae, Angleitner, & Riemann, 1998; McCrae & Costa, 1996).

These Big Five personality dimensions—*extroversion, emotional stability, agreeableness, conscientiousness* (sometimes called dependability), and *openness to experience* (sometimes called *culture* or intellect)—along with their thirty associated facets, are not an exhaustive listing of all aspects of personality. Rather, they represent a broad sample of important traits (Costa & McCrae, 1992, 1995). Nevertheless, they do seem to describe most important individual differences in personality (see **Table 10–1**: The "Big Five" Dimensions of Personality). Support for the universal nature of the five-factor theory comes from a variety of sources. It appears that the traits exist across cultures (McCrae & Costa, 1997) and that they have a strong genetic basis (McCrae, Costa, & John, 1998) (see *Understanding Ourselves: The Genetic Basis of Personality Traits*).

It is interesting that these same personality traits apparently exist in a number of species besides humans. The Big Five, along with dominance

Big Five
Five traits or basic dimensions currently thought to be of central importance in describing personality.

TABLE 10-1	THE "BIG FIVE" DIMENSIONS OF PERSONALITY
Traits	**Facets of Each Big Five Trait**
Extroversion	warmth, gregariousness, assertiveness, activity, excitement-seeking, positive emotions
Agreeableness	trust, straightforwardness, altruism, compliance, modesty, tender-mindedness
Conscientiousness/Dependability	competence, order, dutifulness, achievement-striving, self-discipline, deliberation
Emotional Stability	anxiety, hostility, depression, self-consciousness, impulsiveness, vulnerability
Openness to Experience/Culture/Intellect	fantasy, aesthetics, feelings, actions, ideas, values

Source: Adapted from Jang, K. L., Livesley, W. J., McCrae, R. R., Angleitner, A., & Riemann, R. (1998). Heritability of facet-level traits in a cross-cultural twin sample: Support for a hierarchical model of personality. *Journal of Personality and Social Psychology*, 74, 1556–1565. Table 3, p. 1560. Copyright © 1998 by the American Psychological Association. Adapted with permission.

UNDERSTANDING OURSELVES

The Genetic Basis of Personality Traits

Recent evidence shows that not only the Big Five but also many of their individual facets are strongly influenced by heredity. Although some early theorists (Eysenck, 1947) suggested that physiological mechanisms underlie basic personality traits, only recently has solid evidence begun to support this idea (Eaves, Heath, Neale, Hewitt, & Martin, 1993; Heath, Cloninger, & Martin, 1994; Jang, Livesley, McCrae, Angleitner, & Riemann, 1998; Plomin, 1994).

Behavior genetic research relies strongly on twin studies to tease apart the relative contribution of heredity and environment. Genetic and environmental influences have been found to be similar in both Canadian and German sets of twins. In other words, genes seem

to affect personality, and they seem to do so to the same extent in at least two different cultures (Jang et al., 1998).

Researchers have also found that the Big Five dimensions are all substantially heritable, and to an equal degree (Loehlin, McCrae, Costa, & John, 1998). For the Big Five traits, heritability ranges from 41 percent to 61 percent (Jang, Livesley, & Vernon, 1996). What are the implications of these findings? There are several, although it is important to keep in mind that saying a particular trait such as extraversion has a genetic component does not mean that researchers have found a gene for extraversion. Nor are they likely to, because genes represent a code for specific proteins, not complex personality traits. It does mean,

however, that the Big Five traits and their facets may be hardwired into the human species rather than being a product of culture. It also most likely means that complex traits such as extraversion are influenced by many different genes, not just one. That possibility would explain why individual traits are normally distributed throughout the population, such as the physical traits of eye color or hair type, instead of forming distinct types. Many genes—perhaps thousands of them—surely work in combination to account for such complex traits. Though the precise role that genes play in personality is still far from clear, most psychologists would agree that biological factors contribute significantly to the development of most personality traits.

and activity, have been used to describe personality characteristics in species including gorillas, chimpanzees, rhesus and vervet monkeys, hyenas, dogs, cats, and pigs (Gosling & John, 1999).

Finally, the Big Five dimensions of personality may have some important real-world applications—particularly as they relate to employment decisions (Hogan, Hogan, & Roberts, 1996). For example, the dimensions of conscientiousness and emotional stability reliably predicted job performance in a wide variety of occupational settings (Ones, Viswesvaran, & Schmidt, 1993). And, as you would expect, agreeableness and emotional stability predicted performance for employees in customer service positions (McDaniel & Frei, 1994). Thus, the Big Five dimensions of personality show promise as reliable predictors of job performance, especially when other criteria such as technical skills and experience are also considered (Barrick & Mount, 1991; Hogan et al., 1996).

 10.1

A Trait View of Jaylene Smith

How would trait theorists describe Jaylene Smith's personality?

A psychologist working from the trait perspective would infer certain traits from Jay's behavior. When we observe that Jay chose at an early age to become a doctor, did well academically year after year, and graduated first in her medical-school class, it seems reasonable to infer a trait of determination or persistence to account for her behavior. Taking the Big Five perspective, it seems that Jaylene's personality is high in conscientiousness but perhaps low in emotional stability and extroversion. These relatively few traits account for a great deal of Jay's behavior, and they also provide a thumbnail sketch of what Jay is like.

Evaluating Trait Theories

What major contributions have trait theories made to our understanding of personality?

Traits are the language that we commonly use to describe other people (e.g., as shy or insecure or arrogant). Thus, the trait view of personality has considerable commonsense appeal. Moreover, it is easier scientifically to study personality traits than to study such things as self-actualization and unconscious motives. But trait theories have several shortcomings (Eysenck, 1993; Kroger & Wood, 1993). First, they are primarily descriptive: They seek to describe the basic dimensions of personality but generally do not try to explain causes (Funder, 1991). As you can see from the trait view of Jaylene Smith, trait theory tells us little about why she is the way she is.

In addition, some critics argue that it is dangerous to reduce human complexity to just a few traits (Mischel & Shoda, 1995). Moreover, although the Big Five model is well supported by research, some disagreement remains among psychologists about whether a five-factor model is the best way to describe the basic traits of personality (Almagor, Tillegen, & Waller, 1995; Eysenck, 1992; Lubenski, 2000; Mershon & Gorsuch, 1988).

Finally, some psychologists question whether traits can really describe and predict behavior. Are "agreeable" people always agreeable? Are they agreeable in all situations? Of course not. So then, how useful is the trait designation of "agreeable" to begin with? The issue of consistency in human behavior has long intrigued personality theorists who are interested in the interaction of personality traits with the person's social environment. For this group, behavior is a product of the person *and* the situation. That interaction, the blending of the self and the social, is the focus of cognitive–social learning theorists.

 INTERACTIVE LECTURE **10.3**

WEB QUIZ **10.3**

CHECK YOUR UNDERSTANDING

1. Trait theorists assert that people differ according to the degree to which they possess certain _____ _____.
2. Eysenck stated that personality could be reduced to three basic dimensions: ___ ____, ____-____, and ____.
3. What are the Big Five traits?
4. There is evidence that suggests that personality is almost entirely due to environmental factors. Is this statement true (T) or false (F)?

Answers: 1. personality traits. 2. emotional stability, introversion-extroversion, psychoticism. 3. extroversion, agreeableness, conscientiousness, emotional stability, and openness to experience. 4. F.

Cognitive–Social Learning Theories

How can your expectancies affect your current attitudes and behaviors?

Locus of Control and Self-Efficacy

How does one's locus of control affect self-efficacy?

Another way of looking at personality focuses on the set of personal standards unique to each individual, growing out of our own life history.

People with an internal locus of control are convinced they can control their own fate. This student believes that by studying he can be successful in school.

Cognitive–social learning theory argues that behavior stems from the interaction of *cognitions* (how we think about a situation and how we view our behavior in that situation), *learning and past experiences* (including reinforcement, punishment, and modeling), and the *immediate environment*. Albert Bandura (1977, 1986, 1997) asserts that people evaluate a situation according to certain internal **expectancies,** such as personal preferences, and this evaluation affects their behavior. Environmental feedback that follows the actual behavior, in turn, influences future expectancies. In this way, expectancies guide behavior in a given situation, and the results of the behavior in that situation shape expectancies in future situations. For example, two young women trying a video game for the first time may experience the situation quite differently, even if their scores are similarly low. One may find the experience fun and be eager to gain the skills necessary to go on to the next level of games, whereas the other may be disheartened by getting a low score, may assume that she will never be any good at video games, and so may never play again. Similarly, a person who interprets math problems as opportunities to succeed will approach the math SAT with a different expectancy than someone who sees math problems as opportunities to fail.

Note that in our example, the two young women approach the experience with different expectancies. A person's **locus of control** is a prevalent expectancy, or cognitive strategy, by which we evaluate situations (Rotter, 1954). People with an *internal locus* of control are convinced they can control their own fate. They believe that through hard work, skill, and training, they can find reinforcements and avoid punishments. People with an *external locus* of control do not believe that they control their fate. Instead, they are convinced that chance, luck, and the behavior of others determine their destiny and that they are helpless to change the course of their lives (Strickland, 1989). Some evidence suggests that drug use, inactivity among people suffering from depression, and school truancy are linked to an external locus of control (Lefcourt, 1992). In all these cases, people do not believe that making an effort to be active or productive will bring about any positive consequences.

Two of the leading cognitive–social learning theorists, Bandura and Rotter, believe that expectancies become part of a person's *explanatory style*, which, in turn, greatly influences behavior. Explanatory style, for example, separates optimists from pessimists. It is what causes two beginners who get the same score on a video game to respond so differently.

Explanatory style appears to develop early and can significantly affect behavior and life outcomes (Nolen-Hoeksema, Girgus, & Seligman, 1986). In a now-famous study, researchers tracked 99 students from the Harvard graduation classes of 1939 to 1944. The men were interviewed about their experiences and underwent physical checkups every five years. When researchers analyzed the men's interviews for signs of pessimism or optimism, they found that the explanatory style demonstrated in those interviews predicted the state of an individual's health decades later. Those men who were optimists at age 25 tended to be healthier at age 65, whereas the health of the pessimists had begun to deteriorate at about age 45 (Peterson, Vaillant, & Seligman, 1988). Although the reasons for these findings are not yet clear, a separate investigation that used a checklist about health habits found that the pessimists in this study were less careful about their health than were optimists. They tended to smoke and drink more, and reported twice as many colds and visits to doctors.

Explanatory style dovetails with **self-efficacy,** Bandura's way of describing the degree to which we feel we can meet our personal goals. Suppose that

Cognitive–social learning theories
Personality theories that view behavior as the product of the interaction of cognitions, learning and past experiences, and the immediate environment.

Expectancies
In Bandura's view, what a person anticipates in a situation or as a result of behaving in certain ways.

Locus of control
According to Rotter, an expectancy about whether reinforcement is under internal or external control.

Self-efficacy
According to Bandura, the expectancy that one's efforts will be successful.

a math professor has a son and a daughter. Say that the son's mathematical aptitude is low, whereas the daughter is especially gifted in math. Let's say also that both children develop an expectation, a **performance standard,** to do well in mathematics. The son will probably feel incapable of meeting his standard, whereas the daughter will almost certainly feel confident about meeting hers. In Bandura's terms, the son will probably develop a low sense of self-efficacy; he will feel incapable of meeting his life goals. The daughter will likely develop a strong sense of self-efficacy. In turn, these explanatory styles will have a profound effect on their behavior.

In distinguishing between self-efficacy and locus of control, remember that while self-efficacy expectancies are concerned with whether we think that we can actually perform a given act, locus of control expectancies are concerned with whether we think that our actions are linked to reinforcements and punishments.

If all this sounds pessimistic and deterministic, we must point out that Bandura also emphasizes that people have the power of self-determination (1986). For example, the frustrated son in the preceding example might modify his behavior and try to excel in other areas. In this way, performance standards may be modified by experience, affecting future behavior. For Bandura, human personality develops out of this ongoing interaction among personal standards (learned by observation and reinforcement), situations, and behavioral consequences.

A Cognitive–Social Learning View of Jaylene Smith

How would cognitive–social learning theorists describe the factors that shaped Jaylene Smith's personality?

Jaylene may have *learned* to be shy and introverted because she was rewarded for spending much time by herself studying. Her father probably encouraged her devotion to her studies; certainly she earned the respect of her teachers. Moreover, long hours of studying helped her to avoid the discomfort that she felt being around other people for long periods. Reinforcement may also have shaped Jay's self-discipline and her need to achieve academically.

In addition, at least some aspects of Jaylene's personality were formed by watching her parents and brothers and by learning subtle lessons from these family interactions. Her aggressive behavior with boyfriends, for example, may have grown out of seeing her parents fight. As a young child, she may have observed that some people deal with conflict by means of outbursts. Moreover, as Bandura's concept of self-efficacy would predict, Jay surely noticed that her father, a successful medical researcher, enjoyed and prospered in both his career and his family life, whereas her mother's two jobs as homemaker and store manager left her frustrated and tired. This contrast may have contributed to Jay's interest in medicine and to mixed feelings about establishing a close relationship that might lead to marriage.

Evaluating Cognitive–Social Learning Theories

What contributions have cognitive–social learning theories made to our understanding of personality, and what are their limitations?

Cognitive–social learning theories of personality seem to have great potential. They put mental processes back at the center of personality, and they focus on conscious behavior and experience. We can define and scientifically study the key concepts of these theories, such as self-efficacy and locus of control; that is not true of the key concepts of psychodynamic and humanistic theories. Moreover, cognitive–social learning theories help explain why people behave inconsistently, an area in which trait approaches

Performance standards
In Bandura's theory, standards that people develop to rate the adequacy of their own behavior in a variety of situations.

fall short. Cognitive–social learning theories of personality have also spawned useful therapies that help people recognize and change a negative sense of self-efficacy or explanatory style. In particular, as we will see in Chapter 13 (Therapies), these therapies have helped people overcome depression. Self-efficacy theory has also been embraced by management theorists because of its practical implications for work performance. Many studies, conducted over more than twenty years, have shown a positive correlation between self-efficacy and performance in workplaces, schools, and clinical settings.

It is still too early to say how well cognitive–social learning theories account for the complexity of human personality. Some critics point out that the benefit of hindsight allows us to explain any behavior as the product of certain cognitions, but that doesn't mean those cognitions were the *causes*—or at least the sole causes—of the behavior. Just as there is great diversity in the way that psychologists view personality, psychologists also disagree on the best way to measure or assess personality, the topic we turn to next.

INTERACTIVE LECTURE **10.4**

WEB QUIZ **10.4**

CHECK YOUR UNDERSTANDING

1. Cognitive–social learning theorists believe that people internally organize their ____ and ____ to guide their behavior.
2. In Bandura's view, what a person anticipates in a situation or as a result of behaving in certain ways is known as ____.
3. Cognitive–social learning theorists believe that locus of control is a cognitive strategy by which people ____ situations.

Match the following terms with the appropriate definition.

____4. internal locus of control	a. separates optimists from pessimists
____5. external locus of control	b. degree to which we believe we can meet our goals
____6. explanatory style	c. belief that luck controls destiny
____7. self-efficacy	d. belief that people control their own fate

Answers: 1. expectancies, values. 2. expectancies. 3. evaluate. 4. d. 5. c. 6. a. 7. b.

Personality Assessment

How do psychologists measure personality?

In some ways, testing personality is much like testing intelligence. In both cases, we are trying to measure something intangible and invisible. And in both cases, a "good test" is one that is both *reliable* and *valid*: It gives dependable and consistent results, and it measures what it claims to measure (See Chapter 7: Cognition and Mental Abilities). But there are special difficulties in measuring personality.

Because personality reflects *characteristic* behavior, in assessing personality, we are not interested in someone's *best* behavior. We are interested in *typical* behavior—how a person usually behaves in ordinary situations. Further complicating the measurement process, such factors as fatigue, the desire to impress the examiner, and the fear of being tested can profoundly affect a person's behavior in a personality-assessment situation. For the intricate task of measuring personality, psychologists use four basic tools: the personal interview; direct observation of behavior; objective tests; and projective tests. The tools most closely associated with each of the major theories of personality are shown in the Summary Table.

SUMMARY TABLE

THEORIES OF PERSONALITY

Theory	Roots of Personality	Methods of Assessing
Psychodynamic	Unconscious thoughts, feelings, motives, and conflicts; repressed problem from early childhood.	Projective tests, personal interviews.
Humanistic	A drive toward personal growth and higher levels of functioning.	Objective tests, personal interviews.
Trait	Relatively permanent dispositions within the individual that cause the person to think, feel, and act in characteristic ways.	Objective tests.
Social Learning	Determined by past reinforcement and punishment as well as by observing what happens to other people.	Interviews, objective tests, observations.

The Personal Interview

What are the purposes of structured and unstructured interviews?

An interview is a conversation with a purpose: to obtain information from the person being interviewed. Interviews are often used in clinical settings to find out, for example, why someone is seeking treatment and to help diagnose the person's problem. Such interviews are generally *unstructured*—that is, the interviewer asks the client questions about any material that comes up and asks follow-up questions whenever appropriate. The interviewer may also pay attention to the person's behavior—manner of speaking, poise, or tenseness when certain topics are raised. The most effective interviewers are warm, interested in what the respondent has to say, calm, relaxed, and confident (Feshbach & Weiner, 1982).

When conducting systematic research on personality, investigators more often rely on the *structured* interview. Here the order and content of the questions are fixed, and the interviewer adheres to the set format. Although less personal, this kind of interview allows the interviewer to obtain comparable information from everyone interviewed. Generally speaking, structured interviews draw out information about sensitive topics that might not come up in an unstructured interview.

Direct Observation

What are the advantages and limits of the observational method?

Another way to find out how a person usually behaves is to observe that person's actions in everyday situations over a long period. Behaviorists and social learning theorists prefer this method of assessing personality because it allows them to see how situation and environment influence behavior and to note the range of behaviors that the person is capable of exhibiting.

In *direct observation*, observers watch people's behavior firsthand. Ideally, their unbiased accounts of the subjects' behavior paint an accurate picture of that behavior, but an observer runs the risk of misinterpreting the true meaning of an act. For example, the observer may think that children are being hostile when they are merely protecting themselves from the class bully. An expensive and time-consuming method of research, direct observation may also yield faulty results if, as noted earlier, the presence of the observer affects people's behavior. Whatever the method used, systematic observation allows psychologists to look at aspects of personality (e.g., traits, moods, or motives) as they are expressed in real life (Ozer & Reise, 1994).

FIGURE 10–4
Inkblots used in the Rorschach projective test.

Objective tests
Personality tests that are administered and scored in a standard way.

Sixteen Personality Factor Questionnaire
Objective personality test created by Cattell that provides scores on the sixteen traits he identified.

NEO-PI-R
An objective personality test designed to assess the Big Five personality traits.

Minnesota Multiphasic Personality Inventory (MMPI)
The most widely used objective personality test, originally intended for psychiatric diagnosis.

Projective tests
Personality tests, such as the Rorschach inkblot test, consisting of ambiguous or unstructured material.

Objective Tests

Why are objective tests preferred by trait theorists?

To avoid depending on the skills of an interviewer or the interpretive abilities of an observer in assessing personality, psychologists devised **objective tests,** or personality inventories. Generally, these are written tests that are administered and scored according to a standard procedure. The tests are usually constructed so that the person merely chooses a "yes" or "no" response, or selects one answer among many choices. Objective tests are the most widely used tools for assessing personality, but they have two serious drawbacks. First, they rely entirely on self-report. If people do not know themselves well, or cannot be entirely objective about themselves, or want to paint a particular picture of themselves, self-report questionnaire results have limited usefulness (Funder, 1991). In fact, some research indicates that peers who know you well often do a better job characterizing you than you do yourself (Funder, 1995). Second, if people have taken other personality questionnaires, their familiarity with the test format may affect their responses to the present questionnaire. This is a particular problem on college campuses, where students are likely to participate in many research studies that rely on personality inventories (Council, 1993).

Because of their interest in accurately measuring personality traits, trait theorists favor objective tests. Cattell, for example, developed a 374-question personality test called the **Sixteen Personality Factor Questionnaire.** As to be expected, the 16PF (as it is usually called) provides scores on each of the sixteen traits originally identified by Cattell. More recently, objective tests such as the **NEO-PI-R** have been developed to assess the Big Five major personality traits (Costa & McCrae, 1992, 1995). The NEO-PI-R breaks down each of the Big Five traits into six facets and yields scores for each facet and each trait. For each of over 200 questions, the person indicates to what degree he or she disagrees with the statement made. The primary use of the test is to assess the personality of a normal adult.

The most widely used and thoroughly researched objective personality test, however, is the **Minnesota Multiphasic Personality Inventory (MMPI)** (Butcher & Rouse, 1996). The MMPI was originally developed as an aid in diagnosing psychiatric disorders (Hathaway & McKinley, 1942). The person taking the test is asked to answer "true," "false," or "cannot say" to such questions as "Once in a while I put off until tomorrow what I ought to do today," "At times I feel like swearing," and "There are persons who are trying to steal my thoughts and ideas." Some of the items repeat very similar thoughts in different words: For example, "I tire easily" and "I feel weak all over much of the time." This redundancy provides a check on the possibility of false or inconsistent answers.

Researchers have derived several personality scales from this test, including ratings for masculinity-femininity, depression, and hypochondriasis. These elements of the MMPI are highly regarded as useful tools for differentiating among psychiatric populations (Anastasi & Urbina, 1997). The MMPI is also used to differentiate among more normal personality dimensions, such as extroversion-introversion and assertiveness, but with less success.

Projective Tests

What do projective tests try to measure?

Psychodynamic theorists, who believe that people are often unaware of the determinants of their behavior, tend to discount objective personality tests that rely on self-reports. Instead, they prefer **projective tests** of personality. Most projective tests consist of simple ambiguous stimuli that can elicit an unlimited number of responses. The test-taker looks at some essentially meaningless material or at a vague picture. Then the test-taker explains what the material means to him or her. Or the person may be asked to complete a sentence fragment, such as "When I see myself in the mirror, I . . . " The tests offer no clues regarding the "best way" to interpret the material or to complete the sentence.

Projective tests have several advantages: Because these tests are flexible and can even be treated as games or puzzles, people can take them in a relaxed atmosphere, without the tension and self-consciousness that sometimes accompany objective tests. Often, the person being examined doesn't even know the true purpose of the test, so responses are less likely to be faked. Some psychologists believe that the projective test can uncover unconscious thoughts and fantasies, such as latent sexual or family problems. In any event, the accuracy and usefulness of projective tests depend largely on the skill of the examiner in eliciting and interpreting responses.

The **Rorschach test** is the best known and one of the most frequently used projective personality tests (Ball, Archer, & Imhof, 1994; C. E. Watkins, Campbell, Nieberding, & Hallmark, 1995). It is named for Hermann Rorschach, a Swiss psychiatrist who in 1921 published the results of his research on interpreting inkblots as a key to personality (see **Figure 10–4**). Each inkblot design is printed on a separate card and is unique in form, color, shading, and white space. People are asked to specify what they see in each blot. Test instructions are minimal, so people's responses will be completely their own. After interpreting all the blots, the person goes over the cards again with the examiner and explains which part of each blot prompted each response. The MMPI appears to be more valid than the Rorschach (Garb, Florio, & Grove, 1998).

Somewhat more demanding is the **Thematic Apperception Test (TAT).** It consists of 20 cards picturing one or more human figures in deliberately ambiguous situations (see **Figure 10–5**). A person is shown the cards one by one and asked to write a complete story about each picture, including what led up to the scene depicted, what the characters are doing at that moment, what their thoughts and feelings are, and what the outcome will be.

Although various scoring systems have been devised for the TAT (Hibbard, Farmer, Wells, Difillipo, & Barry, 1994), examiners usually interpret the stories in the light of their personal knowledge of the storyteller. One key in evaluating the TAT is whether the person identifies with the hero or heroine of the story or with one of the minor characters. Then the examiner determines what the attitudes and feelings of the character reveal about the storyteller. The examiner also assesses each story for content, language, originality, organization, and consistency. Certain themes, such as the need for affection, repeated failure, or parental domination, may recur in several plots.

Both the Rorschach and the TAT may open up a conversation between a clinician and a person who is reluctant or unable to talk about personal problems. Both tests may also provide useful information about motives, events, or feelings of which the person is unaware. However, because projective tests are often not administered in a standard fashion, their validity and reliability have been called into question (Dawes, 1994; Wierzbicki, 1993). As a result, their use has declined since the 1970s. Still, when interpreted by a skilled examiner, these tests can offer insight into a person's attitudes and feelings.

FIGURE 10–5

A sample item from the Thematic Apperception Test (TAT). In the photo, the person is making up a story to explain the scene in the painting above. The examiner then interprets and evaluates the person's story for what it reveals about her personality.

Source: Reprinted by permission of the publisher from Thematic Apperception Test by Henry A. Murray, Cambridge, MA: Harvard University Press, Copyright © 1943 by the President and Fellows of Harvard College, © 1971 by Henry A. Murray.

Rorschach test
A projective test composed of ambiguous inkblots; the way people interpret the blots is thought to reveal aspects of their personality.

Thematic Apperception Test (TAT)
A projective test composed of ambiguous pictures about which a person is asked to write a complete story.

INTERACTIVE LECTURE **10.5**

WEB QUIZ **10.5** ✔

CHECK YOUR UNDERSTANDING

1. _____ tests require people to fill out questionnaires, which are then scored according to a standardized procedure.

2. In _____ tests of personality, people are shown ambiguous stimuli and asked to describe them or to make up a story about them.

Match the following tests with the appropriate description.

_____3. objective tests

_____4. MMPI

_____5. Rorschach

_____6. TAT

a. most widely used and researched personality test

b. pictures of people in ambiguous situations

c. projective test using pictures of inkblots

d. designed to eliminate researcher bias

Answers: 1. Objective. 2. projective. 3. d. 4. a. 5. c. 6. b.

KEY TERMS

personality, p. 366

Psychodynamic theories

psychodynamic theories, p. 367

unconscious, p. 367

psychoanalysis, p. 367

id, p. 368

pleasure principle, p. 368

ego, p. 368

reality principle, p. 368

superego, p. 369

ego ideal, p. 369

libido, p. 370

fixation, p. 370

oral stage, p. 370

anal stage, p. 370

phallic stage, p. 370

Oedipus complex, p. 370

Electra complex, p. 370

latency period, p. 370

genital stage, p. 370

personal unconscious, p. 371

collective unconscious, p. 371

archetypes, p. 371

persona, p. 371

extroverts, p. 371

introverts, p. 371

compensation, p. 372

inferiority complex, p. 372

neurotic trends, p. 373

Humanistic personality theories

humanistic personality theory, p. 378

actualizing tendency, p. 378

self-actualizing tendency, p. 378

fully functioning person, p. 378

unconditional positive regard, p. 379

conditional positive regard, p. 379

Trait theories

personality traits, p. 380

factor analysis, p. 380

Big Five, p. 381

Cognitive–social learning theories

cognitive–social learning theory, p. 384

expectancies, p. 384

locus of control, p. 384

self-efficacy, p. 384

performance standard, p. 385

Personality assessment

objective tests, p. 388

Sixteen Personality Factor Questionnaire (16PF), p. 388

NEO-PI-R, p. 388

Minnesota Multiphasic Personality Inventory (MMPI), p. 388

projective tests, p. 388

Rorschach test, p. 389

Thematic Apperception Test (TAT), p. 389

CHAPTER REVIEW

Psychodynamic Theories

What ideas do all psychodynamic theories have in common? **Psychodynamic theories** of **personality** consider behavior to be the result of psychological dynamics within the individual. Often these dynamics are **unconscious** processes.

When Freud proposed that the sexual instinct is the basis of behavior, how was he defining "sexual instinct"? Freud used the term *sexual instinct* to refer to the desire for virtually any form of pleasure. Freud called energy generated by the sexual instinct **libido.** As infants mature, their libido becomes focused on different sensitive parts of the body. A **fixation** occurs if a child is deprived of or receives too much pleasure from the part of the body that dominates one of the five developmental stages—**oral, anal, phallic, latency,** and **genital**—and some sexual energy may lodge in that part of the body. Strong attachment to the parent of the opposite sex and jealousy of the parent of the same sex—which develops during the phallic stage—is termed the **Oedipus complex** in boys and the **Electra complex** in girls. At the end of the phallic stage, the child enters the latency period, characterized by a loss of interest in sexual behavior. Finally, at puberty, the individual enters the genital stage of mature sexuality.

How did Carl Jung's view of the unconscious differ from Freud's? Freud saw the **id** as a "seething cauldron" of excitations, but Jung viewed the unconscious as the **ego's** source of strength. He believed that the unconscious consisted of two distinct components: the **personal unconscious,** encompassing an individual's repressed thoughts, forgotten experiences, and undeveloped ideas; and the **collective unconscious,** a subterranean river of memories and behavior patterns flowing to us from previous generations. Over the millennia, the human mind has developed certain thought forms, called **archetypes,** which give rise to mental images or mythological representations.

What did Alfred Adler believe was the major determinant of personality? Adler believed that people possess innate positive motives and strive toward personal and social perfection. He originally proposed that the principal determinant of personality was the individual's attempt to **compensate** for actual physical weakness, but he later modified his theory to stress the importance of *feelings* of inferiority, whether or not those feelings are justified. Adler concluded that strivings for superiority and perfection, both in one's own life and in the society in which one lives, are crucial to personality development.

What major contributions did Karen Horney make to the psychodynamic perspective? For Horney, *anxiety*—a person's reaction to real or imagined dangers or threats—is a stronger motivating force than the sexual drive, or libido. Anxious adults adopt one of three coping strategies, or **neurotic trends**—moving toward people (submission), moving against people (aggression), and moving away from people (detachment). By emphasizing that culture and not anatomy determines many of the personality traits that differentiate women from men, Horney also challenged the prevailing notion of her time that biological imperatives underlie the personality characteristics of men and women.

Erikson's theory focused less on unconscious conflict and more on what factors? Erikson argued that the quality of the parent-child relationship affects the development of personality because out of this interaction, the child either feels competent and valuable and is able to form a secure sense of identity, or feels incompetent and worthless and fails to build a secure identity. Erikson proposed that each person moves through eight stages of development, each involving a more successful versus a less successful adjustment.

How would a psychodynamic theorist view the personality of Jayline Smith? Freud would probably conclude that Jay had not successfully resolved her Electra complex. Erikson might suggest that Jay has problems achieving intimacy (Stage 6) because she had failed to develop satisfactory relations with other people earlier in her life.

How do modern psychologists view the contributions and limitations of the psychodynamic perspective? Psychodynamic theories have had a profound impact on the way we view ourselves and others, but some of Freud's theories have been criticized as unscientific and culture-bound, based on the anecdotal accounts of individuals who felt troubled enough to seek treatment. Further, research does not show a clear link between unconscious processes and personality. As a therapy, psychoanalysis has been shown to be beneficial in some cases but no more so than are other therapies.

Humanistic Personality Theories

What are the major ways that humanistic personality theory differs from psychodynamic theories? Freud and many of his followers believed that personality grows out of the resolution of unconscious conflicts and developmental crises from the past. **Humanistic personality theory** emphasizes that we are positively motivated and progress toward higher levels of functioning, and it stresses people's potential for growth and change in the present.

According to Rogers, how can thinking of yourself as self-assured help you to become so? Rogers contended that every person is born with certain innate potentials and the **actualizing tendency** to realize our biological potential as well as our conscious sense of who we are. A **fully functioning person** is one whose self-concept closely matches the person's inborn capabilities, and is encouraged when a child is raised in an atmosphere characterized by **unconditional positive regard.**

How would humanistic theorists view the development of Jaylene Smith's personality? Humanistic theorists would focus on the difference between Jay's self-concept and her actual capacities. Her inability to become what she "most truly is" would account for her anxiety, loneliness, and general dissatisfaction. Rogers would suspect that throughout Jay's life, acceptance and love came from satisfying other people's ideas of what she should become.

What have humanistic theories contributed to our understanding of personality? There is a lack of scientifically derived evidence for humanistic theories of personality. In addition, these theories are criticized for taking too rosy a view of human nature and for fostering self-centeredness. Research on humanistic therapies, however, particularly Rogers's client-centered therapy, has shown that humanistic theorists do promote self-acceptance.

Trait Theories

What is the key focus of trait theories? Trait theorists reject the notion that there are just a few distinct personality types. Instead, they insist that each person possesses a unique constellation of fundamental **personality traits,** which can be inferred from how the person behaves.

What five basic traits describe most differences in personality? Recent research suggests that there may be just five overarching and universal personality traits: extroversion, agreeableness, conscientiousness, emotional stability, and openness to experience (also called culture or intellect).

How would trait theorists describe Jaylene Smith's personality? Trait theorists would probably ascribe Jaylene's high achievements to the traits of determination or persistence. Sincerity, motivation, intelligence, anxiety, and introversion would also describe Jay. In terms of Big Five factors, she would be considered high in conscientiousness, but lower in emotional stability and extroversion.

What major contributions have trait theorists made to our understanding of personality? Trait theories are primarily descriptive and provide a way of classifying personalities, but they do not explain why someone's personality developed as it did. Unlike psychodynamic and humanistic theories, however, trait theories are relatively easy to test experimentally, and research con-

firms the value of the five-factor model, referred to as the **"Big Five,"** in pinpointing personality. Also, although most personality theories assume that behavior is consistent across situations and over a lifetime, a number of psychologists believe that situational variables have a significant effect on behavior.

Cognitive–Social Learning Theories

How can your expectancies affect your current attitudes and behaviors? **Cognitive–social learning theories** of personality view behavior as the product of the interaction of cognitions, learning and past experiences, and the immediate environment. Albert Bandura maintains that certain internal **expectancies** determine how a person evaluates a situation and that this evaluation has an effect on the person's behavior.

How does one's locus of control affect self-efficacy? According to Rotter, people with an internal **locus of control**—one type of expectancy—believe that they can control their own fate through their actions. Expectancies prompt people to conduct themselves according to unique performance standards, individually determined measures of excellence by which they judge their behavior. Those who succeed in meeting their own internal **performance standards** develop an attitude that Bandura calls **self-efficacy.**

How would cognitive–social learning theorists describe the factors that shaped Jaylene Smith's personality? These theorists would assert that Jaylene learned to be shy because she was rewarded for the many hours she spent alone studying. Reinforcement would also have shaped her self-discipline and high need to achieve. By watching her parents, Jay could have learned to respond to conflicts with aggressive outbursts.

What contributions have cognitive–social learning theories made to our understanding of personality, and what are their limitations? Cognitive–social learning theories avoid the narrowness of trait and behavioral theories, as well as the reliance on case studies and anecdotal evidence that weakens psychodynamic and humanistic theories. Expectancies and locus of control can be tested scientifically, and they have proved to be useful concepts for predicting health and depression. Correlations such as these, however, do not provide evidence for causes of behavior.

Personality Assessment

How do psychologists measure personality? Psychologists use four different methods to assess personality: the personal interview, direct observation of behavior, **objective tests,** and **projective tests.** Factors such as the desire to impress the examiner, fatigue, and fear of being tested can profoundly affect the reliability and validity of such tests, though researchers are attempting to eliminate potential errors from such sources.

What are the purposes of structured and unstructured interviews? During an unstructured interview, the interviewer asks questions about any material that comes up during the conversation as well as follow-up questions where appropriate, but the behavior of the interviewer may affect the results. In a structured interview, the order and the content of the questions are fixed, and the interviewer does not deviate from the format, so it may not address some of the issues that come up in an unstructured interview. Structured interviews are more likely to be used for systematic research on personality because they solicit comparable information from all interviewees.

What are the advantages and limits of the observational method? Direct observation of a person over a period of time to determine the environmental influence on that person's behavior has the advantage of not relying on people's self-reports of their behavior. However, the subject's behavior may be affected by the observer's presence in ways that can be misinterpreted.

Why are objective tests preferred by trait theorists? Objective personality tests ask respondents to answer "yes-no" questions about their own behavior and thoughts. Cattel's **Sixteen Personality Factor Questionnaire (16PF)** provides scores on sixteen basic personality traits, whereas the **NEO-PI-R** reports scores for each of the Big Five traits and their associated facets. The **Minnesota Multiphasic Personality Inventory (MMPI)** is typically used as an aid to diagnose mental disorders, and it includes questions that measure the truthfulness of a person's response.

What do projective tests try to measure? Psychodynamic theorists, who believe that much behavior is determined by unconscious processes, tend to discount tests that rely on self-reports. They are more likely to use projective tests, which consist of ambiguous stimuli that can draw out an unlimited number of interpretations based on these unconscious processes. Two such tests are the **Rorschach Test** and the **Thematic Apperception Test (TAT).**

CRITICAL THINKING AND APPLICATIONS

1. Explain how Jung, Adler, Horney, and Erikson modified Freud's psychodynamic theory of personality.

2. Twelve-step programs such as Alcoholics Anonymous welcome people back into the program without judging them, no matter how many times they have "gone out again." This approach is consistent with which concept in Carl Rogers's theory? Why?

3. One of the key issues addressed by personality theorists is consistency: Does a person behave the same way across different situations, or does behavior vary with circumstances?

4. Look back at the case study of Jaylene Smith. Which theory or theories do you think best explains her behavior? Why do you feel this way?

5. What are the major forms of personality assessment? Which do you consider the most valuable? the least valuable? Why?

WEB QUIZ **10.6** ✔   **Go to the Morris 6e Companion Website to take a practice chapter exam.**

11 Stress and Health Psychology

"AT ABOUT 15 MINUTES TO 9, ANNE PROSSER, 29, RODE THE ELEVATOR TO THE 90TH floor of Tower 1 [of the World Trade Center] where her global banking office was. As the doors opened, she heard what seemed like an explosion. She didn't know it, but the first plane had just hit several floors above her. 'I got thrown to the ground before I got to our suite,' she said. 'I crawled inside. Not everybody was at work.' She said she tried to leave but there was so much debris in the air she couldn't breathe. Rescuers finally steered her to a stairway. . . . Ten or so blocks north of the towers, the smoke had been outrun and it began to dissipate into the air. People stopped, turned and looked downtown. As the air cleared, an unthinkable site presented itself: empty space where a 110-story tower had been. People gasped. They trembled. They sobbed. 'It can't be,' an elderly woman said. 'It just can't be. Where did it go? Oh, lord, where did it go?' Many of the onlookers stayed put, frozen in horror. Slowly, the next thought crept into their consciousness: The other tower would come down too. . . . People started walking briskly north until the premonition became real—another horrifying eruption, as one floor after another seemed to detonate. Another giant cloud, soot, smoke streaming through the avenues. Again, people ran. Many of them stopped at Canal Street and watched the smoke dissolve. People cried at what they saw: a crystalline sky with nothing in it. 'Oh my God,' Tim Lingenfelder said, 'there's nothing there.' That was when he lost it and began to cry. People stood, numb, transfixed by what had to be a mirage. 'All that were left of the buildings that you could see were the steel girders in like a triangular sail shape,' said Ross Milanytch. 'The dust was about an inch and a half thick on the ground.' Onlookers gathered in clumps and tried to understand. People with cars opened the doors and turned on the radios, and knots of people leaned close to hear what was happening. The news came across of the plane at the Pentagon, the plane in Pittsburgh. 'It's like Pearl Harbor,' said a middle-aged man at a small parking lot on Canal Street. 'It's Pearl Harbor. It's war.' 'It's sickos,' someone else said. 'Sickos.' 'This is America,' a man said. 'How can it happen in America? How?'" (http://www.nytimes.com/2001/09/12/nyregion/12REAC.html)

Nightmares/Day Terrors A 40-year-old cancer survivor received bone-marrow transplants to treat his leukemia. Three years later, tests found no evidence that the leukemia had returned. Yet he had flashbacks of receiving radiation treatment whenever he heard the sound of a generator. Colors that reminded him of the hospital triggered nausea, sweating, and chills. He often woke in the middle of the night, not knowing whether he was at home or in the hospital. He forbade his family to bring a Christmas tree into the house because the scent reminded him of the pine-scented lotion he used while undergoing treatment. Like some other cancer survivors, he was diagnosed with posttraumatic stress disorder—a diagnosis usually applied to soldiers, hostages, and others who have lived through extreme and unusual experiences. (Adapted from Rabasca, 1999a, p. 28)

The Ghetto "There's nothing out there. What they're doing, they're selling drugs, they're working here and there, they're living off of different women, you know, off each other. . . . You got men out there that are trying to survive and get educated, but the ones in my community, the ones that I see, education's the farthest thing from [their minds]. . . . They hear all this stuff on TV, and they just don't have any hope for the future." (Harry, 1995; in Johnson, Levine, & Doolittle, 1999, p. 58)

What do witnesses to terrorism, the recovered cancer patient, and the unemployed ghetto resident share? The common denominator in their stories is stress. When people feel threatened physically or psychologically, when they wonder if they can cope with the demands of their environment, when their heart pounds and their stomach feels queasy, they are experiencing stress. In this context, the term **stress** refers to psychological tension or strain—the uncomfortable emotional and bodily responses to stressful situations. **Adjustment** is any attempt—successful or not—to cope with stress, to balance our needs against the demands of the environment, to weigh our desires against realistic possibilities, and to manage as well as we can.

Stress is part of life. We all feel stressed when the car breaks down, when we loose our wallet, when our computer crashes, or when we're under pressure to meet a deadline and there just aren't enough hours in the day to get everything done. Sometimes, we must cope with acute stress, such as the death of a parent or spouse. But, stress isn't always "bad"; it can have positive as well as negative consequences. Indeed, most people would be bored with an existence that held no challenges or surprises. Moreover, stress may stimulate effort and spark creativity. Deadlines prompt us to get to work; emergencies require us to draw on inner and outer (social and physical) resources, including some that we didn't

know we had; and loss may lead to introspection and insight. Even when a situation is hopeless and a happy ending is impossible, people often report that they have grown, acquired new coping skills and resources, and perhaps experienced a spiritual or religious transformation as a result of stressful experiences (Folkman & Moskowitz, 2000).

Of course, individuals vary in terms of how much stress they can tolerate. Some people are at their best when working under pressure, against strong opposition; others need calm and quiet. Too much stress, over too long a period, may contribute to both physical and psychological problems.

Health psychology focuses on how the mind and body interact. Specifically, health psychologists seek to understand how psychological factors influence wellness and illness. Numerous studies have found that people suffering from acute or chronic stress are more vulnerable to everything from the common cold to cancer (S. Cohen et al., 1998; Spiegel & Kato, 1996). But why do some people who are under constant stress remain healthy, whereas others become sick? What explains differences in the ways people cope with illness, respond to treatment, or deal with disabilities? Can personality traits influence recovery from surgery or serious illness? How can we help individuals to manage, reduce, or overcome stress? As you will learn, new research is uncovering the biological mechanisms that link stress to lowered immunity and poor health. The challenge for health psychologists is to find ways both to prevent stress from becoming physically and emotionally debilitating and to *promote* healthy behavior and well-being.

This chapter begins by looking at the common, everyday sources of stress in our lives and why some individuals seem particularly vulnerable to stress and others are stress-hardy and resilient. Next, we look at how people cope with stress, and we explore the relationship between stress and our body's response to it. Last, we consider what psychologists mean when they say that a person is well-adjusted.

Sources of Stress

What are stressors?

The term **stressor** refers to any environmental demand that creates a state of tension or threat and requires change or adaptation. Many situations prompt us to change our behavior in some way, but only some cause stress. Consider, for example, stopping at a traffic signal that turns red. Normally, this involves no stress. But now imagine that you are rushing to an important appointment and the red light will surely make you late. Here, stress is triggered because the situation not only requires adaptation but also produces tension and distress as well. Stress is not limited to dangerous situations or even to unpleasant situations. Good things can also cause stress, because they "require change or adaptation if an individual is to meet his or her needs" (Morris, 1990, p. 72). For example, a wedding is often a stressful as well as an exciting event. A promotion at work is gratifying, but it demands that we relate to new people in new ways, learn to carry more responsibility, and perhaps work longer hours.

Some events, such as wars and natural disasters, are inherently stressful. Danger is real, lives are threatened, and often there is little or nothing people can do to save themselves. But even in inherently stressful situations, the time of greatest stress is not when danger is actually present. *Anticipating* the danger is actually the time of greatest stress. Parachutists, for example, are most afraid as the time for the jump approaches. Once in line, unable to turn back, they calm down. During the most dangerous part of the jump—in free fall, waiting for their chutes to open—they are much less frightened (Epstein, 1982).

Change

Why is change so stressful for most people?

All the stressful events we've discussed so far involve change. Most people have a strong preference for order, continuity, and predictability in their lives. Therefore, anything—good or bad—that requires change can be experienced as stressful. The more change required, the more stressful the situation.

Questionnaires, such as the College Life Stress Inventory (CLSI), have been constructed to measure the amount of change, and hence the amount of stress, that is present in an individual's life (Renner & Macklin, 1998). As you can see in **Table 11–1,** both positive and negative life events can cause stress, and the more of these life events you are experiencing, the higher is your overall "stress rating."

Although there is considerable individual variation in how well people adapt to life changes such as those represented in the CLSI, in general, very high scores correspond to an enhanced risk of developing a stress-induced illness. In Renner and Macklin's work, college students' scores on the CLSI ranged from a low of 182 to a high of 2,571, but two-thirds had scores between 800 and 1,700. You may find it interesting to compute your score and see how you compare.

Everyday Hassles

How can everyday hassles contribute to stress?

Many of the items on the College Life Stress Inventory concern stress that arises from fairly dramatic, relatively infrequent events. However, many psychologists have pointed out that much stress is generated by "hassles," life's petty annoyances, irritations, and frustrations (Lazarus, DeLongis,

All major life changes involve a certain amount of stress. This is partly because major life changes typically bring strong emotion, and even joy and elation can arouse the body and begin to take a toll on its resources. Major life events can also be stressful because any new experience requires some adjustment.

Stress
A state of psychological tension or strain.

Adjustment
Any effort to cope with stress.

Health psychology
A subfield of psychology concerned with the relationship between psychological factors and physical health and illness.

Stressor
Any environmental demand that creates a state of tension or threat and requires change or adaptation.

TABLE 11-1   COLLEGE LIFE STRESS INVENTORY

Copy the "stress rating" number into the column titled "Your Items" for any item that has happened to you in the last year, and then add up these numbers for your total.

Event	Stress Ratings	Your Items
Being raped	100	
Finding out that you are HIV-positive	100	
Being accused of rape	98	
Death of a close friend	97	
Death of a close family member	96	
Contracting a sexually transmitted disease (other than AIDS)	94	
Concerns about being pregnant	91	
Finals week	90	
Concerns about your partner being pregnant	90	
Oversleeping for an exam	89	
Flunking a class	89	
Having a boyfriend or girlfriend cheat on you	85	
Ending a steady dating relationship	85	
Serious illness in a close friend or family member	85	
Financial difficulties	84	
Writing a major term paper	83	
Being caught cheating on a test	83	
Drunk driving	82	
Sense of overload in school or work	82	
Two exams in one day	80	
Cheating on your boyfriend or girlfriend	77	
Getting married	76	
Negative consequences of drinking or drug use	75	
Depression or crisis in your best friend	73	
Difficulties with parents	73	
Talking in front of a class	72	
Lack of sleep	69	
Change in housing situation (hassles, moves)	69	
Competing or performing in public	69	
Getting in a physical fight	66	
Difficulties with a roommate	66	
Job changes (applying, new job, work hassles)	65	
Declaring a major or having concerns about future plans	65	
A class you hate	62	
Drinking or use of drugs	61	
Confrontations with professors	60	
Starting a new semester	58	
Going on a first date	57	
Registration	55	
Maintaining a steady dating relationship	55	
Commuting to campus or work, or both	54	
Peer pressures	53	
Being away from home for the first time	53	
Getting sick	52	
Concerns about your appearance	52	
Getting straight A's	51	
A difficult class that you love	48	
Making new friends; getting along with friends	47	
Fraternity or Sorority rush	47	
Falling asleep in class	40	
Attending an athletic event (e.g., football game)	20	
Total		_____

Source: Renner, M. J., & Macklin, R. S. (1998). A life stress instrument for classroom use. *Teaching of Psychology, 25*(1), p. 47. Copyright © 1998 by Lawrence Erlbaum Associates, Inc. Reprinted with permission.

Folkman, & Gruen, 1985; Ruffin, 1993; Whisman & Kwon, 1993). Such seemingly minor matters as a having a zipper break, waiting in long lines, or having a petty argument with a friend take their toll. Lazarus believes that big events matter so much because they trigger numerous little hassles that eventually overwhelm us with stress. People who have recently suffered a major traumatic event are more likely than other people to be plagued by minor stressors or hassles (Pillow, Zautra, & Sandler, 1996). "It is not the large dramatic events that make the difference," notes Lazarus, "but what happens day in and day out, whether provoked by major events or not" (1981, p. 62). Both major and minor events are stressful because they lead to feelings of pressure, frustration, and conflict.

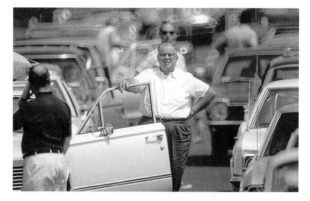

Much of the stress we experience in our lives arises not from major traumas but from small everyday hassles such as traffic jams, petty arguments, and equipment that fails when we need it most.

Pressure Pressure occurs when we feel forced to speed up, intensify, or shift direction in our behavior, or when we feel compelled to meet a higher standard of performance (Morris, 1990). Pressure on the job or in school is a familiar example. Psychologists who study the effects of corporate "downsizing," which requires that production levels are maintained but with fewer workers, often find that these workers report increased stress and depression, increased injuries on the job, and lower job satisfaction. This pressure also contributes to poor job performance (Clay, 1999; Kaminski, 1999). In our private lives, trying to live up to social and cultural norms about what we *should* be doing, as well as our family's and friends' expectations, also adds pressure to meeting our personal needs.

Frustration Frustration occurs when a person is prevented from reaching a goal because something or someone stands in the way. An example of an all-too-common response to frustration is "road rage," the aggressive driving that occurs when ordinarily nonviolent people feel frustrated by traffic congestion and other pressures. Road rage has become more common and more deadly: As many as 9 in 10 drivers have been the "victims" of road rage (James & Nahl, 2000), and road rage contributes to 1,500 to 2,000 injuries and fatalities each year (U.S. House of Representatives, 1997). Some psychologists view road rage as a behavioral syndrome that is rooted in exaggerated forms of cultural norms, especially our annoyance with delays and winner-take-all view of competition (James & Nahl, 2000).

Morris (1990) identified five sources of frustration that are especially common in American life. *Delays* are annoying because our culture puts great stock in the value of time. *Lack of resources* is frustrating to those Americans who cannot afford the new cars or lavish vacations they desire. *Losses*, such as the end of a love affair or a cherished friendship, cause frustration because they often make us feel helpless, unimportant, or worthless. *Failure* generates intense frustration—and accompanying guilt—in our competitive society. We imagine that if we had done things differently, we might have succeeded; thus, we usually feel personally responsible for our setbacks and tend to assume that others blame us for not trying harder or being smarter. *Discrimination* also frustrates us: Being denied opportunities or recognition simply because of one's sex, age, religion, or skin is extremely frustrating.

Conflict Of all life's troubles, conflict is probably the most common. A boy does not want to go to his aunt's for dinner, but neither does he want to listen to his parents complain if he stays home. A student finds that both the required courses she wanted to take this semester are given at the same hours on the same days. **Conflict** arises when we face two or more incompatible demands, opportunities, needs, or goals. We can never completely

Pressure
A feeling that one must speed up, intensify, or change the direction of one's behavior or live up to a higher standard of performance.

Frustration
The feeling that occurs when a person is prevented from reaching a goal.

Conflict
Simultaneous existence of incompatible demands, opportunities, needs, or goals.

resolve conflict. We must either give up some of our goals, modify some of them, delay our pursuit of some of them, or resign ourselves to not attaining all of our goals. Whatever we do, we are bound to experience some frustration, thereby adding to the stressfulness of conflicts.

In the 1930s, Kurt Lewin described two opposite tendencies of conflict: approach and avoidance. When something attracts us, we want to approach it; when something frightens us, we try to avoid it. Lewin (1935) showed how different combinations of these tendencies create three basic types of conflict: approach/approach conflict, avoidance/avoidance conflict, and approach/avoidance conflict (see the Summary Table).

Approach/approach conflict occurs when a person is simultaneously attracted to two appealing goals. A student who has been accepted at two equally desirable colleges or universities is an example. The stress that occurs in approach/approach conflict is that in choosing one desirable option, we must give up the other.

The reverse is **avoidance/avoidance conflict,** in which we confront two undesirable or threatening possibilities, neither of which has any positive attributes. When faced with an avoidance/avoidance conflict, people usually try to escape the situation altogether. If escape is impossible, their coping method depends on how threatening each alternative is. Most often they vacillate between choosing one threat or the other, like a baseball player's being caught in a rundown between first and second base. In no-exit situations, people sometimes simply wait for events to resolve their conflict for them.

An **approach/avoidance conflict,** in which a person is both attracted to and repelled by the same goal, is the most common form of conflict. The closer we come to a goal with good and bad features, the stronger grow our desires both to approach and to avoid, but the tendency to avoid increases more rapidly than the tendency to approach. In an approach/avoidance conflict, therefore, we approach the goal until we reach the point at which the tendency to approach equals the tendency to avoid the goal. Afraid to go any closer, we stop and vacillate, making no choice at all, until the situation changes.

Self-Imposed Stress

How do we create stress?

So far, we have considered sources of stress outside the individual. Sometimes, however, people create problems for themselves quite apart from stressful events in their environment. Some psychologists argue that many people carry around a set of irrational, self-defeating beliefs that add unnecessarily to the normal stresses of living (Ellis & Harper, 1975). For ex-

Approach/approach conflict
According to Lewin, the result of simultaneous attraction to two appealing possibilities, neither of which has any negative qualities.

Avoidance/avoidance conflict
According to Lewin, the result of facing a choice between two undesirable possibilities, neither of which has any positive qualities.

Approach/avoidance conflict
According to Lewin, the result of being simultaneously attracted to and repelled by the same goal.

SUMMARY TABLE

TYPES OF CONFLICT

Type of Conflict	Nature of Conflict
Approach/Approach	You are attracted to two incompatible goals at the same time.
Avoidance/Avoidance	Repelled by two undesirable alternatives at the same time, you are inclined to escape, but other factors often prevent such an escape.
Approach/Avoidance	You are both repelled by, and attracted to, the same goal.

ample, some people believe that "it is essential to be loved or approved by almost everyone for everything I do." For such people, any sign of disapproval will be a source of considerable stress. Others believe that "I must be competent, adequate, and successful at everything I do." For them, the slightest sign of failure or inadequacy means that they are worthless human beings. Still other people believe that "it is disastrous if everything doesn't go the way I would like." These people feel upset, miserable, and unhappy when things don't go perfectly. As we will see in the next chapter, self-defeating thoughts like these can contribute to depression (Beck, 1976, 1984).

Stress and Individual Differences

Do people who are resistant to stress share certain traits?

Just as some people create more stress for themselves than others do, some people cope well with major life stresses, whereas others are thrown by even minor problems. What accounts for these differences? How much stress we experience depends partly on the way we interpret our situation. Self-confident people who feel capable of coping with life will feel less stress in a given situation than will those who lack self-assurance (Kessler, Price, & Wortman, 1985). Also, seeing a challenging situation as an opportunity for success, rather than for failure is typically associated with positive emotions such as eagerness, excitement, and confidence (Folkman & Moskovitz, 2000). For example, students who know they can study when they have to and who have done well on exams in the past tend to be calmer the night before an important test than students who have done poorly on previous exams.

People's overall view of the world is also related to how well they can cope with stress. *Optimists* tend to appraise events as challenges rather than threats and are, in general, better able to cope with stressful events than are *pessimists*, who are more likely to dwell on failure (Peterson, 2000). Similarly, people with an *internal locus of control* see themselves as being able to affect their situations. As a consequence, they are more likely to see difficult circumstances as challenges rather than as threats. Those with an *external locus of control* are more likely to appraise events negatively, since they perceive themselves as helpless victims of circumstances and believe that they cannot affect their situations (Ryan & Deci, 2000).

Hardiness and Resilience　　People with a trait we call *hardiness* tolerate stress exceptionally well or seem to thrive on it (Kobasa, 1979). They also feel that they control their own destinies and are confident about being able to cope with change (see also Kessler, Price, & Wortman, 1985). Conversely, individuals who have little confidence that they can master new situations and can exercise control over events feel powerless and apathetic (Peterson, Maier, & Seligman, 1993b). (Recall our discussion of learned helplessness in Chapter 5, Learning.) Even when change offers new opportunities for taking charge of their situation, they remain passive.

Psychologists are also interested in resilience: the ability to "bounce back," recovering one's self-confidence, good spirits, and hopeful attitude, after extreme or prolonged stress. Resilience may partially explain why some children who grow up in adverse circumstances (such as extreme poverty, dangerous neighborhoods, abusive parents, and/or exposure to drugs and alcohol) become well-adjusted adults, whereas others remain troubled—and frequently get into trouble—throughout their lives. On the basis of research that followed high-risk children into adulthood, it appears that two ways to foster resilience are mentor programs (such as Big Brother/Big Sister, which teams an adult volunteer with a needy child) and

Why do some children living in adverse conditions remain troubled throughout their lives while more resilient children in the same circumstances become well-adjusted adults? Here, the children of migrant workers in Beijing, China play in front of their ramshackle housing.

after-school programs that offer a range of activities (Werner, 1996; Brown, cited in Huang, 1998).

In contrast, *defensive coping* refers to various forms of self-deception that provide a means of protecting our self-esteem and reducing stress (Cramer, 2000). For example, people may convince themselves that they are not really threatened or that they do not really want something they cannot get.

INTERACTIVE LECTURE **11.1**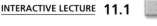

WEB QUIZ **11.1** ✓

> **CHECK YOUR UNDERSTANDING**

1. _____ is any environment demand that creates a state of tension or threat and requires change or adaptation.

2. _____ is an attempt—successful or not—to balance our desires against the demands of the environment, to weigh our needs against realistic possibilities, and to cope as well as we can within the limits of our situation.

3. Indicate whether the following statements are true (T) or false (F).

_____ a. Stress is always a response to negative events in our life.

_____ b. Stressful events almost always involve changes in our lives.

_____ c. Big events in life are always much more stressful than everyday hassles.

Match each type of conflict with the appropriate definition.

_____ 4. approach/approach   _____ a. choosing between two undesired yet unavoidable alternatives

_____ 5. avoidance/avoidance   _____ b. attracted to and repelled by the same goal

_____ 6. approach/avoidance   _____ c. attracted to two goals at once

Answers: 1. Stressor. 2. Adjustment. 3. a. (F); b. (T); c. (F). 4. c. 5. a. 6. b.

Coping with Stress

What is the difference between direct coping and defensive coping?

Whatever its source, stress requires that we cope: that is, make cognitive and behavioral efforts to manage psychological stress (Lazarus, 1993). Psychologists distinguish between two general types of adjustment: direct coping and defensive coping. Direct coping refers to any action we take to change an uncomfortable situation. When our needs or desires are frustrated, for example, we attempt to remove the obstacles between ourselves and our goal, or we give up. Similarly, when we are threatened, we try to eliminate the source of the threat, either by attacking it or by escaping from it.

Direct Coping

What are three strategies that deal directly with stress?

When we are threatened, frustrated, or in conflict, we have three basic choices for coping directly: *confrontation, compromise*, or *withdrawal*. We can meet a situation head-on and intensify our efforts to get what we want (confrontation). We can give up some of what we want and perhaps persuade others to give up part of what they want (compromise). Or we can admit defeat and stop fighting (withdrawal) (see *Understanding Ourselves*: *Coping with Stress at College*.)

Take the case of a woman who has worked hard at her job for years but has not been promoted. She learns that the reason for her not being promoted is her stated unwillingness to move temporarily from the company's main office to a branch office in another part of the country to acquire more experience. Her unwillingness to move stands between her and her goal of advancing in her career. She has several choices, which we will explore.

Confrontation   Acknowledging to oneself that there is a problem for which a solution must be found, attacking the problem head-on, and pushing resolutely toward one's goal is called **confrontation.** The hallmark of the "confrontational style" is making intense efforts to cope with stress and to accomplish one's aims (Morris, 1990). Doing so may involve learning skills, enlisting other people's help, or just trying harder. Or it may require steps to change either oneself or the situation. The woman who wants to advance her career might decide that if she wants to move up in the company, she will have to relocate. Or she might challenge the assumption that working at the branch office would give her the kind of experience that her supervisor thinks she needs. She might try to persuade her boss that even though she has never worked in a branch office, she nevertheless has acquired enough experience to handle a better job in the main office. Or she might remind her supervisor of the company's stated goal of promoting more women to top-level positions.

Confrontation may also include expressions of anger. Anger may be effective, especially if we really have been treated unfairly and if we express our anger with restraint instead of exploding in rage.

Compromise   **Compromise** is one of the most common and effective ways of coping directly with conflict or frustration. We often recognize that we cannot have everything we want and that we cannot expect others to do just what we would like them to do. In such cases, we may decide to settle for less than we originally sought. A young person who has always wanted to become a veterinarian may discover in college that she has less aptitude for biology than she thought. She changes her career plan but decides to devote much of her energy to finding homes for abandoned animals.

Withdrawal   In some circumstances, the most effective way of coping with stress is to withdraw from the situation. A person at an amusement park who is overcome by anxiety just looking at a roller coaster may simply move on to a less threatening ride or may even leave the park. The woman whose promotion depends on temporarily relocating might just quit her job and join another company.

When we realize that our adversary is more powerful than we are, that there is no way we can effectively modify ourselves or the situation, that

---

Confrontation
Acknowledging a stressful situation directly and attempting to find a solution to the problem or attain the difficult goal.

Compromise
Deciding on a more realistic solution or goal when an ideal solution or goal is not practical.

UNDERSTANDING OURSELVES

Coping with Stress at College

It is two weeks before finals, and you have two papers to write and four exams to study for. You are very worried. You are not alone. There are many techniques you can teach yourself to help cope with the pressures of college life.

1. Plan ahead, do not procrastinate, and get things done well before deadlines. Start work on large projects well in advance.

2. Exercise; do whatever activity you enjoy.

3. Listen to your favorite music, watch a television show, or go to a movie as a study break.

4. Talk to other people.

5. Meditate or use other relaxation techniques.

6. Seek out a stress-reduction workshop. Many colleges and universities offer these.

One very effective technique is to make a list of *everything* you have to do, right down to doing the laundry, getting birthday cards for family and friends, and so on. Then star the highest-priority tasks—the ones that *really* have to be done first or those that will take a long time. Use your available time to work on *only* those tasks. Cross off high-priority tasks as they are done, add new tasks as they arrive, and continually adjust the priorities so that the most critical tasks are always starred.

This technique serves various purposes. It removes the fear that you'll forget something important, because everything you can think of is on a single sheet of paper. It helps you realize that things are not as overwhelming as they might otherwise seem (the list is finite, and there are probably only a few things that truly are high-priority tasks). It lets you focus your energy on the most important tasks and makes it easy to avoid spending time on less important things that might drift into your attention. Finally, it assures you that you are doing everything possible to do the most important things in your life, and if you don't manage to do them all, you can truly say, "There's no way I could have done any better; it simply wasn't possible in the time available." Actually, that will seldom be the case. Usually the highest-priority tasks get done and the lower-priority tasks simply wait, often for weeks or months, after which you wonder how important they really are if they always come out on the bottom of the totem pole.

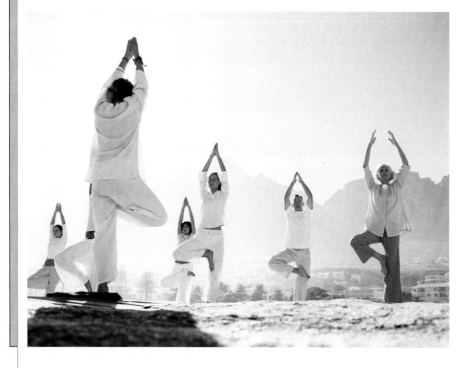

Doing yoga exercises regularly is a direct way of coping with stress that can enhance feelings of well being while improving balance and flexibility.

there is no possible compromise, and that any form of aggression would be self-destructive, **withdrawal** is a positive and realistic response. In seemingly hopeless situations, such as submarine and mining disasters, few people panic (Mintz, 1951). Believing that there is nothing they can do to save themselves, they give up. If in fact a situation is hopeless, resignation may be the most effective way of coping with it.

Perhaps the greatest danger of coping by withdrawal is that the person will come to avoid all similar situations. The person who grew extremely anxious looking at the roller coaster may refuse to go to an amusement park or a carnival again. The woman who did not want to take a job at her company's branch office may not only quit her present job but may leave without even looking for a new one. In such cases, coping by withdrawal can become maladaptive avoidance. Moreover, people who have given up on a situation are in a poor position to take advantage of an effective solution if one should come along.

Withdrawal, in whatever form, is a mixed blessing. Although it can be an effective method of coping, it has built-in dangers. The same characteristic tends to be true of defensive coping, to which we now turn.

Defensive Coping

What are the major ways of coping defensively?

Thus far we have been speaking of coping with stress that arises from recognizable sources. But there are times when we either cannot identify or cannot deal directly with the source of our stress. For example, you return to a parking lot to discover that your car has been damaged. In other cases, a problem is so emotionally threatening that it cannot be faced directly: Perhaps someone close to you is terminally ill, or after four years of hard work, you have failed to gain admission to medical school and may have to abandon your plan to become a doctor.

In such situations, people may turn to **defense mechanisms** as a way of coping. Defense mechanisms are techniques for *deceiving* oneself about the causes of a stressful situation to reduce pressure, frustration, conflict, and anxiety. The self-deceptive nature of such adjustments led Freud to conclude that they are entirely unconscious, but not all psychologists agree that they always spring from unconscious conflicts over which we have little or no control. Often we realize that we are pushing something out of our memory or are otherwise deceiving ourselves. For example, all of us have blown up at someone when we *knew* we were really angry at someone else. Whether defense mechanisms operate consciously or unconsciously, they provide a means of coping with stress that might otherwise be unbearable (see Summary Table).

Denial   **Denial** is the refusal to acknowledge a painful or threatening reality. Although denial is a positive response in some situations, in other situations, it clearly is not. Frequent drug users who insist that they are merely "experimenting" with drugs are using denial. So is the student who expects an exam to be easy and to earn a high grade, even though he or she hasn't studied and unconsciously expects to fail.

Repression   The most common mechanism for blocking out painful feelings and memories is **repression,** a form of forgetting that excludes painful thoughts from consciousness. Soldiers who break down in the field often block out the memory of the experiences that led to their collapse (Grinker & Spiegel, 1945). Many psychologists believe that repression is a symptom that the person is struggling against impulses (such as aggression) that conflict with conscious values. For example, most of us were taught in child-

Withdrawal
Avoiding a situation when other forms of coping are not practical.

Defense mechanisms
Self-deceptive techniques for reducing stress, including denial, repression, projection, identification, regression, intellectualization, reaction formation, displacement, and sublimation.

Denial
Refusal to acknowledge a painful or threatening reality.

Repression
Excluding uncomfortable thoughts, feelings, and desires from consciousness.

SUMMARY TABLE ————————————————————

DEFENSE MECHANISMS

Denial	Refusing to acknowledge a painful or threatening reality: Ray, whose best friend has just been killed in a car accident, insists that it is a case of mistaken identity and that his friend is still alive.
Repression	Excluding uncomfortable thoughts from consciousness: Lisa, whose grandmother died of breast cancer, is at higher-than-average risk for developing breast cancer herself; still, she routinely forgets to get a mammogram.
Projection	Attributing one's repressed motives, feelings, or wishes to others: Marilyn is unfairly passed over for a promotion; she denies that she is angry about this situation but is certain that her supervisor is angry with her.
Identification	Taking on the characteristics of someone else to avoid feeling inadequate: Anthony, uncertain of his own attractiveness, takes on the dress and mannerisms of a popular teacher.
Regression	Reverting to childlike behavior and defenses: Furious because his plan to reorganize his division has been rejected, Bob throws a tantrum.
Intellectualization	Thinking abstractly about stressful problems as a way of detaching oneself from them: After learning that she has not been asked to a classmate's costume party, Tina coolly discusses the ways in which social cliques form and the ways that they serve to regulate and control school life.
Reaction formation	Expression of exaggerated ideas and emotions that are the opposite of one's repressed beliefs or feelings: At work, Michael loudly professes that he would never take advantage of a rival employee, though his harassing behavior indicates quite the opposite.
Displacement	Shifting repressed motives from an original object to a substitute object: Infuriated at his instructor's unreasonable request that he rewrite his term paper but afraid to say anything for fear that he will make the instructor angry, Nelson comes home and yells at his housemates for telling him what to do.
Sublimation	Redirecting repressed motives and feelings into more socially acceptable channels: The child of parents who never paid attention to him, Bill is running for public office.

hood that violence and aggression are wrong. This conflict between our feelings and our values can create stress, and one way of coping defensively with that stress is to repress our feelings—to block out completely any awareness of our underlying anger and hostility.

Denial and repression are the most basic defense mechanisms. In denial we block out situations we can't cope with; in repression we block out unacceptable impulses or thoughts. These psychic strategies form the bases for several other defensive ways of coping.

Projection   If a problem cannot be denied or completely repressed, we may be able to distort its nature so that we can handle it more easily through **projection,** the attribution of one's repressed motives, ideas, or feelings onto others. We ascribe feelings to someone else that we do not want to acknowledge as our own, thus locating the source of our conflict outside ourselves. A corporate executive who feels guilty about the way he rose to power may project his own ruthless ambition onto his colleagues. He simply is doing his job, he believes, whereas his associates are all crassly ambitious and consumed with power.

Projection
Attributing one's repressed motives, feelings, or wishes to others.

Identification   The reverse of projection is **identification:** taking on the characteristics of someone else so that we can vicariously share in that person's triumphs and overcome feeling inadequate. The admired person's actions, that is, become a substitute for our own. A parent with unfulfilled career ambitions may share emotionally in a son's or daughter's professional success. When the child is promoted, the parent may feel personally triumphant. Identification is often used as a form of self-defense in situations in which a person feels utterly helpless.

Parents who themselves have never been stars at anything may identify with their child's outstanding achievements, taking pride in them as if they were their own.

Regression   People under stress may revert to childlike behavior through a process called **regression.** Why do people regress? Some psychologists say that it is because an adult cannot stand feeling helpless. Children, on the other hand, feel helpless and dependent every day, so becoming more childlike can make total dependency or helplessness more bearable.

Regression is sometimes used as a manipulative strategy, too, albeit an immature and inappropriate one. Adults who cry or throw temper tantrums when their arguments fail may expect those around them to react sympathetically, as their parents did when they were children.

Intellectualization   The defense mechanism known as **intellectualization** is a subtle form of denial in which we detach ourselves from our feelings about our problems by analyzing them intellectually and thinking of them almost as if they concerned other people. Parents who start out intending to discuss their child's difficulties in a new school and then find themselves engaged in a sophisticated discussion of educational philosophy may be intellectualizing a very upsetting situation. They appear to be dealing with their problems, but in fact they are not, because they have cut themselves off from their disturbing emotions.

Reaction Formation   The term **reaction formation** refers to a behavioral form of denial in which people express, with exaggerated intensity, ideas and emotions that are the opposite of their own. *Exaggeration* is the clue to this behavior. The woman who extravagantly praises a rival may be covering up jealousy over her opponent's success. Reaction formation may also be a way of convincing oneself that one's motives are pure. The man who feels ambivalent about being a father may devote a disproportionate amount of time to his children in an attempt to prove to *himself* that he is a good father.

Displacement   **Displacement** involves the redirection of repressed motives and emotions from their original objects to substitute objects. The man who has always wanted to be a father may feel inadequate when he learns that he cannot have children. As a result, he may become extremely attached to a pet or to a niece or nephew. In another example of displacement, the woman who must smile and agree with her boss all day may come home and yell at her husband or children.

Sublimation   **Sublimation** refers to transforming repressed motives or feelings into more socially acceptable forms. Aggressiveness, for instance, might be channeled into competitiveness in business or sports. A strong and persistent desire for attention might be transformed into an interest in acting or politics. From the Freudian perspective, sublimation is not only necessary

Identification
Taking on the characteristics of someone else to avoid feeling incompetent.

Regression
Reverting to childlike behavior and defenses.

Intellectualization
Thinking abstractly about stressful problems as a way of detaching oneself from them.

Reaction formation
Expression of exaggerated ideas and emotions that are the opposite of one's repressed beliefs or feelings.

Displacement
Shifting repressed motives and emotions from an original object to a substitute object.

Sublimation
Redirecting repressed motives and feelings into more socially acceptable channels.

but also desirable. People who can transform their sexual and aggressive drives into more socially acceptable forms are clearly better off, for they are able at least partially to gratify instinctual drives with relatively little anxiety and guilt. Moreover, society benefits from the energy and effort that such people channel into the arts, literature, science, and other socially useful activities.

Does defensive coping mean that a person is immature, unstable, or on the edge of a "breakdown"? Is direct coping adaptive, and is defensive coping maladaptive? Not necessarily (Cramer, 2000). In some cases of prolonged and severe stress, lower-level defenses may not only contribute to our overall ability to adjust but also may even become essential to survival. Defenses are "essential for softening failure, alleviating tension and anxiety, repairing emotional hurt, and maintaining our feelings of adequacy and worth" (Coleman, Glaros, and Morris 1987; p. 190). Defenses can also be adaptive for coping with more serious problems. In the short run, especially if there are few other options, defenses may reduce anxiety and thus allow for the highest possible level of adaptation. Over the long run, however, defenses can hinder successful adjustment. Defense mechanisms are maladaptive when they interfere with a person's ability to deal directly with a problem or when they create more problems than they solve.

Socioeconomic and Gender Differences in Coping with Stress

Who experiences the most stress?

Individuals use various coping strategies in different combinations and in different ways to deal with stressful events. It is tempting to conclude that styles of coping, like personality, reside within the individual. Yet a good deal of research indicates that how much stress people encounter and how they cope depend to a significant degree on the environment in which they live (S. E. Taylor & Repetti, 1997).

Consider the impact of socioeconomic status on stress and coping. In poor neighborhoods, addressing even the basic tasks of living is stressful. Housing is often substandard and crowded; there are fewer stores, and they offer lower-quality goods; crime and unemployment rates are likely to be high; and schools have lower teacher-student ratios, high staff turnover, and more part-time teachers. In short, poor people have to deal with more stress than people who are financially better off (N. Adler et al., 1994; S. Cohen & Williamson, 1988; Kessler, 1979). Moreover, some data indicate that people in low-income groups cope less effectively with stress and that, as a result, stressful events have a harsher impact on their emotional lives (Kessler, 1979). Psychologists have offered several possible explanations for these data. People in lower socioeconomic classes often have fewer means for coping with hardship and stress (Pearlin & Schooler, 1978). Low-income people also have fewer people to turn to and fewer community resources to draw on for support during stressful times (Liem & Liem, 1978). In addition, people living in poverty may believe to a greater extent than other people that external factors are responsible for what happens to them and that they have little personal control over their lives. Finally, some evidence suggests that members of low-income groups are more likely to have low self-esteem and to doubt their ability to master difficult situations. All these factors help explain why stress often takes a greater toll on people in lower socioeconomic classes.

Are there gender differences in coping with stress? At present, the answer seems to be "maybe." One study of victims of Hurricane Andrew found that although women reported experiencing more stress than men, men and women turned out to be affected equally when stress was measured physiologically (Adler, 1993b). In another study of 300 dual-earner couples, women and men felt equally stressed by the state of their marriage, their jobs, and how well their children were doing. However, the women in this study experienced greater stress than men when problems developed in long-term relationships, largely because they were more committed to their personal and professional relationships than the men were (Barnett, Brennan, & Marshall, 1994). Some research indicates that when faced with equally stressful situations, men and women generally use quite similar coping strategies (Porter & Stone, 1995). However, other research suggests that in at least some circumstances, men and women may use rather different coping strategies (Ptacek, Smith, & Dodge, 1994; see also Anshel, Porter, & Quek, 1998; Narayanan, Shanker, & Spector, 1999). For example, one recent study (Nolen-Hoeksema, 1999) found that when men are down or depressed, they are more likely than women to turn to alcohol; when women are blue, sad, or mad, they are more likely to ruminate about the problem, revisiting negative emotions and the events that led up to them in their minds.

A new line of research suggest that gender differences in responding to stress may be the result of evolutionary adaptations (S. E. Taylor et al., 2000). In simple terms, when our hunter/gatherer ancestors were threatened with danger, it may have been most adaptive for the species if men responded with aggression and women responded by guarding the children. This "tend-and-befriend" response may provide a partial explanation for why women under stress are more likely than men to seek contact and support from others rather than to behave aggressively.

These children in a low-income neighborhood of Chicago probably experience more stress in their lives than their middle- and upper-class peers.

INTERACTIVE LECTURE **11.2**

WEB QUIZ **11.2**

CHECK YOUR UNDERSTANDING

1. There are two general types of coping: _____ and _____.
2. Confronting problems, compromising, or withdrawing from the situation entirely are all forms of _____ coping.
3. _____ coping is a means of dealing with situations that people feel unable to resolve.

Match the following defense mechanisms with the appropriate definition.

_____ 4. denial | a. a form of forgetting
_____ 5. repression | b. detachment from problems through rational, logical analysis
_____ 6. projection | c. reversion to less mature, even childlike behavior
_____ 7. identification | d. exaggerated expression of emotions or ideas that are the opposite of what we really feel or believe
_____ 8. regression | e. redirection of motives or emotions to other objects
_____ 9. intellectualization | f. refusal to acknowledge that a painful or threatening situation exists
_____ 10. reaction formation | g. attributing one's motives and feelings to others
_____ 11. displacement | h. redirection of motives or emotions into more socially acceptable forms
_____ 12. sublimation | i. taking on the characteristics of someone else to share that person's successes and avoid feelings of personal inadequacy

Answers: 1. direct, defensive. 2. direct. 3. Defensive. 4. f. 5. a. 6. g. 7. i. 8. c. 9. b. 10. d. 11. e. 12. h.

How Stress Affects Health

What long-lasting effects of stress do we need to be concerned with?

"We know that 50 percent of deaths are directly related to human behaviors, and yet we spend too little time doing research and implementing programs related to them," said David Satcher, U.S. Surgeon General (Satcher, 1999, p. 16). Physicians and psychologists agree that stress management is an essential part of programs to prevent disease and promote health. To understand how our body responds to stress, we must first examine how we react to danger. Suppose you are walking alone down an unfamiliar street late at night when you notice that a suspicious stranger is following you. Suddenly your heart begins to pound, your respiration increases, and you develop a queasy feeling in your stomach. What is happening to you? The hypothalamus, a center deep in your brain, is reacting to your perception of danger by organizing a generalized response that affects several organs throughout your body (see **Figure 11–1**). Almost immediately the hypothalamus stimulates the sympathetic branch of the autonomic nervous system and the adrenal glands to release stress hormones such as *adrenaline* and *norepinephrine* into the blood. This process in turn leads to increases in heart rate, blood pressure, respiration, and perspiration. Other organs also respond; for example, the liver increases the available sugar in the blood for extra energy, and the bone marrow increases the white blood cell count to combat infection. Conversely, the rate of some bodily functions decreases; for example, the rate of digestion slows down, thus accounting for the queasy feeling in the stomach.

The noted physiologist Walter Cannon (1929) first described the basic elements of this sequence of events as a *fight-or-flight* response, because it appeared that its primary purpose was to prepare an animal to respond to external threats by either attacking or fleeing from them. Cannon also observed that this physiological mobilization occurred uniformly regardless of the nature of the threat. For instance, the fight-or-flight response can be triggered by physical trauma, fear, emotional arousal, or simply having a *really* bad incident happen at work or school. The adaptive significance of the fight-or-flight response in people was obvious to Cannon, in that it assured the survival of early humans when faced with danger.

Extending Cannon's theory of the fight-or-flight response, the Canadian physiologist Hans Selye (pronounced Say-lee) (1907–1982) contended that we react to physical and psychological stress in three stages that he collectively called the **general adaptation syndrome (GAS)** (Selye, 1956, 1976). These three stages are alarm reaction, resistance, and exhaustion.

Stage 1, *alarm reaction*, is the first response to stress. It begins when the body recognizes that it must fend off some physical or psychological danger. Emotions run high. Activity of the sympathetic nervous system is increased, resulting in the release of hormones from the adrenal gland. We become more sensitive and alert, our respiration and heartbeat quicken, our muscles tense, and we experience other physiological changes as well. All of these changes help us to mobilize our coping resources in order to regain self-control. At the alarm stage we might use either direct or defensive coping strategies. If neither of these approaches reduces the stress, we eventually enter the second stage of adaptation.

General adaptation syndrome (GAS) According to Selye, the three stages the body passes through as it adapts to stress: alarm reaction, resistance, and exhaustion.

FIGURE 11–1

The physiological response to stress. When the body is confronted with a stressful situation, the hypothalamus stimulates the sympathetic nervous system and the adrenal glands to release stress hormones. Other organs, including the stomach and liver, also respond.

Source: Mollica, R. F. (2000, June). Invisible wounds. *Scientific American*, p. 54. Figure by Laurie Grace. Reprinted with permission.

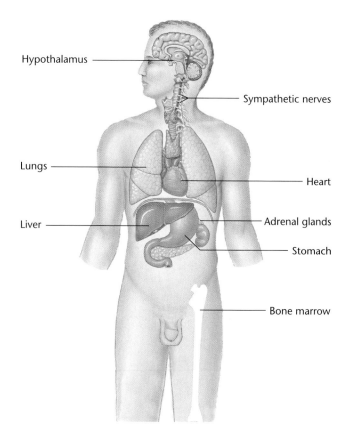

Hypothalamus

Sympathetic nerves

Lungs

Heart

Liver

Adrenal glands

Stomach

Bone marrow

During Stage 2, *resistance*, physical symptoms and other signs of strain appear as we struggle against increasing psychological disorganization. We intensify our use of both direct and defensive coping techniques. If we succeed in reducing the stress, we return to a more normal state. But if the stress is extreme or prolonged, we may turn in desperation to inappropriate coping techniques and cling to them rigidly, despite the evidence that they are not working. When that happens, physical and emotional resources are further depleted, and signs of psychological and physical wear and tear become even more apparent.

In the third stage, *exhaustion*, we draw on increasingly ineffective defense mechanisms in a desperate attempt to bring the stress under control. Some people lose touch with reality and show signs of emotional disorder or mental illness at this stage. Others show signs of "burnout," including the inability to concentrate, irritability, procrastination, and a cynical belief that nothing is worthwhile (Freudenberger, 1983; Maslach & Leiter, 1982, 1997). Physical symptoms such as skin or stomach problems may erupt, and some victims of burnout turn to alcohol or drugs to cope with the stress-induced exhaustion. If the stress continues, the person may suffer irreparable physical or psychological damage or even death.

Selye's contention that stress can be linked to physical illness has been well-supported by research. But how can psychological stress lead to or influence physical illness? First, when a person experiences stress, his heart, lungs, nervous system, and other physiological systems are forced to work harder. The human body is not designed to be exposed for long periods to the powerful biological changes that accompany alarm and mobilization; so when stress is prolonged, people are more likely to experience some kind of physical disorder. Second, stress has a powerful negative effect on the body's immune system, and prolonged stress can destroy the body's ability to defend itself from disease. Stress, too, may lead to unhealthy behavior, such as smoking, drinking, overeating, or skipping meals, not getting enough exercise, and avoiding regular medical checkups, that can also lead to illness and poor overall health.

Live! **psych 11.1**

Stress and Heart Disease

How is Type A behavior related to heart disease?

Stress is a major contributing factor in the development of coronary heart disease (CHD), the leading cause of death and disability in the United States (McGinnis, 1994). Heredity also affects the likelihood of developing CHD, but even among identical twins, the incidence of CHD is closely linked to attitudes toward work, problems in the home, and the amount of leisure time available (Kringlen, 1981). Generally, life stress and social isolation are significant predictors of mortality among those who have suffered heart attacks for whatever reason (Ruberman, Weinblatt, Goldberg, & Chaudhary, 1984).

Mental stress on the job is linked to CHD, as is individual personality. A great deal of research has been done, for example, on people who exhibit the *Type A behavior pattern*—that is, who respond to life events with impatience, hostility, competitiveness, urgency, and constant striving (M. Friedman & Rosenman, 1959). Type A people are distinguished from more easygoing *Type B* people. The two cardiologists who first identified the characteristics of Type As were convinced that this behavior pattern was most likely to surface in stressful situations.

A number of studies have shown that Type A behavior predicts CHD (Booth-Kewley & Friedman, 1987; T. Q. Miller, Tuner, Tindale, Posavac, & Dugoni, 1991). For example, when Type A

Evidence appears to show that the chronic anger and hostility associated with Type A behavior can predict heart disease.

personalities were being evaluated, subjected to harassment or criticism, or playing video games, their heart rate and blood pressure were much higher than those of Type B personalities under the same circumstances (Lyness, 1993). Both high heart rate and high blood pressure are known to contribute to CHD.

Other studies maintain that the link between Type A behavior and CHD is less direct—that the tendency toward Type A behavior may influence people to engage in behaviors, such as smoking or overeating, that directly contribute to heart disease (K. A. Matthews, 1988). On the basis of the preponderance of evidence, however, it seems clear that *chronic anger* and *hostility* (both components of Type A behavior) do indeed predict heart disease (T. Q. Miller, Smith, Turner, Guijavo, & Hallet, 1996). For example, people who scored high on an anger scale were 2.5 times more likely to have heart attacks or sudden cardiac deaths than their calmer peers (J. C. Williams et al., 2000). Counseling designed to diminish the intensity of time urgency and hostility in patients with Type A behavior has been moderately successful in reducing the incidence of CHD (Friedman et al., 1996).

Depression, too, appears to increase the risk of heart disease and premature death (McCabe, Schneiderman, Field, & Wellens, 2000; Schwartzman & Glaus, 2000). Here, the link to heart disease is through the long-term exposure to stress-produced hormones that, over time, damage the heart and blood vessels. Because long-term stress increases the likelihood of developing CHD, reducing stress has become part of the treatment used to slow the progress of atherosclerosis, or blockage of the arteries, which can lead to a heart attack. Both a very low-fat diet and stress-management techniques, such as yoga and deep relaxation, have been effective in treating this disease (Ornish, 1990).

Stress and the Immune System

Why do so many students get sick during finals?

Scientists have long suspected that stress also affects the functioning of the immune system. Recall that the immune system is strongly affected by hormones and signals from the brain. The relatively new field of **psychoneuroimmunology (PNI)** studies the interaction between stress on the one hand and immune, endocrine, and nervous system activity on the other (Ader & Cohen, 1993; Azar, 1999a; Maier, Watkins, & Fleshner, 1994). To the extent that stress disrupts the functioning of the immune system, it can impair health (S. Cohen & Herbert, 1996). Chronic stress, such as caring for an elderly parent, living in poverty, depression (Oltmanns & Emery, 1998), or even the stress associated with college exams (O'Leary, 1990) have been linked to suppressed functioning of the immune system.

Increased stress may make us more susceptible to upper respiratory infections, such as the common cold (Cohen, 1996). For example, volunteers who reported being under severe stress and who had experienced two or more major stressful events during the previous year were more likely to develop a cold when they were exposed to a cold virus (Cohen, Tyrrell, & Smith, 1991). A control group of volunteers who reported lower levels of stress were less likely to develop cold symptoms even though they were equally exposed to the virus.

Psychoneuroimmunologists have also established a possible relationship between stress and cancer. Stress does not cause cancer, but it apparently impairs the immune system so that cancerous cells are better able to establish themselves and spread throughout the body. Current animal research is focused on finding the exact cellular mechanisms that link stress

Psychoneuroimmunology (PNI)
A new field that studies the interaction between stress on the one hand and immune, endocrine, and nervous system activity on the other.

to cancer (e.g., Ben-Eliyahu, Yirmiya, Shavit, & Liebeskind, 1990; Quan et al., 1999).

Establishing a direct link between stress and cancer in humans is more difficult. However, research does show a correlation between stress and incidence of cancer. For example, people who developed cancer generally reported a number of stressful life events in the year before diagnosis (O'Leary, 1990). They were also likely to be fatigued and to feel helpless. Given clear links between stress and other disorders, a link to cancer seems probable, but the scientific jury is still out.

Apart from shedding light on the role of stress in cancer, many medical practitioners agree that psychologists can also play a vital role in improving the quality of life for cancer patients, and perhaps prevent premature death (McGuire, 1999; Rabasca, 1999a). Being diagnosed with cancer is, in itself, stressful, as are the treatments for most forms of cancer. Chemotherapy and radiation treatments can suppress immune function, so patients who are depressed at their diagnosis must then deal with a double blow to the immune system. Cancer therapy now often includes stress-reduction components such as group therapy (Kissane et al., 1997; Spiegel, 1995).

11.2

Staying Healthy

What steps can people take to stay healthy?

Totally avoiding stress is, of course, impossible. So what can we do to effectively manage the stress we do experience? Psychological research has provided us with some answers.

Calm Down   Stress may be part of life, but there are proven ways to reduce the negative impact of stress on your body and your health. *Exercise* is one. Running, walking, biking, swimming, or whatever aerobic exercise you enjoy doing regularly lowers your resting heart rate and blood pressure, so that your body does not react as strongly to stress and recovers more quickly. Moreover, numerous studies show that people who exercise regularly and are physically fit have higher self-esteem than those who do not; are less likely to feel anxious, depressed, or irritable; and have fewer aches and pains, as well as fewer colds (Biddle, 2000; Sonstroem, 1997).

Relax   *Relaxation training* is another stress buster. A number of studies indicate that relaxation techniques improve immune functioning (Andersen, Kiecolt-Glaser, & Glaser, 1994). Relaxation is more than flopping on the couch with the TV zapper, however. Healthful physical relaxation requires lying quietly and alternately tensing and relaxing every voluntary muscle in your body—from your head to your toes—in part to learn how to recognize muscle tension, in part to learn how to relax your body. Breathing exercises can have the same effect: if you are tense, deep, rhythmic breathing is difficult, but learning to do so relieves bodily tension. (See also Chapter 4, States of Consciousness, for a discussion of meditation, and Chapter 5, Learning, for a discussion of biofeedback, both of which can be useful in relaxing and reducing stress.)

Reach Out   A strong network of friends and family who provide social support can help to maintain good health, even though we don't fully understand why (Uchino, Cacioppo, & Kiecolt-Glaser, 1996). Most people can remember times when others made a difference in their lives by giving them good advice, helping them to feel better about themselves, providing assistance with chores and responsibilities or financial help, or simply by "hanging out" with them (Uchino, Uno, & Holt-Lunstad, 1999; R. B. Williams et al., 1992). Some researchers contend that social support may directly affect our response to stress and health by producing physiological changes in endocrine, cardiac, and immune functioning (Uchino et al., 1996).

Health psychologists are also investigating the role religion may play in reducing stress and bolstering health (Smith, 2000). For example, recent research has found that elderly people who pray or attend religious services regularly enjoy better health and markedly lower rates of depression than those who do not (Koenig, 1997; Koenig et al., 1997). However, critics maintain that, at best, the studies connecting health to faith demonstrate correlation, not cause and effect: The explanation may be that people who enjoy good health are more likely to pray and attend religious services (Sloan, Bagiella, & Powell, 1999).

Finally, *altruism*—reaching out and giving to others because this brings *you* pleasure—is one of the more effective ways to reduce stress (Vaillant, 2000). Caring for others tends to take our minds off our own problems, to make us realize that there are others who are worse off than we are, and to foster the feeling that we're involved in something larger than our own small slice of life (Folkman, Chesney, & Christopher-Richards, 1994).

Learn to Cope Effectively   How you appraise events in your environment—and how you appraise your ability to cope with potentially unsettling, unpredictable events—can minimize or maximize stress and its impact on health.

Proactive coping is the psychological term for anticipating stressful events and taking advance steps to avoid them or to minimize their impact (Aspinwall & Taylor, 1997). Proactive coping does not mean "expect the worst"; constant vigilance actually increases stress and may damage health. Rather, proactive coping means "Be prepared." This may include recognizing potential stress in advance and making realistic plans. For example, a recent widower makes plans to spend the holidays with friends. A woman who is moving to a new city finds out as much as she can about her new location before she moves—whether her friends have friends there, where she can participate in activities she enjoys, what are the places and groups or organizations where she might meet people who share her interests, and so on.

Even if you cannot change or escape stressful circumstances, you can change the way you think about things. *Positive reappraisal* helps people to make the best of a tense or painful situation. A low grade can be seen as a warning sign, not a catastrophe; a job that you hate provides information on what you really want in your career.

Finally, one of the most effective, stress-relieving forms of reappraisal is *humor*. King Solomon advised, "a merry heart doeth good like medicine" (Proverbs 17:22). Journalist Norman Cousins (1981) attributed his recovery from a life-threatening disease to regular "doses" of laughter. Watching classic comic films, he believed, reduced both his pain and the inflammation in his tissues. He wrote the following:

> What was significant about the laughter . . . was not just the fact that it provides internal exercise for a person flat on his or her back—a form of jogging for the innards—but that it creates a mood in which the other positive emotions can be put to work, too. In short it helps make it possible for good things to happen. (pp. 145–146)

Health psychologists agree (e.g., Salovey, Rothman, Detweiler, & Steward, 2000; Vaillant, 2000): A healthy body and a sense of humor go hand-in-hand.

INTERACTIVE LECTURE   **11.3**

CHECK YOUR UNDERSTANDING

WEB QUIZ **11.3**

Match the following terms with the appropriate definition.

_____ 1. alarm reaction
      a. signs of psychic and physical wear and tear begin to show

_____ 2. resistance
      b. body recognizes that it must fend off danger

_____ 3. exhaustion
      c. "burnout" can occur here

4. _____ is the term given to the set of characteristics, such as hostility and a sense of urgency, that many people believe make a person more susceptible to coronary heart disease.

5. Indicate whether the following statements are true (T) or false (F).

_____a. Research so far has been unable to find a relationship between stress and the strength of the body's immune system.

_____b. Prolonged psychological stress can make certain diseases worse.

_____c. Increased stress may make us more susceptible to the common cold.

_____d. Prolonged stress has been shown to increase vulnerability to cancer.

_____e. People who attend religious services regularly do not enjoy better health than those who do not attend regularly.

Answers: 1. b. 2. a. 3. c. 4. Type A behavior pattern. 5. a. (F); b. (T); c. (T); d. (T); e. (F).

Sources of Extreme Stress

What are some sources of extreme stress, and what impact do they have?

Extreme stress has a variety of sources, ranging from unemployment to wartime combat, from violent natural disaster to rape. Extreme stress marks a radical departure from everyday life, such that a person cannot carry on as before and, in some cases, never fully recovers. What are some major causes of stress? What effect do they have on people? How do people cope?

Unemployment Joblessness is a major source of stress. In fact, when the jobless rate rises, there is also an increase in first admissions to psychiatric hospitals, infant mortality, deaths from heart disease, alcohol-related diseases, and suicide (Brenner, 1973, 1979; Rayman & Bluestone, 1982). In a study of aircraft workers who lost their jobs, many of the workers reported suffering from high blood pressure, alcoholism, heavy smoking, and anxiety. Other studies have found that family strain increases. "Things just fell apart," one worker said after both he and his wife suddenly found themselves unemployed.

Finally, two studies have shown that death rates go up and psychiatric symptoms worsen not just during periods of unemployment but also during short, rapid upturns in the economy (Brenner, 1979; Eyer, 1977). This finding lends support to the view that change, whether good or bad, causes stress.

Divorce and Separation "The deterioration or ending of an intimate relationship is one of the more potent of stressors and one of the more frequent reasons why people seek psychotherapy" (Coleman et al., 1988, p. 155). After a breakup, both partners often feel they have failed at one of life's most important

A scene from an unemployment office. As unemployment rates rise, so do first admissions to psychiatric hospitals, deaths from heart disease, and suicides.

endeavors, but strong emotional ties often continue to bind the pair. If only one spouse wants to end the marriage, the one initiating the divorce may feel sadness and guilt at hurting his or her partner; the rejected spouse may feel anger, humiliation, and guilt over his or her role in the failure. Even if the decision to separate was mutually agreed on, ambivalent feelings of love and hate can make life turbulent. Adults are not the only ones who are stressed by divorce, of course. A national survey of the impact of divorce on children (Cherlin, 1992) found that a majority suffer intense emotional stress at the time of divorce; although most recover within a year or two (especially if the custodial parent establishes a stable home and their parents do not fight about child rearing), a minority experience long-term problems (see also Wallerstein, Blakesley, & Lewis, 2000.)

Bereavement   For decades it was widely held that following the death of a loved one, people go through a necessary period of intense grief during which they work through their loss and, about a year later, pick up and go on with their lives. Psychologists (Janis, Mahl, & Holt, 1969) and physicians as well as the public at large have endorsed this cultural wisdom. But some have challenged this view of loss (C. G. Davis, Wortman, Lehman, & Silver, 2000; Wortman & Silver, 1989).

According to Wortman, the first myth about bereavement is that people should be intensely distressed when a loved one dies, which suggests that people who are not devastated are behaving abnormally, perhaps pathologically. Often, however, people have prepared for the loss, said their good-byes, and feel little remorse or regret; indeed, they may be relieved that their loved one is no longer suffering. The second myth—that people need to work through their grief—may lead family, friends, and even physicians consciously or unconsciously to encourage the bereaved to feel or act distraught. Moreover, physicians may deny those mourners who are deeply disturbed needed antianxiety or antidepressant medication "for their own good." The third myth holds that people who find meaning in the death, who come to a spiritual or existential understanding of why it happened, cope better than those who do not. In reality, people who do not seek greater understanding are the best adjusted and least depressed. The fourth myth—that people should recover from a loss within a year or so—is perhaps the most damaging. Parents trying to cope with the death of an infant and adults whose spouse or child died suddenly in a vehicle accident continue to experience painful memories and wrestle with depression years later. But because they have not recovered "on schedule," members of their social network may become unsympathetic. Unfortunately, the people who need support most may hide their feelings because they do not want to make other people uncomfortable and fail to seek treatment because they, too, believe they should recover on their own.

Not all psychologists agree with this "new" view of bereavement. But most agree that research on loss must take into account individual (and group or cultural) differences, as well as variations in the circumstances surrounding a loss (Bonanno & Kaltman, 1999; Harvey & Miller, 1998).

Catastrophes   Catastrophes, natural and otherwise—including floods, earthquakes, violent storms, fires, and plane crashes—produce certain psychological reactions common to all stressful events. At first, in the *shock stage*, "the victim is stunned, dazed, and apathetic" and sometimes even "stuporous, disoriented, and amnesic for the traumatic event." Then, in the *suggestible stage*, victims are passive and quite ready to do whatever rescuers tell them to do. In the third phase, the *recovery stage*, emotional balance is regained, but anxiety often persists, and victims may need to recount their experiences over and over again (Morris, 1990). In later stages, survivors may feel irrationally guilty because they lived while others died.

Combat and Other Threatening Personal Attacks Wartime experiences often cause soldiers intense and disabling combat stress that persists long after they have left the battlefield. Similar reactions—including bursting into rage over harmless remarks, sleep disturbances, cringing at sudden loud noises, psychological confusion, uncontrollable crying, and silently staring into space for long periods—are also frequently seen in survivors of serious accidents, especially children, and of violent crimes such as rapes and muggings. **Figure 11–2** shows the traumatic effects of war on the civilian population, based on composite statistics obtained after recent civil wars (Mollica, 2000).

Posttraumatic Stress Disorder

What experiences can lead to posttraumatic stress disorder?

Severely stressful events can cause a psychological disorder known as **posttraumatic stress disorder (PTSD).** Dramatic nightmares in which the victim reexperiences the terrifying event exactly as it happened are common, as are daytime flashbacks, in which the victim relives the trauma. Often, victims of PTSD withdraw from social life and from job and family responsibilities. Posttraumatic stress disorder can set in immediately after a traumatic event or within a short time. But sometimes, months or years may go by in which the victim seems to have recovered from the experience, and then, without warning, psychological symptoms appear, then may disappear only to recur repeatedly; some people suffer for years (Kessler, Sonega, Bromet, Hughes, & Nelson, 1995). Exposure to events reminiscent of the original trauma intensify symptoms of PTSD (Moyers, 1996).

Combat veterans appear to be especially vulnerable to PTSD. More than one-third of the men who took part in heavy combat in Vietnam showed signs of serious PTSD. Veterans of World War II also experienced PTSD; after more than half a century, many still have nightmares from which they awake sweating and shaking (Gelman, 1994). Therapists also have begun to report that some veterans who seemed healthy and well adjusted throughout their postwar lives suddenly develop symptoms of PTSD when they retire (Sleek, 1998). And, of course, soldiers are not the only victims of war. Psychologists are beginning to study the effects of war on civilian

After the attacks on the World Trade Center of September 11, 2001, rescue workers at the site returned every day for months to search for victims, many of whom were their friends and coworkers in the police and fire departments. The extreme trauma of the attacks and their aftermath caused many to suffer from post traumatic stress syndrome.

Posttraumatic stress disorder (PTSD) Psychological disorder characterized by episodes of anxiety, sleeplessness, and nightmares resulting from some disturbing past event.

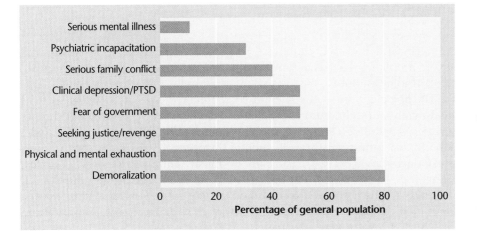

FIGURE 11–2

Mental trauma in societies at war. In societies that have undergone the stress of war, nearly everyone suffers some psychological reaction, ranging from serious mental illness to feelings of demoralization. Rates of clinical depression are as high as 50 percent.

Source: Mollica, R. F. (2000, June). Invisible wounds. *Scientific American*, p. 54. Figure by Laurie Grace. Reprinted by permission of Laurie Grace.

UNDERSTANDING OURSELVES

Traumatic Stress: Recovering From Disasters and Other Traumatic Events

The September 11, 2001, terrorist attacks in New York City and Washington, D.C., were the type of events that we thought could never happen. Like other types of disasters, they were unexpected, sudden, and overwhelming. In some cases, there are no outwardly visible signs of physical injury, but there is nonetheless a serious emotional toll. It is common for people who have experienced traumatic situations to have very strong emotional reactions. Understanding normal responses to these abnormal events can aid you in coping effectively with your feelings, thoughts, and behaviors, and can help you along the path to recovery.

What happens to people after a disaster or another kind of traumatic event?

Shock and denial are typical responses to terrorism, disasters, and other kinds of trauma, especially shortly after the event. Both shock and denial are normal protective reactions. Shock is a sudden and often an intense disturbance of your emotional state that may leave you feeling stunned or dazed. Denial involves your not acknowledging that something very stressful has happened, or not experiencing fully the intensity of the event. You may temporarily feel numb or disconnected from life. As the initial shock subsides, reactions vary from one person to another. The following, however, are normal responses to a traumatic event:

- Feelings become intense and sometimes are unpredictable. You may become more irritable than usual, and your mood may change back and forth dramatically. You might be especially anxious or nervous, or even become depressed.

- Thoughts and behavior patterns are affected by the trauma. You might have repeated and vivid memories of the event. These flashbacks may occur for no apparent reason and may lead to physical reactions such as rapid heartbeat or sweating. You may find it difficult to concentrate or make decisions, or become more easily confused. Sleep and eating patterns also may be disrupted.

- Recurring emotional reactions are common. Anniversaries of the event, such as at one month or one year, as well as reminders such as aftershocks from earthquakes or the sounds of sirens, can trigger upsetting memories of the traumatic experience. These triggers may be accompanied by fears that the stressful event will be repeated.

- Interpersonal relationships often become strained. Greater conflict, such as more frequent arguments with family members and coworkers, is common. On the other hand, you may become withdrawn and isolated and may avoid your usual activities.

- Physical symptoms may accompany the extreme stress. For example, headaches, nausea, and chest pain may result and may require medical attention. Preexisting medical conditions may worsen because of the stress.

How do people respond differently over time?

It is important for you to realize that there is not one standard pat-

survivors and find that they, too, sometimes experience long-lasting and severe problems, such as exhaustion, hatred, mistrust, and the symptoms of PTSD (Mollica, 2000).

Yet not everyone who is exposed to severely stressful events such as heavy combat or childhood sexual abuse develops PTSD. Individual characteristics—including gender (Curle & Williams, 1996; Rabasca, 1999b), personality, a family history of mental disorders (Friedman, Schnurr, & McDonagh-Coyle, 1994), substance abuse among relatives (Gurvits, Gilbertson, Lasko, Orr, & Pittman, 1997), and even preexisting neurological disorders—appear to predispose some people to PTSD more than others. Both men and women who have a history of emotional problems are more tern of reaction to the extreme stress of traumatic experiences. Some people respond immediately, whereas others have delayed reactions—sometimes months or even years later. Some have adverse effects for a long period of time, whereas others recover rather quickly. And reactions can change over time. Some who have suffered from trauma are energized initially by the event to help them with the challenge of coping, only later to become discouraged or depressed. A number of factors tend to affect the length of time required for recovery, including the following:

- *The degree of intensity and loss.* Events that last longer and pose a greater threat and in which loss of life or substantial loss of property is involved often take longer to resolve.

- *A person's general ability to cope with emotionally challenging situations.* Individuals who have handled well other difficult, stressful circumstances may find it easier to cope with the trauma.

- *Other stressful events preceding the traumatic experience.* Individuals faced with other emotionally challenging situations, such as serious health problems or family-related difficulties, may have more intense reactions to the new stressful event and need more time to recover.

How should I help my family and myself?

There are a number of steps you can take to help restore emotional well-being and a sense of control following a terrorist act, a disaster, or another kind of traumatic experience, including the following:

- Give yourself time to heal. Anticipate that this will be a difficult period in your life. Allow yourself to mourn the losses you have experienced.

- Ask for support from people who care about you and who will listen and empathize with your situation.

- Communicate your experience in whatever ways feel comfortable to you—such as by talking with family or close friends or by keeping a diary.

- Find out about local support groups that often are available, such as for those who have suffered from natural disasters or for women who are victims of rape.

- Try to find groups led by appropriately trained and experienced professionals.

- Engage in healthy behaviors to enhance your ability to cope with excessive stress. Eat well-balanced meals and get plenty of rest. If you experience ongoing difficulties with sleep, you may be able to find some relief through relaxation techniques. Avoid alcohol and drugs.

- Establish or reestablish routines such as eating meals at regular times and following an exercise program.

- Avoid major life decisions such as switching careers or jobs if possible, because these activities tend to be highly stressful.

Source: http://helping.apa.org/daily/traumaticstress.html

likely to experience severe trauma and to develop PTSD as a consequence of trauma (Breslau, Davis, & Andreski, 1995).

Recovery from posttraumatic stress disorder depends a great deal on the amount of emotional support that survivors receive from family, friends, and the community. Treatment consists of helping those who have experienced severe trauma to come to terms with their terrifying memories. Immediate treatment near the site of the trauma coupled with the expectation that the individual will return to everyday life is often effective. Reliving the traumatic event in a safe setting is also crucial to successful treatment. This helps desensitize people to the traumatic memories haunting them (Oltmanns & Emery, 1995). In *Understanding Ourselves:*

INTERACTIVE LECTURE **11.4**

Traumatic Stress, we focus on the effects and recovery from traumatic stress.

WEB QUIZ **11.4**

CHECK YOUR UNDERSTANDING

1. Indicate whether the following statements are true (T) or false (F).

____a. Change that results from "good" events like marriage or job promotion does not produce stress.

____b. Most children whose parents divorce experience serious and long-term problems.

____c. If people who are bereaved following the death of a spouse or child have not recovered by the end of one year, this outcome indicates that they are coping abnormally.

2. In extreme cases, severely stressful events can cause a psychological disorder known as ____ ____ ____.

3. Indicate whether the following statements are true (T) or false (F).

____a. Catastrophes, natural and otherwise—including floods, earthquakes, violent storms, fires, and plane crashes—produce different psychological reactions than do other kinds of stressful events.

____b. Posttraumatic stress disorder always becomes evident immediately.

____c. Combat veterans appear to be especially vulnerable to PTSD.

____d. People with a history of emotional problems are more likely to develop PTSD.

Answers: 1. a. (F); b. (F); c. (F). 2. Posttraumatic stress disorder. 3. a. (F); b. (F); c. (T); d. (T).

The Well-Adjusted Person

What qualities describe a well-adjusted person?

We noted at the beginning of the chapter that adjustment is any effort to cope with stress. Psychologists disagree, however, about what constitutes *good* adjustment. Some think it is the ability to live according to social norms. Thus, a woman who grows up in a small town, attends college, teaches for a year or two, and then settles down to a peaceful family life might be considered well adjusted because she is living by the predominant values of her community.

Other psychologists disagree strongly with this view. They argue that society is not always right. Thus, if we accept its standards blindly, we renounce the right to make individual judgments. Barron (1963) argues that well-adjusted people enjoy the difficulties and ambiguities of life, treating them as challenges to be overcome. Such people are aware of their strengths and weaknesses; this awareness enables them to live in harmony with their inner selves.

We may also evaluate adjustment by using specific criteria, such as the following (Morris, 1990), to judge an action:

1. Does the action realistically meet the demands of the situation, or does it simply postpone resolving the problem?

2. Does the action meet the individual's needs?

3. Is the action compatible with the well-being of others?

Abraham Maslow, whose hierarchy of needs was discussed in Chapter 8, believes that well-adjusted people attempt to "actualize" themselves. That is, they live in a way that enhances their own growth and fulfillment,

UNDERSTANDING The World Around Us

Why Are Some People Happier Than Others?

What is the nature of happiness? For psychologists, happiness is just one aspect of *subjective well-being* (SWB). In addition to happiness, SWB includes having more positive than negative emotions and having feelings of overall life satisfaction.

To understand the roots of happiness and feelings of well-being, researchers looked first at external events and the demographic characteristics of happy people. But after decades of research and despite what "common sense" might suggest, they found that external events and demographic characteristics have very little influence on SWB (DeNeve & Cooper, 1998; Diener, Suh, Lucas, & Smith, 1999). More specifically, they found no correlation between age, gender, or intelligence and happiness (DeNeve & Cooper, 1998; Diener & Suh, 1998; Diener et al., 1999). They did find that people who are married, wealthy, well educated, and in good health tend to be happier than others, but the difference is often a small one (Breetvelt & Van Dam,

1991; Brickman, Coates, & Janoff-Bulman, 1978; Diener et al., 1999).

If these variables don't have a major effect on happiness, then what does account for SWB? Increasingly, researchers are coming to believe that the keys to happiness are the goals that people have, their ability to adapt to conditions around them, and their personalities. Con-

> Personality is a strong and consistent predictor of well-being over a period of years.

sistent with this view is the fact that personality is a strong and consistent predictor of well-being over a period of years (DeNeve & Cooper, 1998; Diener et al., 1999). Also, people who are happy in one area of their lives (such as at work) tend to be happy in other areas as well. Thus, researchers believe that stable personality factors predispose people to

feel happy or unhappy in a wide range of situations, though current life events significantly influence happiness at any given moment.

Using the Big Five trait model described in Chapter 10, Personality, DeNeve and Cooper (1998) found that happy people and those reporting more positive than negative emotions tend to be high on extraversion and low on neuroticism. They also found that people who are satisfied with their lives tend to be high on conscientiousness and low on neuroticism. To a lesser extent, people high in agreeableness also tend to be more satisfied with their lives. Thus, happy people in general tend to be enthusiastic, accommodating, understanding, flexible, gregarious, energetic, confident, optimistic, and affectionate.

Why personality should predict happiness so well is not yet known. Some evidence suggests that people may be genetically predisposed to be happy or unhappy (Lykken & Tellegen, 1996). Exactly how genes might affect happiness is currently being explored (Buss, 2000).

regardless of what others might think. According to Maslow, well-adjusted people are unconventional and creative thinkers, perceive people and events realistically, and set goals for themselves. They also tend to form deep, close relationships with a few chosen individuals.

As we have seen, there are many standards for judging whether an individual is well adjusted. A person deemed well adjusted by one standard might not be considered well adjusted by other standards. (See *Understanding the World Around Us*.) The same principle holds true when we try to specify what behaviors are "abnormal"—the topic of the next chapter.

INTERACTIVE LECTURE **11.5**

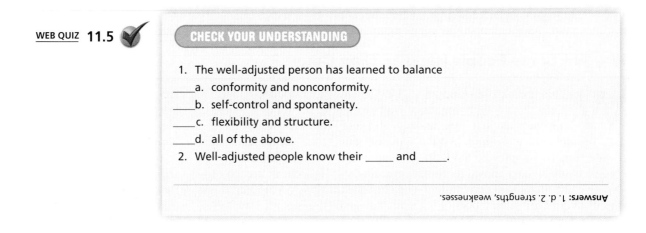

WEB QUIZ **11.5**

CHECK YOUR UNDERSTANDING

1. The well-adjusted person has learned to balance
   ____a. conformity and nonconformity.
   ____b. self-control and spontaneity.
   ____c. flexibility and structure.
   ____d. all of the above.
2. Well-adjusted people know their _____ and _____.

Answers: 1. d. 2. strengths, weaknesses.

KEY TERMS

stress, p. 397
adjustment, p. 397
health psychology, p. 397
stressor, p. 397

Sources of stress
pressure, p. 399
frustration, p. 399
conflict, p. 399
approach/approach conflict, p. 400

avoidance/avoidance conflict, p. 400
approach/avoidance conflict, p. 400

Coping with stress
confrontation, p. 403
compromise, p. 403
withdrawal, p. 405
defense mechanisms, p. 405

denial, p. 405
repression, p. 405
projection, p. 406
identification, p. 407
regression, p. 407
intellectualization, p. 407
reaction formation, p. 407
displacement, p. 407
sublimation, p. 407

How stress affects health
general adaptation syndrome (GAS), p. 410
psychoneuroimmunology, p. 412

Sources of extreme stress
posttraumatic stress disorder (PTSD), p. 417

CHAPTER REVIEW

Sources of Stress

What are stressors? We experience **stress** when we are faced with a tense or threatening situation that requires us to change or adapt our behavior (a **stressor**). Some life-and-death situations, like war and natural disasters, are inherently stressful. Even events that are usually viewed as positive, like a wedding or a job promotion, can be stressful, because they require change or adaptation. How we adjust to the stresses in our lives affects our health, since prolonged or severe stress can contribute to physical and psychological disorders. **Health psychologists** try to find ways to prevent stress from becoming debilitating and to promote healthy behaviors.

Why is change so stressful for most people? Because most people have a strong desire to maintain order in their lives, any event, either good or bad, that involves change will be experienced as stressful.

How can everyday hassles contribute to stress? Many psychologists believe day-to-day petty annoyances and irritations—such as being stuck in traffic, misplacing car keys, and getting into trivial arguments—to be as stressful as major life events because, although seemingly minor, these incidents give rise to feelings of pressure, frustration, conflict, and anxiety.

When we experience **pressure** from either internal or external forces, we feel forced to intensify our efforts or to perform at higher levels. Internal forces include meeting our personal standards; external forces include competition or imposed standards in jobs, grades, and parental demands.

We feel frustrated when someone or something stands between us and our goal. Five basic sources of **frustration** are delays, lack of resources, losses, failure, and discrimination.

Conflict arises when we are faced with two or more incompatible demands, opportunities, needs, or goals.

Someone who is simultaneously attracted to two incompatible goals experiences an **approach/approach conflict,** in which the person must either make a choice between the two goals or opportunities or modify them so as to take some advantage of both goals. The reverse of this problem is **avoidance/avoidance conflict,** in which a person confronts two undesirable or threatening possibilities. People usually try to escape this kind of conflict, but if escape is impossible, they cope in one of several ways, often by vacillating between the two possibilities. Also difficult to resolve is an **approach/avoidance conflict,** in which a person is both attracted to and repelled by the same goal or opportunity. Because both the desire to approach and the desire to avoid the goal grow stronger as the person in this dilemma nears the goal, the situation eventually reaches a point at which the tendency to approach equals the tendency to avoid. The person then vacillates until he or she finally makes a decision or until the situation changes.

How do we create stress? Sometimes we subject ourselves to stress by internalizing a set of irrational, self-defeating beliefs that add unnecessarily to the normal stresses of living and that are independent of outside forces.

Do people who are resistant to stress share certain traits? People who cope well with stress tend to be self-confident and optimistic. They also see themselves as being able to affect their situations, a trait referred to as having an internal locus of control.

Suzanne Kobasa suggests that stress-resistant people share a trait called *hardiness*—a tendency to experience difficult demands as challenging rather than threatening. People who feel that they have some control over an event are far less susceptible to stress than are those who feel powerless in the same situation. *Resilience*, the ability to bounce back after a stressful event, is also related to positive adjustment.

Coping with Stress

What is the difference between direct coping and defensive coping? People generally adjust to stress in one of two ways: *Direct coping* describes any action people take to change an uncomfortable situation, whereas *defensive coping* denotes the various ways people convince themselves—through a form of self-deception—that they are not really threatened or do not really want something they cannot get.

What are three strategies that deal directly with stress? When we cope directly with a particular threat or conflict, we do it in one of three ways: **confrontation, compromise,** or **withdrawal.** When we confront a stressful situation and admit to ourselves that there is a problem that needs to be solved, we may learn new skills, enlist other people's aid, or try harder to reach our goal. Confrontation may also include expressions of anger. Compromise usually requires adjusting expectations or desires; the conflict is resolved by settling for less than what was originally sought. Sometimes the most effective way of coping with a stressful situation is to distance oneself from it. The danger of withdrawal, however, is that it may become a maladaptive habit.

What are the major ways of coping defensively? When a stressful situation arises and there is little that can be done to deal with it directly, people often turn to **defense mechanisms** as a way of coping. Defense mechanisms are ways of deceiving ourselves about the causes of stressful events, thus reducing conflict, frustration, pressure, and anxiety. **Denial** is the refusal to acknowledge a painful or threatening reality. **Repression** is the blocking out of unacceptable thoughts or impulses from consciousness. When we cannot deny or repress a particular problem, we might resort to **projection**—attributing our repressed motives or feelings to others, thereby locating the source of our conflict outside ourselves. **Identification** is another form of defensive coping and may occur in situations in which people feel completely powerless. People who adopt this technique take on the characteristics of a powerful person in order to gain a sense of control. People under severe stress sometimes revert to childlike behavior, called **regression.** Because adults can't stand feeling helpless, becoming more childlike can make total dependency or helplessness more tolerable. Sometimes people **intellectualize** their problems in order emotionally to distance themselves from a particularly disturbing situation. **Reaction formation** refers to a behavioral form of denial in which people express with exaggerated intensity ideas and emotions that are the opposite of their own. Through **displacement,** repressed motives and feelings are redirected from their original objects to substitute objects. **Sublimation** involves transforming repressed emotions into more socially accepted forms.

Although defensive coping can contribute to our overall ability to adjust to difficult circumstances, it can also lead to maladaptive behavior if it interferes with the person's ability to deal constructively with a difficult situation.

Who experiences the most stress? How people handle stress is determined to a significant degree by environment in which they live. People in low-income groups often experience more stress and also have fewer means of coping, lower self-concepts, and an external locus of control. Men and women may cope differently with stress. One view suggest that evolution has shaped behavior such that men are more likely to cope by behaving aggressively, whereas women seek contact and support from others.

How Stress Affects Health

What long-lasting effects of stress do we need to be concerned with? Physiologist Hans Selye contends that people react to physical and psychological stress in three stages that he called the **general adaptation syndrome (GAS).** In Stage 1, *alarm reaction*, the body recognizes that it must fight off some physical or psychological danger. This recognition results in quickened respiration and heart rate, increased sensitivity and alertness, and a highly charged emotional state—a physical adaptation that augments our coping resources and helps us to regain self-control. If neither direct nor defensive coping mechanisms succeed in reducing the stress, we move on to Selye's second stage of adaptation. During this *resistance stage*, physical symptoms of strain appear as we intensify our efforts to cope both directly and defensively. If these attempts to regain psychological equilibrium fail, psychological disorganization rages out of control until we reach *exhaustion*, Selye's third stage. In this phase, we use increasingly ineffective defense mechanisms to bring the stress under control. At this point, some people lose touch with reality, whereas others show signs of "burnout," such as shorter attention spans, irritability, procrastination, and general apathy.

How is Type A behavior related to heart disease? Stress is known to be an important factor in the development of coronary heart disease. Type A behavior pattern—a set of stressful characteristics that includes hostility, urgency, competitiveness, and striving—has been linked to a greater likelihood of coronary heart disease.

Why do so many students get sick during finals? Stress—such as that experienced by students during examination periods—can suppress the functioning of the immune system, the focus of the relatively new field of **psychoneuroimmunology (PNI).** Stress can also increase one's susceptibility to the common cold, and it appears to be linked to the development of some forms of cancer.

What steps can people take to stay healthy? When stress cannot be avoided, people may be able to cope by exercising regularly and learning to relax. Having a strong network of friends and family that provide social support is also related to healthier adjustment. For example, people who are religious and who are altruistic typically experience less stress, although the mechanism involved is not clear. Finally, people can improve their ability to cope by taking steps to minimize the impact of stressful events (proactive coping), by making the best of difficult situations (positive reappraisal), and by maintaining a sense of humor.

Sources of Extreme Stress

What are some sources of extreme stress, and what impact do they have? Stress derives from a number of sources, including unemployment, divorce and separation, bereavement, combat, and catastrophes. One of the impediments to effective coping occurs when the grieving person feels compelled to adjust in socially prescribed ways that do not provide effective relief.

What experiences can lead to posttraumatic stress disorder? Extreme traumas may result in **posttraumatic stress disorder (PTSD),** a disabling emotional disorder whose symptoms include anxiety, sleeplessness, and nightmares. Combat veterans and people with a history of emotional problems are especially vulnerable to PTSD.

The Well-Adjusted Person

What qualities describe a well-adjusted person? Psychologists are of several minds on what constitutes good adjustment. Some believe that well-adjusted people live according to social norms, having learned to control socially forbidden impulses and to limit their goals to those that society allows. Others disagree, arguing that well-adjusted people enjoy overcoming challenging situations and that this ability leads to growth and self-fulfillment. Finally, some psychologists use specific criteria to evaluate a person's ability to adjust, such as how well the adjustment solves the problem and satisfies both personal needs and the needs of others.

CRITICAL THINKING AND APPLICATIONS

1. Because conflict is considered a major source of stress, what strategies could help reduce conflict?

2. Are defense mechanisms bad for you, or do they foster good health? Give an example of defensive coping.

3. What psychological or physical wear and tear do you show when you experience stress, such as during final exams?

4. How would you help children who live in a violent community?

5. In what areas of your life are you well adjusted, and in what areas could you improve?

WEB QUIZ **11.6** ✓ **Go to the Morris 6e Companion Website to take a practice chapter exam.**

12 Psychological Disorders

OVERVIEW

WHEN IS BEHAVIOR ABNORMAL? THE ANSWER TO THIS QUESTION IS MORE complicated than it may seem. There is no doubt that the man on the street corner claiming to be Jesus Christ or the woman insisting that aliens from outer space are trying to kill her is behaving abnormally. But what about the members of a religious cult who follow through on a suicide pact? A business executive who drinks three martinis every day for lunch? A young woman who feels depressed much of the time but still functions effectively at her job?

Perspectives on Psychological Disorders

How does a mental-health professional define a psychological disorder?

Society, the individual, and mental-health professionals all use different standards to distinguish normal behavior from psychological disorders (see **Table 12–1**). Society's main standard is whether behavior conforms to the existing social order. The individual's primary criterion is his or her own sense of well-being. The mental health professional looks chiefly at *personality characteristics, personal discomfort* (the experience of inner distress), and *life functioning* (success in meeting society's expectations for performance in work, school, or social relationships). Serious personal discomfort and inadequate life functioning often go together, complicating the definition of psychological disorder. Consider the imbalance between personal discomfort and life functioning in each of the following examples:

- A young executive is in a state of profound euphoria. He feels exhilarated, invulnerable, and all-powerful. He suddenly decides he's been caught up in a "rat race," quits his job, withdraws his life savings from the bank, and hands out the money on the street corner, telling startled passersby that "it's only paper."
- A 40-year-old successful computer programmer who lives alone feels insecure when relating to others. She makes little eye contact, rarely initiates a conversation, and almost always acts "jittery." Inwardly she feels so tense and restless that she avoids being around people. Often she finds it difficult to sleep at night.
- A 14-year-old boy has been uncontrollable at home and disruptive in school since early childhood. He abuses alcohol and other drugs, and he frequently steals from stores. As part of his initiation into a gang, he fires a semiautomatic pistol into the air while driving through the territory of a rival gang.

Is each of these brief vignettes an example of a psychological disorder? The answer depends, in part, on whose perspective you adopt. The euphoric young executive certainly feels happy, and the adolescent gang member does not think that he has a psychological problem. Although society would label their actions disordered, from their own perspectives

TABLE 12-1   PERSPECTIVES ON PSYCHOLOGICAL DISORDERS

	Standards/Values	Measures
Society	Orderly world in which people assume responsibility for their assigned social roles (e.g., breadwinner, parent), conform to prevailing mores, and meet situational requirements.	Observations of behavior, extent to which a person fulfills society's expectations and measures up to prevailing standards.
Individual	Happiness, gratification of needs.	Subjective perceptions of self-esteem, acceptance, and well-being.
Mental health professional	Sound personality structure characterized by growth, development, autonomy, environmental mastery, ability to cope with stress, adaptation.	Clinical judgment, aided by behavioral observations and psychological tests of such variables as self-concept; sense of identity; balance of psychic forces; unified outlook on life; resistance to stress; self-regulation; the ability to cope with reality; the absence of mental and behavioral symptoms; adequacy in love, work, and play; adequacy in interpersonal relationships.

Source: H. H. Strupp and S. W. Hadley (1977). "A tripartite model of mental health and therapeutic outcomes with special reference to negative effects on psychotherapy," in *American Psychologist, 32*, 187–196. Copyright © 1977 by the American Psychological Association. Adapted by permission of the authors.

Is this young man abnormal? Psychologists would say no, as long as his behavior does not lead to personal discomfort or inadequate life functioning.

neither suffers from the sort of personal discomfort that can define psychological disorder. The opposite is true of the computer programmer. Society might judge her behavior as odd but "normal," because it does not violate any essential social rules and she is functioning adequately. Nevertheless, she is experiencing much discomfort, and from her own perspective, something is seriously wrong.

Although the individual's perspective and society's view conflict in these cases, mental health professionals would assert that all three people are displaying psychological disorders. For clinicians, a psychological disorder exists either when behavior is maladaptive for life functioning or when it causes serious personal discomfort *or both*. But now imagine that the cases are slightly different. What if the young executive takes a trip around the world or gives his savings to a worthy charity instead of handing out money on the street? What if the programmer is not very anxious and honestly prefers being a "loner"? What if the teenager had been basically a "good kid" until he got involved with the gang members, who pressure him to do things he knows are wrong?

These questions bring us to a second, essential point about the definition of psychological disorders. Normal and abnormal behavior often differ only in degree. It is tempting to divide mental health and mental illness into categories that are *qualitatively different* from each other—like apples and oranges. It is often more accurate, however, to think of mental illness as being *quantitatively different* (that is, different in degree) from normal behavior.

To understand the distinction between these two approaches to classification, think about how we classify people's weight. There are no absolute dividing lines between normal and abnormal weight—between someone who is underweight or overweight and someone of normal weight. Because the distinction between normal and abnormal weight is a matter of degree, the dividing line between "normal" and "abnormal" is somewhat arbitrary. Still, it is often useful to divide the dimension of weight into categories such as "obese," "overweight," "normal," "thin," and "skinny." In the same way, abnormal behavior differs only *quantitatively* from normal behavior, but it is often useful to divide the dimension "normal-abnormal" into discrete categories. Nevertheless, it is important to remember that the line separating normal from abnormal behavior is somewhat arbitrary and that cases are always much easier to judge when they fall at the extreme end of a dimension than when they fall near the "dividing line." Remember, too, that individuals, society, and mental health professionals do not always view abnormality from the same viewpoint.

Historical Views of Psychological Disorders

How has the view of psychological disorders changed over time?

We can only speculate about what was considered an emotional disorder thousands of years ago. Mysterious behaviors were probably attributed to supernatural powers, and madness was a sign that spirits had possessed a person. Sometimes "possessed" people were seen as sacred; their visions were considered messages from the gods. At other times, their behavior indicated possession by evil spirits, signaling danger to the community. It is likely that this supernatural view of psychological disorders dominated all early societies.

The roots of a more naturalistic view can be traced to ancient Greece. The Greek physician Hippocrates (ca. 450–ca. 377 B.C.), for example, maintained that madness was like any other sickness—a natural event arising from natural causes. Hippocrates's theories encouraged a systematic search for the causes of mental illness and implied that disturbed people should be treated with the same care and sympathy that are given to people suffering from physical ailments.

During the Middle Ages, Europeans reverted to the supernatural view (although more naturalistic accounts were kept alive in Arab cultures). The emotionally disturbed person was thought to be a witch or to be possessed by the devil. Exorcisms, ranging from the mild to the hair-raising, were performed, and many people endured horrifying tortures. Some people were even burned at the stake.

The systematic, naturalistic approach to mental illness would not resurface until the eighteenth century, but by the late Middle Ages, there was a move away from viewing the mentally ill as witches and demon-possessed, and they were increasingly confined to public and private asylums. Although these institutions were founded with good intentions, most were little more than prisons. In the worst cases, inmates were chained down and deprived of food, light, or air in order to "cure" them.

Little was done to ensure humane standards in mental institutions until 1793, when Philippe Pinel became director of the Bicêtre Hospital in Paris. Under his direction the hospital was drastically reorganized: Patients were released from their chains and allowed to move about the hospital grounds, rooms were made more comfortable and sanitary, and questionable and violent medical treatments were abandoned. Pinel's reforms were soon followed by similar efforts in England and, somewhat later, in the United States.

The most notable American reformer was Dorothea Dix (1802–1887), a schoolteacher from Boston who led a nationwide campaign for humane treatment of mentally ill people. Under her influence the few existing asylums in the United States were gradually turned into hospitals, but these hospitals often failed to provide the compassionate care that Dix had envisioned.

In the seventeenth century, French physicians tried various devices to cure their patients of "fantasy and folly."

The basic reason for the failed—and sometimes abusive—treatment of mentally disturbed people throughout history has been the lack of understanding of the nature and causes of psychological disorders. Although our knowledge is still inadequate, important advances in understanding abnormal behavior can be traced to the late nineteenth and early twentieth centuries, when three influential but conflicting models of abnormal behavior emerged: the biological model, the psychoanalytic model, and the cognitive-behavioral model.

The Biological Model

How can biology influence the development of psychological disorders?

The **biological model** holds that psychological disorders are caused by physiological malfunctions—for example, of the nervous system or the endocrine glands—often steming from hereditary factors. There is growing evidence that genetic factors are involved in mental disorders as diverse as schizophrenia, depression, and anxiety and that the biochemistry of the nervous system is linked to some cases of depression and schizophrenia.

The Psychoanalytic Model

What did Freud and his followers believe was the underlying cause of psychological disorders?

Freud and his followers developed the **psychoanalytic model** at the end of the nineteenth and during the first half of the twentieth century (see Chapter 10). According to this model, behavior disorders are symbolic expressions of unconscious conflicts, which can usually be traced to childhood. For example, a man who behaves toward women in a violent way may be unconsciously expressing rage at his mother for being unaffectionate toward him during his childhood. The psychoanalytic model argues that in order to resolve their problems effectively, people must become aware that the source of their problems lies in their childhood and infancy.

Although Freud and his followers profoundly influenced both the mental health disciplines and Western culture, only weak and scattered scientific evidence supports their psychoanalytic theories about the causes and effective treatment of mental disorders.

The Cognitive–Behavioral Model

According to the cognitive-behavioral model, what causes abnormal behavior?

A third model of abnormal behavior grew out of twentieth-century research on learning and cognition. The **cognitive-behavioral model** suggests that psychological disorders, like all behavior, result from learning. From this perspective, fear, anxiety, sexual deviations, and other maladaptive behaviors are learned—and they can be unlearned.

The cognitive-behavioral model stresses both internal and external learning processes in the development and treatment of psychological disorders. For example, a bright student who believes that he is academically inferior to his classmates and can't perform well on a test may not put much effort into studying. Naturally, he performs poorly, and his poor test score both punishes his minimal efforts and confirms his belief that he is academically inferior. This student is caught up in a vicious cycle (Turk & Salovey, 1985). A cognitive-behavior therapist might try to modify both the young man's dysfunctional studying behavior and his inaccurate and maladaptive cognitive processes.

The cognitive-behavioral model has led to innovations in the treatment of psychological disorders, but the model has been criticized for its limited

Biological model
View that psychological disorders have a biochemical or physiological basis.

Psychoanalytic model
View that psychological disorders result from unconscious internal conflicts.

Cognitive-behavioral model
View that psychological disorders result from learning maladaptive ways of thinking and behaving.

perspective, especially its emphasis on environmental causes and treatments.

The Diathesis-Stress Model and Systems Theory

Why do some people with a family history of a psychological disorder develop the disorder, whereas other family members do not?

Each of the three major competing theories is useful in explaining the causes of certain types of disorders. The most exciting recent developments, however, emphasize integration of the various theoretical models to discover specific causes and specific treatments for different mental disorders.

The **diathesis-stress model** is one promising approach to integration. This model suggests that a biological predisposition called a **diathesis** must combine with some kind of stressful circumstance before the predisposition to a mental disorder shows up as behavior (D. Rosenthal, 1970). According to this model, some people are biologically prone to developing a particular disorder under stress, whereas others are not.

The **systems approach** examines how biological, psychological, and social risk factors combine to produce psychological disorders. It is also known as the *biopsychosocial model.* According to this model, emotional problems are "lifestyle diseases" that, much like heart disease and many other physical illnesses, result from a combination of biological risks, psychological stresses, and social pressures and expectations. Just as heart disease can result from a combination of genetic predisposition, personality styles, poor health habits (such as smoking) and stress, in the systems approach, psychological problems result from several risk factors that influence one another. In this chapter, we follow the systems approach in examining the causes and treatments of abnormal behavior.

Classifying Abnormal Behavior

Why is it useful to have a manual of psychological disorders?

For nearly forty years, the American Psychiatric Association (APA) has issued a manual describing and classifying the various kinds of psychological disorders. This publication, the Diagnostic and Statistical Manual of Mental Disorders (DSM), has been revised four times. The fourth edition, DSM-IV, was published in 1994.

The DSM-IV provides a complete list of mental disorders, with each category painstakingly defined in terms of significant behavior patterns so that diagnoses based on it will be reliable (Nathan & Langenbucher, 1999). Although the manual provides careful descriptions of symptoms of different disorders to improve consistent diagnosis, it is generally silent on cause and treatment. The DSM has gained increasing acceptance because its detailed criteria for diagnosing mental disorders have made diagnosis much more reliable. Today it is the most widely used classification of psychological disorders.

The Prevalence of Psychological Disorders

How common are mental disorders?

Starting in 1980, the National Institute of Mental Health did an ambitious and wide-ranging study of the prevalence of psychological disorders, which involved interviewing nearly 20,000 people around the country. The results were surprising: Overall, 32 percent of Americans suffer from one or more serious mental disorders during their lifetime, and at any given time, more than 15 percent of the population are experiencing a mental disorder (Robins & Regier, 1991). The most common problem is drug abuse, with

Diathesis-stress model
View that people biologically predisposed to a mental disorder (those with a certain diathesis) will tend to exhibit that disorder when particularly affected by stress.

Diathesis
Biological predisposition.

Systems approach
View that biological, psychological, and social risk factors combine to produce psychological disorders. Also known as the biopsychosocial model of psychological disorders.

abuse of alcohol being more prevalent than abuse of all other drugs combined. More than 13 percent of adults over 18 experience alcoholism at some point in their lives. Anxiety disorders are the next most common psychological disorder. Mood disorders, principally depression, are a problem for almost 8 percent of the population at some point in their lives. In contrast, schizophrenia afflicts only 1.5 percent of the population (but note that this represents more than 3 million people).

As you read about these disorders, you may notice that you occasionally experience some of the symptoms being described. This is a natural and normal response and does not indicate that you have the disorder being described. As noted earlier, behavior exists on a continuum, and abnormal behavior is often just highly exaggerated normal behavior that is displayed in inappropriate situations.

INTERACTIVE LECTURE 12.1

WEB QUIZ 12.1 ✓

CHECK YOUR UNDERSTANDING

1. For mental health professionals, behavior that interferes with a person's ability to ____ or that causes serious ____ or both is considered a symptom of a psychological disorder.

2. It is likely that people in early societies believed that ____ forces caused abnormal behavior.

3. There is growing evidence that ____ factors are involved in mental disorders as diverse as schizophrenia, depression, and anxiety.

Match the following model of abnormal behavior with the appropriate description.

____ 4. biological model   a. Abnormal behaviors result from unconscious internal conflicts.

____ 5. psychoanalytic model   b. Abnormal behavior is the product of biological, psychological, and social-risk factors.

____ 6. biopsychosocial model   c. Abnormal behavior is the result of learning and can be unlearned.

____ 7. cognitive-behavioral model   d. Abnormal behavior is caused by heredity, the malfunctioning of the nervous system, or endocrine dysfunction.

8. Two models that attempt to integrate the various other theoretical models to explain specific causes and specific treatments for different mental disorders are the ____ - ____ model and the ___ model.

9. The line separating normal from abnormal behavior is somewhat arbitrary. Is this statement true (T) or false (F)?

10. About one-third of Americans suffer from one or more serious mental disorders during their lifetime. Is this statement true (T) or false (F)?

Answers: 1. function, personal discomfort. 2. supernatural. 3. genetic. 4. d. 5. a. 6. b. 7. c. 8. diathesis-stress, systems. 9. T. 10. T.

Mood Disorders

How do mood disorders differ from ordinary mood changes?

Mood disorders are characterized by disturbances in mood or in prolonged emotional state, sometimes referred to as *affect*. Most people have a wide emotional range; they can be happy or sad, animated or quiet, cheerful or discouraged, overjoyed or miserable, depending on the circumstances. In some people with mood disorders, this range is greatly

Mood disorders
Disturbances in mood or prolonged emotional state.

restricted. They seem stuck at one or the other end of the emotional spectrum—either consistently excited and euphoric or consistently sad—regardless of the circumstances of their lives. Other people with a mood disorder alternate between the extremes of euphoria and sadness.

Depression

How does clinical depression differ from ordinary sadness?

The most common mood disorder is **depression,** a state in which a person feels overwhelmed with sadness. Depressed people lose interest in the things they normally enjoy. Intense feelings of worthlessness and guilt leave them unable to feel pleasure. They are tired and apathetic, sometimes to the point of being unable to make the simplest decisions. Many depressed people feel as if they have failed utterly in life, and they tend to blame themselves for their problems. Seriously depressed people often have insomnia and lose interest in food and sex. They may have trouble thinking or concentrating—even to the extent of finding it difficult to read a newspaper. In fact, difficulty in concentrating and subtle changes in short-term memory are sometimes the first signs of the onset of depression (Williams et al., 2000). In very serious cases, depressed people may be plagued by suicidal thoughts or may even attempt suicide (Cicchetti & Toth, 1998).

We want to point out that *clinical depression* is different from the "normal" kind of depression that all people experience from time to time. It is entirely normal to become sad when a loved one has died, when romantic relationships end, when you have problems on the job or at school—even when the weather is bad or you don't have a date for Saturday night. Most psychologically healthy people also get "the blues" occasionally for no apparent reason. But in all of these instances, either the mood disturbance is a normal reaction to a "real world" problem (for example, grief), or it passes quickly. Only when depression is long-lasting and goes well beyond the typical reaction to a stressful life event is it classified as a mood disorder (APA, 1994). (See *Understanding Ourselves*).

DSM-IV distinguishes between two forms of depression: *Major depressive disorder* is an episode of intense sadness that may last for several months; in contrast, *dysthymia* involves less intense sadness (and related symptoms) but persists with little relief for a period of two years or more. Depression is two to three times more prevalent in women than in men (Simpson, Nee, & Endicott, 1997; Weissman & Olfson, 1995).

Suicide

What factors are related to a person's likelihood of committing suicide?

More than 30,000 people in the United States commit suicide annually (Moscicki, 1995). More women than men attempt suicide, but more men succeed, partly because men tend to choose violent and lethal means, such as guns.

Although the largest number of suicides occurs among older white males, since the 1960s the rates of suicide attempts have been rising among adolescents and young adults (**Figure 12–1**). In fact, adolescents account for 12 percent of all suicide attempts in the United States, and suicide is the third leading cause of death in that age group (Centers for Disease Control and Prevention, 1999; Hoyert et al., 1999). We cannot as yet explain the increase, though the stresses of leaving home, meeting the demands of college or career, and surviving loneliness or broken romantic attachments seem to be particularly great at this stage of life. Although external problems such as unemployment and financial strain may also contribute to personal problems, suicidal behavior is most common among adolescents

Most people feel unhappy and low now and then, but depression goes much deeper than mere unhappiness. Clinically depressed people lose interest in the things that usually give them pleasure. Typically, they feel overwhelmed by sadness, loss, and guilt.

Depression
A mood disorder characterized by overwhelming feelings of sadness, lack of interest in activities, and perhaps excessive guilt or feelings of worthlessness.

UNDERSTANDING OURSELVES

Recognizing Depression

Almost everyone from time to time feels depressed. Failing a major exam, breaking up with a boyfriend or girlfriend, even leaving home and friends to attend college can all produce a temporary state of "the blues." More significant life events can have an even greater impact: the loss of one's job or of a loved one can produce a sense of hopelessness about the future that feels very much like a slide into depression.

But the preceding instances would typically be considered "normal" reactions to negative life events. You may wonder, at what point do these normal responses cross the line into clinical depression? How do clinicians determine whether the hopelessness and despair being expressed by a person constitute a major depressive episode or just a period of sadness that will eventually get better on its own?

The DSM-VI provides the framework for making this distinction. First, clinical depression is characterized by depressed mood, by the loss of interest and pleasure in usual activities, or both. Clinicians also look for some significant impairment or distress in social, occupational, or other important areas of functioning. People suffering from depression not only feel sad or empty but also have significant problems in carrying on a normal lifestyle.

Doctors look, too, for other explanations of the symptoms: Could they be due to substance abuse or the side effects of medication that the person is taking? Could they be the result of a medical condition, such as hypothyroidism (the inability of the thyroid gland to produce an adequate amount of its hormones)? Could the symptoms be better interpreted as an intense grief reaction?

If the symptoms do not seem to be explained by the preceding causes, how do clinicians make a diagnosis of depression? The DSM-IV notes that at least five of the following symptoms, including at least one of the first two, must be present:

1. **Depressed mood:** Does the person feel sad or empty for most of the day, most every day, or do others observe these symptoms?

2. **Loss of interest in pleasure:** Has the person lost interest in performing normal activities, such as working or going to social events? Does the person seem to be "just going through the motions" of daily life without deriving any pleasure from them?

3. **Significant weight loss or gain:** Has the person gained or lost more than 5 percent of body weight in a month? Has the person lost interest in eating or complain that food has lost its taste?

4. **Sleep disturbances:** Is the person having trouble sleeping? Or, conversely, is the person sleeping too much?

5. **Disturbances in motor activities:** Do others notice a change in the person's activity level? Does the person just "sit around," or does the behavior reflect agitation or unusual restlessness?

6. **Fatigue:** Does the person complain of being constantly tired and having no energy?

7. **Feelings of worthlessness or excessive guilt:** Does the person express feelings such as "you'd be better off without me around" or "I'm evil and I ruin everything for everybody I love"?

8. **Inability to concentrate:** Does the person complain of memory problems ("I just can't remember anything anymore") or the inability to focus attention on simple tasks, such as reading a newspaper?

9. **Recurrent thoughts of death:** Does the person talk about committing suicide or express the wish that he or she were dead?

When these symptoms are present and are not due to other medical conditions, a diagnosis of major depression is typically the result, and appropriate treatment can be prescribed. As you will learn in Chapter 13: Therapies, appropriate diagnosis is the first step in the effective treatment of psychological disorders.

Source: Diagnostic and Statistical Manual of Mental Disorders, Fourth Edition.

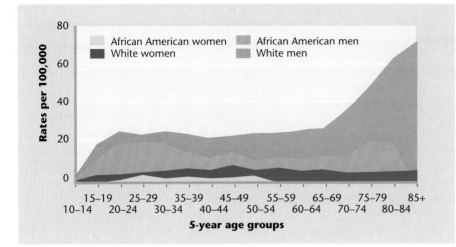

FIGURE 12–1

Gender and race differences in the suicide rate across the life span. The suicide rate for white males, who commit the largest number of suicides at all ages, shows a sharp rise beyond the age of 65. In contrast, the suicide rate for African American females, which is the lowest for any group, remains relatively stable throughout the life span.

Source: Suicide and Life-Threatening Behavior by Moscicki, E. K. Copyright © 1995 by Guilford Publications Inc. Reproduced with permission of Guilford Publications, Inc. in the format Textbook via Copyright Clearance Center.

with psychological problems. Several myths concerning suicide can be quite dangerous:

Myth: Someone who talks about committing suicide will never do it.

Fact: Most people who kill themselves have talked about it. Such comments should always be taken seriously.

Myth: Someone who has tried suicide and failed is not serious about it.

Fact: Any suicide attempt means that the person is deeply troubled and needs help immediately. A suicidal person will try again, picking a more deadly method the second or third time around.

Myth: Only people who are life's losers—those who have failed in their careers and in their personal lives—commit suicide.

Fact: Many people who kill themselves have prestigious jobs, conventional families, and a good income. Physicians, for example, have a suicide rate several times higher than that for the general population; in this case, the tendency to suicide may be related to their work stresses.

People considering suicide are overwhelmed with hopelessness. They feel that things cannot get better and see no way out of their difficulties. This perception is depression in the extreme, and it is not a state of mind that someone can easily be talked out of. Telling a suicidal person that things aren't really so bad does no good; in fact, the person may only view this as further evidence that no one understands his or her suffering. But most suicidal people do want help, however much they may despair of obtaining it. If a friend or family member seems at all suicidal, getting professional help is urgent. A community mental health center is a good starting place, as are the national suicide hotlines.

Mania and Bipolar Disorder

What is mania, and how is it involved in bipolar disorder?

Another mood disorder, which is less common than depression, is **mania**, a state in which the person becomes euphoric or "high," extremely active, excessively talkative, and easily distracted. People suffering from mania may become grandiose—that is, their self-esteem is greatly inflated. They typically have unlimited hopes and schemes but little interest in realistically carrying them out. People in a manic state sometimes become aggressive and hostile toward others as their self-confidence grows more and more ex-

Mania
A mood disorder characterized by euphoric states, extreme physical activity, excessive talkativeness, distractedness, and sometimes grandiosity.

aggerated. At the extreme, people going through a manic episode may become wild, incomprehensible, or violent until they collapse from exhaustion.

The mood disorder in which both mania and depression are present is known as bipolar disorder. In people with **bipolar disorder,** periods of mania and depression alternate (each lasting from a few days to a few months), sometimes with periods of normal mood in between. Occasionally bipolar disorder occurs in a mild form, with moods of unrealistically high spirits followed by moderate depression. Research suggests that bipolar disorder is much less common than depression and, unlike depression, occurs equally in men and women. Bipolar disorder also seems to have a stronger biological component than depression: It is more strongly linked to heredity and is most often treated with drugs (Gershon, 1990).

Causes of Mood Disorders

What causes some people to experience extreme mood changes?

Most psychologists believe that mood disorders result from a combination of risk factors. Biological factors seem to be most important in some cases—for example, bipolar disorder—whereas psychological factors appear to be chiefly responsible in other cases—for example, depression following the experience of a loss (Katz & McGuffin, 1993). Social factors seem to be most important in still other cases—for example, some instances of depression among women. Nevertheless, although researchers have identified many of the causative factors, they still do not yet know exactly how these elements interact to cause a mood disorder.

Biological Factors   Genetic factors can play an important role in the development of depression (Meneka, Watson, & Clark, 1998), particularly in bipolar disorder. The strongest evidence comes from studies of twins (see Chapter 2, The Biological Basis of Behavior). If one identical twin is clinically depressed, the other twin (with identical genes) is likely to become clinically depressed also. Among fraternal twins (who share only about half their genes), if one twin is clinically depressed, the risk for the second twin is much lower (McGuffin, Katz, Watkins, & Rutherford, 1996).

Just what is it that genetically predisposes some people to a mood disorder? Research has linked mood disorders to chemical imbalances in the brain, principally to high and low levels of certain neurotransmitters. These chemicals influence the transmission of nerve impulses from one cell to another (see Chapter 2), and when their levels are altered with medication, mood disorders can often be effectively treated (Delgado, Price, Heninger, & Charney, 1992).

Despite the links between biology and mood disorders, high or low levels of neurotransmitters may not result from a genetic risk for mood disorders. In fact, the chemical imbalance in the brain associated with depression could be caused by stressful life events: Just as biology affects psychological experience, psychological experience can alter our biological functioning.

Psychological Factors   Although a number of psychological factors are thought to play a role in causing severe depression, in recent years the research has focused on the contribution of maladaptive **cognitive distortions.** According to Aaron Beck (1967, 1976, 1984), during childhood and adolescence some people undergo wrenching experiences such as the loss of a parent, severe difficulties in gaining parental or social approval, or humiliating criticism from teachers and other adults. One response to such experience is to develop a negative self-concept—a

Bipolar disorder
A mood disorder in which periods of mania and depression alternate, sometimes with periods of normal mood intervening.

Cognitive distortions
An illogical and maladaptive response to early negative life events that leads to feelings of incompetence and unworthiness that are reactivated whenever a new situation arises that resembles the original events.

feeling of incompetence or unworthiness that has little to do with reality but that is maintained by a distorted and illogical interpretation of real events. When a new situation arises that resembles the situation under which the self-concept was learned, these same feelings of worthlessness and incompetence may be activated, resulting in depression.

Although critics point out that these negative responses may be the result of depression rather than its cause (Hammen, 1985), considerable research supports Beck's view of depression (Alloy, Abramson, & Francis, 1999; Alloy, Abramson, & Whitehouse, 1999). Therapy based on Beck's theories has proved quite successful in treating depression (see Chapter 13).

Social Factors Many social factors have been linked with mood disorders, particularly difficulties in interpersonal relationships. In fact, some theorists have suggested that the link between depression and troubled relationships explains the fact that depression is two to three times more prevalent in women than in men (Culbertson, 1997; Weissman & Olfson, 1995), since women tend to be more relationship-oriented than men are in our society (Gilligan, 1982). Yet not every person who experiences a troubled relationship becomes depressed. As the systems approach would predict, it appears that a genetic predisposition or cognitive distortion is necessary before a distressing close relationship or other significant life stressor will result in a mood disorder.

 INTERACTIVE LECTURE **12.2**

WEB QUIZ **12.2**

CHECK YOUR UNDERSTANDING

1. The two extremes represented by mood disorders are ____ and ____.
2. The most common mood disorder is____.
3. ____ is a mood disorder in which the person becomes euphoric or "high," extremely active, excessively talkative, and easily distracted.
4. The mood disorder in which both mania and depression alternate is known as ____ ____.
5. Biological research indicates that mood disorders may be linked to a ____ ____ in the brain.
6. According to Beck, excessive criticism during childhood and adolescence may lead to a negative self-concept and the ____ ____ typical of depression.
7. Indicate whether the following statements are true (T) or false (F).
   ____ a. People with a mood disorder always alternate between the extremes of euphoria and sadness.
   ____ b. More men attempt suicide, but more women actually kill themselves.
   ____ c. Most psychologists now believe that mood disorders result from a combination of risk factors.

Answers: 1. mania; depression. 2. depression. 3. mania. 4. bipolar disorder. 5. chemical imbalance. 6. cognitive distortions. 7. a. (F); b. (F); c. (T).

Anxiety Disorders

How does an anxiety disorder differ from ordinary anxiety?

All of us are afraid from time to time, but we usually know why we are fearful. Our fear is caused by something appropriate and identifiable, and it passes with time. In the case of **anxiety disorders,** however, either the

Anxiety disorders
Disorders in which anxiety is a characteristic feature or the avoidance of anxiety seems to motivate abnormal behavior.

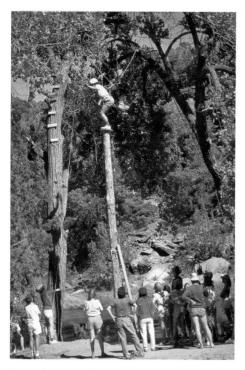

Fear of heights is an example of a specific phobia. In this photo, people are learning to overcome this phobia through desensitization therapy.

Specific phobia
Anxiety disorder characterized by an intense, paralyzing fear of something.

Social phobia
An anxiety disorder characterized by excessive, inappropriate fears connected with social situations or performances in front of other people.

Agoraphobia
An anxiety disorder that involves multiple, intense fears of crowds, public places, and other situations that require separation from a source of security such as the home.

Panic disorder
An anxiety disorder characterized by recurrent panic attacks in which the person suddenly experiences intense fear or terror without any reasonable cause.

person does not know why he or she is afraid, or the anxiety is inappropriate to the circumstances. In either case, the person's fear and anxiety just don't seem to make sense.

Specific Phobias

Into what three categories are phobias usually grouped?

One recent national survey found that anxiety disorders are more common than any other form of mental disorder (Kessler et al., 1994). Anxiety disorders can be subdivided into several diagnostic categories, including the **specific phobias.** A specific phobia is an intense, paralyzing fear of something that perhaps should be feared, but the fear is excessive and unreasonable. In fact, the fear in a specific phobia is so great that it leads the person to avoid routine or adaptive activities and thus interferes with life functioning. For example, it is appropriate to be a bit fearful as an airplane takes off or lands, but people with a phobia about flying refuse to get on or even go near an airplane. Other common phobias focus on animals, heights, closed places, blood, needles, and injury. About 10 percent of people in the United States suffer from at least one specific phobia.

Most people feel some mild fear or uncertainty in many social situations, but when these fears interfere significantly with life functioning, they are considered to be **social phobias.** Intense fear of public speaking is a common form of social phobia. In other cases, simply talking with people or eating in public causes such severe anxiety that the phobic person will go to great lengths to avoid these situations.

Agoraphobia is much more debilitating than social phobia. This term comes from Greek and Latin words that literally mean "fear of the marketplace," but the disorder typically involves multiple, intense fears, such as the fear of being alone, of being in public places from which escape might be difficult, of being in crowds, of traveling in an automobile, or of going through tunnels or over bridges. The common element in all of these situations seems to be a great dread of being separated from sources of security, such as the home or a loved one with whom the person feels safe.

Agoraphobia can greatly interfere with life functioning: Some sufferers are so fearful that they will venture only a few miles from home, whereas others will not leave their homes at all. Although agoraphobia is less common than social phobia (it affects about 3 percent of the population), because of the severity of its effects, it is more likely to cause the sufferer to seek treatment (Robins & Regier, 1991).

Panic Disorder

How does a panic attack differ from fear?

Another type of anxiety disorder is **panic disorder,** characterized by recurring episodes of a sudden, unpredictable, and overwhelming fear or terror. Panic attacks occur without any reasonable cause and are accompanied by feelings of impending doom, chest pain, dizziness or fainting, sweating, difficulty breathing, and fear of losing control or dying. Panic attacks usually last only a few minutes, but they may recur for no apparent reason. For example, consider the following description:

A 31-year-old stewardess . . . had suddenly begun to feel panicky, dizzy, had trouble breathing, started to sweat, and trembled uncontrollably. She excused herself and sat in the back of the plane and within ten minutes the symptoms had subsided. Two similar episodes had occurred in the past: the first, four years previously, when the plane had encountered mild turbulence; the second, two years earlier, during an otherwise uneventful flight, as in this episode. (Spitzer et al., 1981, p. 219)

Panic attacks not only cause tremendous fear while they are happening but also leave a dread of having another panic attack that can persist for days or even weeks after the original episode. In some cases, this dread is so overwhelming that it can lead to the development of agoraphobia: To prevent a recurrence, people may avoid any circumstance that might cause anxiety, clinging to people or situations that help keep them calm.

Other Anxiety Disorders

How do generalized anxiety disorder and obsessive-compulsive disorder differ from specific phobias?

In the various phobias and in panic attacks, there is a specific source of anxiety, such as fear of heights, fear of social situations, or fear of being in crowds. In contrast, **generalized anxiety disorder** is defined by prolonged vague but intense fears that are not attached to any particular object or circumstance. Generalized anxiety disorder perhaps comes closest to the everyday meaning attached to the term *neurotic*. Its symptoms include the inability to relax, muscle tension, rapid heartbeat or pounding heart, apprehensiveness about the future, constant alertness to potential threats, and sleeping difficulties.

A very different form of anxiety disorder is **obsessive-compulsive disorder**, or **OCD.** *Obsessions* are involuntary thoughts or ideas that keep recurring despite the person's attempts to stop them, whereas *compulsions* are repetitive, ritualistic behaviors that a person feels compelled to perform (Patrick, 1994). Obsessive thoughts are often horrible and frightening. One patient, for example, reported that "when she thought of her boyfriend, she wished he were dead"; when her mother went down the stairs, she "wished she'd fall and break her neck"; when her sister spoke of going to the beach with her infant daughter, she "hoped that they would both drown" (Carson & Butcher, 1992, p. 190). Truly compulsive behaviors may be equally dismaying to the person who feels driven to perform them. They often take the form of washing or cleaning, as if the compulsive behavior were the person's attempt to "wash away" the contaminating thoughts. One patient reported that her efforts to keep her clothes and body clean eventually took up six hours of her day, and even then, "washing my hands wasn't enough, and I started to use rubbing alcohol" (Spitzer et al., 1981, p. 137).

Another common type of compulsion is checking: repeatedly performing some kind of behavior to make sure that something was or was not done. For example, a person might feel compelled to check dozens of times whether the doors are locked before going to bed.

People who experience obsessions and compulsions often do not seem particularly anxious, so why is this disorder considered an anxiety disorder? The answer is that if such people try to stop their irrational behavior—or if someone else tries to stop them—they experience severe anxiety. In other words, the obsessive-compulsive behavior seems to have developed to keep anxiety under control.

Finally, two types of anxiety disorder are clearly caused by some specific highly stressful event. Some people who have lived through fires, floods, tornadoes, or disasters such as an airplane crash experience repeated episodes of fear and terror after the event itself is over. If the anxious reaction occurs soon after the event, the diagnosis is *acute stress*

Generalized anxiety disorder
An anxiety disorder characterized by prolonged vague but intense fears that are not attached to any particular object or circumstance.

Obsessive-compulsive disorder (OCD)
An anxiety disorder in which a person feels driven to think disturbing thoughts or to perform senseless rituals.

Extreme stress can cause acute stress disorder. The soldier at left has just learned that his close friend was killed by friendly fire during the Gulf War.

disorder. If it takes place long after the event is over, the diagnosis is likely to be *posttraumatic stress disorder,* discussed in Chapter 11 (Oltmanns & Emery, 1998). Posttraumatic stress disorder is characterized by hyperarousal, avoidance of situations that recall the trauma, and "reexperiencing"—reliving the traumatic event in detail. There are two kinds of traumatic experience that are particularly likely to lead to acute or posttraumatic stress disorder: military combat and rape.

Causes of Anxiety Disorders

What can the cognitive perspective and the biological perspective tell us about the causes of anxiety?

Recall from Chapter 5, Learning, that phobias are often learned after only one fearful event; they are extremely hard to shed, and there is a limited and predictable range of phobic objects. People are more likely to be injured in an automobile accident than by a snake or spider bite, yet snake and spider phobias are far more common than car phobias. It may be that phobias are prepared responses; that is, through evolution we may have become biologically predisposed to associate certain stimuli with intense fears (Marks & Nesse, 1994; Öhman, 1996). Consider a young boy who is savagely attacked by a large dog. Because of this experience, he is now terribly afraid of all dogs. Other children who witnessed the attack or only heard about it may also come to fear dogs. In that way, a realistic fear can be transformed into a phobia.

From a more cognitive perspective, people who feel that they are not in control of stressful events in their lives are more likely to experience anxiety than those who believe that they have control over such events. For example, African Americans who live in high-crime areas have a higher incidence of anxiety disorders than other Americans (Neal & Turner, 1991). In the same situation, though, some people develop unrealistic fears, whereas others do not. Why?

Psychologists working from the biological perspective point to heredity, arguing that we can inherit a predisposition to anxiety disorders (Eysenck, 1970; Sarason & Sarason, 1987). In fact, anxiety disorders tend to run in families (Kendler, Neale, Kessler, Heath, & Eaves, 1992; Torgersen, 1983; Weissman, 1993), although the evidence linking specific kinds of anxiety disorders to genetic factors is less clear (Oltmanns & Emery, 1998).

Finally, we need to consider the vital role that internal psychological conflicts play in producing feelings of anxiety. From the Freudian perspective, defense mechanisms protect us from unacceptable impulses or thoughts (usually sexual or aggressive in nature), but at a cost in anxiety. For example, psychoanalytic theorists view phobias as the result of displacement in which people redirect strong feelings from whatever originally aroused them toward something else (see Chapter 11). Thus, a woman who is afraid of her spouse but represses these feelings might redirect her fear toward elevators or spiders. Although we may doubt the validity of specific psychoanalytic interpretations of phobias, inner conflicts—as well as defenses and other internal distortions of these conflicts—certainly seem to play a role in the development of anxiety and its associated disorders.

INTERACTIVE LECTURE **12.3**

WEB QUIZ **12.3**

CHECK YOUR UNDERSTANDING

Match the following terms with the appropriate description.

____ 1. specific phobia

____ 2. social phobia

____ 3. agoraphobia

____ 4. panic attack

____ 5. generalized anxiety disorder

____ 6. obsessive-compulsive disorder

a. great dread of being separated from sources of security

b. an unreasonable, paralyzing fear of something

c. a sudden, unpredictable, and overwhelming experience of intense fear or terror without any reasonable cause

d. feeling driven to think disturbing thoughts or to perform meaningless rituals

e. excessive inappropriate fears connected with social situations or performances in front of other people

f. prolonged vague but intense fears not attached to any particular object or circumstance

7. The fear in a specific phobia often interferes with life functioning. Is this statement true (T) or false (F)?

8. People who experience obsessions and compulsions appear highly anxious. Is this statement true (T) or false (F)?

9. Research indicates that people who feel that they are not in control of stressful events in their lives are more likely to experience ____ than those who believe that they have control over such events.

10. According to the psychoanalytic view, anxiety results from ____ ____.

11. The belief that we inherit the tendency to develop some phobias more easily than others argues that these phobias are ____ ____.

Answers: 1. b. 2. e. 3. a. 4. c. 5. f. 6. d. 7. T. 8. F. 9. anxiety. 10. unconscious conflicts. 11. prepared responses.

Psychosomatic and Somatoform Disorders

What is the difference between psychosomatic disorders and somatoform disorders?

The term *psychosomatic* perfectly captures the interplay of *psyche* (mind) and *soma* (body), which characterizes these disorders. A **psychosomatic disorder** is a real, physical disorder, but one that has, at least in part, a psychological cause. Tension headaches are an example of a psychosomatic disorder. They are caused by muscle contractions brought on by stress. The headache is real, but it is called "psychosomatic" because psychological factors (such as stress and anxiety) appear to play an important role in causing the symptoms. People suffering from tension headaches are often taught relaxation techniques that relieve stress and reduce muscle tension.

Scientists used to believe that psychological factors contributed to the development of some physical illnesses, principally headaches, allergies, asthma, and high blood pressure, but not others, such as infectious diseases. Today modern medicine leans toward the idea that all physical ailments are to some extent "psychosomatic"—in the sense that stress, anxiety, and various states of emotional arousal alter body chemistry, the

Psychosomatic disorders
Disorders in which there is real physical illness that is largely caused by psychological factors such as stress and anxiety.

"You know, Burkhart, if you're so damn afraid of the flu maybe you should just stay home."

functioning of bodily organs, and the body's immune system (which is vital in fighting infections). Because virtually every physical disease can be linked to psychological stress, DSM-IV does not contain a separate list of psychosomatic disorders.

Psychosomatic disorders involve genuine physical illnesses, but in **somatoform disorders,** physical symptoms occur without any identifiable physical cause. Common complaints are back pain, dizziness, abdominal pain, and sometimes anxiety and depression. People suffering from somatoform disorders believe that they are physically ill and describe symptoms that sound like physical illnesses, but medical examinations reveal no organic problems. Nevertheless, people who suffer from these disorders are not consciously seeking to mislead others about their physical condition. The symptoms are real to them and are not under voluntary control (APA, 1994).

One of the more dramatic forms of somatoform disorder involves complaints of paralysis, blindness, deafness, seizures, loss of feeling, or pregnancy. In these **conversion disorders,** no physical causes appear, yet the symptoms are very real. Yet another somatoform disorder is **hypochondriasis.** Here the person interprets some small symptom—perhaps a cough, a bruise, or perspiration—as a sign of a serious disease. Although the symptom may actually exist, there is no evidence that the serious illness does. Repeated assurances have little effect, and the person is likely to visit one doctor after another, searching for a medical authority who will share his or her conviction.

Body dysmorphic disorder, or imagined ugliness, is a recently diagnosed and poorly understood type of somatoform disorder. Cases of body dysmorphic disorder can be very striking. One man, for example, felt that people stared at his "pointed ears" and "large nostrils" so much that he eventually could not face going to work, so he quit his job. Clearly, people who become that preoccupied with their appearance cannot lead a normal life. Ironically, most people who suffer body dysmorphic disorder are not ugly. They may be average looking or even attractive, but they are unable to evaluate their looks realistically. Many people with this disorder seek physical treatment (such as plastic surgery) rather than psychotherapy.

Somatoform disorders (especially conversion disorders) present a challenge for psychological theorists because they seem to involve some kind of unconscious processes. Freud concluded that the physical symptoms were often related to traumatic experiences buried in a patient's past. Cognitive-behavioral theorists look for ways in which the symptomatic behavior is being rewarded.

From the biological perspective, research has shown that at least some diagnosed somatoform disorders actually were real physical illnesses that were overlooked or misdiagnosed. For example, some cases of "conversion disorder" eventually proved to be neurological problems such as epilepsy or multiple sclerosis (Shalev & Munitz, 1986). Nevertheless, most cases of conversion disorder cannot be explained by current medical science. These cases pose as much of a theoretical challenge today as they did when conversion disorders captured Freud's attention more than a century ago.

Somatoform disorders
Disorders in which there is an apparent physical illness for which there is no organic basis.

Conversion disorders
Somatoform disorders in which a dramatic specific disability has no physical cause but instead seems related to psychological problems.

Hypochondriasis
A somatoform disorder in which a person interprets insignificant symptoms as signs of serious illness in the absence of any organic evidence of such illness.

Body dysmorphic disorder
A somatoform disorder in which a person becomes so preoccupied with his or her imagined ugliness that normal life is impossible.

INTERACTIVE LECTURE **12.4**

CHECK YOUR UNDERSTANDING

Match the following terms with the appropriate description.

____ 1. somatoform disorder   a. the person's interpretation of some small symptom as a sign of a serious disease

____ 2. body dysmorphic disorder   b. recurring physical symptoms for which no organic cause is found

____ 3. conversion disorders   c. imagined ugliness

____ 4. hypochondriasis   d. condition in which sufferers have healthy muscles and nerves, yet their symptoms of paralysis, blindness, deafness, seizures, loss of feeling, or pregnancy are real

5. Indicate whether the following statements are true (T) or false (F).

____a. Modern medicine leans toward the idea that all physical ailments are to some extent "psychosomatic."

____b. People who suffer from somatoform disorders do not consciously seek to mislead others about their physical condition.

____c. Research has shown that at least some diagnosed somatoform disorders actually were real physical illnesses that were overlooked or misdiagnosed.

____d. Most cases of conversion disorder can be explained by current medical science.

Answers: 1. b. 2. c. 3. d. 4. a. 5. a. (T); b. (T); c. (T); d. (F).

Dissociative Disorders

What do dissociative disorders have in common?

Dissociative disorders are among the most puzzling forms of mental disorders, both to the observer and to the sufferer. *Dissociation* means that part of an individual's personality appears to be separated from the rest. The disorder usually involves memory loss and a complete, though generally temporary, change in identity. Rarely, several distinct personalities appear in one person.

Loss of memory without an organic cause can occur as a reaction to an extremely stressful event or period. During World War II, for example, some hospitalized soldiers could not recall what their names were, where they lived, where they were born, or how they came to be in battle. But war and its horrors are not the only causes of *dissociative amnesia*. The person who betrays a friend in a business deal or the victim of rape may also forget, selectively, what has happened. Sometimes an amnesia victim leaves home and assumes an entirely new identity, although this phenomenon, known as *dissociative fugue*, is very unusual.

In **dissociative identity disorder,** commonly known as *multiple personality disorder,* several distinct personalities emerge at different times. Although this dramatic disorder has been the subject of popular fiction and films, most psychologists believe it to be extremely rare, although in recent years the number of cases appears to be increasing (Eich, Macaulay, Loewenstein, & Dihle, 1997). In the true multiple personality, the various personalities are distinct people with their own names, identities, memories, mannerisms, speaking voices, and even IQs. Sometimes the personalities are so separate that they don't know they inhabit a body with other "people." At other times, the personalities do know of the existence of other "people" and even make disparaging remarks about them. Typically, the personalities contrast sharply with one another, as if each one represents different aspects of the same person—one being the more socially acceptable, "nice" side of the person and the other being the darker, more uninhibited or "evil" side.

Dissociative disorders
Disorders in which some aspect of the personality seems separated from the rest.

Dissociative identity disorder
(Also called multiple personality disorder) Disorder characterized by the separation of the personality into two or more distinct personalities.

When she was found by a Florida park ranger, Jane Doe was suffering from amnesia. She could not recall her name, her past, or how to read and write. She never regained her memory of the past.

Depersonalization disorder
A dissociative disorder whose essential feature is that the person suddenly feels changed or different in a strange way.

INTERACTIVE LECTURE **12.5**

The origins of dissociative identity disorder are still not understood. One theory suggests that it develops as a response to childhood abuse. The child learns to cope with abuse by a process of dissociation—by having the abuse, in effect, happen to "someone else," that is, to a personality who is not conscious most of the time (Putnam, Guroff, Silberman, Barban, & Post, 1986). The fact that one or more of the multiple personalities in almost every case is a child (even when the patient is an adult) seems to support this idea, and clinicians report a history of child abuse in more than three-quarters of their cases of dissociative identity disorder (Ross, Norton, & Wozney, 1989).

Other clinicians suggest that dissociative identity disorder is not a real disorder at all but an elaborate kind of role playing—faked in the beginning and then perhaps genuinely believed in by the patient (Mersky, 1992; Rieber, 1998). Some intriguing biological data show that in at least some patients, however, the various personalities have different blood pressure readings, different responses to medication, different allergies, different vision problems (necessitating a different pair of glasses for each personality), and different handedness—all of which would be difficult to feign. Each personality may also exhibit distinctly different brain-wave patterns (Putnam, 1984).

A far less dramatic (and much more common) dissociative disorder is **depersonalization disorder,** in which the person suddenly feels changed or different in a strange way. Some people feel that they have left their bodies, whereas others find that their actions have suddenly become mechanical or dreamlike. This kind of feeling is especially common during adolescence and young adulthood, when our sense of ourselves and our interactions with others change rapidly. Only when the sense of depersonalization becomes a long-term or chronic problem or when the alienation impairs normal social functioning can this be classified a dissociative disorder (APA, 1994).

Dissociative disorders, like conversion disorders, seem to involve some kind of unconscious processes. Trauma is one important psychological factor in the onset of amnesia and fugue and appears to play a role in the development of dissociative identity disorder (Oltmanns & Emery, 1998). The loss of memory is real in amnesia, fugue, and in many cases of multiple personality disorder. Patients often lack awareness of their own memory loss and cannot overcome memory impairments despite their desire and effort to do so. Biological factors may also play a role. Dissociation and amnesia are commonly associated with aging and disorders such as Alzheimer's disease, and dissociative experiences are a common consequence of the ingestion of drugs such as LSD. Nevertheless, all of these observations are only leads in the mystery of what causes dissociative disorders.

WEB QUIZ **12.5**

CHECK YOUR UNDERSTANDING

1. ___ ___ usually involve memory loss and a complete—though generally temporary—change in identity.

Match the following terms with the appropriate description.

____ 2. dissociative amnesia   a. loss of memory without an organic cause, possibly in reaction to intolerable experiences

____ 3. dissociative fugue   b. state in which the person suddenly feels changed or different in a strange way that becomes a long-term or chronic problem

____ 4. depersonalization disorder   c. a highly unusual amnesia during which the victim leaves home and assumes an entirely new identity

5. Clinicians report a history of child abuse in over three-quarters of their cases of dissociative identity disorder. Is this statement true (T) or false (F)?

6. Biological factors may play a role in some cases of dissociation and amnesia. Is this statement true (T) or false (F)?

Answers: 1. Dissociative disorders. 2. a. 3. c. 4. b. 5. T. 6. T.

Sexual and Gender-Identity Disorders

What are the three main types of sexual disorders?

Ideas about what is normal and abnormal in sex vary with the times—and the individual. Alfred Kinsey and his associates showed years ago that many Americans enjoy a variety of sexual activities, some of which were, and still are, forbidden by law (1948, 1953). As psychologists became more aware of the diversity of "normal" sexual behaviors, they increasingly narrowed their definition of abnormal sexual behavior. Today the DSM-IV recognizes only three main types of sexual disorders: sexual dysfunction, paraphilias, and gender-identity disorders.

Sexual dysfunction is the loss or impairment of the ordinary physical responses of sexual function. In men this usually takes the form of *erectile disorder* (ED), the inability to achieve or maintain an erection. In women it often takes the form of *female sexual arousal disorder*, the inability to become sexually excited or to reach orgasm. (These conditions were once called "impotence" and "frigidity," respectively, but professionals in the field have rejected these terms as too negative and judgmental.) Occasional problems with achieving or maintaining an erection in men or with lubrication or reaching orgasm in women are common. Only when the condition is frequent or constant and when enjoyment of sexual relationships becomes impaired should it be considered serious. The incidences of ED are quite high, even among otherwise healthy men. In one survey, 25 percent of 40- to 70-year-old men had moderate ED. Less than half the men in this age group reported having no ED (Lamberg, 1998). A new medication—*sildenafil citrate*, known popularly as *Viagra*—is extremely effective in treating ED (Dinsmore et al., 1999; Goldstein et al., 1998; Marks, Duda, Dorey, Macairan, & Santos, 1999; also see Meston & Frohlich, 2000), but although Viagra does help a man keep an erection, it will not produce an erection unless a man is also sexually aroused. For this reason, some specialists advise physicians first to address the psychological factors that may underlie sexual dysfunction before prescribing Viagra (Lamber, 1998).

A second group of sexual disorders, known as **paraphilias,** involves the use of unconventional sex objects or situations to obtain sexual arousal. Most people have unusual sexual fantasies at some time, and this kind of fantasizing can be a healthy stimulant of normal sexual enjoyment. **Fetishism**—the repeated use of a nonhuman object such as a shoe or underwear as the preferred or exclusive method of achieving sexual excitement—is considered a sexual disorder, however. Fetishes are typically articles of women's clothing or items made out of rubber or leather (Junginger, 1997; Mason, 1997). Most people who practice fetishism are male, and the fetish frequently begins during adolescence. At least one theorist has suggested that fetishes derive from unusual learning experiences: As their sexual drive develops during adolescence, some boys learn to associate arousal with inanimate objects, perhaps as a result of early sexual exploration while masturbating or because of difficulties in social relationships (Wilson, 1987).

Sexual dysfunction
Loss or impairment of the ordinary physical responses of sexual function.

Paraphilias
Sexual disorders in which unconventional objects or situations cause sexual arousal.

Fetishism
A paraphilia in which a nonhuman object is the preferred or exclusive method of achieving sexual excitement.

Pedophilia
Desire to have sexual relations with children as the preferred or exclusive method of achieving sexual excitement.

Gender-identity disorders
Disorders that involve the desire to become, or the insistence that one really is, a member of the other biological sex.

Gender-identity disorder in children
Rejection of one's biological gender in childhood, along with the clothing and behavior that society considers appropriate to that gender.

INTERACTIVE LECTURE **12.6** ➡️

WEB QUIZ **12.6** ✔️

One of the most serious paraphilias is **pedophilia,** which is technically defined as "recurrent, intense sexually arousing fantasies, sexual urges, or behaviors involving sexual activity with a prepubescent child" (APA, 1994, p. 528). Child sexual abuse is shockingly common in the United States, and the abuser usually is someone close to the child, not a stranger.

Pedophiles are almost invariably men under age 40 (Barbaree & Seto, 1997). Although there is no single cause of pedophilia, some of the most common explanations are that pedophiles cannot adjust to the adult sexual role and have been interested exclusively in children as sex objects since adolescence; they turn to children as sexual objects in response to stress in adult relationships in which they feel inadequate; or they have records of unstable social adjustment and generally commit sexual offenses against children in response to a temporary aggressive mood. Studies also indicate that the majority of pedophiles have histories of sexual frustration and failure, tend to perceive themselves as immature, and are rather dependent, unassertive, lonely, and insecure.

Gender-identity disorders involve the desire to become—or the insistence that one really is—a member of the other sex. Some little boys, for example, want to be girls instead. They may reject boys' clothing, desire to wear their sister's clothes, and play only with girls and with toys that are considered "girls' toys." Similarly, some girls wear boys' clothing and play only with boys and "boys' toys." When such children are uncomfortable being a male or a female and are unwilling to accept themselves as such, the diagnosis is **gender-identity disorder in children.**

The causes of gender-identity disorders are not known. Both animal research and the fact that these disorders are often apparent from early childhood suggest that biological factors, such as prenatal hormonal imbalances, are major contributors. Family dynamics and learning experiences, however, may also be contributing factors.

CHECK YOUR UNDERSTANDING

1. ____ ____ is the loss or impairment of the ordinary physical responses of sexual function.
2. In men ____ ____ is the inability to achieve or maintain an erection.
3. In women ____ ____ ____ ____ is the inability to become sexually excited or to reach orgasm.
4. ____ involve the use of unconventional sex objects or situations to obtain sexual arousal.
5. The repeated use of a nonhuman object as the preferred or exclusive method of achieving sexual excitement is known as ____.
6. ____ is recurrent, intense sexually arousing fantasies, sexual urges, or behaviors involving sexual activity with a prepubescent child.
7. ____ ____ ____ involve the desire to become—or the insistence that one really is—a member of the other biological sex.

Answers: 1. Sexual dysfunction. 2. erectile disorder or erectile dysfunction. 3. female sexual arousal disorder. 4. paraphilias. 5. fetishism. 6. Pedophilia. 7. Gender-identity disorders.

Personality Disorders

Which personality disorder creates the most significant problems for society?

In Chapter 10 we saw that personality is the individual's unique and enduring pattern of thoughts, feelings, and behavior. We also saw that despite having certain characteristic views of the world and ways of doing things, people normally can adjust their behavior to fit different situations. But some people, starting at some point early in life, develop inflexible and maladaptive ways of thinking and behaving that are so exaggerated and rigid that they cause serious distress to themselves or problems to others. People with such **personality disorders** range from harmless eccentrics to cold-blooded killers. A personality disorder may also coexist with one of the other problems already discussed in this chapter; that is, someone with a personality disorder may also become depressed, develop sexual problems, and so on.

One group of personality disorders is characterized by odd or eccentric behavior. For example, people who exhibit **schizoid personality disorder** lack the ability or desire to form social relationships and have no warm or tender feelings for others. Such loners cannot express their feelings and appear cold, distant, and unfeeling. Moreover, they often seem vague, absentminded, indecisive, or "in a fog." Because their withdrawal is so complete, persons with schizoid personality disorder seldom marry and may have trouble holding jobs that require them to work with or relate to others (APA, 1994).

People with **paranoid personality disorder** also appear to be odd. Although they often see themselves as rational and objective, they are guarded, secretive, devious, scheming, and argumentative. They are suspicious and mistrustful even when there is no reason to be; they are hypersensitive to any possible threat or trick; and they refuse to accept blame or criticism even when it is deserved.

A cluster of personality disorders characterized by anxious or fearful behavior includes dependent personality disorder and avoidant personality disorder. People with **dependent personality disorder** are unable to make decisions on their own or to do things independently. Rather, they rely on parents, a spouse, friends, or others to make the major choices in their lives and usually are extremely unhappy being alone. Their underlying fear seems to be that they will be rejected or abandoned by important people in their lives. In **avoidant personality disorder,** the person is timid, anxious, and fearful of rejection. It is not surprising that this social anxiety leads to isolation, but unlike the schizoid type, the person with avoidant personality disorder *wants* to have close relationships with others.

Another cluster of personality disorders is characterized by dramatic, emotional, or erratic behavior. People with **narcissistic personality disorder,** for example, display a grandiose sense of self-importance and a preoccupation with fantasies of unlimited success. Such people believe that they are extraordinary, need constant attention and admiration, display a sense of entitlement, and tend to exploit others. They are given to envy and arrogance, and they lack the ability to really care for anyone else (APA, 1994).

Borderline personality disorder is characterized by marked instability in self-image, mood, and interpersonal relationships. People with this personality disorder tend to act impulsively and often in self-destructive ways. They feel uncomfortable being alone and often manipulate self-destructive impulses in an effort to control or solidify their personal relationships.

Borderline personality disorder is both common and serious. The available evidence indicates that although it runs in families, genetics does not seem to play an important role in its development (Oltmanns & Emery, 1998). Instead, studies point to the influence of dysfunctional relationships with parents, including a marked lack of supervision, frequent exposure to domestic violence, and physical and sexual abuse (Guzder, Paris, Zelkowitz, & Marchessault, 1996).

One of the most widely studied personality disorders is **antisocial personality disorder.** People who exhibit this disorder lie, steal, cheat, and

Personality disorders
Disorders in which inflexible and maladaptive ways of thinking and behaving learned early in life cause distress to the person or conflicts with others.

Schizoid personality disorder
Personality disorder in which a person is withdrawn and lacks feelings for others.

Paranoid personality disorder
Personality disorder in which the person is inappropriately suspicious and mistrustful of others.

Dependent personality disorder
Personality disorder in which the person is unable to make choices and decisions independently and cannot tolerate being alone.

Avoidant personality disorder
Personality disorder in which the person's fears of rejection by others lead to social isolation.

Narcissistic personality disorder
Personality disorder in which the person has an exaggerated sense of self-importance and needs constant admiration.

Borderline personality disorder
Personality disorder characterized by marked instability in self-image, mood, and interpersonal relationships.

Antisocial personality disorder
Personality disorder that involves a pattern of violent, criminal, or unethical and exploitative behavior and an inability to feel affection for others.

People with antisocial personality disorder will lie, cheat, or kill without regret. Ted Bundy, shown here, was a serial killer who expressed no remorse for murdering as many as fifty women.

show little or no sense of responsibility, although they often seem intelligent and charming at first. The "con man" exemplifies many of the features of the antisocial personality, as does the person who compulsively cheats business partners because she or he knows their weak points. Antisocial personalities rarely show any anxiety or guilt about their behavior. Indeed, they are likely to blame society or their victims for the antisocial actions that they themselves commit.

People with antisocial personality disorder, like the man in the following description, are responsible for a good deal of crime and violence:

Although intelligent, [G.] was a poor student and was frequently accused of stealing from his schoolmates. At the age of 14, he stole a car, and at the age of 20, he was imprisoned for burglary. After he was released, he spent another two years in prison for drunk driving and then eleven years for a series of armed robberies. Released from prison yet one more time in 1976, he tried to hold down several jobs but succeeded at none of them. He moved in with a woman whom he had met one day earlier, but he drank heavily (a habit that he had picked up at age 10) and struck her children until she ordered him out of the house at gunpoint. "It seems like things have always gone bad for me," he later said. "It seems like I've always done dumb things that just caused trouble for me." (Spitzer, Skodal, Gibbon, & Williams, 1983, p. 68)

On psychiatric evaluation, this man was found to have a superior IQ of 129 and considerable general knowledge. He slept and ate well and showed no significant changes of mood. He admitted to having "made a mess of life" but added that "I never stew about the things I have done." This person, Gary Gilmore, was executed for murder in 1977.

Approximately 3 percent of American men and less than 1 percent of American women suffer from antisocial personality disorder. It is not surprising that prison inmates show high rates of personality disorder: One study identified it in 50 percent of the populations of two prisons (Hare, 1983). Not all people with antisocial personality disorder are convicted criminals, however. Many manipulate others for their own gain while avoiding the criminal justice system.

Antisocial personality disorder seems to result from a combination of biological predisposition, difficult life experiences, and an unhealthy social environment (Moffitt, 1993). Some findings suggest that heredity is a risk factor for the later development of antisocial behavior (Lyons et al., 1995). Impulsive violence and aggression have also been linked with abnormal levels of certain neurotransmitters (Virkkunen, 1983). Although none of this research is definitive, the weight of evidence suggests that some people with antisocial personalities are less responsive to stress and thus are more likely to engage in thrill-seeking behaviors that may be harmful to themselves or others (Patrick, 1994). And, because they respond less emotionally to stress, punishment does not affect them as it does other people (Hare, 1993). Another intriguing explanation for the cause of antisocial personality disorder is that it arises as a consequence of damage to the prefrontal region of the brian during infancy (Anderson, Bechara, Damasio, Tranel, & Damasio, 1999).

Some psychologists feel that emotional deprivation in early childhood predisposes people to antisocial personality disorder. The child for whom no one cares, say psychologists, cares for no one. Respect for others is the basis of our social code, but when you cannot see things from another person's perspective, behavior "rules" seem like nothing more than an assertion of adult power to be defied.

Family influences may also prevent the normal learning of rules of conduct in the preschool and school years. A child who has been rejected by one or both parents is not likely to develop adequate social skills or appropriate social behavior. Further, the high incidence of antisocial behavior in people with an antisocial parent suggests that antisocial behavior may be partly learned and partly inherited. Once serious misbehavior begins in childhood, there is an almost predictable progression: The child's conduct leads to rejection by peers and failure in school, followed by affiliation with other children who have behavior problems. By late childhood or adolescence, the deviant patterns that will later show up as a full-blown antisocial personality disorder are well established (Patterson, DeBaryshe, & Ramsey, 1989).

Cognitive theorists emphasize that in addition to the failure to learn rules and develop self-control, moral development may be arrested among children who are emotionally rejected and inadequately disciplined. For example, between the ages of about 7 and 11, all children are likely to respond to unjust treatment by behaving unjustly toward someone else who is vulnerable. At about age 13, when they are better able to reason in abstract terms, most children begin to think more in terms of fairness than vindictiveness, especially if new cognitive skills and moral concepts are reinforced by parents and peers (M. W. Berkowitz & Gibbs, 1983).

 INTERACTIVE LECTURE **12.7**

 WEB QUIZ **12.7**

CHECK YOUR UNDERSTANDING

1. Lifelong patterns of relatively "normal" but rigid and maladaptive behaviors are called
___ a. schizophrenia
___ b. personality disorders
___ c. anxiety disorders

Match the following personality disorders with the appropriate description.

___ 2. schizoid personality disorder   a. shows instability in self-image, mood, and relationships

___ 3. paranoid personality disorder   b. is fearful and timid

___ 4. dependent personality disorder   c. is mistrustful even when there is no reason

___ 5. avoidant personality disorder   d. shows little sense of responsibility

___ 6. narcissistic personality disorder   e. exhibits extreme dramatic behavior and self-centeredness

___ 7. borderline personality disorder   f. lacks the ability to form social relationships

___ 8. antisocial personality disorder   g. is unable to make own decisions

Answers: 1. b. 2. f. 3. c. 4. g. 5. b. 6. e. 7. a. 8. d.

Schizophrenic Disorders

How is schizophrenia different from multiple-personality disorder?

A common misconception is that *schizophrenia* means "split personality." But, as we have seen, split personality (or multiple personality) is actually a dissociative identity disorder. The misunderstanding comes from the fact that the root *schizo* derives from the Greek verb meaning "to split." What is split in schizophrenia is not so much personality as the connections among thoughts.

Schizophrenic disorders
Severe disorders in which there are disturbances of thoughts, communications, and emotions, including delusions and hallucinations.

Psychotic (psychosis)
Behavior characterized by a loss of touch with reality.

Insanity
Legal term for mentally disturbed people who are not considered responsible for their criminal actions.

Hallucinations
Sensory experiences in the absence of external stimulation.

Delusions
False beliefs about reality that have no basis in fact.

Disorganized schizophrenia
Schizophrenic disorder in which bizarre and childlike behaviors are common.

Catatonic schizophrenia
Schizophrenic disorder in which disturbed motor behavior is prominent.

Schizophrenic disorders are severe conditions marked by disordered thoughts and communications, inappropriate emotions, and bizarre behavior that lasts for months or even years. People with schizophrenia are out of touch with reality, which is to say that they are **psychotic.** *Psychosis* is sometimes confused with insanity, but the terms are not synonymous. **Insanity** is the legal term for people who are found not to be responsible for their criminal actions (see *Understanding the World Around Us*).

People with schizophrenia often suffer from **hallucinations,** false sensory perceptions that usually take the form of hearing voices that are not really there (visual, tactile, or olfactory hallucinations are more likely to indicate substance abuse or organic brain damage). They also frequently have **delusions**—false beliefs about reality with no factual basis—that distort their relationships with their surroundings and with other people. Typically these delusions are *paranoid*: People with schizophrenia believe that someone is out to harm them. They may think that a doctor wishes to kill them or that they are receiving radio messages from aliens invading from outer space. They often regard their own bodies—as well as the outside world—as hostile and alien. Because their world is utterly different from the one most of us live in, people with schizophrenia usually cannot live anything like a normal life unless they are successfully treated with medication (see Chapter 13: Therapies). Often they are unable to communicate with others, since when they speak, their words are incoherent. The following case illustrates some of the major characteristics of schizophrenia:

> For many years [a 35-year-old widow] has heard voices, which insult her and cast suspicion on her chastity. . . . The voices are very distinct, and in her opinion, they must be carried by telescope or a machine from her home. Her thoughts are dictated to her; she is obliged to think them, and hears them repeated after her. She . . . has all kinds of uncomfortable sensations in her body, to which something is "done." In particular, her "mother parts" are turned inside out, and people send a pain through her back, lay ice water on her heart, squeeze her neck, injure her spine, and violate her. There are also hallucinations of sight—black figures and the altered appearance of people—but these are far less frequent. (Spitzer et al., 1981, pp. 308–309)

There are actually several kinds of schizophrenic disorders, which have different characteristic symptoms.

Disorganized schizophrenia includes some of the more bizarre symptoms of schizophrenia, such as giggling, grimacing, and frantic gesturing. People suffering from disorganized schizophrenia show a childish disregard for social conventions and may urinate or defecate at inappropriate times. They are active but aimless, and they are often given to incoherent conversations.

In **catatonic schizophrenia,** motor activity is severely disturbed. People in this state may remain immobile, mute, and impassive. They may behave in a robotlike fashion when ordered to move, and they may even let doctors put their arms and legs into uncomfortable positions that they maintain for hours. At the opposite extreme, they may become excessively excited, talking and shouting continuously.

A young schizophrenic patient painted this picture of the monsters he claimed to see in his room.

UNDERSTANDING The World Around Us

The Insanity Defense

Many people attribute particularly horrifying crimes—assassinations of public figures, mass murders, and serial murders, for instance—to mental disturbance, because it seems that anyone who could commit such crimes must be crazy. But if a person is truly "crazy," is the legal system justified in holding him or her responsible for criminal acts? The legal answer to this question is a qualified yes. A mentally ill person is responsible for his or her crimes unless he or she is determined to be insane. What's the difference between being "mentally ill" and being "insane"? *Insanity* is a legal term, not a psychological one. It is typically applied to defendants who, when they committed the offense with which they are charged, were so mentally disturbed that they either could not distinguish right from wrong or could not control the act—it was an "irresistible impulse."

When a defendant is suspected of being mentally disturbed, another important question must be answered before that person is brought to trial: Can he or she understand the charges and participate in a defense in court? The issue of competency to stand trial is determined by a court-appointed expert. The person found to be incompetent is sent to a psychiatric institution, often for an indefinite period. The person judged to be competent is required to stand trial. At this point, the defendant may plead not guilty by reason of insan-

> Was the defendant unable
> to distinguish right
> from wrong?

ity, an assertion that at the time of the crime the defendant lacked substantial capacity to appreciate the criminality of his or her action (to know right from wrong) or to conform to the requirements of the law (to control his or her behavior).

When a defendant enters an insanity plea, the court system relies heavily on the testimony of forensic psychologists and psychiatrists to determine the mental state of the defendant at the time of the crime. Because most such trials feature experts testifying both for the defense and for the prosecution, the jury is often confused about

Theodore J. Kaczynski, the serial terrorist known as the Unabomber, was sought by the FBI for seventeen years. Kaczynski pleaded guilty to three killings to avoid a trial in which his lawyers had planned to argue that he was legally insane.

which side to believe. Furthermore, many people are cynical about professionals who receive large fees to appear in court and to argue that a defendant is or is not sane. The public, skeptical about professional jargon, often feels that psychological testimony allows dangerous criminals to "get off." Actually, those who successfully plead insanity often are confined longer in mental hospitals than they would have been in prison if convicted of their crimes. Therefore, the insanity plea is not an easy way out of responsibility for a crime.

Paranoid schizophrenia is marked by extreme suspiciousness and complex delusions. People with paranoid schizophrenia may believe themselves to be Napoleon or the Virgin Mary, or they may insist that Russian spies with laser guns are constantly on their trail because they have learned some great secret. Because they are less likely to be incoherent or to look or act "crazy," these people can appear more "normal" than people with other schizophrenic disorders if their delusions are compatible with everyday life. They may, however, become hostile or aggressive toward anyone who questions their thinking or delusions. Note that this disorder is far more severe than paranoid personality disorder, which does not involve bizarre delusions or loss of touch with reality.

Finally, **undifferentiated schizophrenia** is the classification developed for people who have several of the characteristic symptoms of schizo-

Paranoid schizophrenia
Schizophrenic disorder marked by extreme suspiciousness and complex, bizarre delusions.

Undifferentiated schizophrenia
Schizophrenic disorder in which there are clear schizophrenic symptoms that don't meet the criteria for another subtype of the disorder.

phrenia—such as delusions, hallucinations, or incoherence—yet do not show the typical symptoms of any other subtype of the disorder.

Because schizophrenia is a very serious disorder, considerable research has been directed at trying to discover its causes. Many studies indicate that schizophrenia has a genetic component (Gottesman, 1991). People with schizophrenia are more likely than other people to have children with schizophrenia, even when those children have lived with adoptive parents since early in life. And if one identical twin suffers from schizophrenia, the chances are almost 50 percent that the other twin will also develop this disorder. In fraternal twins, if one twin has schizophrenia, the chances are only about 17 percent that the other twin will develop it as well.

Recent research suggests that the biological predisposition to schizophrenia may be related to excessive amounts of the neurotransmitter dopamine in the central nervous system. Drugs that relieve schizophrenic symptoms decrease the amount of dopamine in the brain and block dopamine receptors. Some research also indicates that pathology in various structures of the brain may influence the onset of schizophrenia (Weinberger, 1997). Other studies link schizophrenia to some form of early prenatal disturbance (Wolf & Weinberger, 1996). Nevertheless, scientists have found only average differences in brain structure and chemistry between schizophrenic and healthy people (Noga, Bartley, Jones, Torrey, & Weinberger, 1996). As yet, no laboratory tests can diagnose schizophrenia on the basis of brain abnormalities. In fact, studies of identical twins in which only one suffers from schizophrenia have sometimes found more evidence of brain abnormalities in the well twin than in the sick twin.

Studies of identical twins have also been used to identify the importance of environment in causing schizophrenia. Because identical twins are genetically identical and because half of the identical twins of people with schizophrenia do not develop schizophrenia themselves, this severe and puzzling disorder cannot be caused by genetic factors alone. Environmental factors—ranging from disturbed family relations to taking drugs to biological damage that may occur at any age, even before birth—must also figure in determining whether a person will develop schizophrenia. Recall that the systems model would predict that environment and experience can increase or decrease the effects of any inherited tendency. Consequently, identical twins afflicted with psychological disorders will show different degrees of functioning.

Finally, although quite different in emphasis, the various explanations for schizophrenic disorders are not mutually exclusive. Genetic factors are universally acknowledged, but many theorists believe that only a combination of biological, psychological, and social factors produces schizophrenia (Gottesman, 1991). According to the systems model, genetic factors predispose some people to schizophrenia, and family interaction and life stress activate the predisposition.

INTERACTIVE LECTURE **12.8**

WEB QUIZ **12.8**

CHECK YOUR UNDERSTANDING

1. Schizophrenic disorders are characterized by _____ symptoms, or loss of contact with reality.
2. _____ is the legal term for mentally disturbed people who are found not to be responsible for their criminal actions.
3. People with schizophrenia often suffer from _____, false sensory perceptions that usually take the form of hearing voices that are not really there.

Match the following terms with the appropriate description.

____ 4. disorganized schizophrenia

a. is marked by extreme suspiciousness and complex delusions

____ 5. catatonic schizophrenia

b. has bizarre symptoms that may include giggling, grimacing, frantic gesturing, and a childish disregard for social conventions

____ 6. paranoid schizophrenia

c. is marked by a severe disturbance of motor activity

____ 7. undifferentiated schizophrenia

d. is found in people who have several characteristic symptoms of schizophrenia but do not show the typical symptoms of any other subtype

8. Indicate whether the following statements are true (T) or false (F).

____ a. Schizophrenia is almost the same thing as multiple personality.

____ b. Studies indicate that a biological predisposition to schizophrenia may be inherited.

____ c. Laboratory tests can be used to diagnose schizophrenia on the basis of brain abnormalities.

Answers: 1. psychotic. 2. Insanity. 3. hallucinations. 4. b. 5. c. 6. a. 7. d. 8. a. (F); b. (T); c. (F).

Childhood Disorders

Why do stimulants appear to slow down hyperactive children and adults?

Children may suffer from conditions already discussed in this chapter—for example, depression and anxiety disorders. But other disorders are either characteristic of children or are first evident in childhood. The DSM-IV contains a long list of "disorders usually first diagnosed in infancy, childhood, or adolescence." Two of these disorders are attention-deficit/hyperactivity disorder and autistic disorder.

Attention-deficit/hyperactivity disorder (ADHD) was once known simply as *hyperactivity*. The new name reflects the fact that children with the disorder typically have trouble focusing their attention in the sustained way that other children do. Instead, they are easily distracted, often fidgety and impulsive, and almost constantly in motion. Many theorists believe that this disorder—which affects nearly 5 percent of all school-age children and is much more common in boys than girls—is present at birth but becomes a serious problem only after the child starts school. The class setting demands that children sit quietly, pay attention as instructed, follow directions, and inhibit urges to yell and run around. The child with ADHD simply cannot conform to these demands.

We do not yet know what causes ADHD, but most theorists assume that biological factors are very influential (see Filipek et al., 1997; Vaidya et. al., 1998). Family interaction and other social experiences may be more important in preventing the disorder than in causing it. That is, some exceptionally competent parents and patient, tolerant teachers may be able to teach "difficult" children to conform to the demands of schooling. Although some psychologists train the parents of children with ADHD in these management skills, the most frequent treatment for these children is a type of drug known as a *psychostimulant*. Psychostimulants do not work by "slowing down" hyperactive children; rather, they appear to increase the children's ability to focus their attention so that they can attend to the task at hand, which decreases their hyperactivity (Barkley, 1990). Unfortunately, psy-

Attention-deficit/hyperactivity disorder (ADHD)
A childhood disorder characterized by inattention, impulsiveness, and hyperactivity.

chostimulants often produce only short-term benefits, and their use is controversial (Panskepp, 1998).

A very different and profoundly serious disorder that usually becomes evident in the first few years of life is **autistic disorder.** Autistic children fail to form normal attachments to parents, remaining distant and withdrawn into their own separate worlds. As infants, they may even show distress at being picked up or held. As they grow older, they typically do not speak, or they develop a peculiar speech pattern called *echolalia*, in which they repeat the words said to them. Autistic children typically show strange motor behavior, such as repeating body movements endlessly or walking constantly on tiptoe. They don't play as normal children do; they are not at all social and may use toys in odd ways, constantly spinning the wheels on a toy truck or tearing paper into strips. Autistic children often display the symptoms of retardation, but it is hard to test their mental ability because they generally don't talk. The disorder lasts into adulthood in the great majority of cases (recall the character Raymond in the movie *Rain Man*).

We don't know what causes autism, although most theorists believe that it results almost entirely from biological conditions. Some causes of mental retardation, such as fragile X syndrome (see Chapter 7), also seem to increase the risk of autistic disorder. Recent evidence suggests that genetics also plays a strong role in causing the disorder (Bailey et al., 1995; Cook et al., 1998; Lamb, Moore, Bailey, & Monaco, 2000; Rodier, 2000).

INTERACTIVE LECTURE **12.9**

WEB QUIZ **12.9**

CHECK YOUR UNDERSTANDING

1. Children with ____ typically lack the ability to focus their attention in the sustained way that other children do.
2. The most frequent treatment for ADHD is a type of drug known as a ____.
3. Which of the following is *not* a characteristic of children with autistic disorder?
   a. They fail to form normal attachments to parents.
   b. They often have exceptionally high IQs.
   c. They typically show strange motor behavior, such as repeating body movements endlessly.
   d. As they grow older, they often do not develop speech.
4. Indicate whether the following are true (T) or false (F).
   ____a. ADHD is much more common in boys than in girls.
   ____b. Psychostimulants work by "slowing down" hyperactive children.
   ____c. Most theorists believe that autistic disorder results almost entirely from biological conditions.

Answers: 1. attention-deficit/hyperactivity disorder (ADHD). 2. psychostimulant. 3. b. 4. a. (T); b. (F); c. (T).

Gender and Cultural Differences in Abnormal Behavior

What complex factors contribute to different rates of abnormal behavior in men and women?

Throughout this chapter we have rarely examined the differences between men and women despite the oversimplified conclusion of many studies that women have a higher rate of psychological disorders than men do. Prevalence rates of mental disorders vary by a number of factors: gender, age, race, ethnicity, marital status, income, and type of disorder. Furthermore,

Autistic disorder
A childhood disorder characterized by lack of social instincts and strange motor behavior.

how do we determine the "rate of psychological disorders"? Do we count only people admitted to mental hospitals? those who receive a formal diagnosis in an outpatient-treatment setting? Or do we count all those persons in the general population who are judged to suffer from mental disorders even if they have not sought treatment or received a formal diagnosis? These questions illustrate how hard it is to make a firm generalization about differences between the sexes.

We do know that more women than men are treated for mental disorders, but this does not mean that more women than men have mental disorders, for in our society, it is much more acceptable for women to discuss their emotional difficulties and to seek professional help (Lerman, 1996). Perhaps mental disorders are equally common among men—or even more common—but men do not typically go to therapists and therefore are not counted in the studies.

In our culture, when men display abnormal behavior, they are more likely to drink too much or act aggressively; when women display abnormal behavior, they are more likely to become fearful, passive, hopeless, and "sick" (Basow, 1986).

We saw in Chapter 11 that the effects of stress are greater to the extent that a person feels alienated, powerless, and helpless—situations more frequent among women than men. These factors are especially common among minority women, and psychological disorders are more prevalent among these women than among other women (Russo & Sobel, 1981). Once past puberty, women seem to have higher rates of anxiety disorders and depression than men do, and they are more likely than men to seek professional help for their problems. Greater stress—partly owing to socialization and lower status rather than psychological "weakness"—apparently accounts for this statistic, however. Marriage and family life, associated with lower rates of mental disorders among men, introduce additional stress into the lives of women, particularly young women (ages 25–45), and in some instances this added stress translates into a psychological disorder.

The idea that culture plays a role in the prevalence of mental disorders is supported by evidence that the frequency and nature of at least some disorders varies significantly around the world (Lopez & Guarnaccia, 2000). It is interesting that those disorders that have a strong genetic component (such as schizophrenia) do not differ much from culture to culture or among men and women. Those that appear to be more dependent on cultural expectations (such as ADHD) show wider variations among different cultural groups and among men and women (Weisz, McCarty, Eastman, Chaiyasit, & Suwanlert, 1997).

The differences between men and women, and among various cultural groups around the world, support the systems view of abnormal behavior. Psychological disorders typically develop as a result of complex and interacting biological, psychological, and social factors.

INTERACTIVE LECTURE **12.10**

WEB QUIZ **12.10**

CHECK YOUR UNDERSTANDING

1. Mental disorders for which there seems to be a strong _____ component are distributed fairly equally between the sexes.
2. More women than men are treated for mental disorders. Is this statement true (T) or false (F)?
3. There is greater cultural variation in those abnormal behaviors with strong genetic causes. Is this statement true (T) or false (F)?

Answers: 1. biological. 2. T. 3. F.

KEY TERMS

CHAPTER REVIEW

Perspectives on Psychological Disorders

How does a mental health professional define a psychological disorder? Mental health professionals define a psychological disorder as a condition that either seriously impairs a person's ability to function in life or creates a high level of inner distress (or sometimes both). This view does not mean that the category "disordered" is always easy to distinguish from the category "normal." In fact, it may be more accurate to view abnormal behavior as merely quantitatively different from normal behavior.

How has the view of psychological disorders changed over time? In early societies, abnormal behavior was often attributed to supernatural powers. The roots of a more naturalistic view can be traced to Hippocrates, who maintained that madness was like any other sickness, arising from natural causes. This approach fell into disfavor in the Middle Ages, when possession by devils became the predominant explanation of psychological disorders. A naturalistic view didn't resurface until the eighteenth century. In modern times, three approaches

have helped to advance our understanding of abnormal behavior: the biological, the psychoanalytic, and the cognitive-behavioral.

How can biology influence the development of psychological disorders? The **biological model** holds that abnormal behavior is caused by some physiological malfunction, especially of the brain. It is assumed that these malfunctions are often hereditary in origin. Although there is evidence that genetic/biochemical factors are indeed involved in some psychological disorders, biology alone cannot account for most mental illnesses.

What did Freud and his followers believe was the underlying cause of psychological disorders? The **psychoanalytic model** originating with Freud holds that abnormal behavior is a symbolic expression of unconscious conflicts that generally can be traced to childhood.

According to the cognitive-behavioral model, what causes abnormal behavior? The **cognitive-behavior model** states that psychological disorders arise when people learn maladaptive ways of thinking and acting. What has been learned can be unlearned, however.

Cognitive-behavior therapists therefore strive to modify their patients' dysfunctional behaviors and distorted, self-defeating processes of thought.

Why do some people with a family background of a psychological disorder develop the disorder, whereas other family members do not? The **diathesis-stress model** is one promising approach to answering this question. As an attempt to integrate the biological perspective with environmentally based ones, it holds that psychological disorders develop when a **diathesis** (or biological predisposition) is set off by stressful circumstances. Another attempt at integrating causes is the **systems approach.** It contends that psychological disorders are "lifestyle diseases" that arise from a combination of biological risk factors, psychological stresses, and societal pressures on people. This approach, too, can help to explain why a family background of a disorder doesn't always mean that the disorder will develop.

Why is it useful to have a manual of psychological disorders? For nearly forty years, the American Psychiatric Association has published the *Diagnostic and Statistical Manual of Mental Disorders (DSM)*. The current fourth edition, known as DSM-IV, provides careful descriptions of the symptoms of different disorders so that diagnoses based on them will be reliable from one mental health professional to another. The DSM-IV includes little on causes and treatments.

How common are mental disorders? According to research, 32 percent of Americans will suffer from one or more mental disorders in their lifetime, and 15 percent of the population is so affected at any given point in time. Drug abuse is the most common disorder, followed by anxiety disorders and then mood disorders.

Mood Disorders

How do mood disorders differ from ordinary mood changes? Most people have a wide emotional range, but in some people with **mood disorders,** this range is greatly restricted. They seem stuck at one or the other end of the emotional spectrum, or they may alternate back and forth between periods of mania and depression.

How does clinical depression differ from ordinary sadness? The most common mood disorder is **depression,** a state in which a person feels overwhelmed with sadness, loses interest in activities, and displays other symptoms, such as excessive guilt or feelings of worthlessness. The DSM-IV distinguishes between two forms of clinical depression. *Major depressive disorder* is an

episode of intense sadness that may last for several months; in contrast, *dysthymia* involves less intense sadness but persists with little relief for a period of two years or more.

What factors are related to a person's likelihood of committing suicide? More women than men attempt suicide, but more men succeed. Suicide rates among American adolescents and young adults have been rising, and suicide is the third leading cause of death among adolescents. A common feeling associated with suicide is hopelessness, which is also typical of depression.

What is mania, and how is it involved in bipolar disorder? People suffering from **mania** become euphoric ("high"), extremely active, excessively talkative, and easily distractible. They typically have unlimited hopes and schemes but little interest in realistically carrying them out. At the extreme, they may collapse from exhaustion. Manic episodes rarely appear by themselves; rather, they usually alternate with depression. Such a mood disorder, in which both mania and depression are alternately present and are sometimes interrupted by periods of normal mood, is known as **bipolar disorder.**

What causes some people to experience extreme mood changes? Mood disorders can result from a combination of biological, psychological, and social factors. Biological factors—including genetics and chemical imbalances in the brain—seem to play an important role in the development of depression and especially bipolar disorder. The psychological factor of **cognitive distortions** (unrealistically negative views about the self) occurs in many depressed people, although it is uncertain whether these distortions cause the depression or are caused by it. Finally, social factors, such as troubled relationships, have also been linked with mood disorders.

Anxiety Disorders

How does an anxiety disorder differ from ordinary anxiety? Normal fear is caused by something identifiable, and the fear subsides with time. In the case of **anxiety disorder,** however, either the person doesn't know why he or she is afraid, or the anxiety is inappropriate to the circumstances.

Into what three categories are phobias usually grouped? A **specific phobia** is an intense, paralyzing fear of something that it is unreasonable to fear so excessively. A **social phobia** is excessive, inappropriate fear connected with social situations or performances in front of other people. **Agoraphobia** is a less common and much more debilitating type of anxiety disorder that involves multiple, intense fears such as the fear of being alone or of being in public places or other situations that require separation from a source of security.

How does a panic attack differ from fear? **Panic disorder** is characterized by recurrent panic attacks, which are sudden, unpredictable, and overwhelming experiences of intense fear or terror without any reasonable cause.

How do generalized anxiety disorder and obsessive-compulsive disorder differ from specific phobias? **Generalized anxiety disorder** is defined by prolonged vague but intense fears that, unlike phobias, are not attached to any particular object or circumstance. In contrast, **obsessive-compulsive disorder** involves either involuntary thoughts that recur despite the person's attempt to stop them or compulsive rituals that a person feels compelled to perform. Two other types of anxiety disorder are caused by highly stressful events. If the anxious reaction occurs soon after the event, the diagnosis is *acute stress disorder*; if it occurs long after the event is over, the diagnosis is *posttraumatic stress disorder*.

What can the cognitive perspective and the biological perspective tell us about the causes of anxiety? Psychologists with a biological perspective propose that a predisposition to anxiety disorders may be inherited because these types of disorders tend to run in families. Cognitive psychologists suggest that people who believe that they have no control over stressful events in their lives are more likely to suffer from anxiety disorders than other people are. There are also views of anxiety disorders based on evolutionary and psychoanalytic perspectives. Evolutionary psychologists hold that we are predisposed by evolution to associate certain stimuli with intense fears and that this is the origin of many phobias. Psychoanalytic thinkers focus on inner psychological conflicts and the defense mechanisms they trigger as the sources of anxiety disorders.

Psychosomatic and Somatoform Disorders

What is the difference between psychosomatic disorders and somatoform disorders? **Psychosomatic disorders** are illnesses that have a valid physical basis but are largely caused by psychological factors such as excessive stress and anxiety. In contrast, **somatoform disorders** are characterized by physical symptoms without any identifiable physical cause. Examples are **conversion disorder** (a dramatic specific disability without organic cause),

hypochondriasis (insistence that minor symptoms mean serious illness), and **body dysmorphic disorder** (imagined ugliness in some part of the body).

Dissociative Disorders

What do dissociative disorders have in common? In **dissociative disorders,** some part of a person's personality or memory is separated from the rest. Dissociative amnesia involves the loss of at least some significant aspects of memory. When an amnesia victim leaves home and assumes an entirely new identity, the disorder is known as *dissociative fugue*. In **dissociative identity disorder,** commonly known as *multiple personality disorder*, a person has several distinct personalities that emerge at different times. In **depersonalization disorder,** the person suddenly feels changed or different in a strange way.

Sexual and Gender-Identity Disorders

What are the three main types of sexual disorders? DSM-IV recognizes three main types of sexual disorders. One is **sexual dysfunction**—loss or impairment of the ability to function effectively during sex. In men this may take the form of erectile disorder (inability to achieve or keep an erection), and in women it often occurs as female sexual arousal disorder (inability to become sexually excited or to reach orgasm). Another main class of sexual disorders consists of the **paraphilias,** in which the person has sexual interest in unconventional objects or situations. One example is **fetishism,** or repeated use of a nonhuman object to achieve sexual excitement. Another is **pedophilia,** or sexual arousal that involves a prepubescent child. **Gender-identity disorders** make up the third main type of sexual disorders. These involve the desire to become, or the insistence that one really is, a member of the other sex.

Personality Disorders

Which personality disorder creates the most significant problems for society? **Personality disorders** are enduring, inflexible, and maladaptive ways of thinking and behaving that are so exaggerated and rigid that they cause serious inner distress or conflicts with others. One group of personality disorders is characterized by odd or eccentric behavior. For example, people who exhibit **schizoid personality disorder** lack the ability or desire to form social relationships and have no warm feelings for other people; those with **paranoid personality**

disorder are inappropriately suspicious of others. Another cluster of personality disorders is characterized by anxious or fearful behavior. Examples are **dependent personality disorder** (the inability to think or act independently) and **avoidant personality disorder** (social anxiety leading to isolation). A third group of personality disorders is characterized by dramatic, emotional, or erratic behavior. For instance, people with **narcissistic personality disorder** have a highly overblown sense of self-importance, whereas those with **borderline personality disorder** show much instability in self-image, mood, and interpersonal relationships. Finally, people with **antisocial personality disorder** chronically lie, steal, and cheat with little or no remorse. Because this disorder is responsible for a good deal of crime and violence, it creates the greatest problems for society.

Schizophrenic Disorders

How is schizophrenia different from multiple-personality disorder? In multiple-personality disorder, consciousness is split into two or more distinctive personalities, each of which is coherent and intact. This condition is different from **schizophrenic disorders,** which involve dramatic disruptions in thought and communication, inappropriate emotions, and bizarre behavior that lasts for years. People with schizophrenia are out of touch with reality and usually cannot live anything like a normal life unless successfully treated with medication. They often suffer from **hallucinations** (false sensory perceptions) and **delusions** (false beliefs about reality). Subtypes of schizophrenic disorders include **disorganized schizophrenia** (childish disregard for social conventions), **catatonic schizophrenia** (mute immobility or excessive excitement), **paranoid schizophrenia** (extreme suspiciousness related to complex delusions), and **undifferentiated schizophrenia** (characterized by a diversity of symptoms).

Childhood Disorders

Why do stimulants appear to slow down hyperactive children and adults? DSM-IV contains a long list of disorders usually first diagnosed in infancy, childhood, or adolescence. Two of them discussed in this chapter are **attention-deficit/hyperactivity disorder (ADHD)** and **autistic disorder.** Children with ADHD are highly distractible, often fidgety and impulsive, and almost constantly in motion. The psychostimulants frequently prescribed for ADHD appear to slow such children down because they increase the ability to focus attention on routine tasks. Autistic disorder is a profound problem identified in the first few years of life. It is characterized by a failure to form normal social attachments, severe speech impairment, and strange motor behaviors.

Gender and Cultural Differences in Abnormal Behavior

What complex factors contribute to different rates of abnormal behavior in men and women? Although nearly all psychological disorders affect both men and women, there are some gender differences in the degree to which some disorders are found. Men are more likely to suffer from substance abuse and antisocial personality disorder; and women show higher rates of depression, agoraphobia, simple phobia, obsessive-compulsive disorder, and somatization disorder. In general, gender differences are less likely to be seen in disorders that have a strong biological component. This tendency is also seen cross-culturally, where cultural differences are observed in disorders not heavily influenced by genetic and biological factors. These gender and cultural differences support the systems view that biological, psychological, and social forces interact as causes of abnormal behavior.

CRITICAL THINKING AND APPLICATIONS

1. Imagine that a halfway house for the mentally ill is proposed to be built in a residential neighborhood but that many of the residents are frightened by the prospect of living near recovering mentally ill people. Should they be able to prevent the house from being built? Why, or why not?

2. Do feelings of depression and anxiety indicate that a person is suffering from a mood disorder?

3. How do you feel about the rehabilitation of prisoners, given the fact that antisocial personality disorder may occur in 50 percent of prison populations?

WEB QUIZ **12.11**   Go to the Morris 6e Companion Website to take a practice chapter exam.

13 Therapies

I N CHAPTER 1 WE INTRODUCED THE CONCEPT OF **PSYCHOTHERAPY,** techniques to treat personality and behavior disorders. Literally hundreds of variations are practiced by several different types of mental health professionals. Some types of psychotherapy occur outside the therapist's office, as clients confront their fears in real life. Other psychotherapies treat couples or entire families, and still others treat groups of people with similar problems or goals. Despite the popular image of the clinical, detached analyst, most psychotherapists are warm, understanding, and willing to offer at least some direct information and advice.

In addition to holding inaccurate views of therapists, many people are confused about the effectiveness of psychotherapy. Some who have gone through therapy claim that it changed their lives; others complain that it made little difference. The public's perception of the effectiveness of psychotherapy is particularly important now that health care costs have escalated and treatments of psychological disorders are being monitored more closely in terms of their costs and outcomes. The future of psychotherapy rests in demonstrating its effectiveness.

In this chapter, we survey the major types of therapies, including individual therapies and group therapies. We discuss these in the order in which they were developed: insight therapies, which began in the early twentieth century; behavior therapies, which became popular in the 1960s and 1970s; and the even more recent cognitive therapies. We also examine research that compares the effectiveness of different approaches, and we explore the role of medication and other biological treatments. Finally, we discuss the important issues of caring for the seriously disturbed, and we consider the factor of human diversity when providing treatments.

Insight Therapies

What do insight therapies have in common?

Several of the individual psychotherapies used in both private practice and institutions fall under the heading of **insight therapies.** Although the various insight therapies differ in their details, their common goal is to give people a better awareness and understanding of their feelings, motivations, and actions in the hope that this will lead to better adjustment (Pine, 1998). In this section we consider three major insight therapies: psychoanalysis, client-centered therapy, and Gestalt therapy.

Psychoanalysis

How does "free association" in psychoanalysis help a person to become aware of hidden feelings?

Psychoanalysis is designed to bring hidden feelings and motives to conscious awareness so that the person can deal with them more effectively.

In Freudian psychoanalysis, the client is instructed to talk about whatever comes to mind, with as little editing as possible and without inhibiting or controlling thoughts and fantasies. This process is called **free association.**

Psychotherapy
The use of psychological techniques to treat personality and behavior disorders.

Insight therapies
A variety of individual psychotherapies designed to give people a better awareness and understanding of their feelings, motivations, and actions in the hope that this will help them to adjust.

Psychoanalysis
The theory of personality Freud developed as well as the form of therapy he invented.

Free association
A psychoanalytic technique that encourages the person to talk without inhibition about whatever thoughts or fantasies come to mind.

The consulting room where Freud met his clients. Note the position of Freud's chair at the head of the couch. In order to encourage free association, the psychoanalyst has to function as a blank screen onto which the client can project his or her feelings. To accomplish this, Freud believed, the psychoanalyst has to stay out of sight of the client.

Freud believed that the resulting "stream of consciousness" would provide insight into the person's unconscious mind. During the early stages of psychoanalysis, the analyst remains impassive, mostly silent, and out of the person's sight. In classical psychoanalysis, the client lies on a couch while the neutral analyst sits behind the client. The analyst's silence is a kind of "blank screen" onto which the person eventually projects unconscious thoughts and feelings.

Eventually clients may test their analyst by talking about desires and fantasies that they have never revealed to anyone else. But the analyst maintains neutrality throughout, showing little of his or her own feelings and personality. When clients discover that their analyst is not shocked or disgusted by their revelations, they are reassured and transfer to their analyst feelings they have toward authority figures from their childhood. This process is known as **transference.** It is said to be *positive transference* when the person feels good about the analyst.

As people continue to expose their innermost feelings, they begin to feel increasingly vulnerable. They want reassurance and affection, but their analyst remains silent. Their anxiety builds. Threatened by their analyst's silence and by their own thoughts, clients may feel cheated and perhaps accuse their analyst of being a money-grabber. Or they may suspect that their analyst is really disgusted by their disclosures or is laughing about them behind their backs. This *negative transference* is thought to be a crucial step in psychoanalysis, for it presumably reveals negative feelings toward authority figures and resistance to uncovering repressed emotions.

As therapy progresses, the analyst takes a more active role and begins to *interpret* or suggest alternative meanings for clients' feelings, memories, and actions. The goal of interpretation is to help people to gain **insight**—to become aware of what was formerly outside their awareness. As what was unconscious becomes conscious, clients may come to see how their childhood experiences have determined how they currently feel and act. Analysts encourage their clients to confront childhood events and to recall them fully. As these clients relive their childhood traumas, they become able to resolve conflicts they could not resolve in the past. *Working through* old conflicts is thought to provide people with the chance to review and revise the feelings and beliefs that underlie their problems. In the following therapy session, the analyst helps a woman gain insight into why she tends to suppress emotions and often to act ill. The woman discovers a link between these behaviors and childhood fears regarding her mother, which she has transferred to the analyst.

Transference
The client's carrying over to the analyst feelings held toward childhood authority figures.

Insight
Awareness of previously unconscious feelings and memories and how they influence present feelings and behavior.

Therapist: (summarizing and restating) It sounds as if you would like to let loose with me, but you are afraid of what my response would be.

Patient: I get so excited by what is happening here. I feel I'm being held back by needing to be nice. I'd like to blast loose sometimes, but I don't dare.

Therapist: Because you fear my reaction?

Patient: The worst thing would be that you wouldn't like me. You wouldn't speak to me friendly; you wouldn't smile; you'd feel you can't treat me and discharge me from treatment. But I know this isn't so; I know it.

Therapist: Where do you think these attitudes come from?

Patient: When I was 9 years old, I read a lot about great men in history. I'd quote them and be dramatic, I'd want a sword at my side; I'd dress like an Indian. Mother would scold me: Don't frown; don't talk so much. Sit on your hands, over and over again. I did all kinds of things. I was a naughty child. She told me I'd be hurt. Then, at 14, I fell off a horse and broke my back. I had to be in bed. Mother told me on the day I went riding not to, I'd get hurt because the ground was frozen. I was a stubborn, self-willed child. Then I went against her will and suffered an accident that changed my life, a fractured back. Her attitude was, "I told you so." I was put in a cast and kept in bed for months.

Therapist: You were punished, so to speak, by this accident.

Patient: But I gained attention and love from Mother for the first time. I felt so good. I'm ashamed to tell you this: Before I healed, I opened the cast and tried to walk, to make myself sick again so I could stay in bed longer.

Therapist: How does that connect up with your impulse to be sick now and stay in bed so much?

Patient: Oh. . . . (*pause*)

Therapist: What do you think?

Patient: Oh, my God, how infantile, how ungrownup (*pause*). It must be so. I want people to love me and be sorry for me. Oh, my God. How completely childish. It is, *is* that. My mother must have ignored me when I was little, and I wanted so to be loved.

Therapist: So that it may have been threatening to go back to being self-willed and unloved after you got out of the cast (*interpretation*).

Patient: It did. My life changed. I became meek and controlled. I couldn't get angry or stubborn afterward.

Therapist: Perhaps if you go back to being stubborn with me, you would be returning to how you were before, that is, active, stubborn, but unloved.

Patient: (*excitedly*) And, therefore, losing your love. I need you, but after all, you aren't going to reject me. But the pattern is so established now that the threat of the loss of love is too overwhelming with everybody, and I've got to keep myself from acting selfish or angry. (Wolberg, 1977, pp. 560–561)

Only a handful of people who seek therapy go into traditional psychoanalysis, as this woman did. As Freud himself recognized, analysis requires great motivation to change and an ability to deal rationally with whatever the analysis uncovers. Moreover, traditional analysis may take five years or longer, with three, sometimes five, sessions a week. Few people can afford this kind of treatment. Fewer still possess the verbal and analytical skills necessary to discuss thoughts and feelings in this detailed way. And many want more immediate help for their problems. Moreover, for those with severe disorders, psychoanalysis is not effective.

Many therapists today believe that traditional psychoanalysis has become outdated. Since Freud invented psychoanalysis around the turn of the century, psychodynamic personality theory has changed significantly, as we saw in Chapter 10, Personality. Many of these changes have led to modified psychoanalytic techniques as well as to different approaches to therapy. For example, although Freud felt that to understand the present, one must understand the past, most neo-Freudians encourage their clients to cope directly with current problems in addition to, or as a way of, addressing unresolved conflicts from the past. Neo-Freudians also favor face-to-face discussions, and most take an active role in analysis from the start by interpreting their client' statements freely and suggesting topics for discussion.

Client-Centered Therapy

Why did Carl Rogers call his approach to therapy "client-centered"?

Carl Rogers, the founder of **client-centered** (or **person-centered**) **therapy,** took bits and pieces of the neo-Freudians' views and revised and rearranged them into a radically different approach to therapy. According

Client-centered (or person-centered) therapy
Nondirectional form of therapy developed by Carl Rogers that calls for unconditional positive regard of the client by the therapist with the goal of helping client become fully functioning.

Carl Rogers (far right) leading a group therapy session. Rogers was the founder of client-centered therapy.

to Rogers, the goal of therapy is to help people to become fully functioning, to open them up to all of their experiences and to all of themselves. Such inner awareness is a form of insight, but for Rogers, insight into current feelings was more important than insight into unconscious wishes with roots in the distant past. Rogers called his approach to therapy *client-centered* because he placed the responsibility for change on the person with the problem. Rogers's ideas about therapy are quite specific. He believed that people's defensiveness, rigidity, anxiety, and other signs of discomfort stem from their experiences of conditional positive regard. They have learned that love and acceptance are contingent on conforming to what other people want them to be. The cardinal rule in person-centered therapy is for the therapist to express *unconditional positive regard*—that is, to show true acceptance of clients no matter what they may say or do. Rogers felt that this was a crucial first step toward getting clients to accept themselves.

Rather than taking an objective approach, Rogerian therapists try to understand things from the clients' point of view. They are also emphatically *nondirective*. They do not suggest reasons why clients feel as they do or how they might better handle a difficult situation. Instead, they try to reflect clients' statements, sometimes asking questions and sometimes hinting at feelings that clients have not put into words. Rogers felt that when therapists provide an atmosphere of openness and genuine respect, clients can find themselves, as the man in this session starts to do as he explores his debilitating lack of confidence.

Client: I guess I do have problems at school. . . . You see, I'm chairman of the Science Department, so you can imagine what kind of a department it is.

Therapist: You sort of feel that if you're in something that it can't be too good. Is that . . .

Client: Well, it's not that I . . . It's just that I'm . . . I don't think that I could run it.

Therapist: You don't have any confidence in yourself?

Client: No confidence, no confidence in myself. I never had any confidence in myself. I—like I told you—like when even when I was a kid I didn't feel I was capable and I always wanted to get back with the intellectual group.

Therapist: This has been a long-term thing, then. It's gone on a long time.

Client: Yeah, the *feeling* is—even though I know it isn't, it's the feeling that I have that—that I haven't got it, that—that—that—people will find out that I'm dumb or—or . . .

Therapist: Masquerade.

Client: Superficial, I'm just superficial. There's nothing below the surface. Just superficial generalities, that . . .

Therapist: There's nothing really deep and meaningful to you. (Hersher, 1970, pp. 29–32).

Rogers was not interested in comparing his therapy with others, nor was he concerned simply with statistics on outcomes (such as the percentage of clients who experienced emotional improvements). Rather, he wanted to discover those processes in client-centered therapy that were associated with positive results. Rogers's interest in the *process* of therapy resulted in important and lasting contributions to the field. For example, research has shown that a therapist's warmth and understanding increase success, no matter what therapeutic approach is used (Frank & Frank, 1991).

Gestalt Therapy

How is Gestalt therapy different from psychoanalysis?

Gestalt therapy is largely an outgrowth of the work of Frederick (Fritz) Perls at the Esalen Institute in California. Perls began his career as a psychoanalyst but later turned vehemently against Freud and psychoanalytic techniques. Gestalt therapy emphasizes the here and now and encourages face-to-face confrontations.

Gestalt therapy is designed to help people become more genuine or "real" in their day-to-day interactions. It may be conducted with individuals or with groups ("encounter groups"). The therapist is active and directive, and the emphasis is on the *whole* person (the term *Gestalt* means "whole"). The therapist's role is to "fill in the holes in the personality to make the person whole and complete again" (Perls, 1969, p. 2).

Gestalt therapists try to make people aware of their feelings by using a variety of techniques. For example, they tell people to "own their feelings" by talking in an active rather than a passive way ("I feel angry when he's around" instead of "He makes me feel angry when he's around"). They also ask people to speak to a part of themselves that they imagine to be sitting next to them in an empty chair. This *empty-chair technique* and others are illustrated in the following excerpt.

Therapist: Try to describe just what you are aware of at each moment as fully as possible. For instance, what are you aware of now?

Client: I'm aware of wanting to tell you about my problem, and also a sense of shame—yes, I feel very ashamed right now.

Therapist: Okay. I would like you to develop a dialogue with your feeling of shame. Put your shame in the empty chair over here (*indicates chair*), and talk to it.

Client: Are you serious? I haven't even told you about my problem yet.

Therapist: That can wait—I'm perfectly serious, and I want to know what you have to say to your shame.

Client: (*awkward and hesitant at first, but then becoming looser and more involved*) Shame, I hate you. I wish you would leave me—you drive me crazy, always reminding me that I have a problem, that I'm perverse, different, shameful—even ugly. Why don't you leave me alone?

Therapist: Okay, now go to the empty chair, take the role of shame, and answer yourself back.

Client: (*moves to the empty chair*) I am your constant companion—and I don't *want* to leave you. I would feel lonely without you, and I don't hate you. I pity you, and I pity your attempts to shake me loose, because you are doomed to failure.

Gestalt therapy
An insight therapy that emphasizes the wholeness of the personality and attempts to reawaken people to their emotions and sensations in the here and now.

Therapist: Okay, now go back to your original chair and answer back.

Client: (*once again as himself*) How do you know I'm doomed to failure? (*Spontaneously shifts chairs now, no longer needing direction from the therapist; answers himself back, once again in the role of shame.*) I know that you're doomed to failure because *I* want you to fail and because I control your life. You can't make a single move without me. For all you know, you were born with me. You can hardly remember a single moment when you were without me, totally unafraid that I would spring up and suddenly remind you of your loathsomeness. (Shaffer, 1978, pp. 92–93)

In this way the client becomes more aware of conflicting inner feelings and, with insight, can become more genuine. As we have seen, psychoanalysis, client-centered therapy, and Gestalt therapy differ in their techniques, but all use talk to help people become more aware of their feelings and conflicts, and all involve fairly substantial amounts of time. We turn now to more recent developments in therapy that seek to limit the amount of time people spend in therapy.

Recent Developments

What are some recent developments in insight therapies?

Although Freud, Rogers, and Perls originated the three major forms of insight therapy, others have developed hundreds of variations on this theme. Most involve a therapist who is far more active and emotionally engaged with clients than traditional psychoanalysts thought fit. These therapists give clients direct guidance and feedback, commenting on what they are told rather than just listening to their clients in a neutral manner. Most of these newer therapies are also much shorter-term than traditional psychoanalysis. Insight remains the goal of so-called **short-term psychodynamic therapy,** but the treatment is usually timelimited—for example, to twenty-five sessions. This trend is based on research showing that most people (75 percent) experience improvement in this time frame (Howard, Kopta, Krause & Orlinsky, 1986), even though longer therapy may often be even more beneficial (Seligman, 1995). Finally, with the trend to a time-limited framework, insight therapies have become more symptom-oriented, trying to help clients correct the *immediate* problems in their lives. They see people as less at the mercy of early childhood events than Freud did. Although they do not discount childhood experiences, they focus on the client's current life situation and relationships.

Short-term psychodynamic therapy Insight therapy that is time-limited and focused on trying to help clients correct the immediate problems in their lives.

INTERACTIVE LECTURE **13.1**

WEB QUIZ **13.1**

CHECK YOUR UNDERSTANDING

1. Which of the following is the major goal of working through problems in psychoanalysis?
   a. free association
   b. positive transference
   c. countertransference
   d. insight
2. Insight therapies focus on giving people
   a. skills to change their behavior.
   b. clearer understanding of their feelings, motives, and actions.
   c. an understanding of perceptual processes.
   d. an understanding of biological influences on behavior.

3. Which of the following is not a type of insight therapy?
   a. client-centered therapy
   b. psychoanalysis
   c. Gestalt therapy
   d. Beck's cognitive therapy
4. ____ ____ is a technique in psychoanalysis whereby the client lets thoughts flow without interruption or inhibition.
5. The process called ____ involves having clients project their feelings toward authority figures onto their therapist.
6. Rogerian therapists show that they value and accept their clients by providing them with ____ ____ regard.
7. Indicate whether the following statements are true (T) or false (F).
   ____ a. Psychoanalysis is based on the belief that problems are symptoms of inner conflicts dating back to childhood.
   ____ b. Rogers's interest in the process of therapy was one avenue of exploration that did not prove very fruitful.
   ____ c. In Gestalt therapy, the therapist is active and directive.
   ____ d. Gestalt therapy emphasizes the client's problems in the here and now.

Answers: 1. d. 2. b. 3. d. 4. Free association. 5. transference. 6. unconditional positive. 7. a. (T); b. (F); c. (T); d. (T).

Behavior Therapies

What do behaviorists believe should be the focus of psychotherapy?

Behavior therapies sharply contrast with insight-oriented approaches. They concentrate on changing people's *behavior* rather than on discovering insights into their thoughts and feelings. Behavior therapies are based on the belief that all behavior, both normal and abnormal, is learned. People suffering from hypochondriasis *learn* that they get attention when they are sick; people with paranoid personalities *learn* to be suspicious of others. It is also assumed that maladaptive behaviors *are* the problem, not symptoms of deeper underlying causes. If behavior therapists can teach people to behave in more appropriate ways, they believe that they have cured the problem. The therapist does not need to know exactly how or why a client learned to behave abnormally in the first place. The job of the therapist is simply to teach the person new, more satisfying ways of behaving on the basis of scientifically studied principles of learning, such as classical conditioning, operant conditioning, and modeling.

Using Classical Conditioning Techniques

How can classical conditioning be used as the basis of treatment?

As you saw in Chapter 5, Learning, *classical conditioning* involves the repeated pairing of a neutral stimulus with one that evokes a certain reflex response. Eventually the formerly neutral stimulus alone comes to elicit the same response. The approach is one of learned stimulus-response associations. Several variations on classical conditioning have been used to treat psychological problems.

Desensitization, Extinction, and Flooding Systematic desensitization, a method for gradually reducing fear and anxiety, is one of the oldest behavior therapy techniques (Wolpe, 1990). The method works by gradually associat-

Behavior therapies
Therapeutic approaches that are based on the belief that all behavior, normal and abnormal, is learned, and that the objective of therapy is to teach people new, more satisfying ways of behaving.

Systematic desensitization
A behavioral technique for reducing a person's fear and anxiety by gradually associating a new response (relaxation) with stimuli that have been causing the fear and anxiety.

The clients in these photographs are overcoming a simple phobia: fear of snakes. After practicing a technique of deep relaxation, clients in desensitization therapy work from the bottom of their hierarchy of fears up to the situation that provokes the greatest fear or anxiety. Here, clients progress from handling rubber snakes (top left) to viewing live snakes through a window (top center) and finally to handling live snakes. This procedure can also be conducted vicariously in the therapist's office, where clients combine relaxation techniques with imagining anxiety-provoking scenes.

ing a new response (relaxation) with stimuli that have been causing anxiety. For example, an aspiring politician might seek therapy because he is anxious about speaking to crowds. The therapist explores the kinds of crowds that are most threatening: Is an audience of 500 worse than one of 50? Is it harder to speak to men than it is to women? Is there more anxiety facing strangers than a roomful of friends? From this information the therapist develops a *hierarchy of fears*—a list of situations from the least to the most anxiety-provoking. The therapist then teaches the client how to relax, including both mental and physical techniques of relaxation. Once the person has mastered deep relaxation, she or he begins work at the bottom of the hierarchy of fears. The person is told to relax while imagining the least threatening situation on the list, then the next most threatening, and so on, until the most fear-arousing one is reached and the client can still remain calm.

Numerous studies show that systematic desensitization helps many people overcome their fears and phobias (Wolpe, 1990). The key to its success may not be the learning of a new conditioned relaxation response but rather the *extinction* of the old fear response through mere exposure. Recall from Chapter 5, Learning, that in classical conditioning, extinction occurs when the learned, conditioned stimulus is repeatedly presented without the unconditioned stimulus following. Thus, if a person repeatedly imagines a frightening situation without actually encountering danger, the fear associated with that situation should gradually decline.

Desensitization is most effective when clients gradually confront their fears in the real world rather than merely in their imaginations. People who are deathly afraid of flying, for example, might first simply drive to an airport. When they are able to do this without anxiety, they may move on to walking near a plane on the ground. When they can do that calmly, they may go inside a stationary plane. Eventually they may take a short flight. This commonsense approach of working step-by-step through a hierarchy of fears in real life is probably familiar to you. For example, folk wisdom says that if you fall off a horse, the best way to get over your fear of riding is to get right back on the horse and continue to ride until the fear is gone. That's an example of desensitization in the real world.

The technique of *flooding* is a less familiar and more frightening method of desensitization. It involves full-intensity exposure to a feared stimulus for a prolonged period of time (O'Leary & Wilson, 1987; Wolpe, 1990). For example, someone with a powerful fear of snakes might be forced to handle dozens of snakes, or someone with an overwhelming fear of spiders might be forced to stroke a tarantula and allow it to crawl up an arm. If you think that flooding is an unnecessarily harsh method, keep in mind how debilitating many untreated anxiety disorders can be (see Chapter 12).

Aversive conditioning
Behavioral therapy techniques aimed at eliminating undesirable behavior patterns by teaching the person to associate them with pain and discomfort.

Aversive Conditioning Another classical conditioning technique is **aversive conditioning,** in which pain and discomfort are associated with the behavior that the client wants to unlearn. Aversive conditioning has been used with limited success to treat alcoholism, obesity, smoking, and some psychosexual disorders. For example, the taste and smell of alcohol are sometimes paired with drug-induced nausea and vomiting. Before long, clients feel sick just seeing a bottle of liquor. A follow-up study of nearly 800 people who completed alcohol-aversion treatment found that 63 percent had maintained continuous abstinence for at least twelve months (Wiens & Menustik, 1983). The long-term effectiveness of this technique has been questioned. When the punishment no longer follows, the undesired behavior may reemerge. In addition, aversive conditioning is a controversial technique because of its unpleasant nature.

Therapies Based on Operant Conditioning

How could "behavior contracting" change an undesirable behavior?

In *operant conditioning*, a person learns to behave in a certain way because that behavior is reinforced, or rewarded. One therapy based on the principle of reinforcement is called **behavior contracting**. The therapist and the client agree on behavioral goals and on the reinforcement that the client will receive when he or she reaches those goals. These goals and reinforcements are often written in a contract that binds both the client and the therapist, as if by legal agreement. For instance, a contract to help a person stop smoking might read: "For each day that I smoke fewer than 20 cigarettes, I will earn 30 minutes of time to go bowling. For each day that I exceed the goal, I will lose 30 minutes from the time that I have accumulated."

Another therapy based on operant conditioning is called the token economy. **Token economies** are usually used in schools and hospitals, where controlled conditions are most feasible (O'Leary & Wilson, 1987). People are rewarded with tokens or points for behaviors that are considered appropriate and adaptive. The tokens or points can be exchanged for desired items and privileges. On the ward of a mental hospital, for example, improved grooming habits might earn points that can be used to purchase special foods or weekend passes. Token economies have proved effective in modifying the behavior of people who are resistant to other forms of treatment, such as people with chronic schizophrenia (Paul, 1982; Paul & Lentz, 1977). The positive changes in behavior, however, do not always generalize to everyday life outside the hospital or clinic, where adaptive behavior is not always reinforced and maladaptive behavior is punished.

Therapies Based on Modeling

What are some therapeutic uses of modeling?

Modeling—the process of learning a behavior by watching someone else perform it—can also be used to treat problem behaviors. For instance, one group of researchers helped people to overcome a snake phobia by showing films in which models confronted snakes and gradually moved closer and closer to them (Bandura, Blanchard, & Ritter, 1969). Similar techniques have succeeded in reducing such common phobias as fear of dental work (Melamed, Hawes, Heiby, & Glick, 1975). Moreover, a combination of modeling and positive reinforcement was successful in helping people with schizophrenia to learn and use appropriate behavior both inside and outside the hospital (Bellack, Hersen, & Turner, 1976). Modeling has also been used to teach people with mental retardation job skills and appropriate responses to problems encountered at work (LaGreca, Stone, & Bell, 1983).

Behavior contracting
Form of operant conditioning therapy in which the client and therapist set behavioral goals and agree on reinforcements that the client will receive on reaching those goals.

Token economy
An operant conditioning therapy in which people earn tokens (reinforcers) for desired behaviors and exchange them for desired items or privileges.

Modeling
A behavior therapy in which the person learns desired behaviors by watching others perform those behaviors.

 INTERACTIVE LECTURE **13.2**

WEB QUIZ **13.2** ✓

CHECK YOUR UNDERSTANDING

1. In contrast to ____ therapies, which seek to increase clients' self-awareness, ____ therapies teach people more appropriate ways of acting.
2. The behavioral technique of ____ ____ trains people to remain relaxed and calm in the presence of a formerly feared stimulus.
3. The behavior therapy known as ____ conditioning discourages undesirable behaviors by associating them with discomfort.
4. The therapeutic use of rewards to encourage desired behavior is based on a form of learning called ____ ____.
5. When client and therapist agree on a written set of behavioral goals and a specific schedule of reinforcement when each goal is met, they are using a technique called ____ ____.
6. Therapy based on classical conditioning involves learning desired behaviors by watching others perform those actions. Is this statement true (T) or false (F)?
7. A ____ ____ is an operant conditioning technique in which people earn some tangible item for desired behavior, which can then be exchanged for more basic rewards and privileges.
8. Extinction occurs when a conditioned stimulus is repeatedly presented without the unconditioned stimulus being present. Is this statement true (T) or false (F)?
9. The technique of ____ involves intense and prolonged exposure to something feared.

Answers: 1. insight, behavior. 2. systematic desensitization. 3. aversive. 4. operant conditioning. 5. behavior contracting. 6. F. 7. token economy. 8. T. 9. flooding.

Cognitive Therapies

How can people overcome irrational and self-defeating beliefs about themselves?

Cognitive therapies are based on the belief that if people can change their distorted ideas about themselves and the world, they can also change their problem behaviors and make their lives more enjoyable. The task facing cognitive therapists is to identify such erroneous ways of thinking and to correct them. This focus on learning new ways of thinking shares many similarities with behavior therapies, which also focus on learning. In fact, many professionals consider themselves to be *cognitive behavior therapists*—therapists who combine both cognitive and behavior therapies (Brewin, 1996). Three popular forms of cognitive therapy are stress inoculation therapy, rational-emotive therapy, and Aaron Beck's cognitive approach.

Stress-Inoculation Therapy

How can self-talk help us deal with difficult situations?

As we go about our lives, we talk to ourselves constantly—proposing courses of action, commenting on our performance, expressing wishes, and so on. **Stress-inoculation therapy** makes use of this self-talk to help people cope with stressful situations (Meichenbaum & Cameron, 1982). The client is taught to suppress any negative, anxiety-evoking thoughts and to replace them with positive, "coping" thoughts. Take a student with exam anxiety who faces every test telling herself, "Oh no, another test. I'm so nervous. I'm sure I won't think calmly enough to remember the answers. If

Cognitive therapies
Psychotherapies that emphasize changing clients' perceptions of their life situation as a way of modifying their behavior.

Stress-inoculation therapy
A type of cognitive therapy that trains clients to cope with stressful situations by learning a more useful pattern of self-talk.

An overly critical self image can lead to a spiral of unrealistic expectations, feelings of failure, sweeping negative generalizations, and depression. Cognitive therapists try to help clients toward more realistic expectations and evaluations of themselves.

only I'd studied more. If I don't get through this course, I'll never graduate!" This pattern of thought is highly dysfunctional because it only makes anxiety worse. With the help of a cognitive therapist, the student learns a new pattern of self-talk: "I studied hard for this exam, and I know the material well. I looked at the textbook last night and reviewed my notes. I should be able to do well. If some questions are hard, they won't all be, and even if it's tough, my whole grade doesn't depend on just one test." Then the person tries out the new strategy in a real situation, ideally one of only moderate stress (like a short quiz). Finally, the person is ready to use the strategy in a more stressful situation (like a final exam). Stress-inoculation therapy works by turning the client's thought patterns into a kind of vaccine against stress-induced anxiety.

Rational-Emotive Therapy

What irrational beliefs do many people hold?

Another type of cognitive therapy, **rational-emotive therapy (RET),** developed by Albert Ellis (1973), is based on the view that most people in need of therapy hold a set of irrational and self-defeating beliefs. They believe that they should be competent at *everything*, liked by *everyone, always* treated fairly, quick to find solutions to *every* problem, and so forth. Such beliefs involve absolutes—"musts" and "shoulds"—that allow for no exceptions, no room for making mistakes. When people with such irrational beliefs come up against real-life struggles, they often experience excessive psychological distress. For example, when a college student who believes that he must be liked by everyone isn't invited to join a certain fraternity, he may view the rejection as a catastrophe and become deeply depressed rather than just feeling disappointed.

Rational-emotive therapists confront such dysfunctional beliefs vigorously, using a variety of techniques, including persuasion, challenge, commands, and theoretical arguments (Ellis & MacLaren, 1998). Studies have shown that RET often does enable people to reinterpret their negative beliefs and experiences in a more positive light, decreasing the likelihood of becoming depressed (Blatt, Zuroff, Quinlan, & Pilkonis, 1996; Bruder et al., 1997).

Rational-emotive therapy (RET)
A directive cognitive therapy based on the idea that clients' psychological distress is caused by irrational and self-defeating beliefs and that the therapist's job is to challenge such dysfunctional beliefs.

Beck's Cognitive Therapy

How can cognitive therapy be used to combat depression?

One of the most important and promising forms of cognitive therapy for treating depression is known simply as **cognitive therapy.** Sometimes it is referred to as "Beck's cognitive therapy," after Aaron Beck who developed it (1967), to avoid confusion with the broader category of cognitive therapies.

Beck believes that depression results from inappropriately self-critical patterns of thought about the self. Such people have unrealistic expectations, magnify their failures, make sweeping negative generalizations about themselves from little evidence, notice only negative feedback from the outside world, and interpret anything less than total success as failure. This negative chain of thinking may often spiral downward from small setbacks, until the person concludes that he or she is worthless. According to Beck, this downward spiral of negative, distorted thoughts is at the heart of depression.

Beck's assumptions about the cause of depression are very similar to those underlying RET, but the style of treatment differs considerably. Cognitive therapists are much less challenging and confrontational than rational-emotive therapists. Instead, they try to help clients examine each dysfunctional thought in a supportive but objectively scientific manner ("Are you *sure* your whole life will be totally ruined if you break up with Frank? What is your evidence for that? Didn't you once tell me how happy you were *before* you met him?"). Like RET, Beck's cognitive therapy tries to lead the person to more realistic and flexible ways of thinking.

Cognitive therapy
Therapy that depends on identifying and changing inappropriately negative and self-critical patterns of thought.

INTERACTIVE LECTURE **13.3**

WEB QUIZ **13.3**

CHECK YOUR UNDERSTANDING

1. Developing new ways of thinking that lead to more adaptive behavior lies at the heart of all ____ therapies.

2. A therapist believes that her client suffers from self-defeating beliefs about himself as a result of unrealistic expectations. The focus of therapy is to change these beliefs to more rational ones. The therapist is probably using ____-____ therapy techniques.

3. ____-____ therapy trains clients to cope with stressful situations by learning a more positive pattern of self-talk.

4. Rational-emotive therapy, founded by Albert ____, assumes that most people in need of therapy hold a set of irrational and self-defeating beliefs.

5. An important form of cognitive therapy used to combat depression was developed by Aaron ____.

6. The immediate focus in cognitive therapies is to help clients change their behaviors. Is this statement true (T) or false (F)?

7. Which of the following statements is an irrational belief, according to rational-emotive therapy?

   a. I must be good at whatever I do.

   b. Everyone should like me.

   c. If this person leaves me, it will be the worst thing that ever happened to me.

   d. All of the above.

Answers: 1. cognitive. **2.** rational-emotive. **3.** Stress-inoculation. **4.** Ellis. **5.** Beck. **6.** F. **7.** d.

Group Therapies

What are some advantages of group therapies?

Some therapists believe that treating several people simultaneously is preferable to treating each alone. Such **group therapy** allows both client and therapist to see how the person acts around others. If a person is painfully anxious and tongue-tied, chronically self-critical, or hostile and aggressive, these tendencies will show up quickly in a group.

Group therapies have other advantages, too. A good group offers social support, a feeling that one is not the only person in the world with problems. Group members can also help one another learn useful new behaviors (how to express feelings, how to disagree without antagonizing others). Interactions in a group can lead people toward insights into their own behavior, such as why they are so defensive or feel compelled to complain constantly. Finally, because group therapy consists of several clients "sharing" a therapist, it is less expensive for each participant than individual therapy is (Yalom, 1995).

There are many kinds of group therapy. Some groups follow the general outlines of the therapies we've already mentioned. Others are oriented toward a very specific goal, such as stopping smoking, drinking, or overeating. And some have a single but more open-ended goal—for example, a happier marriage. The *self-help group* is a particularly popular form of group therapy today.

Self-Help Groups

Why are self-help groups so popular?

Because an estimated 40 to 45 million Americans suffer some kind of psychological problem and because the cost of individual treatment can be so high, more and more people faced with life crises are turning to low-cost self-help groups. Most such groups are small, local gatherings of people who share a common problem or predicament and who provide mutual assistance. Alcoholics Anonymous is perhaps the best-known self-help group, but self-help groups are available for virtually every life problem.

Do these self-help groups work? In many cases they apparently do. Alcoholics Anonymous has developed a reputation for helping people cope with alchoholism. Most group members express strong support for their groups (Riordan & Beggs, 1987), and studies have demonstrated that they can indeed be effective (Galanter, 1984; Pisani, Fawcett, Clark, & McGuire, 1993). Such groups also help to prevent more serious psychological disorders by reaching out to people who are near the limits of their ability to cope with stress. The social support they offer is particularly important in an age when divorce, geographic mobility, and other factors have reduced the ability of the family to comfort people. A list of some self-help organizations is included in the *Understanding Ourselves* box on page 474.

Family Therapy

Who is the client in family therapy?

Family therapy is another form of group therapy (Lebow & Gurman, 1995; Molineux, 1985). Family therapists believe that it is a mistake to treat a client in a vacuum, making no attempt

Group therapy can help to identify problems that a person has interacting with other people. The group also offers social support, helping people to feel less alone with their problems.

Group therapy
Type of psychotherapy in which clients meet regularly to interact and help one another achieve insight into their feelings and behavior.

Family therapy
A form of group therapy that sees the family as at least partly responsible for the individual's problems and that seeks to change all family members' behaviors to the benefit of the family unit as well as the troubled individual.

Family therapy is often valuable even when only one family member has a clear psychological disorder.

UNDERSTANDING OURSELVES

How to Find Help

The attitude that seeking help for psychological problems is a sign that you are "crazy" or "not strong enough" to help yourself is very common in our society. But the fact is that tens of thousands of people are helped by psychological counseling and therapy every year. These people include business executives, artists, sports heroes, celebrities—and students. Therapy is a common, useful aid in coping with daily life.

College is a time of stress and anxiety for many people. The pressure of work, the competition for grades, the exposure to many different kinds of people with unfamiliar views, the tension of relating to peers—all these factors take a psychological toll, especially for students away from home for the first time. Most colleges and universities have their own counseling services, and many of them are as sophisticated as the best clinics in the country. Most communities also have mental health programs. As an aid to a potential search for the right counseling service, we include here a list of some of the other available resources for people who would like the advice of a mental health professional. Many of these services have national offices that will provide you with local branches and the appropriate people to contact in your area.

For Alcohol and Drug Abuse

National Clearinghouse for Alcohol and Drug Information
Rockville, MD
(301) 468-2600

General Service Board
Alcoholics Anonymous, Inc.
New York, NY
(212) 870-3400

For Those with a Friend or Relative Who Has an Alcohol Problem

Al-Anon Family Groups
Virginia Beach, VA
(888) 4alanon (meeting information)
(757) 563-1600 (personal assistance)
Web site: www.alanon.alateen.org

National Association for Children of Alcoholics
Rockville, MD
(301) 468-0985

For Eating Abuses

Overeaters Anonymous
(323) 460-2459

to meet the person's parents, spouse, and children, for if one person in the family is having problems, it is often a signal that the entire family needs assistance. Family therapists do not try to reshape the personalities of family members (Gurman & Kniskern, 1991). Instead, the primary goals of family therapy are improving family communication, encouraging family members to become more empathetic, getting them to share responsibilities, and reducing conflict within the family. To achieve these goals, all family members must believe that they will benefit from changes in their behavior.

Although family therapy is especially appropriate when there are problems between husband and wife or parents and children, it is increasingly being used when only one family member has a clear psychological disorder, such as schizophrenia, agoraphobia, or in some cases, depression (Lebow & Gurman, 1995). The goal of treatment in these circumstances is to help the mentally healthy members of the family cope more effectively with the impact of the disorder on the family unit. The improved coping of the well-adjusted family members may in turn help the troubled person. Family therapy is also called for when a person's progress in individual therapy is slowed by the family (often because other family members have trouble adjusting to that person's improvement).

Unfortunately, not all families benefit from family therapy. Sometimes the problems are too entrenched. In the other cases, important family members may be absent or unwilling to cooperate. In still others, one fam-

For Depression and Suicide

Mental Health Counseling Hotline
New York, NY
(212) 734-5876

International Association for Suicide
Prevention
(213) 381-5111

Heartbeat (for survivors of suicides)
Colorado Springs, CO
(719) 596-2575

For Sexual and Sex-Related Problems

Sex Information and Education
Council of the United States
(SIECUS)
New York, NY
(212) 819-9770

National Organization for Women
Legislative Office
Washington, DC
(202) 331-0066

National Clearinghouse on Marital
and Date Rape
Berkeley, CA
(510) 524-1582 (fee required)

For Physical Abuse

Child Abuse Listening and
Mediation (CALM)
Santa Barbara, CA
(805) 965-2376
(805) 692-4011 (hotline)

For Stress

Anxiety Disorders Association
of America
Rockville, MD
(301) 231-8368

For Help in Selecting a Therapist

National Mental Health Consumer
Self-Help Clearinghouse
(215) 751-1810
Mental Health Help Line
(212) 222-7666

For General Information on Mental Health and Counseling

The National Alliance for the
Mentally Ill
Arlington, VA
(703) 524-7600

The National Mental Health
Association
Alexandria, VA
(703) 684-7722

The American Psychiatric
Association
Washington, DC
(202) 682-6000

The American Psychological
Association
Washington, DC
(202) 336-5500

The National Institute of Mental
Health
Rockville, MD
(301) 443-4513

---

ily member monopolizes sessions, making it hard for anyone else's views to be heard. In all these cases, a different therapeutic approach is needed.

Couple Therapy

What are some techniques used in couple therapy?

A third form of group therapy is **couple therapy,** which is designed to assist partners who are having difficulties with their relationship. In the past, this therapy was generally called *marital therapy*, but the term "couple therapy" is considered more appropriate today because it captures the broad range of partners who may seek help (Oltmanns & Emery, 1998).

Most couple therapists concentrate on improving patterns of communication and mutual expectations. In *empathy training*, for example, each member of the couple is taught to share inner feelings and to listen to and understand the partner's feelings before responding to them. This technique requires that people spend more time listening, trying to grasp what is really being said, and less time in self-defensive rebuttal. Other couple therapists use behavioral techniques. For example, a couple might be helped to develop a schedule for exchanging specific caring actions, such as helping with chores around the house, making time to share a special meal together, or remembering special occasions with a gift or card. This approach may not sound very romantic, but proponents of it say it can break a cycle of dissatisfaction and hostility in a relationship and so is an

Couple therapy
A form of group therapy intended to help troubled partners improve their problems of communication and interaction.

INTERACTIVE LECTURE **13.4**

important step in the right direction (Margolin, 1987). Couple therapy for both partners is generally more effective than therapy for only one of them (Dunn & Schwebel, 1995).

WEB QUIZ **13.4**

CHECK YOUR UNDERSTANDING

1. Which of the following is an advantage of group therapy?
   a. The client has the experience of interacting with other people in a therapeutic setting.
   b. It often reveals a client's problems more quickly than individual therapy.
   c. It can be cheaper than individual therapy.
   d. All of the above.
2. A form of therapy that sees an individual's problems as related to relationships within the family system is called ____ therapy.
3. Marital therapy is now called ____ therapy to include a broader range of partners who may seek help together.
4. Group therapy is always the preferred type of therapy. Is this statement true (T) or false (F)?
5. A widely popular form of group therapy today is the ____-____ group.

Answers: 1. d. 2. family. 3. couple. 4. F. 5. self-help.

Effectiveness of Psychotherapy

How much better off is a person who receives psychotherapy than one who gets no treatment at all?

We have noted that some psychotherapies are generally effective, but how much better are they than no treatment at all? Researchers have found that roughly twice as many people improve with formal therapy than with no treatment at all (Borkovec & Costello, 1993; Lambert, Shapiro, & Bergin, 1986). Furthermore, many people who do not receive formal therapy get therapeutic help from friends, clergy, physicians, and teachers. Thus, the recovery rate for people who receive *no* therapeutic help at all is quite possibly even less than one-third. Other attempts to study the effectiveness of psychotherapy have generally agreed that psychotherapy is effective (Lipsey & Wilson, 1993; Shapiro & Shapiro, 1982; Wampold et al., 1997), although its value appears to be related to a number of other factors. For instance, psychotherapy works best for relatively mild psychological problems (Kopta, Howard, Lowry, & Beutler, 1994) and seems to provide the greatest benefits to people who really *want* to change (Orlinsky & Howard, 1994). There also seems to be greater improvement among people who have undergone long-term therapy than among those who have received short-term treatments (Seligman, 1995). This last finding is illustrated in **Figure 13–1.**

Another important question is whether some forms of psychotherapy are more effective than others. Is behavior therapy, for example, more effective than insight therapy? In general, the answer seems to be "not much" (Garfield, 1983; Michelson, 1985; Smith, Glass, & Miller, 1980; Wampold et al., 1997). Most of the benefits of treatment seem to come from being in *some* kind of therapy, regardless of the particular type.

As we have seen, the various forms of psychotherapy are based on very different views about what causes mental disorders and, at least on the sur-

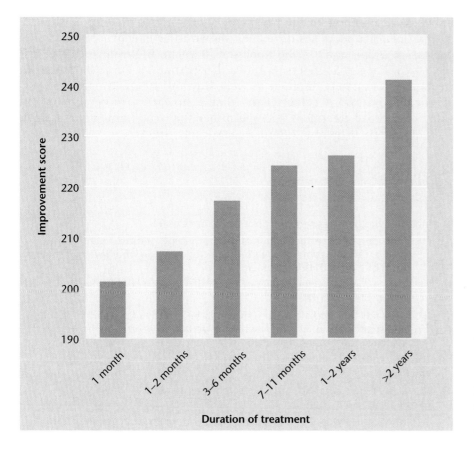

FIGURE 13–1

Duration of therapy and improvement.
One of the most dramatic results of the *Consumer Reports* (1995) study on the effectiveness of psychotherapy was the strong relationship between reported improvement and the duration of therapy.

Source: Adapted from Seligman, M. E. P. (1995). The effectiveness of psychotherapy: The *Consumer Reports* study. *American Psychologist, 50*, 965–974. Copyright © 1995 by the American Psychological Association. Adapted with permission.

face, approach the treatment of mental disorders in different ways. Why, then, is there no difference in their effectiveness? To answer this question, some psychologists have focused their attention on what the various forms of psychotherapy have in common rather than emphasizing their differences (Barker, Funk, & Houston, 1988; Roberts, Kewman, Mercer, & Hovell, 1993). First, all forms of psychotherapy provide people with an *explanation for their problems*. Along with this explanation often comes a new perspective providing people with specific actions to help them cope more effectively. Second, most forms of psychotherapy offer people *hope*. Because most people who seek therapy have low self-esteem and feel demoralized and depressed, hope and the expectation for improvement increase their feelings of self-worth. And third, all major types of psychotherapy engage the client in a *therapeutic alliance* with a therapist. Although their therapeutic approaches may differ, effective therapists are warm, empathetic, and caring people who understand the importance of establishing a strong emotional bond with their clients that is built on mutual respect and understanding (Blatt, Zuroff, Quinlan, & Pilkonis, 1996). Together, these nonspecific factors common to all forms of psychotherapy appear, at least in part, to explain why most people who receive any form of therapy show some benefits as compared with those who receive no therapeutic help at all.

Still, some kinds of psychotherapy seem to be particularly appropriate for certain people and problems (see Nathan & Gorman, 1998). Insight therapy, for example, seems to be best suited to people seeking profound self-understanding, relief of inner conflict and anxiety, or better relationships with others. Behavior therapy is apparently most appropriate for treating specific anxieties or other well-defined behavioral problems, such as sexual dysfunctions. Family therapy is generally more effective than individual counseling for the treatment of drug abuse (Stanton & Shadish, 1997). Cognitive therapies have been shown to be effective treatments for depression (Elkin et al., 1989; Robinson, Berman, & Neimeyer, 1990; also see Kopta, Lueger, Saunders, & Howard, 1999) and seem to be promising treatments for anxiety disorders as well (Howard, 1999). The trend in psychotherapy is toward **eclecticism**—that is, toward a recognition of the value of a broad treatment package rather than commitment to a single form of therapy (Norcross, Alford, & DeMichele, 1994).

INTERACTIVE LECTURE **13.5**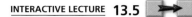

WEB QUIZ **13.5** ✓

CHECK YOUR UNDERSTANDING

1. Indicate whether the following are true (T) or false (F).

____ a. In studies of the effectiveness of psychotherapy, "no treatment" control groups can sometimes inadvertently include people who have had some form of help with their problem.

____ b. The consensus among studies of the effectiveness of psychotherapy is that psychotherapy is effective.

____ c. Behavior therapies have been shown to be effective for treating phobias and specific anxieties, where as cognitive therapies have been shown to be effective for treating depression.

2. There is a trend among psychotherapists to combine treatment techniques in what is called ____.

3. Most researchers agree that psychotherapy helps about ____ - ____ of the people treated.

4. 4. Psychotherapy works best for relatively ____ disorders, as compared with ____ ones.

Answers: 1. a. (T); b. (T); c. (T). 2. eclecticism. 3. two-thirds. 4. mild, severe.

Biological Treatments

What are biological treatments, and who can provide them?

Biological treatments—a group of approaches including medication, electroconvulsive therapy, and psychosurgery—may be used to treat psychological disorders in addition to, or instead of, psychotherapy. Clients and therapists select biological treatments for several reasons. First, some people are too agitated, disoriented, or unresponsive to be helped by psychotherapies. Second, biological treatment is virtually always used for disorders that have a strong biological component. Third, biological treatment is often used for people who are dangerous to themselves and to others. The only mental health professionals licensed to offer biological treatments are psychiatrists, who are physicians, but therapists who are not medical doctors often work with physicians who prescribe medication for their clients. In many cases where biological treatments are used, psychotherapy is also recommended. For example, medication and psychotherapy used together work better for treating major depression and for preventing a recurrence than either treatment used alone (Keller et al., 2000; Reynolds et al., 1999).

Drug Therapies

What are some of the drugs used to treat psychological disorders?

Medication is frequently and effectively used to treat a number of different psychological problems (see **Table 13–1**). In fact, Prozac, a drug used to

---

Eclecticism
Psychotherapeutic approach that recognizes the value of a broad treatment package over a rigid commitment to one particular form of therapy.

Biological treatments
A group of approaches, including medication, electroconvulsive therapy, and psychosurgery, that are sometimes used to treat psychological disorders in conjunction with, or instead of, psychotherapy.

TABLE 13-1 MAJOR TYPES OF PSYCHOACTIVE MEDICATIONS

Therapeutic Use	Chemical Structure*	Trade Name*
Antipsychotics	Phenothiazines	Thorazine
Antidepressants	Tricyclics	Elavil
	MAO inhibitors	Nardil
	SSRIs	Paxil, Prozac, Zoloft
Psychostimulants	Amphetamines	Dexedrine
	Other	Ritalin
Antimanic	Carbamazepine	Tegretol
Antianxiety	Benzodiazepines	Valium
Sedatives	Barbiturates	
Antipanic	Tricyclics	Tofranil
Antiobsessional	Tricyclics	Anafranil

* The chemical structures and especially the trade names listed in this table are often just one example of the many kinds of medications available for the specific therapeutic use.
Source: Klerman et al., 1994.

treat depression, today is one of the best-selling of all prescribed medications. Two major reasons for the widespread use of drug therapies today are the development of several very effective psychoactive medications and the fact that drug therapies can cost less than psychotherapy. Another reason, critics charge, is our society's "pill mentality" (take a medicine to fix any problem). The medications used to treat psychological disorders are prescribed not only by psychiatrists but even more commonly by primary-care physicians such as family practitioners, pediatricians, and gynecologists.

Antipsychotic Drugs Before the mid-1950s, drugs were not widely used to treat psychological disorders, because the only available sedatives induced sleep as well as calm. Then the major tranquilizers *reserpine* and the *phenothiazines* were introduced. In addition to alleviating anxiety and aggression, both drugs reduce psychotic symptoms, such as hallucinations and delusions; for that reason, they are called **antipsychotic drugs.** Antipsychotic drugs are prescribed primarily for very severe psychological disorders, particularly schizophrenia. They are very effective for treating schizophrenia's "positive symptoms," like hallucinations, but less effective for the "negative symptoms," like social withdrawal. Antipsychotic drugs work by blocking the brain's receptors for dopamine, a major neurotransmitter. The better that a drug blocks these receptors, the more effective it is (Oltmanns & Emery, 1998).

Antipsychotics can sometimes have dramatic effects (Grinspoon, Ewalt, & Schader, 1972). People who take them can go from being perpetually frightened, angry, confused, and plagued by auditory and visual hallucinations to being totally free of such symptoms. But antipsychotic drugs can also have a number of undesirable side effects (Kane & Lieberman, 1992; McKim, 1997). Blurred vision and constipation are among the common complaints, as are temporary neurological impairments such as muscular rigidity or tremors. A very serious potential side effect is *tardive dyskinesia*, a permanent disturbance of motor control, particularly of the face (uncontrollable smacking of the lips, for instance), which can be only partially alleviated with other drugs (Diaz, 1997). The risk of tardive dyskinesia increases with the length of time antipsychotics are taken, a fact that leads

Antipsychotic drugs
Drugs used to treat very severe psychological disorders, particularly schizophrenia.

The antidepressant drugs, Zoloft and Prozac, are among the most prescribed medications in the United States.

to another important point. Antipsychotic drugs do not cure schizophrenia; they only alleviate the symptoms while the person is taking the drug. Therefore, most people with schizophrenia must take antipsychotics for years—perhaps for the rest of their lives (Mueser & Glynn, 1995; Oltmanns & Emery, 1998).

Another problem is that antipsychotics are of little value in treating the problems of social adjustment that people with schizophrenia face outside an institutional setting. And because many discharged people fail to take their medications, relapse is common. The relapse rate can be reduced if drug therapy is effectively combined with psychotherapy.

Antidepressant Drugs   A second group of drugs, known as *antidepressants*, are used to combat depression. Until the end of the 1980s, there were only two main types of antidepressant drugs: *monoamine oxidase inhibitors (MAO inhibitors)* and *tricyclics* (named for their chemical properties). Both types of drugs work by increasing the concentration of the neurotransmitters serotonin and norepinephrine in the brain (McKim, 1997). Both are effective for most people with serious depression, but both produce a number of serious and troublesome side effects. The MAO inhibitors require careful dietary restriction, as they can be lethal in combination with some foods. The tricyclics often cause blurred vision, dry mouth, dizziness, low blood pressure, constipation, and other problems. Because of the seriousness of these side effects, the search has continued for better antidepressant drugs.

In 1988, Prozac came onto the market. This drug works by reducing the uptake of serotonin in the nervous system, thus increasing the amount of serotonin active in the brain at any given moment. For this reason, Prozac is part of a group of psychoactive drugs known as *selective serotonin reuptake inhibitors* (SSRIs) (see Chapter 2, The Biological Basis of Behavior). Prozac has fewer side effects than MAO inhibitors or tricyclics and has been heralded in the popular media as a "wonder drug" for the treatment of depression. Its widespread use is considered testimony to its effectiveness. We must be cautious in jumping to such conclusions, however. Prozac undoubtedly has helped many depressed people, but often because of its placebo effect—that is, Prozac frequently works because people believe it will work (Brown, 1998). This fact underscores the very important point that the success of an antidepressant medication does not mean that depression is caused by a "chemical imbalance in the brain." The fact that aspirin relieves headaches does not mean that a lack of aspirin is the cause of headaches. Although antidepressants clearly play an important role in the treatment of depression, some therapists are concerned that too many people are trying to solve their emotional problems with a pill rather than through their own efforts to cope with life more effectively. Moreover, as we noted earlier, medication and psychotherapy work better together against major depression than either does alone (Keller et al., 2000).

Lithium   Bipolar disorder, or manic-depression, is frequently treated with lithium carbonate. Lithium is not a drug but a naturally occurring salt that helps level out the wild and unpredictable mood swings of manic depression. Although it is effective in approximately 75 percent of cases, lithium is often prescribed along with antidepressants because it is slow to take effect (Solomon, Keitner, Miller, Shea, & Keller, 1995). We do not know exactly how lithium works, but recent studies with mice indicate that it may act to stabilize the levels of specific neurotransmitters in the brain (Dixon & Hokin, 1998).

Other Medications   Several other medications can be used to alleviate the symptoms of various psychological problems (see **Table 13–1**). *Psycho-*

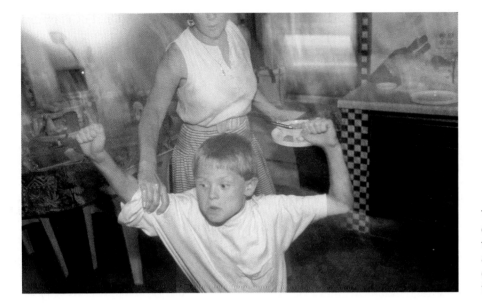

Treating attention deficit hyperactivity disorder (ADHD) with drugs, such as Ritalin, has become a controversial practice, and the disorder itself is still poorly understood. Here, a young boy suffering from ADHD is restrained by his mother.

stimulants, for example, heighten alertness and arousal. Some psychostimulants, such as Ritalin, are commonly used to treat children with attention-deficit/hyperactivity disorder (Adesman, 2000). In these cases, they have a calming rather than a stimulating effect. As with the antidepressants, some professionals worry that psychostimulants are being overused. The White House drew attention to this issue in March 2000, citing recent research showing that the number of children between 2 and 4 years of age taking stimulants and antidepressants more than doubled in recent years (Zito et al., 2000) (see **Figure 13–2**). *Antianxiety medications,* such as Valium, are commonly prescribed as well. Quickly producing a sense of calm and mild euphoria, they are often used to reduce general tension and stress. Because they are potentially addictive, however, they must be used with caution. Another class of drugs, the *sedatives,* produce both calm and drowsiness, and they are used to treat agitation or to induce sleep. These drugs, too, can become addictive. Finally, for reducing episodes of panic and alleviating obsessive-compulsive symptoms, certain types of *antidepressant medications* are effective (Klerman et al., 1994).

Electroconvulsive Therapy

How is the electroconvulsive therapy of today different from that of the past?

Electroconvulsive therapy (ECT) is most often used for cases of prolonged and severe depression that do not respond to other forms of treatment (Olfson, Marcus, Sackeim, Thompson, & Pincus, 1998). The technique of ECT remained largely unchanged for many years. One electrode was placed on each side of the person's head, and a mild current was turned on for a very short time (about 1.5 seconds). The electrical current passed from one side of the brain to the other, producing a brief convulsion, followed by a temporary loss of consciousness. Muscle relaxants administered in advance prevented dangerously violent contractions. When patients awoke several minutes later, they normally had amnesia for the period immediately before the procedure and remained confused for the next hour or so. With repeated treatments, people often became disoriented, but this condition usually cleared after treatment concluded. Treatment normally consisted of ten or fewer sessions of ECT.

Electroconvulsive therapy (ECT) Biological therapy in which a mild electrical current is passed through the brain for a short period, often producing convulsions and temporary coma; used to treat severe, prolonged depression.

FIGURE 13–2

Use of psychiatric medications among preschoolers. A study of 151,675 preschoolers in one Midwestern Medicaid group found that the use of psychiatric medications, particularly stimulants such as Ritalin, increased greatly in recent years.

Source: data from *Journal of the American Medical Association,* figure by Associated Press as found in *The Charlotte Observer,* Feb. 23, 2000. Reprinted with permission.

Recently an important modification was made to traditional ECT. In this new procedure, called *unilateral ECT*, the electrical current is passed through only one side of the brain. Unilateral ECT produces fewer side effects, such as memory impairment and confusion, and is only slightly less effective than the traditional method (Diaz, 1997; Khan, 1993). Another modification uses less powerful electric currents for shorter durations (only 0.04 of a second), which also seems to lessen the severity of side effects.

No one knows exactly why ECT works, but evidence clearly demonstrates its effectiveness. In addition, the fatality rate for ECT is markedly lower than for people taking antidepressant drugs (Henry, Alexander, & Sener, 1995). Still, ECT has many critics, and its use remains controversial. The procedure often produces memory loss, and it is certainly capable of damaging the brain. For these reasons, ECT is best considered a "last resort" treatment when all other methods have failed.

Psychosurgery

What is psychosurgery, and how is it used today?

Psychosurgery refers to brain surgery performed to change a person's behavior and emotional state. This is a drastic step, especially because the effects of psychosurgery are difficult to predict. In a *prefrontal lobotomy*, the frontal lobes of the brain are severed from the deeper centers beneath them. The assumption is that in extremely disturbed people, the frontal lobes intensify emotional impulses from the lower brain centers (chiefly the thalamus and hypothalamus). Unfortunately, lobotomies can work with one person and fail completely with another—possibly producing permanent, undesirable side effects, such as the inability to inhibit impulses or a near-total absence of feeling.

Prefrontal lobotomies are rarely performed today. In fact, very few psychosurgical procedures are done nowadays except as desperate measures to control such conditions as intractable psychoses, epilepsy that does not respond to other treatments, severe obsessive-compulsive disorders (Baer, Rauch, & Ballantine, 1995), and pain in a terminal illness.

Psychosurgery
Brain surgery performed to change a person's behavior and emotional state; a biological therapy rarely used today.

INTERACTIVE LECTURE **13.6**

WEB QUIZ **13.6**

CHECK YOUR UNDERSTANDING

1. The only mental health professionals licensed to provide drug therapy are ____.
2. All of the following are biological therapies except
   a. RET.
   b. ECT.
   c. drug therapy.
   d. psychosurgery.
3. Prozac, tricyclics, and monoamine oxidase inhibitors are all medications used for treating ____.
4. One reason for the widespread use of drug therapy is that it costs less than psychotherapy. Is this statement true (T) or false (F)?
5. Most antipsychotic drugs work by
   a. increasing acetylcholine in the brain.
   b. increasing serotonin in the brain.
   c. inhibiting the function of the hypothalamus.
   d. blocking dopamine receptors in the brain.

6. Which of the following is true of psychosurgery?
    a. It never produces undesirable side effects.
    b. It is useless in controlling pain.
    c. It is widely used today.
    d. Its effects are hard to predict.

7. Electroconvulsive therapy is considered _____ effective in treating cases of severe depression.
    a. hardly ever
    b. mildly
    c. highly

8. Match the following medications with the neurotransmitter(s) that each is believed to influence.

    _____ monoamine oxidase inhibitors   a. norepinephrine

    _____ tricyclics   b. serotonin

    _____ Prozac   c. epinephrine

    _____ lithium

9. Because of its potential negative side effects, ECT is considered a treatment of last resort. Is this statement true (T) or false (F)?

10. Bipolar disorder (also called manic-depressive illness) is often treated with _____.

Answers: 1. psychiatrists. 2. a. 3. depression. 4. T. 5. d. 6. d. 7. c. 8. monoamine oxidase inhibitors: a and b; tricyclics: a and b; Prozac: b; lithium: b and c. 9. T. 10. lithium.

Caring for the Seriously Disturbed and Preventing Disorders

How were people with severe psychological disorders cared for in the past?

For the severely mentally ill, hospitalization has been the treatment of choice in the United States for the past 150 years. Several different kinds of hospitals offer care to the mentally ill. General hospitals admit many people suffering from mental disorders, usually for short-term stays until they can be released to their families or to other institutional care. Private hospitals—some nonprofit and some for-profit—offer services to people with adequate insurance. And for veterans with psychological disorders there are Veterans Administration hospitals.

When most people think of "mental hospitals," however, large, state-run institutions come to mind. These public hospitals, many with beds for thousands of patients, were often built in rural areas in the nineteenth century, the idea being that a country setting would calm patients and help to restore their mental health. Whatever the good intentions were behind the establishment of these hospitals, for most of their history they have not provided adequate care or therapy for their residents. Perpetually underfunded and understaffed, state hospitals have often been little more than warehouses for victims of serious mental illness who were unwanted by their families. Except for new arrivals, who were often intensively treated in the hope of quickly discharging them, patients received little therapy besides drugs, and most spent their days watching television or staring into space. Under these conditions, many patients became completely apathetic and accepted a permanent "sick role."

The development of effective drug therapies starting in the 1950s led to a number of changes in state hospitals (Shorter, 1997). For one thing, people who were agitated could now be sedated with drugs. Although the drugs often

Lacking adequate funding and staff, mental hospitals frequently failed to provide adequate treatment to their residents. Beginning in the 1950s and 1960s, the policy of deinstitutionalization led to the release of many individuals, who, without proper follow-up care, ended up living on the streets. Although not all homeless people are mentally ill, estimates suggest that between 10 and 47 percent of homeless persons suffer from some type of mental disorder.

Deinstitutionalization
Policy of treating people with severe psychological disorders in the larger community, or in small residential centers such as halfway houses, rather than in large public hospitals.

produced lethargy, this was considered an improvement over the use of physical restraints. The second major, and more lasting, result of the new drug therapies was the widespread release of people with severe psychological disorders back into the community—a policy called **deinstitutionalization.** As you will see, this created new problems, both for patients and for society.

Deinstitutionalization

What problems have resulted from deinstitutionalization?

The advent of antipsychotic drugs in the 1950s created a favorable climate for deinstitutionalization. The practice of placing people in smaller, more humane facilities or returning them under medication to care within the community intensified during the 1960s and 1970s. By 1975, 600 regional mental health centers accounted for 1.6 million cases of outpatient care.

In recent years, however, deinstitutionalization has created serious problems. Discharged people often find poorly funded community mental health centers—or none at all. Many of these former patients are not prepared to live in the community, and they receive little guidance in coping with the mechanics of daily life. Those who return home can become a burden to their families, especially when they don't get adequate follow-up care. Residential centers, such as halfway houses, vary in quality, but many provide poor care and minimal contact with the outside world. Insufficient sheltered housing forces many former patients into nonpsychiatric facilities—often rooming houses located in dirty, unsafe, isolated neighborhoods. The patients are further burdened by the social stigma of mental illness, which may be the largest single obstacle to their rehabilitation. Moreover, although outpatient care is presumed to be a well-established national policy objective in mental health, health insurance typically discourages outpatient care by requiring substantial copayments and limiting the number of treatment visits.

The full effects of deinstitutionalization are unknown. Few follow-up studies have been done on discharged patients, who are difficult to keep track of for long periods. But it is obvious that deinstitutionalization, though a worthy ideal, has had dire effects on patients and society. Many patients who were released were unable to obtain follow-up care or to find housing and were incapable of looking after their own needs. Consequently, many have ended up on the streets. Without supervision, they have stopped taking the drugs that made their release possible in the first place and have again become psychotic. Every major U.S. city now has a population of homeless mentally ill men and women living in makeshift shelters or sleeping in doorways, bus stations, parks, and other public spaces. This situation is tragic not only for the mentally ill homeless, who, often incoherent, are easy prey for criminals. It is also contributing to the coarsening of our society, since the public, finding the constant presence of "crazies" among them unpleasant, has begun to lose compassion for both the homeless and the mentally ill and thus to pressure public officials to "get them off the street." Most mental health professionals now agree that many chronically ill patients should not be released to live "in the community" without better planning, more funding, more community support, and readily available short-term rehospitalization for those who require it.

Alternative Forms of Treatment

Are there any alternatives to deinstitutionalization other than rehospitalizing patients?

For the past two decades, Charles Kiesler has argued for a shift from the focus on institutionalization to forms of treatment that avoid hospitalization altogether (Kiesler & Simpkins, 1993). Kiesler (1982b) examined ten controlled studies in which seriously disturbed people were randomly assigned either to hospitals or to an alternative program. The alternative programs took many forms: training people living at home to cope with daily activities; assignment to a small, homelike facility in which staff and residents shared responsibility for residential life; placement in a hostel offering therapy and crisis intervention; providing family-crisis therapy and day-care treatment; providing visits from public-health nurses, combined with medication; and offering intensive outpatient counseling combined with medication. All of these alternatives involved daily professional contact and skillful preparation of the community to receive the patients. Even though the hospitals to which some people in these studies were assigned provided very good patient care—probably substantially above average for institutions in the United States—nine out of the ten studies found that the outcome was more positive for alternative treatments than for the more expensive hospitalization. Moreover, the people who received alternative care were less likely to undergo hospitalization later, thus suggesting that hospitalizing those with mental illness is a self-perpetuating process. Many such people "could be treated in alternative settings more effectively and less expensively," Kiesler concludes (1982, p. 358).

Prevention

What is the difference between primary, secondary, and tertiary prevention?

Yet another approach to serious mental illness is trying to prevent it in the first place. Such *prevention* requires finding and eliminating the conditions that cause or contribute to mental disorders and substituting conditions that foster well-being. Prevention takes three forms: primary, secondary, and tertiary.

Primary prevention refers to efforts to improve the overall environment so that new cases of mental disorders do not develop. Family planning and genetic counseling are two examples of primary prevention programs. They assist prospective parents to think through such questions as how many children to have and when. They also provide testing to diagnose genetic defects in embyros, and they direct parents to treatments, including fetal surgery, that may be able to alleviate those defects before the baby is born. Other primary prevention programs aim at increasing personal and social competencies in a wide variety of groups. For example, there are programs designed to help mothers encourage problem-solving skills in their children and programs to enhance competence and adjustment among the elderly. Current campaigns to educate young people about drugs, violence, and date rape are other examples of primary prevention (Avery-Leaf, Cano, Cascardi, & O'Leary, 1995; Reppucci, Woolard, & Fried, 1999).

Secondary prevention involves identifying groups at high risk for mental disorders—for example, abused children, people who have recently divorced, and those who have been laid off from their jobs. The main thrust of secondary prevention is *intervention* with such high-risk groups—that is, detecting maladaptive behavior early and treating it promptly. One form of intervention is *crisis intervention*, which includes such programs as suicide hotlines. Another is the establishment of short-term crisis facilities at which a therapist can provide face-to-face counseling and support.

The main objective of **tertiary prevention** is to help people adjust to community life after release from a mental hospital. For example, hospitals often grant passes to encourage people to leave the institution for short periods of time before their release. Other tertiary prevention measures are

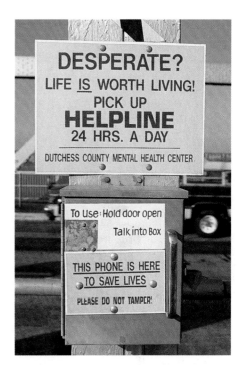

Suicide hotlines and other crisis intervention programs are secondary prevention measures designed to serve individuals and groups at high risk for mental disorders.

Primary prevention
Techniques and programs to improve the social environment so that new cases of mental disorders do not develop.

Secondary prevention
Programs to identify groups that are at high risk for mental disorders and to detect maladaptive behavior in these groups and treat it promptly.

Tertiary prevention
Programs to help people adjust to community life after release from a mental hospital.

halfway houses, where people find support and skills training during the period of transition between hospitalization and full integration into the community, and nighttime and outpatient programs that provide supportive therapy while people live at home and hold down a full-time job. Tertiary prevention also includes efforts to educate the community that the person will reenter.

Preventing behavior disorders has been the ideal of the mental health community since at least 1970, when the final report of the Joint Commission on Mental Health of Children called for a new focus on prevention in mental health work. Ironically, because preventive programs are usually long-range and indirect, they are often the first mental health programs to be eliminated in times of economic hardship. Such cuts, predicated on cost effectiveness, exemplify the old adage about being penny-wise and pound-foolish.

INTERACTIVE LECTURE **13.7**

WEB QUIZ **13.7**

CHECK YOUR UNDERSTANDING

1. The practice of treating severely mentally ill people in large, state-run facilities is known as ____.
2. Many people released from mental hospitals have ended up homeless and on the streets. Is this statement true (T) or false (F)?
3. Which of the following were factors that helped promote deinstitutionalization?
   a. the development of effective antipsychotic drugs
   b. the establishment of a network of community mental health centers
   c. federal budget cuts in the 1960s
   d. all of the above
4. Alternative treatments to hospitalizing people with severe mental disorders are less effective than hospitalization but have the benefit of costing less. Is this statement true (T) or false (F)?
5. Match the following with the appropriate form of prevention.

   ____ halfway houses   a. primary prevention
   ____ educational TV commercials   b. secondary prevention
   ____ hotlines   c. tertiary prevention
   ____ crisis intervention
   ____ genetic counseling

Answers: 1. institutionalization. 2. T. 3. a and b. 4. F. 5. halfway houses: c; educational TV commercials: a; hotlines: b; crisis intervention: b; genetic counseling: a.

Client Diversity and Treatment

Are there particular groups of people who may require special approaches in the treatment of psychological problems?

A major topic of this book is human diversity, the wide range of differences that exist in human beings. Although we all share certain basic human characteristics, as individuals and as groups we also have our own distinctive traits, our own distinctive ways of responding to the world. Do such human differences affect the treatment of psychological problems? Two areas that researchers have explored to answer this question are gender differences and cultural differences.

Gender and Treatment

How can gender stereotypes be avoided in treatment?

In Chapter 12, Psychological Disorders, we saw that there are some significant gender differences in the prevalence of many psychological disorders. In part, this is because women have traditionally been more willing than men to admit that they have psychological problems and need help to solve them. Moreover, psychotherapy is more socially accepted for women than for men (Williams, 1987). However, in recent years, the number of males willing to seek psychotherapy and counseling has increased (Pollack & Levant, 1998). The researchers attribute this increase to the changing roles of men in today's society: Men are increasingly expected to provide financial as well as emotional support for their families.

If there are gender differences in the prevalence of psychological disorders, are there gender differences in their treatment as well? In most respects, the treatment given women is the same as that given men, a fact that has become somewhat controversial in recent years (Enns, 1993). Because most therapists are male and most vocational and rehabilitation programs are male-oriented, some critics of "equal treatment" have claimed that women in therapy are often encouraged to adopt traditional, male-oriented views of what is "normal" or "appropriate." For instance, male therapists tend to urge women to adapt or conform passively to their surroundings. They also tend to be insufficiently sensitive to the fact that much of the stress that women experience comes from trying to cope with a world in which they are not treated equally (Brown & Ballou, 1992). For all these reasons, there has been an increase recently in the number of "feminist therapists." These therapists help their female clients to become aware of the extent to which their problems derive from external controls and inappropriate sex roles, to become more conscious of and attentive to their own needs and goals, and to develop a sense of pride in their womanhood rather than passively accepting or identifying with the status quo.

Although in *most* respects women receive the same kinds of treatment that men receive, there is one very important difference: Women receive a disproportionate share of the drugs prescribed for psychological disorders. Overall, more than 70 percent of all prescriptions written by psychiatrists are for women, although women account for only 58 percent of their office visits (Basow, 1986; Russo, 1985). Similarly, women receive 70 to 80 percent of all antidepressant medications, even though they make up only two-thirds of all cases of depressive disorders. We don't yet know the reasons for this sex bias in drug prescriptions, but it has become a source of considerable concern. Professionals' willingness to prescribe drugs to women may encourage women to see their problems as having physical causes. Moreover, the readiness to prescribe drugs for women at least partly accounts for women's tendency to abuse prescription drugs more often than men do (Russo, 1985).

As researchers continue to explore these various issues, the American Psychological Association has established a set of guidelines regarding treatment of women in psychotherapy:

1. The conduct of therapy should be free of constrictions based on gender-defined roles, and the options explored between client and practitioner should be free of sex-role stereotypes.

2. Psychologists should recognize the reality, variety, and implications of sex-discriminatory practices in society and should facilitate client examination of options in dealing with such practices.

Because most traditional therapeutic programs are male-oriented, many female clients seek out female therapists who are more sensitive to their situation.

3. The therapist should be knowledgeable about current empirical findings on sex roles, sexism, and individual differences resulting from the client's gender-defined identity.

4. The theoretical concepts used by the therapist should be free of sex bias and sex-role stereotypes.

5. The psychologist should demonstrate acceptance of women as equal to men by using language free of derogatory labels.

6. The psychologist should avoid establishing the source of personal problems within the client when they are more properly attributable to situational or cultural factors.

7. The psychologist and a fully informed client mutually should agree on aspects of the therapy relationship such as treatment modality, time factors, and fee arrangements.

8. Although the importance of the availability of accurate information to a client's family is recognized, the privilege of communication about diagnosis, prognosis, and progress ultimately resides with the client, not with the therapist.

9. If authoritarian processes are used as a technique, the therapy should not have the effect of maintaining or reinforcing the stereotypic dependency of women.

10. The client's assertive behaviors should be respected.

11. The psychologist whose female client is subjected to violence in the form of physical abuse or rape should recognize and acknowledge that the client is the victim of a crime.

12. The psychologist should recognize and encourage exploration of a woman client's sexuality and should recognize her right to define her own sexual preferences.

13. The psychologist should not have sexual relations with a woman client nor treat her as a sex object. (APA, 1978)

Culture and Treatment

How can a therapist interact appropriately with clients from different cultures?

Imagine the following scenario: As a Native American client is interviewed by a psychologist, the client stares at the floor. He answers questions politely, but during the entire consultation, he looks away continually, never meeting the doctor's eye. This body language might lead the psychologist to suppose that the man is depressed or has low self-esteem. Unless, that is, the psychologist knows that in the person's culture, avoiding eye contact is a sign of respect.

This example shows that our ideas of what constitutes normal behavior are culture-bound. When psychotherapist and client come from different cultures, misunderstandings of speech, body language, and customs are almost inevitable (Helms & Cook, 1999). Even when client and therapist are of the same nationality and speak the same language, there can be striking differences if they belong to different racial and ethnic groups (Casas, 1995). Some black people, for example, are wary of confiding in a white therapist—so much so that their wariness is sometimes mistaken for paranoia. For this reason, many black people seek out a black therapist, a tendency that is becoming more common as larger numbers of black middle-class people enter therapy (Williams, 1989).

One of the challenges for U.S. therapists in recent years has been to treat refugees from foreign countries, many of whom have fled such horri-

Many African American clients are more comfortable dealing with a therapist of the same racial background.

fying circumstances at home that they arrive in the United States exhibiting posttraumatic stress disorder. These refugees must overcome not only the effects of past trauma but also the new stresses of settling in a strange country, which often include separation from their families, ignorance of the English language, and inability to practice their traditional occupations. Therapists in such circumstances must learn something of their clients' culture. Often they have to conduct interviews through an interpreter—hardly an ideal circumstance for therapy.

Therapists need to recognize that some disorders that afflict people from other cultures may not exist in Western culture at all. For example, *Taijin Kyofusho* (roughly translated as "fear of people") involves a morbid fear that one's body or actions may be offensive to others. Because this disorder is rarely seen outside Japan, American therapists require specialized training to identify it.

Ultimately, however, the best solution to the difficulties of serving a multicultural population is to train therapists of many different backgrounds so that members of ethnic, cultural, and racial minorities can choose therapists of their own group if they wish to do so (Bernal & Castro, 1994). Research has shown that psychotherapy is more likely to be effective when the client and the therapist share a similar cultural background (Sue et al., 1994). Similarly, efforts aimed at preventing mental illness in society must also be sensitive to cultural diversity. Many intervention programs have proved unsuccessful because they failed to take into account the appropriate cultural norms and values of the group being served (Reppucci, Woolard, & Fried, 1999). To be effective, treatment approaches must reflect the beliefs and cultural practices of the person's ethnic group.

INTERACTIVE LECTURE **13.8**

WEB QUIZ **13.8**

CHECK YOUR UNDERSTANDING

Indicate whether the following statements are true (T) or false (F).

____ 1. Men are more likely to be in psychotherapy than women.

____ 2. Women receive a disproportionate share of the drugs prescribed for psychological problems.

____ 3. An important point in the APA guidelines regarding the treatment of women in psychotherapy is that the therapy be free of constrictions based on gender roles and stereotypes.

____ 4. Our ideas about what constitutes normal behavior are culture-bound.

____ 5. Trained mental health professionals rarely misinterpret the body language of a client from another culture.

____ 6. Research has shown that psychotherapy is more likely to be effective when the client and therapist share similar cultural backgrounds.

Answers: 1. F. 2. T. 3. T. 4. T. 5. F. 6. T.

KEY TERMS

CHAPTER REVIEW

Insight Therapies

What do insight therapies have in common? Insight therapy is a major category of treatment for psychological problems. Insight therapies have in common the goal of providing people with better awareness and understanding of their feelings, motivations, and actions in the hope that this will lead to better adjustment. Three examples of insight therapies are psychoanalysis, client-centered therapy, and Gestalt therapy.

How does "free association" in psychoanalysis help a person to become aware of hidden feelings? Psycho-analysis is based on the belief that psychological problems stem from feelings and conflicts repressed during childhood. One way of uncovering what has been repressed is through the process of **free association,** in which the client discloses whatever thoughts or fantasies come to mind without editing or otherwise inhibiting them. As therapy progresses, the analyst takes a more active role and begins to interpret or suggest meanings for their clients' feelings, memories, and actions.

Why did Carl Rogers call his approach to therapy "client-centered"? The insight therapy founded by Carl Rogers is built on the idea that treatment for psychological problems should be based on the client's view of the world rather than on the therapist's. For that reason, it is called **client-centered** or **person-centered therapy.** The therapist's most important task is to provide unconditional positive regard for clients so that they will learn to accept themselves.

How is Gestalt therapy different from psychoanalysis? Gestalt therapy, which grew out of the work of Fritz Perls, is designed to help people become more aware of their feelings and thus more genuine. Unlike Freud, who sat quietly out of sight while his clients free-associated to dredge up memories from the past, Perls believed that therapy should emphasize the here and now and face-to-face confrontations. The Gestalt therapist is much more active and directive than the psychoanalyst, and the focus is on the *whole* person.

What are some recent developments in insight therapies? Contemporary insight therapists are more active than traditional psychoanalysts, giving clients direct guidance and feedback. They are also more focused on clients' immediate problems than on their childhood traumas. An especially significant development is the trend to **short-term psychodynamic therapy,** which recognizes that most people can be successfully treated within a limited time frame.

Behavior Therapies

What do behaviorists believe should be the focus of psychotherapy? Behavior therapies are based on the belief that all behavior, normal and abnormal, is learned and that the goal of therapy is to teach people more satisfying ways of behaving. To behaviorists, the focus of psychotherapy should be the problem behaviors themselves, not some deeper, underlying conflicts that are presumably causing those behaviors.

How can classical conditioning be used as the basis of treatment? When therapies attempt to evoke new conditioned responses to old stimuli, they are using classical conditioning as a basis for treatment. One example is a technique called **systematic desensitization,** in which people learn to remain in a deeply relaxed state while confronting situations that they fear. Flooding, which exposes phobic people to feared situations at full intensity for a prolonged period, is a harsh but effective method of desensitization. In **aversive conditioning,** the goal is to eliminate undesirable behavior by associating it with pain and discomfort.

How could "behavior contracting" change an undesirable behavior? Therapies based on operant conditioning encourage or discourage behaviors by reinforcing or punishing them. In the technique called **behavior contracting,** client and therapist agree on certain behavioral goals and on the reinforcement that the client will receive on reaching them. To improve your study habits by using behavioral contracting, you might reward yourself with pizza or a movie for a certain number of hours spent reading and taking careful notes. In another technique, which is called the **token economy,** tokens that can be exchanged for rewards are used for positive reinforcement.

What are some therapeutic uses of modeling? In **modeling**, a person learns new behaviors by watching others perform them. Modeling has been used to teach fearless behaviors to phobic people, job skills to mentally retarded people, and more appropriate ways of responding to those suffering from schizophrenia.

Cognitive Therapies

How can people overcome irrational and self-defeating beliefs about themselves? **Cognitive therapies** focus not so much on maladaptive behaviors as on maladaptive ways of thinking. By changing people's distorted, self-defeating ideas about themselves and the world, cognitive therapies help to encourage better coping skills and adjustment.

How can self-talk help us to deal with difficult situations? The things we say to ourselves as we go about our daily lives can encourage either success or failure, a self-confident outlook or acute anxiety. **Stress-inoculation therapy** takes advantage of this fact by teaching clients how to use self-talk to "coach" themselves through stressful situations.

What irrational beliefs do many people hold? **Rational-emotive therapy (RET)** is based on the idea that people's emotional problems derive from a set of irrational and self-defeating beliefs that they hold about themselves and the world. They think in terms of absolutes—they must be liked by *everyone*, competent at *everything*, *always* treated fairly, *never* stymied by a problem. The therapist vigorously challenges these beliefs until the client comes to see just how irrational and dysfunctional these beliefs are.

How can cognitive therapy be used to combat depression? Aaron Beck believes that depression results from negative patterns of thought—patterns that are strongly and inappropriately self-critical. The depression-prone person magnifies failures and makes sweeping negative generalizations about the self based on little evidence. Beck's **cognitive therapy** tries to help such people think more objectively and positively about themselves and their life situations.

Group Therapies

What are some advantages of group therapies? **Group therapies** are based on the idea that psychological problems are at least partly interpersonal and are therefore best approached in a group. Group therapies offer a circle of support for clients, shared insights into problems, and the opportunity to obtain psychotherapy at a lower cost. Among the many different kinds of group therapy are self-help groups, family therapy, and couple therapy.

Why are self-help groups so popular? As the cost of private psychotherapy has risen, self-help groups have become increasingly popular because of their low cost. In such groups, people share their concerns and feelings with others who are experiencing similar problems. Alcoholics Anonymous is a very effective self-help group.

Who is the client in family therapy? **Family therapy** is based on the idea that a person's psychological problems are to some extent family problems also. Therefore, the therapist treats the entire family rather than just the individual reportedly having difficulties. The major goals are to improve communication and empathy and to reduce conflict within the family.

What are some techniques used in couple therapy? **Couple therapy** concentrates on improving patterns of communication and interaction between couples. Like family therapy, it attempts to change relationships, not just individuals. Empathy training and scheduled exchanges of rewards are two of the techniques used to turn a hostile, unsatisfying relationship around.

Effectiveness of Psychotherapy

How much better off is a person who receives psychotherapy than one who gets no treatment at all? Most researchers agree that psychotherapy helps about two-thirds of the people treated. Although there is some debate over how many untreated people also recover, the consensus is that those who get therapy are generally better off than those who don't. Each kind of therapy, however, works better for some problems than for others. The general trend in psychotherapy is toward **eclecticism**, the use of whatever treatment works best for a particular problem.

Biological Treatments

What are biological treatments, and who can provide them? **Biological treatments**—including medication, electroconvulsive therapy, and psychosurgery—are sometimes used when psychotherapy does not work or when a client has a disorder for which biological treatment is known to be safe and effective. Medication, especially, is very often used in conjunction with psychotherapy. Psychiatrists (who are also physicians) are the only mental health professionals licensed to offer biological treatments.

What are some of the drugs used to treat psychological disorders? Drugs are the most common form of biological therapy. **Antipsychotic drugs** are valuable in treating schizophrenia. They do not cure the disorder, but they reduce its symptoms, although side effects can be severe. Antidepressant drugs alleviate depression, though some also have serious side effects. Many other types of medications are used to treat psychological disorders, including antimanic and antianxiety drugs, sedatives, and psychostimultants for children with attention-deficit/hyperactivity disorder.

How is the electroconvulsive therapy of today different from that of the past? **Electroconvulsive therapy (ECT)** is used for cases of severe depression that do not respond to other treatments. An electric current briefly passed through the brain of the patient produces convulsions and temporary loss of consciousness, but afterward depression often lifts. Newer forms of ECT are given to only one side of the brain, use less powerful currents, and are applied for a shorter time.

What is psychosurgery, and how is it used today? **Psychosurgery** is brain surgery performed to change a person's behavior and emotional state. It is rarely used today, and then only as a last, desperate measure on people who have severe and intractable problems and don't respond to any other form of treatment.

Caring for the Seriously Disturbed and Preventing Disorders

How were people with severe psychological disorders cared for in the past? In the past, institutionalization in large mental hospitals was the most common approach to caring for people with serious mental disorders. Patients were given shelter and some degree of treatment, but a great many were never able to be released. Then, with the advent of antipsychotic drugs, a trend began toward **deinstitutionalization**, or integrating people with serious mental disorders back into the community.

What problems have resulted from deinstitutionalization? The idea behind deinstitutionalization was that people would be cared for in a community setting, but community mental health centers and other support services proved inadequate to the task. As a result, many former patients stopped taking their medication, became homeless, and ended up suffering from psychosis and living on the streets. Thus, although deinstitutionalization may have been a good idea in principle, in practice it has not worked out well for many patients or for society.

Are there any alternatives to deinstitutionalization other than rehospitalizing patients? Alternatives to hospitalization include living in the family with adequate supports provided to all family members; living in small, homelike facilities in which residents and staff share responsibilities; and providing intensive outpatient counseling or frequent visits from public health nurses. Most alternative treatments involve some medication and skillful preparation of the family and community. Most studies have found more positive outcomes for alternative treatments than for hospitalization.

What is the difference between primary, secondary, and tertiary prevention? Prevention refers to efforts to reduce the incidence of mental illness before it arises.

Primary prevention consists of improving the social environment through assistance to parents, education, and family planning. **Secondary prevention** involves identifying high-risk groups and directing service to them. **Tertiary prevention** involves helping hospitalized patients return to the community.

Client Diversity and Treatment

Are there particular groups of people who may require special approaches in the treatment of psychological problems? Given that human beings differ as much as they do, it isn't surprising that a one-size-fits-all concept isn't always appropriate in the treatment of psychological problems. In recent years the special needs of women and people from other cultures have particularly occupied the attention of mental health professionals.

How can gender stereotypes be avoided in treatment? Women are more likely than men to be in psychotherapy, and they are more likely to be given psychoactive medication. Because, in traditional therapy, women are often expected to conform to gender stereotypes in order to be pronounced "well," many women have turned to "feminist therapists." The American Psychological Association has issued guidelines to ensure that women receive treatment that is not tied to traditional ideas about appropriate behavior for the sexes.

How can a therapist interact appropriately with clients from different cultures? When client and therapist come from different cultural backgrounds or belong to different racial or ethnic groups, misunderstandings can arise in therapy. The APA has issued guidelines to help psychologists deal more effectively with our ethnically and culturally diverse population. Following these guidelines is an important step toward avoiding cultural misunderstandings.

CRITICAL THINKING AND APPLICATIONS

1. How do you think free association leads to insights in traditional psychoanalysis?

2. What are some of the major differences between insight therapies and behavior therapies in the treatment of psychological disorders? Do you agree with the behavioral view that undesirable behaviors are the problem, not symptoms of some underlying cause? Why, or why not?

3. In what ways does cognitive therapy build on behavior therapy?

4. Do you think that deinstitutionalization of people with serious mental disorders was a good idea? Why, or why not?

5. Does drug therapy encourage better results from psychotherapy, or does it interfere with psychotherapy because it takes away the discomfort that motivated the person to seek help? Discuss the reasons for your answer.

WEB QUIZ **13.9** ✔ **Go to the Morris 6e Companion Website to take a practice chapter exam.**

14 Social Psychology

N 1939, WHEN THE GERMANS OCCUPIED WARSAW, POLAND, THE NAZI ARMY segregated the city's Jews into a ghetto surrounded by barbed wire. Deeply concerned about the fate of her Jewish friends, a 16-year-old Catholic girl named Stefania Podgórska made secret expeditions into the ghetto with gifts of food, clothing, and medicine. When the Jewish son of her former landlord made a desperate flight from the ghetto to avoid being deported to a concentration camp, Stefania agreed to hide him in her apartment. At one point, Stefania and her sister sheltered thirteen Jews in their attic at the same time that two German soldiers were bivouacked in their small apartment.

In May 1991, the "hidden children" of the Holocaust gathered with their friends and relatives to pay tribute to twenty-two Christian rescuers who literally saved their lives during World War II.

Gustave Collet, one of the people honored, was a Belgian soldier during World War II who helped hundreds of Jewish children by hiding them in the sanctuary of a Catholic church. According to Gustave, "We all are the sons of the same Father, and there is no reason there should be differences."

Gisela Sohnlein, a student during World War II and a member of the Dutch underground, helped save thousands of Jewish children. In 1943, she was arrested by Nazi soldiers and spent a year and a half in a concentration camp. According to Gisela, "We didn't feel like rescuers at all. We were just ordinary students doing what we had to do."

Wanda Kwiatkowska-Biernacka was 20 when she falsely claimed that a 1-month-old Jewish baby was her illegitimate child. (Lipman, 1991)

Are these people heroes, or, as Gisela Sohnlein stated, were they simply doing what had to be done? Why did they do what so many millions of other people failed to do? What caused many people to acquiesce in the murder of millions of innocent people? Were they following orders? What brought about such hatred?

Social psychologists address questions like these. **Social psychology** is the scientific study of how a person's thoughts, feelings, and behaviors are influenced by the behavior and characteristics of other people, whether real, imagined, or inferred. All the topics in this chapter—from attitude change to group decision making, from conformity to mob action—involve the influence of one or more persons on other people. We begin this chapter by exploring the social forces that are at work when people form impressions of and make judgments about one another, in addition to examining the factors that influence interpersonal attraction.

Social Cognition

What do forming impressions, explaining others' behavior, and experiencing interpersonal attraction have in common?

Part of the process of being influenced by other people involves organizing and interpreting information about them so as to form first impressions, to try to understand their behavior, and to determine to what extent we are attracted to them. This taking in and assessing of information about other

Social psychology
The scientific study of the ways in which the thoughts, feelings, and behaviors of one individual are influenced by the real, imagined, or inferred behavior or characteristics of other people.

If you were to hail this taxi in New York City, based on your assumptions about cab drivers you might never guess that this man from the Middle East holds an advanced degree in biology and is looking for a job at a university. Schemas can be useful, but they can also keep us from finding out what lies beneath the surface.

people is called **social cognition**. Social cognition is a major area of interest to social psychologists.

Forming Impressions

How do we form first impressions of people?

Forming first impressions of people is more complex than you may think. You must direct your attention to various aspects of the person's appearance and behavior and then make a rapid assessment of what those characteristics mean. How do you do this process? What cues do you focus on? And how accurate are the impressions you form? The concept of *schemata* helps to answer these questions.

Schemata   When we meet someone for the first time, we notice a number of things about that person—clothes, gestures, manner of speaking, body build, facial features. We then draw on these cues to fit the person into a category. No matter how little information we have or how contradictory it is, no matter how many times in the past our initial impressions have been wrong, we still categorize people after meeting them only briefly. Associated with each category is a **schema**—a set of beliefs and expectations based on past experience that is presumed to apply to all members of that category (Fiske & Taylor, 1991). Schemata (the plural of schema) flesh out our impressions after we have pegged people into categories. For example, if a woman is wearing a white coat and has a stethoscope around her neck, you could reasonably categorize her as a doctor. Associated with this category is a schema of various beliefs and expectations: highly trained professional, knowledgeable about diseases and their cures, qualified to prescribe medication, and so on. By applying this schema, you expect that this particular woman has these traits.

But schemata can also lead us astray. They can lure us into "seeing" things about a person that we don't actually observe. For instance, most of us associate the traits of shyness, quietness, and the preoccupation of one's own thoughts with the schema *introvert*. If we notice that Melissa is shy, we are likely to categorize her as an introvert. Later we may "remember" that she also seemed preoccupied with her own thoughts. In other words, thinking of Melissa as an introvert saves us the trouble of taking into account all the subtle shadings of her personality. But this kind of thinking can easily lead to errors if we attribute to Melissa qualities that belong to the schema but not to her.

Over time, as we continue to interact with people, we add new information about them to our mental files. Our later experiences, however, generally do not influence us nearly so much as our earliest impressions. This phenomenon is called the **primacy effect.** For example, if you already like a new acquaintance, you may excuse something that annoys you later. Conversely, if someone makes an early *bad* impression, subsequent evidence of that person's good qualities will do little to change your feelings. The primacy effect reflects a desire to lessen our mental effort. We humans have been called "cognitive misers" (Fiske & Taylor, 1991). Instead of exerting ourselves to interpret every detail that we learn about a person, we are stingy with our mental efforts. Once we have formed an impression about someone, we keep it, even if that impression was formed by jumping to conclusions or through prejudice (Fiske, 1995).

If people are specifically warned to beware of first impressions, or if they are encouraged to interpret information about others slowly and carefully, the primacy effect can be weakened or even eliminated (Luchins, 1957; Stewart, 1965). Generally speaking, however, the first impression is the

Social cognition
Knowledge and understanding concerning the social world and the people in it (including oneself).

Schema
A set of beliefs or expectations about something that is based on past experience.

Primacy effect
The fact that early information about someone weighs more heavily than later information in influencing one's impression of that person.

lasting impression, and it can affect our behavior even when it is inaccurate. In one study, pairs of participants played a competitive game (Snyder & Swann, 1978). The researchers told one member of each pair that his or her partner was either hostile or friendly. The players who were led to believe that their partner was hostile behaved differently toward the partner than did the players led to believe that their partner was friendly. In turn, those treated as hostile actually began to display hostility. In fact, these people continued to show hostility later on, when they were paired with new players who had no expectations about them at all. The expectation of hostility, it seems, produced actual aggressiveness, and this behavior persisted. When we bring about expected behavior in another person in this way, our impression becomes a **self-fulfilling prophecy.**

Considerable scientific research has shown how teacher expectations can take the form of a self-fulfilling prophecy and can influence student performance in the classroom (Cooper, 1993; Harris & Rosenthal, 1985; Osborne, 1997; Weinstein, Madison, & Kuklinski, 1995). This finding has been named the *Pygmalion effect* after the mythical sculptor who created the statue of a woman and then brought it to life. Although the research does not suggest that high teacher expectations can turn an "F" student into an "A" student, it does show that both high and low expectations can exert a powerful influence on student achievement. One study, for example, compared the performance of "at risk" ninth-grade students who had been assigned to regular classrooms with that of students assigned to experimental classrooms that received a year-long intervention aimed at increasing teachers' expectations. After one year, the students in the experimental classrooms had higher grades in English and history than the students who were not in the intervention classrooms. Two years later, the experimental students were less likely to drop out of high school (Weinstein et al., 1991).

Stereotypes   Just as schemata shape our impressions of others, so do stereotypes. A **stereotype** is a set of characteristics presumed to be shared by all members of a social category. A stereotype is actually a special kind of schema, one that is simplistic but very strongly held, and not necessarily based on much firsthand experience. A stereotype can involve almost any distinguishing feature of a person—age, sex, race, occupation, place of residence, or membership in a certain group (Hilton & Von Hipple, 1996).

When our first impression of a person is governed by a stereotype, we tend to infer things about that person solely on the basis of some key distinguishing feature and to ignore facts that are inconsistent with the stereotype, no matter how apparent they are. As a result, we may perceive things about the person selectively or inaccurately, thereby perpetuating our initial stereotype. For example, once you have categorized someone as male or female, you may rely more on your stereotype of that gender than on your own observations of how the person acts. Because women are traditionally stereotyped as more emotional and submissive, and men as more rational and assertive (Deaux & Kite, 1993; Williams & Best, 1990), you may come to see these traits in men and women more than they really exist.

Recent studies (Macrae & Bodenhausen, 2000) indicate that sorting people into categories is not automatic or inevitable. People are more likely to apply stereotyped schemata in a chance encounter than in a structured, task-oriented situation (such as a classroom or the office); more likely to pay attention to individual signals than to stereo-

Self-fulfilling prophecy
The process in which a person's expectation about another elicits behavior from the second person that confirms the expectation.

Stereotype
A set of characteristics presumed to be shared by all members of a social category.

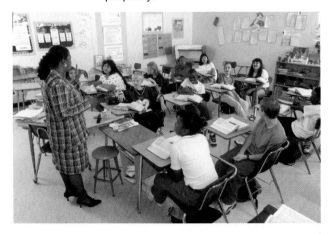

Suppose you are a new teacher entering this classroom on the first day of school in September. Do you have any expectations about children of any ethnic or racial groups that might lead to a self-fulfilling prophecy?

types when they are pursuing a goal; and consciously or unconsciously to suppress stereotypes that violate social norms. For example, a man who has operated according to stereotyped schemata may expect women in gender-typed roles, such as a nurse or secretary or his wife, to be warm and gentle, but may not hold these expectations toward women he meets in his work life or in their professional roles (as lawyer, executive, or telephone repair person).

Attribution

How do we decide why people act as they do?

Suppose that you run into a friend at the supermarket. You greet him warmly, but he barely acknowledges you, mumbles "Hi," and walks away. You feel snubbed and try to figure out why he acted like that. Did he behave that way because of something in the situation? Did you say something to offend him? Was he somehow embarrassed by meeting you at the particular time and place? Or is his behavior more correctly attributed to something within him—to some personal trait such as moodiness or arrogance?

Explaining Behavior   Social interaction is filled with occasions such as this—occasions that invite us to make judgments about the causes of behavior. Especially when something unexpected or unpleasant occurs, we wonder about it and try to understand it. Social psychologists' observations about how we go about attributing causes to behavior form the basis of **attribution theory.**

An early attribution theorist, Fritz Heider (1958), argued that we attribute behavior to either internal or external causes, but not both. Thus you might conclude that a classmate's lateness was caused by his laziness (a personal factor, or an internal attribution) *or* by traffic congestion (a situational factor, or an external attribution).

How do we decide whether to attribute a given behavior to causes inside or outside a person? According to another influential attribution theorist, Harold Kelley (1967), we rely on three kinds of information about the behavior: distinctiveness, consistency, and consensus. For example, if your instructor asks you to stay briefly after class so that she can talk with you, you will probably try to figure out what lies behind her request by asking yourself three questions.

First, how *distinctive* is the instructor's request? Does she often ask students to stay and talk (low distinctiveness), or is such a request unusual (high distinctiveness)? If she often asks students to speak with her, you will probably conclude that she has personal reasons for talking with you. But if her request is highly distinctive, you will probably conclude that something about you, not her, underlies her request.

Second, how *consistent* is the instructor's behavior? Does she regularly ask you to stay and talk (high consistency), or is this a first for you (low consistency)? If she has consistently made this request of you before, you will probably guess that this occasion is like those others. But if her request is inconsistent with past behavior, you will probably wonder whether some particular event—perhaps something you said in class—motivated her to request a private conference.

Finally, what degree of *consensus* among teachers exists regarding this behavior? Do your other instructors ask you to stay and talk with them (high consensus), or is this instructor unique in making such a request (low consensus)? If it is common for your instructors to ask to speak with you, this instructor's request is probably due to some external factor. But if she is the only instructor ever to ask to speak privately with you, it must be

Attribution theory
The theory that addresses the question of how people make judgments about the causes of behavior.

something about this particular person—an internal motive or a concern—that accounts for her behavior (Iacobucci & McGill, 1990).

If you conclude that the instructor has her own reasons for wanting to speak with you, you may feel mildly curious for the remainder of class until you can find out what she wants. But if you think external factors—like your own actions—have prompted her request, you may worry about whether you are in trouble and nervously wait for the end of class.

Biases Unfortunately, the causal attributions we make are often vulnerable to *biases*. For instance, imagine that you are at a party and you see an acquaintance, Ted, walk across the room carrying several plates of food and a drink. As he approaches his chair, Ted spills food on himself. You may attribute the spill to Ted's personal characteristics—he is clumsy. Ted, however, is likely to make a very different attribution. He will likely attribute the spill to an external factor—he was carrying too many other things. Your explanation for this behavior reflects the **fundamental attribution error**—the tendency to attribute the behavior of others to causes within themselves (Gilbert & Malone, 1995; Ross, 1977; Ross & Nisbett, 1991).

The fundamental attribution error is part of the *actor-observer bias*—the tendency to explain the behavior of others as caused by internal factors, while attributing *one's own* behavior to *external* forces (Fiske & Taylor, 1991). Thus Ted, the actor, attributed his own behavior to an external source, whereas you, the observer, attributed the behavior to an internal one. Recall the examples used to introduce this chapter—those who risked their own safety to help others in Nazi-occupied Europe. From the perspective of an observer, we tend to attribute this behavior to personal qualities. Indeed, Robert Goodkind, chairman of the foundation that honored the rescuers, called for parents to "inculcate in our children the values of altruism and moral courage as exemplified by the rescuers." Clearly, Goodkind was making an internal attribution for the heroic behavior. The rescuers themselves, however, attribute their actions to external factors: "We were only ordinary students who did what we had to do."

A related class of biases is called **defensive attribution.** These types of attributions occur when we are motivated to present ourselves well, either to impress others or to feel good about ourselves (Agostinelli, Sherman, Presson, & Chassin, 1992). One example of a defensive attribution is the *self-serving bias,* which is a tendency to attribute our successes to our personal attributes while chalking up our failures to external forces beyond our control (Schlenker, Weigold, & Hallam, 1990; Schlenker & Weigold, 1992). Students do this all the time. They tend to regard exams on which they do well as good indicators of their abilities and exams on which they do poorly as bad indicators (Davis & Stephan, 1980). Similarly, teachers are more likely to assume responsibility for students' successes than for their failures (Arkin, Cooper, & Kolditz, 1980).

A second type of defensive attribution comes from thinking that people get what they deserve: Bad things happen to bad people, and good things happen to good people. This is called the **just-world hypothesis** (Lerner, 1980). When misfortune strikes someone, we often jump to the conclusion that the person deserved it, rather than giving full weight to situational factors that may have been responsible. Why do we behave this way? One reason is that doing so gives us the comforting illusion that such a thing could never happen to us. By reassigning the blame for a terrible misfortune from a chance event (something that could happen to us) to the victim's own negligence (a trait that *we*, of course, do not share), we delude ourselves into believing that we could never suffer such a fate (Chaiken & Darley, 1973).

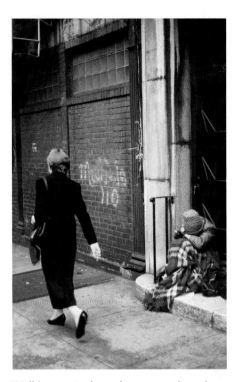

Walking past a homeless person is easier for us if we assume that the person brought this sad condition on himself. By ignoring situational factors that may have been responsible, we protect ourselves from the troubling thought that homelessness, or some other terrible misfortune, might happen to us. This kind of attribution error is called the just-world hypothesis.

Fundamental attribution error
The tendency of people to overemphasize personal causes for other people's behavior and to underemphasize personal causes for their own behavior.

Defensive attribution
The tendency to attribute our successes to our own efforts or qualities and our failures to external factors.

Just-world hypothesis
Attribution error based on the assumption that bad things happen to bad people and good things happen to good people.

Attribution across Cultures Historically, most of the research on attribution theory has been conducted in Western cultures. Do the basic principles of attribution theory apply to people in other cultures as well? The answer is no. In general, East Asians are more likely to attribute both their own and other people's behavior to external, situational factors than to internal dispositions (Choi, Nisbett & Norenzayan, 1999). For example, in one study, Japanese students studying in the United States usually explained failure as a lack of effort (an internal attribution) and attributed their successes to the assistance that they received from others (an external attribution) (Kashima & Triandis, 1986). This process is the reverse of the self-serving bias. Similarly, the fundamental attribution error may not be universal. In some other cultures, people are much less likely to attribute behavior to internal personal characteristics; they place more emphasis on the role of external, situational factors in explaining both their own behavior and that of others (Cousins, 1989; Markus & Kitayama, 1991; Menon, Morris, Chiu, & Hong, 1998; J. Miller, 1984).

14.1

Interpersonal Attraction

Do "birds of a feather flock together," or do "opposites attract"?

A third aspect of social cognition has to do with interpersonal attraction. When people meet, what determines whether they will like each other? This is the subject of much speculation and even mystification, with popular explanations running the gamut from fate to compatible astrological signs. Romantics believe that irresistible forces propel them toward an inevitable meeting with their beloved, but social psychologists take a more hardheaded view. They have found that attraction and the tendency to like someone else are closely linked to such factors as *proximity, physical attractiveness, similarity, exchange,* and *intimacy.*

Proximity **Proximity** is usually the most important factor in determining attraction (Berscheid & Reis, 1998). The closer two people live to each other, the more likely they are to interact; the more frequent their interaction, the more they will tend to like each other. Conversely, two people separated by considerable geographic distance are not likely to run into each other and thus have little chance to develop a mutual attraction. The proximity effect has less to do with simple convenience than with the security and comfort we feel with people and things that have become familiar. Familiar people are predictable and safe—thus more likable (Bornstein, 1989).

Physical Attractiveness Physical attractiveness can powerfully influence the conclusions that we reach about a person's character. We actually give attractive people credit for more than their beauty. We presume them to be more intelligent, interesting, happy, kind, sensitive, moral, and successful than people who are not perceived as attractive. They are also thought to make better spouses and to be more sexually responsive (Dion, 1972; Feingold, 1992; Zuckerman, Miyake, & Elkin, 1995).

Not only do we tend to credit physically attractive people with a wealth of positive qualities, but we also tend to like them more than we do less attractive people. One reason is that physical attractiveness itself is generally considered a positive attribute (Baron & Byrne, 1991). We often perceive beauty as a valuable asset that can be exchanged for other things in social interactions. We may also believe that beauty has a "radiating effect"—that the glow of a companion's good looks enhances our own public image (Kernis & Wheeler, 1981).

Proximity
How close two people live to each other.

Whatever its origins, our preoccupation with physical attractiveness has material consequences. Attractive people tend to be happier, make more money, and are more likely to be treated leniently by teachers (McCall, 1997). In addition, research has found that mothers of more attractive infants tend to show their children more affection and to play with them more often than mothers of unattractive infants (Langlois, Ritter, Casey, & Sawin, 1995). In general, we tend to give good-looking people the benefit of the doubt: If they don't live up to our expectations during the first encounter, we give them a second chance, ask for or accept a second date, or seek further opportunities for interaction. These reactions can give attractive people substantial advantages in life and can lead to self-fulfilling prophecies. Physically attractive people may come to think of themselves as good or lovable because they are continually treated as if they are. Conversely, unattractive people may begin to see themselves as bad or unlovable because they have always been regarded that way—even as children. But attractiveness isn't everything. In the abstract, people might prefer extremely attractive individuals, but in reality they usually choose friends and partners who are close to their own level of attractiveness (Harvey & Pauwells, 1999).

Wonderful or just beautiful? Physically attractive people are often perceived to have a host of other attractive qualities. Here, in a scene from the movie, *Shakespeare in Love*, Joseph Feines and Gwyneth Paltrow play characters whose good looks draw them instantly together.

Similarity Similarity of attitudes, interests, values, backgrounds, and beliefs underlies much interpersonal attraction (P. M. Buss, 1985; Tan & Singh, 1995). When we know that someone shares our attitudes and interests, we tend to have more positive feelings toward that person (Byrne, 1961). The higher the proportion of attitudes that two people share, the stronger the attraction between them (Byrne & Nelson, 1965). We value similarity because it is important to us to have others agree with our choices and beliefs. By comparing our opinions with those of other people, we clarify our understanding of and reduce our uncertainty about social situations. Finding that others agree with us strengthens our convictions and boosts our self-esteem (Suls & Fletcher, 1983).

If similarity is such a critical determinant of attraction, what about the notion that opposites attract? Aren't people sometimes attracted to others who are completely different from them? Extensive research has failed to confirm this notion. In long-term relationships, where attraction plays an especially important role, people overwhelmingly prefer to associate with people who are similar to themselves (D. M. Buss, 1985).

In some cases in which people's attraction seems to be founded on their "differentness," their critical qualities are not opposites but complements. Complementary traits are needs or skills that complete or balance each other (Dryer & Horowitz, 1997; Hendrick & Hendrick, 1992). For example, a person who likes to care for and fuss over others will be most compatible with a mate who enjoys receiving such attention. These people are not really opposites, but their abilities and desires complement each other to their mutual satisfaction. Complementarity almost always occurs between people who share similar goals and values and are willing to adapt to each other. True opposites are unlikely even to meet each other, much less interact long enough to achieve such compatibility.

Self-disclosure—revealing personal experiences and opinions—is essential to all close relationships.

Exchange   According to the *reward theory of attraction,* we tend to like people who make us feel rewarded and appreciated. But the relationship between attraction and rewards is subtle and complex. For example, Aronson's gain-loss theory of attraction (1994) suggests that *increases* in rewarding behavior influence attractiveness more than constant rewarding behavior does. Say that you were to meet and talk with someone at three successive parties, and during these conversations, that person's behavior toward you changed from polite indifference to overt flattery. You would be inclined to like this person more than if she or he had immediately started to praise you during the first conversation and kept up the stream of praise each time you met. The reverse also holds true: We tend to dislike people whose opinion of us changes from good to bad even more than we dislike those who consistently display a low opinion of us.

The reward theory of attraction is based on the concept of **exchange.** In social interactions, people make exchanges. For example, you may agree to help a friend paint his apartment in exchange for his preparing dinner for you. Every exchange involves both rewards (you get a free dinner; he gets his apartment painted) and costs (you have to paint first; he then has to cook you dinner). As long as both parties find their interactions more rewarding than costly, their exchanges will continue (Clore & Byrne, 1974; Lott & Lott, 1974). People seem to "keep score" in their interactions, especially in the early stages of relationships (M. S. Clark & Mills, 1979).

Exchanges work only insofar as they are fair or equitable. A relationship is based on **equity** when what one person "gets out of it" is equal to what the other gets (Walster, Walster, & Berscheid, 1978; van Yperen & Buunk, 1990). When exchanges are consistently unfair, the one who reaps fewer rewards feels cheated, and the one who gains is apt to feel guilty. This result may undermine the attraction that once drew the two people together.

Intimacy   When does liking someone become something more? *Intimacy* is the quality of genuine closeness and trust achieved in communication with another person. When people communicate, they do more than just interact—they share deep-rooted feelings and ideas. When you are first getting to know someone, you communicate about "safe," superficial topics like the weather, sports, or shared activities. As you get to know each other better over time, your conversation progresses to more personal subjects: your personal experiences, memories, hopes and fears, goals and failures (Altman & Taylor, 1973).

Intimate communication is based on the process of *self-disclosure* (Prager, 1995). As you talk with friends, you disclose or reveal personal experiences and opinions that you might conceal from strangers. Because self-disclosure is possible only when you trust the listener, you will seek—and usually receive—a reciprocal disclosure to keep the conversation balanced. For example, after telling your roommate about something that embarrassed you, you may expect him or her to reveal a similar episode; you might even ask directly, "Has anything like that ever happened to you?" Such reciprocal intimacy keeps you "even" and makes your relationship more emotionally satisfying (Collins & Miller, 1994). The pacing of disclosure is important. If you "jump levels" by revealing too much too soon—or to someone who is not ready to make a reciprocal personal response—the other person will retreat, and communication will go no further. People become closer and stay closer through a continuing reciprocal pattern of each person's trying to know the other and allowing the other to know him or her (Harvey & Pauwells, 1999).

Exchange
The concept that relationships are based on trading rewards among partners.

Equity
Fairness of exchange achieved when each partner in the relationship receives the same proportion of outcomes to investments.

INTERACTIVE LECTURE **14.1**

WEB QUIZ **14.1**

CHECK YOUR UNDERSTANDING

1. The scientific study of how a person's thoughts, feelings, and behaviors are influenced by the behavior and characteristics of other people, whether real, imagined, or inferred, is called ___ ___.

2. ___ ___ refers to the process of taking in and assessing information about other people.

3. Associated with the many categories into which we "peg" people are sets of beliefs and expectations called ___ that are assumed to apply to all members of a category. When these are quite simplistic but deeply held, they are often referred to as ___.

4. When the first information we receive about a person weighs more heavily in forming an impression than later information does, we are experiencing the ___ effect.

5. Understanding how we make inferences about why people act as they do is part of ___ theory.

6. According to Fritz Heider, we usually attribute someone's behavior to

   a. internal and external causes both at the same time.

   b. either internal or external causes, but not both at the same time.

   c. external causes only.

   d. internal causes only.

7. Match the following biases in attributing causes to behavior with the appropriate definition.

   ___ fundamental attribution error

   ___ actor-observer bias

   ___ self-serving bias

   ___ just-world hypothesis

   a. attributing the behavior of others to internal causes and one's own behavior to external causes

   b. attributing our success to ourselves and our failures to factors beyond our control

   c. assuming that people must deserve the bad things that happen to them

   d. the tendency to attribute the behavior of others to personal characteristics

8. Which of the following is a basis for interpersonal attraction? (There can be more than one correct answer.)

   a. proximity

   b. similarity

   c. exchange

   d. attraction of true opposites

   e. all of the above

Answers: 1. social psychology. 2. Social cognition. 3. schemata, stereotypes. 4. primacy. 5. attribution. 6. b. 7. fundamental attribution error: d; actor-observer bias: a; self-serving bias: b; just-world hypothesis: c. 8. a, b, and c.

Attitudes

Why are attitudes important?

The phrase "I don't like his attitude" is a telling one. People are often told to "change your attitude" or make an "attitude adjustment." An **attitude** is a relatively stable organization of beliefs, feelings, and tendencies toward something or someone—called an attitude object. Attitudes are important mainly because they often influence our behavior. Discrimination, for example, is often caused by prejudiced attitudes. Psychologists wonder how attitudes are formed and how they can be changed.

Attitude
Relatively stable organization of beliefs, feelings, and behavior tendencies directed toward something or someone—the attitude object.

The Nature of Attitudes

What are the three major components of attitudes?

An attitude has three major components: *evaluative beliefs* about the object, *feelings* about the object, and *behavior tendencies* toward the object. Beliefs include facts, opinions, and our general knowledge. Feelings encompass love, hate, like, dislike, and similar sentiments. Behavior tendencies refer to our inclinations to act in certain ways toward the object—to approach it, avoid it, and so on. For example, our attitude toward a political candidate includes our beliefs about the candidate's qualifications and positions on crucial issues and our expectations about how the candidate will vote on those issues. We also have feelings about the candidate—like or dislike, trust or mistrust. And because of these beliefs and feelings, we are inclined to behave in certain ways toward the candidate—to vote for or against the candidate, to contribute time or money to the candidate's campaign, to make a point of attending or staying away from rallies for the candidate, and so forth.

As we will see shortly, these three aspects of an attitude are very often consistent with one another. For example, if we have positive feelings toward something, we tend to have positive beliefs about it and to behave positively toward it. This tendency does not mean, however, that our every action will accurately reflect our attitudes. For example, our feelings about going to dentists are often negative, yet most of us make an annual visit anyway. Let's look more closely at the relationship between attitudes and behavior.

Attitudes and Behavior   The relationship between attitudes and behavior is not always straightforward. Variables such as what the strength of the attitude is, how easily it comes to mind, how salient a particular attitude is in a given situation, and how relevant the attitude is to the particular behavior in question help to determine whether a person will act in accordance with an attitude (Eagly, 1992; Eagly & Chaiken, 1998; Kraus, 1995).

Personality traits are also important. Some people consistently match their actions to their attitudes (R. Norman, 1975). Others have a tendency to

Children may learn prejudice from their parents or from other adults, but attitudes can be changed.

override their own attitudes in order to behave properly in a given situation. As a result, attitudes predict behavior better for some people than for others (M. Snyder & Tanke, 1976). People who rate highly on **self-monitoring** are especially likely to override their attitudes to behave in accordance with others' expectations. Before speaking or acting, high self-monitors observe the situation for clues about how they should react. Then they try to meet those "demands" rather than behave according to their own beliefs or sentiments. In contrast, low self-monitors express and act on their attitudes with great consistency, showing little regard for situational clues or constraints. Thus, a high self-monitor who disagrees with the politics of a fellow dinner guest may keep her thoughts to herself in an effort to be polite and agreeable, whereas a low self-monitor who disagrees might dispute the speaker openly, even though doing so might disrupt the social occasion (Snyder, 1987).

One of the best antidotes to prejudice is contact among people of different racial groups. Working on class projects together, for example, can help children to overcome negative stereotypes about others.

Attitude Development   How do we acquire our attitudes? Where do they come from? Many of our most basic attitudes derive from early, direct personal experience. Children are rewarded with smiles and encouragement when they please their parents, and they are punished through disapproval when they displease them. These early experiences give children enduring attitudes (Oskamp, 1991). Attitudes are also formed by imitation. Children mimic the behavior of their parents and peers, acquiring attitudes even when no one is deliberately trying to shape them.

But parents are not the only source of attitudes. Teachers, friends, and even famous people are also important in shaping our attitudes. New fraternity or sorority members, for example, may model their behavior and attitudes on upper-class members. A student who idolizes a teacher may adopt many of the teacher's attitudes toward controversial subjects, even if they run counter to attitudes of parents or friends.

The mass media, particularly television, also have a great impact on attitude formation. Television bombards us with messages—not merely through its news and entertainment but also through commercials. Without experience of their own against which to measure the merit of these messages, children are particularly susceptible to the influence of television on their attitudes.

Prejudice and Discrimination

How does a person develop a prejudice toward someone else?

Although the terms *prejudice* and *discrimination* are often used interchangeably, they actually refer to different concepts. **Prejudice**—an attitude—is an unfair, intolerant, or unfavorable view of a group of people. **Discrimination**—a behavior—is an unfair act or a series of acts directed against an entire group of people or individual members of that group. To discriminate is to treat an entire class of people in an unfair way.

Prejudice and discrimination do not always occur together. It is possible to be prejudiced against a particular group without openly behaving in a hostile or discriminatory manner toward its members. A racist store owner may smile at a black customer, for example, to disguise opinions that could hurt his business. Likewise, many institutional practices can be discriminatory even though they are not based on prejudice. For example, regulations establishing a minimum height requirement for police officers may discriminate against women and certain ethnic groups whose average height falls below the arbitrary standard, even though the regulations do not stem from sexist or racist attitudes.

Self-monitoring
The tendency for an individual to observe the situation for cues about how to react.

Prejudice
An unfair, intolerant, or unfavorable attitude toward a group of people.

Discrimination
An unfair act or series of acts taken toward an entire group of people or individual members of that group.

Prejudice   Like attitudes in general, prejudice has three components: beliefs, feelings, and behavioral tendencies. Prejudicial beliefs are virtually always negative stereotypes, and as mentioned earlier, reliance on stereotypes can lead to erroneous thinking about other people. When a prejudiced white employer interviews an African American, for example, the employer may attribute to the job candidate all the traits associated with the African-American stereotype. Qualities of the candidate that do not match the stereotype are likely to be ignored or quickly forgotten (Allport, 1954). For example, the employer whose stereotype includes the belief that African Americans are lazy may belittle the candidate's hard-earned college degree by thinking, "I never heard of that college. It must be an easy school."

This thinking, which is similar to the fundamental attribution error, is known as the *ultimate attribution error*. This error refers to the tendency for a person with stereotyped beliefs about a particular group of people to make internal attributions for their shortcomings and external attributions for their successes. In the preceding example, the employer is making an external attribution (an easy school) for the college success of the African-American job seeker. The other side of the ultimate attribution error is to make internal attributions for the failures of people who belong to groups we dislike. For instance, many white Americans believe that lower average incomes among black Americans compared to whites is due to lack of ability or low motivation (Kluegel, 1990).

Along with stereotyped beliefs, prejudiced attitudes are usually marked by strong emotions, such as dislike, fear, hatred, or loathing. For example, on learning that a person whom they like is a homosexual, heterosexuals may suddenly view the person as undesirable, sick, a sinner, or a pervert. (See Herek, 2000.)

Sources of Prejudice   Many theories attempt to sort out the causes and sources of prejudice. According to the **frustration-aggression theory,** prejudice is the result of people's frustrations (Allport, 1954). As you saw in Chapter 8, Motivation and Emotion, under some circumstances frustration can spill over into anger and hostility. People who feel exploited and oppressed often cannot vent their anger against an identifiable or proper target, so they displace their hostility onto those even "lower" on the social scale than themselves. The result is prejudice and discrimination. The people who are the victims of this displaced aggression become *scapegoats* and are blamed for the problems of the times.

African Americans have been scapegoats for the economic frustrations of some lower-income whites who feel powerless to improve their own condition. Latinos, Asian Americans, Jews, and women are also scapegoated—at times by African Americans. Like kindness, greed, and all other human qualities, prejudice is not restricted to a particular race or ethnic group.

Another theory locates the source of prejudice in a bigoted or an **authoritarian personality** (Adorno et al., 1950). Authoritarian people tend to be rigidly conventional. They favor following the rules and abiding by tradition and are hostile to those who defy social norms (Stone, Lederer, & Christie, 1993). They respect and submit to authority and are preoccupied with power and toughness. Looking at the world through a lens of rigid categories, they are cynical about human nature, fearing, suspecting, and rejecting all groups other than those to which they belong. Prejudice is only one expression of their suspicious, mistrusting views.

There are also cognitive sources of prejudice. As we saw earlier, people are "cognitive misers" who try to simplify and organize their social thinking as much as possible. Too much simplification—*oversimplification*—leads to

Frustration-aggression theory
The theory that under certain circumstances people who are frustrated in their goals turn their anger away from the proper, powerful target and toward another, less powerful target that is safer to attack.

Authoritarian personality
A personality pattern characterized by rigid conventionality, exaggerated respect for authority, and hostility toward those who defy society's norms.

erroneous thinking, stereotypes, prejudice, and discrimination. For example, a stereotyped view of women as indecisive or weak will prejudice an employer against hiring a qualified woman as a manager. Belief in a just world—where people get what they deserve and deserve what they get—also oversimplifies one's view of the victims of prejudice as somehow "deserving" their plight (Fiske & Neubers, 1990).

In addition, prejudice and discrimination may have their roots in people's attempts to conform. If we associate with people who express prejudices, we are more likely to go along with their ideas than to resist them. The pressures of social conformity help to explain why children quickly absorb the prejudices of their parents and playmates long before they have formed their own beliefs and opinions on the basis of experience. Peer pressure often makes it "cool" or acceptable to express certain biases rather than to behave tolerantly toward members of other social groups.

Racism is the belief that members of certain racial or ethnic groups are *innately* inferior. Racists believe that intelligence, industry, morality, and other valued traits are biologically determined and therefore cannot be changed. Racism leads to either/or thinking: Either you are one of "us," or you are one of "them." An *in-group* is any group of people who feel a sense of solidarity and exclusivity in relation to nonmembers. An *out-group*, in contrast, is a group of people who are outside this boundary and are viewed as competitors, enemies, or different and unworthy of respect. These terms can be applied to opposing sports teams, rival gangs, and political parties, or to entire nations, regions, religions, and ethnic or racial groups. According to the *in-group bias*, members see themselves not just as different but also as superior to members of out-groups. In extreme cases, members of an in-group may see members of an out-group as less than human and feel hatred that may lead to violence, civil war, and even genocide.

The most blatant forms of racism in the United States have declined in the last several decades. For example, nine out of ten whites say that they would vote for a black president. Despite a good deal of political rhetoric, 49 percent of whites say that they support maintaining or increasing current affirmative action programs (*USA Today*, 1997). But racism still exists in subtle forms. For example, more than 60 percent of whites say that they approve of interracial marriage but would be "uncomfortable" if someone in their family married an African American. Many whites support racial integration of schools but become "uneasy" if the percentage of black students in their child's class or school approaches 50 percent (Jaynes & Williams, 1989). Thus, it is not surprising that blacks and whites have different views of how blacks are treated in our society. In a 1997 survey, two out of three whites agreed with the statement "Blacks have as good a chance as white people . . . to get any job they are qualified for"; about the same proportion of blacks disagreed (see **Figure 14–1** for other differences from the same survey).

How can we use our knowledge of prejudice, stereotypes, and discrimination to reduce prejudice and its expression? Three strategies appear promising: recategorization, controlled processing, and improving contact between groups (see *Understanding the World Around You* for a discussion of how these strategies can be used to reduce ethnic conflict).

- When we *recategorize*, we try to expand our schema of a particular group—say, by viewing people from different races or genders as sharing similar qualities. These more inclusive schemata become *superordinate categories*. For instance, both Catholics and Protestants in the United States tend to view themselves as Christians rather than as separate competing groups (as in Northern Ireland). If people can create such superordinate categories, they can often reduce stereotypes

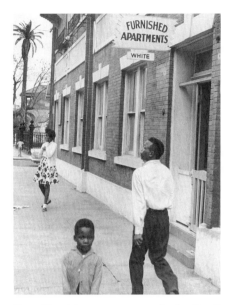

Signs like this were common in the South before the civil rights movement.

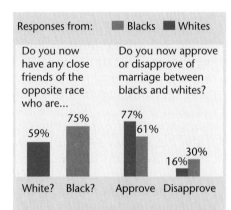

Responses from:	■ Blacks ■ Whites	

Do you now have any close friends of the opposite race who are...

White? 59%
Black? 75%

Do you now approve or disapprove of marriage between blacks and whites?

Approve 77% / 61%
Disapprove 16% / 30%

Are blacks treated less fairly than whites... (Percentage saying 'yes')

	Blacks	Whites
On the job?	45%	14%
On public transportation?	25%	12%
In neighborhood shops?	42%	18%
In stores downtown or in malls?	46%	19%
In restaurants?	42%	16%
By police?	60%	30%

FIGURE 14–1

Racial attitudes in the United States. As the figure illustrates, blacks and whites have different views of how blacks are treated in this country.

Source: Gelles, R. J., & Levine, A. (1999). *Sociology: An Introduction*, 6th Edition, fig. 9-7, p. 338; data from *USA Today*, June 11, 1997, p. 9a.

Racism
Prejudice and discrimination directed at a particular racial group.

UNDERSTANDING The World Around US

Ethnic Conflict and Violence

With the end of the Cold War, interethnic conflict has become the dominant form of war (Mays et al., 1998; Rouhana & Bar-Tal, 1998). Bosnia, Croatia, East Timor, Russia, Turkey, Iraq, Ireland, Israel, Sri Lanka . . . the list of countries torn by ethnic conflict goes on and on, and civilian deaths continue to increase by the thousands. Why does such conflict arise, and why is it so difficult to resolve?

Ethnic conflict has no single cause. In part, ethnic conflict "is often rooted in histories of colonialism, ethnocentrism, racism, political oppression, human rights abuses, social injustice, poverty, and environmental degradation" (Mays et al., 1998, p. 737). But these structural problems are only part of the story, determining primarily who fights whom. The rest of the story is to be found in psychological processes such as intense group loyalty, personal and social identity, shared memories, polarization and deep-rooted prejudice, and societal beliefs (Cairns & Darby, 1998; Mays et al., 1998; Rouhana & Bar-Tal, 1998). In other words, structural problems don't have the same effect if people are not prepared to hate and fear others. This hate and fear largely determine the extent to which ethnic conflict becomes violent (Des Forges, 1995; Ross, 1993; Smith, 1998).

Looking more closely at some of the psychological forces at work,

> Structural problems don't have the same effect if people are not prepared to hate and fear others.

propaganda often plays a significant role by portraying opponents in the most negative fashion possible, thus perpetuating racism, prejudice, and stereotypes. In Rwanda, for example, Tutsis (who were almost exterminated by the resulting violence with Hutus) for years were accused in the mass media of having committed horrible crimes and of plotting the mass murder of Hutus, none of which was true (Smith, 1998). When ethnic violence is protracted, *shared collective memories* become filled with instances of violence, hostility, and victimization. Prejudices are thus reinforced, and people increasingly come to view the conflict as inevitable and their differences as irreconcilable (Rouhana & Bar-Tal, 1998).

Personal and social identity can also contribute to ethnic conflict. Because group memberships contribute to self-image, if the groups to which you belong are maligned or threatened, then to some extent you are personally maligned and threatened. If you are unable to leave those groups, then you are pressured to defend them in order to enhance your own feelings of self-esteem (Cairns & Darby, 1998). In this way, what starts out as ethnic conflict quickly becomes a highly personal threat.

Finally, widespread *societal beliefs* about the conflict and the parties to the conflict also play a role in prolonged ethnic conflicts. Four especially important societal beliefs are "Our goals are just," "The opponent has no legitimacy," "We can do no wrong," and "We are the victims" (Rouhana & Bar-Tal, 1998). These societal beliefs "provide a common social prism through which society members view the conflict. Once formed, they become incorporated into an ethos and are reflected in

and prejudice (Dovidio & Gaertner, 1999; Hewstone, Islam, & Judd, 1993).

- It is also possible to train ourselves to be more "mindful" of people who differ from us. For example, a group of sixth-graders was taught to be more understanding of the handicapped by having them view slides of handicapped people and to think about their situations, answering such questions as "How might a handicapped person drive a car?" The group showed far less prejudice toward the handicapped after this procedure (Langer, Bashner, & Chanowitz, 1985). Apparently, tolerance can be taught. Some researchers believe that we all learn the stereotypes in our culture, so the primary difference between someone who is prejudiced and someone who is not is the ability to suppress prejudiced beliefs through

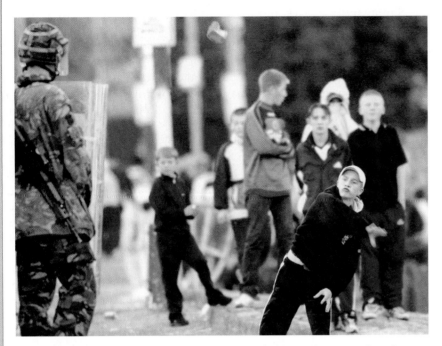

A Protestant youth in Belfast, Northern Ireland throws rocks at British police sent to calm violence between Catholics and Protestants.

the group's language, stereotypes, images, myths, and collective memories" (Rouhana & Bar-Tal, 1998, p. 765). The result is a form of "cognitive freezing" in which people selectively seek out and process information in a way that perpetuates the societal beliefs. This cognitive freezing heightens fear, anger, and hatred—the emotions that are the basis of ethnic violence.

It follows that attempts to build peace cannot address only structural problems. Attempts to redistribute resources more equitably, to reduce oppression and victimization, and to increase social justice are essential, but they will succeed only if attention is also given to important psychological processes.

Concerted efforts must be made to increase tolerance and improve intergroup relations while also developing new, nonviolent means for resolving conflicts (Mays et al., 1998; Smith, 1998). The strategies of recatgegorization, controlled processing, and contact between groups (see p. 507) have helped reduce the level of ethnic conflict in some countries (Smith, 1998). But cognitive changes must also be made: Societal beliefs must be changed, and new beliefs must be developed that are more consistent with conflict resolution and peaceful relationships. In addition, multidisciplinary techniques will need to be developed if programs are to be fully effective in addressing conflicts in different cultures. As one group of experts put it, "It is both risky and ethnocentric to assume that methods developed in Western contexts can be applied directly in different cultures and contexts. Research on different cultural beliefs and practices and their implications for ethnopolitical conflict analysis and prevention is essential if the field of psychology is going to be successful in its contributions" (Mays et al., 1998, p. 739).

controlled processing (Devine, 1989; Devine, Monteith, Zuwerink, & Elliot, 1991).

- Finally, we can reduce prejudice and tensions between groups by bringing them together (Pettigrew, 1998). This was one of the intentions of the famous 1954 U.S. Supreme Court's decision in *Brown v. Board of Education of Topeka, Kansas*, which mandated that public schools become racially integrated. Intergroup contact alone is not enough, however (Taylor & Moghaddam, 1994). It *can* work to undermine prejudicial attitudes if certain conditions are met:

1. *Group members must have equal status.* When blacks and whites were first integrated in the army and in public housing, they had relatively equal status, so prejudice between them was greatly reduced (Petti-

Prejudice and discrimination can be reduced when members of different groups are brought together in a cooperative effort. This diverse group of teenagers is collecting food for needy people.

14.2

grew, 1969). School desegregation has been less than successful because the structure of our school system tends to reward the economic and academic advantages of white children, giving them an edge over black schoolchildren (E. G. Cohen, 1984).

2. *People need to have one-on-one contact with members of the other group.* Simply putting black and white students together in a classroom does not change attitudes. Personal contact such as that which occurs among friends at lunch and after school is more effective.

3. *Members of the two groups must cooperate rather than compete.* Perhaps because it provides the kind of personal contact just mentioned, as well as common ground and equal status, working together to achieve a goal helps to break down prejudice. Integrated sports teams are one example. Cooperative learning techniques have also proved to be effective in overcoming prejudice in schools (D. W. Johnson, Johnson, & Maruyama, 1984; Madden & Slavin, 1983).

4. *Social norms should encourage intergroup contact.* In many cases, school desegregation took place in a highly charged atmosphere. Busloads of black children arrived at their new schools only to face the protests of angry white parents. These conditions did not promote genuine intergroup contact. In situations in which contact is encouraged by social norms, prejudiced attitudes are less likely.

In all of these suggestions, the primary focus is on changing behavior, not on changing attitudes directly. But changing behavior is often a first step toward changing attitudes. This is not to say that attitude change follows automatically. Attitudes can be difficult to budge because they are often so deeply rooted. Completely eliminating deeply held attitudes, then, can be very difficult. That is why social psychologists have concentrated so much effort on techniques that encourage attitude change. The following section examines some of the major findings in the psychological research on attitude change.

Changing Attitudes

What factors encourage someone to change an attitude?

A man watching television on Sunday afternoon ignores scores of beer commercials but listens to a friend who recommends a particular brand. A political speech convinces one woman to change her vote in favor of the candidate but leaves her next-door neighbor determined to vote against him. Why would a personal recommendation have greater persuasive power than an expensively produced television commercial? How can two people with similar initial views derive completely different messages from the same speech? What makes one attempt to change attitudes fail and another succeed? Are some people more resistant to attitude change than others? We begin answering these questions by looking at the process of persuasion.

The Process of Persuasion   To be persuaded, you must first pay attention to the message; then you must comprehend it; finally, you must accept it as convincing. Consider how advertising accomplishes the first step of grabbing your attention. As the competition has stiffened, advertisers have become increasingly creative in seizing your attention. For example, ads that arouse emotions, especially feelings you want to act on, can be memorable and thus persuasive (Engel, Black, & Miniard, 1986). Humor, too, is an effective way to keep you watching or reading an ad that you would otherwise ignore (Scott, Klein, & Bryant, 1990).

Other ads "hook" the audience by involving them in a narrative. A commercial might open with a dramatic scene or situation—for example, two

LAST CALL.

When closing time comes around, don't get behind the wheel.
Get in front of a phone. Call a friend, or call a cab. **MADD**
Mothers Against Drunk Driving

For an ad to affect our behavior, it must first attract our attention.

people seemingly "meant" for each other but not yet making eye contact—and the viewer stays tuned to find out what happens. Some commercials even feature recurring characters and story lines so that each new commercial in the series is really the latest installment in a soap opera. Even ads that are annoying can still be effective in capturing attention, because people tend to notice them when they appear (Aaker & Bruzzone, 1985).

With so many clever strategies focused on seizing and holding your attention, how can you shield yourself from unwanted influences and resist persuasive appeals? One strategy for resisting persuasion is to analyze ads to identify which attention-getting strategies are at work. Make a game of deciphering the advertisers' "code" instead of falling for the ad's appeal. And raise your standards for the kinds of messages that are worthy of your attention and commitment.

The Communication Model   The second and third steps in persuasion—comprehending and then accepting the message—are influenced by both the message itself and the way in which it is presented. The *communication model* of persuasion spotlights four key elements to achieve these goals: the source, the message itself, the medium of communication, and characteristics of the audience. Persuaders manipulate each of these factors in the hopes of changing your attitudes.

The effectiveness of a persuasive message first depends on its *source*, the author or communicator who appeals to the audience to accept the message. Here credibility makes a big difference (McGuire, 1985). For example, we are less likely to change our attitude about the oil industry's antipollution efforts if the president of a major refining company tells us about them than if we hear the same information from an impartial commission appointed to study the situation.

The credibility of the source is most important when we are not inclined to pay attention to the message (Cooper & Croyle, 1984; Petty & Cacioppo, 1981, 1986a). In cases in which we have some interest in the message, the message itself plays the greater role in determining whether we change our attitudes (Petty & Cacioppo, 1986b). The more arguments a message makes in support of a position, the more effective that message is (Calder, Insko, & Yandell, 1974). Novel arguments are more persuasive than rehashes of old standbys that have been heard many times before. Fear sometimes works well, too, especially in convincing people to get tetanus shots (Dabbs & Leventhal, 1966), to drive safely (Leventhal & Niles, 1965), and to take care of their teeth (Evans et al., 1970). But if a message generates too much fear, it will turn off the audience and be ignored (Worchel, Cooper, & Goethals, 1991). In addition, messages designed to persuade are more successful when they present both sides of an argument. A two-sided presentation generally makes the speaker seem less biased and thus enhances his or her credibility. We have greater respect and trust for a communicator who acknowledges that there is another side to a controversial issue.

When it comes to choosing an effective *medium* of persuasion, writing is best suited to making people understand complex arguments, whereas videotaped or live presentations are more effective with an audience that already grasps the gist of an argument (Chaiken & Eagly, 1976). Most effective, however, are face-to-face appeals or the lessons of our own experience. Salespeople who sell products door-to-door rely on the power of personal contact.

The most critical factors in changing attitudes—and the most difficult to control—have to do with the *audience*. Attitudes are most resistant to change if (1) the audience has a strong commitment to its present attitudes, (2) those attitudes are shared by others, and (3) the attitudes were instilled during early childhood by such pivotal groups as the family. The *discrepancy* between the content of the message and the present attitudes of the audience also affects how well the message will be received. Up to a point, the greater the difference between the two, the greater the likelihood of attitude change, as long as the person delivering the message is considered an expert on the topic. If the discrepancy is too great, however, the *audience* may reject the new information altogether, even though it comes from an expert. Finally, certain personal characteristics make some people more susceptible to attitude change than others. People with low self-esteem are more easily influenced, especially when the message is complex and hard to understand. Highly intelligent people tend to resist persuasion because they can think of counterarguments more easily.

In the final analysis, the most effective means of changing attitudes—especially important attitudes, behaviors, or lifestyle choices—may be self-persuasion (Aronson, 1999). In contrast to traditional, direct techniques of persuasion, people are put in situations in which they are motivated to persuade themselves to change their attitudes or behavior. For example, many educators hoped that school integration—by itself—would reduce racial prejudices. But often the reverse proved true: although they attended the same schools and classes, black and white children tended to "self-segregate." When children were assigned to small, culturally diverse study groups, in which they were forced to cooperate, attitudes changed—albeit slowly. Insults and put-downs, often ethnically based, decreased. Having learned both to teach and to listen to "others," students emerged from the experience with fewer group stereotypes and greater appreciation of individual differences. And this outcome, in turn, made them less likely to stereotype others. In a nutshell, working with diverse individuals who did not fit preconceived notions made it difficult to maintain prejudice because of cognitive dissonance.

Cognitive dissonance
Perceived inconsistency between two cognitions.

Cognitive Dissonance Theory   One of the more fascinating approaches to understanding the process of attitude change is the theory of **cognitive**

dissonance, developed by Leon Festinger (1957). Cognitive dissonance exists whenever a person has two contradictory cognitions, or beliefs, at the same time. "I am a considerate and loyal friend" is one cognition; so is "Yesterday I repeated some juicy gossip I heard about my friend Chris." These two cognitions are dissonant—each one implies the opposite of the other. According to Festinger, cognitive dissonance creates unpleasant psychological tension, which motivates us to try to resolve the dissonance in some way.

Sometimes changing one's attitude is the easiest way to reduce the discomfort of dissonance. I cannot easily change the fact that I have repeated gossip about a friend; therefore, it is easier to change my attitude toward my friend. If I conclude that Chris is not really a friend but simply an acquaintance, then my new attitude now fits my behavior—spreading gossip about someone who is *not* a friend does not contradict the fact that I am loyal and considerate to those who *are* my friends.

Discrepant behavior that contradicts an attitude does not necessarily bring about attitude change, however, because there are other ways a person can reduce cognitive dissonance. One alternative is to *increase the number of consonant elements*—that is, the thoughts that are consistent with one another. For example, I might recall the many times I defended Chris when others were critical of him. Now my repeating a little bit of gossip seems less at odds with my attitude toward Chris as a friend. Another option is to reduce the importance of one or both dissonant cognitions. For instance, I could tell myself, "The person I repeated the gossip to was Terry, who doesn't really know Chris very well. Terry doesn't care and won't repeat it. It was no big deal, and Chris shouldn't be upset about it." By reducing the significance of my disloyal action, I reduce the dissonance that I experience and so make it less necessary to change my attitude toward Chris.

But why would someone engage in behavior that goes against an attitude in the first place? One answer is that cognitive dissonance is a natural part of everyday life. Simply choosing between two or more desirable alternatives leads inevitably to dissonance. Suppose you are in the market for a computer but can't decide between an IBM and a Macintosh. If you choose one, all of its bad features and all the good aspects of the other contribute to dissonance. After you have bought one of the computers, you can reduce the dissonance by changing your attitude: You might decide that the other keyboard wasn't "quite right" and that some of the "bad" features of the computer you bought aren't so bad after all.

You may also engage in behavior at odds with an attitude because you are enticed to do so. Perhaps someone offers you a small bribe or reward: "I will pay you 25 cents just to try my product." Curiously, the larger the reward, the smaller the change in attitude that is likely to result. When rewards are large, dissonance is at a minimum, and attitude change is small, if it happens at all. Apparently, when people are convinced that there is a good reason to do something that goes against their beliefs ("I'll try almost anything in exchange for a large cash incentive"), they experience little dissonance, and their attitudes are not likely to shift, even though their behavior may change for a time. If the reward is small, however—just barely enough to induce behavior that conflicts with one's attitude—dissonance will be great, maximizing the chances of attitude change: "I only got 25 cents to try this product, so it couldn't have been the money that attracted me. I must really like this product after all." The trick is to induce the behavior that goes against an attitude while leaving people feeling personally responsible for the dissonant act. In that way, they are more likely to change their attitudes than if they feel they were blatantly induced to act in a way that contradicted their attitudes (J. Cooper, 1971; Kelman, 1974).

<u>INTERACTIVE LECTURE</u>   **14.2**

WEB QUIZ **14.2** ✓

CHECK YOUR UNDERSTANDING

1. A(n) _____ is a fairly stable organization of beliefs, feelings, and behavioral tendencies directed toward some object, such as a person or group.

2. The best way to predict behavior is to measure attitudes. Is this statement true (T) or false (F)?

3. Prejudice is to _____ as discrimination is to _____.
   a. an unfavorable attitude; an unfair act
   b. tolerance; oppression
   c. an unfair act; an unfavorable attitude
   d. oppression; tolerance

4. Which of the following can be an effective way to reduce prejudice (there can be more than one correct answer)?
   a. equal status contact
   b. one-on-one contact
   c. cooperative group projects
   d. social norms that encourage contact
   e. all of the above

5. The message that most likely will result in a change in attitude is one with
   a. high fear from a highly credible source.
   b. high fear from a moderately credible source.
   c. moderate fear from a highly credible source.
   d. moderate fear from a moderately credible source.

6. When trying to change someone's opinion, it is generally better to
   a. present only your side of an argument.
   b. present only criticisms of the opposing viewpoint.
   c. present both sides of an argument.

7. _____ _____ exists whenever a person has two contradictory beliefs at the same time. The cognitive conflict is often resolved through attitude change.

Answers: 1. attitude. 2. F. 3. a. 4. e. 5. c. 6. c. 7. Cognitive dissonance.

Social Influence

What are some areas in which the power of social influence is highly apparent?

In a sense, all social psychology is the study of **social influence**—of how people's thoughts, feelings, and actions are affected by the behavior and characteristics of others. In some areas that social psychologists study, however, the power of social influence is even more apparent than usual. Among these are the study of cultural influences and of conformity, compliance, and obedience.

Cultural Influences

How does your culture influence how you dress or what you eat?

Culture exerts an enormous influence on our attitudes and behavior, and culture is itself a creation of people. As such, culture is a major form of social influence. Consider for a moment the many aspects of day-to-day living that are derived from culture:

Social influence
The process by which others individually or collectively affect one's perceptions, attitudes, and actions.

- *Your culture dictates how you dress.* A Saudi woman covers her face before venturing outside her home; a North American woman freely displays her face, arms, and legs; and women in some other societies go about completely naked (Myers, 1992).
- *Culture specifies what you eat—and what you do not eat.* Americans do not eat dog meat, the Chinese eat no cheese, and the Hindus refuse to eat beef. Culture further guides *how* you eat: with a fork, chopsticks, or your bare hands.
- *People from different cultures seek different amounts of personal space.* Latin Americans, French people, and Arabs get closer to one another in most face-to-face interactions than do Americans, English people, or Swedes (Aiello, 1987; E. T. Hall, 1966).

To some extent, culture influences us through formal instruction. For example, your parents might have reminded you from time to time that certain actions are considered "normal" or the "right way" to behave. But more often we learn cultural lessons through modeling and imitation, with reinforcement also involved. We are rewarded (reinforced) for doing as our companions and fellow citizens do in most situations—for going along with the crowd. This social learning process is one of the chief mechanisms by which a culture transmits its central lessons and values. In the course of comparing and adapting our own behavior to that of others, we learn the norms of our culture. A **norm** is a culturally shared idea or expectation about how to behave. As in the preceding examples, norms are often steeped in tradition and strengthened by habit.

Cultures seem strange to us if their norms are very different from our own. It is tempting to conclude that *different* means "wrong," simply because unfamiliar patterns of behavior can make us feel uncomfortable. To transcend our differences and get along better with people from other cultures, we must find ways to overcome such discomfort. One technique for understanding other cultures is the *cultural assimilator,* a strategy for perceiving the norms and values of another group (Baron, Graziano & Stangor, 1991; Brislin, Cushner, Cherries, & Yong, 1986). This technique teaches by example, asking students to explain why a member of another culture has behaved in a particular way. For example, why do the members of a Japanese grade school class silently follow their teacher single file through a park on a lovely spring day? Are they afraid of being punished for disorderly conduct if they do otherwise? Are they naturally placid and compliant? Once you understand that Japanese children are raised to value the needs and feelings of others over their own selfish concerns, their orderly, obedient behavior seems much less perplexing. Cultural assimilators encourage us to remain open-minded about others' norms and values by challenging such cultural truisms as "Our way is the right way."

Conformity

What increases the likelihood that someone will conform?

Accepting the norms of one's culture should not be confused with conformity. For instance, millions of Americans drink coffee in the morning, but they do not do so because they are conforming. They drink coffee because through cultural experience, they have learned to like and desire it. **Conformity,** in contrast, implies a conflict between an individual and a group—a conflict that is resolved when the individual yields her or his own preferences or beliefs to the norms or expectations of the larger group.

Since the early 1950s, when Solomon Asch conducted the first systematic study of the subject, conformity has been a major topic

Norm
A shared idea or expectation about how to behave.

Conformity
Voluntarily yielding to social norms, even at the expense of one's preferences.

Why do Japanese schoolchildren behave in such an orderly way? How does your answer compare with the discussion of cultural influences?

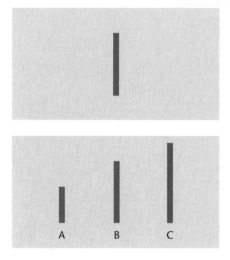

FIGURE 14-2

Asch's experiment on conformity. In Asch's experiment on conformity, participants were shown a comparison card like the top one and asked to indicate which of the three lines on the bottom card was the most similar. Participants frequently chose the wrong line in order to conform to the group choice.

of research in social psychology. Asch demonstrated in a series of experiments that under some circumstances, people will conform to group pressures even if this action forces them to deny obvious physical evidence. His studies ostensibly tested visual judgment by asking people to choose from a card with several lines of differing lengths the line most similar to the line on a comparison card (see **Figure 14–2**). The lines were deliberately drawn so that the comparison was obvious and the correct choice was clear. All but one of the participants were confederates of the experimenter. On certain trials these confederates deliberately gave the same wrong answer. This procedure put the lone dissenter on the spot: Should he conform to what he knew to be a wrong decision and agree with the group, thereby denying the evidence of his own eyes, or should he disagree with the group, thereby risking the social consequences of nonconformity?

Overall, participants conformed on about 35 percent of the trials. There were large individual differences, however, and in subsequent research, experimenters discovered that two sets of factors influence the likelihood that a person will conform: characteristics of the situation and characteristics of the person.

The *size* of the group is one situational factor that has been studied extensively. Asch (1951) found that the likelihood of conformity increased with group size until four confederates were present. After that point, the number of others made no difference to the frequency of conformity.

Another important situational factor is the degree of *unanimity* in the group. If just one confederate broke the perfect agreement of the majority by giving the correct answer, conformity among participants in the Asch experiments fell from an average of 35 percent to about 25 percent (Asch, 1956). Apparently, having just one "ally" eases the pressure to conform. The ally does not even have to share the person's viewpoint—just breaking the unanimity of the majority is enough to reduce conformity (Allen & Levine, 1971).

The *nature of the task* is still another situational variable that affects conformity. For instance, conformity has been shown to vary with the difficulty and ambiguity of a task. When the task is difficult or poorly defined, conformity tends to be higher (Blake, Helson, & Mouton, 1956). In an ambiguous situation, people are less sure of their own opinion and more willing to conform to the majority view.

Personal characteristics also influence conforming behavior. The more a person is attracted to the group, expects to interact with its members in the future, holds a position of relatively low status, and does not feel completely accepted by the group, the more that person tends to conform. The fear of rejection apparently motivates conformity when a person scores high on one or more of these factors.

Sometimes we can be misled by what we think are group norms and conform to what is not, in fact, a norm. Perception, more than reality, for example, could be influencing the dangerous practice of "binge drinking," discussed in the *Understanding Ourselves* box.

Conformity across Cultures   A Chinese proverb states that "if one finger is sore, the whole hand will hurt." In a collectivist culture such as China, community and harmony are very important. Although members of all societies show a tendency to conform, you might suspect that members of collectivist cultures conform more frequently to the will of a group than do members of noncollectivist cultures. Psychologists who have studied this question have used tests similar to those that Asch used in his experiments. They have found that levels of conformity in collectivist cultures are in fact frequently higher than those found by Asch. In col-

UNDERSTANDING OURSELVES

Beliefs and Binge Drinking

Her friends believe that Leslie Baltz, a senior honors student at the University of Virginia, was following a school tradition of the "fourth-year fifth"—drinking a fifth of liquor to celebrate the last home football game. When friends found her unconscious that evening, they rushed her to the hospital. But it was too late. She died the next day, another victim of alcohol poisoning through binge drinking (Winerip, 1998).

Binge drinking, defined as taking five or more alcoholic drinks in a row, has been identified as the number one health hazard for college students (Wechsler, Fulop, Padilla, Lee, & Patrick, 1997). Not only do binge drinkers risk their lives, but also their drinking has been linked to higher rates of drunk driving, unplanned and unsafe sexual activity, physical and sexual assault, unintentional in-

juries, interpersonal problems, physical or cognitive impairment, and poor academic performance (Wechsler, Davenport, Dowdall, Moeykens, & Castillo, 1994).

> When students realize that binge drinking is less common than they think, they are considerably less likely to try it themselves.

So alarming are the consequences of alcohol abuse that the creation of alcohol task forces and education programs has become a growth industry on college campuses. Yet attempts to reduce binge drinking by teaching social skills, increasing awareness of support

systems, improving coping skills, and raising self-esteem have met with relatively little success. What more can be done?

It may be as simple as making students aware that most of their peers do *not* indulge in binge drinking and relying on their tendency to conform to social norms. However serious the problem may be, binge drinking is not as prevalent as many students believe it to be. In some surveys, students estimate that as many as 70 percent of their classmates binge drink (Gose, 1997). Yet a national survey indicates that the actual figure may be closer to 38 percent (Winerip, 1998). When students realize that binge drinking is less common than they think, they are considerably less likely to try it themselves (Donaldson et al., 1994; Gose, 1997; Haines & Spear, 1996; Hansen, 1993; Hansen & Graham, 1991).

lectivist societies as diverse as Fiji, Zaire, Hong Kong, Lebanon, Zimbabwe, Kuwait, Japan, and Brazil, conformity rates ranged from 25 percent to 51 percent (P. B. Smith & Bond, 1994). The rate is typically higher in farming societies (where members are more dependent on one another for long-term group survival) than in hunting and gathering societies (where people must exercise a good deal of independence to survive) (Berry, 1967).

So what conclusions can we draw about conformity? The fact that rates of conformity in the Asch situation are relatively high across a variety of cultures suggests that a universal tendency to conform may exist. But conformity is often greater in collectivist societies, implying that culture can heighten (or lessen) any tendency toward it. There are also situational factors that can make conformity more or less likely, and these, too, can vary depending on a person's culture. Japanese people, for example, often deliberately oppose a majority opinion (even a correct one) when the other members of a group are strangers—something they are much less likely to do when the group is made up of friends (Frager, 1970; Williams & Sogon, 1984). As psychologists learn more about the differences between cultures, they will better understand what is universal about human behavior and what is culturally determined.

 14.3

Compliance

How could a salesperson increase a customer's compliance in buying a product?

Conformity is a response to pressure exerted by norms that are generally left unstated. In contrast, **compliance** is a change of behavior in response to an explicitly stated request. One technique for inducing compliance is the so-called *foot-in-the-door effect*. Every salesperson knows that the moment a prospect allows the sales pitch to begin, the chances of making a sale improve greatly. The same effect operates in other areas of life: Once people have granted a small request, they are more likely to comply with a larger one.

In the most famous study of this phenomenon, Freedman and Fraser (1966) approached certain residents of Palo Alto, California, posing as members of a committee for safe driving. They asked residents to place a large, ugly sign reading "Drive Carefully" in their front yards. Only 17 percent agreed to do so. Then other residents were asked to sign a petition calling for more safe-driving laws. When these same people were later asked to place the ugly "Drive Carefully" sign in their yards, an amazing 55 percent agreed. Compliance with the first small request more than tripled the rate of compliance with the larger request.

Why does the foot-in-the-door technique work so well? One possible explanation is that agreeing to the token act (signing the petition) realigns the person's self-perception to that of someone who more strongly favors the cause. When presented with the larger request, the person then feels obligated to comply (Cialdini & Trost, 1998).

Another strategy commonly used by salespeople is the lowball procedure (Cialdini & Trost, 1998). The first step is to induce a person to agree to do something. The second step is to raise the cost of compliance. Among new-car dealers, lowballing works like this: The dealer persuades the customer to buy a new car by reducing the price well below that offered by competitors. Once the customer has agreed to buy the car, however, the terms of the sale shift abruptly (for example, the trade-in value promised by the used-car manager is cut) so that in the end the car is more costly than it would be at other dealerships. Despite the added costs, many customers follow through on their commitment to buy. Although the original inducement was the low price (the "lowball" that the salesperson originally pitched), once committed, the buyer remains committed to the now pricier car.

Under certain circumstances, a person who has refused to comply with one request may be more likely to comply with a second. For example, if saying no to the first request made you feel guilty, you may say yes to something else. This phenomenon has been dubbed the *door-in-the-face effect* (Cialdini, 1995). In one study, researchers approached students and asked them to make an unreasonably large commitment: Would they counsel delinquent youths at a detention center for two years? Nearly everyone declined, thus effectively "slamming the door" in the researcher's face. But when later asked to make a much smaller commitment—supervising children during a trip to the zoo—many of the same students quickly agreed. The door-in-the-face effect may work because people interpret the smaller request as a concession and feel pressured to comply.

Obedience

How does the "power of the situation" affect obedience?

Compliance is agreement to change behavior in response to a request. **Obedience** is compliance with a command. Like compliance, it is a response to an explicit message; in this case, however, the message is a direct order, generally from a person in authority, such as a police officer, princi-

Compliance
Change of behavior in response to an explicit request from another person or group.

Obedience
Change of behavior in response to a command from another person, typically an authority figure.

Nazi concentration camps are a shocking example of the extremes to which people will go to obey orders. How do you explain the behaviors of the people who ran these camps?

pal, or parent, who can back up the command with some sort of force if necessary. Obedience embodies social influence in its most direct and powerful form.

Several studies by Stanley Milgram, mentioned in Chapter 1, The Science of Psychology, showed how far many people will go to obey someone in authority (Milgram, 1963). People who agreed to participate in what they believed was a learning experiment administered what they thought were severe electrical shocks to the "learners." Milgram's research has been replicated in different cultures and with both male and female participants (Smith & Bond, 1999). What factors influence the degree to which people will do what they are told? Studies in which people were asked to put a dime in a parking meter by people wearing uniforms show that one important factor is the amount of power vested in the person giving the orders. People obeyed a guard whose uniform looked like that of a police officer more often than they obeyed a man dressed either as a milkman or as a civilian. Another factor is surveillance. If we are ordered to do something and then left alone, we are less likely to obey than if we are being watched, especially if the act seems unethical to us. Milgram, for instance, found that his "teachers" were less willing to give severe shocks when the experimenter was out of the room.

Milgram's experiments revealed other factors that influence a person's willingness to follow orders. When the victim was in the same room as the "teacher," obedience dropped sharply. When another "teacher" was present, who refused to give shocks, obedience also dropped. But when responsibility for an act was shared, so that the person was only one of many doing it, the degree of obedience was much greater.

Why do people willingly obey an authority figure, even if doing so means violating their own principles? Milgram (1974) suggested that people come to see themselves as the agents of *another* person's wishes and therefore as not responsible for the obedient actions or their consequences. Once this shift in self-perception has occurred, obedience follows, because in their own minds, they have relinquished control of their actions.

An alternative explanation is that perhaps obedient participants do not succumb to situational forces but rather fail to *perceive* the situation correctly (Nissani, 1990). Thus in Milgram's study, the participants began with the belief that the experiment would be safe and that the experimenter would be trustworthy. The real emotional struggle for the obedient participants, then, may not have been in deciding whether to obey malevolent orders but in recognizing that a trusted authority figure proved to be treacherous.

INTERACTIVE LECTURE **14.3**

WEB QUIZ **14.3** ✓

CHECK YOUR UNDERSTANDING

1. Match the following terms with the appropriate definition.

____ social influence

____ compliance

____ obedience

____ conformity

   a. voluntarily yielding to social norms, even at the expense of one's own preferences

   b. a change of behavior in response to a command from another person

   c. a change of behavior in response to an explicit request from another person or from a group

   d. any actions performed by one or more persons to change the attitudes, behavior, or feelings of others

2. A ____ is a shared idea or expectation about how to behave.

3. Solomon Asch found that the likelihood of a person's conforming [increased/decreased] as the group size expanded to four people.

4. Which of the following are factors that influence the likelihood that a person will conform?

   a. the degree of unanimity in the group

   b. the difficulty or ambiguity of the task that the group faces

   c. strong attachment to the group

   d. the group's gender makeup

5. Research shows that compliance is often higher in collectivist cultures than in noncollectivist ones. Is this statement true (T) or false (F)?

6. Once people have granted a small request, they are more likely to comply with a larger one. This is called the ____-____-____-____ effect.

7. Many people are willing to obey an authority figure, even if doing so means violating their own principles. Is this statement true (T) or false (F)?

Answers: 1. social influence: d; compliance: c; obedience: b; conformity: a. **2.** norm. **3.** increased. **4.** a, b, and c. **5.** T. **6.** foot-in-the-door. **7.** T.

Social Action

Do we behave differently when other people are present?

The various kinds of social influence that we have just discussed may take place even when no one else is physically present. We refrain from playing our stereo at full volume when our neighbors are sleeping, comply with jury notices that we received in the mail, and obey traffic signals even when no one is on the road to enforce them. We now turn to processes that *do* depend on the presence of others. Specifically, we examine processes that occur when people interact one on one and in groups. One of these social actions is called *deindividuation*.

Deindividuation

What negative outcomes can result from deindividuation?

We have seen several cases of social influence in which people act differently in the presence of others from the way they would if they were alone. The most striking and frightening instance of this phenomenon is *mob behavior*. Some well-known violent examples of mob behavior are the beatings and lynchings of African Americans, the looting that sometimes accompanies urban rioting, and the wanton destruction of property that mars otherwise peaceful protests and demonstrations. One reason for such behavior is that people lose their personal sense of responsibility in a group, especially in a group subjected to intense pressures and anxiety. This process is called **deindividuation,** because people respond not as individuals but as anonymous parts of a larger group. In general the more anonymous that people feel in a group, the less responsible that they feel as individuals.

But deindividuation only partly explains mob behavior. Another contributing factor is that, in a group, one dominant and persuasive person can convince people to act through a *snowball effect*: If the persuader convinces just a few people, those few will convince others, who will convince still others, and the group becomes an unthinking mob. Moreover, large groups provide *protection*. Anonymity makes it difficult to press charges. If two, or even ten, people start smashing windows, they will probably be arrested. If a thousand people do so, very few of them will be caught or punished.

Helping Behavior

What factors make us more inclined to help a person in need?

Research on deindividuation seems to support the unfortunate—and inaccurate—notion that when people get together, they become more destructive and irresponsible than they would be individually. But human society depends on people's willingness to work together and help one another. In fact, instances of cooperation and mutual assistance are just as abundant as examples of human conflict and hostility. One need only recall the behavior of people all over the country in the aftermath of the September 11, 2001, terrorist attacks on the World Trade Center and the Pentagon to find hundreds of examples of people working together and helping each other (Ballie, 2001). If, as we saw in Chapter 8, Motivation and Emotion, our willingness to harm others is influenced by social forces, so is our willingness to help others.

What are some of the social forces that can promote helping behavior? One is perceived self-interest. We offer our boss a ride home from the office because we know that our next promotion depends on how much she likes us. We volunteer to feed a neighbor's cat while he is away because we want him to do the same for us. But when helpful actions are not linked to such personal gain, they are considered **altruistic behavior.** A person who acts in an altruistic way does not expect any recognition or reward in return, except perhaps the good feeling that comes from helping someone in need. Many people direct altruistic acts, including many charitable contributions, at strangers and make them anonymously (M. L. Hoffman, 1977). (See *Understanding the World Around Us* to gain additional insight into the factors that influenced Gentiles to help Jewish victims of the Holocaust.)

Under what conditions is helping behavior most likely to occur? Like other things that social psychologists study, helping is influenced by two sets of factors: those in the situation and those in the individual.

The most important situational variable is the *presence of other people*. In a phenomenon called the **bystander effect,** the likelihood that a person will help someone else in trouble *decreases* as the number of bystanders present increases (Clarkson, 1996). In one experiment, people filling out a question-

Deindividuation
A loss of personal sense of responsibility in a group.

Altruistic behavior
Helping behavior that is not linked to personal gain.

Bystander effect
The tendency for an individual's helpfulness in an emergency to decrease as the number of passive bystanders increases.

After the attacks on the World Trade Center and the Pentagon on September 11, 2001, strangers reached out to help each other with physical and financial support.

naire heard a taped "emergency" in the next room, complete with a crash and screams. Of those who were alone, 70 percent offered help to the unseen female victim, but of those who waited with a companion—a stranger who did nothing to help—only 7 percent offered help (Latané & Rodin, 1969).

Another key aspect of the situation is its *ambiguity*. Any factors that make it harder for others to recognize a genuine emergency reduce the probability of altruistic actions (Clark & Word, 1974). The *personal characteristics* of bystanders also affect helping behavior. Not all bystanders are equally likely to help a stranger. Increasing the amount of personal responsibility that one person feels for another boosts the likelihood that help will be extended (Moriarty, 1975). The amount of *empathy* that we feel toward another person affects our willingness to help, too (Krebs, 1975). *Mood* also makes a difference: A person in a good mood is more likely to help another in need than is someone who is in a neutral or bad mood (Salovey, Mayer, & Rosenhan, 1991; Isen & Levin, 1972). In addition, helping behavior is increased when people don't *fear embarrassment* by offering assistance that isn't really needed (McGovern, 1976). Finally, when others are watching, people who score high on the need for approval are more likely to help than are low scorers (Satow, 1975).

Helping Behavior across Cultures People often assume that there is a "helping personality" or a set of traits that determines who is helpful and who is not. This is unlikely. Several conditions, both individual and situational, combine to determine when help will be offered. Similarly, it's doubtful that there is such a thing as a "helpful culture"—that is, a society, nation, or group whose members are invariably "more helpful" than those of other groups. Psychologists have instead focused on the cultural factors that make helping more or less likely to take place.

Individualism/collectivism is an important dimension in this area: It seems plausible that members of individualist cultures feel less obligated to help other people than do members of collectivist cultures. A study using Indian and American participants investigated this possibility (Miller, Bersoff, & Harwood, 1990). Participants were presented with helping scenarios involving either a stranger, a friend, or a close relative whose need was either minor, moderate, or extreme. There were no cultural differences in cases of extreme need; members of both cultures reported being equally willing to help. But the two groups differed in cases of minor needs. Almost three times as many Indians (from a collectivist culture) as Americans (from an individualist culture) felt obligated to help in a scenario involving

UNDERSTANDING The World Around Us

Altruism and the Holocaust

This chapter began with the story of a 16-year-old Catholic girl, Stefania Podgórska, and others, who hid Jewish children from the Nazis throughout Nazi-occupied Europe. Only a few thousand non-Jews risked their lives to rescue Jews from persecution, deportation, and death. Why did they do what so many millions of others failed to do? What qualities enabled them to behave so altruistically and bravely?

In 1981, several researchers who set out to find answers to questions like these combined their efforts two years later in the Altruistic Personality Project. By 1985, the project had published findings based on interviews with 25 rescuers and 50 survivors, as well as historical documents about the activities of others (Fogelman & Wiener, 1985). The people with whom the researchers spoke came from several countries and differed widely in education and vocation. The rescuers did, however, share some characteristics. For one thing, most had an uncommon capacity for perseverance and a strong belief in their own competence to risk and survive danger. For another, they preferred not to see themselves as heroes but instead considered their behavior to be natural.

Although no single personality characteristic emerged, researchers could identify some common threads. For example, rescuers tended to fall into one of two

> Most had . . . a strong belief in their own competence to risk and survive danger.

groups: those who were motivated by deeply rooted moral values and felt ethically bound to rescue victims, and those who were attached personally to the victims and sometimes identified with them emotionally. These findings support the contention of social psychologist Carol Gilligan (1982) that there are fundamentally two forms of moral reasoning: one based on a sense of justice and the other based on a sense of responsibility and caring.

Morally motivated rescuers often harbored intense anti-Nazi attitudes. For some, religious belief played a paramount role in their lives. These rescuers also tended to help victims regardless of whether they liked or disliked them. Many of them belonged to families with traditions of concern for others outside the family, and many stated that their behavior was strongly guided by their parents' values. Stefania cited her parents' belief in religious tolerance.

In contrast, emotionally motivated rescuers frequently had strong personal attachments to the people whom they helped—neighbors, for instance. Some helped people whom they scarcely knew but with whom they identified. In certain cases, the empathy sprang from the rescuer's belief that he or she was also vulnerable to persecution. "It is easy to understand what the Jews felt," explained one Ukrainian rescuer, "because Jews and the Ukrainians were in similar positions everywhere" (Fogelman & Wiener, 1985, p. 63).

---

a close friend or a stranger asking for minor assistance. Even within collectivist cultures, however, the prediction of when help will be offered can be problematic (Triandis, 1994). Some members of collectivist societies are reluctant to offer help to anyone outside their in-group. They are therefore less likely to help strangers. Other cultures treat a stranger as a member of their group until that person's exact status can be determined.

Groups and Decision Making

How is making a decision in a group different from making a decision on your own?

There is a tendency in our society to turn important decisions over to groups. In the business world key decisions are often made around a conference table rather than behind one person's desk. In politics, major policy decisions are seldom vested in just one person. Groups of advisers, cabinet officers, committee members, or aides meet to deliberate and forge a course of action. In the courts, a defendant may request a trial by jury, and for some serious crimes, jury trial is required by law. The nine-member U.S. Supreme Court renders group decisions on legal issues affecting the entire nation.

Many people trust these group decisions more than decisions made by individuals. And yet the dynamics of social interaction within groups sometimes conspire to make group decisions *less* sound than those made by someone acting alone. Social psychologists are intrigued by how this outcome happens.

Polarization in Group Decision Making   People often assume that an individual acting alone is more likely to take risks than a group considering the same issue. This assumption remained unchallenged until the early 1960s. At that time, James Stoner (1961) designed an experiment to test the idea. He asked participants individually to counsel imaginary people who had to choose between a risky but potentially rewarding course of action and a conservative but less rewarding alternative. Next, the participants met in small groups to discuss each decision until they reached unanimous agreement. Surprisingly, the groups consistently recommended a riskier course of action than the people working alone did. This phenomenon is known as the **risky shift.**

The risky shift is simply one aspect of a more general group phenomenon called **polarization**—the tendency for people to become more extreme in their attitudes as a result of group discussion. Polarization begins when group members discover during discussion that they share views to a greater degree than they realized. Then, in an effort to be seen in a positive light by the others, at least some group members become strong advocates for what is shaping up to be the dominant sentiment in the group. Arguments leaning toward one extreme or the other not only reassure people that their initial attitudes are correct but also intensify those attitudes so that the group as a whole becomes more extreme in its position. So, if you want a group decision to be made in a cautious, conservative direction, you should make sure that the members of the group hold cautious and conservative views in the first place. Otherwise, the group decision may polarize in the opposite direction.

The Effectiveness of Groups   The adage "Two heads are better than one" reflects the common assumption that members of a group will pool their abilities and arrive at a better decision than will individuals working alone. In fact, groups are more effective than individuals only under certain circumstances. For one thing, their success depends on the task that they are faced with. If the requirements of the task match the skills of the group members, the group is likely to be more effective than any single individual.

Even if task and personnel are perfectly matched, however, the ways in which group members *interact* may reduce the group's efficiency. For example, high-status individuals tend to exert more influence in groups, so if they do not possess the best problem-solving skills, group decisions may suffer (Torrance, 1954). Another factor affecting group interaction and effectiveness is group size. The larger the group, the more likely it is to include someone who has the skills needed to solve a difficult problem. On the other hand, it is much harder to coordinate the activities of a large group. In addition, large groups may be more likely to encourage *social loafing*, the tendency of group members to exert less effort on the assumption that others in the group will do the work. Finally, the quality of group decision making also depends on the *cohesiveness* of a group. When the people in a group like one another and feel committed to the goals of the group, cohesiveness is high. Under these conditions, members may work hard for the group, spurred on by high morale. But cohesiveness can undermine the quality of group decision mak-

Risky shift
Greater willingness of a group than an individual to take substantial risks.

Polarization
Shift in attitudes by members of a group toward more extreme positions than the ones held before group discussion.

ing. If the group succumbs to *groupthink*, according to Irving Janis (1982), strong pressure to conform prevents its members from criticizing the emerging group consensus. In such a group, amiability and morale supersede judgment. Members with doubts may hesitate to express them. The result may be disastrous decisions—such as the Bay of Pigs invasion, the Watergate cover-up, or the go-ahead for the *Challenger* space flight (Kruglanski, 1986).

Group Leadership   Every group has a leader, but how do group leaders come to the fore? For many years, the predominant answer was the **great person theory,** which states that leaders are extraordinary people who assume positions of influence and then shape events around them. In this view, people like George Washington, Winston Churchill, and Nelson Mandela were "born leaders"—who would have led any nation at any time in history.

Most historians and psychologists now regard this theory as naive, because it ignores social and economic factors. An alternative theory holds that leadership emerges when the right person is in the right place at the right time. For instance, in the later 1950s and early 1960s, Dr. Martin Luther King, Jr., rose to lead the black civil rights movement. Dr. King was clearly a "great person"—intelligent, dynamic, eloquent, and highly motivated. Yet had the times not been right (for instance, had he lived thirty years earlier) it is doubtful that he would have been as successful as he was.

And there is probably even more to becoming a leader than either the great person theory or the right-place-at-the-right-time perspective implies. According to what is called the *transactional view*, a sizable number of factors interact to determine who emerges as a leader. The leader's traits, certain aspects of the situation in which the group finds itself, and the response of the group and the leader to each other are all important considerations.

These same considerations are also important in determining how effective a leader turns out to be. Personal characteristics, for example, such as leadership style, are significant only in relation to other aspects of the group and its situation. This point is stressed in Fred Fiedler's *contingency model* of leader effectiveness. According to Fiedler (1978, 1993), some leaders are *task-oriented*—that is, concerned mainly with getting the group's goals accomplished—whereas others are *relationship-oriented*—concerned mainly with fostering group cohesiveness and harmony. Which style is more effective depends on the particular situation, such as the clarity of the tasks to be accomplished, the quality of leader-member relations, and the amount of power that the leader exercises. When the situation is very favorable for the leader (clear tasks, good relations with members, much power held), a task-oriented style is usually more effective. This is also true when conditions are very *un*favorable (when tasks are vague, relations with members are poor, and little power is exercised). It is when conditions for the leader are somewhere between these two extremes that a relationship-oriented leader becomes most successful, according to Fiedler's research. In Fiedler's view there is no such thing as an ideal leader for all situations. "It is simply not meaningful to speak of an effective or ineffective leader," he writes. "We can only speak of a leader who tends to be effective in one situation and ineffective in another" (Fiedler, 1967, p. 261).

Leadership across Cultures   The distinction between task-oriented and relationship-oriented leaders seems to be a main operating principle in most work groups in the United States. Someone who is explicitly appointed manager or crew chief is charged with making sure that the job gets done, whereas someone else usually emerges informally to act as the relationship-oriented specialist who tells jokes, remembers everyone's birthday, smooths disputes, and generally maintains morale (Bales, 1951). In the Western world, this division of leadership often operates in informal social groups as well. Yet it is not

One theory of leadership holds that the particularly effective leader is the right person in the right place at the right time. For the American civil rights movement, Martin Luther King, Jr., was such a leader.

Great person theory
The theory that leadership is a result of personal qualities and traits that qualify one to lead others.

the only approach to leadership. Consider a collectivist culture that values cooperation and interdependence among group members. In such an environment, it is unlikely that individuals would emerge to serve specific functions within a group. Although one member may be named "the manager," there is less need for individuals to have clearly defined roles as "this type of leader" or "that type of leader." All members see themselves as working together to accomplish the group's goals.

Leadership in American businesses is currently being transformed through the introduction of a management style that has proved successful in Japan and other Eastern collectivist cultures (J. W. Dean & Evans, 1994; McFarland, Senn, & Childress, 1993). This approach emphasizes decision-making input from all group members, small work teams that promote close cooperation, and a style of leadership in which managers receive much the same treatment as any other employee. In the West, it is not uncommon for executives to have their own parking spaces, dining facilities, fitness and social clubs, as well as separate offices and independent schedules. Most Japanese executives consider this privileged style of management very strange. In many Eastern cultures, managers and executives share the same facilities as their workers, hunt for parking spaces like everyone else, and eat and work side by side with their employees. It is interesting that the Japanese model has effectively combined the two leadership approaches—task-oriented and relationship-oriented—into a single overall style. By being a part of the group, the leader can simultaneously work toward and direct the group's goals, while also contributing to the group's morale and social climate. Combining these roles is an effective strategy for Japanese leaders in such diverse workplaces as banks, bus companies, shipyards, coal mines, and government offices (Misumi, 1985).

Organizational Behavior

Can psychology help to increase worker output and satisfaction?

The places where we work and the various organizations to which we belong shape much of our behavior. **Industrial organizational (I/O) psychology** spotlights the influence on human interaction of large, complex organizational settings, with special emphasis on behavior in the workplace.

Productivity   I/O psychologists focus on practical problems, such as how to reduce employee turnover, improve worker morale, and increase productivity. One of the first studies of the relationship between productivity and working conditions was conducted in the late 1920s by Elton Mayo and his colleagues, who gradually increased the lighting in the Western Electric Hawthorne plant in Cicero, Illinois. The researchers were testing the hypothesis that better lighting would boost worker output. But their results showed something else entirely: Productivity increased with better lighting, too much lighting, and too little lighting. In what has become known as the **Hawthorne effect,** the workers' efficiency rose no matter what was done to their conditions, simply because of the attention that the researchers were giving to them.

The methods of Mayo's team have since come under criticism (Parsons, 1974), but their study was one of the first to highlight the importance of psychological and social factors on behavior in the workplace. Since the 1930s, I/O psychologists have attempted to analyze that relationship in more specific terms. For example, workers whose jobs call for a greater variety of skills are more likely to think of their work as meaningful and to exhibit increased motivation and satisfaction, and workers whose jobs entail more autonomy generally produce work of a higher quality (Melamed, Ben-Avi, Luz, & Green, 1995). Thus motivation, satisfaction, and productivity in the workplace can all be improved by making the right changes in job components.

Industrial/organizational (I/O) psychology
The area of psychology concerned with the application of psychological principles to the problems of human organizations, especially work organizations.

Hawthorne effect
The principle that people will alter their behavior because of researchers' attention and not necessarily because of any specific treatment condition.

Research by I/O psychologists has also found that small, cohesive work groups are more productive than large, impersonal ones. Putting this idea into practice, managers of assembly-line workers have developed the autonomous work group, replacing the massive assembly line with small groups of workers who produce an entire unit (a whole car, for instance) and periodically alternate their tasks. Additional benefits derived from this approach include greater worker satisfaction, higher-quality output, and decreased absenteeism and turnover (Pearson, 1992).

Communication and Responsibility   The way in which communications are handled within an organization also has an impact on organizational efficiency and the attitudes of its members. A system in which members communicate with just one person in authority—a centralized system—typically works well in solving simple problems. Complex problems, in contrast, are better handled in a decentralized way, with group members freely communicating with one another (Porter & Roberts, 1976).

I/O psychologists have also examined the issue of assigning responsibility for key decisions to work groups. Although some groups make better decisions than others, group decision making in general enhances member satisfaction (Cotton, 1993). If people believe that they had an input into a decision, they are more satisfied with the outcome and their membership in the group. Increasing the number of people who participate in the decision-making process does not, however, lead to increased productivity. Increasingly, corporations are turning to I/O psychologists for advice on issues ranging from helping employees balance work and family to teaching employees at all levels communications skills and building communications networks (Murray, 1999).

INTERACTIVE LECTURE   14.4

WEB QUIZ   14.4

CHECK YOUR UNDERSTANDING

1. _____ is a process by which people feel anonymous in a large group.

2. In a mob, one dominant person can often convince other people to engage in an action they wouldn't otherwise do as a result of the _____ effect.

3. _____ behavior is helping other people with no expectation of personal gain.

4. According to the bystander effect, the likelihood that someone will help another person in trouble increases with the number of passive bystanders present. Is this statement true (T) or false (F)?

5. If group members are inclined to take risks, their group decision is likely to be riskier than decisions arrived at by each individual acting alone. This phenomenon is known as the _____ _____.

6. A shift in attitudes by the members of a group toward more extreme positions than those they held before group discussion is called group _____.

7. The poor decisions made in the Watergate cover-up, the Challenger space flight, and the Bay of Pigs invasion were due primarily to a process called _____.

8. Which is most important in determining who will lead a group?

   a. the personal characteristics of potential leaders

   b. the situation in which the group finds itself

   c. both personal traits and situational factors interacting with each other

9. Motivation, satisfaction, and productivity in the workplace can all be increased by making the right changes in how jobs are structured. Is this statement true (T) or false (F)?

Answers: 1. Deindividuation. 2. snowball. 3. Altruistic. 4. F. 5. risky shift. 6. polarization. 7. groupthink. 8. c. 9. T.

KEY TERMS

CHAPTER REVIEW

Social Cognition

What do forming impressions, explaining others' behavior, and experiencing interpersonal attraction have in common? Forming impressions, explaining others' behavior, and experiencing interpersonal attraction are all examples of social cognition. **Social cognition** is the process of taking in and assessing information about other people. It is one way in which we are influenced by the thoughts, feelings, and behaviors of others.

How do we form first impressions of people? When forming impressions of others, we rely on schemata, or sets of expectations and beliefs about categories of people. Impressions are also affected by the order in which information is acquired. First impressions are the strongest (the **primacy effect**), probably because we prefer not to expend a great deal of cognitive effort analyzing large amounts of subsequent data. This same preference also encourages us to form impressions using simplistic but strongly held schemata called **stereotypes.**

How do we decide why people act as they do? **Attribution theory** holds that people seek to understand human behavior by attributing it either to causes within the person or causes in the situation. Biases in perception can lead to the **fundamental attribution error,** in which we overemphasize personal traits in attributing causes to others' behavior. **Defensive attribution** motivates us to explain our own actions in ways that protect our self-esteem. We tend to attribute our successes to internal factors and our failures to external ones. The **just-world hypothesis** may lead us to blame the victim when bad things happen to other people.

Do "birds of a feather flock together," or do "opposites attract"? When it comes to interpersonal attraction, the adage "Birds of a feather flock together" has more validity than "Opposites attract." People who are similar in attitudes, interests, backgrounds, and values tend to like one another. **Proximity** is another factor that promotes liking. The more we are in contact with certain people, the more we tend to like them. We also tend to like people who make us feel appreciated and rewarded, an idea based on the concept of **exchange.**

Attitudes

Why are attitudes important? An **attitude** is a relatively stable organization of beliefs, feelings, and tendencies toward something or someone—called an attitude object. Attitudes are important because they often influence behavior. We cannot always tell people's attitudes from their actions, however.

What are the three major components of attitudes? The three major components of attitudes are (1) evaluative beliefs about the attitude object, (2) feelings about that object, and (3) behavioral tendencies toward it. These three components are very often (but not always) consistent with one another.

How does a person develop a prejudice toward someone else? **Prejudice** is an unfair negative attitude directed toward a group and its members, whereas **discrimination** is behavior based on prejudice. One explanation of prejudice is the **frustration–aggression**

theory, which states that people who feel exploited and oppressed displace their hostility toward the powerful onto people who are "lower" on the social scale than they are. Another theory links prejudice to the **authoritarian personality,** a rigidly conformist and bigoted personality type marked by exaggerated respect for authority and hostility toward those who defy society's norms. A third theory proposes a cognitive source of prejudice—oversimplified or stereotyped thinking about categories of people. Finally, conformity to the prejudices of one's social group can help to explain prejudice.

What factors encourage someone to change an attitude? Attitudes can change in response to new experiences, including efforts at persuasion. The first step in persuasion is to get the audience's attention. Then the task is to get the audience to comprehend and accept the message. According to the communication model, persuasion is a function of the source, the message itself, the medium of communication, and the characteristics of the audience. Attitudes may also be changed when new actions, beliefs, or perceptions contradict preexisting attitudes, called **cognitive dissonance.**

Social Influence

What are some areas in which the power of social influence is highly apparent? **Social influence** is the process by which people's thoughts, feelings, and actions are affected by the behavior and characteristics of other people. In some topics that social psychologists study, the power of social influence is even more apparent than usual. Among these are the study of cultural influences and of conformity, compliance, and obedience.

How does your culture influence how you dress or what you eat? The culture in which you are immersed has an enormous influence on your thoughts and actions. Culture dictates differences in diet, dress, and personal space. The fact that you eat pizza and shun rattlesnake meat, dress in jeans and a T-shirt instead of a loincloth or sari, and feel uncomfortable when others stand very close to you when they speak are all results of culture. In the course of adapting our behavior to that of others, we learn the **norms** of our culture, as well as its beliefs and values.

What increases the likelihood that someone will conform? Voluntarily yielding one's preferences, beliefs, or judgments to those of a larger group is called **conformity.** Research by Solomon Asch and others has shown that characteristics of both the situation and the person influence the likelihood of conforming. There are also cultural influences on the tendency to conform, with people in collectivist cultures often being more prone to conformity than those in noncollectivist ones.

How could a salesperson increase a customer's compliance in buying a product? **Compliance** is a change in behavior in response to an explicit request from someone else. One technique to encourage compliance is the foot-in-the-door approach, or getting people to go along with a small request in order to make them more likely to comply with a larger one. For instance, a salesperson might get you to agree to try a product "free" for thirty days in order to make you more likely to buy the product later. Another technique is the lowball procedure: initially offering a low price to win commitment, and then gradually escalating the cost. Also effective is the door-in-the-face tactic, or initially making an unreasonable request, which is bound to be turned down but will perhaps generate enough guilt to make compliance with another request more likely.

How does the "power of the situation" affect obedience? Classic work by Stanley Milgram showed that many people were willing to obey orders to administer harmful shocks to other people. This **obedience** to an authority figure was more likely when certain situational factors were present. For example, people found it harder to disobey when the authority figure issuing the order was nearby. They were also more likely to obey the command when the person being given the shock was some distance from them. According to Milgram, obedience is brought on by the constraints of the situation.

Social Action

Do we behave differently when other people are present? Conformity, compliance, and obedience may take place even when no one else is physically present, but other processes of social influence depend on the presence of others. Among these are deindividuation, the bystander effect, group decision making, and organizational behavior.

What negative outcomes can result from deindividuation? Immersion in a large, anonymous group may lead to **deindividuation,** the loss of a sense of personal responsibility for one's actions. Deindividuation can sometimes lead to violence or other forms of irresponsible behavior. The greater the sense of anonymity, the more this effect occurs.

What factors make us more inclined to help a person in need? Helping someone in need without expectation of a reward is called **altruistic behavior.** Altruism is influenced by situational factors such as the presence of other people. According to the **bystander effect,** a person is less apt to offer assistance when other potential helpers are present. Conversely, being the only person to spot someone in trouble tends to encourage helping. Also encouraging helping are an unambiguous emergency situation and certain personal characteristics, such as empathy for the victim and being in a good mood.

How is making a decision in a group different from making a decision on your own? Research on the **risky shift** and the broader phenomenon of group **polarization** shows that group decision making actually increases tendencies toward extreme solutions, encouraging members to lean toward either greater risk or greater caution. People deliberating in groups may also display social loafing, or a tendency to exert less effort on the assumption that others will do most of the work. And in very cohesive groups, there is a tendency toward groupthink, or an unwillingness to criticize the emerging group consensus even when it seems misguided.

Can psychology help to increase worker output and satisfaction? **Industrial/organizational (I/O) psychology** studies behavior in organizational settings such as the workplace. Research in this field shows that worker output and satisfaction can be raised by a variety of situational changes. For instance, worker output often increases simply because of attention from others, a phenomenon called the **Hawthorne effect.** Research findings have led organizations to establish autonomous work groups to replace less efficient assembly-line arrangements. Productivity and morale may also be improved by increasing worker responsibility and facilitating communication in the workplace.

CRITICAL THINKING AND APPLICATIONS

1. What is a self-fulfilling prophecy? How does this concept apply to human relationships? Can you think of instances from your own experience when self-fulfilling prophecies seemed to be at work?

2. Think of an advertisement that influenced your decision to buy something. What kind of message did the ad convey? How was this message communicated? Why did you respond to it? Were you aware at the time that the ad was designed to elicit this response? Is advertising inherently dishonest and manipulative, or does it sometimes serve a useful purpose?

WEB QUIZ **14.5** ✓   **Go to the Morris 6e Companion Website to take a practice chapter exam.**

Measurement and Statistical Methods

Most of the experiments described in this book involve measuring one or more variables and then analyzing the data statistically. The design and scoring of all the tests we have discussed are also based on statistical methods. **Statistics** is a branch of mathematics. It provides techniques for sorting out quantitative facts and ways of drawing conclusions from them. Statistics let us organize and describe data quickly; they guide the conclusions we draw and help us to make inferences.

Statistical analysis is essential to conducting an experiment or designing a test, but statistics can only handle numbers—groups of them. To use statistics, the psychologist first must measure things—count and express them in quantities.

Scales of Measurement

No matter what we are measuring—height, noise, intelligence, attitudes—we have to use a scale. The data we want to collect determine the scale we use, and, in turn, the scale we use helps to determine the conclusions we can draw from our data.

Nominal Scales   A nominal scale is a set of arbitrarily named or numbered categories. If we decide to classify a group of people by the color of their eyes, we are using a **nominal scale.** We can count how many people have blue eyes, how many have green eyes, how many have brown eyes, and so on, but we cannot say that one group has more or less eye color than the other. The colors are simply different. Because a nominal scale is more of a way of classifying than of measuring, it is the least informative kind of scale. If we want to compare our data more precisely, we will have to use a scale that tells us more.

Ordinal Scales   If we list horses in the order in which they finish a race, we are using an **ordinal scale.** On an ordinal scale, data are ranked from first to last according to some criterion. An ordinal scale tells the order, but nothing about the distances between what is ranked first and second or ninth and tenth. It does not tell us how much faster the winning horse ran than the horses that placed or showed. If a person ranks her preferences for

Statistics
A branch of mathematics that psychologists use to organize and analyze data.

Nominal scale
A set of categories for classifying objects.

Ordinal scale
Scale indicating order or relative position of items according to some criterion.

various kinds of soup—pea soup first, then tomato, then onion, and so on—we know what soup she likes most and what soup she likes least, but we have no idea how much better she likes tomato than onion, or whether pea soup is far more favored than either one of them. Because we do not know the distances between the items ranked on an ordinal scale, we cannot add or subtract ordinal data. If mathematical operations are necessary, we need a still more informative scale.

Interval Scales   An **interval scale** is often compared to a ruler that has been broken off at the bottom—it only goes from, say, 5½ to 12. The intervals between 6 and 7, 7 and 8, 8 and 9, and so forth are equal, but there is no zero. A thermometer is an interval scale—even though a certain degree registered on a Fahrenheit or Centigrade thermometer specifies a certain state of cold or heat, there is no such thing as no temperature at all. One day is never twice as hot as another; it is only so many equal degrees hotter.

An interval scale tells us how many equal-size units that one thing lies above or below another thing of the same kind, but it does not tell us how many times bigger, smaller, taller, or fatter one thing is than another. An intelligence test cannot tell us that one person is three times as intelligent as another, only that he or she scored so many points above or below someone else.

Ratio Scales   We can only say that a measurement is two times as long as another or three times as high when we use a **ratio scale,** one that has a true zero. For instance, if we measure the snowfall in a certain area over several winters, we can say that six times as much snow fell during the winter in which we measured a total of 12 feet as during a winter in which only 2 feet fell. This scale has a zero—there may be no snow.

Measurements of Central Tendency

Usually, when we measure a number of instances of anything—from the popularity of television shows to the weights of 8-year-old boys to the number of times a person's optic nerve fires in response to electrical stimulation—we get a distribution of measurements that range from smallest to largest or lowest to highest. The measurements will usually cluster around some value near the middle. This value is the **central tendency** of the distribution of the measurements.

Suppose, for example, that you want to keep 10 children busy tossing rings around a bottle. You give them three rings to toss each turn, the game has 6 rounds, and each player scores 1 point every time he or she gets the ring around the neck of the bottle. The highest possible score is 18. The distribution of scores might end up like this: 11, 8, 13, 6, 12, 10, 16, 9, 12, 3.

What could you quickly say about the ring-tossing talent of the group? First, you could arrange the scores from lowest to highest: 3, 6, 8, 9, 10, 11, 12, 12, 13, 16. In this order, the central tendency of the distribution of scores becomes clear. Many of the scores cluster around the values between 8 and 12. There are three ways to describe the central tendency of a distribution. We usually refer to all three as the *average*.

The arithmetical average is called the **mean**—the sum of all of the scores in the group divided by the number of scores. If you add up all the scores and divide by 10, the total number of scores in this group of ring tossers, you find that the mean for the group is 10.

The **median** is the point that divides a distribution in half—50 percent of the scores fall above the median, and 50 percent fall below. In the ring-

Interval scale
Scale with equal distances between the points or values, but without a true zero.

Ratio scale
Scale with equal distances between the points or values and with a true zero.

Central tendency
Tendency of scores to congregate around some middle value.

Mean
Arithmetical average calculated by dividing a sum of values by the total number of cases.

Median
Point that divides a set of scores in half.

tossing scores, 5 scores fall at 10 or below, 5 at 11 or above. The median is thus halfway between 10 and 11—10.5.

The point at which the largest number of scores occurs is called the **mode.** In our example, the mode is 12. More people scored 12 than any other number.

Differences Between the Mean, Median, and Mode

If we take many measurements of anything, we are likely to get a distribution of scores in which the mean, median, and mode are all about the same—the score that occurs most often (the mode) will also be the point that half the scores are below and half above (the median). And the same point will be the arithmetical average (the mean). This is not always true, of course, and small samples rarely come out so symmetrically. In these cases, we often have to decide which of the three measures of central tendency—the mean, the median, or the mode—will tell us what we want to know.

For example, a shopkeeper wants to know the general incomes of passersby so that he can stock the right merchandise. He might conduct a rough survey by standing outside his store for a few days from 12:00 to 2:00 and asking every tenth person who walks by to check a card showing the general range of his or her income. Suppose that most of the people checked the ranges between $15,000 and $25,000 a year. A couple of the people, however, made a lot of money—one checked $100,000–$150,000, and the other checked the $200,000-or-above box. The mean for the set of income figures would be pushed higher by those two large figures and would not really tell the shopkeeper what he wants to know about his potential customers. In this case, he would be wiser to use the median or the mode.

Suppose that instead of meeting two people whose incomes were so great, he noticed that people from two distinct income groups walked by his store—several people checked the box for $15,000–$17,000, and several others checked $23,000–$25,000. The shopkeeper would find that his distribution was bimodal. It has two modes—$16,000 and $24,000. This might be more useful to him than the mean, which could lead him to think his customers were a unit with an average income of about $20,000.

Another way of approaching a set of scores is to arrange them into a **frequency distribution**—that is, to select a set of intervals and count how many scores fall into each interval. A frequency distribution is useful for large groups of numbers; it puts the number of individual scores into more manageable groups.

Suppose that a psychologist tests memory. She asks 50 college students to learn 18 nonsense syllables, then records how many syllables each student can recall 2 hours later. She arranges her raw scores from lowest to highest in a rank distribution:

2	6	8	10	11	14
3	7	9	10	12	14
4	7	9	10	12	15
4	7	9	10	12	16
5	7	9	10	13	17
5	7	9	11	13	
6	8	9	11	13	
6	8	9	11	13	
6	8	10	11	13	

Mode
Point at which the largest number of scores occurs.

Frequency distribution
A count of the number of scores that fall within each of a series of intervals.

The scores range from 2 to 17, but 50 individual scores are too cumbersome to work with. So the psychologist chooses a set of 2-point intervals and tallies the number of scores in each interval:

Interval	Tally	Frequency
1–2	|	1
3–4	|||	3
5–6	|||| |	6
7–8	|||| ||||	9
9–10	|||| |||| |||	13
11–12	|||| |||	8
13–14	|||| ||	7
15–16	||	2
17–18	|	1

Now the psychologist can tell at a glance what the results of her experiment were. Most of the students had scores near the middle of the range, and very few had scores in the high or low intervals. She can see these results even better if she uses the frequency distribution to construct a bar graph—a **frequency histogram.** Marking the intervals along the horizontal axis and the frequencies along the vertical axis would give her the graph shown in **Figure A–1.** Another way is to construct a **frequency polygon,** a line graph. A frequency polygon drawn from the same set of data is shown in **Figure A–2.** Note that the figure is not a smooth curve, as the points are connected by straight lines. With many scores, however, and with small intervals, the angles would smooth out, and the figure would resemble a rounded curve.

Frequency histogram
Type of bar graph that shows frequency distributions.

Frequency polygon
Type of line graph that shows frequency distributions.

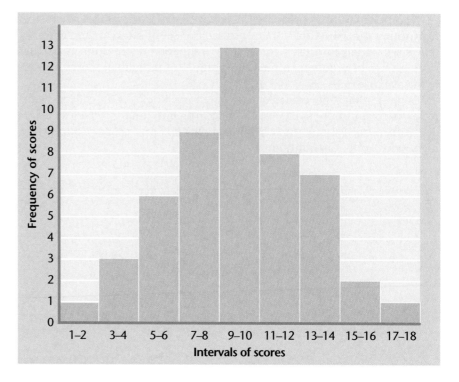

FIGURE A–1

A frequency histogram for a memory experiment. The bars indicate the frequency of scores within each interval.

FIGURE A–2

A frequency polygon drawn from data used in Figure A–1. The dots, representing the frequency of scores in each interval, are connected by straight lines.

The Normal Curve

Ordinarily, if we take enough measurements of almost anything, we get a *normal distribution*. Tossing coins is a favorite example of statisticians. If you tossed 10 coins into the air 1,000 times and recorded the heads and tails on each toss, your tabulations would reveal a normal distribution. Five heads and 5 tails would occur most often, 6 heads/4 tails and 4 heads/6 tails would be the next most frequent, and so on down to the rare all heads or all tails.

Plotting a normal distribution on a graph yields a particular kind of frequency polygon, called a **normal curve. Figure A–3** shows data on the heights of 1,000 men. Superimposed over the gray bars that reflect the actual data is an "ideal" normal curve for the same data. Note that the curve is absolutely symmetrical—the left slope parallels the right slope exactly. Moreover, the mean, median, and mode all fall on the highest point on the curve.

Normal curve

Hypothetical bell-shaped distribution curve that occurs when a normal distribution is plotted as a frequency polygon.

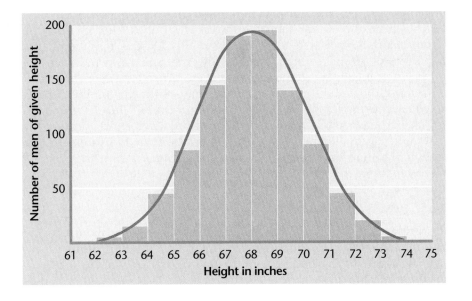

FIGURE A–3

A normal curve, based on measurements of the heights of 1,000 adult males.

Source: From Hill, 1966.

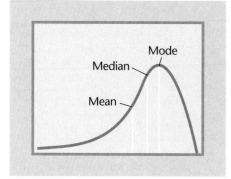

FIGURE A–4

A skewed distribution.   Most of the scores are gathered at the high end of the distribution, causing the hump to shift to the right. Because the tail on the left is longer, we say that the curve is skewed to the left. Note that the *mean*, *median*, and *mode* are different.

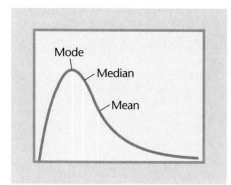

FIGURE A–5

In this distribution most of the scores are gathered at the low end, so the curve is skewed to the right. The *mean, median*, and *mode* do not coincide.

Range
Difference between the largest and smallest measurements in a distribution.

Standard deviation
Statistical measure of variability in a group of scores or other values.

The normal curve is a hypothetical entity. No set of real measurements shows such a smooth gradation from one interval to the next, or so purely symmetrical a shape. But because so many things do approximate the normal curve so closely, the curve is a useful model for much that we measure.

Skewed Distributions

If a frequency distribution is asymmetrical—if most of the scores are gathered at either the high end or the low end—the frequency polygon will be *skewed*. The hump will sit to one side or the other, and one of the curve's tails will be disproportionately long.

If a high school mathematics instructor, for example, gives her students a sixth-grade arithmetic test, we would expect nearly all the scores to be quite high. The frequency polygon would probably look like the one in **Figure A–4.** But if a sixth-grade class is asked to do advanced algebra, the scores would probably be quite low. The frequency polygon would be very similar to the one shown in **Figure A–5.**

Note, too, that the mean, median, and mode fall at different points in a skewed distribution, unlike in the normal curve, where they coincide. Usually, if you know that the mean is greater than the median of a distribution, you can predict that the frequency polygon will be skewed to the right. If the median is greater than the mean, the curve will be skewed to the left.

Measures of Variation

Sometimes it is not enough to know the distribution of a set of data and what their mean, median, and mode are. Suppose that an automotive safety expert feels that too much damage occurs in tail-end accidents because automobile bumpers are not all the same height. It is not enough to know what the average height of an automobile bumper is. The safety expert also wants to know about the variation in bumper heights: How much higher is the highest bumper than the mean? How do bumpers of all cars vary from the mean? Are the latest bumpers closer to the same height?

Range

The simplest measure of variation is the **range**—the difference between the largest and smallest measurements. Perhaps the safety expert measured the bumpers of 1,000 cars 2 years ago and found that the highest bumper was 18 inches from the ground, and the lowest was only 12 inches from the ground. The range was thus 6 inches—18 minus 12. This year the highest bumper is still 18 inches high, and the lowest is still 12 inches from the ground. The range is still 6 inches. Moreover, our safety expert finds that the means of the two distributions are the same—15 inches off the ground. But look at the two frequency polygons in **Figure A–6**—there is still something the expert needs to know, as the measurements cluster around the mean in drastically different ways. To find out how the measurements are distributed around the mean, our safety expert has to turn to a slightly more complicated measure of variation—the standard deviation.

The Standard Deviation

The **standard deviation,** in a single number, tells us much about how the scores in any frequency distribution are dispersed around the mean. Calculating the standard deviation is one of the most useful and widely employed statistical tools.

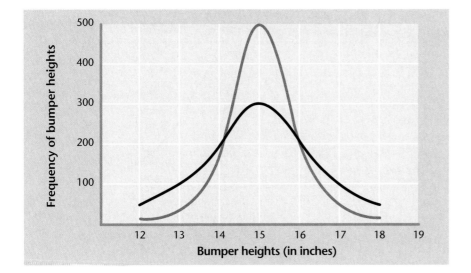

FIGURE A–6

Frequency polygons for two sets of measurements of automobile bumper heights. Both are normal curves, and in each distribution the *mean, median,* and *mode* are 15. But the variation from the mean is different, causing one curve to be flattened and the other to be much more sharply peaked.

To find the standard deviation of a set of scores, we first find the mean. Then we take the first score in the distribution, subtract it from the mean, square the difference, and jot it down in a column to be added up later. We do the same for all the scores in the distribution. Then we add up the column of squared differences, divide the total by the number of scores in the distribution, and find the square root of that number. **Figure A–7** shows the calculation of the standard deviation for a small distribution of scores.

In a normal distribution, however peaked or flattened the curve, about 68 percent of the scores fall between 1 standard deviation above the mean and 1 standard deviation below the mean (see **Figure A–8**). Another 27 percent fall between 1 standard deviation and 2 standard deviations on either side of the mean, and 4 percent more between the second and third standard deviations on either side. Overall, then, more than 99 percent of the scores fall between 3 standard deviations above and 3 standard deviations below the mean. This makes the standard deviation useful for comparing two different normal distributions.

Number of scores = 10		Mean = 7
Scores	Difference from mean	Difference squared
4	$7 - 4 = 3$	$3^2 = 9$
5	$7 - 5 = 2$	$2^2 = 4$
6	$7 - 6 = 1$	$1^2 = 1$
6	$7 - 6 = 1$	$1^2 = 1$
7	$7 - 7 = 0$	$0^2 = 0$
7	$7 - 7 = 0$	$0^2 = 0$
8	$7 - 8 = -1$	$-1^2 = 1$
8	$7 - 8 = -1$	$-1^2 = 1$
9	$7 - 9 = -2$	$-2^2 = 4$
10	$7 - 10 = -3$	$-3^2 = 9$

$$\text{Sum of squares} = 30$$
$$\div$$
$$\text{Number of scores} = 10$$
$$\text{Variance} = 3$$
$$\text{Standard deviation} = \sqrt{3} = 1.73$$

FIGURE A–7

Step-by-step calculation of the *standard deviation* for a group of 10 scores with a mean of 7.

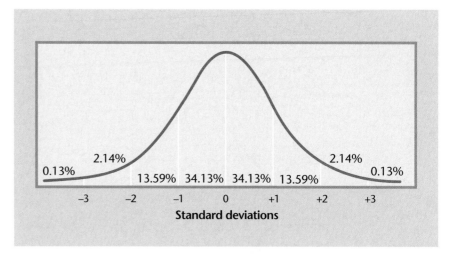

FIGURE A–8

A normal curve, divided to show the percentage of scores that fall within each *standard deviation* from the *mean*.

Now let us see what the standard deviation can tell our automotive safety expert about the variations from the mean in the two sets of data. The standard deviation for the cars measured 2 years ago is about 1.4. A car with a bumper height of 16.4 is 1 standard deviation above the mean of 15; one with a bumper height of 13.6 is 1 standard deviation below the mean. Because the engineer knows that the data fall into a normal distribution, he or she can figure that about 68 percent of the 1,000 cars he or she measured will fall somewhere between these two heights: 680 cars will have bumpers between 13.6 and 16.4 inches high. For the more recent set of data, the standard deviation is just slightly less than 1. A car with a bumper height of about 14 inches is 1 standard deviation below the mean; a car with a bumper height of about 16 is 1 standard deviation above the mean. Thus, in this distribution, 680 cars have bumpers between 14 and 16 inches high. This tells the safety expert that car bumpers are becoming more similar, although the range of heights is still the same (6 inches), and the mean height of bumpers is still 15.

Measures of Correlation

Measures of central tendency and measures of variation can be used to describe a single set of measurements—like the children's ring-tossing scores—or to compare two or more sets of measurements—like the two sets of bumper heights. Sometimes, however, we need to know whether two sets of measurements are in any way associated with each other—whether they are *correlated*. Is parental IQ related to children's IQ? Does the need for achievement relate to the need for power? Is watching violence on television related to aggressive behavior?

One fast way to determine whether two variables are correlated is to draw a **scatter plot.** We assign one variable (X) to the horizontal axis of a graph, the other variable (Y) to the vertical axis. Then we plot a person's score on one characteristic along the horizontal axis, and his or her score on the second characteristic along the vertical axis. Where the two scores intersect, we draw a dot. When several scores have been plotted in this way, the pattern of dots tells whether the two characteristics are in any way correlated with each other.

If the dots on a scatter plot form a straight line running between the lower left-hand corner and the upper right-hand corner, as they do in **Figure A–9a,** we have a perfect positive correlation—a high score on one

Scatter plot
Diagram showing the association between scores on two variables.

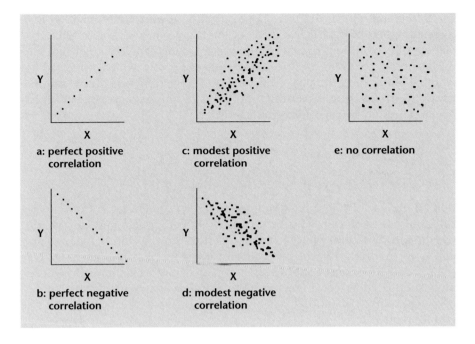

a: perfect positive correlation

c: modest positive correlation

e: no correlation

b: perfect negative correlation

d: modest negative correlation

FIGURE A–9

Scatter plots provide a picture of the strength and direction of a correlation.

of the characteristics is always associated with a high score on the other. A straight line running between the upper-left-hand corner and the lower-right-hand corner, as in **Figure A–9b,** is the sign of a perfect negative correlation—a high score on one of the characteristics is always associated with a low score on the other. If the pattern formed by the dots is cigar shaped in either of these directions, as in **Figure A–9c** and **d,** we have a modest correlation—the two characteristics are related but not highly correlated. If the dots spread out over the whole graph, forming a circle or a random pattern, as they do in **Figure A–9e,** there is no correlation between the two characteristics.

A scatter plot can give us a general idea whether a correlation exists and how strong it is. To describe the relation between two variables more precisely, we need a **correlation coefficient**—a statistical measure of the degree to which two variables are associated. The correlation coefficient tells us the degree of association between two sets of matched scores—that is, to what extent high or low scores on one variable tend to be associated with high or low scores on another. It also provides an estimate of how well we can predict from a person's score on one characteristic how high he or she will score on another. If we know, for example, that a test of mechanical ability is highly correlated with success in engineering courses, we could predict that success on the test would also mean success as an engineering major.

Correlation coefficients can run from +1.0 to −1.0. The highest possible value (+1.0) indicates a perfect positive correlation—high scores on one variable are always and systematically related to high scores on a second variable. The lowest possible value (−1.0) means a perfect negative correlation—high scores on one variable are always and regularly related to low scores on the second variable. In life, most things are far from perfect, so most correlation coefficients fall somewhere between +1.0 and −1.0. A correlation smaller than ±0.20 is considered very low, from ±0.20 to ±0.40 is low, from ±0.40 to ±0.60 is moderate, from ±0.60 to ±0.80 is high, and from ±0.80 to ±1.0 is very high. A correlation of zero indicates that there is no correlation between two sets of scores—no regular relation between them at all.

Correlation coefficient
Statistical measure of the strength of association between two variables.

Correlation tells us nothing about causality. If we found a high positive correlation between participation in elections and income levels, for example, we still could not say that being wealthy made people vote or that voting made people wealthy. We would still not know which came first or whether some third variable explained both income levels and voting behavior. Correlation tells us only that we have found some association between scores on two specified characteristics.

Using Statistics to Make Predictions

Behind the use of statistics is the hope that we can generalize from our results and use them to predict behavior. We hope, for example, that we can use the record of how well a group of rats run through a maze today to predict how another group of rats will do tomorrow, that we can use a person's scores on a sales aptitude test to predict how well she or he will sell life insurance, that we can measure the attitudes of a relatively small group of people about pollution control to indicate what the attitudes of the whole country are.

First we have to determine whether our measurements are representative and whether we can have confidence in them. In Chapter 1 we discussed this problem when we considered the problem of proper sampling.

Probability

Errors based on inadequate sampling procedures are somebody's fault. Other kinds of errors occur randomly. In the simplest kind of experiment, a psychologist will gather a representative sample, split it randomly into two groups, and then apply some experimental manipulation to one of the groups. Afterward the psychologist will measure both groups and determine whether the experimental group's score is now different from the score of the control group. But even if there is a large difference between the scores of the two groups, it may still be wrong to attribute the difference to the manipulation. Random effects might influence the results and introduce error.

Statistics give the psychologist many ways to determine precisely whether the difference between the two groups is really significant, whether something other than chance produced the results, and whether the same results would be obtained with different subjects. These probabilities are expressed as measures of **significance.** If the psychologist computes the significance level for the results as 0.05, he or she knows that there are 19 chances out of 20 that the results are not due to chance. But there is still 1 chance in 20—or a 0.05 likelihood—that the results are due to chance. A 0.01 significance level would mean that there is only 1 chance in 100 that the results are due to chance.

Significance
Probability that results obtained were due to chance.

GLOSSARY

Absolute threshold The least amount of energy that can be detected as a stimulation 50 percent of the time.

Achievement motive The need to excel, to overcome obstacles.

Actualizing tendency According to Rogers, the drive of every organism to fulfill its biological potential and become what it is inherently capable of becoming.

Adaptation An adjustment of the senses to the level of stimulation they are receiving.

Additive color mixing The process of mixing lights of different wavelengths to create new hues.

Adjustment Any effort to cope with stress.

Adoption studies Research carried out on children, adopted at birth by parents not related to them, to determine the relative influence of heredity and environment on human behavior.

Adrenal glands Two endocrine glands located just above the kidneys.

Aerial perspective Monocular cue to distance and depth based on the fact that more distant objects are likely to appear hazy and blurred.

Afferent neurons Neurons that carry messages from sense organs to the spinal cord or brain.

Affiliation motive The need to be with others.

Afterimage Sense experience that occurs after a visual stimulus has been removed.

Aggression Behavior aimed at doing harm to others; also, the motive to behave aggressively.

Agoraphobia An anxiety disorder that involves multiple, intense fears of crowds, public places, and other situations that require separation from a source of security such as the home.

Alcohol Depressant that is the intoxicating ingredient in whiskey, beer, wine, and other fermented or distilled liquors.

Algorithm A step-by-step method of problem solving that guarantees a correct solution.

All-or-none law Principle that the action potential in a neuron does not vary in strength; either the neuron fires at full strength, or it does not fire at all.

Altered states of consciousness Mental states that differ noticeably from normal waking consciousness.

Altruistic behavior Helping behavior that is not linked to personal gain.

Alzheimer's disease A neurological disorder, most commonly found in late adulthood, characterized by progressive losses in memory and cognition and by changes in personality.

Amphetamines Stimulant drugs that initially produce "rushes" of euphoria often followed by sudden "crashes" and, sometimes, severe depression.

Amplitude The magnitude of a wave; in sound, the primary determinant of loudness.

Anal stage Second stage in Freud's theory of personality development, in which a child's erotic feelings center on the anus and on elimination.

Anorexia nervosa A serious eating disorder that is associated with an intense fear of weight gain and a distorted body image.

Antipsychotic drugs Drugs used to treat very severe psychological disorders, particularly schizophrenia.

Antisocial personality disorder Personality disorder that involves a pattern of violent, criminal, or unethical and exploitative behavior and an inability to feel affection for others.

Anxiety disorders Disorders in which anxiety is a characteristic feature or the avoidance of anxiety seems to motivate abnormal behavior.

Apnea Sleep disorder characterized by breathing difficulty during the night and feelings of exhaustion during the day.

Approach/approach conflict According to Lewin, the result of simultaneous attraction to two appealing possibilities, neither of which has any negative qualities.

Approach/avoidance conflict According to Lewin, the result of being simultaneously attracted to and repelled by the same goal.

Archetypes In Jung's theory of personality, thought forms common to all human beings, stored in the collective unconscious.

Arousal theory Theory of motivation that propose that organisms seek an optimal level of arousal.

Association areas Areas of the cerebral cortex where incoming messages from the separate senses are combined into meaningful impressions and outgoing messages from the motor areas are integrated.

Attachment Emotional bond that develops in the first year of life that makes human babies cling to their caregivers for safety and comfort.

Attention The selection of some incoming information for further processing

Attention-deficit/hyperactivity disorder (ADHD) A childhood disorder characterized by inattention, impulsiveness, and hyperactivity.

Attitude Relatively stable organization of beliefs, feelings, and behavior tendencies directed toward something or someone—the attitude object.

Attribution theory The theory that addresses the question of how people make judgments about the causes of behavior.

Auditory nerve The bundle of axons that carries signals from each ear to the brain.

Authoritarian personality A personality pattern characterized by rigid conventionality, exaggerated respect for authority, and hostility toward those who defy society's norms.

Autistic disorder A childhood disorder characterized by lack of social instincts and strange motor behavior.

Autokinetic illusion The perception that a stationary object is actually moving.

Autonomic nervous system The part of the peripheral nervous system that carries messages between the central nervous system and the internal organs.

Autonomy Sense of independence; a desire not to be controlled by others.

Availability A heuristic by which a judgment or decision is based on information that is most easily retrieved from memory.

Aversive conditioning Behavioral therapy techniques aimed at eliminating undesirable behavior patterns by teaching the person to associate them with pain and discomfort.

Avoidance/avoidance conflict According to Lewin, the result of facing a choice between two undesirable possibilities, neither of which has any positive qualities.

Avoidance training Learning a desirable behavior to prevent the occurrence of something unpleasant, such as punishment.

Avoidant personality disorder Personality disorder in which the person's fears of rejection by others lead to social isolation.

Axon Single long fiber extending from the cell body; it carries outgoing messages.

Babbling A baby's vocalizations, consisting of repetition of consonant-vowel combinations.

Barbiturates Potentially deadly depressants, first used for their sedative and anticonvulsant properties, now used only to treat such conditions as epilepsy and arthritis.

Basilar membrane Vibrating membrane in the cochlea of the inner ear; it contains sense receptors for sound.

Behavior contracting Form of operant conditioning therapy in which the client and therapist set behavioral goals and agree on reinforcements that the client will receive on reaching those goals.

Behavior genetics Study of the relationship between genetics and behavior.

Behavior therapies Therapeutic approaches that are based on the belief that all behavior, normal and abnormal, is learned, and that the objective of therapy is to teach people new, more satisfying ways of behaving.

Behaviorism School of psychology that studies only observable and measurable behavior.

Big Five Five traits or basic dimensions currently thought to be of central importance in describing personality.

Binaural cue Cue to sound location that involves both ears working together.

Binocular cues Visual cues requiring the use of both eyes.

Biofeedback A technique that uses monitoring devices to provide precise information about internal physiological processes, such as heart rate or blood pressure, to teach people to gain voluntary control over these functions.

Biographical (or retrospective) study A method of studying developmental changes by reconstructing people's past through interviews and inferring the effects of past events on current behaviors.

Biological model View that psychological disorders have a biochemical or physiological basis.

Biological treatments A group of approaches, including medication, electroconvulsive therapy, and psychosurgery, that are sometimes used to treat psychological disorders in conjunction with, or instead of, psychotherapy.

Biopsychosocial theory The theory that the interaction of biological, psychological, and cultural factors influence the intensity and duration of pain.

Bipolar cells Neurons that have only one axon and one dendrite; in the eye, these neurons connect the receptors on the retina to the ganglion cells.

Bipolar disorder A mood disorder in which periods of mania and depression alternate, sometimes with periods of normal mood intervening.

Blind spot The place on the retina where the axons of all the ganglion cells leave the eye and where there are no receptors.

Blocking A process whereby prior conditioning prevents conditioning to a second stimulus even when the two stimuli are presented simultaneously.

Body dysmorphic disorder A somatoform disorder in which a person becomes so preoccupied with his or her imagined ugliness that normal life is impossible.

Borderline personality disorder Personality disorder characterized by marked instability in self-image, mood, and interpersonal relationships.

Brainstorming A problem-solving strategy in which an individual or a group produces numerous ideas and evaluates them only after all ideas have been collected.

Brightness The nearness of a color to white as opposed to black.

Brightness constancy The perception of brightness as the same, even though the amount of light reaching the retina changes.

Bulimia An eating disorder characterized by binges of eating followed by self-induced vomiting.

Bystander effect The tendency for an individual's helpfulness in an emergency to decrease as the number of passive bystanders increases.

Cannon-Bard theory States that the experience of emotion occurs simultaneously with biological changes.

Case study Intensive description and analysis of a single individual or just a few individuals.

Catatonic schizophrenia Schizophrenic disorder in which disturbed motor behavior is prominent.

Central nervous system Division of the nervous system that consists of the brain and spinal cord.

Cerebellum Structure in the hindbrain that controls certain reflexes and coordinates the body's movements.

Cerebral cortex The outer surface of the two cerebral hemispheres that regulates most complex behavior.

Childhood amnesia The difficulty adults have remembering experiences from their first 2 years of life.

Chromosomes Pairs of threadlike bodies within the cell nucleus that contain the genes.

Chunking The grouping of information into meaningful units for easier handling by short-term memory.

Classical (or Pavlovian) conditioning The type of learning in which a response naturally elicited by one stimulus comes to be elicited by a different, formerly neutral stimulus.

Client-centered (or person-centered) therapy Nondirectional form of therapy developed by Carl Rogers that calls for unconditional positive regard of the client by the therapist with the goal of helping the client become fully functioning.

Cliques Groups of adolescents with similar interests and strong mutual attachment.

Cocaine Drug derived from the coca plant that, although producing a sense of euphoria by stimulating the sympathetic nervous system, also leads to anxiety, depression, and addictive cravings.

Cochlea Part of the inner ear containing fluid that vibrates, which in turn causes the basilar membrane to vibrate.

Cognition The processes whereby we acquire and use knowledge.

Cognitive dissonance Perceived inconsistency between two cognitions.

Cognitive distortions An illogical and maladaptive response to early negative life events that leads to feelings of incompetence and unworthiness that are reactivated whenever a new situation arises that resembles the original events.

Cognitive learning Learning that depends on mental processes that are not directly observable.

Cognitive map A learned mental image of a spatial environment that may be called on to solve problems when stimuli in the environment change.

Cognitive psychology School of psychology devoted to the study of mental processes in the broadest sense.

Cognitive theory States that emotional experience depends on one's perception or judgment of the situation one is in.

Cognitive therapies Psychotherapies that emphasize changing clients' perceptions of their life situation as a way of modifying their behavior.

Cognitive therapy Therapy that depends on identifying and changing inappropriately negative and self-critical patterns of thought.

Cognitive-behavioral model View that psychological disorders result from learning maladaptive ways of thinking and behaving.

Cognitive–social learning theories Personality theories that view behavior as the product of the interaction of cognitions, learning and past experiences, and the immediate environment.

Cohort A group of people born during the same period in historical time.

Collective unconscious In Jung's theory of personality, the level of the unconscious that is inherited and common to all members of a species.

Color blindness Partial or total inability to perceive hues.

Color constancy An inclination to perceive familiar objects as retaining their color despite changes in sensory information.

Compensation According to Adler, the person's effort to overcome imagined or real personal weaknesses.

Compensatory model A rational decision-making model in which choices are systematically evaluated on various criteria.

Compliance Change of behavior in response to an explicit request from another person or group.

Compromise Deciding on a more realistic solution or goal when an ideal solution or goal is not practical.

Concept A mental category for classifying objects, people, or experiences.

Concrete-operational stage In Piaget's theory, the stage of cognitive development between 7 and 11 years of age in which the individual can attend to more than one thing at a time and understand someone else's point of view, though thinking is limited to concrete matters.

Conditional positive regard In Rogers's theory, acceptance and love that are dependent on behaving in certain ways and on fulfilling certain conditions.

Conditioned response (CR) After conditioning, the response an organism produces when a conditioned stimulus is presented.

Conditioned stimulus (CS) An originally neutral stimulus that is paired with an unconditioned stimulus and eventually produces the desired response in an organism when presented alone.

Conditioned taste aversion Conditioned avoidance of certain foods even if there is only one pairing of conditioned and unconditioned stimuli.

Cones Receptor cells in the retina responsible for color vision.

Confirmation bias The tendency to look for evidence in support of a belief and to ignore evidence that would disprove a belief.

Conflict Simultaneous existence of incompatible demands, opportunities, needs, or goals.

Conformity Voluntarily yielding to social norms, even at the expense of one's preferences.

Confrontation Acknowledging a stressful situation directly and attempting to find a solution to the problem or attain the difficult goal.

Consciousness Our awareness of various cognitive processes, such as sleeping, dreaming, concentrating, and making decisions.

Content validity Refers to a test's having an adequate sample of questions measuring the skills or knowledge it is supposed to measure.

Contingency A reliable "if-then" relationship between two events such as a CS and a US.

Control group In a controlled experiment, the group not subjected to a change in the independent variable; used for comparison with the experimental group.

Convergence A visual depth cue that comes from muscles controlling eye movement as the eyes turn inward to view a nearby stimulus.

Convergent thinking Thinking that is directed toward one correct solution to a problem.

Conversion disorders Somatoform disorders in which a dramatic specific disability has no physical cause but instead seems related to psychological problems.

Cornea The transparent protective coating over the front part of the eye.

Corpus callosum A thick band of nerve fibers connecting the left and right cerebral cortex.

Correlational research Research technique based on the naturally occurring relationship between two or more variables.

Counterfactual thinking Thinking about alternative realities and things that never happened.

Couple therapy A form of group therapy intended to help troubled partners improve their problems of communication and interaction.

Creativity The ability to produce novel and socially valued ideas or objects.

Criterion-related validity Validity of a test as measured by a comparison of the test score and independent measures of what the test is designed to measure.

Critical period A time when certain internal and external influences have a major effect on development; at other periods, the same influences will have little or no effect.

Cross-sectional study A method of studying developmental changes by comparing people of different ages at about the same time.

Culture The tangible goods and the values, attitudes, behaviors, and beliefs that are passed from one generation to another.

Culture-fair tests Intelligence tests designed to eliminate cultural bias by minimizing skills and values that vary from one culture to another.

Dark adaptation Increased sensitivity of rods and cones in darkness.

Daydreams Apparently effortless shifts in attention away from the here-and-now into a private world of make-believe.

Decibel Unit of measurement for the loudness of sounds.

Defense mechanisms Self-deceptive techniques for reducing stress, including denial, repression, projection, identification, regression, intellectualization, reaction formation, displacement, and sublimation.

Defensive attribution The tendency to attribute our successes to our own efforts or qualities and our failures to external factors.

Deindividuation A loss of personal sense of responsibility in a group.

Deinstitutionalization Policy of treating people with severe psychological disorders in the larger community, or in small residential centers such as halfway houses, rather than in large public hospitals.

Delusions False beliefs about reality that have no basis in fact.

Dendrites Short fibers that branch out from the cell body and pick up incoming messages.

Denial Refusal to acknowledge a painful or threatening reality.

Deoxyribonucleic acid (DNA) Complex molecule in a double-helix configuration that is the main ingredient of chromosomes and genes and that forms the code for all genetic information.

Dependent personality disorder Personality disorder in which the person is unable to make choices and decisions independently and cannot tolerate being alone.

Dependent variable In an experiment, the variable that is measured to see how it is changed by manipulations in the independent variable.

Depersonalization disorder A dissociative disorder whose essential feature is that the person suddenly feels changed or different in a strange way.

Depressants Chemicals that slow down behavior or cognitive processes.

Depression A mood disorder characterized by overwhelming feelings of sadness, lack of interest in activities, and perhaps excessive guilt or feelings of worthlessness.

Desensitization therapy A conditioning technique designed to gradually reduce anxiety about a particular object or situation.

Developmental psychology The study of the changes that occur in people from birth through old age.

Diathesis Biological predisposition.

Diathesis-stress model View that people biologically predisposed to a mental disorder (those with a certain diathesis) will tend to exhibit that disorder when particularly affected by stress.

Dichromats People (and animals) that are blind to either red-green or yellow-blue.

Difference threshold or just noticeable difference (jnd) The smallest change in stimulation that can be detected 50 percent of the time.

Discrimination An unfair act or series of acts taken toward an entire group of people or individual members of that group.

Disorganized schizophrenia Schizophrenic disorder in which bizarre and childlike behaviors are common.

Displacement Shifting repressed motives and emotions from an original object to a substitute object.

Display rules Culture-specific rules that govern how, when, and why expressions of emotion are appropriate.

Dissociative disorders Disorders in which some aspect of the personality seems separated from the rest.

Dissociative identity disorder (Also called multiple personality disorder) Disorder characterized by the separation of the personality into two or more distinct personalities.

Divergent thinking Thinking that meets the criteria of originality, inventiveness, and flexibility.

Dominant gene Member of a gene pair that controls the appearance of a certain trait.

Double-blind procedure Chemically inactive substance used for comparison with active drugs in experiments on the effects of drugs.

Dreams Vivid visual and auditory experiences that occur primarily during REM periods of sleep.

Drive State of tension or arousal that motivates behavior.

Drive-reduction theory States that motivated behavior is aimed at reducing a state of bodily tension or arousal and at returning the organism to homeostasis.

Eclecticism Psychotherapeutic approach that recognizes the value of a broad treatment package over a rigid commitment to one particular form of therapy.

Efferent neurons Neurons that carry messages from the spinal cord or brain to the muscles and glands.

Ego Freud's term for the part of the personality that mediates between environmental demands (reality), conscience (superego), and instinctual needs (id); now often used as a synonym for "self."

Egocentric Unable to see things from another's point of view.

Ego ideal The part of the superego that consists of standards of what one would like to be.

Elaborative rehearsal The linking of new information in short-term memory to familiar material stored in long-term memory.

Electroconvulsive therapy (ECT) Biological therapy in which a mild electrical current is passed through the brain for a short period, often producing convulsions and temporary coma; used to treat severe, prolonged depression.

Elevation Monocular cue to distance and depth based on the fact that the higher on the horizontal plane an object is, the farther away it appears.

Embryo A developing human between 2 weeks and 3 months after conception.

Emotion Feeling, such as fear, joy, or surprise, that underlies behavior.

Emotional intelligence According to Goleman, a form of intelligence that refers to how effectively people perceive and understand their own emotions and the emotions of others, and can regulate and manage their emotional behavior.

Emotional memory Learned emotional responses to various stimuli.

Endocrine glands Glands of the endocrine system that release hormones into the bloodstream.

Episodic memory The portion of long-term memory that stores personally experienced events.

Equity Fairness of exchange achieved when each partner in the relationship receives the same proportion of outcomes to investments.

Ethnicity A common cultural heritage—including religion, language, or ancestry—that is shared by a group of individuals.

Evolutionary psychology An approach to, and subfield of, psychology that is concerned with the evolutionary origins of behaviors and mental process, their adaptive value, and the purposes they continue to serve.

Exchange The concept that relationships are based on trading rewards among partners.

Existential psychology School of psychology that focuses on the meaninglessness and alienation of modern life, and how these factors lead to apathy and psychological problems.

Expectancies In Bandura's view, what a person anticipates in a situation or as a result of behaving in certain ways.

Experimental group In a controlled experiment, the group subjected to a change in the independent variable.

Experimental method Research technique in which an investigator deliberately manipulates selected events or circumstances and then measures the effects of those manipulations on subsequent behavior.

Experimenter bias Expectations by the experimenter that might influence the results of an experiment or its interpretation.

Explicit memory Memory for information that we can readily express in words and are aware of having; these memories can be intentionally retrieved from memory.

Extinction A decrease in the strength or frequency, or stopping, of a learned response because of failure to continue pairing the US and CS (classical conditioning) or withholding of reinforcement (operant conditioning).

Extrinsic motivation A desire to perform a behavior to obtain an external reward or avoid punishment.

Extrovert According to Jung, a person who usually focuses on social life and the external world instead of on his or her internal experience.

Factor analysis A statistical technique that identifies groups of related objects, used by Cattell to identify clusters of traits.

Family studies Studies of heritability in humans based on the assumption that if genes influence a certain trait, close relatives should be more similar on that trait than distant relatives.

Family therapy A form of group therapy that sees the family as at least partly responsible for the individual's problems and that seeks to change all family members' behaviors to the benefit of the family unit as well as the troubled individual.

Feature detectors Specialized brain cells that only respond to particular elements in the visual field such as movement or lines of specific orientation.

Feminist theory Feminist theories offer a wide variety of views on the social roles of women and men, the problems and rewards of those roles, and prescriptions for changing those roles.

Fetal alcohol syndrome (FAS) A disorder that occurs in children of women who drink alcohol during pregnancy that is characterized by facial deformities, heart defects, stunted growth, and cognitive impairments.

Fetishism A paraphilia in which a nonhuman object is the preferred or exclusive method of achieving sexual excitement.

Fetus A developing human between 3 months after conception and birth.

Fixation According to Freud, a partial or complete halt at some point in the individual's psychosexual development.

Fixed-interval schedule A reinforcement schedule in which the correct response is reinforced after a fixed length of time since the last reinforcement.

Fixed-ratio schedule A reinforcement schedule in which the correct response is reinforced after a fixed number of correct responses.

Flashbulb memory A vivid memory of a certain event and the incidents surrounding it even after a long time has passed.

Formal-operational stage In Piaget's theory, the stage of cognitive development between 11 and 15 years of age in which the individual becomes capable of abstract thought.

Fovea The area of the retina that is the center of the visual field.

Framing The perspective from which we interpret information before making a decision.

Fraternal twins Twins developed from two separate fertilized ova and therefore different in genetic makeup.

Free association A psychoanalytic technique that encourages the person to talk without inhibition about whatever thoughts or fantasies come to mind.

Frequency The number of cycles per second in a wave; in sound, the primary determinant of pitch.

Frequency theory Theory that pitch is determined by the frequency with which hair cells in the cochlea fire.

Frontal lobe Part of the cerebral cortex that is responsible for voluntary movement; it is also important for attention, goal-directed behavior, and appropriate emotional experiences.

Frustration The feeling that occurs when a person is prevented from reaching a goal.

Frustration-aggression theory The theory that under certain circumstances people who are frustrated in their goals turn their anger away from the proper, powerful target and toward another, less powerful target that is safer to attack.

Fully functioning person According to Rogers, an individual whose self-concept closely resembles his or her inborn capacities or potentials.

Functional fixedness The tendency to perceive only a limited number of uses for an object, thus interfering with the process of problem solving.

Functionalism Theory of mental life and behavior that is concerned with how an organism uses its perceptual abilities to function in its environment.

Fundamental attribution error The tendency of people to overemphasize personal causes for other people's behavior and to underemphasize personal causes for their own behavior.

Ganglion cells Neurons that connect the bipolar cells in the eyes to the brain.

Gate control theory The theory that a "neurological gate" in the spinal cord controls the transmission of pain messages to the brain.

Gender The psychological and social meanings attached to being biologically male or female.

Gender constancy The realization that gender does not change with age.

Gender identity A little girl's knowledge that she is a girl, and a little boy's knowledge that he is a boy.

Gender stereotypes General beliefs about characteristics that men and women are presumed to have.

Gender-identity disorder in children Rejection of one's biological gender in childhood, along with the clothing and behavior that society considers appropriate for that gender.

Gender-identity disorders Disorders that involve the desire to become, or the insistence that one really is, a member of the other biological sex.

Gender-role awareness Knowledge of what behavior is appropriate for each gender.

General adaptation syndrome (GAS) According to Selye, the three stages the body passes through as it adapts to stress: alarm reaction, resistance, and exhaustion.

Generalized anxiety disorder An anxiety disorder characterized by prolonged vague but intense fears that are not attached to any particular object or circumstance.

Genes Elements that control the transmission of traits; they are found on the chromosomes.

Genetics Study of how traits are transmitted from one generation to the next.

Genital stage In Freud's theory of personality development, the final stage of normal adult sexual development, which is usually marked by mature sexuality.

Gestalt psychology School of psychology that studies how people perceive and experience objects as whole patterns.

Gestalt therapy An insight therapy that emphasizes the wholeness of the personality and attempts to reawaken people to their emotions and sensations in the here and now.

Giftedness Refers to superior IQ combined with demonstrated or potential ability in such areas as academic aptitude, creativity, and leadership.

Glial cells (or glia) Cells that insulate and support neurons by holding them together, provide nourishment and remove waste products, prevent harmful substances from passing into the brain, and form the myelin sheath.

Golgi tendon organs Receptors that sense movement of the tendons, which connect muscle to bone.

Gonads The reproductive glands—testes in males and ovaries in females.

Graded potential A shift in the electrical charge in a tiny area of a neuron.

Grammar The language rules that determine how sounds and words can be combined and used to communicate meaning within a language.

Great person theory The theory that leadership is a result of personal qualities and traits that qualify one to lead others.

Group tests Written intelligence tests administered by one examiner to many people at one time.

Group therapy Type of psychotherapy in which clients meet regularly to interact and help one another achieve insight into their feelings and behavior.

Growth spurt A rapid increase in height and weight that occurs during adolescence.

Hallucinations Sensory experiences in the absence of external stimulation.

Hallucinogens Any of a number of drugs, such as LSD and mescaline, that distort visual and auditory perception.

Hawthorne effect The principle that people will alter their behavior because of researchers' attention and not necessarily because of any specific treatment condition.

Health psychology A subfield of psychology concerned with the relationship between psychological factors and physical health and illness.

Hertz (Hz) Cycles per second; unit of measurement for the frequency of sound waves.

Heuristics Rules of thumb that help in simplifying and solving problems, although they do not guarantee a correct solution.

Higher-order conditioning Conditioning based on previous learning; the conditioned stimulus serves as an unconditioned stimulus for further training.

Hill climbing A heuristic problem-solving strategy in which each step moves you progressively closer to the final goal.

Hindbrain Area containing the medulla, pons, and cerebellum.

Hindsight The tendency to vision outcomes as inevitable and predictable after we know the outcome.

Holophrases One-word sentences commonly used by children under 2 years of age.

Homeostasis State of balance and stability in which the organism functions effectively.

Hormones Chemical substances released by the endocrine glands; they help regulate bodily activities.

Hues The aspects of color that correspond to names such as red, green, and blue.

Human genome The full complement of genes within a human cell.

Humanistic personality theory Any personality theory that asserts the fundamental goodness of people and their striving toward higher levels of functioning.

Humanistic psychology School of psychology that emphasizes nonverbal experience and altered states of consciousness as a means of realizing one's full human potential.

Hypnosis Trancelike state in which a person responds readily to suggestions.

Hypochondriasis A somatoform disorder in which a person interprets insignificant symptoms as signs of serious illness in the absence of any organic evidence of such illness.

Hypothalamus Forebrain region that governs motivation and emotional responses.

Hypotheses Specific, testable predictions derived from a theory.

Identical twins Twins developed from a single fertilized ovum and therefore identical in genetic makeup at the time of conception.

Identification Taking on the characteristics of someone else to avoid feeling incompetent.

Identity crisis A period of intense self-examination and decision making; part of the process of identity formation.

Identity formation Erickson's term for the development of a stable sense of self necessary to make the transition from dependence on others to dependence on oneself.

Id In Freud's theory of personality, the collection of unconscious urges and desires that continually seek expression.

Image A mental representation of a sensory experience.

Imaginary audience Elkind's term for adolescents' delusion that they are constantly being observed by others.

Implicit memory Memory for information that we cannot readily express in words and may not be aware of having; these memories cannot be intentionally retrieved from memory.

Imprinting The tendency in certain species to follow the first moving thing (usually its mother) it sees after it is born or hatched.

Incentive External stimulus that prompts goal-directed behavior.

Independent variable In an experiment, the variable that is manipulated to test its effects on the other, dependent variables.

Industrial/organizational (I/O) psychology The area of psychology concerned with the application of psychological principles to the problems of human organizations, especially work organizations.

Inferiority complex In Adler's theory, the fixation on feelings of personal inferiority that results in emotional and social paralysis.

Information-processing model A computerlike model used to describe the way humans encode, store, and retrieve information.

Insanity Legal term for mentally disturbed people who are not considered responsible for their criminal actions.

Insight 1) Awareness of previously unconscious feelings and memories and how they influence present feelings and behavior. 2) Learning that occurs rapidly as a result of understanding all the elements of a problem.

Insight therapies A variety of individual psychotherapies designed to give people a better awareness and understanding of their feelings, motivations, and actions in the hope that this will help them to adjust.

Insomnia Sleep disorder characterized by difficulty in falling asleep or remaining asleep throughout the night.

Instinct Inborn, inflexible, goal-directed behavior that is characteristic of an entire species.

Intellectualization Thinking abstractly about stressful problems as a way of detaching oneself from them.

Intelligence A general term referring to the ability or abilities involved in learning and adaptive behavior.

Intelligence quotient (IQ) A numerical value given to intelligence that is determined from the scores on an intelligence test; based on a score of 100 for average intelligence.

Intermittent pairing Pairing the conditioned stimulus and the unconditioned stimulus on only a portion of the learning trials.

Interneurons (or association neurons) Neurons that carry messages from one neuron to another.

Interposition Monocular distance cue in which one object, by partly blocking a second object, is perceived as being closer.

Intrinsic motivation   A desire to perform a behavior that stems from the behavior performed.

Introvert   According to Jung, a person who usually focuses on his or her own thoughts and feelings.

Ions   Electrically charged particles found both inside and outside the neuron.

Iris   The colored part of the eye that regulates the size of the pupil.

James-Lange theory   States that stimuli cause physiological changes in our bodies, and emotions result from those physiological changes.

Just-world hypothesis   Attribution error based on the assumption that bad things happen to bad people and good things happen to good people.

Kinesthetic senses   Senses of muscle movement, posture, and strain on muscles and joints.

Language acquisition device   A hypothetical neural mechanism for acquiring language that is presumed to be "wired into" all humans.

Language   A flexible system of communication that uses sounds, rules, gestures, or symbols to convey information.

Latency period   In Freud's theory of personality, a period in which the child appears to have no interest in the other sex; occurs after the phallic stage.

Latent learning   Learning that is not immediately reflected in a behavior change.

Law of effect (principle of reinforcement)   Thorndike's theory that behavior consistently rewarded will be "stamped in" as learned behavior, and behavior that brings about discomfort will be "stamped out."

Learned helplessness   Failure to take steps to avoid or escape from an unpleasant or aversive stimulus that occurs as a result of previous exposure to unavoidable painful stimuli.

Learning   The process by which experience or practice results in a relatively permanent change in behavior or potential behavior.

Learning set   The ability to become increasingly more effective in solving problems as more problems are solved.

Lens   The transparent part of the eye behind the pupil that focuses light onto the retina.

Libido   According to Freud, the energy generated by the sexual instinct.

Light adaptation   Decreased sensitivity of rods and cones in bright light.

Limbic system   Ring of structures that plays a role in learning and emotional behavior.

Linear perspective   Monocular cue to distance and depth based on the fact that two parallel lines seem to come together at the horizon.

Linguistic relativity hypothesis   Whorf's idea that patterns of thinking are determined by the specific language one speaks.

Locus of control   According to Rotter, an expectancy about whether reinforcement is under internal or external control.

Longitudinal study   A method of studying developmental changes by evaluating the same people at different points in their lives.

Long-term memory (LTM)   The portion of memory that is more or less permanent, corresponding to everything we "know."

Lysergic acid diethylamide (LSD)   Hallucinogenic or "psychedelic" drug that produces hallucinations and delusions similar to those occurring in a psychotic state.

Mania   A mood disorder characterized by euphoric states, extreme physical activity, excessive talkativeness, distractedness, and sometimes grandiosity.

Marijuana   A mild hallucinogen that produces a "high" often characterized by feelings of euphoria, a sense of well-being, and swings in mood from gaiety to relaxation; may also cause feelings of anxiety and paranoia.

Maturation   An automatic biological unfolding of development in an organism as a function of the passage of time.

Means-end analysis   A heuristic strategy that aims to reduce the discrepancy between the current situation and the desired goal at a number of intermediate points.

Meditation   Any of the various methods of concentration, reflection, or focusing of thoughts undertaken to suppress the activity of the sympathetic nervous system.

Memory   The ability to remember the things that we have experienced, imagined, and learned.

Menarche   First menstrual period.

Menopause   The time in a woman's life when menstruation ceases.

Mental representations   Mental images or symbols (such as words) used to think about or remember an object, a person, or an event.

Mental retardation   Condition of significantly subaverage intelligence combined with deficiencies in adaptive behavior.

Mental set   The tendency to perceive and to approach problems in certain ways.

Midbrain   Region between the hindbrain and the forebrain; it is important for hearing and sight, and it is one of several places in the brain where pain is registered.

Midlife crisis   A time when adults discover they no longer feel fulfilled in their jobs or personal lives and attempt to make a decisive shift in career or lifestyle.

Midlife transition   According to Levinson, a process whereby adults assess the past and formulate new goals for the future.

Minnesota Multiphasic Personality Inventory (MMPI)   The most widely used objective personality test, originally intended for psychiatric diagnosis.

Mnemonics   Techniques that make material easier to remember.

Modeling   A behavior therapy in which the person learns desired behaviors by watching others perform those behaviors.

Monaural cue   Cue to sound location that requires just one ear.

Monochromats   Organisms that are totally color-blind.

Monocular cues   Visual cues requiring the use of one eye.

Mood disorders   Disturbances in mood or prolonged emotional state.

Morphemes   The smallest meaningful units of speech, such as simple words, prefixes, and suffixes.

Motion parallax   Monocular distance cue in which objects closer than the point of visual focus seem to move in the direction opposite to the viewer's moving head, and objects beyond the focus point appear to move in the same direction as the viewer's head.

Motive   Specific need or desire, such as hunger, thirst, or achievement, that prompts goal-directed behavior.

Motor (or efferent) neurons   Neurons that carry messages from the spinal cord or brain to the muscles and glands.

Myelin sheath   White fatty covering found on some axons.

Narcissistic personality disorder   Personality disorder in which the person has an exaggerated sense of self-importance and needs constant admiration.

Narcolepsy   Hereditary sleep disorder characterized by sudden nodding off during the day and sudden loss of muscle tone following moments of emotional excitement.

Natural selection   The mechanism proposed by Darwin in his theory of evolution, which states that organisms best adapted to their environment tend to survive, transmitting their genetic characteristics to succeeding generations, whereas organisms with less adaptive characteristics tend to vanish from the earth.

Naturalistic observation   Research method involving the systematic study of animal or human behavior in natural settings rather than in the laboratory.

Negative reinforcer   Any event whose reduction or termination increases the likelihood that ongoing behavior will recur.

Neonates   Newborn babies.

NEO-PI-R   An objective personality test designed to assess the Big Five personality traits.

Nerve (or tract)   Group of axons bundled together.

Neural impulse (or action potential)   The firing of a nerve cell.

Neural plasticity   The ability of the brain to change in response to experience.

Neurogenesis   The growth of new neurons.

Neurons   Individual cells that are the smallest unit of the nervous system.

Neurotic trends   Horney's term for irrational strategies for coping with emotional problems and minimizing anxiety.

Neurotransmitters   Chemicals released by the synaptic vesicles that travel across the synaptic space and affect adjacent neurons.

Non-REM (NREM) sleep   Non-rapid-eye-movement stages of sleep that alternate with REM stages during the sleep cycle.

Norm   A shared idea or expectation about how to behave.

Obedience   Change of behavior in response to a command from another person, typically an authority figure.

Object permanence   The concept that things continue to exist even when they are out of sight.

Objective tests   Personality tests that are administered and scored in a standard way.

Observational (or vicarious) learning   Learning by observing other people's behavior.

Observer bias   Expectations or biases of the observer that might distort or influence his or her interpretation of what was actually observed.

Obsessive-compulsive disorder   An anxiety disorder in which a person feels driven to think disturbing thoughts or to perform senseless rituals.

Occipital lobe   Part of the cerebral hemisphere that receives and interprets visual information.

Oedipus complex and Electra complex   According to Freud, a child's sexual attachment to the parent of the opposite sex and jealousy toward the parent of the same sex; generally occurs in the phallic stage.

Olfactory bulb   The smell center in the brain.

Operant behavior   Behavior designed to operate on the environment in a way that will gain something desired or avoid something unpleasant.

Operant (or instrumental) conditioning   The type of learning in which behaviors are emitted (in the presence of specific stimuli) to earn rewards or avoid punishments.

Opiates   Drugs, such as opium and heroin, derived from the opium poppy, that dull the senses and induce feelings of euphoria, well-being, and relaxation. Synthetic drugs resembling opium derivatives are also classified as opiates.

Opponent-process theory   Theory of color vision that holds that three sets of color receptors (yellow-blue, red-green, black-white) respond to determine the color you experience.

Optic chiasm   The point near the base of the brain where some fibers in the optic nerve from each eye cross to the other side of the brain.

Optic nerve   The bundle of axons of ganglion cells that carries neural messages from each eye to the brain.

Oral stage   First stage in Freud's theory of personality development, in which the infant's erotic feelings center on the mouth, lips, and tongue.

Organ of Corti   Structure on the surface of the basilar membrane that contains the receptor cells for hearing.

Oval window   Membrane across the opening between the middle ear and inner ear that conducts vibrations to the cochlea.

Overtones   Tones that result from sound waves that are multiples of the basic tone; primary determinant of timbre.

Pancreas   Organ lying between the stomach and small intestine; it secretes insulin and glucagon to regulate blood-sugar levels.

Panic disorder   An anxiety disorder characterized by recurrent panic attacks in which the person suddenly experiences intense fear or terror without any reasonable cause.

Paranoid personality disorder   Personality disorder in which the person is inappropriately suspicious and mistrustful of others.

Paranoid schizophrenia   Schizophrenic disorder marked by extreme suspiciousness and complex, bizarre delusions.

Paraphilias   Sexual disorders in which unconventional objects or situations cause sexual arousal.

Parasympathetic division   Branch of the autonomic nervous system; it calms and relaxes the body.

Parathyroids   Four tiny glands embedded in the thyroid; they secrete parathormone.

Parietal lobe   Part of the cerebral cortex that receives sensory information from throughout the body.

Participants   Individuals whose reactions or responses are observed in an experiment.

Pedophilia   Desire to have sexual relations with children as the preferred or exclusive method of achieving sexual excitement.

Peer group   A network of same-aged friends and acquaintances who give one another emotional and social support.

Perception   The brain's interpretation of sensory information so as to give it meaning.

Perceptual constancy   A tendency to perceive objects as stable and unchanging despite changes in sensory stimulation.

Performance standards   In Bandura's theory, standards that people develop to rate the adequacy of their own behavior in a variety of situations.

Performance tests   Intelligence tests that minimize the use of language.

Peripheral nervous system   Division of the nervous system that connects the central nervous system to the rest of the body.

Persona   According to Jung, our public self, the mask we put on to represent ourselves to others.

Personal fable   Elkind's term for adolescents' delusion that they are unique, very important, and invulnerable.

Personal unconscious   In Jung's theory of personality, one of the two levels of the unconscious; it contains the individual's repressed thoughts, forgotten experiences, and undeveloped ideas.

Personality disorders   Disorders in which inflexible and maladaptive ways of thinking and behaving learned early in life cause distress to the person or conflicts with others.

Personality traits   Dimensions or characteristics on or in which people differ in distinctive ways.

Personality   An individual's unique pattern of thoughts, feelings, and behaviors that persists over time and across situations.

Phallic stage   Third stage in Freud's theory of personality development, in which erotic feelings center on the genitals.

Pheromones   Chemicals that communicate information to other organisms through smell.

Phi phenomenon   Apparent movement caused by flashing lights in sequence, as on theater marquees.

Phonemes   The basic sounds that make up any language.

Pineal gland   A gland located roughly in the center of the brain that appears to regulate activity levels over the course of a day.

Pitch   Auditory experience corresponding primarily to frequency of sound vibrations, resulting in a higher or lower tone.

Pituitary gland   Gland located on the underside of the brain; it produces the largest number of the body's hormones.

Placebo   Experimental design useful in studies of the effects of drugs, in which neither the subject nor the researcher knows at the time of administration which subjects are receiving an active drug and which are receiving an inactive substance.

Placebo effect   Pain relief that occurs when a person believes a pill or procedure will reduce pain. The actual cause of the relief seems to come from endorphins.

Place theory   Theory that pitch is determined by the location of greatest vibration on the basilar membrane.

Pleasure principle   According to Freud, the way in which the id seeks immediate gratification of an instinct.

Polarization   1) Shift in attitudes by members of a group toward more extreme positions than the ones held before group discussion. 2) The condition of a neuron when the inside is negatively charged relative to the outside; for example, when the neuron is at rest.

Polygenic inheritance   Process by which several genes interact to produce a certain trait; responsible for our most important traits.

Positive psychology   An emerging field of psychology that focuses on positive experiences, including subjective well-being, self-determination, the relationship between positive emotions and physical health, and the factors that allow individuals, communities, and societies to flourish.

Positive reinforcer   Any event whose presence increases the likelihood that ongoing behavior will recur.

Posttraumatic stress disorder (PTSD)   Psychological disorder characterized by episodes of anxiety, sleeplessness, and nightmares resulting from some disturbing past event.

Prejudice   An unfair, intolerant, or unfavorable attitude toward a group of people.

Prenatal development   Development from conception to birth.

Preoperational stage   In Piaget's theory, the stage of cognitive development between 2 and 7 years of age in which the individual becomes able to use mental representations and language to describe, remember, and reason about the world, though only in an egocentric fashion.

Preparedness A biological readiness to learn certain associations because of their survival advantages.

Pressure A feeling that one must speed up, intensify, or change the direction of one's behavior or live up to a higher standard of performance.

Primacy effect The fact that early information about someone weighs more heavily than later information in influencing one's impression of that person.

Primary drive An unlearned drive, such as hunger, that is based on a physiological state.

Primary motor cortex The section of the frontal lobe responsible for voluntary movement.

Primary prevention Techniques and programs to improve the social environment so that new cases of mental disorders do not develop.

Primary reinforcer A reinforcer that is rewarding in itself, such as food, water, and sex.

Primary somatosensory cortex Area of the parietal lobe where messages from the sense receptors are registered.

Principle of conservation The concept that the quantity of a substance is not altered by reversible changes in its appearance.

Proactive interference The process by which information already in memory interferes with new information.

Problem representation The first step in solving a problem; it involves interpreting or defining the problem.

Procedural memory The portion of long-term memory that stores information relating to skills, habits, and other perceptual-motor tasks.

Projection Attributing one's repressed motives, feelings, or wishes to others.

Projective tests Personality tests, such as the Rorschach inkblot test, consisting of ambiguous or unstructured material.

Prototype According to Rosch, a mental model containing the most typical features of a concept

Proximity How close two people live to each other.

Psychoactive drugs Chemical substances that change moods and perceptions.

Psychoanalysis The theory of personality Freud developed as well as the form of therapy he invented.

Psychoanalytic model View that psychological disorders result from unconscious internal conflicts.

Psychobiology The area of psychology that focuses on the biological foundations of behavior and mental processes.

Psychodynamic theories Personality theories contending that behavior results from psychological factors that interact within the individual, often outside conscious awareness.

Psychology The scientific study of behavior and mental processes.

Psychoneuroimmunology (PNI) A new field that studies the interaction between stress on the one hand and immune, endocrine, and nervous system activity on the other.

Psychosomatic disorders Disorders in which there is real physical illness that is largely caused by psychological factors such as stress and anxiety.

Psychosurgery Brain surgery performed to change a person's behavior and emotional state; a biological therapy rarely used today.

Psychotherapy The use of psychological techniques to treat personality and behavior disorders.

Psychotic (psychosis) Behavior characterized by a loss of touch with reality.

Puberty The onset of sexual maturation, with accompanying physical development.

Punisher A stimulus that follows a behavior and decreases the likelihood that the behavior will be repeated.

Punishment Any event whose presence decreases the likelihood that ongoing behavior will recur.

Pupil A small opening in the iris through which light enters the eye.

Race A subpopulation of a species, defined according to an identifiable characteristic (that is, geographic location, skin color, hair texture, genes, facial features, and so forth).

Racism Prejudice and discrimination directed at a particular racial group.

Random sample Sample in which each potential participant has an equal chance of being selected.

Rational-emotive therapy (RET) A directive cognitive therapy based on the idea that clients' psychological distress is caused by irrational and self-defeating beliefs and that the therapist's job is to challenge such dysfunctional beliefs.

Reaction formation Expression of exaggerated ideas and emotions that are the opposite of one's repressed beliefs or feelings.

Reality principle According to Freud, the way in which the ego seeks to satisfy instinctual demands safely and effectively in the real world.

Receptor cell A specialized cell that responds to a particular type of energy.

Receptor sites Locations on a receptor neuron into which a specific neurotransmitter fits like a key into a lock.

Recessive gene Member of a gene pair that can control the appearance of a certain trait only if it is paired with another recessive gene.

Regression Reverting to childlike behavior and defenses.

Reinforcer A stimulus that follows a behavior and increases the likelihood that the behavior will be repeated.

Reliability Ability of a test to produce consistent and stable scores.

REM (paradoxical) sleep Sleep stage characterized by rapid eye movements and increased dreaming.

Representative sample Sample carefully chosen so that the characteristics of the participants correspond closely to the characteristics of the larger population.

Representativeness A heuristic by which a new situation is judged on the basis of its resemblance to a stereotypical model.

Repression Excluding uncomfortable thoughts, feelings, and desires from consciousness.

Response generalization Giving a response that is somewhat different from the response originally learned to that stimulus.

Resting potential Electrical charge across a neuron membrane resulting from more positive ions concentrated on the outside and more negative ions on the inside.

Reticular formation (RF) Network of neurons in the hindbrain, the midbrain, and part of the forebrain whose primary function is to alert and arouse the higher parts of the brain.

Retina The lining of the eye containing receptor cells that are sensitive to light.

Retinal disparity Binocular distance cue based on the difference between the images cast on the two retinas when both eyes are focused on the same object.

Retroactive interference The process by which new information interferes with information already in memory.

Retrograde amnesia The inability to recall events preceding an accident or injury, but without loss of earlier memory.

Risky shift Greater willingness of a group than an individual to take substantial risks.

Rods Receptor cells in the retina responsible for night vision and perception of brightness.

Rorschach test A projective test composed of ambiguous inkblots; the way people interpret the blots is thought to reveal aspects of their personality.

Rote rehearsal Retaining information in memory simply by repeating it over and over.

Saturation The vividness or richness of a hue.

Schedule of reinforcement In operant conditioning, the rule for determining when and how often reinforcers will be delivered.

Schema (skee-mah; plural: schemata) A set of beliefs or expectations about something that is based on past experience.

Schizoid personality disorder Personality disorder in which a person is withdrawn and lacks feelings for others.

Schizophrenic disorders Severe disorders in which there are disturbances of thoughts, communications, and emotions, including delusions and hallucinations.

Scientific method An approach to knowledge that relies on collecting data, generating a theory to explain the data, producing testable hypotheses based on the theory, and testing those hypotheses empirically.

Secondary drive A learned drive, such as ambition, that is not based on a physiological state.

Secondary prevention Programs to identify groups that are at high risk for mental disorders and to detect maladaptive behavior in these groups and treat it promptly.

Secondary reinforcer A reinforcer whose value is acquired through association with other primary or secondary reinforcers.

Self-actualizing tendency According to Rogers, the drive of human beings to fulfill their self-concepts, or the images they have of themselves.

Self-efficacy According to Bandura, the expectancy that one's efforts will be successful.

Self-fulfilling prophecy The process in which a person's expectation about another elicits behavior from the second person that confirms the expectation.

Self-monitoring The tendency for an individual to observe the situation for cues about how to react.

Semantic memory The portion of long-term memory that stores general facts and information.

Sensation The basic experience of stimulating the body's senses.

Sensory (or afferent) neurons Neurons that carry messages from sense organs to the spinal cord or brain.

Sensory registers Entry points for raw information from the senses.

Sensory-motor stage In Piaget's theory, the stage of cognitive development between birth and 2 years of age in which the individual develops object permanence and acquires the ability to form mental representations.

Serial position effect The finding that when asked to recall a list of unrelated items, performance is better for the items at the beginning and end of the list.

Sex-typed behavior Socially prescribed ways of behaving that differ for boys and girls.

Sexual dysfunction Loss or impairment of the ordinary physical responses of sexual function.

Shadowing Monocular cue to distance and depth based on the fact that shadows often appear on the parts of objects that are more distant.

Shape constancy A tendency to see an object as the same shape no matter what angle it is viewed from.

Shaping Reinforcing successive approximations to a desired behavior.

Short-term memory (STM) Working memory; briefly stores and processes selected information from the sensory registers

Short-term psychodynamic therapy Insight therapy that is time-limited and focused on trying to help clients correct the immediate problems in their lives.

Sixteen Personality Factor Questionnaire Objective personality test created by Cattell that provides scores on the sixteen traits he identified.

Size constancy The perception of an object as the same size regardless of the distance from which it is viewed.

Skinner box A box often used in operant conditioning of animals; it limits the available responses and thus increases the likelihood that the desired response will occur.

Social cognition Knowledge and understanding concerning the social world and the people in it (including oneself).

Social influence The process by which others individually or collectively affect one's perceptions, attitudes, and actions.

Social learning theorists Psychologists whose view of learning emphasizes the ability to learn by observing a model or receiving instructions, without firsthand experience by the learner.

Social phobia An anxiety disorder characterized by excessive, inappropriate fears connected with social situations or performances in front of other people.

Social psychology The scientific study of the ways in which the thoughts, feelings, and behaviors of one individual are influenced by the real, imagined, or inferred behavior or characteristics of other people.

Socialization Process by which children learn the behaviors and attitudes appropriate to their family and culture.

Somatic nervous system The part of the peripheral nervous system that carries messages from the senses to the central nervous system and between the central nervous system and the skeletal muscles.

Somatoform disorders Disorders in which there is an apparent physical illness for which there is no organic basis.

Sound A psychological experience created by the brain in response to changes in air pressure that are received by the auditory system.

Sound waves Changes in pressure caused when molecules of air or fluid collide with one another and then move apart again.

Specific phobia Anxiety disorder characterized by an intense, paralyzing fear of something.

Spinal cord Complex cable of neurons that runs down the spine, connecting the brain to most of the rest of the body.

Split-half reliability A method of determining test reliability by dividing the test into two parts and checking the agreement of scores on both parts.

Spontaneous recovery The reappearance of an extinguished response after the passage of time, without training.

Stereoscopic vision Combination of two retinal images to give a three-dimensional perceptual experience.

Stereotype A set of characteristics presumed to be shared by all members of a social category.

Stimulants Drugs, including amphetamines and cocaine, that stimulate the sympathetic nervous system and produce feelings of optimism and boundless energy.

Stimulus control Control of conditioned responses by cues or stimuli in the environment.

Stimulus discrimination Learning to respond to only one stimulus and to inhibit the response to all other stimuli.

Stimulus generalization The transfer of a learned response to different but similar stimuli.

Stimulus motive Unlearned motive, such as curiosity or contact, that prompts us to explore or change the world around us.

Stress A state of psychological tension or strain.

Stressor Any environmental demand that creates a state of tension or threat and requires change or adaptation.

Stress-inoculation therapy A type of cognitive therapy that trains clients to cope with stressful situations by learning a more useful pattern of self-talk.

Stretch receptors Receptors that sense muscle stretch and contraction.

Stroboscopic motion Apparent movement that results from flashing a series of still pictures in rapid succession, as in a motion picture.

Structuralism School of psychology that stresses the basic units of experience and the combinations in which they occur.

Subgoals Intermediate, more manageable goals used in one heuristic strategy to make it easier to reach the final goal.

Sublimation Redirecting repressed motives and feelings into more socially acceptable channels.

Substance abuse A pattern of drug use that diminishes the ability to fulfill responsibilities at home or at work or school, that results in repeated use of a drug in dangerous situations, or that leads to legal difficulties related to drug use.

Substance dependence A pattern of compulsive drug-taking that results in tolerance, withdrawal symptoms, or other specific symptoms for at least a year.

Subtractive color mixing The process of mixing pigments, each of which absorbs some wavelengths of light and reflects others.

Superego According to Freud, the social and parental standards the individual has internalized; the conscience and the ego ideal.

Survey research Research technique in which questionnaires or interviews are administered to a selected group of people.

Sympathetic division Branch of the autonomic nervous system; it prepares the body for quick action in an emergency.

Synapse Area composed of the axon terminal of one neuron, the synaptic space, and the dendrite or cell body of the next neuron.

Synaptic space (or synaptic cleft) Tiny gap between the axon terminal of one neuron and the dendrites or cell body of the next neuron.

Synaptic vesicles   Tiny sacs in a terminal button that release chemicals into the synapse.

Systematic desensitization   A behavioral technique for reducing a person's fear and anxiety by gradually associating a new response (relaxation) with stimuli that have been causing the fear and anxiety.

Systems approach   View that biological, psychological, and social risk factors combine to produce psychological disorders. Also known as the biopsychosocial model of psychological disorders.

Taste buds   Structures on the tongue that contain the receptor cells for taste.

Temperament   Characteristic patterns of emotional reactions and emotional self-regulation.

Temporal lobe   Part of the cerebral hemisphere that helps regulate hearing, balance and equilibrium, and certain emotions and motivations.

Terminal button (or synaptic knob)   Structure at the end of an axon terminal branch.

Tertiary prevention   Programs to help people adjust to community life after release from a mental hospital.

Texture gradient   Monocular cue to distance and depth based on the fact that objects seen at greater distances appear to be smoother and less textured.

Thalamus   Forebrain region that relays and translates incoming messages from the sense receptors, except those for smell.

Thematic Apperception Test (TAT)   A projective test composed of ambiguous pictures about which a person is asked to write a complete story.

Theory   Systematic explanation of a phenomenon; it organizes known facts, allows us to predict new facts, and permits us to exercise a degree of control over the phenomenon.

Theory of multiple intelligences   Howard Gardner's theory that there is not one intelligence, but rather many intelligences, each of which is relatively independent of the others.

Threshold of excitation   The level an impulse must exceed to cause a neuron to fire.

Thyroid gland   Endocrine gland located below the voice box; it produces the hormone thyroxin.

Timbre   The quality or texture of sound; caused by overtones.

Token economy   An operant conditioning therapy in which people earn tokens (reinforcers) for desired behaviors and exchange them for desired items or privileges.

Transference   The client's carrying over to the analyst feelings held toward childhood authority figures.

Triarchic theory of intelligence   Sternberg's theory that intelligence involves mental skills (componential aspect), insight and creative adaptability (experiential aspect), and environmental responsiveness (contextual aspect).

Trichromatic theory   The theory of color vision that holds that all color perception derives from three different color receptors in the retina (usually red, green, and blue receptors).

Trichromats   People (and animals) that have normal color vision.

Twin studies   Studies of identical and fraternal twins to determine the relative influence of heredity and environment on human behavior.

Unconditional positive regard   In Rogers's theory, the full acceptance and love of another person regardless of our behavior.

Unconditioned response (UR)   A response that takes place in an organism whenever an unconditioned stimulus occurs.

Unconditioned stimulus (US)   A stimulus that invariably causes an organism to respond in a specific way.

Unconscious   In Freud's theory, all the ideas, thoughts, and feelings of which we are not and normally cannot become aware.

Undifferentiated schizophrenia   Schizophrenic disorder in which there are clear schizophrenic symptoms that don't meet the criteria for another subtype of the disorder.

Validity   Ability of a test to measure what it has been designed to measure.

Variable-interval schedule   A reinforcement schedule in which the correct response is reinforced after varying lengths of time following the last reinforcement.

Variable-ratio schedule   A reinforcement schedule in which a varying number of correct responses must occur before reinforcement is presented.

Vestibular senses   The senses of equilibrium and body position in space.

Vicarious reinforcement or vicarious punishment   Reinforcement or punishment experienced by models that affects the willingness of others to perform the behaviors they learned by observing those models.

Visual acuity   The ability to distinguish fine details visually.

Volley principle   Refinement of frequency theory; it suggests that receptors in the ear fire in sequence, with one group responding, then a second, then a third, and so on, so that the complete pattern of firing corresponds to the frequency of the sound wave.

Waking consciousness   Mental state that encompasses the thoughts, feelings, and perceptions that occur when we are awake and reasonably alert.

Wavelengths   The different energies represented in the electromagnetic spectrum.

Weber's law   The principle that the jnd for any given sense is a constant fraction or proportion of the stimulation being judged.

Wechsler Adult Intelligence Scale–Third Edition (WAIS-III)   An individual intelligence test developed especially for adults; measures both verbal and performance abilities.

Wechsler Intelligence Scale for Children–Third Edition (WISC-III)   An individual intelligence test developed especially for school-aged children; measures verbal and performance abilities and also yields an overall IQ score.

Withdrawal   Avoiding a situation when other forms of coping are not practical.

Working backward   A heuristic strategy in which one works backward from the desired goal to the given conditions.

Yerkes-Dodson law   States that there is an optimal level of arousal for the best performance of any task; the more complex the task, the lower the level of arousal that can be tolerated before performance deteriorates.

REFERENCES

Aaker, D.A., & Bruzzone, D.E. (1985). Causes of irritation in advertising. *Journal of Marketing, 49,* 47–57.

Aaronson, D., & Scarborough, H.S. (1976). Performance theories for sentence coding: Some quantitative evidence. *Journal of Experimental Psychology: Human Perception and Performance, 2,* 56–70.

Aaronson, D., & Scarborough, H.S. (1977). Performance theories for sentence coding: Some quantitative models. *Journal of Verbal Learning and Verbal Behavior, 16,* 277–304.

Abbar, M., Courltet, P., Bellivier, F., Leboyer, M., Boulenger, J.P., Castelhau, D., Ferrcira, M., Lambercy, C., Mouthon, D., Paoloni-Giacobino, A., Vessaz, M., Malafosse, A., Buresi, C., (2001). Suicide attempts and the tryptophan hydroxylase gene. *Molecular Psychiatry, 6,* 268–273.

Abramov, I., & Gordon, J. (1994). Color appearance: On seeing red or yellow, or green, or blue. *Annual Review of Psychology, 45,* 451–485.

Achter, J.A., Lubinski, D., & Benbow, C.P. (1996). Multipotentiality among intellectually gifted: "It was never there and already it's vanishing." *Journal of Counseling Psychology, 43,* 65–76.

Ackerman, D. (1995). *A natural history of the senses.* New York: Vintage.

Acredolo, L.P., & Hake, J.L. (1982). Infant perception. In B.B. Wolman (ed.), *Handbook of developmental psychology* (pp. 244–283). Englewood Cliffs, NJ: Prentice Hall.

Adams, G.R., & Gullota, T. (1983). *Adolescent life experiences.* Monterey, CA: Brooks/Cole.

Adams, J.L. (1980). *Conceptual blockbusting: A guide to better ideas* (2nd ed.). New York: Norton.

Adams, K., & Johnson-Greene, D. (1995). *PET and neuropsychological performance among chronic alcoholics.* Paper presented at the annual meeting of the American Psychological Association, New York.

Adelmann, P.K., & Zajonc, R.B. (1989). Facial efference and the experience of emotion. *Annual Review of Psychology, 40,* 249–280.

Ader, R., & Cohen, N. (1993). Ps. *of Psychology, 44,* 53–85.

Adesman, A. (2000, April). Does my child need Ritalin? *Newsweek,* p. 81.

Adler, N., Boyce, T., Chesney, M.A., Cohen, S., Folkman, S., Kahn, R.I., & Syme, S.L. (1994). Socioeconomic status and health. The challenge of the gradient. *American Psychologist, 49,* 15–24.

Adorno, T.W., Frenkel-Brunswick, E., Levinson, D.J., & Sanford, R.N. (1950). *The authoritarian personality.* New York: Harper & Row.

Agostinelli, G., Sherman, S.J., Presson, C.C., & Chassin, L. (1992). Self-protection and self-enhancement biases in estimates of population prevalence. *Personality and Social Psychology Bulletin, 18*(5), 631–642.

Agras, W.S., & Kraemer, H. (1983). The treatment of anorexia nervosa. Do different treatments have different outcomes? *Psychiatric Annals, 13,* 928–935.

Aiken, L.R. (1988). *Psychological testing and assessment* (6th ed.). Boston: Allyn & Bacon.

Ainsworth, M.D. (1989). Attachments beyond infancy. *American Psychologist, 44,* 709–716.

Ainsworth, M.D., Blehar, M.C., Waters, E., & Wall, S. (1978). *Patterns of attachment.* New York: Halstead Press.

Ainsworth, M.D.S. (1977). Attachment theory and its utility in cross-cultural research. In P.H. Leiderman, S.R. Tulkin, & A. Rosenfields (eds.), *Culture and infancy: Variation in the human experience.* New York: Academic Press.

Albus, M. (1989). Cholecystokinin. *Progress in Neuro-Psychopharmacology and Biological Psychiatry, 12*(Suppl.), 5–21.

Alexander, C.N., Robinson, P., & Rainforth, N. (1994). Treating and preventing alcohol, nicotine, and drug abuse through Transcendental Meditation: A review and statistical meta-analysis. *Alcoholism Treatment Quarterly* [Special Issue], *11*(1–2), 13–87.

Allen, L.S., & Gorski, R.A. (1992). Sexual orientation and size of the anterior commissure in the human brain. *Proceedings of the National Academy of Sciences, 89,* 7199–7202.

Allen, V.L., & Levine, J.M. (1971). Social support and conformity: The role of independent assessment of reality. *Journal of Experimental Social Psychology, 7,* 48–58.

Alloy, L.B., Abramson, L.Y., & Francis, E.L. (1999). Do negative cognitive styles confer vulnerability to depression? *Current Directions in Psychological Science, 8,* 128–132

Alloy, L.B., Abramson, L.Y., Whitehouse, W.G., Hogan, M.E., Tashman, N.A., Steinberg, D.L., Rose, D.T., & Donovan, P. (1999). Depressogenic cognitive styles: Predictive validity, information processing and personality characteristics, and developmental origins. *Behaviour Research and Therapy, 37,* 503–531.

Allport, G.W. (1954). *The nature of prejudice.* New York: Anchor.

Allport, G.W., & Odbert, H.S. (1936). Trait-names: A psycholexical study. *Psychological Monographs, 47*(1, Whole No. 211).

Almagor, M., Tellegen, A., & Waller, N.G. (1995). The big seven model: A cross-cultural replication and further explorations of the basic dimensions of natural language descriptors. *Journal of Personality and Social Psychology, 69,* 300–307.

Altabe, M.N., & Thompson, J.K. (1994). Body image. In *Encyclopedia of human behavior* (Vol. 1, pp. 407–414). San Diego, CA: Academic Press.

Altman, I., & Taylor, D.A. (1973). *Social penetration: The development of interpersonal relationships.* New York: Holt, Rinehart & Winston.

Altman, L.K. (1995, April 18). Research dispels myth that brain in adults is unable to renew itself. *New York Times,* p. B9.

Aluja-Fabregat, A., & Torrubia-Beltri, R. (1998). Viewing mass media violence, perception of violence, personality and academic achievement. *Personality and Individual Differences, 25,* 973–989.

Amen, D.G., Stubblefield, M., Carmichael, B., & Thisted, R. (1996). Brain SPECT findings and aggressiveness. *Annals of clinical psychiatry, 8*(3), 129–137.

American Academy of Pediatrics. (1999, August 2). *AAP discourages television for very young children.* Press release.

American Psychiatric Association (APA). (1994). *Diagnostic and statistical manual of mental disorders* (4th ed.). Washington, DC: American Psychiatric Press.

American Psychiatric Association (APA). (1994). *Diagnostic and statistical manual of mental disorders* (4th ed.). Washington, DC: Author.

American Psychological Association (APA). (2000, November). Facts & figures. *Monitor on Psychology*, p. 10.

America's Children: Key National Indicators of Well-Being. (2000). A report from the National Maternal and Child Health Clearinghouse. Retrieved November 10, 2000, from the World Wide Web: http://childstats.gov

Anastasi, A., & Urbina, S. (1997). *Psychological testing* (7th ed.). Upper Saddle River, NJ: Prentice Hall.

Anch, A.M., Browman, C.P., Mitler, M.M., & Walsh, J.K. (1988). *Sleep: A scientific perspective.* Englewood Cliffs, NJ: Prentice Hall.

Anderson, C.A. (1997). Effects of violent movies and trait hostility on hostile feelings and aggressive thoughts. *Aggressive Behavior, 23,* 161–178.

Anderson, D.R. (1998). Educational television is not an oxymoron. *Annals of Public Policy Research, 557,* 24–38.

Anderson, D.R., Huston, A.C., Wright, J.C., & Collins, P.A. (1998). Initial findings on the long term impact of Sesame Street and educational television for children: The Recontact Study. In R. Noll & M. Price (Eds.), *A communications cornucopia: Markle Foundation essays on information policy* (pp. 279–296). Washington, DC: Brookings Institution.

Anderson, S.W., Bechara, A., Damasio, H., Tranel, D., & Damasio, A.R. (1999). Impairment of social and moral behavior related to early damage in human prefrontal contex. *Nature Neuroscience, 2,* 1032–1037.

Andrews, J.A., & Lewinsohn, P.M. (1992). Suicidal attempts among older adolescents: Prevalence and co-occurrence with psychiatric disorders. *Journal of the American Academy of Child and Adolescent Psychiatry, 31,* 655–662.

Angier, N. (1992, May 20). Is there a male menopause? Jury is still out. *New York Times,* p. A1.

Angier, N. (1995, June 20). Does testosterone equal aggression? Maybe not. *New York Times,* p. 1.

Anshel, M.H., Porter, A., & Quek, J-J. (1998). Coping with acute stress in sports as a function of gender: An exploratory study. *Journal of Sport Behavior, 21,* 363–376.

Aranya, N., Kushnir, T., & Valency, A. (1986). Organizational commitment in a male dominated profession. *Human Relations, 39,* 433–438.

Archer, J. (1996). Sex differences in social behavior: Are the social role and evolutionary explanations compatible? *American Psychologist, 51*(9), 909–917.

Arias, C., Curet, C.A., Moyano, H.F., Joekes, S., & Blanch, N. (1993). Echolocation: A study of auditory functioning in blind and sighted subjects. *Journal of Visual Impairment and Blindness, 87,* 73–77.

Arkin, R.M., Cooper, H., & Kolditz, T. (1980). A statistical review of literature concerning the self-serving attribution bias in interpersonal influence situations. *Journal of Personality, 48,* 435–448.

Arnett, J. (1991, April). *Sensation seeking and egocentrism as factors in reckless behaviors among a college-age sample.* Paper presented at the meeting of the Society for Research in Child Development, Seattle, WA.

Arnett, J. (1995). The young and the reckless: Adolescent reckless behavior. *American Psychological Society, 4*(3), 67–71.

Arnett, J.J. (1999). Adolescent storm and stress, reconsidered. *American Psychologist, 54,* 317–326.

Arnett, J.J. (2000). Emerging adulthood: A theory of development from the late teens through the twenties. *American Psychologist, 55,* 469–480.

Aronoff, G.M. (ed.). (1993). *Evaluation and treatment of chronic pain* (2nd ed.). Baltimore, MD: Williams & Wilkins.

Aronson, E. (1994). *The social animal* (7th ed.). New York: Freeman.

Aronson, E. (1999). The power of self-persuasion. *American Psychologist, 54,* 875–884.

Ary, D.V., Duncan, T.E., Duncan, S.C., & Hops, H. (1999). Adolescent problem behavior: The influence of parents and peers. *Behaviour Research and Therapy, 37,* 217–230.

Asch, S.E. (1951). Effects of group pressure upon the modification and distortion of judgments. In H. Guetzkow (ed.), *Groups, leadership, and men.* Pittsburgh: Carnegie Press.

Asch, S.E. (1956). Studies of independence and conformity: I. A minority of one against a unanimous majority. *Psychological Monographs, 70*(9, Whole No. 416).

Ashley, R. (1975, October 17). The other side of LSD. *New York Times Magazine,* pp. 40ff.

Aslin, R.N., & Smith, L.B. (1988). Perceptual development. *Annual Review of Psychology, 39,* 435–473.

Aspinwall, L.G., & Taylor, S.E. (1997). A stitch in time: Self-regulation and proactive coping. *Psychological Bulletin, 121,* 417–436.

Aston, R. (1972). Barbiturates, alcohol and tranquilizers. In S.J. Mule & H. Brill (eds.), *The chemical and biological aspects of drug dependence.* Cleveland, OH: CRC Press.

Atchley, R.C. (1982). Retirement as a social institution. *Annual Review of Sociology, 8,* 263–287.

Aved, B.M., Irwin, M.M., Cummings, L.S., & Findeisen, N. (1993). Barriers to prenatal care for low-income women. *Western Journal of Medicine, 158*(5), 493–498.

Avery-Leaf, S., Cano, A., Cascardi, M., & O'Leary, K.D. (1995). *Evaluation of a dating violence prevention program.* Paper presented at the International Family Violence Research Conference, Durham, NH.

Azar, B. (1997b, December). Maternal emotions may influence fetal behaviors. *APA Monitor,* p. 17.

Azar, B. (1999a, March). "Decade of Behavior" moves forward. *APA Monitor,* p. 16.

Baars, B.J., & McGovern, K. (1994). Consciousness. In V.S. Ramachandran (Ed.), *Encyclopedia of human behavior* (Vol. 1, pp. 687–699). San Diego, CA: Academic Press.

Babkoff, H., Caspy, T., Mikulincer, M., & Sing, H.C. (1991). Monotonic and rhythmic influences: A challenge for sleep deprivation research. *Psychological Bulletin, 109,* 411–428.

Baddeley, A.D. (1986). *Working memory.* Oxford: Clarendon Press.

Baddeley, A.D. (1987). Amnesia. In R.L. Gregory (ed.), *The Oxford companion to the mind* (pp. 20–22). Oxford: Oxford University Press.

Baddeley, A.D. (1994). The magical number seven: Still magic after all these years? *Psychological Review, 101,* 353–356.

Baddeley, A.D., & Hitch, G.J. (1994). Developments in the concept of working memory. *Neuropsychology, 6,* 485–493.

Baer, L., Rauch, S.L., & Ballantine, T. (1995). Cingulotomy for intractable obsessive-compulsive disorder: Prospective long-term follow-up of 18 patients. *Archives of General Psychiatry, 52,* 384–392.

Bailey, A., LeCouteur, A., Gottesman, I., Bolton, P., Simonoff, E., Yuzda, E., & Rutter, M. (1995). Autism as a strongly genetic disorder: Evidence from a British twin study. *Psychological Medicine, 25*(1), 63–77.

Baillargeon, R. (1994). How do infants learn about the physical world? *American Psychological Society, 3*(5), 133–140.

Balaguer, A., & Markman, H. (1994). Mate selection. In *Encyclopedia of human behavior* (Vol. 3, pp. 127–135).

Bales, R.F. (1951). *Interaction Process Analysis: A method for the study of small groups.* Reading, MA: Addison-Wesley.

Ball, J.D., Archer, R.P., & Imhof, E.A. (1994). Time requirements of psychological testing: A survey of practitioners. *Journal of Personality Assessment, 63,* 239–249.

Ballie, R. (2001). Teen drinking more dangerous than previously thought. *Monitor on Psychology, 32,* 12.

Bandura, A. (1962). Social learning through imitation. In M.R. Jones (ed.), *Nebraska Symposium on Motivation.* Lincoln: University of Nebraska Press.

Bandura, A. (1965). Influence of models' reinforcement contingencies on the acquisition of imitative responses. *Journal of Personality and Social Psychology, 1,* 589–595.

Bandura, A. (1973). *Aggression: A social learning analysis.* Englewood Cliffs, NJ: Prentice Hall.

Bandura, A. (1977). *Social learning theory.* Englewood Cliffs, NJ: Prentice Hall.

Bandura, A. (1986). *Social foundations of thought and action: A social cognitive theory.* Englewood Cliffs, NJ: Prentice Hall.

Bandura, A. (1997). *Self-efficacy: The exercise of control.* New York: Freeman.

Bandura, A., Blanchard, E.B., & Ritter, B. (1969). Relative efficacy of desensitization and modeling approaches for inducing behavioral, affective, and attitudinal changes. *Journal of Personality and Social Psychology, 13,* 173–199.

Banich, M.T. (1998). Integration of information between the cerebral hemispheres. *Current Directions in Psychological Science, 7,* 32–37.

Barbaree, H.E., & Marshall, W.L. (1991). The role of male sexual arousal in rape: Six models. *Journal of Consulting and Clinical Psychology, 59,* 621–630.

Barbaree, H.E., & Seto, M.C. (1997). Pedophilia: Assessment and treatment. In D.R. Laws & W.T. O'Donohue (eds.), *Handbook of sexual deviance: Theory and application.* New York: Guilford.

Barber, B.L., & Eccles, J.E. (1992). Long-term influence of divorce and single parenting on adolescent family- and work-related values, behaviors and aspirations. *Psychological Bulletin, 111,* 108–126.

Barglow, P., Vaughn, B.E., & Molitor, N. (1987). Effects of maternal absence due to employment on the quality of infant-mother attachment in a low-risk sample. *Child Development, 58,* 945–954.

Barinaga, M. (2000a, March 3). Asilomar revisited: Lessons for today. *Science, 287,* 1584–1585.

Barker, S.L., Funk, S.C., & Houston, B.K. (1988). Psychological treatment versus nonspecific factors: A meta-analysis of conditions that engender comparable expectations for improvement. *Clinical Psychology Review, 8,* 579–594.

Barkley, R.A. (1990). *Hyperactive children: A handbook for diagnosis and treatment* (2nd ed.). New York: Guilford.

Barnett, R.C., Brennan, R.T., & Marshall, N.L. (1994). Gender and relationship between parent role quality and psychological distress. A study of men and women in dual-earner couples. *Journal of Family Issues, 15,* 229–252.

Barnett, W.S. (1998). Long-term effects on cognitive development and school success. In W.S. Barnett & S.S. Boocock (Eds.), *Early care and education for children in poverty* (pp. 11–44). Albany, NY: State University of New York Press.

Baron, R.A., & Byrne, D. (1991). *Social psychology: Understanding human interaction* (6th ed.). Boston: Allyn & Bacon.

Barret, G.V., & Depinet, R.L. (1991). A reconsideration of testing for competence rather than for intelligence. *American Psychologist, 46,* 1012–1024.

Barrett-Connor, E., & Bush, T.L. (1991). Estrogen and coronary heart disease in women. *Journal of the American Medical Association, 265,* 1861–1867.

Barrick, M.R., & Mount, M.K. (1991). The Big Five personality dimensions and job performance: A meta-analysis. *Personnel Psychology, 44,* 1–26.

Barron, F. (1963). *Creativity and psychological health.* Princeton, NJ: Van Nostrand.

Barron, F., & Harrington, D.M. (1981). Creativity, intelligence, and personality. *Annual Review of Psychology, 32,* 439–476.

Bartlett, F.C. (1932). *Remembering: A study in experimental and social psychology.* New York: Macmillan.

Bartoshuk, L.M., & Beauchamp, G.K. (1994). Chemical senses. *Annual Review of Psychology, 45,* 419–449.

Baruch, F., & Barnett, R. (1986). Role quality, multiple role involvement, and psychological well-being in mid-life women. *Journal of Personality and Social Psychology, 51,* 578–585.

Basow, S.A. (1986). *Gender stereotypes: Traditions and alternatives* (2nd ed.). Pacific Grove, CA: Brooks/Cole.

Bassetti, C., & Aldrich, M.S. (1996). Narcolepsy. *Neurological Clinics, 14,* 545–571.

Bauer, P.J. (1996). What do infants recall of their lives? Memory for specific events by one- to two-year-olds. *American Psychologist, 51*(1), 29–41.

Baumeister, R.F., & Leary, M.R. (1995). The need to belong: Desire for interpersonal attachments as a fundamental human motivation. *Psychological Bulletin, 117,* 497–529.

Baumrind, D. (1972). Socialization and instrumental competence in young children. In W.W. Hartup (ed.), *The young child: Reviews of research* (Vol. 2). Washington, DC: National Association for the Education of Young Children.

Baumrind, D. (1985). Research using intentional deception. *American Psychologist, 40,* 165–174.

Bayley, N. (1956). Individual patterns of development. *Child Development, 27,* 45–74.

Beatty, S.E., & Hawkins, D.I. (1989). Subliminal stimulation: Some new data and interpretation. *Journal of Advertising, 18,* 4–8.

Bechara, A., et al. (1997). Deciding advantageously before knowing the advantageous strategy. *Science, 275,* 1293–1295.

Beck, A.T. (1967). *Depression: Clinical, experimental and theoretical aspects.* New York: Harper (Hoeber).

Beck, A.T. (1976). *Cognitive therapy and emotional disorders.* New York: International Universities Press.

Beck, A.T. (1984). Cognition and therapy. *Archives of General Psychiatry, 41,* 1112–1114.

Beck, R. (1983). *Motivation: Theories and principles* (2nd ed.). Englewood Cliffs, NJ: Prentice Hall.

Begley, S. (May 3, 1999). Why the young kill. *Newsweek,* pp. 32–35.

Beirne-Smith, M., Patton, J., & Ittenbach, R. (1994). *Mental retardation* (4th ed.). New York: Macmillan.

Bellack, A.S., Hersen, M., & Turner, S.M. (1976). Generalization effects of social skills training in chronic schizophrenics: An experimental analysis. *Behavior Research and Therapy, 14,* 391–398.

Belsky, J., Lang, M.E., & Rovine, M. (1985). Stability and change in marriage across the transition to parenthood: A second study. *Journal of Marriage and the Family, 97,* 855–865.

Belsky, J., & Rovine, M. (1988). Nonmaternal care in the first year of life and infant parent attachment security. *Child Development, 59,* 157–167.

Belsky, J., Spritz, B., & Crnic, K. (1996). Infant attachment security and affective-cognitive information processing at age 3. *American Psychological Society, 7*(2), 111–114.

Bem, D.J., & Honorton, C. (1994). Does psi exist? Replicable evidence for an anomalous information transfer. *Psychological Bulletin, 115,* 4–18.

Bem, S.L. (1989). Genital knowledge and gender constancy in preschool children. *Child Development, 60,* 649–662.

Ben-Eliyahu, S., Yirmiya, R., Shavit, Y., & Liebeskind, J.C. (1990). Stress-induced suppression of natural killer cell cytotoxicity in the rat: A naltrexone-insensitive paradigm. *Behavioral Neuroscience, 104,* 235–238.

Benin, M.H., & Agostinelli, J. (1988). Husbands' and wives' satisfaction with the division of labor. *Journal of Marriage and the Family, 50,* 349–361.

Benjamin, L.T., Jr. (2000). The psychology laboratory at the turn of the 20th century. *American Psychologist, 55,* 318–321.

Bennett, D.A., & Knopman, D.S. (1994). Alzheimer's disease: A comprehensive approach to patient management. *Geriatrics, 49*(8), 20–26.

Benson, H. (1975). *The relaxation response.* New York: William Morrow.

Benton, D., & Roberts, G. (1988). Effect of vitamin and mineral supplementation on intelligence of a sample of schoolchildren. *Lancet, 1,* 14–144.

Berger, R.J. (1969). The sleep and dream cycle. In A. Kales (ed.), *Sleep: Physiology and pathology.* Philadelphia: Lippincott.

Berkowitz, M.W., & Gibbs, J.C. (1983). Measuring the developmental features of moral discussion. *Merrill-Palmer Quarterly, 29,* 399–410.

Berlin, B., & Kay, P. (1969). *Basic color terms: Their universality and evolution.* Berkeley: University of California Press.

Bernal, M.E., & Castro, F.G. (1994). Are clinical psychologists prepared for service and research with ethnic minorities? *American Psychologist, 49*(9), 797–805.

Berry, J.W., Portinga, Y.H., Segall, M.H., & Dasen, P.R. (1992). *Cross-cultural psychology: Research and applications.* New York: Cambridge University Press.

Berry, J.W. (1967). Independence and conformity in subsistence level societies. *Journal of Personality and Social Psychology, 7,* 415–518.

Berscheid, E., & Reis, H.T. (1998). Attraction and close relationships. In D. Gilbert, S.T. Fiske, & G. Lindzey (Eds.), *Handbook of social psychology* (4th ed., Vol. 2, pp. 193–381). New York: McGraw-Hill.

Bertenthal, B.I., Campos, J.J., & Kermoian, R. (1994). An epigenetic perspective on the development of self-produced locomotion and its consequences. *American Psychological Society, 3*(5), 140–145.

Bertrand, S., & Masling, J. (1969). Oral imagery and alcoholism. *Journal of Abnormal Psychology, 74,* 50–53.

Betancourt, H., & López, S.R. (1993). The study of culture, ethnicity, and race in American psychology. *American Psychologist, 48,* 629–637.

Bettencourt, B.A., & Miller, N. (1996). Gender differences in aggression as a function of provocation: A meta-analysis. *Psychological Bulletin, 119*(3), 422–427.

Biddle, S. (2000). Exercise, emotions, and mental health. In Y. Hanin (Ed.), *Emotions in sport* (pp. 267–291). Champaign, IL: Human Kinetics.

Birchler, G.R., & Fals-Stewart, W.S. (1994). Marital dysfunction. In *Encyclopedia of human behavior* (Vol. 3, pp. 103–113). San Diego, CA: Academic Press.

Birren, J.E. (1983). Aging in America: Role for psychology. *American Psychologist, 38,* 298–299.

Birren, J.E., & Fisher, L.M. (1995). Aging and speed of behavior: Possible consequences for psychological functioning. *Annual Review of Psychology, 46,* 329–353.

Bjorklund, D.F. (1989). *Children's thinking, developmental function and individual differences.* Pacific Grove, CA: Brooks/Cole.

Bjornson, C.R.R., Rietze, R.L., Reynolds, B.A., Magli, M.C., & Vescovi, A.L. (1999, January 22). Turning brain into blood: A hematopoietic fate adopted by adult neural stem cells in vivo. *Science, 283,* 534–537.

Blagrove, M., & Akehurst, L. (2000). Effects of sleep loss on confidence-accuracy relationships for reasoning and eyewitness memory. *Journal of Experimental Psychology: Applied, 6,* 59–73.

Blake, R.R., Helson, H., & Mouton, J. (1956). The generality of conformity behavior as a function of factual anchorage, difficulty of task and amount of social pressure. *Journal of Personality, 25,* 294–305.

Blakeslee, S. (1994, October 5). Yes, people are right. Caffeine is addictive. *New York Times.*

Blanchard, E.B., Appelbaum, K.A., Radnitz, C.L., Morrill, B., Michultka, D., Kirsch, C., Guarnier, P., Hillhouse, J., Evans, D.D., & Jaccard, J. (1990). A controlled evaluation of thermal biofeedback and thermal biofeedback combined with cognitive therapy in the treatment of vascular headache. *Journal of Consulting & Clinical Psychology, 58,* 216–224.

Blanck, D.C., Bellack, A.S., Rosnow, R.L., Rotheram-Borus, M.J., & Schooler, N.R. (1992). Scientific rewards and conflicts of ethical choices in human subjects research. *American Psychologist, 47,* 959–965.

Blatt, S.J., Zuroff, D.C., Quinlan, D.M., & Pilkonis, P. (1996). Interpersonal factors in brief treatment of depression: Further analysis of the NIMH Treatment of Depression Collaborative Research Program. *Journal of Consulting and Clinical Psychology, 64,* 162–171.

Block, J. (1971). *Lives through time.* Berkeley, CA: Bancroft.

Block, J., & Robbins, R.W. (1993). A longitudinal study of consistency and change in self-esteem from early adolescence to early adulthood. *Child Development, 64,* 902–923.

Blood, A.J., & Zatorre, R.J. (2001). Intensely pleasurable responses to music correlate with activity in brain regions implicated in reward and emotion. *Proceedings from the National Academy of Sciences, USA, 98,* 11818–11823.

Bloom, L. (1970). *Language development: Form and function in emerging grammar.* Cambridge, MA: MIT Press.

Blouin, J.L., Dombroski, B.A., Nath, S.K., Lasseter, V.K., Wolyniec, P.S., Nestadt, G., Thornquist, M., Ullrich, G., McGrath, J., Kasch, L., Lamacz, M., Thomas, M.G., Gehrig, C., Radhakrishnan, U., Snyder, S.E., Balk, K.G., Neufeld, K., Swartz, K.L., DeMarchi, N., Papadimitriou, G.N., Dikeos, D.G., Stefanis, C.N., Chakravarti, A., Childs, B., Pulver, A.E. (1998). Schizophrenia susceptibility loci on chromosomes 13q32 and 8p21. *Nature Genetics, 20,* 70–73.

Blum, J.M. (1979). *Pseudoscience and mental ability: The origins and fallacies of the IQ controversy.* New York: Monthly Review Press.

Blumenthal, A.L. (1975). A reappraisal of Wilhelm Wundt. *American Psychologist, 30,* 1081–1088.

Blundell, J.E., & Halford, J.C.G. (1998). Serotonin and appetite regulation: Implications for the pharmacological treatment of obesity. *CNS Drugs, 9,* 473–495.

Bok, S. (1999). *Mayhem: Violence as public entertainment.* Cambridge, MA: Perseus Books.

Bolles, R.C. (1972). Reinforcement, expectancy, and learning. *Psychological Review, 79,* 394–409.

Bolos, A.M., Dean, M., Lucas-Derse, S., Ramsburg, M., Brown, G.L., & Goldman, D. (1990). Population and pedigree studies reveal a lack of association between the dopamine D2 receptor gene and alcoholism. *JAMA, Journal of the American Medical Association, 264,* 3156–3160.

Bonanno, G.A., & Kaltman, S. (1999). Toward an integrative perspective on bereavement. *Psychological Bulletin, 125,* 760–776.

Bond, M.H., Wan, K.C., Leung, K., & Giacolone, R.A. (1985). How are responses to verbal insult related to cultural collectivism and power distance? *Journal of Cross-Cultural Psychology, 16,* 111–127.

Boomsma, D.I., Koopmans, J.R., Van Doornen, L.J.P., & Orlebeke, J.M. (1994). Genetic and social influences on starting to smoke: A study of Dutch adolescent twins and their parents. *Addiction, 89,* 219–226.

Booth-Kewley, S., & Friedman, H.S. (1987). Psychological predictors of heart disease: A quantitative review. *Psychological Bulletin, 101,* 343–362.

Boring, E.G., Langfeld, H.S., & Weld, H.P. (1976). *Foundations of psychology.* New York: Wiley.

Borkovec, T.D., & Costello, E. (1993). Efficacy of applied relaxation and cognitive-behavioral therapy in the treatment of generalized anxiety disorder. *Journal of Consulting and Clinical Psychology, 61,* 611–619.

Bornstein, R.F. (1989). Exposure and affect: Overview and meta-analysis of research, 1968–1987. *Psychological Reports, 106,* 265–289.

Botwin, M.D., & Buss, D.M. (1989). The structure of act report data: Is the five factor model of personality recaptured? *Journal of Personality and Social Psychology, 56,* 988–1001.

Bouchard, C., Tremblay, A., Despres, J.P., Nadeau, A., Lupien, P.J., Theriault, G., Dussault, J., Moorjani, S., Pinault, S., & Fournier, G. (1990). The response to long-term overfeeding in identical twins. *New England Journal of Medicine, 322,* 1477–1482.

Bouchard, T.J., Jr. (1984). Twins reared together and apart: What they tell us about human diversity. In S.W. Fox (Ed.), *Individuality and determinism* (pp. 147–178). New York: Plenum.

Bouchard, T.J., Jr., Lykken, D.T., McGue, M., Segal, N.L., & Tellegren, A. (1990). Sources of human psychological differences: The Minnesota study of twins reared apart. *Science, 250,* 223–228.

Bourgois, P. (1999). *Participant observation study of indirect paraphernalia sharing/HIV risk in a network of heroin injectors.* Retrieved September 17, 2000, from the World Wide Web: http://165.112.78.61/CEWG/ethno.html

Bourne, L.E., Dominowski, R.L., Loftus, E.F., & Healy, A.F. (1986). *Cognitive process* (2nd ed.). Englewood Cliffs, NJ: Prentice Hall.

Bouton, M.E. (1993). Context, time and memory retrieval in the interference paradigms of Pavlovian conditioning. *Psychological Bulletin, 114,* 80–99.

Bouton, M.E. (1994). Context, ambiguity and classical conditioning. *Current Directions in Psychological Science, 3,* 49–52.

Bower, G.H., & Mann, T. (1992). Improving recall by recoding interfering material at the time of recall. *Journal of Experimental Psychology: Learning, Memory, and Cognition, 18,* 1310–1320.

Bowlby, J. (1982). *Attachment and loss* (2nd ed.). New York: Basic Books. (Original work published in 1969.)

Bradley, C. (1997). Generativity-stagnation: Development of a status model. *Developmental Review, 17,* 262–290.

Brainerd, C.J. (1978). The stage question in cognitive-developmental theory. *Behavioral and Brain Sciences, 2,* 172–213.

Brainerd, C.J. (1996). Piaget: A centennial celebration. *American Psychological Society, 7*(4), 191–225.

Brandon, T.H. (1994). Negative affect as motivation to smoke. *Current Directions in Psychological Science, 3,* 33–37.

Braun, A.R., Balkin, T.J., Wesensten, N.J., Gwadry, F., Varga, M., Baldwin, P., Carson, R.E., Belenky, G., & Herscovitch, P. (1998, January 2). Dissociated pattern of activity in visual cortices and their projections during human rapid eye movement sleep. *Science, 279,* 91–95.

Bredemeier, B., & Shields, D. (1985, October). Values and violence in sports today. *Psychology Today,* pp. 23–32.

Breetvelt, I.S., & Van Dam, F.S.A.M. (1991). Underreporting by cancer patients: The case of response-shift. *Social Science and Medicine, 32,* 981–987.

Brenner, M.H. (1973). *Mental illness and the economy.* Cambridge, MA: Harvard University Press.

Brenner, M.H. (1979). Influence of the social environment on psychopathology: The historic perspective. In J.E. Barrett (ed.), *Stress and mental disorder.* New York: Raven Press.

Breslau, N., Davis, G.C., & Andreski, P. (1995). Risk factors for PTSD-related traumatic events: A prospective analysis. *American Journal of Psychiatry, 152,* 529–535.

Brewin, C.R. (1996). Theoretical foundations of cognitive-behavior therapy for anxiety and depression. *Annual Review of Psychology, 47,* 33–57.

Brickman, P., Coates, D., & Janoff-Bulman, R. (1978). Lottery winners and accident victims: Is happiness relative? *Journal of Personality and Social Psychology, 36,* 917–927.

Broadbent, D.E. (1958). *Perception and communication.* New York: Pergamon.

Brobert, A.G., Wessels, H., Lamb, M.E., & Hwang, C.P. (1997). Effects of day care on the development of cognitive abilities in 8-year-olds: A longitudinal study. *Developmental Psychology, 33,* 62–69.

Brody, L. (1985). Gender differences in emotional development: A review of theories and research. In A.J. Stewart & M.B. Lykes (eds.), *Gender and personality: Current perspectives on theory and research* (pp. 14–61). Durham, NC: Duke University Press.

Broida, J., Tingley, L., Kimball, R., & Miele, J. (1993). Personality differences between pro- and anti-vivisectionists. *Society and Animals, 1,* 129–144.

Bronfenbrenner, U. (1986). Ecology of the family as a context for human development: Research perspectives. *Developmental Psychology, 22,* 723–742.

Brooks-Gunn, J. (1993). *Adolescence.* Paper presented at the meeting of the Society for Research in Child Development, Kansas City, MO.

Brooks-Gunn, J., & Lewis, M. (1984). The development of early visual self-recognition. *Developmental Review, 4,* 215–239.

Brown, B., & Grotberg, J.J. (1981). Head Start: A successful experiment. *Courrier.* Paris: International Children's Centre.

Brown, L.S., & Ballou, M. (1992). *Personality and psychopathology: Feminists reappraisals.* New York: Guilford.

Brown, R. (1958). *Words and things.* New York: Free Press/Macmillan.

Brown, W.A. (1998, August 23). The power of the placebo. *Charlotte Observer,* p. 1E.

Browne, A. (1993). Violence against women by male partners: Prevalence, outcomes and policy implications. *American Psychologist, 48,* 1077–1087.

Bruch, H. (1980). *The golden cage: The enigma of anorexia nervosa.* New York: Random House.

Bruder, G.E., Stewart, M.W., Mercier, M.A., Agosti, V., Leite, P., Donovan, S., & Quitkin, F.M. (1997). Outcome of cognitive-behavioral therapy for depression: Relation to hemispheric dominance for verbal processing. *Journal of Abnormal Psychology, 106,* 138–144.

Brumberg, J.J. (1988). *Fasting girls: The emergence of anorexia nervosa as a modern disease.* Cambridge, MA: Harvard University Press.

Brunner, H.G., Nelen, M., Breakefield, X.O., Ropers, H.H., & Van Oost, B.A. (1993a). Abnormal behavior associated with a point mutation in the structural gene for monoamine oxidase A. *Science, 262,* 578–580.

Bushman, B.J., Baumeister, R.F., & Stack, A.D. (1999). Catharsis, aggression, and persuasive influence: Self-fulfilling or self-defeating prophecies? *Journal of Personality & Social Psychology, 76,* 367–376.

Bushman, B.J. (1993). Human aggression while under the influence of alcohol and other drugs: An integrative research review. *Current Directions in Psychological Science, 2,* 148–152.

Bushman, B.J., & Baumeister, R.F. (1998). Threatened egotism, narcissism, self-esteem, and direct and displaced aggression: Does self-love or self-hate lead to violence? *Journal of Personality & Social Psychology, 75,* 219–229.

Bushman, B.J., & Cooper, H.M. (1990). Effects of alcohol on human aggression: An integrative research review. *Psychological Bulletin, 107,* 341–354.

Buss, D.M. (1990). The evolution of anxiety and social exclusion. *Journal of Social and Clinical Psychology, 9,* 196–210.

Buss, D.M. (1991). Evolutionary personality psychology. *Annual Review of Psychology, 42,* 459–491.

Buss, D.M. (2000a). The evolution of happiness. *American Psychologist, 55,* 15–23.

Buss, D.M. (2000b). *The dangerous passion: Why jealousy is as necessary as love and sex.* New York: Free Press.

Buss, D.M., & Malamuth, N.M. (Eds.). (1996). *Sex, power, conflict: Evolutionary and feminist perspectives.* New York: Oxford University Press.

Buss, D.M., & Shackelford, T.K. (1997). Human aggression in evolutionary perspective. *Clinical Psychology Review, 17,* 605–619.

Buss, D.M. (1985). Human mate selection. *American Scientist, 73,* 47–51.

Buss, D.M. (1989). Sex differences in human mate preferences: Evolutionary hypotheses tested in 37 cultures. *Behavioral and Brain Sciences, 12,* 1–49.

Butcher, J.N., & Rouse, S.V. (1996). Personality: Individual differences and clinical assessment. *Annual Review of Psychology, 47,* 87–111.

Butler, R.N., & Lewis, M.I. (1982). *Aging and mental health: Positive psychological and biomedical approaches.* St. Louis, MO: Mosby.

Byne, W. (1994). The biological evidence challenged. *Scientific American, 270*(5), 50–55.

Byrne, D. (1961). Interpersonal attraction and attitude similarity. *Journal of Abnormal and Social Psychology, 62,* 713–715.

Cabeza, R., & Nyberg, L. (2000). Imaging cognition II: An empirical review of 275 PET and fMRI studies. *Journal of Cognitive Neuroscience, 12,* 1–47.

Cacioppo, J.T., & Gardner, W.L. (1999). Emotion. *Annual Review of Psychology, 50,* 191–214.

Cairns, E., & Darby, J. (1998). The conflict in Northern Ireland: Causes, consequences, and controls. *American Psychologist, 53,* 754–760.

Calder, B.J., Insko, C.A., & Yandell, B. (1974). The relation of cognitive and memorial processes to persuasion in simulated jury trial. *Journal of Applied Social Psychology, 4,* 62–92.

Califano, J.A., Jr. (1999, August 24). White-Line Fever: What an older and wiser George W. should do. *Washington Post,* p. A17.

Califano, J.A., Jr. (2000, March). *It's the substance abuse, stupid!* Opening remarks. National Center on Addiction and Substance Abuse (CASA) at Columbia University. Retrieved September 15, 2000, from the World Wide Web: http://www.casacolumbia.org

Callahan, R. (2000, January 13). Tall Polish men have tall kids, study says. *Charlotte Observer,* p. 12A.

Cannon, W.B. (1929). *Bodily changes in pain, hunger, fear, and rage,* rev. ed. New York: Appleton-Century.

Capron, C., & Duyme, M. (1989). Assessment of effects of socioeconomic status on IQ in a full cross-fostering study. *Nature (London), 340,* 552–554.

Carlson, N.R. (2000). *Physiology of behavior* (7th ed.). Boston: Allyn & Bacon.

Carlson, V. (1994). Child abuse. In *Encyclopedia of human behavior* (Vol. 1, pp. 561–578). San Diego, CA: Academic Press.

Carpenter, S. (2001). Research confirms the virtue of 'sleeping on it'. *Monitor on Psychology, 32,* 49–51.

Carr, M., Borkowski, J.G., & Maxwell, S.E. (1991). Motivational components of underachievement. *Developmental Psychology, 27,* 108–118.

Carskadon, M.A., & Dement, W.C. (1982). Nocturnal determinants of daytime sleepiness. *Sleep, 5*(Suppl. 2), 73–81.

Carson, R.C., & Butcher, J.N. (1992). *Abnormal psychology and modern life.* New York: HarperCollins.

Carstensen, L. (1995). Evidence for a life-span theory of socioemotional selectivity. *American Psychological Society, 4*(5), 151–156.

Carter, B. (1996, February 7). New report becomes a weapon in the debate over TV violence. *New York Times.*

Carter, R. (1998). *Mapping the mind.* Berkeley: University of California Press.

Casas, J.M. (1995). Counseling and psychotherapy with racial/ethnic minority groups in theory and practice. In B. Bongar & L.E. Beutler (eds.), *Comprehensive handbook of psychotherapy* (pp. 311–335). New York: Oxford University Press.

Caspi, A., & Elder, G.H., Jr. (1986). Life satisfaction in old age: Linking social psychology and history. *Journal of Psychology and Aging, 1,* 18–26.

Caspi, A., Moffitt, T., Newman, D.L., & Silva, P. (1996). Behavioral observations at age 3 years predict adult psychiatric disorders. *Archives of General Psychiatry, 53,* 1033–1039.

Cattell, R.B. (1965). *The scientific analysis of personality.* Baltimore: Penguin.

Cattell, R.B. (1971). *Abilities: Their structure, growth, and action.* Boston: Houghton Mifflin.

Cattell, R.B., & Kline, P. (1977). *The specific analysis of personality and motivation.* New York: Academic Press.

Cavanaugh, J.C. (1990). *Adult development and aging.* Belmont, CA: Wadsworth.

Ceci, S.J., & Williams, W.M. (1997). Schooling, intelligence, and income. *American Psychologist, 52,* 1051–1058.

Celis, W. (1994, June 8). More college women drinking to get drunk. *New York Times,* p. B8.

Centers for Disease Control and Prevention. (1999). Suicide deaths and rates per 100,000 [On-line]. Available: http://www.cdc.gov/ncipc/data/us9794/suic.htm

Chaiken, S., & Eagly, A.H. (1976). Communication modality as a determinant of message persuasiveness and message comprehensibility. *Journal of Personality and Social Psychology, 34,* 605–614.

Chaikin, A.L., & Darley, J.M. (1973). Victim or perpetrator? Defensive attribution of responsibility and the need for order and justice. *Journal of Personality and Social Psychology, 25,* 268–275.

Chait, L.D., & Pierri, J. (1992). Effects of smoked marijuana on human performance: A critical review. In L. Murphy & A. Bartke (eds.), *Marijuana/cannabinoids: Neurobiology and neurophysiology* (pp. 387–424). Boca Raton, FL: CRC Press.

Chance, P. (1992). The rewards of learning. *Phi Delta Kappan, 73,* 200–207.

Chance, P. (1997). Speaking of differences. *Phi Delta Kappan, 78,* 506–507.

Chassin, L., Pitts, S. C., DeLucia, C., & Todd, M. (1999). A longitudinal study of children of alcoholics: Predicting young adult substance use disorders, anxiety, and depression. *Journal of Abnormal Psychology, 108,* 106–119.

Cheour, M., Ceponiene, R., Lehtokoski, A., Luuk, A., Allik, J., Alho, K., & Näätänen, R. (1998). Development of language-specific phoneme representations in the infant brain. *Nature Neuroscience, 1,* 351–353.

Cherlin, A. (1992). *Marriage, divorce, remarriage.* Boston, MA: Harvard University Press.

Cherry, C. (1966). *On human communication: A review, a survey, and a criticism* (2nd ed.). Cambridge, MA: MIT Press.

Chipman, S.F., Krantz, D.H., & Silver, R. (1992). Mathematics anxiety and science careers among able bodied college women. *Psychological Science, 5,* 292–295.

Choi, I., Nisbett, R.E., & Norenzayan, A. (1999). Casual attribution across cultures: Variation and universality. *Psychological Bulletin, 125,* 47–63.

Chomsky, N. (1965). *Aspects of the theory of syntax.* Cambridge, MA: MIT Press.

Chomsky, N. (1986). *Knowledge of language: It's nature, origins and use.* New York: Praeger.

Chwalisz, K., Diener, E., & Gallagher, D. (1988). Autonomic arousal feedback and emotional experience: Evidence from the spinal cord injured. *Journal of Personality and Social Psychology, 54,* 820–828.

Cialdini, R.B. (1995). Principles and techniques of social influence. In A. Tesser (Ed.), *Advanced social psychology* (pp. 257–282). New York: McGraw-Hill.

Cialdini, R.B., & Trost, M. (1998). Social influence: Social norms, conformity, and compliance. In D. Gilbert, S.T. Fiske, & G. Lindzey (Eds.), *Handbook of social psychology* (4th ed., Vol. 2, pp. 151–192). Boston: McGraw-Hill.

Cicchetti, D., & Toth, S.L. (1998). The development of depression in children and adolescents. *American Psychologist, 53,* 221–241.

Clark, G.M. (1998). Research advances for cochlear implants. *Auris Nasus Larynx, 25,* 73–87.

Clark, J.E. (1994). Motor development. In *Encyclopedia of human behavior* (Vol. 3, pp. 245–55). San Diego, CA: Academic Press.

Clark, M.S., & Mills, J. (1979). Interpersonal attraction in exchange and communal relationships. *Journal of Personality and Social Psychology, 37,* 12–24.

Clark, R.D., & Word, L.E. (1974). Where is the apathetic bystander? Situational characteristics of the emergency. *Journal of Personality and Social Psychology, 29,* 279–287.

Clarkson, P. (1996). *To act or not to act: That is the question.* London: Whurr.

Clausen, J.A. (1975). The social meaning of differential physical and sexual maturation. In S.E. Dragastin & G.H. Elder, Jr. (eds.), *Adolescence in the life cycle: Psychological change and social context* (pp. 25–47). New York: Wiley.

Clay, R.A. (1999, January). "Lean production" may also be a lean toward injuries. *APA Monitor,* p. 26.

Cloninger, S.C. (1993). *Theories of personality. Understanding persons.* Englewood Cliffs, NJ: Prentice Hall.

Clore, G.L., & Byrne, D. (1974). A reinforcement-affect model of attraction. In T.L. Huston (ed.), *Foundations of interpersonal attraction* (pp. 143–170). New York: Academic Press.

Cloud, J. (July 6, 1998). Of arms and the boy. *Time,* pp. 58–62.

Cohen, A., & Raffal, R.D. (1991). Attention and feature integration: Illusory conjunctions in a patient with a parietal lobe lesion. *Psychological Science, 2,* 106–110.

Cohen, E.G. (1984). The desegregated school: Problems in status, power and interethnic climate. In N. Miller & M.B. Brewer (eds.), *Groups in contact: The psychology of desegregation* (pp. 77–96). New York: Academic Press.

Cohen, S. (1996). Psychological stress, immunity, and upper respiratory infections. *Current Directions in Psychological Science, 5(3),* 86–88.

Cohen, S., & Herbert, T.B. (1996). Health psychology: Psychological factors and physical disease from the perspective of human psychoneuroimmunology. *Annual Review of Psychology, 47,* 113–142.

Cohen, S., & Williamson, G.M. (1988). Stress and infectious disease in humans. *Psychological Bulletin, 109,* 5–24.

Cohen, S., Frank, E., Doyle, W.J., Skoner, D.P., Rabin, B.S., & Gwaltney, J.M., Jr. (1998). Types of stressors that increase susceptibility to the common cold in healthy adults. *Health Psychology, 17,* 214–223.

Colegrove, F.W. (1982). Individual memories. *American Journal of Psychology, 10,* 228–55. (Original work published in 1899.) (Reprinted in V. Neisser (ed.), *Memory observed: Remembering in natural contexts.* San Francisco: Freeman.)

Coleman, J., Glaros, A., & Morris, C.G. (1987). *Contemporary psychology and effective behavior* (6th ed.). Glenview, IL: Scott, Foresman.

Coley, R.L., & Chase-Lansdale, L. (1998). Adolescent pregnancy and parenthood: Recent evidence and future directions. *American Psychologist, 53,* 152–166.

Collaer, M.L., & Hines, M. (1995). Human behavioral sex differences: A role for gonadal hormones during early development? *American Psychological Associations, 118(1),* 55–107.

Collins, N.L., & Miller, L.C. (1994). Self-disclosure and liking: A meta-analytic review. *Psychological Bulletin, 116,* 457–475.

Collins, R.C. (1993). Head Start: Steps toward a two-generation program strategy. *Young Children, 48*(2), 25–73.

Collins, W.A., Maccoby, E.E., Steinberg, L., Hetherington, E.M., & Bornstein, M.H. (2000). Contemporary research on parenting: The case for nature and nurture. *American Psychologist, 55,* 218–232.

Collins, W.A., Maccoby, E.E., Steinberg, L., Hetherington, E. M., & Bornstein, M. H. (2001). Toward nature WITH nurture. *American Psychologist,* 56, 171–172.

Compas, B.E., Hinden, B.R., & Gerhardt, C.A. (1995). Adolescent development: Pathways and processes of risk and resilience. *Annual Review of Psychology, 46*, 265–293.

Conger, J.J., & Petersen, A.C. (1991). *Adolescence and youth* (4th ed.). New York: HarperCollins.

Connelly, B., Johnston, D., Brown, I.D., Mackay, S., & Blackstock, E.G. (1993). The prevalence of depression in a high school population. *Adolescence, 28*(109), 149–158.

Conrad, R. (1972). Short-term memory in the deaf: A test for speech coding. *British Journal of Psychology, 63*, 173–180.

Conroy, J.W. (1996). The small ICF/MR program: Dimensions of quality and cost. *Mental Retardation, 34*, 13–26.

Conway, M.A. (1996). Failures of autobiographical remembering. In D. Hermann, C. McEvoy, C. Hertzog, P. Hertel, & M.K. Johnson (eds.), *Basic and applied memory research: Theory in context.* Nahwah, NJ: Erlbaum.

Cook, E.H., Courchesne, R.Y., Cox, N.J., Lord, C., Gonen, D., Guter, S.J., Lincoln, A., Nix, K., Haas, R., Leventhal, B.L., & Courchesne, E. (1998). Linkage-disequilibrium mapping of autistic disorder, with 15q11-13 markers. *American Journal of Human Genetics, 62*, 1077–1083.

Cooper, H. (1993). In search of a social fact. A commentary on the study of interpersonal expectations. In P. Blanck (ed.), *Interpersonal expectations: Theory, research, and application* (pp. 218–226). Paris; Cambridge University Press.

Cooper, J. (1971). Personal responsibility and dissonance. *Journal of Personality and Social Psychology, 18*, 354–363.

Cooper, J., & Croyle, R.T. (1984). Attitudes and attitude change. *Annual Review of Psychology, 35*, 395–3426.

Cooper, M.L., Frone, M.R., Russell, M., & Mudar, P. (1995). Drinking to regulate positive and negative emotions: A motivational model of alcohol use. *Journal of Personality & Social Psychology, 69*, 990–1005.

Corder, B., Saunders, A.M., Strittmatter, W.J., Schmechel, D.E., Gaskell, P.C., & Small, D.E. (1993). Gene dose of apolipoprotein E type 4 allele and the risk of Alzheimer's disease in late onset families. *Science, 261*, 921–923.

Coren, S., Porac, C., & Ward, L.M. (1984). *Sensation and perception* (2nd ed.). Orlando, FL: Academic Press.

Cornelius, R.R. (1996). *The science of emotion: Research and tradition in the psychology of emotions.* Upper Saddle River, NJ: Prentice Hall.

Cosmides, L., Tooby, J., & Barkow, J. (1992). *The adapted mind: Evolutionary psychology and the generation of culture.* New York: Oxford.

Costa, P.T., & McCrae, R.R. (1995). Domains and facets: Hierarchical personality assessment using the Revised NEO Personality Inventory. *Journal of Personality Assessment, 64*, 21–50.

Costa, P.T., Jr., & McCrae, R.R. (1992). *Revised NEO Personality Inventory (NEO-PI-R) and NEO Five-Factor Inventory (NEO-FFI) professional manual.* Odessa, FL: Psychological Assessment Resources, Inc.

Cotton, J.L. (1993). *Employee involvement: Methods for improving performance and work attitudes.* Newbury Park, CA: Sage.

Council, J.R. (1993). Context effects in personality research. *Current Directions, 2*, 31–34.

Cousins, N. (1981). *Anatomy of an illness as perceived by the patient.* New York: Bantam.

Cousins, S. (1989). Culture and self-perception in Japan and in the United States. *Journal of Personality and Social Psychology, 56*, 124–131.

Cowan, N. (1988). Evolving conceptions of memory storage, selective attention, and their mutual constraints within the human information-processing system. *Psychological Bulletin, 104*, 163–191.

Cox, D.J., Sutphen, J., Borowitz, S., & Dickens, M.N. (1994). Simple electromyographic biofeedback treatment for chronic pediatric constipation/encopresis: Preliminary report. *Biofeedback & Self Regulation, 19*(1), 41–50.

Craig, A.D., & Bushnell, M.C. (1994). The thermal grill illusion: Unmasking the burn of cold pain. *Science, 265*, 252–255.

Craighead, L. (1990). Supervised exercise in behavioral treatment for moderate obesity. *Behavior Therapy, 20*, 49–59.

Craik, F.I.M. (1994). Memory changes in normal aging. *Current Directions in Psychological Science, 3*, 155–158.

Craik, F.I.M., Moroz, T.M., Moscovitch, M., Stuss, D.T., Winocur, G., Tulving, E., & Kapur, S. (1999). In search of the self: A positron emission tomography study. *Psychological Science, 10*, 26–34.

Cramer, P. (2000). Defense mechanisms in psychology today: Further processes for adaptation. *American Psychologist, 55*, 637–646.

Crandall, C.S. (1994). Prejudice against fat people: Ideology and self-interest. *Journal of Personality and Social Psychology, 66*, 882–894.

Crick, F., & Mitchison, G. (1995). REM sleep and neural nets. *Behavioural Brain Research [Special Issue: The function of sleep], 69*, 147–155.

Cronan, T.A., Walen, H.R., & Cruz, S.G. (1994). The effects of community-based literacy training on Head Start parents. *Journal of Community Psychology, 22*, 248–258.

Cronbach, L.J. (1990). *Essentials of psychological testing* (5th ed.). New York: HarperCollins.

Crovitz, H.F., & Schiffman, H. (1974). Frequency of episodic memories as a function of their age. *Bulletin of the Psychonomic Society, 4*, 517–518.

Crutchfield, R.A. (1955). Conformity and character. *American Psychologist, 10*, 191–198.

Crystal, D.S., et al. (1994). Psychological maladjustments and academic achievement: A cross-cultural study of Japanese, Chinese, and American high school students. *Child Development, 65*, 738–753.

Csikszentmihalyi, M., Rathunde, K., & Whalen, S. (1993). *Talented teenagers: The roots of success and failure.* New York: Cambridge University Press.

Culbertson, F.M. (1997). Depression and gender: An international review. *American Psychologist, 52*, 25–31.

Cumming, E., & Henry, W.E. (1961). *Growing old: The process of disengagement.* New York: Basic Books.

Curle, C.E., & Williams, C. (1996). Post-traumatic stress reactions in children: Gender differences in the incidence of trauma reactions at two years and examination of factors influencing adjustment. *British Journal of Clinical Psychology, 35*, 297–309.

Cutler, D.M. (2001). The reduction in disability among the elderly. *Proc. Natl. Acad. Sci., USA, 98*, 6546–6547.

Czeisler, C.A., Duffy, J.F., & Shanahan, T.L. (1999, June 25). Stability, precision, and near-24-hour period of human circadian pacemaker. *Science, 284,* 2177–2181.

D'Esposito, M., Zarahn, E., & Aguirre, G.K. (1999). Event-related functional MRI: Implications for cognitive psychology. *Psychological Bulletin, 125,* 155–164.

Dabbs, J.M., & Leventhal, H. (1966). Effects of varying the recommendations in a fear-arousing communication. *Journal of Personality and Social Psychology, 4,* 525–531.

Daehler, M.W. (1994). Cognitive development. In *Encyclopedia of human behavior* (Vol. 1, pp. 627–637).

Dahlström, W.G. (1993). Tests: Small samples, large consequences. *American Psychologist, 48,* 393–399.

Daley, S. (1991, January 9). Girls' self-esteem is lost on way to adolescence, new study finds. *New York Times,* Sec. B.

Daly, M., & Wilson, M.I. (1996). Violence against stepchildren. *American Psychological Society, 5*(3), 77–81.

Daniell, H.W. (1971). Smokers' wrinkles: A study in the epidemiology of "Crow's feet." *Annals of Internal Medicine, 75,* 873–880.

Danielle, D.M., Rose, R.J., Viken, R.J., & Kaprio, J. (2000). Pubertal timing and substance use: Associations between and within families across late adolescence. *Developmental Psychology, 36,* 180–189.

Darwin, C.R. (1859). *On the Origin of species.* London.

Davidson, R.J. (1992). Emotion and affective style: Hemispheric substrates. *Psychological Science, 3,* 39–43.

Davies, P.T., & Cummings, E.M. (1994). Marital conflict and child adjustment: An emotional security hypothesis. *Psychological Bulletin, 166*(3), 387–411.

Davis, C.G., Wortman, C.B., Lehman, D.R., & Silver, R.C. (2000). Searching for meaning in loss: Are clinical assumptions correct? *Death Studies, 24,* 497–540.

Davis, M.H., & Stephan, W.G. (1980). Attributions for exam performance. *Journal of Applied Social Psychology, 10,* 235–248.

Dawes, R.M. (1994). *House of cards: The collapse of modern psychotherapy.* New York: Free Press.

DeKay, W.T., & Buss, D.M. (1992). Human nature, individual differences and the importance of context: Perspectives from evolutionary psychology. *Current Directions in Psychological Science, 1,* 184–189.

DeMaris, A., & Rao, K.V. (1992). Premarital cohabitation and subsequent marital stability in the United States: A reassessment. *Journal of Marriage and the Family, 54,* 178–190.

DePaulo, B.M., & Pfeifer, R.L. (1986). On-the-job experience and skill detecting deception. *Journal of Applied Social Psychology, 16,* 249–267.

DeWaal, F.B.M. (1999). The end of nature versus nurture. *Scientific American, 281*(6), 94–99.

DeWitt, K. (1991, August 28). Low test scores renew debate on TV. *New York Times,* p. B8.

Dean, J.W., Jr., & Evans, J.R. (1994). *Total quality: Management, organization, and strategy.* St. Paul, MN: West.

Deaux, K., & Kite, M. (1993). Gender stereotypes. In F.L. Denmark & M.A. Paludi (eds.), *Psychology of women: A handbook of issues and theories* (pp. 107–139). Westport, CT: Greenwood.

Deci, E.L., Koestner, R., & Ryan, R.M. (1999). A meta-analytic review of experiments examining the effects of extrinsic rewards on intrinsic motivation. *Psychological Bulletin, 125,* 627–668.

Dehaene, S., Spelke, E., Stanescu, R., Pinel, P., & Tsivkin, S. (1999, May 7). Sources of mathematical thinking: Behavioral and brain-imaging evidence. *Science, 284,* 970–974.

Deikman, A.J. (1973). Deautomatization and the mystic experience. In R.W. Ornstein (ed.), *The nature of human consciousness.* San Francisco: Freeman.

Dement, W.C. (1974). *Some must watch while some must sleep.* San Francisco: Freeman.

Des Forges, A.L. (1995). The ideology of genocide. *Issue, 23*(2), 44–47.

Detweiler, J.B., Bedell, B.T., Salovey, P., Pronin, E., & Rothman, A.J. (1999). Message framing and sunscreen use: Gain-framed messages motivate beach-goers. *Health Psychology, 18,* 189–196.

Devine, P.G. (1989). Stereotypes and prejudice: Their automatic and controlled components. *Journal of Personality & Social Psychology, 56,* 5–18.

Devine, P.G., Monteith, M.J., Zuwerink, J.R., & Elliot, A.J. (1991). Prejudice with and without compunction. *Journal of Personality & Social Psychology, 60,* 817–830.

DiFranza, J.R., & Lew, R.A. (1995). Effect of maternal cigarette smoking on pregnancy complications and sudden infant death syndrome. *Journal of Family Practice, 40*(4), 385–394.

DiGiovanna, A.G. (1994). *Human aging: Biological perspectives.* New York: McGraw-Hill.

DiMatteo, M.R., & Friedman, H.S. (1982). *Social psychology and medicine.* Cambridge, MA: Oelgeschlager, Gunn, & Hain.

DiPietro, J.A., Hodgson, D.M., Costigan, K.A., & Johnson, T.R. (1996). Fetal antecedents of infant temperament. *Child Development, 67,* 2568–2583.

Diamond, J. (1994). Race without color. *Discover, 15,* 82–92.

Diaz, J. (1997). *How drugs influence behavior: Neuro-behavioral approach.* Upper Saddle River, NJ: Prentice Hall.

Diener, E., & Suh, E. (1998). Age and subjective well-being: An international analysis. *Annual Review of Gerontology and Geriatrics, 17,* 304–324.

Diener, E., Suh, E.M., Lucas, R.E., & Smith, H.L. (1999). Subjective well-being: Three decades of progress. *Psychological Bulletin, 125,* 276–302.

Dill, S. (1994, January 16). Babies' grunts may have meaning. *Associated Press.*

Dillon, S. (1994, October 21). Bilingual education effort is flawed, study indicates. *New York Times,* p. A20.

Dinsmore, W.W., Hodges, M., Hargreaves, C., Osterloh, I.H., Smith, M.D., & Rosen, R.C. (1999). Sildenafil citrate (Viagra) in erectile dysfunction: Near normalization in men with broad-spectrum erectile dysfunction compared with age-matched healthy control subjects. *Urology, 53,* 800–805.

Dion, K.K. (1972). Physical attractiveness and evaluations of children's transgressions. *Journal of Personality and Social Psychology, 24,* 285–290.

Dixon, J.F., & Hokin, L.E. (1998). Lithium acutely inhibits and chronically up-regulates and stabilizes glutamate uptake by presynaptic nerve endings in mouse cerebral cortex. *Proceedings of the National Academy of Sciences, 95,* 8363–8368.

Doherty, W.J., & Jacobson, N.S. (1982). Marriage and the family. In B.B. Wolman (ed.), *Handbook of developmental psychology* (pp. 667–80). Englewood Cliffs, NJ: Prentice Hall.

Domhoff, G.W. (1996). *Finding meaning in dreams: A quantitative approach.* New York: Plenum Press.

Domjan, M. (1987). Animal learning comes of age. *American Psychologist, 42,* 556–564.

Domjan, M., & Purdy, J.E. (1995). Animal research in psychology: More than meets the eye of the general psychology student. *American Psychologist, 50,* 496–503.

Donatelle, R.J., & Davis, L.G. (1993). *Access to health* (2nd ed.). Englewood Cliffs, NJ: Prentice Hall.

Dovidio, J.F., & Gaertner, S.I. (1999). Reducing prejudice: Combating intergroup biases. *Current Directions in Psychological Science, 8,* 101–105.

Downs, H. (1994, August 21). Must we age? *Parade Magazine,* pp. 3, 5, 7.

Dryer, D.C., & Horowitz, L.M. (1997). When do opposites attract? Interpersonal complementarity versus similarity. *Journal of Personality and Social Psychology, 72*(3), 592–603.

Du, L., Faludi, G., Palkovits, M., Demeter, E., Bakish, D., Lapierre, Y.D., Sotonyi, P., & Hrdina, P.D. (1999). Frequency of long allele in serotonin transporter gene is increased in depressed suicide victims. *Biological Psychiatry, 46,* 196–201.

Dubner, R., & Gold, M. (1998, December). *The neurobiology of pain.* Paper presented at the National Academy of Sciences colloquium, Irvine, CA.

Duncan, J., Seitz, R.J., Kolodny, J., Bor, D., Herzog, H., Ahmed, A., Newell, F.N., & Emslie, H. (2000, July 21). A neural basis for general intelligence. *Science, 285,* 457–460.

Dunkle, T. (1982, April). The sound of silence. *Science,* pp. 30–33.

Dunn, R.L., & Schwebel, A.I. (1995). Meta-analytic review of marital therapy outcome research. *Journal of Family Psychology, 9,* 58–68.

Dyk, P.K. (1993). Anatomy, physiology and gender issues in adolescence. In T.P. Gullota, G.R. Adams, & R. Montemayor (eds.), *Adolescent sexuality: Advances in adolescent development* (pp. 35–36). Newbury Park, CA: Sage.

Eagly, A.H. (1992). Uneven progress: Social psychology and the study of attitudes. *Journal of Personality and Social Psychology, 63*(5), 693–710.

Eagly, A.H., & Carli, L.L. (1981). Sex of researchers and sex-typed communications as determinants of sex differences in influenceability: A meta-analysis of social influence studies. *Psychological Bulletin, 90,* 1–20.

Eagly, A.H., & Steffen, V.J. (1986). Gender and aggressive behavior: A meta-analytic review of the social psychological literature. *Psychological Bulletin, 100,* 309–330.

Eaves, L.J., Heath, A.C., Neale, M.C., Hewitt, J.K., & Martin, N.G. (1993). *Sex differences and non-additivity in the effects of genes on personality.* Unpublished manuscript, cited in F. S. Mayer & K. Sutton. (1996). *Personality: An integrative approach.* Upper Saddle River, NJ: Prentice Hall.

Eccles, J., et al. (1993). Development during adolescence: The impact of stage-environment fit on young adolescents' experiences in school and families. *American Psychologist, 2,* 90–101.

Eckerman, C.O., Davis, C.C., & Didow, S.M. (1989). Toddlers' emerging ways of achieving social coordinations with a peer. *Child Development, 60,* 440–453.

Eibl-Eibesfeldt, I. (1972). *Love and hate.* New York: Holt, Rinehart & Winston.

Eich, E., Macaulay, D., Loewenstein, R.J., & Dihle, P.H. (1997). Memory, amnesia, and dissociative identity disorder. *Psychological Science, 8,* 417–422.

Eimas, P.D., & Tartter, V.C. (1979). The development of speech perception. In H.W. Reese & L.P. Lipsitt (eds.), *Advances in child development and behavior* (Vol. 13). New York: Academic Press.

Eisenberg, N., & Lennon, R. (1983). Sex differences in empathy and related capacities. *Psychological Bulletin, 94,* 100–131.

Eisenberger, R., & Cameron, J. (1996). Detrimental effects of reward. *American Psychologist, 51,* 1153–1166.

Eisenman, R. (1994). Birth order, effect on personality and behavior. In *Encyclopedia of human behavior* (Vol. 1, pp. 401–405).

Ekman, P. (1994). Strong evidence for universals in facial expressions: A reply to Russell's mistaken critique. *Psychological Bulletin, 115*(2), 268–287.

Ekman, P., & Davidson, R.J. (1993). Voluntary smiling changes regional brain activity. *Psychological Science, 4,* 342–345.

Ekman, P., & Friesen, W.V. (1971). Constants across cultures in the face and emotion. *Journal of Personality and Social Psychology, 17,* 124–129.

Ekman, P., & Friesen, W.V. (1975). *Unmasking the face.* Englewood Cliffs, NJ: Prentice Hall.

Ekman, P., & O'Sullivan, M. (1991). Who can catch a liar? *American Psychologist, 46,* 913–920.

Ekman, P., Friesen, W.V., & Ellsworth, P. (1972). *Emotion in the human face.* Elmsford, NY: Pergamon.

Ekman, P., Friesen, W.V., O'Sullivan, M., Chan, A., Diacoyanni-Tarlatzis, I., Heider, K., Krause, R., LeCompte, W.A., Pitcairn, T., Ricci-Bitti, P.E., Scherer, K., Tomita, M., & Tzavaras, A. (1987). Universals and cultural differences in the judgments of facial expressions of emotion. *Journal of Personality and Social Psychology, 53,* 712–717.

Ekman, P., Sorenson, E.R., & Friesen, W.V. (1969). Pancultural elements in facial displays of emotion. *Science, 164,* 86–88.

Elbert, T., Pantev, C., Wienbruch, C., Rockstroh, B., & Taub, E. (1995). Increased cortical representation of the fingers of the left hand in string players. *Science, 270,* 305–307.

Eley, T.C., & Stevenson, J. (1999). Exploring the covariation between anxiety and depression symptoms: A genetic analysis of the effects of age and sex. *Journal of Child Psychology & Psychiatry & Allied Disciplines, 40,* 1273–1282.

Eley, T.C., Bishop, D.V.M., Dale, P.S., Oliver, B., Petrill, S.A., Price, T.S., Saudino, K.J., Simonoff, E., Stevenson, J., Plomin, R., & Purcell, S. (1999). Genetic and environmental origins of verbal and performance components of cognitive delay in 2-year olds. *Developmental Psychology, 35,* 1122–1131.

Eley, T.C., Lichenstein, P., & Stevenson, J. (1999). Sex differences in the etiology of aggressive and nonaggressive antisocial behavior: Results from two twin studies. *Child Development, 70,* 155–168.

Elkin, I., Shea, T., Watkins, J.T., Imber, S.D., Sotsky, S.M., Collins, J.F., Glass, D.R., Pikonis, P.A., Leber, W.R., Docherty, J.P., Fiester, S.J., & Parloff, M.B. (1989). National Institute of Mental Health treatment of depression collaborative research program: General effectiveness of treatments. *Archives of General Psychiatry, 46,* 971–982.

Elkind, D. (1968). Cognitive development in adolescence. In J.F. Adams (ed.), *Understanding adolescence.* Boston: Allyn & Bacon.

Elkind, D. (1969). Egocentrism in adolescence. In R.W. Grinder (ed.), *Studies in adolescence* (2nd ed.). New York: Macmillan.

Ellis, A. (1973). *Humanistic psychotherapy: The rational emotive approach.* New York: Julian Press.

Ellis, A., & Harper, R.A. (1975). *A new guide to rational living.* North Hollywood, CA: Wilshire Book Co.

Ellis, A., & MacLaren, C. (1998). *Rational emotive behavior therapy: A therapist's guide.* San Luis Obispo, CA: Impact.

Ellis, L., & Coontz, P.D. (1990). Androgens, brain functioning, and criminality: The neurohormonal foundations of antisociality. In

L. Ellis & H. Hoffman (eds.), *Crime in biological, social, and moral contexts* (pp. 36–49). New York: Praeger Press.

Engel, J.F., Black, R.D., & Miniard, P.C. (1986). *Consumer behavior.* Chicago: Dryden Press.

Epstein, R., Kirshnit, C.E., Lanza, R.P., & Rubin, L.C. (1984). "Insight" in the pigeon: Antecedents and determinants of an intelligent performance. *Nature (London), 308,* 61–62.

Erdley, C.A., & D'Agostino, P.R. (1988). Cognitive and affective components of automatic priming effects. *Journal of Personality and Social Psychology, 54,* 741–747.

Erikson, E.H. (1963). *Childhood and society* (2nd ed.). New York: Norton.

Erikson, E.H. (1968). *Identity: Youth in crisis.* New York: Norton.

Eriksson, P.S., Perfilieva, E., Björk-Eriksson, T., Alborn, A.M., Nordborg, C., Peterson, D.A., & Gage, F.H. (1998). Neurogenesis in the adult human hippocampus. *Nature Medicine, 4,* 1313–1317.

Eron, L.D. (1982). Parent–child interaction, television violence, and aggression of children. *American Psychologist, 37,* 197–211.

Esposito, M.D., Zarahn, E., & Aguirre, G.K. (1999). Event-related functional MRI: Implications for Cognitive Psychology. *Psychological Bulletin, 125,* 155–164.

Evans, L.I., Rozelle, R.M., Lasater, T.M., Dembroski, R.M., & Allen, B.P. (1970). Fear arousal, persuasion and actual vs. implied behavioral change: New perspective utilizing a real-life dental hygiene program. *Journal of Personality and Social Psychology, 16,* 220–227.

Evans, R.B. (1999, December). A century of psychology. *APA Monitor,* pp. 14–30.

Eyer, J. (1977). Prosperity as a cause of death. *International Journal of Health Services, 7,* 125–150.

Eysenck, H.J. (1947). *Dimensions of personality.* London: Routledge & Kegan Paul.

Eysenck, H.J. (1970). *The structure of human personality* (3rd ed.). London: Methuen.

Eysenck, H.J. (1976). *The measurement of personality.* Baltimore, MD: University Park Press.

Eysenck, H.J. (1992). Four ways five factors are *not* basic. *Personality and Individual Differences, 13,* 667–673.

Eysenck, H.J. (1993). Commentary on Goldberg. *American Psychologist, 48,* 1299–1300.

Fagot, B.I. (1994). Parenting. In *Encyclopedia of human behavior* (Vol. 3, pp. 411–419). San Diego, CA: Academic Press.

Fairburn, C.G., & Wilson, G.T. (eds.). (1993). *Binge eating: Nature, assessment and treatment.* New York: Guilford Press.

Fallon, A., & Rozin, P. (1985). Sex differences in perceptions of desirable body states. *Journal of Abnormal Psychology, 84,* 102–105.

Fantz, R.L., Fagan, J.F., & Miranda, S.B. (1975). Early visual selectivity. In L.B. Cohen & P. Salapatek (eds.), *Infant perception: From sensation to cognition* (Vol. 1). New York: Academic Press.

Farber, S. (1981, January). Telltale behavior of twins. *Psychology Today,* pp. 58–62, 79–80.

Farthing, C.W. (1992). *The psychology of consciousness.* Englewood Cliffs, NJ: Prentice Hall.

Featherstone, R.E., Fleming, A.S., & Ivy, G.O. (2000). Plasticity in the maternal circuit: Effects of experience and partum condition on brain astrocyte number in female rats. *Behavioral Neuroscience, 114,* 158–172.

Fehr, B. (1994). Prototype-based assessment of laypeople's views of love. *Personal Relationships, 1,* 309–331.

Feingold, A. (1992). Good-looking oeioke are not what we think. *Psychological Bulletin, 111,* 304–341.

Feinson, M.C. (1986). Aging widows and widowers: Are there mental health differences? *International Journal of Aging and Human Development, 23,* 244–255.

Feldman, R.S., Salzinger, S., Rosario, M., Alvarado, L., Caraballo, L., & Hammer, M. (1995). Parent, teacher, and peer ratings of physically abused and nonmaltreated children's behavior. *Journal of Abnormal Child Psychology, 23*(3), 317–334.

Ferguson, C.A., & Macken, M.A. (1983). The role of play in phonological development. In K.E. Nelson (ed.), *Children's language* (Vol. 4). Hillsdale, NJ: Erlbaum.

Feshbach, S., & Weiner, B. (1982). *Personality.* Lexington, MA: D.C. Heath.

Festinger, L. (1957). *A theory of cognitive dissonance.* Evanston, IL: Row, Peterson.

Fiedler, F.E. (1967). *A theory of leadership effectiveness.* New York: McGraw-Hill.

Fiedler, F.E. (1978). The contingency model and the dynamics of the leadership process. In L. Berkowitz (ed.), *Advances in experimental social psychology* (Vol. 11, pp. 59–112). New York: Academic Press.

Fiedler, F.E. (1993). The leadership situation and the black box contingency theories. In M. Chemers & R. Ayman (eds.), *Leadership theory and research: Perspective and directions* (pp. 1–28). San Diego, CA: Academic Press.

Field, T.M. (1986). Interventions for premature infants. *Journal of Pediatrics, 109,* 183–191.

Filipek, P.A., Semrund-Clikeman, M., Steingard, R.J., Renshaw, P.R., Kennedy, D.N., & Biederman, J. (1997). Volumetric MRI analysis comparing subjects having attention-deficit hyperactivity disorder with normal controls. *Neurology, 48,* 589–601.

Finn, P.R., Sharkansky, E.J., Brandt, K.M., & Turcotte, N. (2000). The effects of familial risk, personality, and expectancies on alcohol use and abuse. *Journal of Abnormal Psychology, 109,* 122–133.

Fischer, K.W., & Henke, R.W. (1996). Infants' construction of actions in context: Piaget's contribution to research on early development. *Psychological Science, 7*(4), 204–210.

Fischhoff, B. (1975). Hindsight & foresight: The effect of outcome knowledge on the judgment under uncertainty. *Journal of Experimental Psychology: Human Perception and Performance, 1,* 288–299.

Fischhoff, B., & Downs, J. (1997). Accentuate the relevant. *Psychological Science, 8,* 154–158.

Fischman, J. (1985, September). Mapping the mind. *Psychology Today,* pp. 18–19.

Fisher, S., & Greenberg, R.P. (1985). *The scientific credibility of Freud's theories and therapy.* New York: Columbia University Press.

Fiske, S.T., & Neuberg, S.L. (1990). A continuum of impression formation, from category-based to individuating processes: Influence of information and motivation on attention and interpretation. In M.P. Zanna (ed.), *Advances in experimental social psychology* (Vol. 23, pp. 399–427). New York: Academic Press.

Fiske, S.T., & Taylor, S.E. (1991). *Social cognition* (2nd ed.). New York: McGraw-Hill.

Flavell, J.H. (1999). Cognitive development: Children's knowledge about the mind. *Annual Review of Psychology, 50,* 21–45.

Flavell, J.F. (1986). The development of children's knowledge about the appearance–reality distinction. *American Psychologist, 41,* 418–425.

Flavell, J.H. (1996). Piaget's legacy. *Psychological Science, 7*(4), 200–204.

Flier, J.S., & Maratos-Flier, E. (1998). Obesity and the hypothalamus: Novel peptides for new pathways. *Cell, 92,* 437–440.

Flynn, J.R. (1999). Searching for justice: The discovery of IQ gains over time. *American Psychologist, 54,* 5–20.

Flynn, J.R. (1987). Massive IQ gains in 14 nations: What IQ tests really measure. *Psychological Bulletin, 101,* 171–191.

Fogelman, E., & Wiener, V.L. (1985, August). The few, the brave, the noble. *Psychology Today,* pp. 60–65.

Folkman, S., & Moskowitz, S.T. (2000). Positive affect and the other side of coping. *American Psychologist, 55,* 647–654.

Folkman, S., Chesney, M.A., & Christopher-Richards, A. (1994). Stress and coping in partners of men with AIDS. *Psychiatric Clinics of North America, 17,* 33–55.

Ford, W.C.L., North, K., Taylor, H., Farrow, A., Hull, M.G.R., & Golding, J. (2000). Increasing paternal age is associated with delayed conception in a large population of fertile couples: Evidence for declining fecundity in older men. *Human Reproduction, 15,* 1703–1708.

Ford-Mitchell, D. (1997, November 12). Daydream your way to better health. *Ann Arbor News,* p. C3.

Forgatch, M.S., & DeGarmo, D.S. (1999). Parenting through change: An effective prevention program for single mothers. *Journal of Consulting and Clinical psychology, 67,* 711–724.

Frager, R. (1970). Conformity and anticonformity in Japan. *Journal of Personality and Social Psychology, 15,* 203–210.

Freedman, J.L., & Fraser, S.C. (1966). Compliance without pressure: The foot-in-the-door technique. *Journal of Personality and Social Psychology, 4,* 195–202.

Freud, S. (1900). The interpretation of dreams. In J. Strachey (ed.), *The standard edition of the complete psychological works of Sigmund Freud* (Vol. 5). London: Hogarth Press.

Frezza, M., di Padova, C., Pozzato, G., Terpin, M., Baraona, E., & Lieber, C.S. (1990). High blood alcohol levels in women: The role of decreased gastric alcohol dehydrogenase activity and first-pass metabolism. *New England Journal of Medicine, 322,* 95–99.

Friedland, R.P., Fritsch, T., Smyth, K.A., Koss, E., Lerner, A.J., Chen, C.H., Petot, G.J., Debanne, S.M., (2001). Patients with Alzheimer's disease have reduced activities in midlife compared with healthy control-group members. *Proc. Natl. Acad. Sci, USA, 98,* 3440–3445.

Friedman, M.J., Schnurr, P.P., & McDonagh-Coyle, A. (1994). Post-traumatic stress disorder in the military veteran. *Psychiatric Clinics of North America, 17,* 265–277.

Friedman, M., & Rosenman, R.H. (1959). Association of specific overt behavior patterns with blood and cardiovascular findings: Blood cholesterol level, blood clotting time, incidence of arcus senilis and clinical coronary artery disease. *JAMA, Journal of the American Medical Association, 169,* 1286–1296.

Friedman, M., Breall, W.S., Goodwin, M.L., Sparagon, B.J., Ghandour, G., & Fleischmann, N. (1996). Effect of Type A behavioral counseling on frequency of episodes of silent myocardial ischemia in coronary patients. *American Heart Journal, 132*(5), 933–937.

Friman, P.C., Allen, K.D., Kerwin, M.L.E., & Larzelere, R. (1993). Changes in modern psychology. *American Psychology, 48,* 658–664.

Frosch, C.A., Mangelsdorf, S.C., McHale, J.L. (2000). Marital behavior and the security of preschooler-parent attachment relationships. *Journal of Family Psychology, 14,* 144–161.

Frumkin, B., & Ainsfield, M. (1977). Semantic and surface codes in the memory of deaf children. *Cognitive Psychology, 9,* 475–493.

Funder, D.C. (1991). Global traits: A neo-Allportian approach to personality. *Psychological Science, 2,* 31–39.

Funder, D.C. (1995). On the accuracy of personality judgment: A realistic approach. *Psychological Review, 102*(4), 652–670.

Furstenberg, F.F., Jr., Brooks-Gunn, J., & Chase-Lansdale, L. (1989). Teenaged pregnancy and childbearing. *American Psychologist, 44,* 313–320.

Gabrieli, J.D., Desmond, J.E., Bemb, J.B., Wagner, A.D., Stone, M.V., Vaidya, C.J. & Glover, G.H. (1996). Functional magnetic resonance imaging of semantic memory processes in the frontal lobes. *Psychological Science, 7,* 278–283.

Gage, F.H. (2000, February 25). Mammalian neural stem cells. *Science, 287,* 1433–1438.

Galanter, M. (1984). Self-help large-group therapy for alcoholism: A controlled study. *Alcoholism, Clinical and Experimental Research, 8*(1), 16–23.

Gallistel, C.R. (1981). Bell, Magendie, and the proposals to restrict the use of animals in neurobehavioral research. *American Psychologist, 36,* 357–360.

Garb, H.N., Florio, C.M., & Grove, W.M. (1998). The validity of the Rorschach and the Minnesota Multiphasic Personality Inventory: Results from meta-analysis. *Psychological Science, 9,* 402–404.

Garbarino, J. (1999). *Lost boys: Why our sons turn violent and how we can save them.* NY: Free Press.

Garber, H., & Heber, R. (1982). Modification of predicted cognitive development in high risk children through early intervention. In D.K. Detterman & R.J. Sternberg (eds.), *How and how much can intelligence be increased?* (pp. 121–137). Norwood, NJ: Ablex.

Gardner, H. (1982). *Developmental psychology* (2nd ed.). Boston: Little, Brown.

Gardner, H. (1983a). *Frames of mind: The theory of multiple intelligences.* New York: Basic Books.

Gardner, H. (1993). *Multiple intelligences: The theory in practice.* New York: Basic Books.

Garfield, S.L. (ed.). (1983). Special section: Meta-analysis and psychotherapy. *Journal of Consulting and Clinical Psychology, 51,* 3–75.

Garfinkel, P.E., & Garner, D.M. (1982). *Anorexia nervosa: A multidimensional perspective.* New York: Brunner/Mazel.

Gécz, J., & Mulley, J. (2000). Genes for cognitive function: Developments on the X. *Genome Research, 10,* 157–163.

Geen, R.G. (1998). Aggression and antisocial behavior. In D. Gilbert, S.T. Fiske, & G. Lindzey (Eds.), *Handbook of social psychology* (4th ed., Vol. 2, pp. 317–356). Boston: McGraw-Hill

Gelman, D. (1990, October 29). A fresh take on Freud. *Newsweek,* pp. 84–86.

Gelman, D. (1994, June 13). Reliving the painful past. *Newsweek,* pp. 20–22.

Gergen, K.J. (1973). The codification of research ethics—views of a Doubting Thomas. *American Psychologist, 28,* 907–912.

Gershon, E.S. (1990). Genetics. In F.K. Goodwin & K.R. Jamison (eds.), *Manic depressive illness* (pp. 373–401). New York: Oxford University Press.

Getzels, J.W. (1975). Problem finding and the inventiveness of solutions. *Journal of Creative Behavior, 9,* 12–18.

Getzels, J.W., & Jackson, P. (1962). *Creativity and intelligence.* New York: Wiley.

Gilbert, D.T., & Malone, P.S. (1995). The correspondence bias. *Psychological Bulletin, 117,* 21–38.

Gilbert, E.H., & DeBlassie, R.R. (1984). Anorexia nervosa: Adolescent starvation by choice. *Adolescence, 19,* 839–853.

Gilbert, L.A. (1994). Current perspectives on dual-career families. *Current Directions in Psychological Science, 3,* 101–105.

Gilligan, C. (1982). *In a different voice: Psychological theory and women's development.* Cambridge, MA: Harvard University Press.

Gilligan, C. (1992). *Joining the resistance: Girls' development in adolescence.* Paper presented at the meeting of the American Psychological Association, Montreal.

Gilovich, T. (1991). *How we know what isn't so: The fallibility of human reason in everyday life.* New York: Free Press.

Ginsberg, H. (1972). *The myth of the deprived child.* Englewood Cliffs, NJ: Prentice Hall.

Glassman, A.H., & Koob, G.F. (1996). Neuropharmacology. Psychoactive smoke. *Nature, 379,* 677–678.

Glenner, G.G. (1994). Alzheimer's disease. In *Encyclopedia of human behavior* (Vol. 1, pp. 103–111). San Diego, CA: Academic Press.

Goerge, R.M., & Lee, B.J. (1997). Abuse and neglect of the children. In R. A. Maynard (Ed.), *Kids having kids: Economic costs and social consequences of teen pregnancy* (pp. 205–230). Washington, DC: Urban Institute Press.

Gold, M.S. (1994). The epidemiology, attitudes, and pharmacology of LSD use in the 1990s. *Psychiatric Annals, 24,* 124–126.

Goldberg, L.R. (1993). The structure of phenotypic personality traits. *American Psychologist, 48,* 26–34.

Goldsmith, H.H., & Harman, C. (1994). Temperament and attachment: Individuals and relationships. *Current Directions in Psychological Sciences, 3*(2), 53–57.

Goldstein, E.B. (1999). *Sensation and perception* (5th ed.). Pacific Grove, CA: Brooks-Cole.

Goldstein, I., Lue, T.F., Padma-Nathan, H., Rosen, R.C., Steers, W.D., & Wicker, P.A. (1998). Oral sildenafil in the treatment of erectile dysfunction. Sildenafil study group. *New England Journal of Medicine, 338,* 1397–1404.

Goleman, D. (1996, February 26). Studies suggest older minds are stronger than expected. *New York Times.*

Goleman, D. (1997). *Emotional Intelligence.* New York: Bantam Books.

Golomb, J., Kluger, A., de Leon, M.J., Ferris, S.H., Convit, A., Mittelman, M.S., Cohen, J., Rusinek, H., DeSanti, S., & George, A.E. (1994). Hippocampal formation size in normal human aging: A correlate of delayed secondary memory performance. *Learning & Memory, 1,* 45–54.

Goode, E. (2000a, August 8). How culture molds habits of thought. *New York Times,* pp. D1, D4.

Goode, E. (2000b, March 14). Human nature: born or made? *New York Times,* pp. F1, F9.

Goode, E. (2000c, May 19). Scientists find a particularly female response to stress. *New York Times.* Available on-line at:www.ny-times.com

Goode, E. (2000d, February 1). Viewing depression as a tool for survival. *New York Times,* p. D7.

Gopnik, A. (1996). The post-Piaget era. *Psychological Science, 7*(4), 221–225.

Gopnik, A., Neltzoff, A.N., & Kuhl, P. (1999). *The scientist in the crib: Minds, brains and how children learn.* New York: William Morrow.

Gordis, E. (1996). Alcohol research: At the cutting edge. *Archives of General psychiatry, 53,* 199–201.

Gose, B. (1997, October 24). Colleges try to curb excessive drinking by saying moderation is okay. *Chronicle of Higher Education,* pp. A61–A62.

Gosling, S.D., & John, O.P. (1999). Personality dimensions in non-human animals: A cross-species review. *Current Directions in Psychological Science, 8,* 69–75.

Gottesman, I.I. (1991). *Schizophrenia genesis: The origins of madness.* New York: Freeman.

Gouzoulis-Mayfrank, E., Daumann, J., Tuchtenhagen, F., Pelz, S., Becker, S., Kunert, H.J., Fimm, B., & Sass, H. (2000). Impaired cognitive performance in drug free users of recreational ecstasy (MDMA). *Journal of Neurology, Neurosurgery and Psychiatry, 68,* 719–725.

Grady, D. (1997, March 21). Importance of a sleep disorder is played down in a British study. *New York Times,* p. A15.

Graham, K. (1997). *Personal history.* New York: Knopf.

Graham, S. (1992). Most of the subjects were white and middle class. *American Psychologist, 47,* 629–639.

Grandey, A.A. (2000). Emotional regulation in the workplace: A new way to conceptualize emotional labor. *Journal of Occupational Health Psychology, 5,* 95–110.

Green, J.P., & Lynn, S.J. (2000). Hypnosis and suggestion-based approaches to smoking cessation: An examination of the evidence. *International Journal of Clinical & Experimental Hypnosis [Special Issue: The Status of Hypnosis as an Empirically Validated Clinical Intervention], 48,* 195–224.

Greene, R.L. (1987). Effects of maintenance rehearsal on human memory. *Psychological Bulletin, 102,* 403–413.

Greenfield, P.M., & Smith, J.H. (1976). *The structure of communication in early language development.* New York: Academic Press.

Greenwald, A.G., & Banaji, M.R. (1995). Implicit social cognition: Attitudes, self-esteem, and stereotypes. *Psychological Review, 102,* 4–27.

Greenwald, A.G. (1992). New Look 3: Unconscious cognition reclaimed. *American Psychologist, 47,* 766–779.

Greenwald, A.G., Spangenberg, E.R., Pratkanis, A.R., & Eskenazi, J. (1991). Double-blind tests of subliminal self-help audiotapes. *Psychological Science, 2,* 119–122.

Griffiths, R.A., & Channon-Little, L.D. (1995). Dissociation, dieting disorders and hypnosis: A review. *European Eating Disorders Review [Special Issue: Dissociation and the Eating Disorders], 3,* 148–159.

Grinker, R.R., & Spiegel, J.P. (1945). *War neurosis.* Philadelphia: Blakiston.

Grinspoon, L., Ewalt, J.R., & Shader, R.I. (1972). *Schizophrenia: Pharmacotherapy and psychotherapy.* Baltimore: Williams & Wilkins.

Gruber, H.E., & Wallace, D.B. (2001). Creative work: The case of Charles Darwin. *American Psychologist, 56,* 346–349.

Guérin, D. (1994). *Fussy infants at risk.* Paper presented at the meeting of the American Psychological Association, Los Angeles.

Guilford, J.P. (1967). *The nature of human intelligence.* New York: McGraw-Hill.

Gunne, L.M., & Anggard, E. (1972). *Pharmical kinetic studies with amphetamines—relationship to neuropsychiatric disorders.* International Symposium on Pharmical Kinetics, Washington, DC.

Gurvits, T.V., Gilbertson, M.W., Lasko, N.B., Orr, S.P., & Pitman, R.K. (1997). Neurological status of combat veterans and adult survivors of sexual abuse PTSD. *Annals of the New York Academy of Sciences, 821,* 468–471.

Guthrie, R. (1976). *Even the rat was white*. New York: Harper & Row.

Guzder, J., Paris, J., Zelkowitz, P., & Marchessault, K. (1996). Risk factors for borderline personality in children. *Journal of the American Academy of Child and Adolescent Psychiatry, 35*, 26–33.

Gwirtsman, H.E. (1984). Bulimia in men: Report of three cases with neuro-endocrine findings. *Journal of Clinical Psychiatry, 45*, 78–81.

Haberlandt, K. (1997). *Cognitive psychology*. Boston: Allyn & Bacon.

Hack, M., Breslau, N., Weissman, B., Aram, D., Klein, N., & Borawski, E. (1991). Effect of very low birth weight and subnormal head size on cognitive abilities at school age. *New England Journal of Medicine, 325*, 231–237.

Haefele, J.W. (1962). *Creativity and innovation*. New York: Reinhold.

Haines, M., & Spear, S.F. (1996). Changing the perception of the norm: A strategy to decrease binge drinking among college students. *Journal of American College Health, 45*, 134–140.

Hall, C.C.I. (1997). Cultural malpractice: The growing obsolescence of psychology with the changing U.S. population. *American Psychologist, 52*, 642–651.

Hall, G.S. (1904). *Adolescence: Its psychology and its relations to physiology, anthropology, sex, crime, religion and education* (Vol. 1). New York: Appleton-Century-Crofts.

Hall, J.A. (1984). *Nonverbal sex differences: Communication accuracy and expressive style*. Baltimore: Johns Hopkins University Press.

Halpern, D.F. (1997). Sex differences in intelligence: Implications for education. *American Psychologist, 52*, 1091–1102.

Halpern, D.F. (1992). *Sex differences in cognitive abilities* (2nd ed.). Hillsdale, NJ: Erlbaum.

Hameroff, S.R., Kaszniak, A.W., & Scott, A.C. (Eds.). (1996). *Toward a science of consciousness: The first Tucson discussions and debates*. Cambridge, MA: MIT Press.

Hammen, C.L. (1985). Predicting depression: A cognitive-behavioral perspective. In P. Kendall (Ed.), *Advances in cognitive-behavioral research and therapy* (Vol. 4, pp. 29–71). New York: Academic Press.

Hammen, C., Gitlin, M., & Altshuler, L. (2000). Predictors of work adjustment in bipolar I patients. A naturalistic longitudinal follow-up. *Journal of Consulting & Clinical Psychology, 68*, 220–225.

Hampson, E., & Kimura, D. (1992). Sexual differentiation and hormonal influences on cognitive function in humans. In J.B. Becker, S.M. Breedlove, & D. Crews (eds.), *Behavioral endocrinology*. Cambridge, MA: MIT Press.

Hampson, J., & Nelson, K. (1993). The relation of maternal language to variation in rate and style of language acquisition. *Journal of Child Language, 20*, 313–342.

Hansel, C.E. (1969). ESP: Deficiencies of experimental method. *Nature, 221*, 1171–1172.

Hansen, W.B. (1993). School-based alcohol prevention programs. *Alcohol, Health and Research World, 17*, 54–60.

Hansen, W.B., & Graham, J.W. (1991). Preventing alcohol, marijuana, and cigarette use among adolescents: Peer pressure resistance training versus establishing conservative norms. *Preventive Medicine, 20*, 414–430.

Harburg, E., Gleiberman, L., DiFranceisco, W., Schork, A. & Weissfeld, L.A. (1990b). Familial transmission of alcohol use: III. Impact of imitation/non-imitation of parent alcohol use (1960) on the sensible/problem drinking of their offspring (1977). *British Journal of Addiction, 85*, 1141–1155.

Hare, R.D. (1983). Diagnosis of antisocial personality disorder in two prison populations. *American Journal of Psychiatry, 140*, 887–890.

Hare, R.D. (1993). *Without conscience: The disturbing world of the psychopaths among us*. New York: Pocket Books.

Harlow, H.F. (1949). The formation of learning sets. *Psychological Review, 56*, 51–65.

Harlow, H.F. (1958). The nature of love. *American Psychologist, 13*, 673–685.

Harlow, H.F., & Zimmerman, R.R. (1959). Affectional responses in the infant monkey. *Science, 130*, 421–432.

Harrell, R.F., Woodyard, E., & Gates, A.I. (1955). *The effect of mother's diet on the intelligence of the offspring*. New York: Teacher's College, Columbia Bureau of Publications.

Harris, J.R. (1998). *The nurture assumption: Why children turn out the way they do*. New York: Free Press.

Harris, J.R., & Liebert, R.M. (1991). *The child: A contemporary view of development* (3rd ed.). Englewood Cliffs, NJ: Prentice Hall.

Harris, M., & Rosenthal, R. (1985). Mediation of the interpersonal expectancy effect: A taxonomy of expectancy situations. In P. Blanck (ed.), *Interpersonal expectations: Theory, research, and application* (pp. 350–378). Paris: Cambridge University Press.

Hart, B., & Risley, T.R. (1995). *Meaningful differences in the everyday experience of young American children*. Baltimore: Brookes.

Hartmann, E. (1983). Two case reports: Night terrors with sleepwalking—A potentially lethal disorder. *Journal of Nervous & Mental Disease, 171*, 503–505.

Harvey, J.H., & Miller, E.D. (1998). Toward a psychology of loss. *Psychological Science, 9*, 429–434.

Harvey, J.H., & Pauwells, B.G. (1999). Recent developments in close-relationships theory. *Current Directions in Psychological Science, 8*, 93–95.

Hathaway, S.R., & McKinley, J.C. (1942). A multiphasic personality schedule (Minnesota): III. The measurement of symptomatic depression. *Journal of Psychology, 14*, 73–84.

Hauri, P. (1982). *Sleep disorders*. Kalamazoo, MI: Upjohn.

Hay, M.S., & Ellig, T.W. (1999). The 1995 Department of Defense sexual harassment survey: Overview and methodology. *Military Psychology [Special Issue: Sexual harassment], 11*, 233–242.

Hazan, C., & Shaver, P. (1987). Romantic love conceptualized as attachment process. *Journal of Personality and Social Psychology, 52*, 511–524.

Hearst, E. (1975). The classical-instrumental distinction: Reflexes, voluntary behavior, and categories of associative learning. In W.K. Estes (ed.), *Handbook of learning and cognitive processes: Vol. 2. Conditioning and behavior theory*. Hillsdale, NJ: Erlbaum.

Heath, A.C., Cloninger, C.R., & Martin, N.G. (1994). Testing a model for the genetic structure of personality: A comparison of the personality systems of Cloninger and Eysenck. *Journal of Personality and Social Psychology, 66*, 762–775.

Heath, A.C., & Martin, N.G. (1993). Genetic models for the natural history of smoking: Evidence for a genetic influence on smoking persistence. *Addictive Behavior, 18*, 19–34.

Heath, R.C. (1972). Pleasure and brain activity in man. *Journal of Nervous and Mental Disease, 154*, 3–18.

Heatherton, T.F., & Baumeister, R.F. (1991). Binge eating as escape from self-awareness. *Psychological Bulletin, 110*, 86–108.

Hebb, D.O. (1955). Drives and the CNS (conceptual nervous system). *Psychological Review, 62*, 243–254.

Heber, R., Garber, H., Harrington, S., & Hoffman, C. (1972). *Rehabilitation of families at risk for mental retardation*. Madison: University of Wisconsin, Rehabilitation Research and Training Center in Mental Retardation.

Hechtman, L. (1989). Teenage mothers and their children: Risks and problems: A review. *Canadian Journal of Psychology, 34*, 569–575.

Hedges, L.V., & Nowell, A. (1995). Sex differences in mental test scores, variability, and numbers of high-scoring individuals. *Science, 269,* 41–45.

Heider, E.R. (1972). Universals in color naming and memory. *Journal of Experimental Psychology, 93,* 10–20.

Heider, E.R., & Oliver, D.C. (1972). The structure of the color space in naming and memory in two languages. *Cognitive Psychology, 3,* 337–354.

Heider, F. (1958). *The psychology of interpersonal relations.* New York: Wiley.

Helgesen, S. (1998). *Everyday revolutionaries: Working women and the transformation of American life.* New York: Doubleday.

Hellige, J.B. (1990). Hemispheric asymmetry. *Annual Review of Psychology, 41,* 55–80.

Hellige, J.B. (1993). *Hemispheric asymmetry: What's right and what's left.* Cambridge, MA: Harvard University Press.

Helmreich, R., & Spence, J. (1978) The Work and Family Orientation Questionnaire: An objective instrument to assess components of achievement motivation and scientific attainment. *Personality and Social Psychology Bulletin, 4,* 222–226.

Helms, J.E. (1992). Why is there no study of cultural equivalence in standardized cognitive ability testing? *American Psychologist, 47,* 1083–1101.

Helms, J.E., & Cook, D.A. (1999). *Using race and culture in counseling and psychotherapy: Theory and process.* Needham Heights, MA: Allyn & Bacon.

Hendrick, S., & Hendrick, C. (1992). *Liking, loving and relating* (2nd ed.). Pacific Grove, CA: Brooks/Cole.

Henriques, J.B., & Davidson, R.J. (1990). Regional brain electrical asymmetries discriminate between previously depressed and healthy control subjects. *Journal of Abnormal Psychology, 99,* 22–31.

Henry, J.A., Alexander, C.A., & Sener, E.K. (1995). Relative mortality from overdose of antidepressants. *British Medical Journal, 310,* 221–224.

Henry, S. (1996, March 7). Keep your brain fit for life. *Parade Magazine,* pp. 8–11.

Herek, G.M. (2000). The psychology of sexual prejudice. *Current Directions in Psychological Science, 9,* 19–22.

Herrnstein, R.J., & Murray, C. (1994). *The bell curve.* New York: Free Press.

Hersher, L. (ed.). (1970). *Four psychotherapies.* New York: Appleton-Century-Crofts.

Herzog, H.A. (1995). Has public interest in animal rights peaked? *American Psychologist, 50,* 945–947.

Hetherington, E.M., Bridges, M., & Insabella, G.M. (1998). What matters? What does not? Five perspectives on the association between marital transitions and children's adjustment. *American Psychologist, 53,* 167–184.

Hewstone, M., Islam, M.R., & Judd, C.M. (1993). Models of cross categorization and intergroup relations. *Journal of Personality and Social psychology, 64,* 779–793.

Hilgard, E.R., Hilgard, J.R., & Kaufmann, W. (1983). *Hypnosis in the relief of pain* (2nd ed.). Los Altos, CA: Kaufmann.

Hill, C.E., Zack, J.S., Wonnell, T.L., Hoffman, M.A., Rochlen, A.B., Goldberg, J.L., Nakayama, E.Y., Heaton, K.J., Kelly, F.A., Eiche, K., Tomlinson, M.J., & Hess, S. (2000). Structured brief therapy with a focus on dreams or loss for clients with troubling dreams and recent loss. *Journal of Counseling Psychology, 47,* 90–101.

Hilton, J., & von Hipple, W. (1996). Stereotypes. *Annual Review of Psychology, 47,* 237–271.

Hobson, J.A. (1994). *The chemistry of conscious states: How the brain changes its mind.* Boston: Little, Brown.

Hochberg, J. (1978). *Perception* (2nd ed.). Englewood Cliffs, NJ: Prentice Hall.

Hochschild, A.R. (1983). *The managed heart.* Berkeley: University of California Press.

Hochschild, A., & Machung, A. (1989). *The second shift: Working parents and the revolution at home.* New York: Viking.

Hoffman, H.S., & DePaulo, P. (1977). Behavioral control by an imprinting stimulus. *American Scientist, 65,* 58–66.

Hoffman, M. (1991). Unraveling the genetics of fragile X syndrome. *Science, 252,* 1070.

Hoffman, M.L. (1977). Personality and social development. *Annual Review of Psychology, 28,* 295–321.

Hoffrage, U., Hertwig, R., & Gigerenzer, G. (2000). Hindsight bias: A by-product of knowledge updating? *Journal of Experimental Psychology: Learning, Memory & Cognition, 26,* 566–581.

Hogan, R., Hogan, J., & Roberts, B.W. (1996). Personality measurement and employment decisions: Questions and answers. *American Psychologist, 51*(5), 469–477.

Holden, C. (2000). Asia stays on top, U.S. in middle in new global rankings. *Science, 290,* 1866.

Holland, C.A., & Rabbitt, P.M.A. (1990). Aging memory: Use versus impairment. *British Journal of Psychology, 82,* 29–38.

Hollister, L.E. (1986). Health aspects of cannibis. *Pharmacological Reviews, 38,* 1–20.

Holmbeck, G.N. (1994). Adolescence. In *Encyclopedia of human behavior* (Vol. 1, pp. 17–28). San Diego, CA: Academic Press.

Hopkins, B., & Westra, T. (1989). Maternal expectations of their infants' development: Some cultural differences. *Developmental Medicine and Child Neurology, 31*(3), 384–390.

Hopkins, B., & Westra, T. (1990). Motor development, maternal expectation, and the role of handling. *Infants Behavior and Development, 13,* 117–122.

Hoptman, M.J., & Davidson, R.J. (1994). How and why do the two cerebral hemispheres interact? *Psychological Bulletin, 116,* 195–219.

Horn, J. (1983). The Texas Adoption Project: Adopted children and their intellectual resemblance to biological and adoptive parents. *Child Development, 54,* 268–275.

Horney, K. (1937). *The neurotic personality of our time.* New York: Norton.

Howard, R.C. (1999). Treatment of anxiety disorders: Does specialty training help? *Professional Psychology: Research & Practice, 30,* 470–473.

Hoyert, D.L., Kochanek, K.D., & Murphy, S.L. (1999). Deaths: Final data for 1997. *National Vital Statistics Reports, 47*(9). Hyattsville, MD: National Center for Health Statistics.

Hsu, L.K. (1996). Epidemiology of the eating disorder. *Psychiatric Clinics of North America, 19*(4), 681–700.

Huang, T. (1998, February 3). Weathering the storms. *Charlotte Observer,* pp. 1–2E.

Hubel, D.H. (1963). The visual cortex of the brain. *Scientific American, 209,* 54–62.

Hubel, D.H., & Livingstone, M.S. (1990). Color and contrast sensitivity in the lateral geniculate body and primary visual cortex of the macaque monkey. *Journal of Neuroscience, 10,* 2223–2237.

Huebner, A.M., Garrod, A., & Snarey, J. (1990). *Moral development in Tibetan Buddhist monks: A cross-cultural study of adolescents and young adults in Nepal.* Paper presented at the meeting of the Society for Research in Adolescence, Atlanta, GA.

Hunt, E., Streissguth, A.P., Kerr, B., & Olson, H.C. (1995). Mothers' alcohol consumption during pregnancy: Effects on spatial-visual reasoning in 14-year-old children. *Psychological Science, 6*(6), 339–342.

Hunt, M. (1994). *The story of psychology.* New York: Anchor/Random House.

Huston, A.C., Watkins, B.A., & Kunkel, D. (1989). Public policy and children's television. *American Psychologist, 44,* 424–433.

Hyde, J.S. (1984a). Children's understanding of sexist language. *Developmental Psychology, 20,* 697–706.

Hyde, J.S. (1984b). How large are gender differences in aggression? A developmental meta-analysis. *Developmental Psychology, 20,* 722–736.

Hyde, J.S., & Linn, M.C. (1988). Gender differences in verbal ability: A meta-analysis. *Psychological Bulletin, 104,* 53–69.

Hyde, J.S., Fennema, E., & Lamon, S.J. (1990). Gender differences in mathematics performance: A meta-analysis. *Psychological Bulletin, 107,* 139–155.

Iacobucci, D., & McGill, A.L. (1990). Analysis of attribution data: Theory testing and effects estimation. *Journal of Personality and Social Psychology, 59*(3), 426–441.

Inciardi, J.A., & Harrison, L.D. (1998). *Heroin in the age of crack cocaine.* Thousand Oaks, CA: Sage.

Inciardi, J.A., Surratt, H.L., & Saum, C.A. (1997). *Cocaine-exposed infants: Social, legal, and public health issues.* Thousand Oaks, CA: Sage.

Irvine, A.B., Biglan, A., Smolkowski, K., Metzler, C.W., & Ary, D.V. (1999). The effectiveness of a parenting skills program for parents of middle school students in small communities. *Journal of Consulting & Clinical Psychology, 67,* 811–825.

Isen, A.M., & Levin, P.F. (1972). The effect of feeling good on helping: Cookies and kindness. *Journal of Personality and Social Psychology, 21,* 384–388.

Ito, T.A., Miller, N., & Pollock, V. (1996). Alcohol and aggression: A meta-analysis on the moderating effects of inhibitory cues, triggering events, and self-focused attention. *Psychological Bulletin, 120,* 60–82.

Iwamasa, G.Y., & Smith, S.K. (1996). Ethnic diversity in behavioral psychology: A review of the literature. *Behavioral Modification, 20,* 45–59.

Izard, C.E. (1992). Basic emotions, relations among emotions, and emotion-cognition relations. *Psychological Review, 99,* 561–565.

Izard, C.E. (1971). *The face of emotion.* New York: Appleton-Century-Crofts.

Izard, C.E. (1980). Cross-cultural perspectives on emotion and emotion communication. In H.C. Triandis & W.J. Lonner (eds.), *Handbook of cross-cultural psychology* (Vol. 3). Boston: Allyn & Bacon.

Izard, C.E. (1994). Innate and universal facial expressions: Evidence from developmental and cross-cultural research. *Psychological Bulletin, 115*(2), 288–299.

Jacobs, G.H. (1993). The distribution and nature of color vision among the mammals. *Biological Review of the Cambridge Philosophical Society, 68,* 413–471.

Jacobsen, P.B., Bovbjerg, D.H., Schwartz, M.D., & Andrykowski, M.A. (1994). Formation of food aversions in patients receiving repeated infusions of chemotherapy. *Behaviour Research & Therapy, 38,* 739–748.

James, L., & Nahl, D. (2000). *Road rage and aggressive driving: Steering clear of highway warfare.* Amherst, NY: Prometheus.

James, W. (1890). *The principles of psychology.* New York: Holt.

Jang, K.L., Livesley, W.J., & Vernon, P.A. (1996). Heritability of the Big Five personality dimensions and their facets: A twin study. *Journal of Personality, 64,* 577–591.

Jang, K.L., Livesley, W.J., McCrae, R.R., Angleitner, A., & Riemann, R. (1998). Heritability of facet-level traits in a cross-cultural twin sample: Support for a hierarchical model of personality. *Journal of Personality and Social Psychology, 74,* 1556–1565.

Janis, I. (1982). *Groupthink: Psychological studies of policy decisions and fiascoes* (2nd ed.). Boston: Houghton Mifflin.

Janis, I.L., Mahl, G.G., & Holt, R.R. (1969). *Personality: Dynamics, development and assessment.* New York: Harcourt Brace Jovanovich.

Janofsky, M. (1994, December 13). Survey reports more drug use by teenagers. *New York Times,* p. A1.

Janos, P.M., & Robinson, N.M. (1985). Psychosocial development in intellectually gifted children. In F. D. Horowitz & M. O'Brien (Eds.), *Gifted and talented: Developmental perspectives* (pp. 149–195). Washington, DC: American Psychological Association.

Jaynes, G.D., & Williams, R.M. (Eds.). (1989). *Common destiny: Blacks and American society.* Washington, DC: National Academy Press.

Jaynes, J.H., & Wlodkowski, R.J. (1990). *Eager to learn: Helping children become motivated and love learning.* San Francisco: Jossey-Bass.

Jenkins, L. (2000). *Biolinguistics.* Cambridge, England: Cambridge University Press.

Jensen, A.R. (1969). How much can we boost IQ and scholastic achievement? *Harvard Educational Review, 39,* 1–123.

Johnson, D. (1990). Can psychology ever be the same again after the human genome is mapped? *Psychological Science, 1,* 331–332.

Johnson, D.M., & Erneling, C.A. (Eds.). (1997). *The future of the cognitive revolution.* New York: Oxford University Press.

Johnson, D.W., Johnson, R.T., & Maruyama, G. (1984). Effects of cooperative learning: A meta-analysis. In N. Miller & M.B. Brewer (eds.), *Groups in contact: The psychology of desegregation* (pp. 187–212). New York: Academic Press.

Johnson, E.S., Levine, A., & Doolittle, F. (1999). *Fathers' fair share: Helping poor men manage child support and fatherhood.* New York: Russell Sage.

Johnson, H.G., Ekman, P., & Friesen, W.V. (1975). Communicative body movements: American emblems. *Semiotica, 15,* 335–353.

Johnson-Greene, D., Adams, K.M., Gilman, S., Kluin, K.J., Junck, L., Martorello, S., & Heumann, M. (1997). Impaired upper limb coordination in alcoholic cerebellar degeneration. *Archives of Neurology, 54,* 436–439.

Jones, C.J., & Meredith, W. (2000). Developmental paths of psychological health from early adolescence to later adulthood. *Psychology & Aging, 15,* 351–360.

Jones, C.P., & Adamson, L.B. (1987). Language use and mother-child-sibling interactions. *Child Development, 58,* 356–366.

Jones, F.D., & Koshes, R.J. (1995). Homosexuality and the military. *American Journal of Psychiatry, 152,* 16–21.

Jones, M.A., & Krisberg, B. (1994) *Images and reality: Juvenile crime, youth violence, and public policy.* San Francisco, CA: National Council on Crime and Delinquency.

Jones, M.C. (1924). Elimination of children's fears. *Journal of Experimental Psychology, 7,* 381–390.

Junginger, J. (1997). Fetishism. In D.R. Laws & W.T. O'Donohue (eds.), *Handbook of sexual deviance: Theory and application*. New York: Guilford.

Kadotani, H., Kadotani, T., Young, T., Peppard, P.E., Finn, L., Colrain, I.M., Murphy, G.M., & Mignot, E., (2001). Association between apolipoprotein E C 4 and sleep-disordered breathing in adults. *Journal of the American Medical Association, 285,* 2888–2890.

Kagan, J. (1989). Temperamental contributions to social behavior. *American Psychologist, 44*(4), 668–674.

Kagan, J. (1994, October 5). The realistic view of biology and behavior. *Chronicle of Higher Education.*

Kagan, J., & Snidman, N. (1991). Infant predictors of inhibited and uninhibited profiles. *Psychological Science, 2*(1), 40–44.

Kagan, J., Arcus, D., & Snidman, N. (1993). The idea of temperament: Where do we go from here? In R. Plomin & G.E. McClearn (eds.), *Nature, nurture, and psychology*. Washington, DC: American Psychological Association.

Kagan, J., Reznick, J.S., Snidman, N., Gibbons, J., & Johnson, M.O. (1988). Childhood derivatives of inhibition and lack of inhibition to the unfamiliar. *Child Development, 59,* 1580–1589.

Kagitcibasi, C. (1997). Individualism and collectivism. In J.W. Berry, Y.H. Poortinga, & J. Kirpatrick (Eds.), *Person, self, and experience: Exploring pacific ethnopsychologies* (pp. 3–32). Berkeley: University of California Press.

Kahneman, D., & Tversky, A. (1996). On the reality of cognitive illusions. *Psychological Review, 103*(3), 582–591.

Kalat, J.W. (1988). *Biological psychology* (3rd ed.). Belmont, CA: Wadsworth.

Kales, J.D., Kales, A., Soldatos, C.R., Caldwell, A.B., Charney, D.S., & Martin, E.D. (1980). Night terrors: Clinical characteristics and personality patterns. *Archives of General Psychiatry, 137,* 1413–1417.

Kamin, L.J. (1969). Selective association and conditioning. In N.J. Mackintosh & W.K. Honig (eds.), *Fundamental issues in associative learning*. Halifax: Dalhousie University Press.

Kaminski, M. (1999). *The team concept: A worker-centered alternative to lean production*. APA Public Interest Directorate. Available online at: www.apa.org/pi/wpo/niosh/abstract22.html

Kane, J., & Lieberman, J. (1992). *Adverse effects of psychotropic drugs*. New York: Guilford Press.

Kantrowitz, B., Rosenberg, D., Rogers, P., Beachy, L., & Holmes, S. (1993, November 1). Heroin makes an ominous comeback. *Newsweek.*

Kaplan, C.A., & Simon, H.A. (1990). In search of insight. *Cognitive Psychology, 22,* 374–419.

Kashima, Y., & Triandis, H.C. (1986). The self-serving bias in attributions as a coping strategy: A cross-cultural study. *Journal of Cross-Cultural Psychology, 17,* 83–98.

Kassebaum, N.L. (1994). Head Start: Only the best for America's children. *American Psychologist, 49,* 123–126.

Kassin, S.M., Tubb, V.A., Hosch, H.M., & Memon, A. (2001). Cases of wrongful conviction often contain erroneous testimony by eyewitnesses. Experts agree that the current state of the literature strongly supports 7 conclusions about the accuracy of eyewitness identification. *American Psychologist, 56,* 405–416

Katz, R., & McGuffin, P. (1993). The genetics of affective disorders. In D. Fowles (ed.), *Progress in experimental personality and psychopathology research*. New York: Springer.

Kaufman, L. (1979). *Perception: The world transformed*. New York: Oxford University Press.

Keck, J.O., Staniunas, R.J., Coller, J.A., Barrett, R.C., & Oster, M.E. (1994). Biofeedback training is useful in fecal incontinence but disappointing in constipation. *Disorders of the Colon and Rectum, 37,* 1271–1276.

Keller, M.B., McCullough, J.P., Klein, D.N., Arnow, B., Dunner, D.L., Gelenberg, A.J., Markowitz, J.C., Nemeroff, C.B., Russell, J.M., Thase, M.E., Trivedi, M.H., Zajecka, J., Blalock, J.A., Borian, F.E., DeBattista, C., Fawcett, J., Hirschfeld, M.A., Jody, D.N., Keitner, G., Kocsis, J.H., Koran, L.M., Kornstein, R.M, Miller, I., Ninan, P.T., Rothbaum, B., Rush, A.J., Schatzberg, A.F., & Vivian, D. (2000). A comparison of Nefazodone, the cognitive behavioral-analysis system of psychotherapy, and their combination for the treatment of chronic depression. *New England Journal of Medicine, 342,* 1462–1470.

Kelley, H.H. (1967). Attribution theory in social psychology. In D. Levine (ed.), *Nebraska Symposium on Motivation*. Lincoln: University of Nebraska Press.

Kelly, J.B. (1982). Divorce: The adult perspective. In B.B. Wolman (ed.), *Handbook of developmental psychology* (pp. 734–750). Englewood Cliffs, NJ: Prentice Hall.

Kelly, K., & Dawson, L. (1994). Sexual orientation. *Encyclopedia of human behavior* (Vol. 4, pp. 183–192). San Diego, CA: Academic Press.

Kelman, H.C. (1974). Attitudes are alive and well and gainfully employed in the sphere of action. *American Psychologist, 230,* 310–324.

Kendler, K.S., Neale, M.C., Kessler, R.C., Heath, A.C., & Eaves, L.J. (1992). Generalized anxiety disorder in women: A population-based twin study. *Archives of General Psychiatry, 49,* 267–272.

Kernis, M.H., & Wheeler, L. (1981). Beautiful friends and ugly strangers: Radiation and contrast effects in perception of same-sex pairs. *Personality and Social Psychology Bulletin, 7,* 617–620.

Kessler, R.C. (1979). Stress, social status, and psychological distress. *Journal of Health and Social Behavior, 20,* 259–272.

Kessler, R.C., McGonagle, K.A., Zhao, S., Nelson, C.R., Highes, M., Eshleman, S., Wittchen, H., & Kendler, K.S. (1994). Lifetime and 12-month prevalence of DSM-III-R psychiatric disorders in the United States: Results from the National Comorbidity Survey. *Archives of General Psychiatry, 51,* 8–19.

Kessler, R.C., Price, R.H., & Wortman, C.B. (1985). Social factors in psychopathology: Stress, social support, and coping processes. *Annual Review of Psychology, 36,* 531–572.

Kessler, R.C., Sonnega, A., Bromet, E., Hughes, M., & Nelson, C.B. (1995). Post-traumatic stress disorder in the national Comorbidity Survey. *Archives of General Psychiatry, 52,* 1057.

Khan, A. (1993). Electroconvulsive therapy: Second edition. *Journal of Nervous and Mental Disease, 181*(9), n.p.

Kiesler, C.A., & Simpkins, C.G. (1993). *The unnoticed majority in psychiatric inpatient care*. New York: Plenum.

Kilpatrick, D.G., Acierno, R., Saunders, B., Resnick, H.S., Best, C.L., & Schnurr, P.P. (2000). Risk factors for adolescent substance abuse and dependence: Data from a national sample. *Journal of Consulting & Clinical Psychology, 68,* 19–30.

Kimberg, D.Y., D'Esposito, M.D., & Farah, M.J. (1997). Cognitive functions in the prefrontal cortex–working memory and executive control. *Current Directions in Psychological Science, 6,* 185–192.

Kimmel, D.C. (1974). *Adulthood and aging*. New York: Wiley.

Kimura, D., & Hampson, E. (1994). Cognitive pattern in men and women is influenced by fluctuations in sex hormones. *Current Directions in Psychological Science, 3* (2), 57–61.

Kingstone, A., Enns, J.T., Mangun, G.R., & Gazzaniga, M.S. (1995). Right-hemisphere memory superiority: Studies of a split-brain patient. *Psychological Science, 6,* 118–121.

Kinsey, A.C., Pomeroy, W.B., & Martin, C.E. (1948). *Sexual behavior in the human male.* Philadelphia: Saunders.

Kinsey, A.C., Pomeroy, W.B., Martin, C.E., & Gebhard, P.H. (1953). *Sexual behavior in the human female.* Philadelphia: Saunders.

Kirsch, I., Montgomery, G., & Saperstein, G. (1995). Hypnosis as an adjunct to cognitive behavioral psychotherapy: A meta analysis. *Journal of Consulting and Clinical Psychology, 63,* 214–220.

Kish, S.J., Furukawa, Y., Ang, L., Vorce, S.P., & Kalasinsky, K.S. (2000). Striatal serotonin is depleted in brain of a human MDMA (Ecstasy) user. *Neurology, 55,* 294–296.

Kissane, D.W., Bloch, S., Miach, P., Smith, G.C., Seddon, A., & Keks, N. (1997). Cognitive-existential group therapy for patients with primary breast cancer–techniques and themes. *Psychooncology, 6*(1), 25–33.

Klatzky, R.L. (1980). *Human memory: Structures and processes* (2nd ed.). San Francisco: Freeman.

Kleim, J.A., Vij, K., Ballard, D.H., & Greenough, W.T. (1997). Learning-dependent synaptic modifications in the cerebellar cortex of the adult rat persist for at least four weeks. *Journal of Neuroscience, 17,* 717–721.

Kleinmuntz, D.N. (1991). Decision making for professional decision makers. *Psychological Science, 2,* 135, 138–141.

Klerman, G.L., Weissman, M.M., Markowitz, J.C., Glick, I., Wilner, P.J., Mason, B., & Shear, M.K. (1994). Medication and psychotherapy. In A.E. Bergin & S.L. Garfield (eds.), *Handbook of psychotherapy and behavior change* (4th ed., pp. 734–782). New York: Wiley.

Kling, K.C., Hyde, J.S., Showers, C.J., & Buswell, B. N. (1999). Gender differences in self-esteem: A meta-analysis. *Psychological Bulletin, 125,* 470–500.

Klingenspor, B. (1994). Gender identity and bulimic eating behavior. *Sex Roles, 31,* 407–432.

Klinger, E. (1990). *Daydreaming: Using waking fantasy and imagery for self-knowledge and creativity.* New York: J.P. Tarcher.

Kluegel, J.R. (1990). Trends in white's explanations of the black–white gap in socioeconomic status, 1977–89. *American Sociological Review, 55,* 512–525.

Knight, G.P., Fabes, R.A., & Higgins, D.A. (1996). Concerns about drawing causal inferences from meta-analyses: An example in the study of gender differences in aggression. *Psychological Bulletin, 119*(3), 410–421.

Knutson, J.R. (1995). Psychological characteristics of maltreated children: Putative risk factors and consequences. *Annual Review of Psychology, 46,* 401–431.

Kobasa, S.C. (1979). Stressful life events, personality, and health: An inquiry into hardiness. *Journal of Personality and Social Psychology, 37,* 1–11.

Koenig, H.G. (1997). *Is religion good for your health? The effects of religion on physical and mental health.* Binghamton, NY: Haworth Press.

Kohlberg, L. (1969). Stage and sequence: The cognitive–developmental approach to socialization. In D.A. Goslin (ed.), *Handbook of socialization theory and research.* Chicago: Rand McNally.

Kohlberg, L. (1979). *The meaning and measurement of moral development* (Clark Lectures). Worcester, MA: Clark University.

Kohlberg, L. (1981). *The philosophy of moral development* (Vol. 1). San Francisco: Harper & Row.

Kohn, A. (1993). *Punished by rewards.* Boston: Houghton Mifflin.

Kokmen, E. (1991). The EURODEM collaborative re-analysis of case-control studies of Alzheimer's disease: Implications for clinical research and practice. *International Journal of Epidemiology, 20*(Suppl. 2), S65–S67.

Kolata, G. (1996a, April 3). Can it be? Weather has no effect on arthritis. *New York Times,* p. B9.

Kolata, G. (1996b, February 27). New era of robust elderly belies the fears of scientists. *New York Times,* p. A1.

Komatsu, L.K. (1992). Recent views of conceptual structure. *Psychological Bulletin, 112,* 500–526.

Komiya, N., Good, G.E., & Sherrod, N.B. (2000). Emotional openness as a predictor of college students' attitudes toward seeking psychological help. *Journal of Counseling Psychology, 47,* 138–143.

Kopta, S.M., Lueger, R.J., Saunders, S.M., & Howard, K.I. (1999). Individual psychotherapy outcome and process research: Challenges leading to greater turmoil or a positive transition? *Annual Review of Psychology, 50,* 441–469.

Kopta, S.M., Howard, K.I., Lowry, J.L., & Beutler, L.E. (1994). Patterns of symptomatic recovery in psychotherapy. *Journal of Consulting and Clinical Psychology, 62,* 1009–1016.

Koss, M.P., & Boeschen, L. (2000). Rape. In A. Kazdin (Ed.), *Encyclopedia of psychology* (Vol.7, pp. 1–6). Washington, DC and Oxford: APA and Oxford University Press.

Krasne, F.B., & Glanzman, D.L. (1995). What we can learn from invertebrate learning. *Annual Review of Psychology, 46,* 585–624.

Kraus, S.J. (1995). Attitudes and the prediction of behavior: A meta-analysis of the empirical literature. *Personality and Social Psychology Bulletin, 21,* 58–75.

Krebs, D. (1975). Empathy and altruism. *Journal of Personality and Social Psychology, 32,* 1134–1140.

Kringlen, E. (1981). *Stress and coronary heart disease. Twin research 3: Epidemiological and clinical studies.* New York: Alan R. Liss.

Kroger, R.O., & Wood, L.A. (1993). Reification, "faking" and the Big Five. *American Psychologist, 48,* 1297–1298.

Krosnick, J.A. (1999). Survey research. *Annual Review of Psychology, 50,* 537–567.

Kruglanski, A.W. (1986, August). Freeze-think and the Challenger. *Psychology Today,* pp. 48–49.

Kuhl, P.K., Williams, K.A., & Lacerda, F. (1992). Linguistic experience alters phonetic perception in infants by 6 months of age. *Science, 255,* 606–608.

Kulik, J., & Brown, R. (1979). Frustration, attribution of blame, and aggression. *Journal of Experimental Social Psychology, 15,* 183–194.

Kunkel, D., Wilson, B.J., Linz, D., Potter, J., Donnerstein, E., Smith, S.L., Blumenthal, E., & Gray, T. (1996). *The national television violence study.* Studio City, CA: Mediascope.

Kupfermann, I. (1991). Hypothalamus and limbic system motivation. In E.R. Kandel, J.H. Schwartz, & T.M. Jessel (eds.), *Principles of neural science* (3rd ed., pp. 750–760). New York: Elsevier.

Kurdek, L.A., Fine, M.A., & Sinclair, R.J. (1995). School adjustment in sixth graders: Parenting transitions, family climate, and peer norm effects. *Child Development, 66,* 430–445.

Kurdek, L.A. (1991). Correlates of relationship satisfaction in cohabiting gay and lesbian couples: Integration of contextual, investment, and problem-solving models. *Journal of Personality & Social Psychology, 61*(6), 910–922.

Kurdek, L.A. (1992). Assumptions versus standards: The validity of two relationship cognitions in heterosexual and homosexual couples *Journal of Family Psychology, 6*(2), 164–170.

LaGreca, A.M., Stone, W.L., & Bell, C.R., III. (1983). Facilitating the vocational-interpersonal skills of mentally retarded individuals. *American Journal of Mental Deficiency, 88,* 270–278.

LaRue, A., & Jarvik, L. (1982). Old age and biobehavioral changes. In B.B. Wolman (ed.), *Handbook of developmental psychology* (pp. 791–806). Englewood Cliffs, NJ: Prentice Hall.

Labouvie-Vief, G. (1986). Modes of knowledge and the organization of development. In M.L. Commons, L. Kohlberg, F.A. Richards, & J. Sinott (eds.), *Beyond formal operations: 3. Models and methods in the study of adult and adolescent thoughts.* New York: Praeger.

Lacayo, R. (April 6, 1998). Toward the root. *Time,* pp. 38–39.

Lachman, S.J. (1984). *Processes in visual misperception: Illusions for highly structured stimulus material.* Paper presented at the 92nd annual convention of the American Psychological Association, Toronto, Canada.

Lachman, S.J. (1996). Processes in perception: Psychological transformations of highly structured stimulus material. *Perceptual and Motor Skills, 83,* 411–418.

Lamb, J.A., Moore, J., Bailey, A., & Monaco, A.P. (2000). Autism: Recent molecular genetic advances. *Human Molecular Genetics, 9,* 861–868.

Lamberg, L. (1998). New drug for erectile dysfunction boon for many, "viagravation" for some. *JAMA: Medical News & Perspectives, 280,* 867–871

Lambert, M.J., Shapiro, D.A., & Bergin, A.E. (1986). The effectiveness of psychotherapy. In S.L. Garfield & A.E. Bergin (eds.), *Handbook of psychotherapy and behavior change* (3rd ed., pp. 157–212). New York: Wiley.

Lambert, W.W., Solomon, R.L., & Watson, P.D. (1949). Reinforcement and extinction as factors in size estimation. *Journal of Experimental Psychology, 39,* 637–641.

Lampl, M., Veidhuis, J.D., & Johnson, M.L. (1992). Saltation and stasis: A model of human growth. *Science, 258,* 801–803.

Lande, R. (1993). The video violence debate. *Hospital and Community Psychiatry, 44,* 347–351.

Landesman, S., & Butterfield, E.C. (1987). Normalization and de-institution of mentally retarded individuals: Controversy and facts. *American Psychologist, 42,* 809–816.

Langer, E.J., Bashner, R.S., & Chanowitz, B. (1985). Decreasing prejudice by increasing discrimination. *Journal of Personality and Social Psychology, 49,* 113–120.

Langlois, J.H., Ritter, J.M., Casey, R.J., & Sawin, D.B. (1995). Infant attractiveness predicts maternal behaviors and attitudes. *Developmental Psychology, 31,* 464–472.

Lantz, M.S., Buchalter, E.N., & McBee, L. (1997). The wellness group: A novel intervention for coping with disruptive behavior in elderly nursing home residents. *Gerontologist, 37,* 551–556.

Larimer, M.E., Lydum, A.R., Anderson, B.K., & Turner, A.P. (1999). Male and female recipients of unwanted sexual contact in a college student sample: Prevalence rates, alcohol use, and depression symptoms. *Sex Roles, 40,* 295–308.

Latané, B., & Rodin, J. (1969). A lady in distress: Inhibiting effects of friends and strangers on bystander intervention. *Journal of Experimental Social Psychology, 5,* 189–202.

Laumann, E.O., Gagnon, J.H., Michael, R.T., & Michaels, S. (1994). *The social organization of sexuality: Sexual practices in the United States.* Chicago: University of Chicago Press.

Lazarus, R.S. (1993). From psychological stress to the emotions: A history of changing outlooks. *Annual Review of Psychology, 44,* 1–21.

Lazarus, R.S. (1982). Thoughts on the relations between emotion and cognition. *American Psychologist, 37,* 1019–1024.

Lazarus, R.S. (1991a). Cognition and motivation in emotion. *American Psychologist, 46,* 352–367.

Lazarus, R.S. (1991b). Progress on a cognitive-motivational-relational theory of emotion. *American Psychologist, 46,* 819–834.

Lazarus, R.S. (1991c). *Emotion and adaptation.* New York: Oxford University Press.

Lazarus, R.S., De Longis, A., Folkman, S., & Gruen, R. (1985). Stress and adaptional outcomes. *American Psychologist, 40,* 770–779.

Leary, W.E. (1990, January 25). Risk of hearing loss is growing, panel says. *New York Times,* Sec. B.

Leary, W.E. (1995, April 21). Young who try suicide may succeed more often. *New York Times.*

Lebow, J.L., & Gurman, A.S. (1995). Research assessing couple and family therapy. *Annual Review of Psychology, 46,* 27–57.

Leccese, A.P. (1991). *Drugs and society.* Englewood Cliffs, NJ: Prentice Hall.

Lefcourt, H.M. (1992). Durability and impact of the locus of control construct. *Psychological Bulletin, 112,* 411–414.

Leibowitz, H.W., & Owens, D.A. (1977). Nighttime driving accidents and selective visual degradation. *Science, 197,* 422–423.

Leigh, R.J. (1994). Human vestibular cortex. *Annals of Neurology, 35,* 383–384.

Lerman, C., Caporaso, N.D., Audrain, J., Main, D., Bowman, E.D., Lockshin, B., Boyd, N.R., & Shields, P.G. (1999). Evidence suggesting the role of specific genetic factors in cigarette smoking. *Health Psychology, 18,* 14–20.

Lerman, H. (1996). *Gender bias in the diagnostic classification of mental disorders.* New York: Basic Books.

Lerner, M.J. (1980). *The belief in a just world: A fundamental delusion.* New York: Plenum.

Lerner, R.M., & Galambos, N.L. (1998). Adolescent development: Challenges and opportunities for research, programs and policies. *Annual Review of Psychology, 49,* 413–446.

Leshner, A.I. (1996). Understanding drug addiction: Implications for treatment. *Hospital Practice, 31,* 7–54.

Lev, M. (1991, May). No hidden meaning here: Survey sees subliminal ads. *New York Times,* Sec. C.

LeVay, S. (1991). A difference in hypothalamic structure between heterosexual and homosexual men. *Science, 253,* 1034–1038.

LeVay, S., & Hamer, D.H. (1994, May). Evidence for a biological influence in male homosexuality. *Scientific American,* pp. 44–49.

Levenson, M.R., & Aldwin, C.M. (1994). Aging, personality, and adaptation. In V. S. Ramachandran (Ed.), *Encyclopedia of human behavior* (Vol. 1, pp. 47–55). San Diego, CA: Academic Press.

Levenson, R.W. (1992). Autonomic nervous system differences among emotions. *Psychological Science, 3,* 23–27.

Leventhal, H., & Niles, P. (1965). Persistence of influence for varying duration of exposure to threat stimuli. *Psychological Reports, 16,* 223–233.

Levine, S., Johnson, D.F., & Gonzales, C.A. (1985). Behavioral and hormonal responses to separation in infant rhesus monkeys and mothers. *Behavioral Neuroscience, 99,* 399–410.

Levinson, D.J. (1978). *The seasons of a man's life.* New York: Knopf.

Levinson, D.J. (1986). A conception of adult development. *American Psychologist, 41,* 3–13.

Levinson, D.J. (1987). *The seasons of a woman's life.* New York: Knopf.

Lewin, K.A. (1935). *A dynamic theory of personality* (K.E. Zener & D.K. Adams, trans.). New York: McGraw-Hill.

Lewin, T. (1994a, May 18). Boys are more comfortable with sex than girls are, survey finds. *New York Times*, p. A10.

Lewin, T. (1995, May 30). The decay of families is global study says. *New York Times*, p. A5.

Lewin, T. (1996, March 27). Americans are firmly attached to traditional roles for sexes, poll finds. *New York Times*, p. A12.

Lewy, A.J., Ahmed, S., Latham, J.J., & Sack R. (1992). Melatonin shifts human circadian rhythms according to a phase-response curve. *Chronobiology International 9*, 380–392.

Lichstein, K.L., Wilson, N.M., & Johnson, C.T. (2000). Psychological treatment of secondary insomnia. *Psychology & Aging, 15*, 232–240.

Lichtenstein, E. (1999). Nicotine Anonymous: Community resource and research implications. *Psychology of Addictive Behaviors, 13*, 60–68.

Liem, R., & Liem, J.V. (1978). Social class and mental illness reconsidered: The role of economic stress and social support. *Journal of Health and Social Behavior, 19*, 139–156.

Liggett, D.R. (2000). *Sport hypnosis*. Champaign, IL: Human Kinetics.

Lightdale, J.R., & Prentice, D.A. (1994). Rethinking sex differences in aggression: Aggressive behavior in the absence of social roles. *Personality and Social Psychology Bulletin, 20*, 34–44.

Lin, L., Umahara, M., York, D.A., & Bray, G.A. (1998). Beta-casomophins stimulate and enterostatin inhibits the intake of dietary fat in rats. *Peptids, 19*, 325–331.

Lindsay, D.S. (1993). Eyewitness suggestibility. *Current Directions in Psychological Science, 2*, 86–89.

Lindsay, D.S., & Johnson, M.K. (1989). The eyewitness suggestibility effect and memory for source. *Memory & Cognition, 17*, 349–358.

Linn, R.L. (1982). Admissions testing on trial. *American Psychologist, 37*, 279–291.

Lipman, S. (1991). *Laughter in Hell: The use of humor during the Holocaust*. Northvale, NJ: J. Aronson.

Lipsey, M., & Wilson, D. (1993). The efficacy of psychological, educational, and behavioral treatment: Confirmation from meta-analysis. *American Psychologist, 48*, 1181–1209.

Lipsky, D.K., & Gartner, A. (1996). Inclusive education and school restructuring. In W. Stainback & S. Stainback (eds.), *Controversial issues confronting special education: Divergent perspectives* (pp. 3–15). Baltimore: Brookes.

Liu, C., Weaver, D.R., Jin, X., Shearman, I.P., Pieschl, R.I., Gribkoff, V.K., & Reppert, S.M. (1997). Molecular dissection of two distinct actions of melatonin on the suprachiasmatic circadian clock. *Neuron, 19*, 99–102.

Livingstone, M.S., & Hubel, D.H. (1988a). Do the relative mapping densities of the magno- and parvocellular systems vary with eccentricity? *Journal of Neuroscience, 8*, 4334–4339.

Livingstone, M.S., & Hubel, D.H. (1988b, May 6). Segregation of form, color, movement, and depth: Anatomy, physiology, and perception. *Science, 340*, 740–749.

Loehlin, J.C. (2001). Behavior genetics and parenting theory. *American Psychologist, 56*, 169–170.

Loehlin, J.C., McCrae, R.R., Costa, P.T., & John, O.P. (1998). Heritability of common and measure-specific components of the Big Five personality traits. *Journal of Research in Personality, 32*, 431–453.

Loehlin, J.C., Horn, J.M., & Willerman, L. (1997). Heredity, environment, and IQ in the Texas adoption study. In R.J. Sternberg & E. Grigorenko (eds.), *Intelligence: Heredity and environment*. New York: Cambridge University Press.

Loehlin, J.C., Willerman, L., & Horn, J.M. (1988). Human behavior genetics. *Annual Review of Psychology, 39*, 101–133.

Loewenstein, G. (1994). The psychology of curiosity: A review and reinterpretation. *Psychological Bulletin, 116*, 75–98.

Loftus, E.F. (1993a). The reality of repressed memories. *American Psychologist, 48*, 518–537.

Loftus, E.F. (1997). Repressed memory accusations: Devastated families and devastated patients. *Applied Cognitive Psychology, 11*(1), 25–30.

Loftus, E.F., & Hoffman, H.G. (1989). Misinformation and memory: The creation of new memories. *Journal of Experimental Psychology: General, 118*, 100–114.

Loftus, E.F., & Palmer, J.C. (1974). Reconstruction of automobile destruction: An example of the interaction between language and memory. *Journal of Verbal Learning and Verbal Behavior, 13*, 585–589.

Loftus, E.F., & Pickrell, J.E. (1995). The formation of false memories. *Psychiatric Annals, 25*, 720–725.

Logue, A.W., Ophir, I., & Strauss, K.E. (1981). The acquisition of taste aversions in humans. *Behavior Research and Therapy, 19*, 319–333.

Lorenz, K. (1935). Der Kumpan inder Umwelt des Vogels. *Journal of Ornithology, 83*, 137–213, 289–413.

Lott, A.J., & Lott, B.E. (1974). The role of reward in the formation of positive interpersonal attitudes. In T.L. Huston (Ed.), *Foundations of interpersonal attraction* (pp. 171–192). New York: Academic Press.

Louie, T.A., Curren, M.T., & Harich, K.R. (2000). "I knew we could win": Hindsight bias for favorable and unfavorable decision outcomes. *Journal of Applied Psychology, 85*, 264–272.

Lubinski, D. (2000). Scientific and social significance of assessing individual differences: "Sinking shafts at a few critical points." *Annual Review of Psychology, 51*, 405–444.

Lubinski, D., & Benbow, C.P. (2000). States of excellence. *American Psychologist, 55*, 137–150.

Luchins, A. (1957). Primacy-recency in impression formation. In C. Hovland, W. Mandell, E. Campbell, T. Brock, A. Luchins, A. Cohen, W. McGuire, I. Janis, R. Feierbend, & N. Anderson (eds.), *The order of presentation in persuasion*. New Haven, CT: Yale University Press.

Lykken, D., & Tellegen, A. (1996). Happiness is a stochastic phenomenon. *Psychological Science, 7*, 186–189.

Lyness, S.A. (1993). Predictors of differences between Type A and B individuals in heart rate and blood pressure reactivity. *Psychological Bulletin, 114*, 266–295.

Lyons, M.J., True, W.R., Eisen, S.A., Goldberg, J., Meyer, J.M., Faraone, S.V., Eaves, L.J., & Tsuang, M.T. (1995). Differential heritability of adult and juvenile antisocial traits. *Archives of General Psychiatry, 52*, 906–915.

Maas, J. (1998). *Power sleep: The revolutionary program that prepares your mind for peak performance*. New York: Villard.

MacDonald, T.K., Fong, G.T., Zanna, M.P., & Martineau, A.M. (2000). Alcohol myopia and condom use: Can alcohol intoxication be associated with more prudent behavior. *Journal of Personality & Social Psychology, 78*, 605–619.

MacDonald, T.K., MacDonald, G., Zanna, M.P., & Fong, G. (2000). Alcohol, sexual arousal and intentions to use condoms in young men: Applying alcohol myopia theory to risky sexual behavior. *Health Psychology, 19*, 290–298.

MacLean, P.D. (1970). The limbic brain in relation to the psychoses. In P. Black (ed.), *Physiological correlates of emotion* (pp. 129–146). New York: Academic Press.

MacLeod, D.I.A. (1978). Visual sensitivity. *Annual Review of Psychology, 29*, 613–645.

Maccoby, E.E. (1998). *The two sexes: Growing up apart, coming together.* Cambridge, MA: Belknap Press.

Maccoby, E.E. (2000). Parenting and its effects on children: On reading and misreading behavior genetics. *Annual Review of Psychology, 51*, 1–27.

Macionis, J.J. (1993). *Sociology* (4th ed.). Englewood Cliffs, NJ: Prentice Hall.

Mackavey, W.R., Malley, J.E., & Stewart, A.J. (1991). Remembering autobiographically consequential experiences: Content analysis of psychologists' accounts of their lives. *Psychology and Aging, 6*, 50–59.

Mackworth, N. (1965). Originality. *American Psychologist, 20*, 51–66.

Macrae, C.N., & Bodenhausen, G.V. (2000). Social cognition: Thinking categorically about others. *Annual Review of Psychology, 51*, 93–120.

Madden, N.A., & Slavin, R.E. (1983). Effects of cooperative learning on the social acceptance of mainstreamed academically handicapped students. *Journal of Special Education, 17*, 171–182.

Maddi, S.R. (1989). *Personality theories: A comparative approach* (5th ed.). Homewood, IL: Dorsey.

Madsen, P.L. (1993). Blood flow and oxygen uptake in the human brain during various states of sleep and wakefulness. *Acta Paediatrica Scandinavica, 148*(Suppl.), 3–27.

Maier, S.F., Watkins, L.R., & Fleshner, M. (1994). Psychoneuroimmunology: The interface between behavior, brain and immunity. *American Psychologist, 49*(12), 1004–1017.

Maisto, A.A., & Hughes, E. (1995). Adaptation to group home living for adults with mental retardation as a function of previous residential placement. *Journal of Intellectual Disability Research, 39*, 15–18.

Maloney, M. P., & Ward, M.P. (1976). *Psychological assessment: A conceptual approach.* New York: Academic Press.

Mandel, D.R., Jusczyk, P.W., & Pisoni, D.B. (1995). Infants' recognition of the sound patterns of their own names. *Psychological Science, 6*, 314–317.

Manton, K.G., Gu, X. (2001). Changes in the prevalence of chronic disability in the United States black and nonblack population above age 65 from 1982 to 1999. *Proc. Natl. Acad. Sci, USA, 98*, 6354–6359.

Maquet, P., Laureys, S., Peigneus, P., Fuchs, S., Petiau, C., Phips, C., Aerts, J., Fiore, G.D., Degueldre, C., Meulemans, T., Luxen, A., Franck, G., VanDerLinden, M., Smith, C., & Axel, C. (2000). Experience-dependent changes in cerebral activation during human REM sleep. *Nature: Neuroscience, 3*, 831–836.

Marano, H.E. (1997, July 1). Puberty may start at 6 as hormones surge. *New York Times*, pp. C1, C6.

Marcia, J.E. (1994). The empirical study of ego identity. In H.A. Bosna, T.L.G. Graafsma., H.D. Grotevant, & D.J. de Levita (Eds.), *Identity and development: An interdisciplinary approach* (pp. 67–80). Thousand Oaks, CA: Sage.

Marcia, J.E. (1980). Identity in adolescence. In J. Adelson (ed.), *Handbook of adolescent psychology.* New York: Wiley.

Marcus, G.F. (1996). Why do children say "breaked"? *American Psychological Society, 5*(3), 81–85.

Margolin, G. (1987). Marital therapy: A cognitive-behavioral-affective approach. In N.S. Jacobson (ed.), *Psychotherapists in clinical practice* (pp. 232–285). New York: Guilford.

Marks, I.M., & Nesse, R.M. (1994). Fear and fitness: An evolutionary analysis of anxiety disorders. *Ethology and Sociobiology, 15*, 247–261.

Marks, L.S., Duda, C., Dorey, F.J., Macairan, M.L., & Santos, P.B. (1999). Treatment of erectile dysfunction with sildenafil. *Urology, 53*, 19–24.

Markus, H.R., & Kitayama, S. (1991). Culture and self: Implications for cognition, emotion, and motivation. *Psychological Review, 98*, 224–253.

Martin, S., (2001). Substance abuse is nation's No. 1 health problem, but there is hope. *Monitor on Psychology, 32*, 10.

Martindale, C. (2001). Oscillations and analogies. *American Psychologist, 56*, 342–345.

Martino, A. (1995, February 5). Mid-life usually brings positive change, not crisis. *Ann Arbor News.*

Maslach, C., & Leiter, M.P. (1997). *The truth about burnout.* San Francisco: Jossey-Bass.

Masling, J., Rabie, L., & Blondheim, S.H. (1967). Obesity, level of aspiration, and Rorshach and TAT measures of oral dependence. *Journal of Consulting Psychology, 31*, 233–239.

Maslow, A.H. (1954). *Motivation and personality.* New York: Harper & Row.

Mason, F.L. (1997). Fetishism: Psychopathology and theory. In D.R. Laws & W.T. O'Donohue (eds.), *Handbook of sexual deviance: Theory and application.* New York: Guilford.

Massaro, D.W., & Cowan, N. (1993). Information processing models: Microscopes of the mind. *Annual Review of Psychology, 44*, 383–425.

Masters, W.H., & Johnson, V.E. (1966). *Human sexual response.* Boston: Little Brown & Co.

Matsumoto, D. (1996). *Culture and psychology.* Pacific Grove, CA: Brooks/Cole.

Matthews, D.B., Best, P.J., White, A.M., Vandergriff, J.L., & Simson, P.E. (1996). Ethanol impairs spatial cognitive processing: New behavioral and electrophysiological findings. *Current Directions in Psychological Science, 5*, 111–115.

Matthews, K.A. (1988). Coronary heart disease and Type A behaviors: Update on and alternative to the Booth-Kewley and Friedman (1987) quantitative review. *Psychological Bulletin, 104*, 373–380.

Mattson, S.N., Riley, E.P., Gramling, L., Delis, D.C., & Jones, K.L. (1998). Neuropsychological comparison of alcohol-exposed children with or without physical features of fetal alcohol syndrome. *Neuropsychology, 12*, 146–153.

Maurer, D., & Maurer, C. (1988). *The world of the newborn.* New York: Basic Books.

Mayer, J.D., & Geher, G. (1996). Emotional intelligence and the identification of emotion. *Intelligence, 22*, 89–113.

Mayer, J.D., & Salovey, P. (1997). What is emotional intelligence? In P. Salovey & D. Sluyter (eds.), *Emotional development, emotional literacy, and emotional intelligence.* New York: Basic Books.

Mays, V.M., Bullock, M., Rosenzweig, M.R., & Wessells, M. (1998). Ethnic conflict: Global challenges and psychological perspectives. *American Psychologist, 53*, 737–742.

Mazzoni, G.A.L., Lombardo, P., Malvagia, S., & Loftus, E.F. (1999). Dream interpretation and false beliefs. *Professional Psychology: Research & Practice, 30*, 45–50.

McBurney, D.H., & Collings, V.B. (1984). *Introduction to sensation/perception* (2nd ed.). Englewood Cliffs, NJ: Prentice Hall.

McCabe, P.M., Schneiderman, N., Field, T., & Wellens, A.R. (2000). *Stress, coping, and cardiovascular disease.* Mahwah, NJ: Erlbaum.

McCall, M. (1997). Physical attractiveness and access to alcohol: What is beautiful does not get carded. *Journal of Applied Social Psychology, 27*(5), 453–462.

McCall, R.B. (1979). *Infants*. Cambridge, MA: Harvard University Press.

McCann, U.D., Szabo, Z., Scheffel, U., Dannals, R.F., & Ricaurte, G.A. (1998). Positron emission tomographic evidence of toxic effect of MDMA ("Ecstasy") on brain serotonin neurons in human beings. *Lancet, 352*, 1443–1437.

McCann, U.D., Slate, S.O., & Ricaurte, G.A. (1996). Adverse reactions with 3,4-methylenedioxymethamphetamine (MDMA; "ecstasy"). *Drug Safety, 15*, 107–115.

McClearn, G.E., Plomin, R., Gora-Maslak, G., & Crabbe, J.C. (1991). The gene chase in behavioral science. *Psychological Science, 2*, 222–229.

McClelland, D.C. (1958). Methods of measuring human motivation. In J. W. Atkinson (Ed.), *Motives in fantasy, action and society: A method of assessment and study*. New York: Van Nostrand.

McClelland, D.C., & Atkinson, J.W. (1948). The projective expression of needs: I. The effect of different intensities of the hunger drive on perception. *Journal of Psychology, 25*, 205–222.

McCloskey, M., & Egeth, H.E. (1983). Eyewitness identification: What can a psychologist tell a jury? *American Psychologist, 38*, 550–563.

McClure, E.B. (2000). A meta-analytic review of sex differences in facial expression processing and their development in infants, children, and adolescents. *Psychological Bulletin, 126*, 424–453

McConnell, R.A. (1969). ESP and credibility in science. *American psychologist, 24*, 531–538.

McCrae, R.R., & Costa, P.T., Jr. (1996). Toward a new generation of personality theories: Theoretical contexts for the five-factor model. In J.S. Wiggins (ed.), *The five-factor model of personality: Theoretical perspectives* (pp. 51–87). New York: Guilford Press.

McCrae, R.R., & Costa, P.T., Jr. (1997). Personality trait structure as a human universal. *American Psychologist, 52*, 509–516.

McDaniel, M.A., & Frei, R.L. (1994). Validity of customer service measures in personnel selection: A review of criterion and construct evidence. (Cited in Hogan, R., Hogan, J., & Roberts, B.W. [1996]. Personality measurement and employment decisions: Questions and answers. *American Psychologist, 51*[5], 469–477.)

McDaniel, M.A., Waddill, P.J., & Shakesby, P.S. (1996). Study strategies, interest, and learning from text: The application of material appropriate processing. In D. Herrmann, C. McEvoy, C. Hertzog, P. Hertel, & M.K. Johnson (eds.), *Basic and applied memory research: Theory in context*. Nahwah, NJ: Erlbaum.

McDonald, J.W. (1999). Repairing the damaged spinal cord. *Scientific American, 281*(3), 65–73.

McElhatton, P.R., Bateman, D.N., Evans, C., Pughe, K.R., & Thomas, S.H.L. (1999). Congenital anomalies after prenatal ecstasy exposure. *Lancet, 354*, 1441–1442.

McFarland, L.J., Senn, L.E., & Childress, J.R. (1993). *21st century leadership: Dialogues with 100 top leaders*. Los Angeles: The Leadership Press.

McGeer, P.L., & McGeer, E.G. (1980). Chemistry of mood and emotion. *Annual Review of Psychology, 31*, 273–307.

McGinnis, M. (1994). The role of behavioral research in national health policy. In S. Blumenthal, K. Matthews, & Weiss (eds.), *New research frontiers in behavioral medicine: Proceeding of the National Conference*. Washington, DC: NIH Publications.

McGovern, L.P. (1976). Dispositional social anxiety and helping behavior under three conditions of threat. *Journal of Personality, 44*, 84–97.

McGrady, A. (1996). Good news–bad press: Applied psychophysiology in cardiovascular disorders *Biofeedback and Self-Regulation, 21*(4), 335–346.

McGue, M. (1993). From proteins to cognitions: The behavioral genetics of alcoholism. In R. Plomin & G. E. McClearn (Eds.), *Nature, nurture & psychology* (pp. 245–268). Washington, DC: American Psychological Association.

McGuffin, P., Katz, R., Watkins, S., & Rutherford, J. (1996). A hospital-based twin register of the heritability of DSM-IV unipolar depression. *Archives of General Psychiatry, 53*, 129–136.

McGuire, M.T., Wing, R.R., Klem, M.L., Lang, W., & Hill, J.O. (1999). What predicts weight regain in a group of successful weight losers? *Journal of Consulting & Clinical Psychology, 67*, 177–185.

McGuire, P.A. (1999, June 6). Psychology and medicine connecting in the war over cancer. *APA Monitor*, pp. 8–9.

McGuire, S. (2001). Are behavioral genetic and socialization research compatible? *American Psychologist, 56*, 171.

McGuire, S. (2001). Are behavioral genetic and socialization research compatible? *American Psychologist, 56*, 171.

McGuire, W.J. (1985). Attitudes and attitude change. In G. Lindzey & E. Aronson (eds.), *Handbook of social psychology*. Reading, MA: Addison-Wesley.

McKay, R. (1997). Stem cells in the nervous system. *Science, 276*, 66–71.

McKim, W.A. (1997). *Drugs and behavior* (3rd ed.). Upper Saddle River, NJ: Prentice Hall.

McMillan, T.M., Robertson, I.H., & Wilson, B.A. (1999). Neurogenesis after brain injury: Implications for neurorehabilitation. *Neuropsychological Rehabilitation, 9*, 129–133.

McNamara, H.J., Long, J.B., & Wike, E.L. (1956). Learning without response under two conditions of external cues. *Journal of Comparative and Physiological Psychology, 49*, 477–480.

McNeil, B.J., Pauker, S.G., Sox, H.C., Jr., & Tversky, A. (1982). On the elicitation of preferences for alternative therapies. *New England Journal of Medicine, 306*, 1259–1262.

Mead, M. (1935). *Sex and temperament in three primitive societies*. New York: Morrow.

Mednick, A. (1993, May). Worlds' women familiar with a day's double shift. *APA Monitor*, p. 32.

Mednick, S.A. (1962). The associative basis of creativity. *Psychological Review, 69*, 220–232.

Meichenbaum, D., & Cameron, R. (1982). Cognitive-behavior therapy. In G.T. Wilson & C.M. Franks (eds.), *Contemporary behavior therapy: Conceptual and empirical foundations*. New York: Guilford.

Melamed, B.G., Hawes, R.R., Heiby, E., & Glick, J. (1975). Use of filmed modeling to reduce uncooperative behavior of children during dental treatment. *Journal of Dental Research, 54*, 797–801.

Melamed, S., Ben-Avi, I., Luz, J., & Green, M. (1995). Objective and subjective work monotony: Effects on job satisfaction, psychological distress, and absenteeism in blue-collar workers. *Journal of Applied Psychology, 80*, 29–42.

Melcher, T.P. (2000). Clarifying the effects of parental substance abuse, child sexual abuse, and parental caregiving on adult adjustment. *Professional Psychology: Research & Practice, 31*, 64–69.

Mellers, B.A., Schwartz, A., & Cooke, A.D.J. (1998). Judgment and decision making. *Annual Review of Psychology, 49*, 447–477.

Meltzoff, A.N., & Gopnik, A. (1997). *Words, thoughts and theories*. Boston, MA: MIT Press.

Meltzoff, A.N., & Moore, M.K. (1985). Cognitive foundations and social functions of imitation and intermodal representation in infancy. In J. Mehler & R. Fox (eds.), *Neonate cognition: Beyond the blooming, fuzzing confusion*. Hillsdale, NJ: Erlbaum.

Melzack, R. (1980). Psychological aspects of pain. In J.J. Bonica (ed.), *Pain*. New York: Raven Press.

Menon, T., Morris, M.W., Chiu, C.Y., & Hong, Y.Y. (1998). *Culture and the perceived autonomy of individuals and groups: American attributions to personal dispositions and Confucian attributions to group*. Unpublished manuscript, Stanford University.

Mershon, B., & Gorsuch, R.L. (1988). Number of factors in the personality sphere: Does increase in factors increase predictability of real-life criteria? *Journal of Personality and Social Psychology, 55*, 675–680.

Mersky, H. (1992). The manufacture of personalities: The production of multiple personality disorder. *British Journal of Psychiatry, 160*, 327–340.

Merzer, M. (1998) Some pilots admit to midair naps. Reprint from *The Spokesman Review*, June 21. http://www.spokane.net/stories/1998/Jun/21/S410433.asp.

Meston, C.M., & Frohlich, M.A. (2000). The neurobiology of sexual function. *Archives of General Psychiatry, 57*, 1012–1030.

Metcalfe, J., Funnell, M., & Gazzaniga, M.S. (1995). Guided visual search is a left-hemisphere process in split-brain patient. *Psychological Science, 6*, 157–173.

Meyer, G.J., Finn, S.E., Eyde, L.D., Kay, G.G., Moreland, K.L., Dies, R.R., Eisman, E.J., Kubiszyn, T.W., & Reed, G.M. (2001). Psychological testing and psychological assessment: A review of evidence and issues. *American Psychologist, 56*, 128–165.

Michael, R.P., Bonsall, R.W., & Warner, P. (1974). Human vaginal secretions: Volatile fatty acid content. *Science, 186*, 1217–1219.

Michael, R.T., Gagnon, J.H., Laumann, E.O., & Kolata, G. (1994). *Sex in America: A definitive survey*. Boston: Little, Brown.

Michelson, L. (ed.). (1985). Meta-analysis and clinical psychology [special issue.] *Clinical Psychology Review, 5*(1).

Middaugh, S.J. (1990). On clinical efficacy: Why biofeedback does—and does not—work. *Biofeedback and Self-Regulation, 15*, 191–208.

Migliaccio, E., Giorgio, M., Mele, S., Pelicci, G., Reboldi, P., Pandolfi, P. P., Lanfrancone, L., & Pelicci, P. G. (1999). The p66shu adaptor protein controls oxidative stress response and life span in mammals. *Nature, 402*, 309–313.

Milgram, S. (1963). Behavioral study of obedience. *Journal of Abnormal and Social Psychology, 67*, 371–378.

Milgram, S. (1974). *Obedience to authority: An experimental view*. New York: Harper & Row.

Miller, J. (1984). Culture and the development of everyday social explanation. *Journal of Personality and Social Psychology, 46*, 961–978.

Miller, J.G., Bersoff, D.M., & Harwood, R.L. (1990). Perceptions of social responsibilities in India and the United States: Moral imperatives or personal decisions? *Journal of Personality and Social Psychology, 58*, 33–47.

Miller, P.A., Kliewer, W., & Burkeman, D. (1993, March). *Effects of maternal socialization on children's learning to cope with divorce*. Paper presented at the biennial meeting of the Society for Research in Child Development, New Orleans, LA.

Miller, T.Q., Turner, C.W., Tindale, R.S., Posavac, E.J., & Dugoni, B.L. (1991). Reasons for the trend toward null findings in research on Type A behavior. *Psychological Bulletin, 110*, 469–485.

Miller, T.Q., Smith, T.W., Turner, C.W., Guijarro, M.L., & Hallet, A.J. (1996). A meta-analytic review of research on hostility and physical health. *Psychological Bulletin, 119*(2), 322–348.

Miller, W.R., & Brown, S.A. (1997). Why psychologists should treat alcohol and drug problems. *American Psychologist, 52*, 1269–1279.

Milner, B. (1959). The memory defect in bilateral hippocampal lesions. *Psychiatric Research Reports, 11*, 43–52.

Milton, J., & Wiseman, R. (1999). Does psi exist? Lack of replication of an anomalous process of information transfer. *Psychological Bulletin, 125*, 387–391.

Minton, H.L., & Schneider, F.W. (1980). *Differential psychology*. Monterey, CA: Brooks/Cole.

Mischel, W., & Shoda, Y. (1995). A cognitive-affective system theory of personality: Reconceptualizing situations, dispositions, dynamics, and invariance in personality structure. *Psychological Review, 102*(2), 246–268.

Mistry, J., & Rogoff, B. (1994). Remembering in cultural context. In W.W. Lonner & R. Malpass (eds.), *Psychology and culture* (pp. 139–144). Boston: Allyn & Bacon.

Misumi, J. (1985). *The behavioral science of leadership: An interdisciplinary Japanese leadership program*. Ann Arbor: University of Michigan Press.

Mittleman, M. (2000, March). *Association between marijuana use and cardiovascular disease*. Paper presented at the conference of the American Heart Association, San Diego.

Moen, P., Kim, J., & Hofmeister, H. (2001). Couples' work/retirement transitions, gender, and marital quality. *Social Psychology Quarterly, 64*, 55–71.

Moffitt, T.W. (1993). Adolescence-limited and life-course-persistent antisocial behavior: A developmental taxonomy. *Psychological Review, 100*, 674–701.

Moghaddam, F.M., Taylor, D.M., & Wright, S.C. (1993). *Social psychology in cross-cultural perspective*. New York: Freeman.

Molineux, J.B. (1985). *Family therapy: A practical manual*. Springfield, IL: Charles C. Thomas.

Mollica, R. F. (2000). Invisible wounds. *Scientific American, 282*(6), 54–57.

Moncrieff, R.W. (1951). *The chemical senses*. London: Leonard Hill.

Montgomery, G.H., DuHamel, K.N., & Redd, W.H. (2000). A meta-analysis of hypnotically induced analgesia: How effective is hypnosis? *International Journal of Clinical & Experimental Hypnosis [Special Issue: The Status of Hypnosis as an Empirically Validated Clinical Intervention], 48*, 138–153.

Moore, K.A., Morrison, D.R., & Greene, A.D. (1997). Effects on the children born to adolescent mothers. In R.A. Maynard (Ed.), *Kids having kids: Economic costs and social consequences of teen pregnancy* (pp. 145–180). Washington, DC: Urban Institute Press.

Moore, R.Y. (1999, June 25). A clock for the ages. *Science, 284*, 2102–2103.

Moore-Ede, M.C., Czeisler, C.A., & Richardson, G.S. (1983). Circadian timekeeping in health and disease: I. Basic properties of circadian pacemakers. *New England Journal of Medicine, 309*, 469–476.

Moriarty, T. (1975). Crime, commitment and the responsive bystander: Two field experiments. *Journal of Personality and Social Psychology, 31*, 370–376.

Morin, C.M., Stone, J., McDonald, K., & Jones, S. (1994). Psychological management of insomnia: A clinical replication series with 100 patients. *Behavior Therapy, 25*, 291–309.

Morris, C. (1990). *Contemporary psychology and effective behavior* (7th ed.). Glenview, IL: Scott, Foresman.

Moscicki, E.K. (1995). Epidemiology of suicidal behavior. *Suicide and Life-Threatening Behavior, 25*, 22–35.

Moyers, F. (1996). Oklahoma City bombing: Exacerbation of symptoms in veterans with PTSD. *Archives of Psychiatric Nursing, 10*(1), 55–59.

Mroczek, D.K., & Kolarz, C.M. (1998). The effect of age on positive and negative affect: A developmental perspective on happiness. *Journal of Personality & Social Psychology, 75*, 1333–1349.

Mueser, K.T., & Glynn, S.M. (1995). *Behavioral family therapy for psychiatric disorders.* Boston: Allyn & Bacon.

Muir, D.W. (1985). The development of infants' auditory spatial sensitivity. In S. Trehub & B. Schneider (Eds.), *Auditory development in infancy.* New York: Plenum.

Mumford, M.D., & Gustafson, S.B. (1988). Creativity syndrome: Integration, application, and innovation. *Psychological Bulletin, 103*, 27–43.

Murray, B. (1999, October). Psychologists can boost the corporate bottom line. *APA Monitor*, p. 17.

Murray, H.G., & Denny, J.P. (1969). Interaction of ability level and interpolated activity in human problem solving. *Psychological Reports, 24*, 271–276.

Murstein, B.J. (1986). *Paths to marriage.* Beverly Hills, CA: Sage.

Muth, E.R., Stern, R.M., Uijtdehaage, S.H.J., & Koch, K.L. (1994). Effects of Asian ancestry on susceptibility to vection-induced motion sickness. In J.Z. Chen & R.W. McCallum (eds.), *Electrogastrography: Principles and applications* (pp. 227–233). New York: Raven Press.

Myers, D.G. (1996). *Social psychology* (5th ed.). New York: McGraw-Hill.

Narayanan, L., Shanker, M., & Spector, P.E. (1999). Stress in the workplace: A comparison of gender and occupations. *Journal of Organizational Behavior, 20*, 63–73.

Nathan, P.E., & Gorman, J.M. (1998). *A guide to treatments that work.* New York: Oxford University Press.

Nathan, P.E., & Langenbucher, J.W. (1999). Psychopathology: Description and classification. *Annual Review of Psychology, 50*, 79–107.

National Advisory Mental Health Council. (1995). Basic behavioral science research for mental health: A national investment emotion and motivation. *American Psychologist, 50*(10), 838–845.

National Household Survey on Drug Abuse. (1998).*Summary of findings from the 1998 National Household Survey on Drug Abuse.* Retrieved September 16, 2000, from the World Wide Web: http://www.samhsa.gov/oas/nhsda/pe1996/rtst1013.htm#E8E 26

National Institute of Health Consensus Development Conference. (1996). Integration of behavioral and relaxation approaches into the treatment of chronic pain and insomnia. NIH technology assessment panel. Reported in the *Journal of the American Medical Association, 276*(4), 313–318.

National Institute on Drug Abuse. (1998). *Marijuana: Facts parents need to know.* Retrieved September 12, 2000, from the World Wide Web: http://165.112.78.61/MarijBroch/Marijparentstxt. html

National Institute on Drug Abuse. (2000a). *Marijuana.* Retrieved September 9, 2000, from the World Wide Web: http://165. 112.78.61/Infofax/marijuana.html

National Institute on Drug Abuse. (2000b). *Methamphetamine.* Retrieved September 14, 2000, from the World Wide Web: http://165.112.78.61/Infofax/methamphetamine.html

National Institute on Drug Abuse. (2000c). *Origins and pathways to drug abuse: Research findings (from 9/98).* Retrieved September 13, 2000, from the World Wide Web: http://165.112.78.61/ ICAW/origins/originsfindings998.html

National Research Council, Panel on Child Abuse and Neglect. (1993). *Understanding child abuse and neglect.* Washington, DC: National Academy Press.

Neal, A., & Turner, S.M. (1991). Anxiety disorders research with African Americans: Current status. *Psychological Bulletin, 109*(3), 400–410.

Neher, A. (1991). Maslow's theory of motivation: A critique. *Journal of Humanistic Psychology, 31*, 89–112.

Nehlig, A., Daval, J.L., & Debry, G. (1992). Caffeine and the central nervous system: Mechanisms of action, biochemical, metabolic and psychostimulant effects. *Brain Research Reviews, 17*, 139–170.

Neisser, U. (1982). *Memory observed: Remembering in natural contexts.* San Francisco: Freeman.

Neitz, J., Geist, T., & Jacobs, G.H. (1989). Color vision in the dog. *Visual Neuroscience, 3*(2), 119–125.

Nelson, C.A., Monk, C.S., Lin, J., Carver, L.C., Thomas, K.M., & Truwit, C.L. (2000). Functional neuroanatomy of spatial working memory in children. *Developmental Psychology, 36*, 109–116.

Nelson, D.L. (1994). Implicit memory. In D.E. Morris & M. Gruneberg (Eds.), *Theoretical aspects of memory* (pp. 130–167). London: Routledge.

Nelson, D.L. (1999). Implicit memory. In D.E. Morris & M. Gruneberg (eds.), *Theoretical aspects of memory.* London: Routledge.

Ness, R.B., Grisso, J.A., Hirschinger, N., Markovic, N., Shaw, L.M., Kay, N.L., & Kline, J. (1999). Cocaine and tobacco use and the risk of spontaneous abortion. *New England Journal of Medicine, 340*, 333–339.

Netting, J. (1999). Wink of an eye. *Scientific American*, 26–27.

Neugarten, B.L. (1977). Personality and aging. In I. Birren & K.W. Schaie (eds.), *Handbook of the psychology of aging.* New York: Van Nostrand.

Neuron, in press. Published online August 3, 2001.

Newman, P.R. (1982). The peer group. In B.B. Wolman (ed.), *Handbook of developmental psychology* (pp. 526–536). Englewood Cliffs, NJ: Prentice Hall.

Niehoff, D. (1999). *The biology of violence (How understanding the brain, behavior, and environment can break the vicious circle of aggression).* NY: Free Press.

Nissani, M. (1990). A cognitive reinterpretation of Stanley Milgram's observations on obedience to authority. *American Psychologist, 45*, 1384–1385.

Nixon, S.J. (1999). Neurocognitive performance in alcoholics: Is polysubstance abuse important? *Psychological Science, 10*, 181–185.

Noga, J.T., Bartley, A.J., Jones, D.W., Torrey, E.F., & Weinberger, D.R. (1996). Cortical gyral anatomy and gross brain dimensions in monozygotic twins discordant for schizophrenia. *Schizophrenia Research, 22*(1), 27–40.

Nolen-Hoeksema, S. (1999, October). Men and women handle negative situations differently, study suggests. *APA Monitor.*

Norcross, J.C., Alford, B.A., & DeMichele, J.T. (1994). The future of psychotherapy: Delphi data and concluding observation. *Psychotherapy, 29*, 150–158.

Norman, R. (1975). Affective-cognitive consistency, attitudes, conformity, and behavior. *Journal of Personality and Social Psychology, 32*, 83–91.

Norris, F.H., & Murrell, S.A. (1990). Social support, life events, and stress as modifiers of adjustment to bereavement by older adults. *Psychology and Aging, 45*, 267–275.

Norris, P.A. (1986). On the status of biofeedback and clinical practice. *American Psychologist, 41*, 1009–1010.

Novak, M.A. (1991, July). "Psychologists care deeply" about animals. *APA Monitor*, p. 4.

O'Connell, A., & Russo, N. (eds.). (1990). *Women in psychology: A bibliographic sourcebook*. Westport, CT: Greenwood Press.

O'Connor, N., & Hermelin, B. (1987). Visual memory and motor programmes: Their use by idiot savant artists and controls. *British Journal of Psychology, 78*, 307–323.

O'Connor, T.G., McGuire, S., Reiss, D., Hetherington, E.M., & Plomin, R. (1998). Co-occurrence of depressive symptoms and antisocial behavior in adolescence: A common genetic liability. *Journal of Abnormal Psychology, 107*, 27–37.

O'Leary, A. (1990). Stress, emotion, and human immune function. *Psychological Bulletin, 108*, 363–382.

O'Leary, K.D., & Wilson, G.T. (1987). *Behavior therapy: Application and outcome*. Englewood Cliffs, NJ: Prentice Hall.

O'Leary, S.G. (1995). Parental discipline mistakes. *American Psychological Society, 4*(1), 11–14.

O'Leary, V.E., & Smith, D. (1988, August). *Sex makes a difference: Attributions for emotional cause*. Paper presented at the meeting of the American Psychological Association, Atlanta, GA.

Offer, D., & Offer, J. (1975). *From teenager to young manhood*. New York: Basic Books.

Office of Educational Research and Improvement. (1988). *Youth indicators, 1988*. Washington, DC: U. S. Government Printing Office.

Ogawa, S., Lubahn, D., Korach, K., & Pfaff, D. (1997). Behavioral effects of estrogen receptor gene disruption in male mice. *Proceedings of the National Academy of Sciences of the U.S.A., 94*, 1476.

Ojemann, G., Ojemann, J., Lettich, E., & Berger, M. (1989). Cortical language localization in left, dominant hemisphere: An electrical stimulation mapping investigation in 117 patients. *Journal of Neurosurgery, 71*, 316–326.

Olds, M.E., & Forbes, J.L. (1981). The central basis of motivation: Intracranial self-stimulation studies. *Annual Review of Psychology, 32*, 523–574.

Olfson, M., Marcus, S., Sackeim, H.A., Thompson, J., & Pincus, H.A. (1998). Use of ECT for the inpatient treatment of recurrent major depression. *American Journal of Psychiatry, 155*, 22–29.

Oltmanns, T.F., & Emery, R.E. (1998). *Abnormal psychology* (2nd ed.). Upper Saddle River, NJ: Prentice Hall.

Olton, D.S., & Samuelson, R.J. (1976). Remembrance of places passed: Spatial memory in rats. *Journal of Experimental Psychology, 2*, 97–115.

Omi, M., & Winant, H. (1994). *Racial formation in the United States: From the 1960s to the 1990s* (2nd ed). New York: Routledge.

Ones, D.S., Viswesvaran, C., & Schmidt, F.L. (1993). Comprehensive meta-analysis of integrity test validation: Findings and implications for personnel selection and theories of job performance. *Journal of Applied Psychology, 78*, 679–703.

Orbuch, T.L., House, J.S., Mero, R.P., & Webster, P.S. (1996). Marital quality over the life course. *Social Psychology Quarterly, 59*, 162–171.

Orlinsky, D.E., & Howard, K.I. (1994). Unity and diversity among psychotherapies: A comparative perspective. In B. Bonger & L.E. Beutler (eds.), *Foundations of psychotherapy: Theory, research, and practice*. New York: Basic Books.

Orlofsky, J.L. (1993). Intimacy status: Theory and research. In J.E. Marcia, A.S. Waterman, D.R. Matteson, S.L. Archer, & J.L. Orlofsky (Eds.), *Ego identity: A handbook for psychosocial research*. New York: Springer-Verlag.

Ortar, G. (1963). Is a verbal test cross-cultural? *Scripta Hierosolymitana, 13*, 219–235.

Osborne, J.W. (1997). Race and academic disidentification. *Journal of Educational Psychology, 89*, 728–735.

Oskamp, S. (1991). *Attitudes and opinions* (2nd ed.). Englewood Cliffs, NJ: Prentice Hall.

Owens, J., Maxim R., McGuinn, M., Nobile, C., Msall, M., & Alario, A. (1999). Television-viewing habits and sleep disturbance in school children. *Pediatrics, 104*, 27.

Ozer, D.J., & Reise, S.P. (1994). Personality assessment. *Annual Review of Psychology, 45*, 357–388.

Pace, R. (1994, July 28). Christy Henrich, 22, gymnast plagued by eating disorders. *New York Times*, p. A12.

Paikoff, R.L., & Brooks-Gunn, J. (1991). Do parent–child relationships change during puberty? *Psychological Bulletin, 110*(1), 47–66.

Panksepp, J. (1998). Attention deficit hyperactivity disorders, psychostimulants, and intolerance of childhood playfulness: A tragedy in the making? *Current Directions in Psychological Science, 7*, 91–98.

Paris, S.G., & Weissberg, J.A. (1986). Young children's remembering in different contexts: A reinterpretation of Istomina's study. *Child Development, 57*, 1123–1129.

Parker, J.G., & Asher, S.R. (1987). Peer relations and later personal adjustment: Are low-accepted children at risk? *Psychological Bulletin, 102*, 357–389.

Parsons, H.M. (1974). What happened to Hawthorne? *Science, 183*, 922–932.

Patrick, C.J. (1994). Emotion and psychopathy: Startling new insights. *Psychophysiology, 31*, 319–330.

Patterson, C.J. (1994). Lesbian and gay families. *Current Directions in Psychological Science, 3*(2), 62–64.

Patterson, D.R., & Ptacek, J.T. (1997). Baseline pain as a moderator of hypnotic analgesia for burn injury treatment. *Journal of Consulting & Clinical Psychology, 65*, 60–67.

Patterson, G.R., & Bank, L. (1989). Some amplifying mechanisms for pathologic processes in families. In M.R. Gunnar & E. Thelen (eds.), *Systems and development: The Minnesota Symposia on Child Psychology* (Vol. 22). Hillsdale, NJ: Erlbaum.

Patterson, G.R., DeBaryshe, B.D., & Ramsey, E. (1989). A developmental perspective on antisocial behavior. *American Psychologist, 44*, 329–335.

Paul, G.L. (1982). The development of a "transportable" system of behavioral assessment for chronic patients. Invited address, University of Minnesota, Minneapolis.

Paul, G.L., & Lentz, R.J. (1977). *Psychosocial treatment of chronic mental patients: Milieu versus social learning programs*. Cambridge, MA: Harvard University Press.

Pavlov, I.P. (1927). *Conditional reflexes* (G.V. Anrep, trans.). London: Oxford University Press.

Pearlin, L.I., & Schooler, C. (1978). The structure of coping. *Journal of Health and Social Behavior, 19*, 2–21.

Pearson, C.A.L. (1992). Autonomous workgroups: An evaluation at an industrial site. *Human Relations, 9*, 905–936.

Pedlow, R., Sanson, A., Prior, M., & Oberklaid, F. (1993). Stability of maternally reported temperament from infancy to 8 years. *Developmental Psychology, 29*, 998–1007.

Pellegrini, A.D., & Galda, L. (1994). Play. In *Encyclopedia of human behavior* (Vol. 3, pp. 535–543). San Diego, CA: Academic Press.

Peplau, L.A., & Cochran, S.D. (1990). A relationship perspective on homosexuality. In D.P. McWhirter, S.A. Sanders, & J.M. Reinisch (eds.), *Homosexuality/heterosexuality: The Kinsey scale and current research*. New York: Oxford University Press.

Perry, B.D., & Pollard, R. (1998). Homeostasis, stress, trauma, and adaptation: A neurodevelopmental view of childhood trauma. *Child Adolescent Psychiatric Clinics of North America, 7,* 33–51.

Perry, D.G., Perry, L.C., & Weiss, R.J. (1989). Sex differences in the consequences that children anticipate for aggression. *Developmental Psychology, 25,* 312–319.

Persky, H. (1983). Psychosexual effects of hormones. *Medical Aspects of Human Sexuality, 17,* 74–101.

Persson-Blennow, I., & McNeil, T.F. (1988). Frequencies and stability of temperament types in childhood. *Journal of the American Academy of Child and Adolescent Psychiatry, 27,* 619–622.

Pert, C.B., & Snyder, S.H. (1973). The opiate receptor: Demonstration in nervous tissue. *Science, 179*(6), 1011–1014.

Peskin, H. (1967). Pubertal onset and ego functioning. *Journal of Abnormal Psychology, 72,* 1–15.

Petersen, R.C., Stevens, J.C., Ganguli, M., Tangalos, E.G., Cummings, J.L., & DeKosky, S.T. (2001). Practice parameter: Early detection of dementia: Mild cognitive impairment (an evidence-based review. *Neurology, 56,* 1133–1142.

Peterson, C. (2000). The future of optimism. *American Psychologist, 55,* 44–55.

Peterson, C., Maier, S.F., & Seligman, M.E.P. (1993a). Explanatory style and helplessness. *Social Behavior and Personality, 20,* 1–14.

Peterson, C., Maier, S.F., & Seligman, M.E.P. (1993b). *Learned helplessness: A theory for the age of personal control.* New York: Oxford University Press.

Peterson, C., Vaillant, G.E., & Seligman, M.E.P. (1988). Explanatory style as a risk factor for illness. *Cognitive Therapy and Research, 12,* 119–132.

Petitto, L.A., & Marentette, P.F. (1991, March 22). Babbling in the manual mode: Evidence for the ontogeny of language. *Science, 251,* 1493–1496.

Pettigrew, T.F. (1998). Intergroup contact theory. *Annual Review of Psychology, 49,* 65–85.

Pettigrew, T.F. (1969). Racially separate or together? *Journal of Social Issues, 25,* 43–69.

Petty, R.E., & Cacioppo, J.T. (1981). *Attitudes and persuasion: Classic and contemporary approaches.* Dubuque, IA: Wm. C. Brown.

Petty, R.E., & Cacioppo, J.T. (1986a). The elaboration likelihood model of persuasion. In L. Berkowitz (ed.), *Advances in experimental social psychology* (Vol. 19). Orlando, FL: Academic Press.

Petty, R.E., & Cacioppo, J.T. (1986b). *Communication and persuasion: Central and peripheral routes to attitude change.* New York: Springer-Verlag.

Phelps, J.A., Davis, J.O., & Schartz, K.M. (1997). Nature, nurture, and twin research strategies. *Current Directions in Psychological Science, 6,* 117–121.

Phelps, L., & Bajorek, E. (1991). Eating disorders of the adolescent: Current issues in etiology, assessment, and treatment. *School Psychology Review, 20,* 9–22.

Phinney, J.S. (1996). When we talk about American ethnic groups, what do we mean? *American Psychologist, 51,* 918–927.

Piaget, J. (1967). *Six psychological studies.* New York: Random House.

Piaget, J. (1969). The intellectual development of the adolescent. In G. Caplan & S. Lebovici (eds.), *Adolescence: Psychosocial perspectives.* New York: Basic Books.

Piaget, J., & Inhelder, B. (1956). *The child's conception of space* (F. J. Langdon & E. L. Lunzer, Trans.). London: Routledge & Kegan Paul.

Pillow, D.R., Zautra, A.J., & Sandler, I. (1996). Major life events and minor stressors: Identifying mediational links in the stress process. *Journal of Personality and Social Psychology, 70,* 381–394.

Pinker, S. (1994). *The language instinct: How the mind creates language.* New York: HarperCollins.

Pinker, S. (1997). *How the mind works.* New York: Norton.

Pinker, S. (1999). *Words and rules: The ingredients of language.* New York: Basic Books.

Pion, G.M., Mednick, M.T., Astin, H.S., Hall, C.C.I., Kenkel, M.B., Keita, G.P., Kohout, J.L., & Kelleher, J.C. (1996). The shifting gender composition of psychology: Trends and implications for the discipline. *American Psychologist, 15*(5), 509–528.

Piontelli, A. (1989). A study on twins before and after birth. *International Review of Psycho-Analysis, 16,* 413–426.

Pisani, V.D., Fawcett, J., Clark, D.C., & McGuire, M. (1993). The relative contributions of medication adherence and AA meeting attendance to abstinent outcome for chronic alcoholics. *Journal of Studies on Alcohol, 54,* 115–119

Platt, J.J. (1997). *Cocaine addiction: Theory, research, and treatment.* Cambridge, MA: Harvard University Press.

Plomin, R. (1994). *Genetics and experience: The interplay between nature and nurture.* Thousand Oaks, CA: Sage.

Plomin, R. (1997). Identifying genes for cognitive abilities and disabilities. In R.J. Sternberg & E. Grigorenko (eds.), *Intelligence: Heredity and environment.* New York: Cambridge University Press.

Plomin, R. (1999). Parents and personality. *Contemporary Psychology, 44,* 269–271.

Plomin, R., & Rende, R. (1991). Human behavioral genetics. *Annual Review of Psychology, 42,* 161–190.

Plomin, R., Corley, R., DeFries, J.C., & Fulker, D.W. (1990). Individual differences in television watching in early childhood: Nature as well as nurture. *Psychological Science 1*(6), 371–377.

Plomin, R., DeFries, J.C., & McClearn, G.E. (1990). *Behavioral genetics: A primer* (2nd ed.). New York: Freeman.

Plomin, R., McClearn, G.E., Smith, D.L., Vignetti, S., Chorney, M.J., Chorney, K., Venditti, C.P., Kasarda, S., Thompson, L.A., Detterman, D.K., Daniels, J., Owen, M.J., & McGuffin, P. (1994). DNA markers associated with high versus low IQ: The IQ quantitative trait loci (QTL) Project, *Behavior Genetics, 24,* 107–119.

Plous, S. (1996). Attitudes toward the use of animals in psychology research and education: Results from a national survey of psychologists. *American Psychologist, 51*(11), 1167–1180.

Plutchik, R. (1980). *Emotion: A psychoevolutionary synthesis.* New York: Harper & Row.

Plutchik, R. (1994). *The psychology and biology of emotion.* New York: HarperCollins.

Pollack, W.S., & Levant, R.F. (1998). *New psychotherapy for men.* New York: Wiley.

Pontieri, F.E., Tanda, G., Orzi, F., & DiChiara, G. (1996). Effects of nicotine on the nucleus accumbens and similarity to those of addictive drugs. *Nature, 382,* 255–257.

Pope, H. (2000). *The Adonis complex: The secret crisis of male obsession.* New York: Free Press.

Porkka-Heiskanen, T., Strecker, R.E., Thakkar, M., Bjørkum, A.A., Greene, R.W., & McCarley, R.W. (1997). Adenosine: A mediator of the sleep-inducing effects of prolonged wakefulness. *Science, 276,* 1265–1268.

Porter, L.S., & Stone, A.A. (1995). Are there really gender differences in coping? A reconsideration of previous results from a daily study. *Journal of Social and Clinical Psychology, 14,* 184–202.

Porter, L.W., & Roberts, K.H. (1976). Communication in organizations. In M.D. Dunnette (ed.), *Handbook of industrial and organizational psychology*. Chicago: Rand McNally.

Powell, N.B., Schechtman, K.B., Riley, R.W., Li, K., Troell, R., Guilleminault, C., (2001). The road to danger: The comparative risks of driving while sleepy. *Laryngoscope, 111*, 887–893.

Power, F.C. (1994). Moral development. In *Encyclopedia of human behavior* (Vol. 3, pp. 203–212). San Diego, CA: Academic Press.

Powers, S.I., Hauser, S.T., & Kilner, L.A. (1989). Adolescent mental health. *American Psychologist, 44*, 200–208.

Prager, K.J. (1995). *The psychology of intimacy*. New York: Guilford Press.

Prentky, R.A., Knight, R.A., & Rosenberg, R. (1988). Validation analyses on a taxonomic system for rapists: Disconfirmation and reconceptualization. *Annals of the New York Academy of Sciences, 528*, 21–40.

Prior, M., Smart, D., Sanson, A., & Obeklaid, F. (1993). Sex differences in psychological adjustment from infancy to 8 years. *Journal of the American Academy of Child and Adolescent Psychiatry, 32*, 291–304.

Ptacek, J.T., Smith R.E., & Dodge, K.L. (1994). Gender differences in coping with stress: When stressor and appraisals do not differ. *Personality and Social Psychology Bulletin, 20*, 421–430.

Puca, A.A., Daly, M.J., Brewster, S.J., Matise, T.C., Barrett, J., Shea-Drinkwater, M., Kang, S., Joyce, E., Nicoli, J., Benson, E., Kunkel, L.M. & Perls, T. (2001). A genome-wide scan for linkages to human exceptional longevity identifies a locus on chromosome 4. *Proceedings from the National Academy of Sciences, USA, 98*, 10505–10508.

Puig, C. (1995, February 27). Children say they imitate anti-social behavior on TV: Survey finds shows influence more than two-thirds.

Putnam, F.W. (1984). The psychophysiological investigation of multiple personality: A review. *Psychiatric Clinics of North America, 7*, 31–39.

Putnam, F.W., Guroff, J.J., Silberman, E.D., Barban, L., & Post, R.M. (1986). The clinical phenomenology of multiple personality disorder: Review of 100 recent cases. *Journal of Clinical Psychology, 47*, 285–293.

Quadrel, M.J., Prouadrel, Fischoff, B., & Davis, W. (1993). Adolescent (In)vulnerability. *American Psychologist, 2*, 102–116.

Quan, N., Zhang, Z.B., Demetrikopoulos, M.K., Kitson, R.P., Chambers, W.H., Goldfarb, R.H., & Weiss, J.M. (1999). Evidence for involvement of B lymphocytes in the surveillance of lung metastases in the rat. *Cancer Research, 59*, 1080–1089.

Rabasca, L. (1999a, June). Improving life for the survivors of cancer. *APA Monitor*, pp. 28–29.

Rabasca, L. (1999b, November). Is it depression? Or could it be a mild traumatic brain injury? *APA Monitor*, pp. 27–28.

Rabasca, L. (2000a, March). Lessons in diversity [and] Helping American Indians earn psychology degrees. *Monitor on Psychology*, 50–53.

Rabasca, L. (2000b, April). Self-help sites: A blessing or a bane? *Monitor on Psychology*, pp. 28–30.

Rabasca, L. (2000c, April). Taking telehealth to the next step. *Monitor on Psychology*, pp. 36–37.

Rabasca, L. (2000d, April). Taking time and space out of service delivery. *Monitor on Psychology*, pp. 40–41.

Ramey, S.L. (1999). Head Start and preschool education: Toward continued improvement. *American Psychologist, 54*, 344–346.

Rasika, S., Alvarez-Buylla, A., & Nottebohm, F. (1999). BDNF mediates the effects of testosterone on the survival of new neurons in an adult brain. *Neuron, 22*, 53–62.

Ree, M.J., & Earles, J.A. (1992). Intelligence is the best predictor of job performance. *Current Directions in Psychological Science, 1*, 86–89.

Reed, S.K. (1992). *Cognition: Theory and applications* (3rd ed.). Pacific Grove, CA: Brooks/Cole.

Reed, S.K. (1996). *Cognition: Theory and applications* (4th ed.). Pacific Grove, CA: Brooks/Cole.

Reinisch, J.M., & Sanders, S.A. (1982). Early barbiturate exposure: The brain, sexually dimorphic behavior and learning. *Neuroscience and Biobehavioral Reviews, 6*(3), 311–319.

Reinish, J.M., Ziemba-Davis, M., & Sanders, S.A. (1991). Hormonal contributions to sexually dimorphic behavioral development in humans. *Psychoneuroendocrinology, 16*, 213–278.

Renner, M.J., & Mackin, R.S. (1998). A life stress instrument for classroom use. *Teaching of Psychology, 25*, 46–48.

Renzulli, J.S. (1978). What makes giftedness? Reexamining a definition. *Phi Delta Kappan, 60*, 180–184, 216.

Reppucci, N.D., Woolard, J.L., & Fried, C.S. (1999). Social, community and preventive interventions. *Annual Review of Psychology 50*, 387–418

Reschly, D.J. (1981). Psychology testing in educational classification and placement. *American Psychologist, 36*, 1094–1102.

Rescorla, R.A. (1966). Predictability and number of pairings in Pavlovian fear conditioning. *Psychonomic Science, 4*, 383–384.

Rescorla, R.A. (1967). Pavlovian conditioning and its proper control procedures. *Psychological Review, 74*, 71–80.

Rescorla, R.A. (1988). Pavlovian conditioning: It's not what you think. *American Psychologist, 43*, 151–160.

Rescorla, R.A., & Solomon, R.L. (1967). Two-process learning theory: Relationships between Pavlovian conditioning and instrumental learning. *Psychological Review, 74*, 151–182.

Reuter-Lorenz, P.A., & Miller, A.C. (November 1998). The cognitive neuroscience of human laterality: Lessons from the bisected brain. *Current Directions in Psychological Science, 7*, 15–20.

Reyna, V.F., & Titcomb, A.L. (1997). Constraints on the suggestibility of eyewitness testimony: A fuzzy-trace theory analysis. In D.G. Payne & F.G. Conrad (eds.), *Intersections in basic and applied memory research*. Mahwah, NJ: Erlbaum.

Reynolds, C.F., Frank, E., Perel, J.M., Imber, S.D., Cornes, C., Miller, M.D., Mazumdar, S., Houck, P.R., Dew, M.A., Stack, J.A., Pollock, B.G., & Kupfer, D.J. (1999). Nortriptyline and interpersonal psychotherapy as maintenance therapies for recurrent major depression. *Journal of the American Medical Association, 281*, 39–45.

Rhue, J.W., Lynn, S.J., & Kirsch, I. (1993). *Handbook of clinical hypnosis*. Washington, DC: American Psychological Association.

Richardson, G.S., Miner, J.D., & Czeisler, C.A. (1989–90). Impaired driving performance in shiftworkers: The role of the circadian system in a multifactional model. *Alcohol, Drugs & Driving, 5*(4), 6(1), 265–273.

Rieber, R.W. (1998, August). *Hypnosis, false memory and multiple personality: A trinity of affinity*. Paper presented at the annual meeting of the American Psychological Association, San Francisco, CA.

Rietze, R.L., Valcanis, H., Booker, G.F., Thomas, T., Voss, A.K., Barlett, P.F. (2001). Purification of pluripotent neural stem cell from the adult mouse brain. *Nature, 412*, 736–739.

Riger, S. (1992). Epistemological debates, feminist voices. *American Psychologist, 47*, 730–740.

Rilling, M. (2000). John Watson's paradoxical struggle to explain Freud. *American Psychologist, 55,* 301–312.

Rini, C.K., Dunkel-Schetter, C., Wadhwa, P.D., & Sandman, C.A. (1999). Psychological adaptation and birth outcomes: The role of personal resources, stress, and sociocultural context in pregnancy. *Health Psychology, 18,* 333–345.

Riordan, R.J., & Beggs, M.S. (1987). Counselors and self-help groups. *Journal of Counseling and Development, 65,* 427–429.

Ripple, C.H., Gilliam, W.S., Chanana, N., & Zigler, E. (1999). Will fifty cooks spoil the broth? The debate over entrusting head start to the states. *American Psychologist, 54,* 327–343.

Roberts, A.H., Kewman, D.G., Mercer, L., & Hovell, M. (1993). The power of nonspecific effects in healing: Implications for psychosocial and biological treatments. *Clinical Psychology Review, 13,* 375–391.

Robins, L.N., & Regier, D.A. (1991). *Psychiatric disorders in America: The Epidemiologic Catchment Area Study.* New York: Free Press.

Robins, R.W., Gosling, S.D., & Craik, K.H. (1999). An empirical analysis of trends in psychology. *American Psychologist, 54,* 117–128.

Robinson, A., & Clinkenbeard, P.R. (1998). Giftedness: An exceptionality examined. *Annual Review of Psychology, 49,* 117–139.

Robinson, L.A., Berman, J.S., & Neimeyer, R.A. (1990). Psychotherapy for the treatment of depression: A comprehensive review of controlled outcome research. *Psychological Bulletin, 108,* 30–49.

Rodier, P.M. (2000). The early origins of autism. *Scientific American, 282*(2), 56–63.

Rodin, J. (1985). Insulin levels, hunger, and food intake: An example of feedback loops in body weight regulation. *Health Psychology, 4,* 1–24.

Roese, N.J. (1997). Counterfactual thinking. *Psychological Bulletin, 121,* 133–148.

Rofe, Y. (1984). Stress and affiliation: A utility theory. *Psychological Review, 91,* 251–268.

Rofe, Y., Hoffman, M., & Lewin, I. (1985). Patient affiliation in major illness. *Psychological Medicine, 15,* 895–896.

Rogers, C.R. (1961). *On becoming a person: A therapist's view of psychotherapy.* Boston: Houghton Mifflin.

Roitbak, A.I. (1993). *Glia and its role in nervous activity.* Saint Petersburg, Russia: Nauka.

Romeo, F. (1984). Adolescence, sexual conflict, and anorexia nervosa. *Adolescence, 19,* 551–557.

Rosch, E.H. (1973). Natural categories. *Cognitive Psychology, 4,* 328–350.

Rosch, E.H. (1978). Principles of categorization. In E.H. Rosch & B.B. Lloyd (eds.), *Cognition and categorization.* Hillsdale, NJ: Erlbaum.

Rosenthal, D. (1970). *Genetic theory and abnormal behavior.* New York: McGraw-Hill.

Rosenzweig, M.R. (1984). Experience, memory, and the brain. *American Psychologist, 39,* 365–376.

Rosenzweig, M.R. (1996). Aspects of the search for neural mechanisms of memory. *Annual Review of Psychology, 47,* 1–32.

Rosenzweig, M.R., & Leiman, A.L. (1982). *Physiological psychology.* Lexington, MA: D.C. Heath.

Ross, C.A., Norton, G.R., & Wozney, K. (1989). Multiple personality disorder: An analysis of 236 cases. *Canadian Journal of Psychiatry, 34,* 413–418.

Ross, L. (1977). The intuitive psychologist and his shortcomings: Distortions in the attribution process. In L. Berkowitz (ed.), *Advances in experimental social psychology* (Vol. 10). New York: Academic Press.

Ross, L., & Nisbett, R.E. (1991). *The person and the situation.* New York: McGraw-Hill.

Ross, M.H. (1993). *The culture of conflict.* New Haven, CT: Yale University Press.

Rottenstreich, Y., & Tversky, A. (1997). Unpacking, repacking, and anchoring: Advances in support theory. *Psychological Review, 104*(2), 406–415.

Rotter, J.B. (1954). *Social learning and clinical psychology.* Englewood Cliffs, NJ: Prentice Hall.

Rouhana, N.N., & Bar-Tal, D. (1998). Psychological dynamics of instractable ethnonational conflicts: The Israeli-Palestinian case. *American Psychologist, 53,* 761–770.

Rovner, S. (1990, December 25). The empty nest myth. *Ann Arbor News,* p. D3.

Rowan, A., & Shapiro, K.J. (1996). Animal rights, a bitten apple. *American Psychologist, 51*(11), 1183–1184.

Rowe, D. C. (2001). The nurture assumption persists. *American Psychologist, 56,* 168–169.

Ruberman, J.W., Weinblatt, E., Goldberg, J.D., & Chaudhary, B.S. (1984). Psychological influences on mortality after myocardial infarction. *New England Journal of Medicine, 311,* 552–559.

Rubin, K.H., Coplan, R.J., Chen, X., & McKinnon, J.E. (1994). Peer relationships and influences in childhood. In *Encyclopedia of human behavior* (Vol. 3, pp. 431–439). San Diego, CA: Academic Press.

Ruble, D.N., Fleming, A.S., Hackel, L.S., & Stangor, C. (1988). Changes in the marital relationship during the transition to first time motherhood: Effects of violated expectations concerning division of household labor. *Journal of Personality and Social Psychology, 55,* 78–87.

Ruffin, C.L. (1993). Stress and health-little hassles vs. major life events. *Australian Psychologist, 28,* 201–208.

Russell, J.A. (1991). Culture and the categorization of emotions. *Psychological Bulletin, 110,* 426–450.

Russell, T.G., Rowe, W., & Smouse, A.D. (1991). Subliminal self-help tapes and academic achievement: An evaluation. *Journal of Counseling and Development, 69,* 359–362.

Russo, N.F. (1985). *A woman's mental health agenda.* Washington, DC: American Psychological Association.

Russo, N.F., & Denmark, F.L. (1987). Contributions of women to psychology. *Annual Review of Psychology, 38,* 279–298.

Russo, N.F., & Sobel, S.B. (1981). Sex differences in the utilization of mental health facilities. *Professional Psychology, 12,* 7–19.

Rutter, M.L. (1997). Nature-nurture integration: An example of antisocial behavior. *American Psychologist, 52,* 390–398.

Ryan, R.M., & Deci, E.L. (2000). Self-determination theory and the facilitation of intrinsic motivation, social development, and well-being. *American Psychologist, 55,* 68–78.

Sack, R.L., Brandes, R.W., Kendall, A.R., & Lewy, A.J. (2001). Entrainment of free-running circadian rhythms by melatonin in blind people. *The New England Journal of Medicine, 343,* 1070–1077.

Sacks, O. (2000). *Seeing voices: A journey into the world of the deaf.* New York: Vintage.

Sadeh, A., Raviv, A., & Gruber, R. (2000). Sleep patterns and sleep disruptions in school-age children. *Developmental Psychology, 36,* 291–301.

Salovey, P., Mayer, J.D., & Rosenhan, D.L. (1991). Mood behavior. In M. S. Clark (Ed.), *Review of personality and social psychol-*

ogy: Prosocial behavior (Vol. 12, pp. 215–237). Newbury Park, CA: Sage.

Salovey, P., Rothman, A.J., Detweiler, J.B., & Steward, W.T. (2000). Emotional states and physical health. *American Psychologist, 55,* 110–121.

Salthouse, T.A. (1991). Mediation of adult age differences in cognition by reductions in working memory and speed of processing. *Psychological Science, 2*(3), 179–183.

Sanford, R.N. (1937). The effects of abstinence from food upon imaginal processes: A further experiment. *Journal of Psychology, 3,* 145–159.

Sarason, I.G., & Sarason, B.R. (1987). *Abnormal psychology: The problem of maladaptive behavior* (5th ed.). Englewood Cliffs, NJ: Prentice Hall.

Sarter, M., Berntson, G.G., & Cacioppo, J.T. (1996). Brain imaging and cognitive neuroscience: Toward strong inference in attributing function to structure. *American Psychologist, 51,* 13–21.

Satow, K.K. (1975). Social approval and helping. *Journal of Experimental Social Psychology, 11,* 501–509.

Sattler, J.M. (1992). *Assessment of children* (3rd ed.). San Diego: Jerome M. Sattler.

Savic, I., Berglund, H., Gulyas, B., and Roland, P. (2001). Smelling of odorous sex hormone-like compounds causes sex differentiated hypothalamic activations in humans.

Scarr, S. (1993). Ebbs and flows of evolution in psychology. *Contemporary Psychology, 38,* 458–462.

Scarr, S. (1999). Freedom of choice for poor families. *American Psychologist, 54,* 144–145.

Scarr, S., & Weinberg, R. (1983). The Minnesota Adoption Study: Genetic differences and malleability. *Child Development, 54,* 260–267.

Schacter, D.L. (1999). The seven sins of memory: Insights from psychology and cognitive neuroscience. *American Psychologist, 54,* 182–203.

Schaie, K.W. (1984). Midlife influences upon intellectual functioning in old age. *International Journal of Behavioral Development, 7,* 463–478.

Schaie, K.W. (1994). The course of adult intellectual development. *American Psychologist, 4,* 304–313.

Schanberg, S.M., & Field, T.M. (1987). Sensory deprivation stress and supplemental stimulation in the rat pup and preterm human neonate. *Child Development, 58,* 1431–1447.

Scherer, K.R., & Wallbott, H.G. (1994). Evidence for universality and cultural variation of differential emotion response patterning. *Journal of Personality and Social Psychology, 66,* 310–328.

Schlenker, B.R., & Weigold, M.F. (1992). Interpersonal processes involving impression regulation and management. *Annual Review of Psychology, 43,* 133–168.

Schlenker, B.R., Weigold, M.F., & Hallam, J.R. (1990). Self-serving attributions in social context: Effects of self-esteem and social pressure. *Journal of Personality and Social Psychology, 58*(5), 855–863.

Schoenthaler, S.J., Amos, S.P., Eysenck, H.J., Peritz, E., & Yudkin, J. (1991). Controlled trial of vitamin-mineral supplementation: Effects on intelligence and performance. *Personality and Individual Differences, 12,* 251–362.

Schwartz, B. (1989). *Psychology of learning and behavior* (3rd ed.). New York: Norton.

Schwartz, G.E. (1974, April). TM relaxes some people and makes them feel better. *Psychology Today,* pp. 39–44.

Schwartz, P. (1994, November 17). Some people with multiple roles are blessedly stressed. *New York Times.*

Schwarz, E.D., & Perry, B.D. (1994). The post-traumatic response in children and adolescents. *Psychiatric clinics of North America, 17,* 311–326.

Schweickert, R., & Boruff, B. (1986). Short-term memory capacity: Magic number or magic spell? *Journal of Experimental Psychology: Learning, Memory, & Cognition, 12*(3), 419–425.

Schweinhart, L.J., Barnes, H.V., & Weikart, D.P. (1993). *Significant benefits: The High/Scope Perry Study through age 27* (Monographs of the High/Scope Educational Research Foundation, No. 10). Ypsilanti, MI: High/Scope Press.

Scott, C., Klein, D.M., & Bryant, J. (1990). Consumer response to humor in advertising: A series of field studies using behavioral observation. *Journal of Consumer Research, 16,* 498–501.

Scott, K.G., & Carran, D.T. (1987). The epidemiology and prevention of mental retardation. *American Psychologist, 42,* 801–804.

Scupin, R. (1995). *Cultural anthropology* (2nd ed.). Englewood Cliffs, NJ: Prentice Hall.

Seamon, J. G., & Kenrick, D. T. (1992). *Psychology.* Englewood Cliffs, NJ: Prentice Hall.

Sears, D.O. (1994). On separating church and lab. *Psychological Science, 5,* 237–339.

Seeley, R.J., & Schwartz, J.C. (1997). The regulation of energy balance: Peripheral hormonal signals and hypothalamic neuropeptides. *Current Directions in Psychological Science, 6,* 39–44.

Segall, M.H., Lonner, W.J., & Berry, J.W. (1998). Cross-cultural psychology as a scholarly discipline: On the flowering of culture in behavioral research. *American Psychologist, 53,* 1011–1110.

Seligman, J., Rogers, P., & Annin, P. (1994, May 2). The pressure to lose. *Newsweek,* pp. 60, 62.

Seligman, M.E.P., & Csikzentmihalyi, M. (2000). Positive psychology. *American Psychologist, 55,* 5–14.

Seligman, M.E.P. (1995). The effectiveness of psychotherapy: The *Consumer Reports* study. *American Psychologist, 50*(12), 965–974.

Seligmann, J., et al. (1992, February 3). The new age of Aquarius. *Newsweek,* p. 65.

Sell, R.L., Wells, J.A., & Wypij, D. (1995). The prevalence of homosexual behavior and attraction in the United States, the United Kingdom and France: Results of national population-based samples. *Archives of Sexual Behavior, 24,* 235–238.

Selman, R. (1981). The child as friendship philosopher. In S.R. Asher & J.M. Gottman (eds.), *The development of children's friendships.* New York: Cambridge University Press.

Selye, H. (1956). *The stress of life.* New York: McGraw-Hill.

Selye, H. (1976). *The stress of life* (rev. ed.). New York: McGraw-Hill.

Semrud-Clikeman, M., & Hynd, G.W. (1990). Right hemispheric dysfunction in nonverbal learning disabilities: Social, academic, and adaptive functioning in adults and children. *Psychological Bulletin, 107,* 196–209.

Seppa, N. (1997, June). Children's TV remains steeped in violence. *APA Monitor,* p. 36.

Shaffer, D.R., (1999). *Developmental psychology: Childhood and adolescence.* Pacific Grove, CA: Brooks/Cole.

Shaffer, J.B.P. (1978). *Humanistic psychology.* Upper Saddle River, NJ: Pearson Education, Inc.

Shalev, A., & Munitz, H. (1986). Conversion without hysteria: A case report and review of the literature. *British Journal of Psychiatry, 148,* 198–203.

Shapiro, D., & Shapiro, D. (1982). Meta-analysis of comparative therapy outcome studies: A replication and refinement. *Psychological Bulletin, 92,* 581–604.

Shapiro, K. (1991, July). Use morality as basis for animal treatment. *APA Monitor*, p. 5.

Shaw, P.J., Cirelli, C., Greenspan, R.J., & Tononi, G. (2000, March 10). Correlates of sleep and waking in drosophila melanogaster. *Science, 287*, 1834–1837.

Shaywitz, S.E., Shaywitz, B.A., Pugh, K.R., Fulbright, R.K., Constable, R.T., Mencl, W.E., Shankweiler, D.P., Liberman, A.M., Skudlarski, P., Fletcher, J.M., Katz, L., Marchione, K.E., Lacadie, C., Gatenb, C., & Gore, J.C. (1998). Functional disruption in the organization of the brain for reading in dyslexia. *Neurobiology, 95*, 2636–2641.

Shepard, R.N. (1978). Externalization of mental images and the act of creation. In B.S. Randhawa & W.E. Coffman (Eds.), *Visual learning, thinking, and communication* (pp. 138–189). New York: Academic Press.

Sherman, R.A. (1996). *Unraveling the mysteries of phantom limb sensations*. New York: Plenum Press.

Shimamura, A.P., Berry, J.M., Mangels, J.A., Rusting, C.L., & Jurica, P.J. (1995). Memory and cognitive abilities in university professors: Evidence for successful aging. *Psychological Science, 6*(5), 271–277.

Shorter, E. (1997). *A history of psychiatry: From the era of the asylum to the age of Prozac*. New York: Wiley.

Shriver, M.D., & Piersel, W. (1994). The long-term effects of intrauterine drug exposure: Review of recent research and implications for early childhood special education. *Topics in Early Childhood Special Education, 14*(2), 161–183.

Siegel, L. (1993). Amazing new discovery: Piaget was wrong. *Canadian Psychology, 34*, 239–245.

Simon, H.A. (1974). How big is a chunk? *Science, 165*, 482–488.

Simpson, H.B., Nee, J.C., & Endicott, J. (1997). First-episode major depression. Few sex differences in course. *Archives of General Psychiatry, 54*(7), 633–639.

Singer, J.L. (1975). *The inner world of daydreaming*. New York: Harper Colophon.

Singer, J.L., & Singer, D.G. (1983). Psychologists look at television: Cognitive, developmental, personality, and social policy implications. *American Psychologist, 38*, 826–834.

Singh, G.K., & Yu, S.M. (1995). Infant mortality in the United States: Trends, differentials, and projections, 1950 through 2010. *American Journal of Public Health, 85*(7), 957–964.

Singular, S. (1982, October). A memory for all seasonings. *Psychology Today*, pp. 54–63.

Sinnott, J.D. (1994). Sex roles. In *Encyclopedia of human behavior* (Vol. 4, pp. 151–158). San Diego, CA: Academic Press.

Skaalvik, E.M., & Rankin, R.J. (1994). Gender differences in mathematics and verbal achievement, self-perception and motivation. *British Journal of Educational Psychology, 64*, 419–428.

Skeels, H.M. (1938). Mental development of children in foster homes. *Journal of Consulting Psychology, 2*, 33–43.

Skeels, H.M. (1942). The study of the effects of differential stimulation on mentally retard children: A follow-up report. *American Journal of Mental Deficiencies, 46*, 340–350.

Skeels, H.M. (1966). Adult status of children with contrasting early life experiences. *Monographs of the Society for Research in Child Development, 31*(3), 1–65.

Skinner, B.F. (1938). *The behavior of organisms*. New York: Appleton-Century-Crofts.

Skinner, B.F. (1987). Whatever happened to psychology as the science of behavior? *American Psychologist, 42*, 780–786.

Skinner, B.F. (1989). The origins of cognitive thought. *American Psychologist, 44*, 13–18.

Skinner, B.F. (1990). Can psychology be a science of mind? *American Psychologist, 45*, 1206–1210.

Skinner, B.F. (1953). Some contributions of an experimental analysis of behavior to psychology as a whole. *American Psychologist, 8*(2), 69–78.

Skinner, B.F. (1957). *Verbal behavior*. Englewood Cliffs, NJ: Prentice Hall.

Skinner, B.F. (1987). Whatever happened to psychology as the science of behavior? *American Psychologist, 42*, 780–786.

Skrzycki, C. (1995, November 24). Is it pure or just pure nonsense? *Washington Post*, pp. F1, F4.

Sloan, R.P., Bagiella, E., & Powell, T. (1999). Religion, spirituality, and medicine. *The Lancet, 353*, 664–667.

Slovic, P. (1995). The construction of preference. *American Psychologist, 50*, 364–371.

Smith, B.W. (2000). Noah revisited: Religious coping by church members and the impact of the 1993 Midwest flood. *Journal of Community Psychology, 28*, 169–186.

Smith, C.T. (1985). Sleep states and learning: A review of the animal literature. *Neuroscience & Biobehavioral Reviews, 9*, 157–168.

Smith, C.T., & Kelly, G. (1988). Paradoxical sleep deprivation applied two days after end of training retards learning. *Physiology & Behavior, 43*, 213–216.

Smith, C.T., & Lapp, L. (1986). Prolonged increase in both PS and number of REMS following a shuttle avoidance task. *Physiology & Behavior, 36*, 1053–1057.

Smith, D. (2000). Smoking increases teen depression. *Monitor on Psychology, 31*, 58.

Smith, D. (2001). Impairment on the job. *Monitor on Psychology, 32*, 52–53.

Smith, D.N. (1998). The psychocultural roots of genocide: Legitimacy and crisis in Rwanda. *American Psychologist, 53*, 743–753.

Smith, M.L., Glass, G.V., & Miller, T.I. (1980). *The benefits of psychotherapy*. Baltimore: Johns Hopkins University Press.

Smith, P.B., & Bond, M.H. (1999). *Social psychology across cultures: Analysis and perspectives* (2nd ed.). Boston: Allyn & Bacon.

Smith, P.B., & Bond, M.H. (1994). *Social psychology across cultures: Analysis and perspectives*. Boston: Allyn & Bacon.

Smollar, J., & Youniss, J. (1989). Transformations in adolescents' perceptions of parents. *International Journal of Behavioral Development, 12*, 71–84.

Snodgrass, S.E. (1992). Further effects of role versus gender on interpersonal sensitivity. *Journal of Personality and Social Psychology, 62*, 154–158.

Snyder, M. (1987). *Public appearances/private realities: The psychology of self-monitoring*. New York: Freeman.

Snyder, M., & Swann, W.B., Jr. (1978). Behavioral confirmation in social interaction: From social perception to social reality. *Journal of Experimental Social Psychology, 14*, 148–162.

Snyder, M., & Tanke, E.D. (1976). Behavior and attitude: Some people are more consistent than others. *Journal of Personality, 44*, 501–517.

Snyder, S.H. (1977). Opiate receptors and internal opiates. *Scientific American, 236*, 44–56.

Solomon, D.A., Keitner, G.I., Miller, I.W., Shea, M.T., & Keller, M.B. (1995). Course of illness and maintenance treatments for patients with bipolar disorder. *Journal of Clinical Psychiatry, 56*, 5–13.

Solomon, P.R., Hirschoff, A., Kelly, B., Relin, M., Brush, M., DeVeaux, R.D., & Pendlebury, W.W. (1998). A 7 minute neurocognitive screening battery highly sensitive to Alzheimer's disease. *Archives of Neurology, 55*, 349–355.

Sommers, C.H. (1994, April 3). The myth of schoolgirls' low self-esteem. *Wall Street Journal*, p. 4.

Sommers-Flanagan, R., Sommers-Flanagan, J., & Davis, B. (1993). What's happening on music television? A gender role content analysis. *Sex Roles, 28*, 745–754.

Sonstroem, R.J. (1997). Physical activity and self-esteem. In W.P. Morgan (Ed.), *Physical activity and mental health* (pp. 127–143). Philadelphia, PA: Taylor & Francis.

Sorensen, R.C. (1973). *Adolescent sexuality in contemporary America*. New York: World.

Spellman, B.A., & Mandel, D.R. (1999). When possibility informs reality: Counterfactual thinking as a cue to causality. *Current Directions in Psychological Science, 8*, 120–123.

Sperling, G. (1960). The information available in brief visual presentations. *Psychological Monographs, 74*, 1–29.

Sperry, R.W. (1964). The great cerebral commissure. *Scientific American, 210*, 42–52.

Sperry, R.W. (1968). Hemisphere disconnection and unity in conscious awareness. *American Psychologist, 23*, 723–733.

Sperry, R.W. (1970). *Perception in the absence of neocortical commissures. In Perception and its disorders* (Res. Publ. A.R.N.M.D., Vol. 48). New York: The Association for Research in Nervous and Mental Disease.

Sperry, R.W. (1988). Psychology's mentalists paradigm and the religion/science tension. *American Psychologist, 43*, 607–613.

Sperry, R.W. (1995). The future of psychology. *American Psychologist, 5*(7), 505–506.

Spiegel, D. (1995). Essentials of psychotherapeutic intervention for cancer patients. *Support Care Cancer, 3*(4), 252–256.

Spiegel, D., & Kato, P. M. (1996). Psychological influences on cancer incidence and progression. *Harvard Review of Psychiatry, 4*, 10–26.

Spitzer, R.L., Skodal, A.E., Gibbon, M., & Williams, J.B.W. (1981). *DSM-III case book*. Washington, DC: American Psychiatric Association.

Spitzer, R.L., Skodal, A.E., Gibbon, M., & Williams, J.B.W. (1983). *Psychopathology: A casebook*. New York: McGraw-Hill.

Spoendlin, H.H., & Schrott, A. (1989). Analysis of the human auditory nerve. *Hearing Research, 43*, 25–38.

Squier, L.H., & Domhoff, G.W. (1998). The presentation of dreaming and dreams in introductory psychology textbooks: A critical examination with suggestions for textbook authors and course instructors. *Dreaming: Journal of the Association for the Study of Dreams, 8*, 149–168.

Squire, S. (1983). *The slender balance: Causes and cures for bulimia, anorexia, and the weight loss/weight gain seesaw*. New York: Putnam.

Sridhar, K.S., Ruab, W.A., & Weatherby, N.L. (1994). Possible role of marijuana smoking as a carcinogen in development of lung cancer at a young age. *Journal of Psychoactive Drugs, 26*, 285–288.

Stack, S. (1994). Divorce. In *Encyclopedia of human behavior* (Vol. 2, pp. 153–63). San Diego, CA: Academic Press.

Stancliffe, R.J. (1997). Community residence size, staff presence and choice. *Mental Retardation, 35*, 1–9.

Stanton, M.D., & Shadish, W.R. (1997). Outcome, attrition, and family-couples treatment for drug abuse: A meta-analysis and review of the controlled, comparative studies. *Psychological Bulletin, 122*, 170–191.

Steele, C.M., & Josephs, R.A. (1990). Alcohol myopia: Its prized and dangerous effects. *American Psychologist, 45*, 921–933.

Steiger, H., Gauvin, L., Jabalpurwala, S., Seguin, J.R., & Stotland, S. (1999). Hypersensitivity to social interactions in bulimic syndromes: Relationships to binge eating. *Journal of Consulting Clinical Psychology, 67*, 765–775.

Steinberg, K.K. et al. (1991). A meta-analysis of the effect of estrogen replacement therapy on the risk of breast cancer. *JAMA, Journal of the American Medical Association, 265*(15), 1985–1990.

Steiner, J.E. (1979). Facial expressions in response to taste and smell stimulation. In H.W. Reese & L.P. Lipsitt (eds.), *Advances in child development and behavior* (Vol. 13). New York: Academic Press.

Steinhauer, J. (1997, July 6). Living together without marriage or apologies *New York Times*, p. A9.

Steinhausen, H.C., Willms, J., & Spohr, H. (1993). Long-term psychopathological and cognitive outcome of children with fetal alcohol syndrome. *Journal of the American Academy of Child and Adolescent Psychiatry, 32*, 990–994.

Stern, L. (1985). *The structures and strategies of human memory*. Homewood, IL: Dorsey Press.

Stern, R.M., & Koch, K.L. (1996). Motion sickness and differential susceptibility. *Current Directions in Psychological Science, 5*, 115–120.

Sternberg, R.J. (1999). The theory of successful intelligence. *Review of General Psychology, 3*, 292–316.

Sternberg, R.J. (2001). What is the common thread of creativity? Its dialectical relation to intelligence and wisdom. *American Psychologist, 56*, 360–362.

Sternberg, R.J. (1985). *Beyond IQ: A triarchic theory of human intelligence*. New York: Cambridge University Press.

Sternberg, R.J. (1986). *Intelligence applied*. Orlando, FL: Harcourt Brace Jovanovich.

Sternberg, R.J., & Kaufman, J.C. (1998). Human abilities. *Annual Review of Psychology, 49*, 479–502.

Stevens, G., & Gardner, S. (1982). *Women of psychology: Expansion and refinement* (Vol. 1). Cambridge, MA: Schenkman.

Stevenson, H.W. (1992). Learning from Asian schools. *Scientific American*, 70–76.

Stevenson, H.W. (1993). Why Asian students still outdistance Americans. *Educational Leadership*, 63–65.

Stevenson, H.W., Chen, C., & Lee, S.-Y. (1993). Mathematics achievement of Chinese, Japanese, and American children: Ten years later. *Science, 259*, 53–58.

Stevenson, H.W., Lee, S.-Y., & Stigler, J.W. (1986). Mathematics achievment of Chinese, Japanese, and American children. *Science, 231*, 693–697.

Stewart, R.H. (1965). Effect of continuous responding on the order effect in personality impression formation. *Journal of Personality and Social Psychology, 1*, 161–165.

Stickgold, R., Rittenhouse, C.D., & Hobson, J.A. (1994). Dream splicing: A new technique for assessing thematic coherence in subjective reports of mental activity. *Consciousness and Cognition, 3*, 114–128.

Stiles, W.B., Shapiro, D.A., & Elliott, R. (1986). Are all psychotherapies equivalent? *American Psychologist, 41*, 165–180. (From Myers, 1992.)

Stock, M.B., & Smythe, P.M. (1963). Does undernutrition during infancy inhibit brain growth and subsequent intellectual development? *Archives of Disorders in Childhood, 38*, 546–552.

Stodghill, R. (1998, June 15). Where'd you learn that? *Time*, 52–59.

Stone, W.F., Lederer, G., & Christie, R. (1993). Introduction: Strength and weakness. In W.F. Stone, G. Lederer, & R. Christie (eds.), *The authoritarian personality today: Strength and weakness*. New York: Springer-Verlag.

Stoner, J.A.F. (1961). *A comparison of individual and group decisions involving risk*. Unpublished master's thesis, School of Industrial Management, MIT.

Strickland, B.R. (2000). Misassumptions, misadventures, and the misuse of psychology. *American Psychologist, 55*, pp. 331–338.

Strickland, B.R. (1989). Internal-external control expectancies. From contingency to creativity. *American Psychologist, 44*, 1–12.

Stumpf, H., & Stanley, J.C. (1998). Stability and change in gender-related differences on the college board advanced placement and achievement tests. *Current Directions in Psychological Research, 7*, 192–196.

Subotnik, R.F., & Arnold, K.D. (1994). *Beyond Terman: Contemporary longitudinal studies of giftedness and talent*. Norwood, NJ: Ablex.

Sue, S., Zane, N., & Young, K. (1994). Research on psychotherapy with culturally diverse populations. In A.E. Bergin & S.L. Garfield (eds.), *Handbook of psychotherapy and behavior change* (4th ed., pp. 783–820). New York: Wiley.

Sullivan, E.V., Rosenbloom, M.J., Lim, K.O., & Pfefferbaum, A. (2000). Longitudinal changes in cognition, gait, and balance in abstinent and relapsed alcoholic men: Relationships to changes in brain structure. *Neuropsychology, 14*, 178–188.

Suls, J., & Fletcher, B. (1983). Social comparison in the social and physical sciences: An archival study. *Journal of Personality and Social Psychology, 44*, 575–580.

Swan, N. (1998). Brain scans open window to view cocaine's effects on the brain. *NIDA Notes, 13*, 12.

Tagano, D.W., Moran, D.J., III, & Sawyers, J.K. (1991). *Creativity in early childhood classrooms*. Washington, DC: National Education Association.

Takaki, A., Nagai, K., Takaki, S., & Yanaihara, N. (1990). Satiety function of neurons containing CCKK-like substance in the dorsal parabrachial nucleus. *Physiology & Behavior, 48*, 865–871.

Takami, S., Getchell, M.L., Chen, Y., Monti-Bloch, L., & Berliner, D.L. (1993). Vomeronasal epithelial cells of the adult human express neuron-specific molecules. *Neuro Report, 4*, 374–378.

Tan, D.T.Y., & Singh, R. (1995). Attitudes and attraction: A developmental study of the similarity-attraction and dissimilarity-repulsion hypotheses. *Personality and Social Psychology Bulletin, 21*(9), 975–986.

Tanner, J.M. (1978). *Foetus into man: Physical growth from conception to maturity*. Cambridge, MA: Harvard University Press.

Tavris, C. (1992). *The mismeasure of woman*. New York: Simon & Schuster.

Taylor, D.M., & Moghaddam, F.M. (1994). *Theories of intergroup relations: International social psychological perspectives*. Westport, CT: Praeger.

Taylor, S.E., & Repetti, R.L. (1997). Health psychology: What is an unhealthy environment and how does it get under the skin? *Annual Review of Psychology, 48*, 411–447.

Taylor, S.E., Klein, L.C., Lewis, B.P., Gruenewald, T.L., Gurung, R.A.R., & Updegraff, J.A. (2000). Biobehavioral responses to stress in females: Tend-and-befriend, not fight-or-flight. *Psychological Review, 107*, 411–429.

Terman, L.M. (1925). *Mental and physical traits of a thousand gifted children: Genetic studies of genius* (Vol. 1). Stanford, CA: Stanford University Press.

Testa, M., Livingston, J.A., & Collins, R.L. (2000). The role of women's alcohol consumption in evaluation of vulnerability to sexual aggression. *Experimental & Clinical Psychopharmacology, 8*, 185–191.

Thelen, E. (1994). Three-month-old infants can learn task-specific patterns of interlimb coordination. *American Psychological Society, 5*(5), 280–288.

Thelen, E. (1995). Motor development: A new synthesis. *American Psychologist, 50*(2), 79–95.

Thomas, A., & Chess, S. (1977). *Temperament and development*. New York: Brunner/Mazel.

Thompson, J.K., & Thompson, C.M. (1986). Body size distortion and self-esteem in asymptomatic, normal weight males and females. *International Journal of Eating Disorders, 5*, 1061–1068.

Thompson, P.M., Vidal, C., Giedd, J.N., Gochman, P., Blumnethal, J., Nicolson, R., Toga, A.W., & Rapoport, J.L. (2001). Mapping adolescent brain changes reveals dynamic wave accelerated gray matter loss in very early-onset schizophrenia. *Proceedings from the National Academy of Sciences, USA, 98*, 11650–11655.

Thompson, R.A., & Ganzel, A.K. (1994). Socioemotional development. In V. S. Ramachandran (Ed)., *Encyclopedia of human behavior* (pp. 275–286). San Diego: Academic Press.

Thorndike, E.L. (1898). Animal intelligence. *Psychological Review Monograph, 2*(4, Whole No. 8).

Thurstone, L.L. (1938). Primary mental abilities. *Psychometric Monographs, 1*.

Tincoff, R., & Jusczyk, P.W. (1999). Some beginnings of word comprehension in 6-month-olds. *Psychological Science, 10*, 172–176.

Tolman, E.C., & Honzik, C.H. (1930). Introduction and removal of reward, and maze performance in rates. University of California Publications in *Psychology, 4*, 257–275.

Tomarken, A.J., Davidson, R.J., & Henriques, J.B. (1990). Resting frontal brain asymmetry predicts affective responses to films. *Journal of Personality and Social Psychology, 59*, 791–801.

Tooby, J., & Cosmides, L. (1990). The past explains the present: Emotional adaptations and the structure of ancestral environments. *Ethology and Sociobiology, 10*, 29–50.

Torgersen, S. (1983). Genetic factors in anxiety disorders. *Archives of General Psychiatry, 40*, 1085–1089.

Torrance, E.P. (1954). Leadership training to improve air-crew group performance. *USAF ATC Instructor's Journal, 5*, 25–35.

Treaster, J.B. (1994, February 1). Survey finds marijuana use is up in high schools. *New York Times*, p. A1.

Treisman, A.M. (1960). Contextual cues in selective listening. *Quarterly Journal of Experimental Psychology, 12*, 242–248.

Treisman, A.M. (1964). Verbal cues, language and meaning in selective attention. *American Journal of Psychology, 77*, 206–219.

Triandis, H.C. (1994). *Culture and social behavior*. New York: McGraw-Hill.

Trice, A.D. (1986). Ethical variables? *American Psychologist, 41*, 482–483.

Tulving, E., Kapur, S., Markowitsch, H.J., Craik, F.I.M., Habib, R., & Houle, S. (1994). Neuroanatomical correlates of retrieval in episodic memory: Auditory sentence recognition. *Proceedings of the National Academy of Sciences of the U.S.A., 91*, 2012–2015.

Tupes, E.C., & Christal, R.W. (1961). *Recurrent personality factors based on trait ratings*. USAF ASD Technical Report, No. 61–97.

Turk, D.C., & Salovey, P. (1985). Cognitive structures, cognitive processes, and cognitive behavior modification: II. Judgments and inferences of the clinician. *Cognitive Therapy and Research, 9*, 19–34.

Turkheimer, E. (1991). Individual and group differences in adoption studies of IQ. *Psychological Bulletin, 110*, 392–405.

Turnbull, C.M. (1961). Observations. *American Journal of Psychology, 1*, 304–308.

U.S. Bureau of the Census. (1990). *Statistical abstract of the United States* (110th ed.). Washington, DC: U. S. Government Printing Office.

U.S. House of Representatives. (1997, July 17). The Subcommittee on Surface Transportation Hearing. *Road rage: Causes and dangers of aggressive driving.* Retrieved November 21, 2000, from the World Wide Web: http://www.house.gov/transportation/press/presss31.htm

Uchino, B.N., Uno, D., & Holt-Lunstad, J. (1999). Social support, psychological processes, and health. *Current Directions in Psychological Science, 8,* 145–148.

Uchino, B.N., Cacioppo, J.T., & Kiecolt-Glaser, J.K. (1996). The relationship between social support and physiological processes: A review with emphasis on underlying mechanisms and implications for health. *Psychological Bulletin, 119*(3), 488–531.

Uhl, G., Blum, K., Nobel, E.P., & Smith, S. (1993). Substance abuse vulnerability and D2 dopamine receptor gene and severe alcoholism. *Trends in Neuroscience, 16,* 83–88.

Ulrich, R., & Azrin, N. (1962). Reflexive fighting in response to aversive stimulation. *Journal of Experimental Analysis of Behavior, 5,* 511–520.

Underwood, G. (1994). Subliminal perception on TV. *Nature, 370,* 103.

Underwood, G. (1996). *Implicit cognition.* New York: Oxford University.

Vaidya, C.J., Austin, G., Kirkorian, G., Ridlehuber, H.W., Desmond, J.E., Glover, G.H., & Gabrieli, J.D.E. (1998). Selective effects of methylphenidate in attention deficit hyperactivity disorder: A functional magnetic resonance study. *Proceedings of the National Academy of Sciences, U.S.A., 96,* 8301–8306.

Vaillant, G.E. (2000). Adaptive mental mechanisms: Their role in positive psychology. *American Psychologist, 55,* 89–98.

Vaillant, G.E. (1977). *Adaptation to life.* Boston: Little, Brown.

Valian, V. (1998). *Why so slow?: The advancement of women.* Cambridge, MA: MIT Press.

Valkenburg, P.M., & van der Voort, T.H.A. (1994). Influence of TV on daydreaming and creative imagination: A review of research. *Psychological Bulletin, 116,* 316–339.

Vallee, B.I. (1998). Alcohol in the Western world. *Scientific American, 278*(6), 80–85.

Van Natta, P., Malin, H., Bertolucci, D., & Kaelber, C. (1985). The influence of alcohol abuse as a hidden contributor to mortality. *Alcohol, 2,* 535–539.

Van Yperen, N.W., & Buunk, B.P. (1990). A longitudinal study of equity and satisfaction in intimate relationships. *European Journal of Social Psychology, 54,* 287–309.

Vaughn, M. (1993, July 22). Divorce revisited. *Ann Arbor News,* p. C4.

Vgontzas, A.N., & Kales, A. (1999). Sleep and its disorders. *Annual Review of medicine, 50,* 387–400.

Virkkunen, M. (1983). Insulin secretion during the glucose tolerance test in antisocial personality. *British Journal of Psychiatry, 142,* 598–604.

Volkow, N.D., Wang, G.J., Fischman, M.W., Foltin, R.W., Fowler, J.S., Abumrad, N.N., Vitkun, S., Logan, J., Gatley, S.J., Pappas, N., Hitzemann, R., & Shea, C.E. (1997). Relationship between subjective effects of cocaine and dopamine transporter occupancy. *Nature, 386,* 827–830.

von Hippel, W., Hawkins, C., & Narayan, S. (1994). Personality and perceptual expertise: Individual differences in perceptual identification. *Psychological Science, 5,* 401–406.

von Hofsten, C., & Fazel-Zandy, S. (1984). Development of visually guided hand orientation in reaching. *Journal of Experimental Child Psychology, 38,* 208–219.

Voyer, D., Voyer, S., & Bryden, M.P. (1995). Magnitude of sex differences in spatial abilities: A meta-analysis and consideration of critical variables. *Psychological Bulletin, 117*(2), 250–270.

Vygotsky, L.S. (1978). *Mind in society: The development of higher mental processes.* Cambridge, MA: Harvard University Press. (Original works published 1930, 1933, and 1935.)

Wachs, T.D., & Smitherman, C.H. (1985). Infant temperament and subject loss in a habituation procedure. *Child Development, 56,* 861–867.

Wadden, T.S., Vogt, R.A., Anderson, R.E., Bartlett, S.F., Foster, G.D., Kuebnel, R.H., Wilk, F., Weinstock, R., Buckenmeyer, P., Berkowitz, R.I., & Steen, S.N. (1997). Exercise in the treatment of obesity: Effects of four interventions on body composition, resting energy expenditure, appetite and mood. *Journal of Consulting and Clinical Psychology, 65,* 269–277.

Wagner, B.M. (1997). Family risk factors for child and adolescent suicidal behavior. *Psychological Bulletin, 121,* 246–298.

Wahlsten, D. (1999). Single-gene influences on brain and behavior. *Annual Review of Psychology, 50,* 599–624.

Waldman, H.B. (1996). Yes, overall crime statistics are down, but juveniles are committing more criminal offenses. *ASDC J. Dent Child, 63*(6), 438–442.

Walk, R.D., & Gibson, E.J. (1961). A comparative and analytical study of visual depth perception. *Psychological Monographs,* No. 75.

Wall, P.D., & Melzack, R. (1996). *The Challenge of Pain* (2nd ed.). Harmondworth, UK: Penguin.

Wall, R.P., & Melzack, R. (eds.). (1989). *Textbook of pain* (2nd ed.). Edinburgh: Churchill Livingston.

Wallerstein, J.S., Blakeslee, S., & Lewis, J. (2000). *The unexpected legacy of divorce: Twenty-five year landmark study.* New York: Hyperion.

Walster, E., Walster, G.W., & Berscheid, E. (1978). *Equity: Theory and research.* Boston: Allyn & Bacon.

Walters, E.E., & Kendler, K.S. (1995). Anorexia nervosa and anorexic-like syndromes in a population-based female twin sample. *American Journal of Psychiatry, 152,* 64–67.

Walton, G.E., & Bower, T.G.R. (1993). Newborns form "prototypes" in less than 1 minute. *Psychological Science, 4,* 203–206.

Walton, G.E., Bower, N.J.A., & Bower, T.G.R. (1992). Recognition of familiar faces by newborns. *Infant Behavior and Development, 15,* 265–269.

Waltz, J.A., Knowlton, B.J., Holyoak, K.J., Boone, K.B., Mishkin, F.S., Santos, M.M., Thomas, C.R., & Miller, B.L. (1999). A system for relational reasoning in human prefrontal cortex. *Psychological Science, 10,* 119–125.

Wampold, B.E., Mondin, G.W., Moody, M., Stich, F., Benson, K., & Ahn, H. (1997). A meta-analysis of outcome studies comparing bona fide psychotherapies: Empirically, "all must have prizes." *Psychological Bulletin, 122,* 203–215.

Warr, P., & Perry, G. (1982). Paid employment and women's psychological well-being. *Psychological Bulletin, 91,* 498–516.

Watkins, C.E., Campbell, V.L., Nieberding, R., & Hallmark, R. (1995). Contemporary practice of psychological assessment by clinical psychologists. *Professional Psychological Research & Practice, 26,* 54–60.

Watson, J.B. (1924). *Behaviorism.* Chicago: University of Chicago Press.

Watson, J.B., & Rayner, R. (1920). Conditioned emotional reactions. *Journal of Experimental Psychology, 3,* 1–14.

Watson, M.W., & Getz, K. (1990). The relationship between Oedipal behaviors and children's family role concepts. *Merrill-Palmer Quarterly, 36,* 487–505.

Weaver, M.T., & McGrady, A. (1995). A provisional model to predict blood pressure response to biofeedback-assisted relaxation. *Biofeedback and Self-Regulation, 20*(3), 229–240.

Webb, W.B., & Levy, C.M. (1984). Effects of spaced and repeated total sleep deprivation. *Ergonomics, 27*, 45–58.

Webb, W.B., & Levy, C.M. (1984). Effects of spaced and repeated total sleep deprivation. *Ergonomics, 27*, 45–58.

Wechsler, H., Davenport, A., Dowdall, G., Moeykens, B., & Castillo, S. (1994). Health and behavioral consequences of binge drinking in college. *Journal of the American Medical Association, 272*, 1672–1677.

Wechsler, H., Fulop, M., Padilla, A., Lee, H., & Patrick, K. (1997). Binge drinking among college students: A comparison of California with other states. *Journal of American College Health, 45*, 273–277.

Wechsler, H., Dowdall, G.W., Davenport, A., & DeJong, W. (2000). *Binge drinking on college campuses: Results of a national study.* Available on-line at: www.hsph.havard.edu/cas

Wedeking, C., Seebeck, T., Bettens, F., & Paepke, A.J. (1995). MHC-dependent mate preferences in humans. *Proceedings of the Royal Society of London, B, 260*, 245–249.

Weinberg, M.K., Tronick, E.Z., Cohn, J.F., & Olson, K.L. (1999). Gender differences in emotional expressivity and self-regulation during early infancy. *Developmental Psychology, 35*, 175–188.

Weinberger, D.R. (1997). The biological basis of schizophrenia: New directions. *Journal of Clinical Psychiatry, 58*(Suppl. 10), 22–27.

Weinstein, R.S., Madison, W., & Kuklinski, M. (1995). Raising expectations in schooling: Obstacles and opportunities for change. *American Educational Research Journal, 32*, 121–160.

Weinstein, R.S., Soule, C.R., Collins, F., Cone, J., Melhorn, M., & Simantocci, K. (1991). Expectations and high school change: Teacher-researcher collaboration to prevent school failure. *American Journal of Community Psychology, 19*, 333–402.

Weinstein, S. (1968). Intensive and extensive aspects of tactile sensitivity as a function of body part, sex, and laterality. In D.R. Kenshalo (ed.), *The skin senses.* Springfield, IL: Charles C. Thomas.

Weissman, M.M. (1993). The epidemiology of personality disorders: A 1990 update. *Journal of Personality Disorders* (Suppl.), 44–62.

Weissman, M.M., & Olfson, M. (1995). Depression in women: Implications for health care research. *Science, 269*, 799–801.

Wells, G.L. (1993). What do we know about eyewitness identification? *American Psychologist, 48*, 553–571.

Werker, F.J., & Desjardins, R.N. (1995). Listening to speech in the 1st year of life: Experiential influences on phoneme perception. *American Psychological Society, 4*(3), 76–81.

Werker, J.F. (1989). Becoming a native listener. *American Scientist, 77*, 54–59.

Werner, E.E. (1996). Vulnerable but invincible: High risk children from birth to adulthood. *European Child & Adolescent Psychiatry, 5*(Suppl. 1), 47–51.

Werner, E.E. (1995). Resilience in development. *American Psychological Society, 4*(3), 81–84.

Westen, D. (1998b). Unconscious thought, feeling and motivation: The end of a century-long debate. In R. F. Bornstein & J. M. Masling (Eds.), *Empirical perspectives on the psychoanalytic unconscious* (pp. 1–43). Washington, DC: American Psychological Association.

Whisman, M.A., & Kwon, P. (1993). Life stress and dysphoria: The role of self-esteem and hopelessness. *Journal of Personality and Social Psychology, 65*, 1054–1060.

Whorf, B.L. (1956). *Language, thought, and reality.* New York: MIT Press–Wiley.

Wielkiewicz, R.M., & Calvert, C.R.X. (1989). *Training and habilitating developmentally disabled people: An introduction.* Newbury Park, CA: Sage.

Wiens, A.N., & Menustik, C.E. (1983). Treatment outcome and patient characteristics in an aversion therapy program for alcoholism. *American Psychologist, 38*, 1089–1096.

Wierzbicki, M. (1993). *Issues in clinical psychology: Subjective versus objective approaches.* Boston: Allyn & Bacon.

Wiggins, J.S. (ed.). (1996). *The five-factor model of personality: Theoretical perspectives.* New York: Guilford Press.

Wilder, B.J., & Bruni, J. (1981). *Seizure disorders: A pharmacological approach to treatment.* New York: Raven Press.

Will, G. (1993, April 6). How do we turn children off to the violence caused by TV? Wise up parents. *Philadelphia Inquirer*, p. A1.

Williams, J.C., Paton, C.C., Siegler, I.C., Eigenbrodt, M.L., Nieto, F.J., & Tyroles, H.A. (2000). Anger proneness predicts coronary heart disease risk: Prospective analysis from the atherosclerosis risk in communities (ARIC) study. *Circulation, 101*, 2034–2039.

Williams, J.E., & Best, D.L. (1990). *Measuring sex stereotypes: A multinational study.* Newbury Park, CA: Sage.

Williams, J.E., & Best, D.L. (1990). *Sex and psyche: Gender and self viewed cross-culturally.* Newbury Park, CA: Sage.

Williams, J.H. (1987). *Psychology of women: Behavior in a biosocial context* (3rd ed.). New York: Norton.

Williams, L. (1989, November 22). Psychotherapy gaining favor among blacks. *New York Times.*

Williams, R.A., Hagerty, B.M., Cimprich, B., Therrien, B., Bay, E., & Oe, H. (2000). Changes in directed attention and short-term memory in attention. *Journal of Psychiatric Research, 34*, 227–238.

Williams, R.B., Barefoot, J.C., Califf, R.M., Haney, T.L., Saunders, W.B., Pryor, D.B., Hatky, M.A., Siegler, I.C., & Mark, D.B. (1992). Prognostic importance of social and economic resources among medically treated patients with angiographically documented coronary artery disease. *Journal of the American Medical Association, 267*, 520–524.

Williams, T.P., & Sogon, S. (1984). Group composition and conforming behavior in Japanese students. *Japanese Psychological Research, 26*, 231–234.

Willis, S.L. (1985). Towards an educational psychology of the elder adult learner: Intellectual and cognitive bases. In J.E. Birren & K.W. Schaie (eds.), *Handbook of the psychology of aging* (2nd ed.). New York: Van Nostrand.

Willis, S.L., & Schaie, K.W. (1986). Training the elderly on the ability factors of spatial orientation and inductive reasoning. *Psychology and Aging, 1*, 239–247.

Wilson, G.D. (1987). An ethological approach to sexual deviation. In G.D. Wilson (ed.), *Variant sexuality: Research and theory* (pp. 84–115). London: Croom Helm.

Winerip, M. (1998, January 4). Binge nights: The emergency on campus. *Education Life (New York Times* supplement), Section 4A, pp. 28–31, 42.

Wing, H. (1969). *Conceptual learning and generalization.* Baltimore, MD: Johns Hopkins University.

Winn, P. (1995). The lateral hypothalamus and motivated behavior: An old syndrome reassessed and a new perspective gained. *Current Directions in Psychological Science, 4*, 182–187.

Winner, E. (1998). *Psychological aspects of giftedness.* New York: Basic Books.

Winner, E. (2000). The origins and ends of giftedness. *American Psychologist, 55*, 159–169.

Winson, J. (1990). The meaning of dreams. *Scientific American, 263*(5), 94–96.

Witkin, A.H., et al. (1962). *Psychological differentiation.* New York: Wiley.

Wolberg, L.R. (1977). *The technique of psychotherapy* (3rd ed.). New York: Grune & Stratton.

Wolf, S.S., & Weinberger, D.R. (1996). Schizophrenia: A new frontier in developmental neurobiology. *Israel Journal of Medical Science, 32*(1), 51–55.

Wolfson, C., Wolfson, D. B., Asgharian, M., M'Lan, C. E., Ostbye, T., Rockwood, K., Hogan, D. B. (2001). Reevaluation of the duration of survival after the onset of dementia. *The New England Journal of Medicine, 344,* 1111–1116.

Wolpe, J. (1973). *The practice of behavior therapy* (2nd ed.). New York: Pergamon.

Wolpe, J. (1982). *The practice of behavior therapy* (3rd ed.). New York: Pergamon.

Wolpe, P.R. (1990). The holistic heresy: Strategies of ideological challenge in the medical profession. *Social Science & Medicine, 31*(8), 913–923.

Wolsko, C., Park, B., Judd, C. M., & Wittenbrink, B. (2000). Framing interethnic ideology: Effects of multicultural and color-blind perspectives on judgments of groups and individuals. *Journal of Personality & Social Psychology, 78,* 635–654.

Wood, J.M., & Bootzin, R.R. (1990). The prevalence of nightmares and their independence from anxiety. *Journal of Abnormal Psychology, 99,* 64–68.

Wood, N.L., & Cowan, N. (1995). The cocktail party phenomenon revisited: Attention and memory in the classic selective listening procedure of Cherry (1953). *Journal of Experimental Psychology: General, 124,* 243–262.

Wood, W., Wong., F.Y., & Chachere, J.G. (1991). Effects of media violence on viewers' aggression in unconstrained social interaction. *Psychological Bulletin, 109,* 371–383.

Woods, S.C., Schwartz, M.W., Baskin, D.G., & Seeley, R.J. (2000). Food intake and the regulation of body weight. *Annual Review of Psychology, 51,* 255–277.

Woods, S.C., Seeley, R.J., Porte, D., Jr., & Schwartz, M.W. (1998). Signals that regulate food intake and energy homeostasis. *Science, 280,* 1378–1383.

Woodward, K.L., & Springen, K. (1992, August 22). Better than a gold watch. *Newsweek,* p. 71.

Worchel, S., Cooper, J., & Goethals, G.R. (1991). *Understanding social psychology* (5th ed.). Pacific Grove, CA: Brooks/Cole.

Wortman, C.B., & Silver, R.C. (1989). The myths of coping with loss. *Journal of Consulting & Clinical Psychology, 57,* 349–357.

Wright, J.C., Anderson, D.R., Huston, A.C., Collins, P.A., Schmitt, K.L., & Linebarger, D.L. (1999). Early viewing of educational television programs: The short- and long-term effects on schooling. *Insights, 2,* 5–8.

Wright, R. (1994). *The moral animal: The new science of evolutionary psychology.* New York: Pantheon.

Wyatt, W.J. (1993, December). Identical twins, emergenesis, and environments. *American Psychologist,* pp. 1294–1295.

Wynn, K. (1995). Infants possess a system of numerical knowledge. *American Psychological Society, 4*(6), 172–177.

Wyrwicka, W. (1988). Imitative behavior: A theoretical view. *Pavlovian Journal of Biological Science, 23,* 125–131.

Yalom, I.D. (1995). *The theory and practice of group psychotherapy* (4th ed.). New York: Basic Books.

Yamamoto, K., & Chimbidis, M.E. (1966). Achievement, intelligence, and creative thinking in fifth grade children: A correlational study. *Merrill-Palmer Quarterly, 12,* 233–241.

Yanovski, S.Z. (1993). Binge eating disorder. Current knowledge and future directions. *Obesity Research, 1,* 306–324.

Yoder, J.D., & Kahn, A.S. (1993). Working toward an inclusive psychology of women. *American Psychologist, 48,* 846–850.

York, J.L., & Welte, J.W. (1994). Gender comparisons of alcohol consumption in alcoholic and nonalcoholic populations. *Journal of Studies on Alcohol, 55,* 743–750.

Young, M.W. (2000). The tick-tock of the biological clock. *Scientific American, 282*(3), 64–71.

Zadra, A., & Donderi, D. C. (2000). Nightmares and bad dreams: Their prevalence and relationship to well-being. *Journal of Abnormal Psychology, 109,* 273–281.

Zajonc, R.B. (1984). On the primacy of affect. *American Psychologist, 39,* 117–129.

Zajonc, R.B., Murphy, S.T., & Inglehart, M. (1989). Feeling and facial efference: Implications of the vascular theory of emotion. *Psychological Review, 96.*

Zaragoza, M.S., & Mitchell, K.J. (1996). Repeated exposure to suggestion and the creation of false memories. *Psychological Science, 7*(5), 294–300.

Zaragoza, M.S., Lane, S.M., Ackil, J.K., & Chambers, K.L. (1997). Confusing real and suggested memories: Source monitoring and eyewitness suggestibility. In N.L. Stein, P.A. Ornstein, B. Tversky, & C. Brainerd (eds.), *Memory for everyday and emotional events.* Mahwah, NJ: Erlbaum.

Zigler, E. (1998). By what goals should Head Start be assessed? *Children's Services: Social Policy, Research, and Practice, 1,* 5–18.

Zigler, E., & Hodapp, R.M. (1991). Behavioral functioning in individuals with mental retardation. *Annual Review of Psychology, 42,* 29–50.

Zigler, E., & Muenchow, S. (1992). *Head Start: The inside story of America's most successful educational experiment.* New York: Basic Books.

Zigler, E., & Styfco, S.J. (1994). Head Start: Criticisms in a constructive context. *American Psychologist, 49,* 127–132.

Zigler, E., & Styfco, S.J. (eds.). (1993). *Head Start and beyond.* New Haven, CT: Yale University Press.

Zigler, E., Styfco, S. J. (2001). Extended childhood intervention prepares children for school and beyond. *Journal of the American Medical Association, 285,* 2378–2380.

Zito, J.M., Safer, D.J., dosReis, S., Gardner, J.F., Boles, M., & Lynch, F. (2000). Trends in the prescribing of psychotropic medications to preschoolers. *Journal of the American Medical Association, 283,* 1025–1030.

Zucker, R.A., & Gomberg, E.S.L. (1990). Etiology of alcoholism reconsidered: The case for a biopsychosocial process. *American Psychologist, 41,* 783–793.

Zuckerman, M. (1979). *Sensation seeking: Beyond the optimal level of arousal.* Hillsdale, NJ: Erlbaum.

Zuckerman, M. (1994). *Behavioral expressions and biosocial bases of sensation seeking.* NY: Cambridge University Press.

Zuckerman, M., Miyake, K., & Elkin, C.S. (1995). Effects of attractiveness and maturity of face and voice on interpersonal impression. *Journal of Research in Personality, 29,* 253–272.

Zuger, A. (1998, July 28). A fistful of aggression is found among women. *New York Times,* p. B8

Zwislocki, J.J. (1981). Sound analysis in the ear: A history of discoveries. *American Scientist, 245,* 184–192.

Page abbreviations are as follows: (T) top, (C) center, (B) bottom, (L) left, and (R) right.

Chapter 1

Opener: Pictor, New York; p. 5 (T) Ellen Senisi/The Image Works, (B) Scott Camazine/Photo Researchers, Inc.; p. 8 The Cartoon Bank © The New Yorker Collection 1997 Donald Reilly from cartoonbank.com. All Rights Reserved; p. 9 (left) Travelpix/Getty Images, Inc., (middle left) Robert Caputo/Stock Boston, (middle right) Arvind Garg/Getty Images, Inc., (right) Frank Siteman/Index Stock Imagery, Inc.; p. 10 B. Daemmrich/The Image Works; p. 12 Keystone Press Agency; p. 13 Library of Congress/Courtesy of the Library of Congress; p. 14 Bildarchiv der Oesterreichische Nationalbibliothek; p. 15 Getty Images Inc.; p. 16 (T) G. Paul Bishop, (B) Chris J. Johnson/Stock Boston; p. 19 (left) Peter Johnson/CORBIS, (right) The Image Works; p. 20 (T) CORBIS, (B) Dr. Elizabeth Loftus/Courtesy of Elizabeth Loftus; p. 22 A. Ramey/Stock Boston; p. 23 Vincent Oliver/Getty Images Inc.; p. 25 (T) Jerry Bauer/Carol Gilligan, (B) Bob Daemmrich/Stock Boston; p. 26 (T) UPI/CORBIS, (B) Paul Conklin/PhotoEdit; p. 28 Breese/Getty Images, Inc.; p. 29 (T) Jeff Greenberg/Index Stock Imagery, Inc., (B) Bill Anderson/Photo Researchers, Inc.; p. 30 R. Lord/The Image Works, p. 38 Alexandra Milgram/From the film *Obedience* copyright 1965 by Stanley Milgram and distributed by Penn State Media Sales. Permission granted by Alexandra Milgram; p. 31 Robert Brenner/PhotoEdit; p. 40 Wade Bruton/Wade Bruton—UNC Charlotte.

Chapter 2

Opener: Roger Tully/Getty Images, Inc.; p. 53 Rick Browne/Stock Boston; p. 54 E.R. Lewis/Y.Y. Zeevi, T.E. Everhart/Edwin R. Lewis, Professor Emeritus; p. 60 (T) Dan McCoy/Rainbow, (B) Library of Congress/Courtesy of the Library of Congress; p. 65 Mazziotta Et/Photo Researchers, Inc.; p. 66 (top) Richard T. Nowitz/Photo Researchers, Inc., (middle) Catherine Pouedras/Science Photo Library/Photo Researchers, Inc., (bottom) Howard Sochurek/Woodfin Camp & Associates; p. 67 Brad Markel/Getty Images, Inc.; p. 69 Bruce Herman/Getty Images, Inc.; p. 74 CNRI/Science Photo Library/Science Source/Photo Researchers, Inc.; p. 75 Jean Claude Revy/Phototake NYC; p. 76 (T) Renate Hiller/Renate Hiller, (B) B. Daemmrich/The Image Works.

Chapter 3

Opener: Tom Schierlitz/Getty Images, Inc.; p. 90 Bob Daemmrich/The Image Works; p. 93 Don Wong/Science Source/Photo Researchers, Inc.; p. 94 Edwin R. Lewis, Professor Emeritus; p. 98 Pearson Education/PH College; p. 99 (T) Fritz Goro/TimePix, (B) Graham-Field, Inc./Ishihara, "Test for Color Deficiency." Courtesy

Kamehara & Co., Ltd. Offered Exclusively in The USA by Graham-Field, Inc., Bay Shore, New York; p. 100 Hart-Davis/Science Photo Library/Photo Researchers, Inc.; p. 105 David Klein/Getty Images, Inc.; p. 106 Dorothy Littell Greco/The Image Works; p. 108 Robbie Jack/CORBIS; p. 110 Nik Kleinberg/Stock Boston; p. 111 (T) Fujifotos/The Image Works, (B) Steve Raymer/CORBIS; p. 113 USDA/APHIS/Animal and Plant Health Inspection Service; p. 114 Kaiser Porcelain Ltd.; p. 115 The Cartoon Bank © The New Yorker Collection 2000 John O'Brien from cartoonbank.com. All Rights Reserved; p. 116 Dirck Halstead/Getty Images, Inc./Pawan Sinha and Tomaso Poggio. Photo © Dirck Halstead/Gamma Liaison; p. 120 Fred Charles/Getty Images, Inc.

Chapter 4

Opener: Tibor Hirsch/Photo Researchers, Inc.; p. 131 The Cartoon Bank © The New Yorker Collection 1993 Dana Fradon from cartoonbank.com. All Rights Reserved; p. 132 Will & Deni McIntyre/Photo Researchers, Inc.; p. 137 Alvis Upitis/Getty Images, Inc.; p. 140 SuperStock, Inc./Marc Chagall (Russian, 1887–1985), "Above the City." Tretyakov Gallery, Moscow, Russia. SuperStock, © Artists Rights Society (ARS), New York; p. 143 The Metropolitan Museum of Art/William Hogarth (1697–1765), "Gin Lane." The Metropolitan Museum of Art, Harris Brisbane Dick Fund, 1932. [32.35(124)]; p. 146 Stephen Ferry/Getty Images, Inc.; p. 150 The Granger Collection; p. 151 www.smokingisugly.com. Reprinted by permission of Christy Turlington; p. 153 The Granger Collection; p. 154 Kal Muller/Woodfin Camp & Associates; p. 159 Carl Frank/Photo Researchers, Inc.; p. 160 Stock Montage, Inc./Historical Pictures Collection.

Chapter 5

Opener: Azzara Steve/Corbis/Sygma; p. 168 Joe Sohm/The Image Works; p. 169 Tom Bean/Getty Images, Inc.; p. 172 The Cartoon Bank © The New Yorker Collection 1978 Sam Gross from cartoonbank.com. All Rights Reserved; p. 173 Walter Dawn/Photo Researchers, Inc.; p. 175 (T) Dubrowsky/Getty Images, Inc., (B) William R. Sallaz/Duomo Photography Incorporated; p. 176 Grant LeDuc/Grant LeDuc; p. 178 The Granger Collection; p. 183 David Ball/Corbis/Stock Market; p. 185 Corbis Digital Stock; p.184 Carroll Seghers/Photo Researchers, Inc.; p. 191 Library of Congress; p. 192 Lawrence Migdale/Photo Researchers, Inc.; p. 193 Albert Bandura. p. 197 Library of Congress, Courtesy of the Library of Congress; p. 190 Hank Morgan/Photo Researchers, Inc.

Chapter 6

Opener: G&V Chapman/Getty Images, Inc.; p. 202 Babor Demjen/Stock Boston; p. 204 Ellen B. Senisi/The Image Works; p. 205 A.

Brucelle/Corbis/Sygma; p. 206 The Cartoon Bank © The New Yorker Collection 1997 Annie Levin from cartoonbank.com. All Rights Reserved.; p. 210 Jeff Isaac/Photo Researchers, Inc.; p. 211 (T) Getty Images, Inc./PhotoDisc, Inc., (B) Spencer Platt/Getty Images, Inc.; p. 212 Michele Burgess/Corbis/Stock Market; p. 219 UPI/CORBIS; p. 221 Laima E. Druskis/Pearson Education/PH College; p. 223 Renee Lynn/Photo Researchers, Inc.; p. 225 Carmen Taylor/AP/Wide World Photos.

Chapter 7

Opener: Hillery Smith Garrison/AP/Wide World Photos; p. 233 The Cartoon Bank © The New Yorker Collection 1994 Sam Gross from cartoonbank.com. All Rights Reserved.; p. 234 Art Resource, N.Y./Picasso, Pablo (1881–1973). Nude with bunch of irises and mirror. 1934. © 162 × 130 cm. Copyright Succession Picasso/ARS, NY Photo: R.G. Ojeda. Musee Picasso, Paris, France; p. 36 Kal Muller/Woodfin Camp & Associates; p. 239 Bob Daemmrich/Stock Boston; p. 244 Spencer Grant/PhotoEdit; p. 245 Stuart Ramson/AP/Wide World Photos; p. 246 CORBIS; p. 250 Thomas Engstrom/Getty Images, Inc/; p. 252 (left) Mimi Forsyth/Mimi Forsyth, (right) Lew Merrim/Photo Researchers, Inc.; p. 255 George Goodwin/George Goodwin; p. 260 (T) Jeff Greenberg/Photo Researchers, Inc., (B) Jacques Chenet/Woodfin Camp & Associates; p. 261 Will Hart/Will Hart; p. 262 (T) Russell D. Curtis/Photo Researchers, Inc., (B) James Schnepf/Getty Images, Inc.; p. 265 Raphael Gaillarde/Getty Images, Inc.; p. 266 Erik Samper/Getty Images, Inc.

Chapter 8

Opener: CORBIS; p. 279 Ellis Herwig/Stock Boston; p. 283 (bottom left) Camermann/The Image Works, (bottom right) W. Hill, Jr./The Image Works; p. 284 AP/Wide World Photos; p. 288 Michele Burgess/Corbis/Stock Market; p. 290 Jim Tuten/Animals Animals/Earth Scenes; p. 291 Skip Nall/Getty Images, Inc./PhotoDisc, Inc.; p. 292 Harlow Primate Laboratory; p. 293 Reuters/CORBIS; p. 296 Catherine Ursillo/Photo Researchers, Inc.; p. 297 Robert Burke/Getty Images, Inc.; p. 300 (T) Zig Leszczynski/Animals Animals/Earth Scenes, (B) Michael S. Yamashita © Michael S. Yamashita/CORBIS; p. 301 (T) Joe McNally Photography, (B) Picture Desk, Inc./Kobal Collection; p. 304 Robert Azzi/Woodfin Camp & Associates; p. 306 Jack Hollingsworth/Getty Images, Inc./PhotoDisc, Inc.; p. 307 (all) Paul Ekman, Ph.D., Professor of Psychology/9C0 1972, Paul Ekman. Reprinted with permission.

Chapter 9

Opener: Art Montes De Oca/Getty Images, Inc.; p. 314 Rose Hartman/CORBIS; p. 316 James W. Hanson, M.D./From the Journal of the American Medical Association, 1976, Vol 235, 1458–1460. Courtesy, James W. Hanson,

NAME INDEX

SUBJECT INDEX